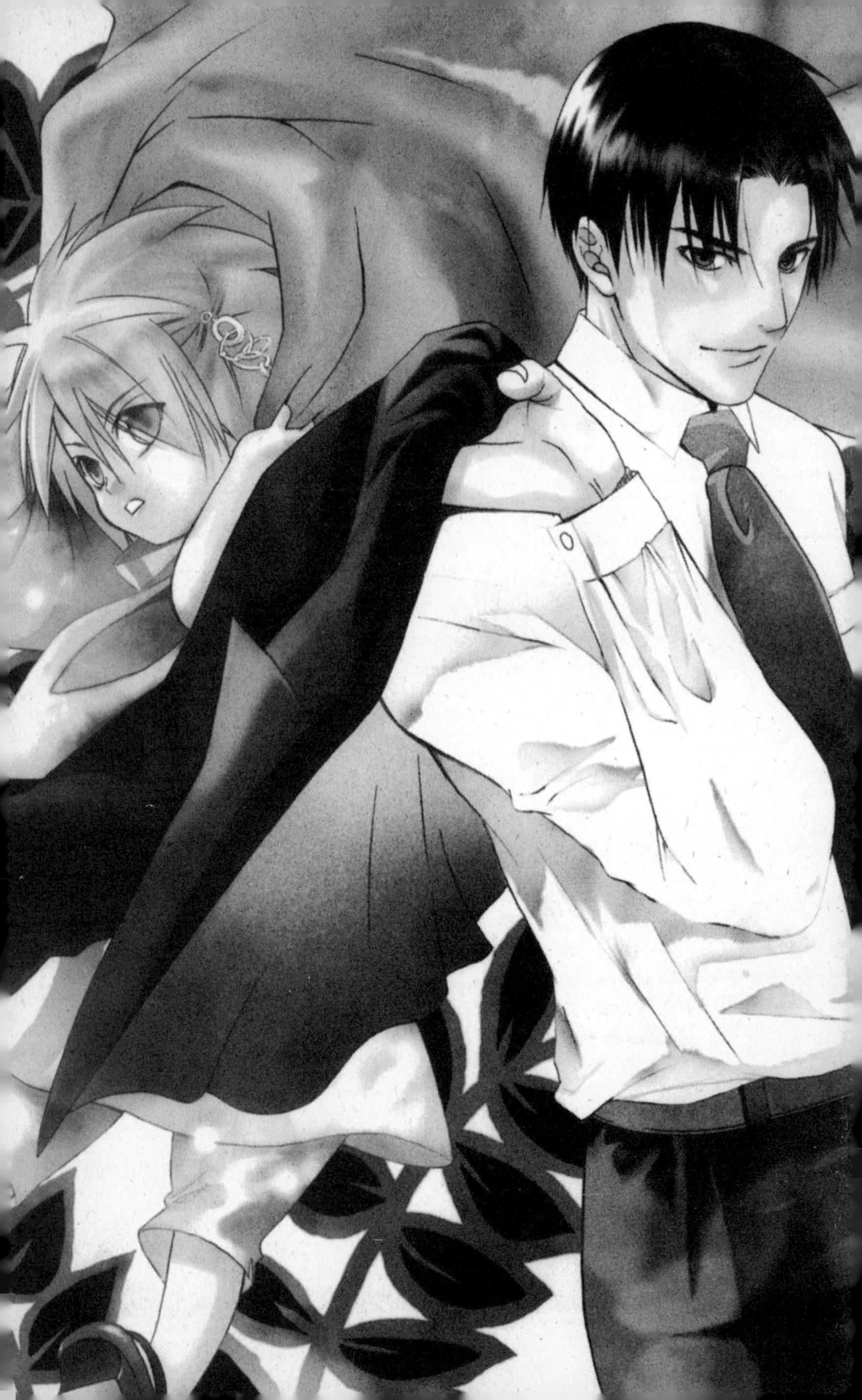

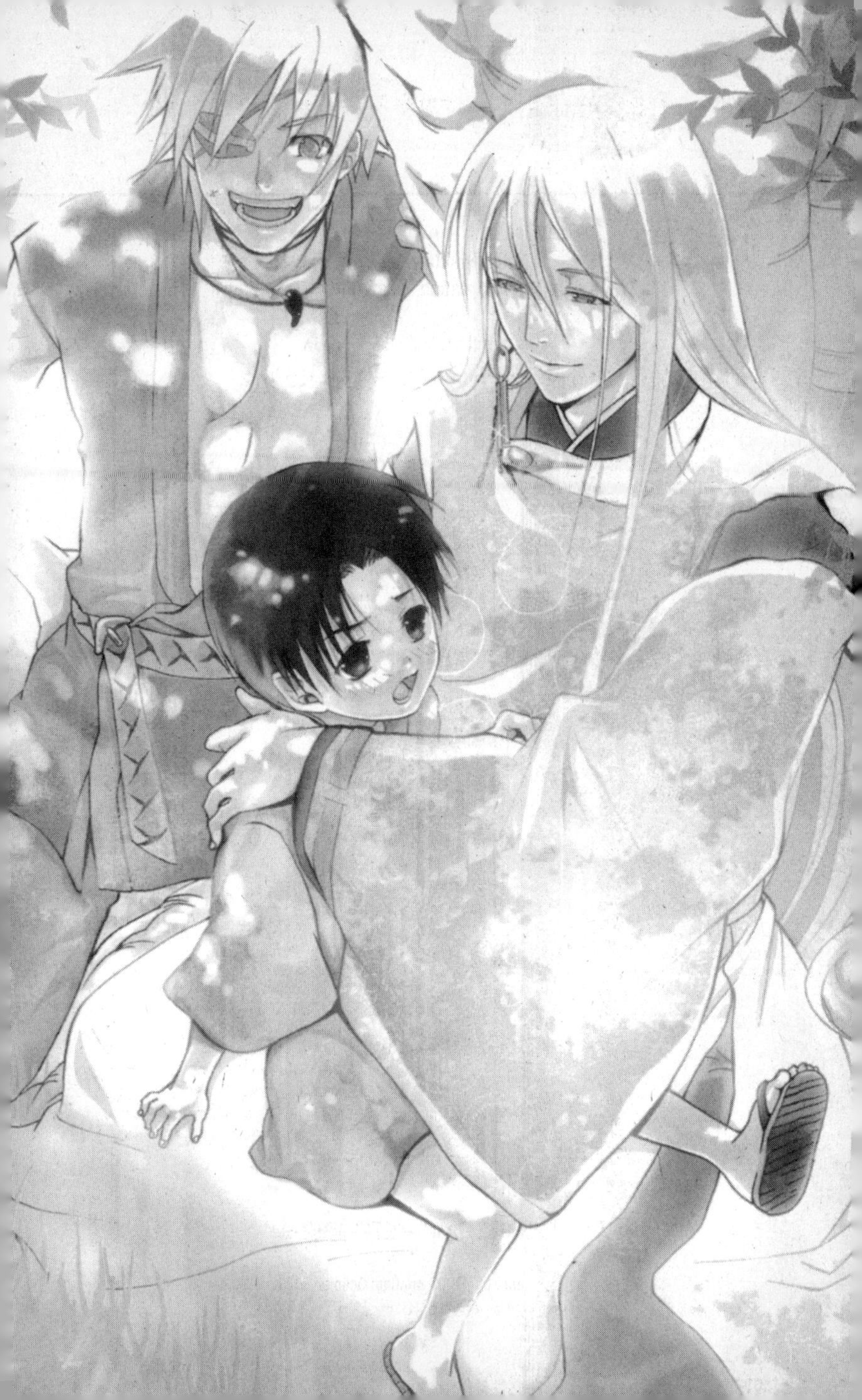

Black Gate
Created by Yukiko Sumiyoshi

Translation - Ajani A. Oloye
English Adaptation - Jay Antani
Retouch and Lettering - Star Print Brokers
Production Artist - Rui Kyo
Graphic Designer - Al-Insan Lashley

Editor - Jill Bentley
Print Production Manager - Lucas Rivera
Managing Editor - Vy Nguyen
Senior Designer - Louis Csontos
Art Director - Al-Insan Lashley
Director of Sales and Manufacturing - Allyson De Simone
Associate Publisher - Marco F. Pavia
President and C.O.O. - John Parker
C.E.O. and Chief Creative Officer - Stu Levy

A  Manga

TOKYOPOP Inc.
5900 Wilshire Blvd. Suite 2000
Los Angeles, CA 90036

E-mail: info@TOKYOPOP.com
Come visit us online at www.TOKYOPOP.com

ISBN: 978-1-4278-1882-9

First TOKYOPOP printing: October 2010
10 9 8 7 6 5 4 3 2 1
Printed in the USA

BLACK GATE

the black gate does not wait for the soul to die

By Yukiko Sumiyoshi

HAMBURG // LONDON // LOS ANGELES // TOKYO

Table of Contents

Volume 1

SOUL.1...................... 9
SOUL.2 47
SOUL.3.................. 75
SOUL.4................105
SOUL.5................143
SOUL.6.................. 179
Afterword............211

Volume 2

SOUL.7................ 219
SOUL.8.................. 253
SOUL.9.................. 285
SOUL.10 318
SOUL.11................357
SOUL.12 393
Afterword............ 435

Volume 3

SOUL.13 439
SOUL.14 469
SOUL.15................ 496
SOUL.16 527
SOUL.17 556
Afterword............627

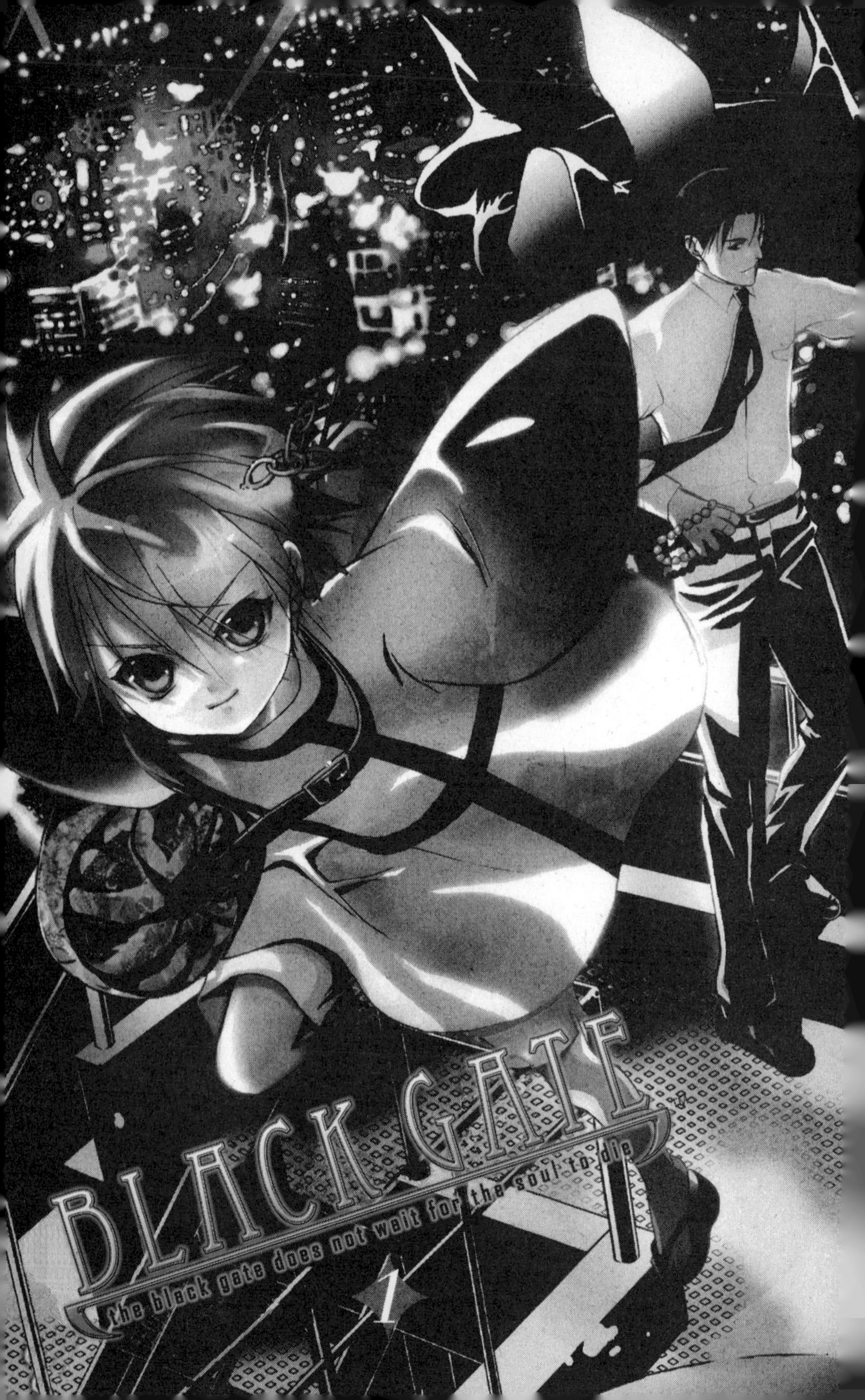
BLACK GATE
the black gate does not wait for the soul to die
1

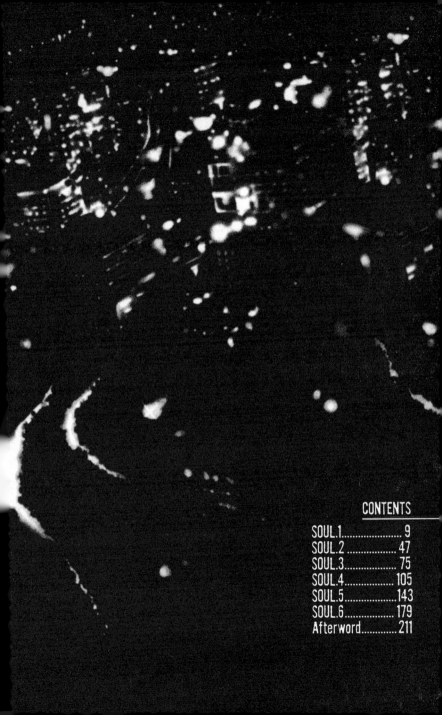

CONTENTS

SOUL.1......................9
SOUL.2 47
SOUL.3..................75
SOUL.4................105
SOUL.5................143
SOUL.6................179
Afterword............211

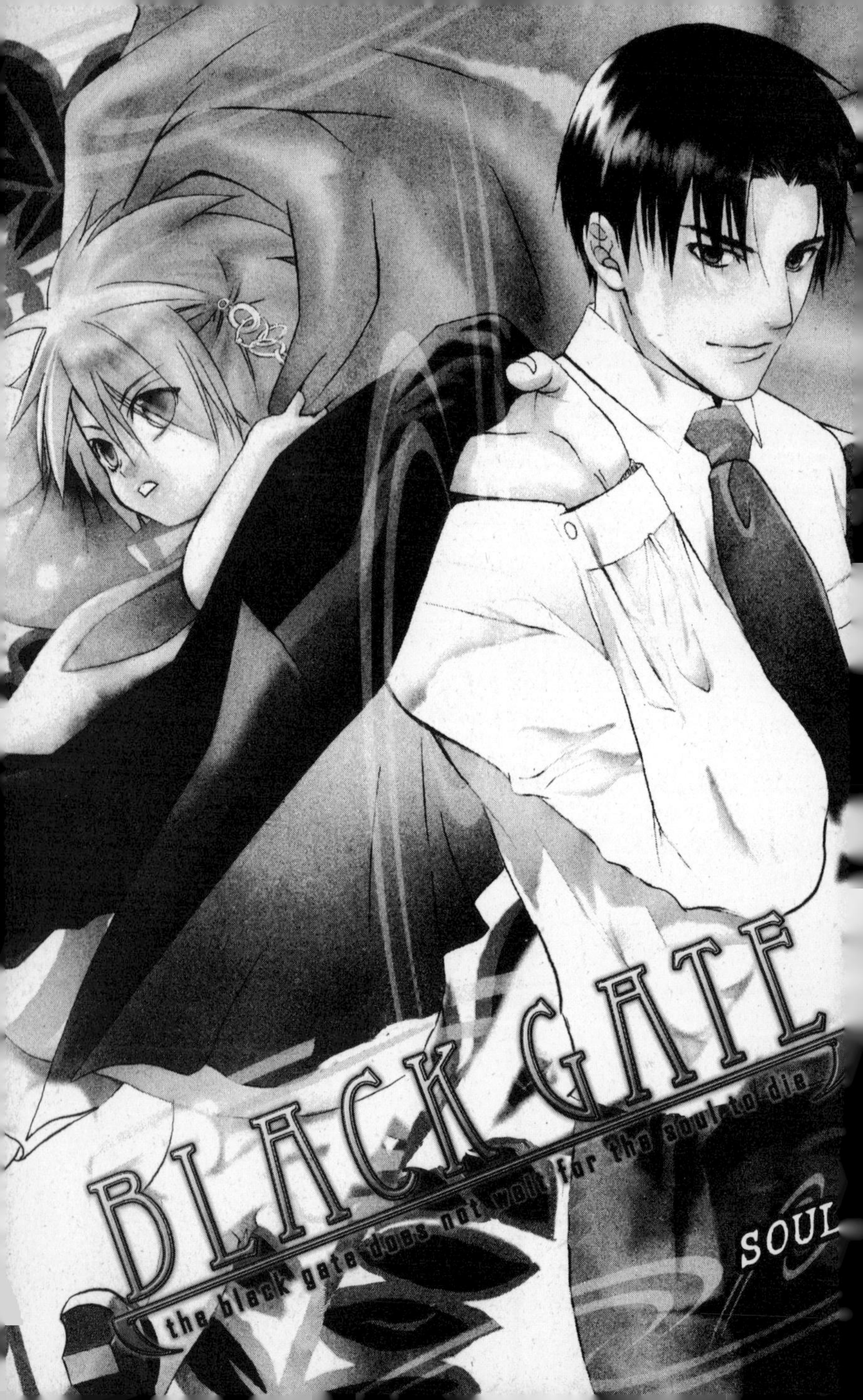
BLACK GATE
the black gate does not wait for the soul to die
SOUL

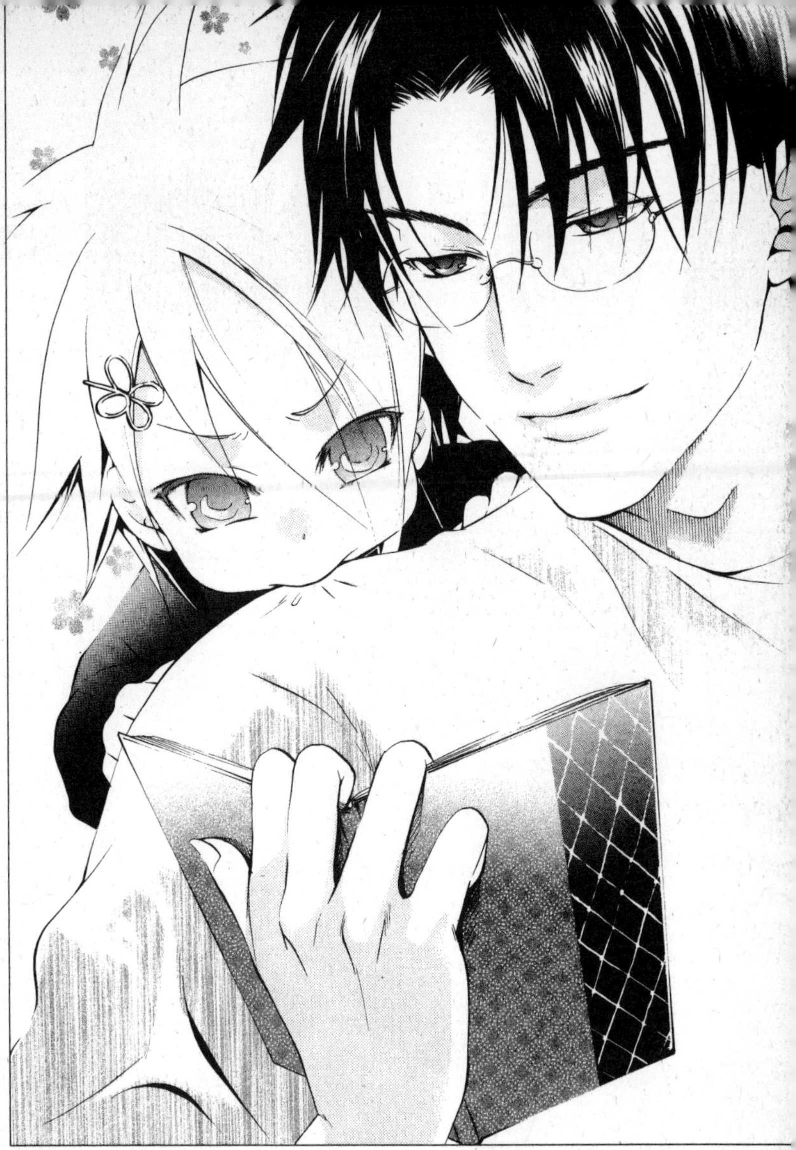

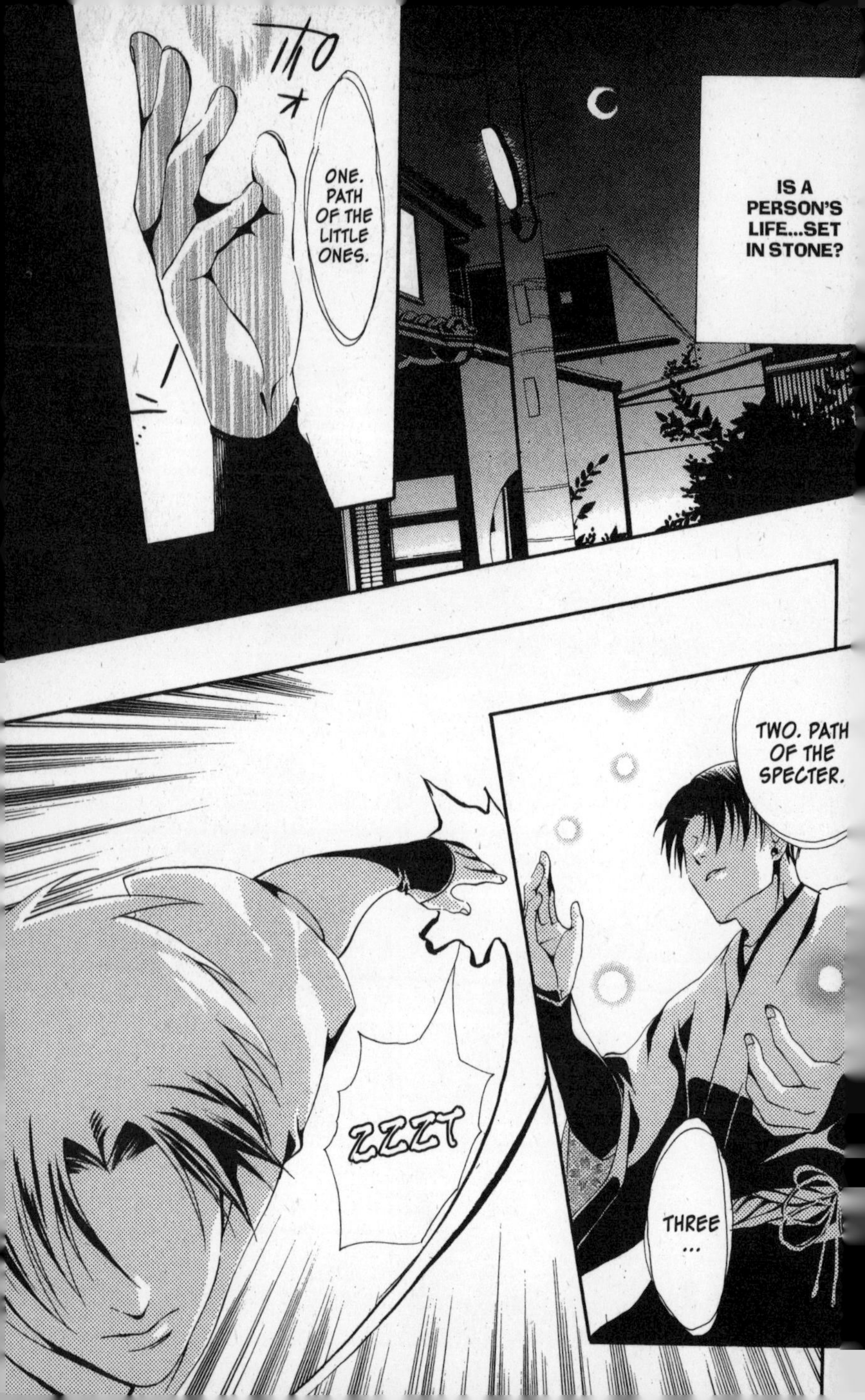
IS A PERSON'S LIFE...SET IN STONE?
ONE. PATH OF THE LITTLE ONES.
TWO. PATH OF THE SPECTER.
THREE ...
ZZZT

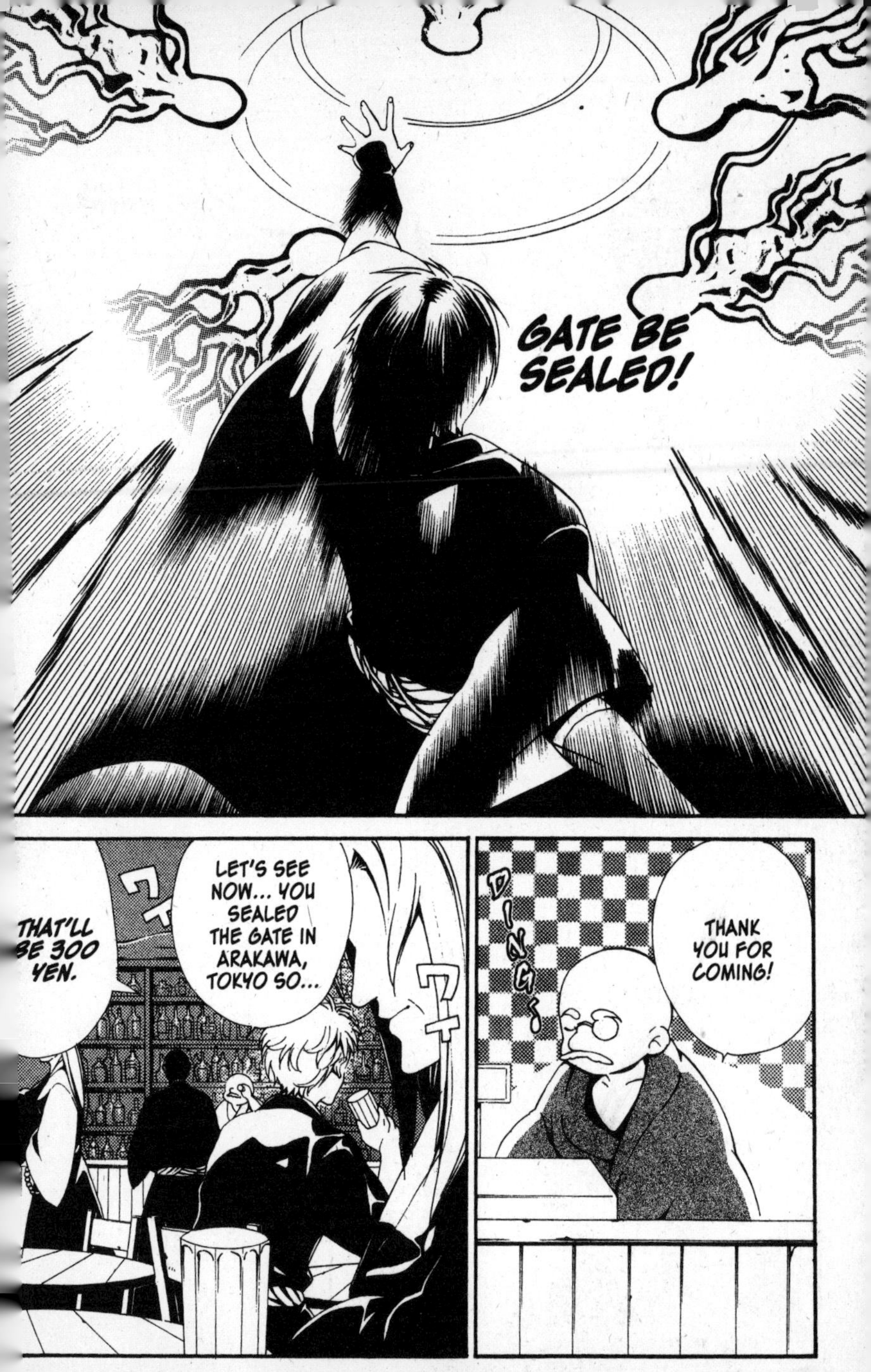
GATE BE SEALED!
DING
THANK YOU FOR COMING!
LET'S SEE NOW... YOU SEALED THE GATE IN ARAKAWA, TOKYO SO...
THAT'LL BE 300 YEN.

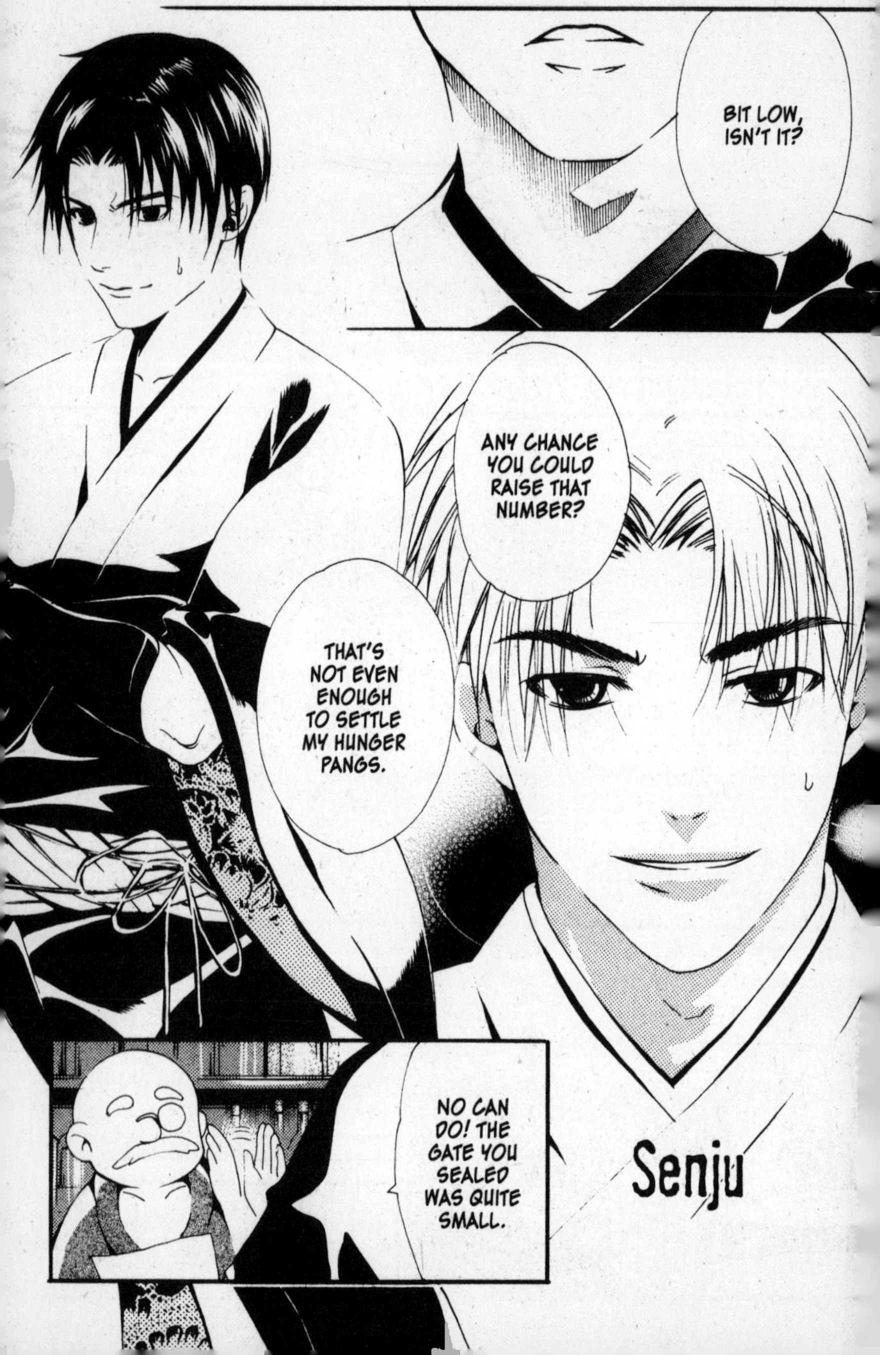
BIT LOW, ISN'T IT?
ANY CHANCE YOU COULD RAISE THAT NUMBER?
THAT'S NOT EVEN ENOUGH TO SETTLE MY HUNGER PANGS.
Senju
NO CAN DO! THE GATE YOU SEALED WAS QUITE SMALL.

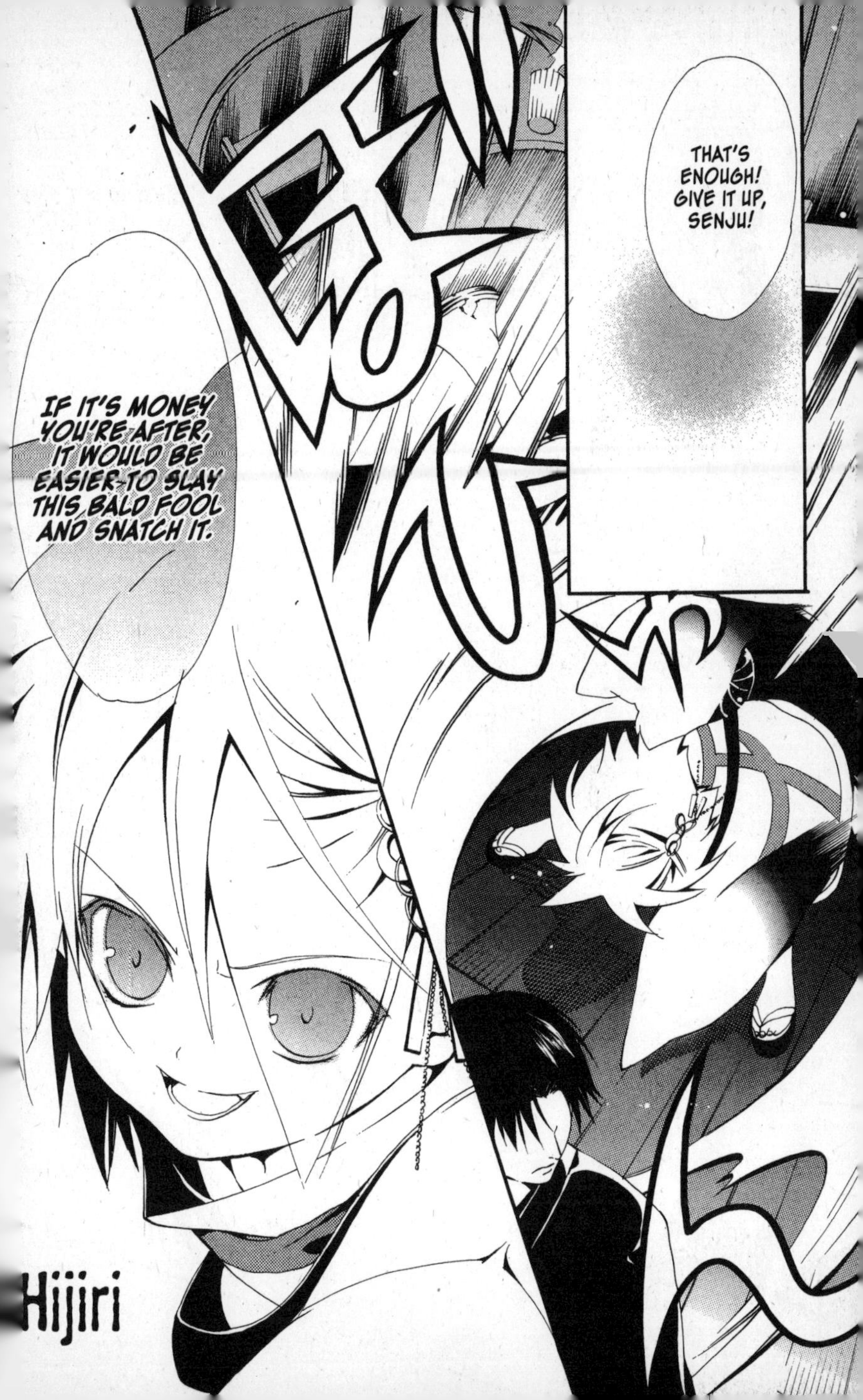
THAT'S ENOUGH! GIVE IT UP, SENJU!
IF IT'S MONEY YOU'RE AFTER, IT WOULD BE EASIER TO SLAY THIS BALD FOOL AND SNATCH IT.
Hijiri

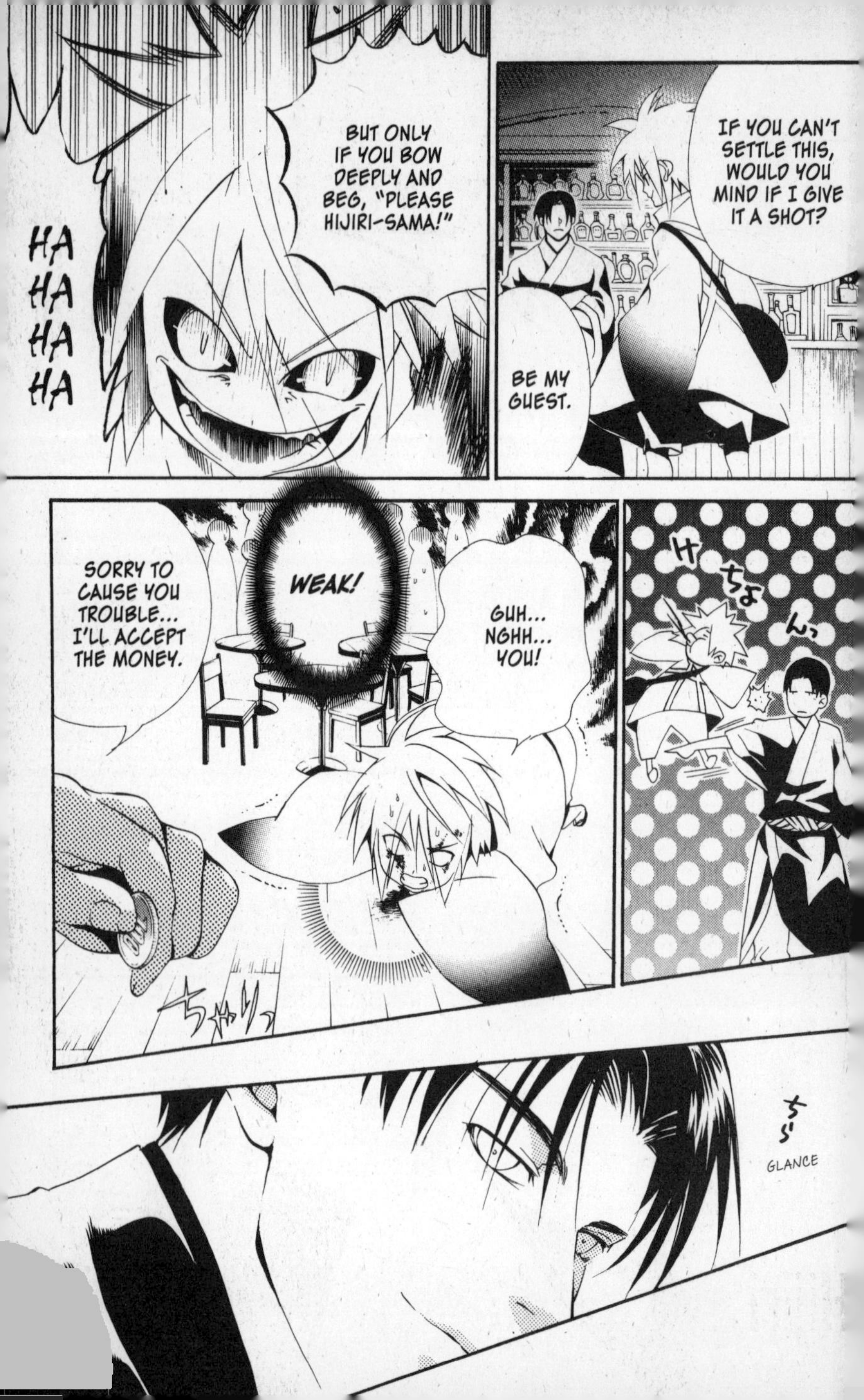
IF YOU CAN'T SETTLE THIS, WOULD YOU MIND IF I GIVE IT A SHOT?
BE MY GUEST.
BUT ONLY IF YOU BOW DEEPLY AND BEG, "PLEASE HIJIRI-SAMA!"
HA HA HA HA
ちょんっ
GUH... NGHH... YOU!
WEAK!
SORRY TO CAUSE YOU TROUBLE... I'LL ACCEPT THE MONEY.
ちゃりっ
ちら
GLANCE

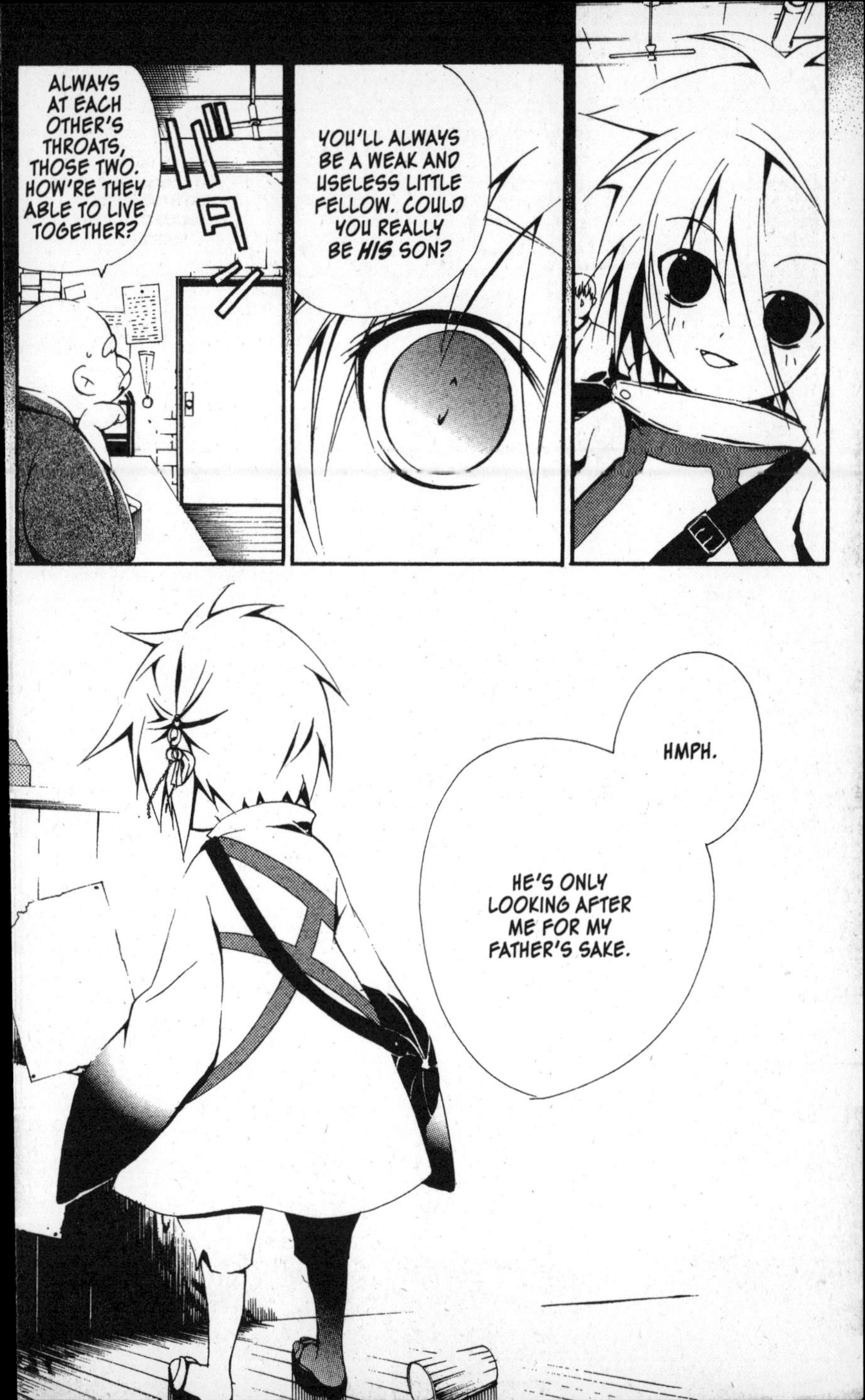
YOU'LL ALWAYS BE A WEAK AND USELESS LITTLE FELLOW. COULD YOU REALLY BE *HIS* SON?
ALWAYS AT EACH OTHER'S THROATS, THOSE TWO. HOW'RE THEY ABLE TO LIVE TOGETHER?
HMPH.
HE'S ONLY LOOKING AFTER ME FOR MY FATHER'S SAKE.

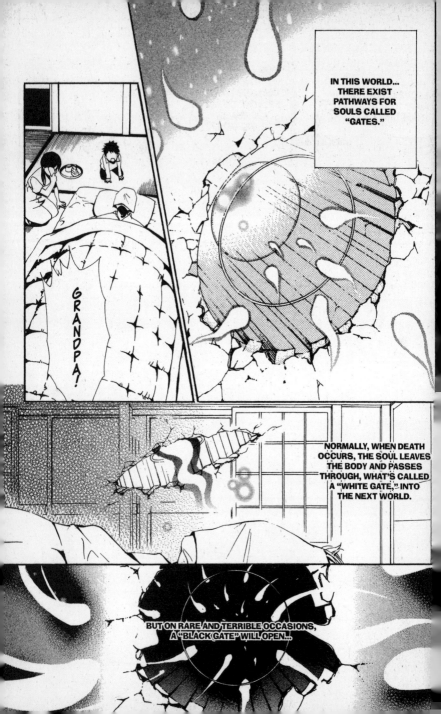

IN THIS WORLD...
THERE EXIST
PATHWAYS FOR
SOULS CALLED
"GATES."

GRANDPA!

NORMALLY, WHEN DEATH
OCCURS, THE SOUL LEAVES
THE BODY AND PASSES
THROUGH, WHAT'S CALLED
A "WHITE GATE," INTO
THE NEXT WORLD.

BUT ON RARE AND TERRIBLE OCCASIONS,
A "BLACK GATE" WILL OPEN...

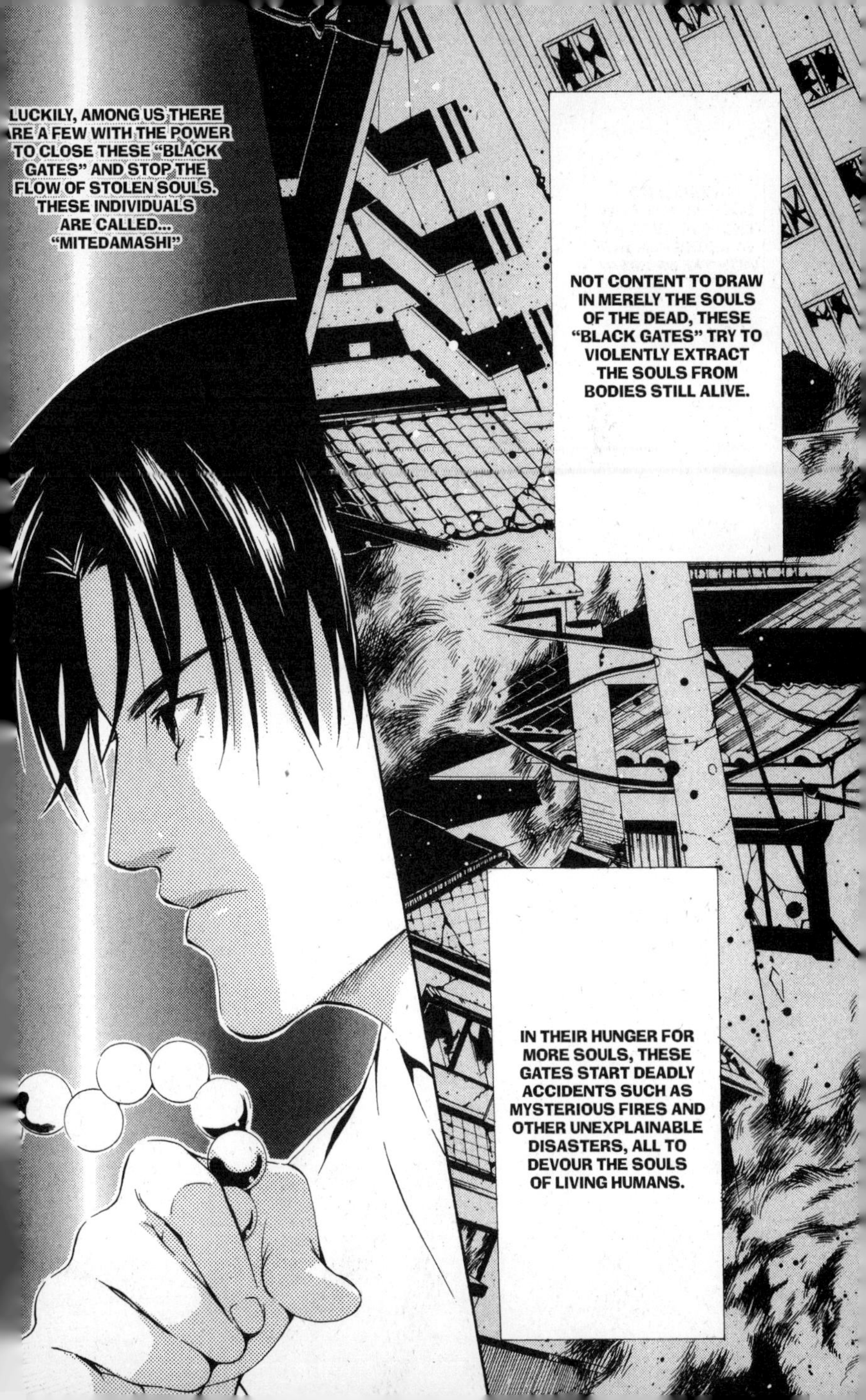
NOT CONTENT TO DRAW IN MERELY THE SOULS OF THE DEAD, THESE "BLACK GATES" TRY TO VIOLENTLY EXTRACT THE SOULS FROM BODIES STILL ALIVE.
IN THEIR HUNGER FOR MORE SOULS, THESE GATES START DEADLY ACCIDENTS SUCH AS MYSTERIOUS FIRES AND OTHER UNEXPLAINABLE DISASTERS, ALL TO DEVOUR THE SOULS OF LIVING HUMANS.
LUCKILY, AMONG US THERE ARE A FEW WITH THE POWER TO CLOSE THESE "BLACK GATES" AND STOP THE FLOW OF STOLEN SOULS. THESE INDIVIDUALS ARE CALLED... "MITEDAMASHI"

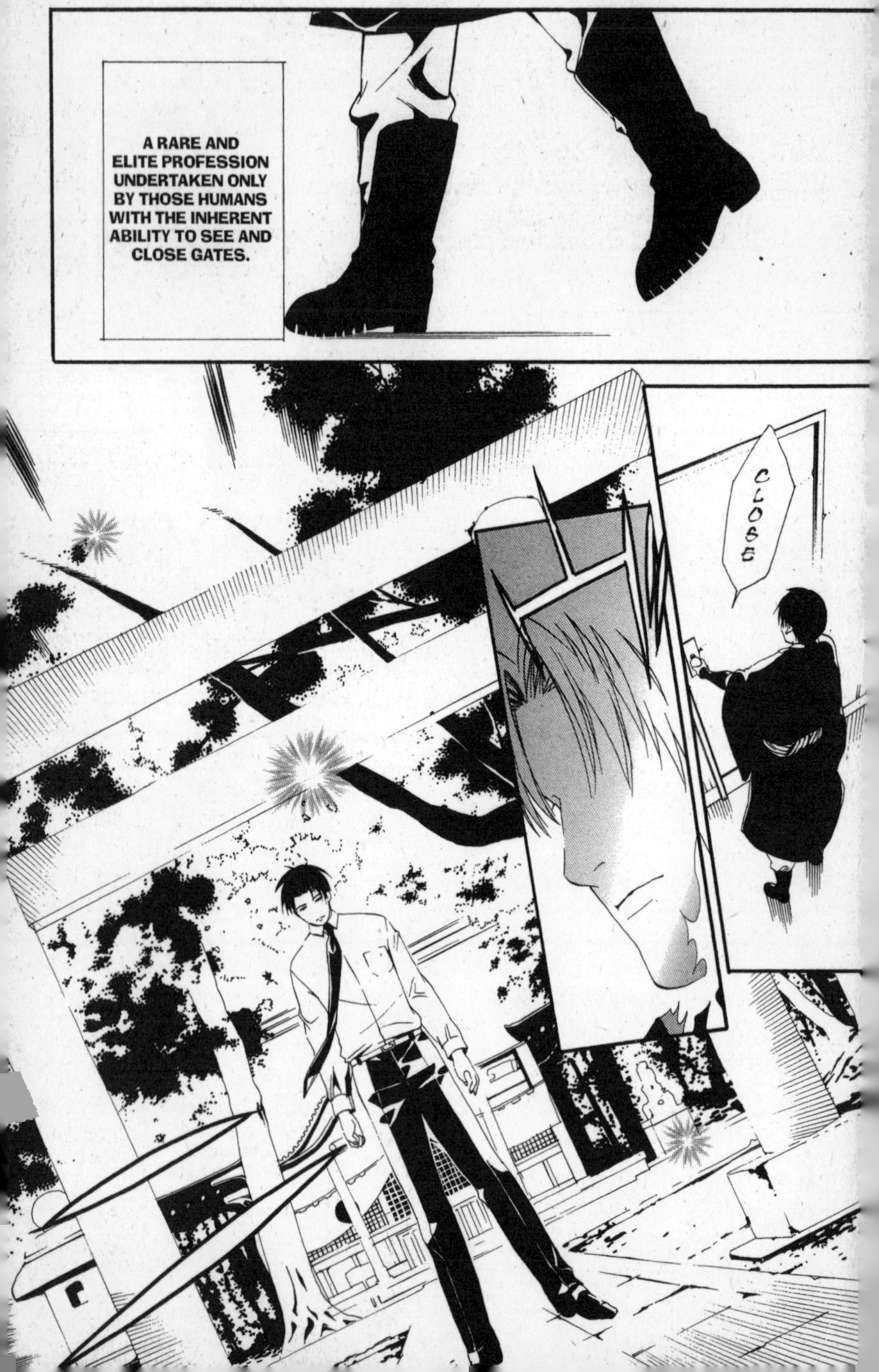
A RARE AND ELITE PROFESSION UNDERTAKEN ONLY BY THOSE HUMANS WITH THE INHERENT ABILITY TO SEE AND CLOSE GATES.
CLOSE

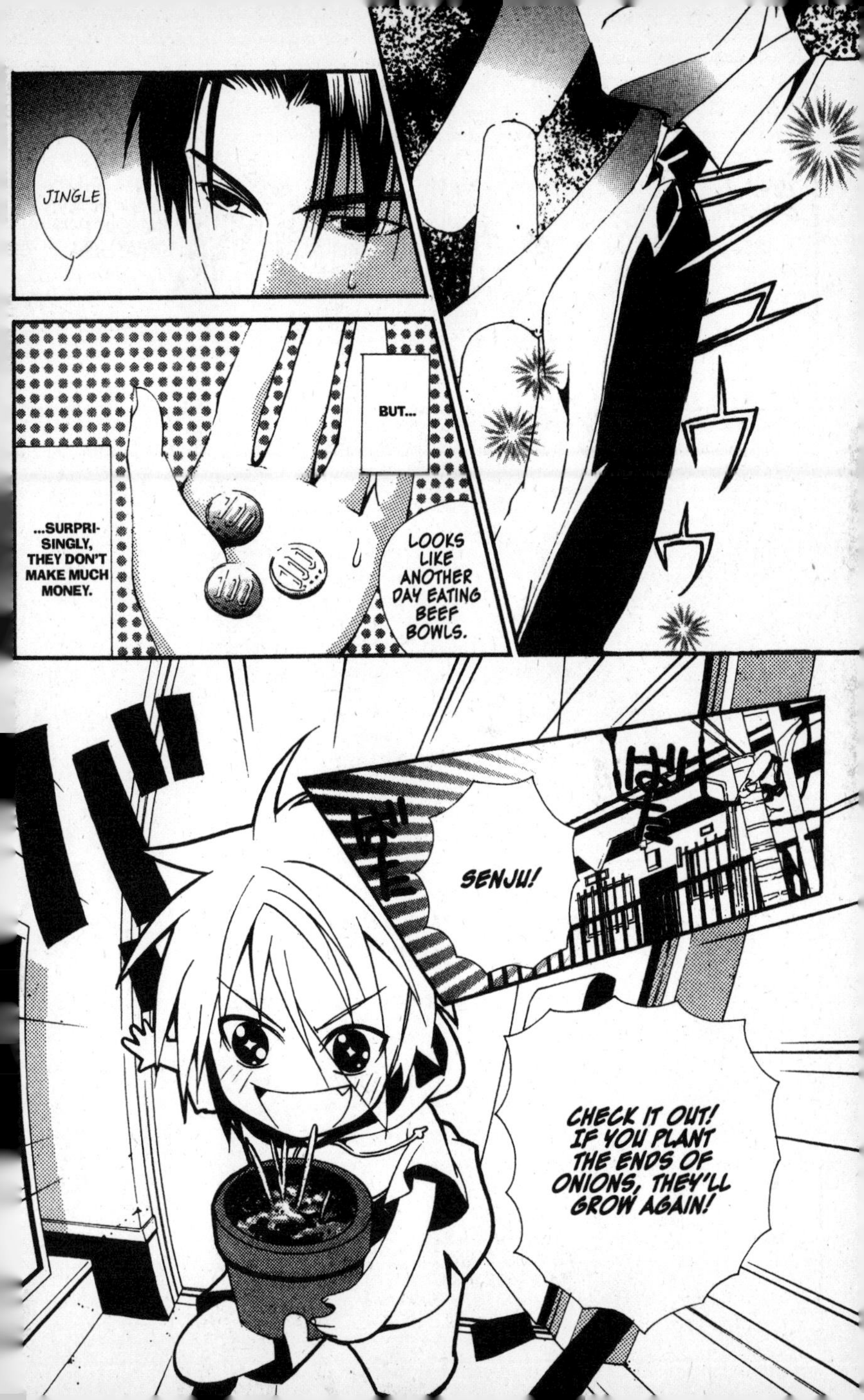
JINGLE
BUT...
LOOKS LIKE ANOTHER DAY EATING BEEF BOWLS.
...SURPRI-SINGLY, THEY DON'T MAKE MUCH MONEY.
SENJU!
CHECK IT OUT! IF YOU PLANT THE ENDS OF ONIONS, THEY'LL GROW AGAIN!

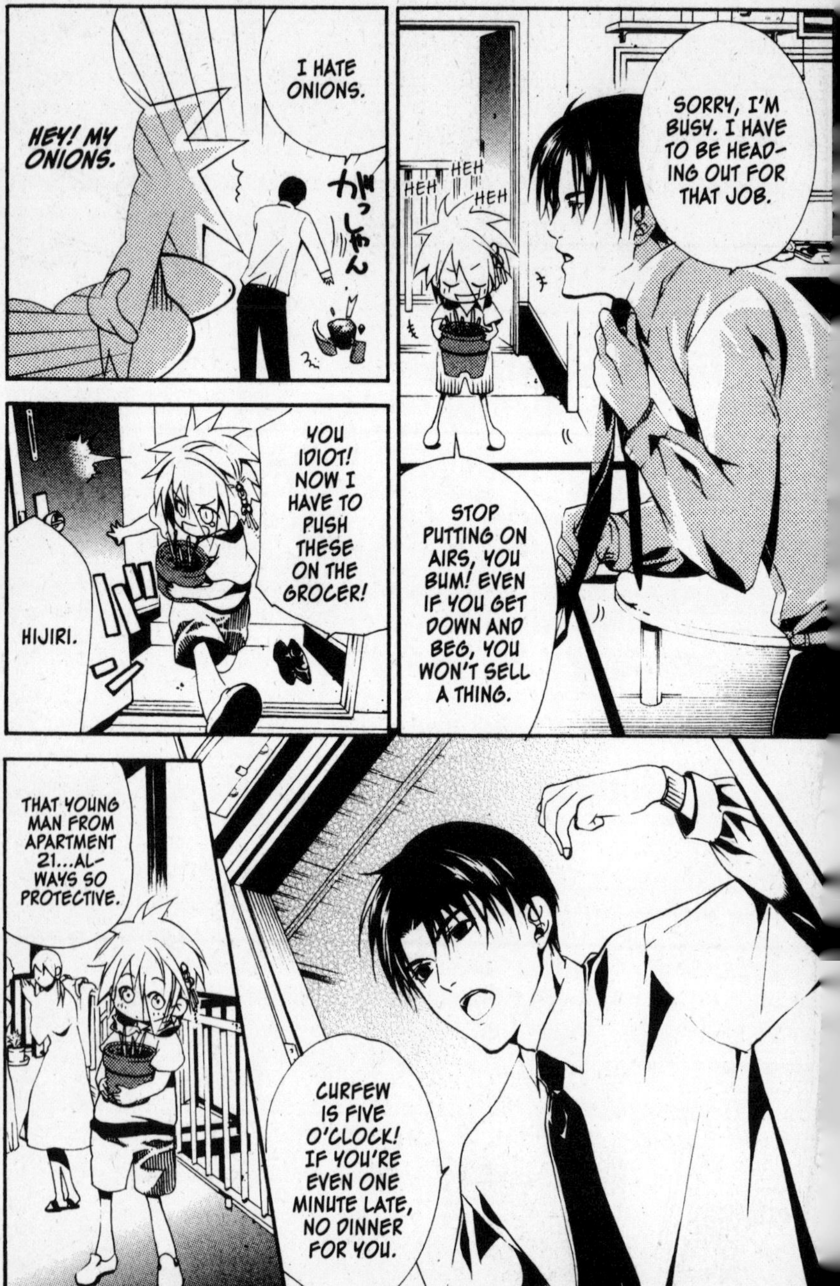
SORRY, I'M BUSY. I HAVE TO BE HEADING OUT FOR THAT JOB.
HEH HEH HEH
STOP PUTTING ON AIRS, YOU BUM! EVEN IF YOU GET DOWN AND BEG, YOU WON'T SELL A THING.
I HATE ONIONS.
がっしゃん
HEY! MY ONIONS.
YOU IDIOT! NOW I HAVE TO PUSH THESE ON THE GROCER!
HIJIRI.
CURFEW IS FIVE O'CLOCK! IF YOU'RE EVEN ONE MINUTE LATE, NO DINNER FOR YOU.
THAT YOUNG MAN FROM APARTMENT 21...ALWAYS SO PROTECTIVE.

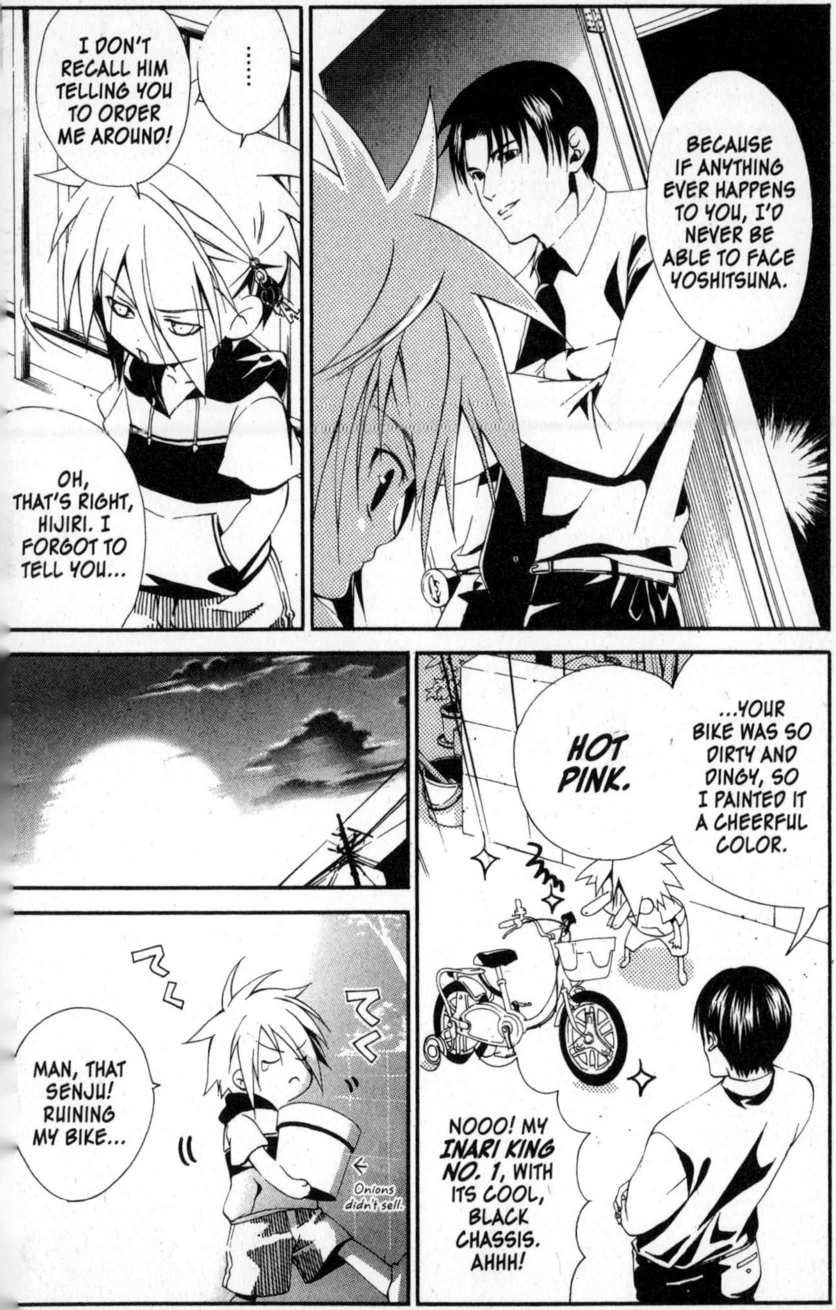
BECAUSE IF ANYTHING EVER HAPPENS TO YOU, I'D NEVER BE ABLE TO FACE YOSHITSUNA.
......
I DON'T RECALL HIM TELLING YOU TO ORDER ME AROUND!
OH, THAT'S RIGHT, HIJIRI. I FORGOT TO TELL YOU...
...YOUR BIKE WAS SO DIRTY AND DINGY, SO I PAINTED IT A CHEERFUL COLOR.
HOT PINK.
NOOO! MY INARI KING NO. 1, WITH ITS COOL, BLACK CHASSIS. AHHH!
MAN, THAT SENJU! RUINING MY BIKE...
Onions didn't sell.

*Inari is a type of sushi. It's rice stuffed into a pocket of sweet, fried tofu.

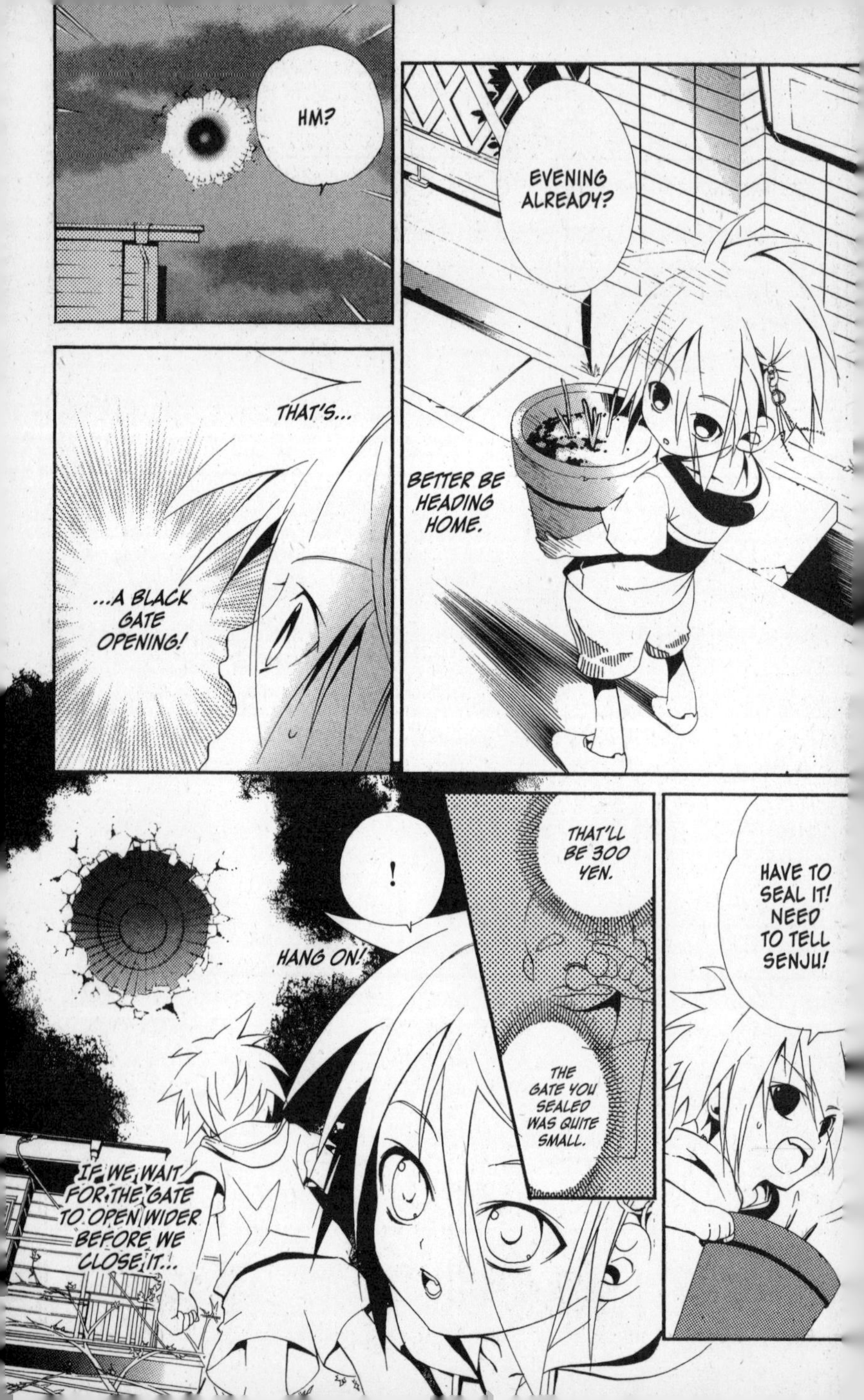
EVENING ALREADY?
BETTER BE HEADING HOME.
HM?
THAT'S...
...A BLACK GATE OPENING!
HAVE TO SEAL IT! NEED TO TELL SENJU!
THAT'LL BE 300 YEN.
THE GATE YOU SEALED WAS QUITE SMALL.
!
HANG ON!
IF WE WAIT FOR THE GATE TO OPEN WIDER BEFORE WE CLOSE IT...

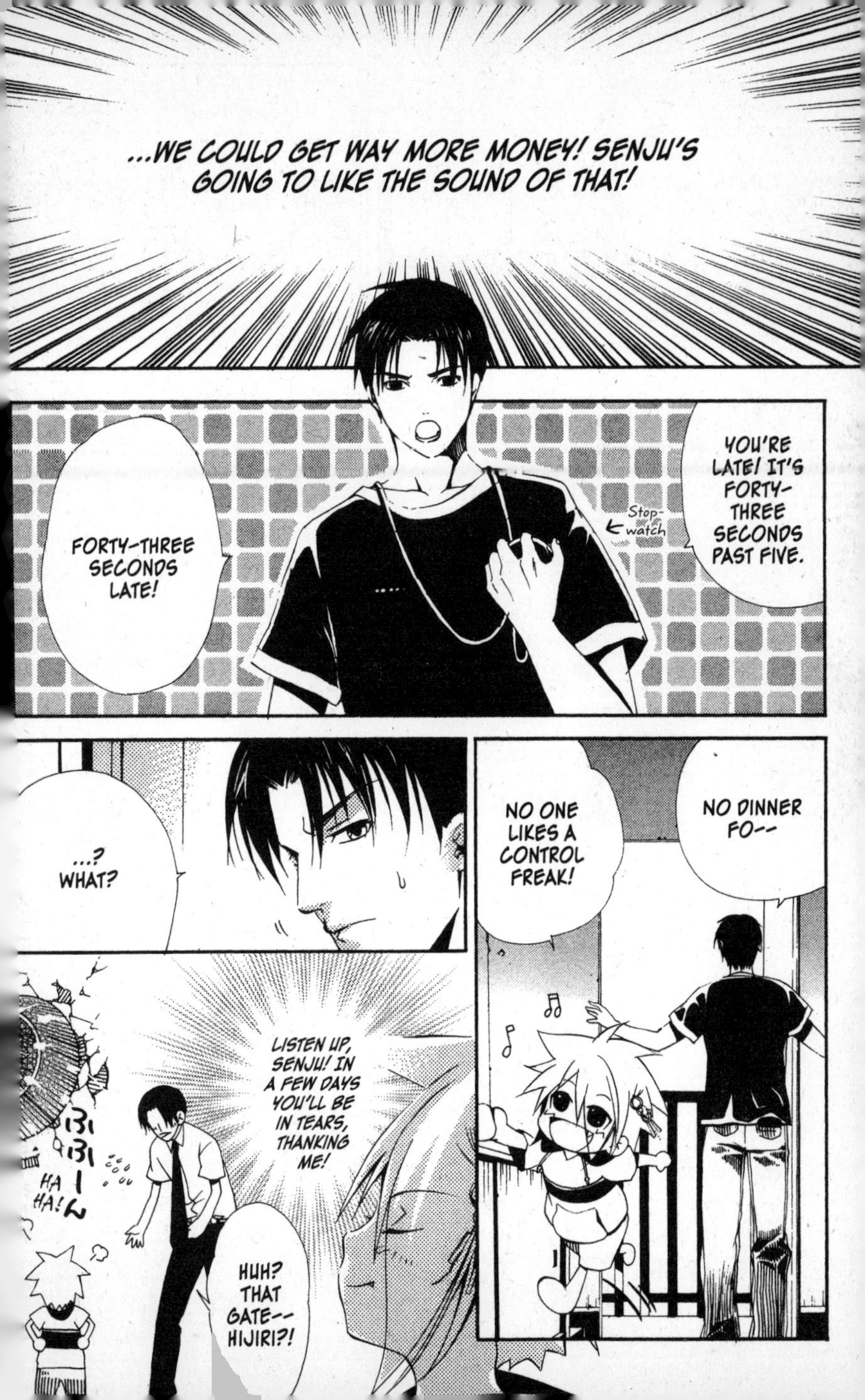
...WE COULD GET WAY MORE MONEY! SENJU'S GOING TO LIKE THE SOUND OF THAT!
YOU'RE LATE! IT'S FORTY-THREE SECONDS PAST FIVE.
Stop-watch
FORTY-THREE SECONDS LATE!
NO DINNER FO--
NO ONE LIKES A CONTROL FREAK!
...? WHAT?
LISTEN UP, SENJU! IN A FEW DAYS YOU'LL BE IN TEARS, THANKING ME!
HUH? THAT GATE--HIJIRI?!
HA HA!

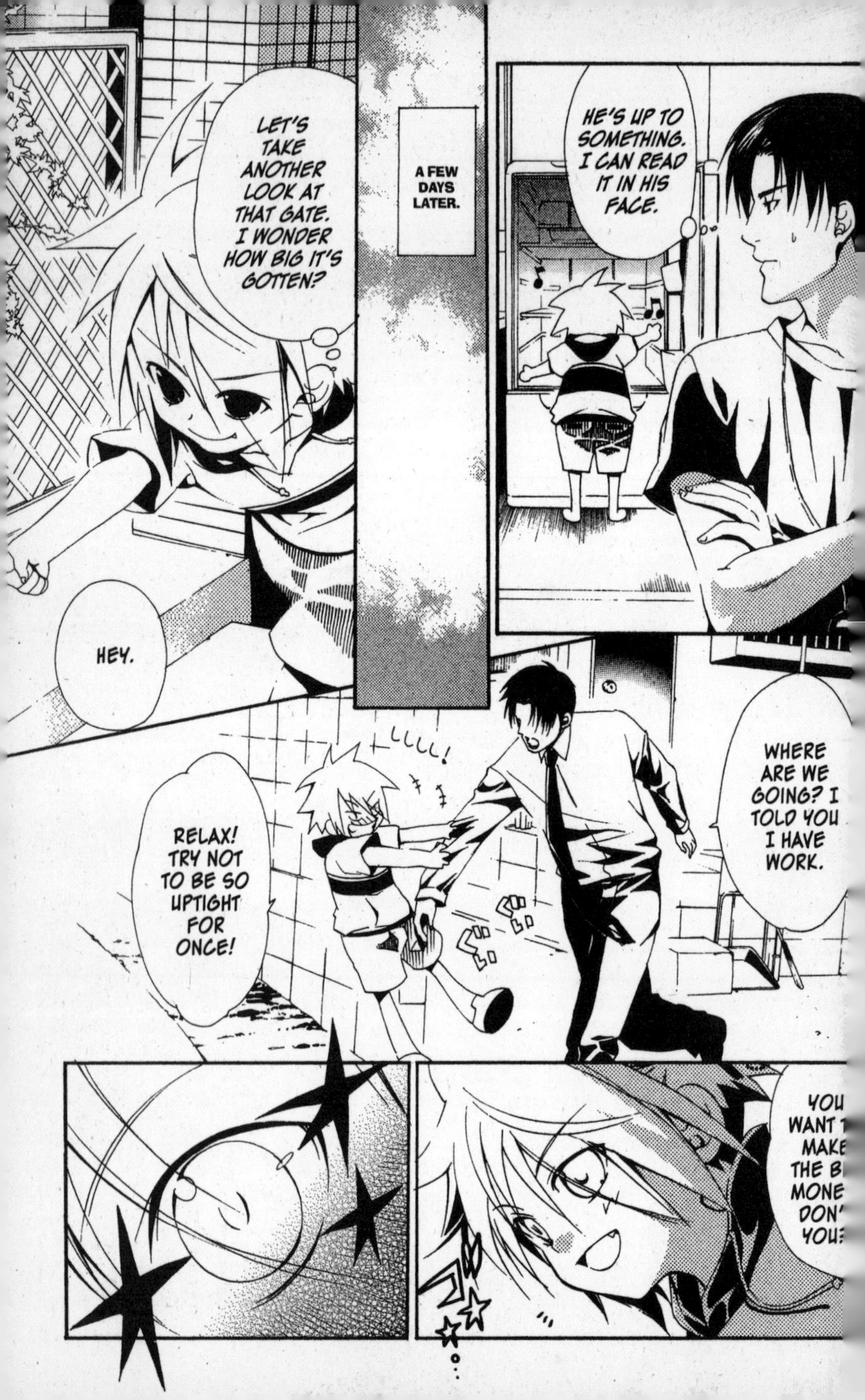
HE'S UP TO SOMETHING. I CAN READ IT IN HIS FACE.
A FEW DAYS LATER.
LET'S TAKE ANOTHER LOOK AT THAT GATE. I WONDER HOW BIG IT'S GOTTEN?
HEY.
WHERE ARE WE GOING? I TOLD YOU I HAVE WORK.
RELAX! TRY NOT TO BE SO UPTIGHT FOR ONCE!
YOU WANT T MAKE THE B MONE DON' YOU?

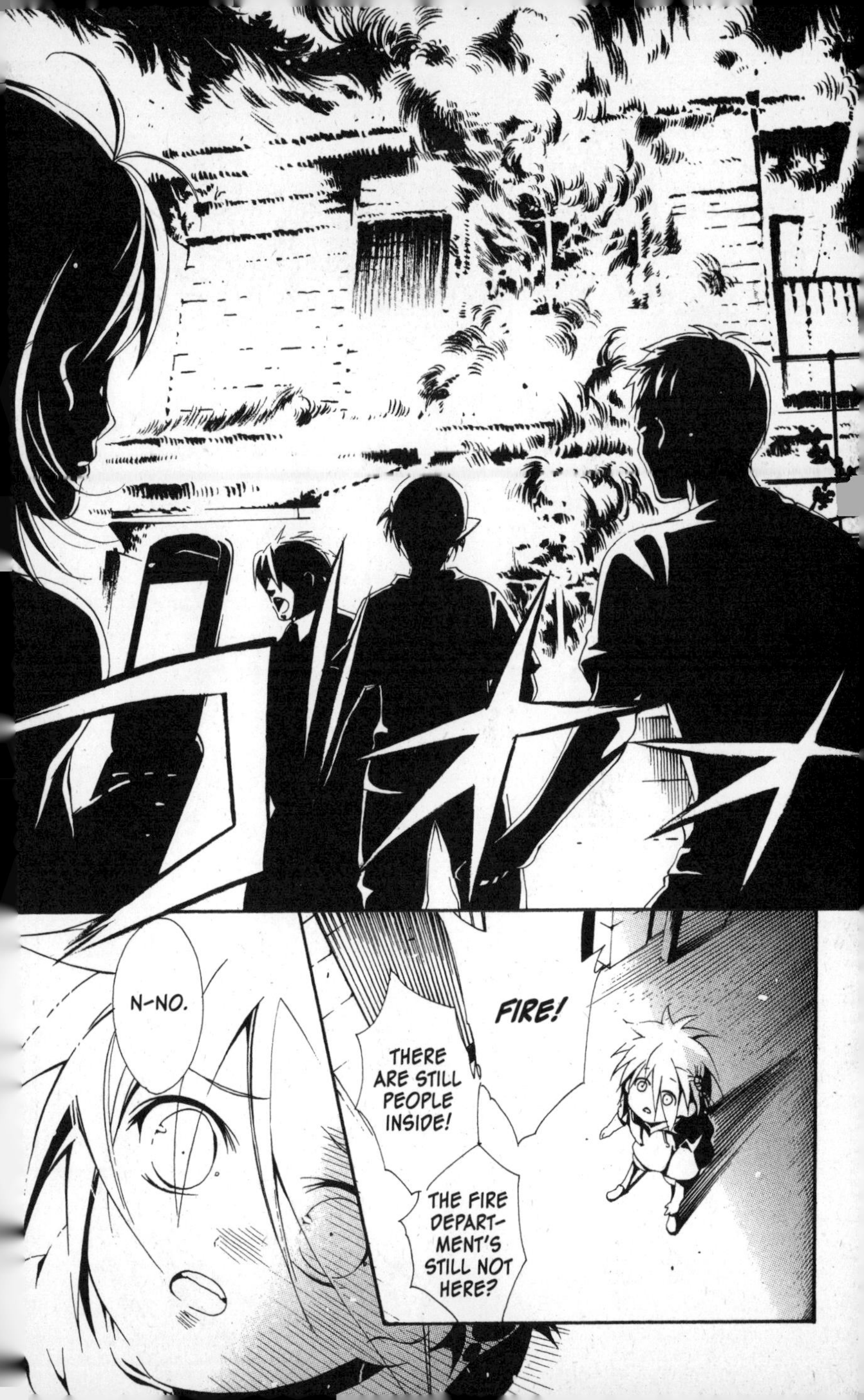
FIRE!
THERE ARE STILL PEOPLE INSIDE!
THE FIRE DEPARTMENT'S STILL NOT HERE?
N-NO.

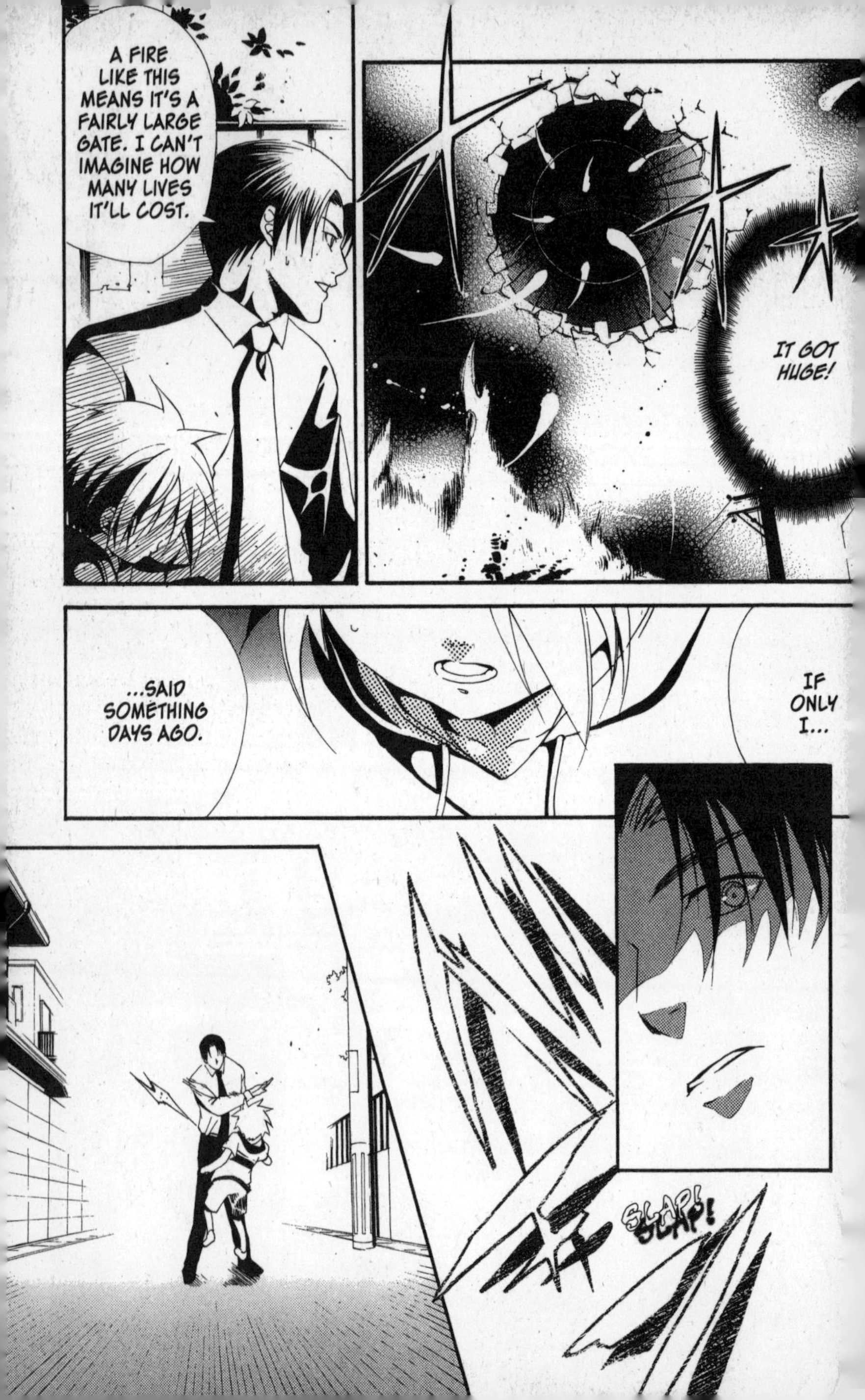
IT GOT HUGE!
A FIRE LIKE THIS MEANS IT'S A FAIRLY LARGE GATE. I CAN'T IMAGINE HOW MANY LIVES IT'LL COST.
IF ONLY I...
...SAID SOMETHING DAYS AGO.
SLAP! SLAP!

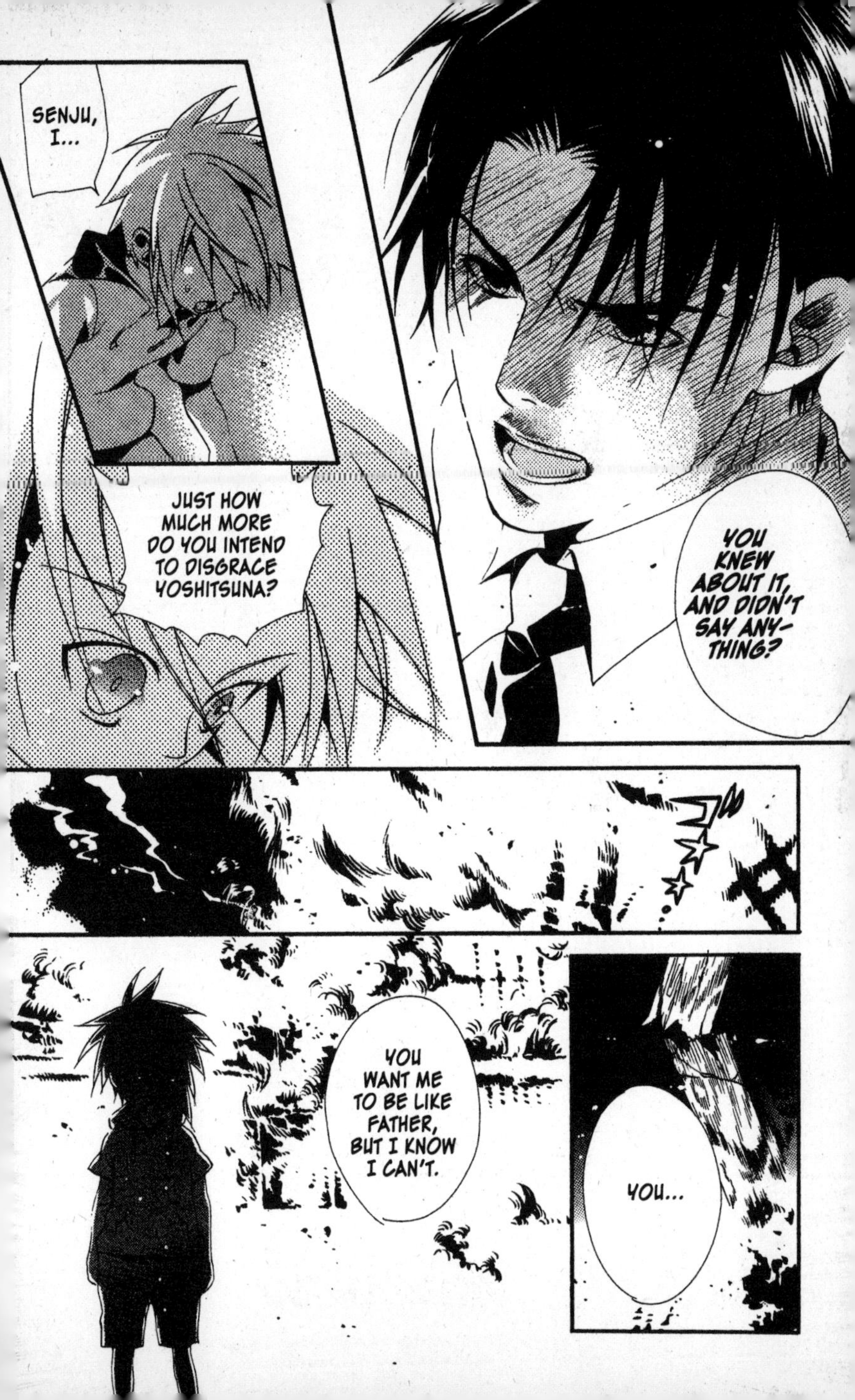
YOU KNEW ABOUT IT, AND DIDN'T SAY ANY-THING?
SENJU, I...
JUST HOW MUCH MORE DO YOU INTEND TO DISGRACE YOSHITSUNA?
YOU...
YOU WANT ME TO BE LIKE FATHER, BUT I KNOW I CAN'T.

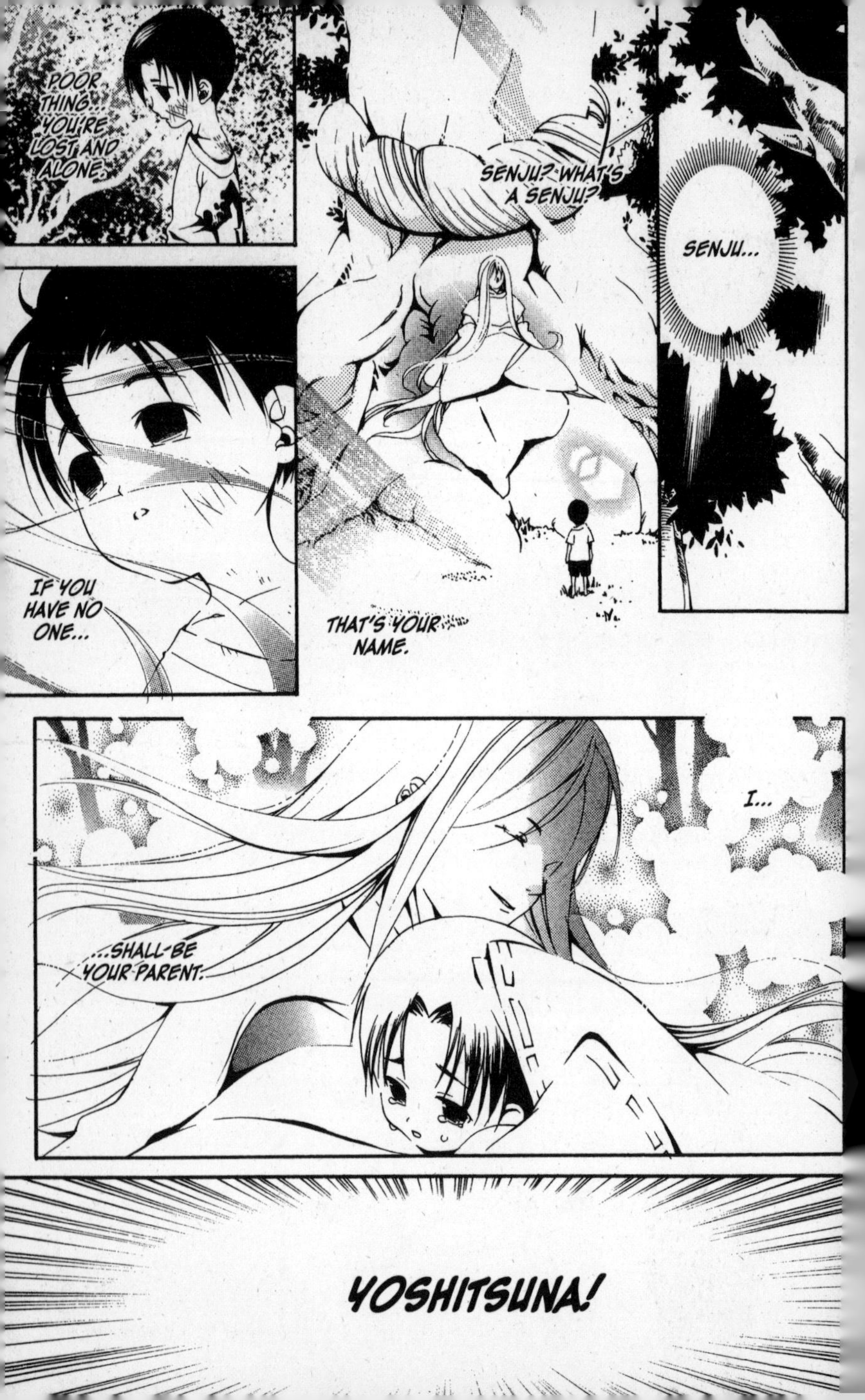
SENJU...
SENJU? WHAT'S A SENJU?
THAT'S YOUR NAME.
POOR THING... YOU'RE LOST AND ALONE.
IF YOU HAVE NO ONE...
I...
...SHALL BE YOUR PARENT.
YOSHITSUNA!

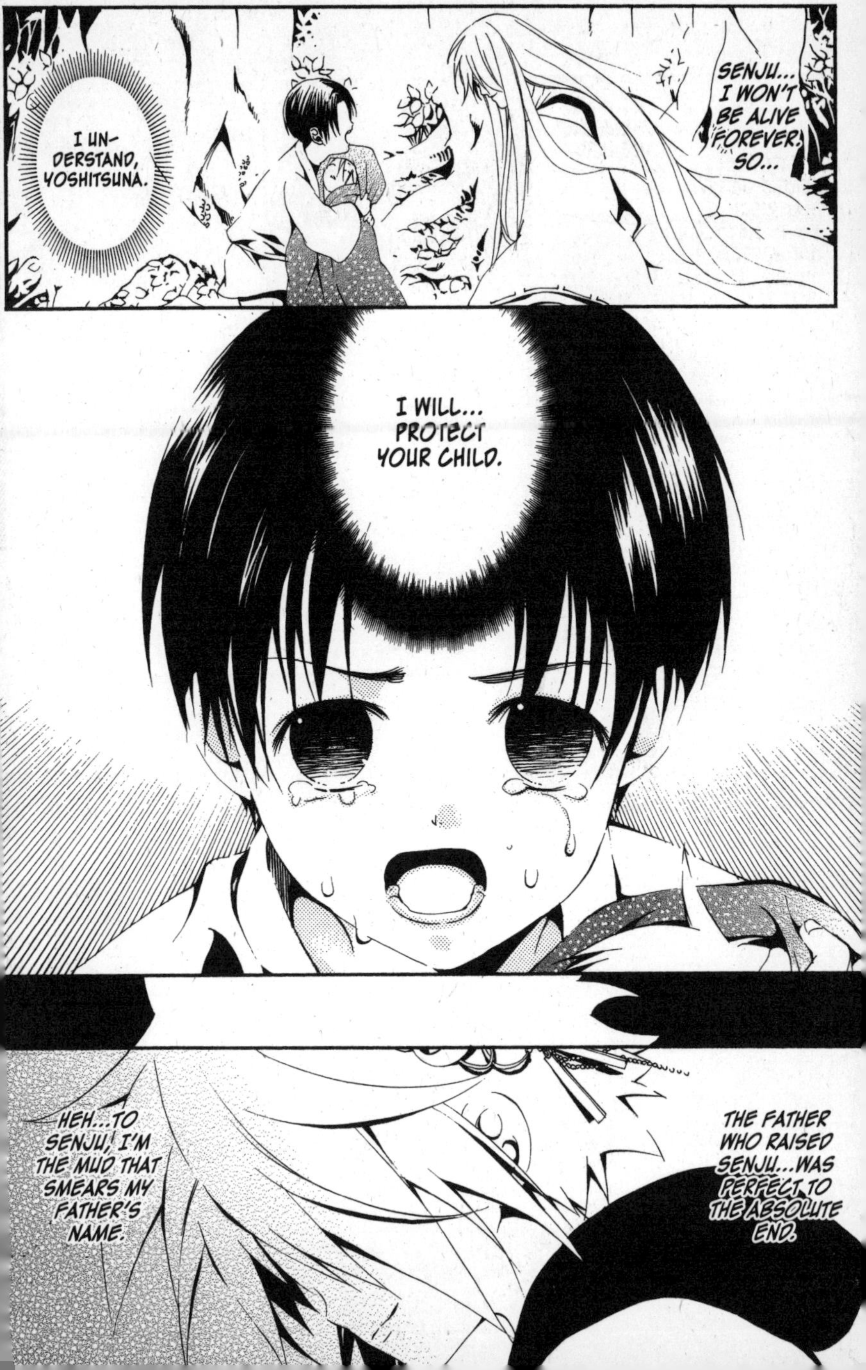
SENJU... I WON'T BE ALIVE FOREVER. SO...
I UN-DERSTAND, YOSHITSUNA.
I WILL... PROTECT YOUR CHILD.
THE FATHER WHO RAISED SENJU...WAS PERFECT TO THE ABSOLUTE END.
HEH...TO SENJU, I'M THE MUD THAT SMEARS MY FATHER'S NAME.

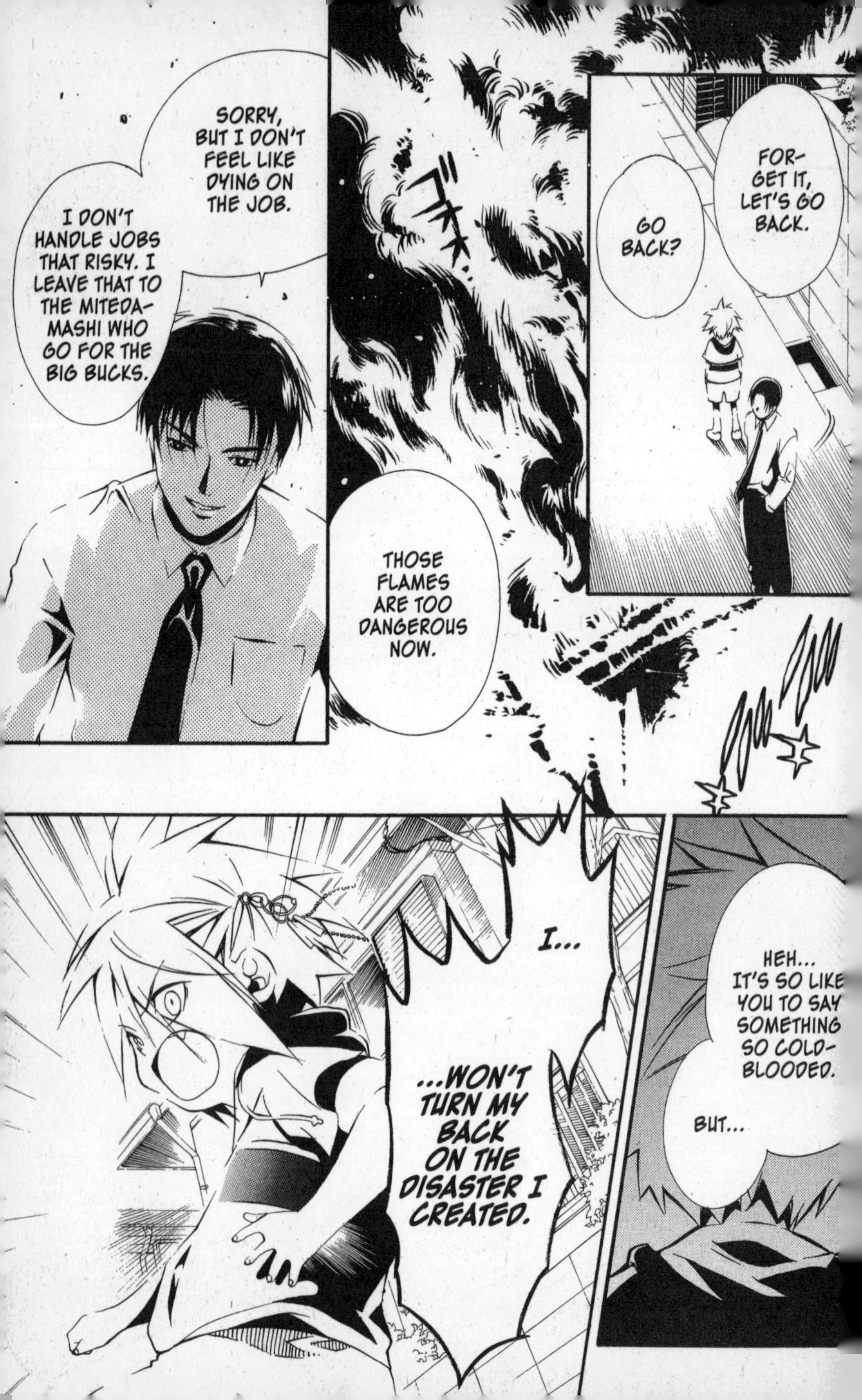
FOR-GET IT, LET'S GO BACK.
GO BACK?
THOSE FLAMES ARE TOO DANGEROUS NOW.
SORRY, BUT I DON'T FEEL LIKE DYING ON THE JOB.
I DON'T HANDLE JOBS THAT RISKY. I LEAVE THAT TO THE MITEDA-MASHI WHO GO FOR THE BIG BUCKS.
HEH... IT'S SO LIKE YOU TO SAY SOMETHING SO COLD-BLOODED.
BUT...
I...
...WON'T TURN MY BACK ON THE DISASTER I CREATED.

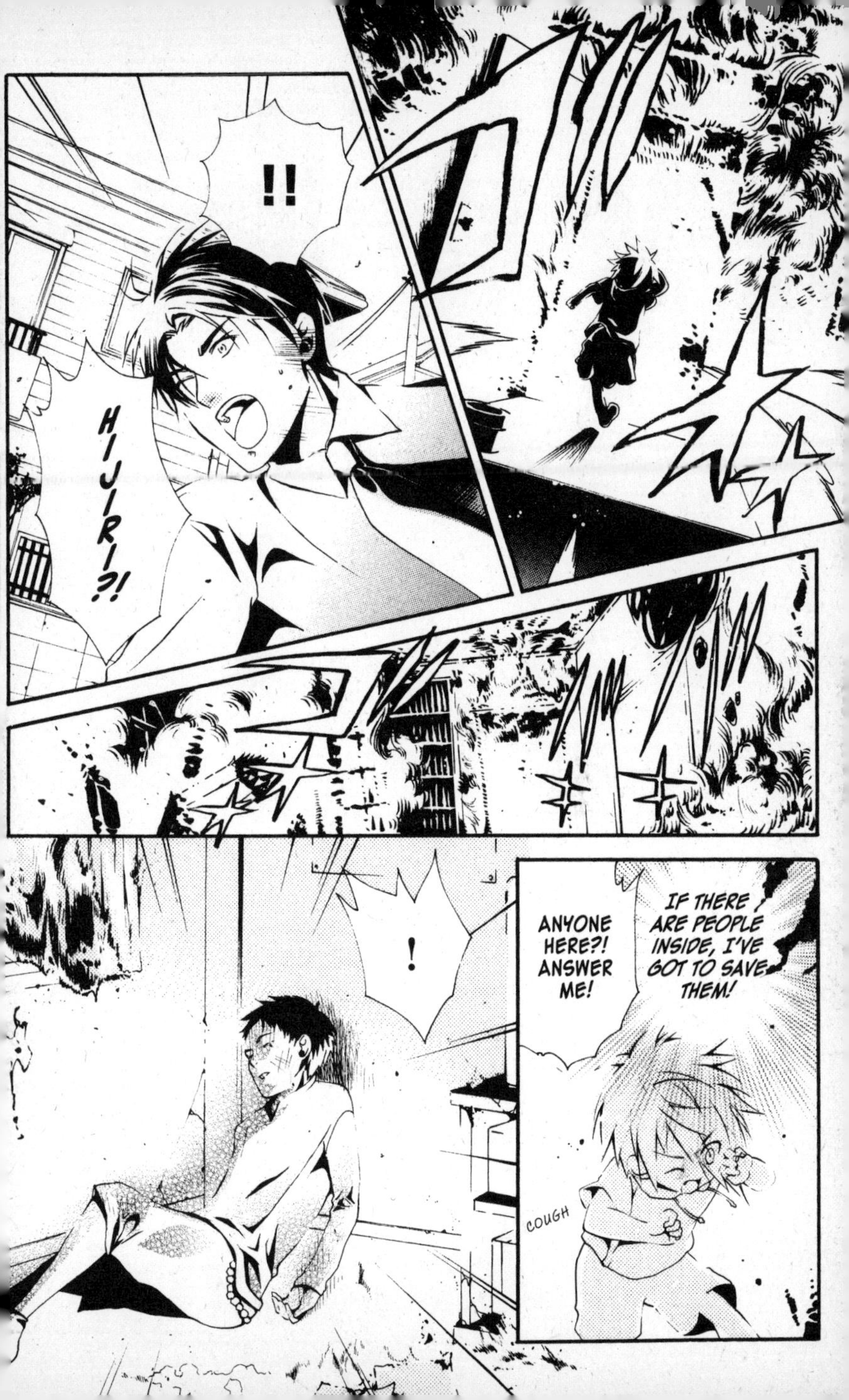
!!
HIJIRI?!
IF THERE ARE PEOPLE INSIDE, I'VE GOT TO SAVE THEM!
ANYONE HERE?! ANSWER ME!
COUGH
!

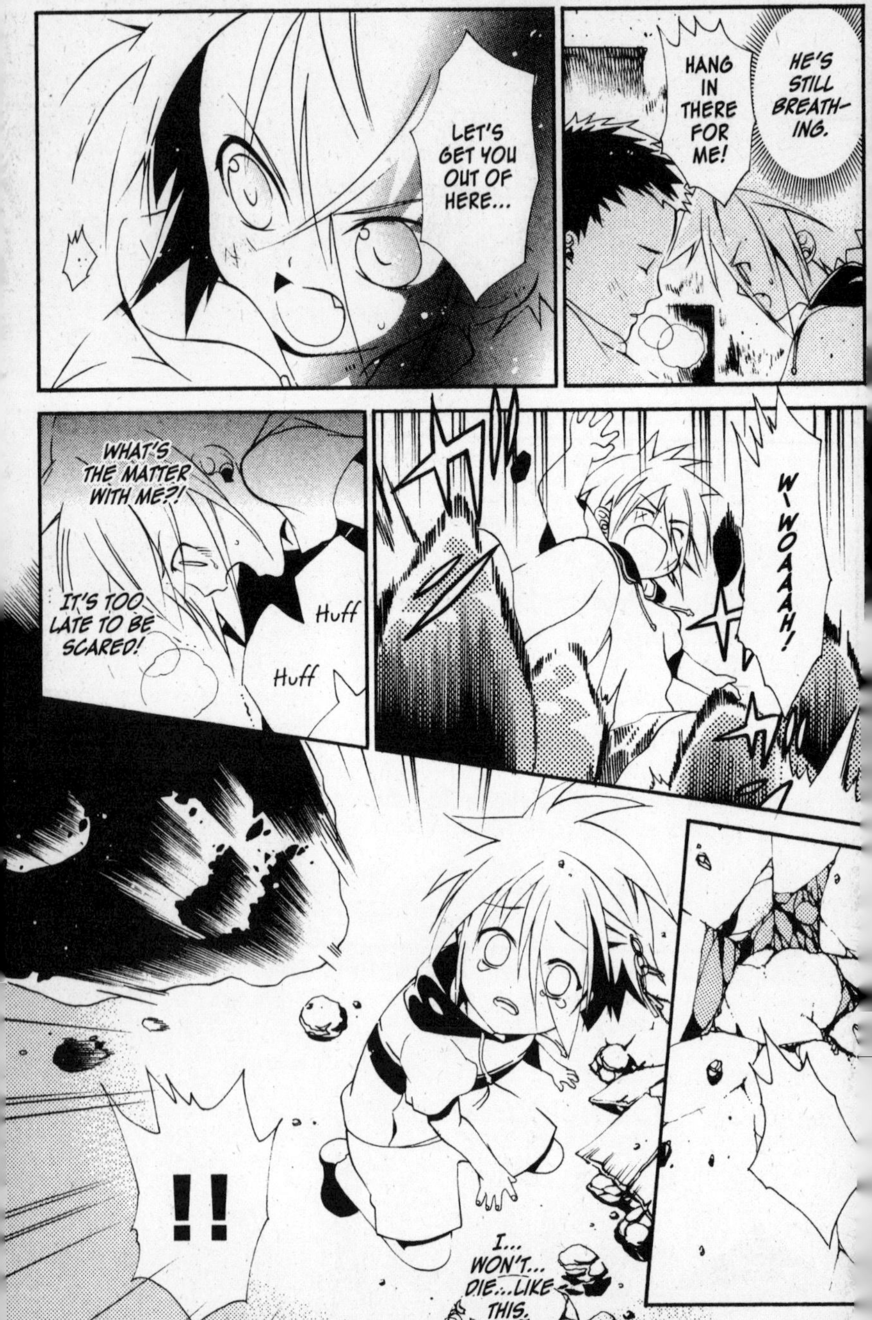
HE'S STILL BREATHING.
HANG IN THERE FOR ME!
LET'S GET YOU OUT OF HERE...
WI-WOAAAH!
WHAT'S THE MATTER WITH ME?!
IT'S TOO LATE TO BE SCARED!
Huff
Huff
I... WON'T... DIE...LIKE THIS.
!!

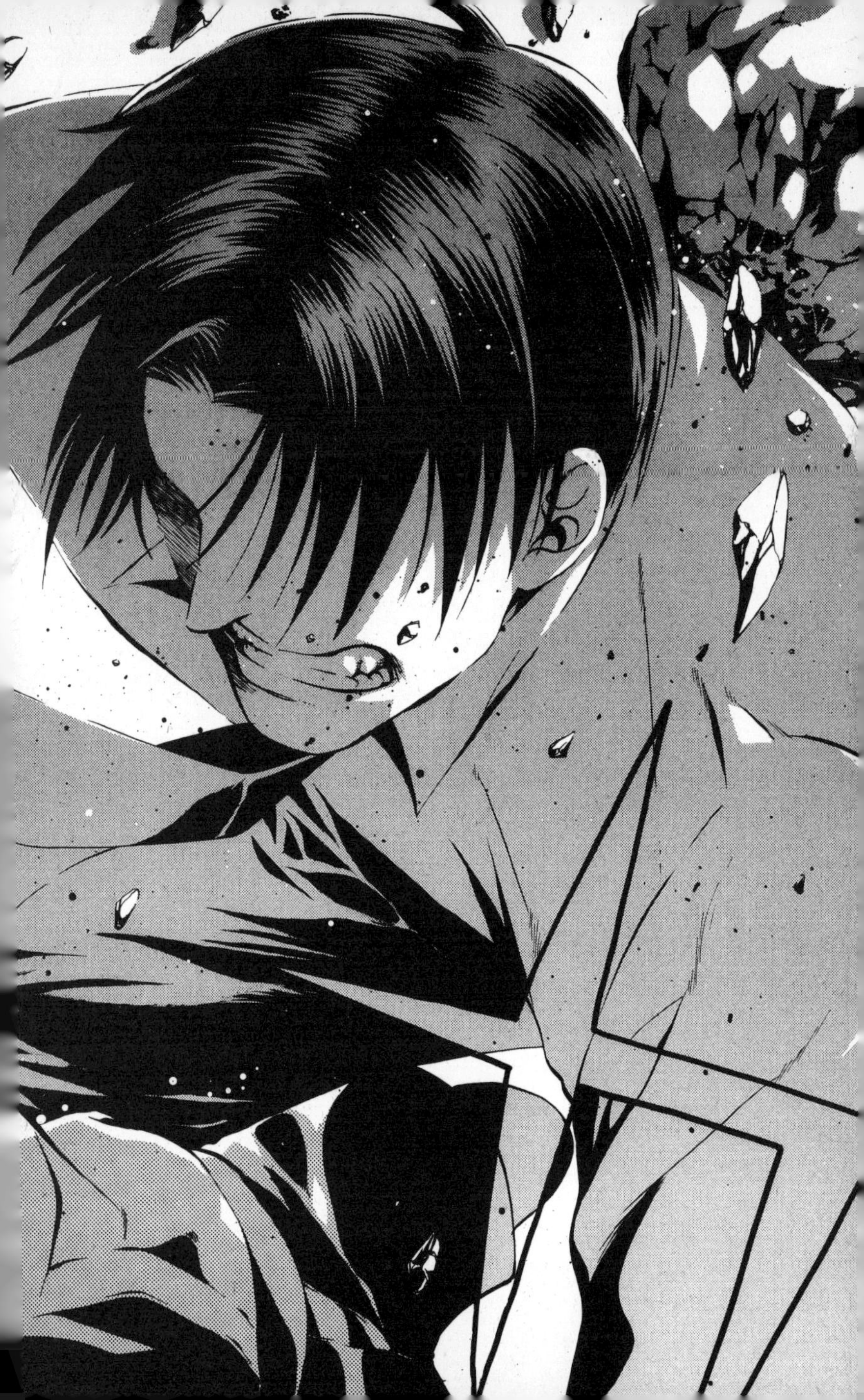

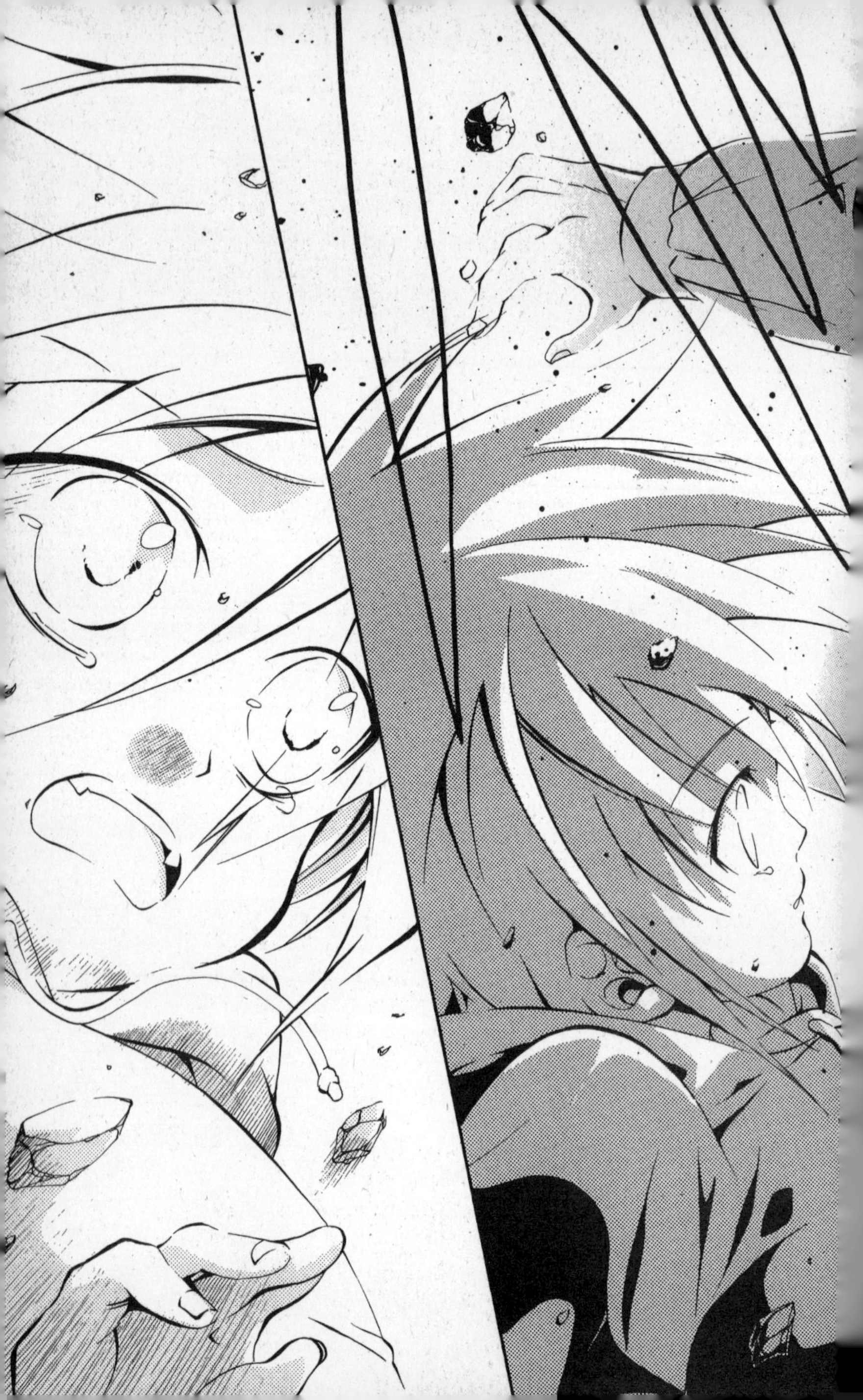

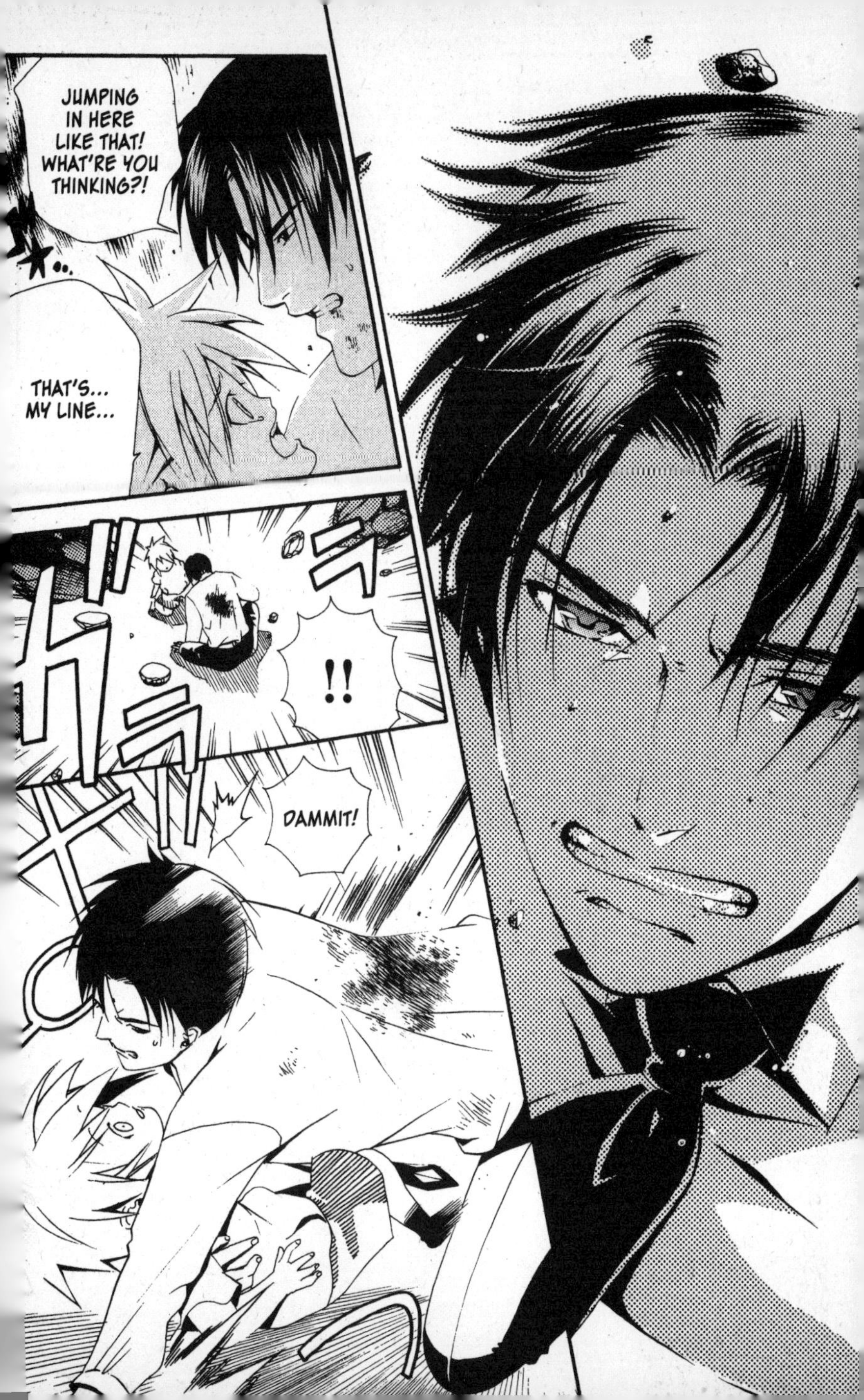
JUMPING IN HERE LIKE THAT! WHAT'RE YOU THINKING?!
THAT'S... MY LINE...
!!
DAMMIT!

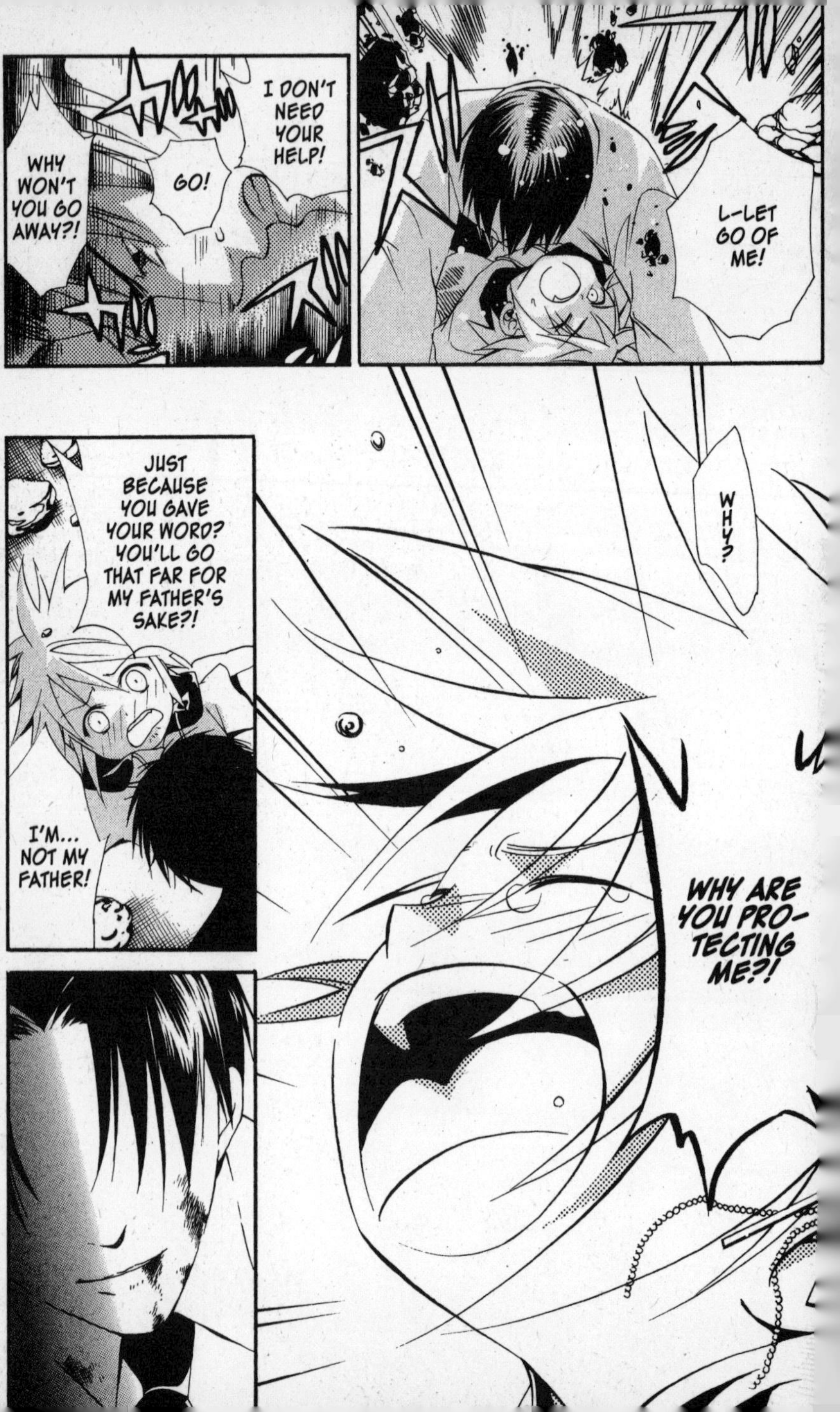
L-LET GO OF ME!
I DON'T NEED YOUR HELP!
GO!
WHY WON'T YOU GO AWAY?!
WHY?
WHY ARE YOU PRO-TECTING ME?!
JUST BECAUSE YOU GAVE YOUR WORD? YOU'LL GO THAT FAR FOR MY FATHER'S SAKE?!
I'M... NOT MY FATHER!

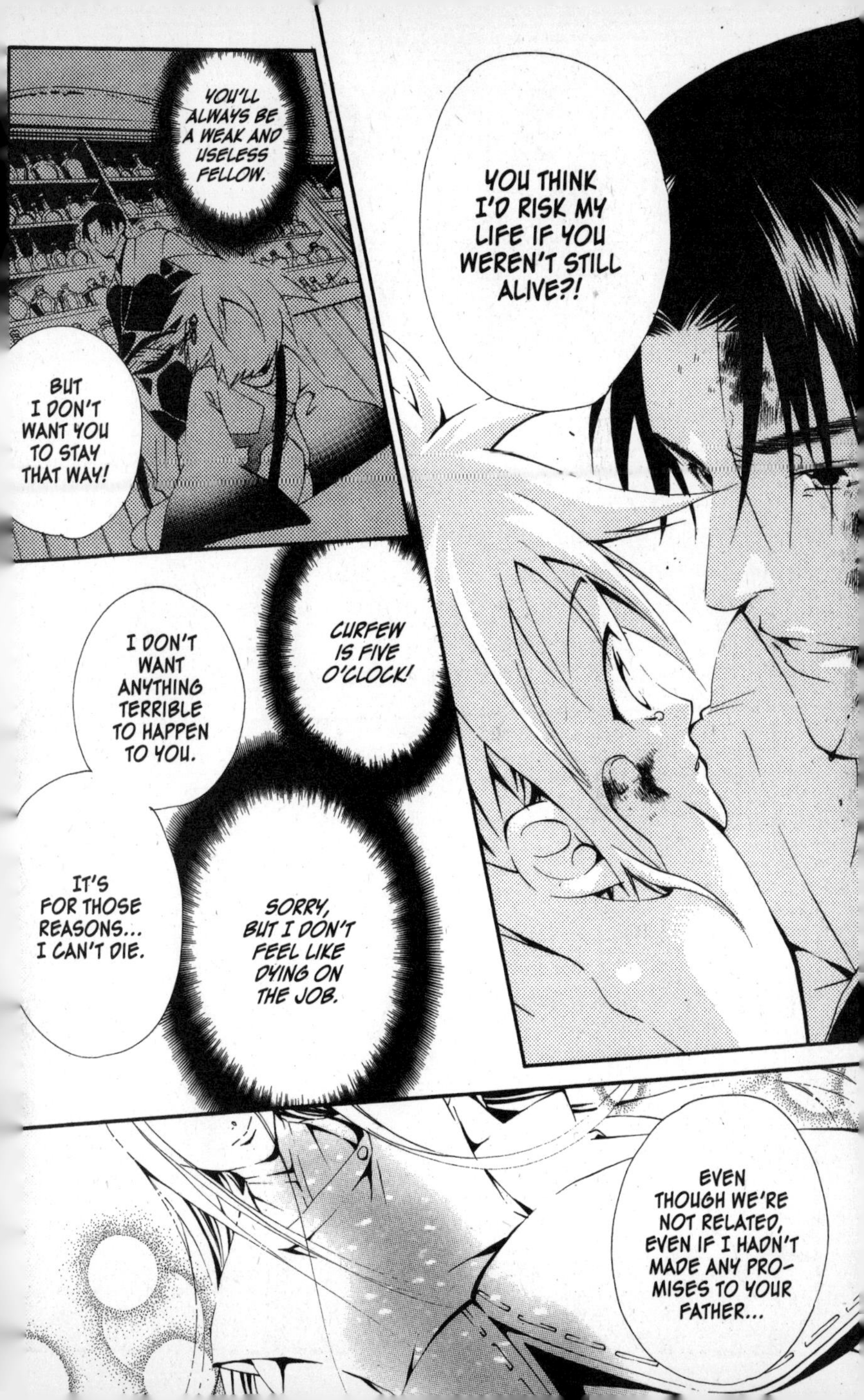

YOU THINK I'D RISK MY LIFE IF YOU WEREN'T STILL ALIVE?!
YOU'LL ALWAYS BE A WEAK AND USELESS FELLOW.
BUT I DON'T WANT YOU TO STAY THAT WAY!
CURFEW IS FIVE O'CLOCK!
I DON'T WANT ANYTHING TERRIBLE TO HAPPEN TO YOU.
SORRY, BUT I DON'T FEEL LIKE DYING ON THE JOB.
IT'S FOR THOSE REASONS... I CAN'T DIE.
EVEN THOUGH WE'RE NOT RELATED, EVEN IF I HADN'T MADE ANY PRO-MISES TO YOUR FATHER...

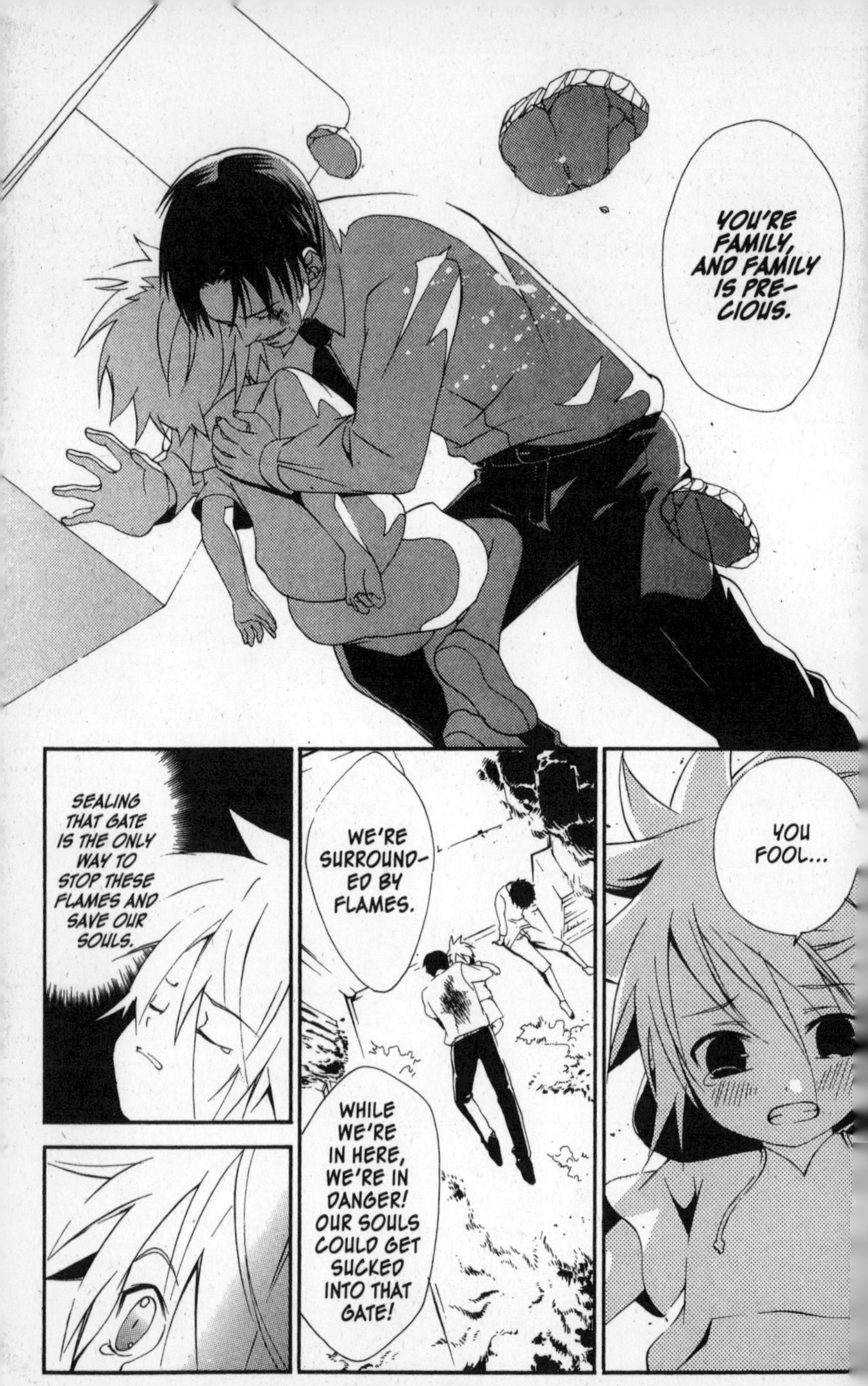
YOU'RE FAMILY, AND FAMILY IS PRE- CIOUS.
YOU FOOL...
WE'RE SURROUND- ED BY FLAMES.
WHILE WE'RE IN HERE, WE'RE IN DANGER! OUR SOULS COULD GET SUCKED INTO THAT GATE!
SEALING THAT GATE IS THE ONLY WAY TO STOP THESE FLAMES AND SAVE OUR SOULS.

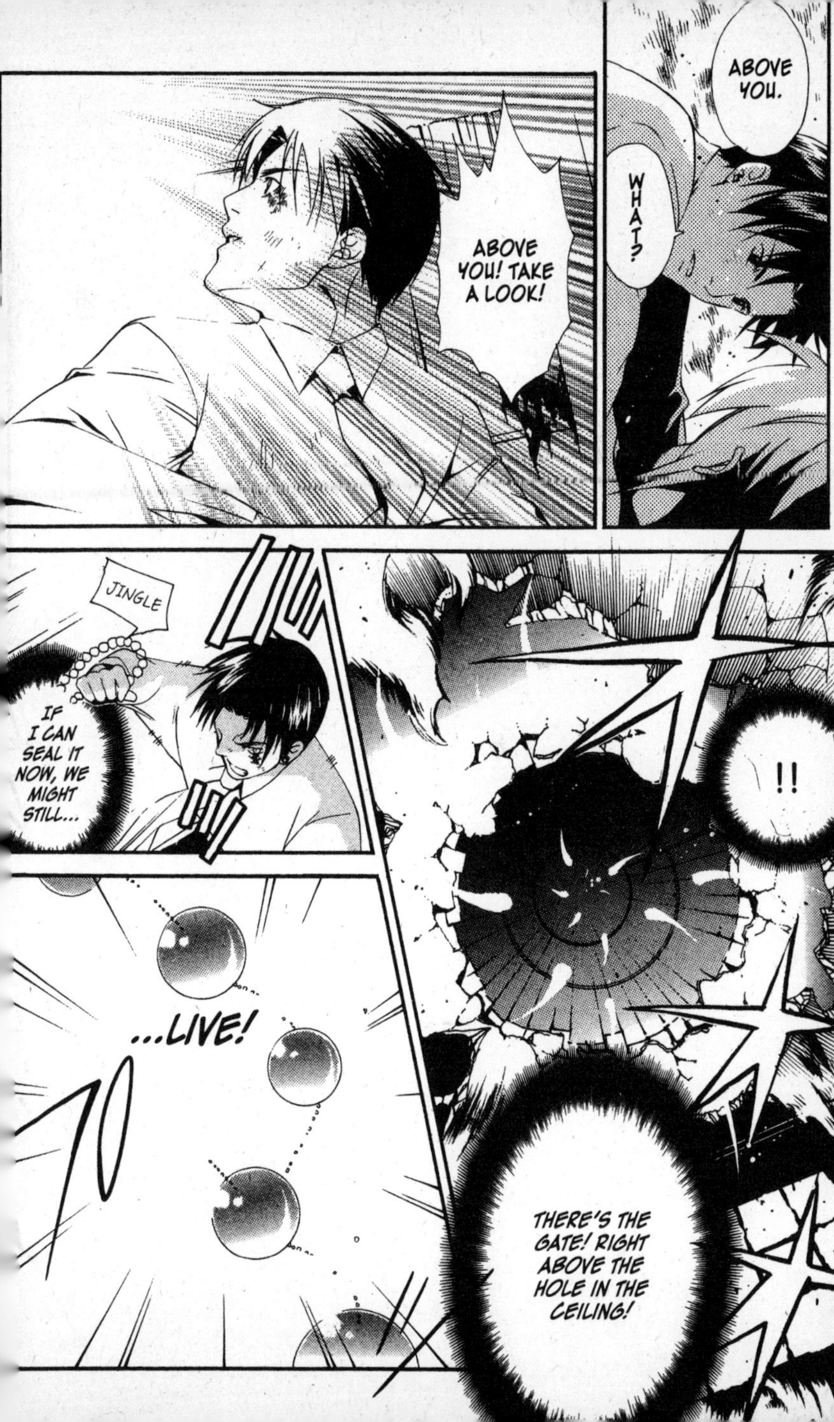
ABOVE YOU.
WHAT?
ABOVE YOU! TAKE A LOOK!
!!
THERE'S THE GATE! RIGHT ABOVE THE HOLE IN THE CEILING!
JINGLE
IF I CAN SEAL IT NOW, WE MIGHT STILL...
...LIVE!

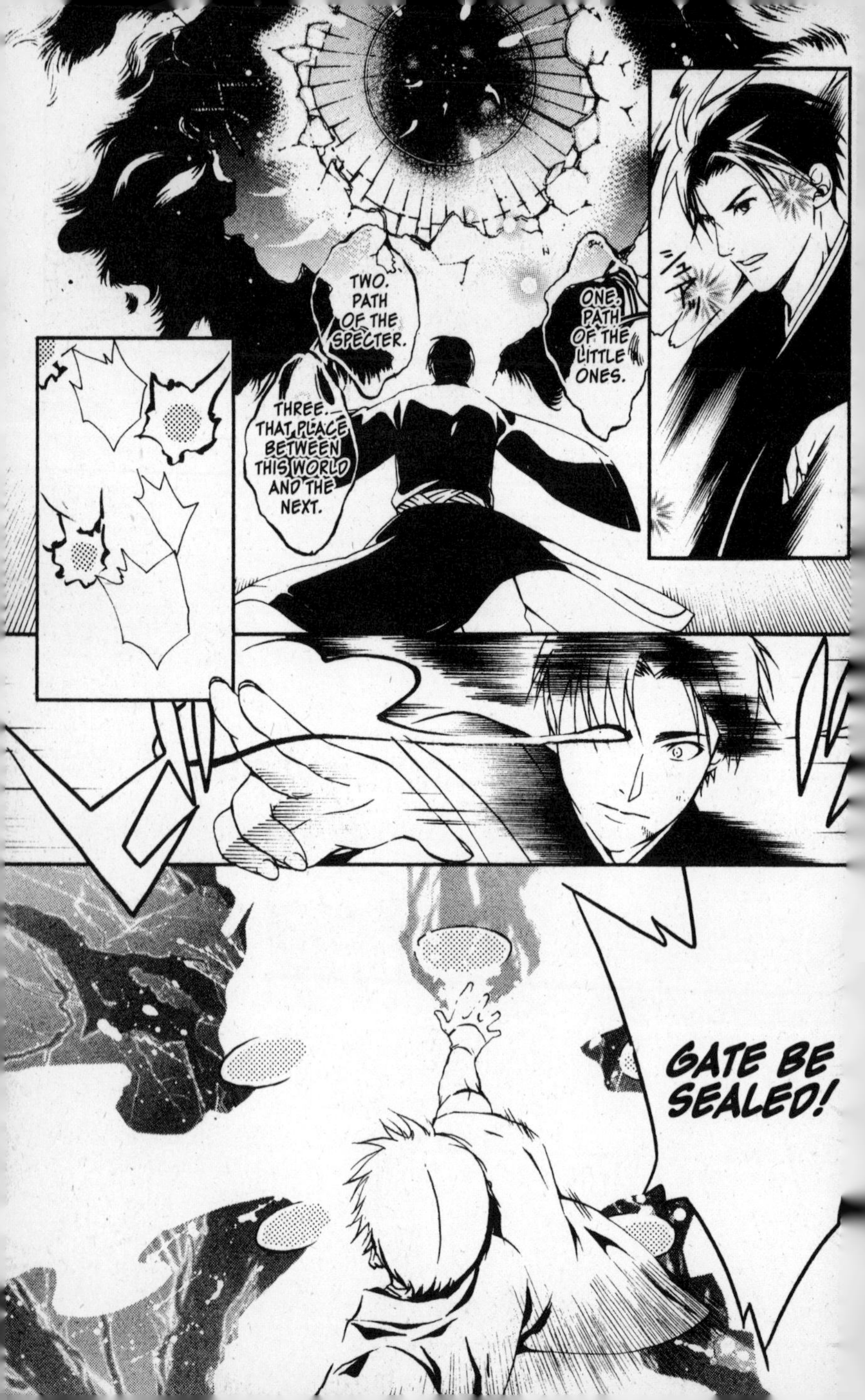
ONE. PATH OF THE LITTLE ONES.
TWO. PATH OF THE SPECTER.
THREE. THAT PLACE BETWEEN THIS WORLD AND THE NEXT.
GATE BE SEALED!

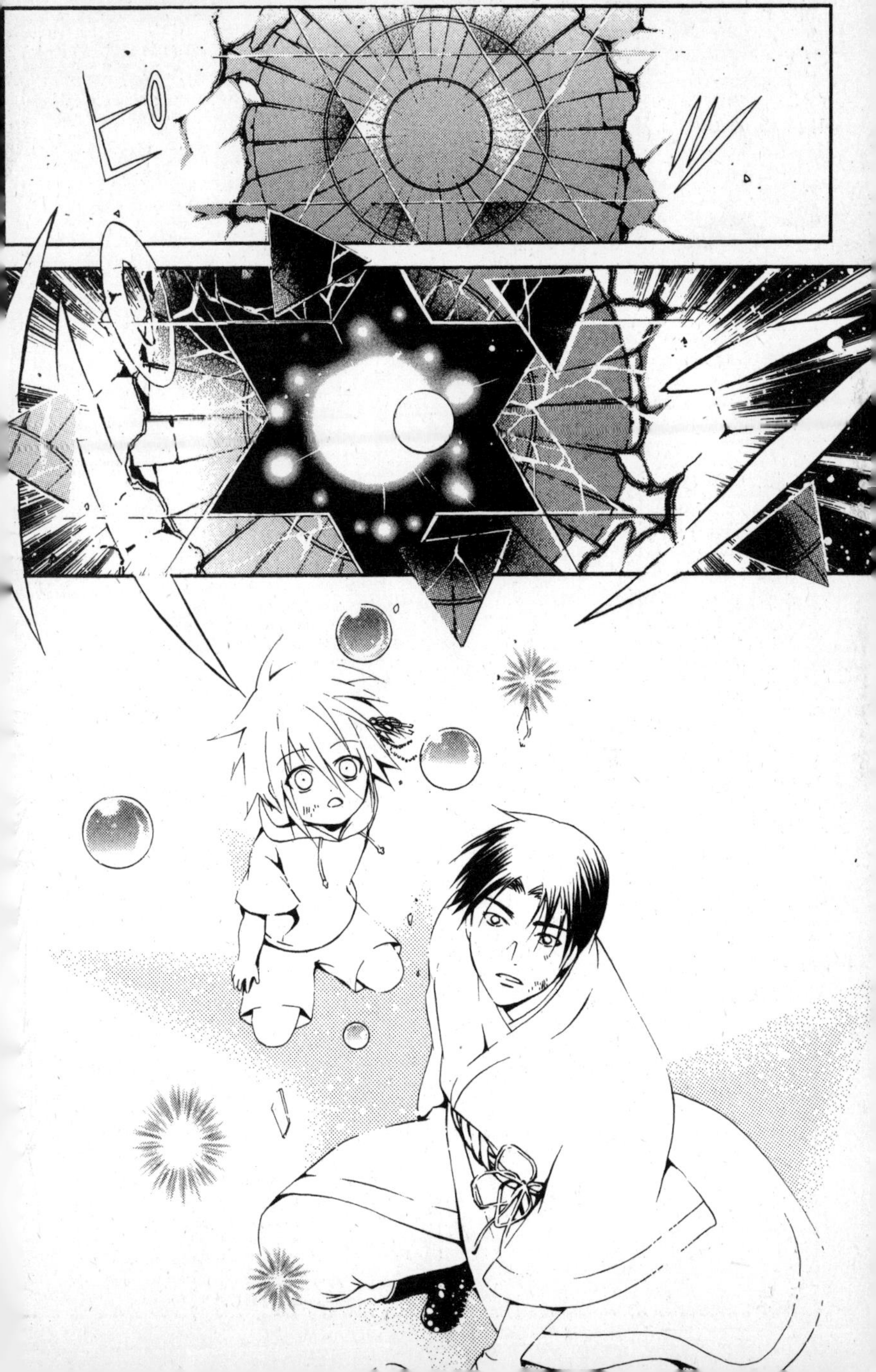

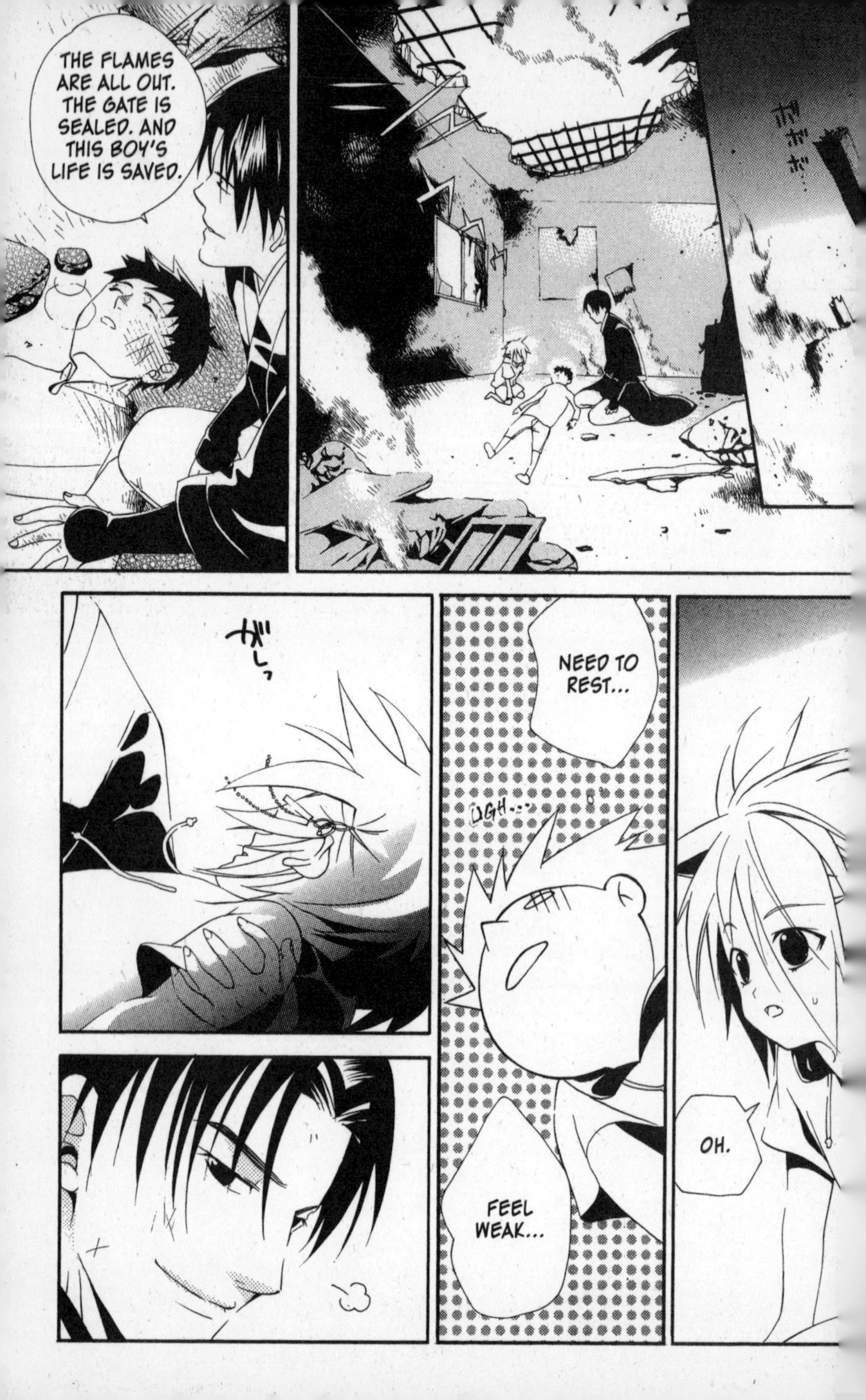
THE FLAMES ARE ALL OUT. THE GATE IS SEALED. AND THIS BOY'S LIFE IS SAVED.
OH.
NEED TO REST...
UGH...
FEEL WEAK...

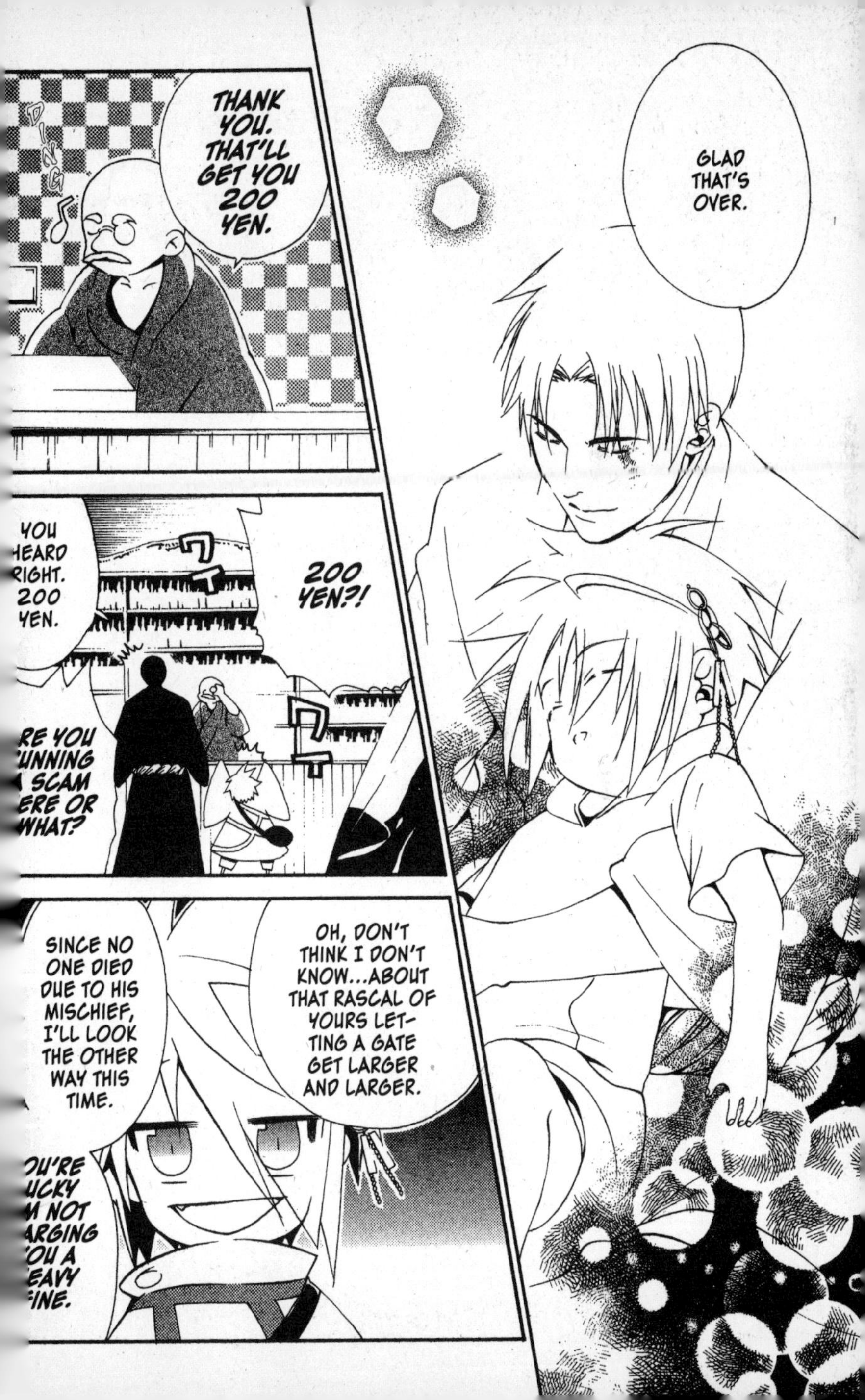
GLAD THAT'S OVER.
DING
THANK YOU. THAT'LL GET YOU 200 YEN.
200 YEN?!
YOU HEARD RIGHT. 200 YEN.
RE YOU UNNING A SCAM ERE OR WHAT?
OH, DON'T THINK I DON'T KNOW...ABOUT THAT RASCAL OF YOURS LETTING A GATE GET LARGER AND LARGER.
SINCE NO ONE DIED DUE TO HIS MISCHIEF, I'LL LOOK THE OTHER WAY THIS TIME.
OU'RE UCKY M NOT ARGING OU A EAVY FINE.

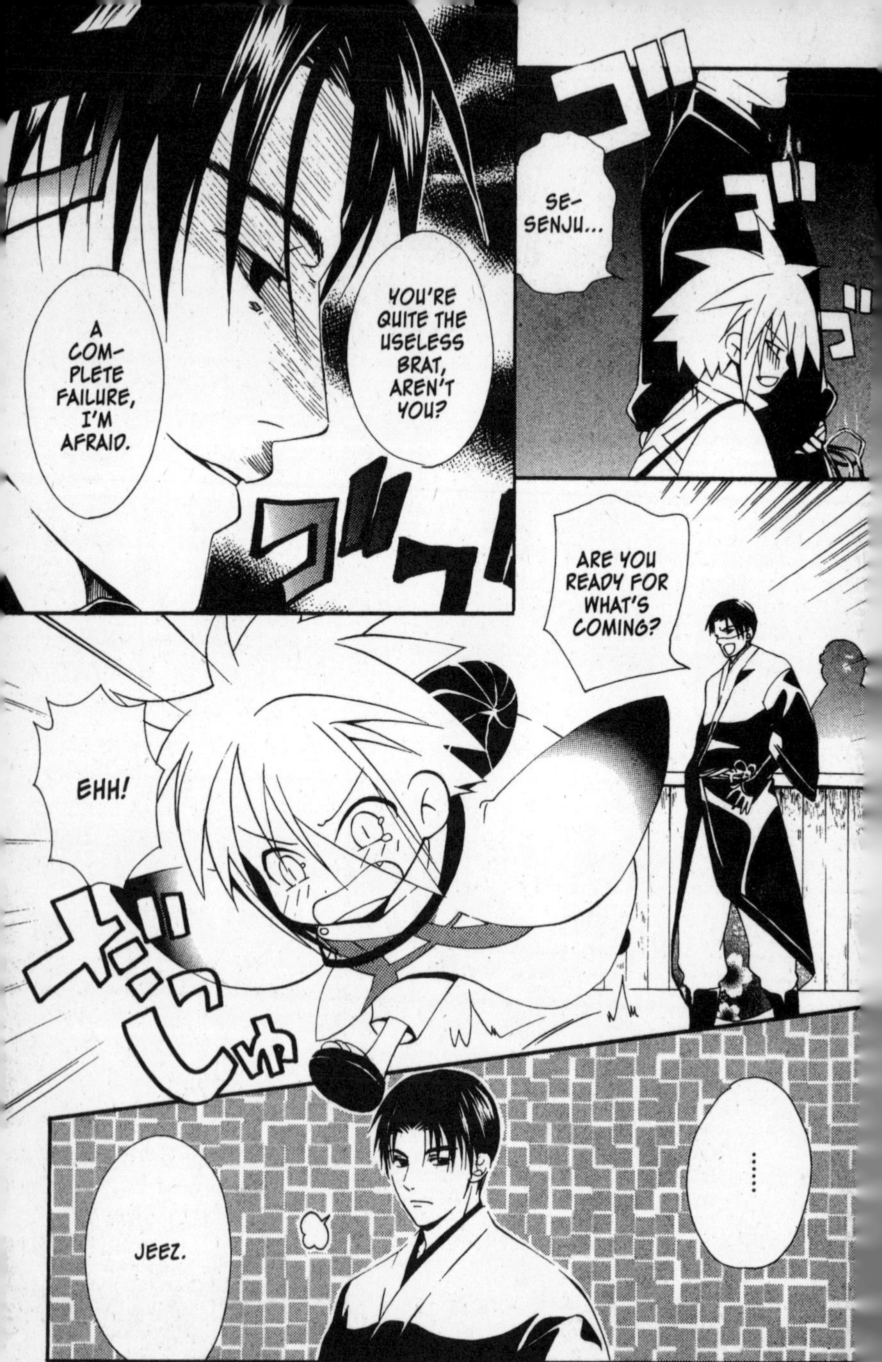
SE-SENJU...
YOU'RE QUITE THE USELESS BRAT, AREN'T YOU?
A COMPLETE FAILURE, I'M AFRAID.
ARE YOU READY FOR WHAT'S COMING?
EHH!
......
JEEZ.

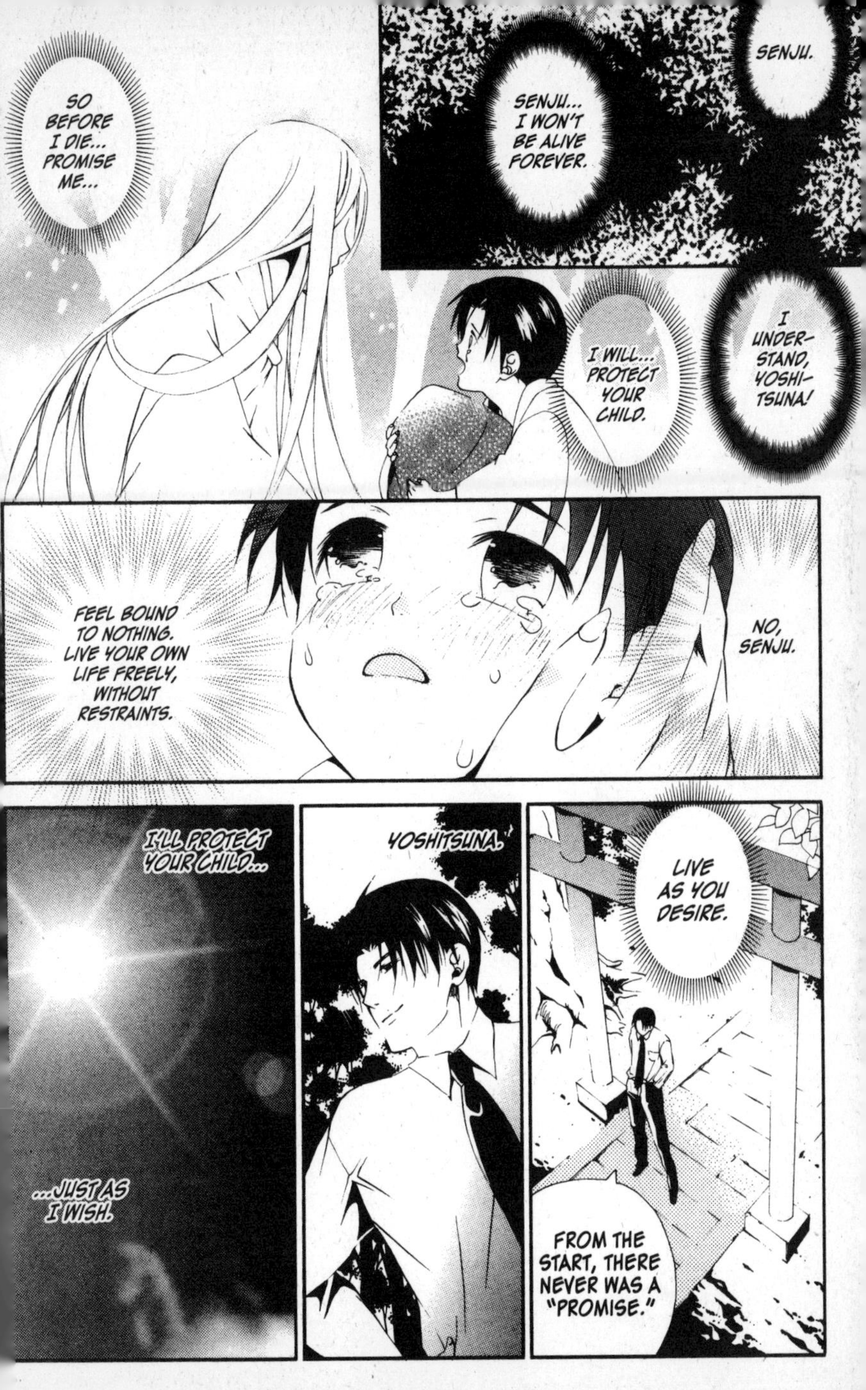
SENJU.
SENJU... I WON'T BE ALIVE FOREVER.
SO BEFORE I DIE... PROMISE ME...
I UNDER-STAND, YOSHI-TSUNA!
I WILL... PROTECT YOUR CHILD.
NO, SENJU.
FEEL BOUND TO NOTHING. LIVE YOUR OWN LIFE FREELY, WITHOUT RESTRAINTS.
LIVE AS YOU DESIRE.
FROM THE START, THERE NEVER WAS A "PROMISE."
YOSHITSUNA.
I'LL PROTECT YOUR CHILD...
...JUST AS I WISH.

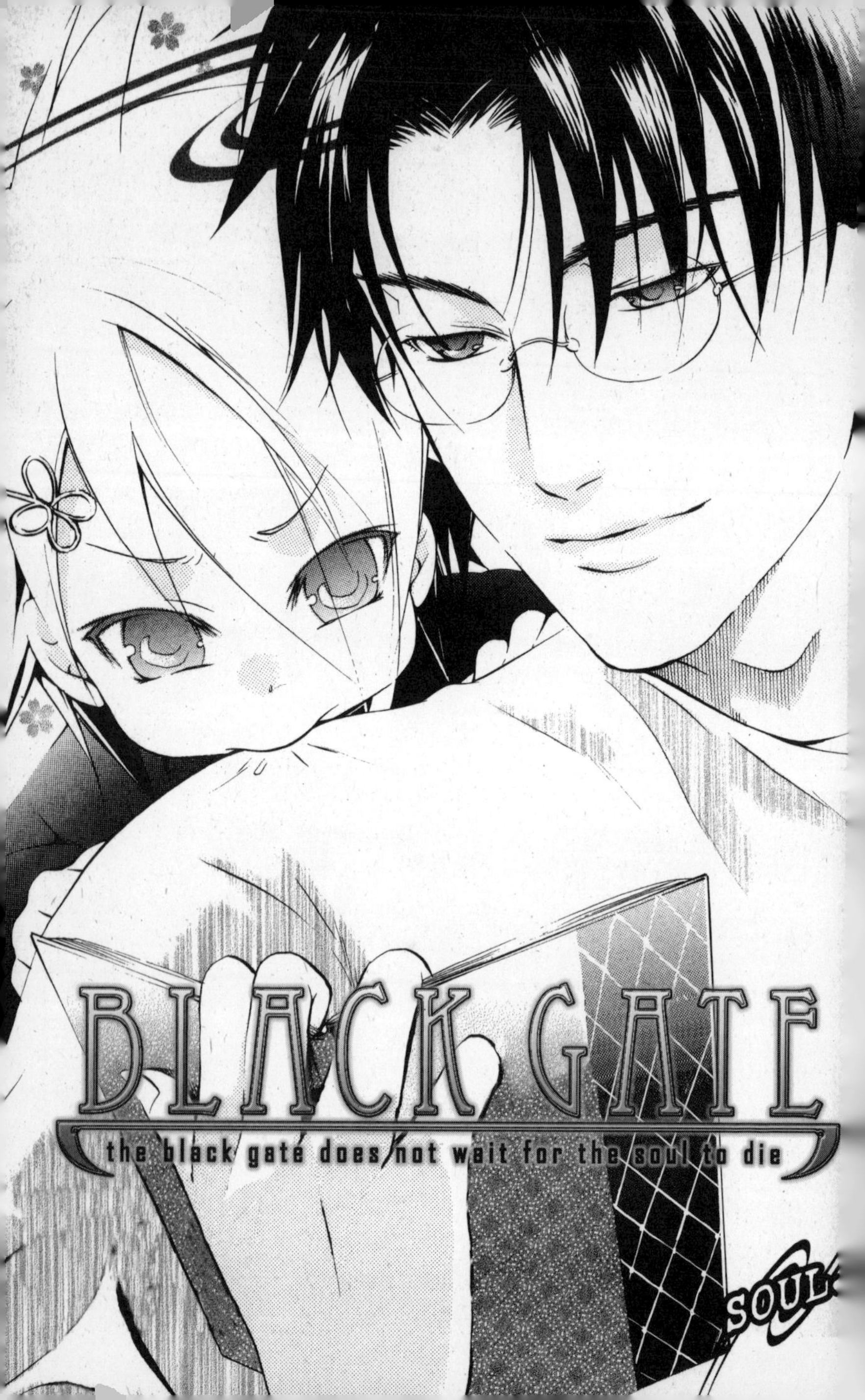
BLACK GATE
the black gate does not wait for the soul to die
SOUL

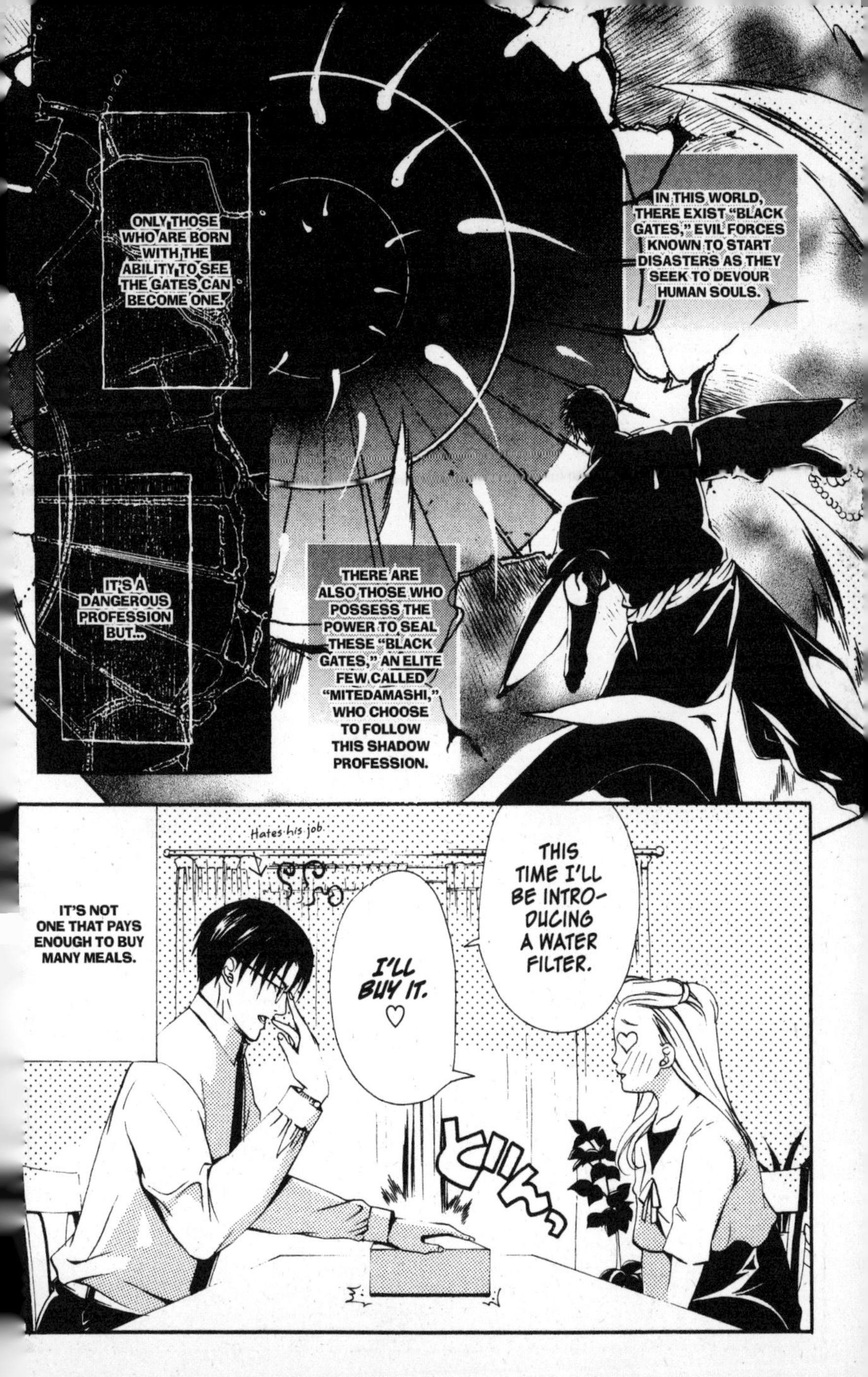
IN THIS WORLD, THERE EXIST "BLACK GATES," EVIL FORCES KNOWN TO START DISASTERS AS THEY SEEK TO DEVOUR HUMAN SOULS.
ONLY THOSE WHO ARE BORN WITH THE ABILITY TO SEE THE GATES CAN BECOME ONE.
THERE ARE ALSO THOSE WHO POSSESS THE POWER TO SEAL THESE "BLACK GATES," AN ELITE FEW CALLED "MITEDAMASHI," WHO CHOOSE TO FOLLOW THIS SHADOW PROFESSION.
IT'S A DANGEROUS PROFESSION BUT...
THIS TIME I'LL BE INTRODUCING A WATER FILTER.
I'LL BUY IT. ♡
Hates his job.
IT'S NOT ONE THAT PAYS ENOUGH TO BUY MANY MEALS.

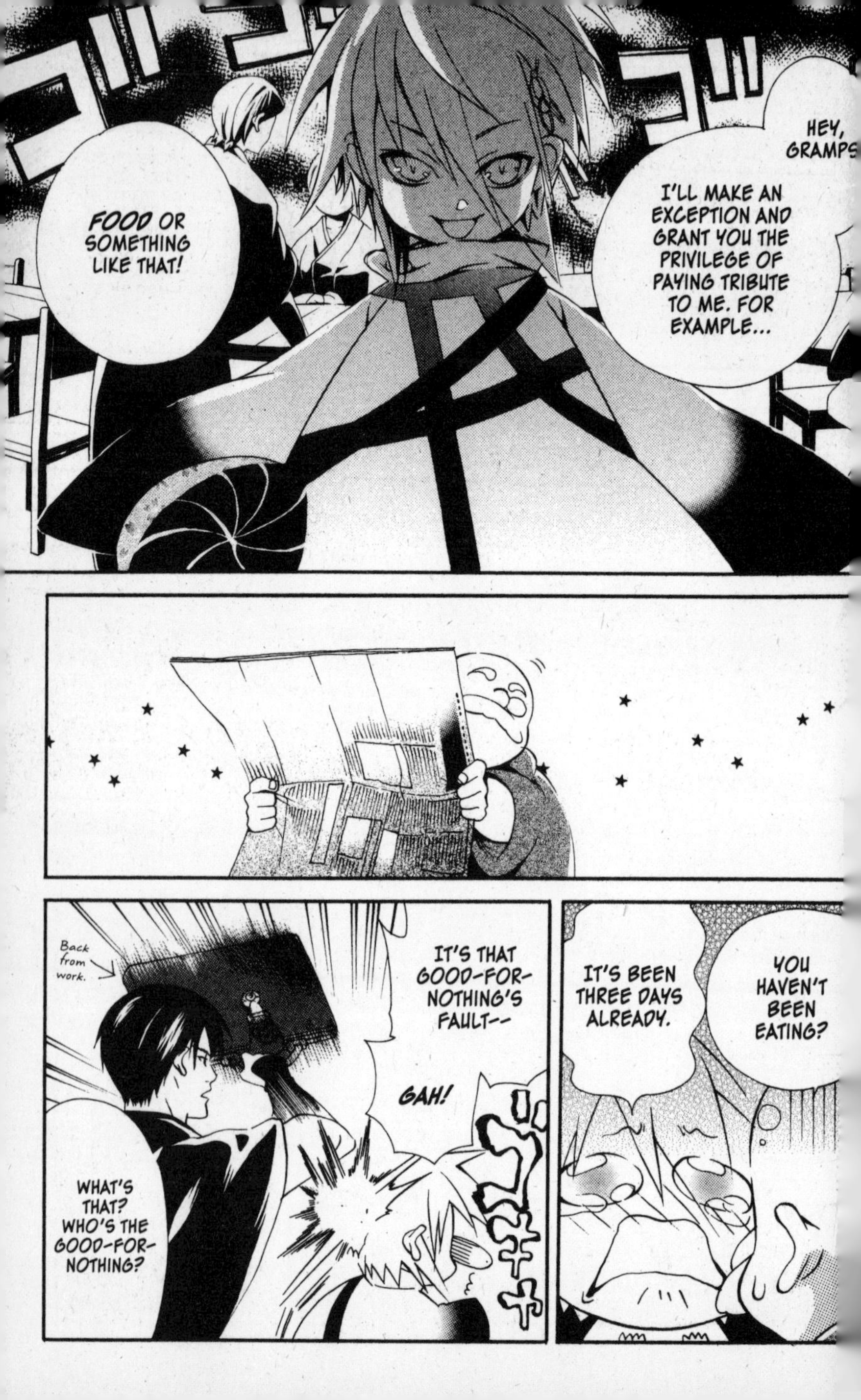
HEY, GRAMPS
I'LL MAKE AN EXCEPTION AND GRANT YOU THE PRIVILEGE OF PAYING TRIBUTE TO ME. FOR EXAMPLE...
FOOD OR SOMETHING LIKE THAT!
YOU HAVEN'T BEEN EATING?
IT'S BEEN THREE DAYS ALREADY.
IT'S THAT GOOD-FOR-NOTHING'S FAULT--
GAH!
Back from work.
WHAT'S THAT? WHO'S THE GOOD-FOR-NOTHING?

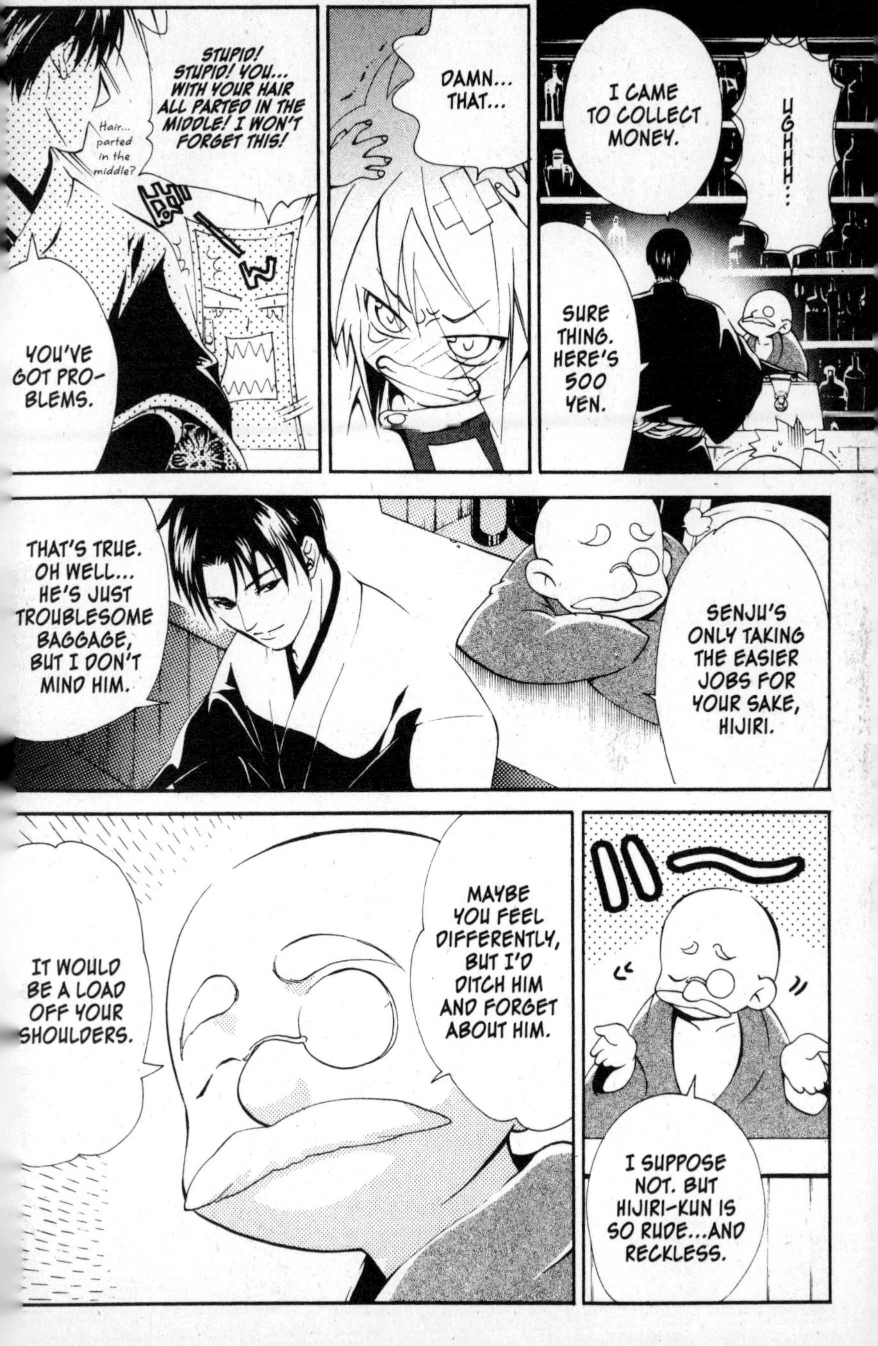
I CAME TO COLLECT MONEY.
UGHHH...
SURE THING. HERE'S 500 YEN.
DAMN... THAT...
STUPID! STUPID! YOU... WITH YOUR HAIR ALL PARTED IN THE MIDDLE! I WON'T FORGET THIS!
Hair... parted in the middle?
YOU'VE GOT PRO-BLEMS.
SENJU'S ONLY TAKING THE EASIER JOBS FOR YOUR SAKE, HIJIRI.
THAT'S TRUE. OH WELL... HE'S JUST TROUBLESOME BAGGAGE, BUT I DON'T MIND HIM.
I SUPPOSE NOT. BUT HIJIRI-KUN IS SO RUDE...AND RECKLESS.
MAYBE YOU FEEL DIFFERENTLY, BUT I'D DITCH HIM AND FORGET ABOUT HIM.
IT WOULD BE A LOAD OFF YOUR SHOULDERS.

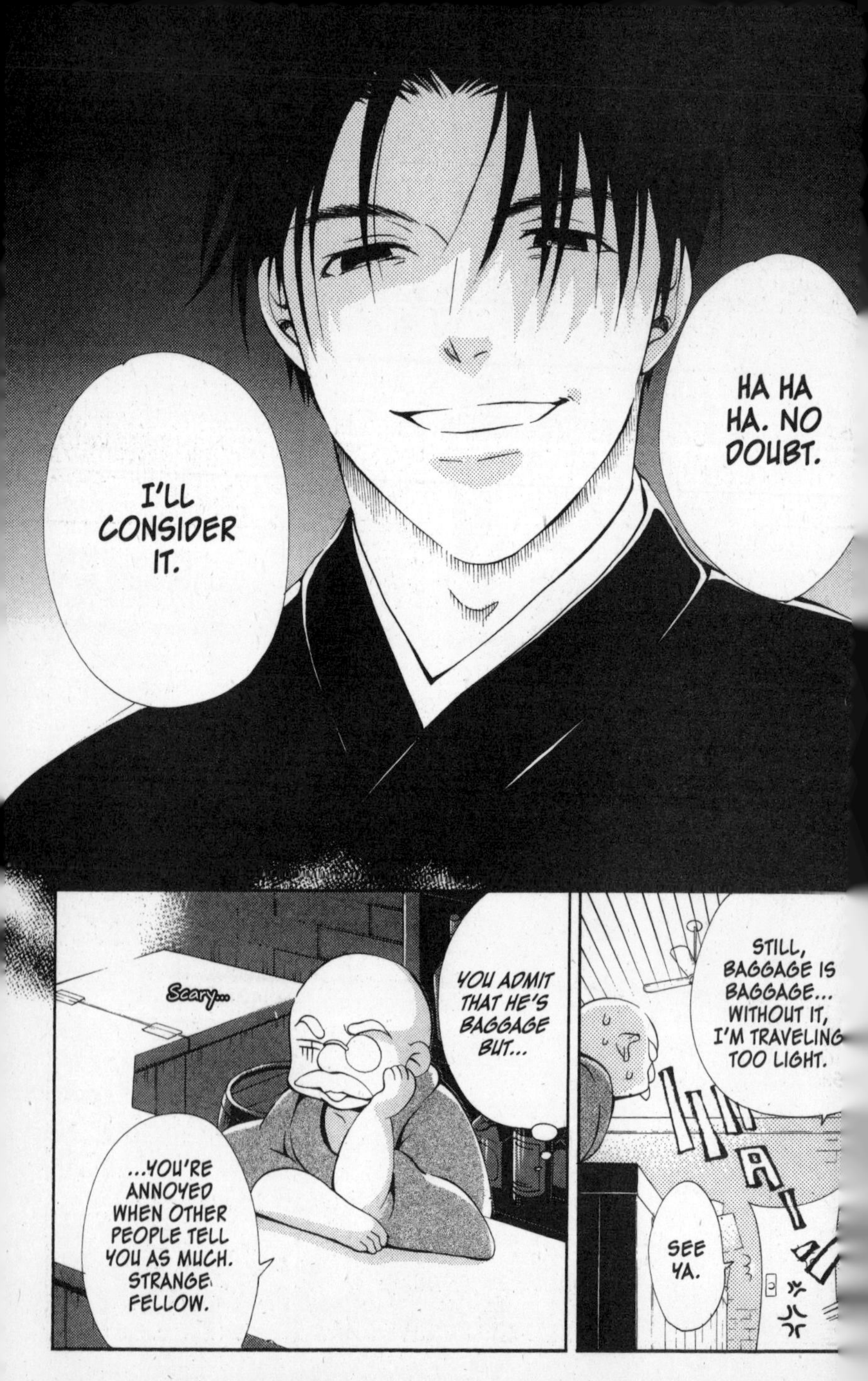
HA HA HA. NO DOUBT.
I'LL CONSIDER IT.
STILL, BAGGAGE IS BAGGAGE... WITHOUT IT, I'M TRAVELING TOO LIGHT.
SEE YA.
YOU ADMIT THAT HE'S BAGGAGE BUT...
...YOU'RE ANNOYED WHEN OTHER PEOPLE TELL YOU AS MUCH. STRANGE FELLOW.
Scary...

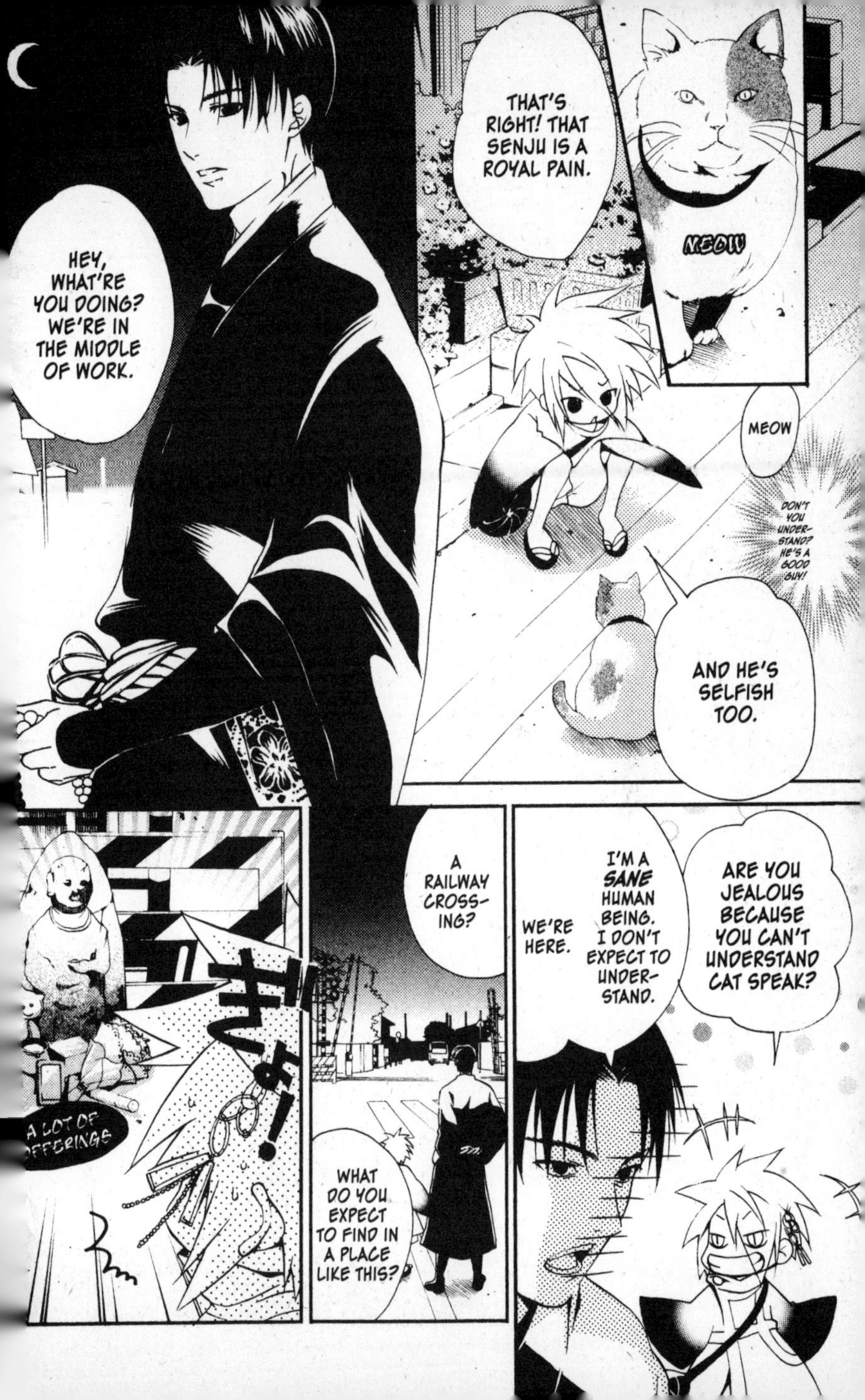
THAT'S RIGHT! THAT SENJU IS A ROYAL PAIN.
MEOW
MEOW
DON'T YOU UNDERSTAND? HE'S A GOOD GUY!
AND HE'S SELFISH TOO.
HEY, WHAT'RE YOU DOING? WE'RE IN THE MIDDLE OF WORK.
ARE YOU JEALOUS BECAUSE YOU CAN'T UNDERSTAND CAT SPEAK?
I'M A SANE HUMAN BEING. I DON'T EXPECT TO UNDERSTAND.
WE'RE HERE.
A RAILWAY CROSS-ING?
WHAT DO YOU EXPECT TO FIND IN A PLACE LIKE THIS?
ぎょ!
A LOT OF OFFERINGS

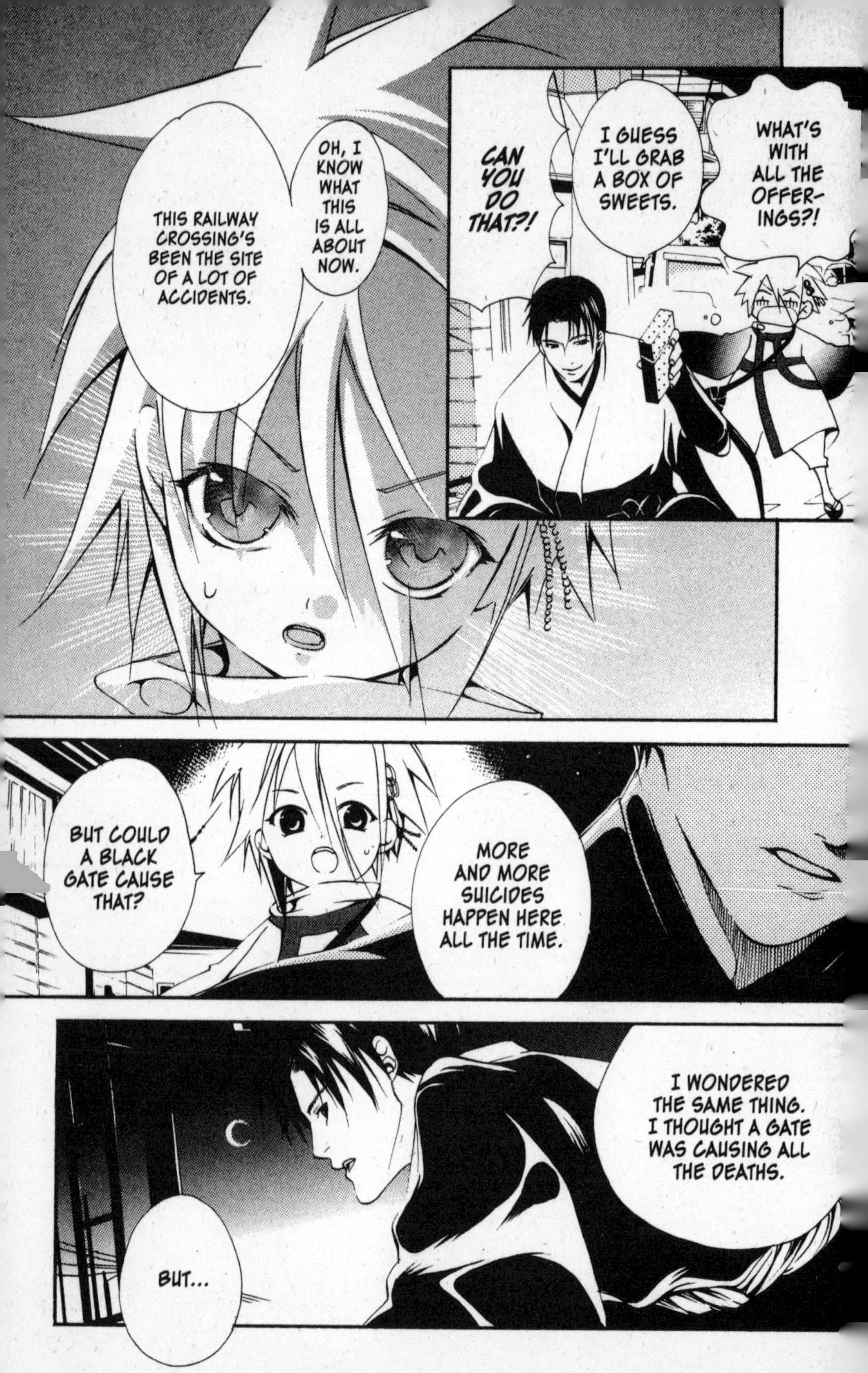
WHAT'S WITH ALL THE OFFERINGS?!
I GUESS I'LL GRAB A BOX OF SWEETS.
CAN YOU DO THAT?!
OH, I KNOW WHAT THIS IS ALL ABOUT NOW.
THIS RAILWAY CROSSING'S BEEN THE SITE OF A LOT OF ACCIDENTS.
MORE AND MORE SUICIDES HAPPEN HERE ALL THE TIME.
BUT COULD A BLACK GATE CAUSE THAT?
I WONDERED THE SAME THING. I THOUGHT A GATE WAS CAUSING ALL THE DEATHS.
BUT...

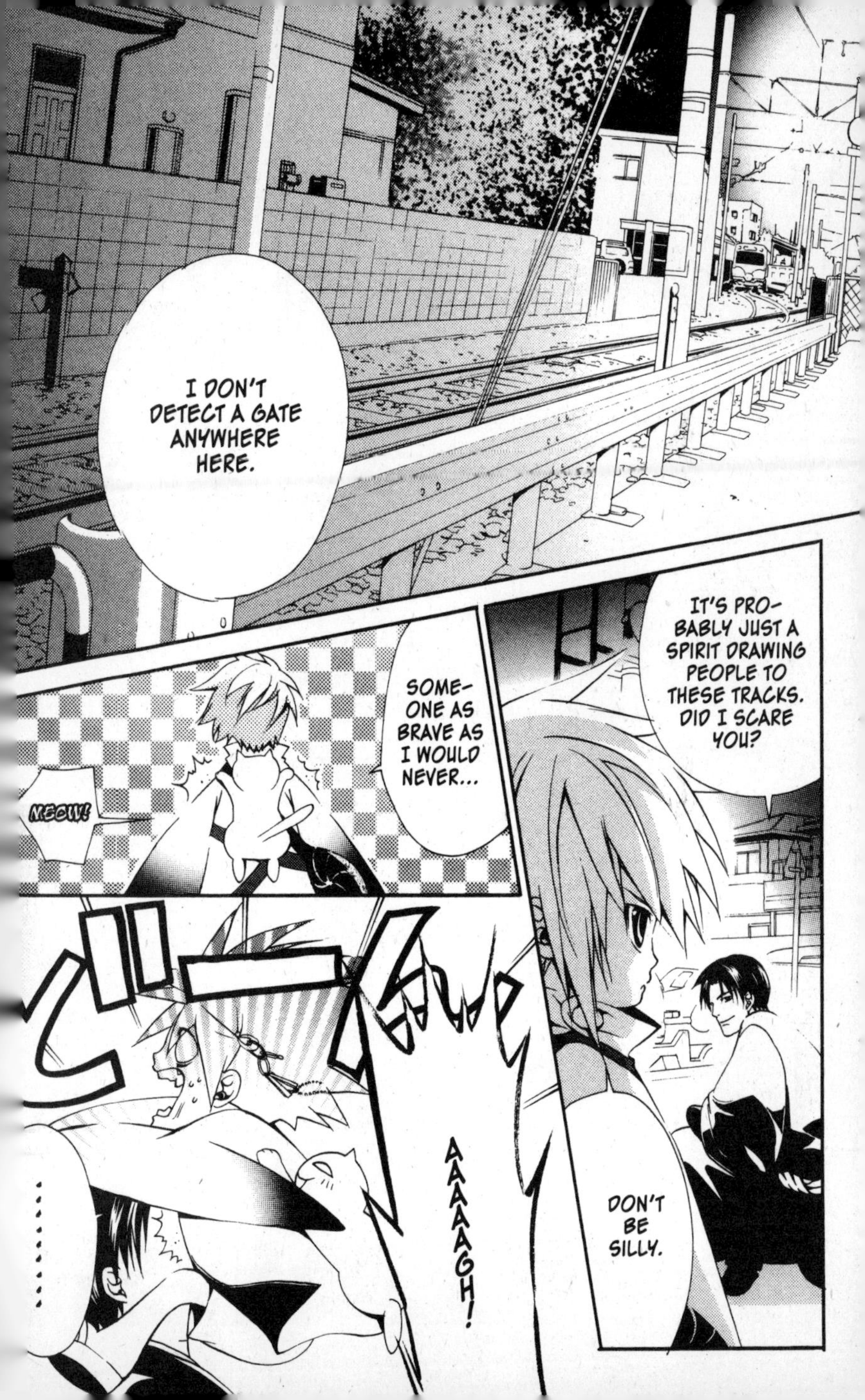
I DON'T DETECT A GATE ANYWHERE HERE.
IT'S PRO-BABLY JUST A SPIRIT DRAWING PEOPLE TO THESE TRACKS. DID I SCARE YOU?
DON'T BE SILLY.
SOME-ONE AS BRAVE AS I WOULD NEVER...
MEOW!
AAAAAGH!
......

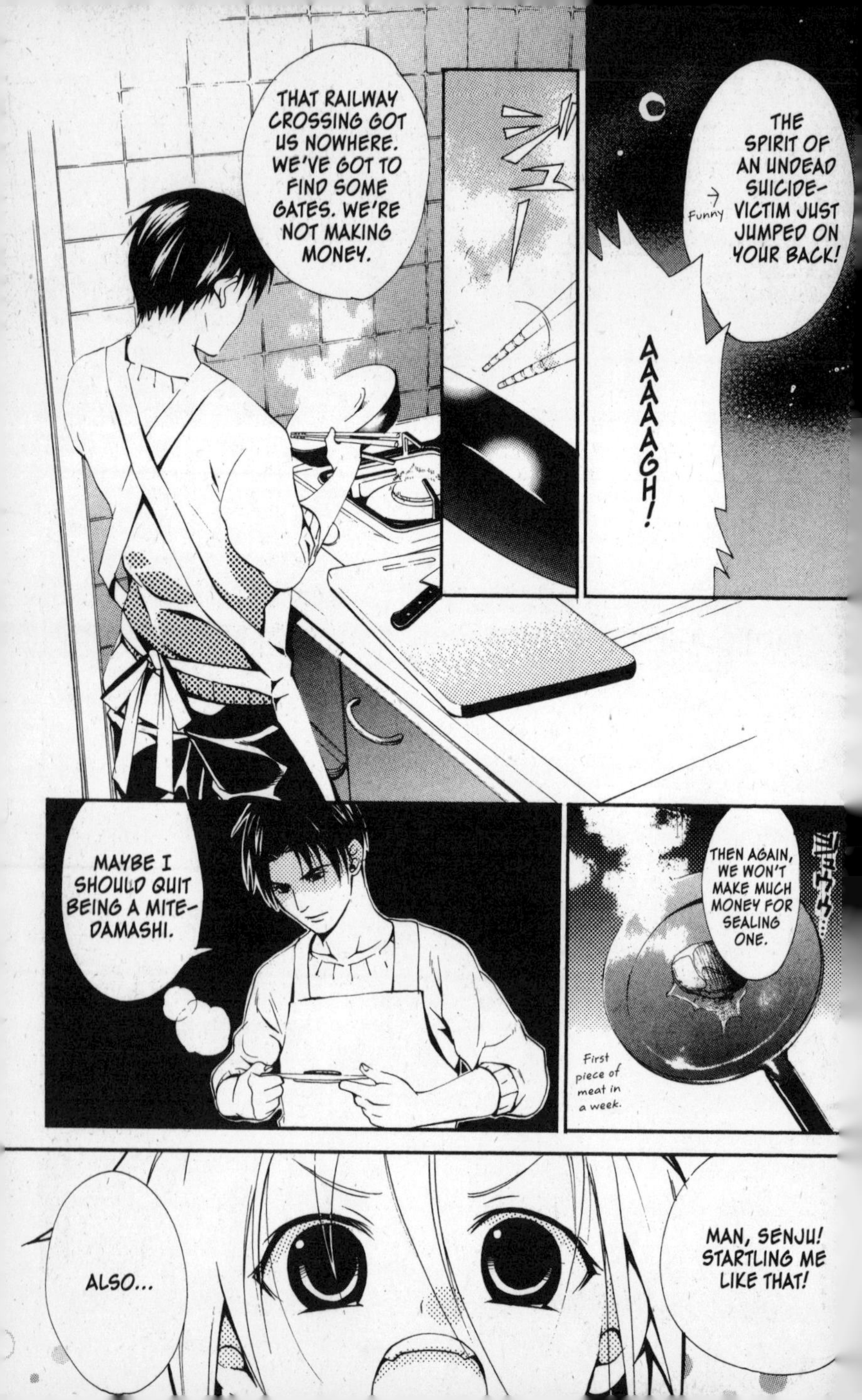
Funny
THE SPIRIT OF AN UNDEAD SUICIDE-VICTIM JUST JUMPED ON YOUR BACK!
AAAAAGH!
THAT RAILWAY CROSSING GOT US NOWHERE. WE'VE GOT TO FIND SOME GATES. WE'RE NOT MAKING MONEY.
THEN AGAIN, WE WON'T MAKE MUCH MONEY FOR SEALING ONE.
First piece of meat in a week.
MAYBE I SHOULD QUIT BEING A MITE-DAMASHI.
MAN, SENJU! STARTLING ME LIKE THAT!
ALSO...

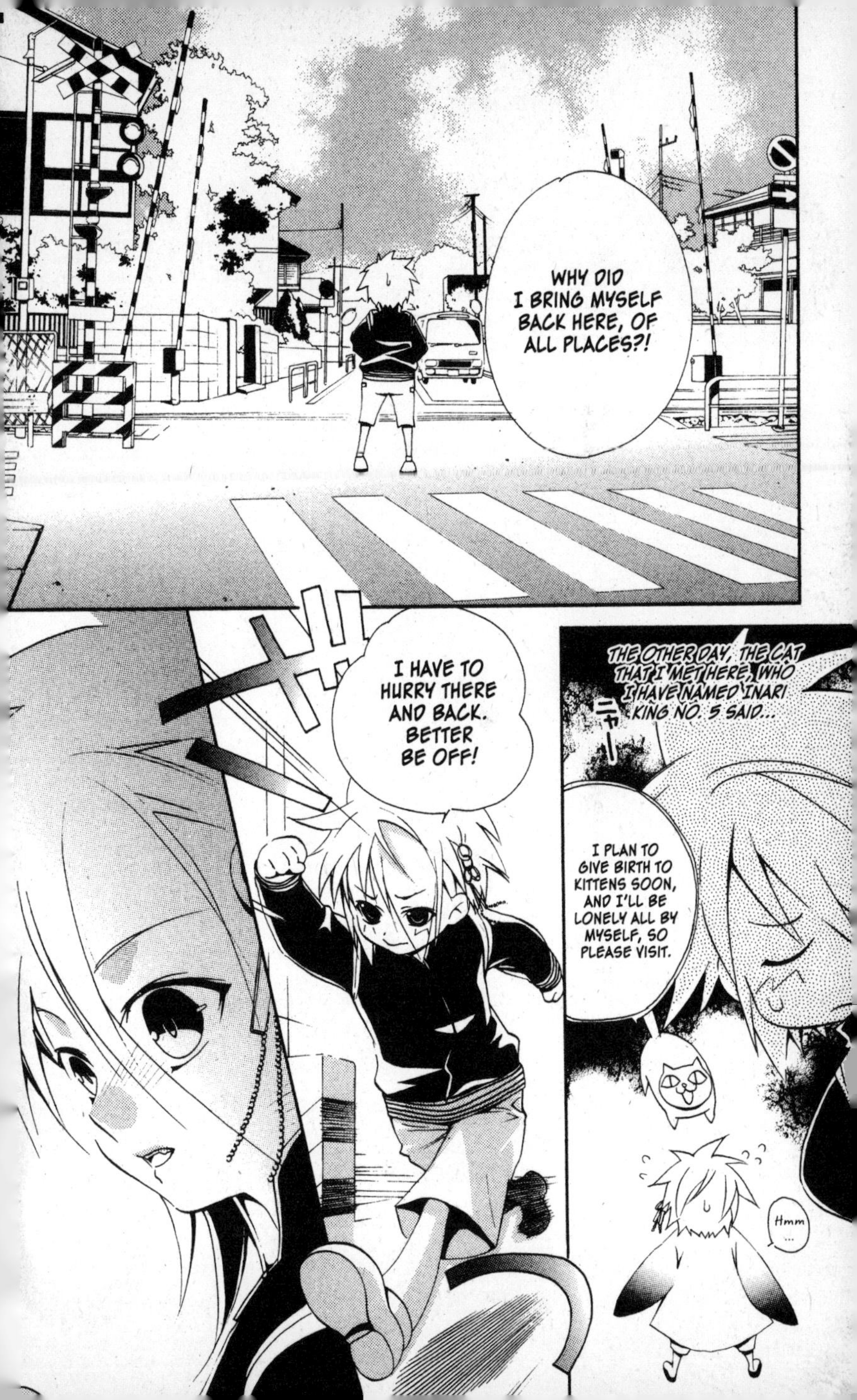
WHY DID I BRING MYSELF BACK HERE, OF ALL PLACES?!
THE OTHER DAY, THE CAT THAT I MET HERE, WHO I HAVE NAMED INARI KING NO. 5 SAID...
ニャー
I PLAN TO GIVE BIRTH TO KITTENS SOON, AND I'LL BE LONELY ALL BY MYSELF, SO PLEASE VISIT.
Hmm ...
I HAVE TO HURRY THERE AND BACK. BETTER BE OFF!

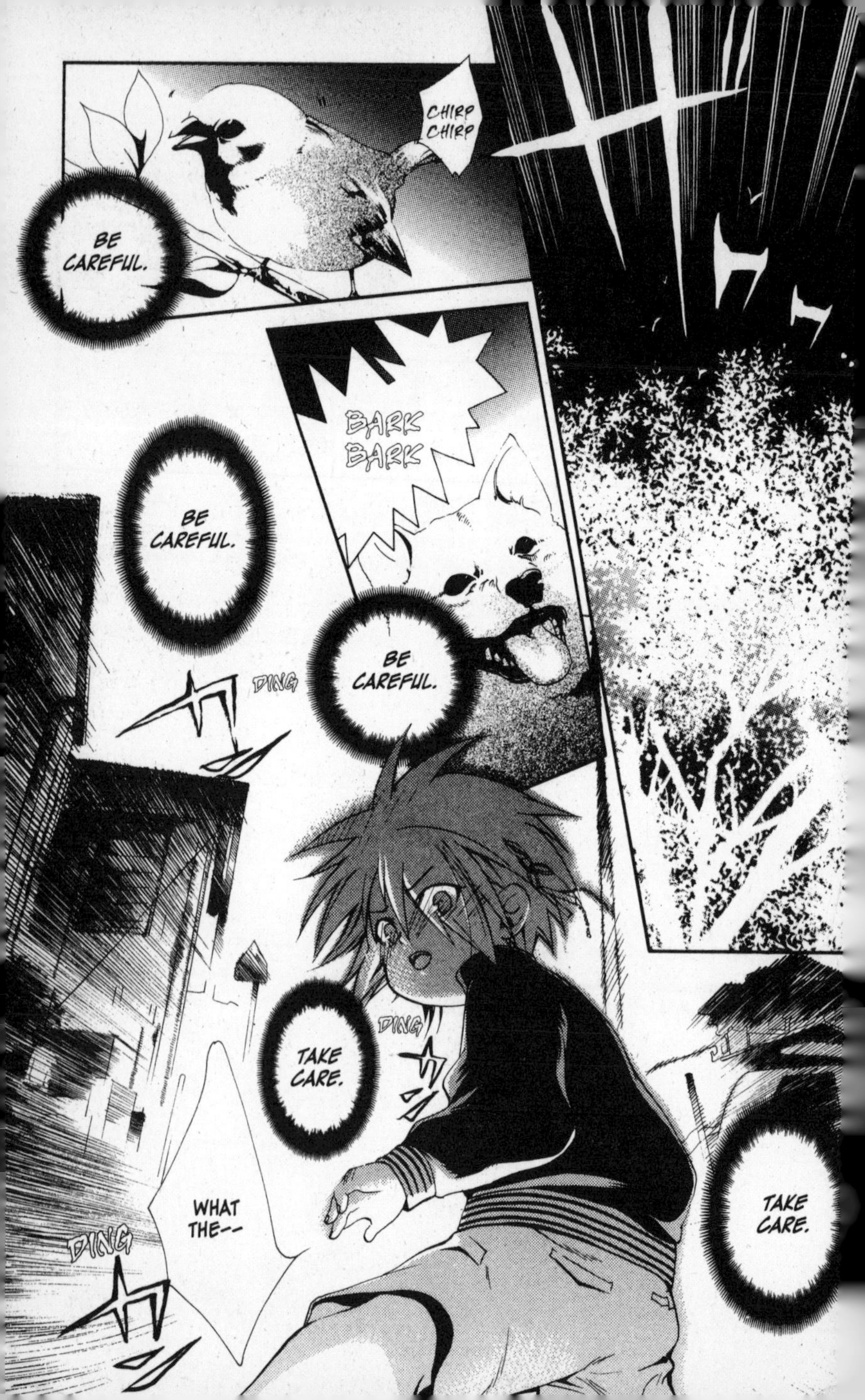
CHIRP CHIRP
BE CAREFUL.
BARK BARK
BE CAREFUL.
BE CAREFUL.
DING
TAKE CARE.
DING
TAKE CARE.
WHAT THE--
DING

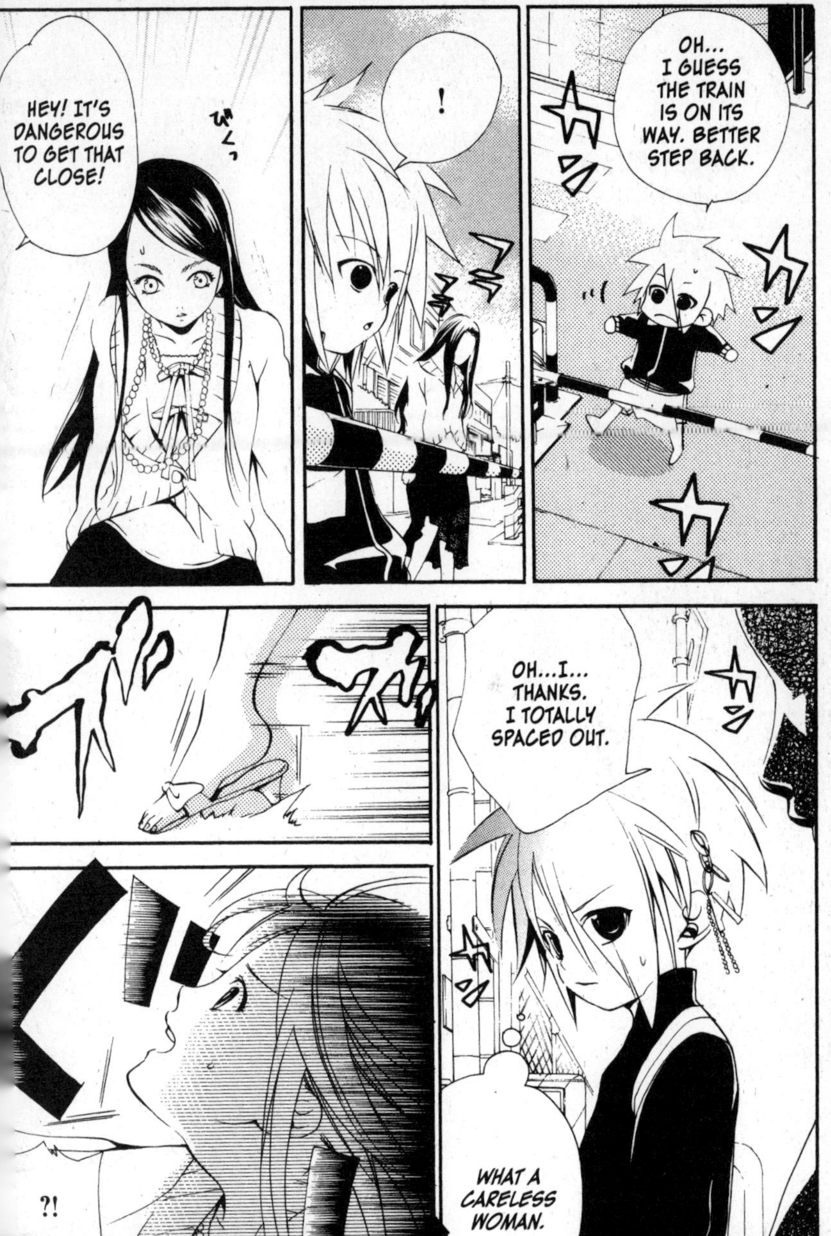
OH... I GUESS THE TRAIN IS ON ITS WAY. BETTER STEP BACK.
!
HEY! IT'S DANGEROUS TO GET THAT CLOSE!
びくっ
OH...I... THANKS. I TOTALLY SPACED OUT.
WHAT A CARELESS WOMAN.
?!

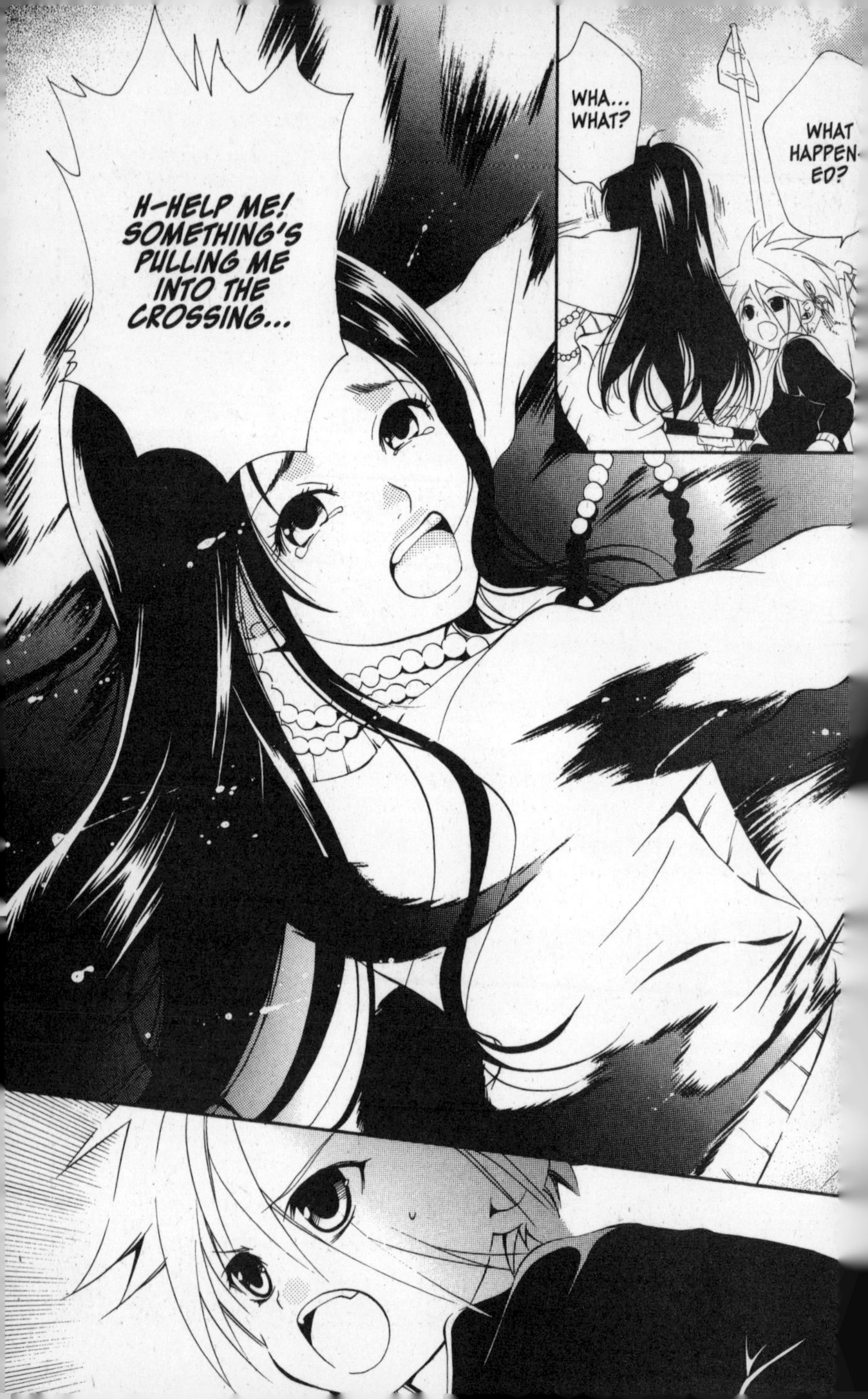
WHAT HAPPEN-ED?
WHA... WHAT?
H-HELP ME! SOMETHING'S PULLING ME INTO THE CROSSING...

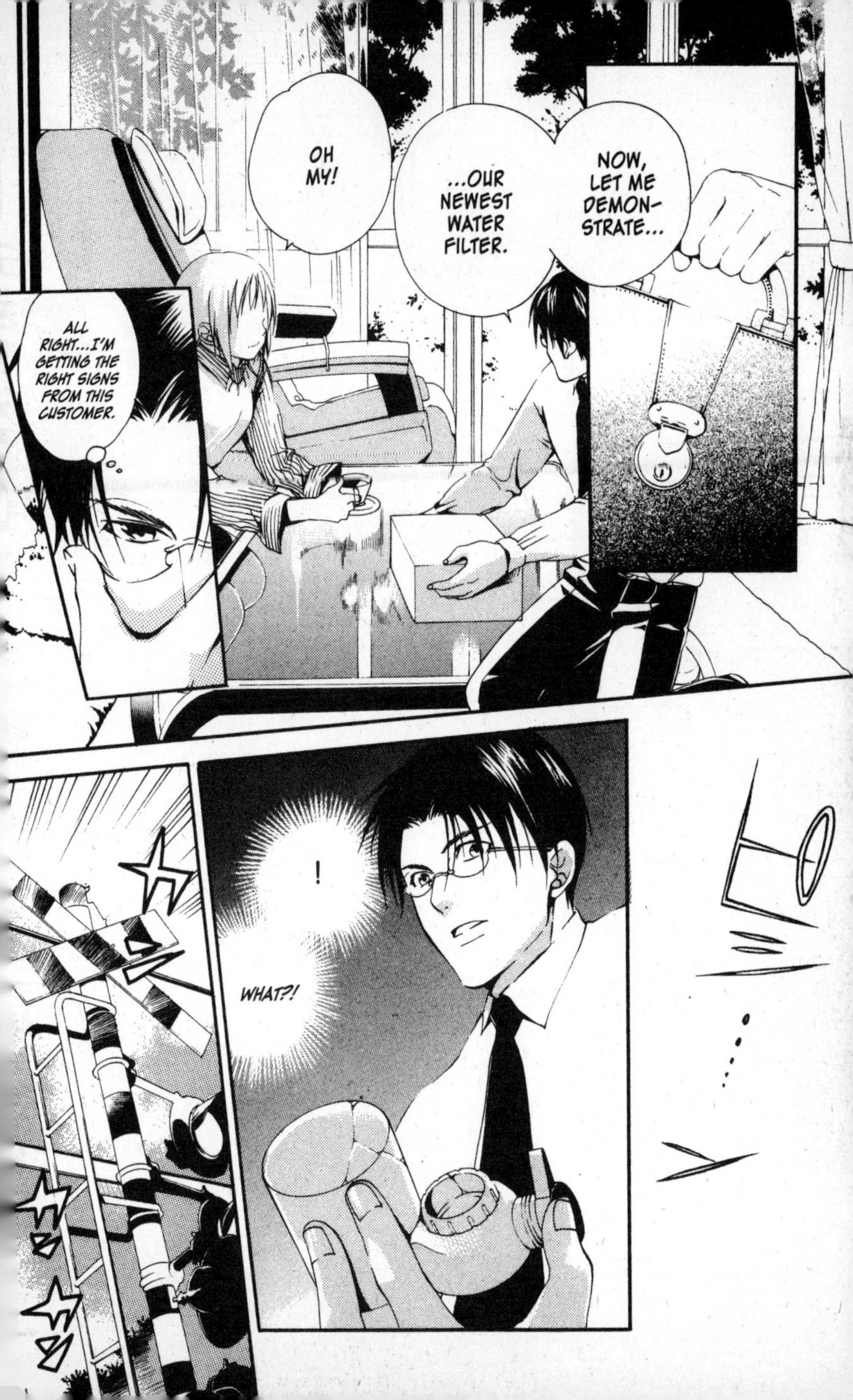
NOW, LET ME DEMON-STRATE...
...OUR NEWEST WATER FILTER.
OH MY!
ALL RIGHT...I'M GETTING THE RIGHT SIGNS FROM THIS CUSTOMER.
!
WHAT?!

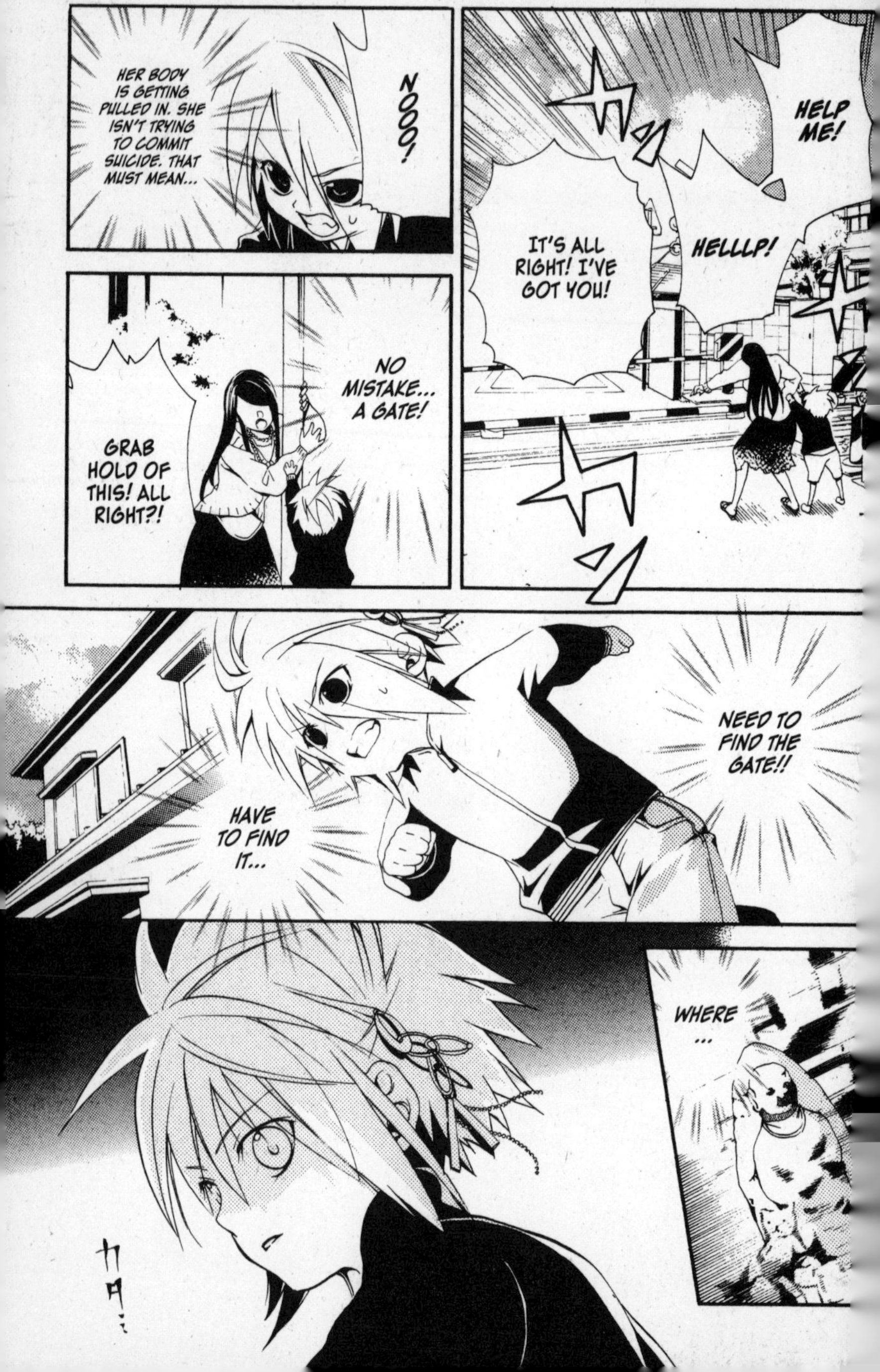
HELP ME!
HELLLP!
IT'S ALL RIGHT! I'VE GOT YOU!
NOOO!
HER BODY IS GETTING PULLED IN. SHE ISN'T TRYING TO COMMIT SUICIDE. THAT MUST MEAN...
NO MISTAKE... A GATE!
GRAB HOLD OF THIS! ALL RIGHT?!
NEED TO FIND THE GATE!!
HAVE TO FIND IT...
WHERE ...
カタ..

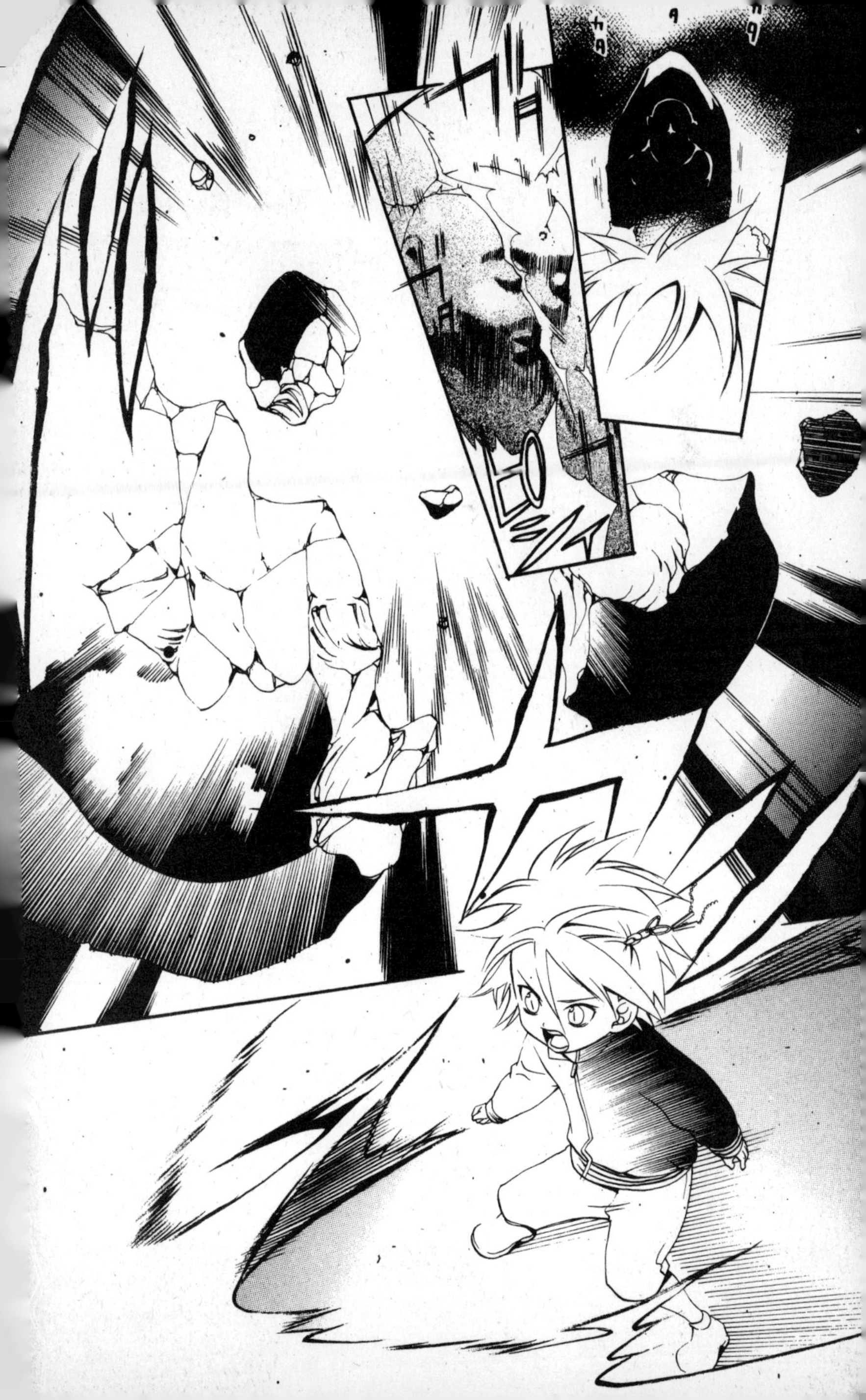
カタ

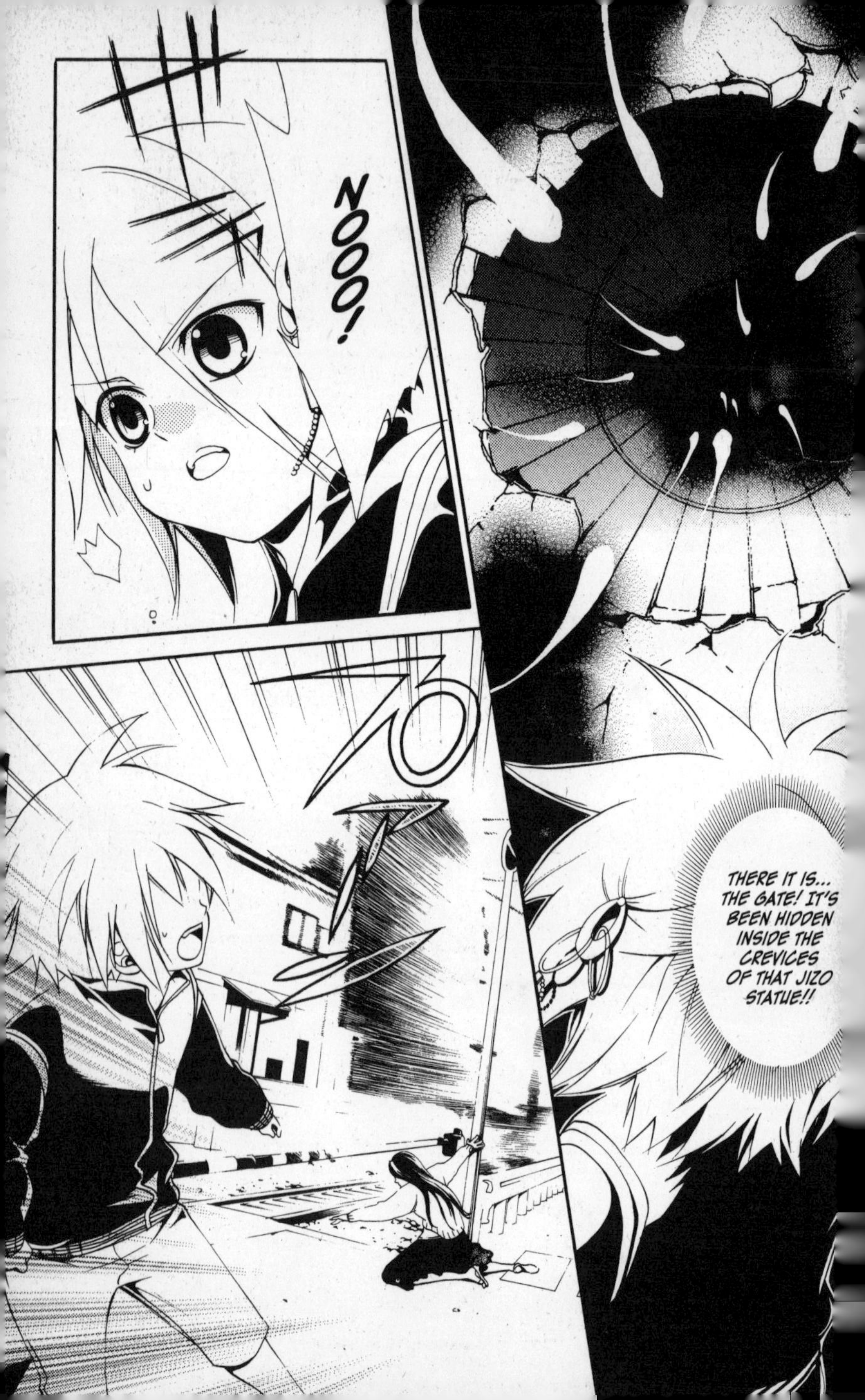
THERE IT IS... THE GATE! IT'S BEEN HIDDEN INSIDE THE CREVICES OF THAT JIZO STATUE!!
NOOOO!

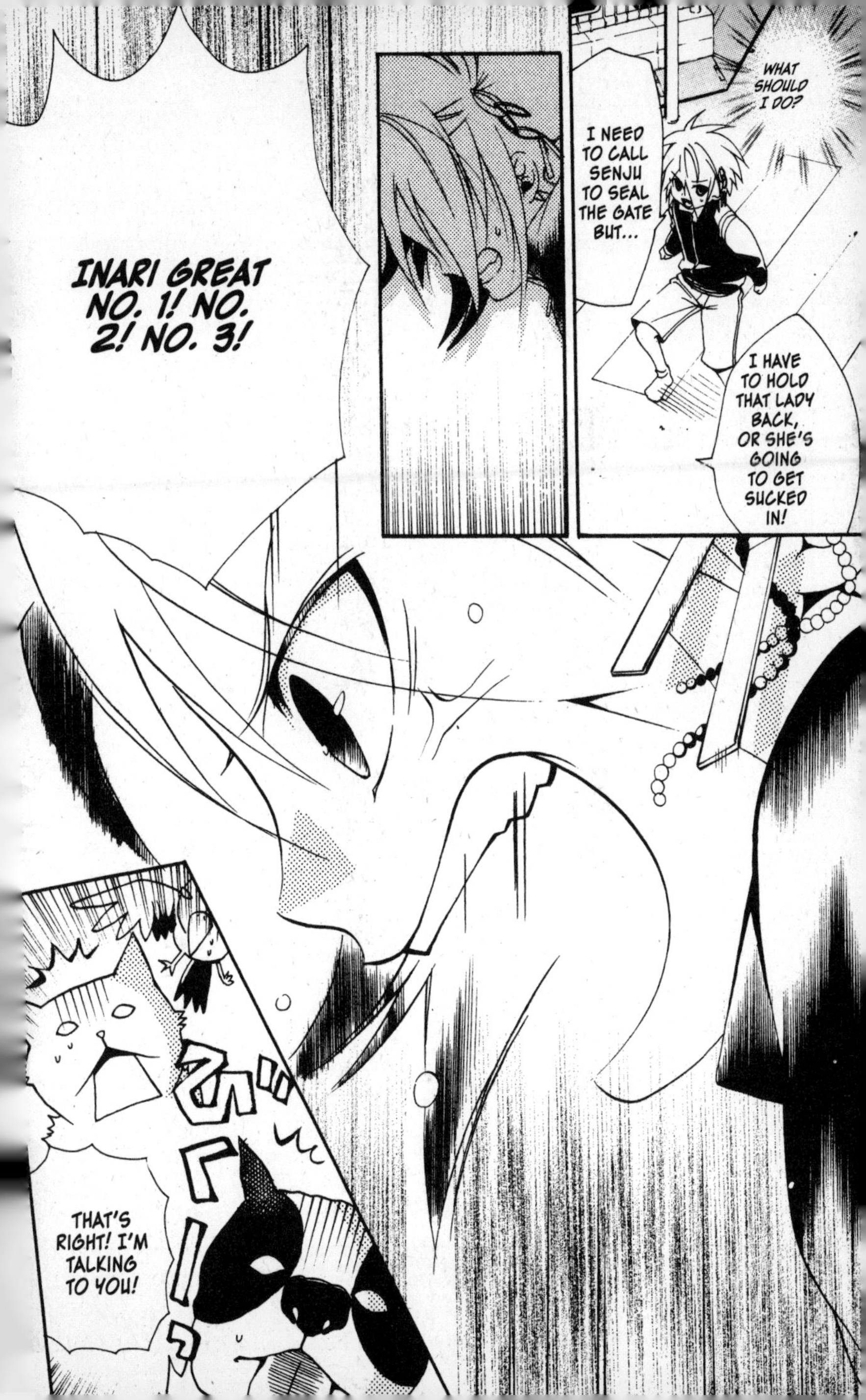
WHAT SHOULD I DO?
I NEED TO CALL SENJU TO SEAL THE GATE BUT...
I HAVE TO HOLD THAT LADY BACK, OR SHE'S GOING TO GET SUCKED IN!
INARI GREAT NO. 1! NO. 2! NO. 3!
THAT'S RIGHT! I'M TALKING TO YOU!

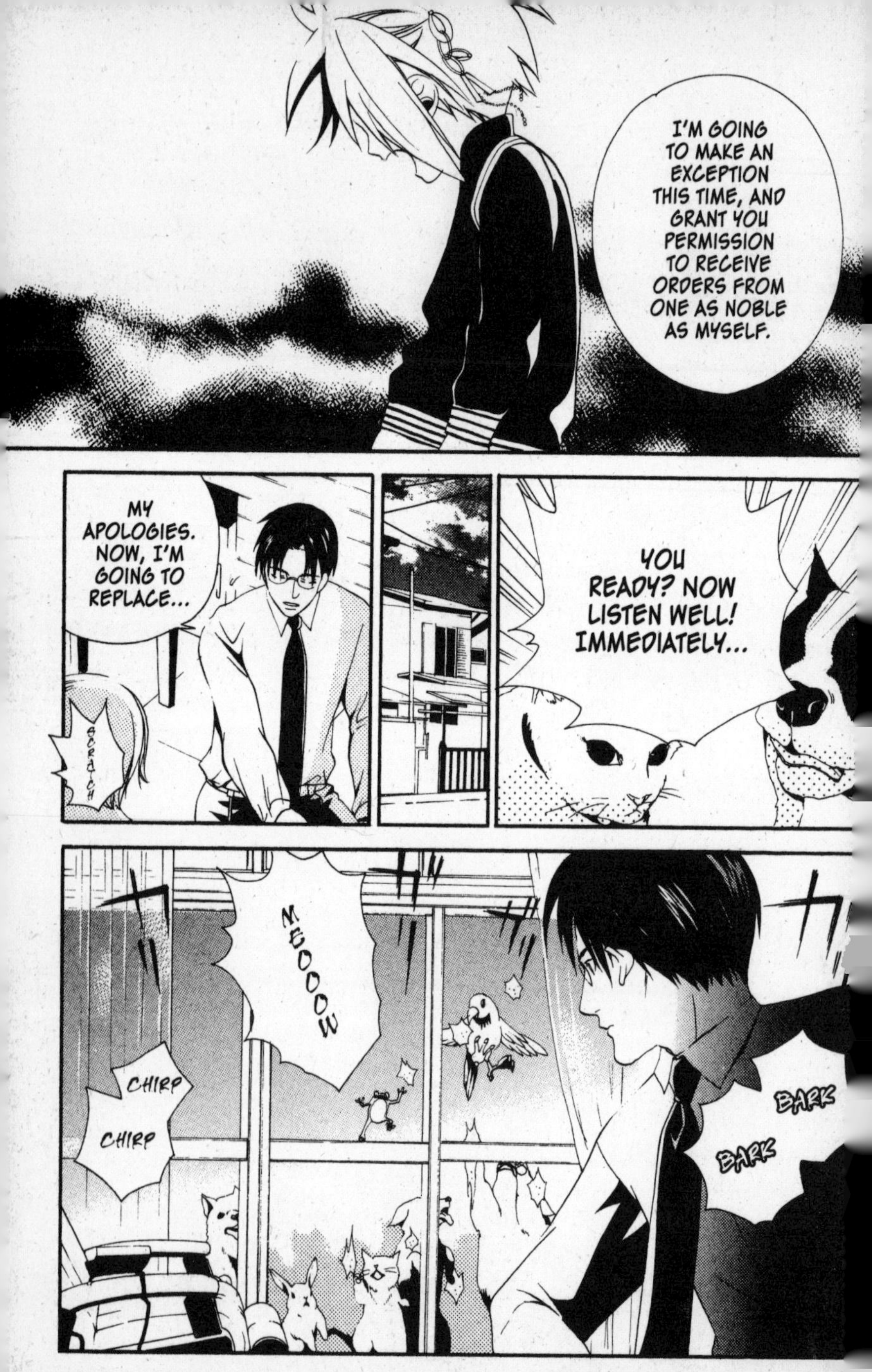
I'M GOING TO MAKE AN EXCEPTION THIS TIME, AND GRANT YOU PERMISSION TO RECEIVE ORDERS FROM ONE AS NOBLE AS MYSELF.
YOU READY? NOW LISTEN WELL! IMMEDIATELY...
MY APOLOGIES. NOW, I'M GOING TO REPLACE...
SCRATCH
BARK
BARK
MEOOOOW
CHIRP
CHIRP

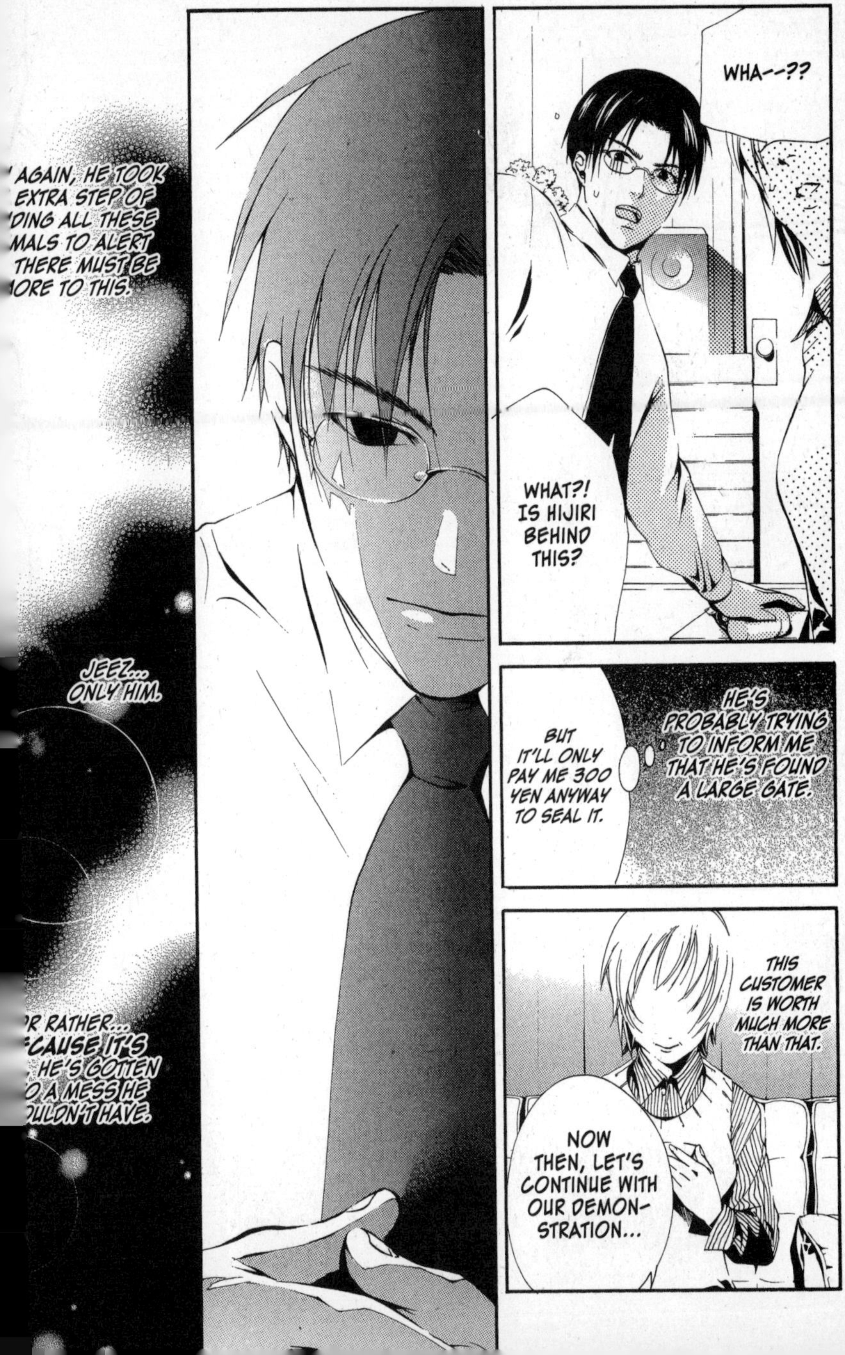
WHA--??
WHAT?! IS HIJIRI BEHIND THIS?
HE'S PROBABLY TRYING TO INFORM ME THAT HE'S FOUND A LARGE GATE.
BUT IT'LL ONLY PAY ME 300 YEN ANYWAY TO SEAL IT.
THIS CUSTOMER IS WORTH MUCH MORE THAN THAT.
NOW THEN, LET'S CONTINUE WITH OUR DEMONSTRATION...
AGAIN, HE TOOK EXTRA STEP OF DING ALL THESE MALS TO ALERT THERE MUST BE ORE TO THIS.
JEEZ... ONLY HIM.
R RATHER... ECAUSE IT'S HE'S GOTTEN O A MESS HE ULDN'T HAVE.

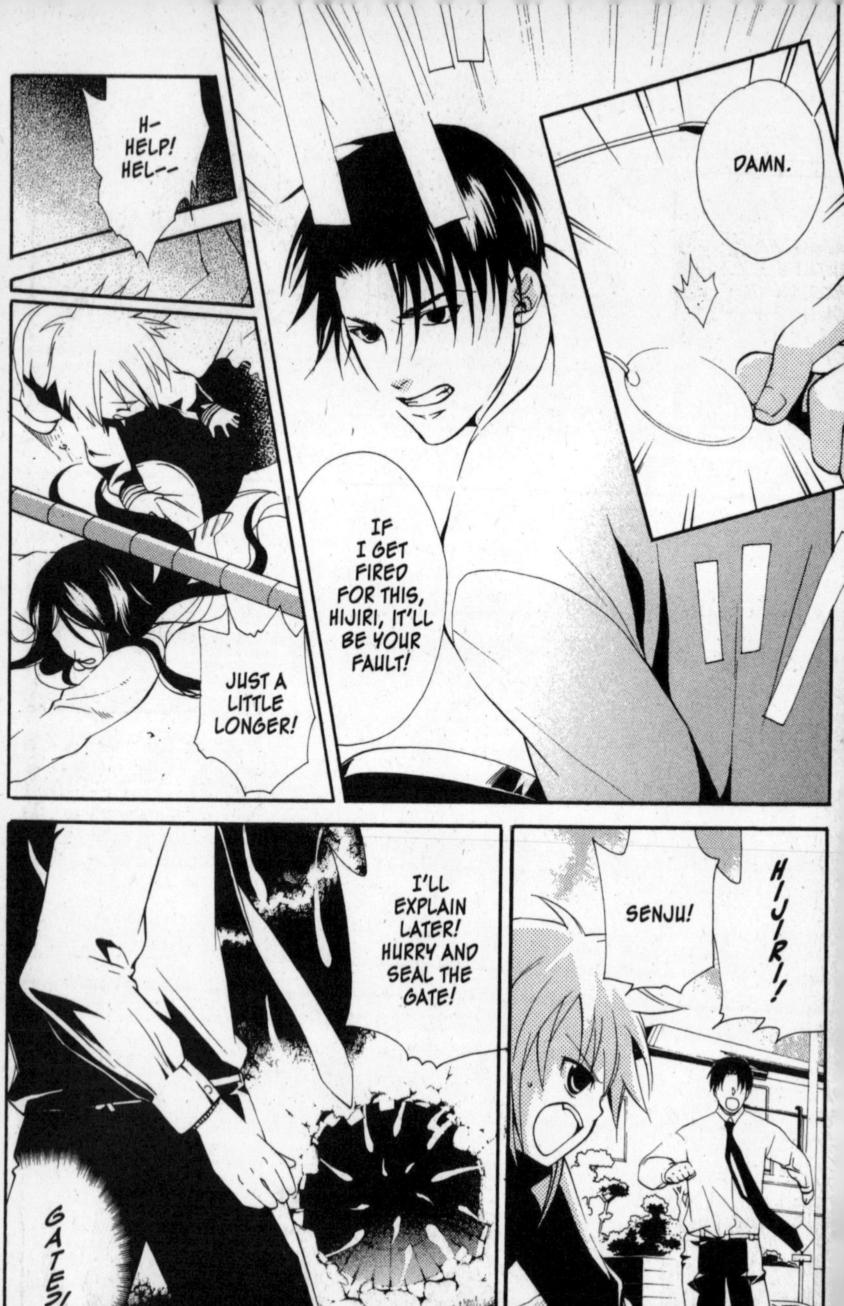
DAMN.
IF I GET FIRED FOR THIS, HIJIRI, IT'LL BE YOUR FAULT!
H-HELP! HEL--
JUST A LITTLE LONGER!
HIJIRI!
SENJU!
I'LL EXPLAIN LATER! HURRY AND SEAL THE GATE!
GATE?!

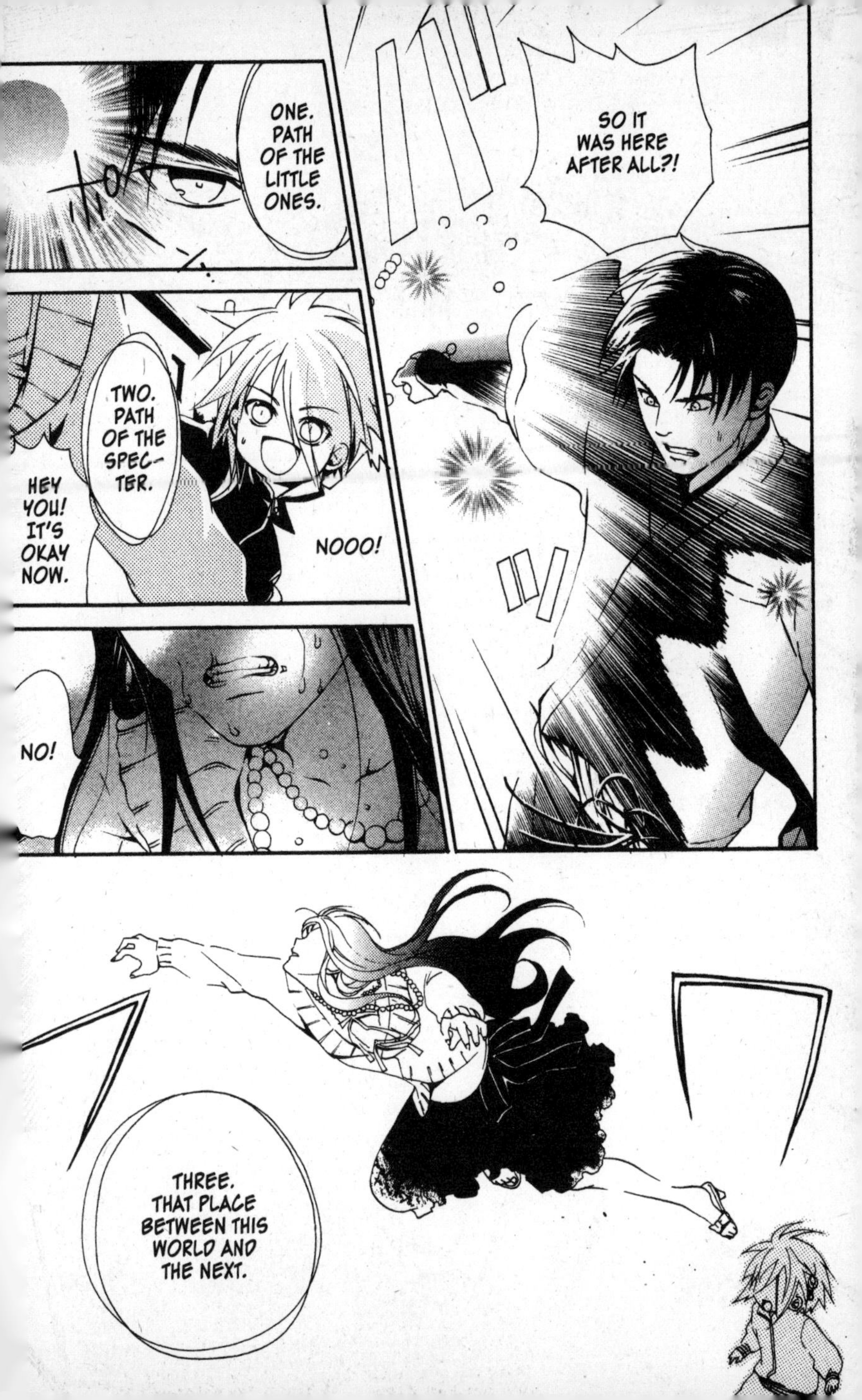
SO IT WAS HERE AFTER ALL?!
ONE. PATH OF THE LITTLE ONES.
TWO. PATH OF THE SPECTER.
NOOO!
HEY YOU! IT'S OKAY NOW.
NO!
THREE. THAT PLACE BETWEEN THIS WORLD AND THE NEXT.

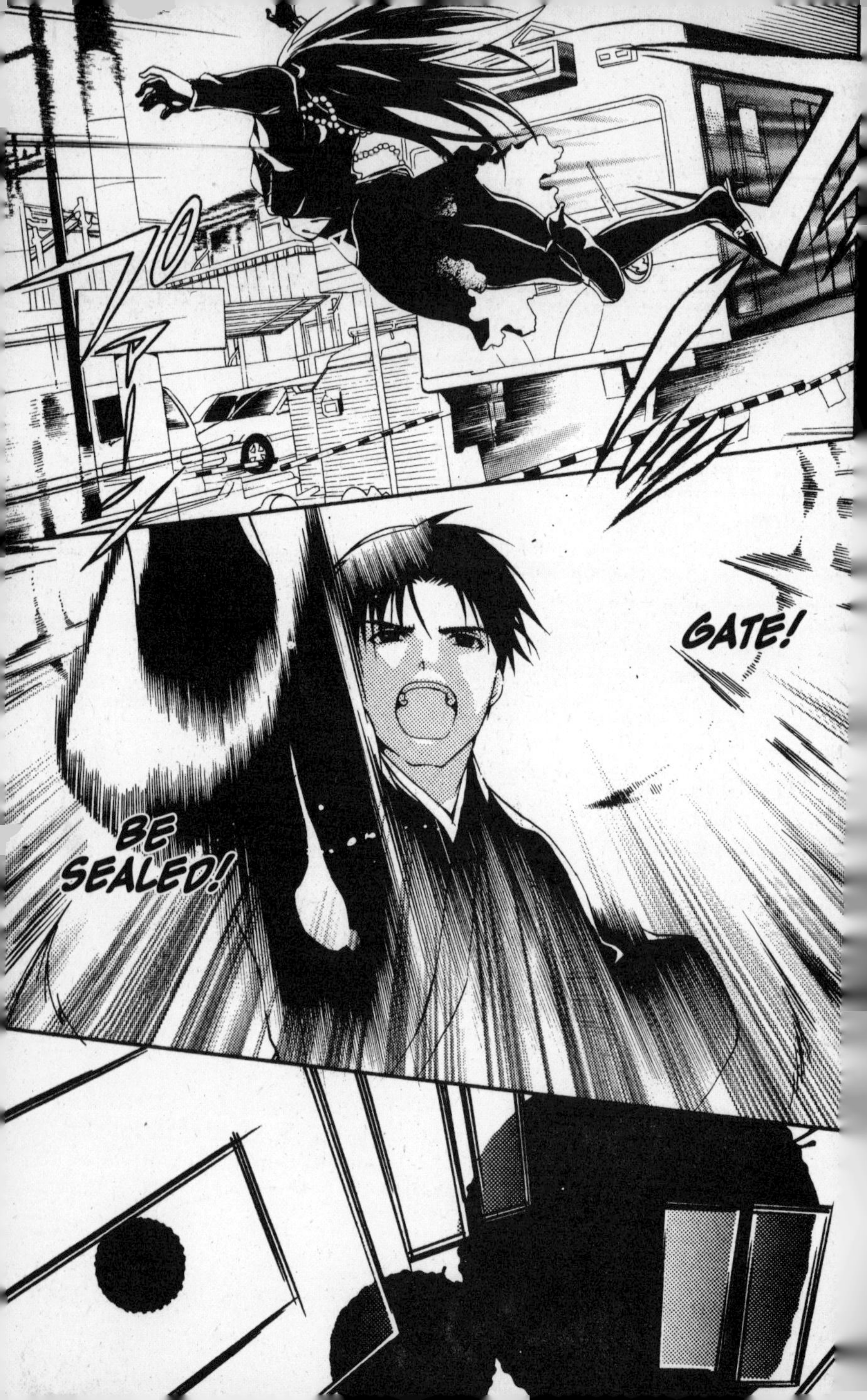
GATE!
BE SEALED!

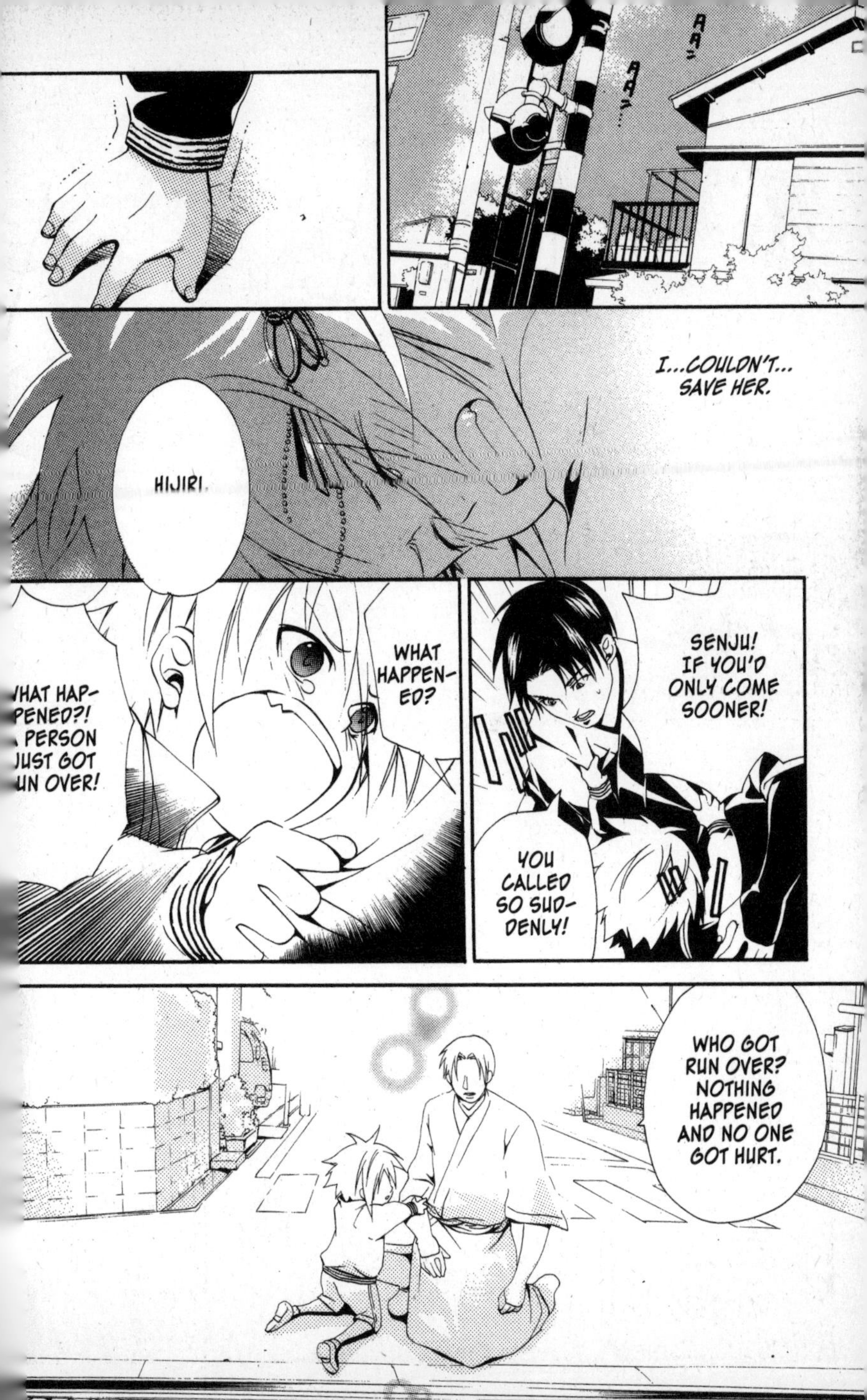
AA~
AA~...
I...COULDN'T... SAVE HER.
HIJIRI.
SENJU! IF YOU'D ONLY COME SOONER!
YOU CALLED SO SUD-DENLY!
WHAT HAPPEN-ED?
HAT HAP-PENED?! PERSON JUST GOT UN OVER!
WHO GOT RUN OVER? NOTHING HAPPENED AND NO ONE GOT HURT.

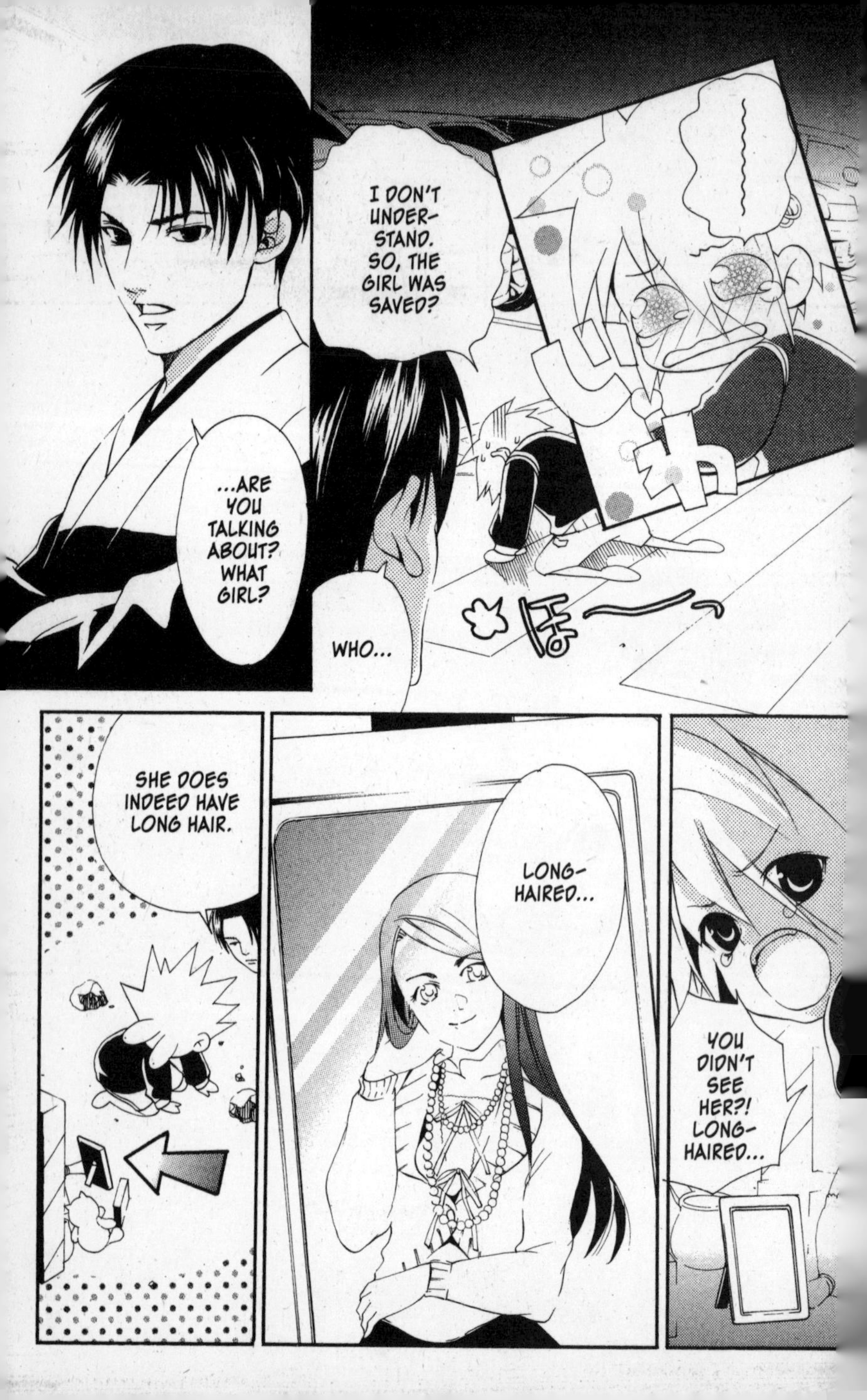
I DON'T UNDER-STAND. SO, THE GIRL WAS SAVED?
WHO...
...ARE YOU TALKING ABOUT? WHAT GIRL?
YOU DIDN'T SEE HER?! LONG-HAIRED...
LONG-HAIRED...
SHE DOES INDEED HAVE LONG HAIR.

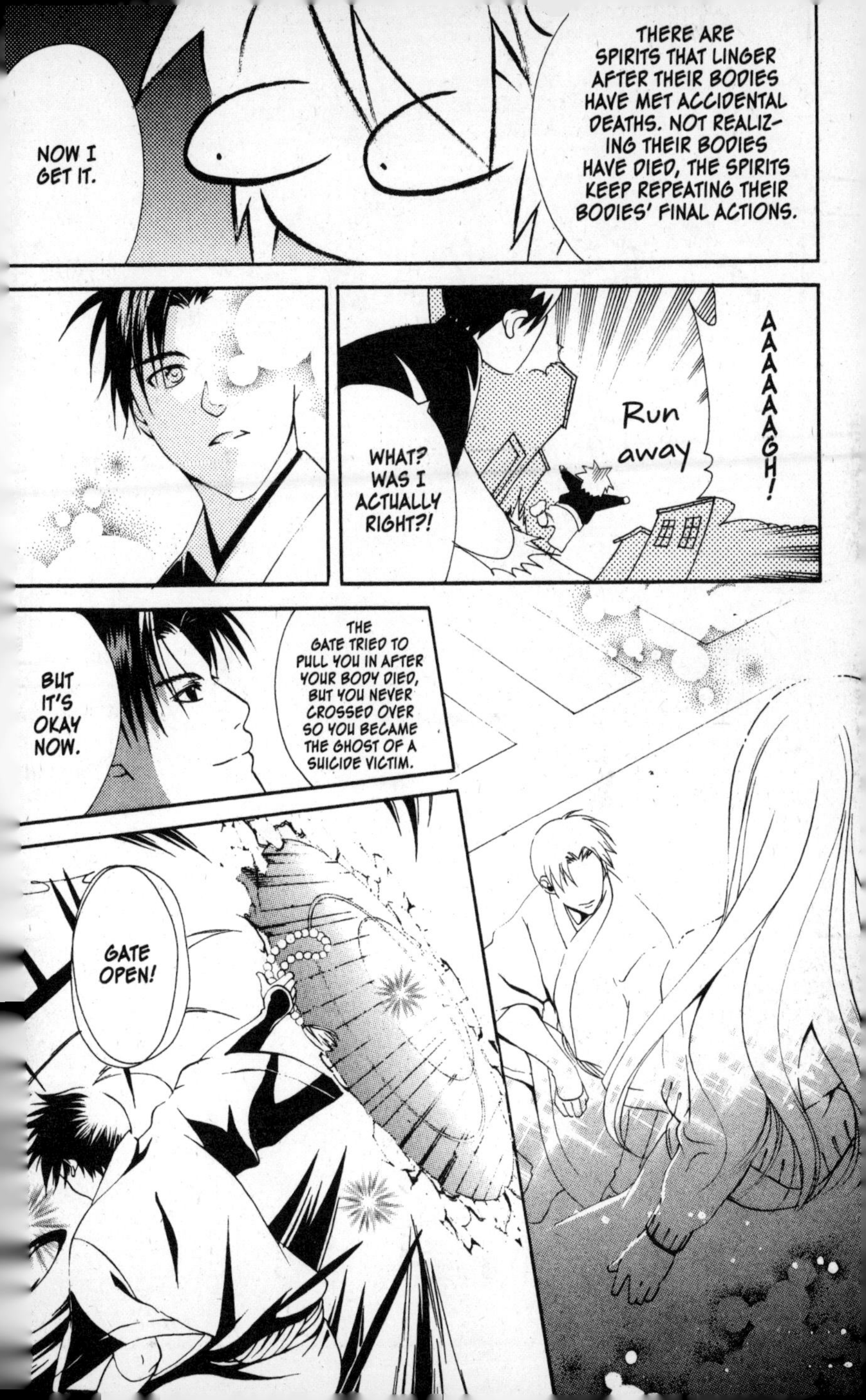
THERE ARE SPIRITS THAT LINGER AFTER THEIR BODIES HAVE MET ACCIDENTAL DEATHS. NOT REALIZING THEIR BODIES HAVE DIED, THE SPIRITS KEEP REPEATING THEIR BODIES' FINAL ACTIONS.
NOW I GET IT.
AAAAAAAGH!
Run away
WHAT? WAS I ACTUALLY RIGHT?!
THE GATE TRIED TO PULL YOU IN AFTER YOUR BODY DIED, BUT YOU NEVER CROSSED OVER SO YOU BECAME THE GHOST OF A SUICIDE VICTIM.
BUT IT'S OKAY NOW.
GATE OPEN!

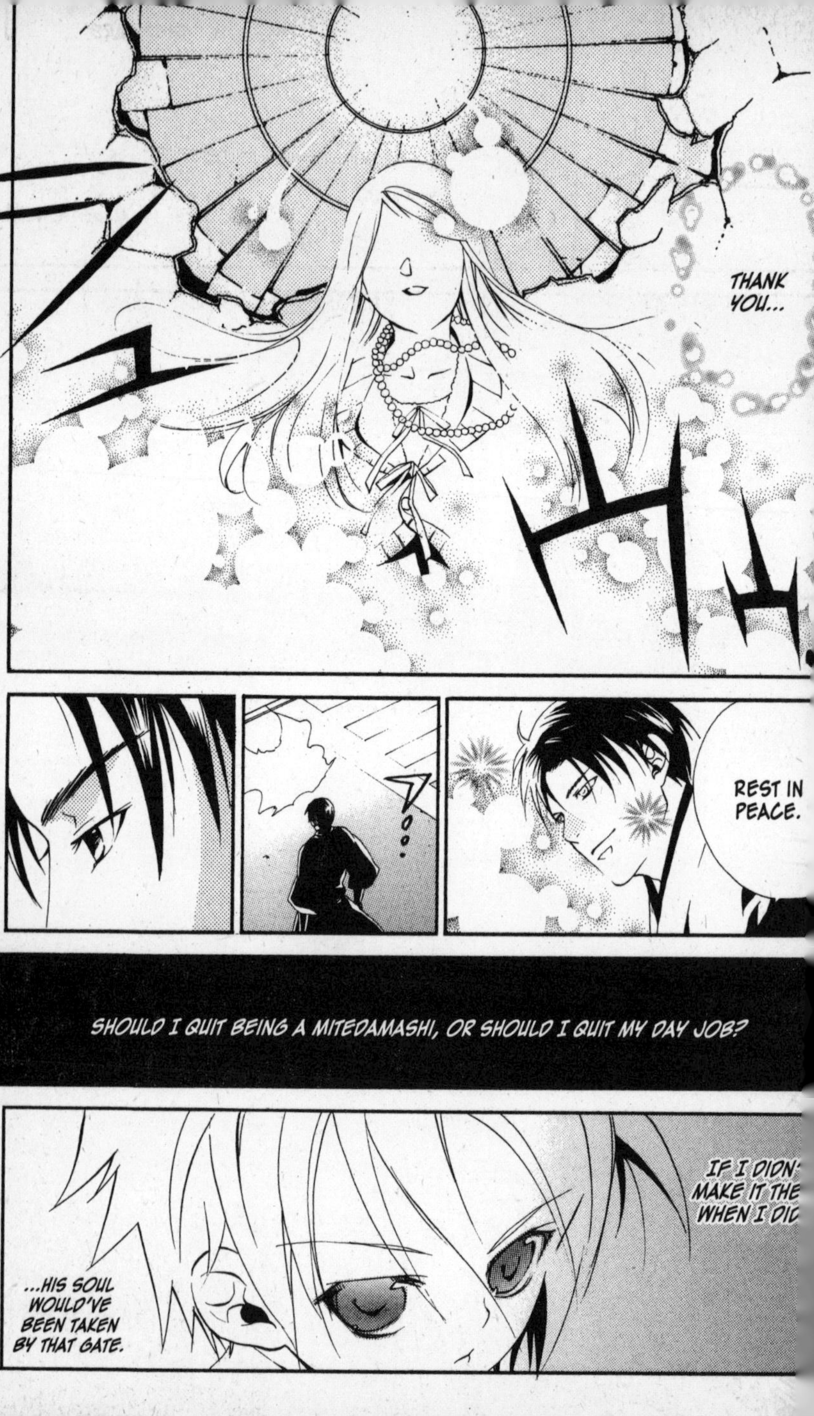
THANK YOU...
REST IN PEACE.
SHOULD I QUIT BEING A MITEDAMASHI, OR SHOULD I QUIT MY DAY JOB?
IF I DIDN' MAKE IT THE WHEN I DID
...HIS SOUL WOULD'VE BEEN TAKEN BY THAT GATE.

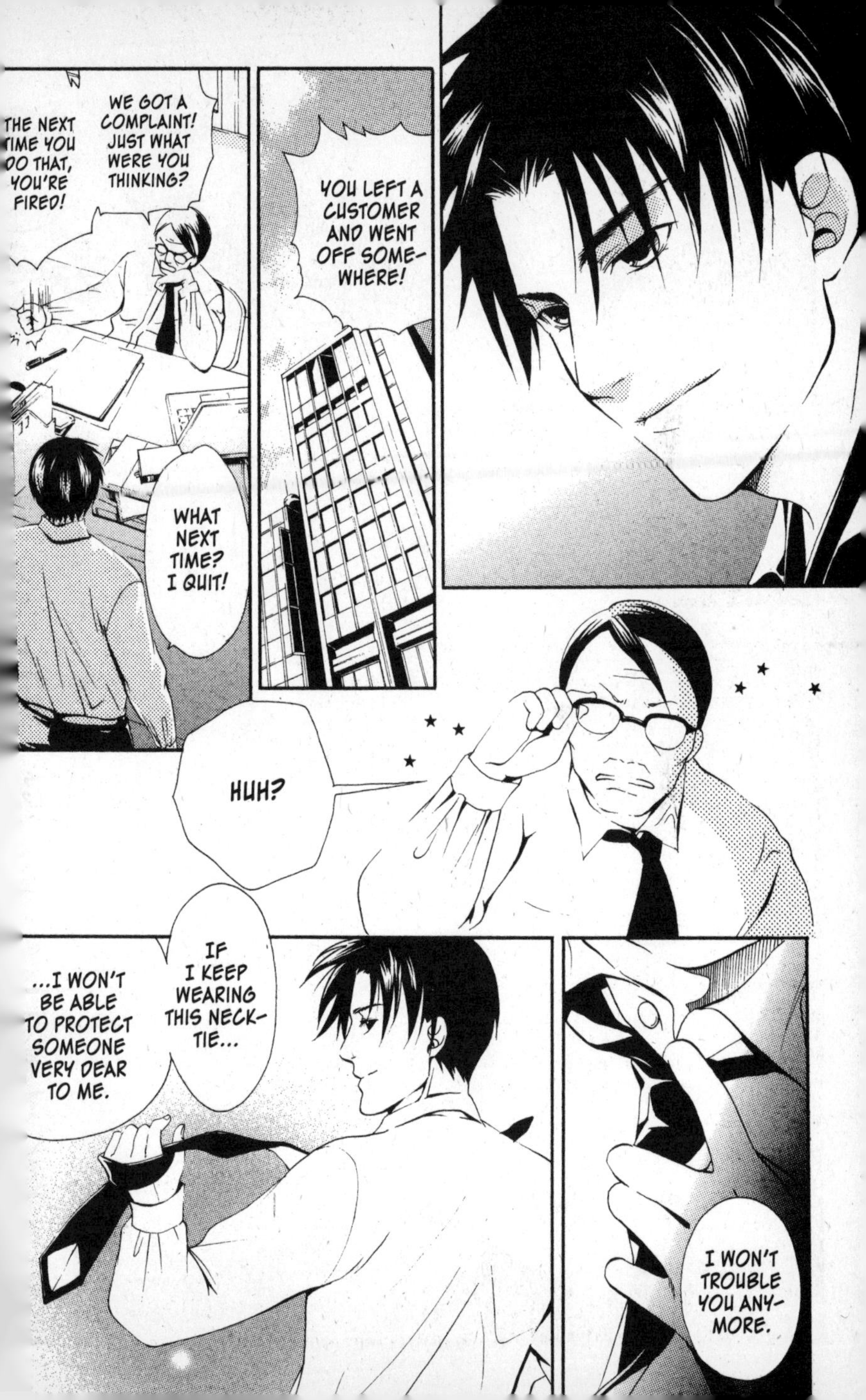
YOU LEFT A CUSTOMER AND WENT OFF SOME-WHERE!
WE GOT A COMPLAINT! JUST WHAT WERE YOU THINKING?
THE NEXT TIME YOU DO THAT, YOU'RE FIRED!
WHAT NEXT TIME? I QUIT!
HUH?
I WON'T TROUBLE YOU ANY-MORE.
IF I KEEP WEARING THIS NECK-TIE...
...I WON'T BE ABLE TO PROTECT SOMEONE VERY DEAR TO ME.

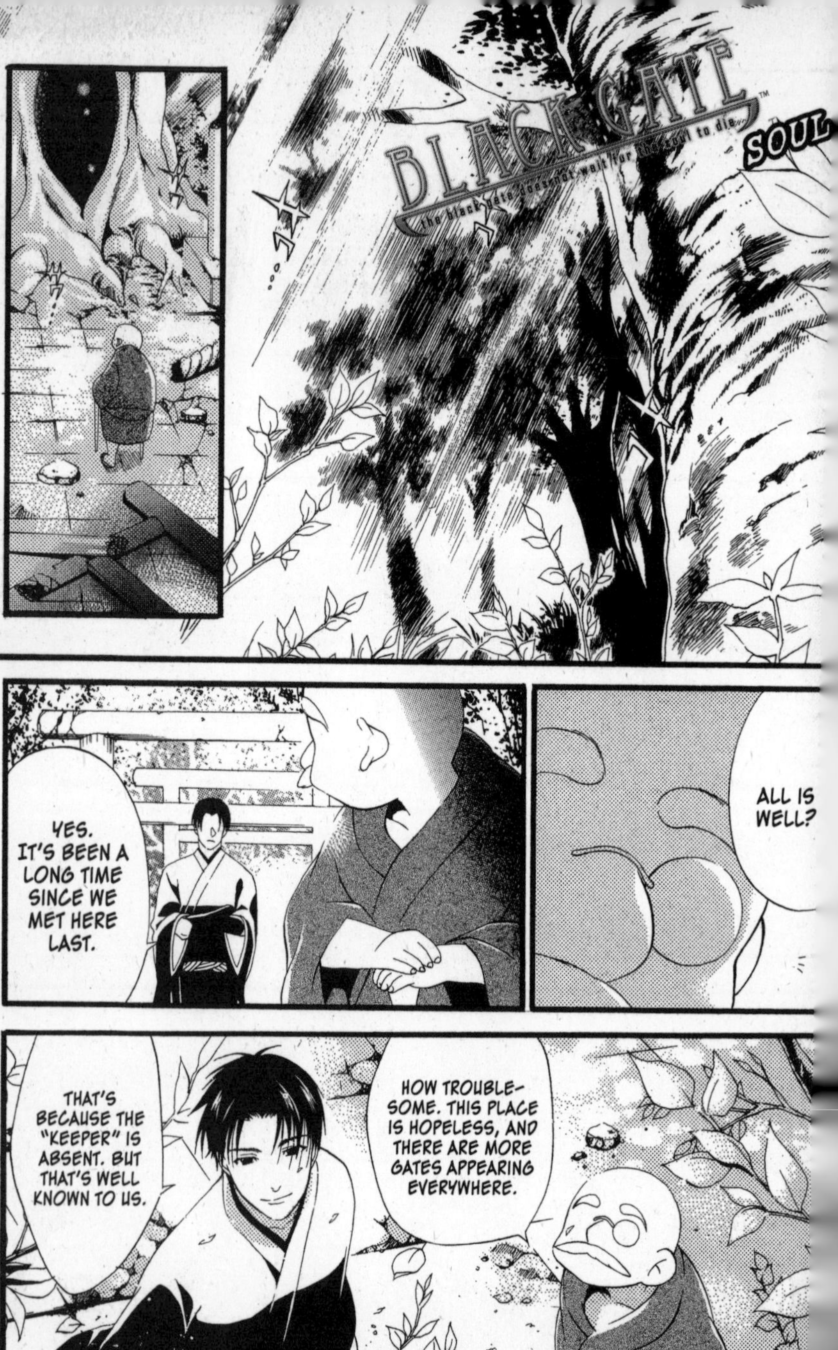
BLACK GATE
SOUL
ALL IS WELL?
YES. IT'S BEEN A LONG TIME SINCE WE MET HERE LAST.
HOW TROUBLE-SOME. THIS PLACE IS HOPELESS, AND THERE ARE MORE GATES APPEARING EVERYWHERE.
THAT'S BECAUSE THE "KEEPER" IS ABSENT. BUT THAT'S WELL KNOWN TO US.

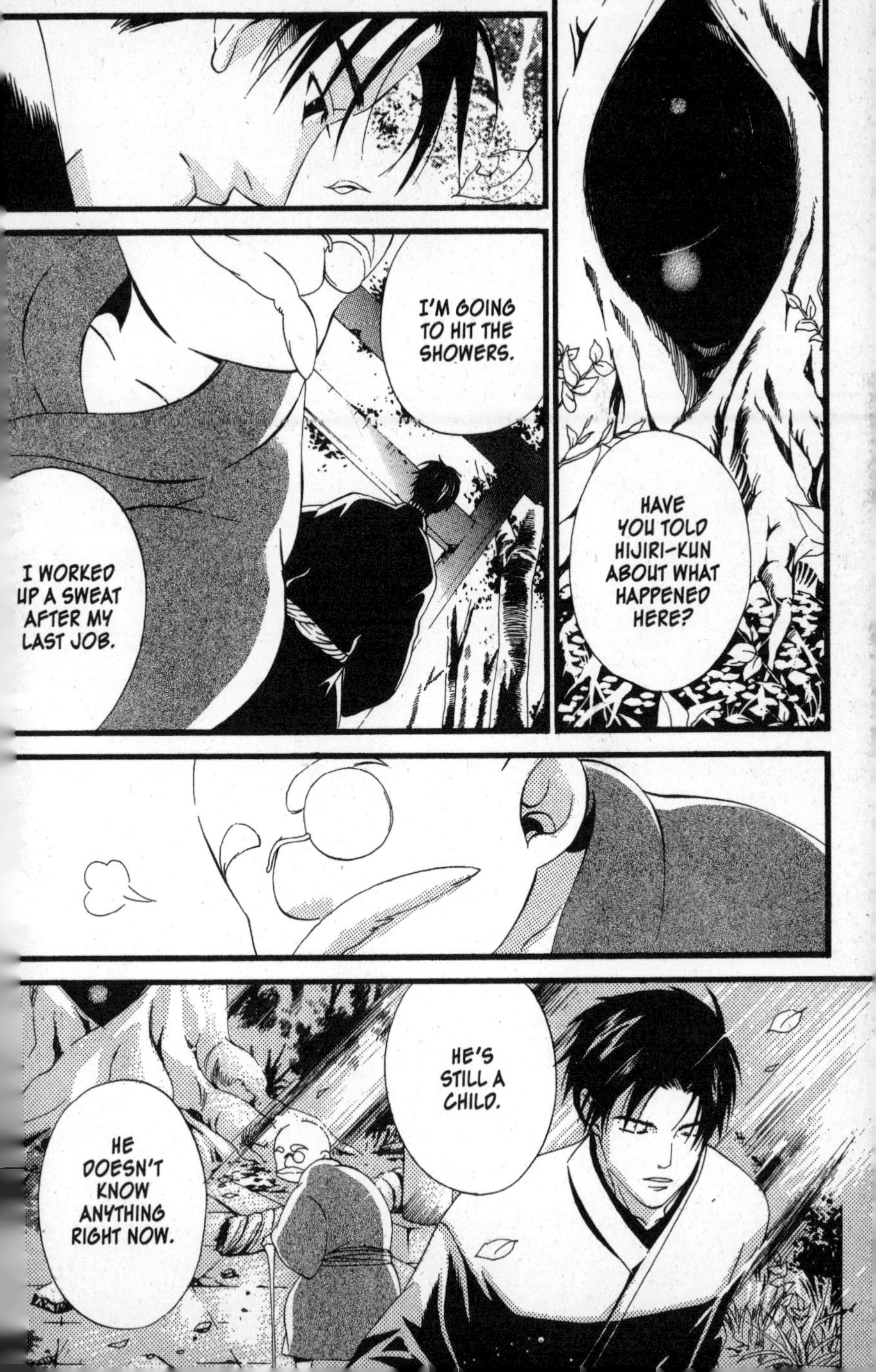
HAVE YOU TOLD HIJIRI-KUN ABOUT WHAT HAPPENED HERE?
I'M GOING TO HIT THE SHOWERS.
I WORKED UP A SWEAT AFTER MY LAST JOB.
HE'S STILL A CHILD.
HE DOESN'T KNOW ANYTHING RIGHT NOW.

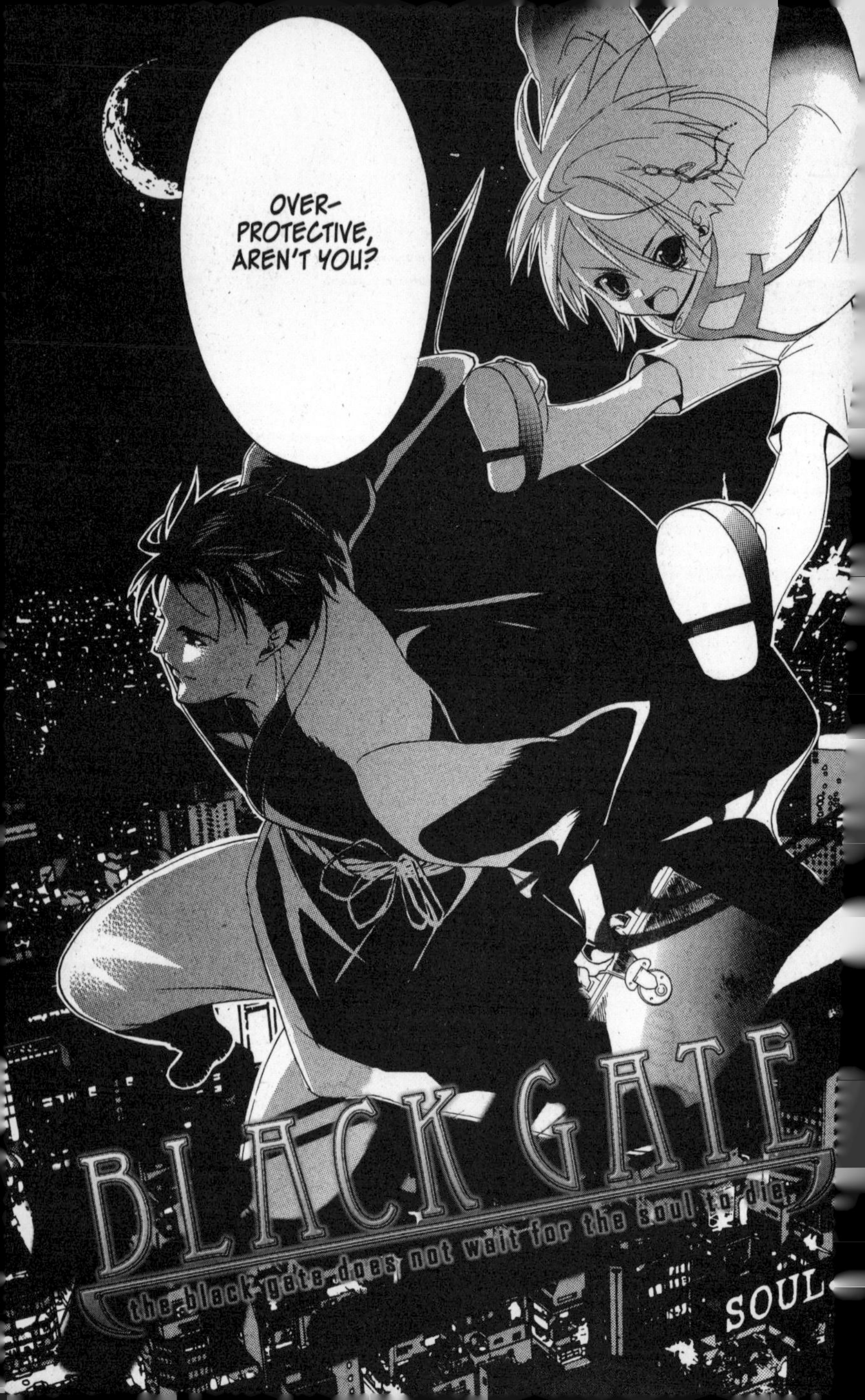
OVER-PROTECTIVE, AREN'T YOU?
BLACK GATE
the black gate does not wait for the soul to die
SOUL

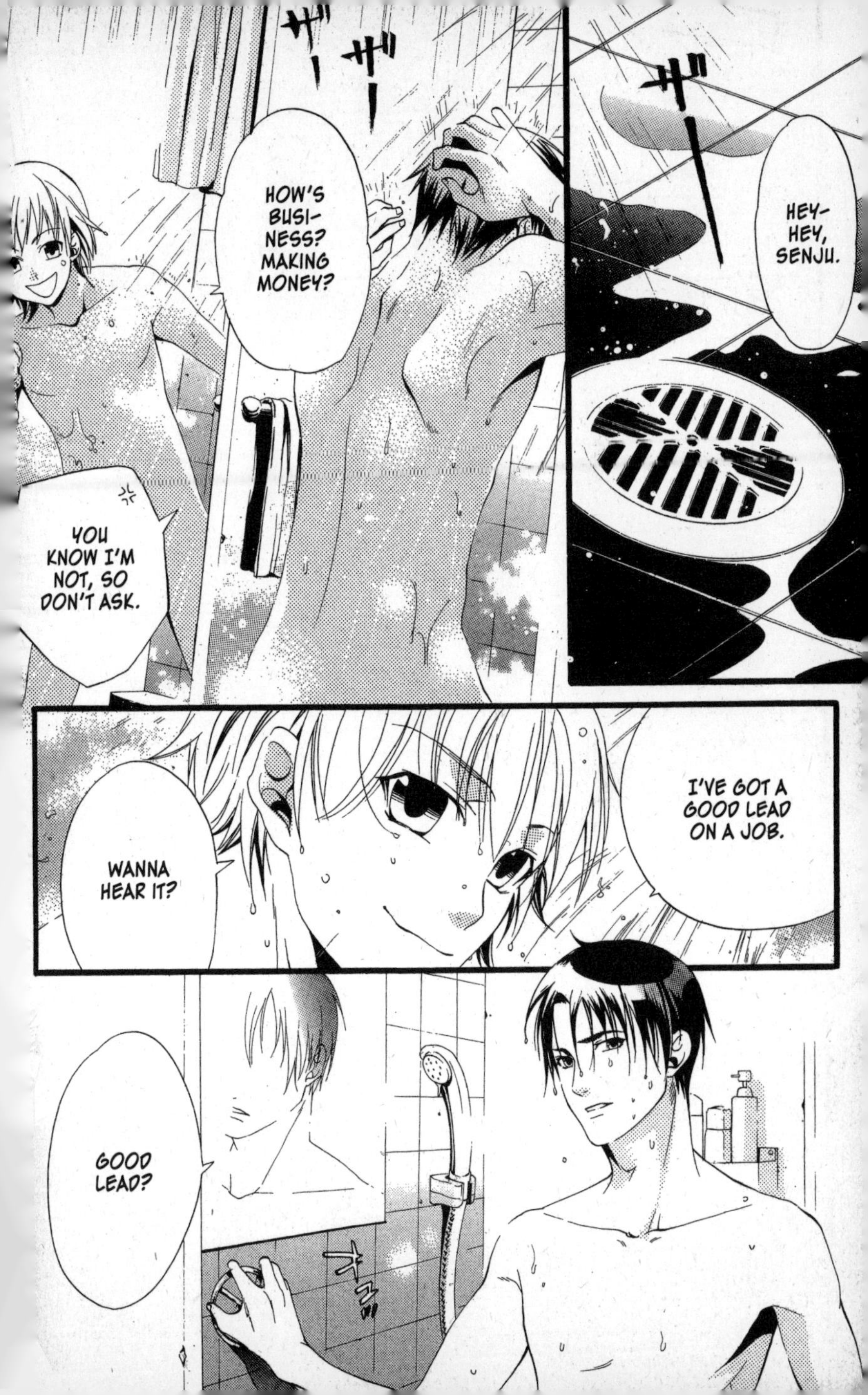
HEY-HEY, SENJU.
HOW'S BUSI-NESS? MAKING MONEY?
YOU KNOW I'M NOT, SO DON'T ASK.
I'VE GOT A GOOD LEAD ON A JOB.
WANNA HEAR IT?
GOOD LEAD?

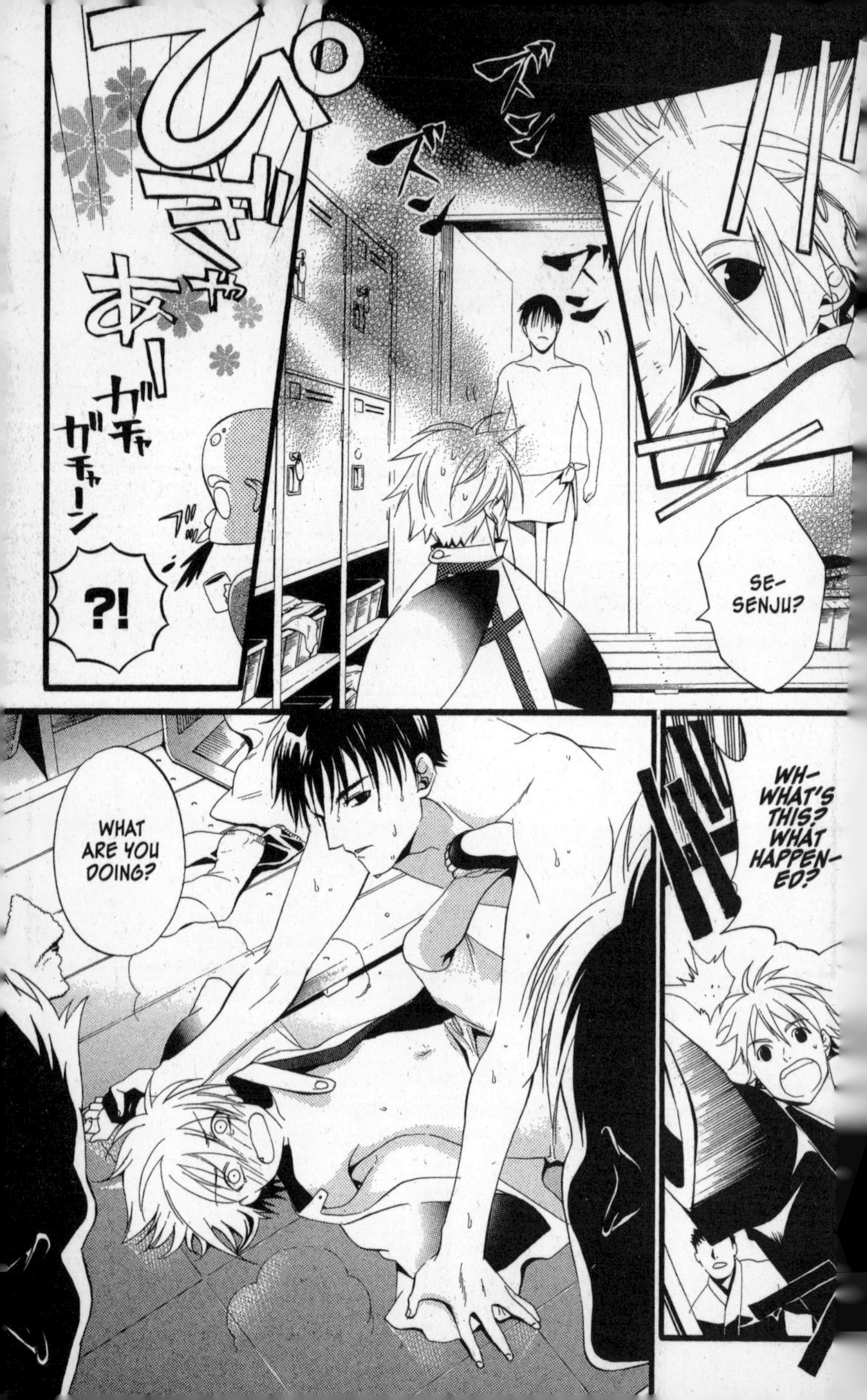
ズドン
ズドン
SE- SENJU?
?!
ガチャガチャーン
WH- WHAT'S THIS? WHAT HAPPENED?
WHAT ARE YOU DOING?

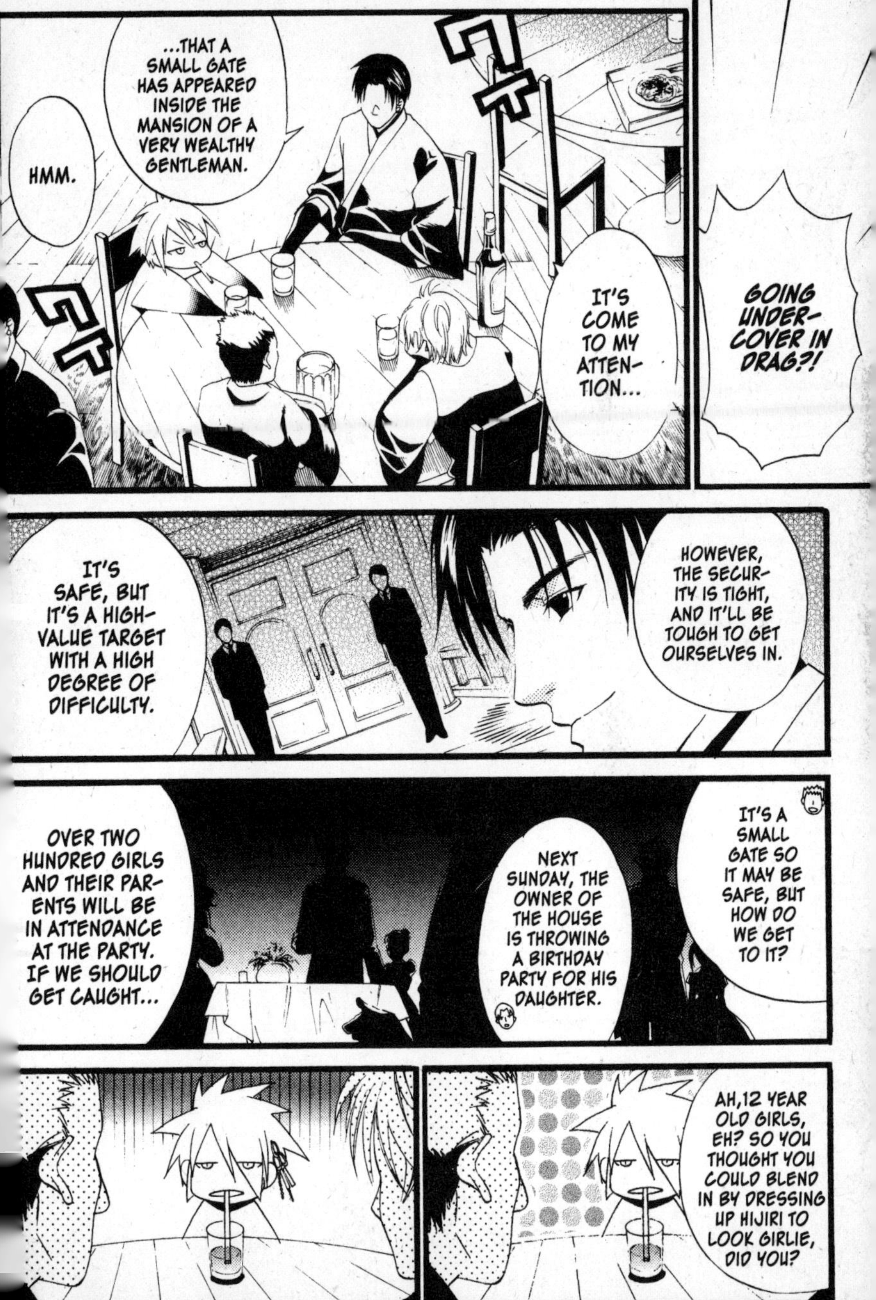
GOING UNDER-COVER IN DRAG?!
IT'S COME TO MY ATTENTION...
...THAT A SMALL GATE HAS APPEARED INSIDE THE MANSION OF A VERY WEALTHY GENTLEMAN.
HMM.
HOWEVER, THE SECURITY IS TIGHT, AND IT'LL BE TOUGH TO GET OURSELVES IN.
IT'S SAFE, BUT IT'S A HIGH-VALUE TARGET WITH A HIGH DEGREE OF DIFFICULTY.
IT'S A SMALL GATE SO IT MAY BE SAFE, BUT HOW DO WE GET TO IT?
NEXT SUNDAY, THE OWNER OF THE HOUSE IS THROWING A BIRTHDAY PARTY FOR HIS DAUGHTER.
OVER TWO HUNDRED GIRLS AND THEIR PARENTS WILL BE IN ATTENDANCE AT THE PARTY. IF WE SHOULD GET CAUGHT...
AH,12 YEAR OLD GIRLS, EH? SO YOU THOUGHT YOU COULD BLEND IN BY DRESSING UP HIJIRI TO LOOK GIRLIE, DID YOU?

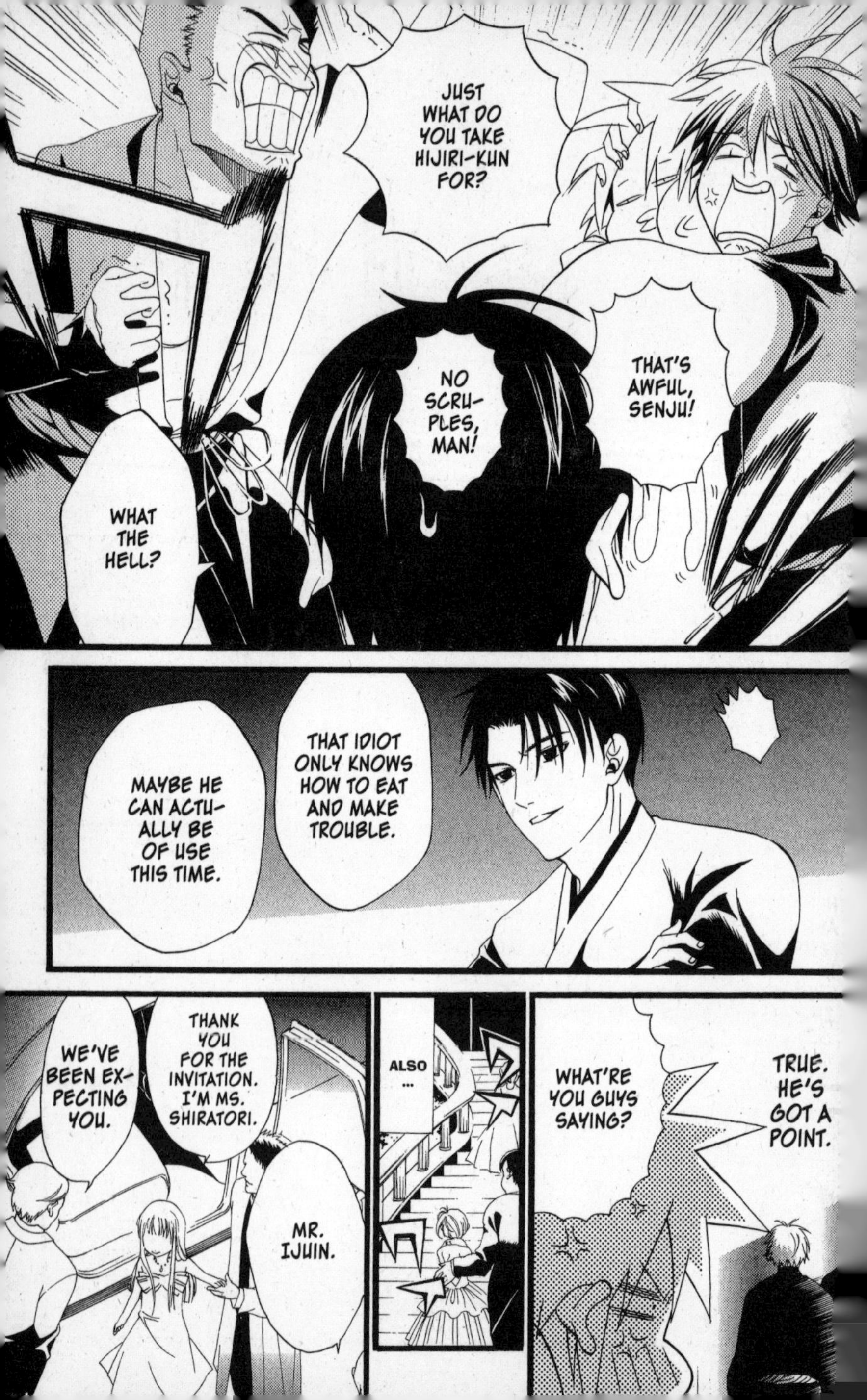
JUST WHAT DO YOU TAKE HIJIRI-KUN FOR?
THAT'S AWFUL, SENJU!
NO SCRU-PLES, MAN!
WHAT THE HELL?
THAT IDIOT ONLY KNOWS HOW TO EAT AND MAKE TROUBLE.
MAYBE HE CAN ACTU-ALLY BE OF USE THIS TIME.
TRUE. HE'S GOT A POINT.
WHAT'RE YOU GUYS SAYING?
ALSO ...
THANK YOU FOR THE INVITATION. I'M MS. SHIRATORI.
WE'VE BEEN EX-PECTING YOU.
MR. IJUIN.

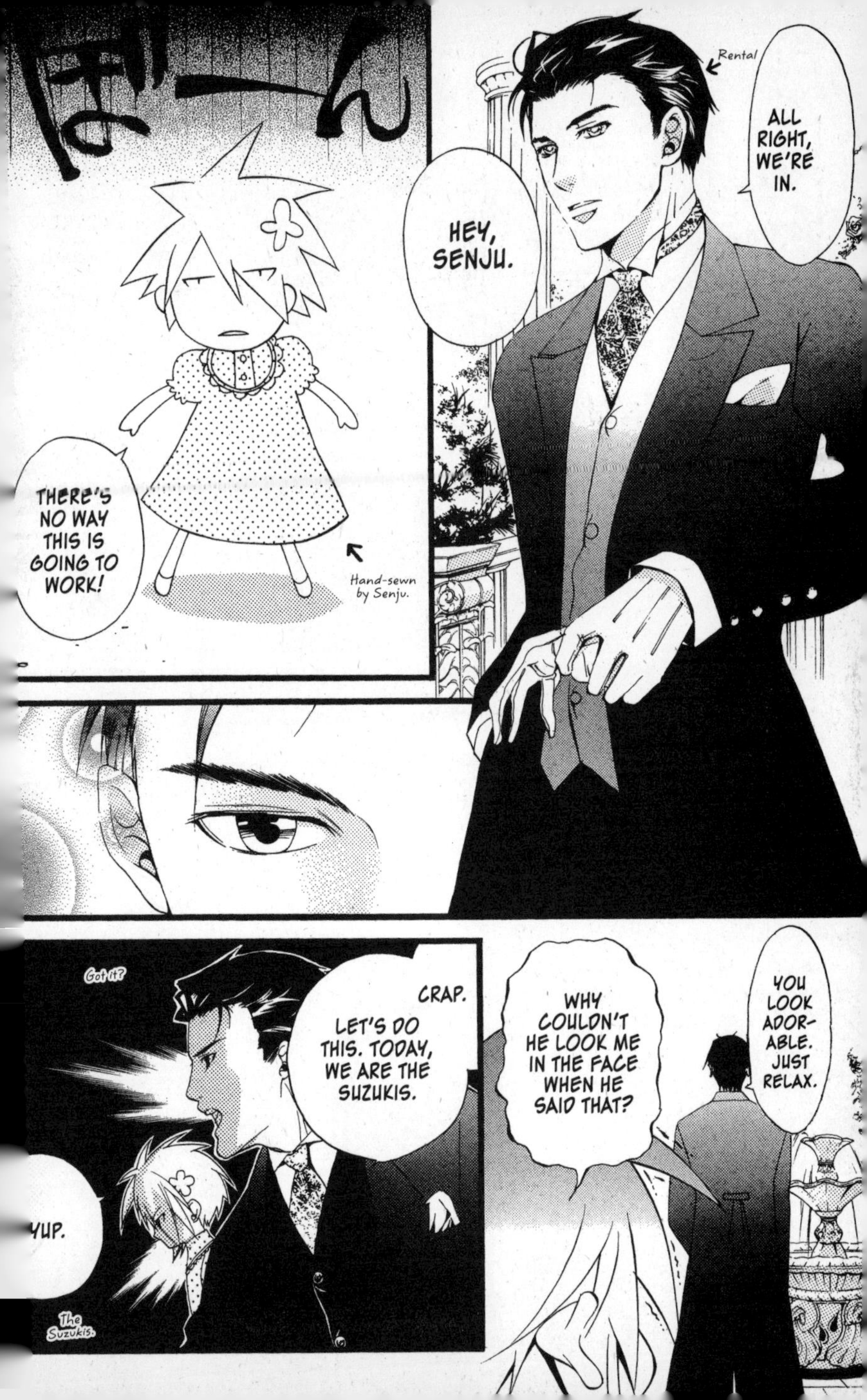
Rental
ALL RIGHT, WE'RE IN.
HEY, SENJU.
ぽーん
Hand-sewn by Senju.
THERE'S NO WAY THIS IS GOING TO WORK!
YOU LOOK ADORABLE. JUST RELAX.
WHY COULDN'T HE LOOK ME IN THE FACE WHEN HE SAID THAT?
CRAP.
LET'S DO THIS. TODAY, WE ARE THE SUZUKIS.
Got it?
YUP.
The Suzukis.

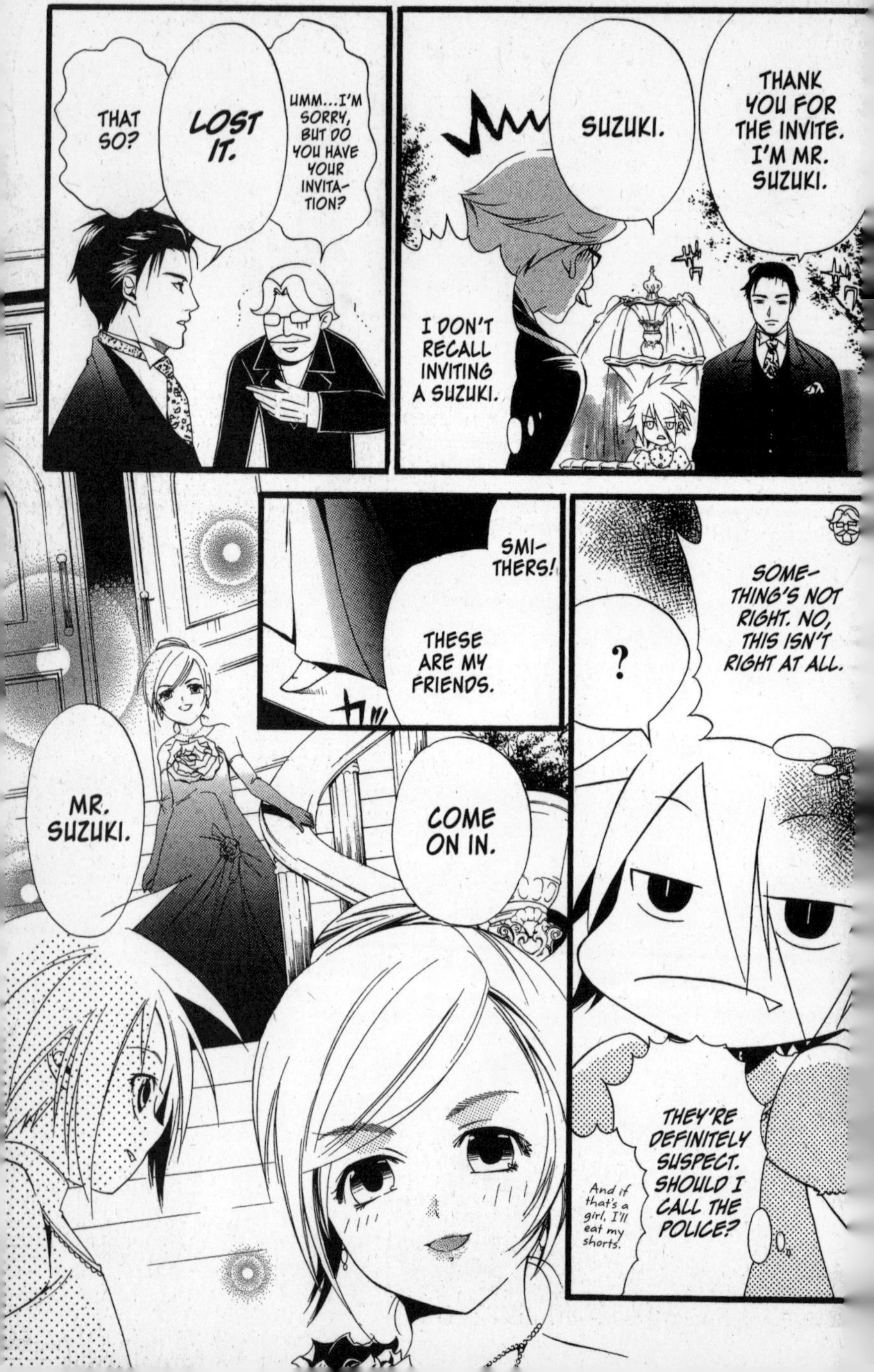
THANK YOU FOR THE INVITE. I'M MR. SUZUKI.
SUZUKI.
I DON'T RECALL INVITING A SUZUKI.
UMM...I'M SORRY, BUT DO YOU HAVE YOUR INVITA-TION?
LOST IT.
THAT SO?
SOME-THING'S NOT RIGHT. NO, THIS ISN'T RIGHT AT ALL.
?
THEY'RE DEFINITELY SUSPECT. SHOULD I CALL THE POLICE?
And if that's a girl, I'll eat my shorts.
SMI-THERS!
THESE ARE MY FRIENDS.
COME ON IN.
MR. SUZUKI.

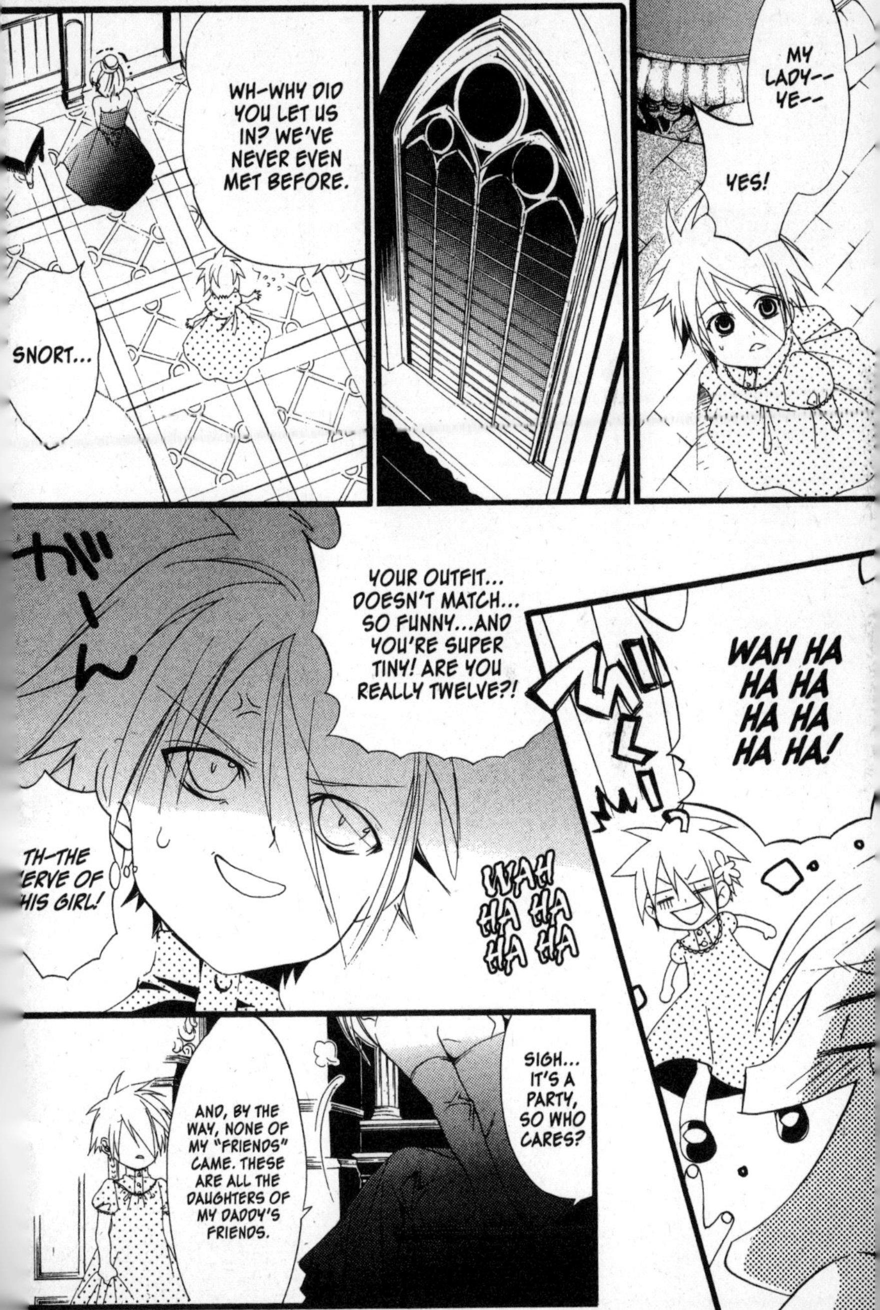
MY LADY-- YE--
YES!
WH-WHY DID YOU LET US IN? WE'VE NEVER EVEN MET BEFORE.
SNORT...
WAH HA HA HA HA HA HA HA!
YOUR OUTFIT... DOESN'T MATCH... SO FUNNY...AND YOU'RE SUPER TINY! ARE YOU REALLY TWELVE?!
WAH HA HA HA HA
TH-THE ERVE OF HIS GIRL!
SIGH... IT'S A PARTY, SO WHO CARES?
AND, BY THE WAY, NONE OF MY "FRIENDS" CAME. THESE ARE ALL THE DAUGHTERS OF MY DADDY'S FRIENDS.

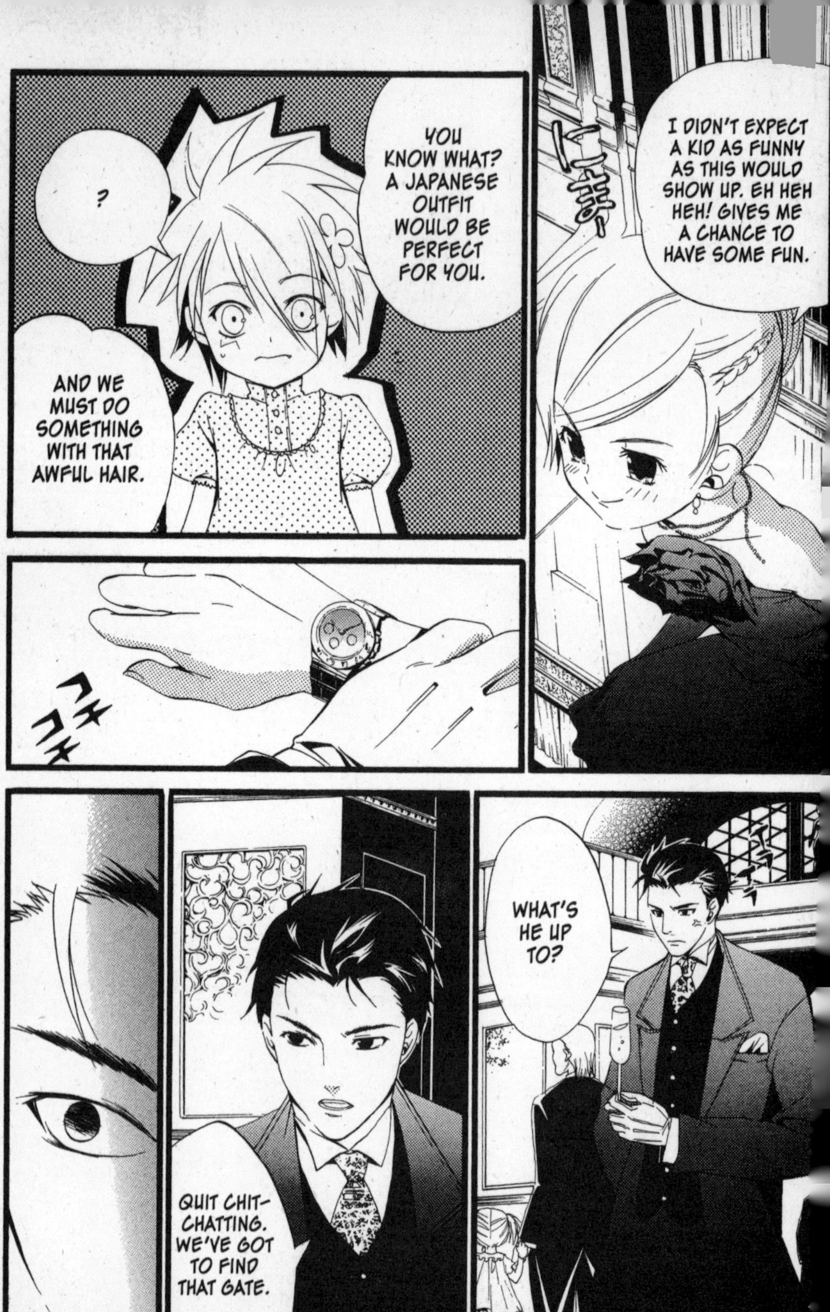

I DIDN'T EXPECT A KID AS FUNNY AS THIS WOULD SHOW UP. EH HEH HEH! GIVES ME A CHANCE TO HAVE SOME FUN.
YOU KNOW WHAT? A JAPANESE OUTFIT WOULD BE PERFECT FOR YOU.
?
AND WE MUST DO SOMETHING WITH THAT AWFUL HAIR.
WHAT'S HE UP TO?
QUIT CHIT-CHATTING. WE'VE GOT TO FIND THAT GATE.

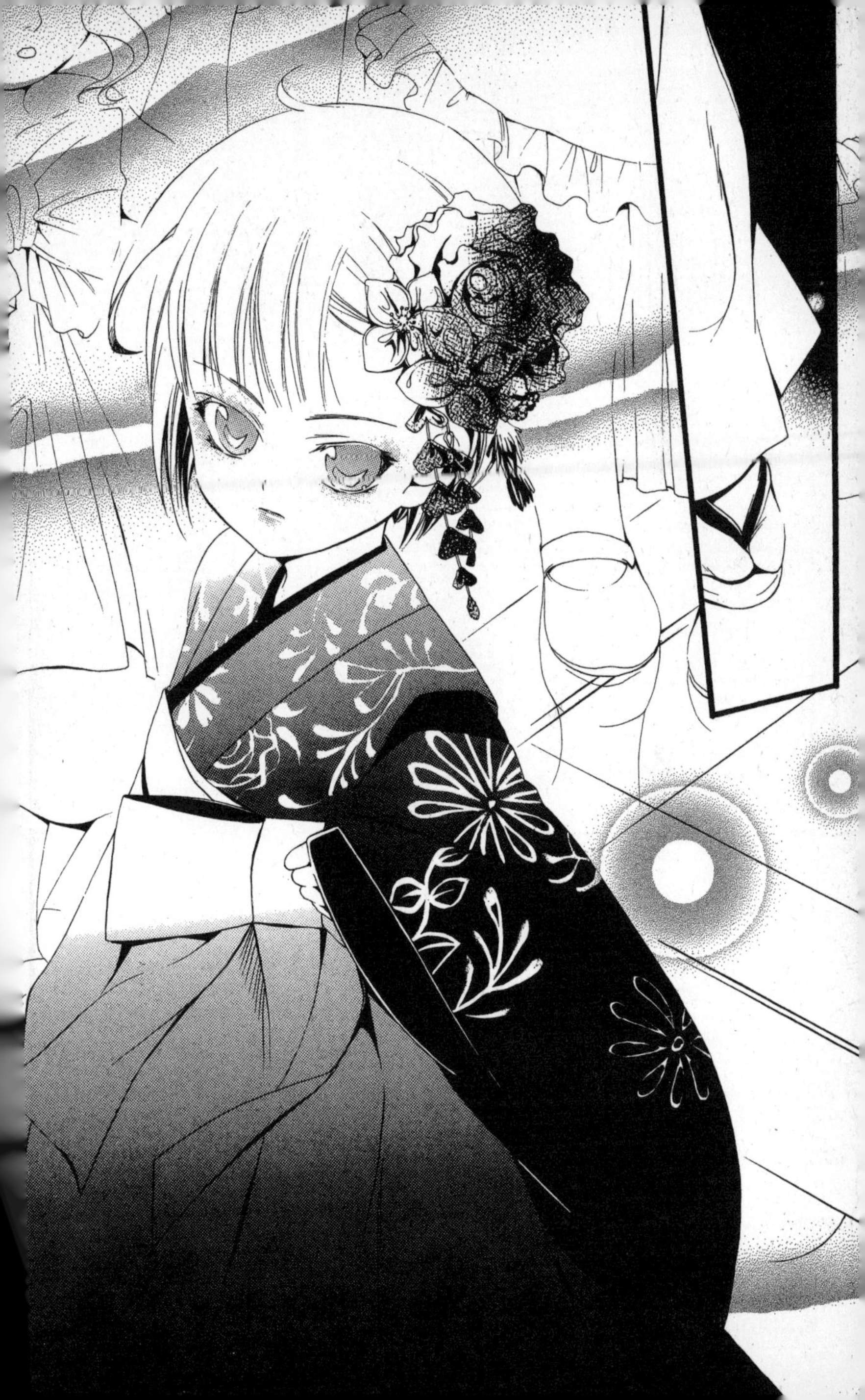

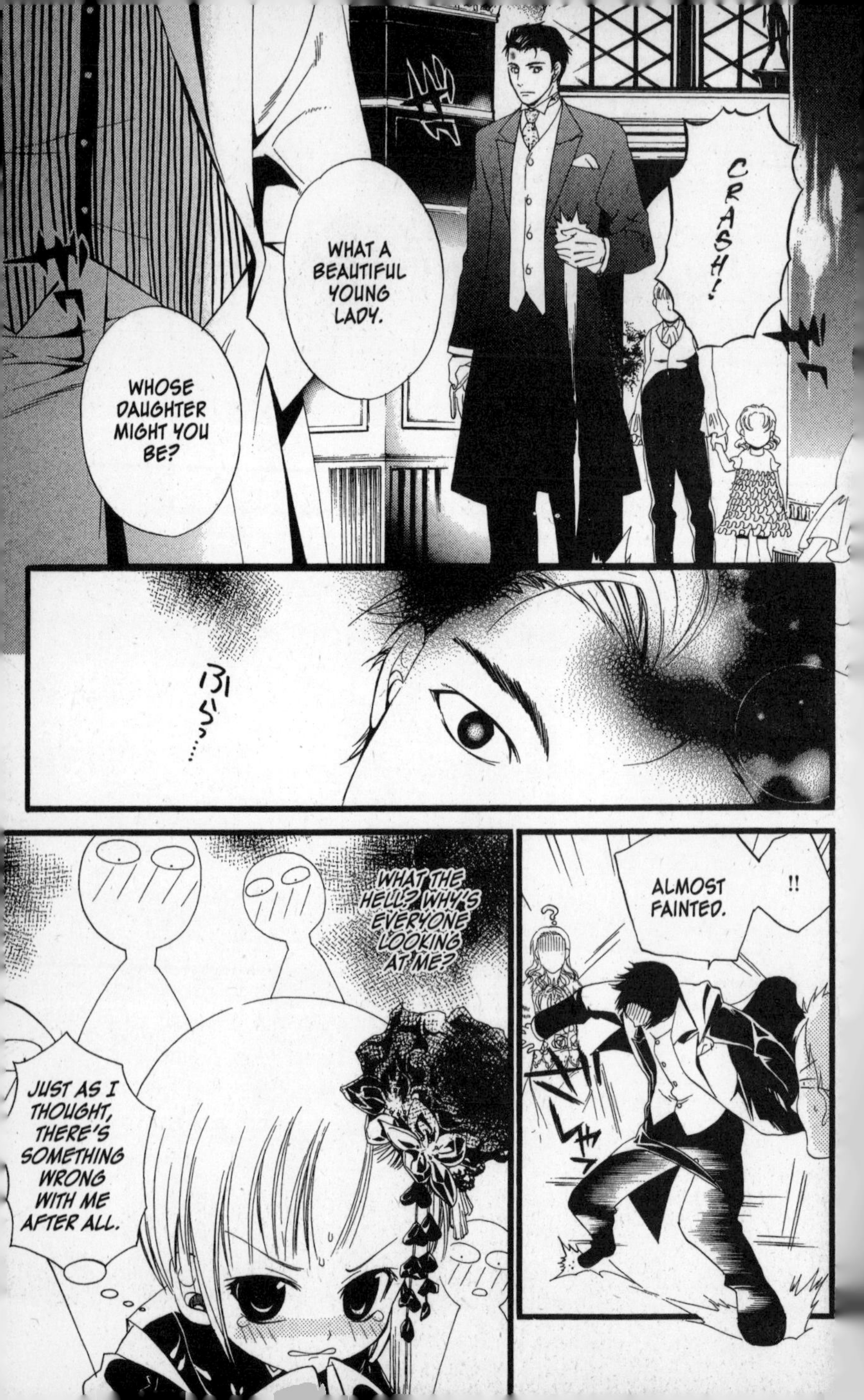
CRASH!
WHAT A BEAUTIFUL YOUNG LADY.
WHOSE DAUGHTER MIGHT YOU BE?
ALMOST FAINTED.
!!
WHAT THE HELL? WHY'S EVERYONE LOOKING AT ME?
JUST AS I THOUGHT, THERE'S SOMETHING WRONG WITH ME AFTER ALL.

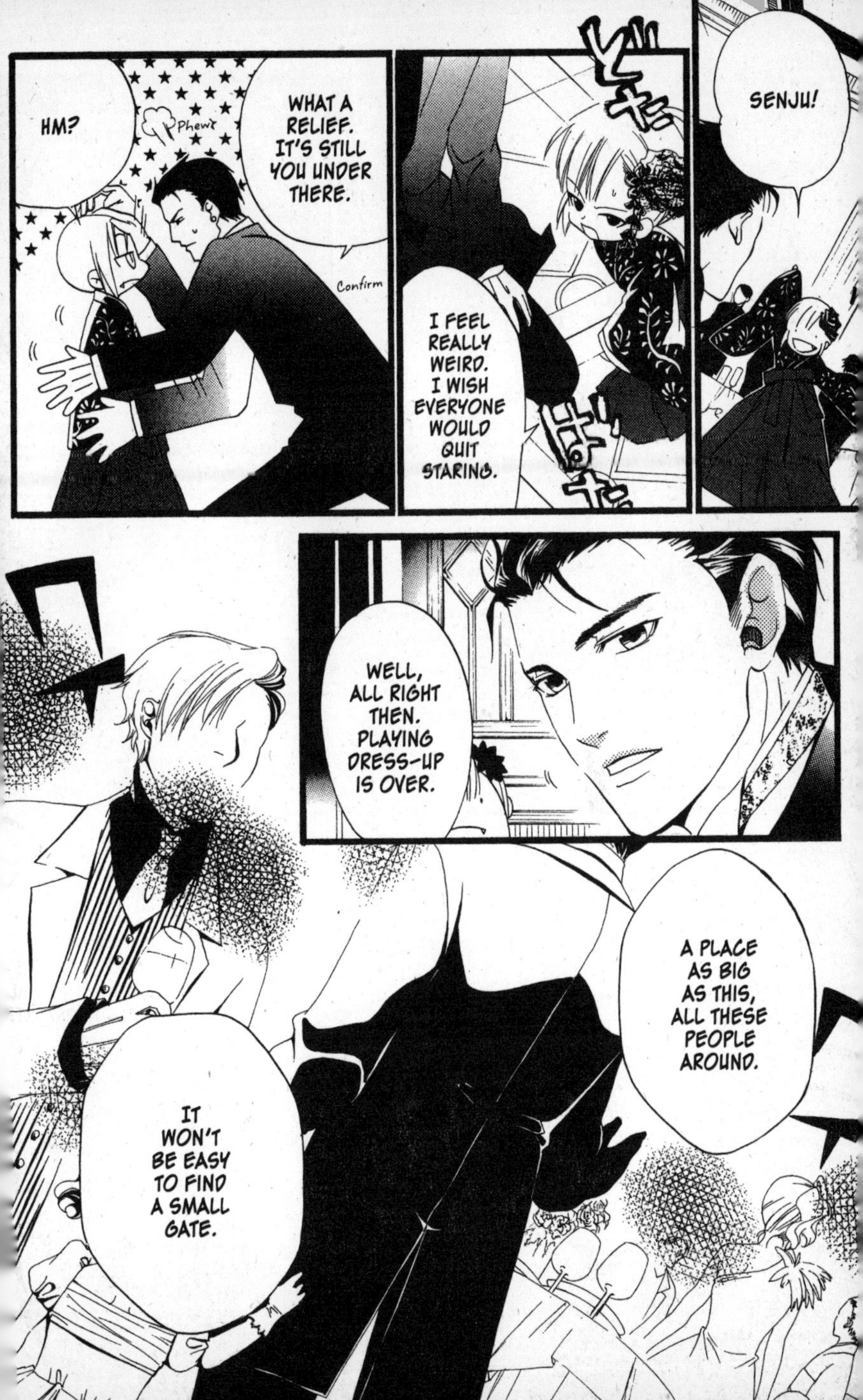
SENJU!
I FEEL REALLY WEIRD. I WISH EVERYONE WOULD QUIT STARING.
WHAT A RELIEF. IT'S STILL YOU UNDER THERE.
Phew
HM?
Confirm
WELL, ALL RIGHT THEN. PLAYING DRESS-UP IS OVER.
A PLACE AS BIG AS THIS, ALL THESE PEOPLE AROUND.
IT WON'T BE EASY TO FIND A SMALL GATE.

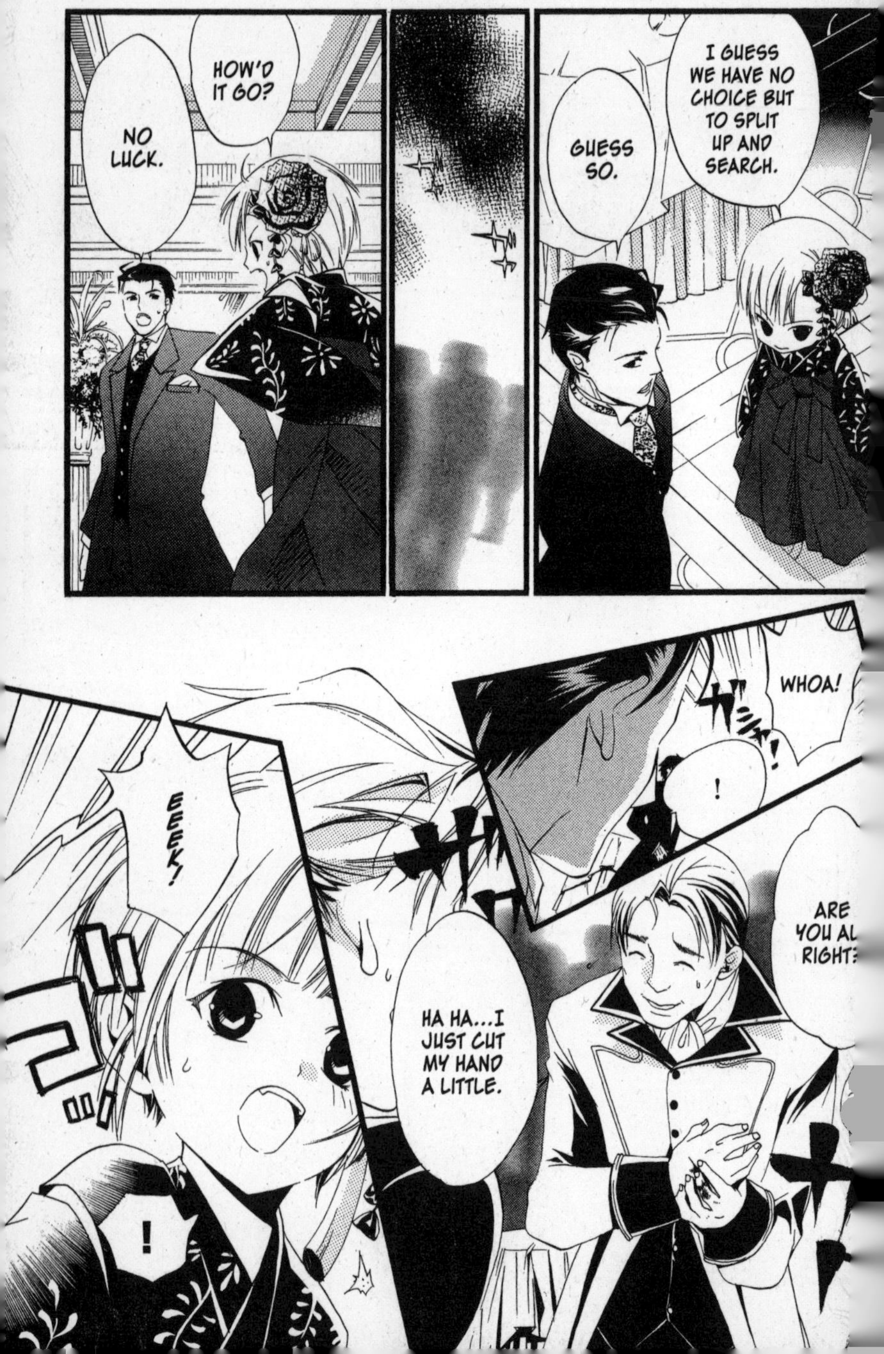
I GUESS WE HAVE NO CHOICE BUT TO SPLIT UP AND SEARCH.
GUESS SO.
HOW'D IT GO?
NO LUCK.
WHOA!
!
ARE YOU AL RIGHT
HA HA...I JUST CUT MY HAND A LITTLE.
EEEK!
!

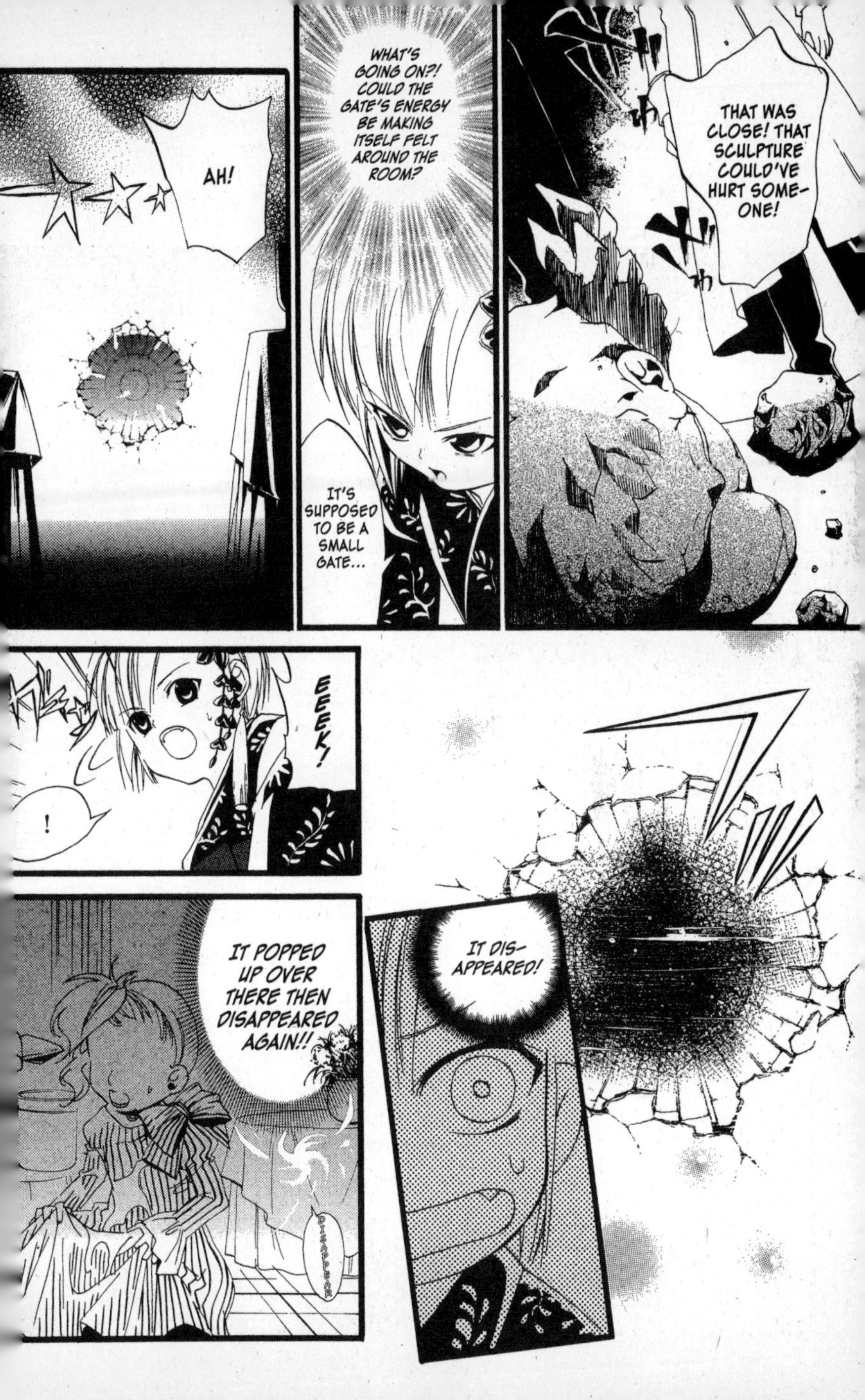
THAT WAS CLOSE! THAT SCULPTURE COULD'VE HURT SOME-ONE!
WHAT'S GOING ON?! COULD THE GATE'S ENERGY BE MAKING ITSELF FELT AROUND THE ROOM?
IT'S SUPPOSED TO BE A SMALL GATE...
AH!
EEEK!
!
IT DIS-APPEARED!
IT POPPED UP OVER THERE THEN DISAPPEARED AGAIN!!
DISAPPEAR

A "MOVING GATE"...

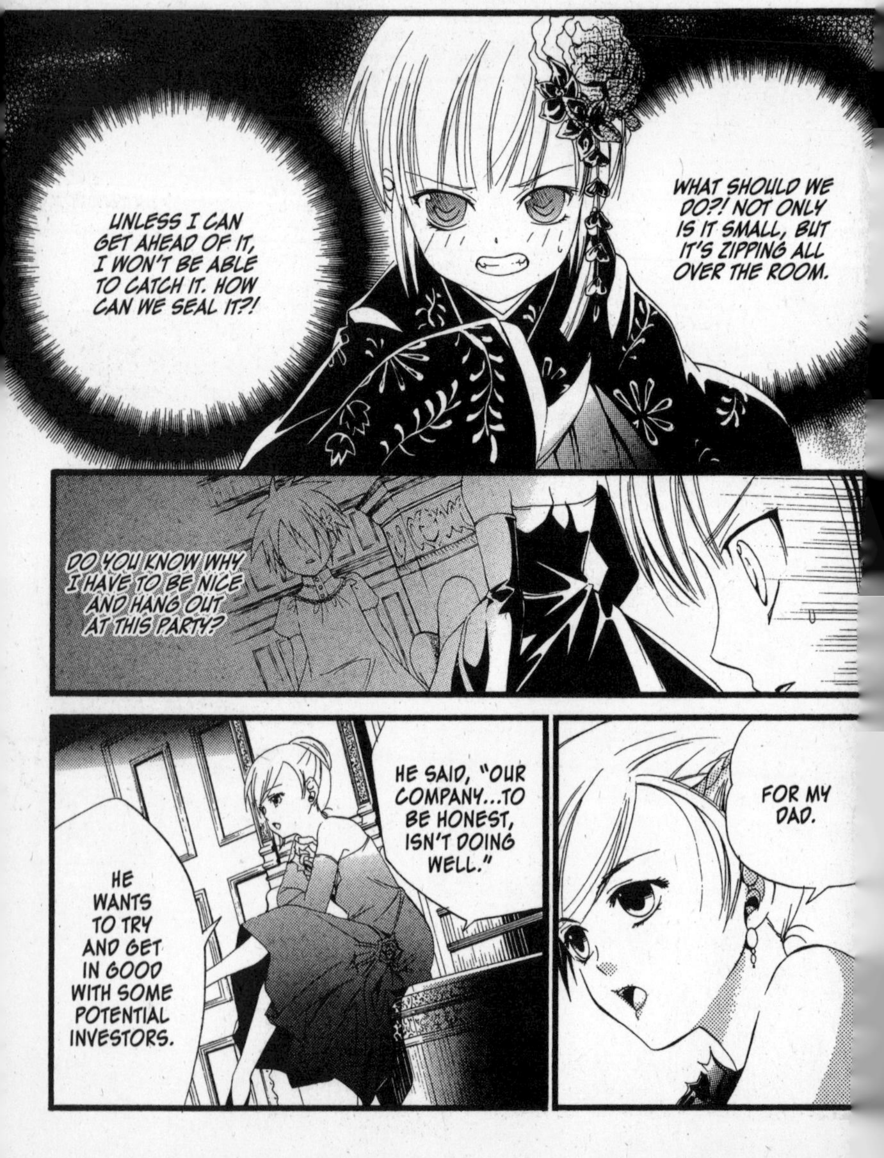
WHAT SHOULD WE DO?! NOT ONLY IS IT SMALL, BUT IT'S ZIPPING ALL OVER THE ROOM.
UNLESS I CAN GET AHEAD OF IT, I WON'T BE ABLE TO CATCH IT. HOW CAN WE SEAL IT?!
DO YOU KNOW WHY I HAVE TO BE NICE AND HANG OUT AT THIS PARTY?
FOR MY DAD.
HE SAID, "OUR COMPANY...TO BE HONEST, ISN'T DOING WELL."
HE WANTS TO TRY AND GET IN GOOD WITH SOME POTENTIAL INVESTORS.

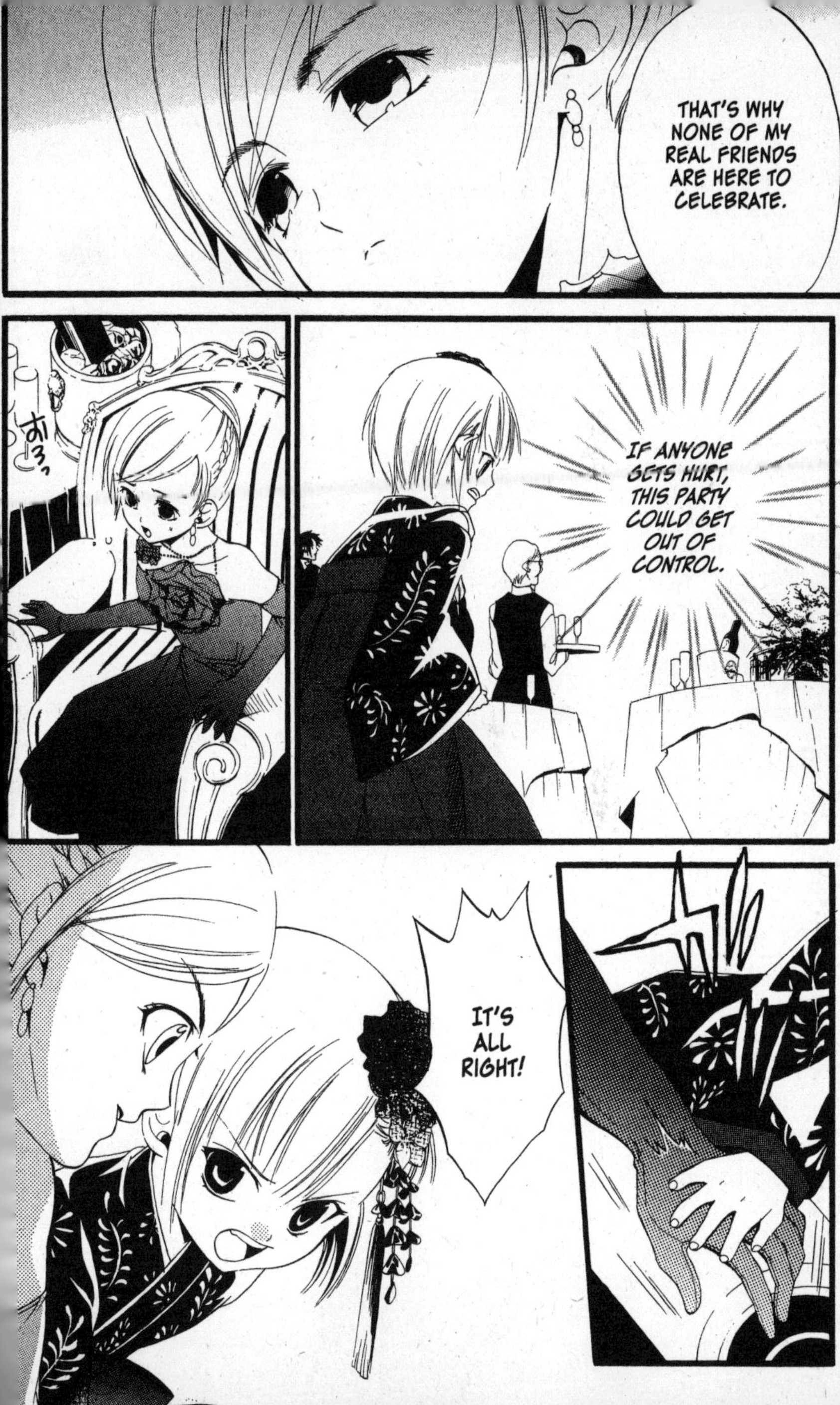
THAT'S WHY NONE OF MY REAL FRIENDS ARE HERE TO CELEBRATE.
IF ANYONE GETS HURT, THIS PARTY COULD GET OUT OF CONTROL.
おろっ
IT'S ALL RIGHT!

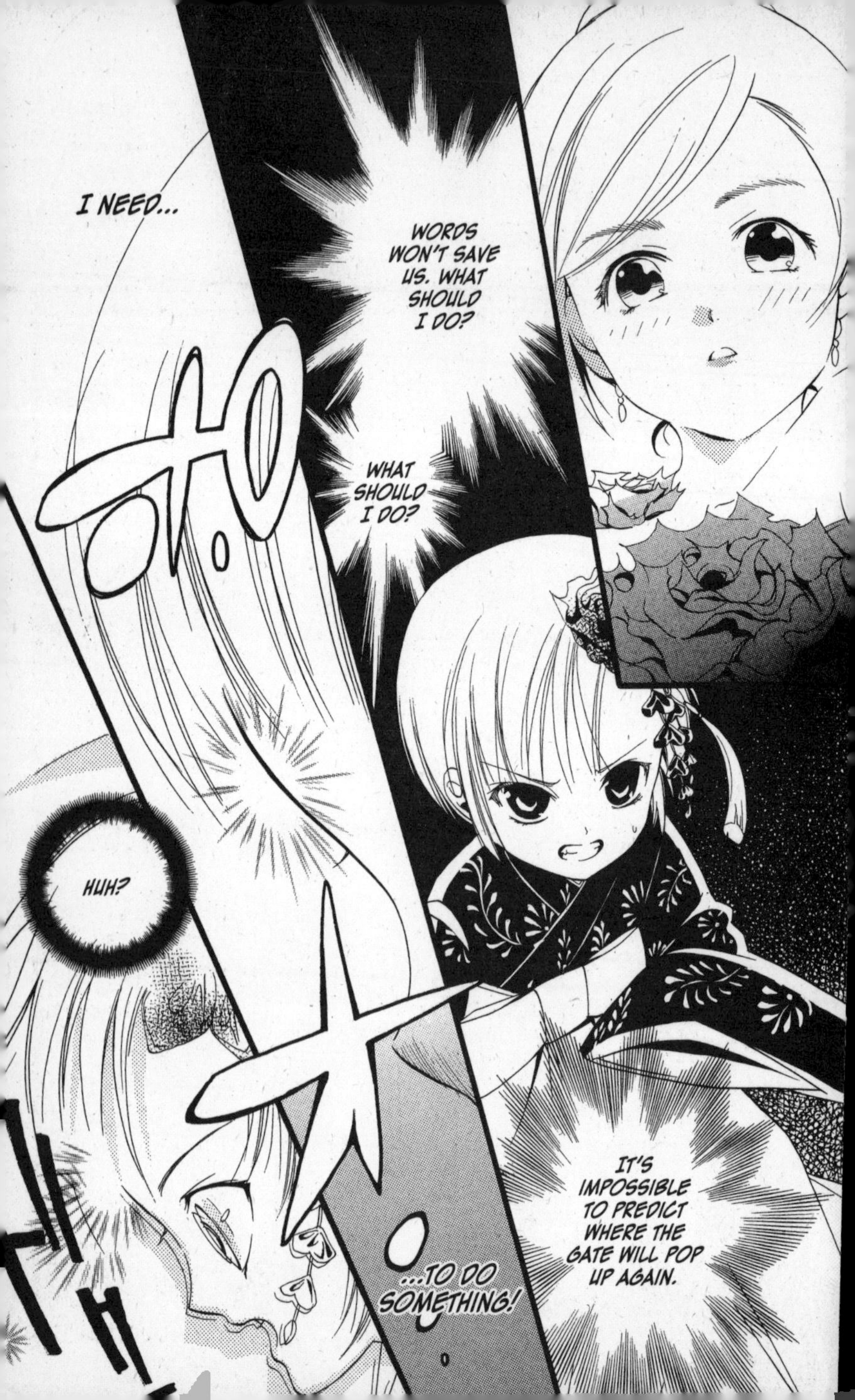
WORDS WON'T SAVE US. WHAT SHOULD I DO?
WHAT SHOULD I DO?
I NEED...
IT'S IMPOSSIBLE TO PREDICT WHERE THE GATE WILL POP UP AGAIN.
...TO DO SOMETHING!
HUH?

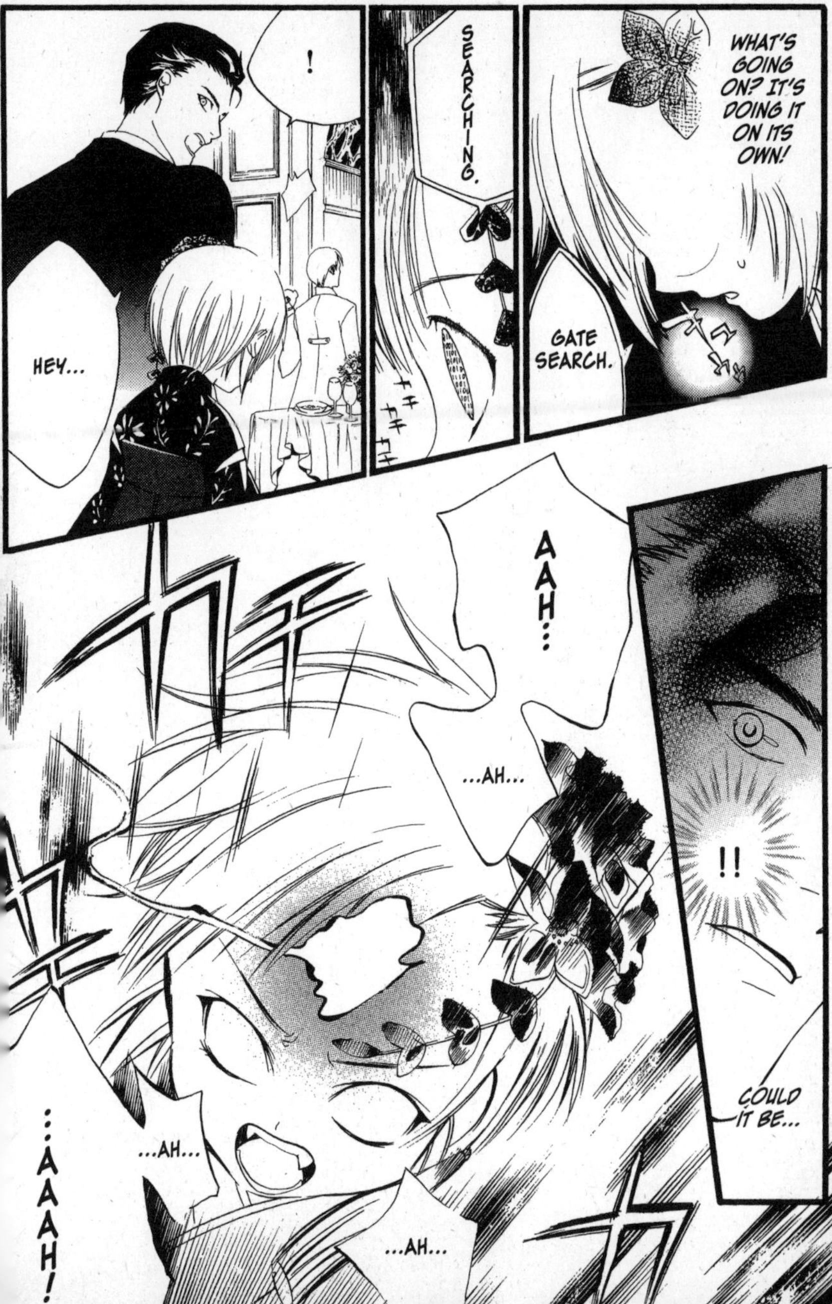
WHAT'S GOING ON? IT'S DOING IT ON ITS OWN!
GATE SEARCH.
SEARCHING.
!
HEY...
!!
COULD IT BE...
AAH...
...AH...
...AH...
...AH...
...AAAAH!

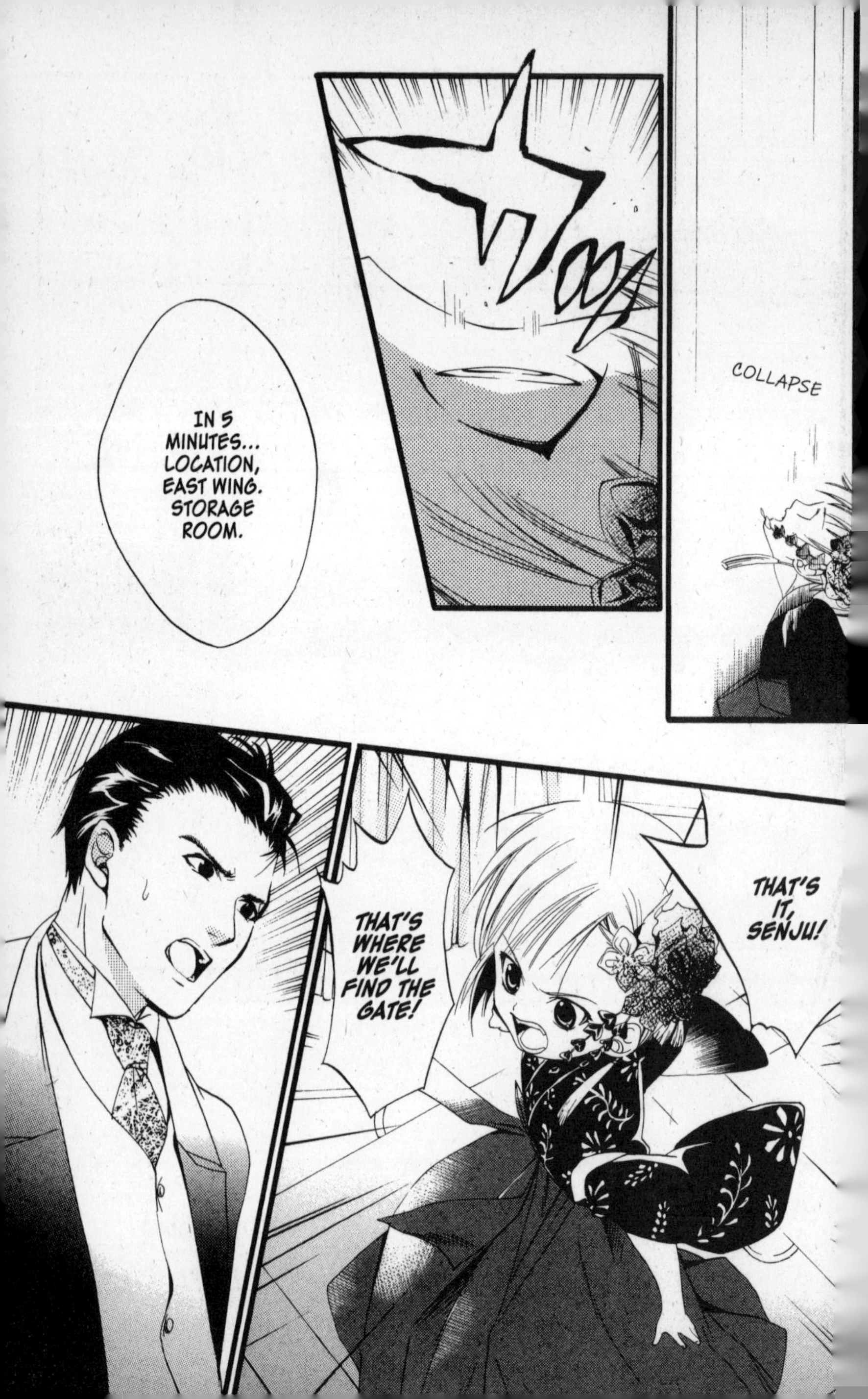
COLLAPSE
IN 5 MINUTES... LOCATION, EAST WING. STORAGE ROOM.
THAT'S IT, SENJU!
THAT'S WHERE WE'LL FIND THE GATE!

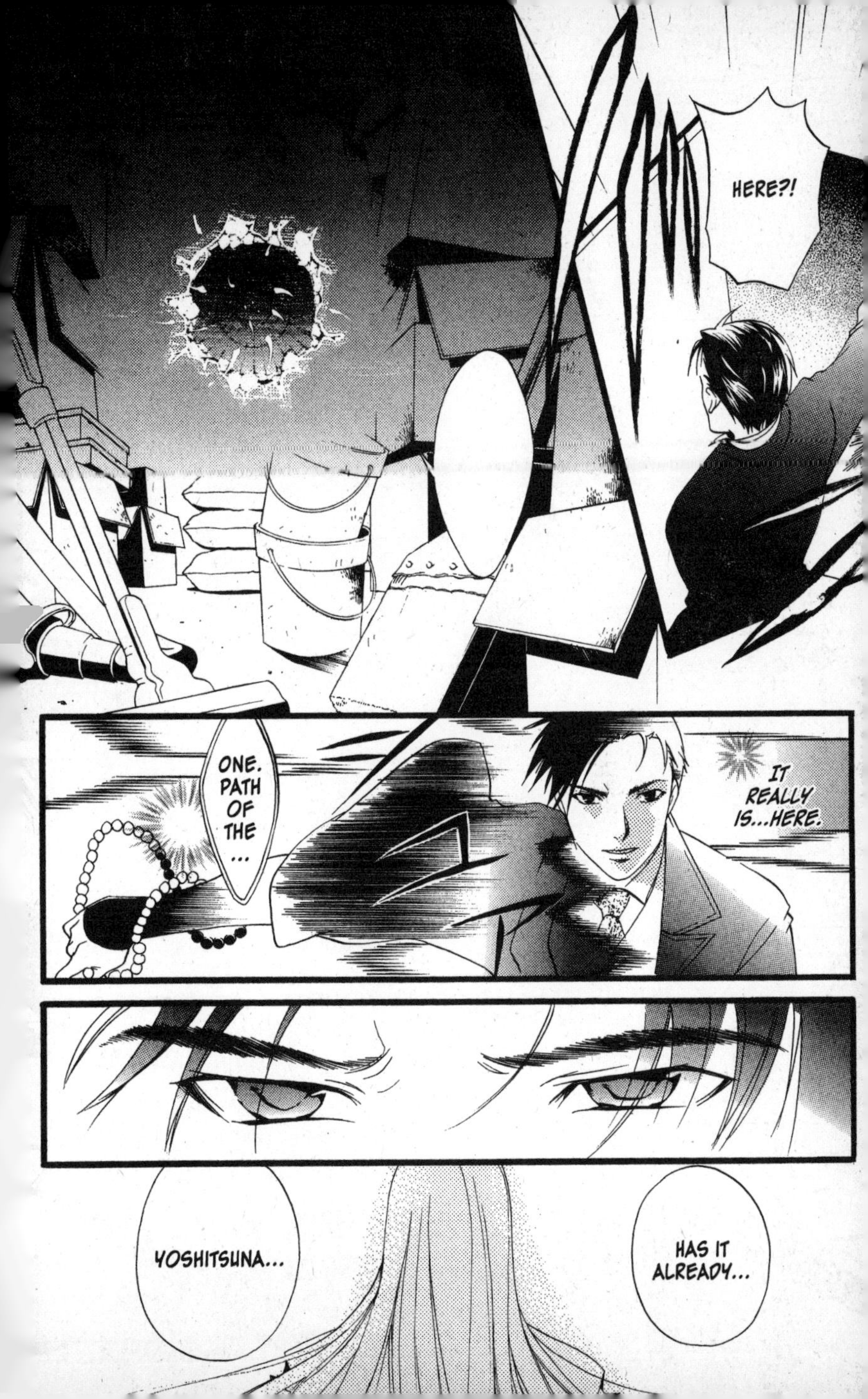
HERE?!
IT REALLY IS...HERE.
ONE. PATH OF THE ...
HAS IT ALREADY...
YOSHITSUNA...

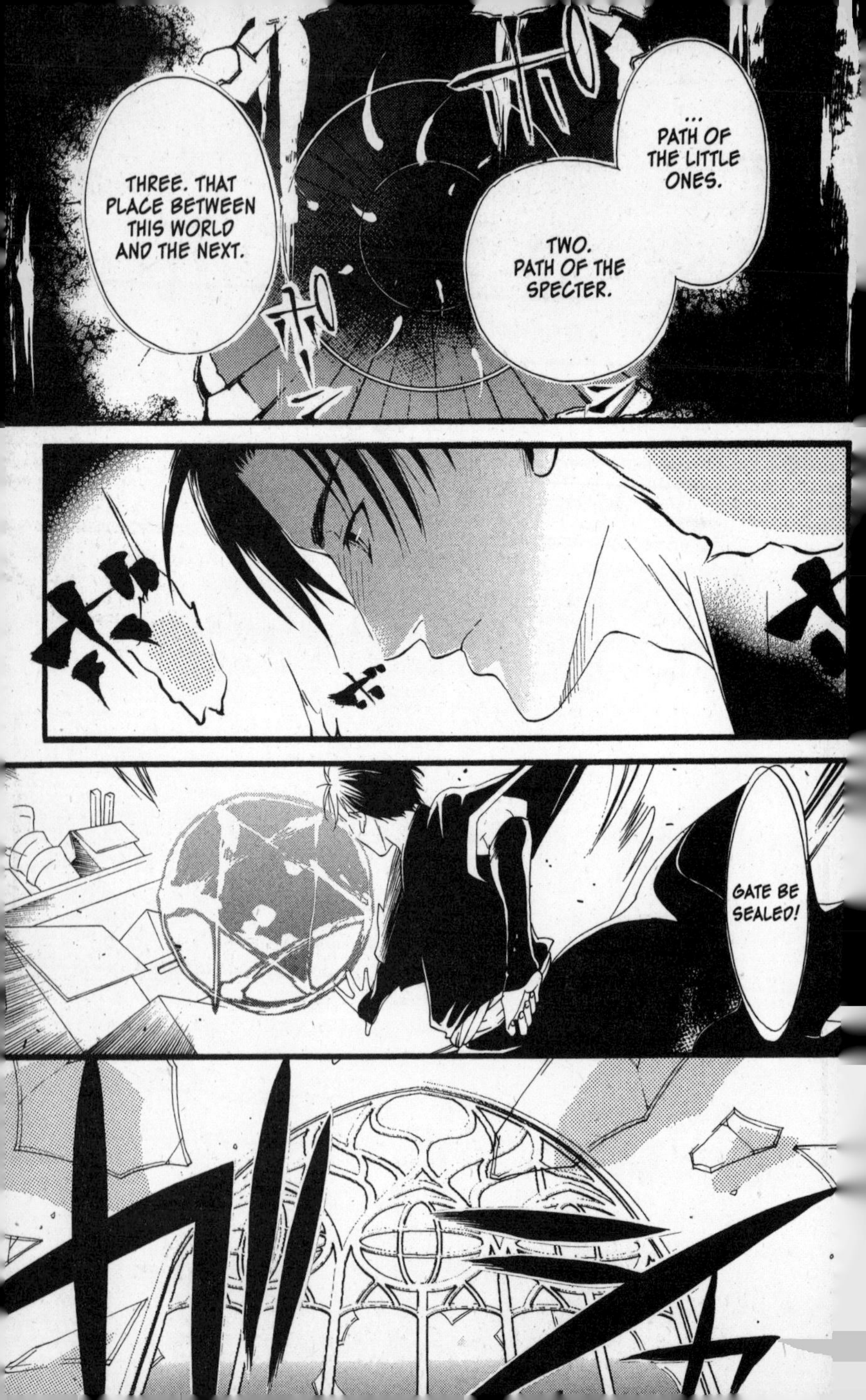
... PATH OF THE LITTLE ONES.
TWO. PATH OF THE SPECTER.
THREE. THAT PLACE BETWEEN THIS WORLD AND THE NEXT.
GATE BE SEALED!

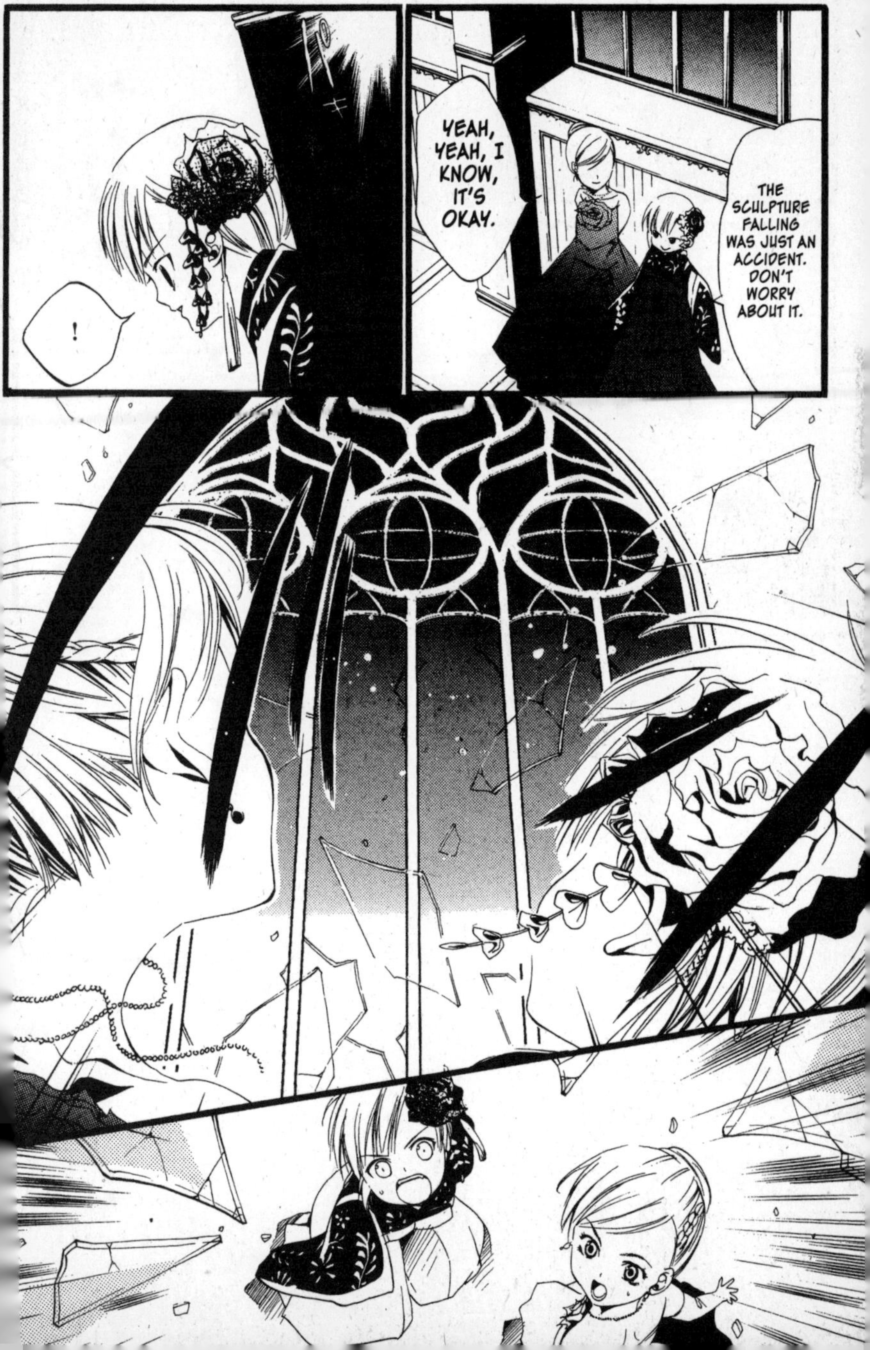
THE SCULPTURE FALLING WAS JUST AN ACCIDENT. DON'T WORRY ABOUT IT.
YEAH, YEAH, I KNOW, IT'S OKAY.
!

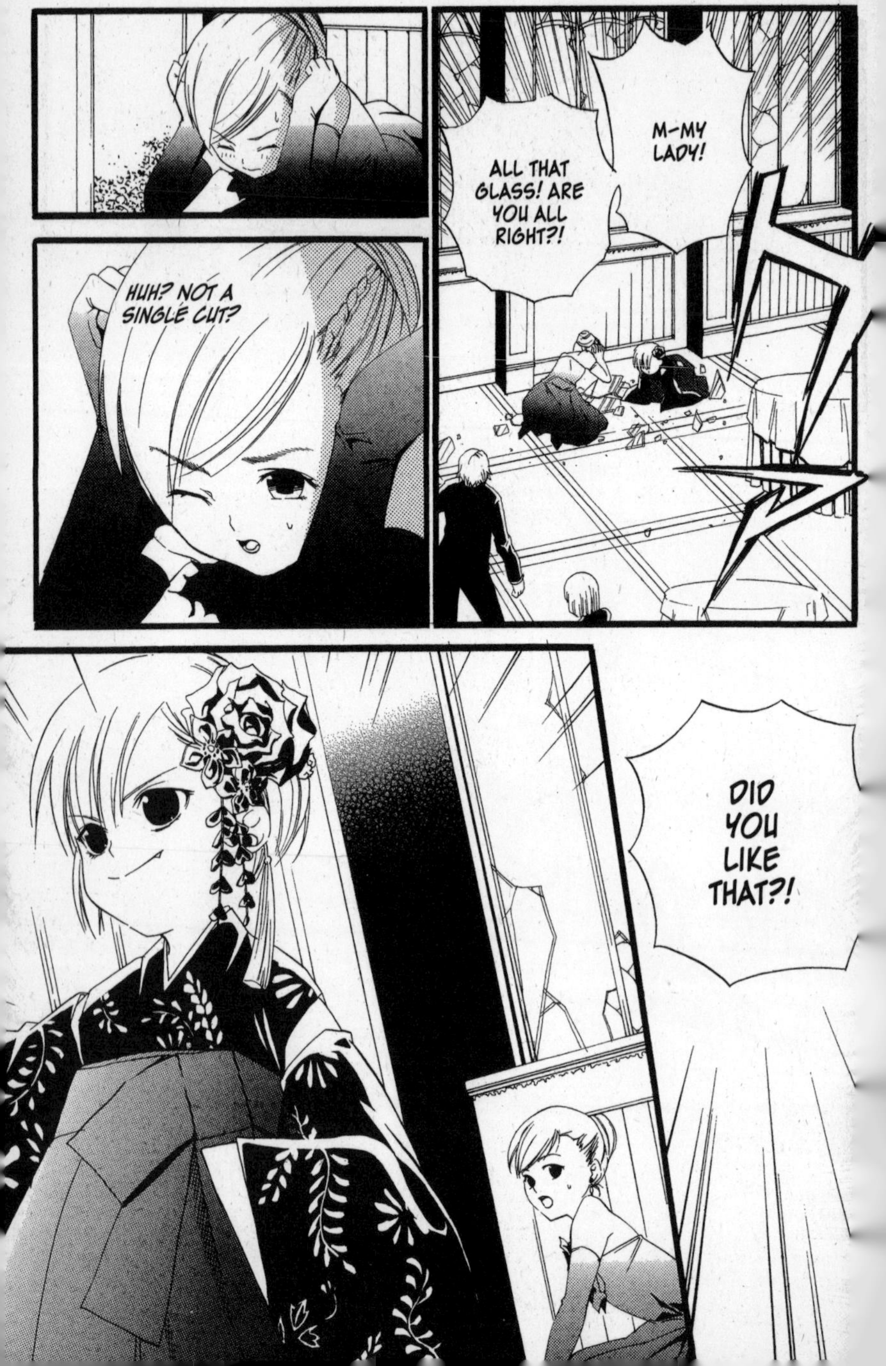
M-MY LADY!
ALL THAT GLASS! ARE YOU ALL RIGHT?!
HUH? NOT A SINGLE CUT?
DID YOU LIKE THAT?!

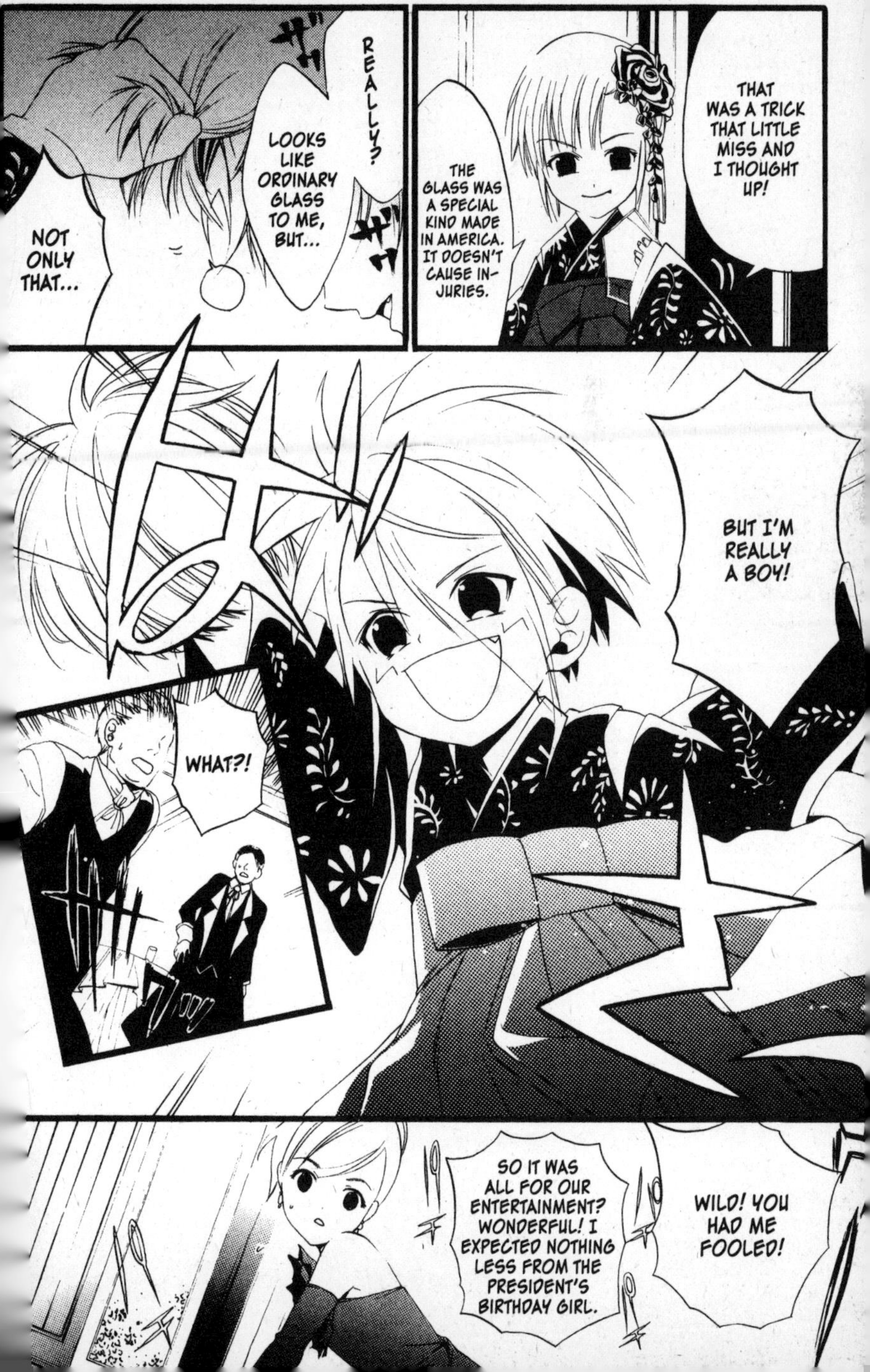
THAT WAS A TRICK THAT LITTLE MISS AND I THOUGHT UP!
THE GLASS WAS A SPECIAL KIND MADE IN AMERICA. IT DOESN'T CAUSE INJURIES.
REALLY?
LOOKS LIKE ORDINARY GLASS TO ME, BUT...
NOT ONLY THAT...
BUT I'M REALLY A BOY!
WHAT?!
WILD! YOU HAD ME FOOLED!
SO IT WAS ALL FOR OUR ENTERTAINMENT? WONDERFUL! I EXPECTED NOTHING LESS FROM THE PRESIDENT'S BIRTHDAY GIRL.

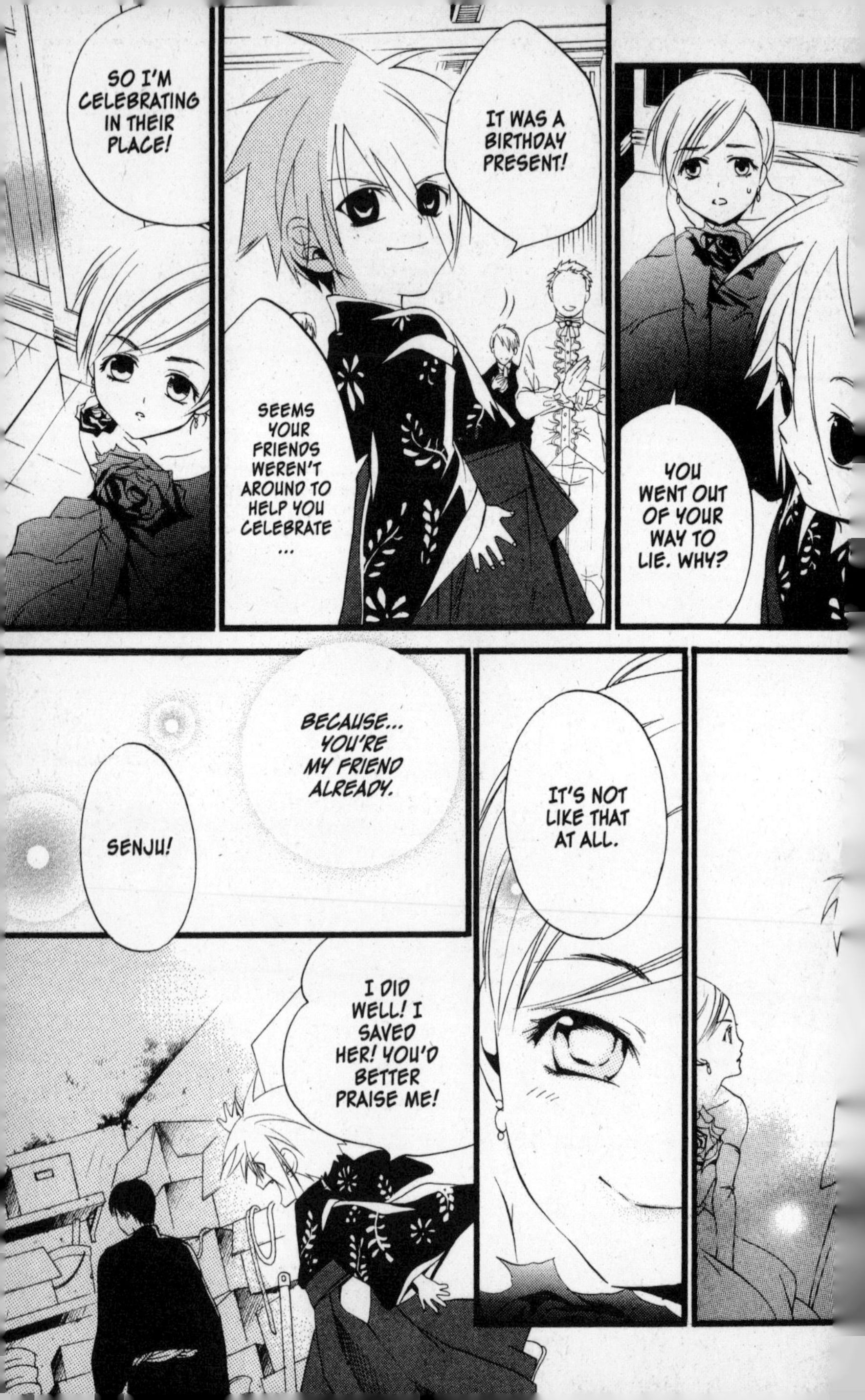
YOU WENT OUT OF YOUR WAY TO LIE. WHY?
IT WAS A BIRTHDAY PRESENT!
SEEMS YOUR FRIENDS WEREN'T AROUND TO HELP YOU CELEBRATE ...
SO I'M CELEBRATING IN THEIR PLACE!
IT'S NOT LIKE THAT AT ALL.
BECAUSE... YOU'RE MY FRIEND ALREADY.
SENJU!
I DID WELL! I SAVED HER! YOU'D BETTER PRAISE ME!

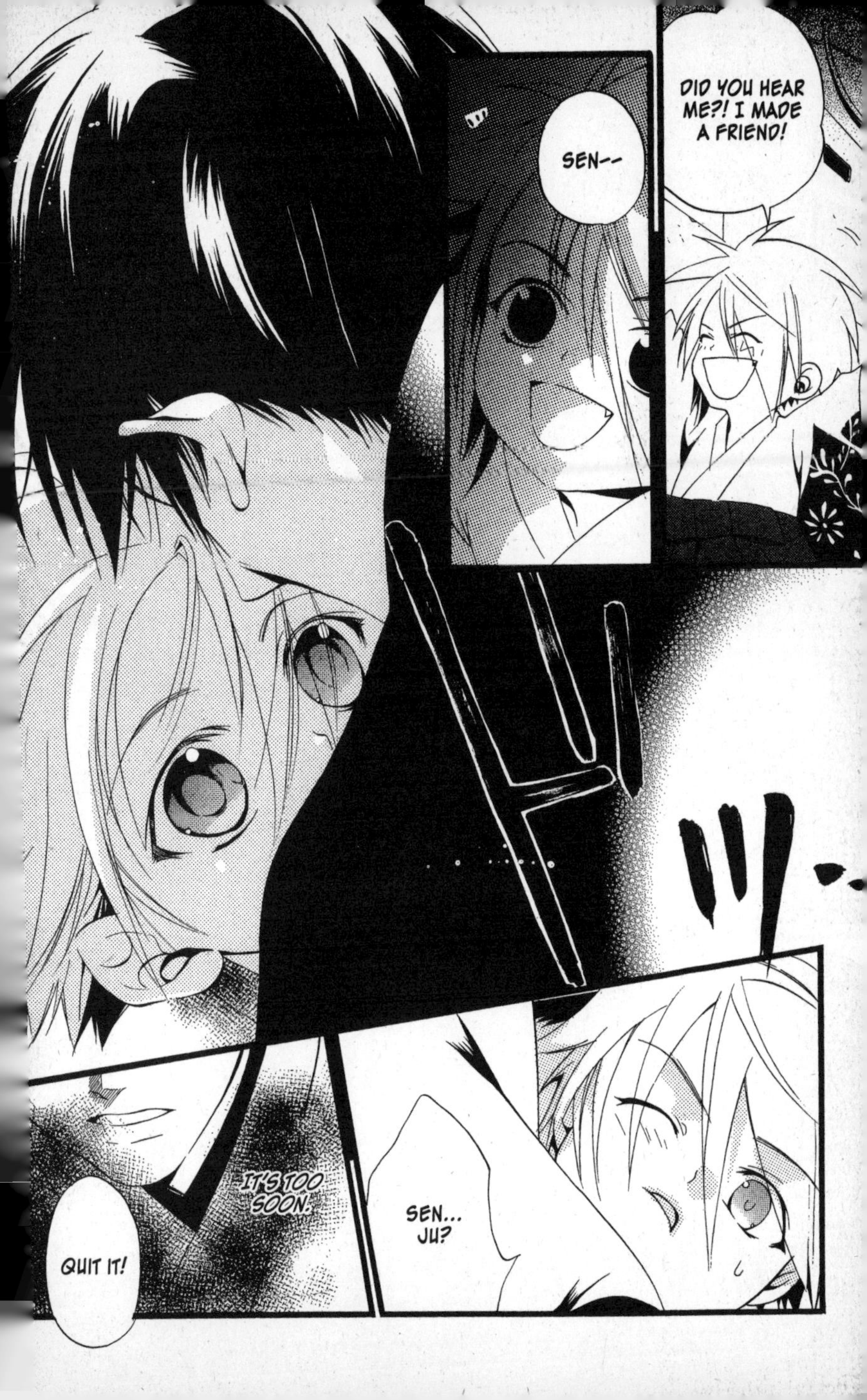
DID YOU HEAR ME?! I MADE A FRIEND!
SEN--
SEN... JU?
IT'S TOO SOON.
QUIT IT!

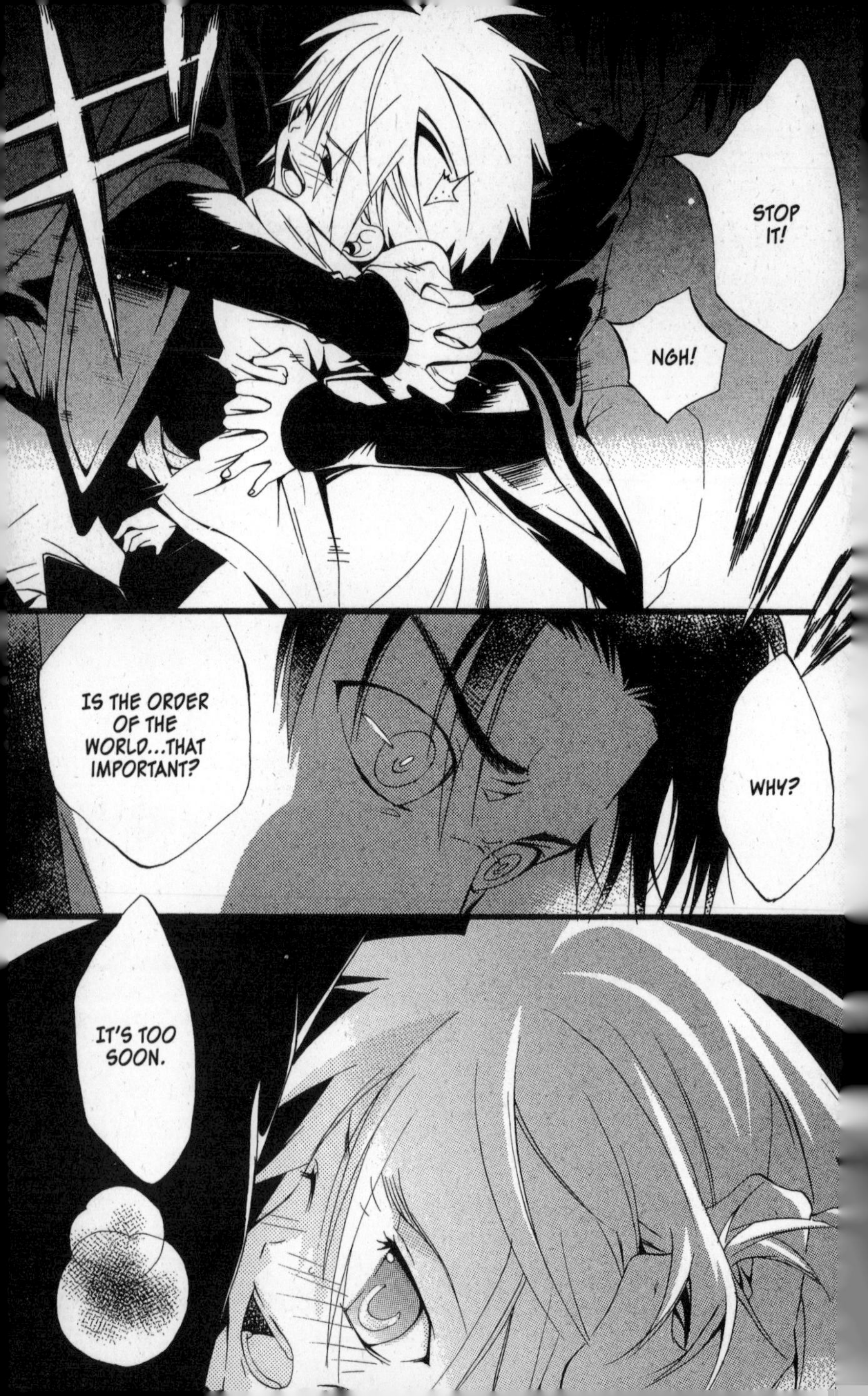
STOP IT!
NGH!
WHY?
IS THE ORDER OF THE WORLD...THAT IMPORTANT?
IT'S TOO SOON.

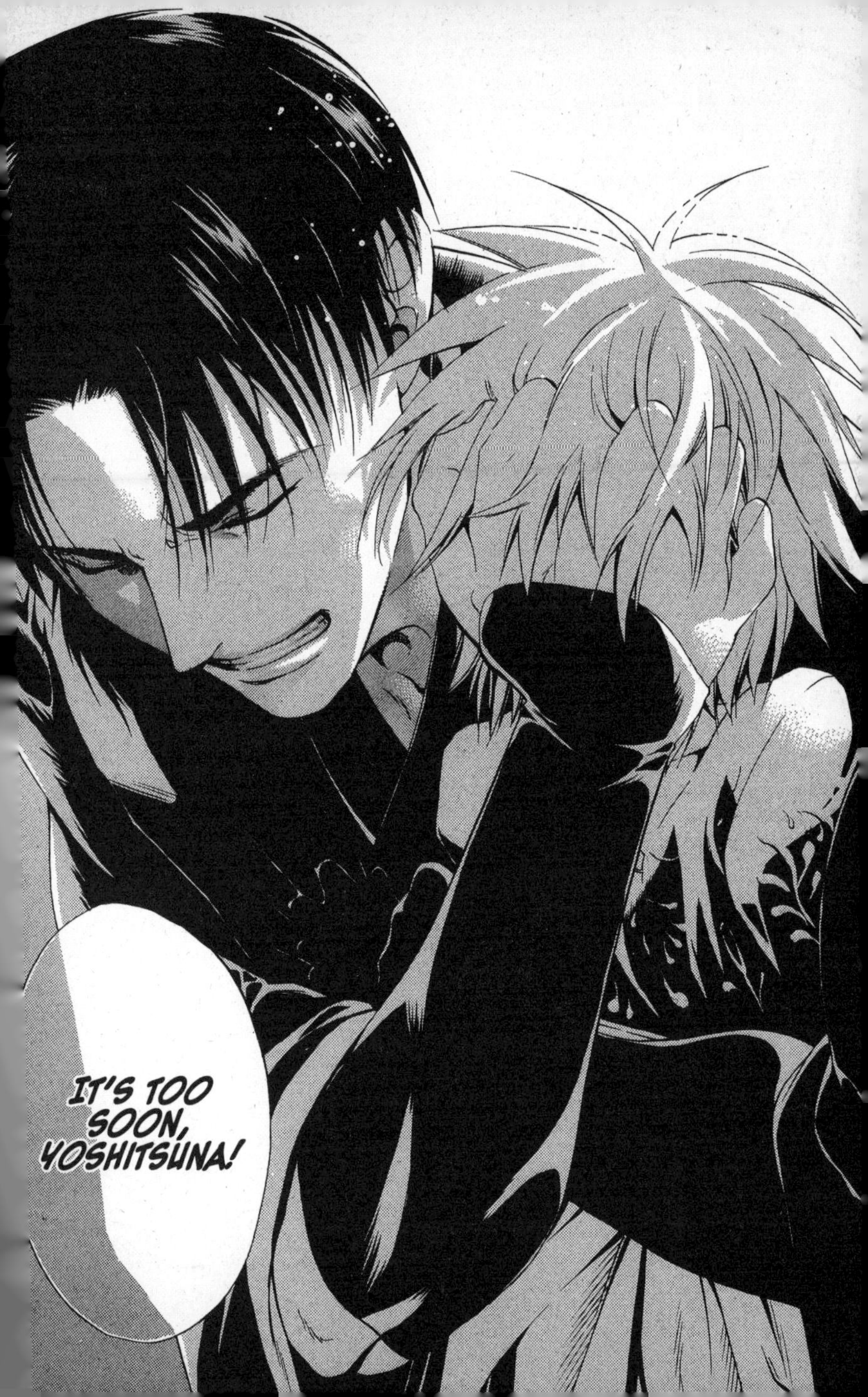
IT'S TOO SOON, YOSHITSUNA!

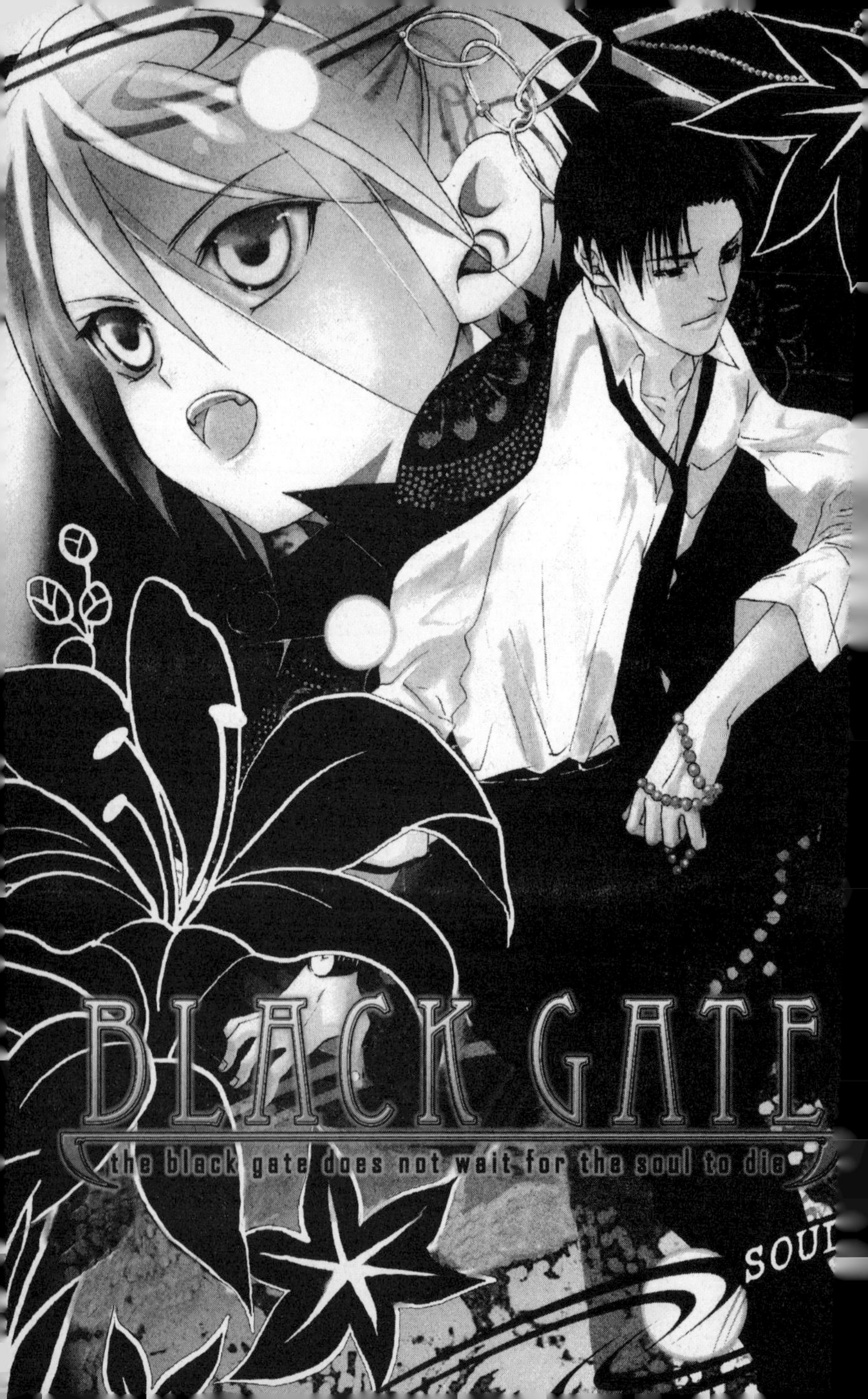
BLACK GATE
the black gate does not wait for the soul to die
SOUL

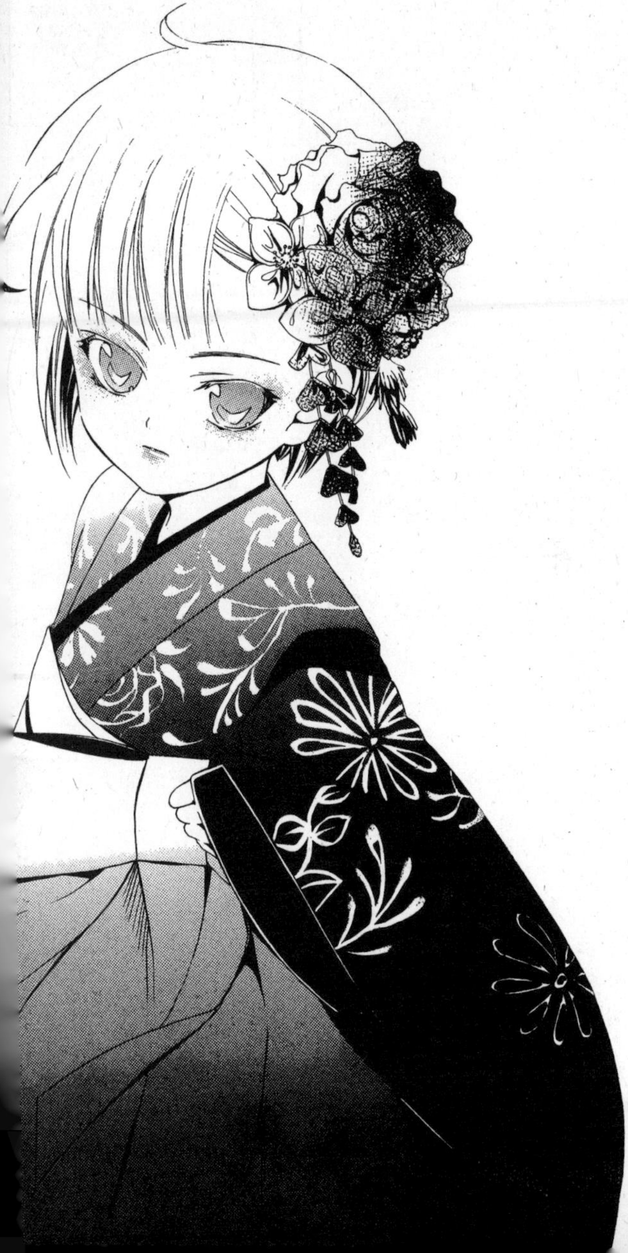

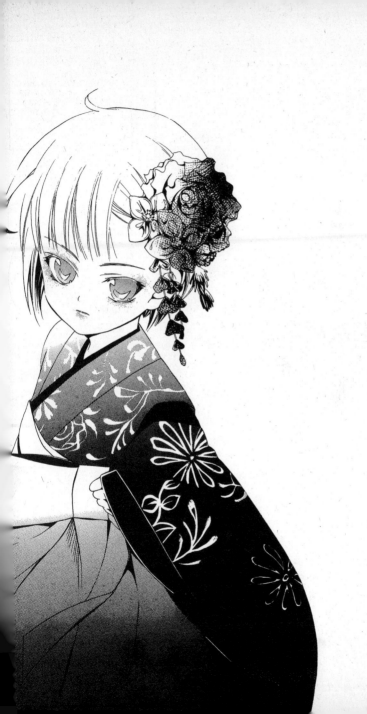

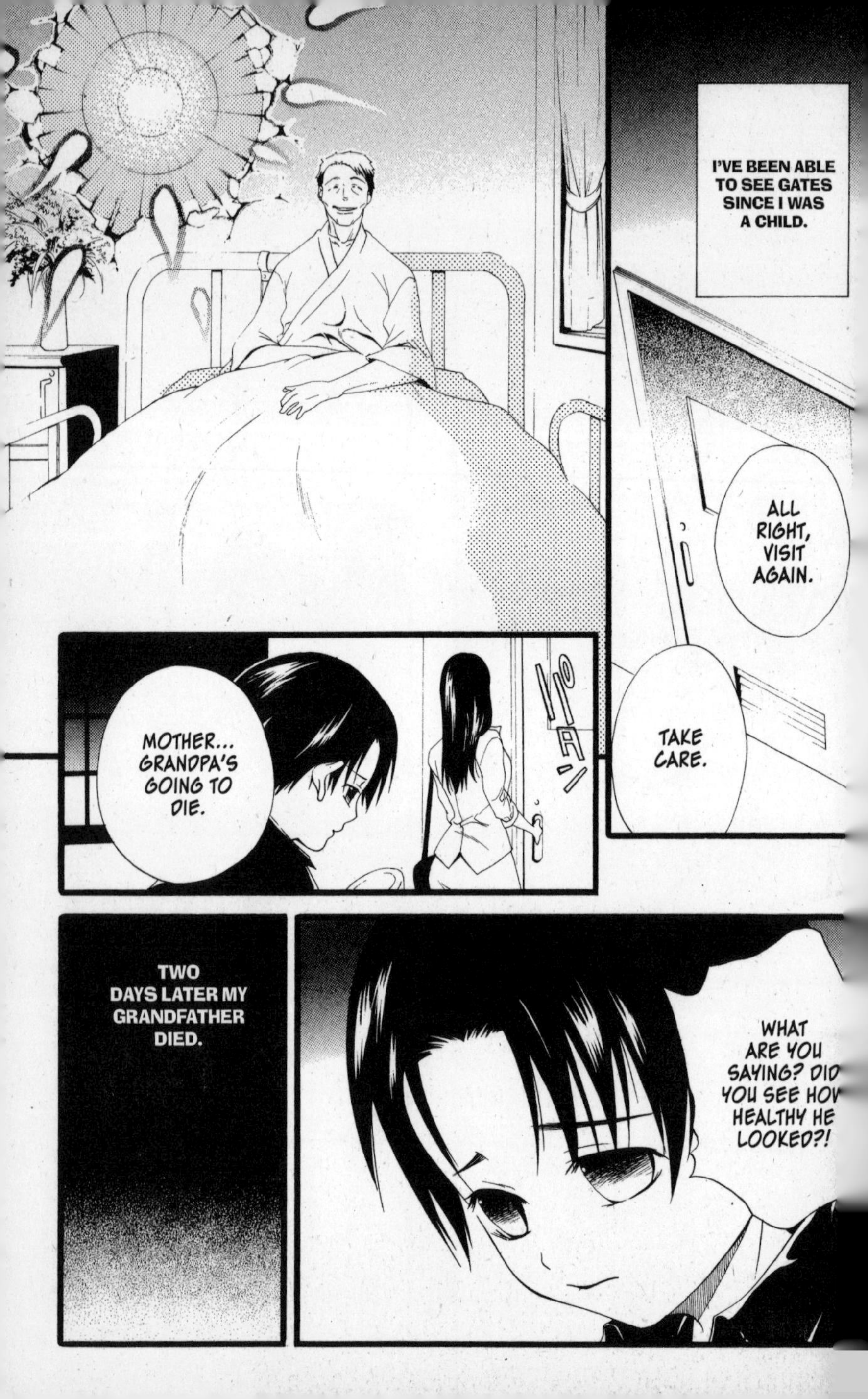
I'VE BEEN ABLE TO SEE GATES SINCE I WAS A CHILD.
ALL RIGHT, VISIT AGAIN.
TAKE CARE.
MOTHER... GRANDPA'S GOING TO DIE.
WHAT ARE YOU SAYING? DID YOU SEE HOW HEALTHY HE LOOKED?!
TWO DAYS LATER MY GRANDFATHER DIED.

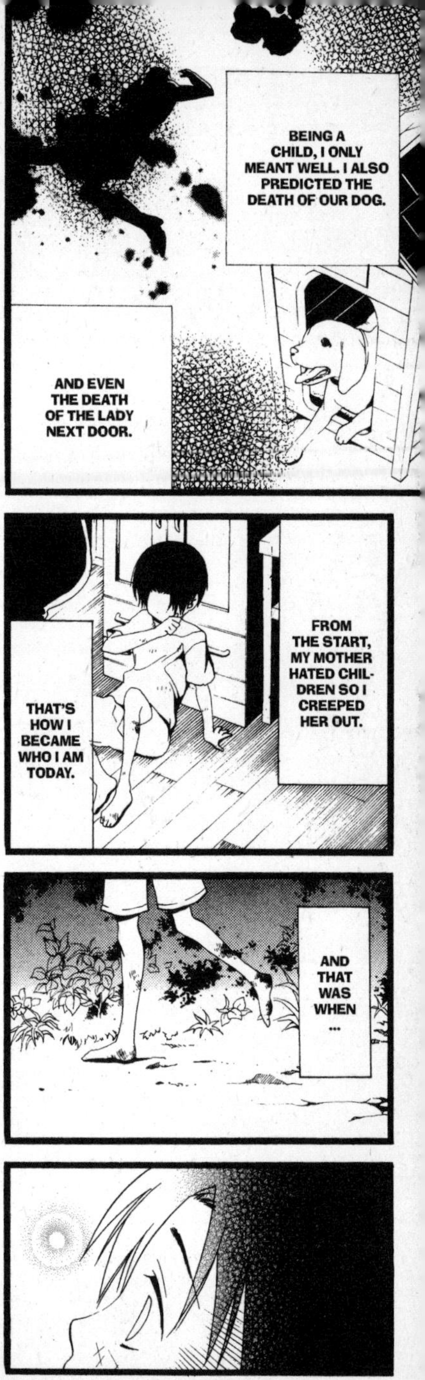
BEING A CHILD, I ONLY MEANT WELL. I ALSO PREDICTED THE DEATH OF OUR DOG.
AND EVEN THE DEATH OF THE LADY NEXT DOOR.
FROM THE START, MY MOTHER HATED CHIL-DREN SO I CREEPED HER OUT.
THAT'S HOW I BECAME WHO I AM TODAY.
AND THAT WAS WHEN ...
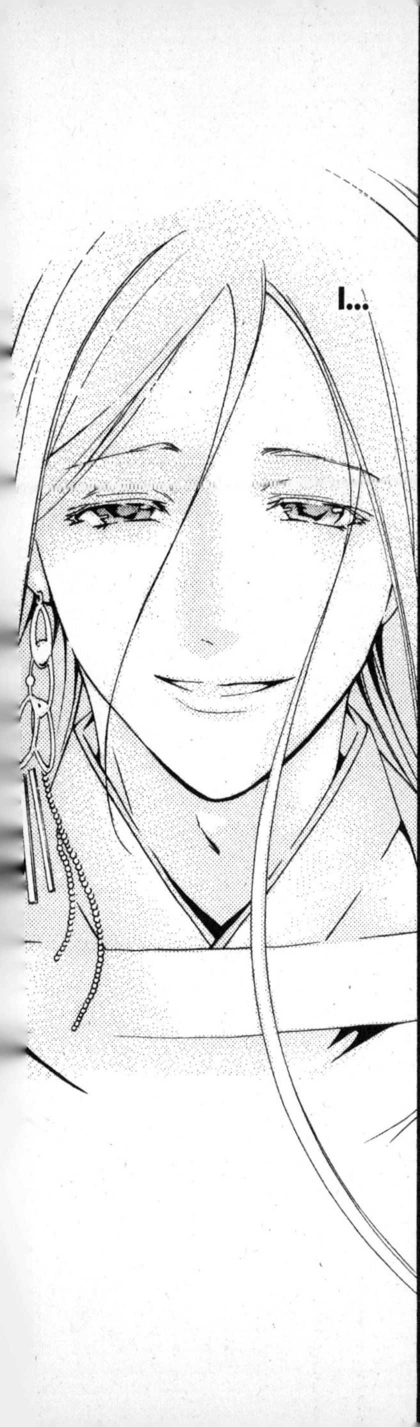
I...

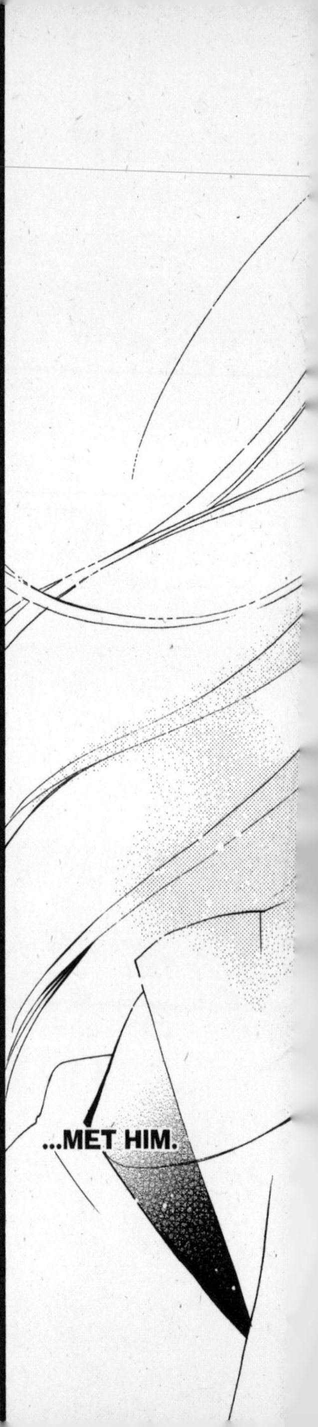
...MET HIM.
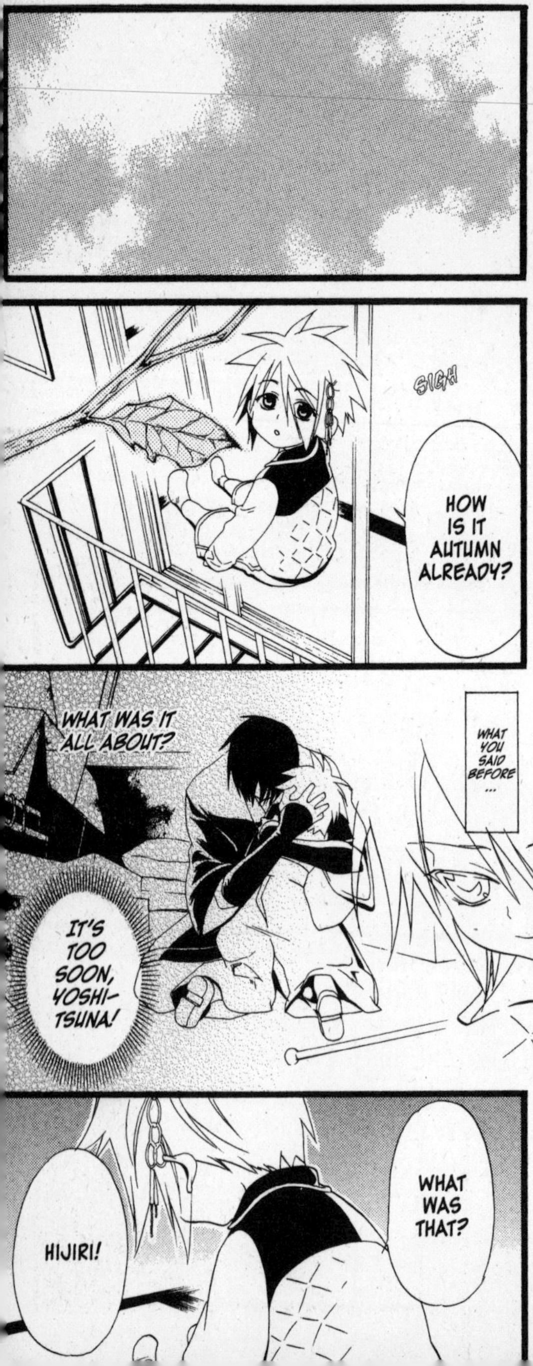
SIGH
HOW IS IT AUTUMN ALREADY?
WHAT YOU SAID BEFORE ...
WHAT WAS IT ALL ABOUT?
IT'S TOO SOON, YOSHI-TSUNA!
WHAT WAS THAT?
HIJIRI!

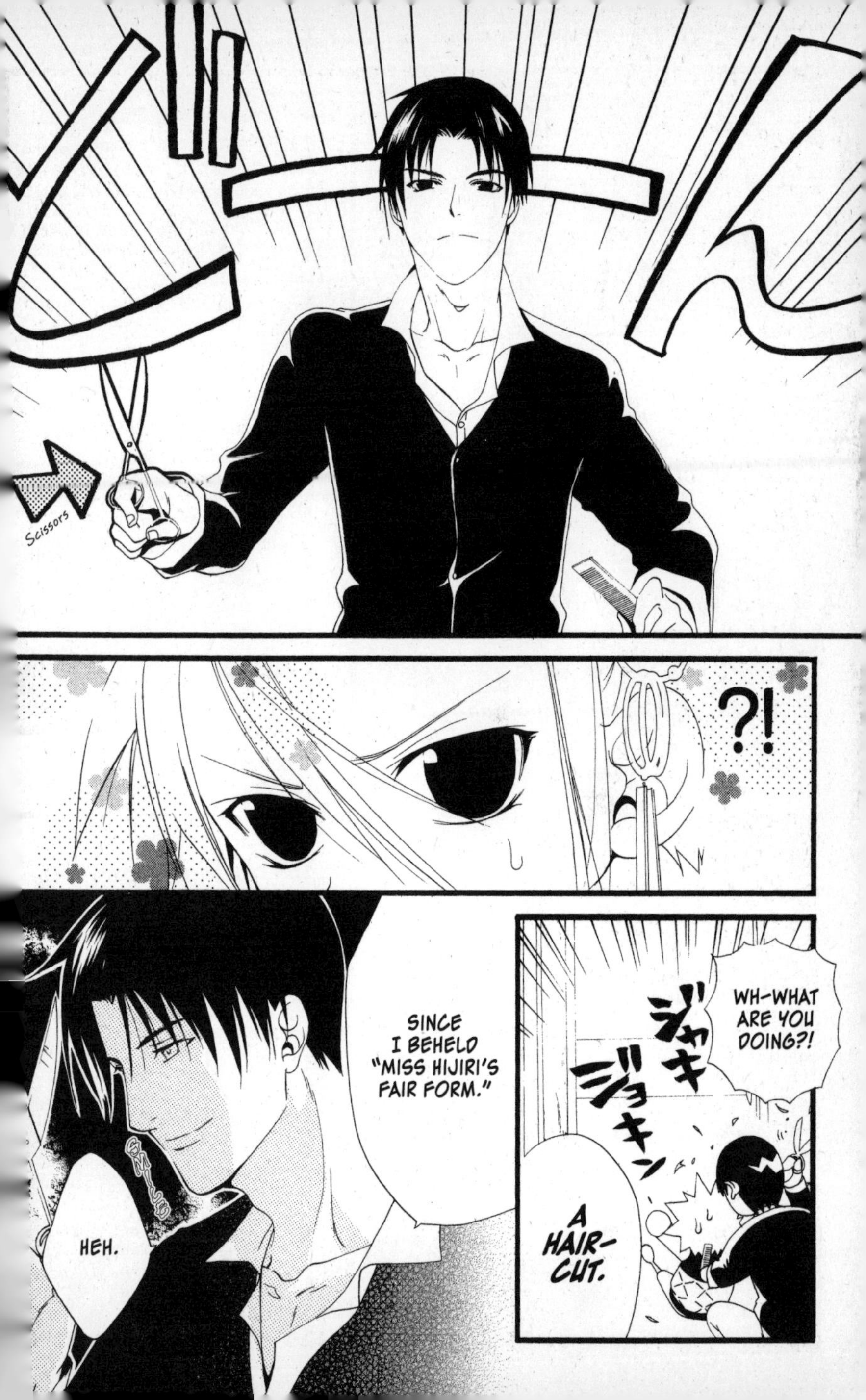

Scissors
?!
WH-WHAT ARE YOU DOING?!
ジャキ
ジョキン
A HAIR-CUT.
SINCE I BEHELD "MISS HIJIRI'S FAIR FORM."
HEH.

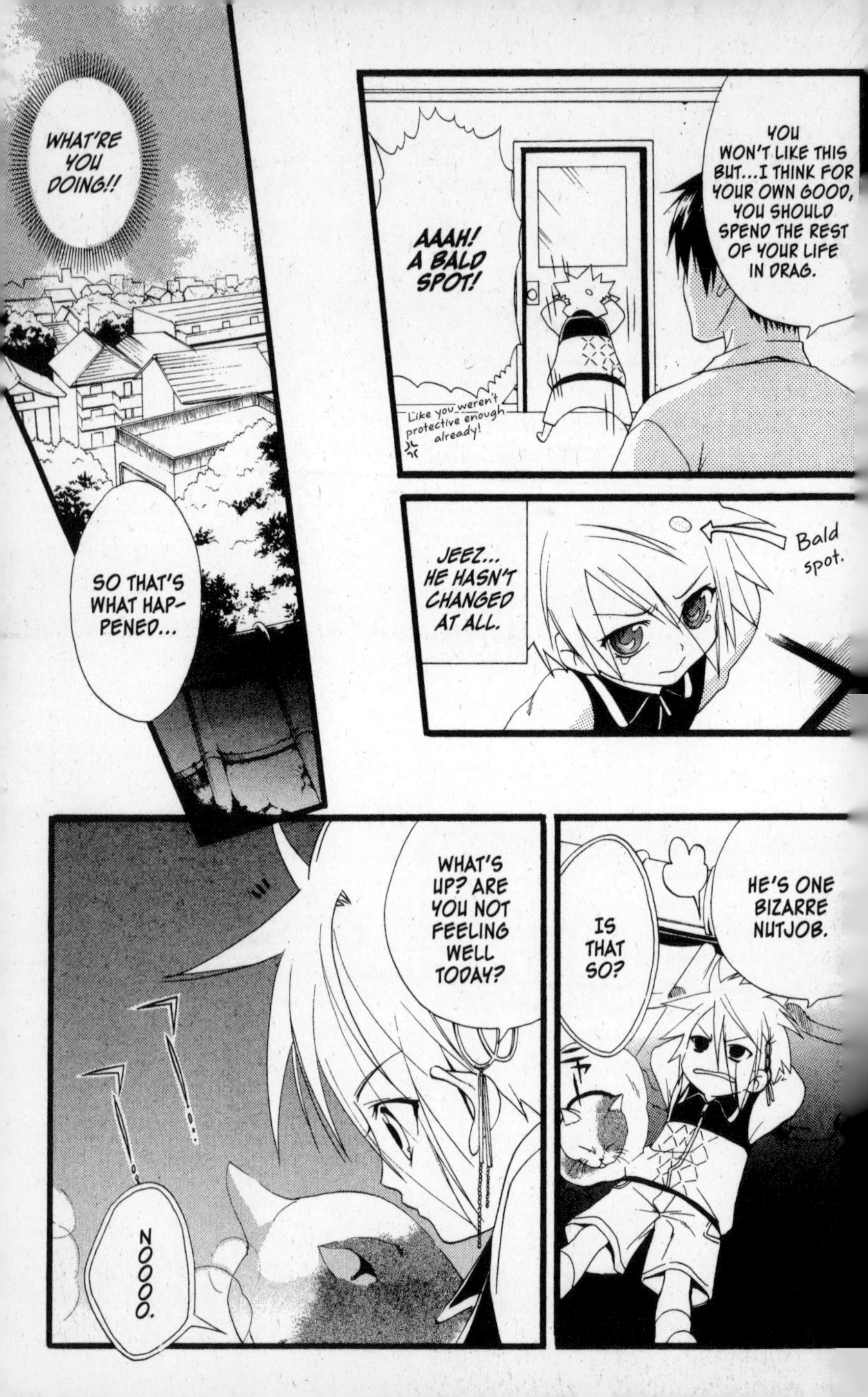
YOU WON'T LIKE THIS BUT...I THINK FOR YOUR OWN GOOD, YOU SHOULD SPEND THE REST OF YOUR LIFE IN DRAG.
AAAH! A BALD SPOT!
Like you weren't protective enough already!
Bald spot.
JEEZ... HE HASN'T CHANGED AT ALL.
WHAT'RE YOU DOING!!
SO THAT'S WHAT HAP-PENED...
HE'S ONE BIZARRE NUTJOB.
IS THAT SO?
WHAT'S UP? ARE YOU NOT FEELING WELL TODAY?
NOOOO.

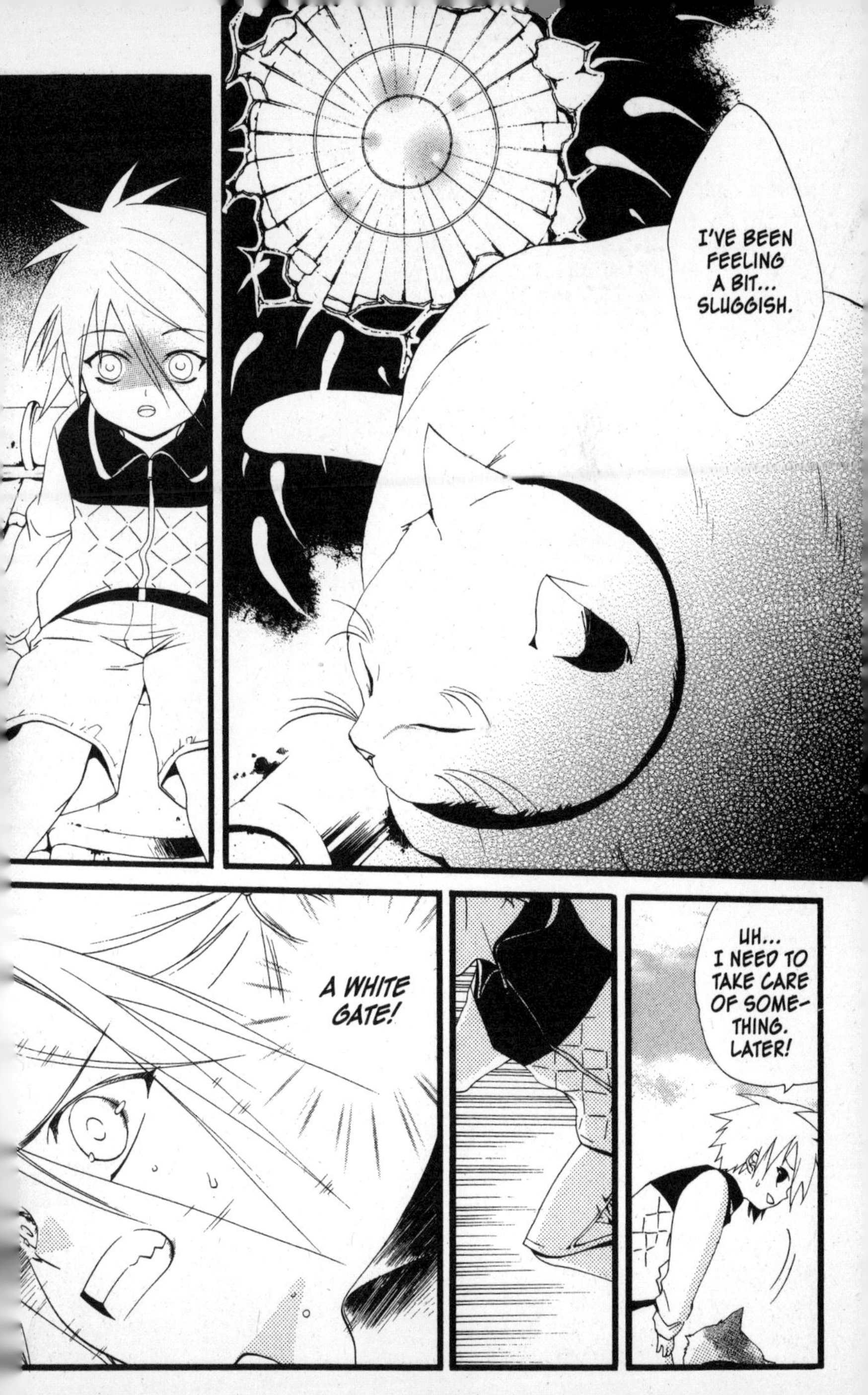
I'VE BEEN FEELING A BIT... SLUGGISH.
UH... I NEED TO TAKE CARE OF SOME-THING. LATER!
A WHITE GATE!

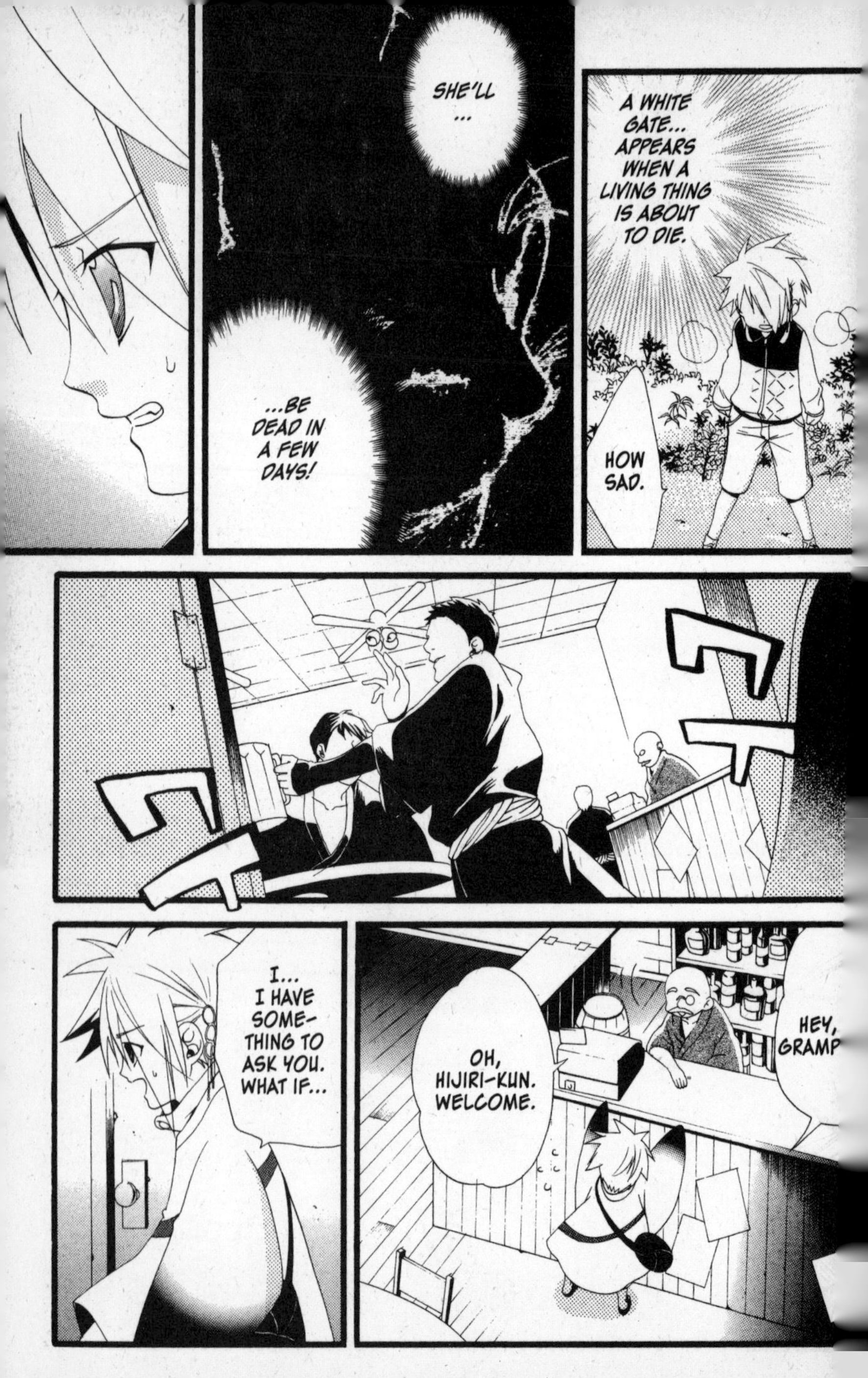
A WHITE GATE... APPEARS WHEN A LIVING THING IS ABOUT TO DIE.
HOW SAD.
SHE'LL ...
...BE DEAD IN A FEW DAYS!
HEY, GRAMP
OH, HIJIRI-KUN. WELCOME.
I... I HAVE SOME-THING TO ASK YOU. WHAT IF...

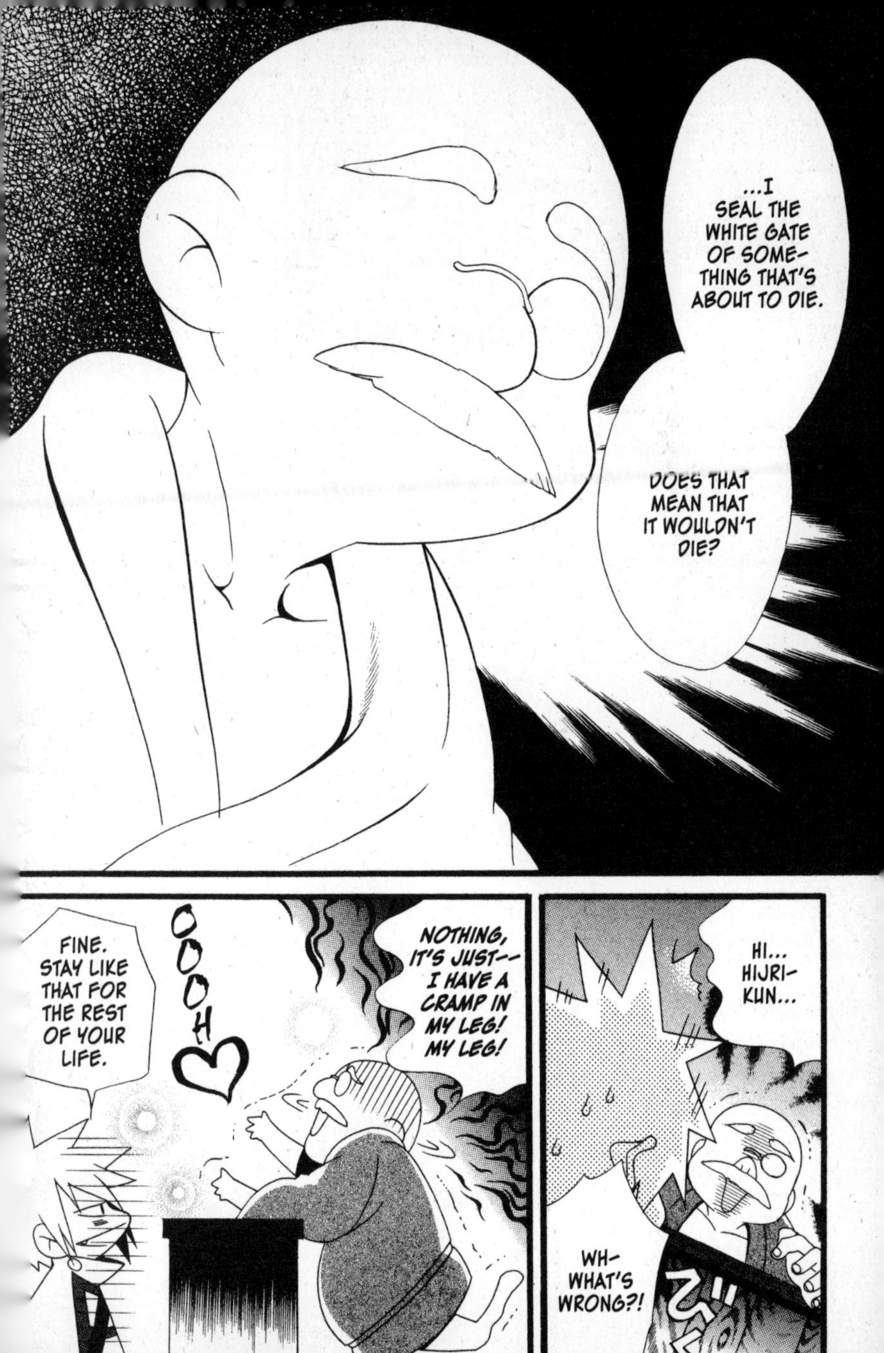
...I SEAL THE WHITE GATE OF SOMETHING THAT'S ABOUT TO DIE.
DOES THAT MEAN THAT IT WOULDN'T DIE?
HI... HIJIRI-KUN...
WH- WHAT'S WRONG?!
NOTHING, IT'S JUST-- I HAVE A CRAMP IN MY LEG! MY LEG!
OOOH ♥
FINE. STAY LIKE THAT FOR THE REST OF YOUR LIFE.

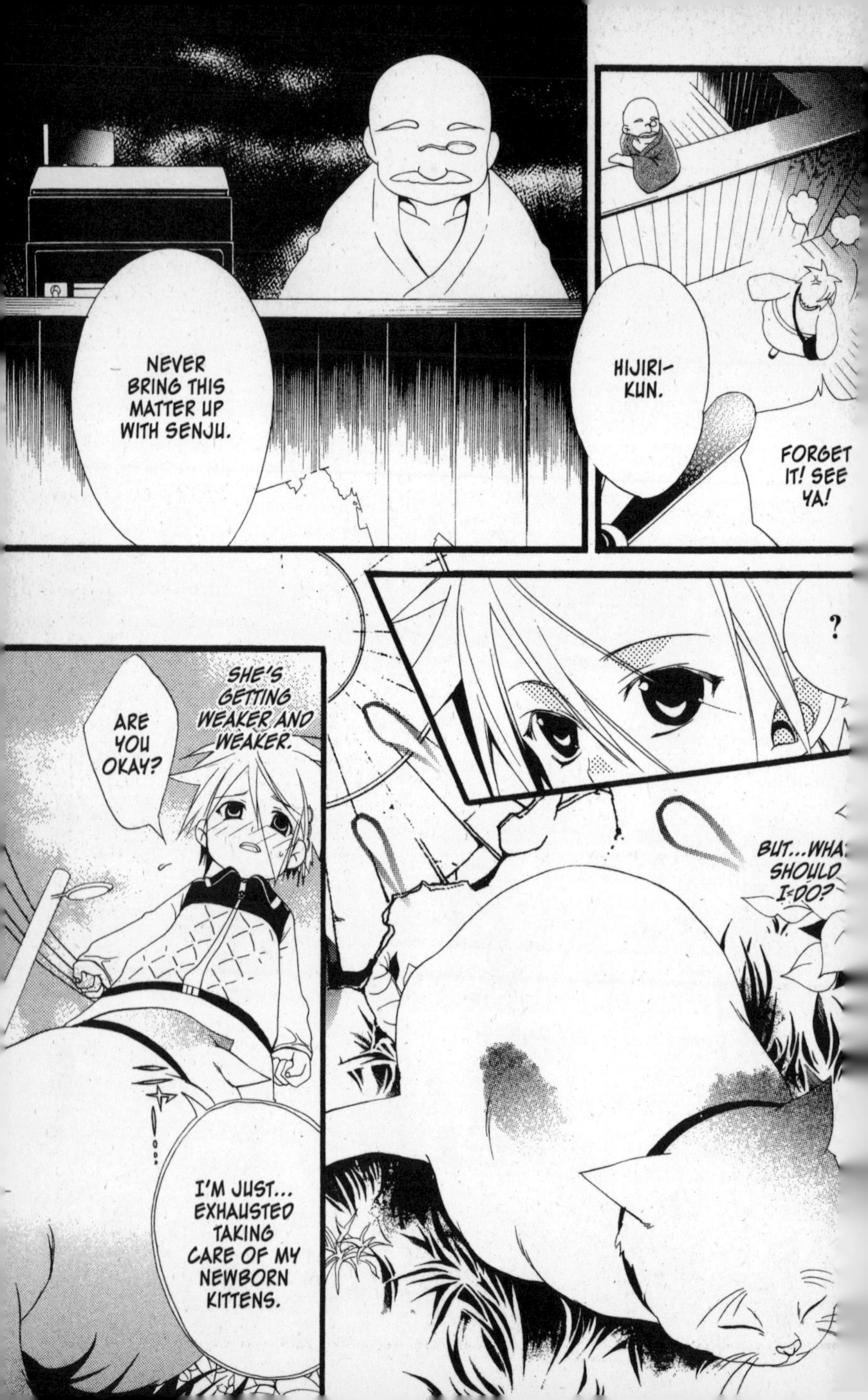
HIJIRI-KUN.
FORGET IT! SEE YA!
NEVER BRING THIS MATTER UP WITH SENJU.
?
BUT...WHAT SHOULD I DO?
SHE'S GETTING WEAKER AND WEAKER.
ARE YOU OKAY?
I'M JUST... EXHAUSTED TAKING CARE OF MY NEWBORN KITTENS.

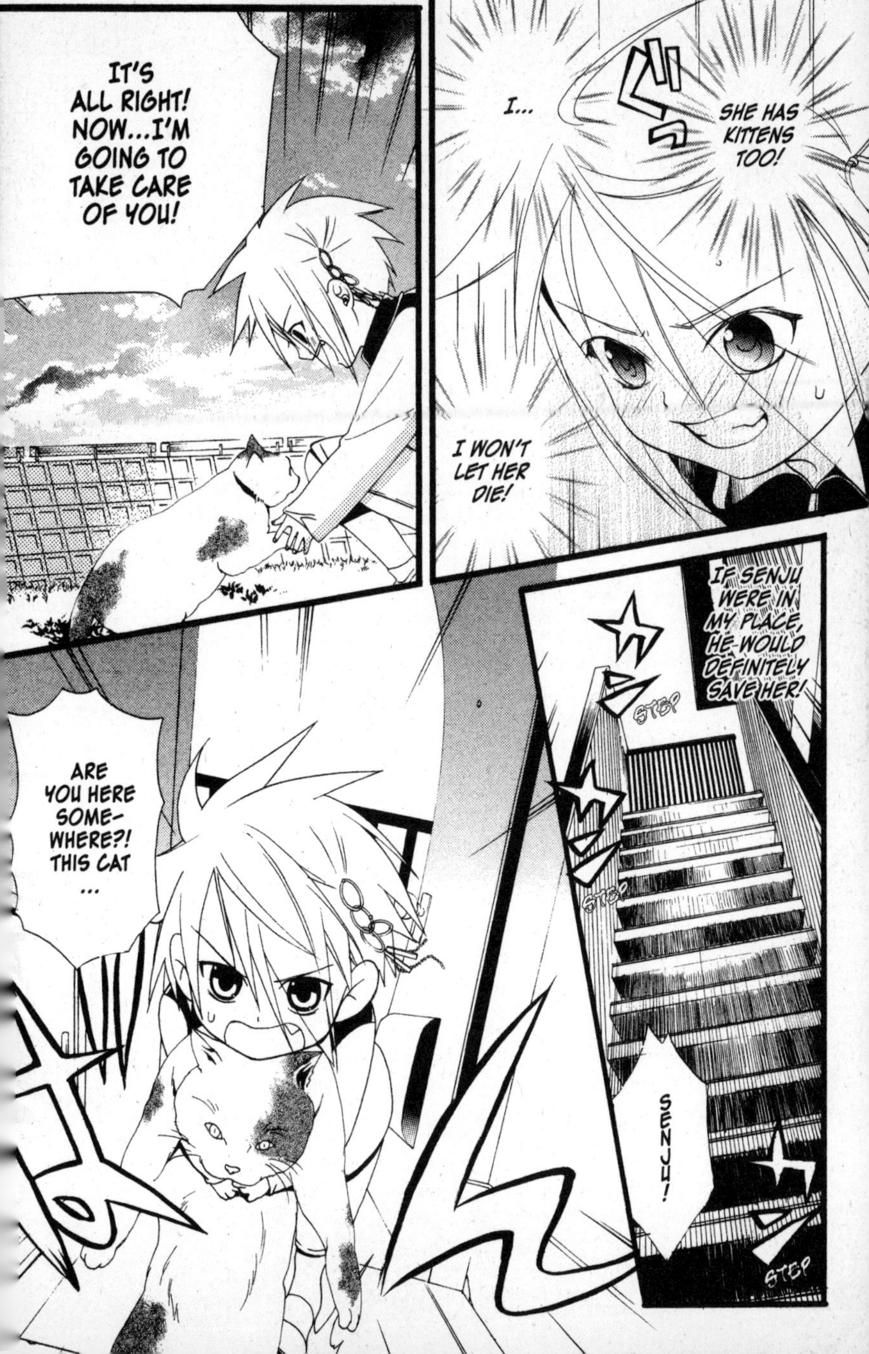
SHE HAS KITTENS TOO!
I...
I WON'T LET HER DIE!
IT'S ALL RIGHT! NOW...I'M GOING TO TAKE CARE OF YOU!
IF SENJU WERE IN MY PLACE, HE WOULD DEFINITELY SAVE HER!
STEP
STEP
SENJU!
STEP
ARE YOU HERE SOME-WHERE?! THIS CAT ...

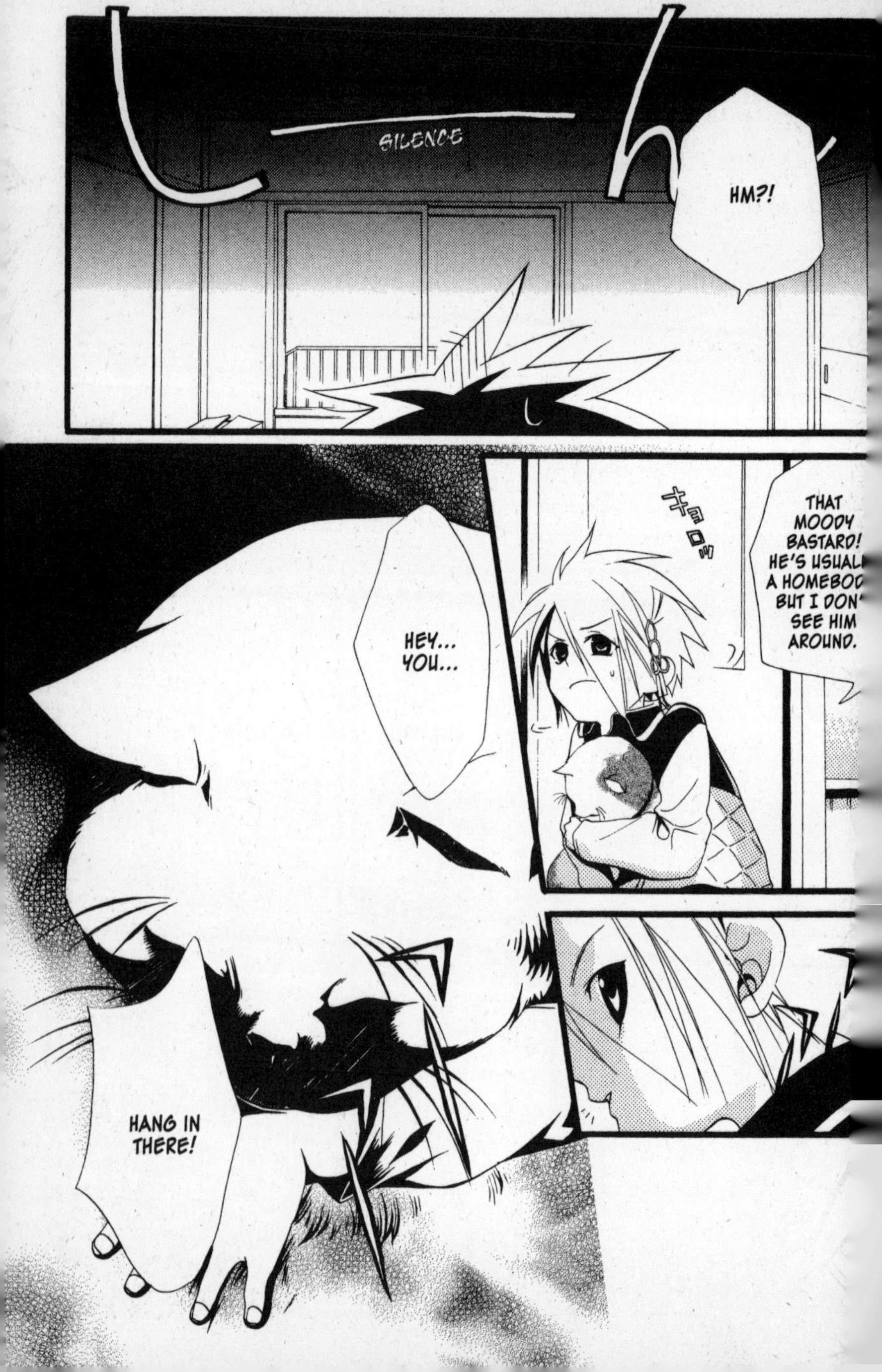
HM?!
SILENCE
THAT MOODY BASTARD! HE'S USUALL A HOMEBOD BUT I DON' SEE HIM AROUND.
キョロッ
HEY... YOU...
HANG IN THERE!

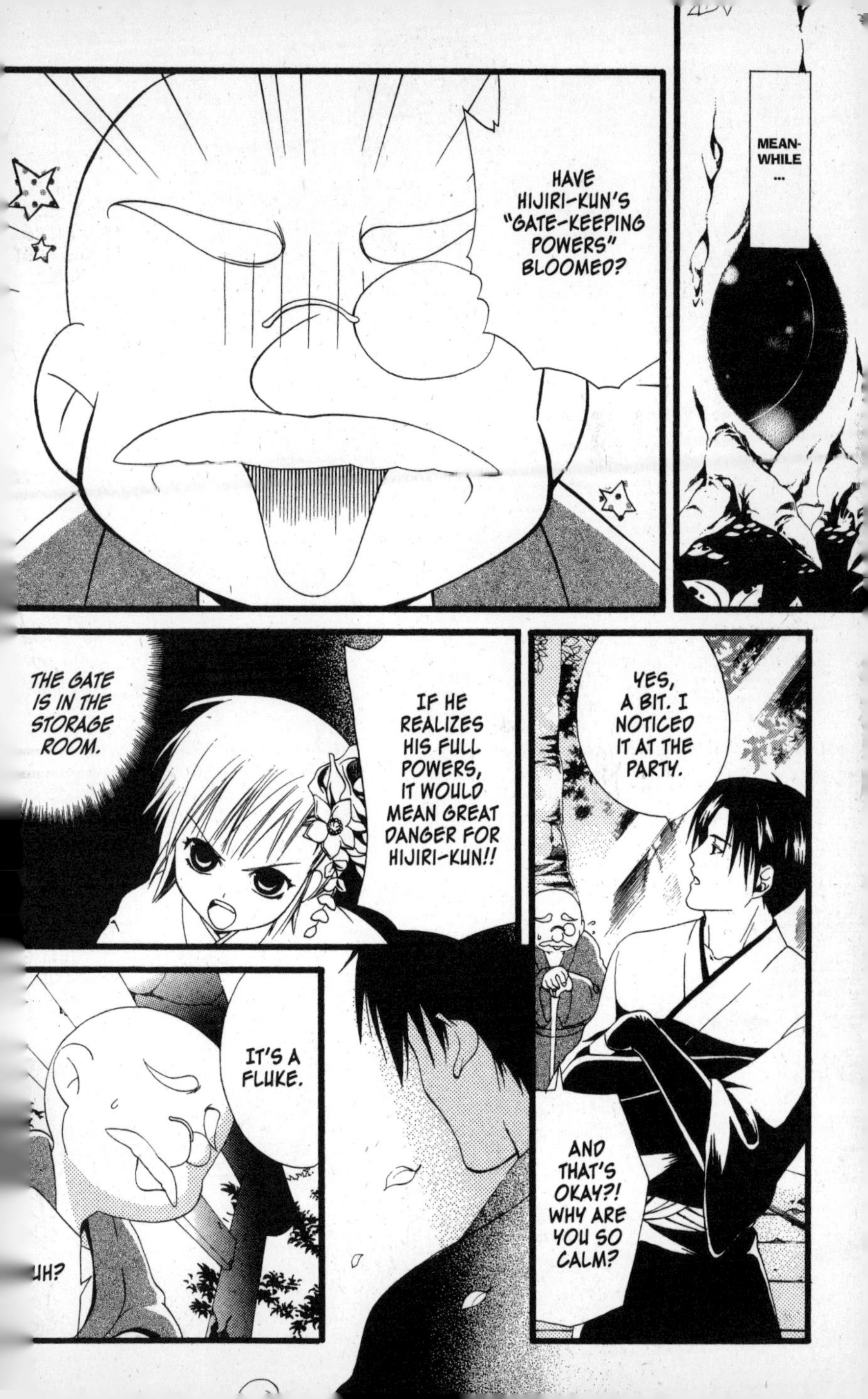
MEAN-WHILE ...
HAVE HIJIRI-KUN'S "GATE-KEEPING POWERS" BLOOMED?
YES, A BIT. I NOTICED IT AT THE PARTY.
AND THAT'S OKAY?! WHY ARE YOU SO CALM?
IF HE REALIZES HIS FULL POWERS, IT WOULD MEAN GREAT DANGER FOR HIJIRI-KUN!!
THE GATE IS IN THE STORAGE ROOM.
IT'S A FLUKE.
UH?

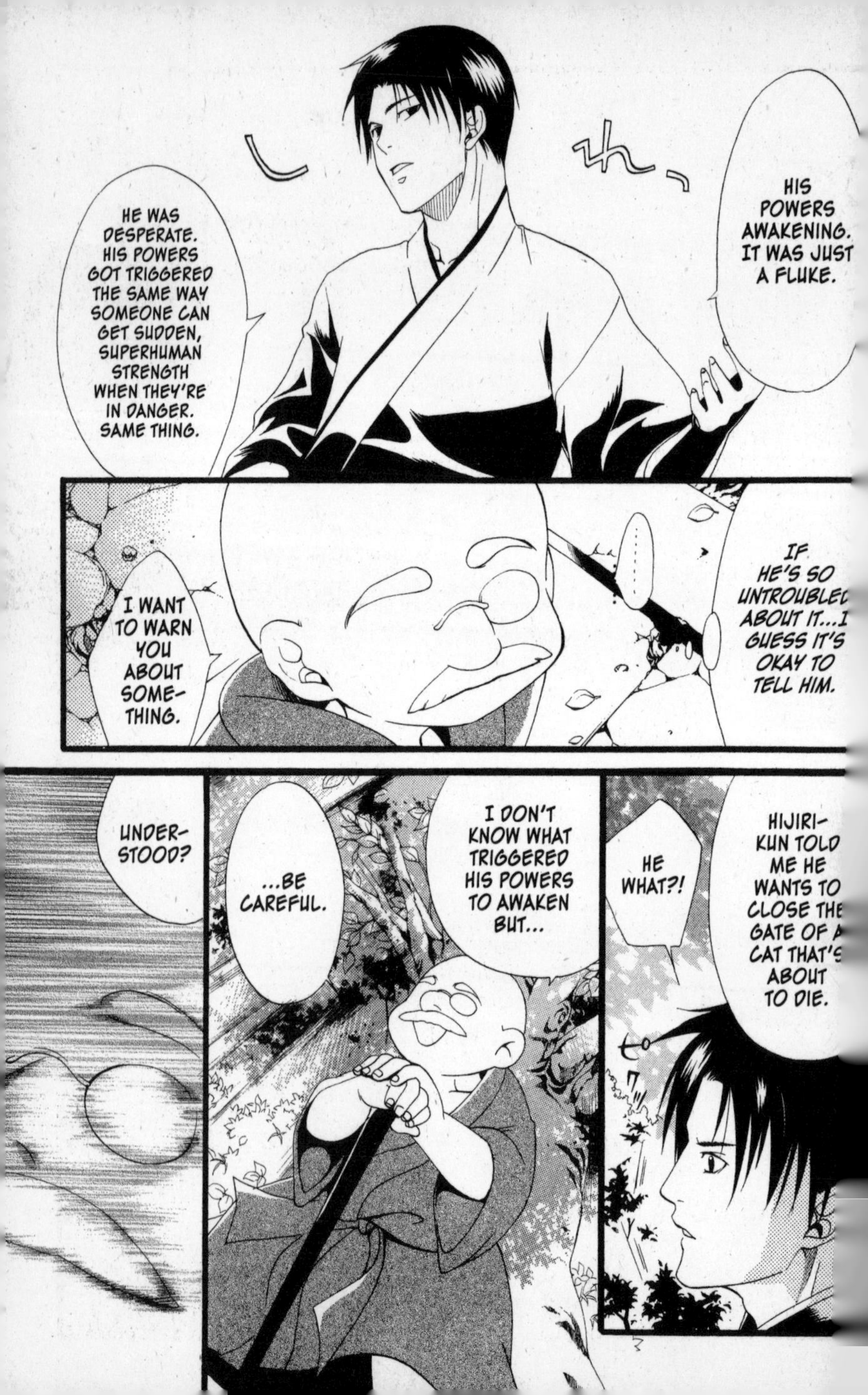
HIS POWERS AWAKENING. IT WAS JUST A FLUKE.
HE WAS DESPERATE. HIS POWERS GOT TRIGGERED THE SAME WAY SOMEONE CAN GET SUDDEN, SUPERHUMAN STRENGTH WHEN THEY'RE IN DANGER. SAME THING.
IF HE'S SO UNTROUBLED ABOUT IT...I GUESS IT'S OKAY TO TELL HIM.
...
I WANT TO WARN YOU ABOUT SOME-THING.
HIJIRI-KUN TOLD ME HE WANTS TO CLOSE THE GATE OF A CAT THAT'S ABOUT TO DIE.
HE WHAT?!
I DON'T KNOW WHAT TRIGGERED HIS POWERS TO AWAKEN BUT...
...BE CAREFUL.
UNDER-STOOD?

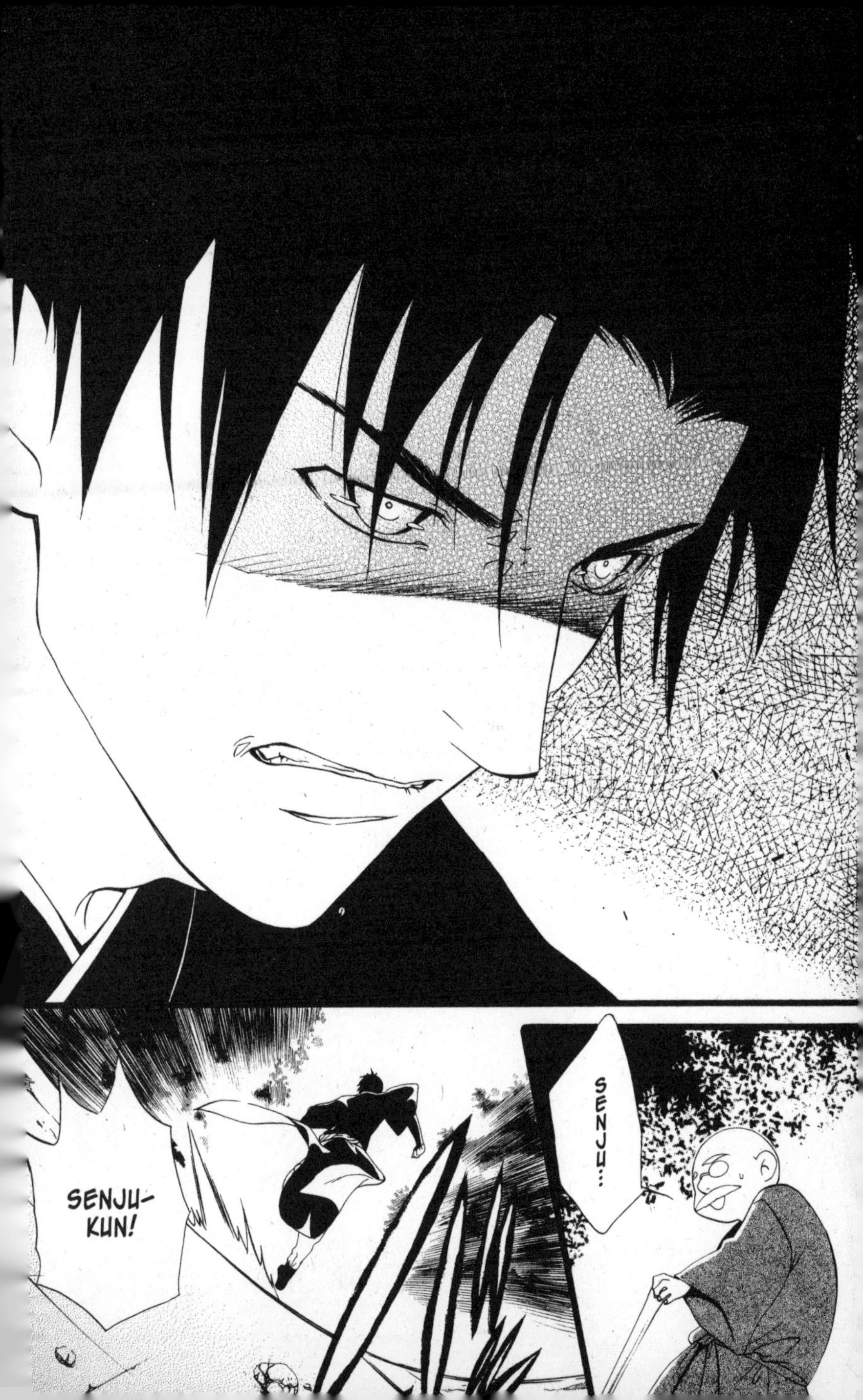
SENJU...
SENJU-KUN!

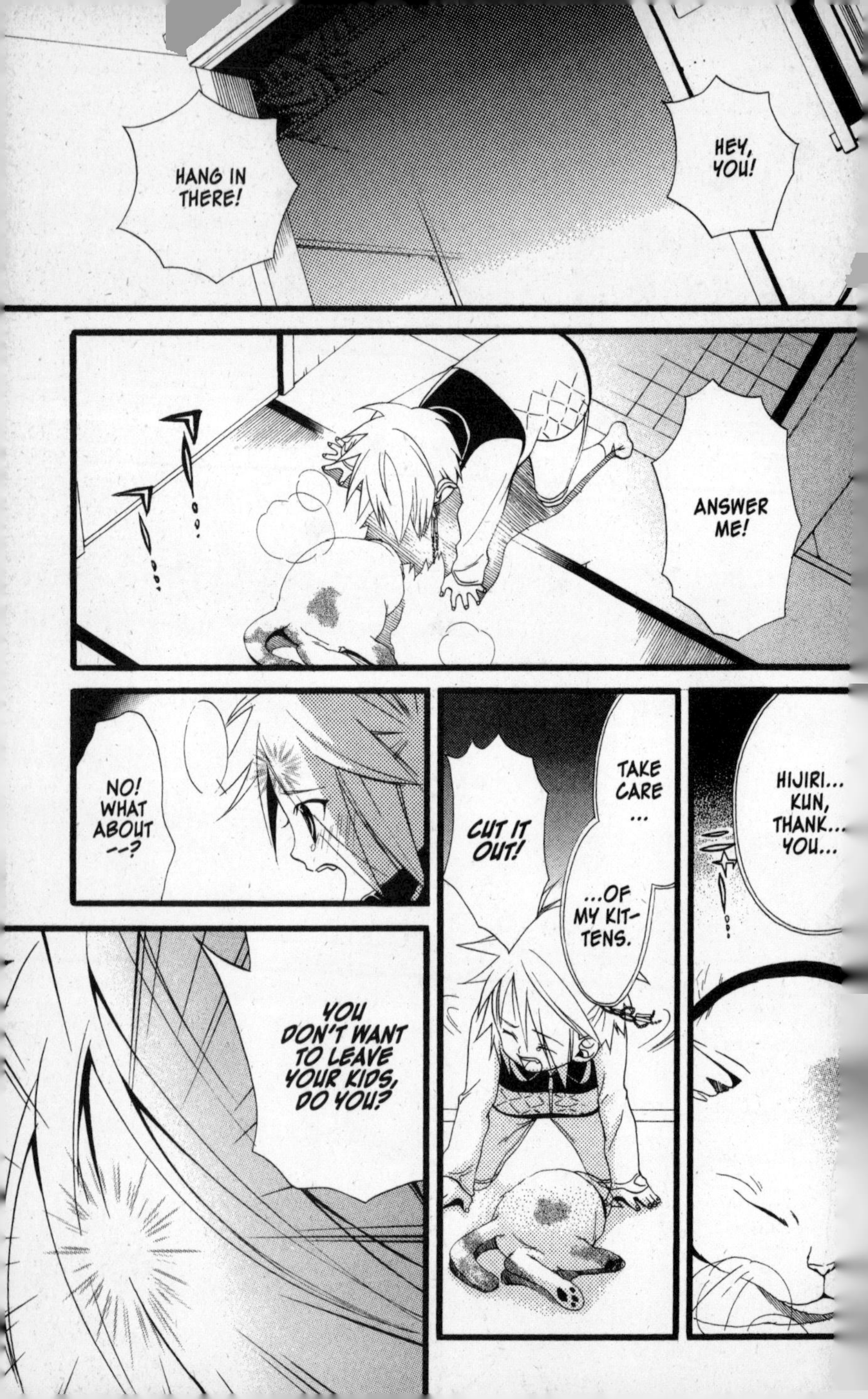
HEY, YOU!
HANG IN THERE!
ANSWER ME!
HIJIRI... KUN, THANK... YOU...
TAKE CARE ...
...OF MY KIT-TENS.
CUT IT OUT!
NO! WHAT ABOUT --?
YOU DON'T WANT TO LEAVE YOUR KIDS, DO YOU?

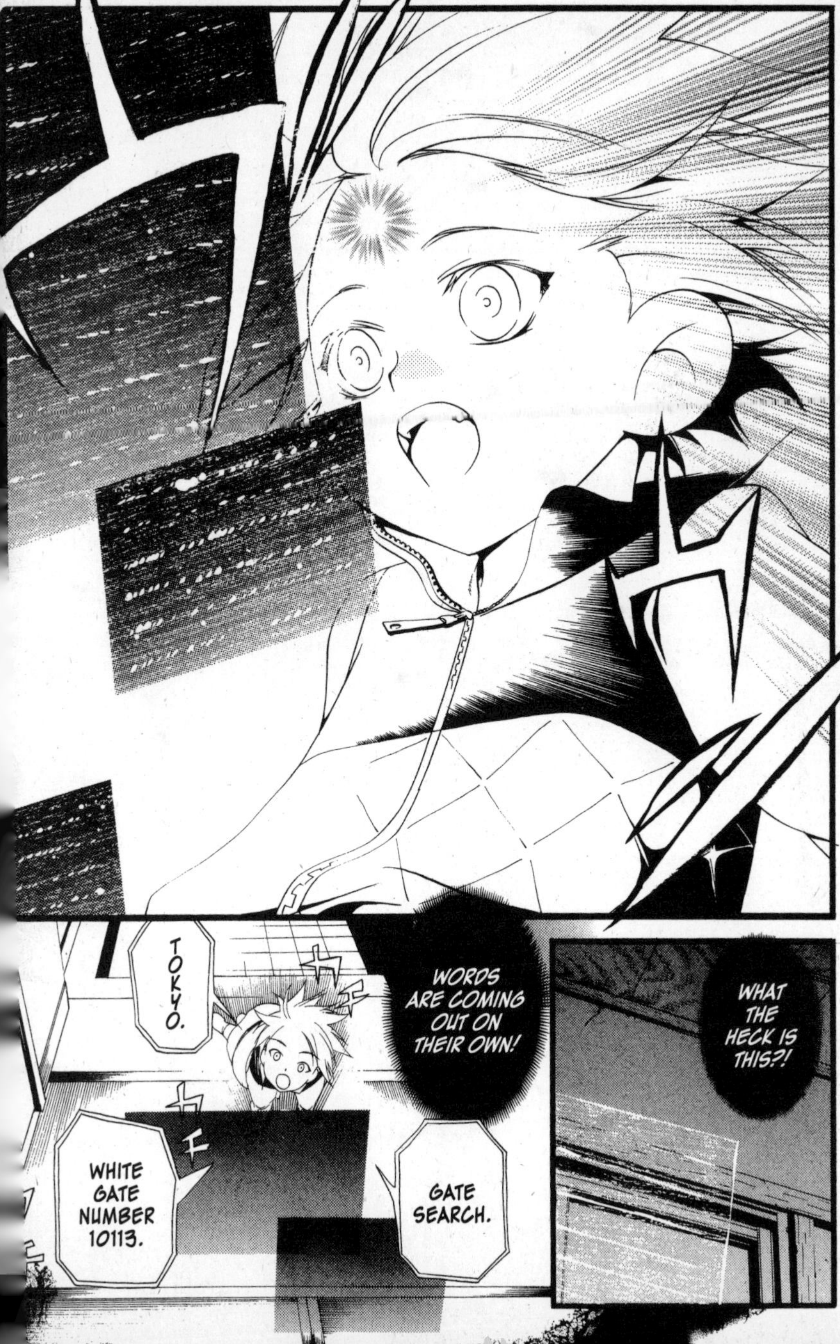
WHAT THE HECK IS THIS?!
WORDS ARE COMING OUT ON THEIR OWN!
TOKYO.
GATE SEARCH.
WHITE GATE NUMBER 10113.

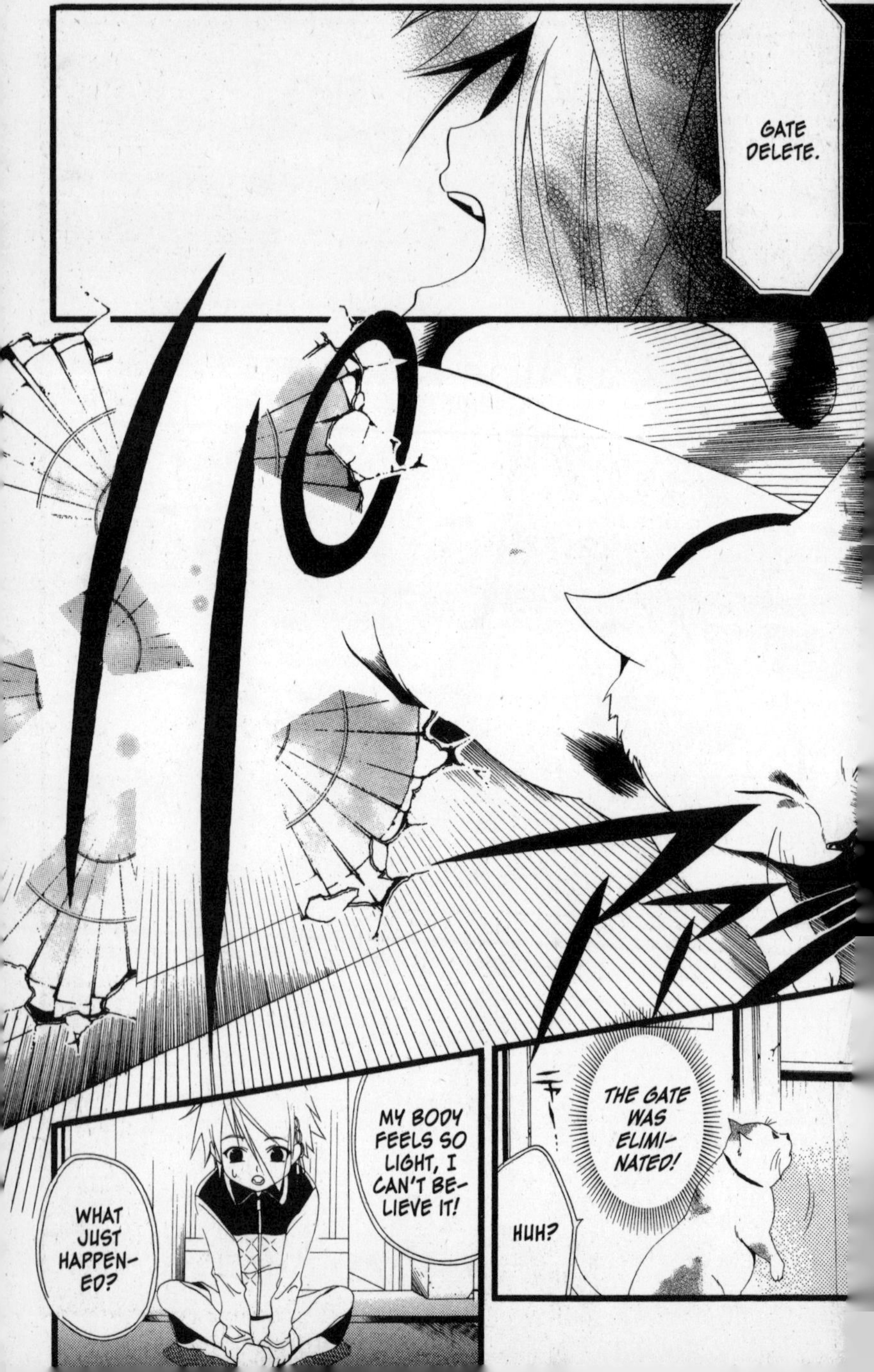
GATE DELETE.
THE GATE WAS ELIMINATED!
HUH?
MY BODY FEELS SO LIGHT, I CAN'T BELIEVE IT!
WHAT JUST HAPPENED?

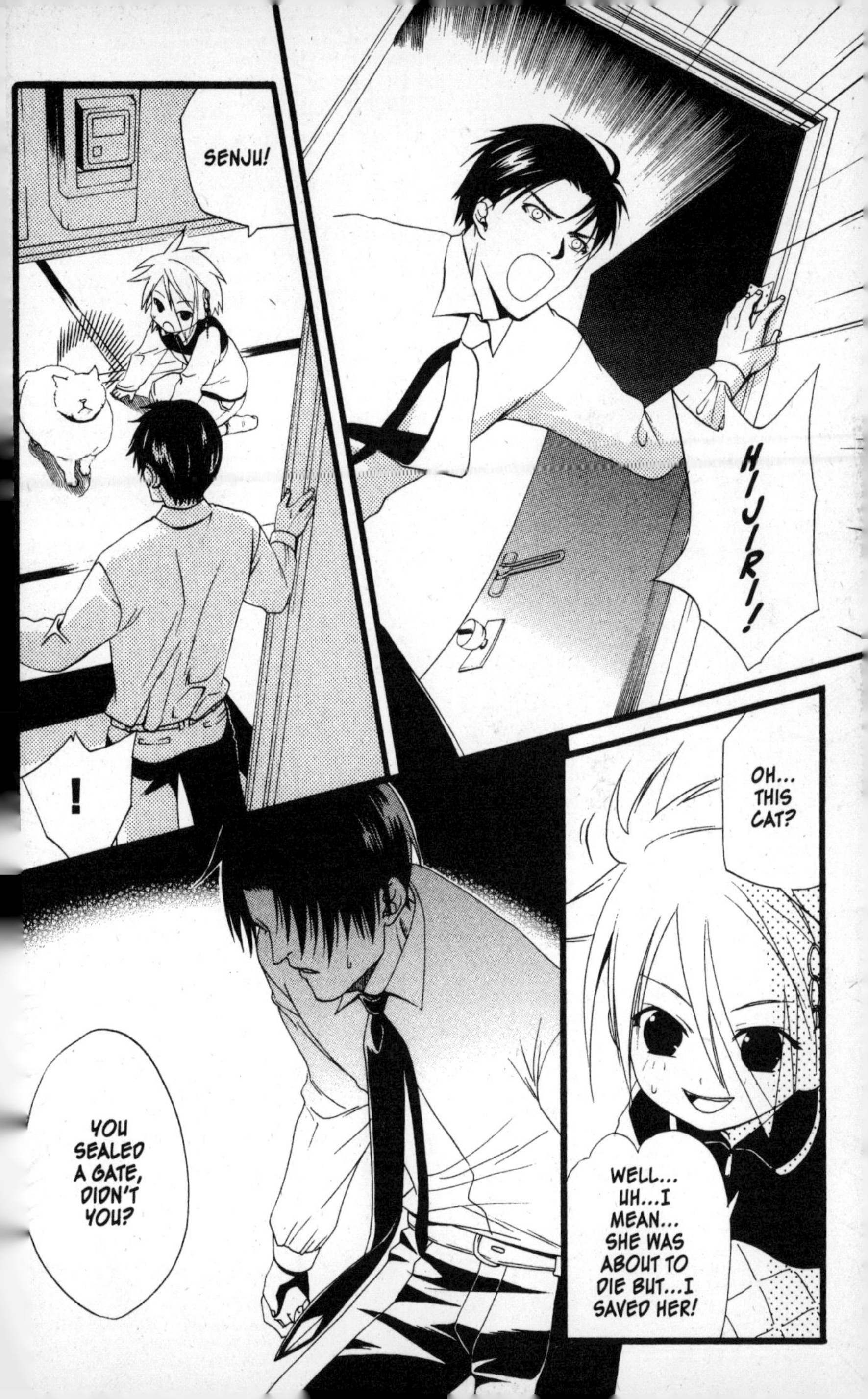
HIJIRI!
SENJU!
!
OH... THIS CAT?
WELL... UH...I MEAN... SHE WAS ABOUT TO DIE BUT...I SAVED HER!
YOU SEALED A GATE, DIDN'T YOU?

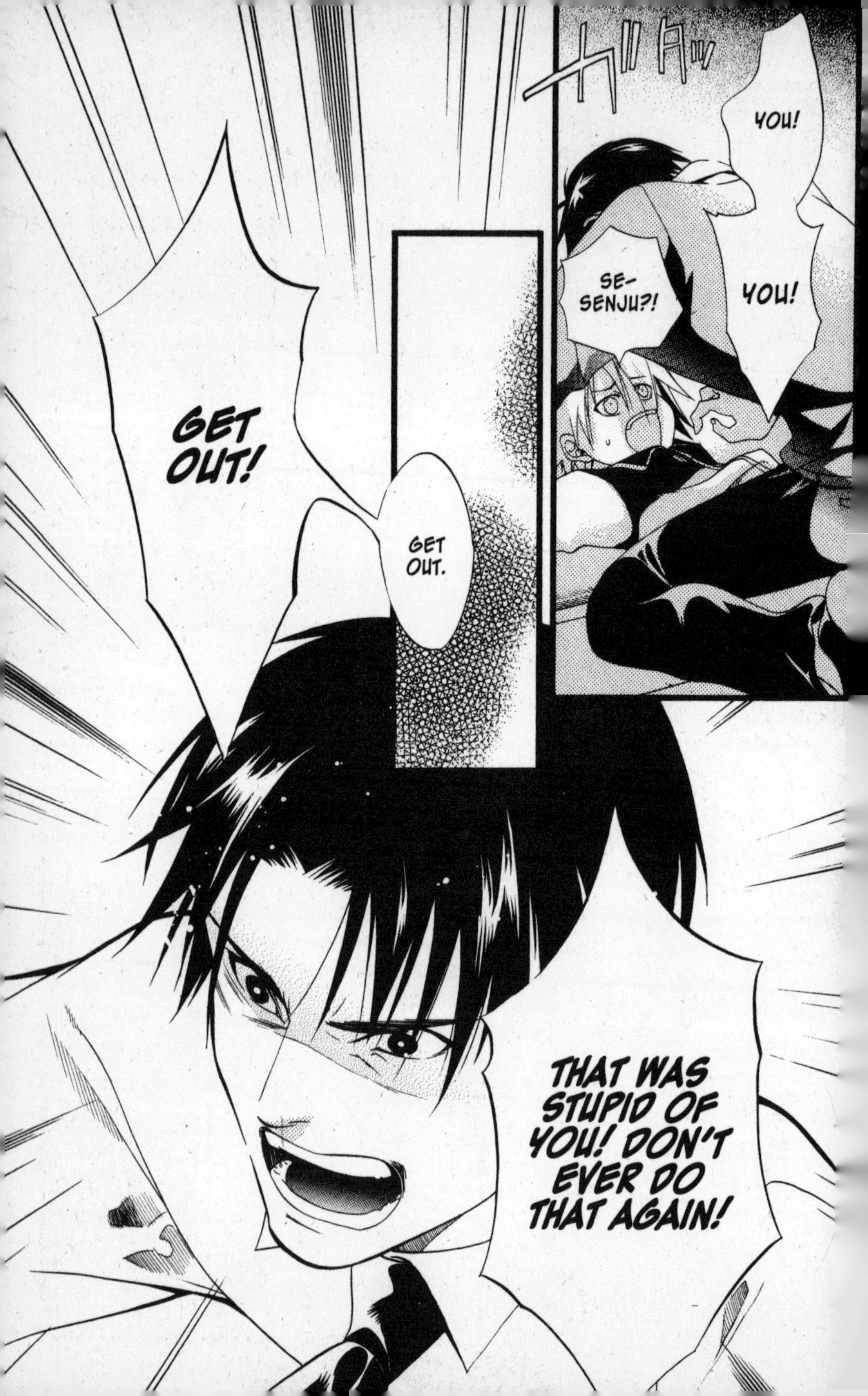
YOU!
YOU!
SE- SENJU?!
GET OUT.
GET OUT!
THAT WAS STUPID OF YOU! DON'T EVER DO THAT AGAIN!

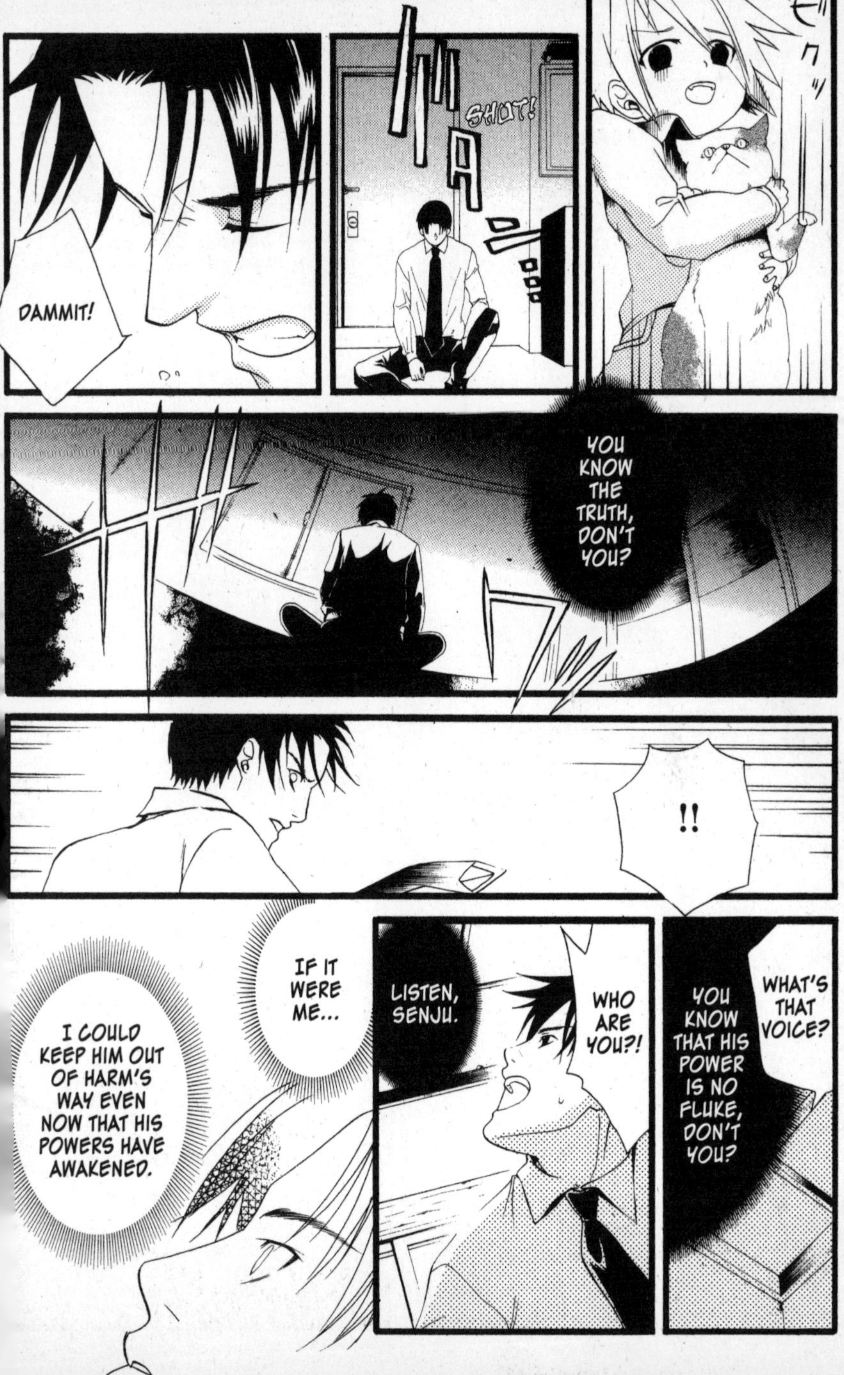
ビクッ
SHUT!
DAMMIT!
YOU KNOW THE TRUTH, DON'T YOU?
!!
WHAT'S THAT VOICE?
YOU KNOW THAT HIS POWER IS NO FLUKE, DON'T YOU?
WHO ARE YOU?!
LISTEN, SENJU.
IF IT WERE ME...
I COULD KEEP HIM OUT OF HARM'S WAY EVEN NOW THAT HIS POWERS HAVE AWAKENED.

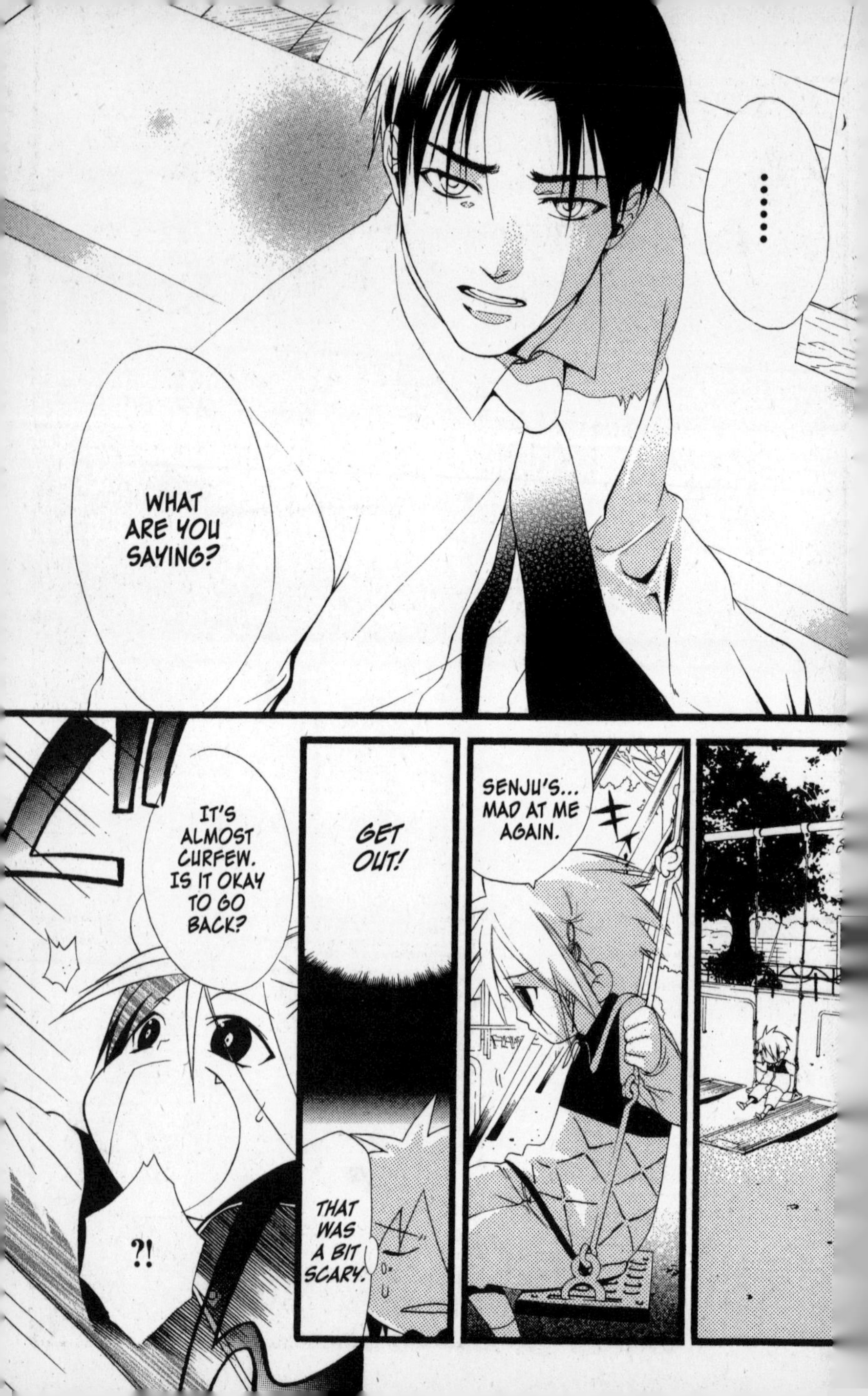
......
WHAT ARE YOU SAYING?
SENJU'S... MAD AT ME AGAIN.
GET OUT!
THAT WAS A BIT SCARY.
IT'S ALMOST CURFEW. IS IT OKAY TO GO BACK?
?!

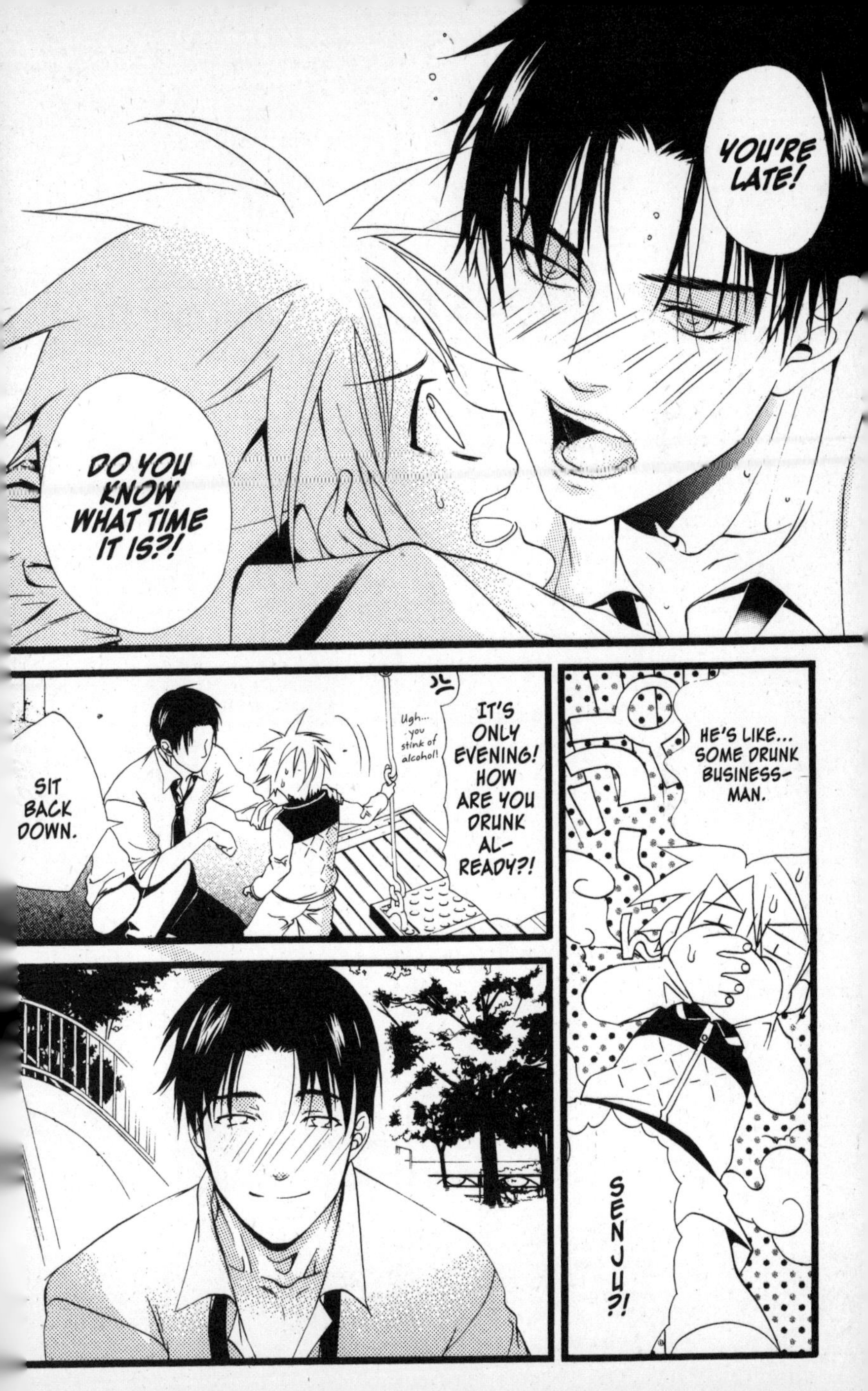
YOU'RE LATE!
DO YOU KNOW WHAT TIME IT IS?!
HE'S LIKE... SOME DRUNK BUSINESS-MAN.
SENJU?!
IT'S ONLY EVENING! HOW ARE YOU DRUNK AL-READY?!
Ugh... you stink of alcohol!
SIT BACK DOWN.

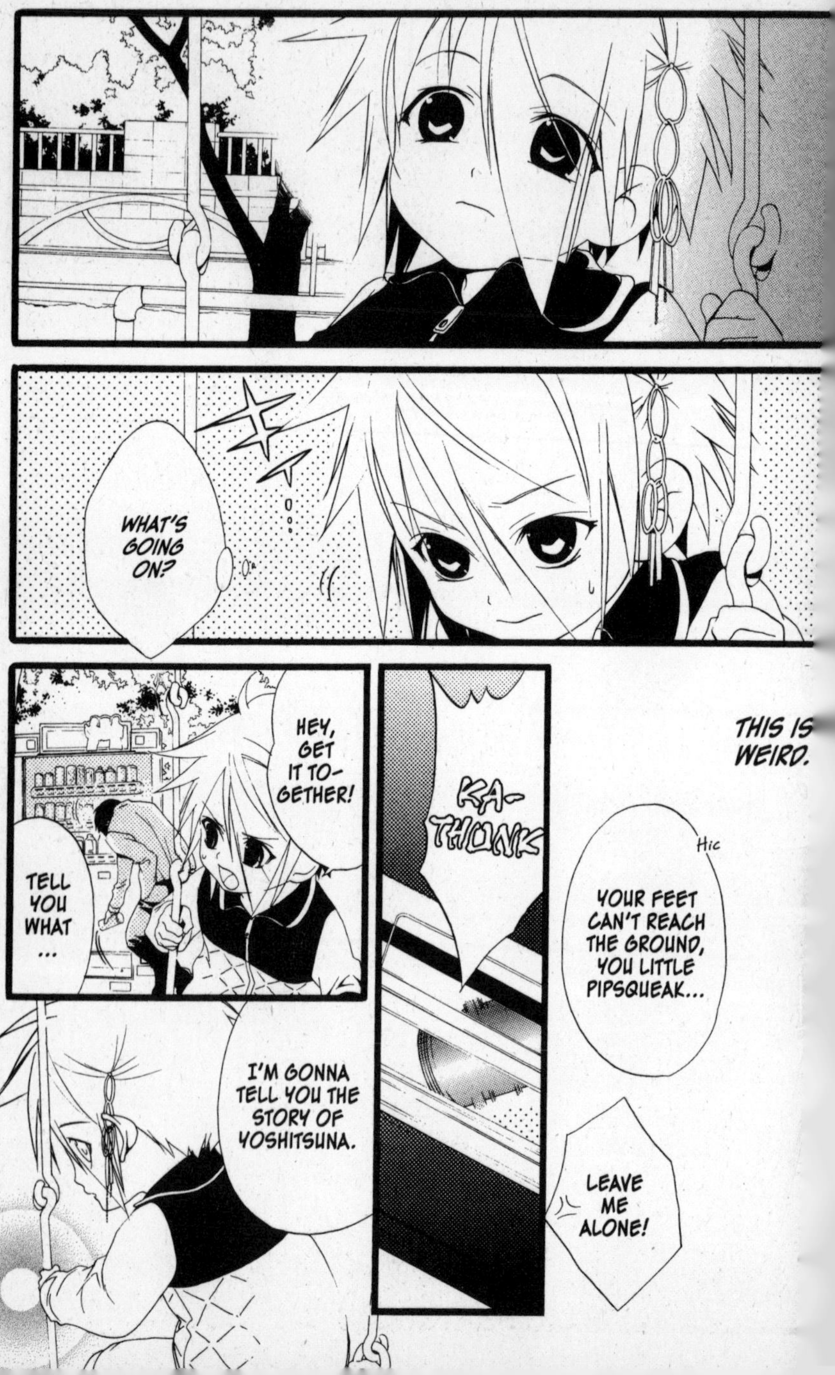
WHAT'S GOING ON?
THIS IS WEIRD.
KA-THONK
Hic
YOUR FEET CAN'T REACH THE GROUND, YOU LITTLE PIPSQUEAK...
LEAVE ME ALONE!
HEY, GET IT TO-GETHER!
TELL YOU WHAT ...
I'M GONNA TELL YOU THE STORY OF YOSHITSUNA.

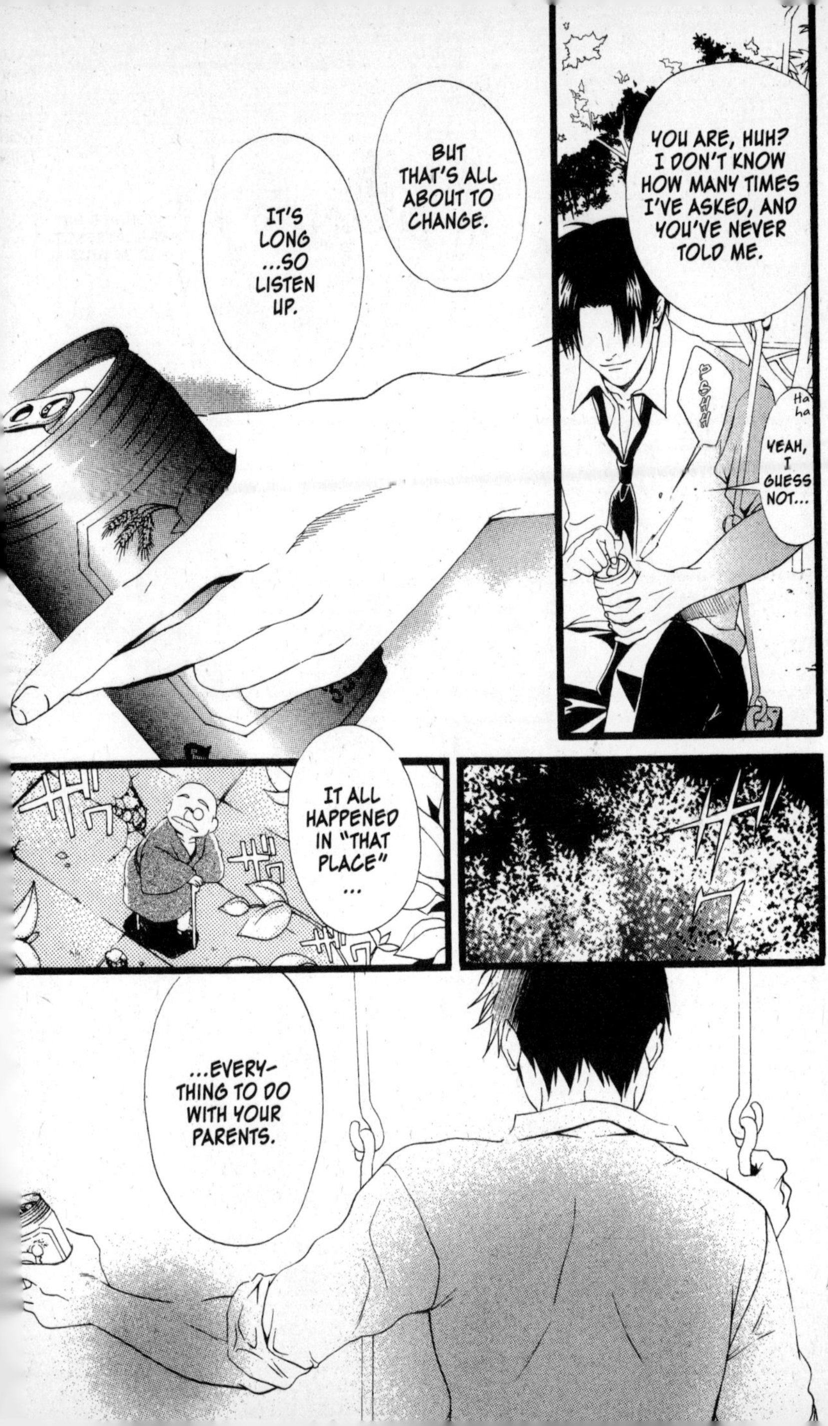
YOU ARE, HUH? I DON'T KNOW HOW MANY TIMES I'VE ASKED, AND YOU'VE NEVER TOLD ME.
PSHH
Ha ha
YEAH, I GUESS NOT...
BUT THAT'S ALL ABOUT TO CHANGE.
IT'S LONG ...SO LISTEN UP.
IT ALL HAPPENED IN "THAT PLACE" ...
...EVERY-THING TO DO WITH YOUR PARENTS.

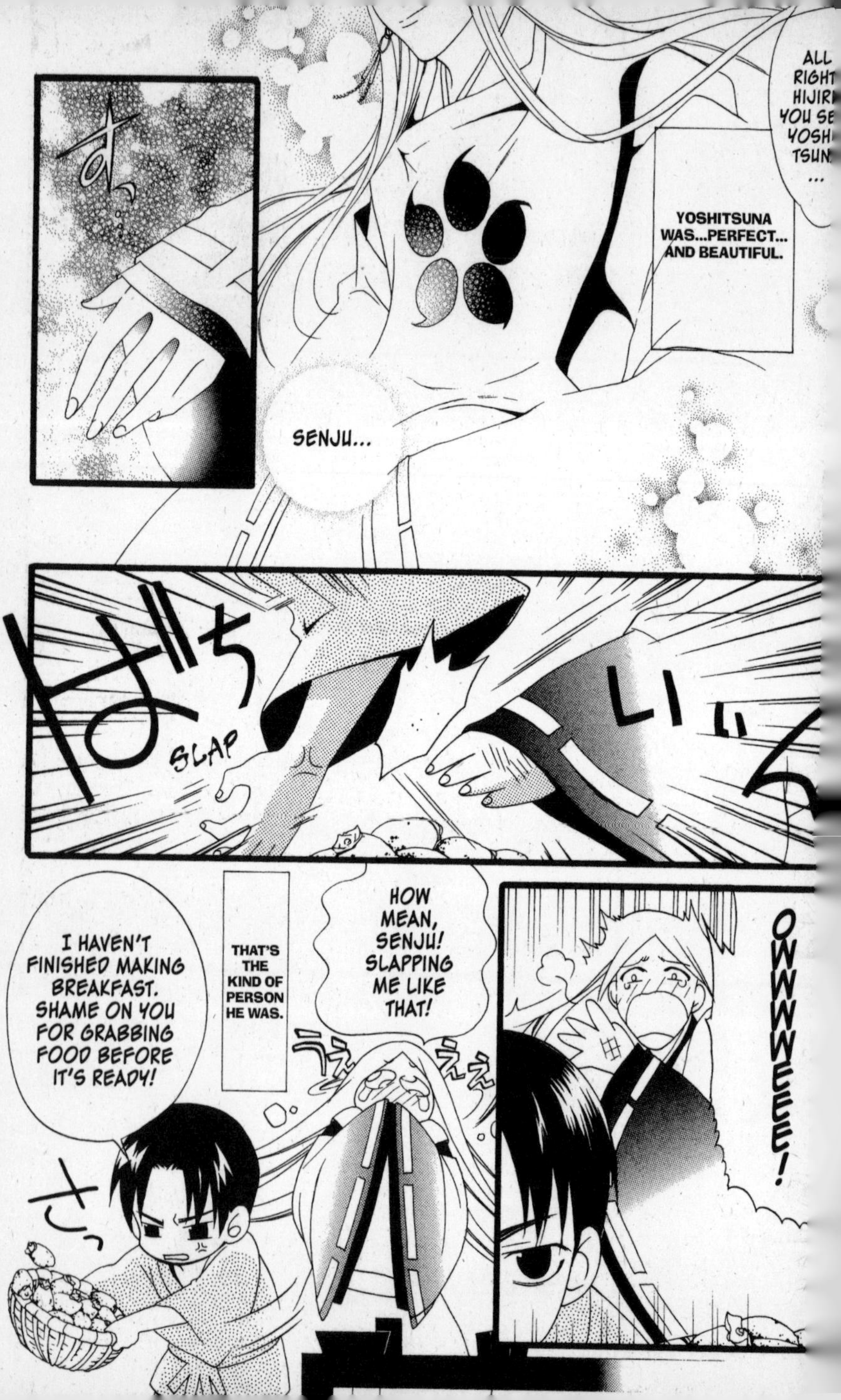
ALL RIGHT HIJIR YOU SE YOSHI TSUN ...
YOSHITSUNA WAS...PERFECT... AND BEAUTIFUL.
SENJU...
すっ
SLAP
OWWWWEEEE!
HOW MEAN, SENJU! SLAPPING ME LIKE THAT!
THAT'S THE KIND OF PERSON HE WAS.
I HAVEN'T FINISHED MAKING BREAKFAST. SHAME ON YOU FOR GRABBING FOOD BEFORE IT'S READY!
さっ

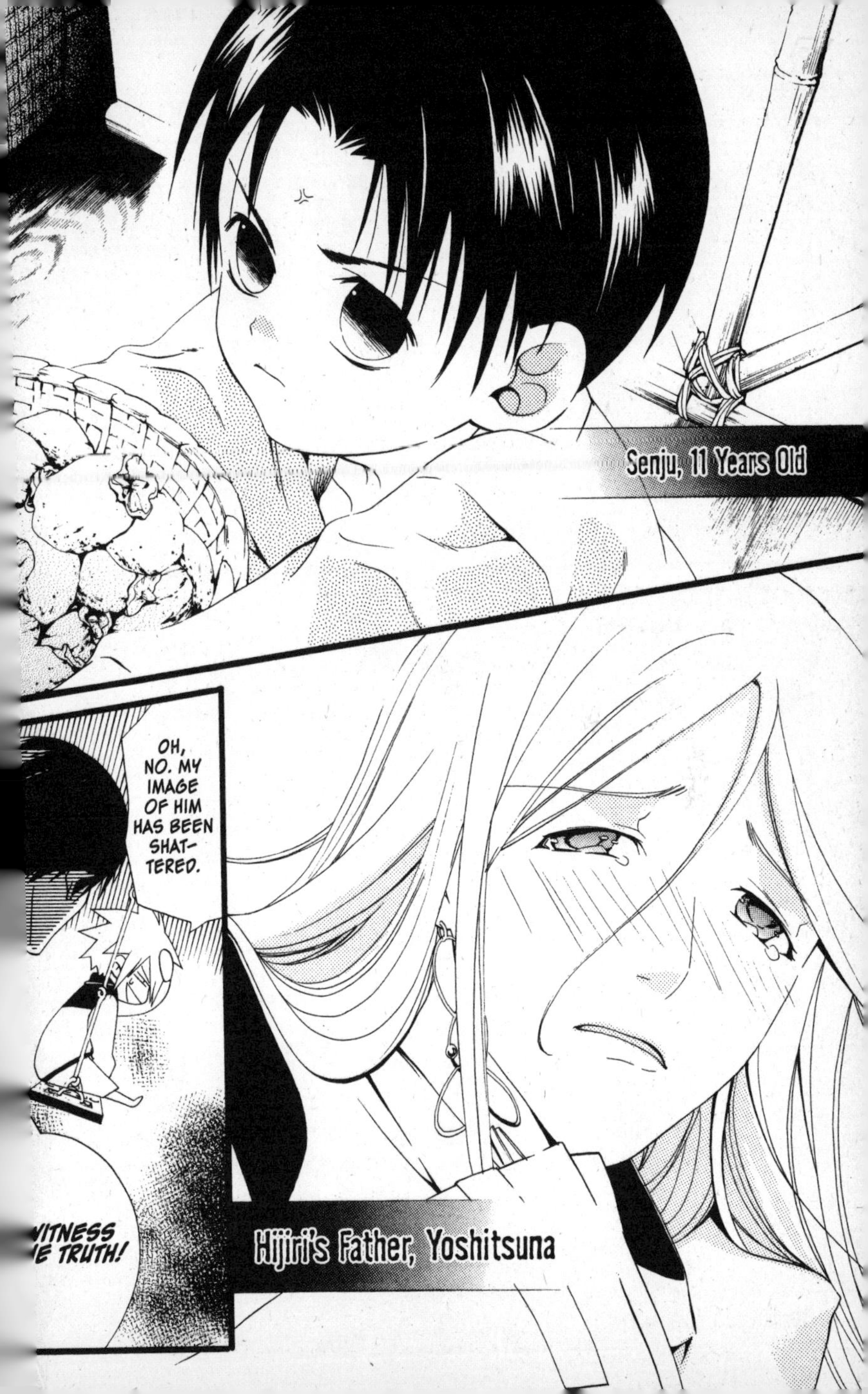
Senju, 11 Years Old
Hijiri's Father, Yoshitsuna
OH, NO. MY IMAGE OF HIM HAS BEEN SHAT-TERED.
WITNESS THE TRUTH!

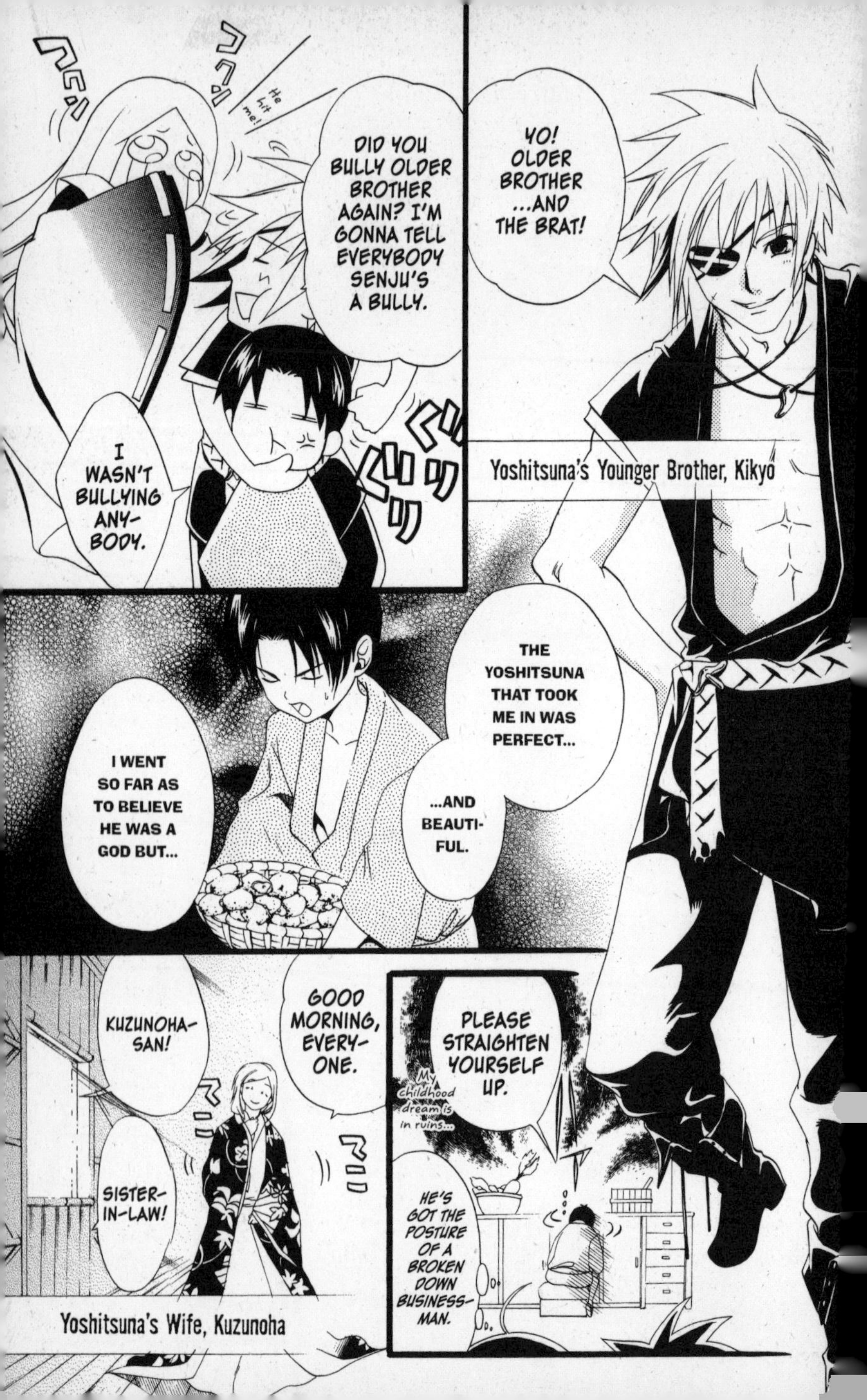
YO! OLDER BROTHER ...AND THE BRAT!
Yoshitsuna's Younger Brother, Kikyo
He hit me!
DID YOU BULLY OLDER BROTHER AGAIN? I'M GONNA TELL EVERYBODY SENJU'S A BULLY.
I WASN'T BULLYING ANY-BODY.
THE YOSHITSUNA THAT TOOK ME IN WAS PERFECT...
...AND BEAUTI-FUL.
I WENT SO FAR AS TO BELIEVE HE WAS A GOD BUT...
PLEASE STRAIGHTEN YOURSELF UP.
My childhood dream is in ruins...
HE'S GOT THE POSTURE OF A BROKEN DOWN BUSINESS-MAN.
GOOD MORNING, EVERY-ONE.
KUZUNOHA-SAN!
SISTER-IN-LAW!
Yoshitsuna's Wife, Kuzunoha

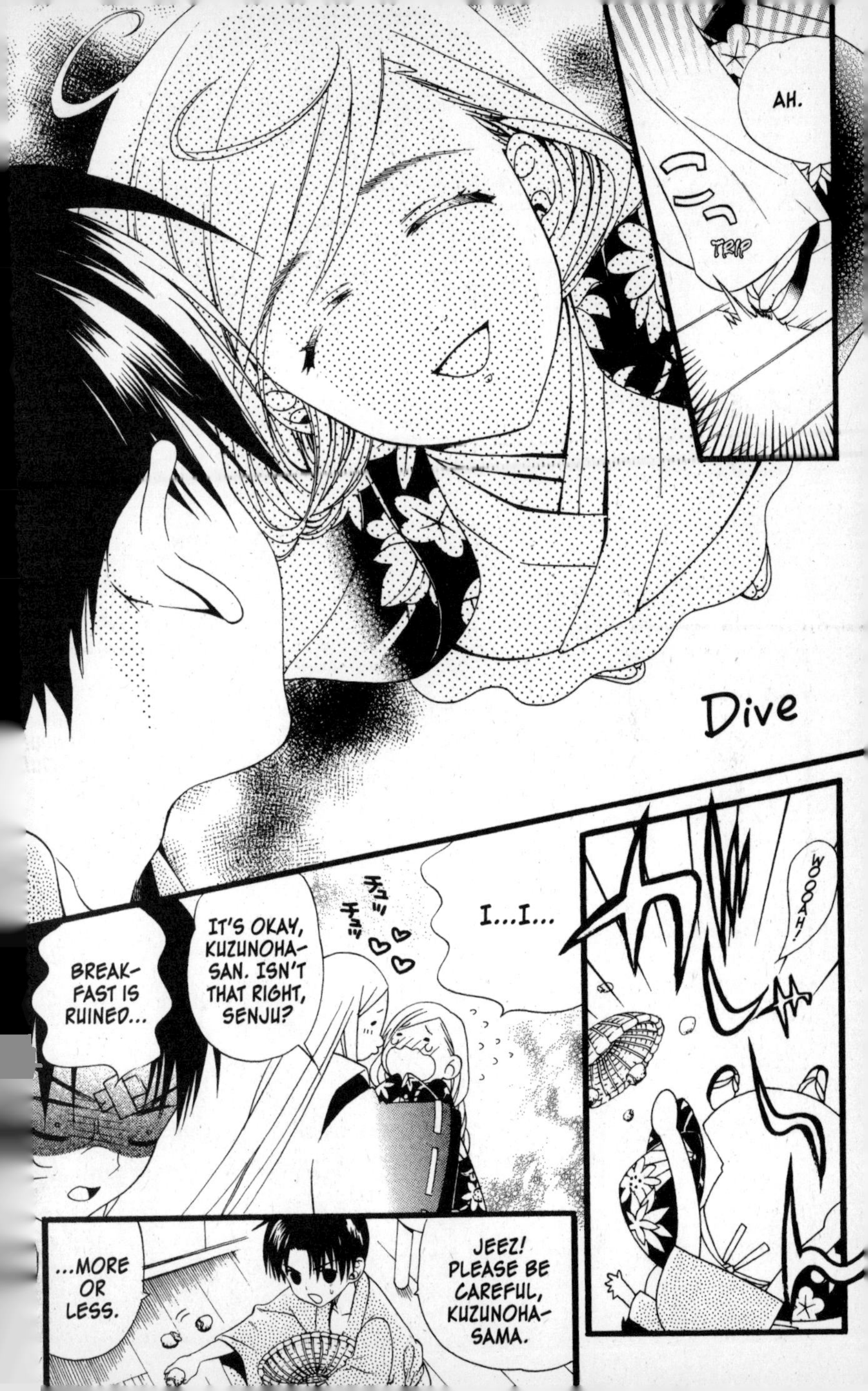
AH.
TRIP
Dive
WOOOAH!
I...I...
チュッ
チュッ
IT'S OKAY, KUZUNOHA-SAN. ISN'T THAT RIGHT, SENJU?
BREAK-FAST IS RUINED...
JEEZ! PLEASE BE CAREFUL, KUZUNOHA-SAMA.
...MORE OR LESS.

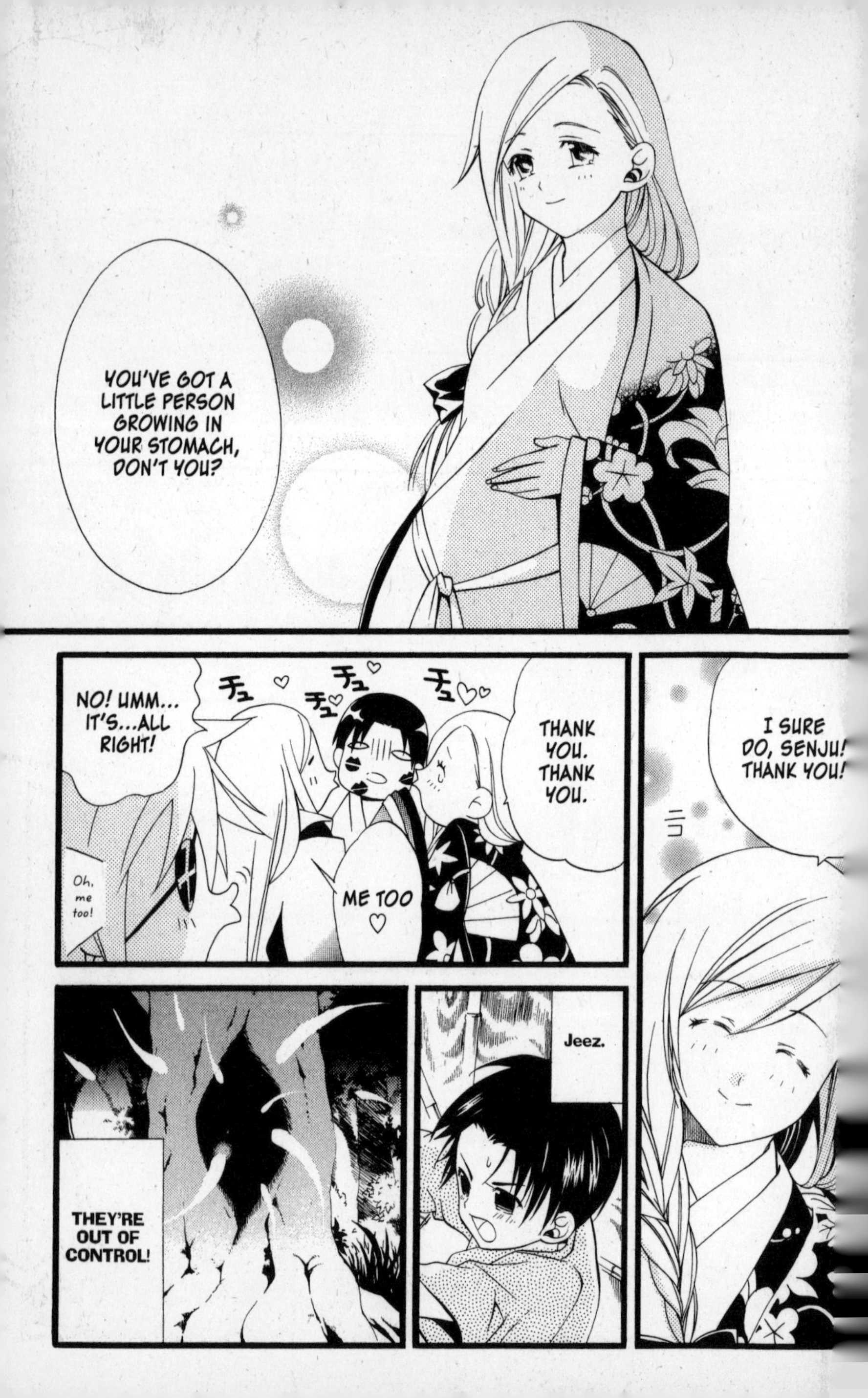
YOU'VE GOT A LITTLE PERSON GROWING IN YOUR STOMACH, DON'T YOU?
I SURE DO, SENJU! THANK YOU!
チュ♡
チュ♡
THANK YOU. THANK YOU.
チュ
チュ♡
NO! UMM... IT'S...ALL RIGHT!
ME TOO ♡
Oh, me too!
Jeez.
THEY'RE OUT OF CONTROL!

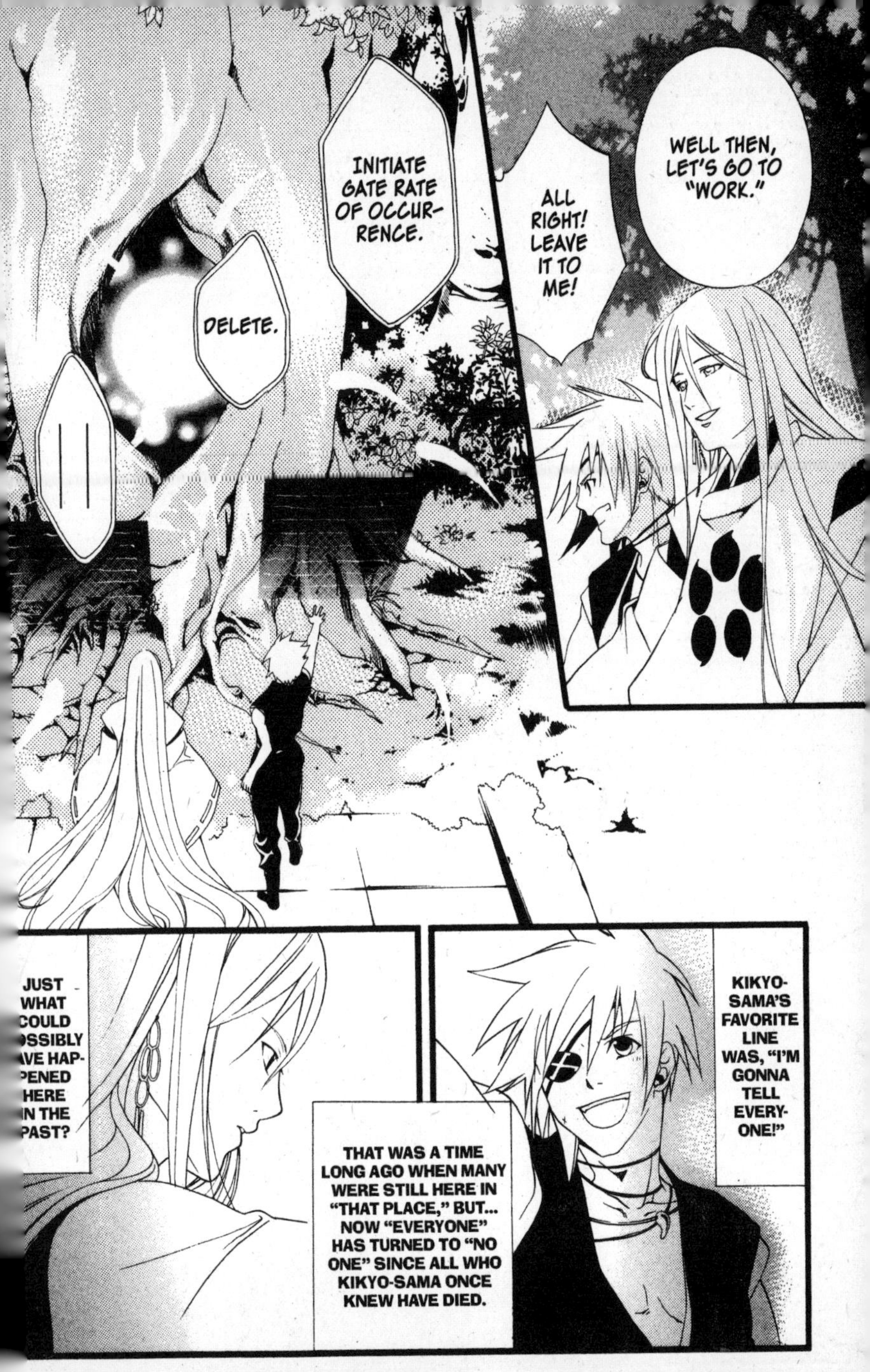
WELL THEN, LET'S GO TO "WORK."
ALL RIGHT! LEAVE IT TO ME!
INITIATE GATE RATE OF OCCUR-RENCE.
DELETE.
KIKYO-SAMA'S FAVORITE LINE WAS, "I'M GONNA TELL EVERY-ONE!"
THAT WAS A TIME LONG AGO WHEN MANY WERE STILL HERE IN "THAT PLACE," BUT... NOW "EVERYONE" HAS TURNED TO "NO ONE" SINCE ALL WHO KIKYO-SAMA ONCE KNEW HAVE DIED.
JUST WHAT COULD OSSIBLY AVE HAP-PENED HERE IN THE PAST?

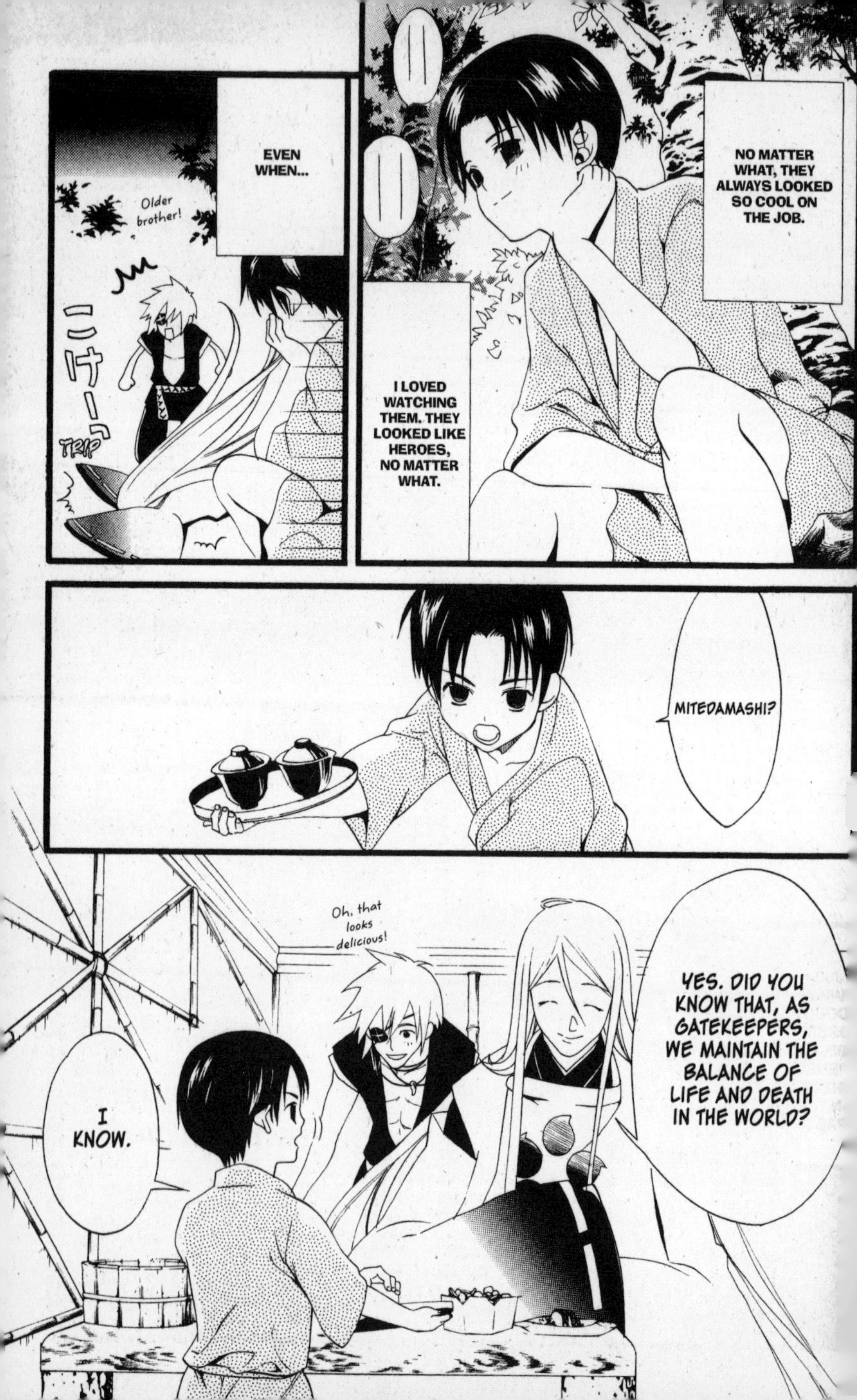
NO MATTER WHAT, THEY ALWAYS LOOKED SO COOL ON THE JOB.
...
...
I LOVED WATCHING THEM. THEY LOOKED LIKE HEROES, NO MATTER WHAT.
EVEN WHEN...
Older brother!
こけーっ
TRIP
MITEDAMASHI?
YES. DID YOU KNOW THAT, AS GATEKEEPERS, WE MAINTAIN THE BALANCE OF LIFE AND DEATH IN THE WORLD?
Oh, that looks delicious!
I KNOW.

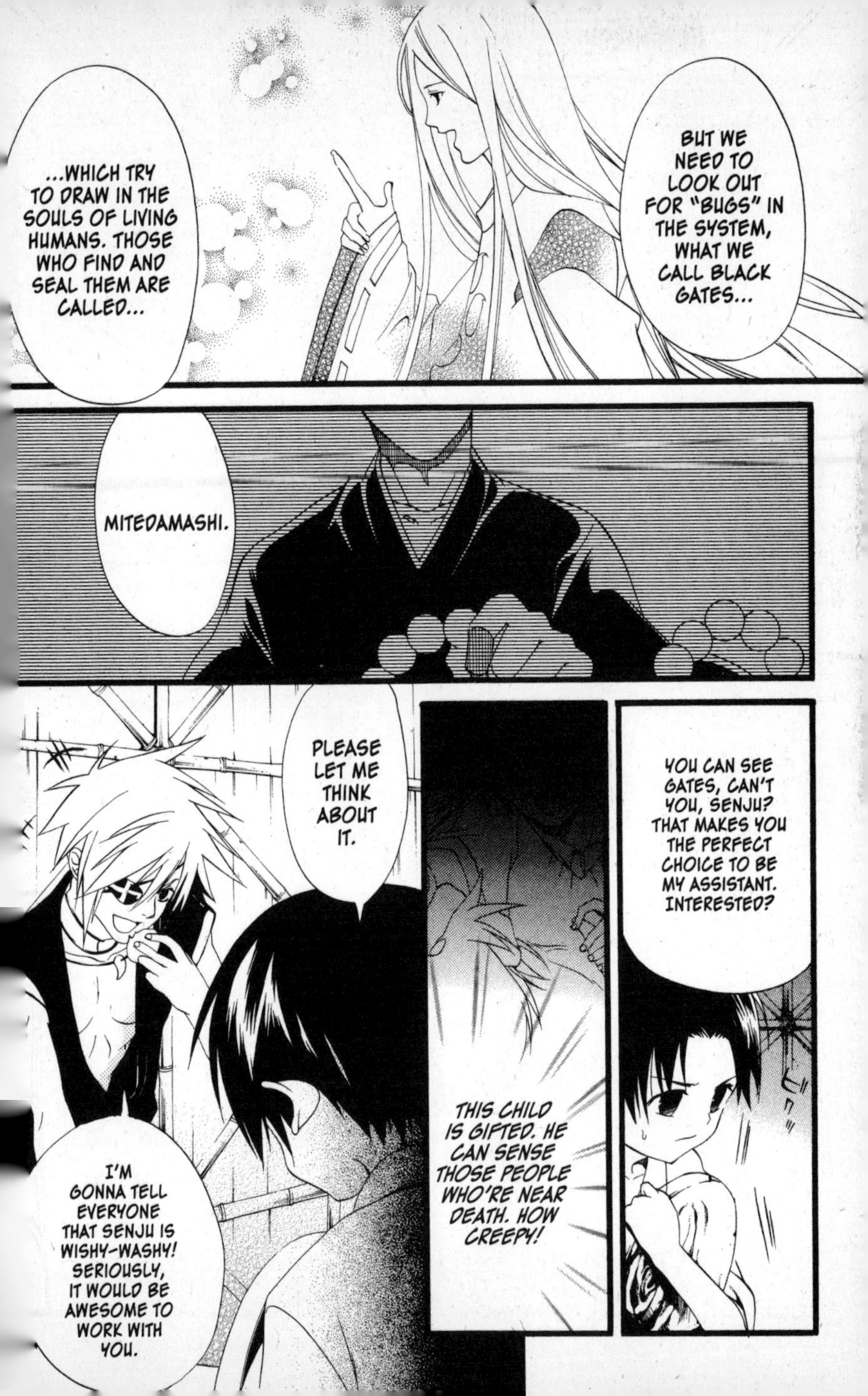
BUT WE NEED TO LOOK OUT FOR "BUGS" IN THE SYSTEM, WHAT WE CALL BLACK GATES...
...WHICH TRY TO DRAW IN THE SOULS OF LIVING HUMANS. THOSE WHO FIND AND SEAL THEM ARE CALLED...
MITEDAMASHI.
YOU CAN SEE GATES, CAN'T YOU, SENJU? THAT MAKES YOU THE PERFECT CHOICE TO BE MY ASSISTANT. INTERESTED?
THIS CHILD IS GIFTED. HE CAN SENSE THOSE PEOPLE WHO'RE NEAR DEATH. HOW CREEPY!
PLEASE LET ME THINK ABOUT IT.
I'M GONNA TELL EVERYONE THAT SENJU IS WISHY-WASHY! SERIOUSLY, IT WOULD BE AWESOME TO WORK WITH YOU.

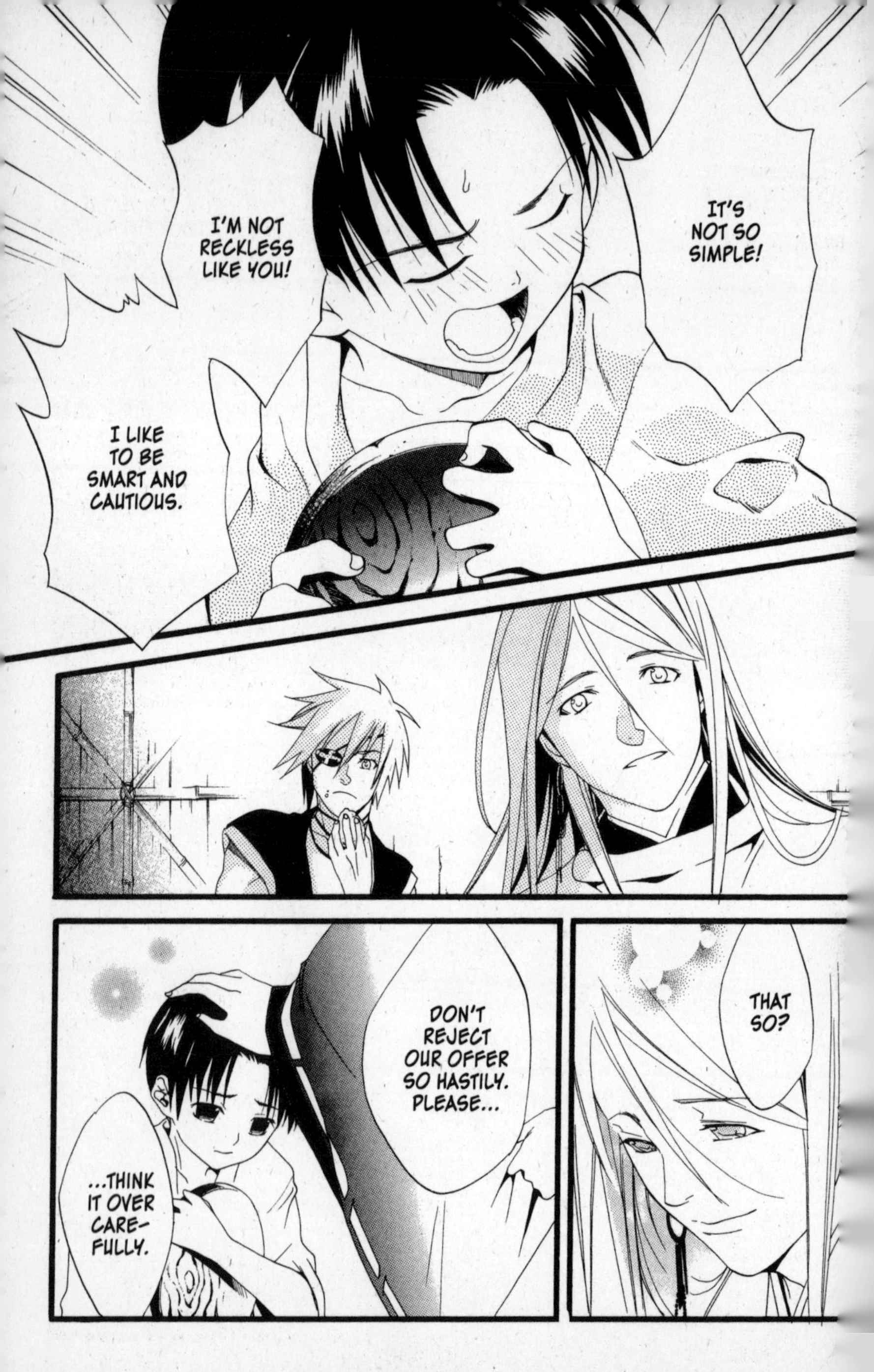
IT'S NOT SO SIMPLE!
I'M NOT RECKLESS LIKE YOU!
I LIKE TO BE SMART AND CAUTIOUS.
THAT SO?
DON'T REJECT OUR OFFER SO HASTILY. PLEASE...
...THINK IT OVER CARE-FULLY.

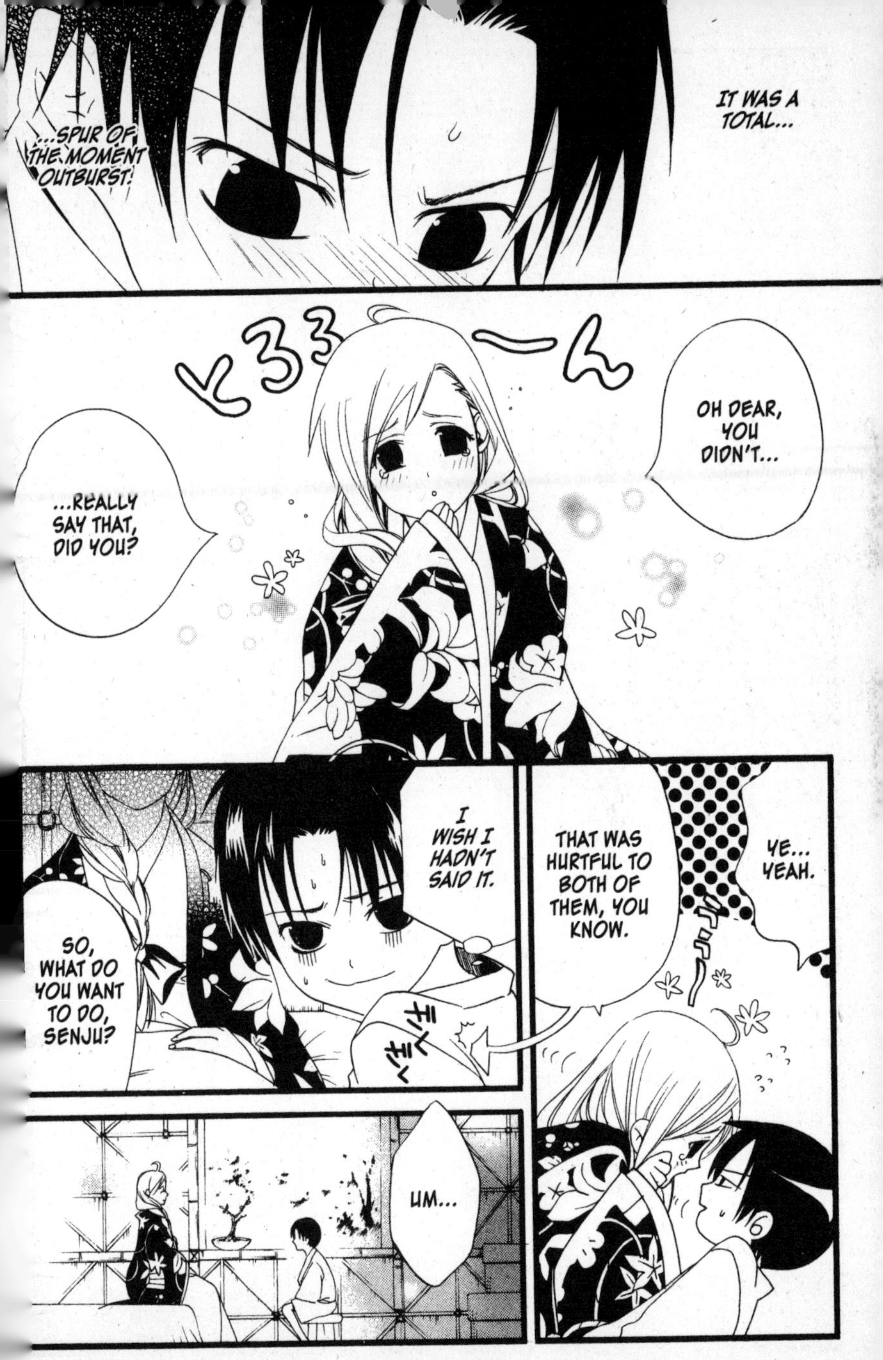

IT WAS A TOTAL...
...SPUR OF THE MOMENT OUTBURST!
くるるーん
OH DEAR, YOU DIDN'T...
...REALLY SAY THAT, DID YOU?
YE... YEAH.
THAT WAS HURTFUL TO BOTH OF THEM, YOU KNOW.
I WISH I HADN'T SAID IT.
SO, WHAT DO YOU WANT TO DO, SENJU?
UM...

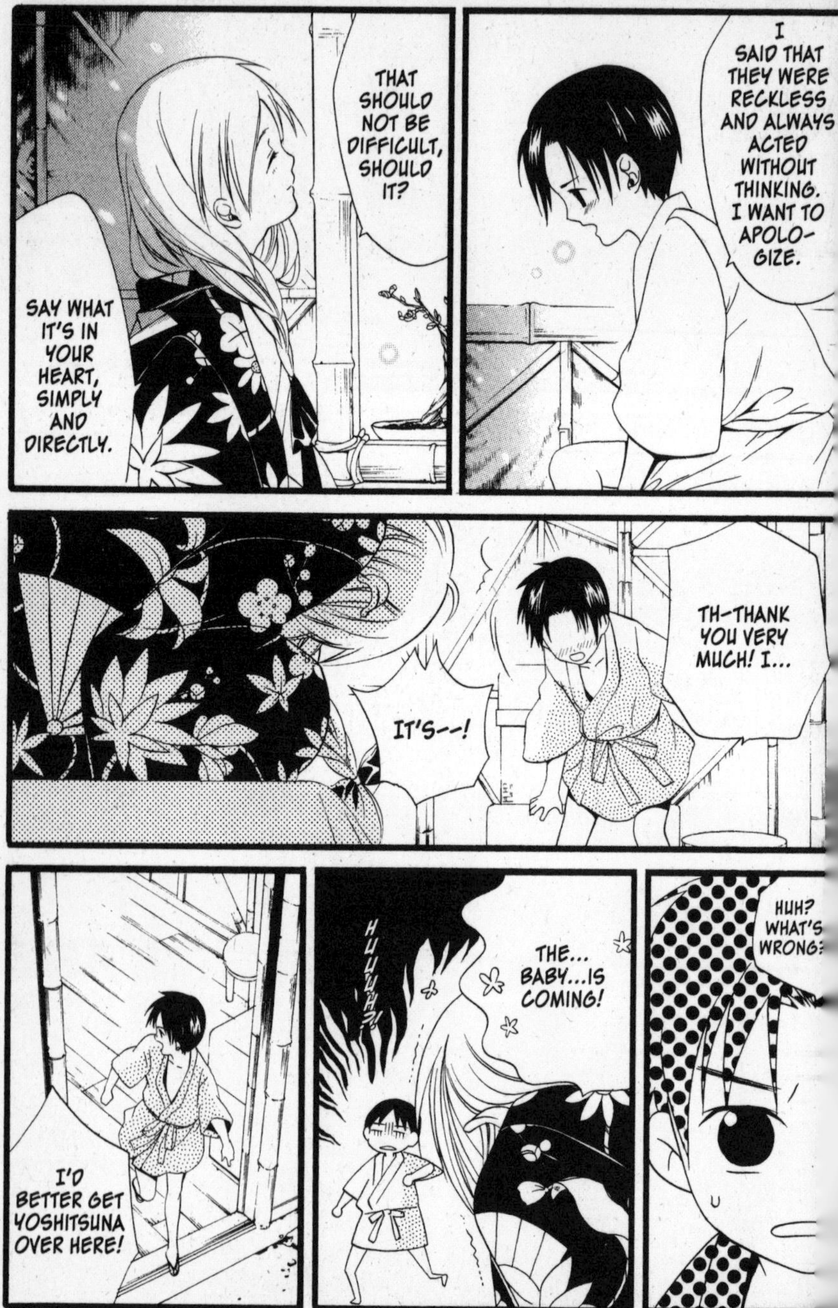
I SAID THAT THEY WERE RECKLESS AND ALWAYS ACTED WITHOUT THINKING. I WANT TO APOLOGIZE.
THAT SHOULD NOT BE DIFFICULT, SHOULD IT?
SAY WHAT IT'S IN YOUR HEART, SIMPLY AND DIRECTLY.
TH-THANK YOU VERY MUCH! I...
IT'S--!
HUH? WHAT'S WRONG?
THE... BABY...IS COMING!
HUUUH?!
I'D BETTER GET YOSHITSUNA OVER HERE!

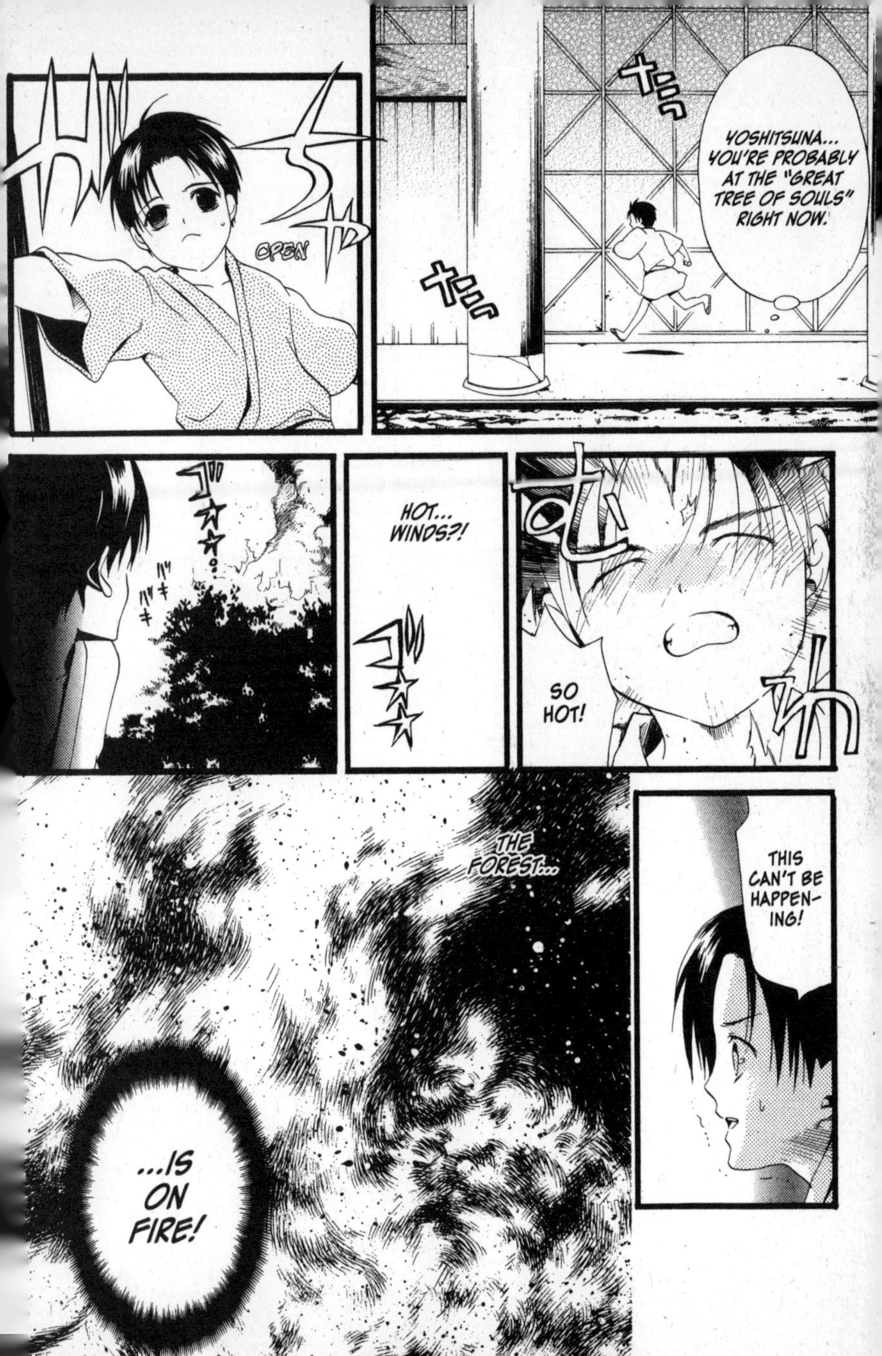
YOSHITSUNA... YOU'RE PROBABLY AT THE "GREAT TREE OF SOULS" RIGHT NOW.
OPEN
SO HOT!
HOT... WINDS?!
THIS CAN'T BE HAPPENING-ING!
THE FOREST...
...IS ON FIRE!

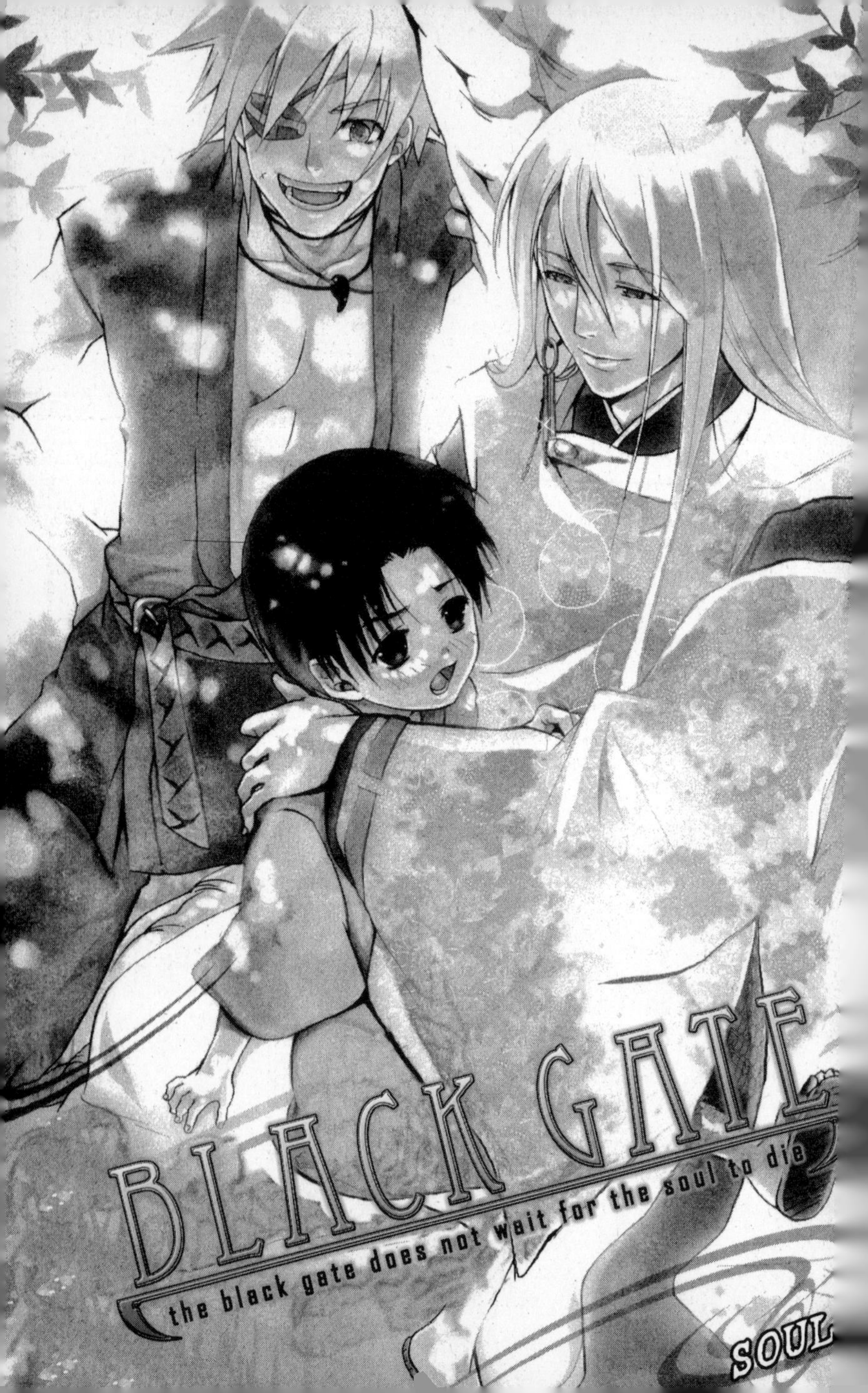
BLACK GATE
the black gate does not wait for the soul to die
SOUL

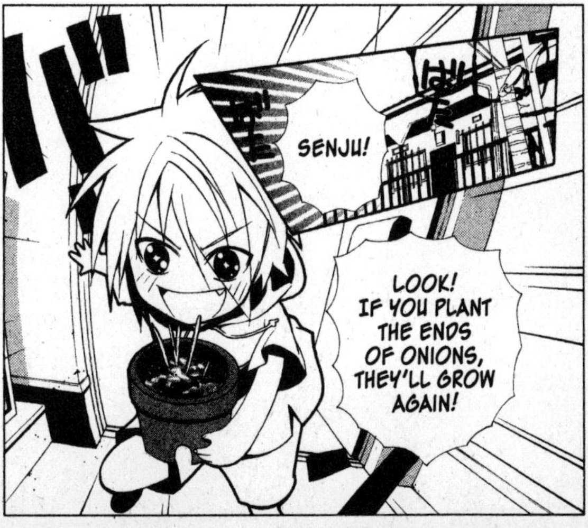
SENJU!
LOOK! IF YOU PLANT THE ENDS OF ONIONS, THEY'LL GROW AGAIN!

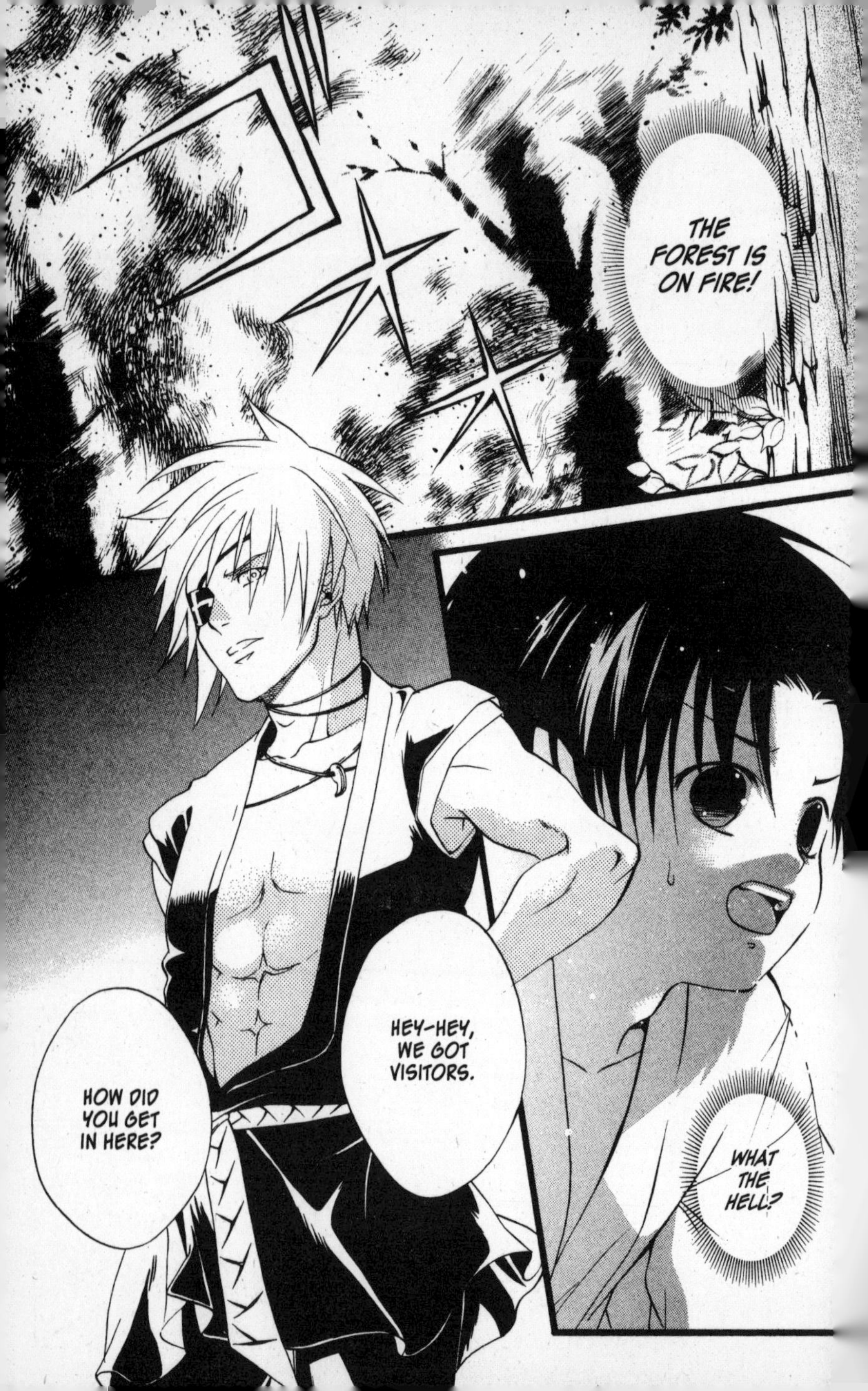
THE FOREST IS ON FIRE!
WHAT THE HELL?
HEY-HEY, WE GOT VISITORS.
HOW DID YOU GET IN HERE?

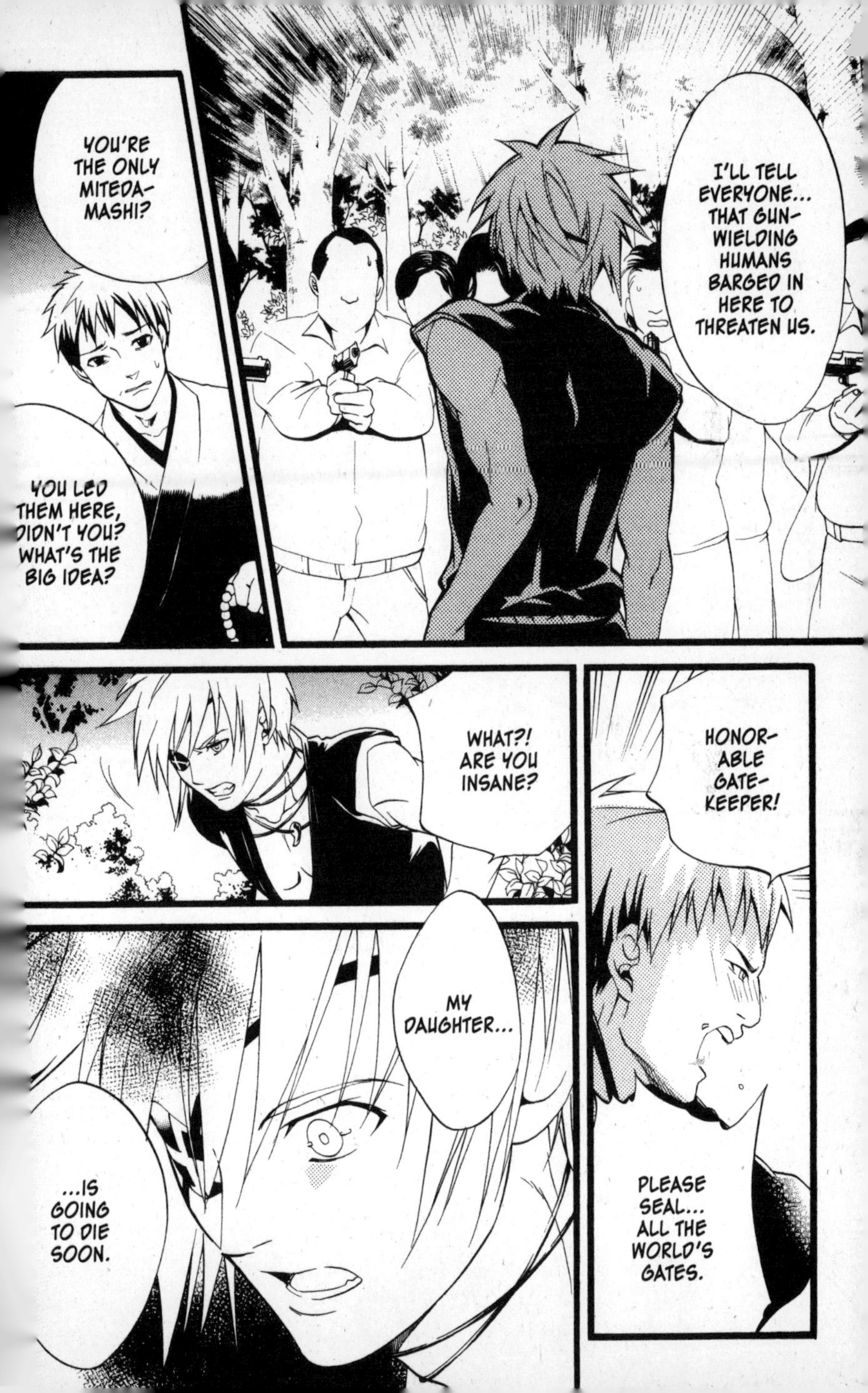
I'LL TELL EVERYONE... THAT GUN-WIELDING HUMANS BARGED IN HERE TO THREATEN US.
YOU'RE THE ONLY MITEDA-MASHI?
YOU LED THEM HERE, DIDN'T YOU? WHAT'S THE BIG IDEA?
HONORABLE GATE-KEEPER!
PLEASE SEAL... ALL THE WORLD'S GATES.
WHAT?! ARE YOU INSANE?
MY DAUGHTER...
...IS GOING TO DIE SOON.

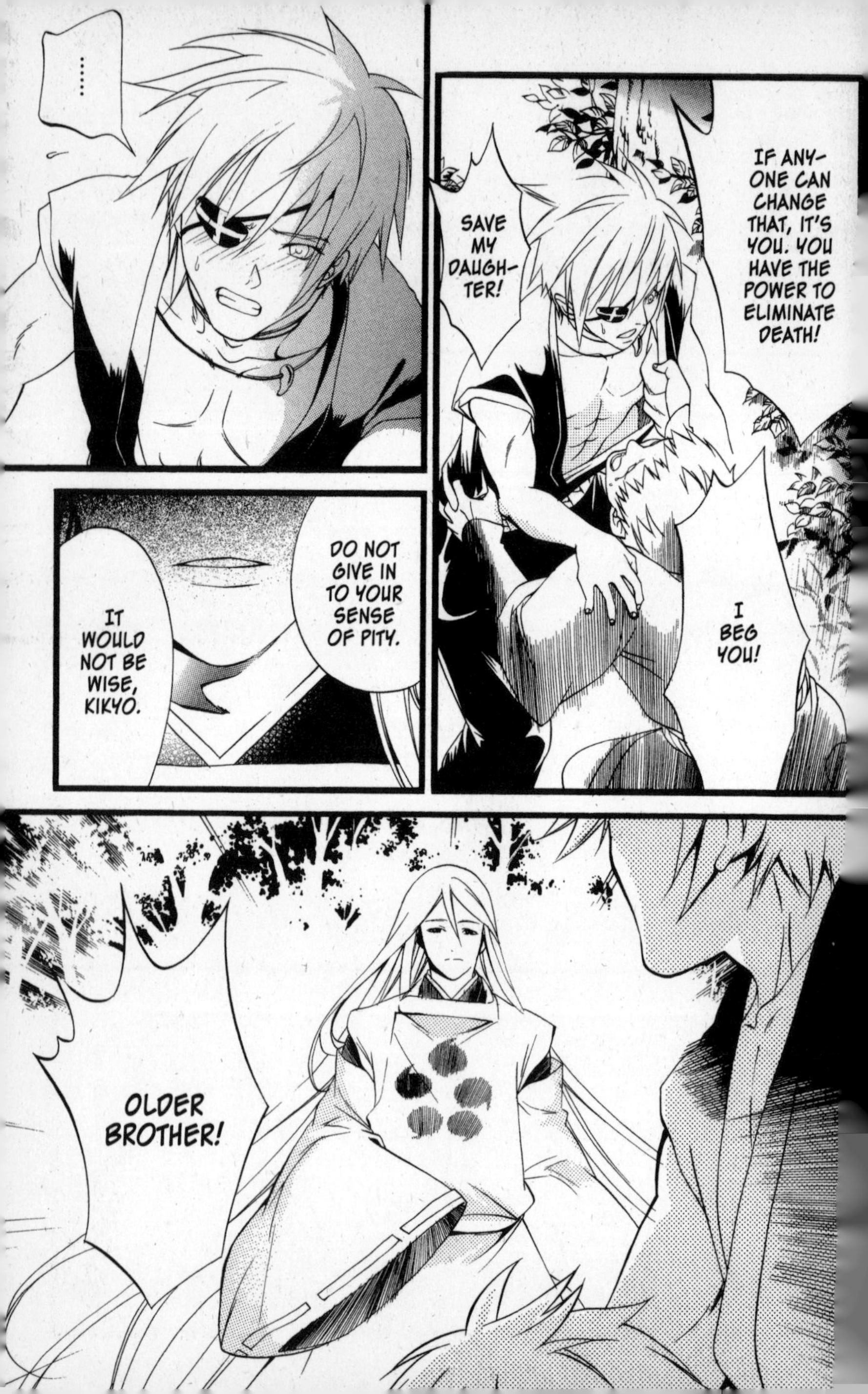
IF ANYONE CAN CHANGE THAT, IT'S YOU. YOU HAVE THE POWER TO ELIMINATE DEATH!
SAVE MY DAUGHTER!
I BEG YOU!
……
DO NOT GIVE IN TO YOUR SENSE OF PITY.
IT WOULD NOT BE WISE, KIKYO.
OLDER BROTHER!

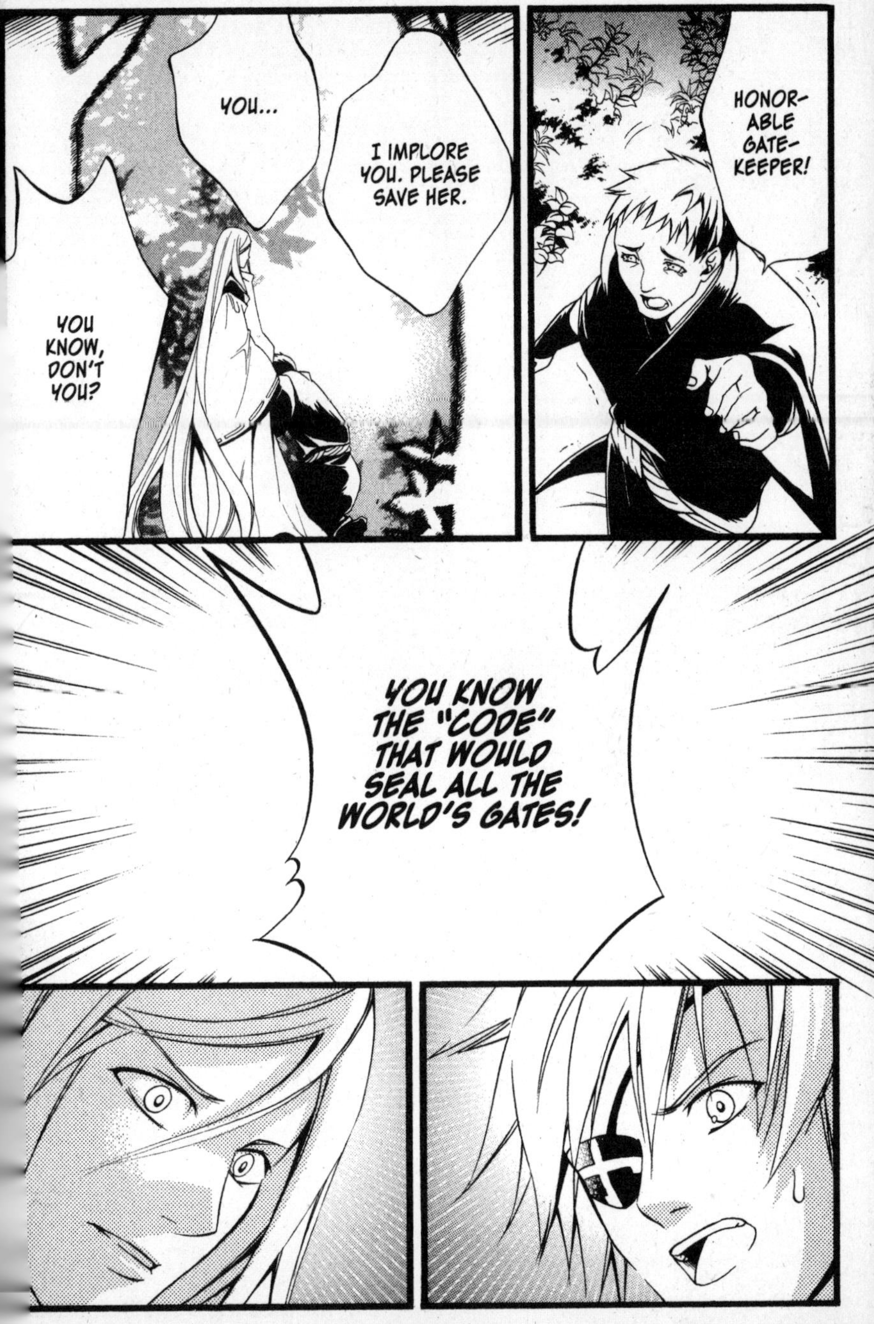
HONORABLE GATEKEEPER!
I IMPLORE YOU. PLEASE SAVE HER.
YOU...
YOU KNOW, DON'T YOU?
YOU KNOW THE "CODE" THAT WOULD SEAL ALL THE WORLD'S GATES!

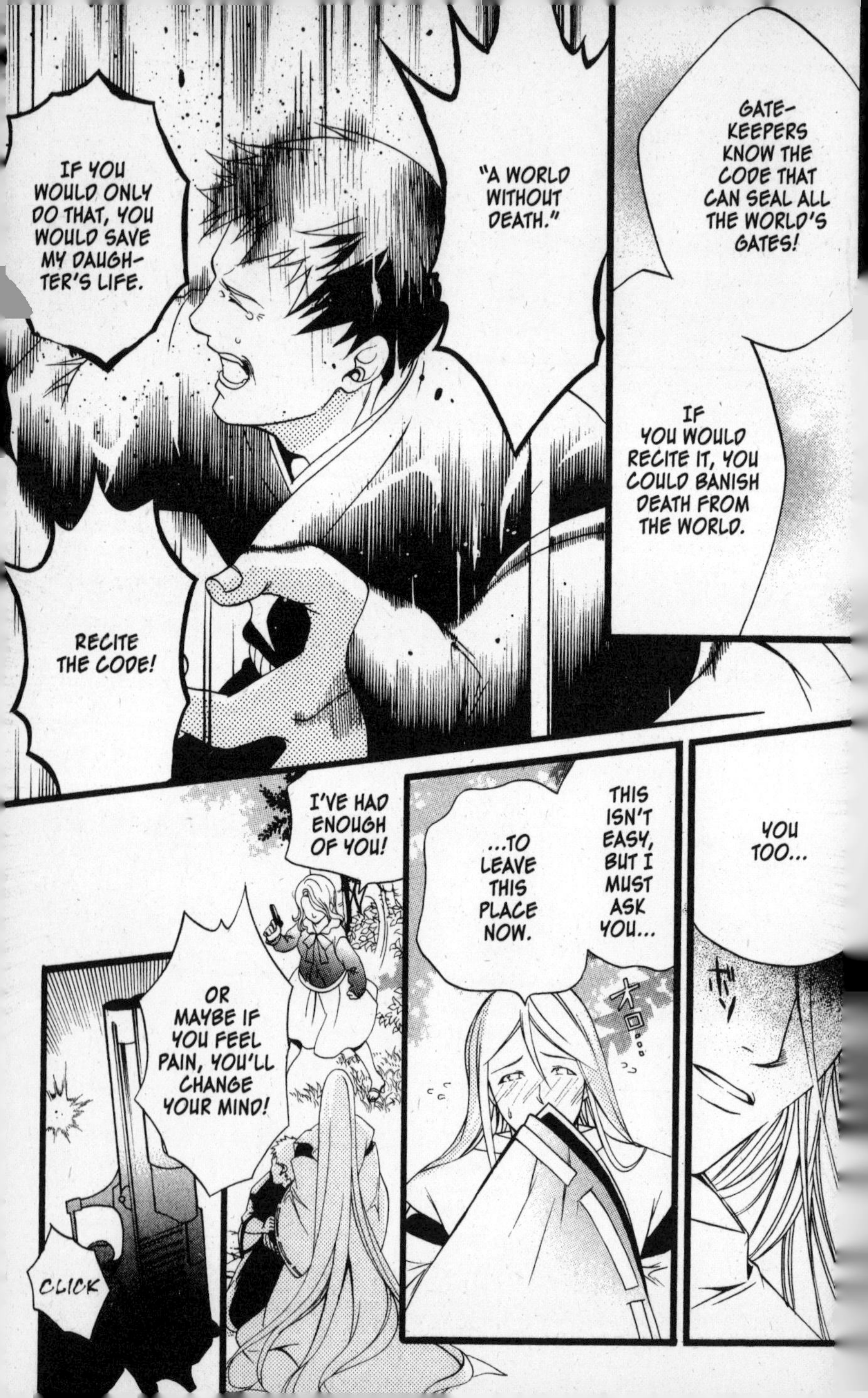
GATE-KEEPERS KNOW THE CODE THAT CAN SEAL ALL THE WORLD'S GATES!
IF YOU WOULD RECITE IT, YOU COULD BANISH DEATH FROM THE WORLD.
"A WORLD WITHOUT DEATH."
IF YOU WOULD ONLY DO THAT, YOU WOULD SAVE MY DAUGH-TER'S LIFE.
RECITE THE CODE!
YOU TOO...
ボッ
THIS ISN'T EASY, BUT I MUST ASK YOU...
...TO LEAVE THIS PLACE NOW.
オロ...
I'VE HAD ENOUGH OF YOU!
OR MAYBE IF YOU FEEL PAIN, YOU'LL CHANGE YOUR MIND!
CLICK

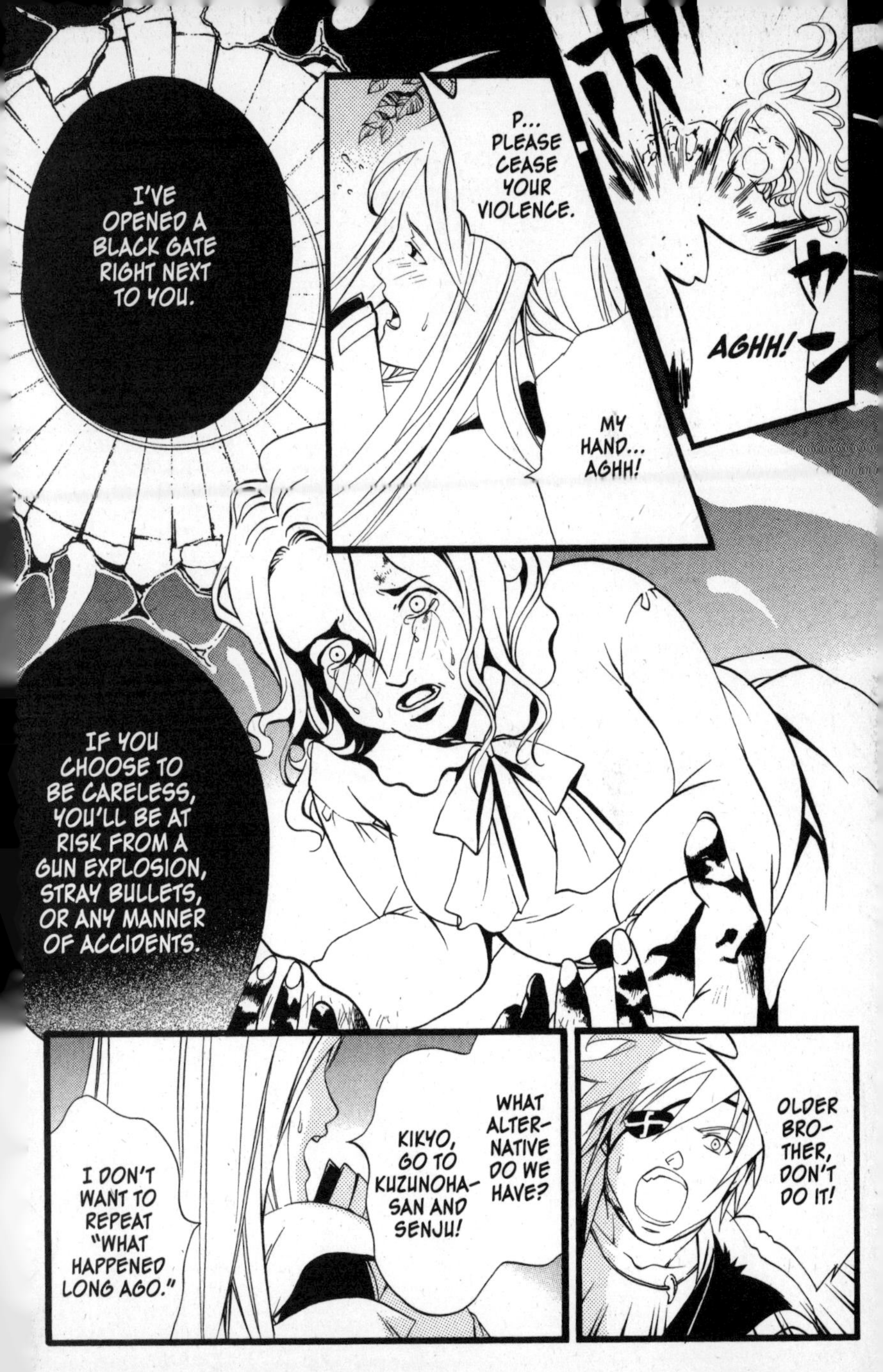
AGHH!
P... PLEASE CEASE YOUR VIOLENCE.
MY HAND... AGHH!
I'VE OPENED A BLACK GATE RIGHT NEXT TO YOU.
IF YOU CHOOSE TO BE CARELESS, YOU'LL BE AT RISK FROM A GUN EXPLOSION, STRAY BULLETS, OR ANY MANNER OF ACCIDENTS.
OLDER BRO-THER, DON'T DO IT!
WHAT ALTER-NATIVE DO WE HAVE?
KIKYO, GO TO KUZUNOHA-SAN AND SENJU!
I DON'T WANT TO REPEAT "WHAT HAPPENED LONG AGO."

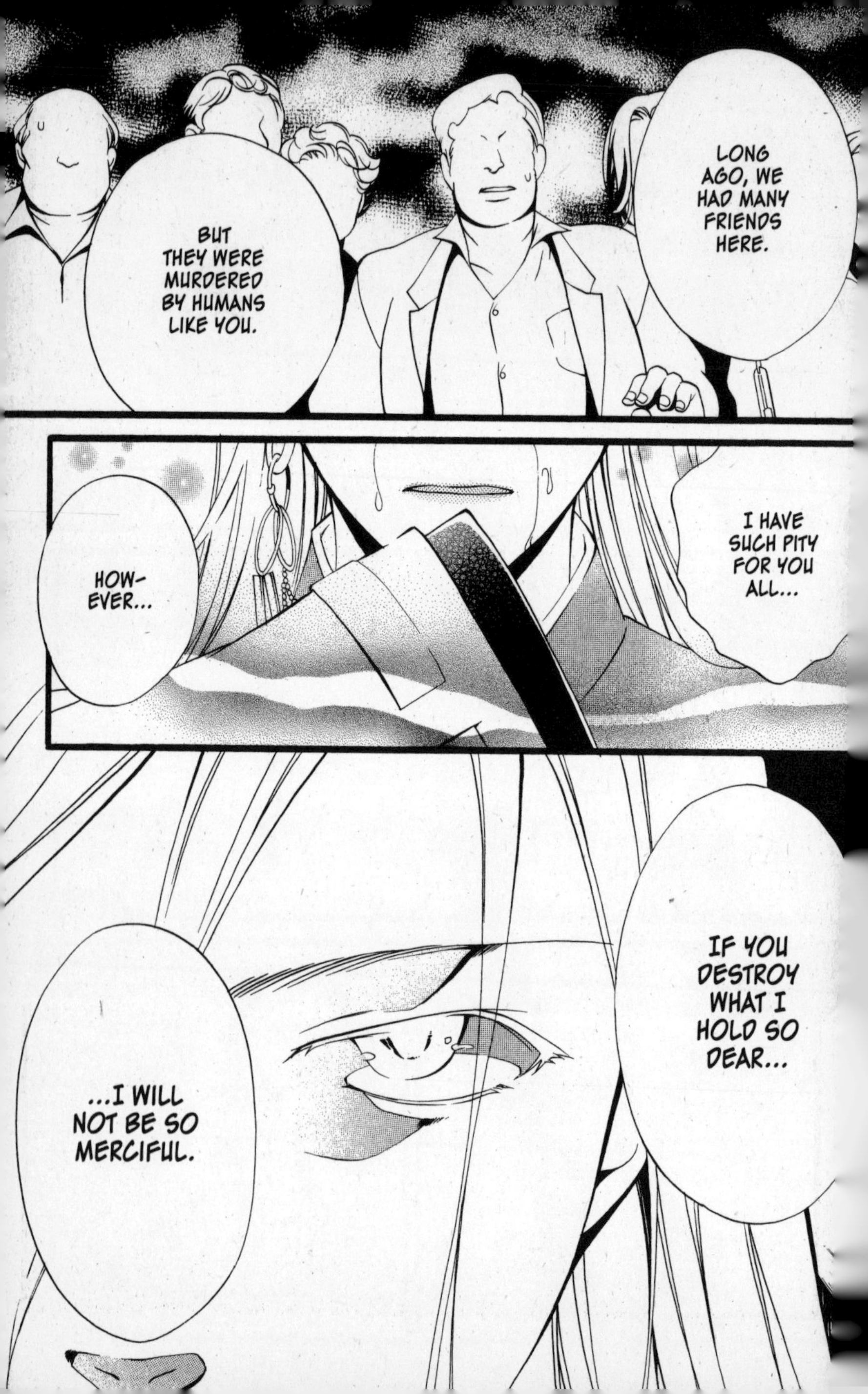
LONG AGO, WE HAD MANY FRIENDS HERE.
BUT THEY WERE MURDERED BY HUMANS LIKE YOU.
I HAVE SUCH PITY FOR YOU ALL...
HOW-EVER...
IF YOU DESTROY WHAT I HOLD SO DEAR...
...I WILL NOT BE SO MERCIFUL.

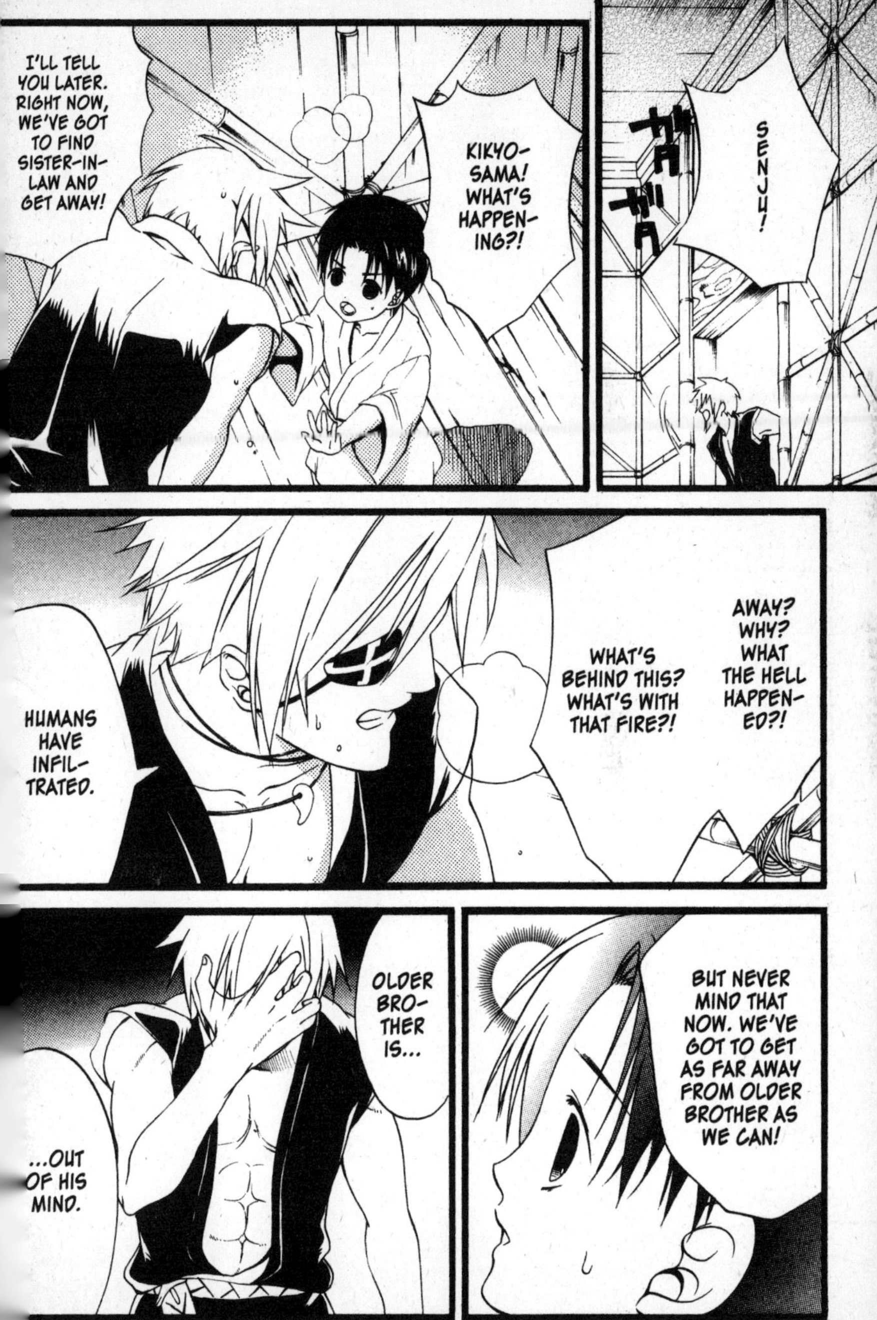
SENJU!
KIKYO-SAMA! WHAT'S HAPPENING?!
I'LL TELL YOU LATER. RIGHT NOW, WE'VE GOT TO FIND SISTER-IN-LAW AND GET AWAY!
AWAY? WHY? WHAT THE HELL HAPPENED?!
WHAT'S BEHIND THIS? WHAT'S WITH THAT FIRE?!
HUMANS HAVE INFILTRATED.
BUT NEVER MIND THAT NOW. WE'VE GOT TO GET AS FAR AWAY FROM OLDER BROTHER AS WE CAN!
OLDER BROTHER IS...
...OUT OF HIS MIND.

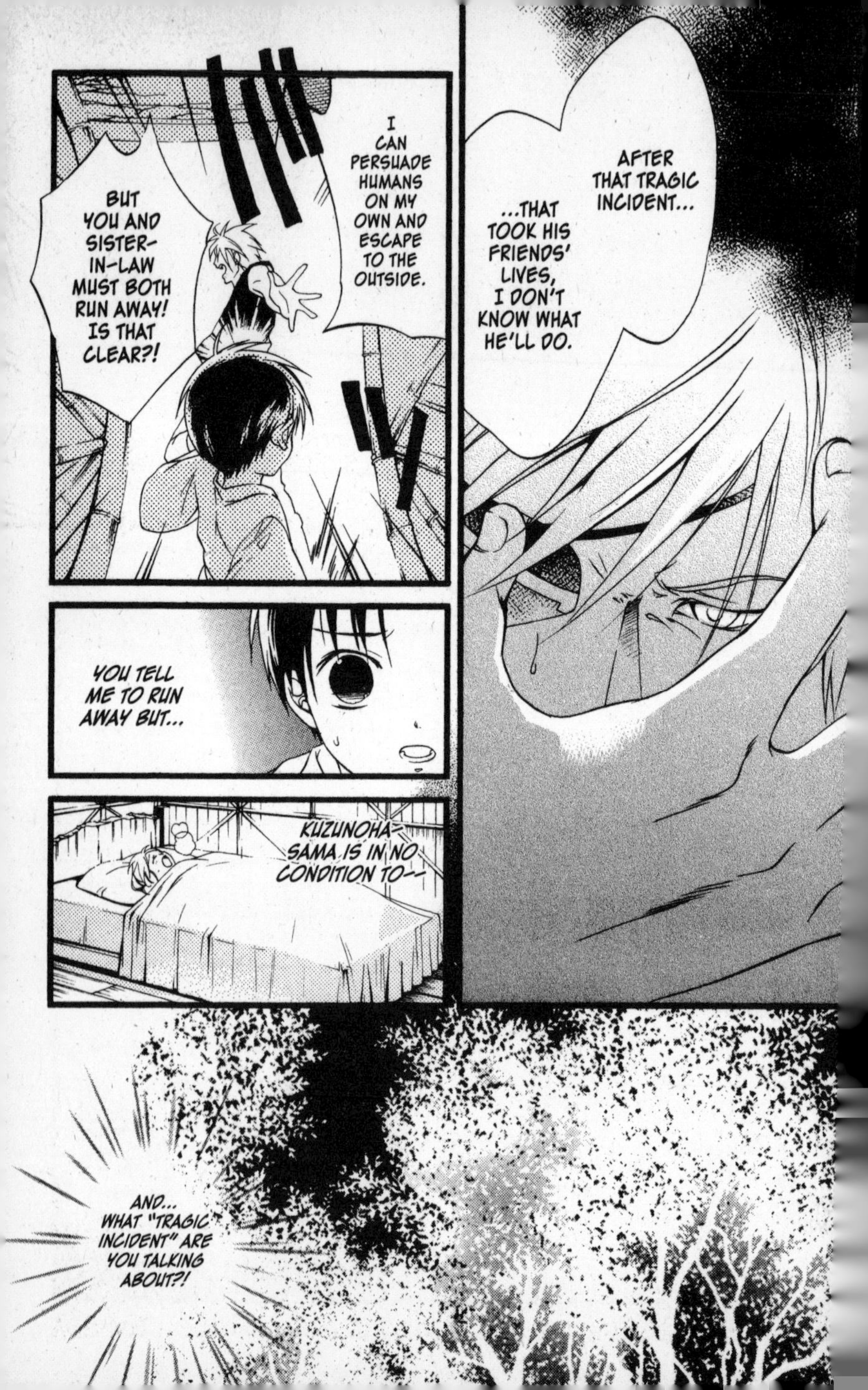
AFTER THAT TRAGIC INCIDENT...
...THAT TOOK HIS FRIENDS' LIVES, I DON'T KNOW WHAT HE'LL DO.
I CAN PERSUADE HUMANS ON MY OWN AND ESCAPE TO THE OUTSIDE.
BUT YOU AND SISTER-IN-LAW MUST BOTH RUN AWAY! IS THAT CLEAR?!
YOU TELL ME TO RUN AWAY BUT...
KUZUNOHA-SAMA IS IN NO CONDITION TO--
AND... WHAT "TRAGIC INCIDENT" ARE YOU TALKING ABOUT?!

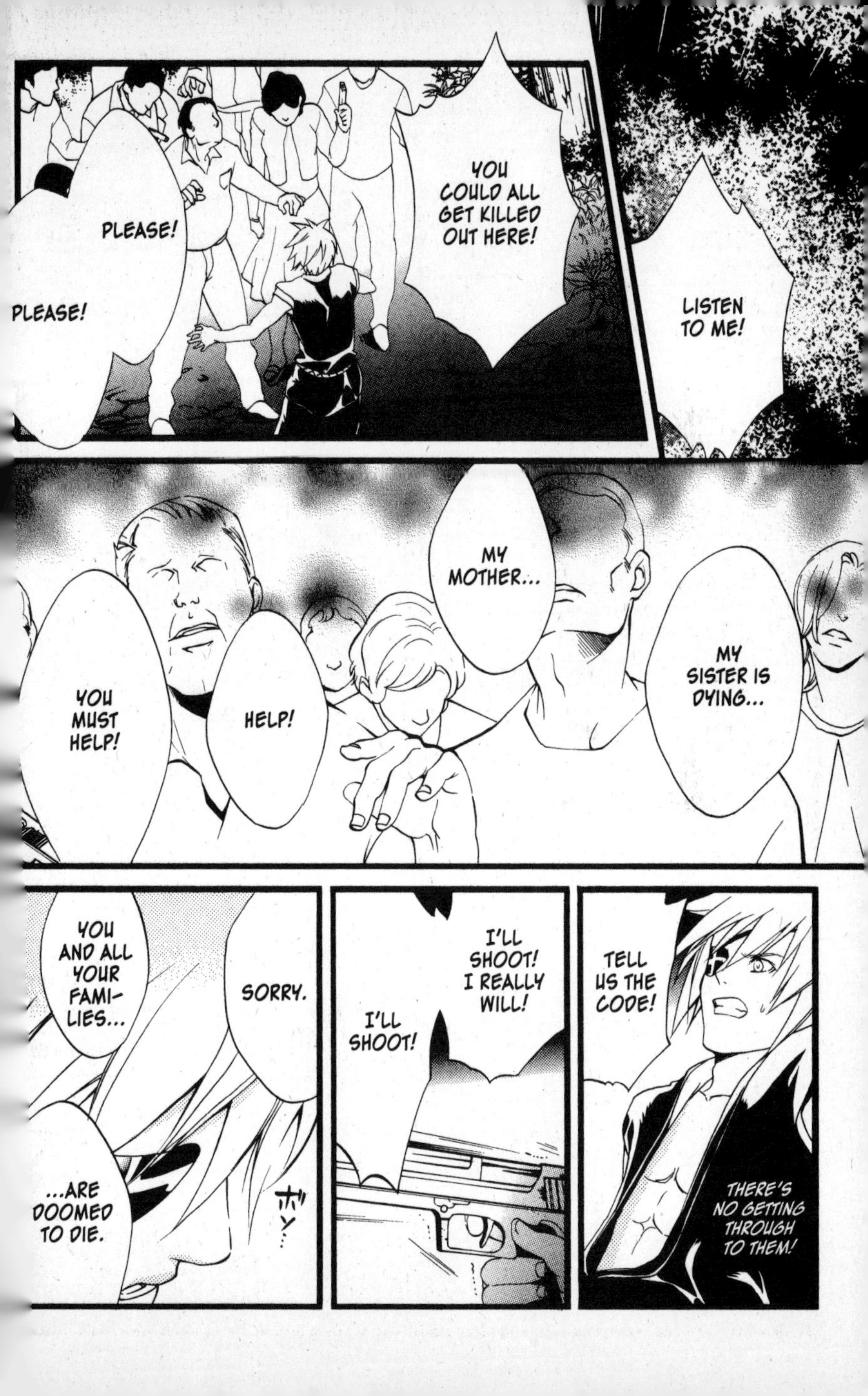
LISTEN TO ME!
YOU COULD ALL GET KILLED OUT HERE!
PLEASE!
PLEASE!
MY SISTER IS DYING...
MY MOTHER...
HELP!
YOU MUST HELP!
TELL US THE CODE!
THERE'S NO GETTING THROUGH TO THEM!
I'LL SHOOT! I REALLY WILL!
I'LL SHOOT!
SORRY.
YOU AND ALL YOUR FAMI-LIES...
...ARE DOOMED TO DIE.
ボッ...

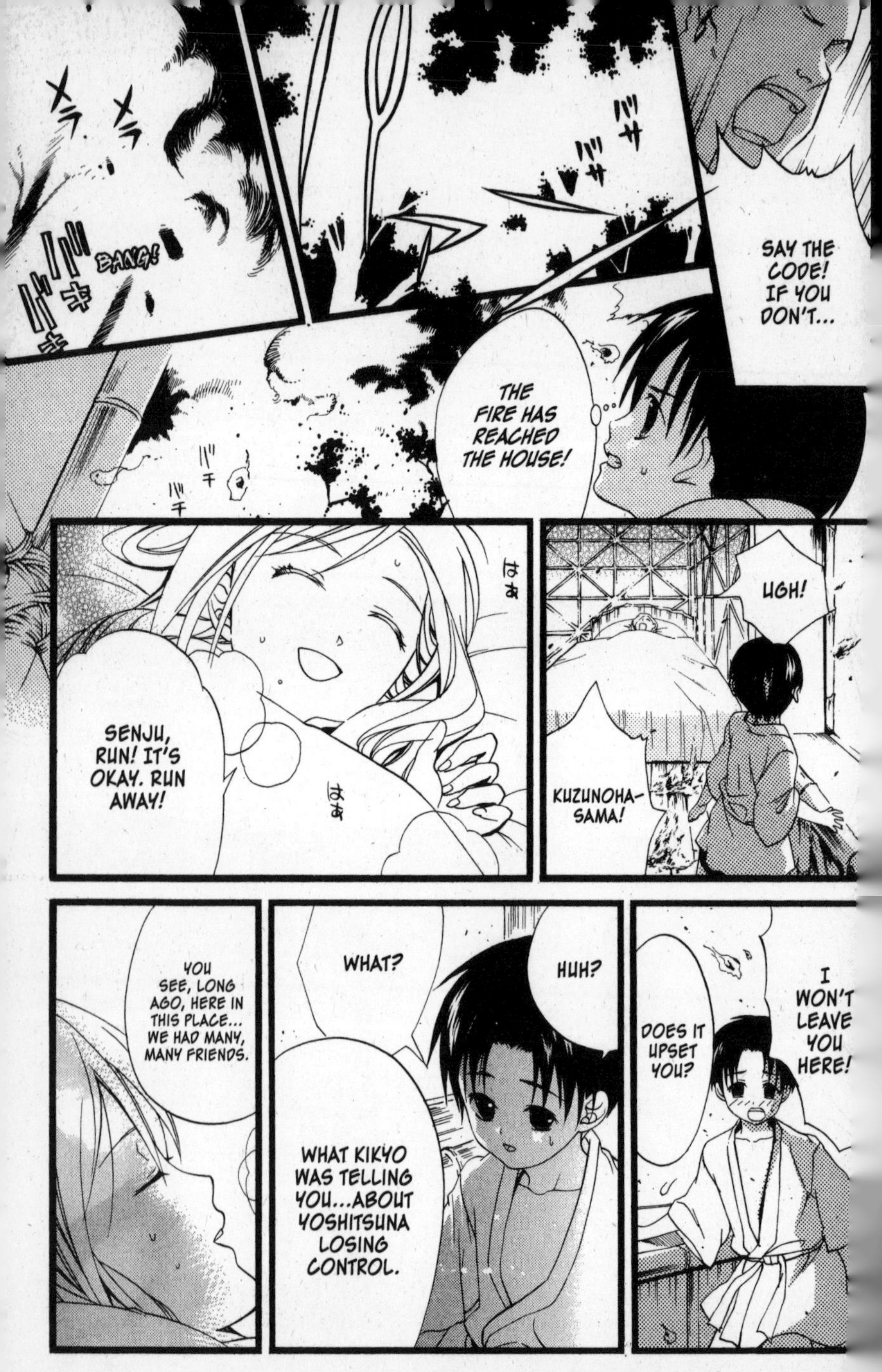
SAY THE CODE! IF YOU DON'T...
バサ
バサ
メラ
メラ
BANG!
THE FIRE HAS REACHED THE HOUSE!
バチ
バチ
UGH!
KUZUNOHA-SAMA!
はあ
SENJU, RUN! IT'S OKAY. RUN AWAY!
はあ
I WON'T LEAVE YOU HERE!
DOES IT UPSET YOU?
HUH?
WHAT?
WHAT KIKYO WAS TELLING YOU...ABOUT YOSHITSUNA LOSING CONTROL.
YOU SEE, LONG AGO, HERE IN THIS PLACE... WE HAD MANY, MANY FRIENDS.

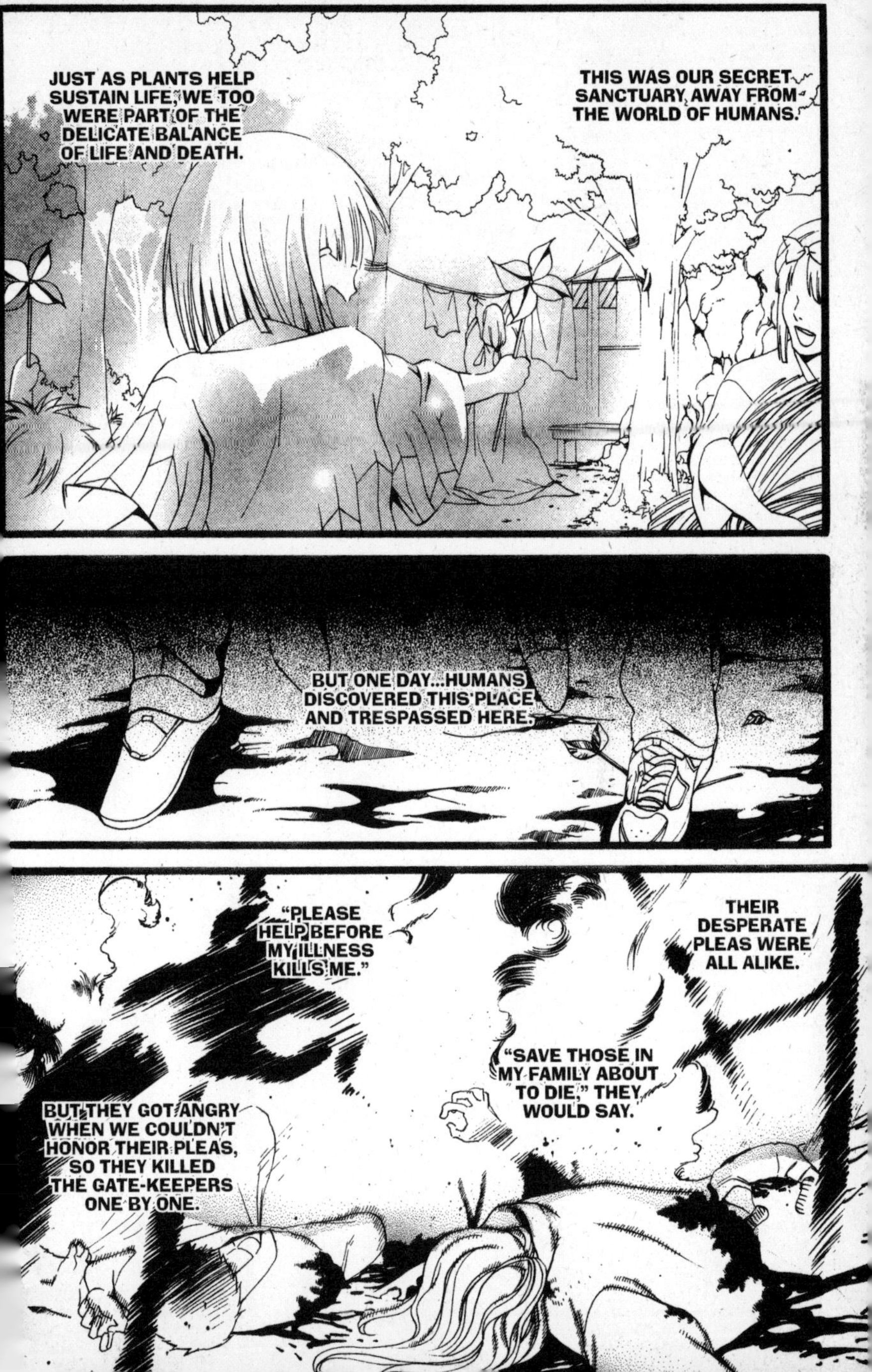
THIS WAS OUR SECRET SANCTUARY, AWAY FROM THE WORLD OF HUMANS.
JUST AS PLANTS HELP SUSTAIN LIFE, WE TOO WERE PART OF THE DELICATE BALANCE OF LIFE AND DEATH.
BUT ONE DAY...HUMANS DISCOVERED THIS PLACE AND TRESPASSED HERE.
THEIR DESPERATE PLEAS WERE ALL ALIKE.
"PLEASE HELP BEFORE MY ILLNESS KILLS ME."
"SAVE THOSE IN MY FAMILY ABOUT TO DIE," THEY WOULD SAY.
BUT THEY GOT ANGRY WHEN WE COULDN'T HONOR THEIR PLEAS, SO THEY KILLED THE GATE-KEEPERS ONE BY ONE.

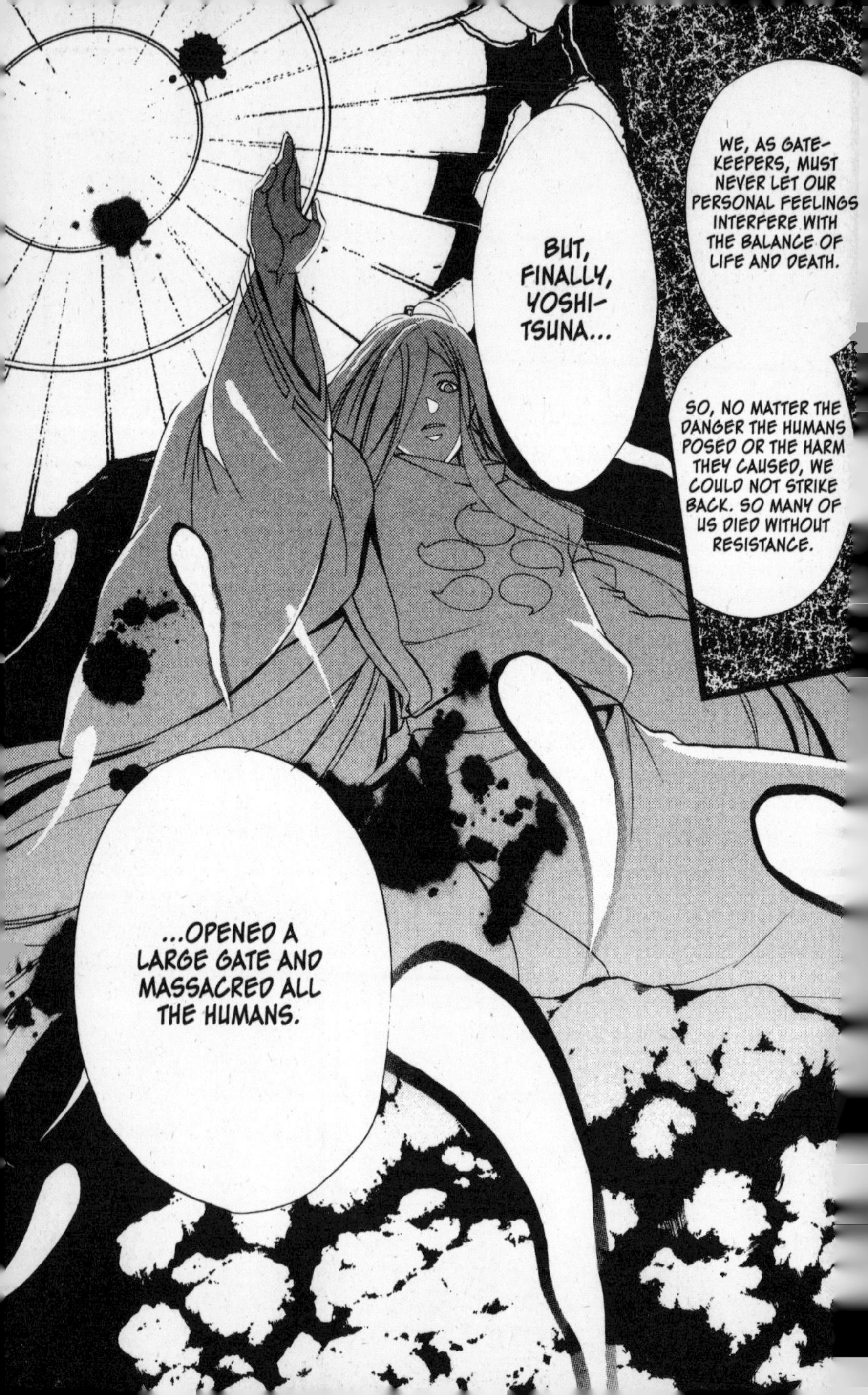
WE, AS GATE-KEEPERS, MUST NEVER LET OUR PERSONAL FEELINGS INTERFERE WITH THE BALANCE OF LIFE AND DEATH.
SO, NO MATTER THE DANGER THE HUMANS POSED OR THE HARM THEY CAUSED, WE COULD NOT STRIKE BACK. SO MANY OF US DIED WITHOUT RESISTANCE.
BUT, FINALLY, YOSHI-TSUNA...
...OPENED A LARGE GATE AND MASSACRED ALL THE HUMANS.

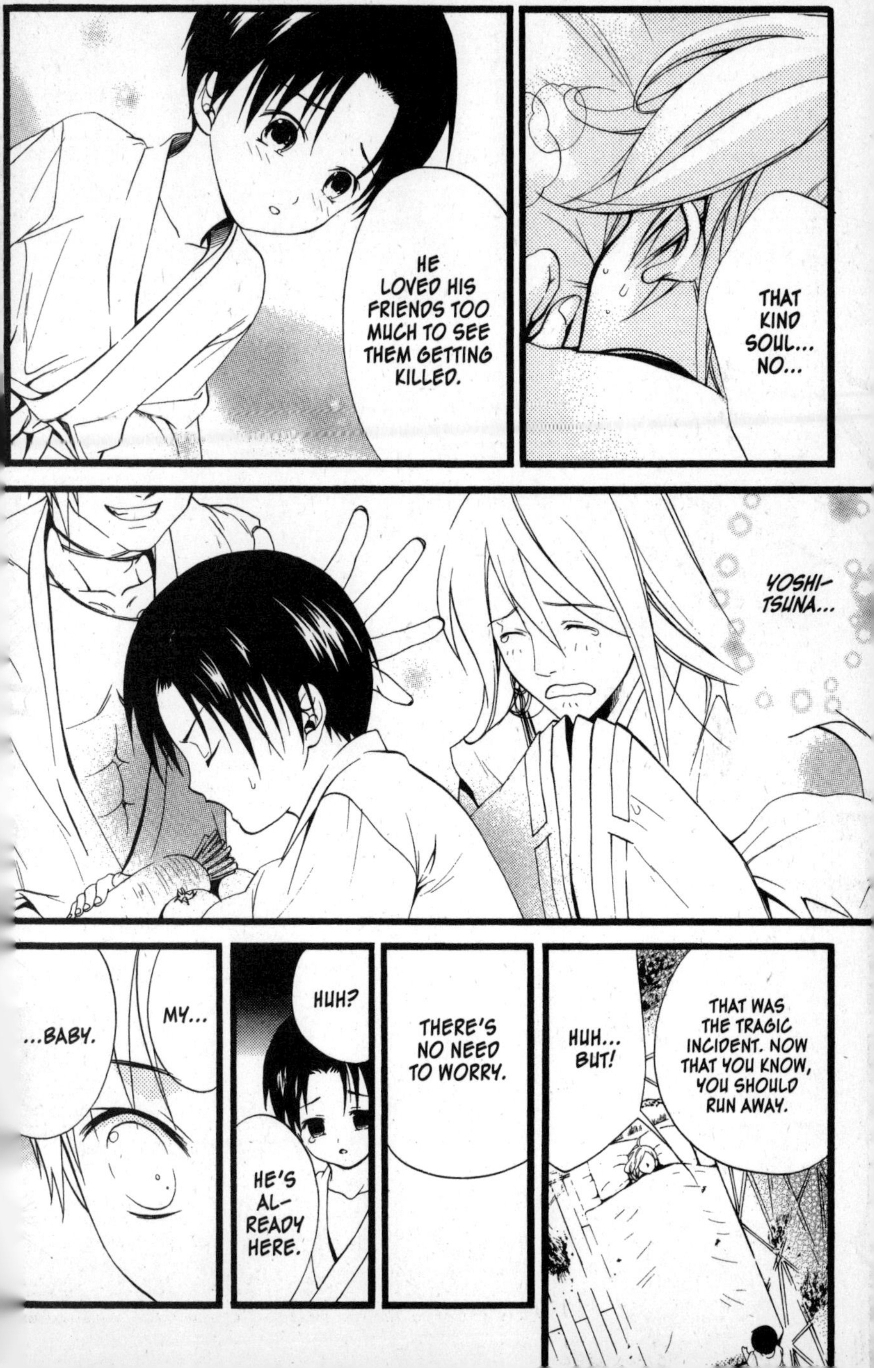
THAT KIND SOUL... NO...
HE LOVED HIS FRIENDS TOO MUCH TO SEE THEM GETTING KILLED.
YOSHI-TSUNA...
THAT WAS THE TRAGIC INCIDENT. NOW THAT YOU KNOW, YOU SHOULD RUN AWAY.
HUH... BUT!
THERE'S NO NEED TO WORRY.
HUH?
HE'S AL-READY HERE.
MY...
...BABY.

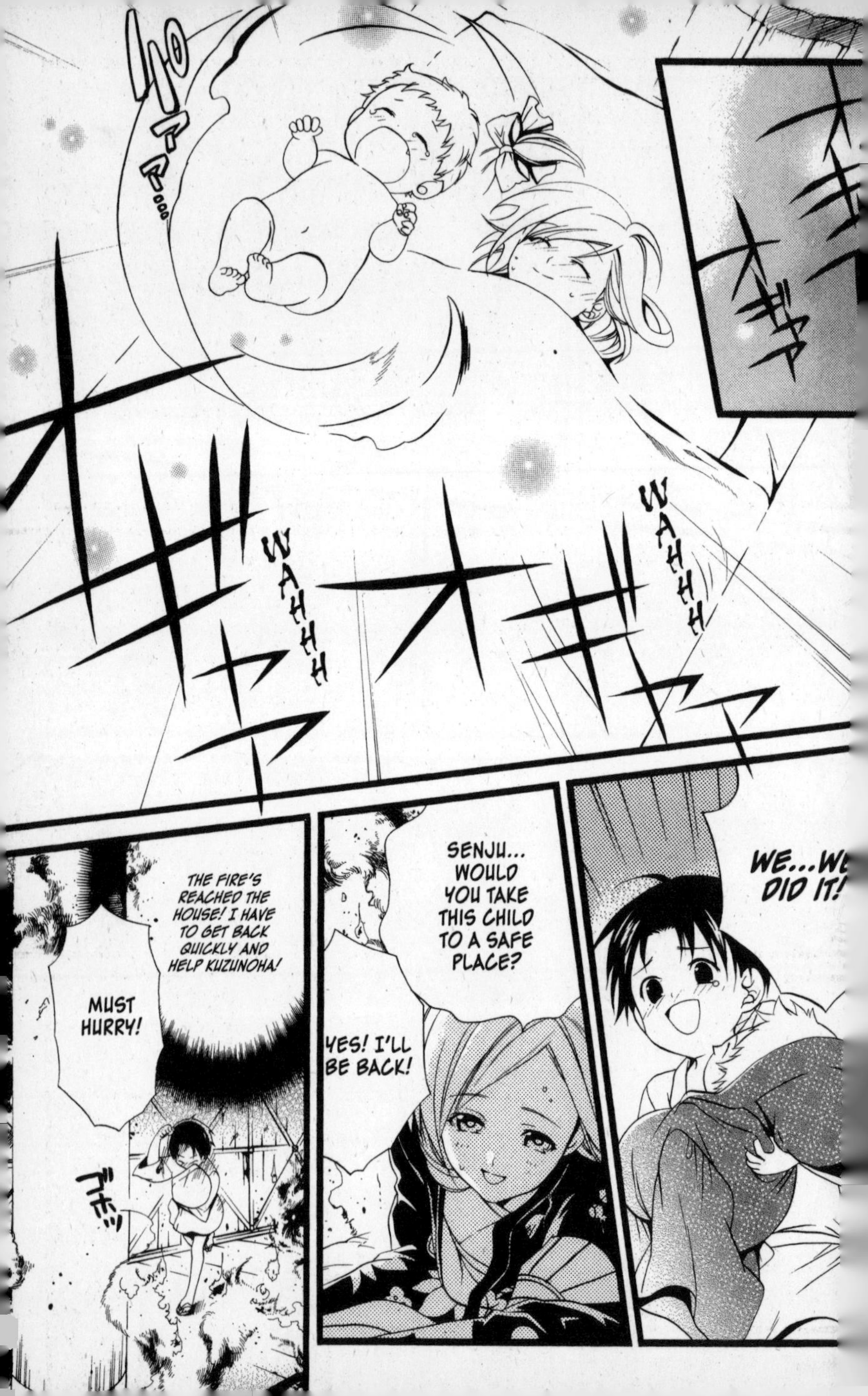
WAHHH
WAHHH
WE...WE DID IT!
SENJU... WOULD YOU TAKE THIS CHILD TO A SAFE PLACE?
YES! I'LL BE BACK!
THE FIRE'S REACHED THE HOUSE! I HAVE TO GET BACK QUICKLY AND HELP KUZUNOHA!
MUST HURRY!
ゴホッ

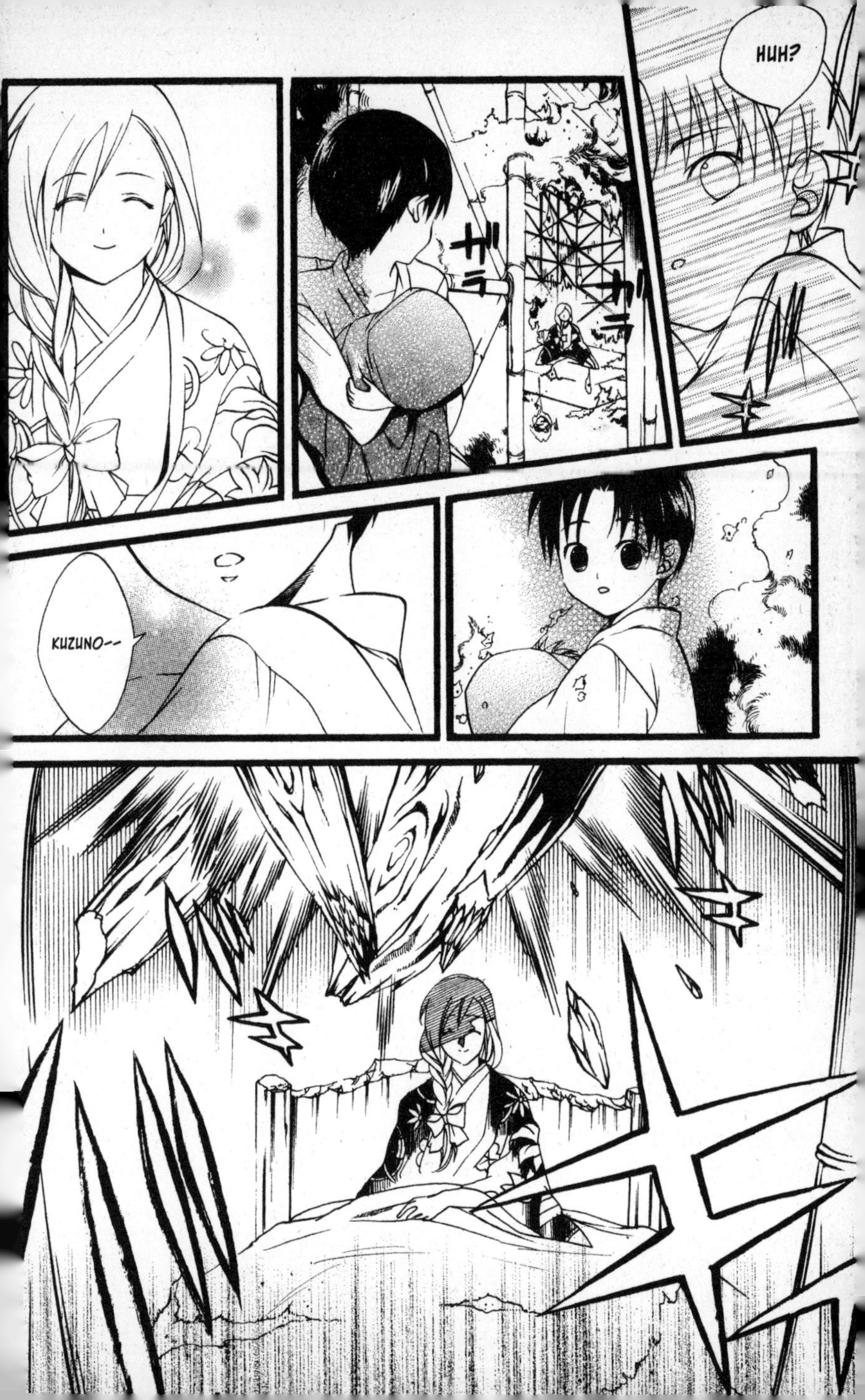
HUH?
ガラ
ガラ
KUZUNO--

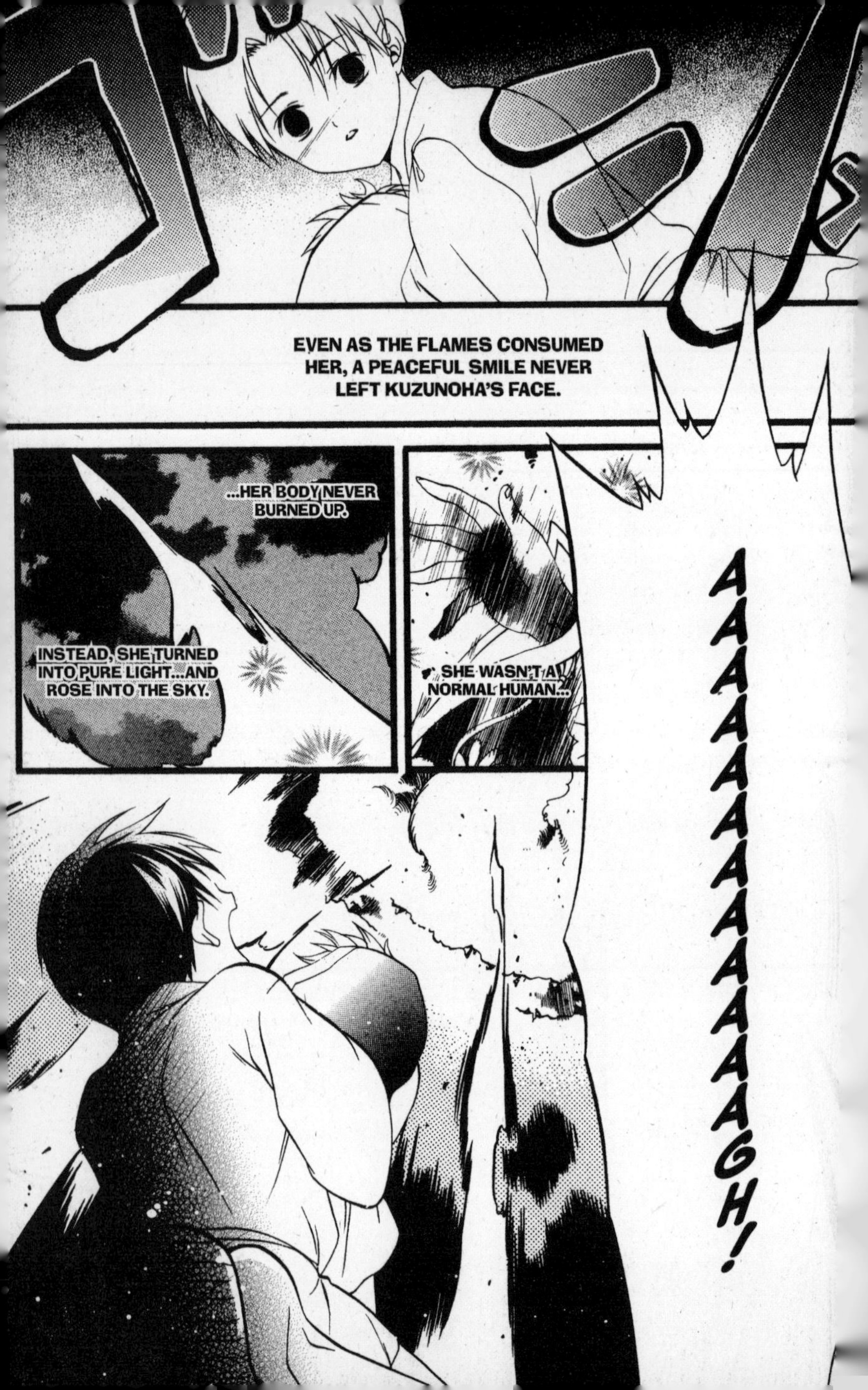
EVEN AS THE FLAMES CONSUMED HER, A PEACEFUL SMILE NEVER LEFT KUZUNOHA'S FACE.
SHE WASN'T A NORMAL HUMAN...
...HER BODY NEVER BURNED UP.
INSTEAD, SHE TURNED INTO PURE LIGHT...AND ROSE INTO THE SKY.
AAAAAAAAAAAAAAGH!

UGH...
UGHH...

KUZU-
NOHA...
SA...

HIC

KUZUNOHA-
SAMA...
UGH...

UGHHH...?

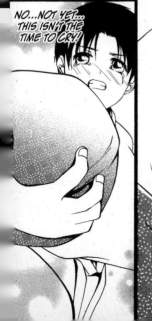

NO...NOT YET...
THIS ISN'T THE
TIME TO CRY!

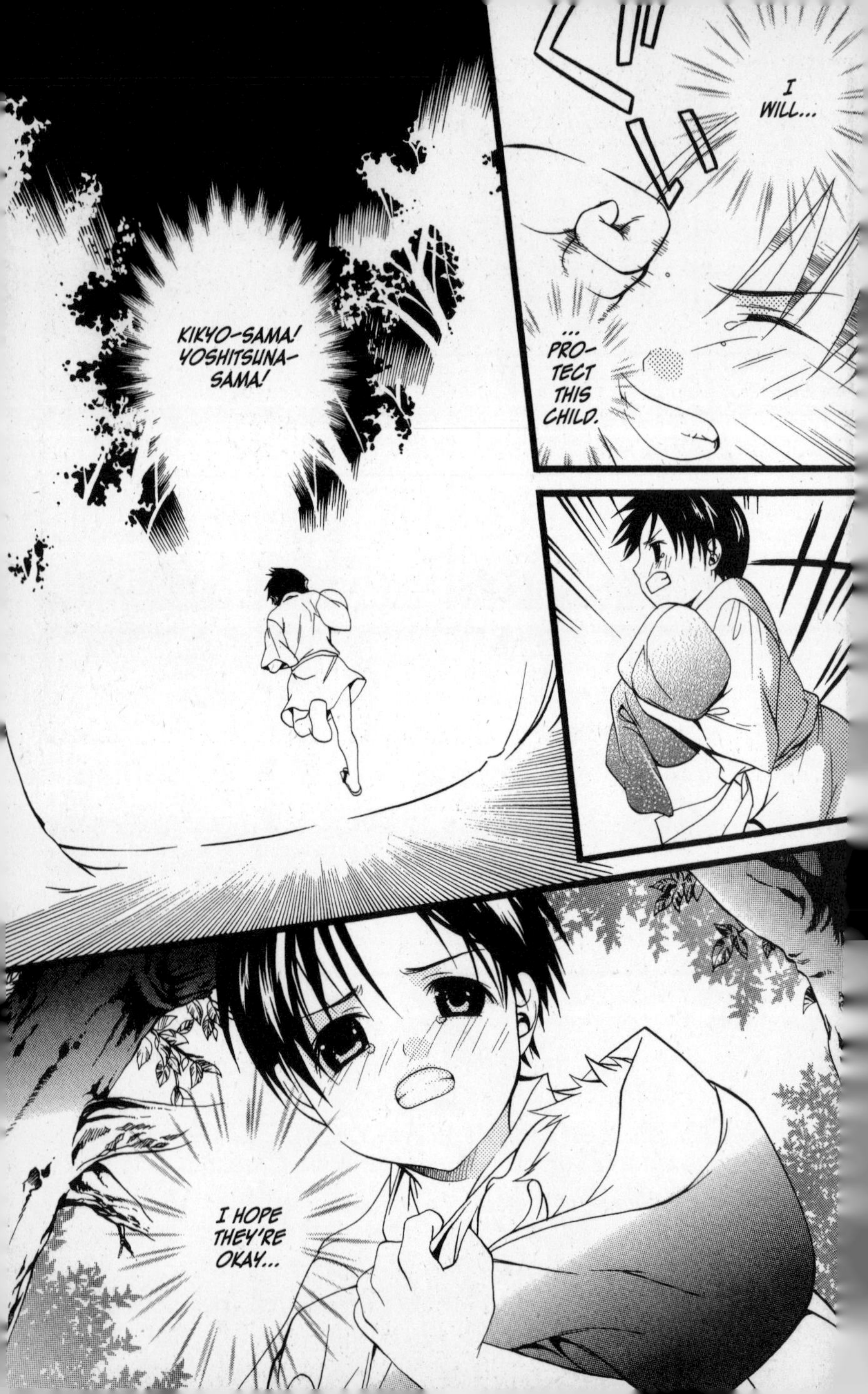
I WILL...
... PROTECT THIS CHILD.
KIKYO-SAMA! YOSHITSUNA-SAMA!
I HOPE THEY'RE OKAY...

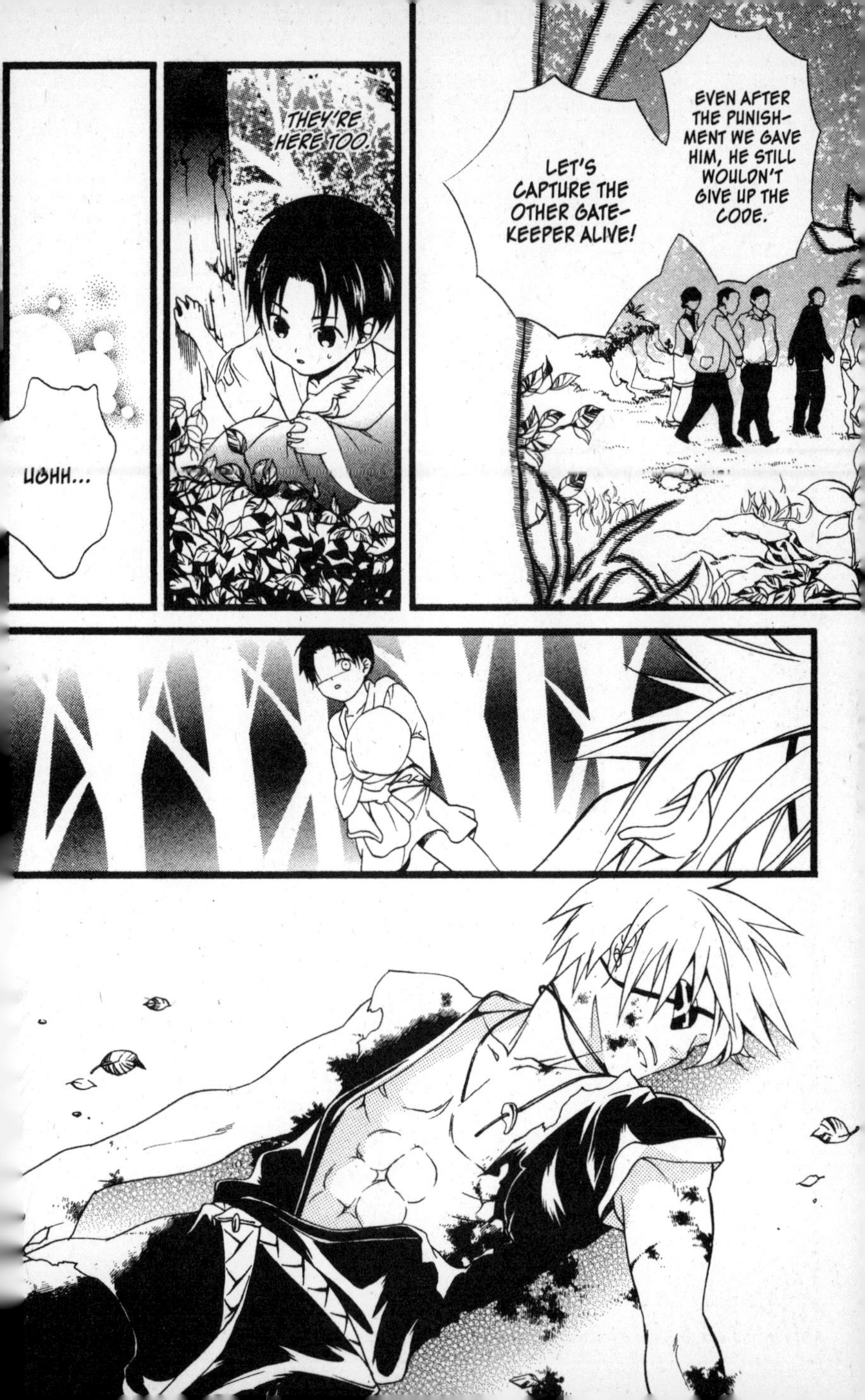
EVEN AFTER THE PUNISH-MENT WE GAVE HIM, HE STILL WOULDN'T GIVE UP THE CODE.
LET'S CAPTURE THE OTHER GATE-KEEPER ALIVE!
THEY'RE HERE TOO.
UGHH...

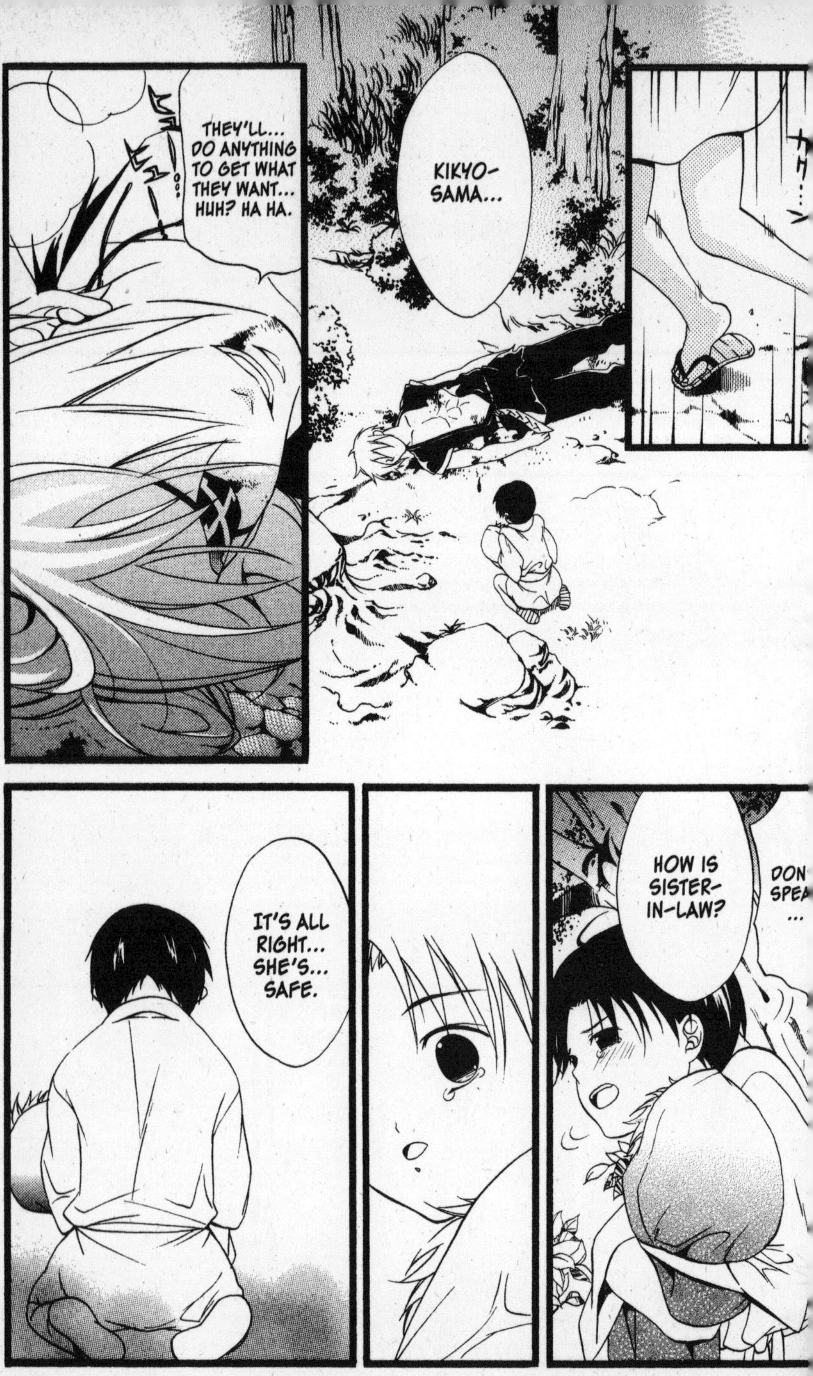
KIKYO-SAMA...
THEY'LL... DO ANYTHING TO GET WHAT THEY WANT... HUH? HA HA.
DON SPEA ...
HOW IS SISTER-IN-LAW?
IT'S ALL RIGHT... SHE'S... SAFE.

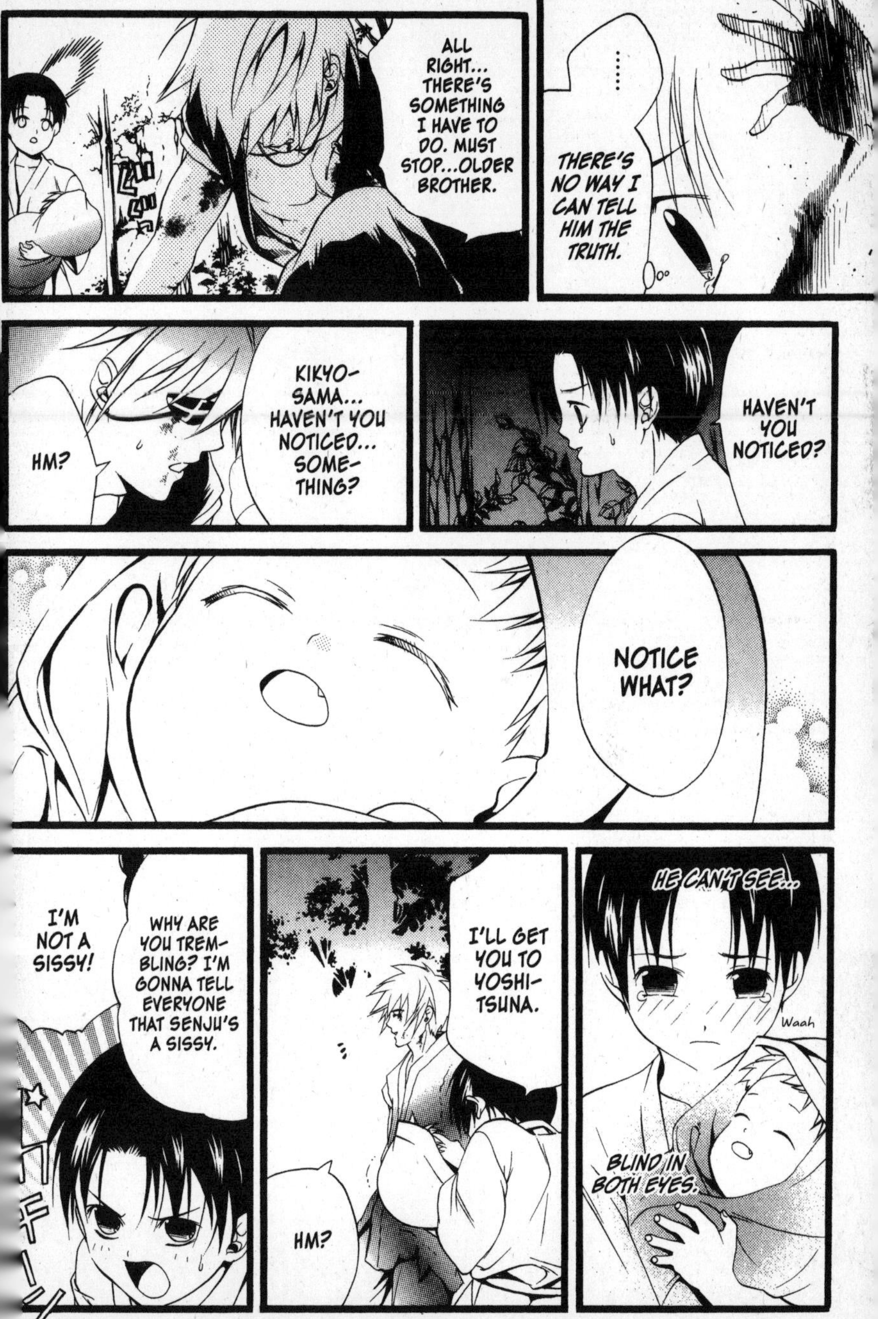
......
THERE'S NO WAY I CAN TELL HIM THE TRUTH.
ALL RIGHT... THERE'S SOMETHING I HAVE TO DO. MUST STOP...OLDER BROTHER.
HAVEN'T YOU NOTICED?
KIKYO-SAMA... HAVEN'T YOU NOTICED... SOME-THING?
HM?
NOTICE WHAT?
HE CAN'T SEE...
Waah
BLIND IN BOTH EYES.
I'LL GET YOU TO YOSHI-TSUNA.
HM?
WHY ARE YOU TREM-BLING? I'M GONNA TELL EVERYONE THAT SENJU'S A SISSY.
I'M NOT A SISSY!

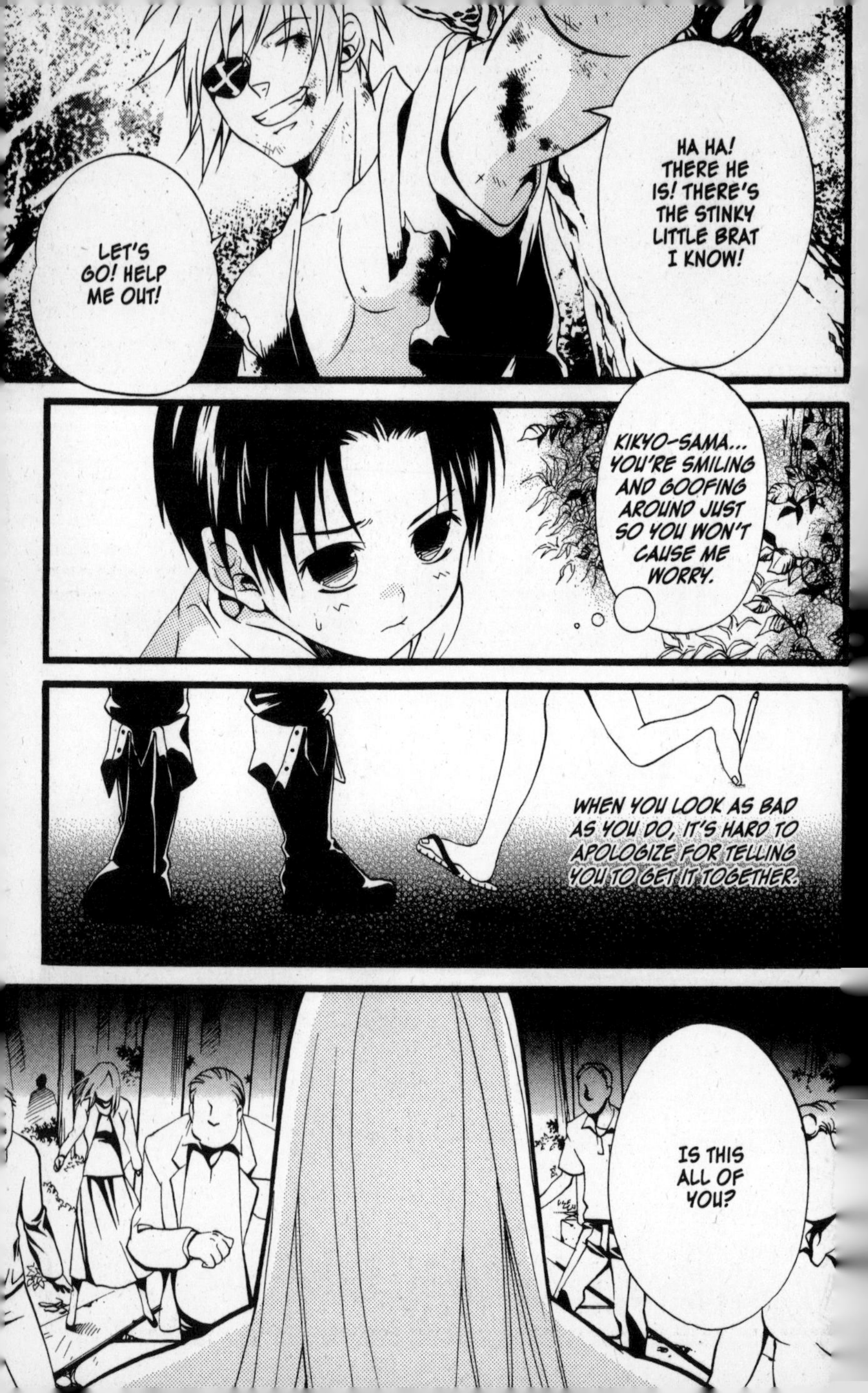
HA HA! THERE HE IS! THERE'S THE STINKY LITTLE BRAT I KNOW!
LET'S GO! HELP ME OUT!
KIKYO-SAMA... YOU'RE SMILING AND GOOFING AROUND JUST SO YOU WON'T CAUSE ME WORRY.
WHEN YOU LOOK AS BAD AS YOU DO, IT'S HARD TO APOLOGIZE FOR TELLING YOU TO GET IT TOGETHER.
IS THIS ALL OF YOU?

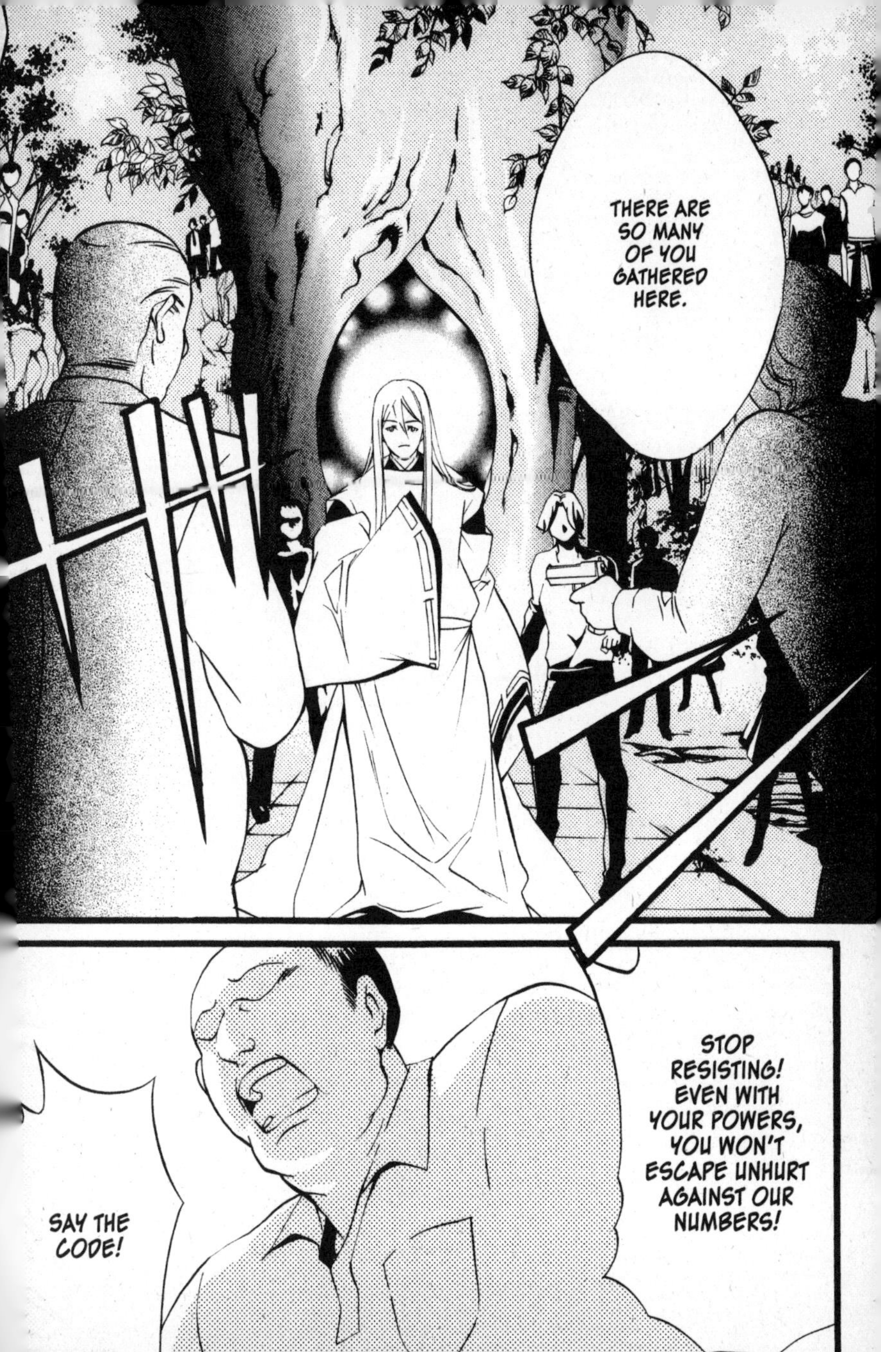
THERE ARE SO MANY OF YOU GATHERED HERE.
STOP RESISTING! EVEN WITH YOUR POWERS, YOU WON'T ESCAPE UNHURT AGAINST OUR NUMBERS!
SAY THE CODE!

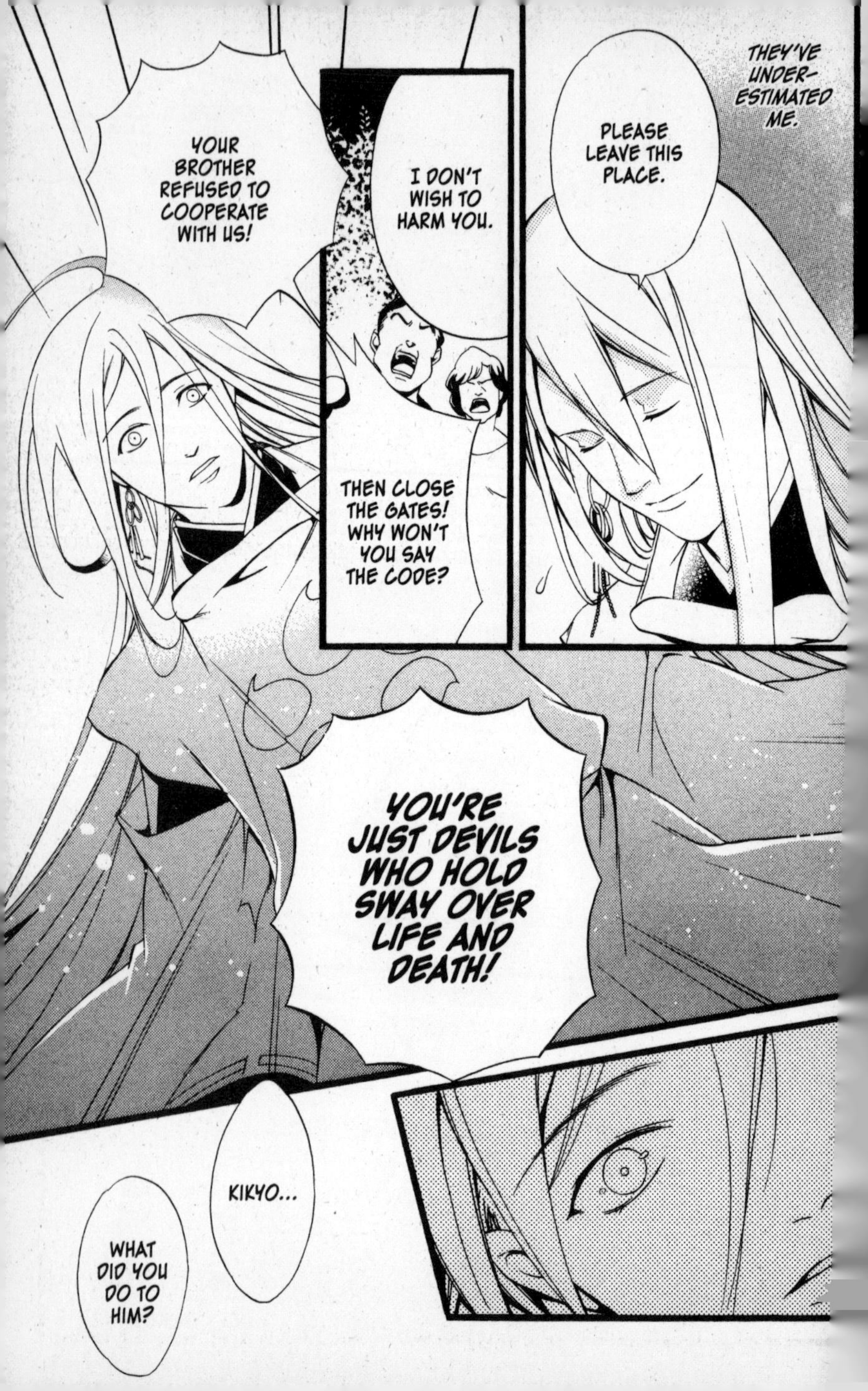
THEY'VE UNDER-ESTIMATED ME.
PLEASE LEAVE THIS PLACE.
I DON'T WISH TO HARM YOU.
THEN CLOSE THE GATES! WHY WON'T YOU SAY THE CODE?
YOUR BROTHER REFUSED TO COOPERATE WITH US!
YOU'RE JUST DEVILS WHO HOLD SWAY OVER LIFE AND DEATH!
KIKYO...
WHAT DID YOU DO TO HIM?

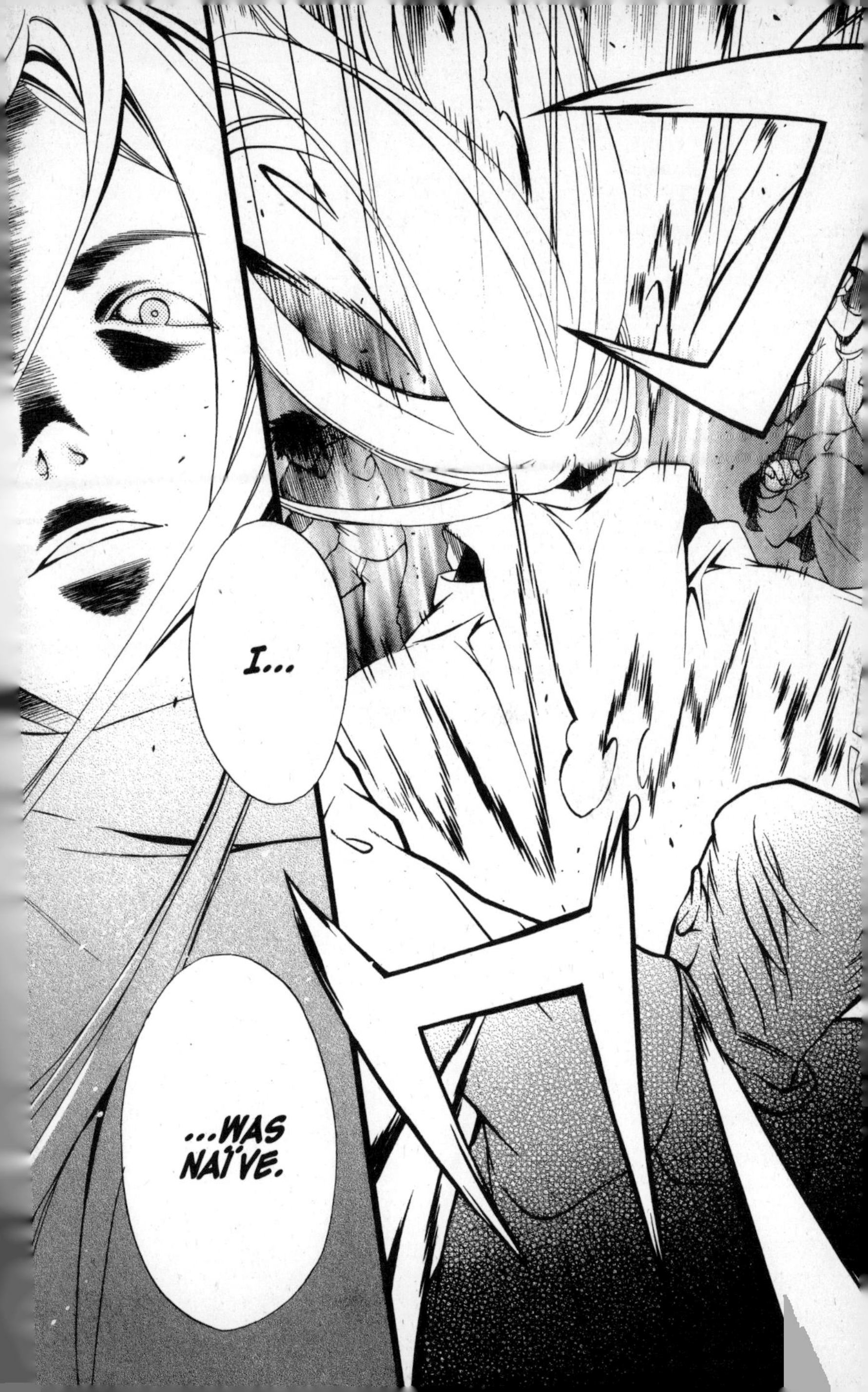
I...
...WAS NAÏVE.

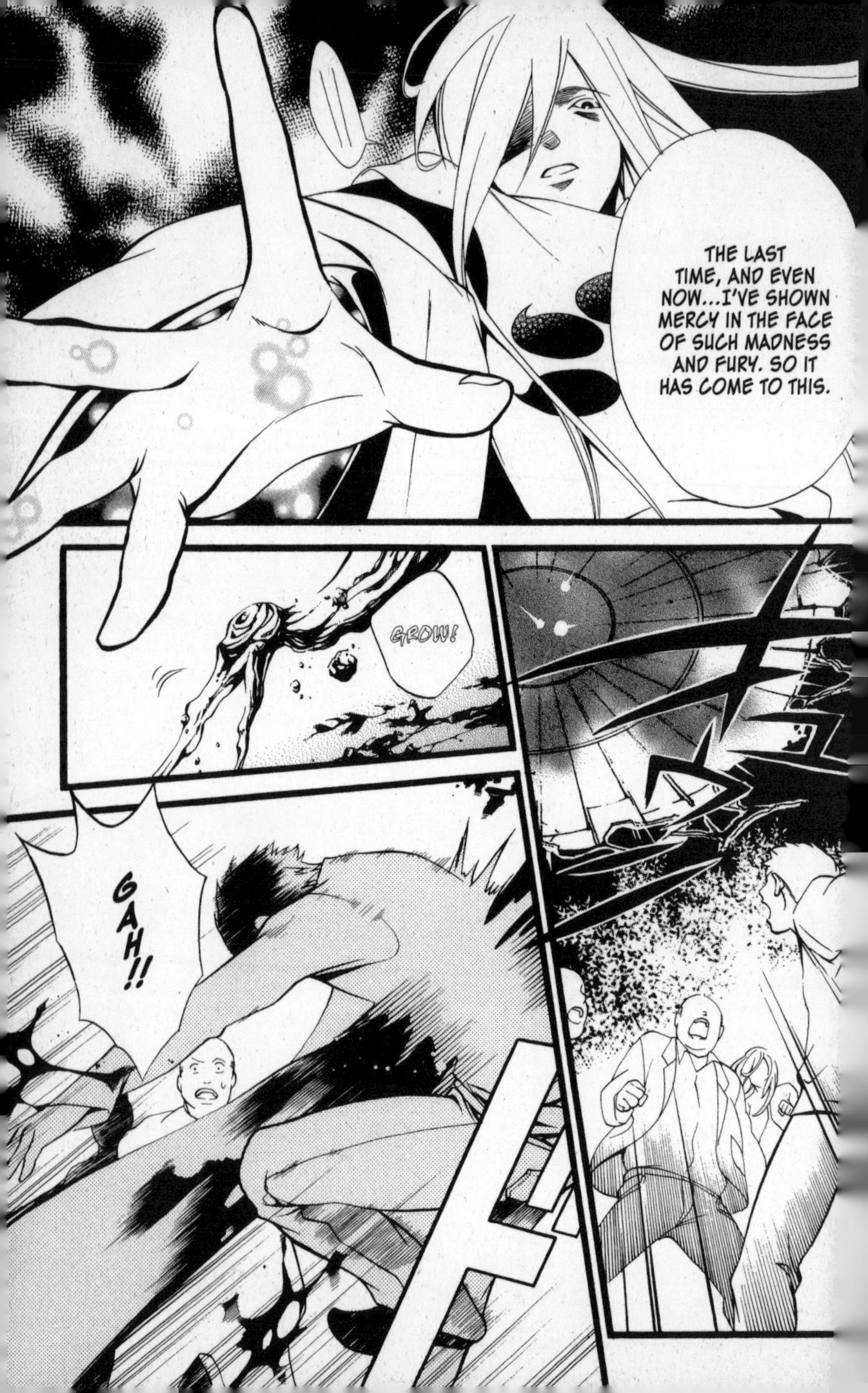
THE LAST TIME, AND EVEN NOW...I'VE SHOWN MERCY IN THE FACE OF SUCH MADNESS AND FURY. SO IT HAS COME TO THIS.
GROW!
GAH!!

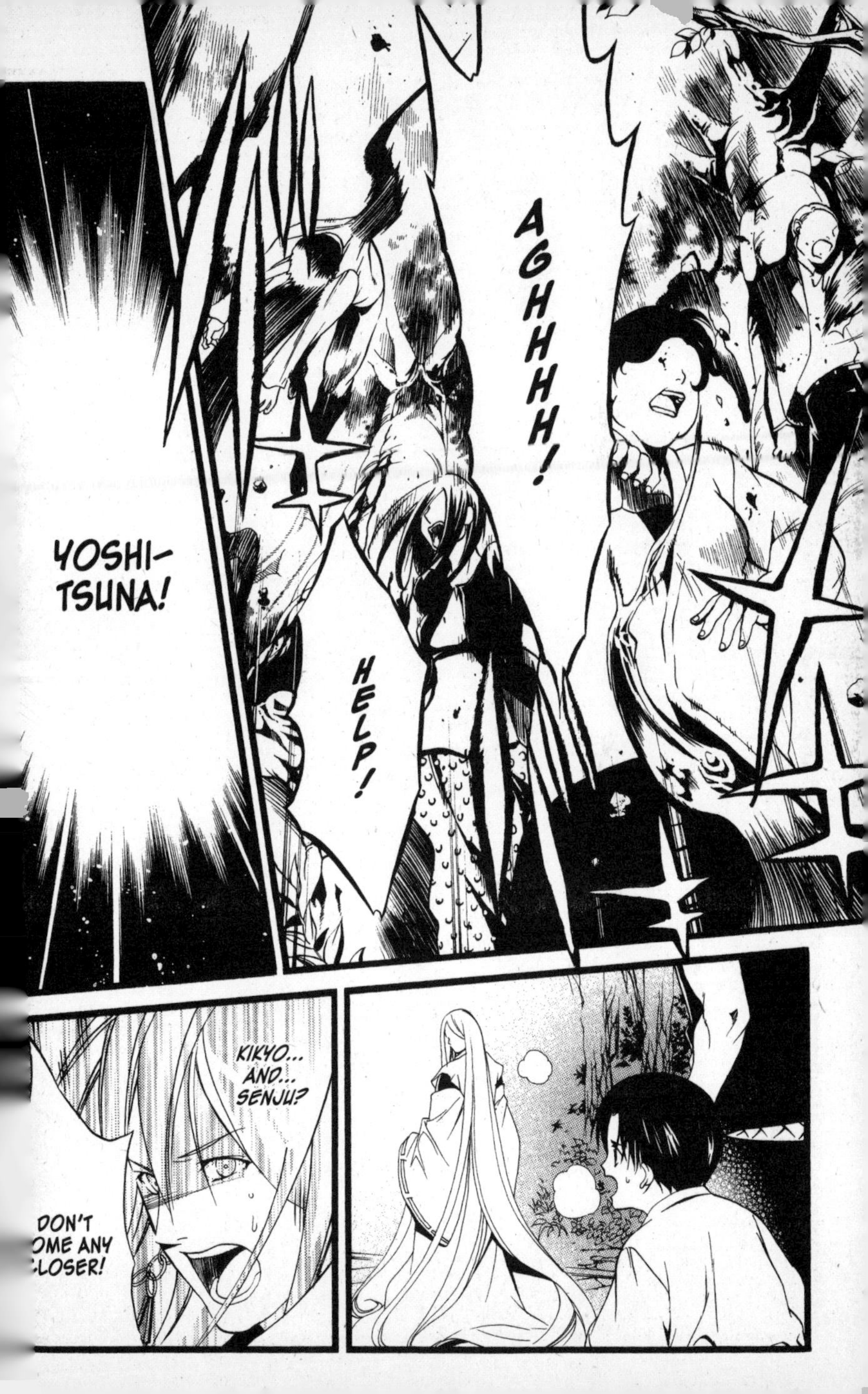
AGHHHH!
HELP!
YOSHI-TSUNA!
KIKYO... AND... SENJU?
DON'T OME ANY LOSER!

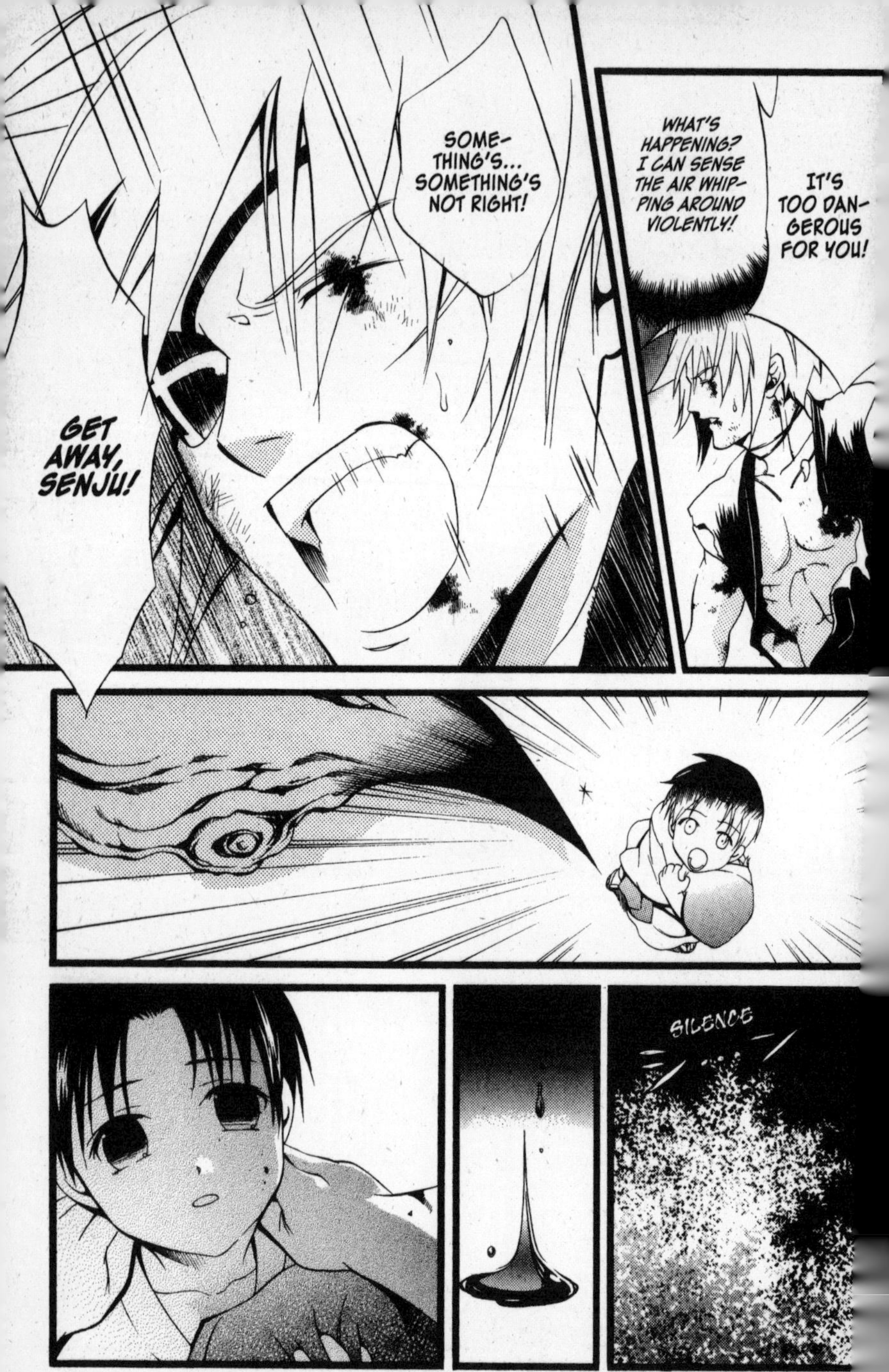
WHAT'S HAPPENING? I CAN SENSE THE AIR WHIPPING AROUND VIOLENTLY!
IT'S TOO DANGEROUS FOR YOU!
SOMETHING'S... SOMETHING'S NOT RIGHT!
GET AWAY, SENJU!
SILENCE

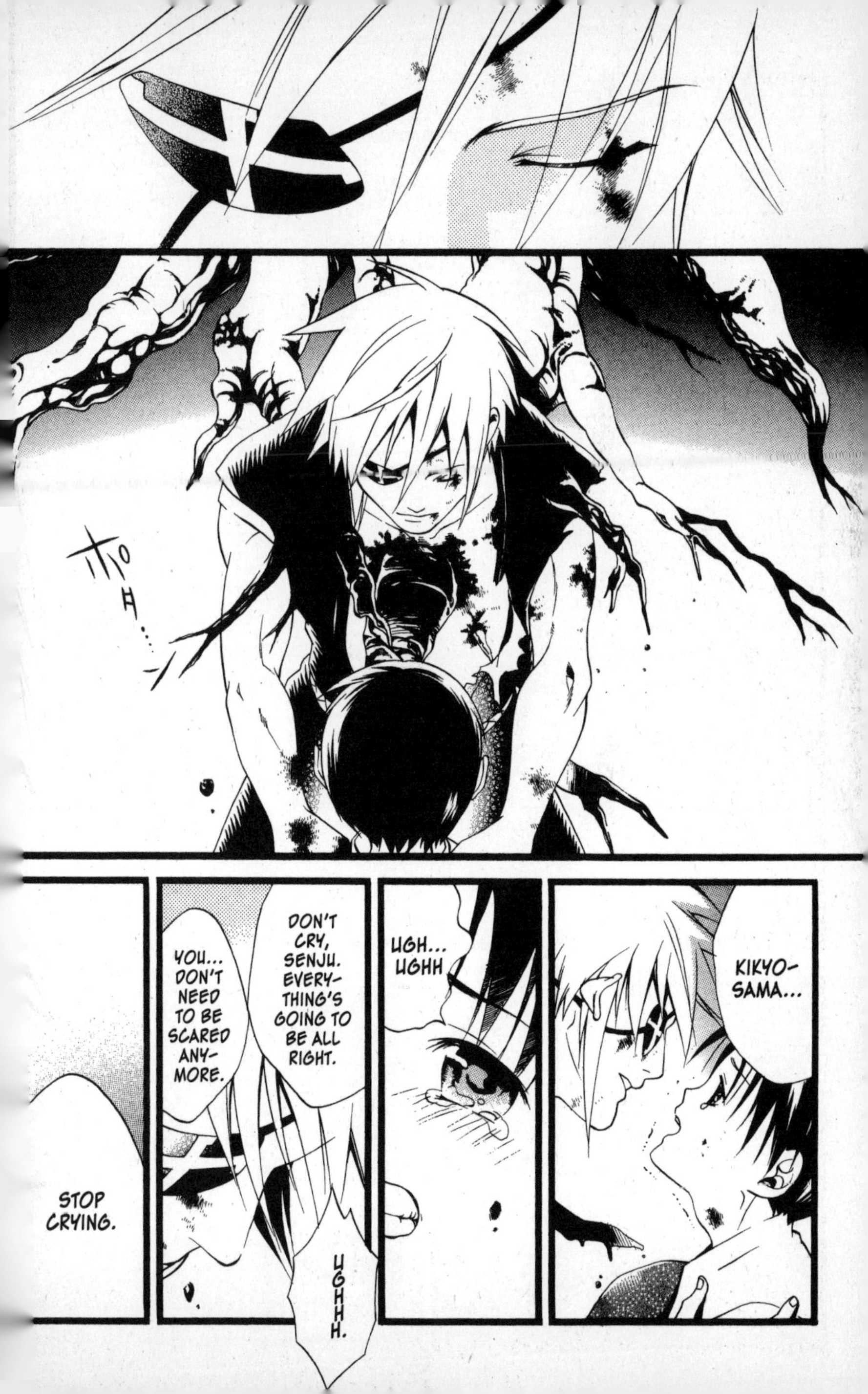
KIKYO-SAMA...
UGH... UGHH
DON'T CRY, SENJU. EVERYTHING'S GOING TO BE ALL RIGHT.
YOU... DON'T NEED TO BE SCARED ANYMORE.
UGHHH.
STOP CRYING.

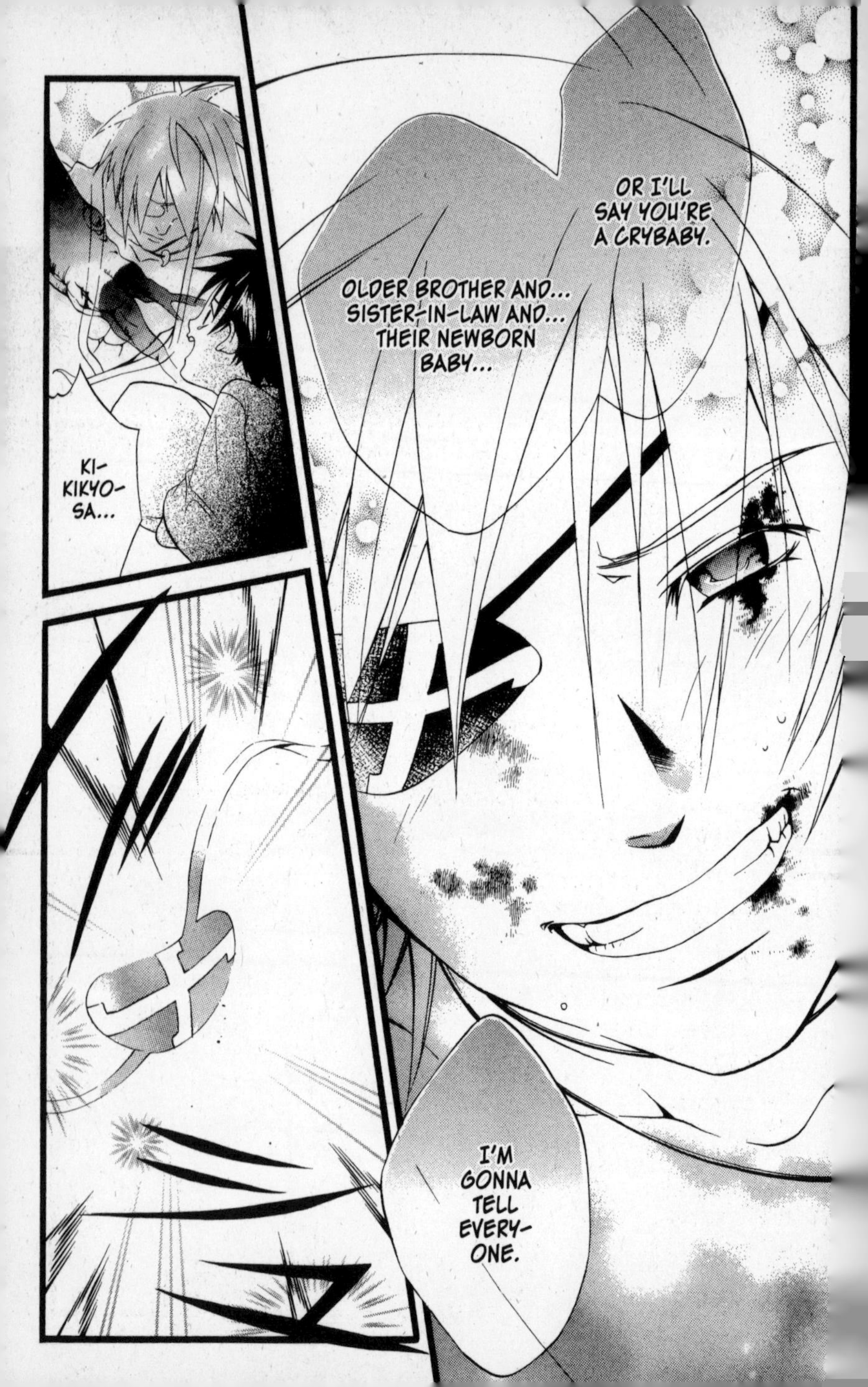
OR I'LL SAY YOU'RE A CRYBABY.
OLDER BROTHER AND... SISTER-IN-LAW AND... THEIR NEWBORN BABY...
I'M GONNA TELL EVERY-ONE.
KI-KIKYO-SA...

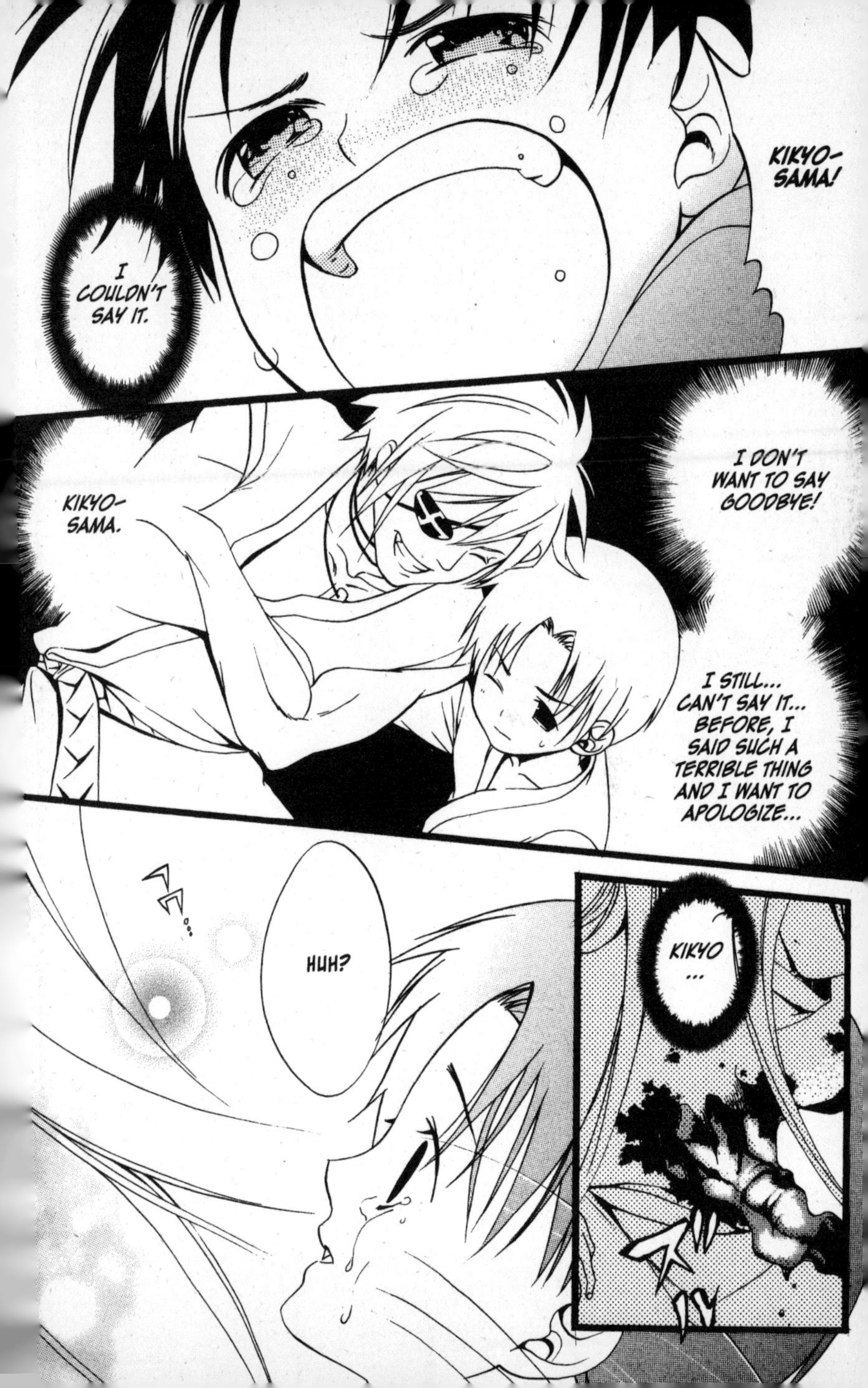
KIKYO-SAMA!
I COULDN'T SAY IT.
I DON'T WANT TO SAY GOODBYE!
I STILL... CAN'T SAY IT... BEFORE, I SAID SUCH A TERRIBLE THING AND I WANT TO APOLOGIZE...
KIKYO-SAMA.
KIKYO ...
HUH?

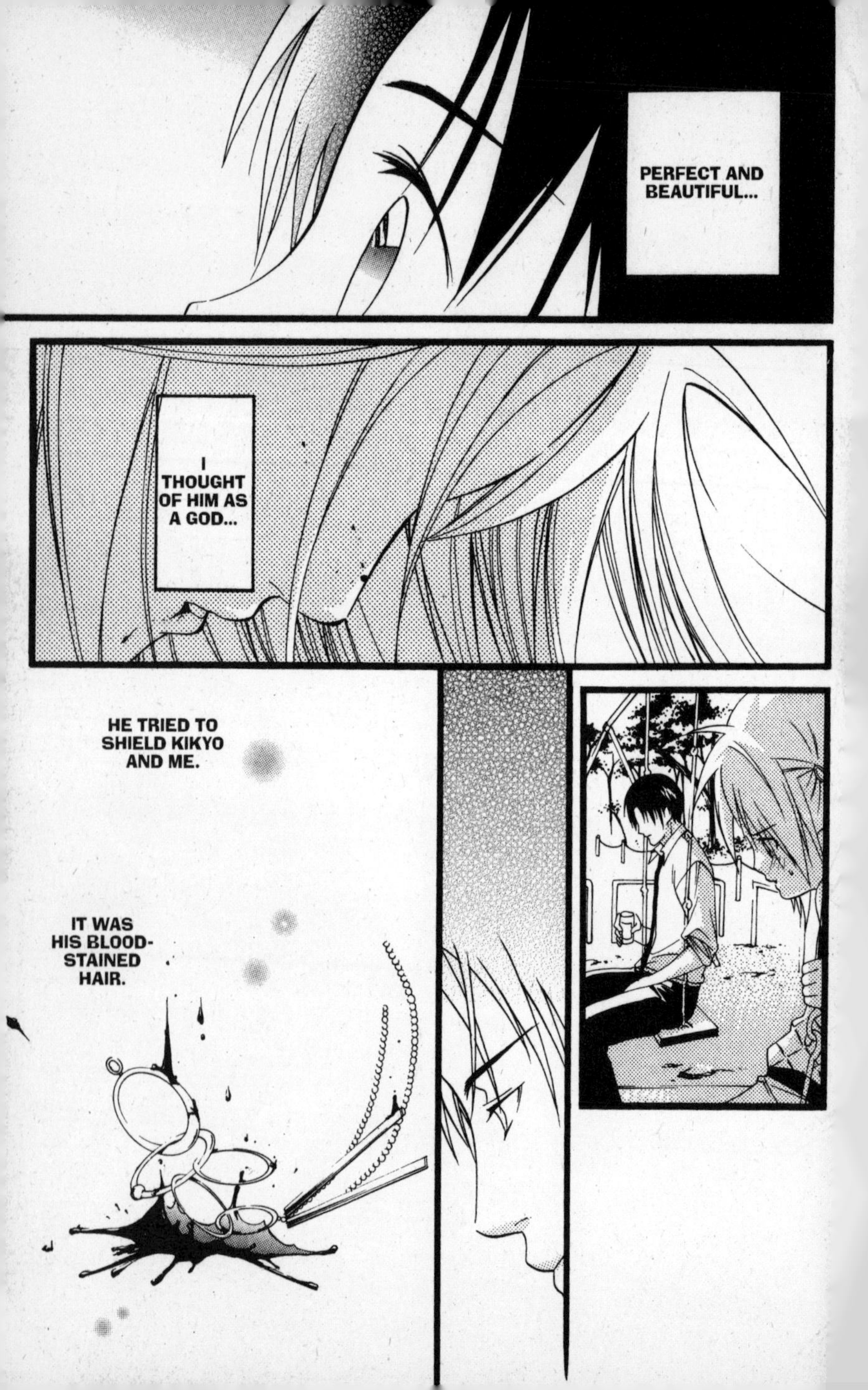
PERFECT AND BEAUTIFUL...
I THOUGHT OF HIM AS A GOD...
HE TRIED TO SHIELD KIKYO AND ME.
IT WAS HIS BLOOD-STAINED HAIR.

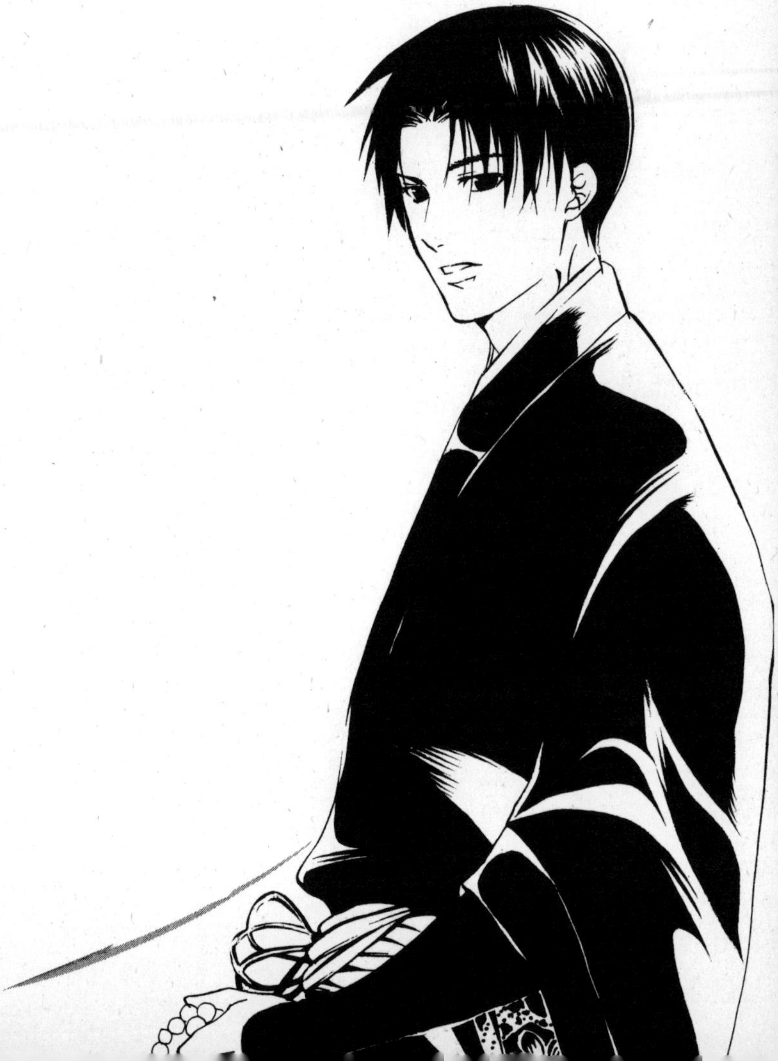

BLACK GATE

the black gate does not wait for the soul to die

PERFECT AND
BEAUTIFUL...

I THOUGHT
OF HIM AS
A GOD...

IT WAS HIS BLOOD-
STAINED HAIR.

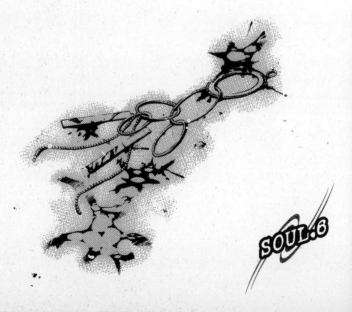

SOUL:6

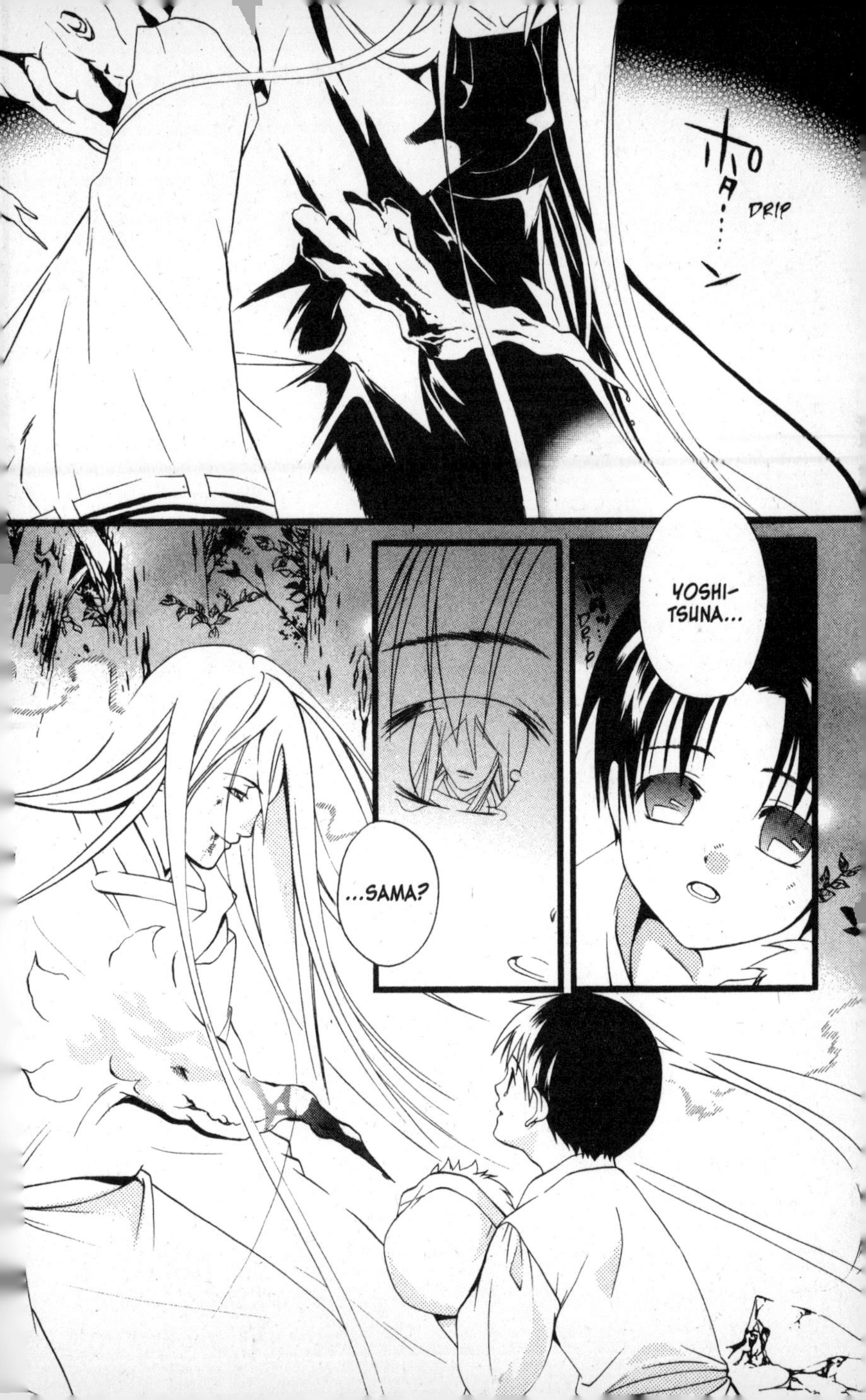
DRIP
YOSHI-TSUNA...
...SAMA?

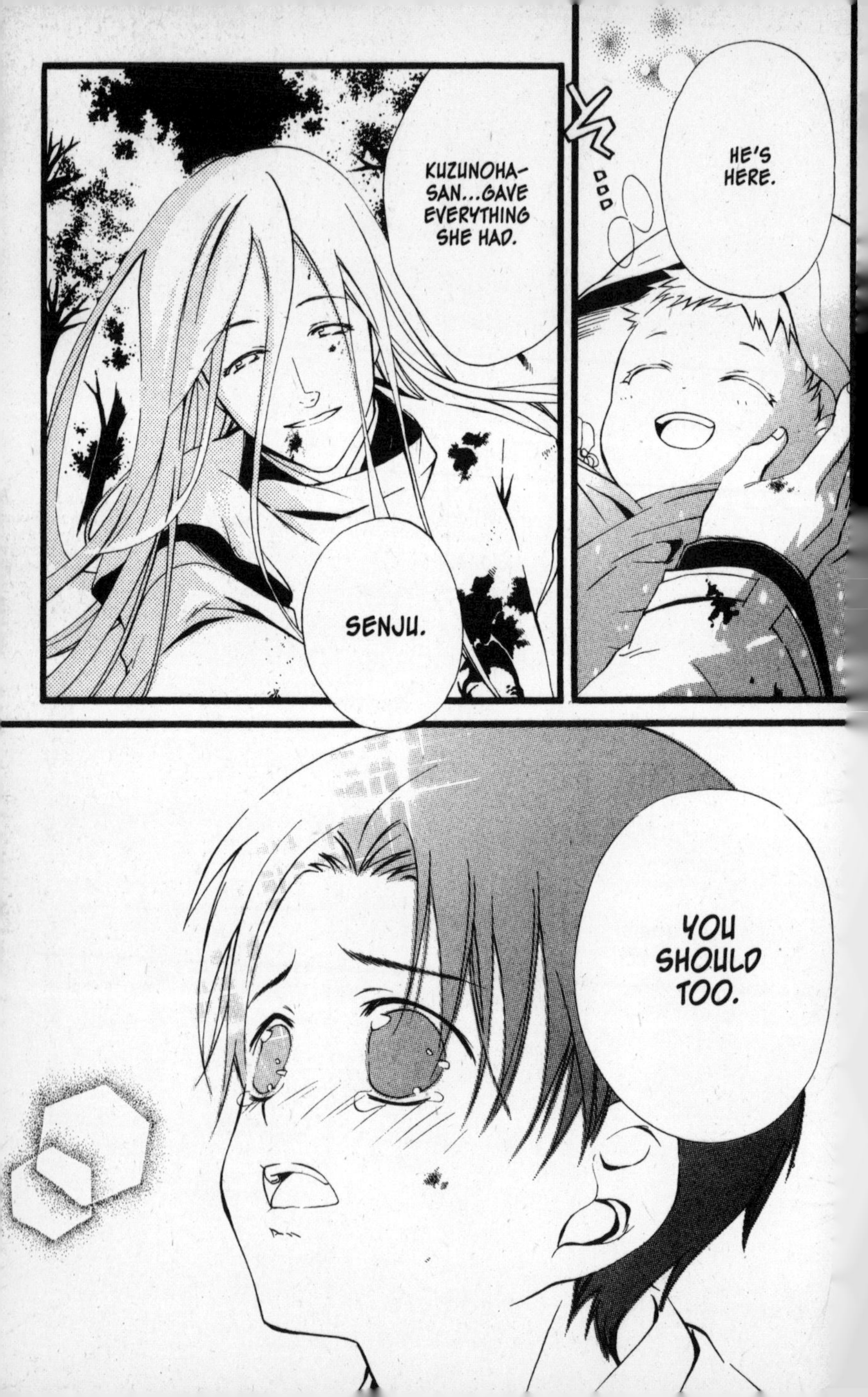
HE'S HERE.
KUZUNOHA-SAN...GAVE EVERYTHING SHE HAD.
SENJU.
YOU SHOULD TOO.

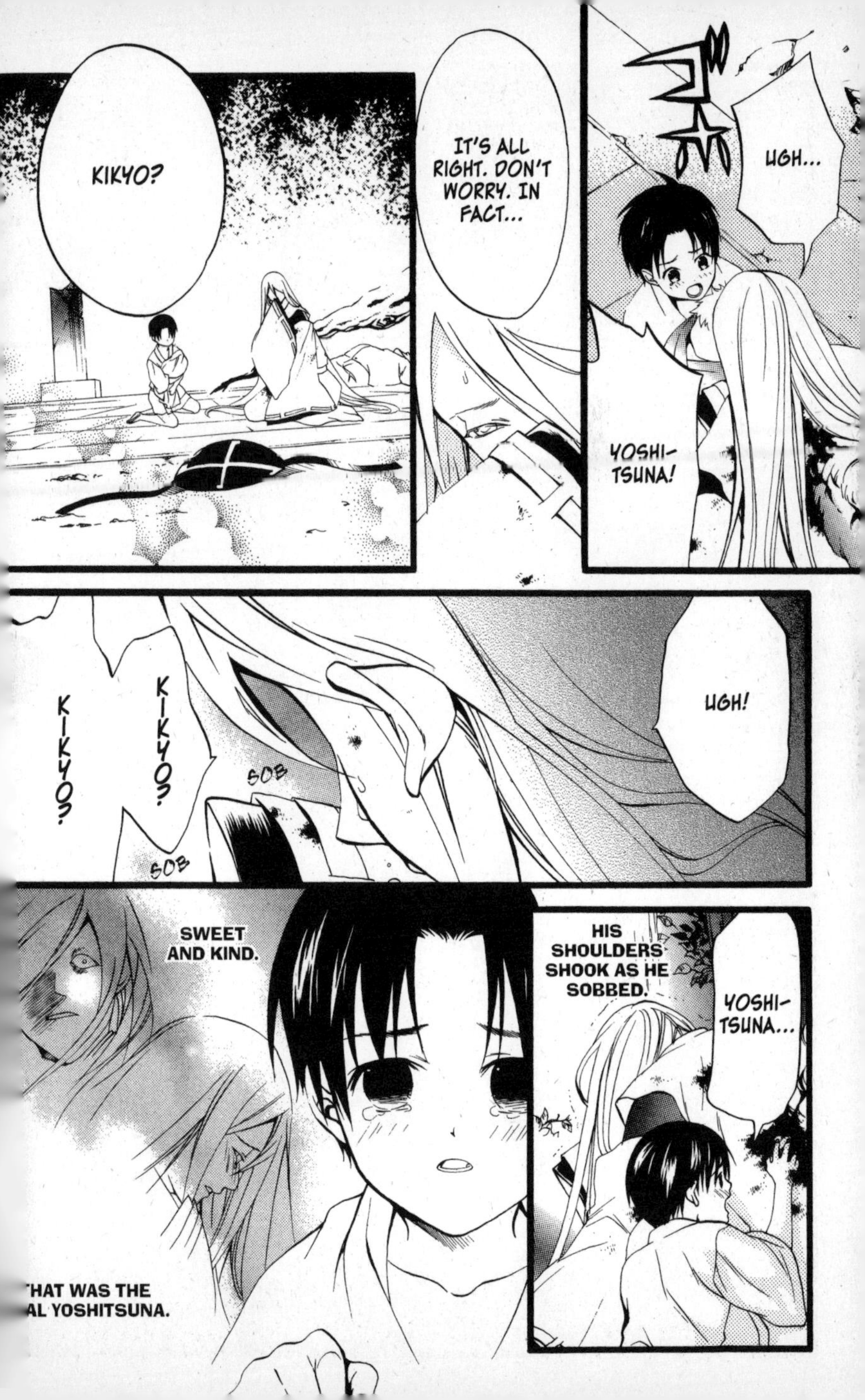
UGH...
YOSHI-TSUNA!
IT'S ALL RIGHT. DON'T WORRY. IN FACT...
KIKYO?
UGH!
SOB
KIKYO?
SOB
KIKYO?
YOSHI-TSUNA...
HIS SHOULDERS SHOOK AS HE SOBBED.
SWEET AND KIND.
THAT WAS THE
AL YOSHITSUNA.

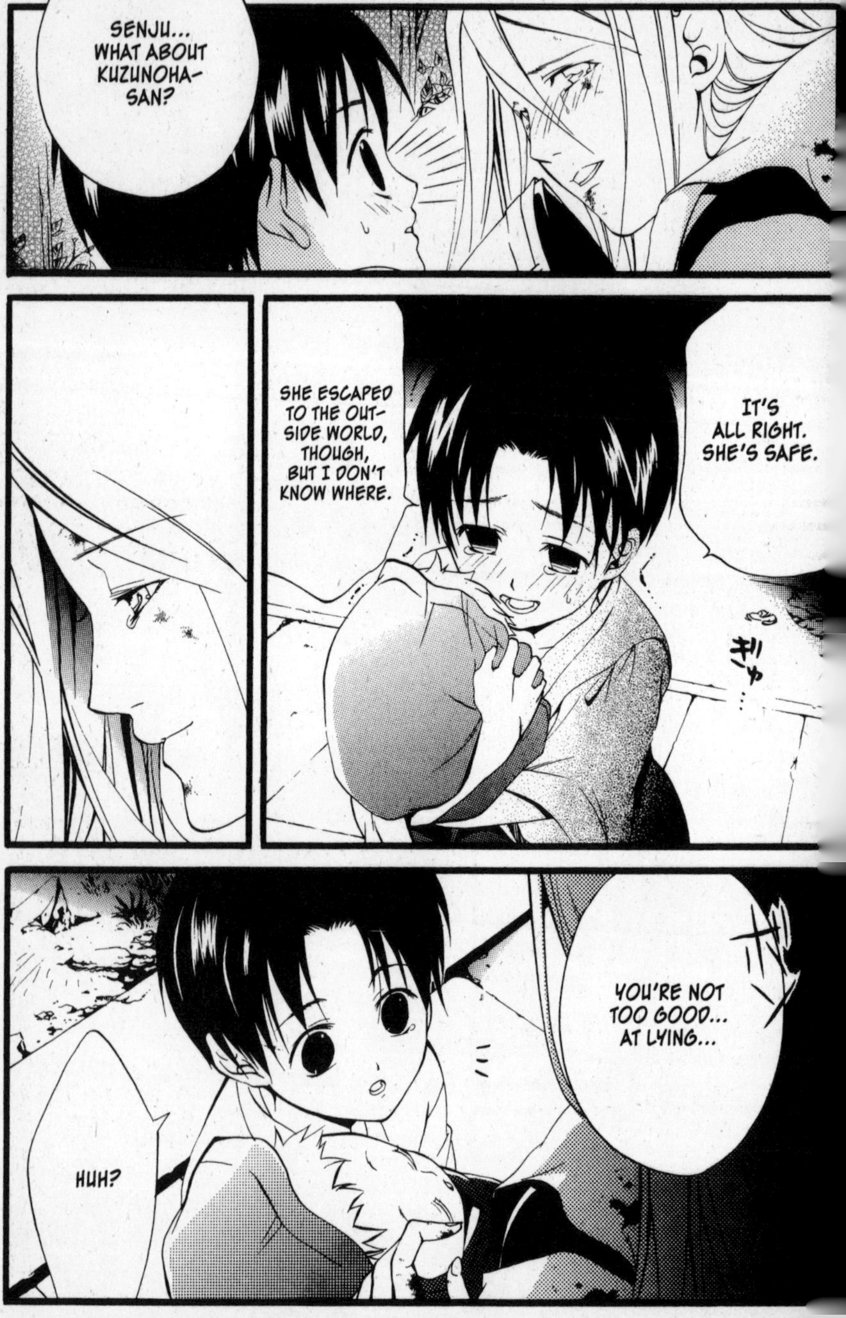
SENJU... WHAT ABOUT KUZUNOHA-SAN?
IT'S ALL RIGHT. SHE'S SAFE.
ぎゅ…
SHE ESCAPED TO THE OUT-SIDE WORLD, THOUGH, BUT I DON'T KNOW WHERE.
YOU'RE NOT TOO GOOD... AT LYING...
HUH?

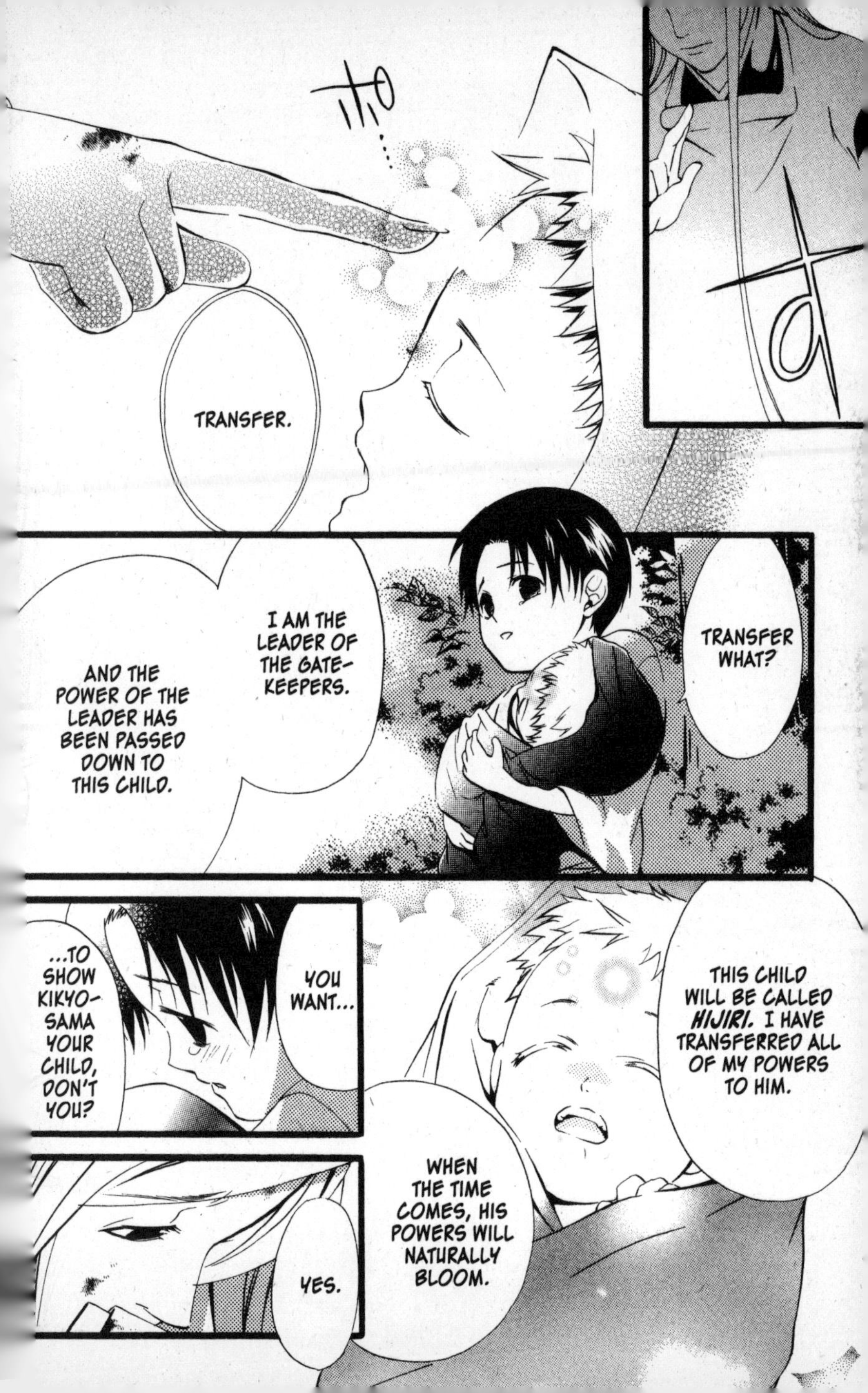
TRANSFER.
TRANSFER WHAT?
I AM THE LEADER OF THE GATE-KEEPERS.
AND THE POWER OF THE LEADER HAS BEEN PASSED DOWN TO THIS CHILD.
THIS CHILD WILL BE CALLED *HIJIRI.* I HAVE TRANSFERRED ALL OF MY POWERS TO HIM.
WHEN THE TIME COMES, HIS POWERS WILL NATURALLY BLOOM.
YOU WANT...
...TO SHOW KIKYO-SAMA YOUR CHILD, DON'T YOU?
YES.

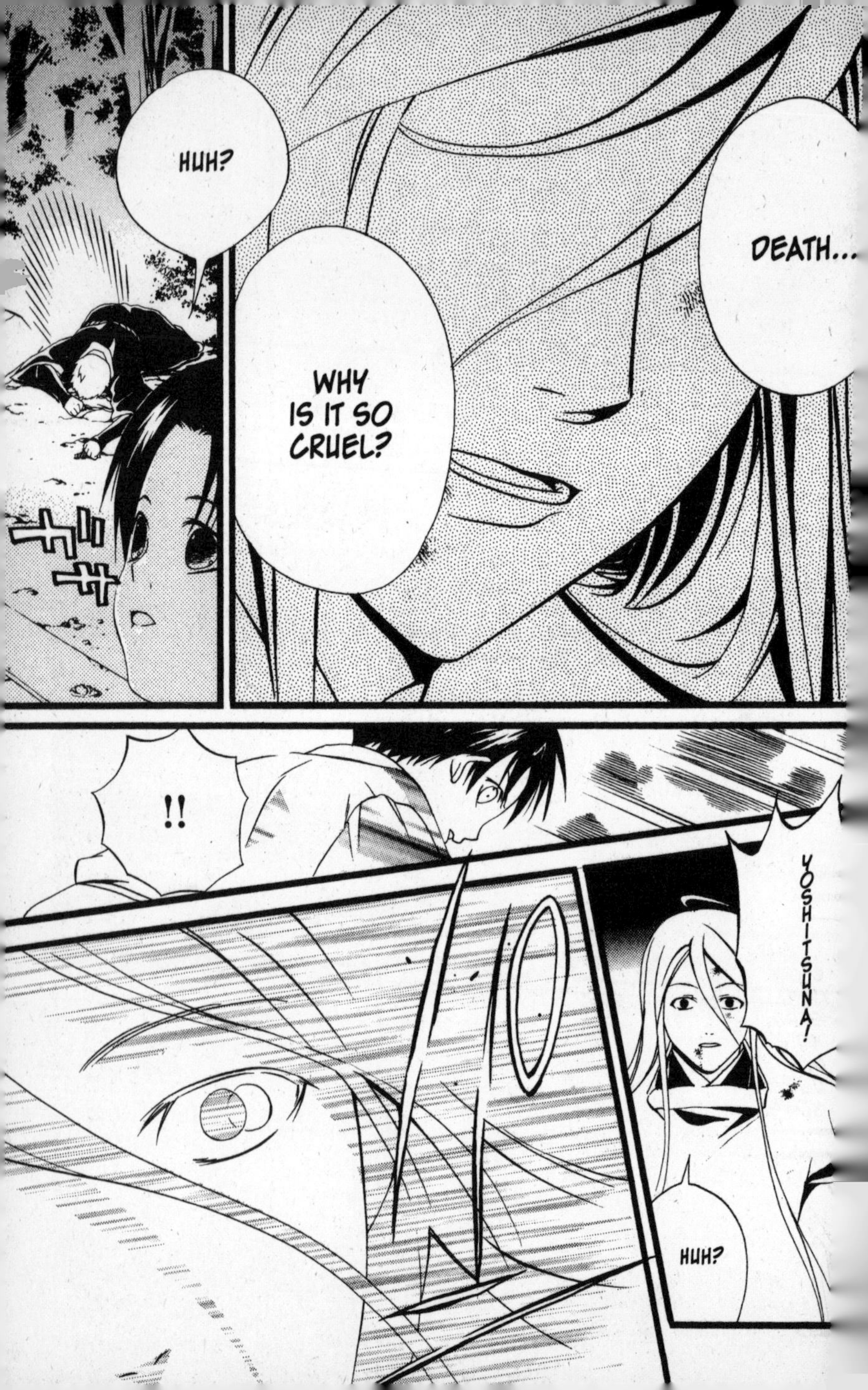
DEATH...
WHY IS IT SO CRUEL?
HUH?
!!
YOSHITSUNA!
HUH?

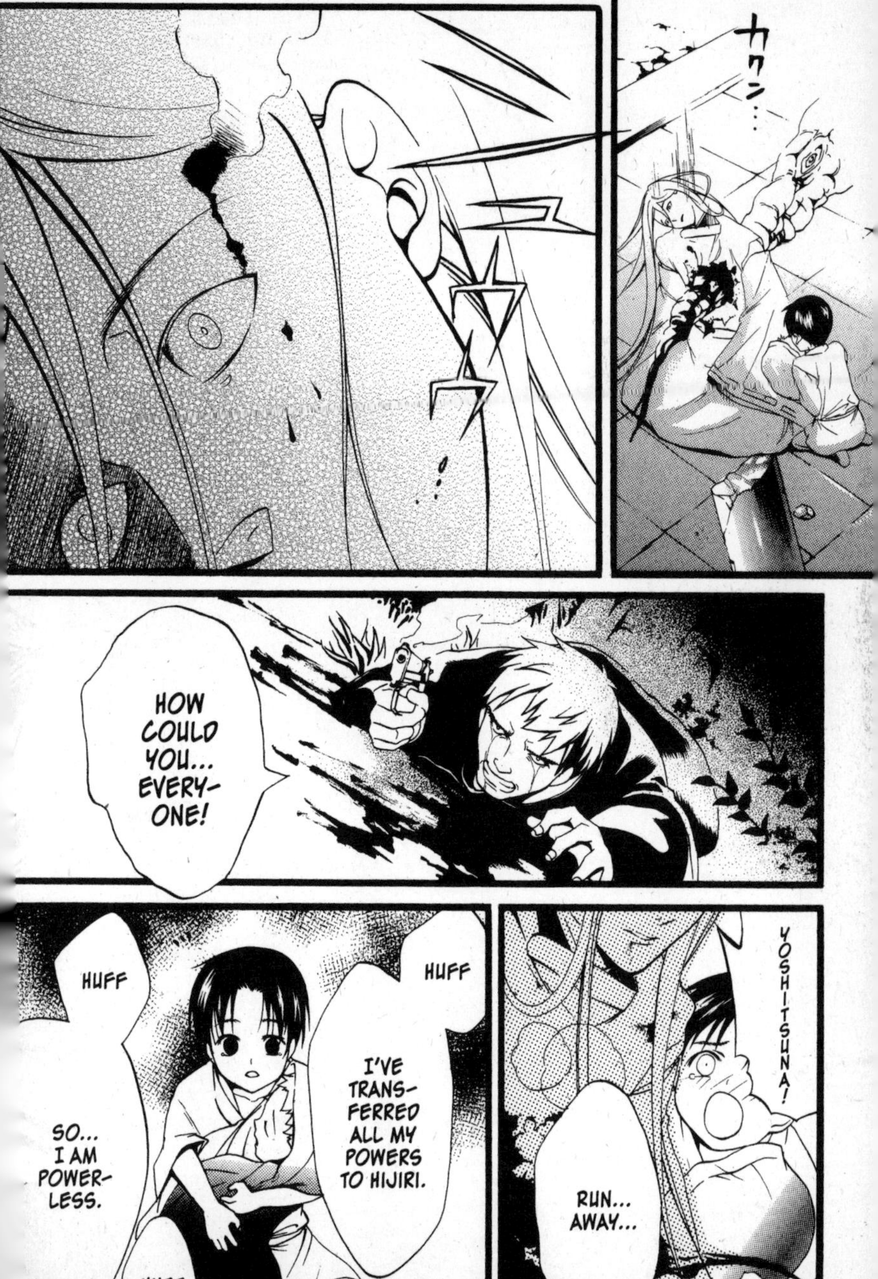
カクン…
HOW COULD YOU... EVERY-ONE!
YOSHITSUNA!
RUN... AWAY...
HUFF
HUFF
I'VE TRANSFERRED ALL MY POWERS TO HIJIRI.
SO... I AM POWERLESS.
HUFF

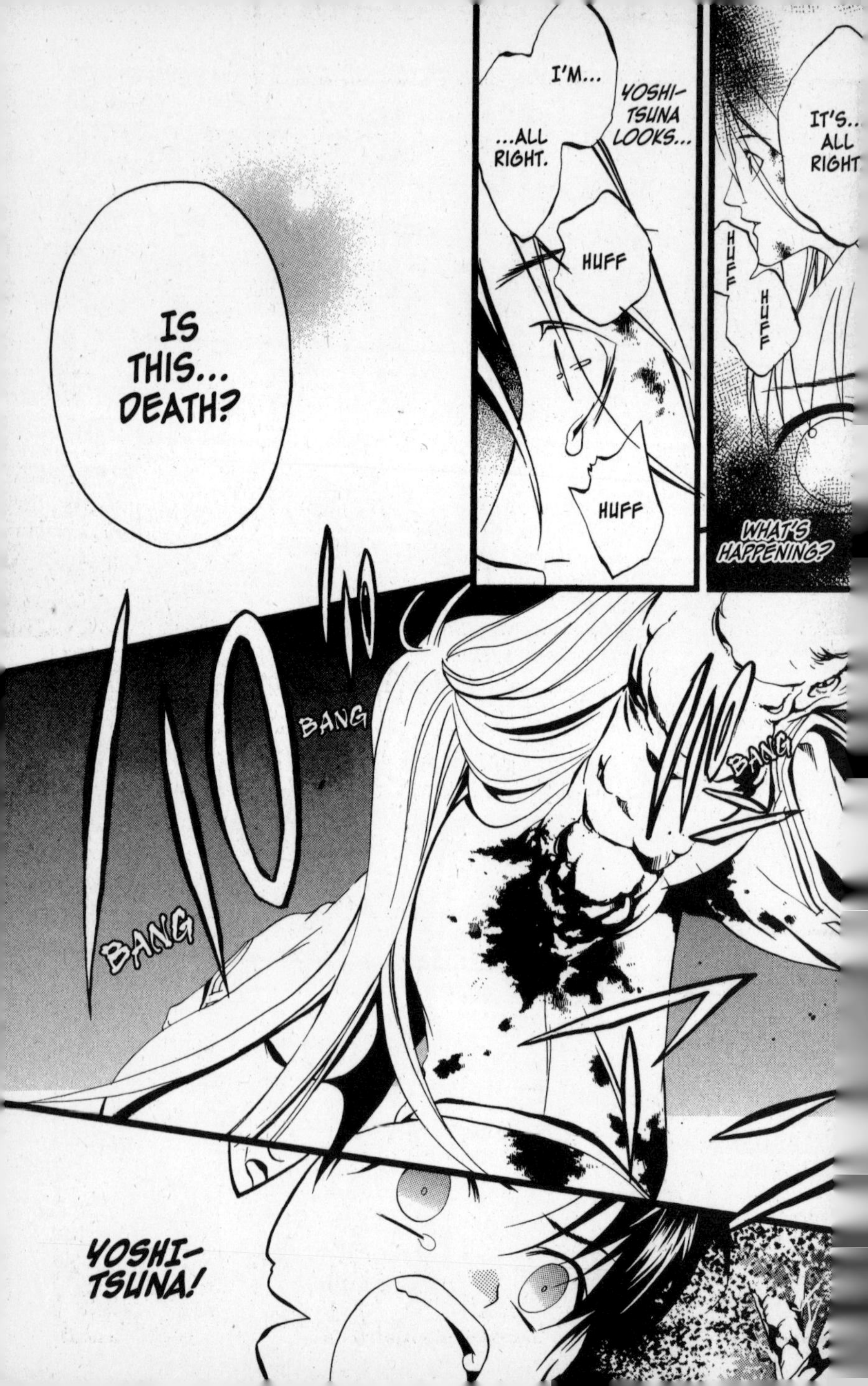
IT'S... ALL RIGHT.
HUFF
HUFF
WHAT'S HAPPENING?
YOSHI-TSUNA LOOKS...
I'M...
...ALL RIGHT.
HUFF
HUFF
IS THIS... DEATH?
BANG
BANG
BANG
YOSHI-TSUNA!

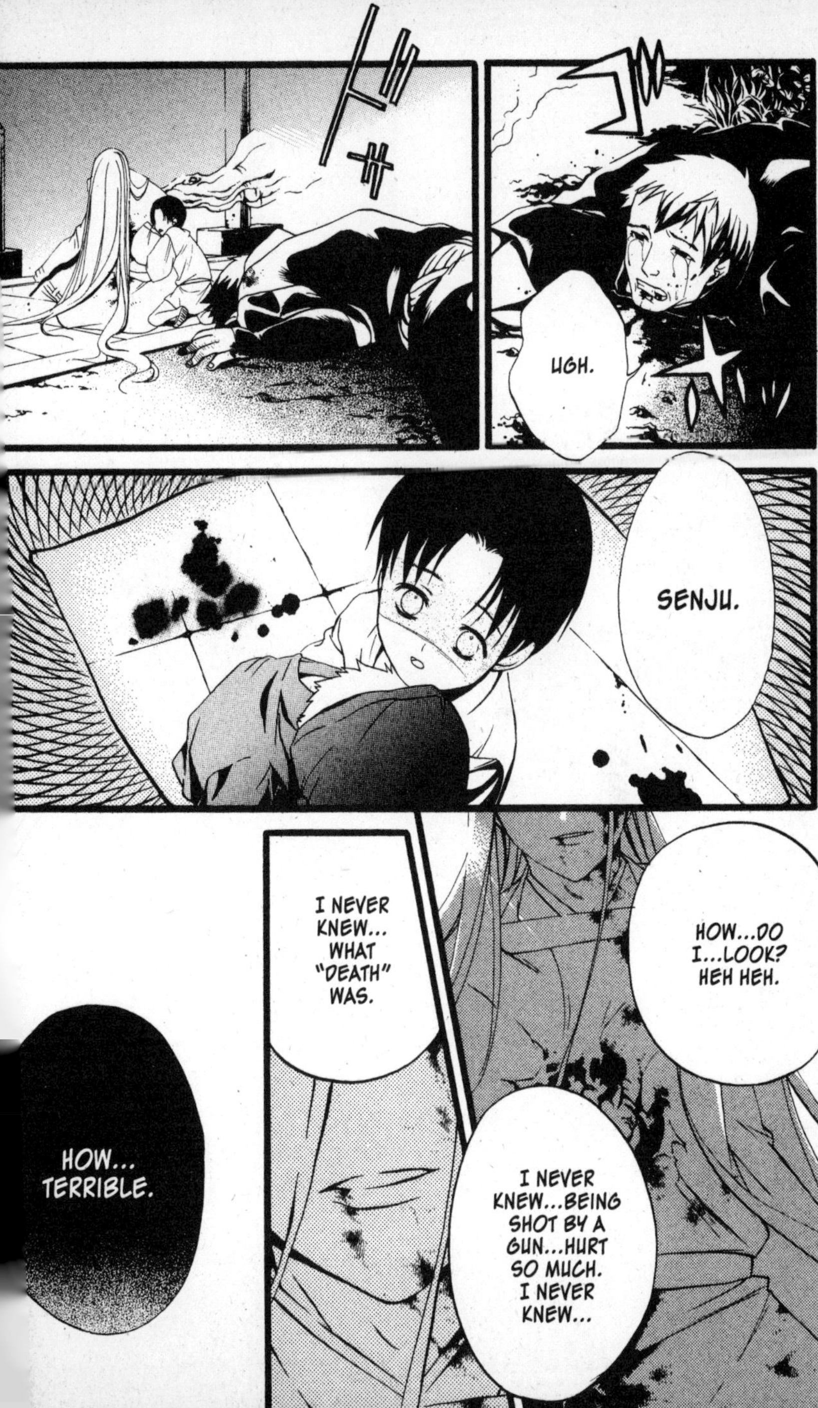
UGH.
SENJU.
HOW...DO I...LOOK? HEH HEH.
I NEVER KNEW... WHAT "DEATH" WAS.
I NEVER KNEW...BEING SHOT BY A GUN...HURT SO MUCH. I NEVER KNEW...
HOW... TERRIBLE.

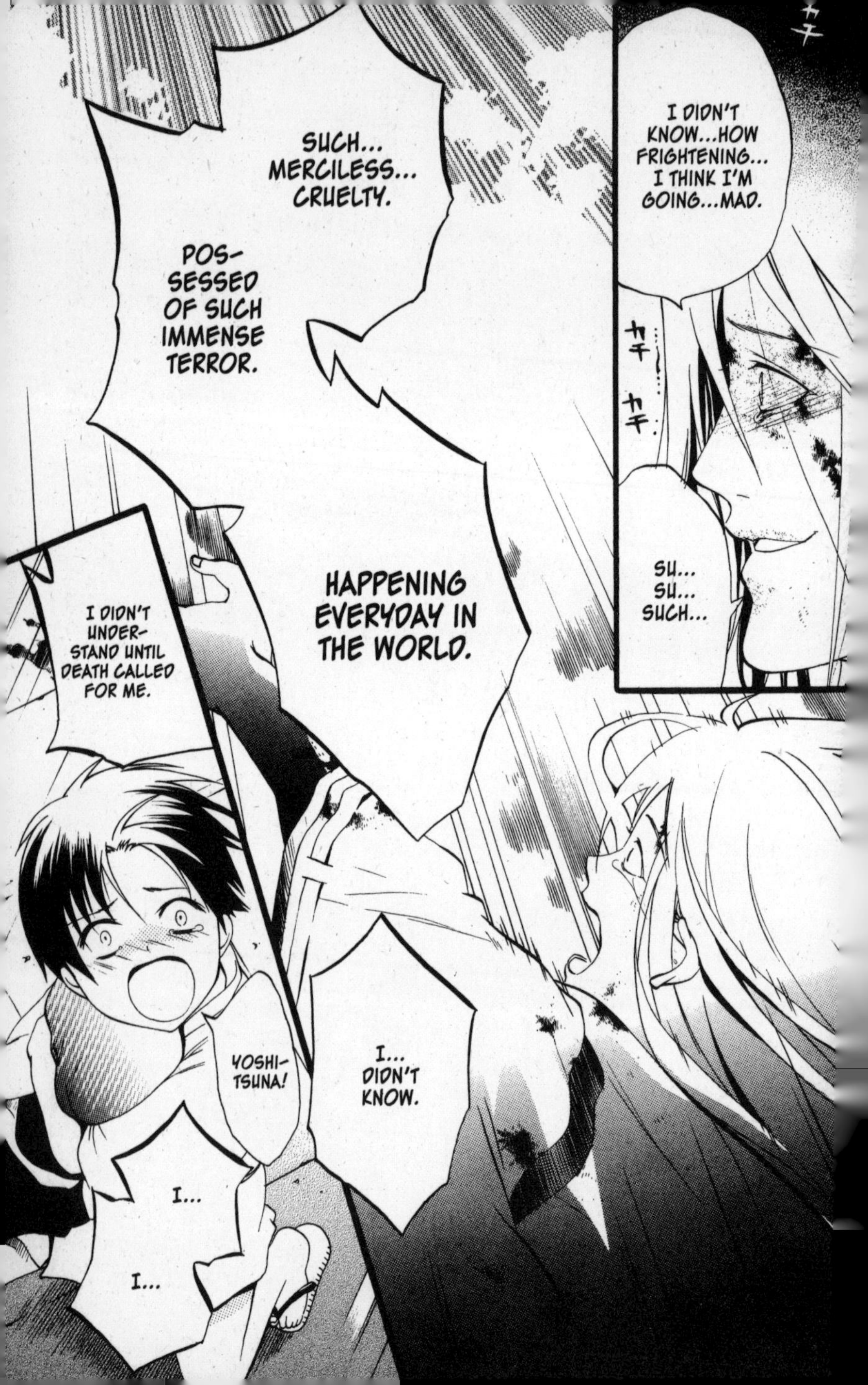

カチ
I DIDN'T KNOW...HOW FRIGHTENING... I THINK I'M GOING...MAD.
カチ
カチ
SU... SU... SUCH...
SUCH... MERCILESS... CRUELTY.
POS-SESSED OF SUCH IMMENSE TERROR.
HAPPENING EVERYDAY IN THE WORLD.
I DIDN'T UNDER-STAND UNTIL DEATH CALLED FOR ME.
I... DIDN'T KNOW.
YOSHI-TSUNA!
I...
I...

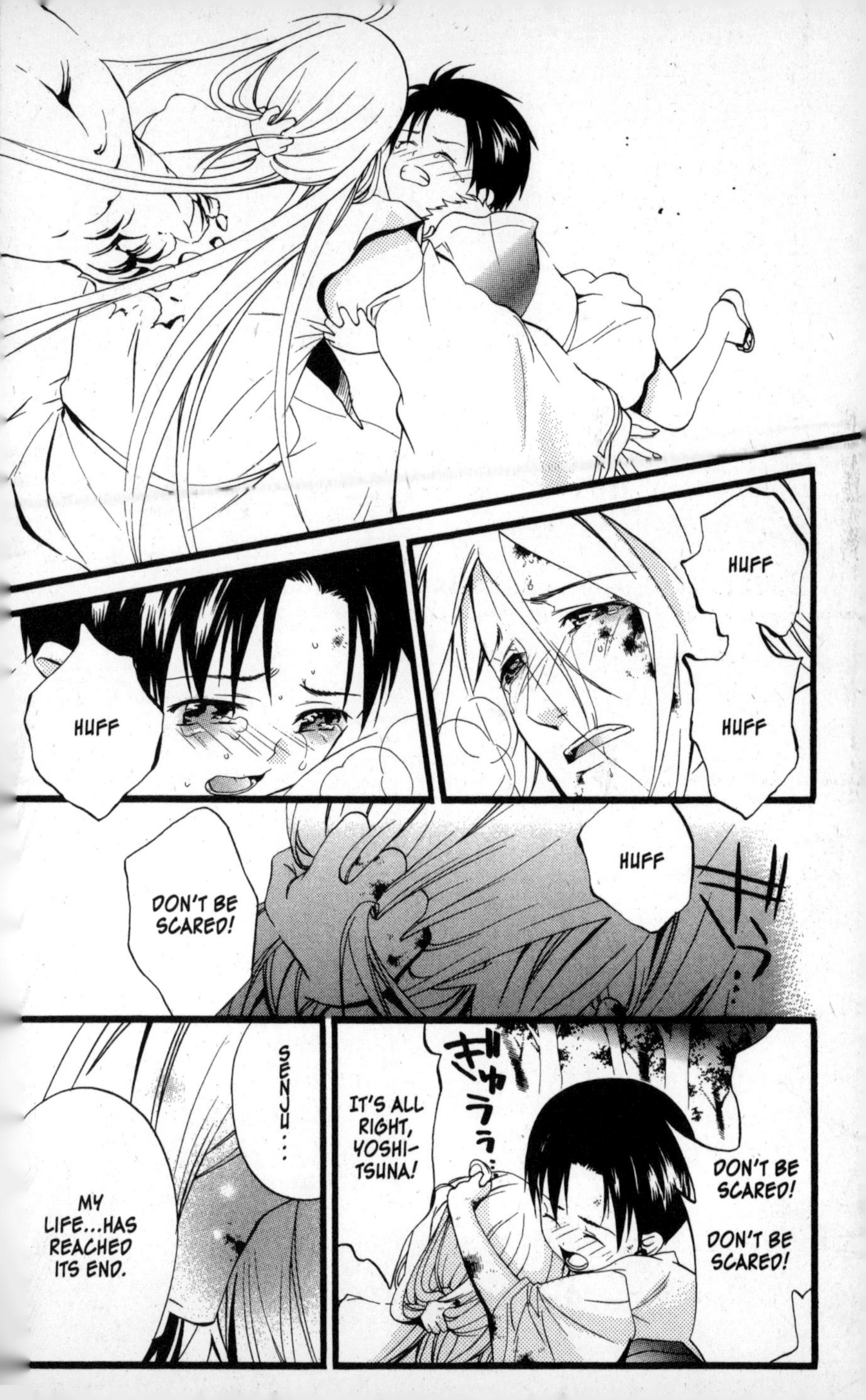
HUFF
HUFF
HUFF
HUFF
DON'T BE SCARED!
IT'S ALL RIGHT, YOSHI-TSUNA!
DON'T BE SCARED!
DON'T BE SCARED!
SENJU...
MY LIFE...HAS REACHED ITS END.

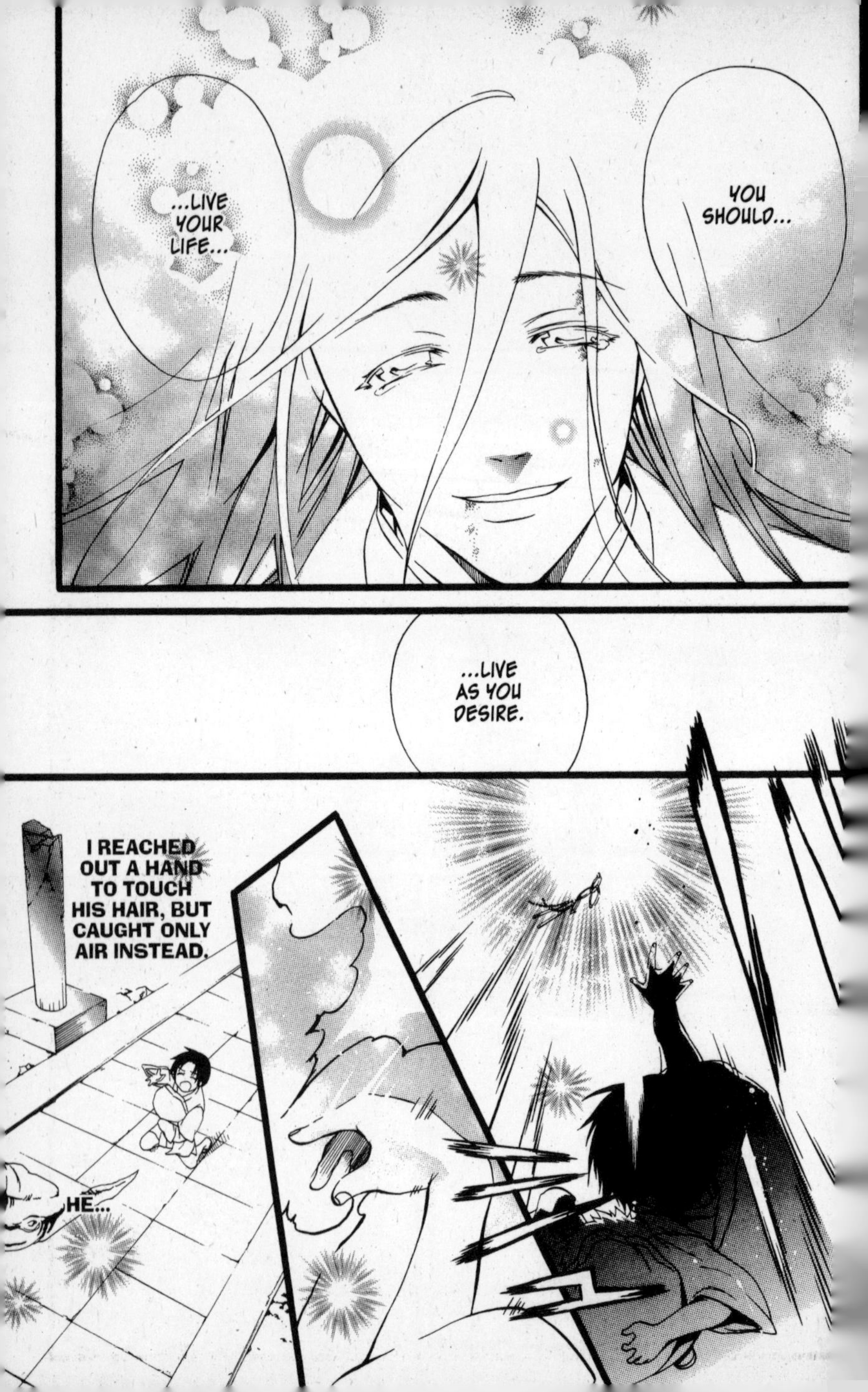
YOU SHOULD...
...LIVE YOUR LIFE...
...LIVE AS YOU DESIRE.
I REACHED OUT A HAND TO TOUCH HIS HAIR, BUT CAUGHT ONLY AIR INSTEAD.
HE...

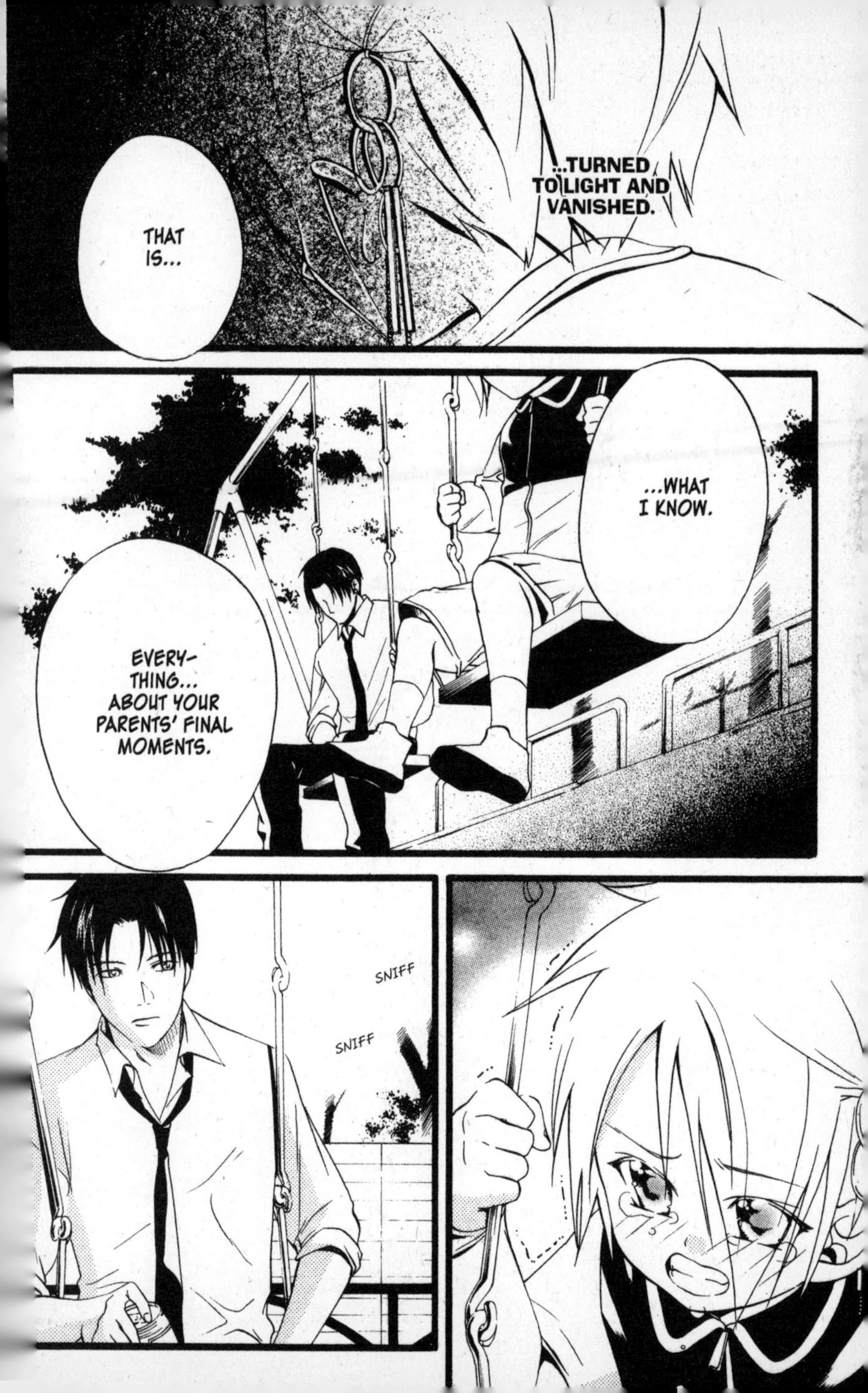
...TURNED TO LIGHT AND VANISHED.
THAT IS...
...WHAT I KNOW.
EVERY-THING... ABOUT YOUR PARENTS' FINAL MOMENTS.
SNIFF
SNIFF

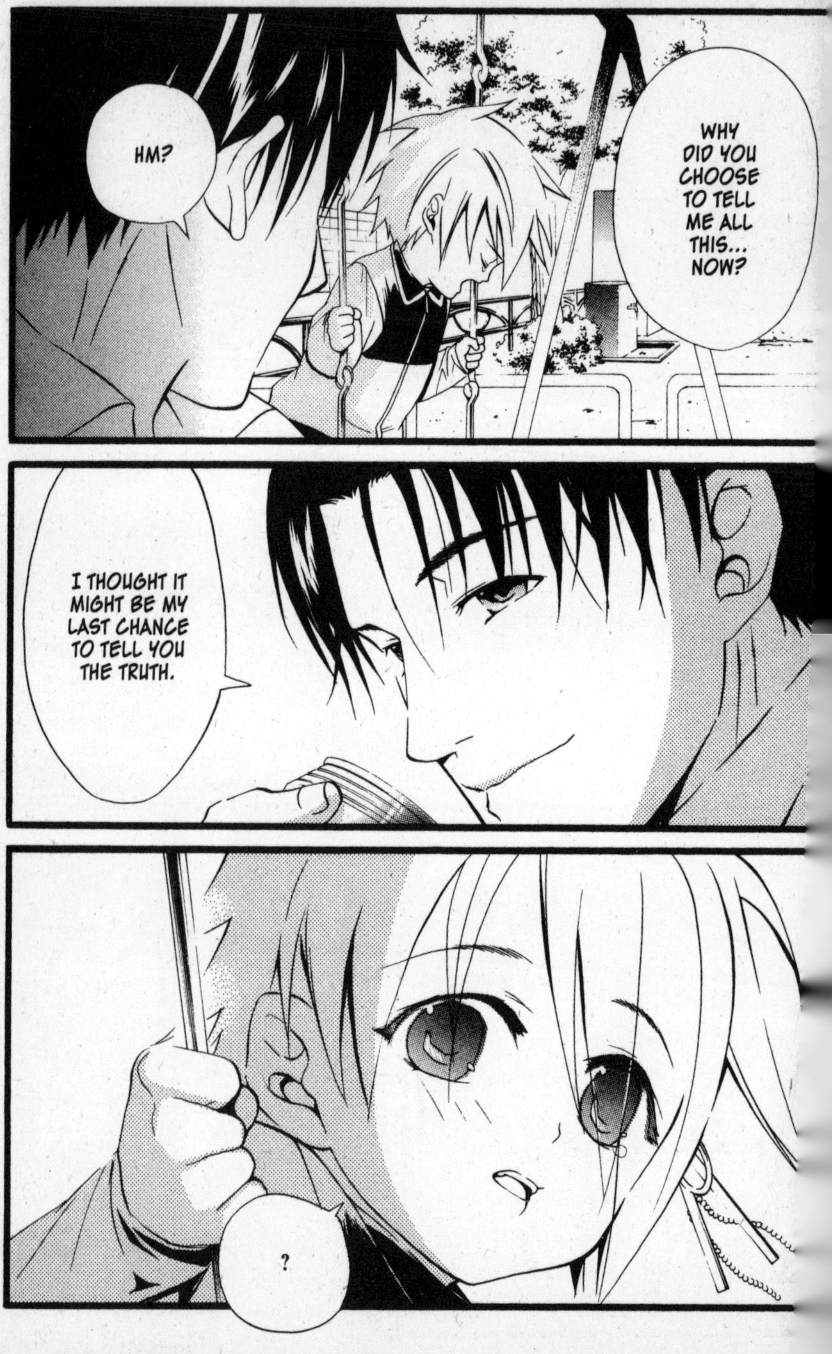
WHY DID YOU CHOOSE TO TELL ME ALL THIS... NOW?
HM?
I THOUGHT IT MIGHT BE MY LAST CHANCE TO TELL YOU THE TRUTH.
?

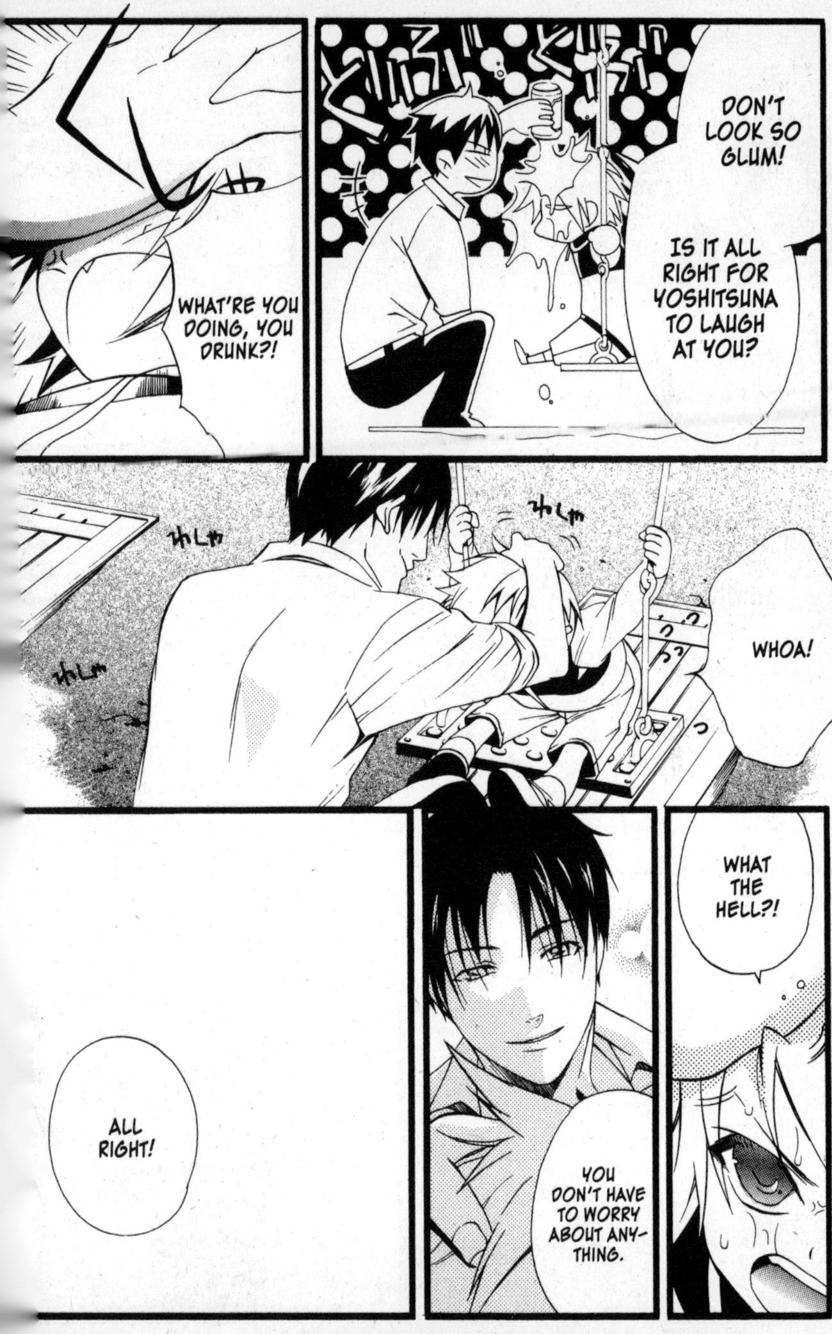
DON'T LOOK SO GLUM!
IS IT ALL RIGHT FOR YOSHITSUNA TO LAUGH AT YOU?
WHAT'RE YOU DOING, YOU DRUNK?!
WHOA!
WHAT THE HELL?!
YOU DON'T HAVE TO WORRY ABOUT ANY-THING.
ALL RIGHT!

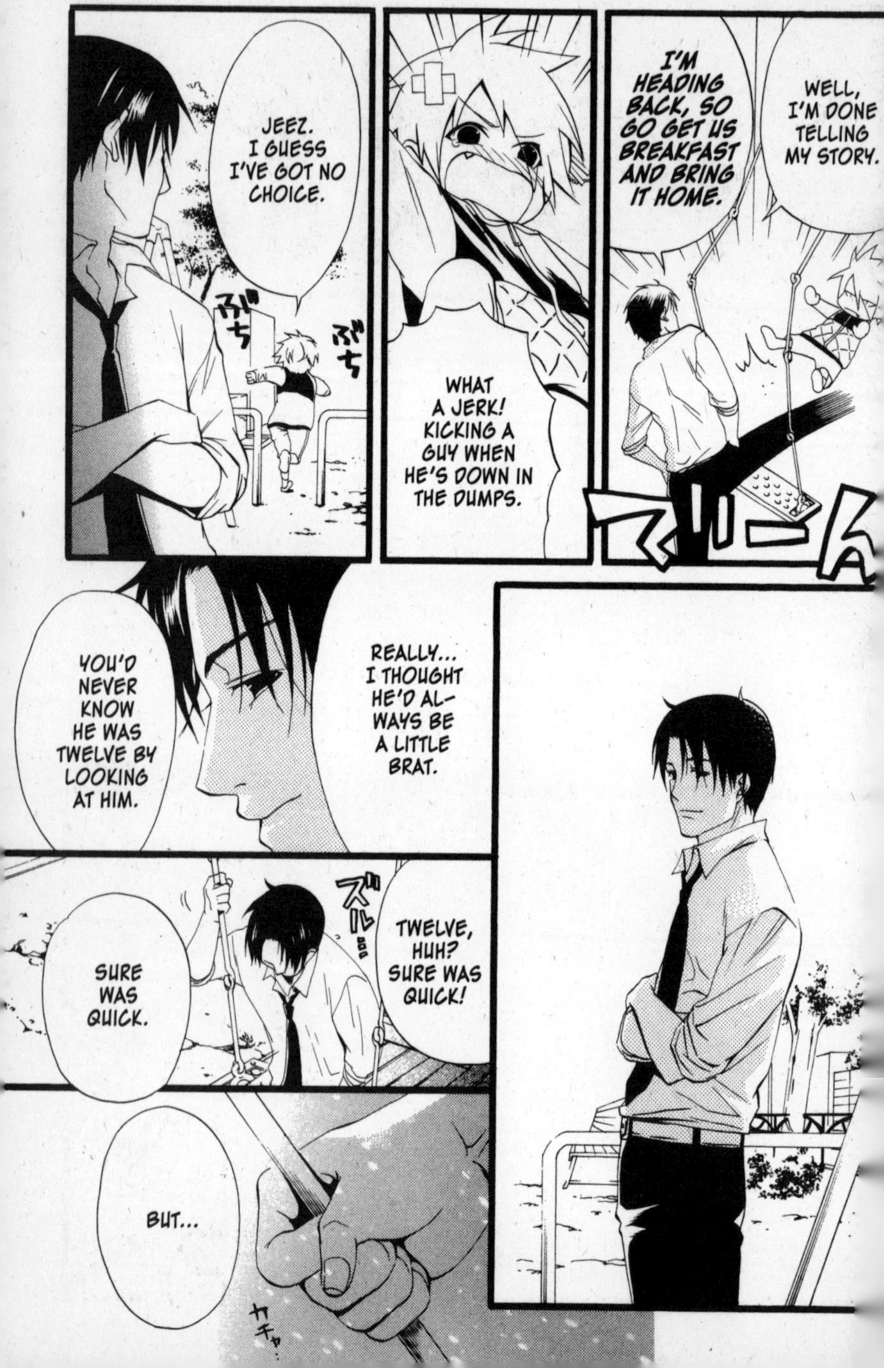
WELL, I'M DONE TELLING MY STORY.
I'M HEADING BACK, SO GO GET US BREAKFAST AND BRING IT HOME.
WHAT A JERK! KICKING A GUY WHEN HE'S DOWN IN THE DUMPS.
JEEZ. I GUESS I'VE GOT NO CHOICE.
ぶち
ぶち
REALLY... I THOUGHT HE'D AL-WAYS BE A LITTLE BRAT.
YOU'D NEVER KNOW HE WAS TWELVE BY LOOKING AT HIM.
TWELVE, HUH? SURE WAS QUICK!
ズル
SURE WAS QUICK.
BUT...
カチャ

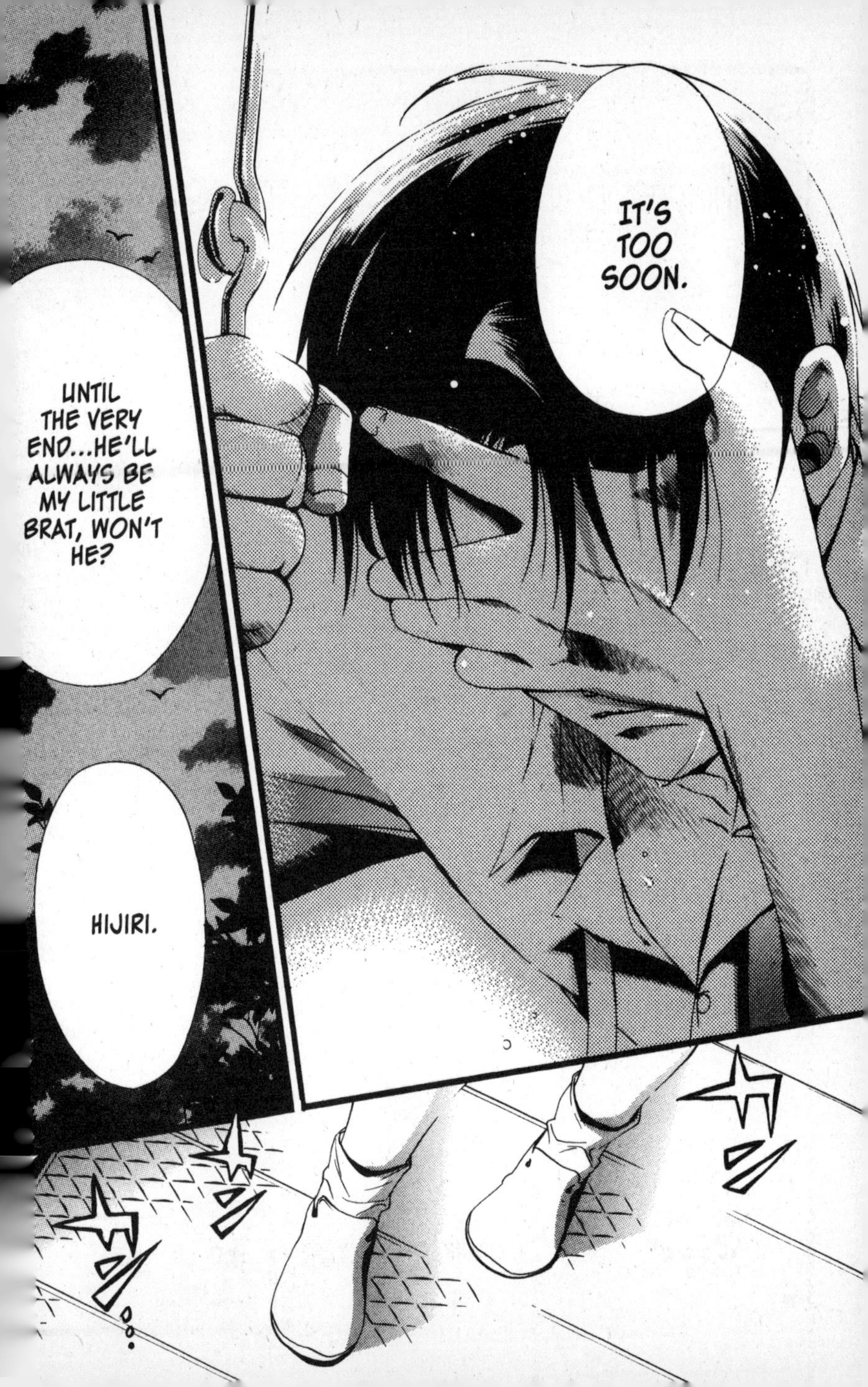
IT'S TOO SOON.
UNTIL THE VERY END...HE'LL ALWAYS BE MY LITTLE BRAT, WON'T HE?
HIJIRI.

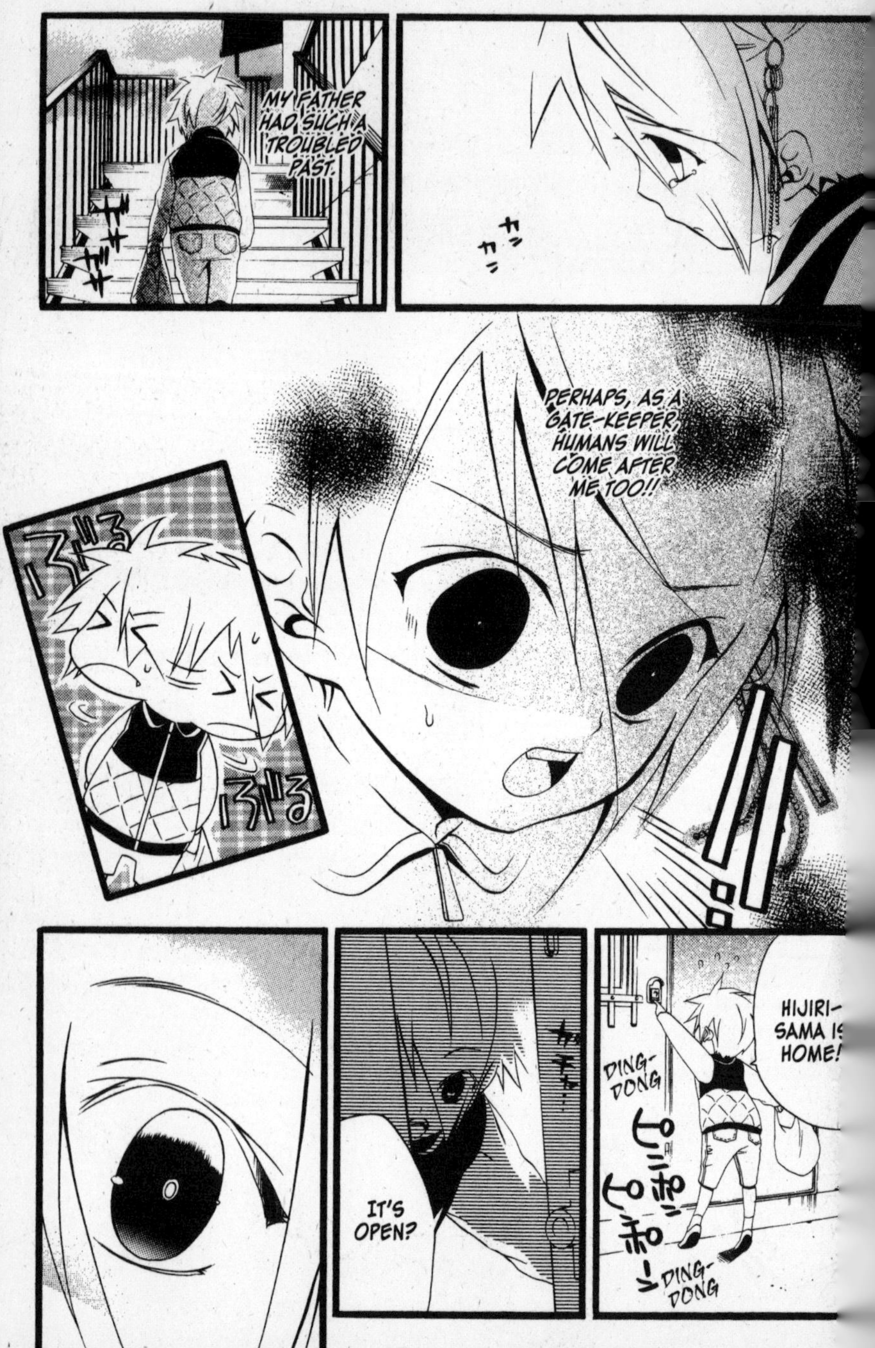

カン
カン
MY FATHER HAD SUCH A TROUBLED PAST.
PERHAPS, AS A GATE-KEEPER, HUMANS WILL COME AFTER ME TOO!!
HIJIRI-SAMA IS HOME!
DING-DONG
DING-DONG
IT'S OPEN?

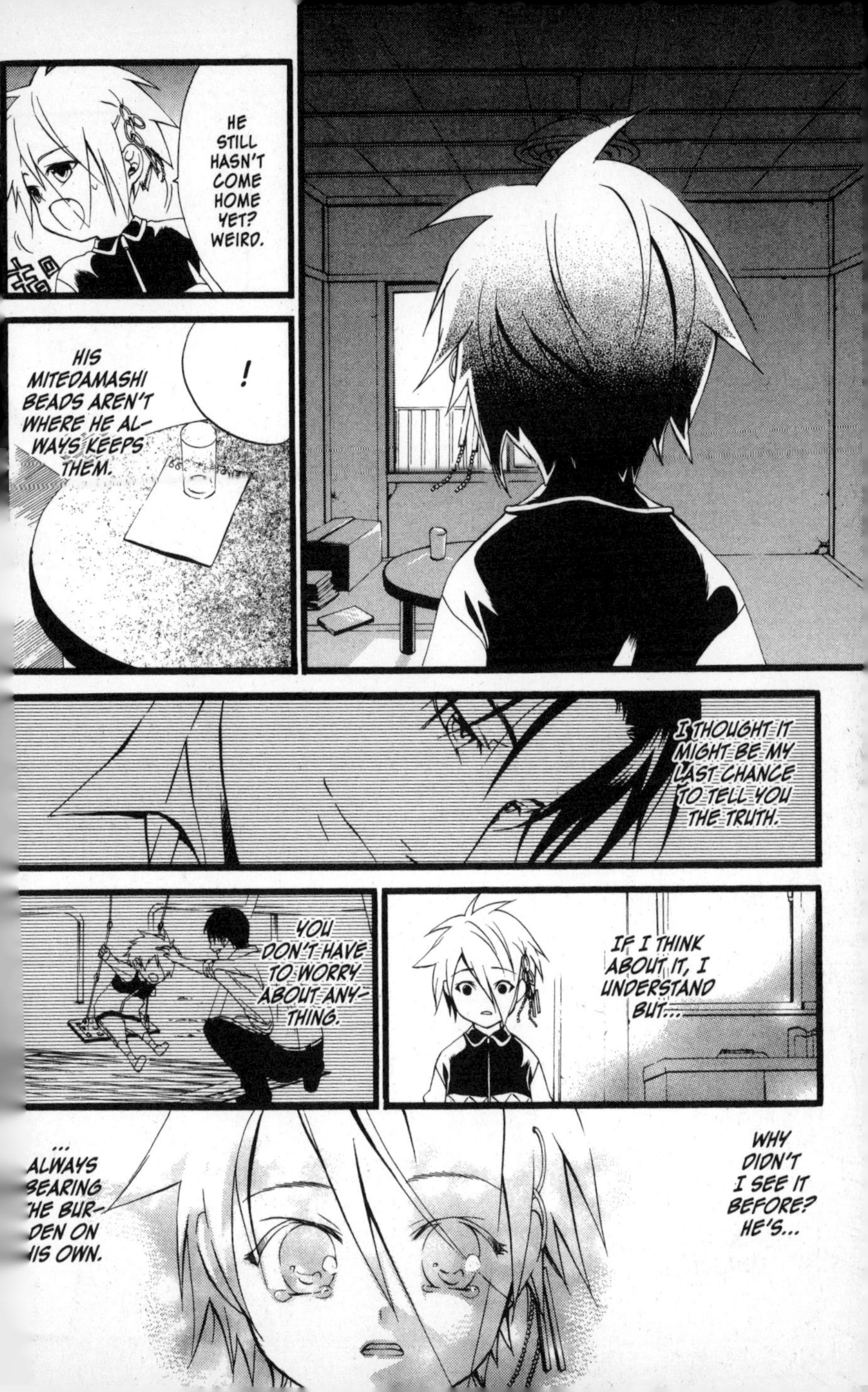
HE STILL HASN'T COME HOME YET? WEIRD.
!
HIS MITEDAMASHI BEADS AREN'T WHERE HE AL-WAYS KEEPS THEM.
I THOUGHT IT MIGHT BE MY LAST CHANCE TO TELL YOU THE TRUTH.
IF I THINK ABOUT IT, I UNDERSTAND BUT...
YOU DON'T HAVE TO WORRY ABOUT ANY-THING.
WHY DIDN'T I SEE IT BEFORE? HE'S...
...ALWAYS BEARING THE BUR-DEN ON HIS OWN.

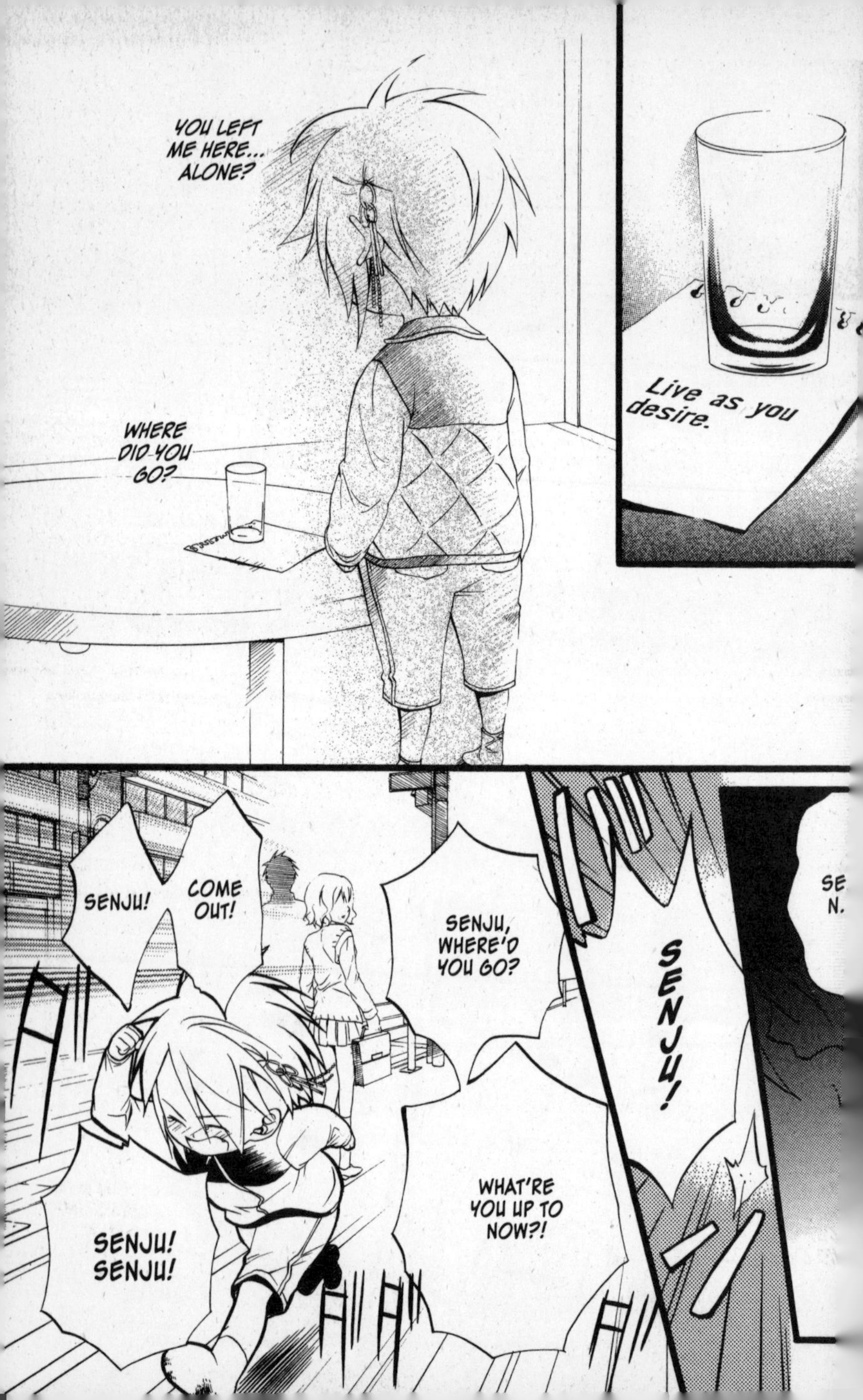
Live as you desire.
YOU LEFT ME HERE... ALONE?
WHERE DID YOU GO?
SE N.
SENJU!
SENJU, WHERE'D YOU GO?
WHAT'RE YOU UP TO NOW?!
COME OUT!
SENJU!
SENJU! SENJU!

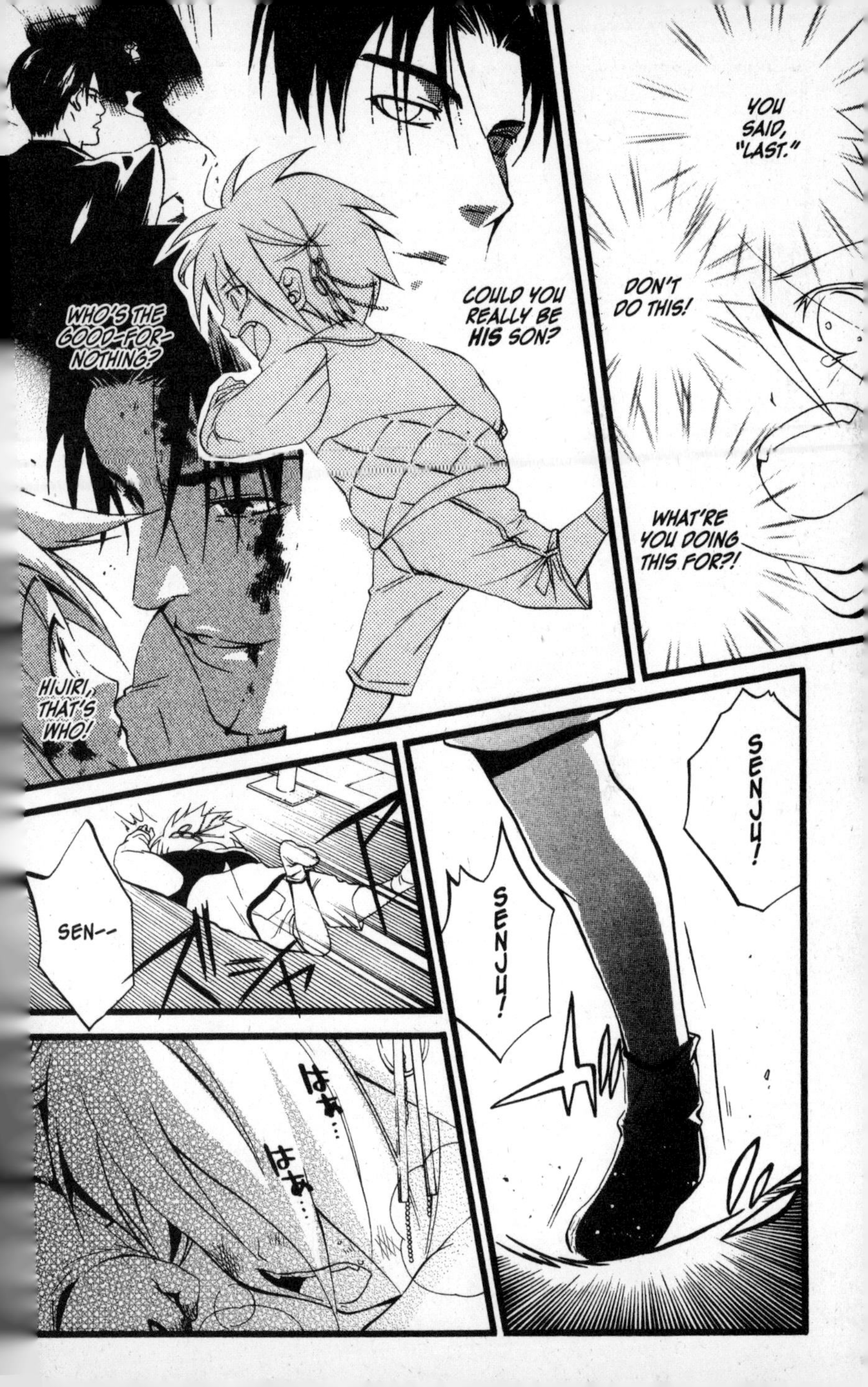
YOU SAID, "LAST."
DON'T DO THIS!
WHAT'RE YOU DOING THIS FOR?!
COULD YOU REALLY BE HIS SON?
WHO'S THE GOOD-FOR-NOTHING?
HIJIRI, THAT'S WHO!
SENJU!
SENJU!
SEN--
はぁ…
はぁ…

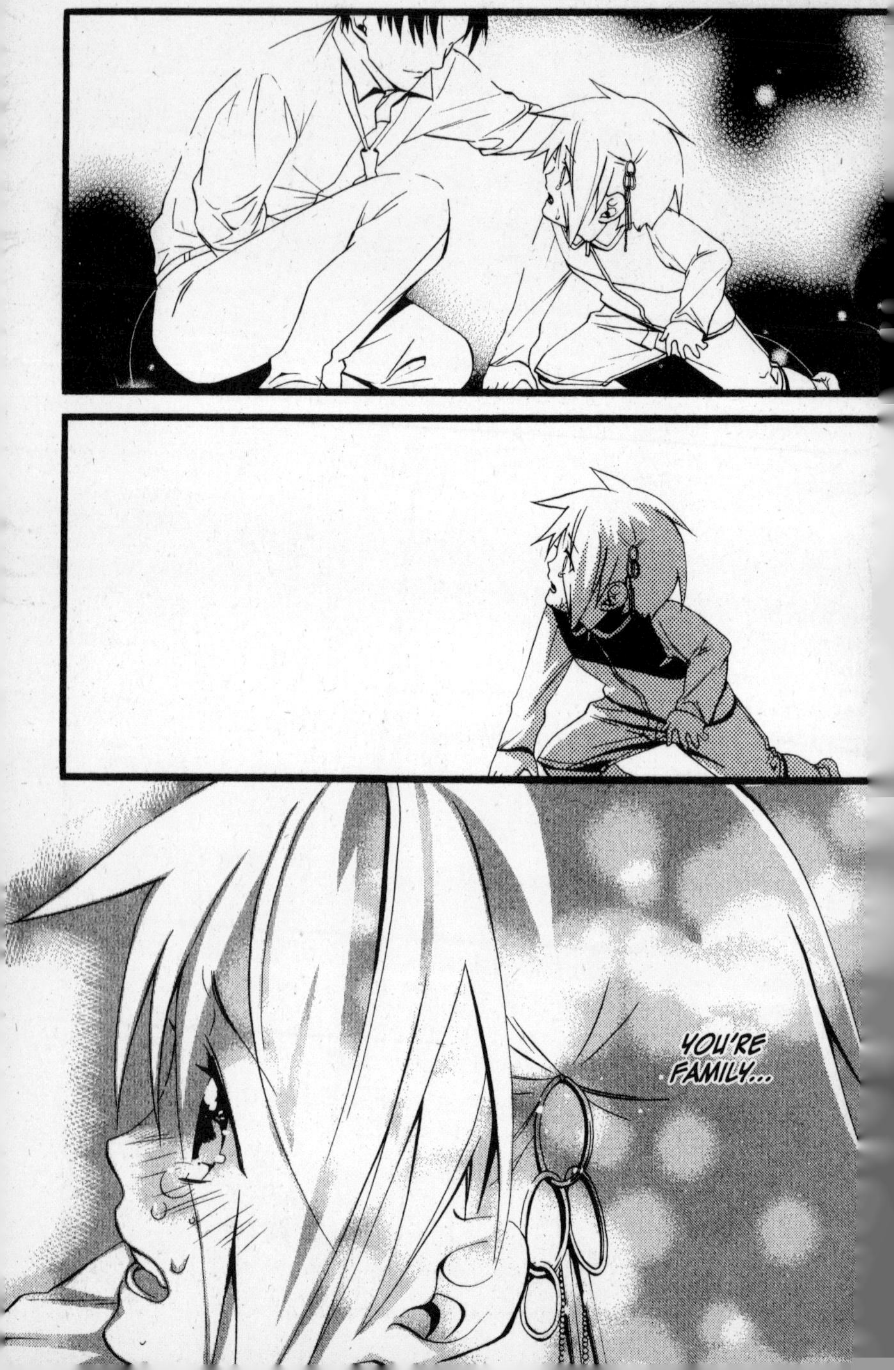
YOU'RE FAMILY...

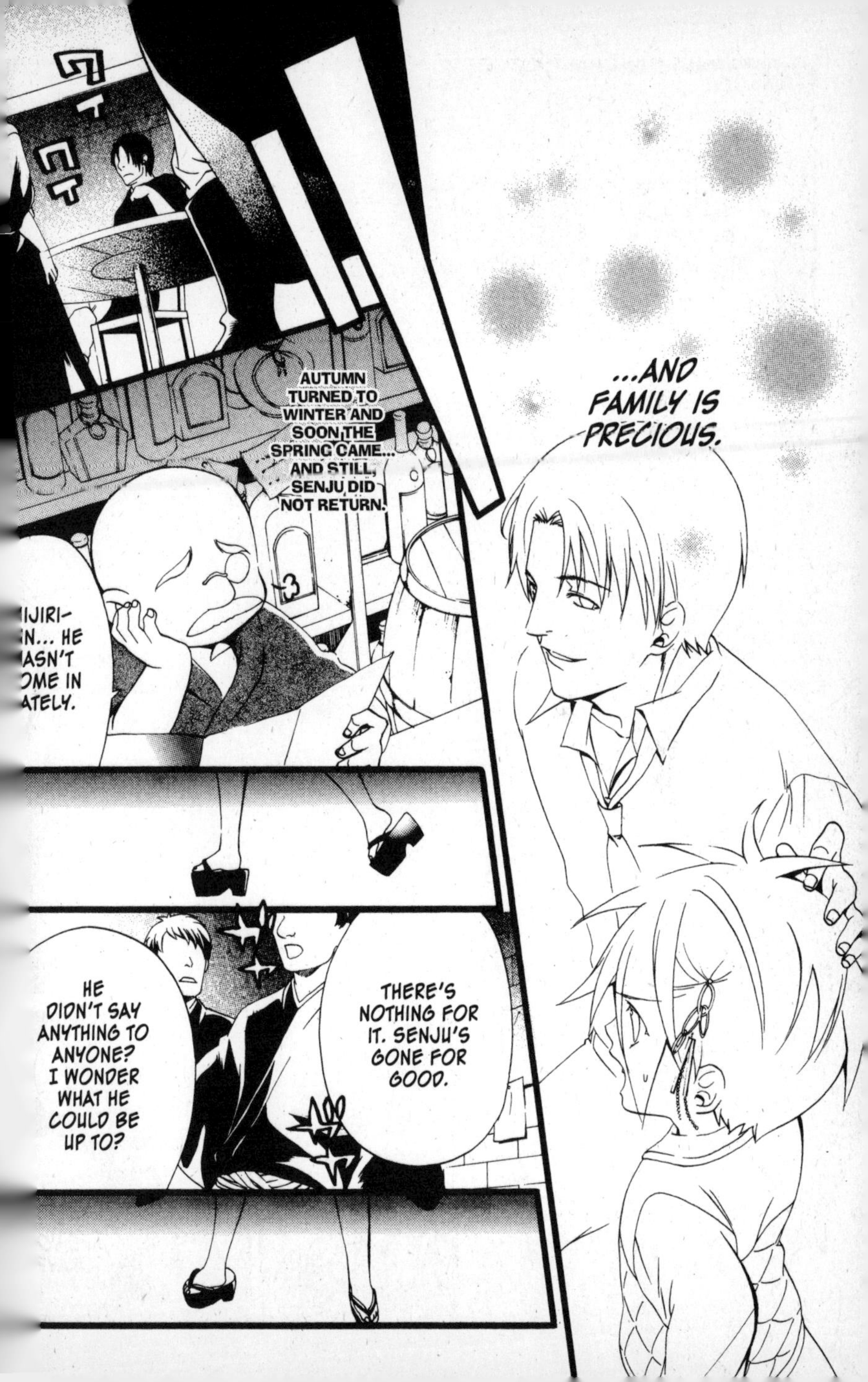
...AND FAMILY IS PRECIOUS.
AUTUMN TURNED TO WINTER AND SOON THE SPRING CAME... AND STILL, SENJU DID NOT RETURN.
IJIRI- N... HE ASN'T OME IN ATELY.
THERE'S NOTHING FOR IT. SENJU'S GONE FOR GOOD.
HE DIDN'T SAY ANYTHING TO ANYONE? I WONDER WHAT HE COULD BE UP TO?

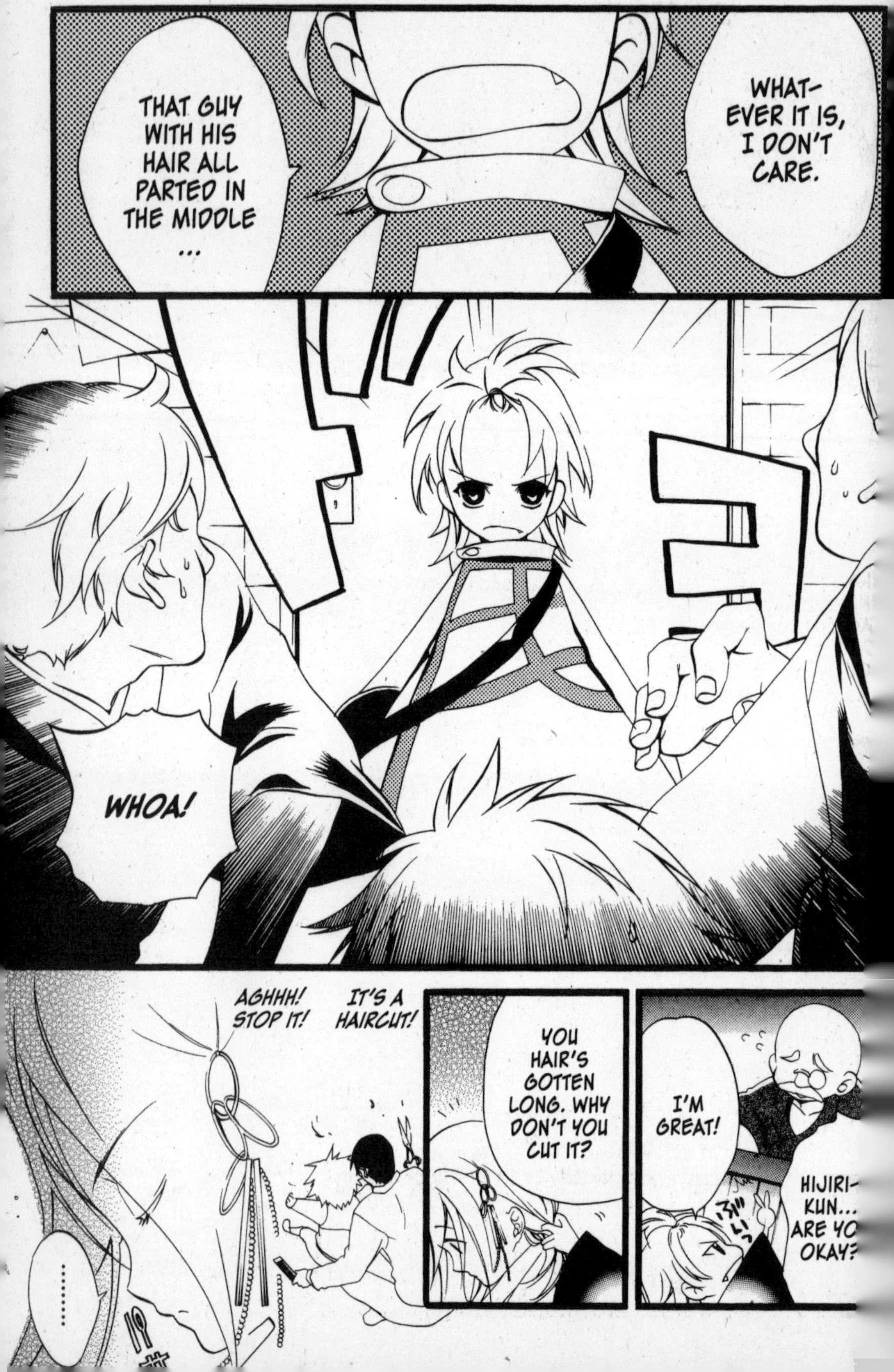
WHAT-EVER IT IS, I DON'T CARE.
THAT GUY WITH HIS HAIR ALL PARTED IN THE MIDDLE ...
WHOA!
HIJIRI-KUN... ARE YO OKAY?
I'M GREAT!
YOU HAIR'S GOTTEN LONG. WHY DON'T YOU CUT IT?
IT'S A HAIRCUT!
AGHHH! STOP IT!
......

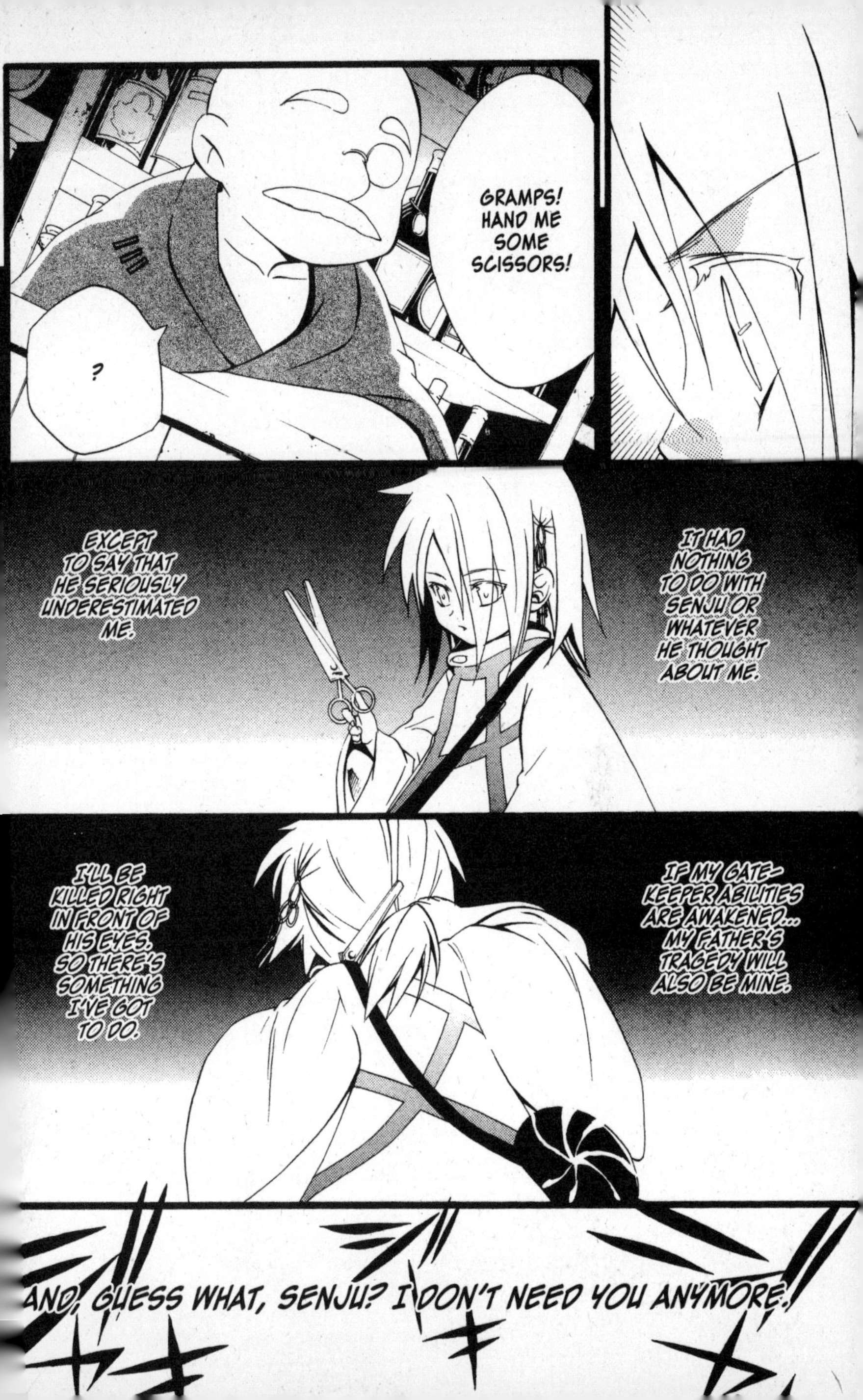
GRAMPS! HAND ME SOME SCISSORS!
?
IT HAD NOTHING TO DO WITH SENJU OR WHATEVER HE THOUGHT ABOUT ME.
EXCEPT TO SAY THAT HE SERIOUSLY UNDERESTIMATED ME.
IF MY GATE-KEEPER ABILITIES ARE AWAKENED... MY FATHER'S TRAGEDY WILL ALSO BE MINE.
I'LL BE KILLED RIGHT IN FRONT OF HIS EYES. SO THERE'S SOMETHING I'VE GOT TO DO.
AND, GUESS WHAT, SENJU? I DON'T NEED YOU ANYMORE!

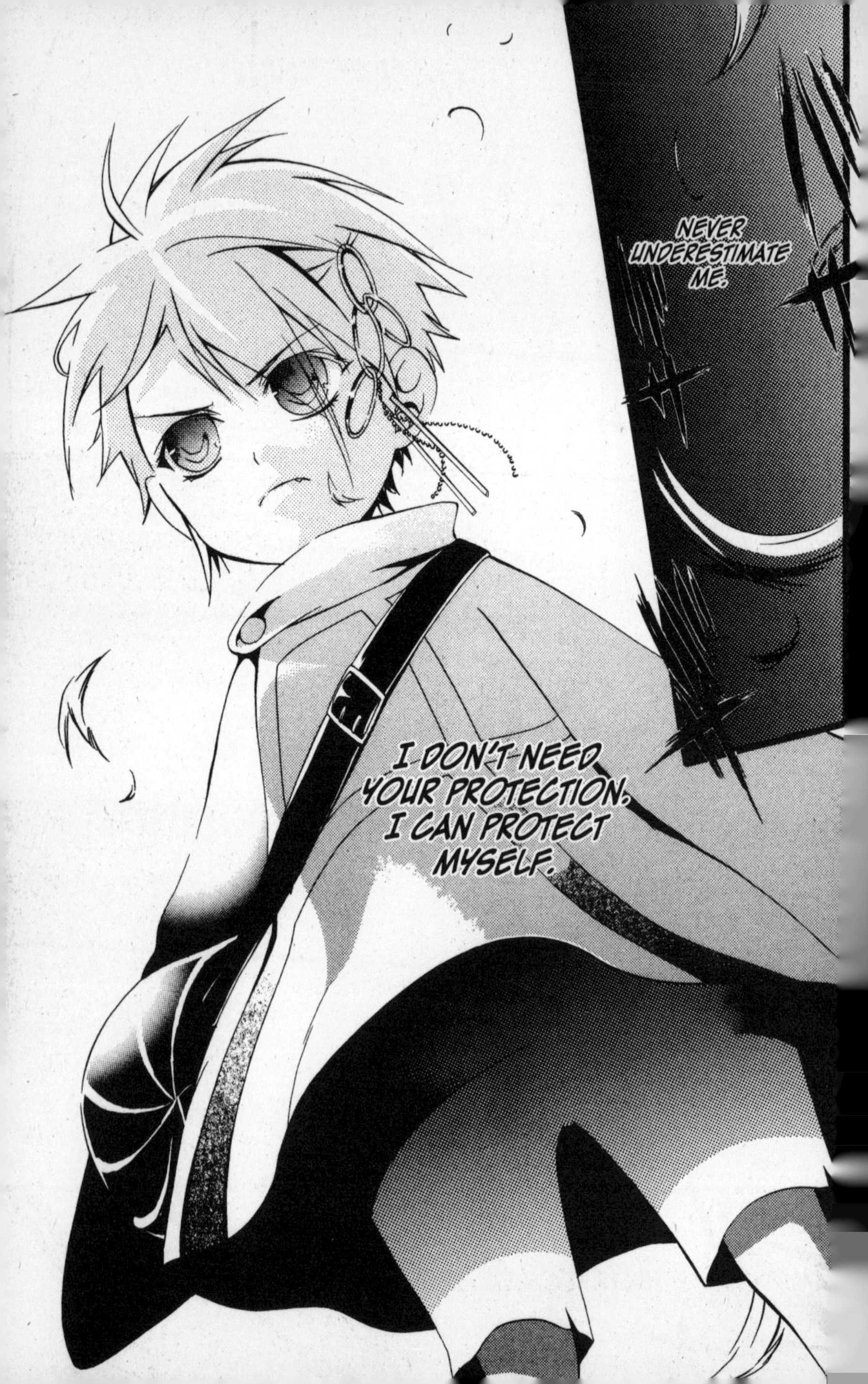
NEVER UNDERESTIMATE ME.
I DON'T NEED YOUR PROTECTION. I CAN PROTECT MYSELF.

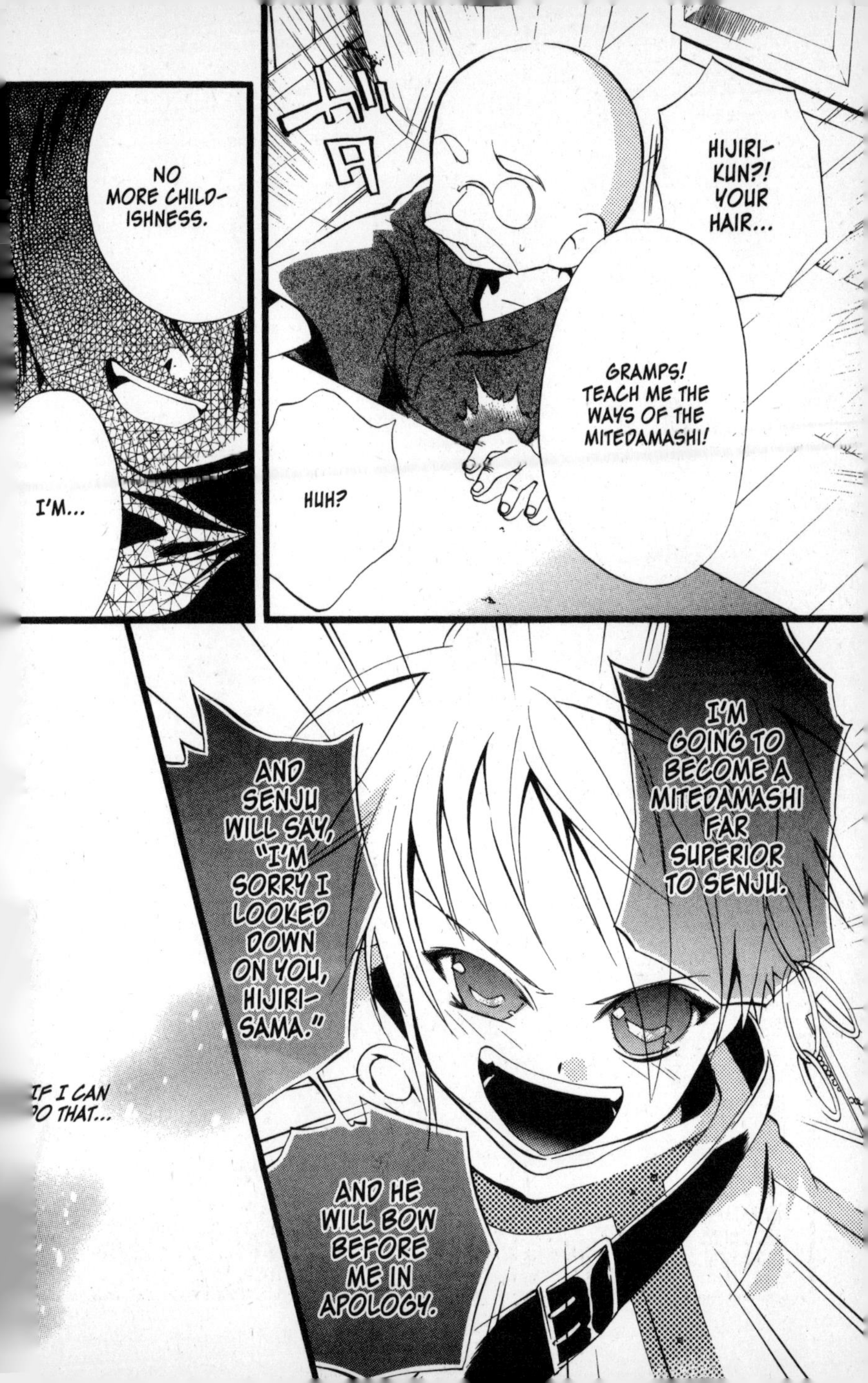
HIJIRI-KUN?! YOUR HAIR...
GRAMPS! TEACH ME THE WAYS OF THE MITEDAMASHI!
HUH?
NO MORE CHILDISHNESS.
I'M...
I'M GOING TO BECOME A MITEDAMASHI FAR SUPERIOR TO SENJU.
AND SENJU WILL SAY, "I'M SORRY I LOOKED DOWN ON YOU, HIJIRI-SAMA."
AND HE WILL BOW BEFORE ME IN APOLOGY.
IF I CAN DO THAT...

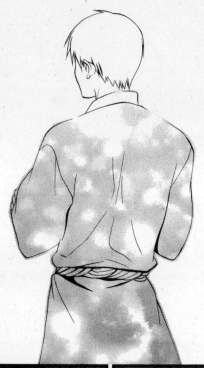

...HE WILL RETURN.

YEAH?

NEVER MIND THE ATTITUDE. OLD MAN HAZAMA'S LOOKING FOR YOU.

HEY, HIJIRI!

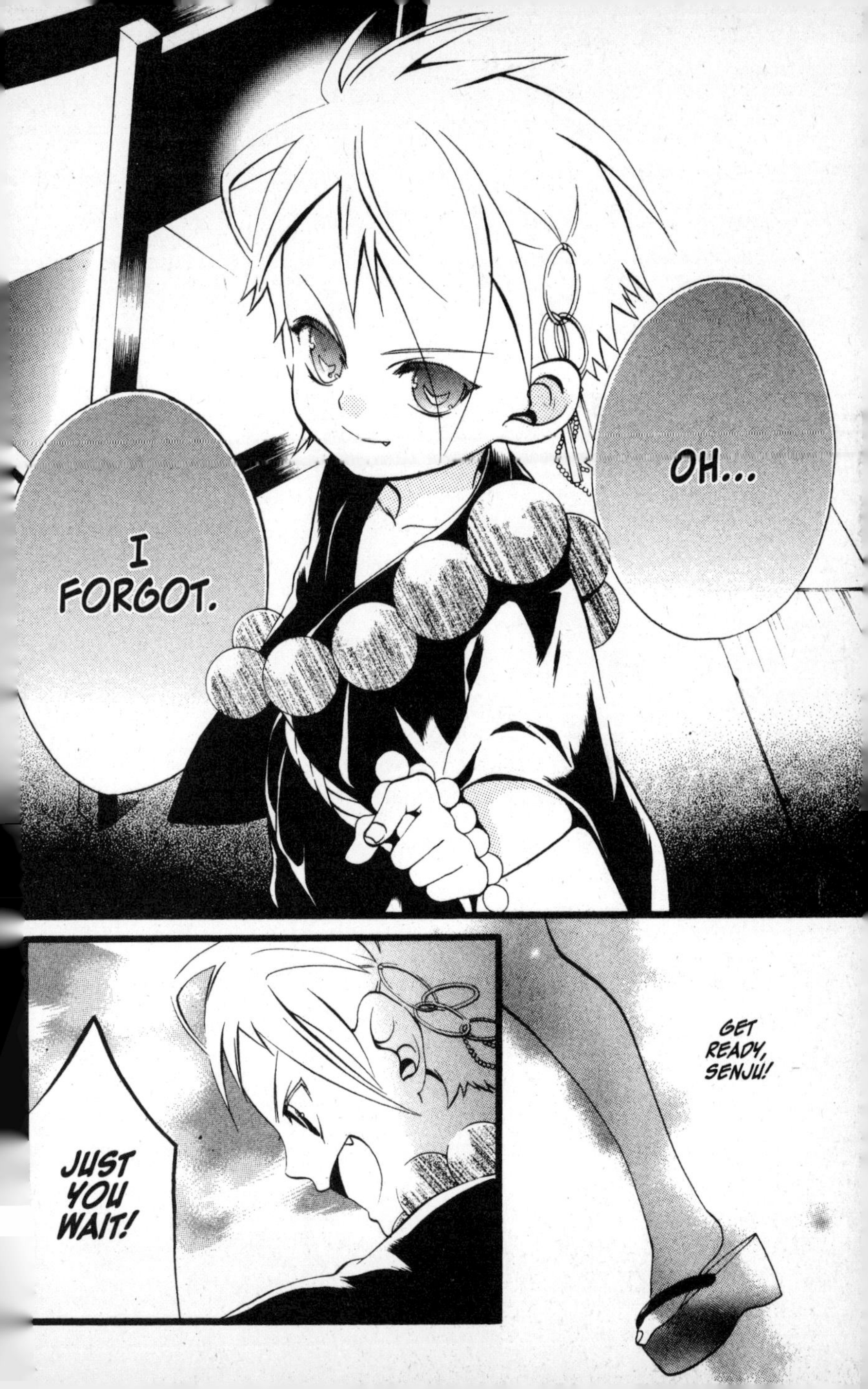
OH...
I FORGOT.
GET READY, SENJU!
JUST YOU WAIT!

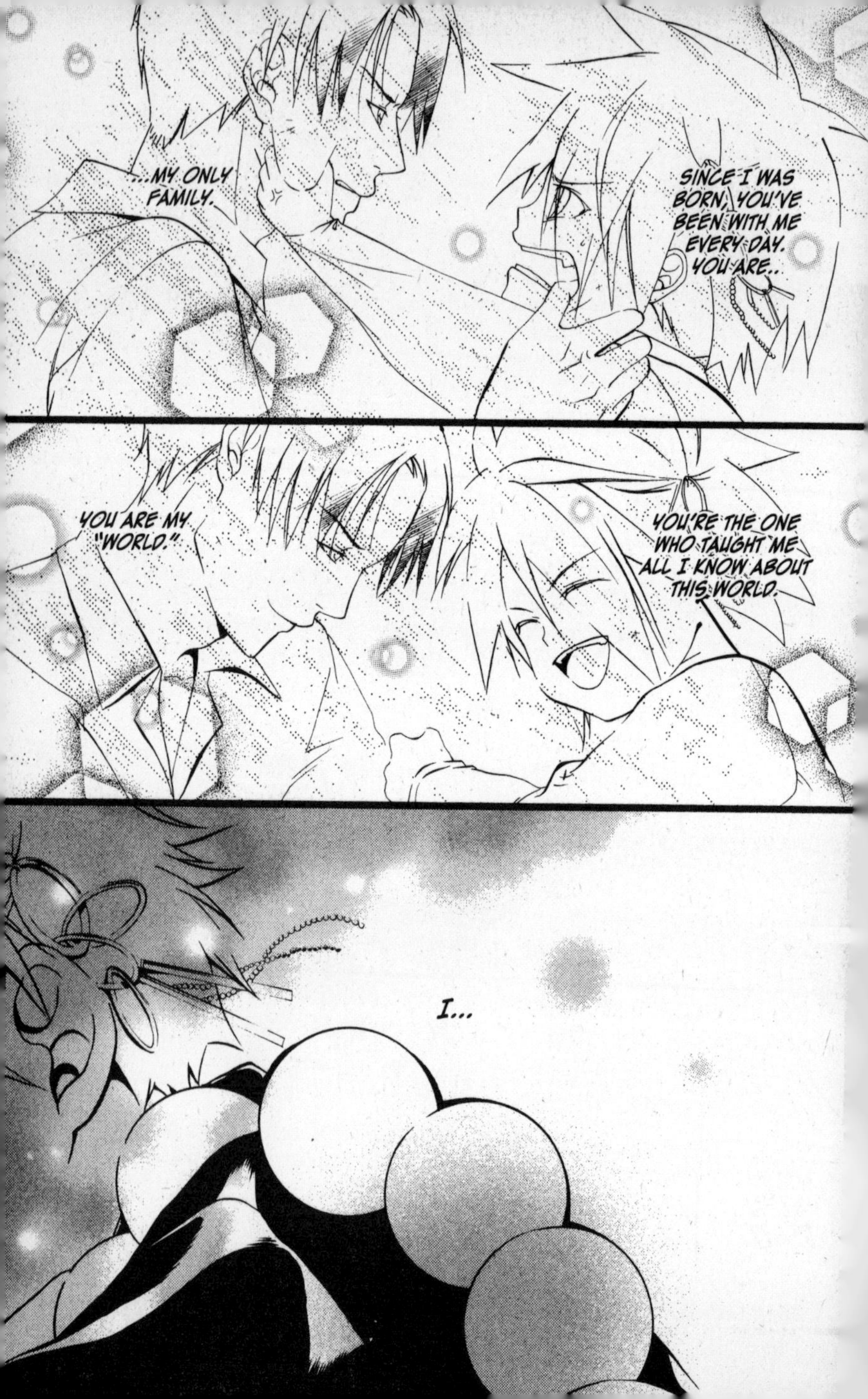
SINCE I WAS BORN, YOU'VE BEEN WITH ME EVERY DAY. YOU ARE...
...MY ONLY FAMILY.
YOU'RE THE ONE WHO TAUGHT ME ALL I KNOW ABOUT THIS WORLD.
YOU ARE MY "WORLD."
I...

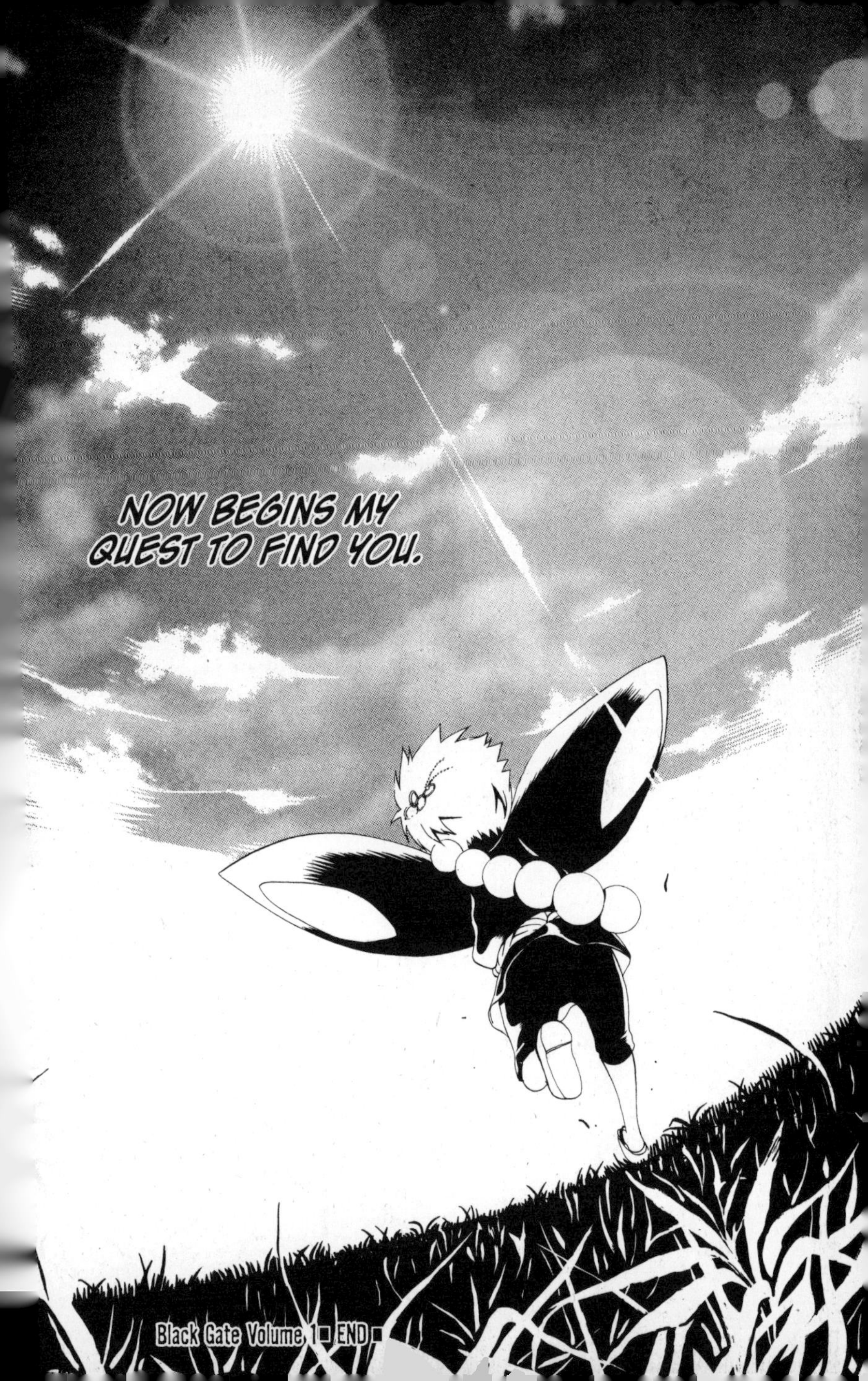
NOW BEGINS MY QUEST TO FIND YOU.
Black Gate Volume 1 END

Afterword

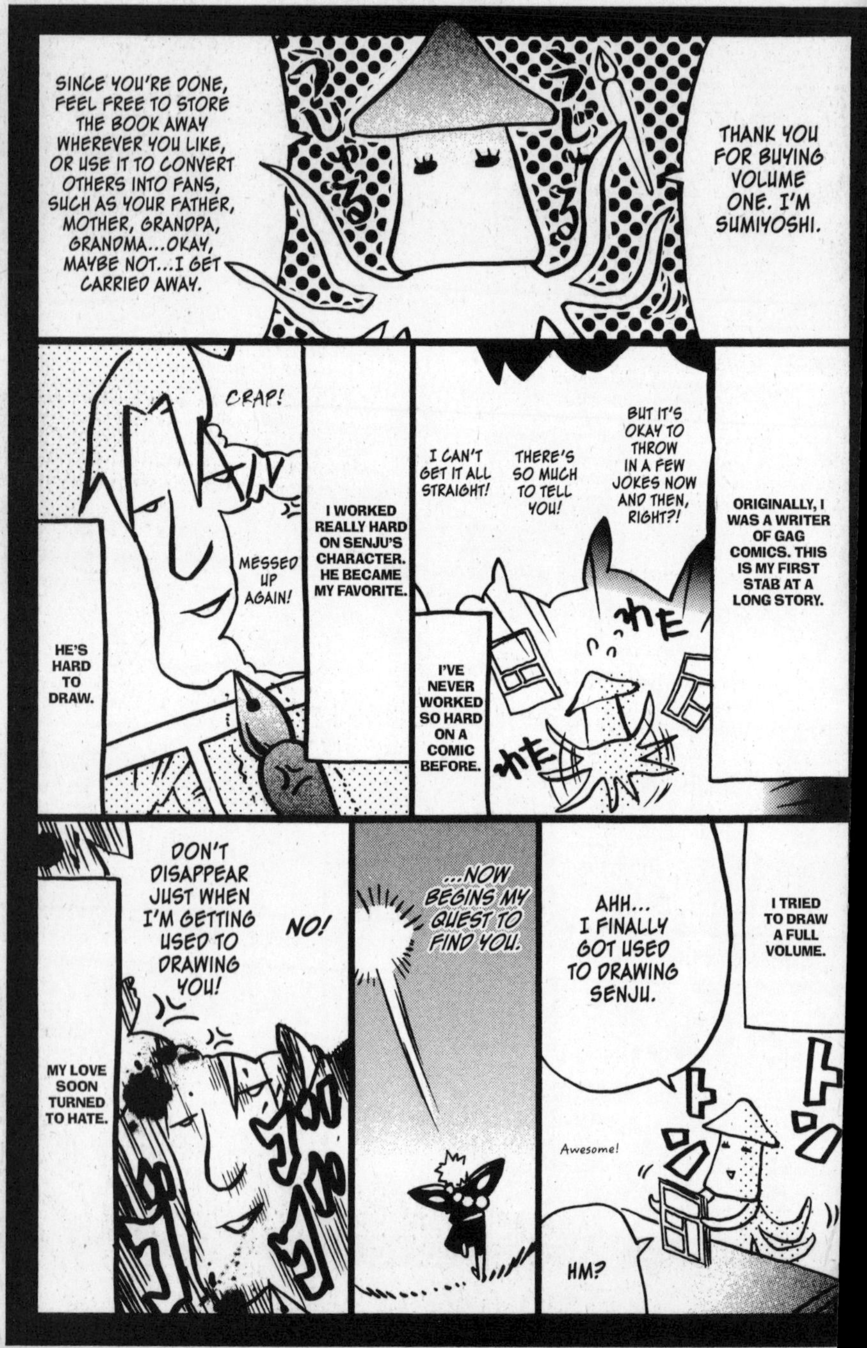
THANK YOU FOR BUYING VOLUME ONE. I'M SUMIYOSHI.
SINCE YOU'RE DONE, FEEL FREE TO STORE THE BOOK AWAY WHEREVER YOU LIKE, OR USE IT TO CONVERT OTHERS INTO FANS, SUCH AS YOUR FATHER, MOTHER, GRANDPA, GRANDMA...OKAY, MAYBE NOT...I GET CARRIED AWAY.
ORIGINALLY, I WAS A WRITER OF GAG COMICS. THIS IS MY FIRST STAB AT A LONG STORY.
BUT IT'S OKAY TO THROW IN A FEW JOKES NOW AND THEN, RIGHT?!
THERE'S SO MUCH TO TELL YOU!
I CAN'T GET IT ALL STRAIGHT!
I'VE NEVER WORKED SO HARD ON A COMIC BEFORE.
I WORKED REALLY HARD ON SENJU'S CHARACTER. HE BECAME MY FAVORITE.
CRAP!
MESSED UP AGAIN!
HE'S HARD TO DRAW.
I TRIED TO DRAW A FULL VOLUME.
AHH... I FINALLY GOT USED TO DRAWING SENJU.
Awesome!
HM?
...NOW BEGINS MY QUEST TO FIND YOU.
DON'T DISAPPEAR JUST WHEN I'M GETTING USED TO DRAWING YOU!
NO!
MY LOVE SOON TURNED TO HATE.

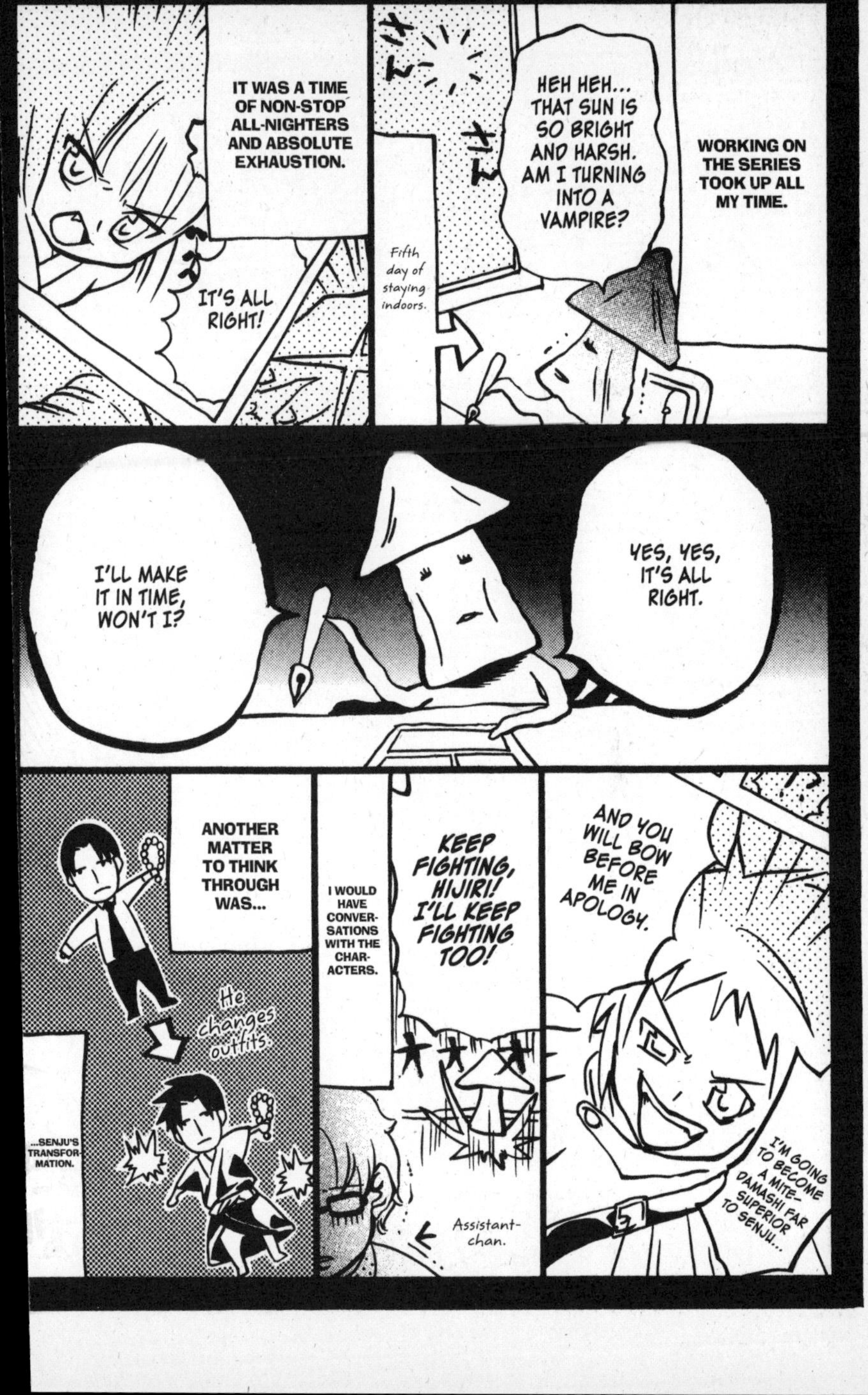
WORKING ON THE SERIES TOOK UP ALL MY TIME.
HEH HEH... THAT SUN IS SO BRIGHT AND HARSH. AM I TURNING INTO A VAMPIRE?
Fifth day of staying indoors.
IT WAS A TIME OF NON-STOP ALL-NIGHTERS AND ABSOLUTE EXHAUSTION.
IT'S ALL RIGHT!
YES, YES, IT'S ALL RIGHT.
I'LL MAKE IT IN TIME, WON'T I?
I'M GOING TO BECOME A MITE-DAMASHI FAR SUPERIOR TO SENJU...
AND YOU WILL BOW BEFORE ME IN APOLOGY.
I WOULD HAVE CONVERSATIONS WITH THE CHARACTERS.
KEEP FIGHTING, HIJIRI! I'LL KEEP FIGHTING TOO!
Assistant-chan.
ANOTHER MATTER TO THINK THROUGH WAS...
He changes outfits.
...SENJU'S TRANSFORMATION.

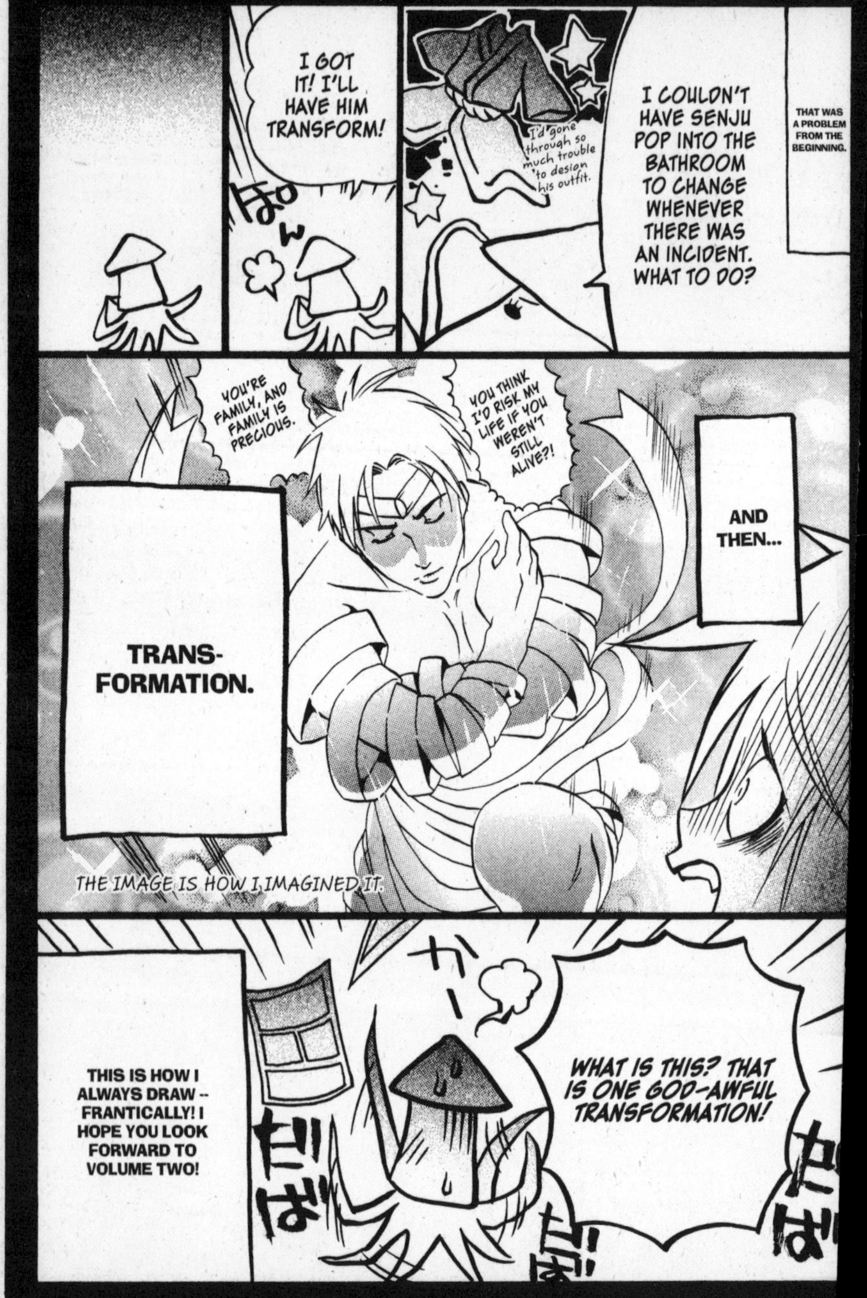
THAT WAS A PROBLEM FROM THE BEGINNING.
I COULDN'T HAVE SENJU POP INTO THE BATHROOM TO CHANGE WHENEVER THERE WAS AN INCIDENT. WHAT TO DO?
I'd gone through so much trouble to design his outfit.
I GOT IT! I'LL HAVE HIM TRANSFORM!
AND THEN...
YOU THINK I'D RISK MY LIFE IF YOU WEREN'T STILL ALIVE?!
YOU'RE FAMILY, AND FAMILY IS PRECIOUS.
TRANS-FORMATION.
THE IMAGE IS HOW I IMAGINED IT.
WHAT IS THIS? THAT IS ONE GOD-AWFUL TRANSFORMATION!
THIS IS HOW I ALWAYS DRAW -- FRANTICALLY! I HOPE YOU LOOK FORWARD TO VOLUME TWO!

Afterword ■End■

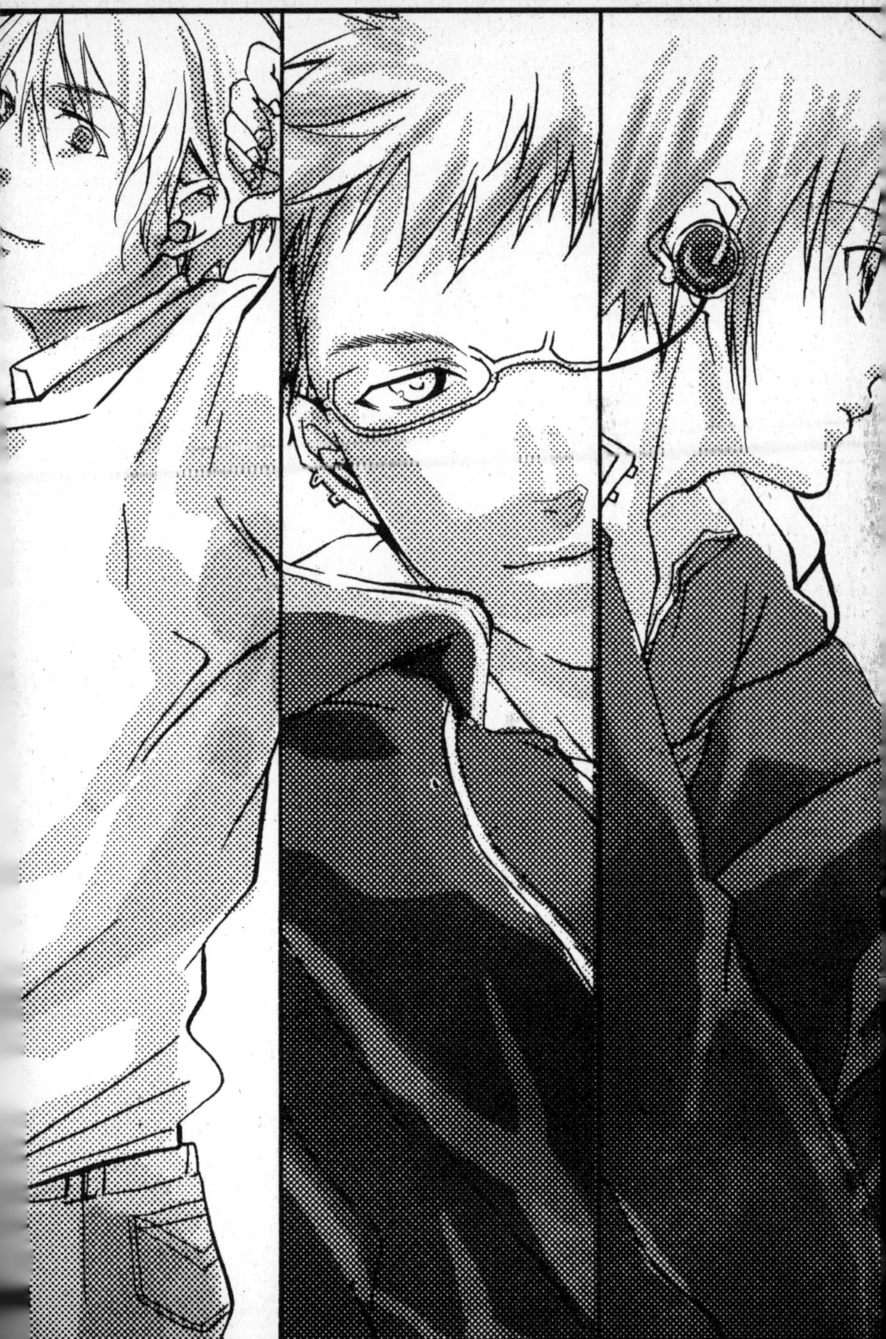

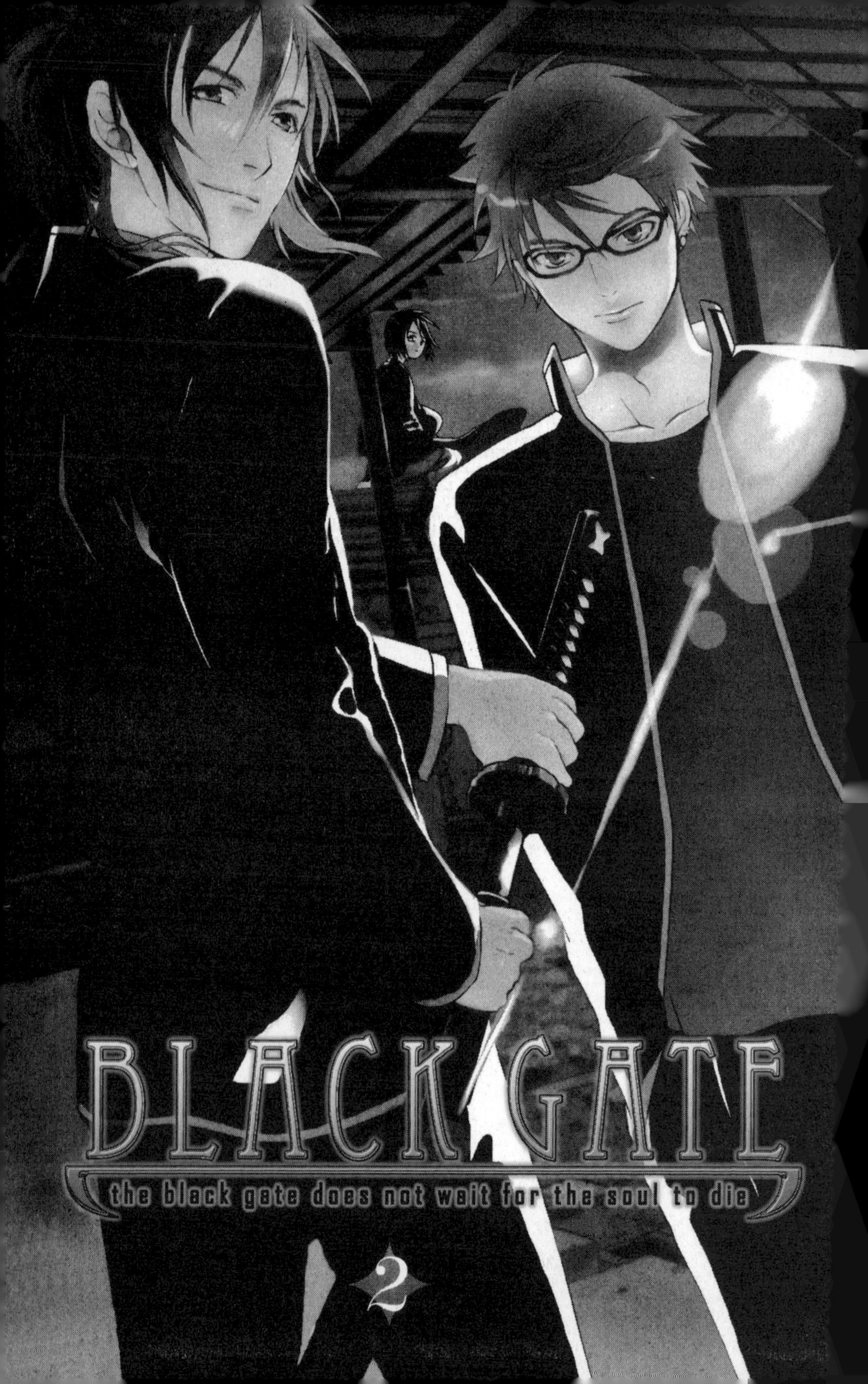

BLACK GATE
the black gate does not wait for the soul to die
2

Characters & Story Guide

The story so far...

BLACK GATE

the black gate does not wait for the soul to die

IN THIS WORLD, THERE EXIST CERTAIN "PATHWAYS FOR THE SOULS," OTHERWISE CALLED "SPIRITUAL PATHWAYS" OR "GATES." NORMALLY, WHEN THE BODY OF A LIVING THING DIES, ITS SOUL SEPARATES FROM THE BODY AND PASSES THROUGH WHAT IS CALLED A "WHITE GATE," ON ITS WAY TO ITS NEXT EXISTENCE. BUT THERE ALSO EXIST "BLACK GATES," WHICH ARE RARE, BUT DANGEROUS. NOT CONTENT SIMPLY WITH THE SOULS OF THOSE WHO HAVE DIED NATURALLY, THESE BLACK GATES ATTEMPT TO FORCEFULLY PULL IN THE SOULS OF THINGS STILL ALIVE. BLACK GATES ARE KNOWN TO START ACCIDENTS SUCH AS MYSTERIOUS FIRES AND OTHER DISASTERS WITH UNKNOWN CAUSES, IN THEIR ATTEMPT TO DEVOUR MORE SOULS.

THERE ARE THOSE AMONG US WITH THE POWER TO SEE AND CLOSE THESE DANGEROUS GATES. THESE RARE INDIVIDUALS ARE CALLED "MITEDAMASHI."

ONE SUCH MITEDAMASHI, SENJU, HAS BEEN THE GUARDIAN TO HIJIRI, A YOUNG BOY AND THE SON OF SENJU'S BENEFACTOR. AS HE'S GROWN OLDER, THE ABILITY TO DETECT AND CLOSE GATES HAS BEGUN TO AWAKEN WITHIN HIJIRI. NOTICING HIJIRI'S POWERS GROWING STRONGER BY THE DAY, SENJU DECIDES TO TELL HIJIRI THE TRUTH OF HIS PARENTS' DEATHS AND HIS OWN ORIGINS.

LONG AGO, HIJIRI'S FATHER, YOSHITSUNA, WAS THE LEADER OF THE GATE-KEEPERS. HE LIVED WITH HIS WIFE, KUZUNOHA, AND HIS YOUNGER BROTHER, KIKYO. TOGETHER, THEY CARED FOR THE HUMAN, SENJU, THEN JUST A YOUNG BOY.

THEIR DAYS OF PEACE, HOWEVER, WERE BRIEF. A MOB OF HUMAN BEINGS, DEMANDING IMMORTALITY, KILLED YOSHITSUNA, KUZUNOHA, AND KIKYO, LEAVING SENJU TO CARE FOR HIJIRI. AFTER TELLING HIJIRI THIS STORY, SENJU LEAVES HIM, VANISHING INTO SOME UNKNOWN DESTINATION.

LEFT TO FEND FOR HIMSELF, HIJIRI DETERMINES TO BECOME A GREAT MITEDAMASHI AND TO SEEK OUT SENJU.

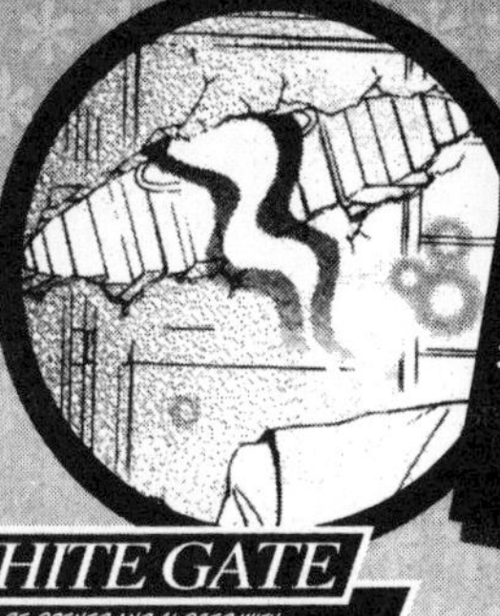

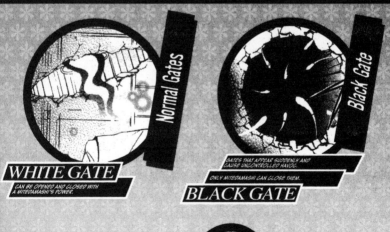

Normal Gates

WHITE GATE

CAN BE OPENED AND CLOSED WITH A MITEDAMASHI'S POWER.

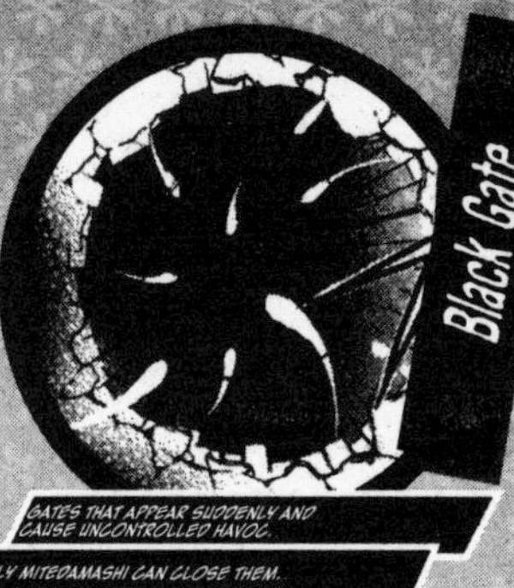

Black Gate

GATES THAT APPEAR SUDDENLY AND CAUSE UNCONTROLLED HAVOC.

ONLY MITEDAMASHI CAN CLOSE THEM.

BLACK GATE

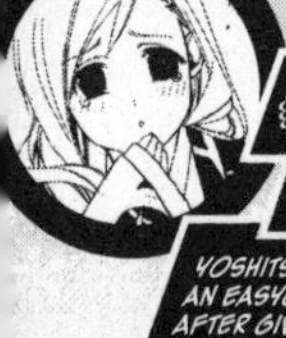

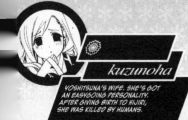

kuzunoha

YOSHITSUNA'S WIFE. SHE'S GOT AN EASYGOING PERSONALITY. AFTER GIVING BIRTH TO HIJIRI, SHE WAS KILLED BY HUMANS.

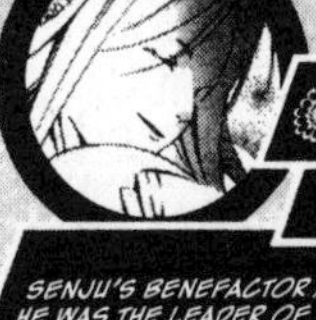

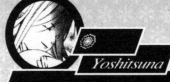

Yoshitsuna

SENJU'S BENEFACTOR AND HIJIRI'S FATHER. HE WAS THE LEADER OF THE GATE-KEEPERS BUT WAS KILLED BY A MOB OF HUMANS DEMANDING IMMORTALITY. BEFORE DYING, HE ENTRUSTED HIJIRI TO SENJU'S PROTECTION.

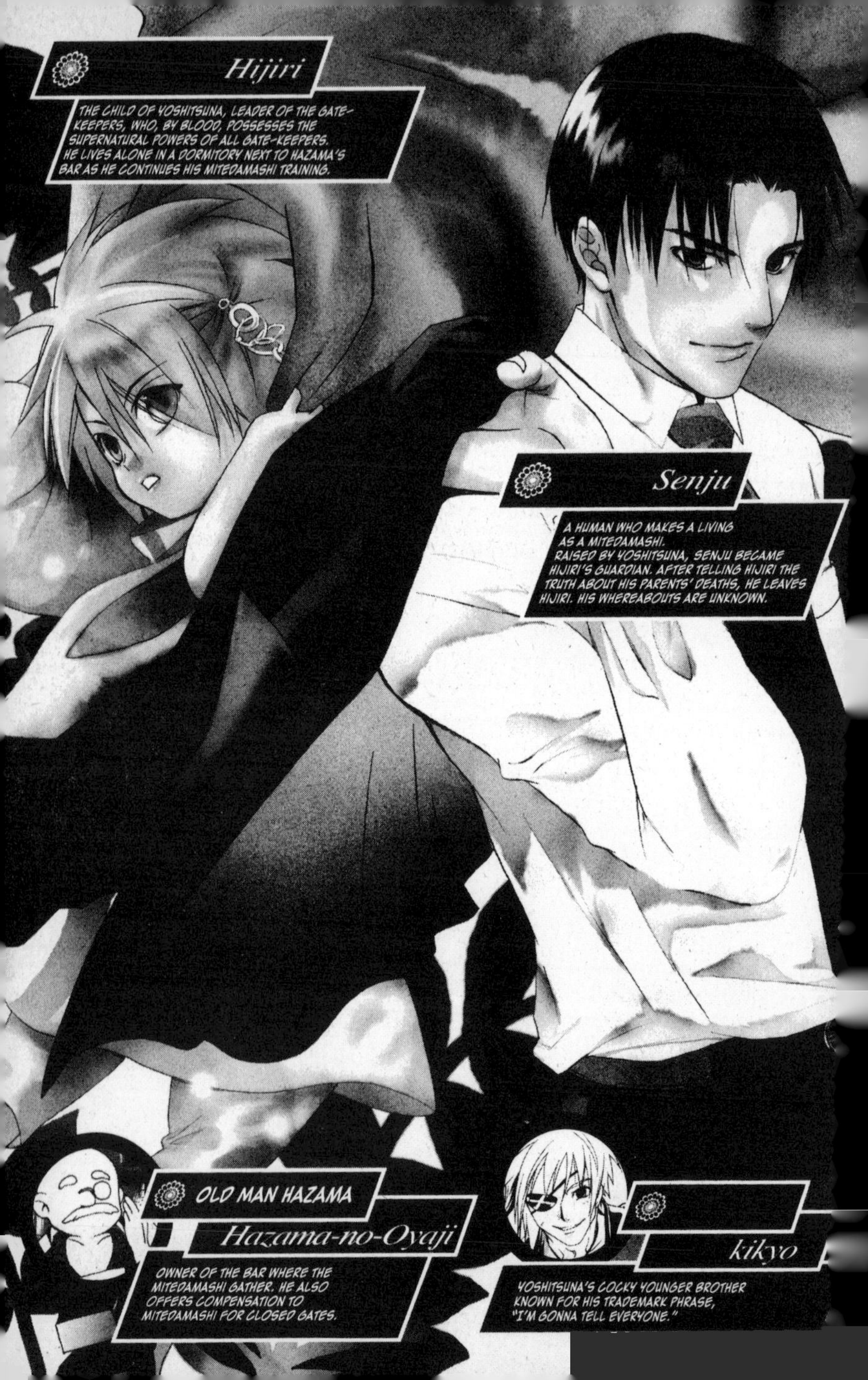
Hijiri
THE CHILD OF YOSHITSUNA, LEADER OF THE GATE-KEEPERS, WHO, BY BLOOD, POSSESSES THE SUPERNATURAL POWERS OF ALL GATE-KEEPERS. HE LIVES ALONE IN A DORMITORY NEXT TO HAZAMA'S BAR AS HE CONTINUES HIS MITEDAMASHI TRAINING.
Senju
A HUMAN WHO MAKES A LIVING AS A MITEDAMASHI. RAISED BY YOSHITSUNA, SENJU BECAME HIJIRI'S GUARDIAN. AFTER TELLING HIJIRI THE TRUTH ABOUT HIS PARENTS' DEATHS, HE LEAVES HIJIRI. HIS WHEREABOUTS ARE UNKNOWN.
kikyo
YOSHITSUNA'S COCKY YOUNGER BROTHER KNOWN FOR HIS TRADEMARK PHRASE, "I'M GONNA TELL EVERYONE."
OLD MAN HAZAMA
Hazama-no-Oyaji
OWNER OF THE BAR WHERE THE MITEDAMASHI GATHER. HE ALSO OFFERS COMPENSATION TO MITEDAMASHI FOR CLOSED GATES.

CONTENTS

SOUL.7 219
SOUL.8 253
SOUL.9 285
SOUL.10 318
SOUL.11 357
SOUL.12 393
Afterword 435

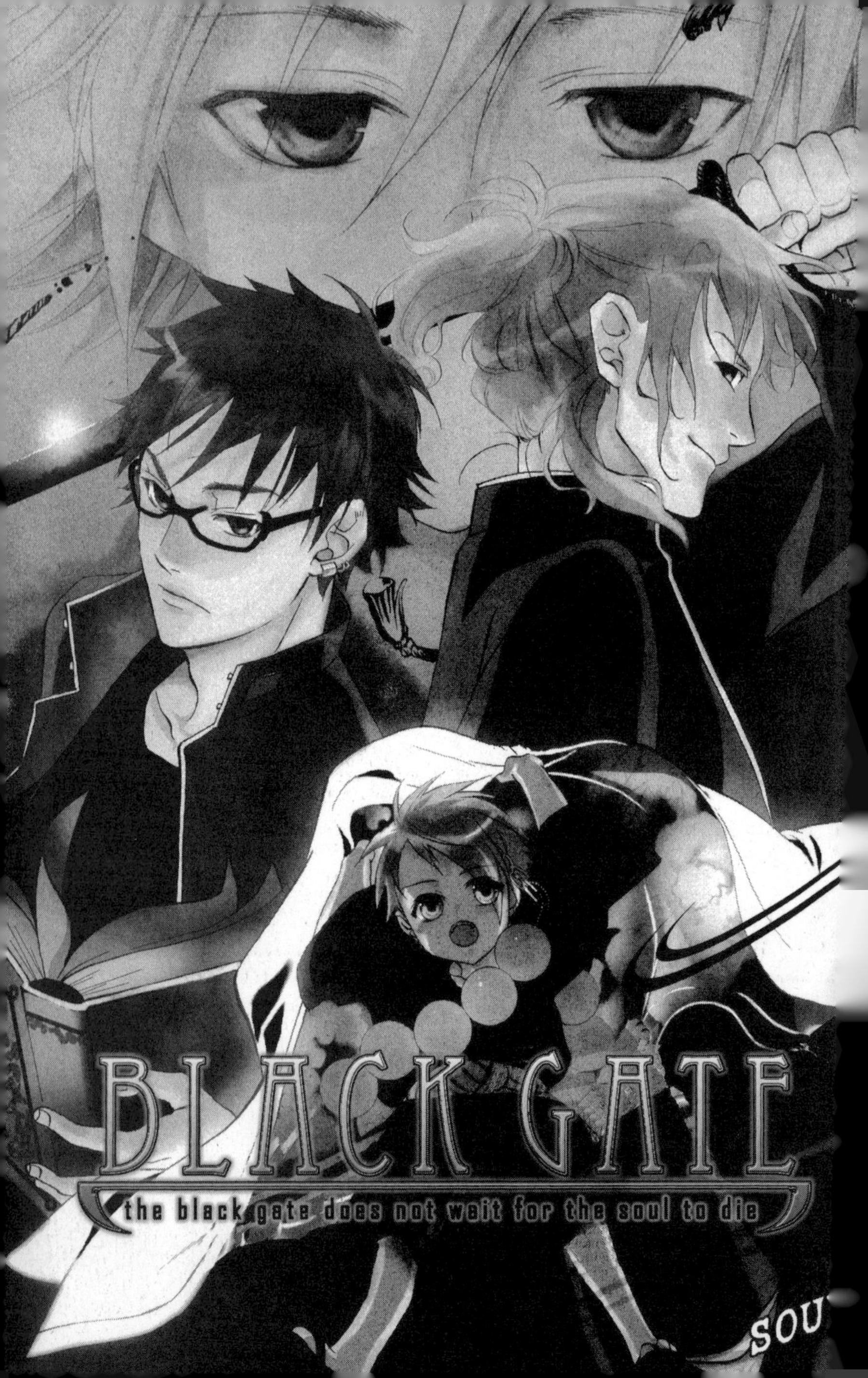
BLACK GATE
the black gate does not wait for the soul to die
SOU

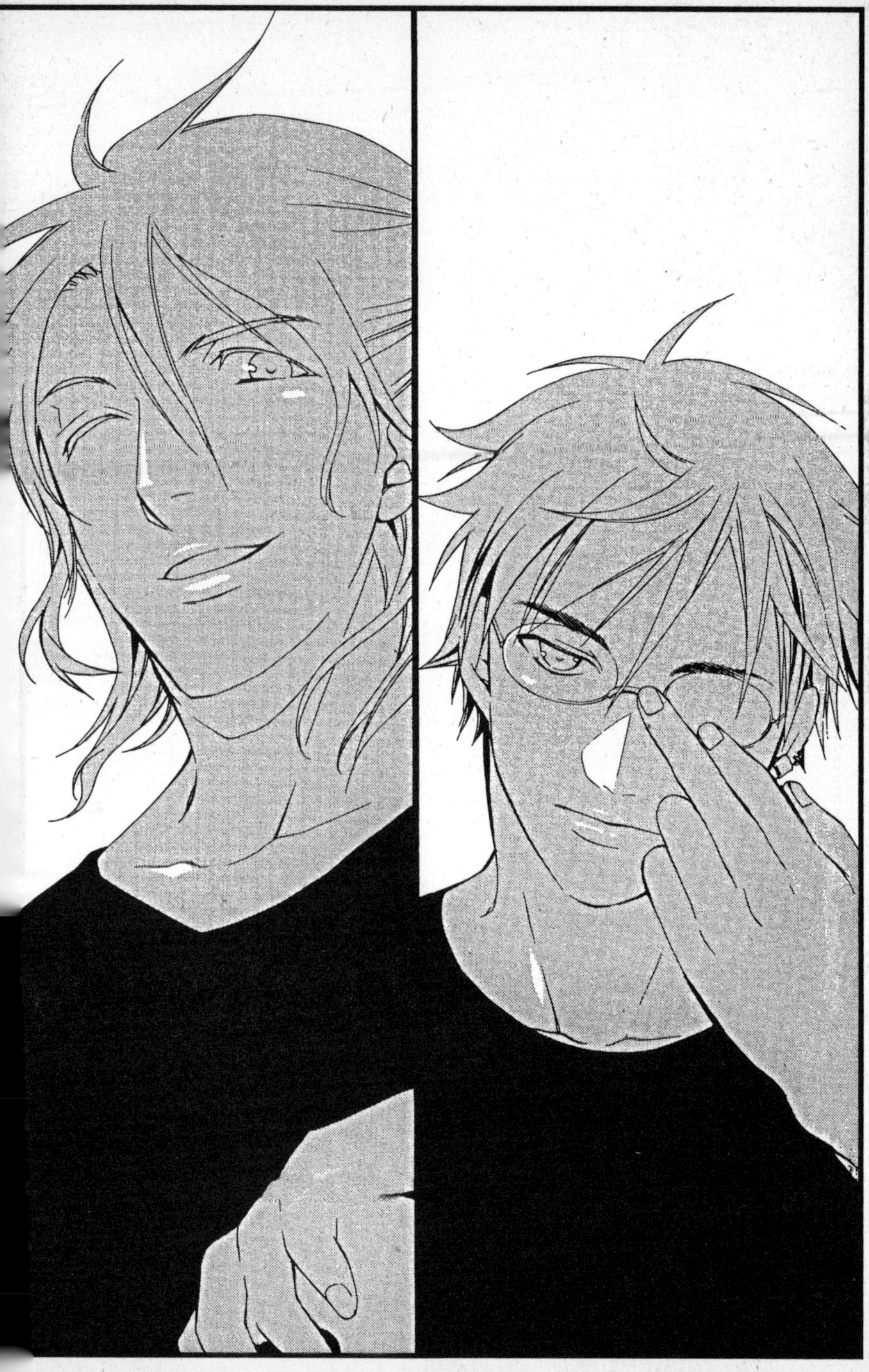

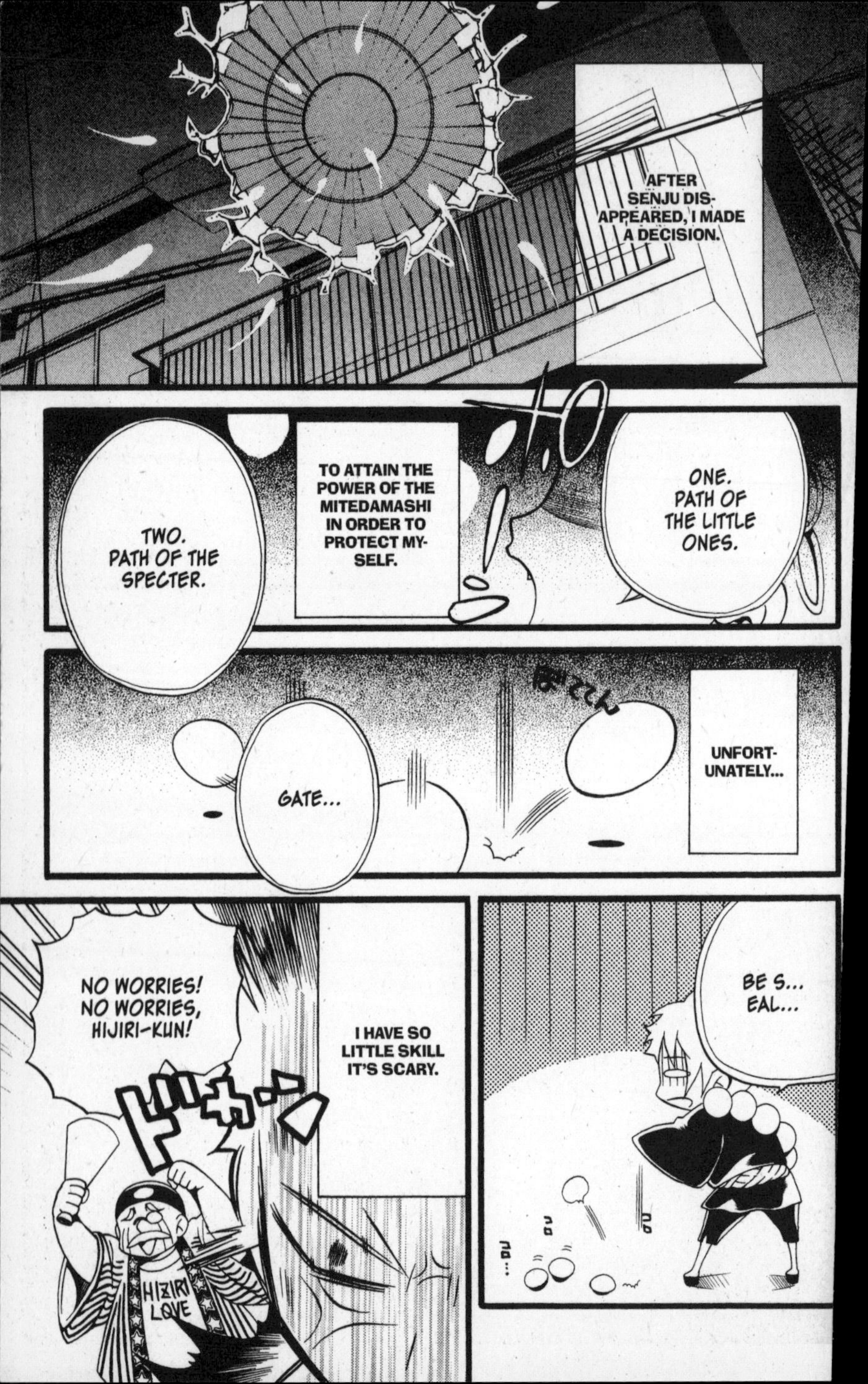
AFTER SENJU DIS-APPEARED, I MADE A DECISION.
ONE. PATH OF THE LITTLE ONES.
TO ATTAIN THE POWER OF THE MITEDAMASHI IN ORDER TO PROTECT MY-SELF.
TWO. PATH OF THE SPECTER.
UNFORT-UNATELY...
GATE...
BE S... EAL...
I HAVE SO LITTLE SKILL IT'S SCARY.
NO WORRIES! NO WORRIES, HIJIRI-KUN!
HIZIRI LOVE

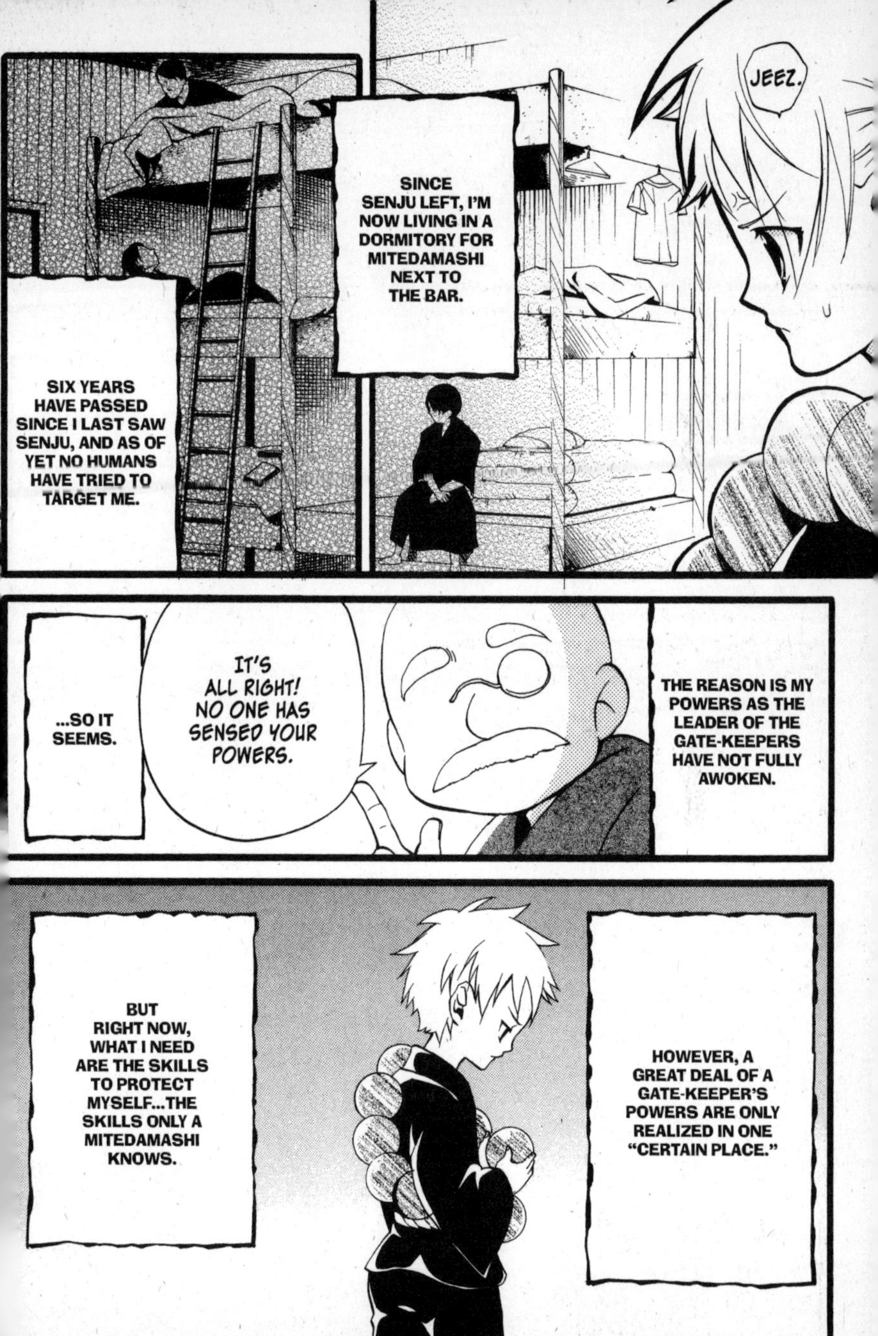
JEEZ.
SINCE SENJU LEFT, I'M NOW LIVING IN A DORMITORY FOR MITEDAMASHI NEXT TO THE BAR.
SIX YEARS HAVE PASSED SINCE I LAST SAW SENJU, AND AS OF YET NO HUMANS HAVE TRIED TO TARGET ME.
THE REASON IS MY POWERS AS THE LEADER OF THE GATE-KEEPERS HAVE NOT FULLY AWOKEN.
IT'S ALL RIGHT! NO ONE HAS SENSED YOUR POWERS.
...SO IT SEEMS.
HOWEVER, A GREAT DEAL OF A GATE-KEEPER'S POWERS ARE ONLY REALIZED IN ONE "CERTAIN PLACE."
BUT RIGHT NOW, WHAT I NEED ARE THE SKILLS TO PROTECT MYSELF...THE SKILLS ONLY A MITEDAMASHI KNOWS.

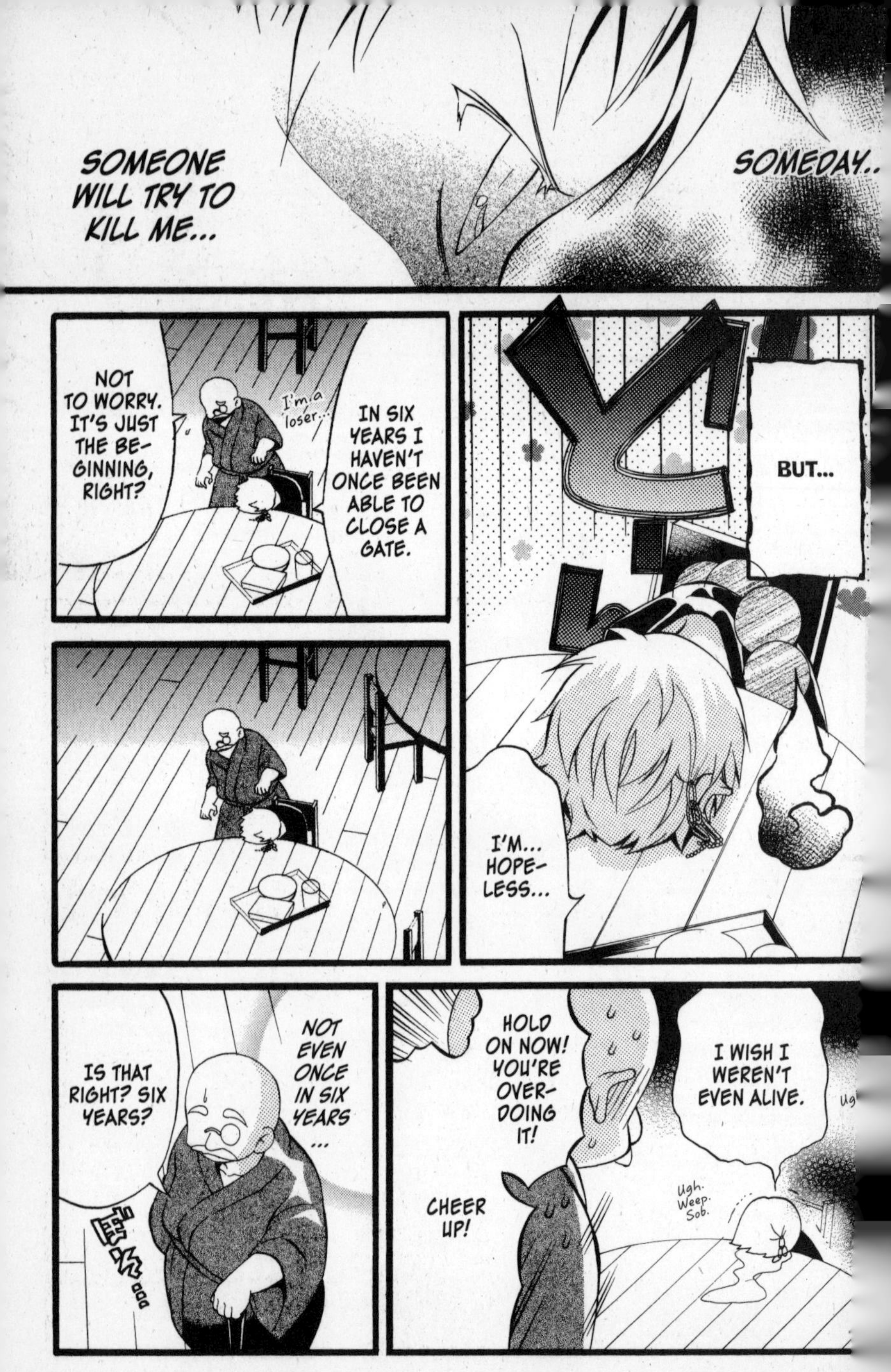
SOMEDAY...
SOMEONE WILL TRY TO KILL ME...
BUT...
I'M... HOPELESS...
IN SIX YEARS I HAVEN'T ONCE BEEN ABLE TO CLOSE A GATE.
I'm a loser...
NOT TO WORRY. IT'S JUST THE BEGINNING, RIGHT?
I WISH I WEREN'T EVEN ALIVE.
HOLD ON NOW! YOU'RE OVERDOING IT!
Ugh. Weep. Sob.
CHEER UP!
NOT EVEN ONCE IN SIX YEARS ...
IS THAT RIGHT? SIX YEARS?

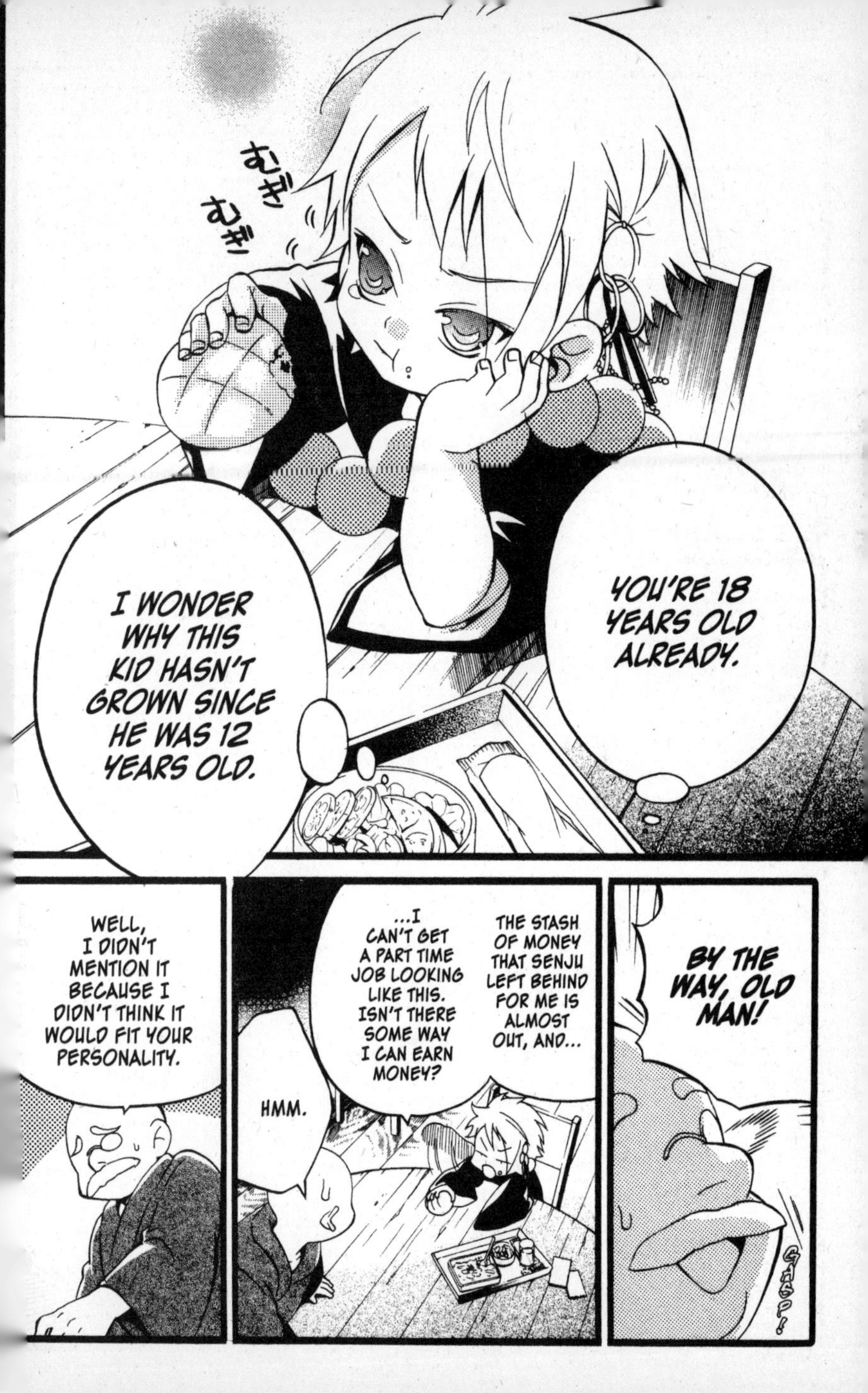
むぎ むぎ
YOU'RE 18 YEARS OLD ALREADY.
I WONDER WHY THIS KID HASN'T GROWN SINCE HE WAS 12 YEARS OLD.
BY THE WAY, OLD MAN!
GASP!
THE STASH OF MONEY THAT SENJU LEFT BEHIND FOR ME IS ALMOST OUT, AND...
...I CAN'T GET A PART TIME JOB LOOKING LIKE THIS. ISN'T THERE SOME WAY I CAN EARN MONEY?
HMM.
WELL, I DIDN'T MENTION IT BECAUSE I DIDN'T THINK IT WOULD FIT YOUR PERSONALITY.

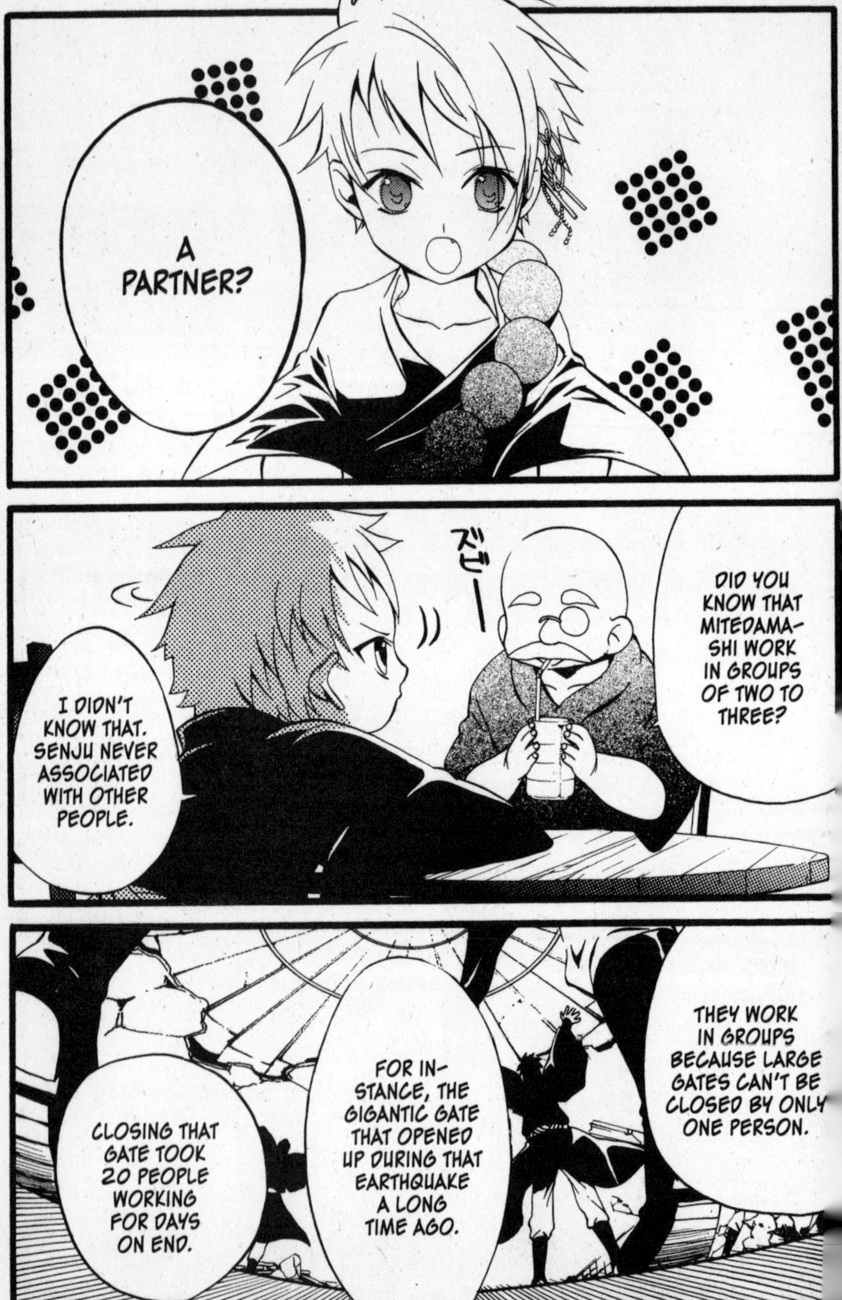
A PARTNER?
DID YOU KNOW THAT MITEDAMA-SHI WORK IN GROUPS OF TWO TO THREE?
ズビー
I DIDN'T KNOW THAT. SENJU NEVER ASSOCIATED WITH OTHER PEOPLE.
THEY WORK IN GROUPS BECAUSE LARGE GATES CAN'T BE CLOSED BY ONLY ONE PERSON.
FOR IN-STANCE, THE GIGANTIC GATE THAT OPENED UP DURING THAT EARTHQUAKE A LONG TIME AGO.
CLOSING THAT GATE TOOK 20 PEOPLE WORKING FOR DAYS ON END.

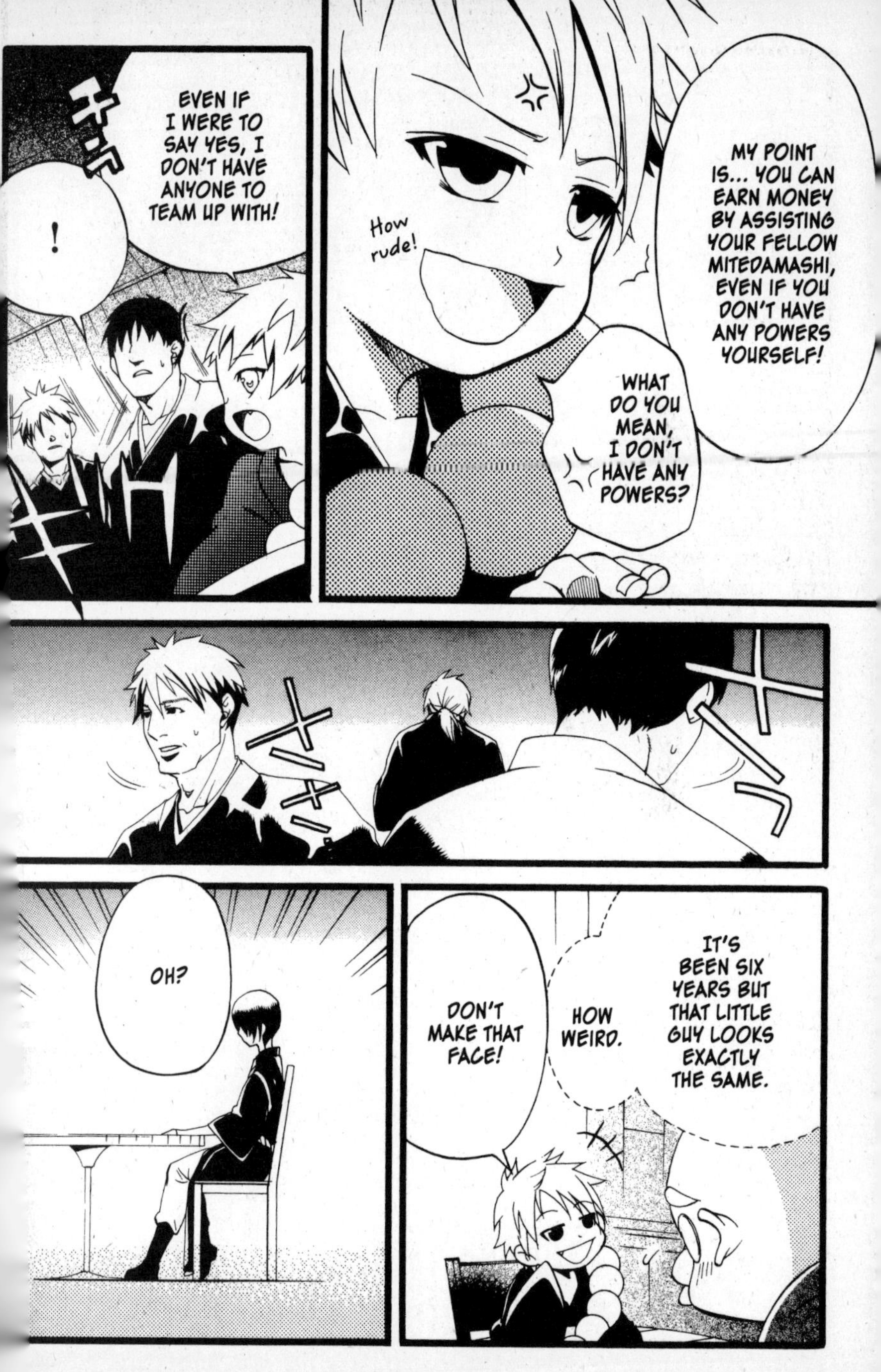
MY POINT IS... YOU CAN EARN MONEY BY ASSISTING YOUR FELLOW MITEDAMASHI, EVEN IF YOU DON'T HAVE ANY POWERS YOURSELF!
How rude!
WHAT DO YOU MEAN, I DON'T HAVE ANY POWERS?
EVEN IF I WERE TO SAY YES, I DON'T HAVE ANYONE TO TEAM UP WITH!
!
IT'S BEEN SIX YEARS BUT THAT LITTLE GUY LOOKS EXACTLY THE SAME.
HOW WEIRD.
DON'T MAKE THAT FACE!
OH?

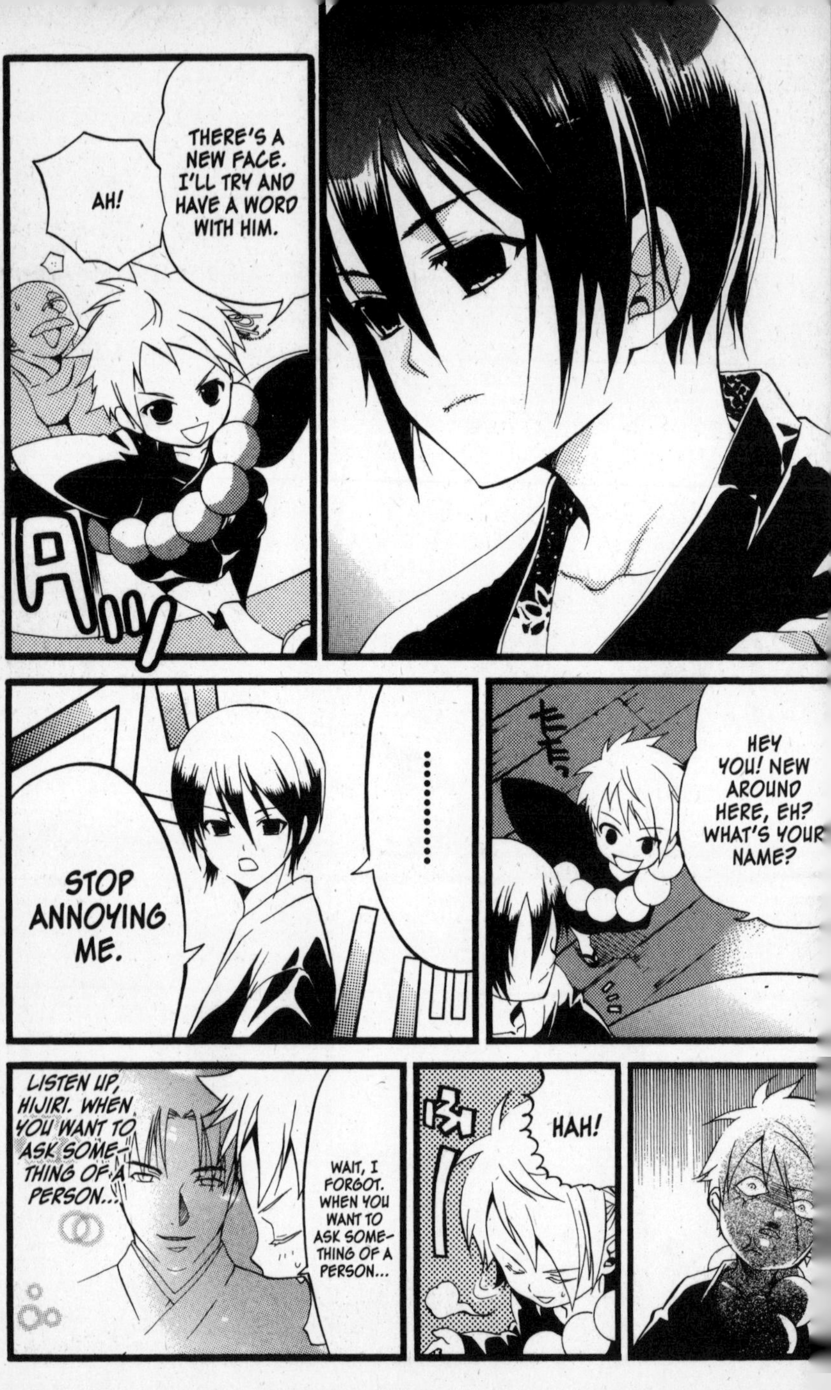
THERE'S A NEW FACE. I'LL TRY AND HAVE A WORD WITH HIM.
AH!
HEY YOU! NEW AROUND HERE, EH? WHAT'S YOUR NAME?
....
STOP ANNOYING ME.
HAH!
WAIT, I FORGOT. WHEN YOU WANT TO ASK SOME-THING OF A PERSON...
LISTEN UP, HIJIRI. WHEN YOU WANT TO ASK SOME-THING OF A PERSON...

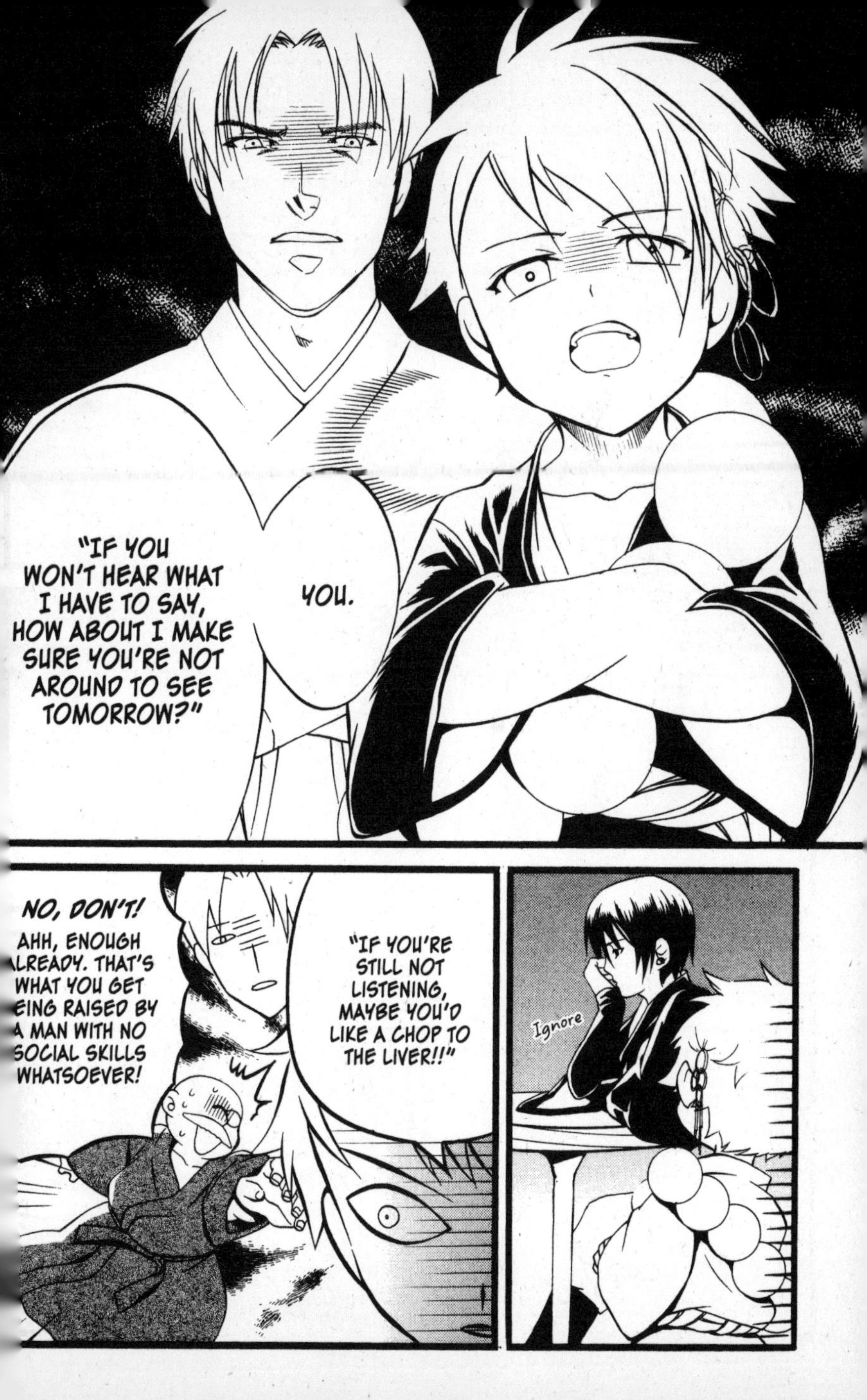
YOU.
"IF YOU WON'T HEAR WHAT I HAVE TO SAY, HOW ABOUT I MAKE SURE YOU'RE NOT AROUND TO SEE TOMORROW?"
Ignore
"IF YOU'RE STILL NOT LISTENING, MAYBE YOU'D LIKE A CHOP TO THE LIVER!!"
NO, DON'T!
AHH, ENOUGH LREADY. THAT'S WHAT YOU GET EING RAISED BY A MAN WITH NO SOCIAL SKILLS WHATSOEVER!

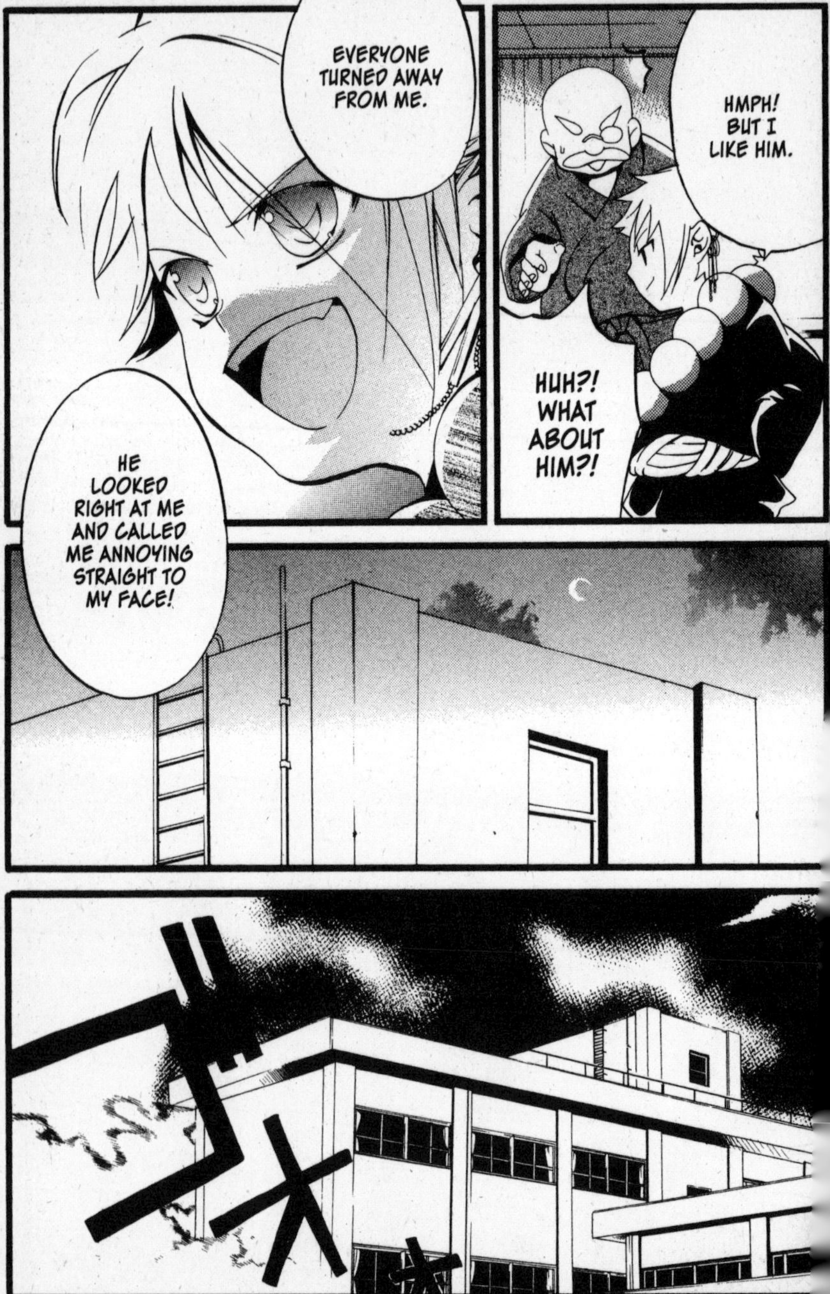
HMPH! BUT I LIKE HIM.
HUH?! WHAT ABOUT HIM?!
EVERYONE TURNED AWAY FROM ME.
HE LOOKED RIGHT AT ME AND CALLED ME ANNOYING STRAIGHT TO MY FACE!

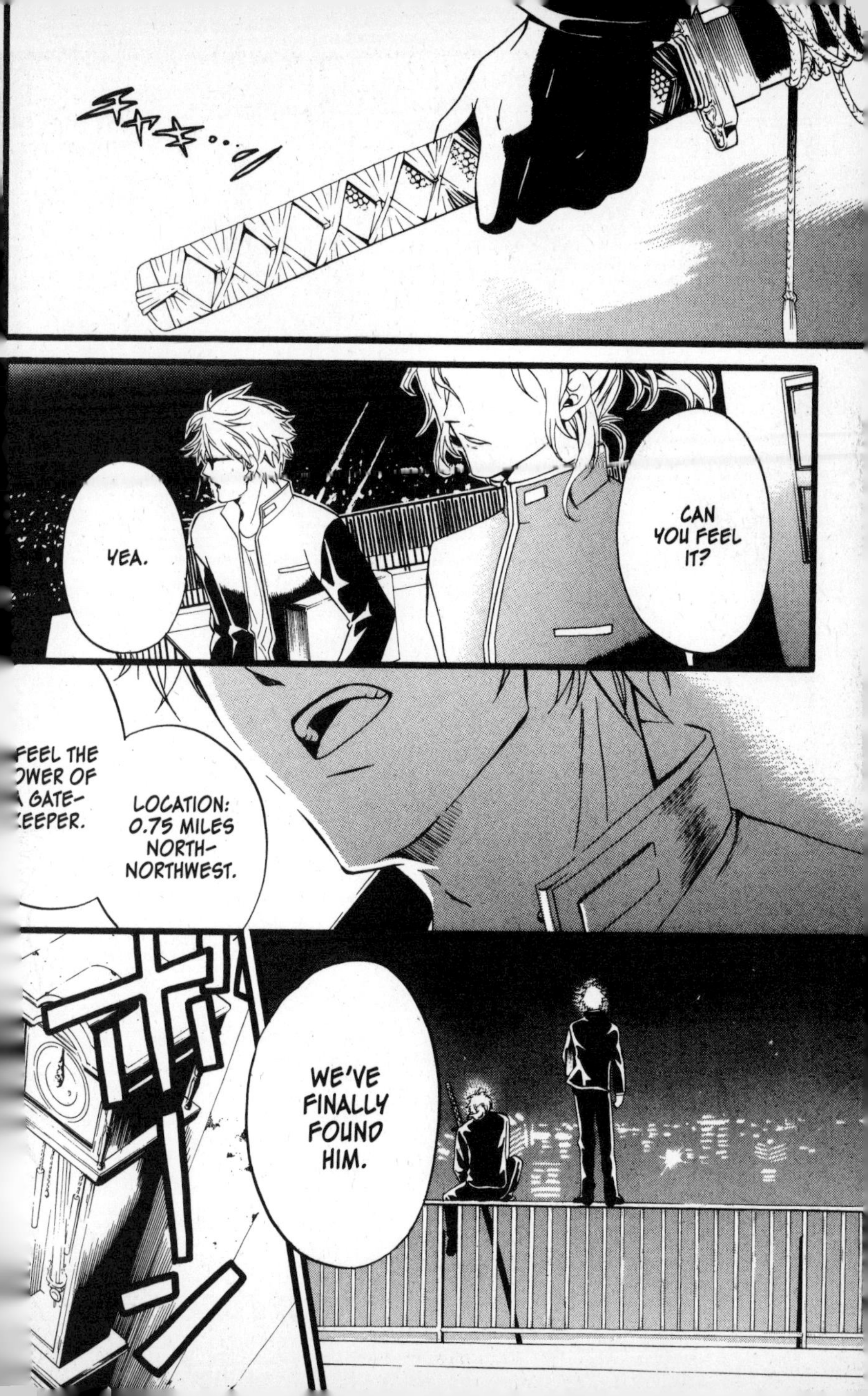
CAN YOU FEEL IT?
YEA.
LOCATION: 0.75 MILES NORTH-NORTHWEST.
FEEL THE OWER OF A GATE- EEPER.
WE'VE FINALLY FOUND HIM.

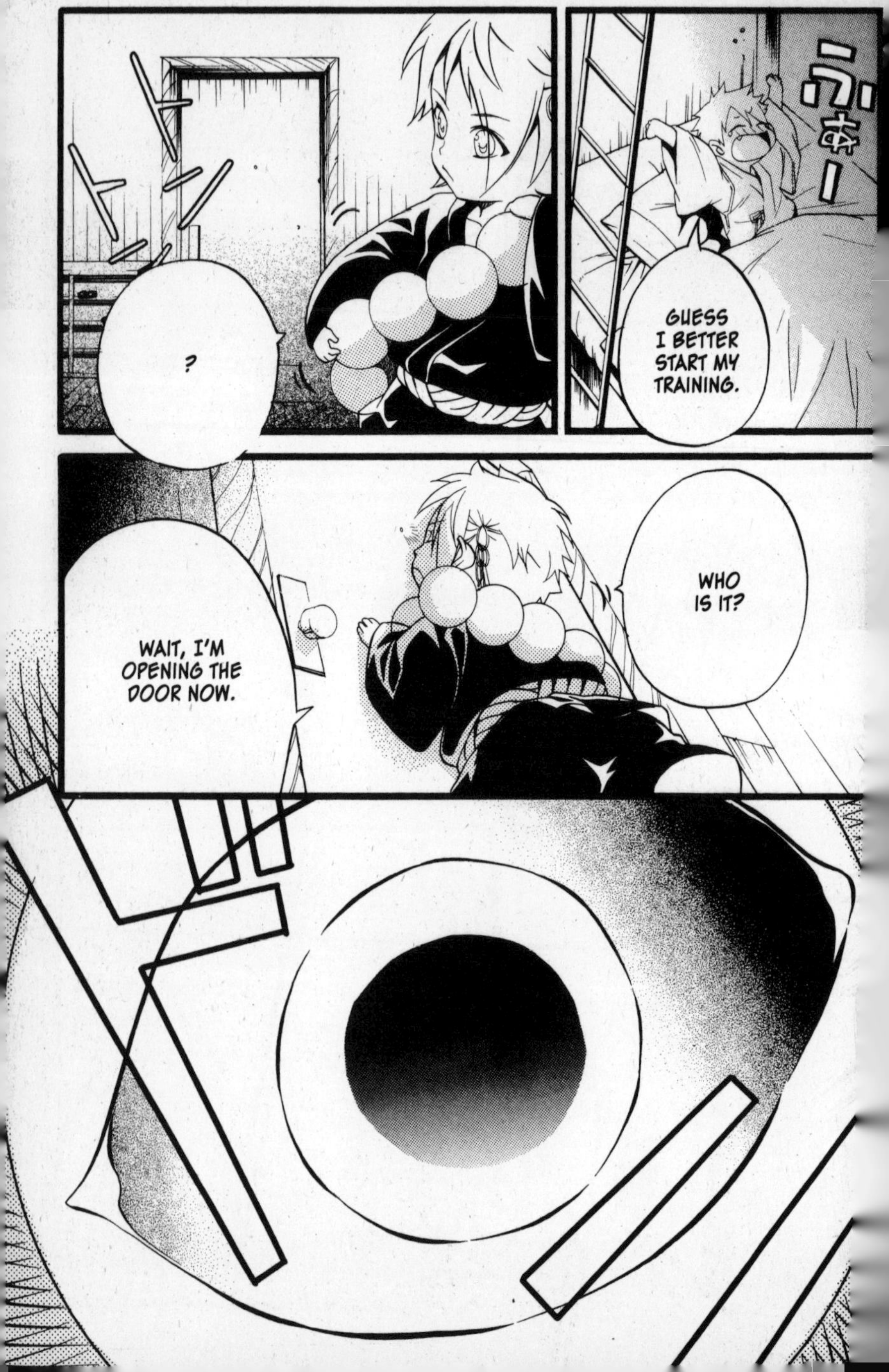
ふぁー
GUESS I BETTER START MY TRAINING.
?
WHO IS IT?
WAIT, I'M OPENING THE DOOR NOW.

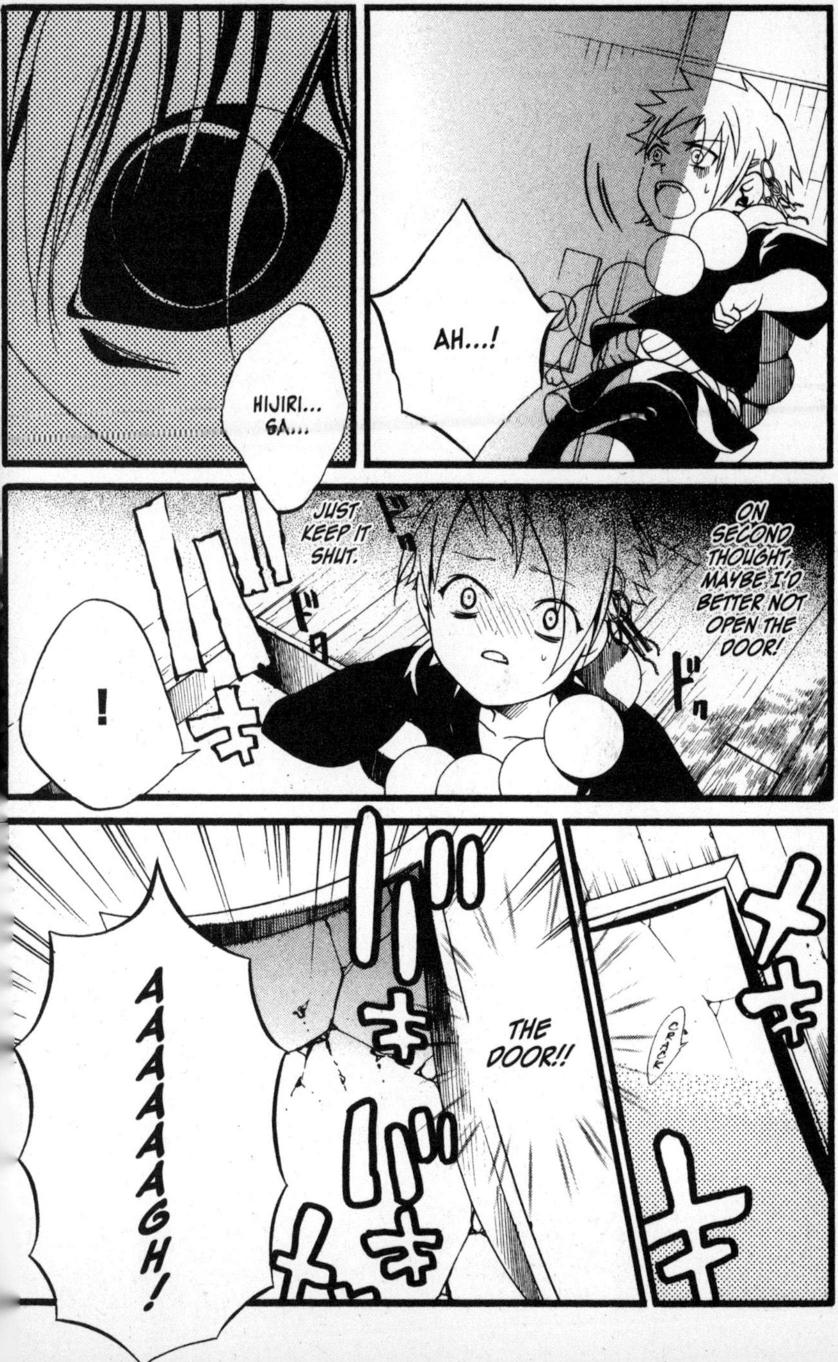
AH...!
HIJIRI... GA...
ON SECOND THOUGHT, MAYBE I'D BETTER NOT OPEN THE DOOR!
JUST KEEP IT SHUT.
!
CRACK
THE DOOR!!
AAAAAAAGH!

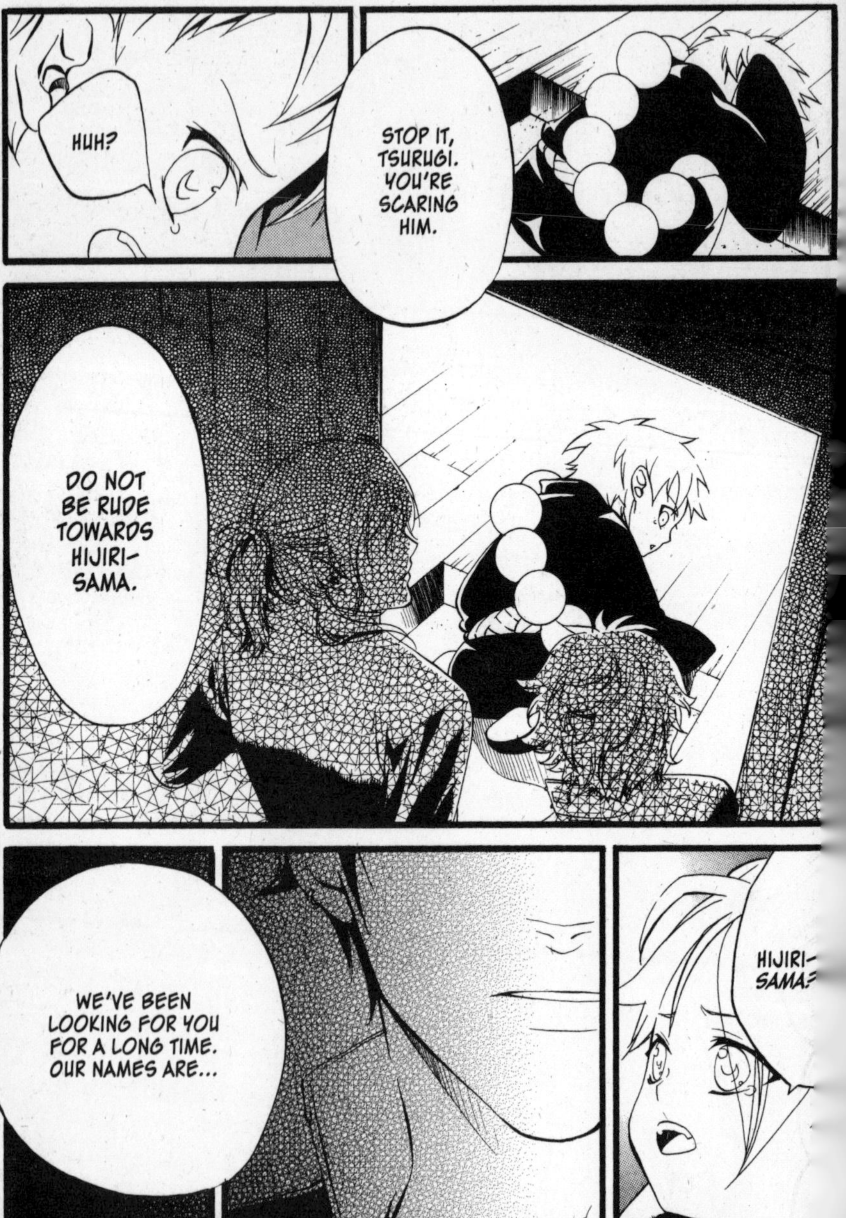
STOP IT, TSURUGI. YOU'RE SCARING HIM.
HUH?
DO NOT BE RUDE TOWARDS HIJIRI-SAMA.
HIJIRI-SAMA?
WE'VE BEEN LOOKING FOR YOU FOR A LONG TIME. OUR NAMES ARE...

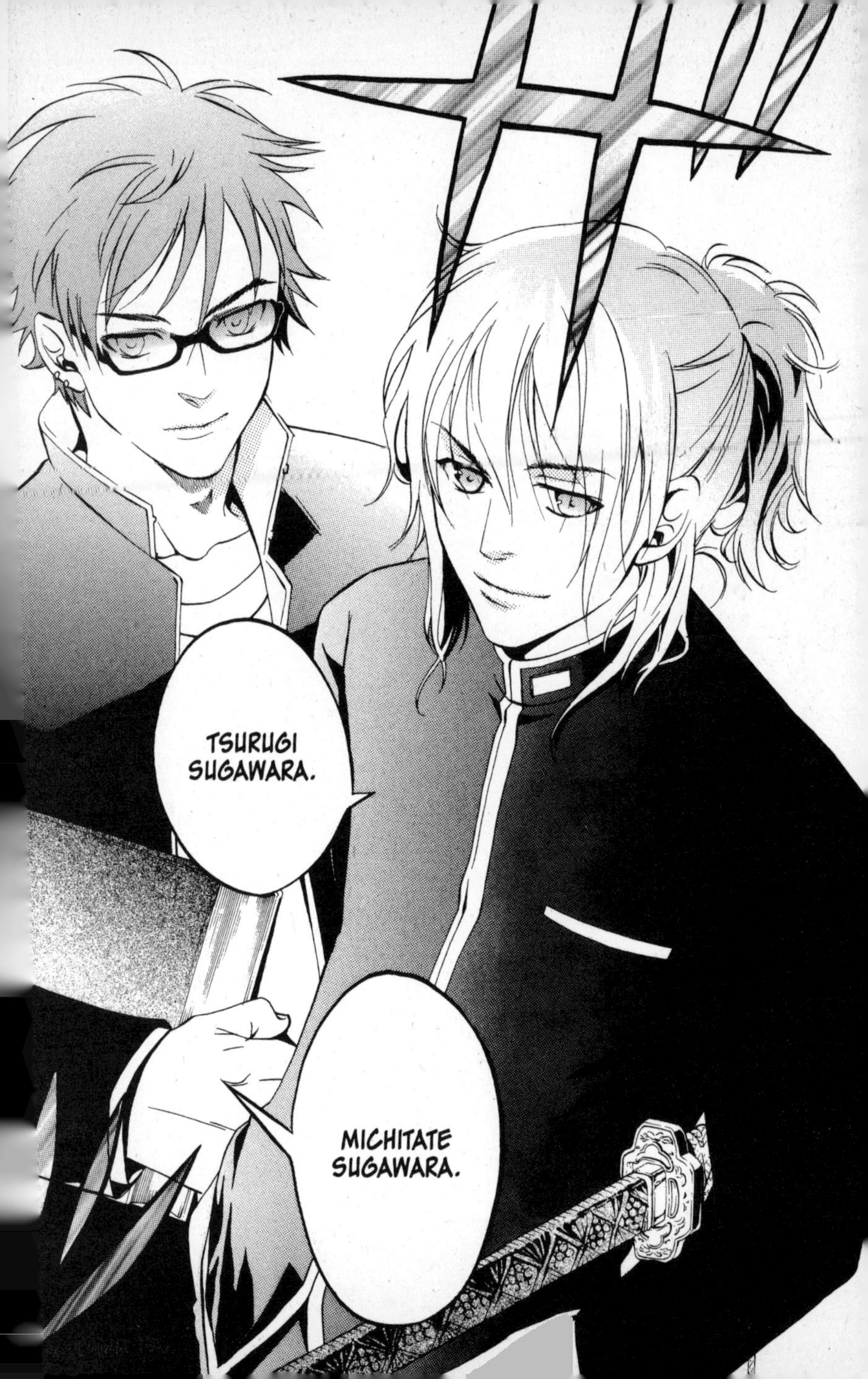
TSURUGI SUGAWARA.
MICHITATE SUGAWARA.

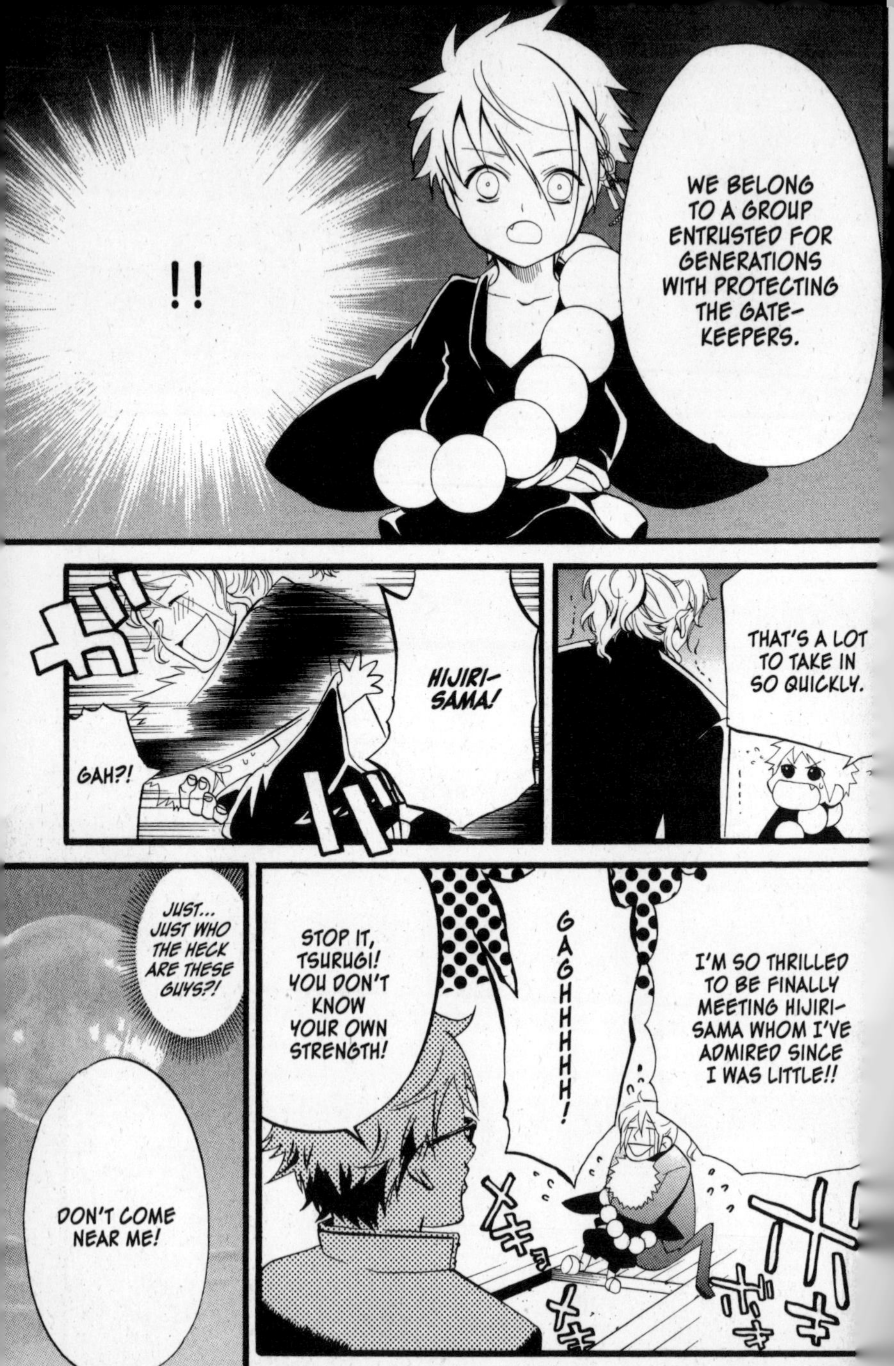
WE BELONG TO A GROUP ENTRUSTED FOR GENERATIONS WITH PROTECTING THE GATE-KEEPERS.
!!
THAT'S A LOT TO TAKE IN SO QUICKLY.
HIJIRI-SAMA!
GAH?!
I'M SO THRILLED TO BE FINALLY MEETING HIJIRI-SAMA WHOM I'VE ADMIRED SINCE I WAS LITTLE!!
GAGHHHHH!
STOP IT, TSURUGI! YOU DON'T KNOW YOUR OWN STRENGTH!
JUST... JUST WHO THE HECK ARE THESE GUYS?!
DON'T COME NEAR ME!

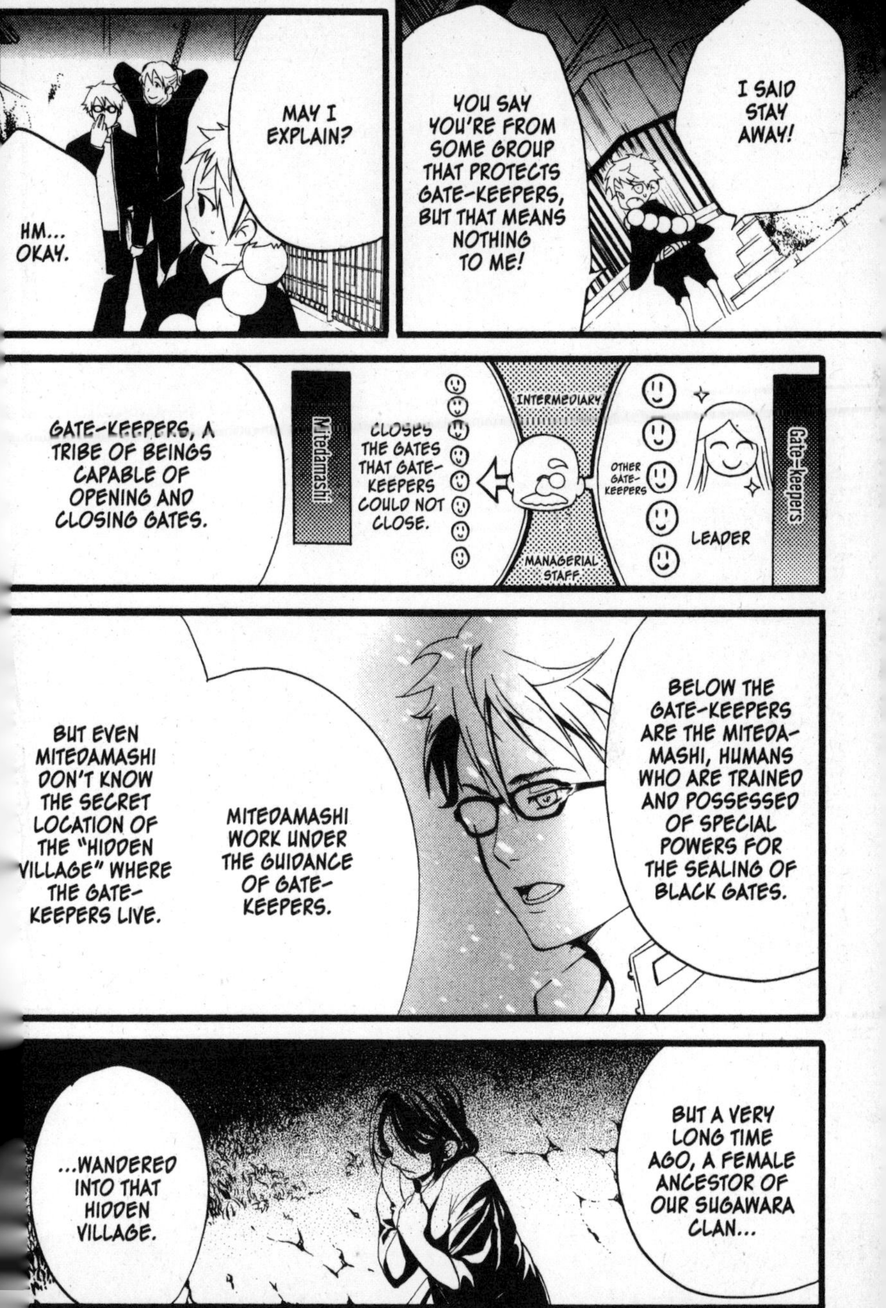
I SAID STAY AWAY!
YOU SAY YOU'RE FROM SOME GROUP THAT PROTECTS GATE-KEEPERS, BUT THAT MEANS NOTHING TO ME!
MAY I EXPLAIN?
HM... OKAY.
Gate-Keepers
LEADER
OTHER GATE-KEEPERS
INTERMEDIARY
MANAGERIAL STAFF
CLOSES THE GATES THAT GATE-KEEPERS COULD NOT CLOSE.
Mitedamashi
GATE-KEEPERS, A TRIBE OF BEINGS CAPABLE OF OPENING AND CLOSING GATES.
BELOW THE GATE-KEEPERS ARE THE MITEDA-MASHI, HUMANS WHO ARE TRAINED AND POSSESSED OF SPECIAL POWERS FOR THE SEALING OF BLACK GATES.
MITEDAMASHI WORK UNDER THE GUIDANCE OF GATE-KEEPERS.
BUT EVEN MITEDAMASHI DON'T KNOW THE SECRET LOCATION OF THE "HIDDEN VILLAGE" WHERE THE GATE-KEEPERS LIVE.
BUT A VERY LONG TIME AGO, A FEMALE ANCESTOR OF OUR SUGAWARA CLAN...
...WANDERED INTO THAT HIDDEN VILLAGE.

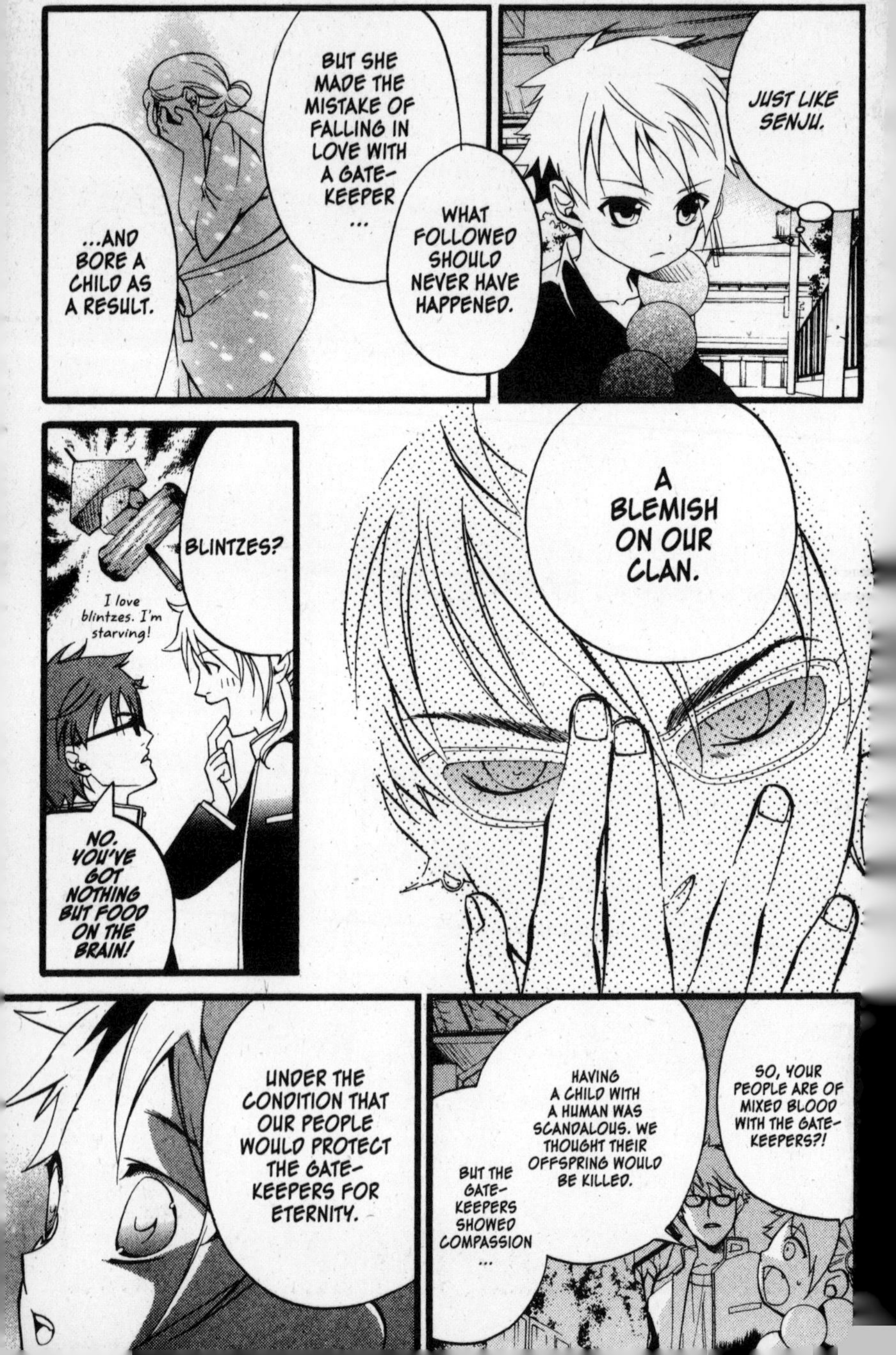
JUST LIKE SENJU.
BUT SHE MADE THE MISTAKE OF FALLING IN LOVE WITH A GATEKEEPER ...
...AND BORE A CHILD AS A RESULT.
WHAT FOLLOWED SHOULD NEVER HAVE HAPPENED.
A BLEMISH ON OUR CLAN.
BLINTZES?
I love blintzes. I'm starving!
NO. YOU'VE GOT NOTHING BUT FOOD ON THE BRAIN!
SO, YOUR PEOPLE ARE OF MIXED BLOOD WITH THE GATEKEEPERS?!
HAVING A CHILD WITH A HUMAN WAS SCANDALOUS. WE THOUGHT THEIR OFFSPRING WOULD BE KILLED.
BUT THE GATEKEEPERS SHOWED COMPASSION ...
UNDER THE CONDITION THAT OUR PEOPLE WOULD PROTECT THE GATEKEEPERS FOR ETERNITY.

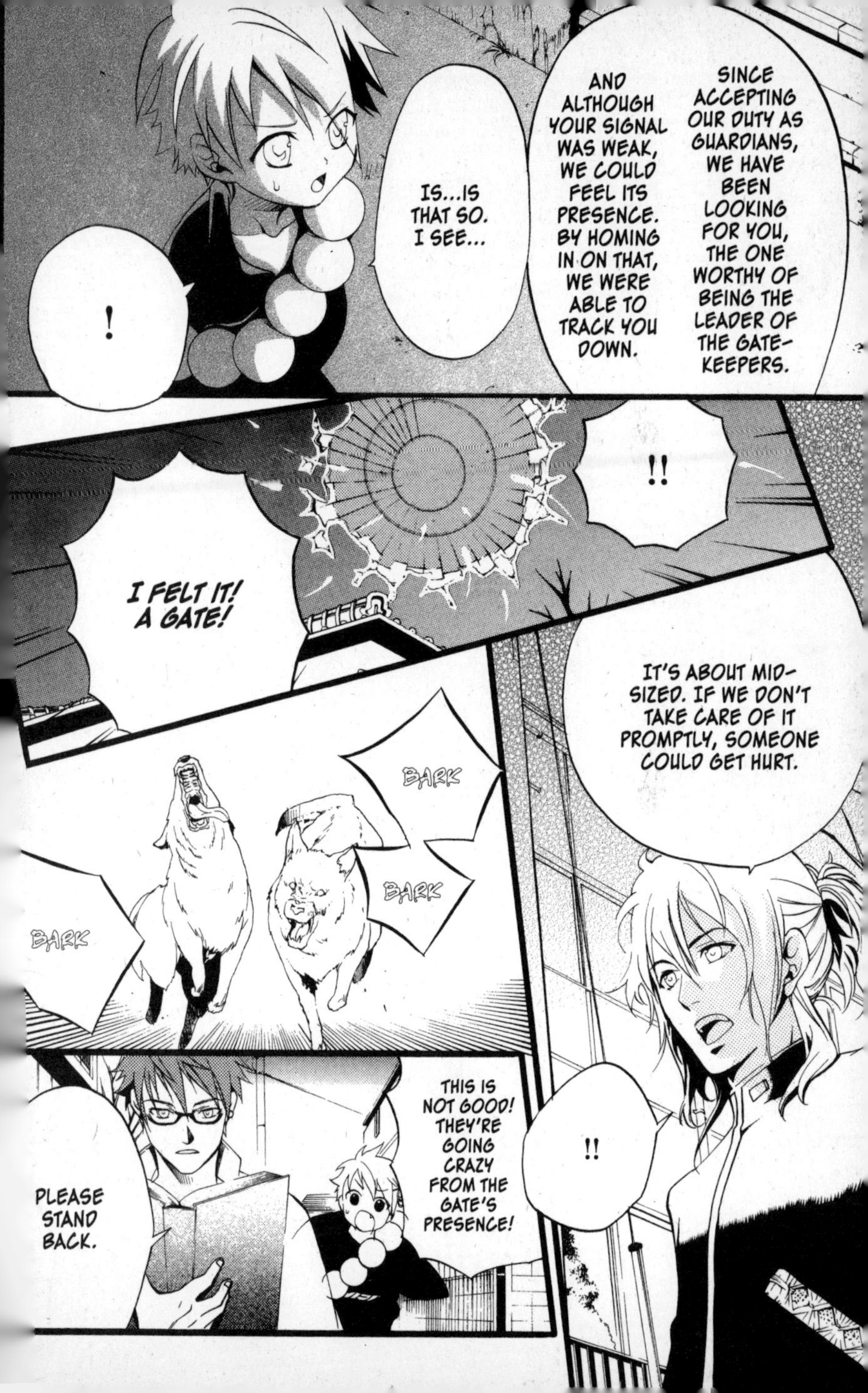
SINCE ACCEPTING OUR DUTY AS GUARDIANS, WE HAVE BEEN LOOKING FOR YOU, THE ONE WORTHY OF BEING THE LEADER OF THE GATE-KEEPERS.
AND ALTHOUGH YOUR SIGNAL WAS WEAK, WE COULD FEEL ITS PRESENCE. BY HOMING IN ON THAT, WE WERE ABLE TO TRACK YOU DOWN.
IS...IS THAT SO. I SEE...
!
!!
I FELT IT! A GATE!
IT'S ABOUT MID-SIZED. IF WE DON'T TAKE CARE OF IT PROMPTLY, SOMEONE COULD GET HURT.
!!
BARK
BARK
BARK
THIS IS NOT GOOD! THEY'RE GOING CRAZY FROM THE GATE'S PRESENCE!
PLEASE STAND BACK.

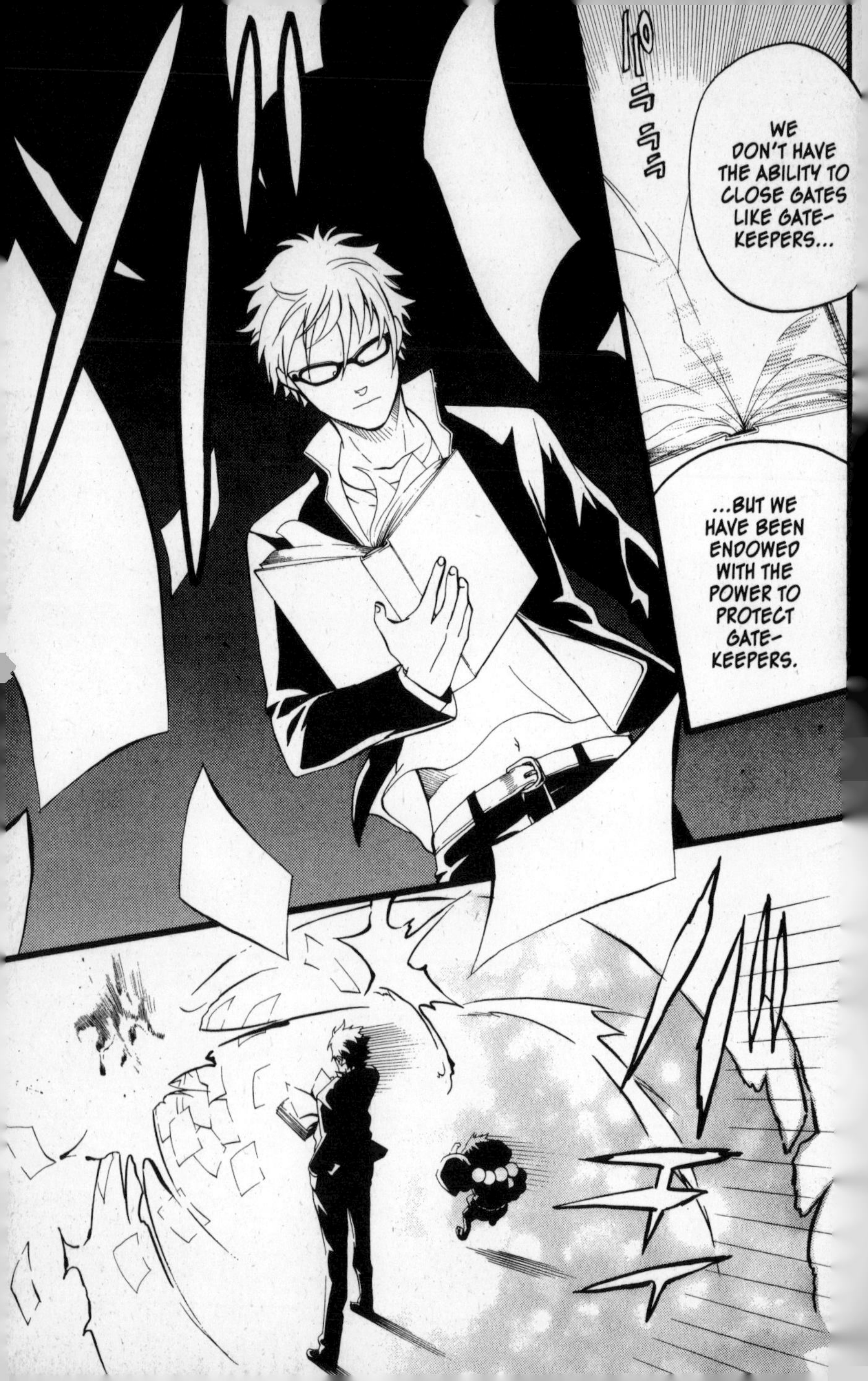
WE DON'T HAVE THE ABILITY TO CLOSE GATES LIKE GATE-KEEPERS...
...BUT WE HAVE BEEN ENDOWED WITH THE POWER TO PROTECT GATE-KEEPERS.

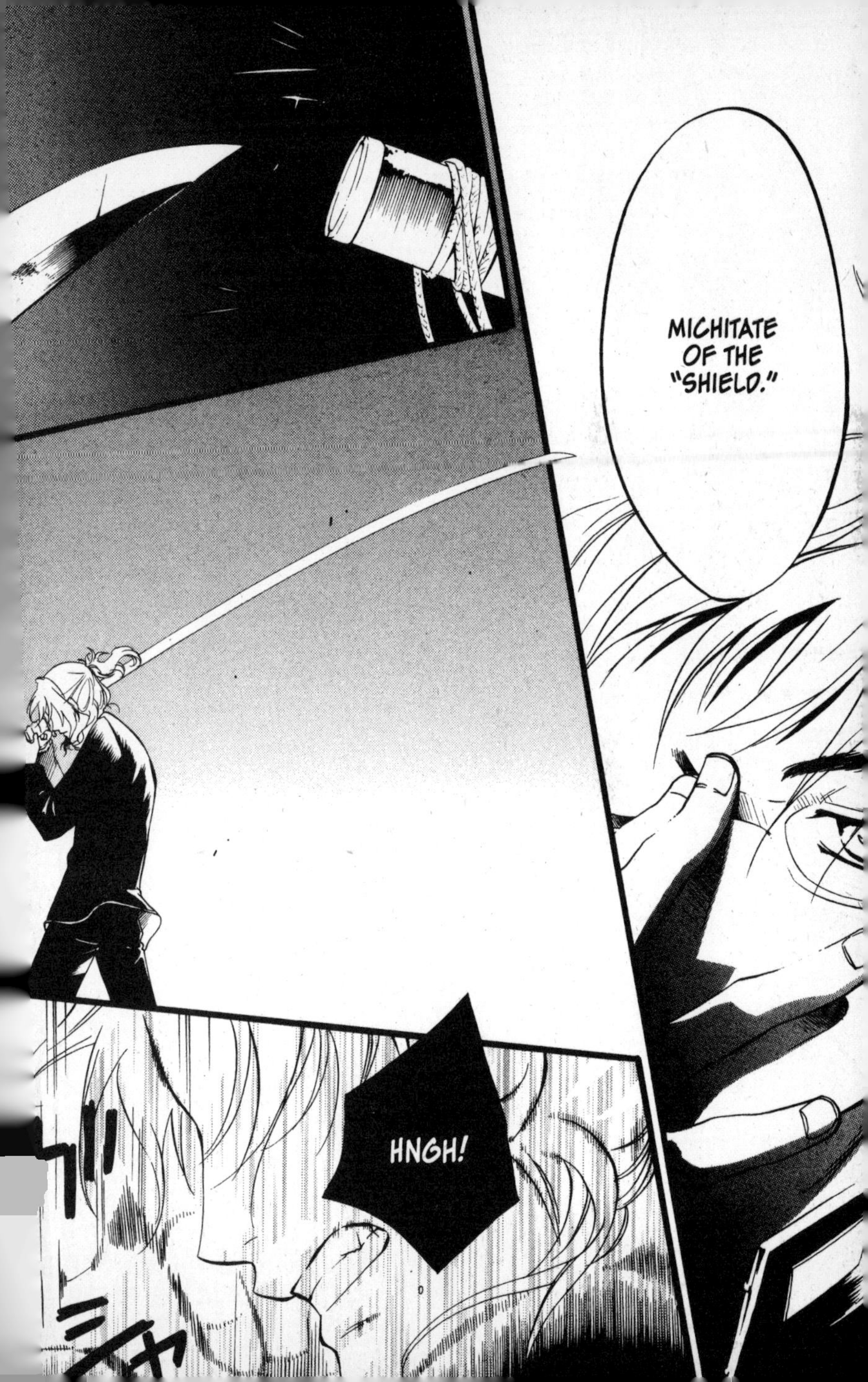
MICHITATE OF THE "SHIELD."
HNGH!

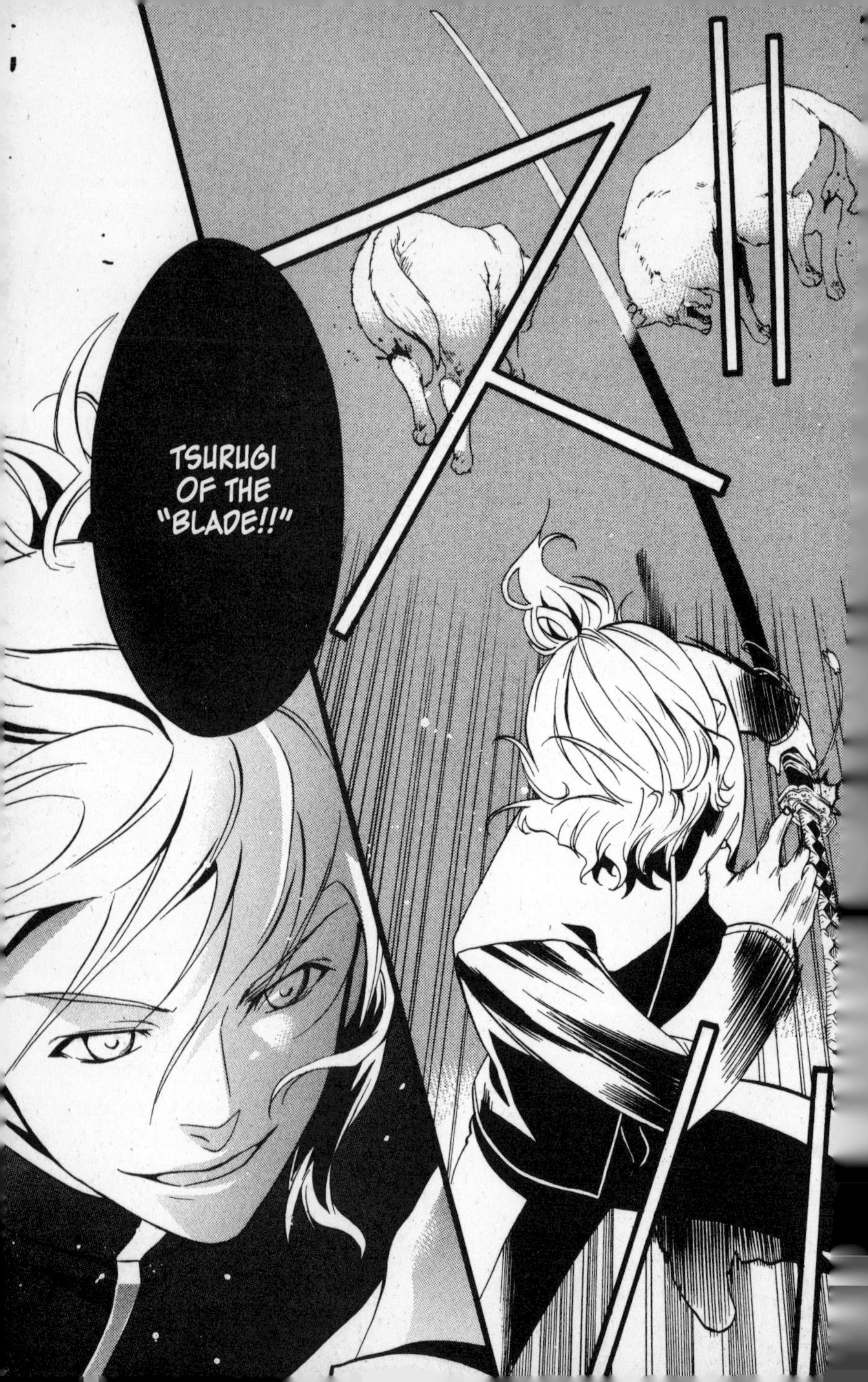
TSURUGI OF THE "BLADE!!"

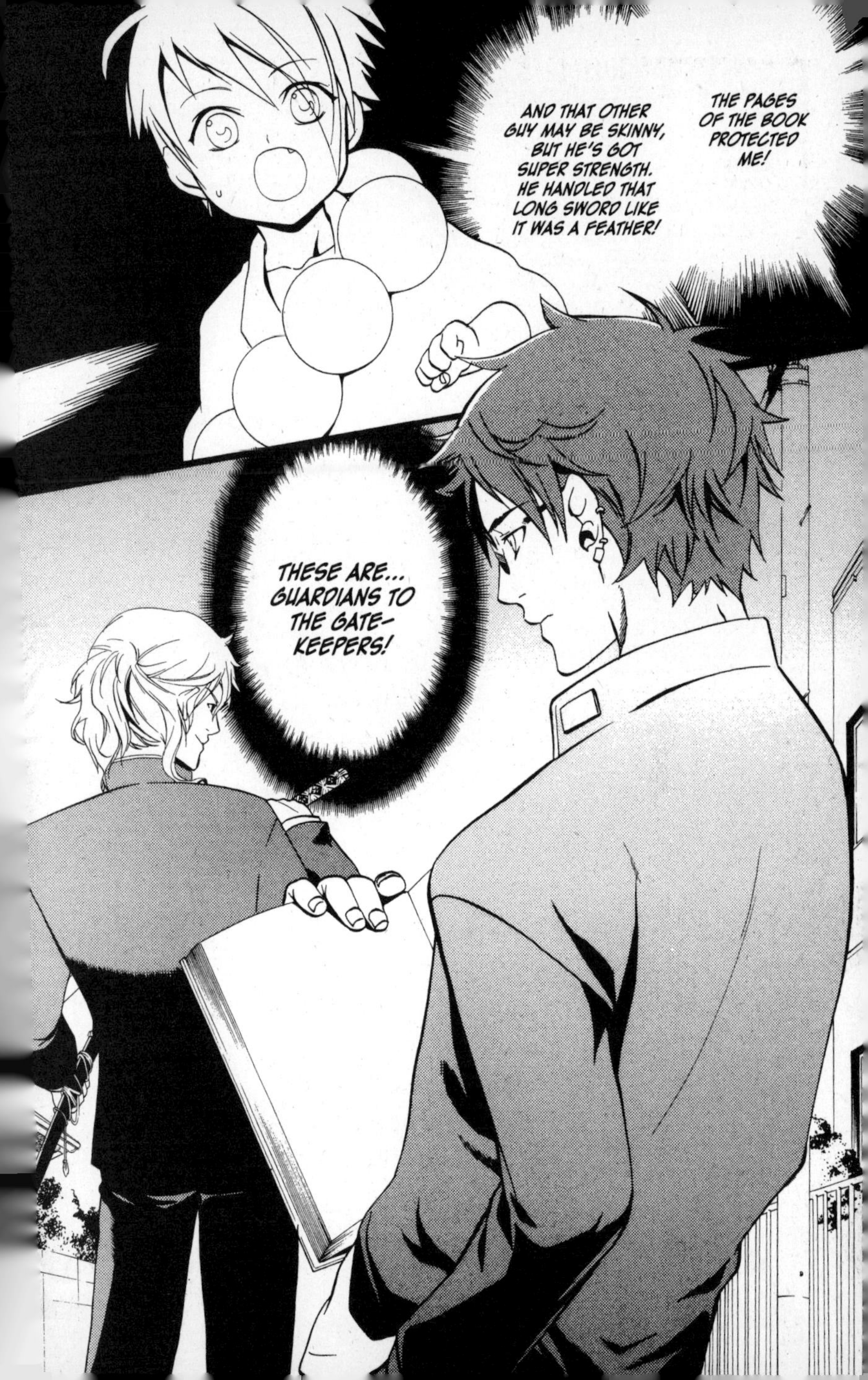
THE PAGES OF THE BOOK PROTECTED ME!
AND THAT OTHER GUY MAY BE SKINNY, BUT HE'S GOT SUPER STRENGTH. HE HANDLED THAT LONG SWORD LIKE IT WAS A FEATHER!
THESE ARE... GUARDIANS TO THE GATE-KEEPERS!

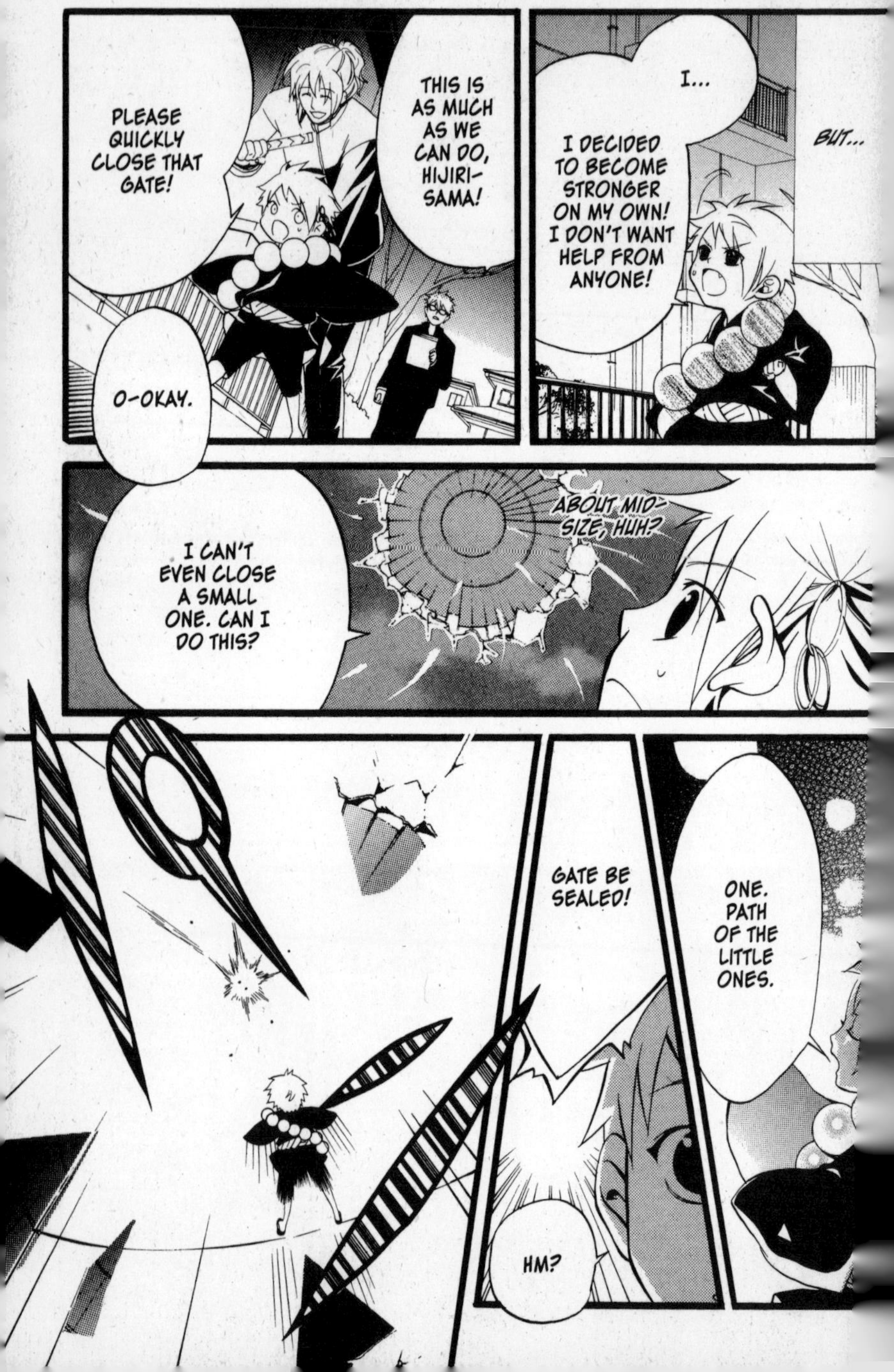
BUT...
I...
I DECIDED TO BECOME STRONGER ON MY OWN! I DON'T WANT HELP FROM ANYONE!
THIS IS AS MUCH AS WE CAN DO, HIJIRI-SAMA!
PLEASE QUICKLY CLOSE THAT GATE!
O-OKAY.
ABOUT MID-SIZE, HUH?
I CAN'T EVEN CLOSE A SMALL ONE. CAN I DO THIS?
ONE. PATH OF THE LITTLE ONES.
GATE BE SEALED!
HM?

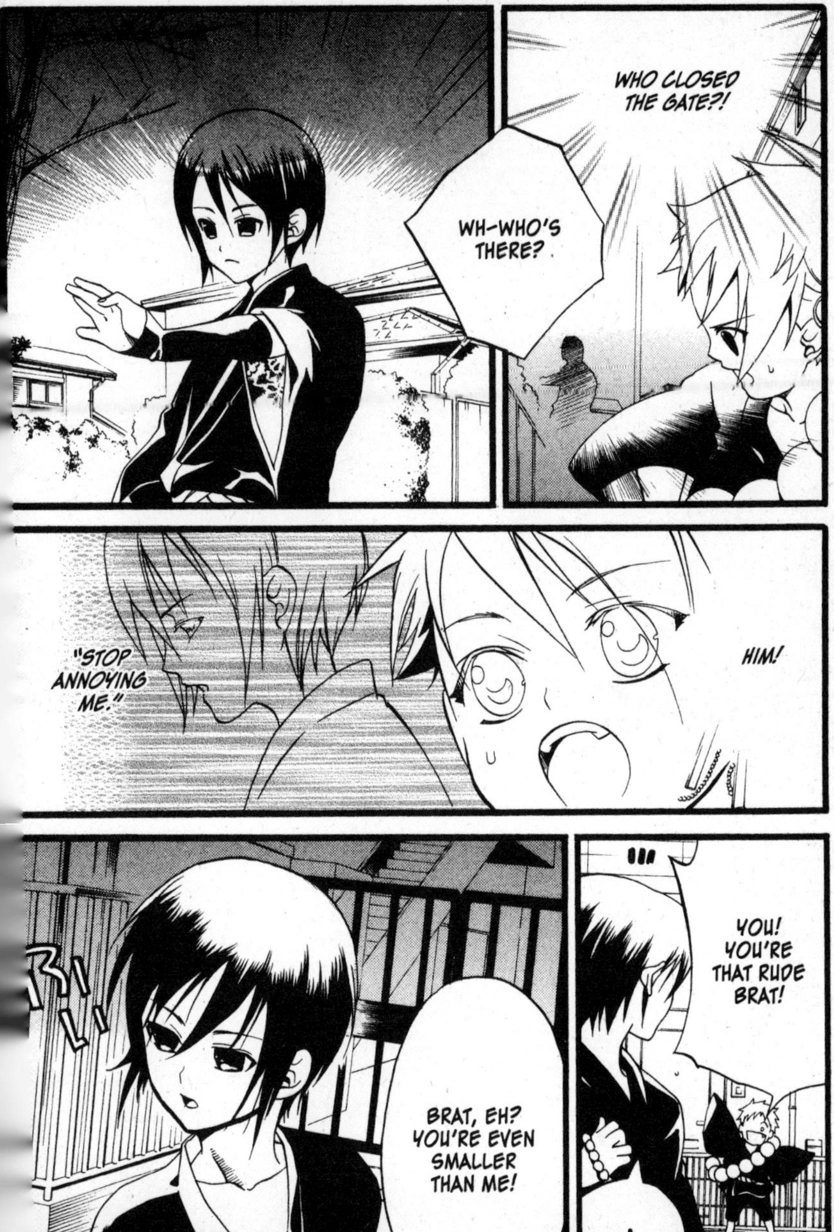
WHO CLOSED THE GATE?!
WH-WHO'S THERE?
HIM!
"STOP ANNOYING ME."
YOU! YOU'RE THAT RUDE BRAT!
!
BRAT, EH? YOU'RE EVEN SMALLER THAN ME!

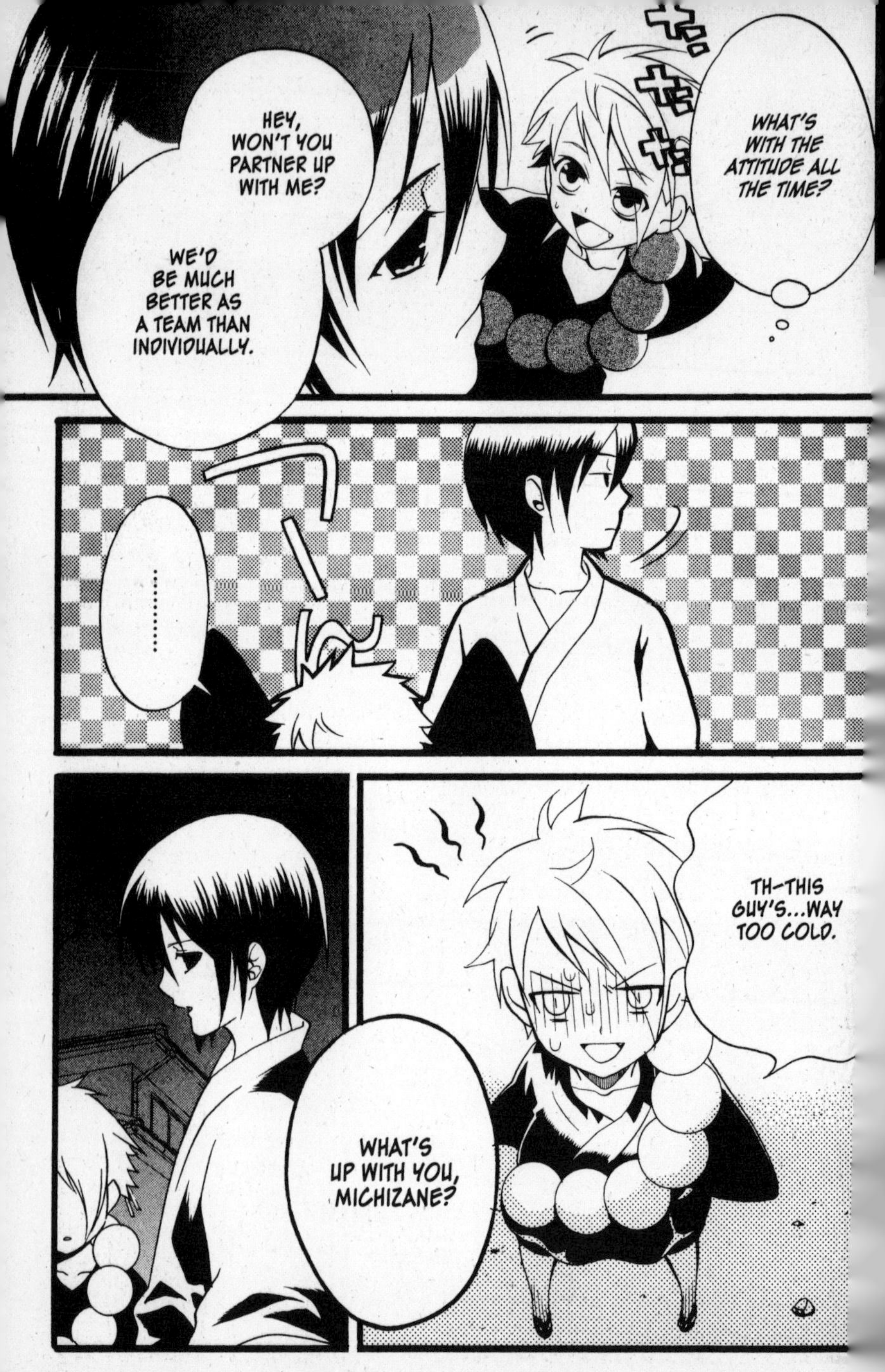
WHAT'S WITH THE ATTITUDE ALL THE TIME?
HEY, WON'T YOU PARTNER UP WITH ME?
WE'D BE MUCH BETTER AS A TEAM THAN INDIVIDUALLY.
……
TH-THIS GUY'S...WAY TOO COLD.
WHAT'S UP WITH YOU, MICHIZANE?

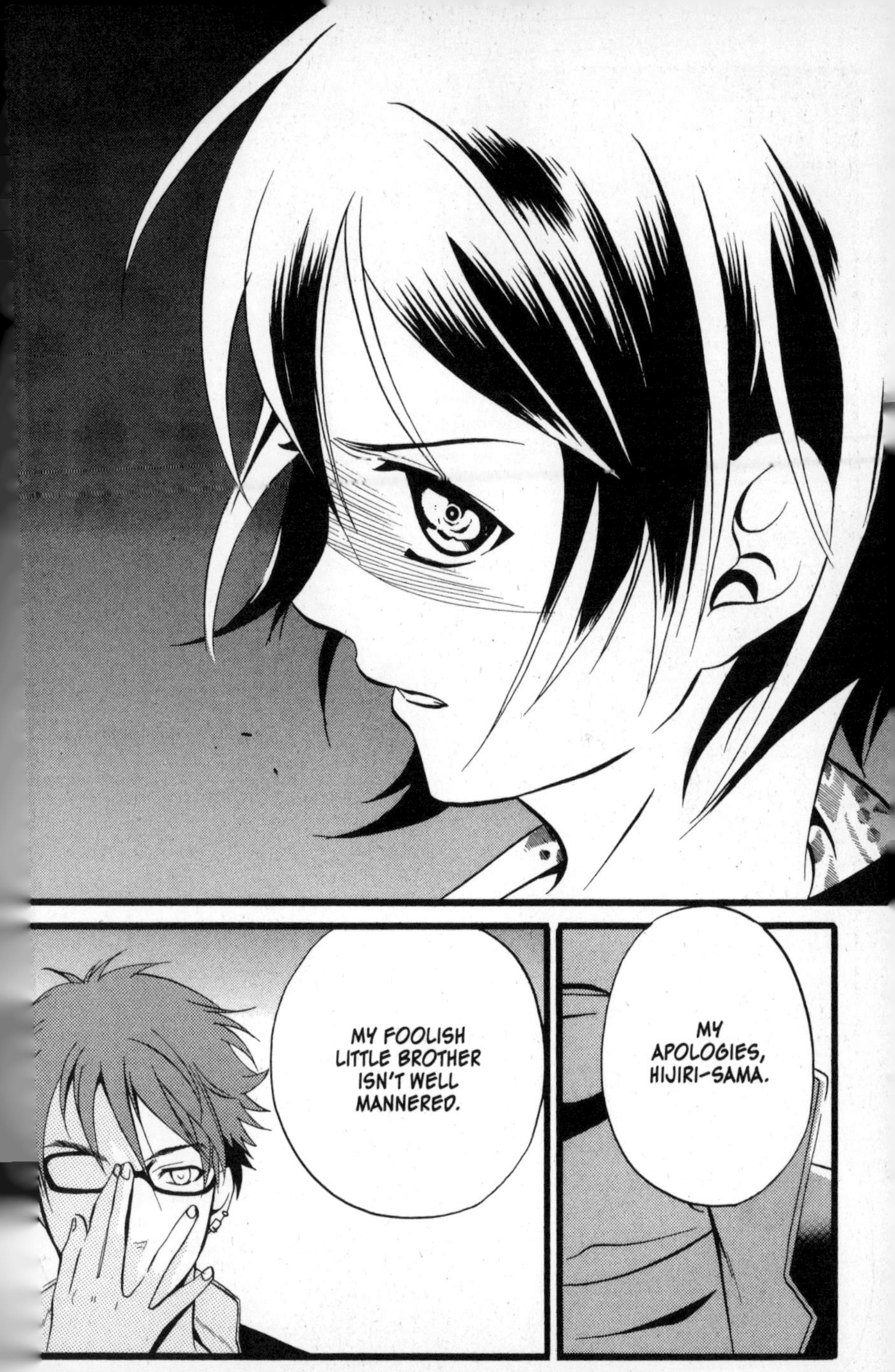
MY APOLOGIES, HIJIRI-SAMA.
MY FOOLISH LITTLE BROTHER ISN'T WELL MANNERED.

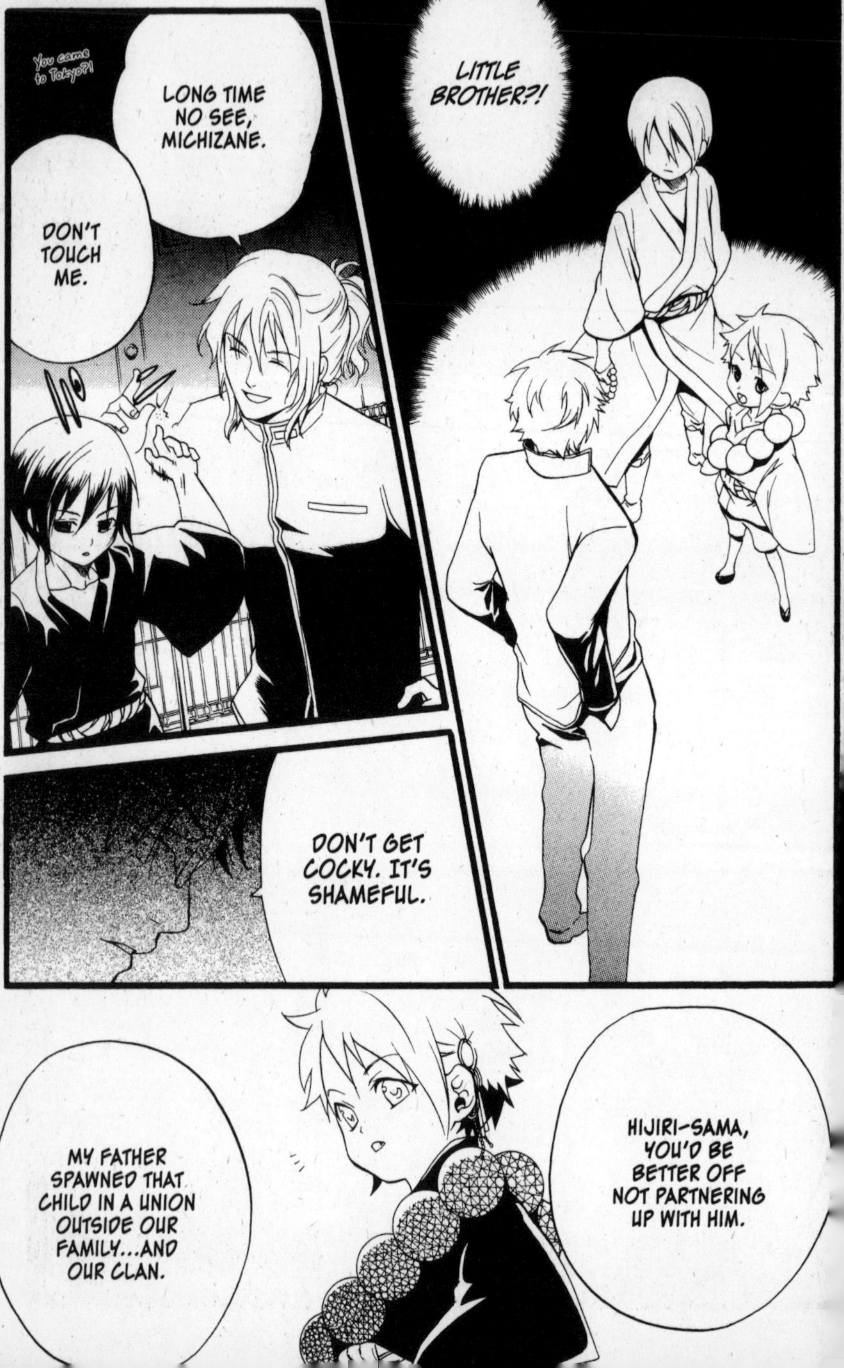
LITTLE BROTHER?!
LONG TIME NO SEE, MICHIZANE.
You came to Tokyo?!
DON'T TOUCH ME.
DON'T GET COCKY. IT'S SHAMEFUL.
HIJIRI-SAMA, YOU'D BE BETTER OFF NOT PARTNERING UP WITH HIM.
MY FATHER SPAWNED THAT CHILD IN A UNION OUTSIDE OUR FAMILY...AND OUR CLAN.

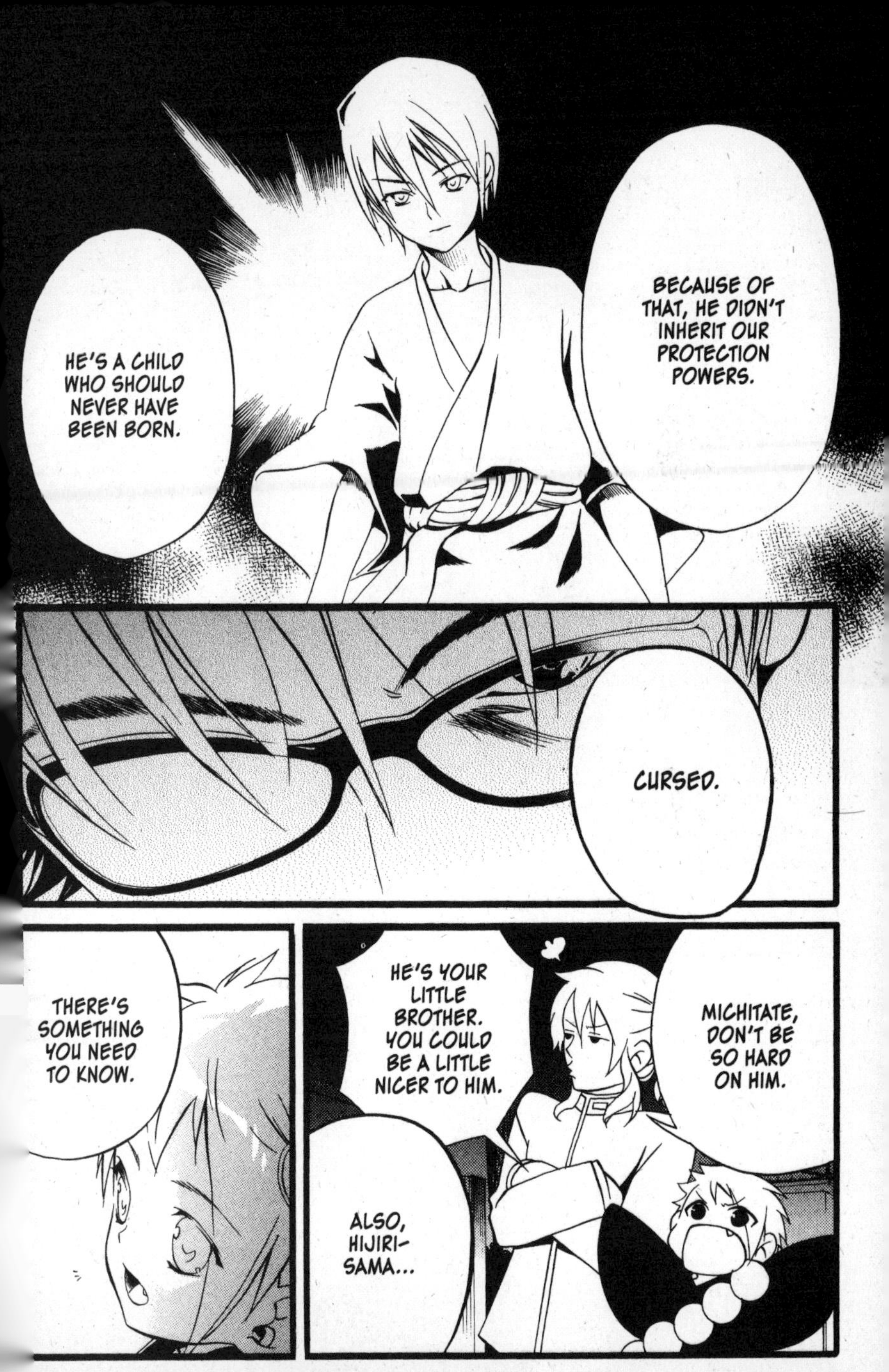
BECAUSE OF THAT, HE DIDN'T INHERIT OUR PROTECTION POWERS.
HE'S A CHILD WHO SHOULD NEVER HAVE BEEN BORN.
CURSED.
MICHITATE, DON'T BE SO HARD ON HIM.
HE'S YOUR LITTLE BROTHER. YOU COULD BE A LITTLE NICER TO HIM.
ALSO, HIJIRI-SAMA...
THERE'S SOMETHING YOU NEED TO KNOW.

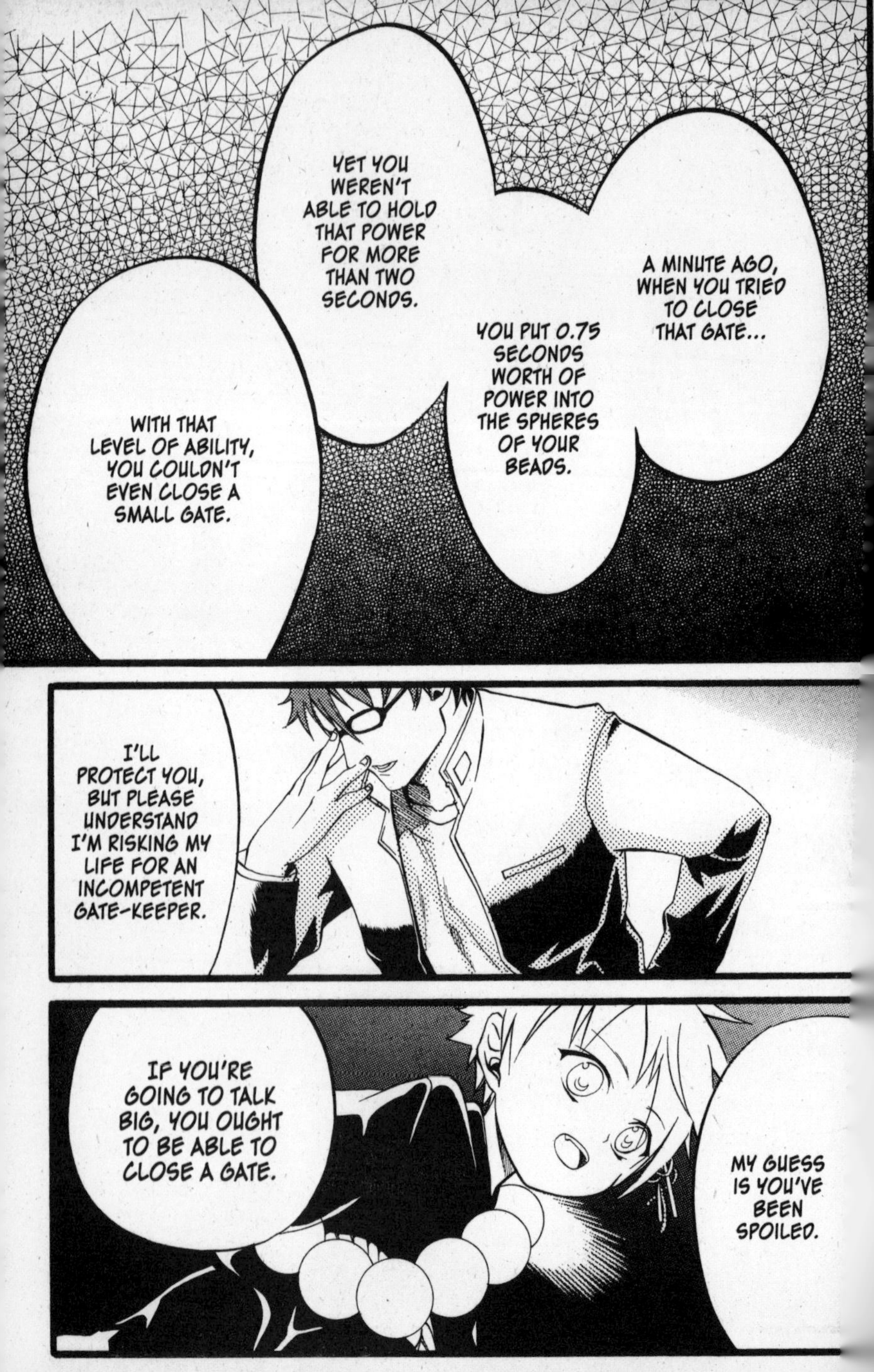
A MINUTE AGO, WHEN YOU TRIED TO CLOSE THAT GATE...
YOU PUT 0.75 SECONDS WORTH OF POWER INTO THE SPHERES OF YOUR BEADS.
YET YOU WEREN'T ABLE TO HOLD THAT POWER FOR MORE THAN TWO SECONDS.
WITH THAT LEVEL OF ABILITY, YOU COULDN'T EVEN CLOSE A SMALL GATE.
I'LL PROTECT YOU, BUT PLEASE UNDERSTAND I'M RISKING MY LIFE FOR AN INCOMPETENT GATE-KEEPER.
MY GUESS IS YOU'VE BEEN SPOILED.
IF YOU'RE GOING TO TALK BIG, YOU OUGHT TO BE ABLE TO CLOSE A GATE.

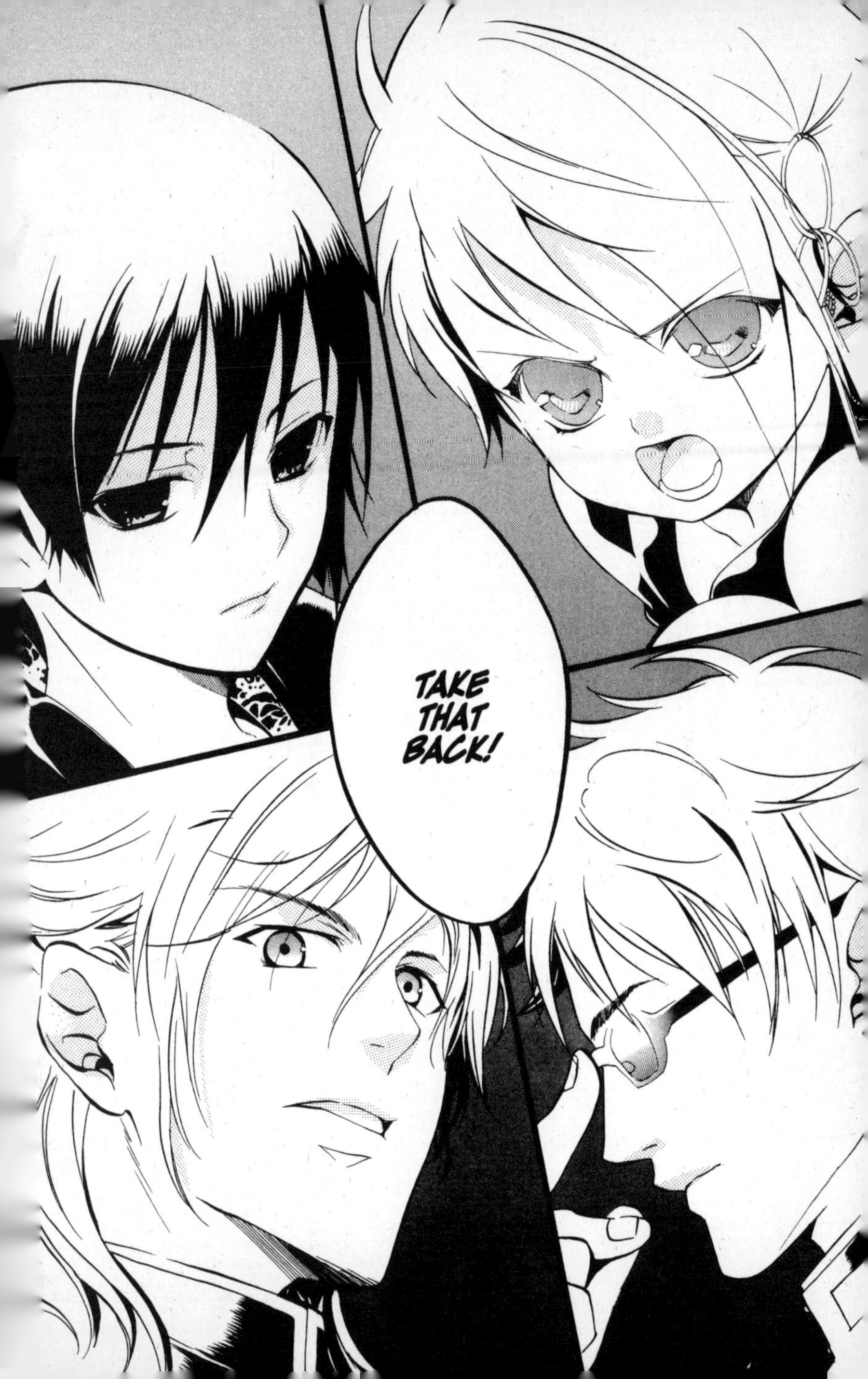
TAKE THAT BACK!

CHARACTER PROFILE:01
HIJIRI

■HIJIRI■

AGE: 18 YEARS OLD (AS
OF VOLUME 2)
HEIGHT: 130 CM
BLOOD TYPE: UNKNOWN
BIRTHDATE: UNKNOWN

THE PROTAGONIST OF THIS CHAPTER. HE IS THE SON OF THE
LATE YOSHITSUNA, THE LEADER OF THE GATE-KEEPERS. HE HA[S]
INHERITED HIS FATHER'S POWERS, BUT HE HIMSELF IS A FAILU[RE]
HE HAS A BOLD ATTITUDE, BUT HIS NATURE IS BASICALLY
THAT OF A BULLIED CHILD. UNTIL SIX YEARS AGO, HE
WAS TEASED AND MADE FUN OF DAILY BY SENJU.
AS A RESULT, HE'S GROWN UP TO BE PRETTY CHICKEN-HEARTE[D]
FOR UNKNOWN REASONS, HIS PHYSICAL APPEARANCE HASN'T
CHANGED IN THE PAST SIX YEARS (THOUGH, ACTUALLY, EVEN
LONGER). BUT HE ISN'T TOO CONCERNED ABOUT THAT.
SINCE HE CAN SPEAK WITH ANIMALS, HE HAS MANY
ANIMAL FRIENDS. HIS FAVORITE FOOD IS FRIED TOFU.
HE BELIEVES THE REASON THAT SENJU SUDDENLY LEFT HIM
IS BECAUSE HE HIMSELF IS WORTHLESS. SO HE BECAME
DEVOTED TO IMPROVING HIMSELF BY TRAINING DAY AND NIGH[T]
UNFORTUNATELY, HIS EFFORTS HAVE THUS FAR BEEN IN VAIN.

■SENJU■

AGE: 29 YEARS OLD (AS OF VOLUME 2)/HEIGHT: 178 CM/BLOOD TYPE: AB/ BIRTHDATE: JANUARY 3RD

BORN IN TOKYO, HE RAISED HIJIRI AFTER HIS REAL PARENTS DIED. HE IS A TWISTED, SELFISH, OVERBEARING HUMAN FULL OF PERSONALITY FAULTS. AS A MITEDAMASHI, HOWEVER, HE POSSESSES CONSIDERABLE TALENT.
FOR THE MOST PART, HE'S NEVER HAD MANY FRIENDS, AND, ON HIS DAYS OFF, HE SPENDS HIS DAYS LARGELY AT HOME. IN THIS REGARD, HIJIRI CALLS HIM A "GLOOMY SHUT-IN." BUT HE DEFENDS HIS STAY-AT-HOME LIFESTYLE, SAYING, "I DON'T HAVE MONEY TO HANG OUT ANYWHERE ELSE."
AT AGE 10, HE WANDERED INTO THE GATE-KEEPERS' HIDDEN VILLAGE, AND FROM THEN UNTIL THE "TRAGIC INCIDENT" OCCURRED, HE LIVED WITH YOSHITSUNA AND HIS CLAN.
THE NAME "SENJU" WAS GIVEN TO HIM BY YOSHITSUNA TO MEAN, "HE WHO CAN CAST OFF HIS PREVIOUS SELF AND HAS A THOUSAND WAYS TO LIVE." HIS BIOLOGICAL PARENTS ALSO GAVE HIM A NAME.
HE RESPECTS YOSHITSUNA, AND, THOUGH THEY ARE UNRELATED, HE HAS GREAT AFFECTION FOR YOSHITSUNA'S SON, HIJIRI.
HE IS A BUSINESSMAN (THOUGH WITH NO BUSINESS SKILLS) WHO, IN HARD TIMES, IS KNOWN TO LIVE ON BEEF BOWLS.
HIS WHEREABOUTS ARE UNKNOWN SINCE HE LEFT HIJIRI AND VANISHED.

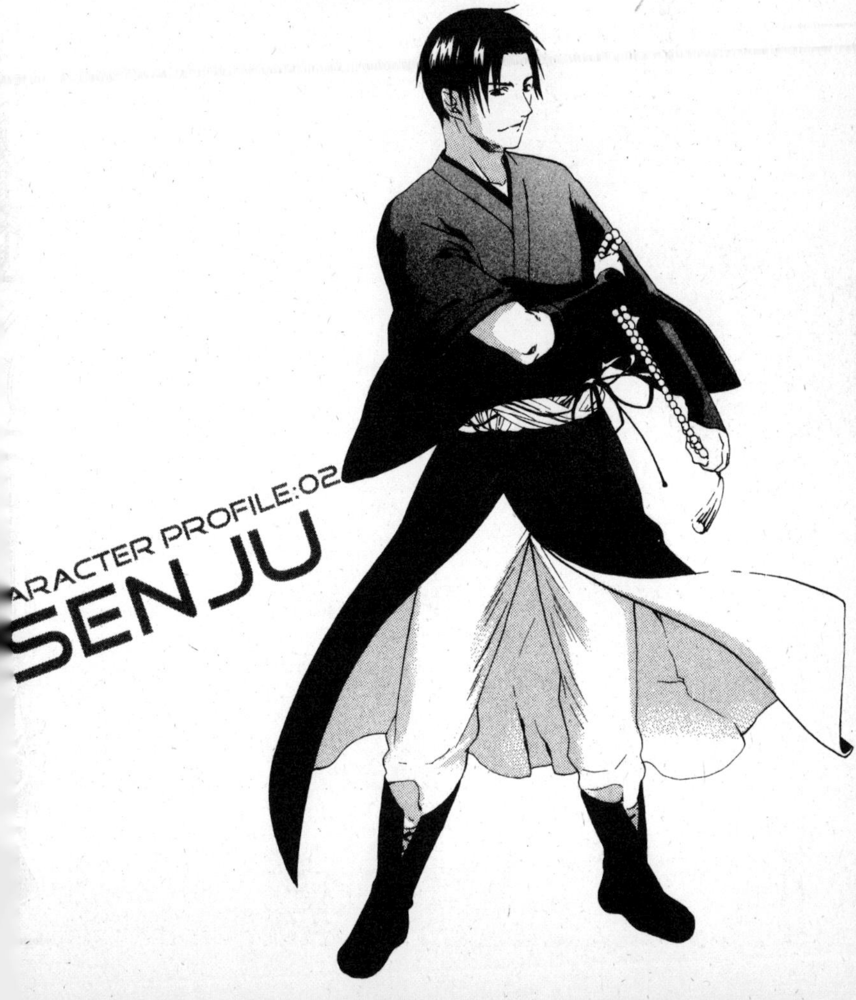
ARACTER PROFILE:02
SENJU

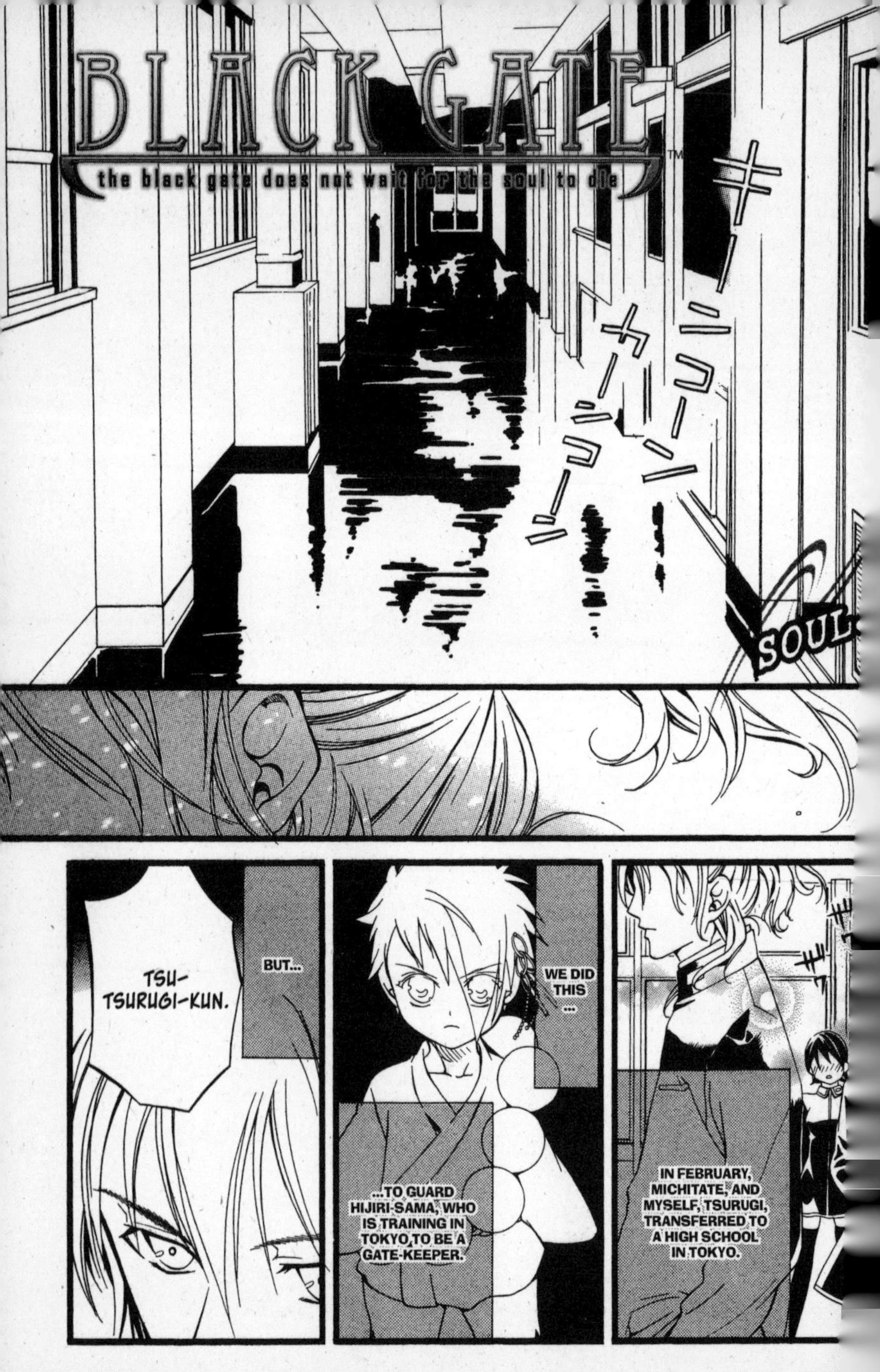
BLACK GATE™
the black gate does not wait for the soul to die
キーンコーン
カーンコーン
SOUL
IN FEBRUARY, MICHITATE, AND MYSELF, TSURUGI, TRANSFERRED TO A HIGH SCHOOL IN TOKYO.
WE DID THIS ...
...TO GUARD HIJIRI-SAMA, WHO IS TRAINING IN TOKYO TO BE A GATE-KEEPER.
BUT...
TSU-TSURUGI-KUN.

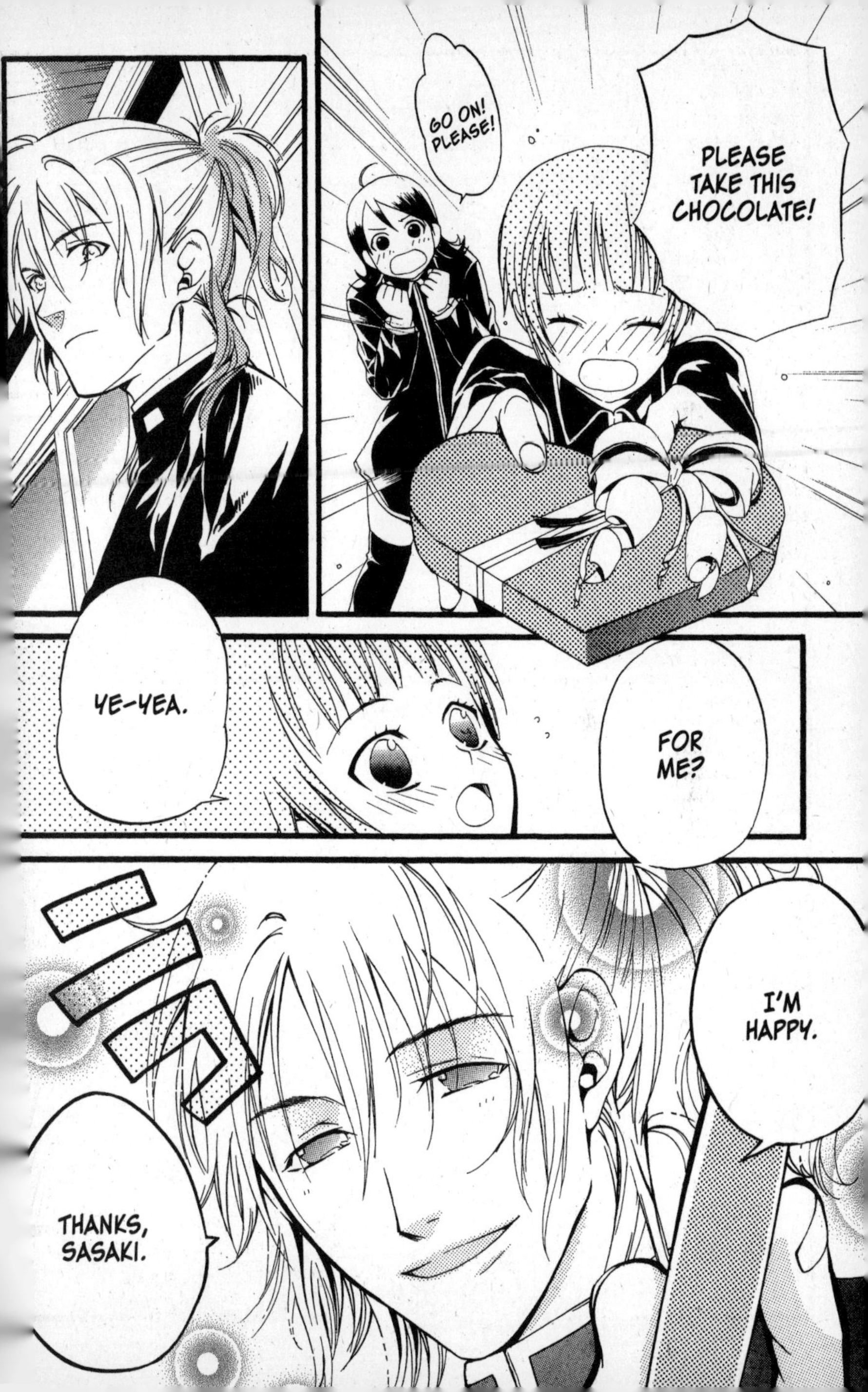
PLEASE TAKE THIS CHOCOLATE!
GO ON! PLEASE!
FOR ME?
YE-YEA.
I'M HAPPY.
THANKS, SASAKI.

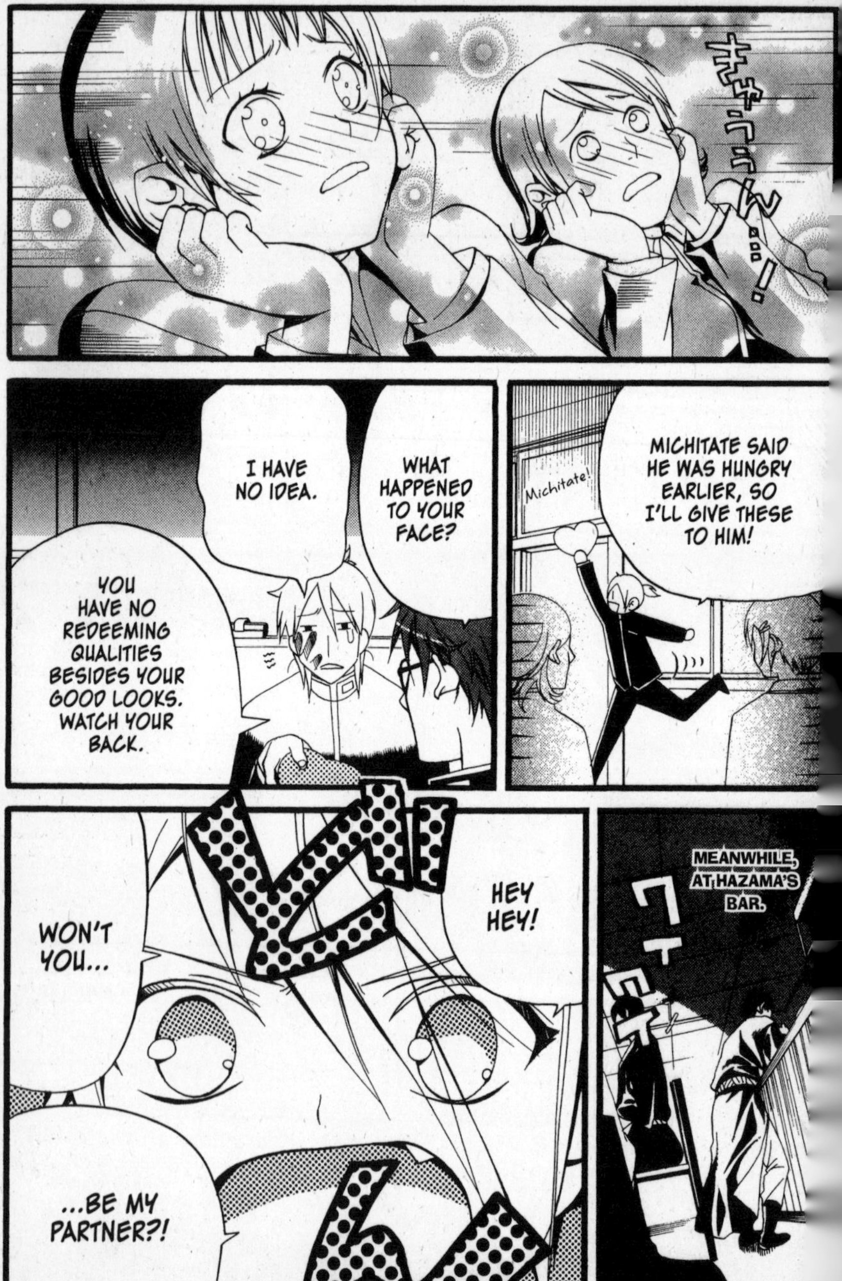
きゃううん…!
MICHITATE SAID HE WAS HUNGRY EARLIER, SO I'LL GIVE THESE TO HIM!
Michitate!
WHAT HAPPENED TO YOUR FACE?
I HAVE NO IDEA.
YOU HAVE NO REDEEMING QUALITIES BESIDES YOUR GOOD LOOKS. WATCH YOUR BACK.
MEANWHILE, AT HAZAMA'S BAR.
HEY HEY!
WON'T YOU...
...BE MY PARTNER?!

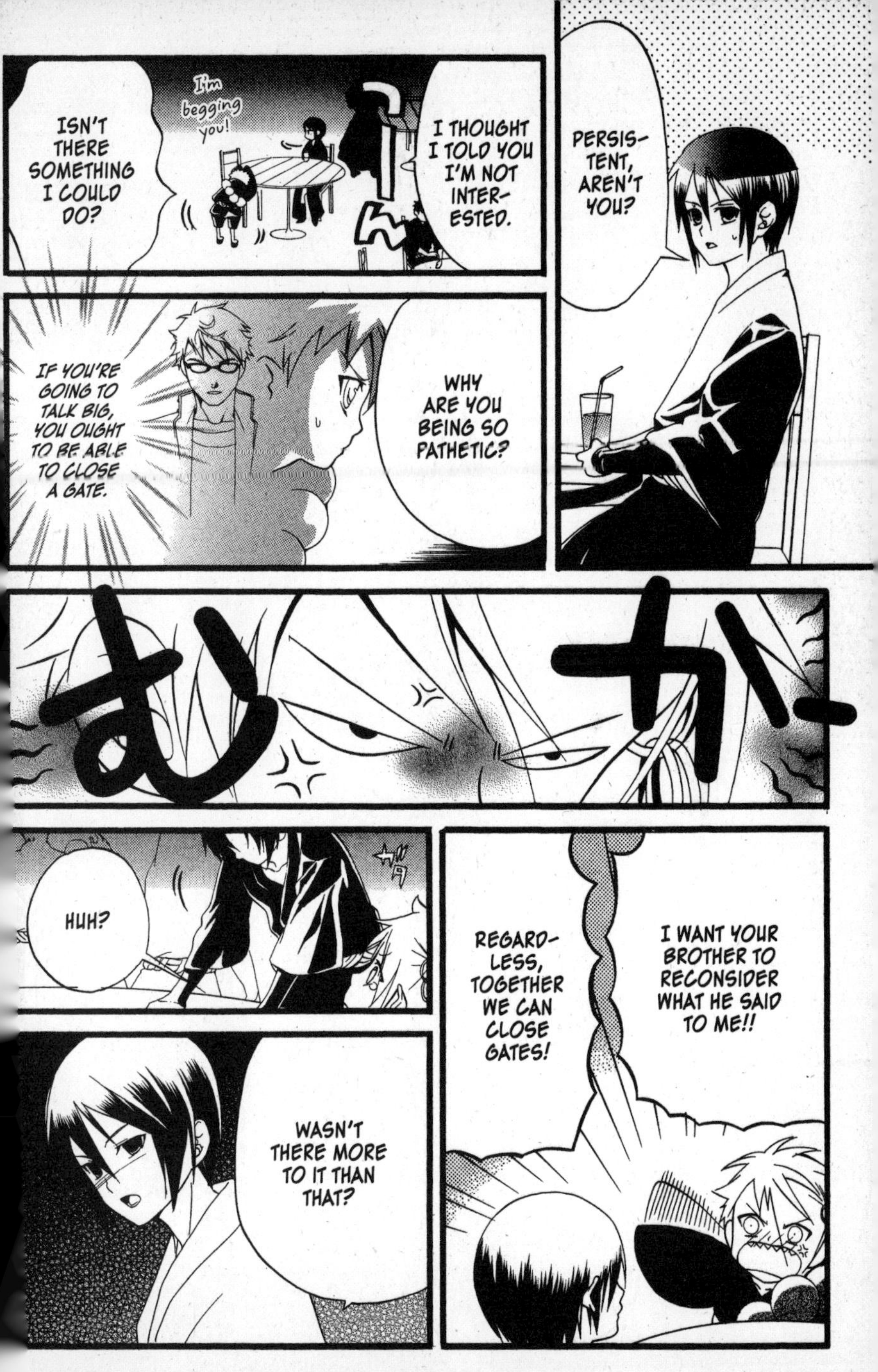
PERSIS-TENT, AREN'T YOU?
I THOUGHT I TOLD YOU I'M NOT INTER-ESTED.
I'm begging you!
ISN'T THERE SOMETHING I COULD DO?
WHY ARE YOU BEING SO PATHETIC?
IF YOU'RE GOING TO TALK BIG, YOU OUGHT TO BE ABLE TO CLOSE A GATE.
むか
I WANT YOUR BROTHER TO RECONSIDER WHAT HE SAID TO ME!!
REGARD-LESS, TOGETHER WE CAN CLOSE GATES!
HUH?
WASN'T THERE MORE TO IT THAN THAT?

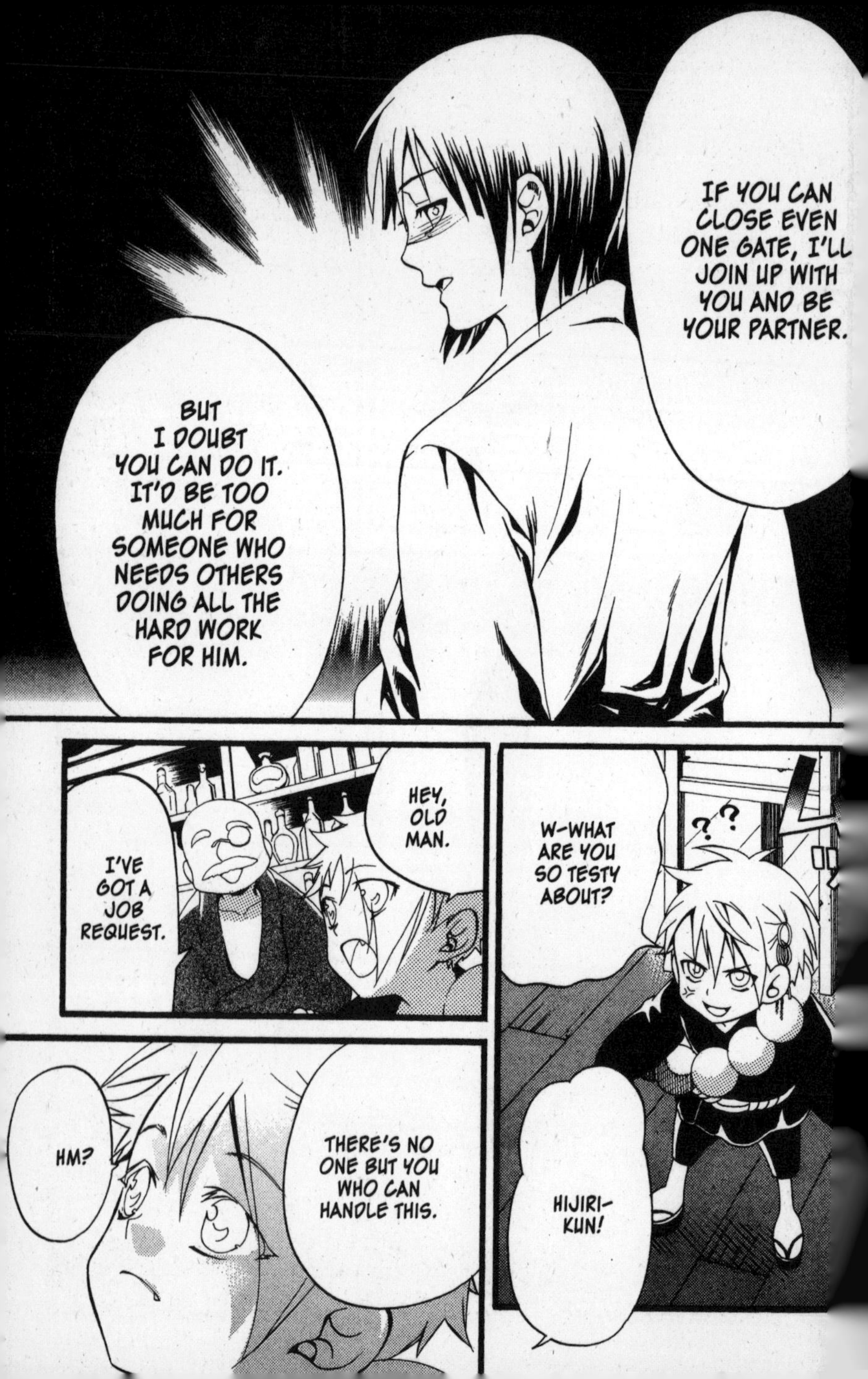
IF YOU CAN CLOSE EVEN ONE GATE, I'LL JOIN UP WITH YOU AND BE YOUR PARTNER.
BUT I DOUBT YOU CAN DO IT. IT'D BE TOO MUCH FOR SOMEONE WHO NEEDS OTHERS DOING ALL THE HARD WORK FOR HIM.
W-WHAT ARE YOU SO TESTY ABOUT?
HIJIRI-KUN!
HEY, OLD MAN.
I'VE GOT A JOB REQUEST.
THERE'S NO ONE BUT YOU WHO CAN HANDLE THIS.
HM?

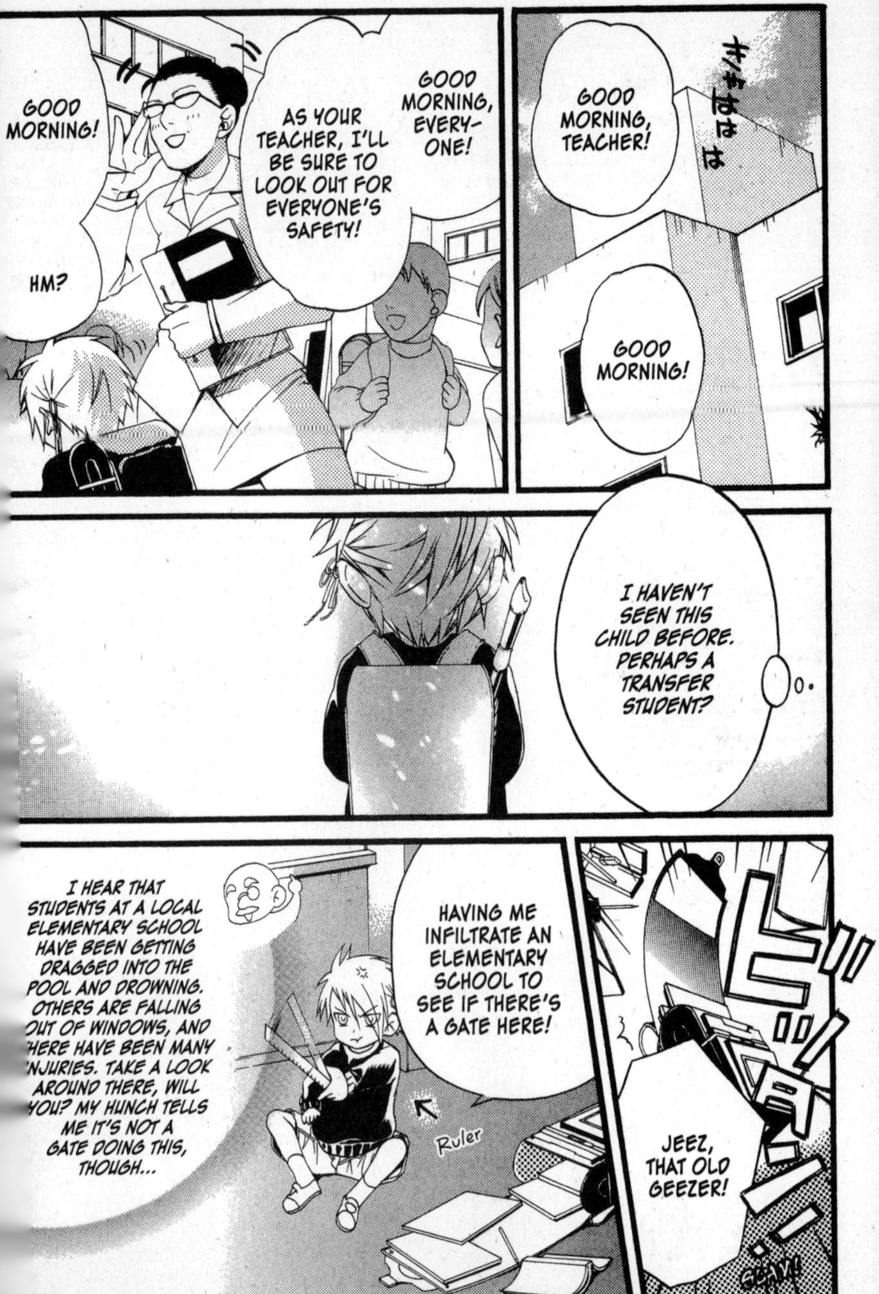

GOOD MORNING, TEACHER!
きゃははは
GOOD MORNING!
GOOD MORNING, EVERYONE!
AS YOUR TEACHER, I'LL BE SURE TO LOOK OUT FOR EVERYONE'S SAFETY!
GOOD MORNING!
HM?
I HAVEN'T SEEN THIS CHILD BEFORE. PERHAPS A TRANSFER STUDENT?
JEEZ, THAT OLD GEEZER!
HAVING ME INFILTRATE AN ELEMENTARY SCHOOL TO SEE IF THERE'S A GATE HERE!
Ruler
I HEAR THAT STUDENTS AT A LOCAL ELEMENTARY SCHOOL HAVE BEEN GETTING DRAGGED INTO THE POOL AND DROWNING. OTHERS ARE FALLING OUT OF WINDOWS, AND THERE HAVE BEEN MANY INJURIES. TAKE A LOOK AROUND THERE, WILL YOU? MY HUNCH TELLS ME IT'S NOT A GATE DOING THIS, THOUGH...

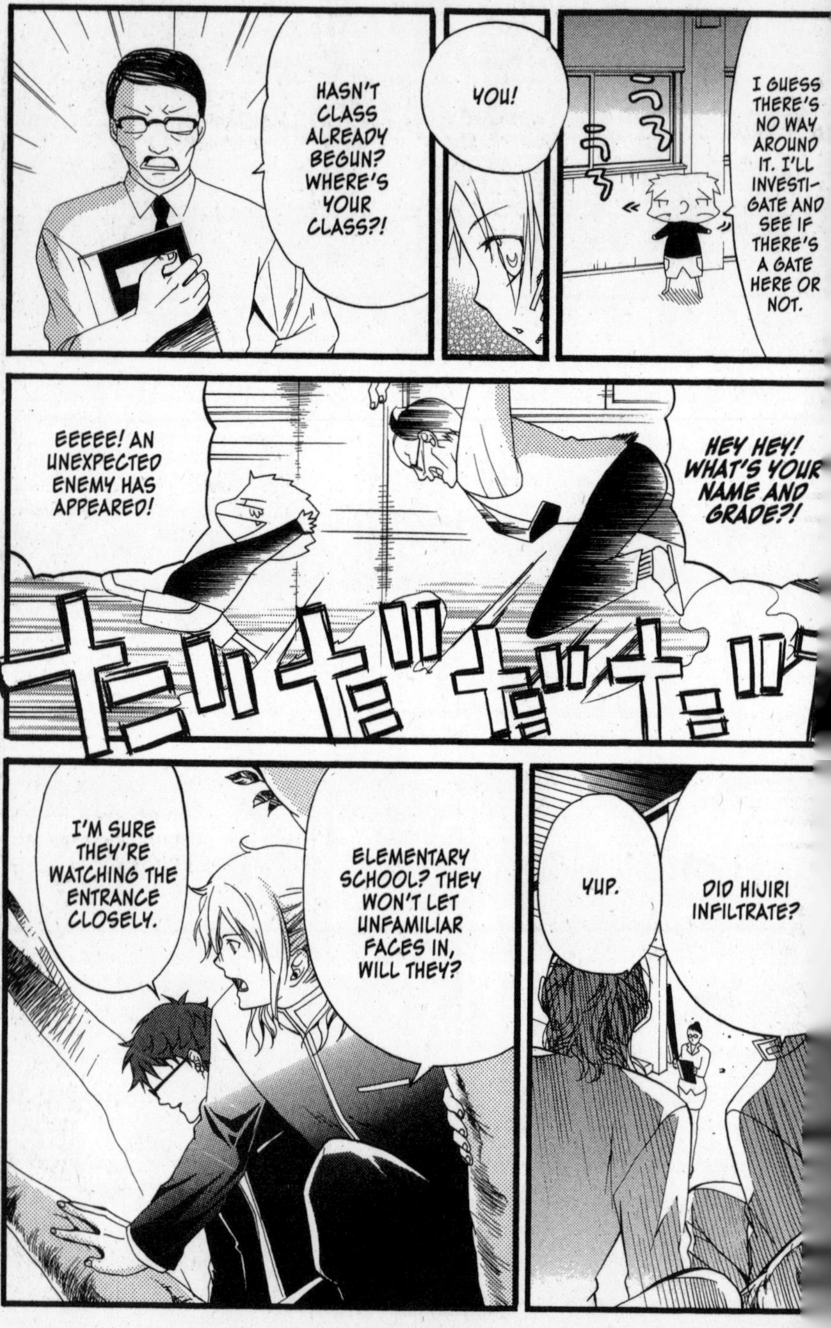
I GUESS THERE'S NO WAY AROUND IT. I'LL INVESTI-GATE AND SEE IF THERE'S A GATE HERE OR NOT.
YOU!
HASN'T CLASS ALREADY BEGUN? WHERE'S YOUR CLASS?!
HEY HEY! WHAT'S YOUR NAME AND GRADE?!
EEEEE! AN UNEXPECTED ENEMY HAS APPEARED!
DID HIJIRI INFILTRATE?
YUP.
ELEMENTARY SCHOOL? THEY WON'T LET UNFAMILIAR FACES IN, WILL THEY?
I'M SURE THEY'RE WATCHING THE ENTRANCE CLOSELY.

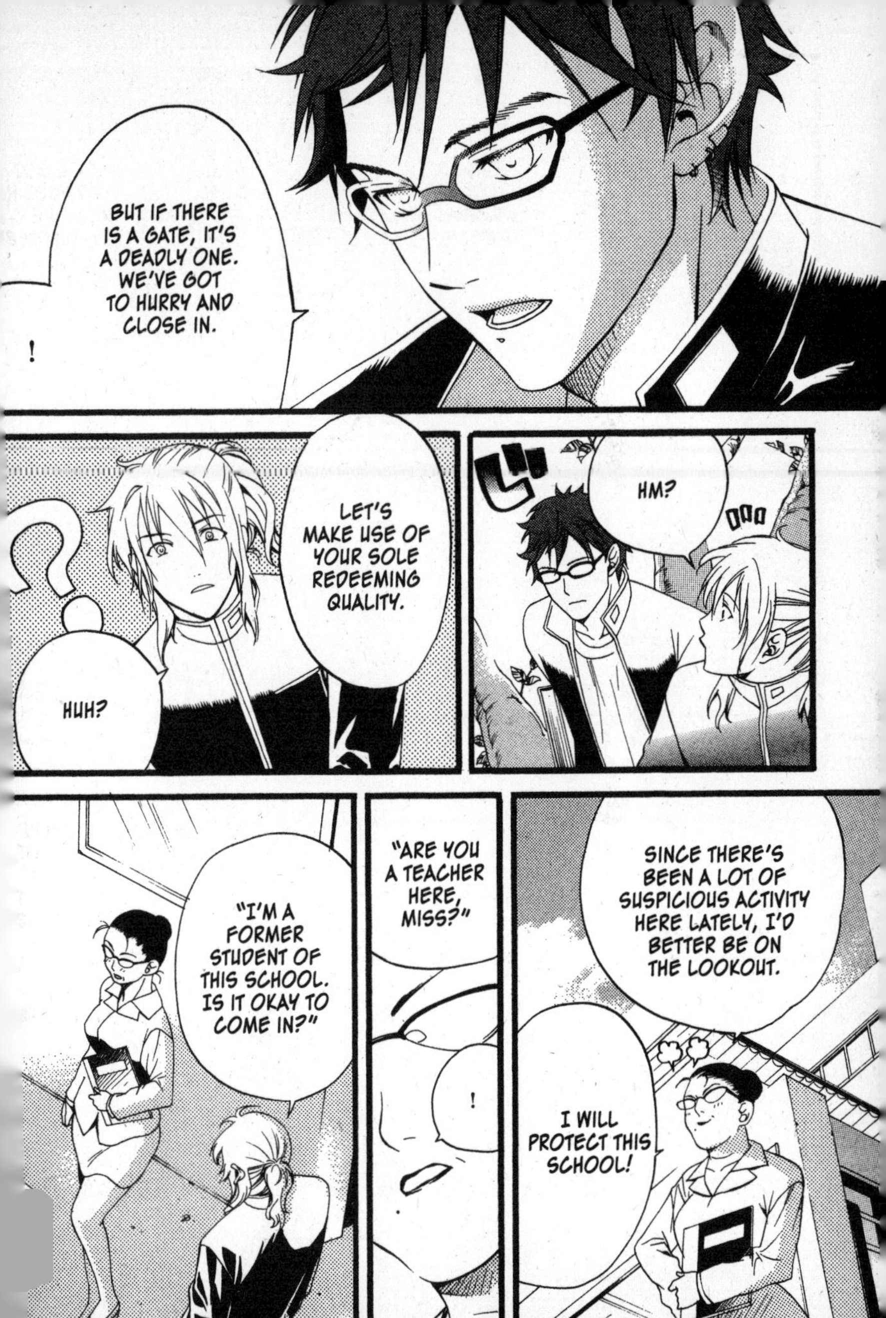
BUT IF THERE IS A GATE, IT'S A DEADLY ONE. WE'VE GOT TO HURRY AND CLOSE IN.
!
HM?
LET'S MAKE USE OF YOUR SOLE REDEEMING QUALITY.
HUH?
SINCE THERE'S BEEN A LOT OF SUSPICIOUS ACTIVITY HERE LATELY, I'D BETTER BE ON THE LOOKOUT.
I WILL PROTECT THIS SCHOOL!
"ARE YOU A TEACHER HERE, MISS?"
!
"I'M A FORMER STUDENT OF THIS SCHOOL. IS IT OKAY TO COME IN?"

uotes because these are lines given to Tsurugi by Michitate.

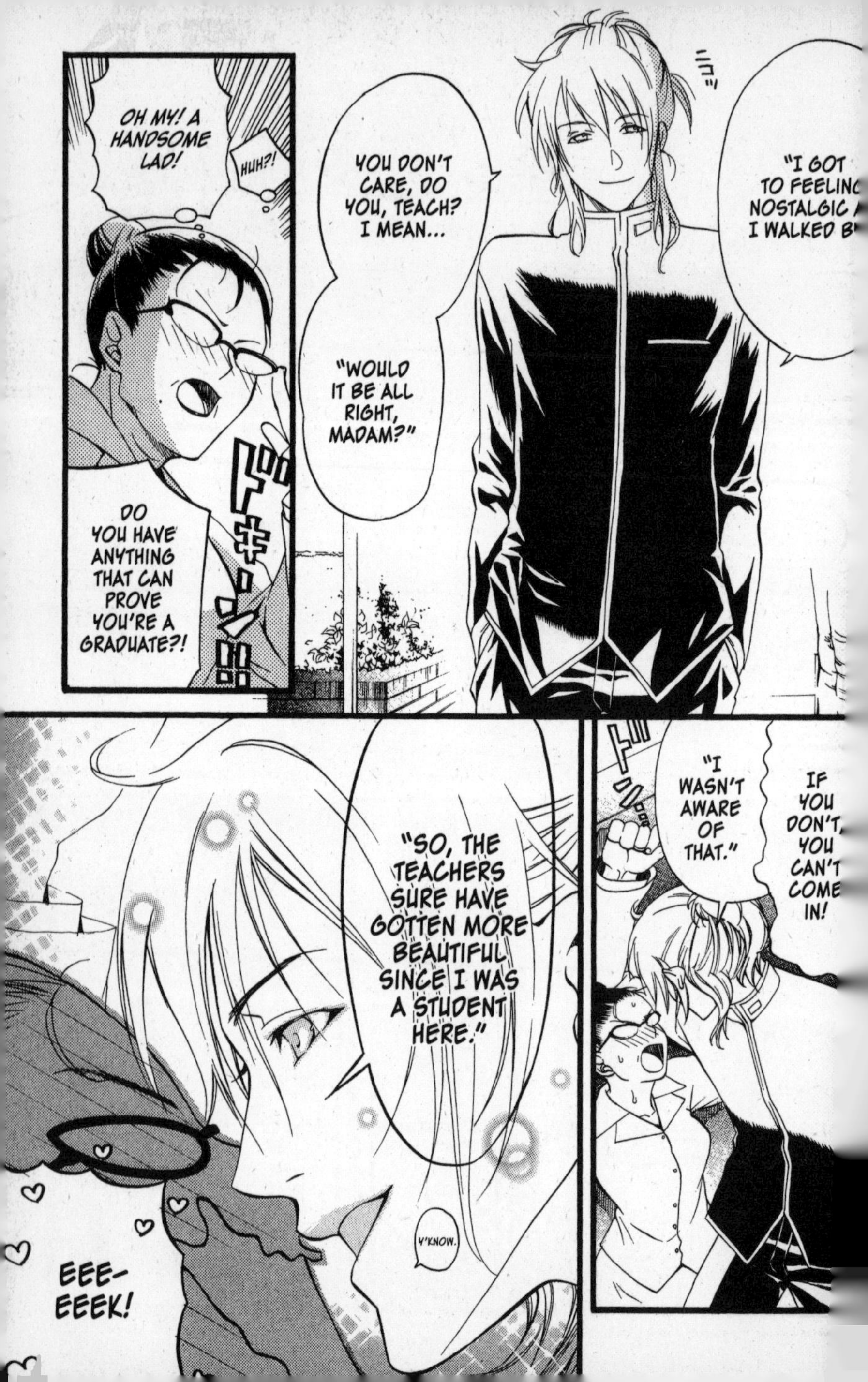

"I GOT TO FEELIN NOSTALGIC I WALKED
YOU DON'T CARE, DO YOU, TEACH? I MEAN...
"WOULD IT BE ALL RIGHT, MADAM?"
OH MY! A HANDSOME LAD!
HUH?!
DO YOU HAVE ANYTHING THAT CAN PROVE YOU'RE A GRADUATE?!
IF YOU DON'T, YOU CAN'T COME IN!
"I WASN'T AWARE OF THAT."
"SO, THE TEACHERS SURE HAVE GOTTEN MORE BEAUTIFUL SINCE I WAS A STUDENT HERE."
Y'KNOW.
EEE-EEEK!

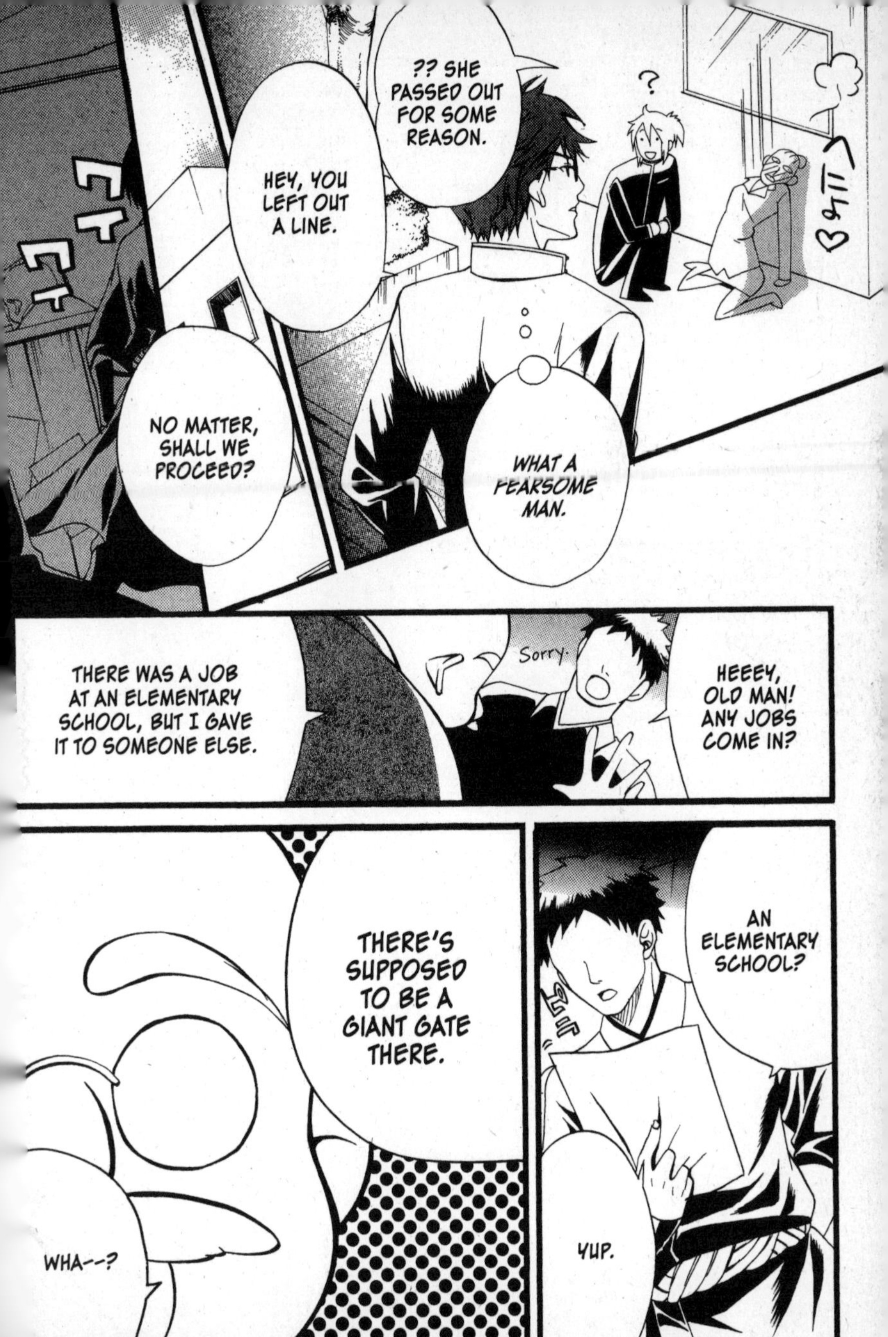

?? SHE PASSED OUT FOR SOME REASON.
HEY, YOU LEFT OUT A LINE.
WHAT A FEARSOME MAN.
NO MATTER, SHALL WE PROCEED?
HEEEY, OLD MAN! ANY JOBS COME IN?
Sorry.
THERE WAS A JOB AT AN ELEMENTARY SCHOOL, BUT I GAVE IT TO SOMEONE ELSE.
AN ELEMENTARY SCHOOL?
YUP.
THERE'S SUPPOSED TO BE A GIANT GATE THERE.
WHA--?

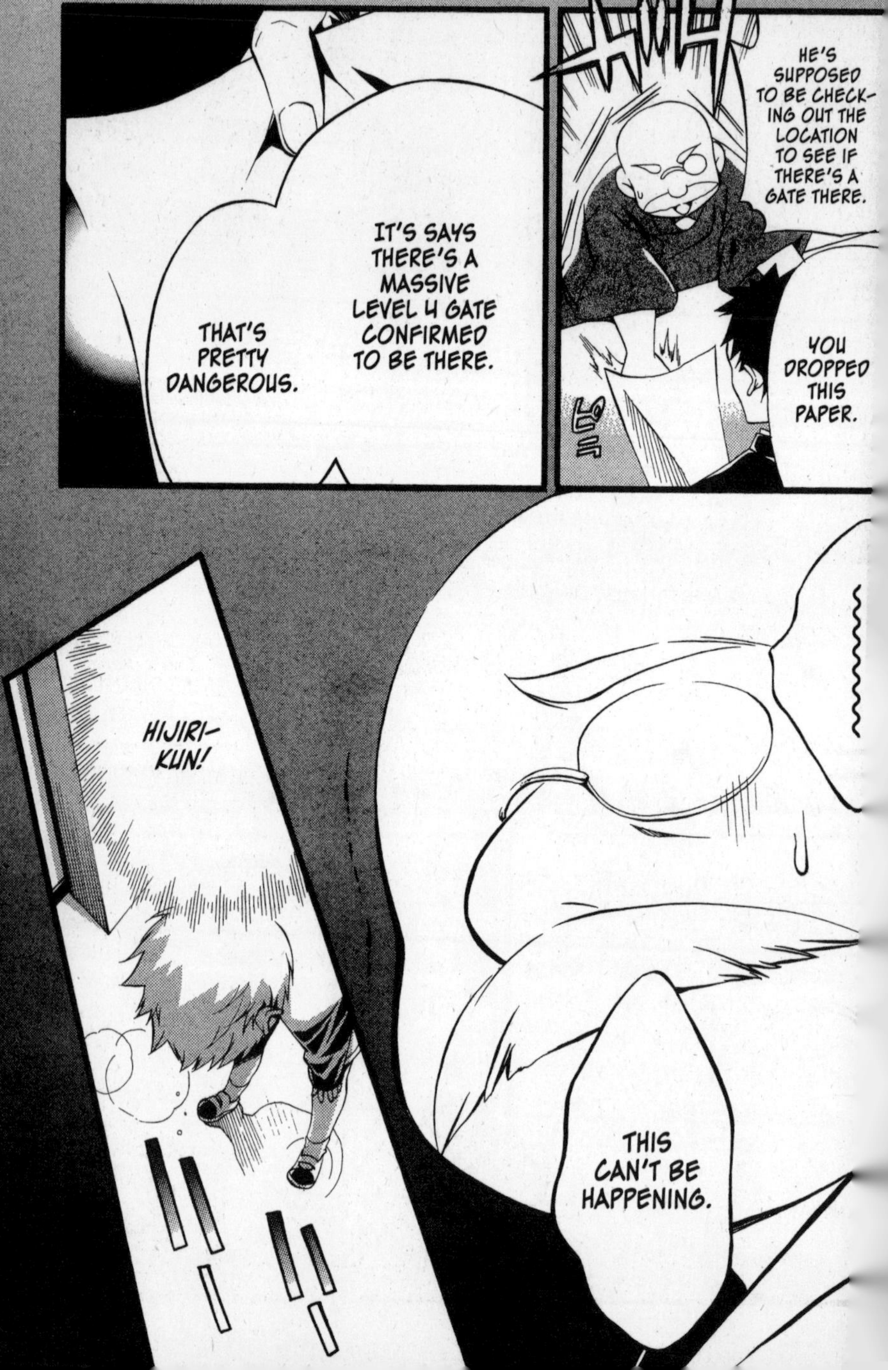
HE'S SUPPOSED TO BE CHECK-ING OUT THE LOCATION TO SEE IF THERE'S A GATE THERE.
YOU DROPPED THIS PAPER.
IT'S SAYS THERE'S A MASSIVE LEVEL 4 GATE CONFIRMED TO BE THERE.
THAT'S PRETTY DANGEROUS.
THIS CAN'T BE HAPPENING.
HIJIRI-KUN!

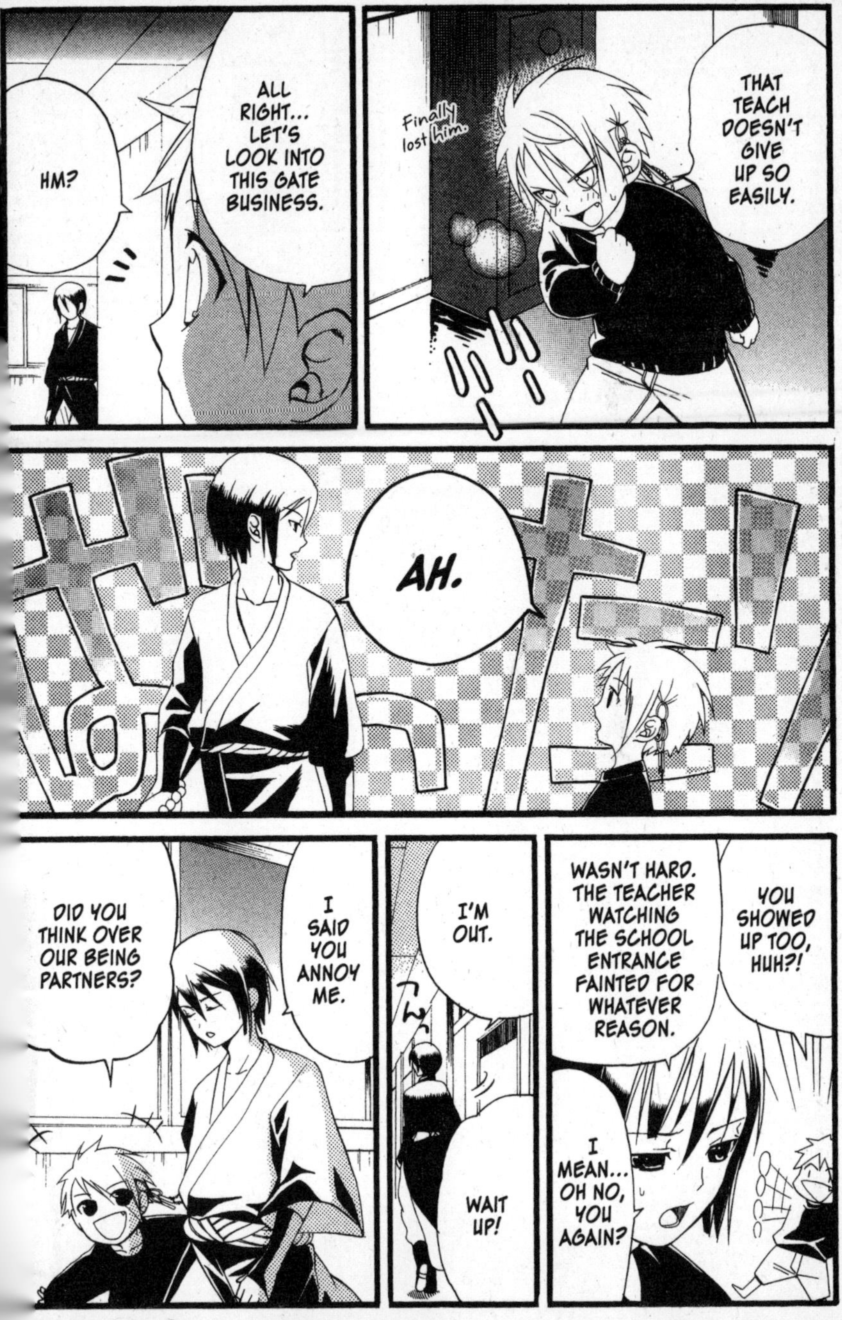
THAT TEACH DOESN'T GIVE UP SO EASILY.
Finally lost him.
ALL RIGHT... LET'S LOOK INTO THIS GATE BUSINESS.
HM?
AH.
YOU SHOWED UP TOO, HUH?!
WASN'T HARD. THE TEACHER WATCHING THE SCHOOL ENTRANCE FAINTED FOR WHATEVER REASON.
I MEAN... OH NO, YOU AGAIN?
I'M OUT.
WAIT UP!
I SAID YOU ANNOY ME.
DID YOU THINK OVER OUR BEING PARTNERS?

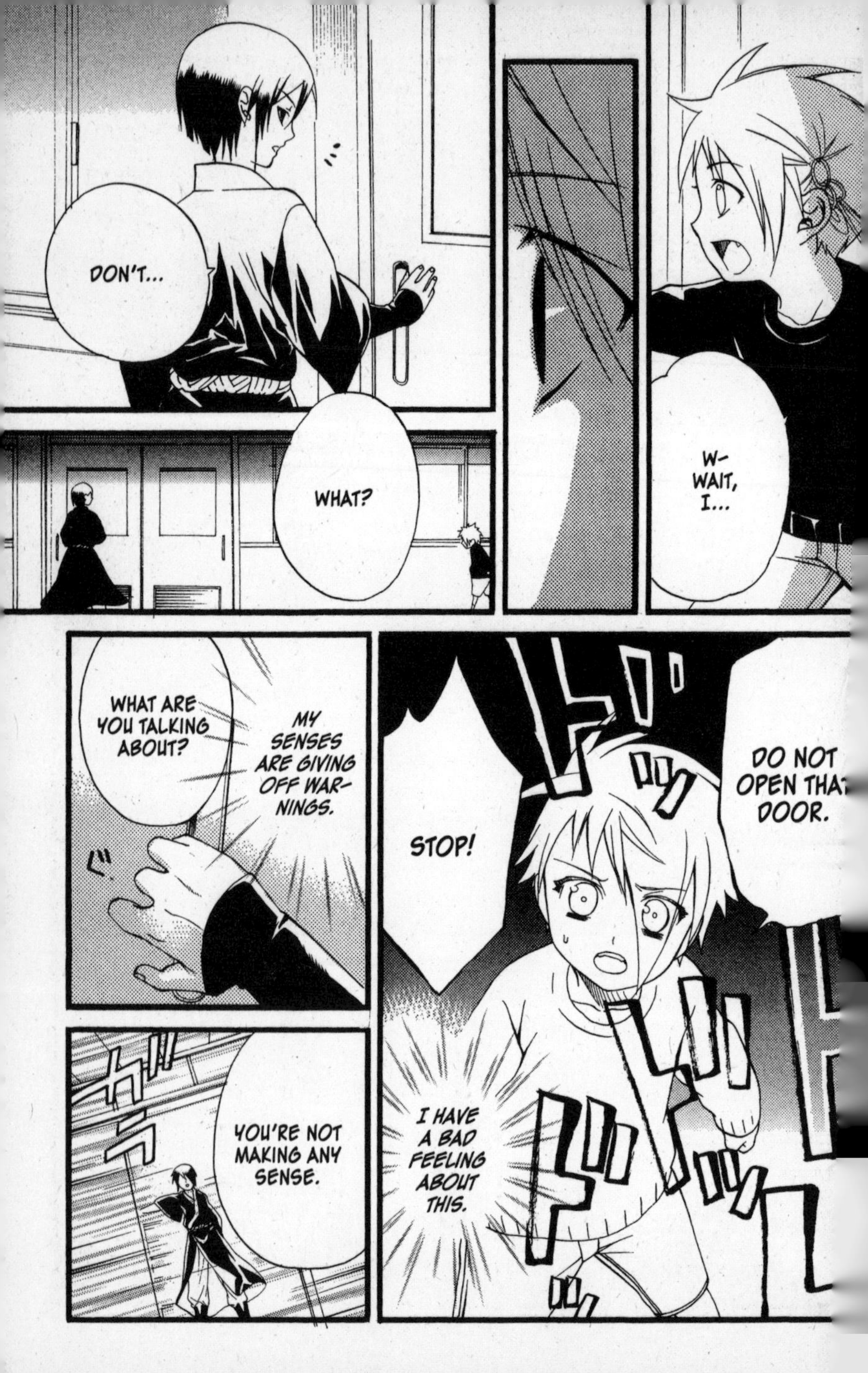
W-WAIT, I...
DON'T...
WHAT?
DO NOT OPEN THAT DOOR.
STOP!
I HAVE A BAD FEELING ABOUT THIS.
WHAT ARE YOU TALKING ABOUT?
MY SENSES ARE GIVING OFF WARNINGS.
YOU'RE NOT MAKING ANY SENSE.

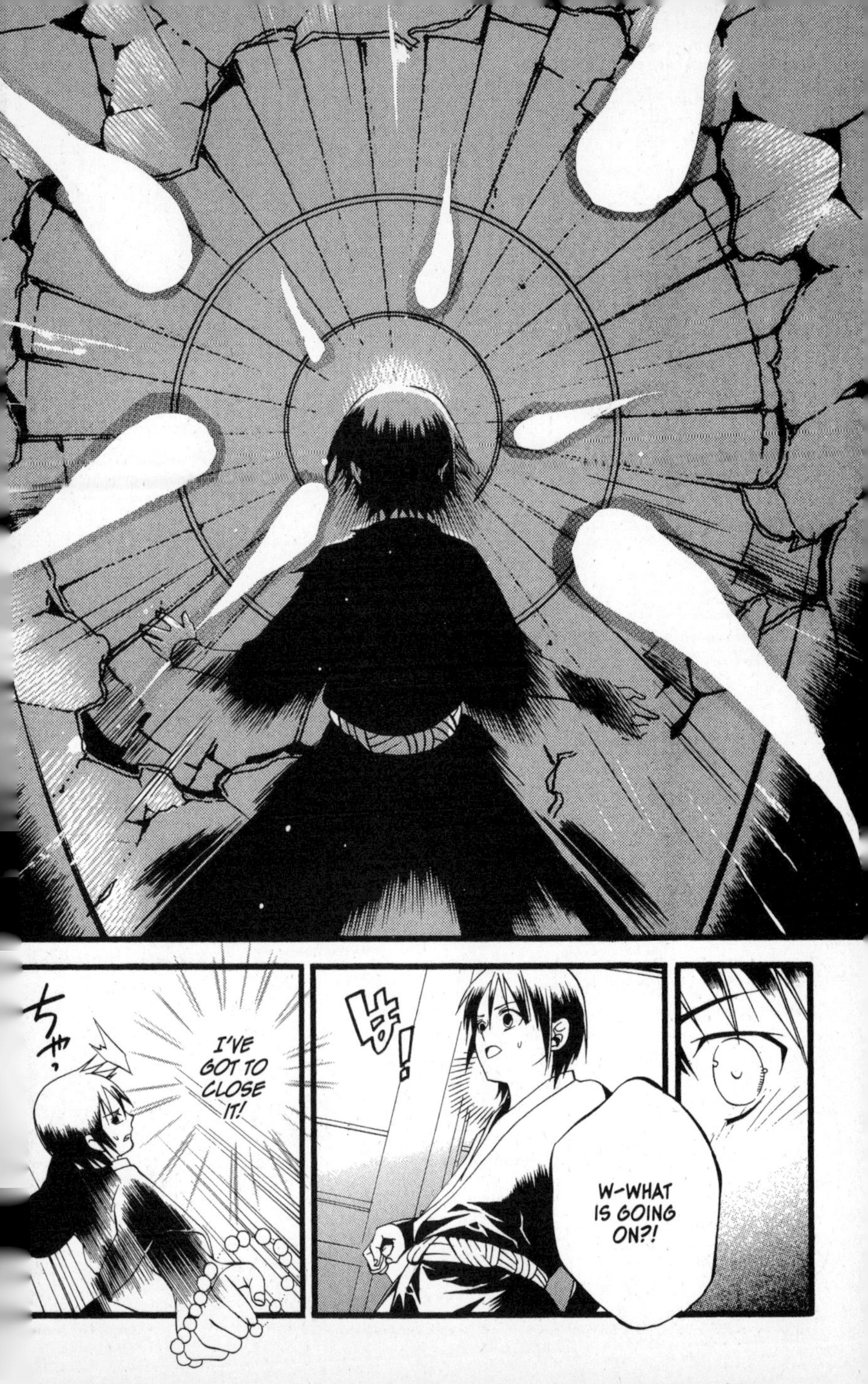
は!
W-WHAT IS GOING ON?!
ちゃ
I'VE GOT TO CLOSE IT!

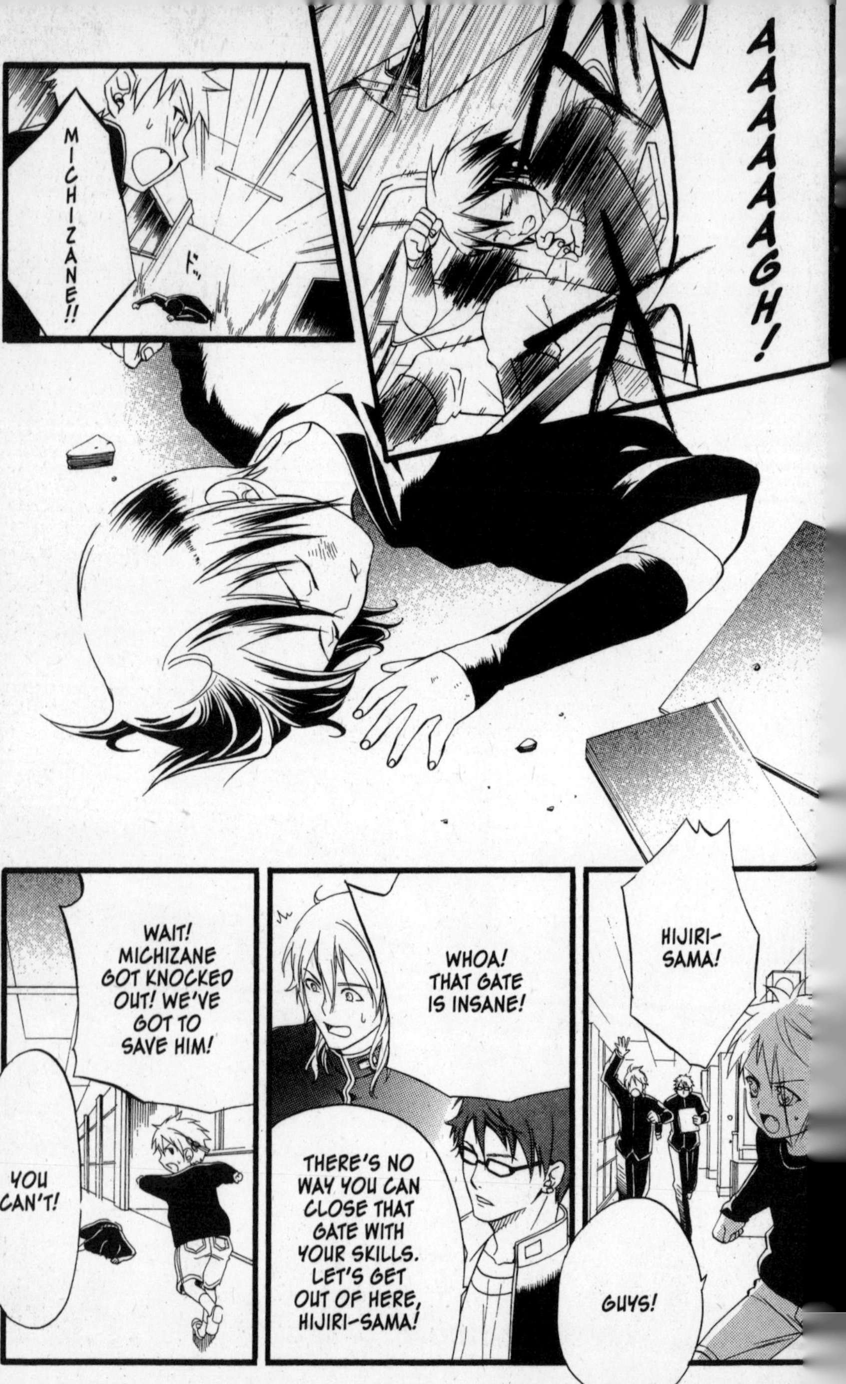
AAAAAAAGH!
MICHIZANE!!
ド…
HIJIRI-SAMA!
GUYS!
WHOA! THAT GATE IS INSANE!
THERE'S NO WAY YOU CAN CLOSE THAT GATE WITH YOUR SKILLS. LET'S GET OUT OF HERE, HIJIRI-SAMA!
WAIT! MICHIZANE GOT KNOCKED OUT! WE'VE GOT TO SAVE HIM!
YOU CAN'T!

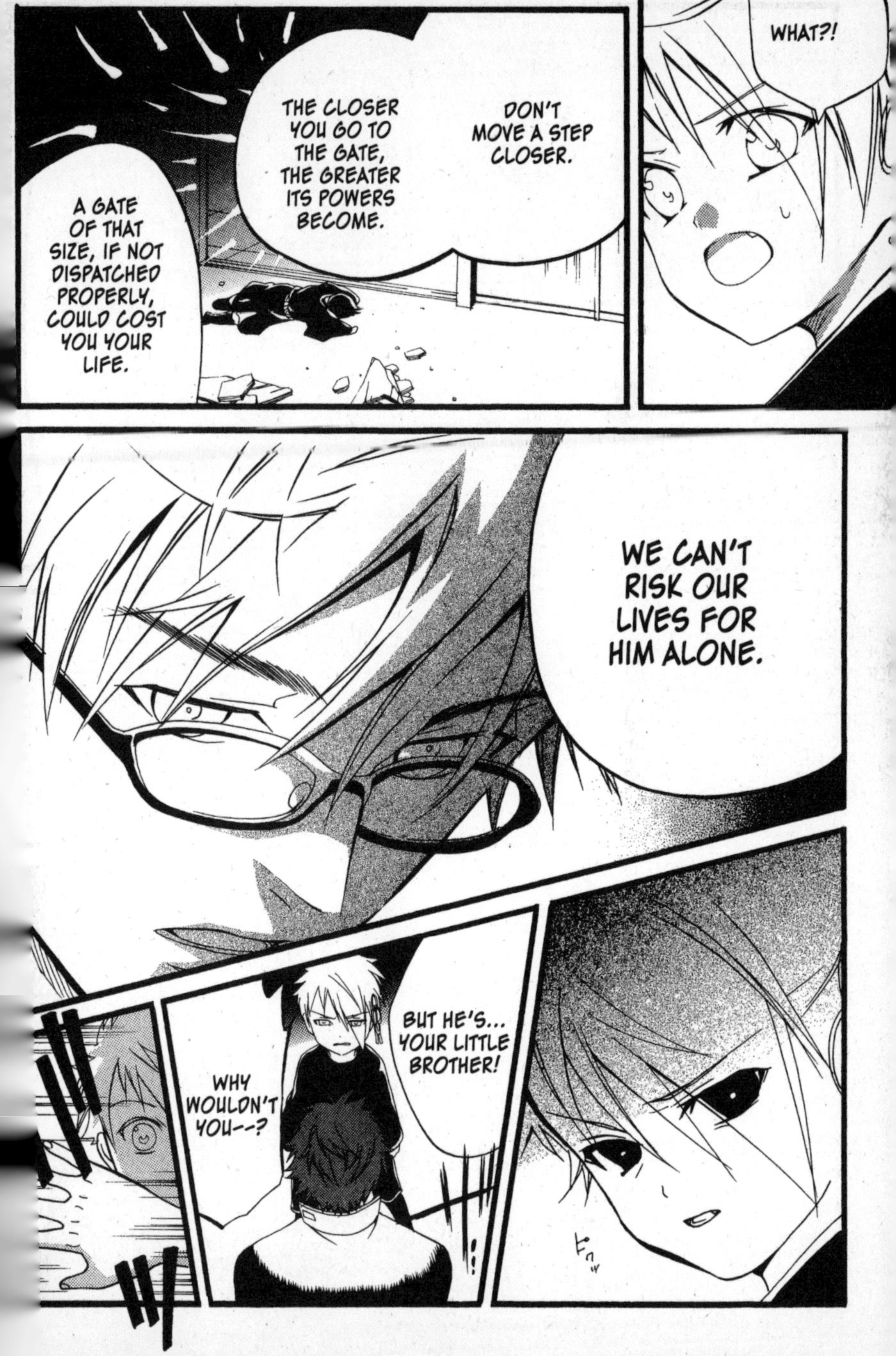
WHAT?!
DON'T MOVE A STEP CLOSER.
THE CLOSER YOU GO TO THE GATE, THE GREATER ITS POWERS BECOME.
A GATE OF THAT SIZE, IF NOT DISPATCHED PROPERLY, COULD COST YOU YOUR LIFE.
WE CAN'T RISK OUR LIVES FOR HIM ALONE.
BUT HE'S... YOUR LITTLE BROTHER!
WHY WOULDN'T YOU--?

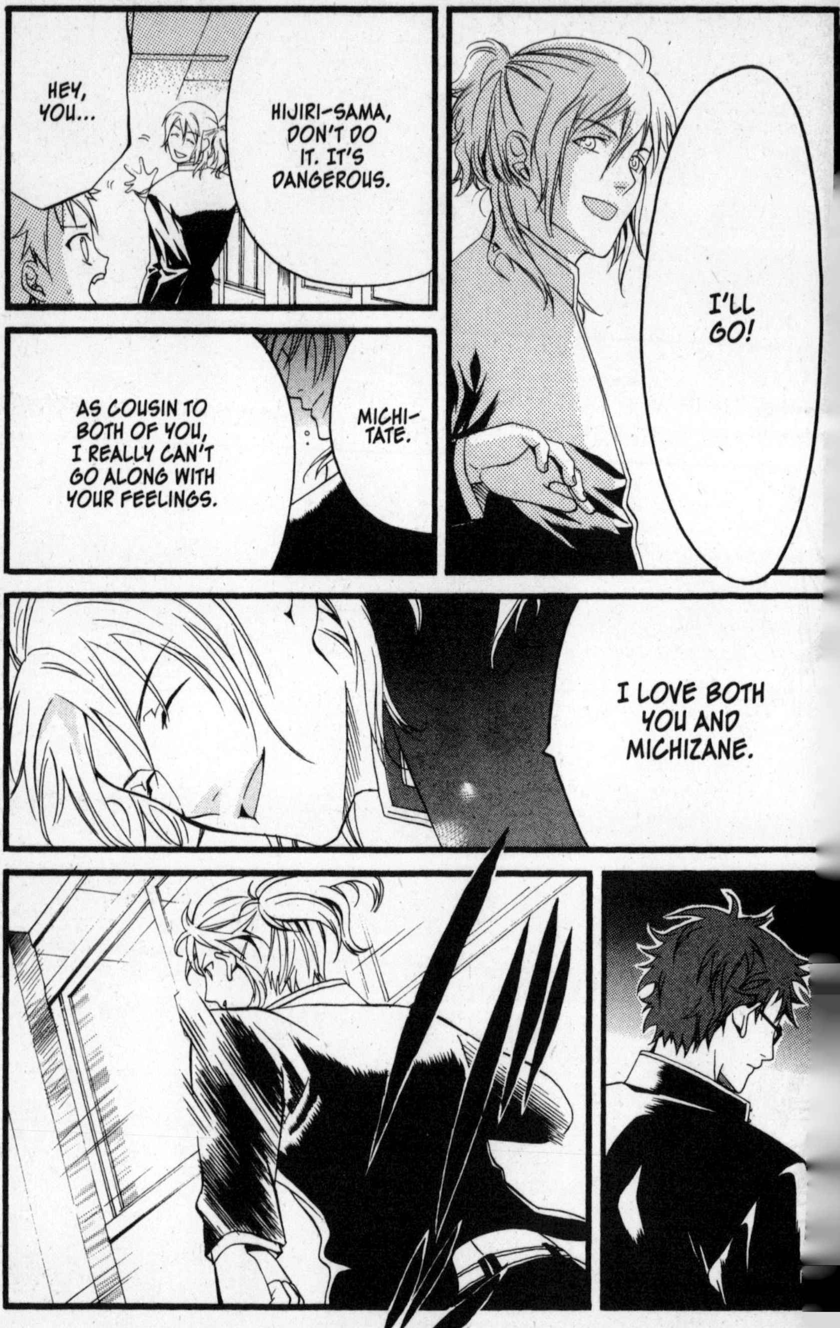
I'LL GO!
HIJIRI-SAMA, DON'T DO IT. IT'S DANGEROUS.
HEY, YOU...
MICHI-TATE.
AS COUSIN TO BOTH OF YOU, I REALLY CAN'T GO ALONG WITH YOUR FEELINGS.
I LOVE BOTH YOU AND MICHIZANE.

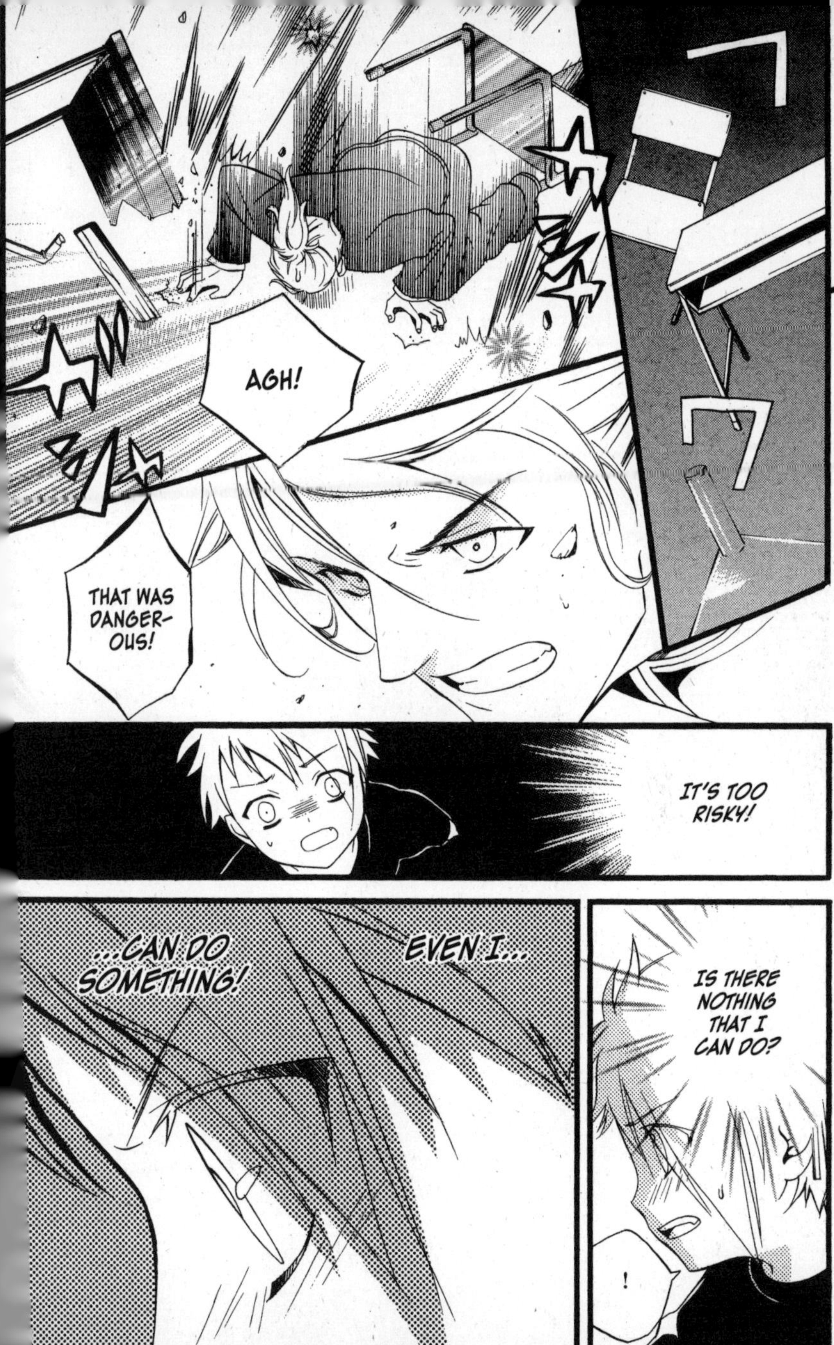
AGH!
THAT WAS DANGER-OUS!
IT'S TOO RISKY!
IS THERE NOTHING THAT I CAN DO?
!
EVEN I...
...CAN DO SOMETHING!

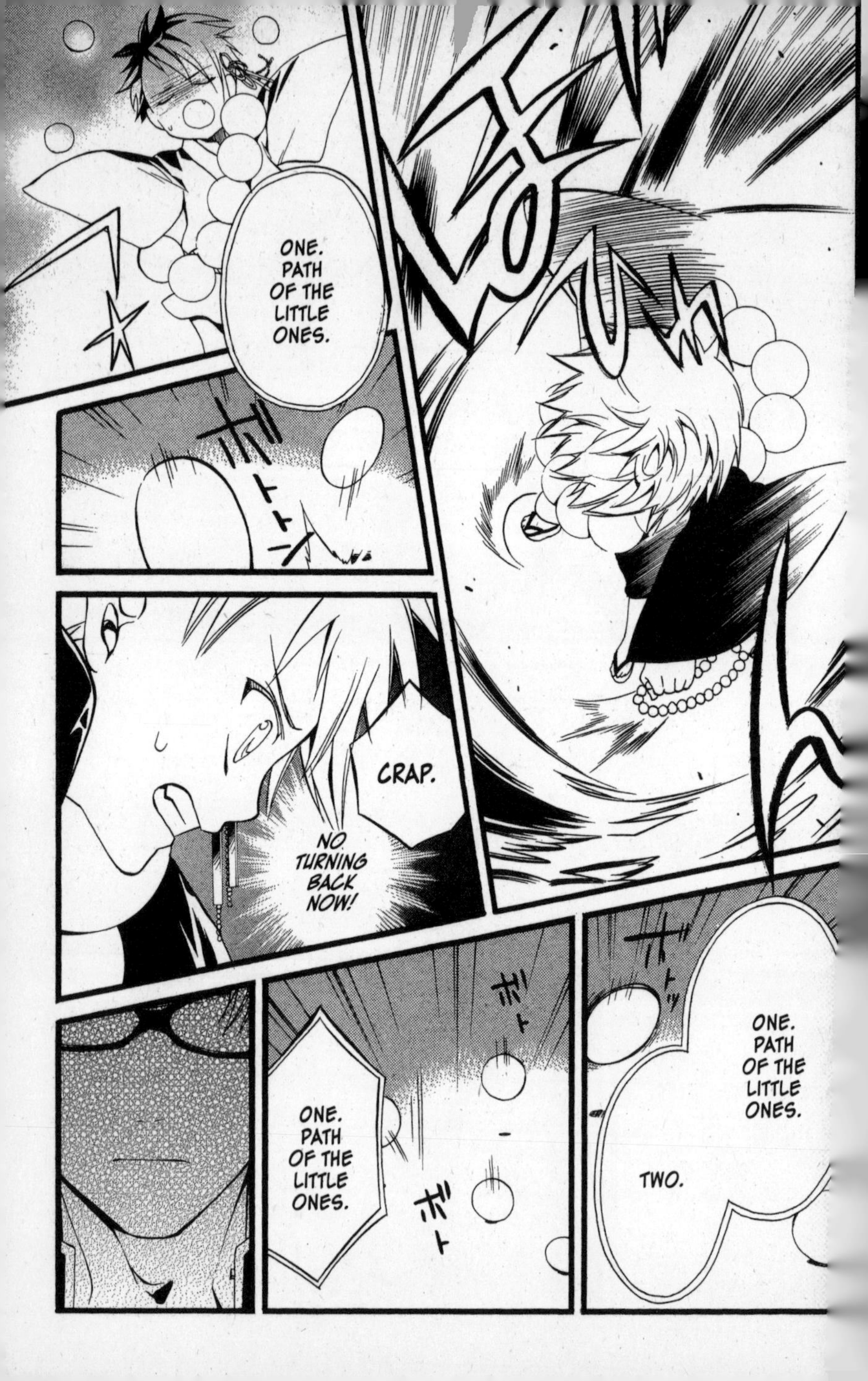
ONE. PATH OF THE LITTLE ONES.
CRAP.
NO TURNING BACK NOW!
ONE. PATH OF THE LITTLE ONES.
TWO.
ONE. PATH OF THE LITTLE ONES.

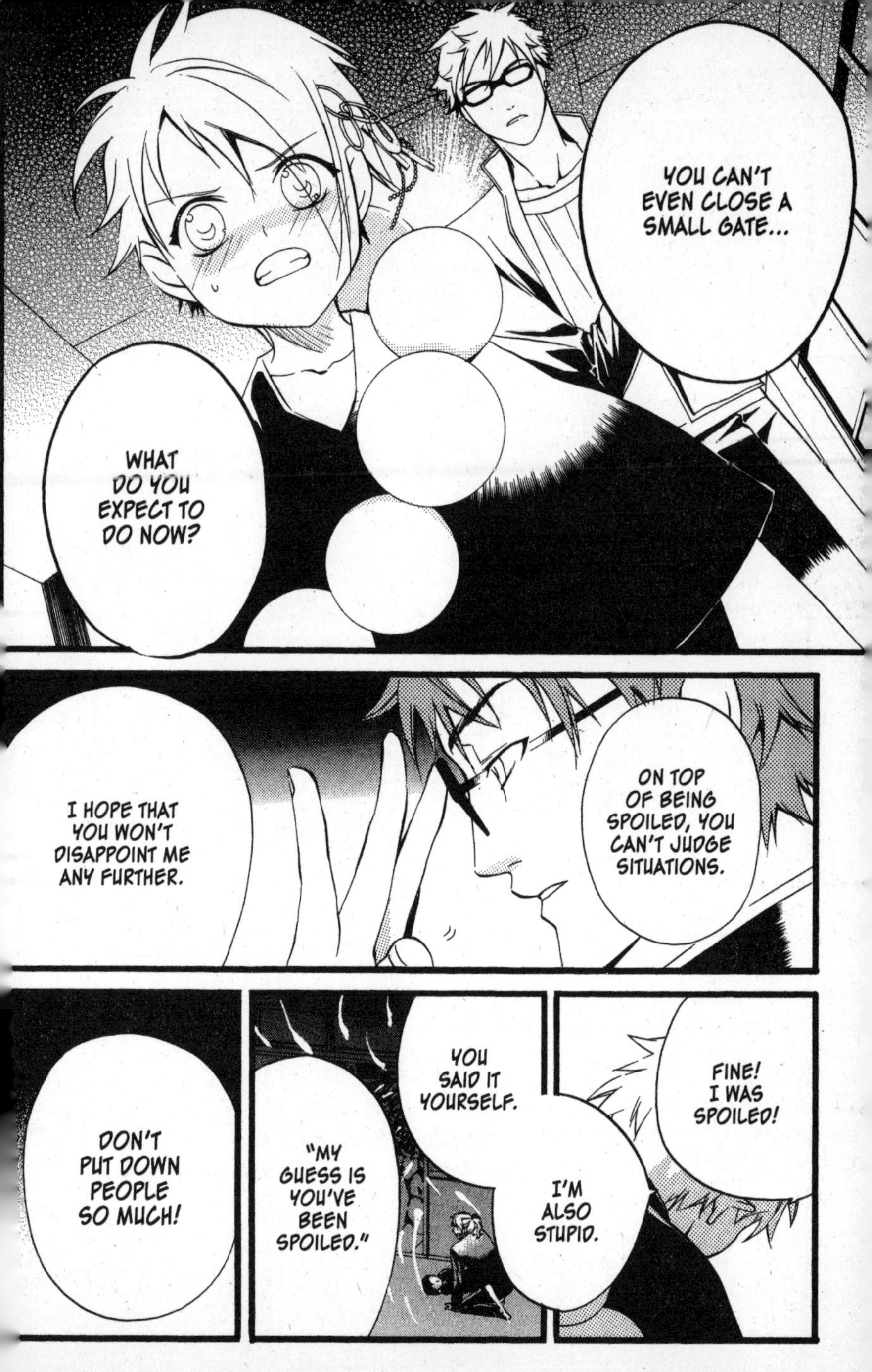
YOU CAN'T EVEN CLOSE A SMALL GATE...
WHAT DO YOU EXPECT TO DO NOW?
ON TOP OF BEING SPOILED, YOU CAN'T JUDGE SITUATIONS.
I HOPE THAT YOU WON'T DISAPPOINT ME ANY FURTHER.
FINE! I WAS SPOILED!
I'M ALSO STUPID.
YOU SAID IT YOURSELF.
"MY GUESS IS YOU'VE BEEN SPOILED."
DON'T PUT DOWN PEOPLE SO MUCH!

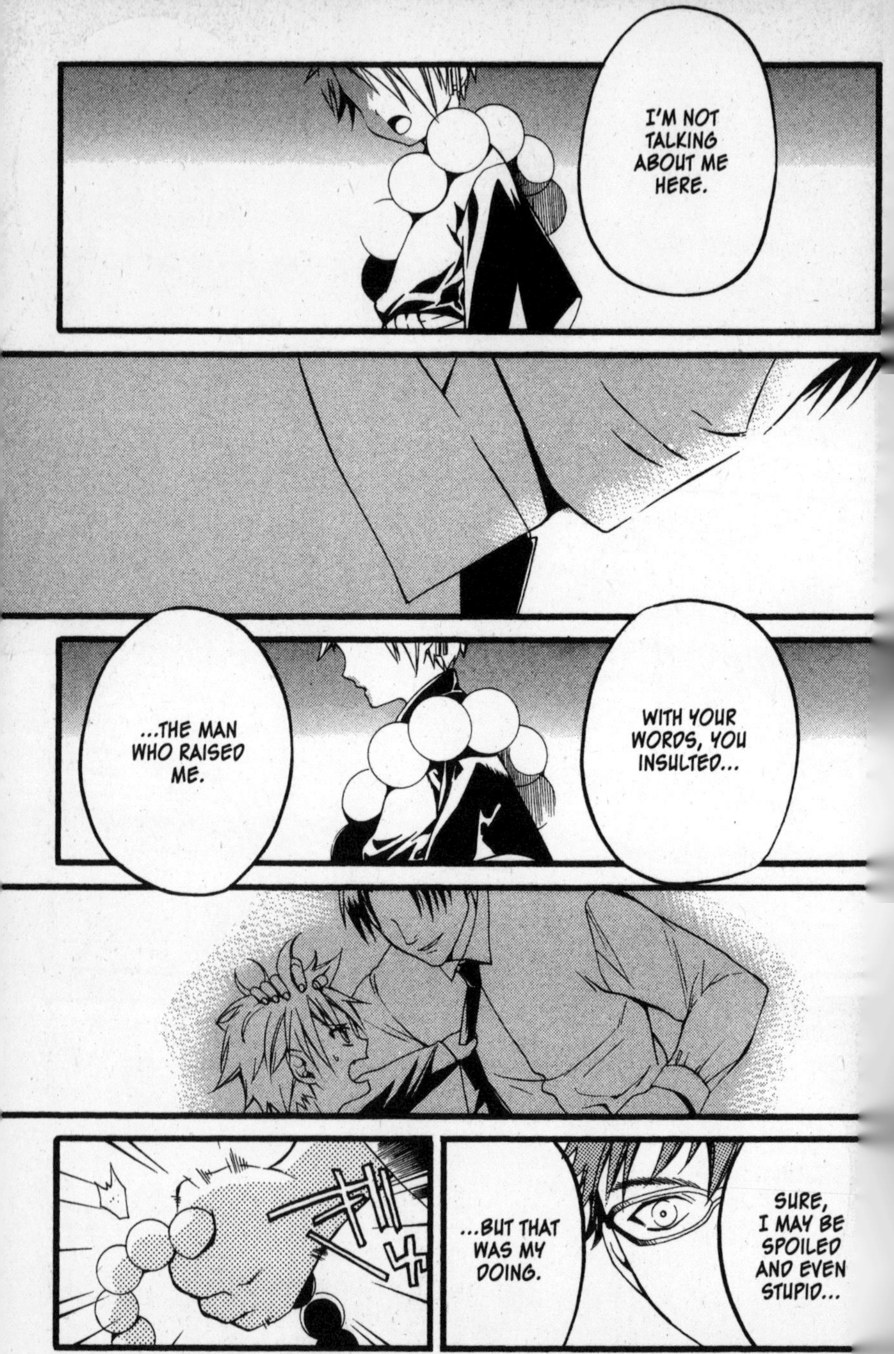
I'M NOT TALKING ABOUT ME HERE.
WITH YOUR WORDS, YOU INSULTED...
...THE MAN WHO RAISED ME.
SURE, I MAY BE SPOILED AND EVEN STUPID...
...BUT THAT WAS MY DOING.

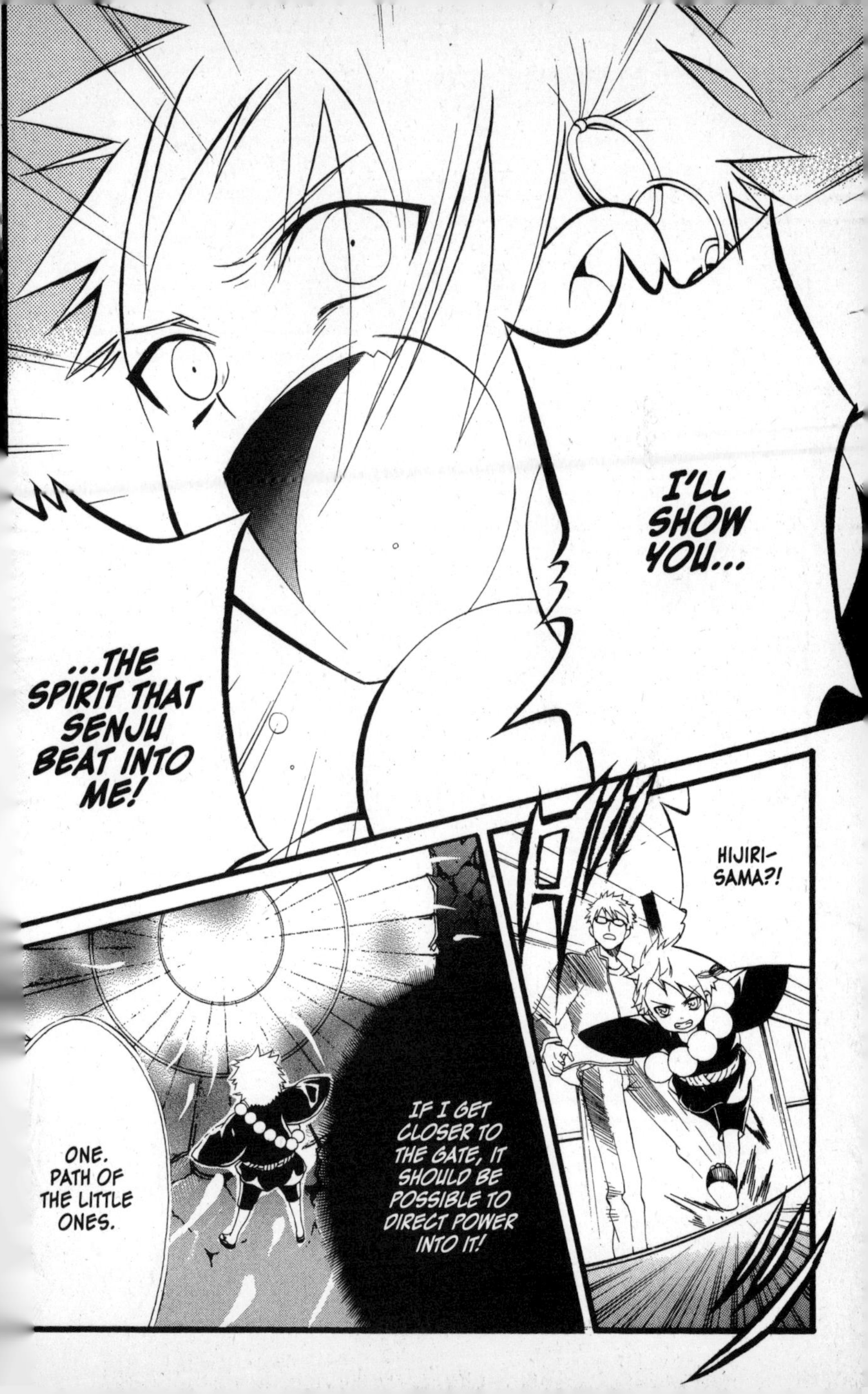
I'LL SHOW YOU...
...THE SPIRIT THAT SENJU BEAT INTO ME!
HIJIRI-SAMA?!
IF I GET CLOSER TO THE GATE, IT SHOULD BE POSSIBLE TO DIRECT POWER INTO IT!
ONE. PATH OF THE LITTLE ONES.

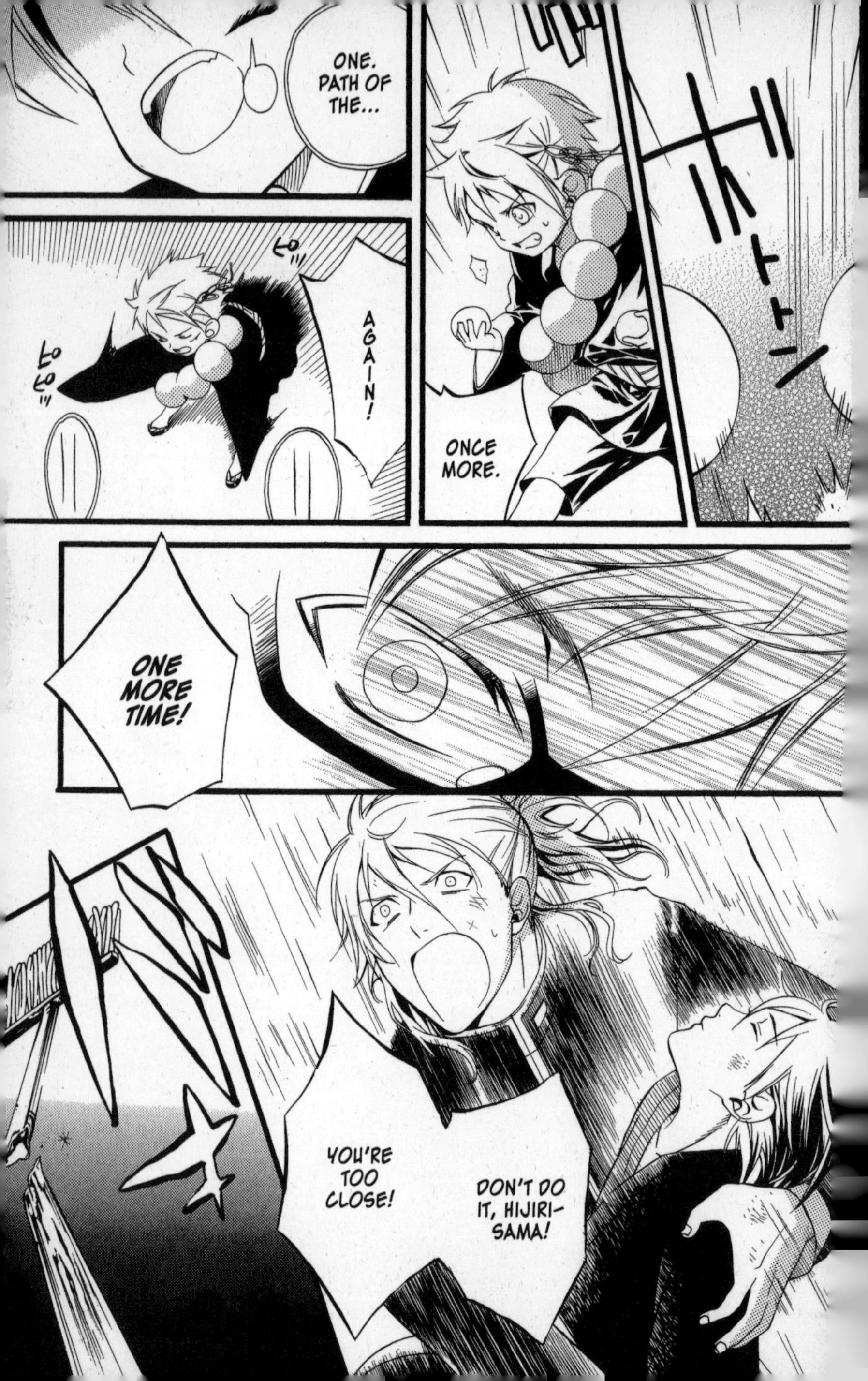
ONCE MORE.
ONE. PATH OF THE...
AGAIN!
ONE MORE TIME!
DON'T DO IT, HIJIRI-SAMA!
YOU'RE TOO CLOSE!

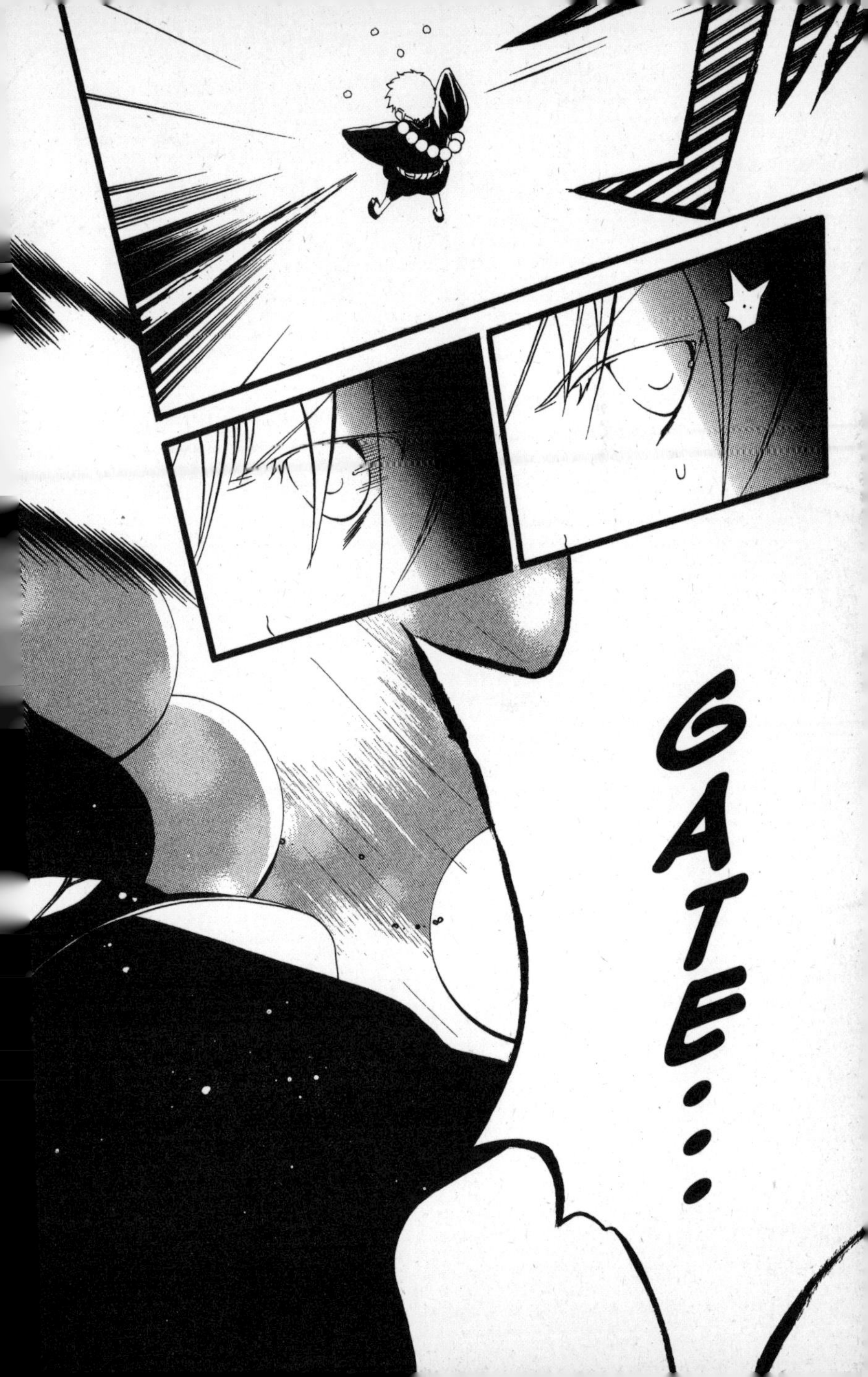
GATE...

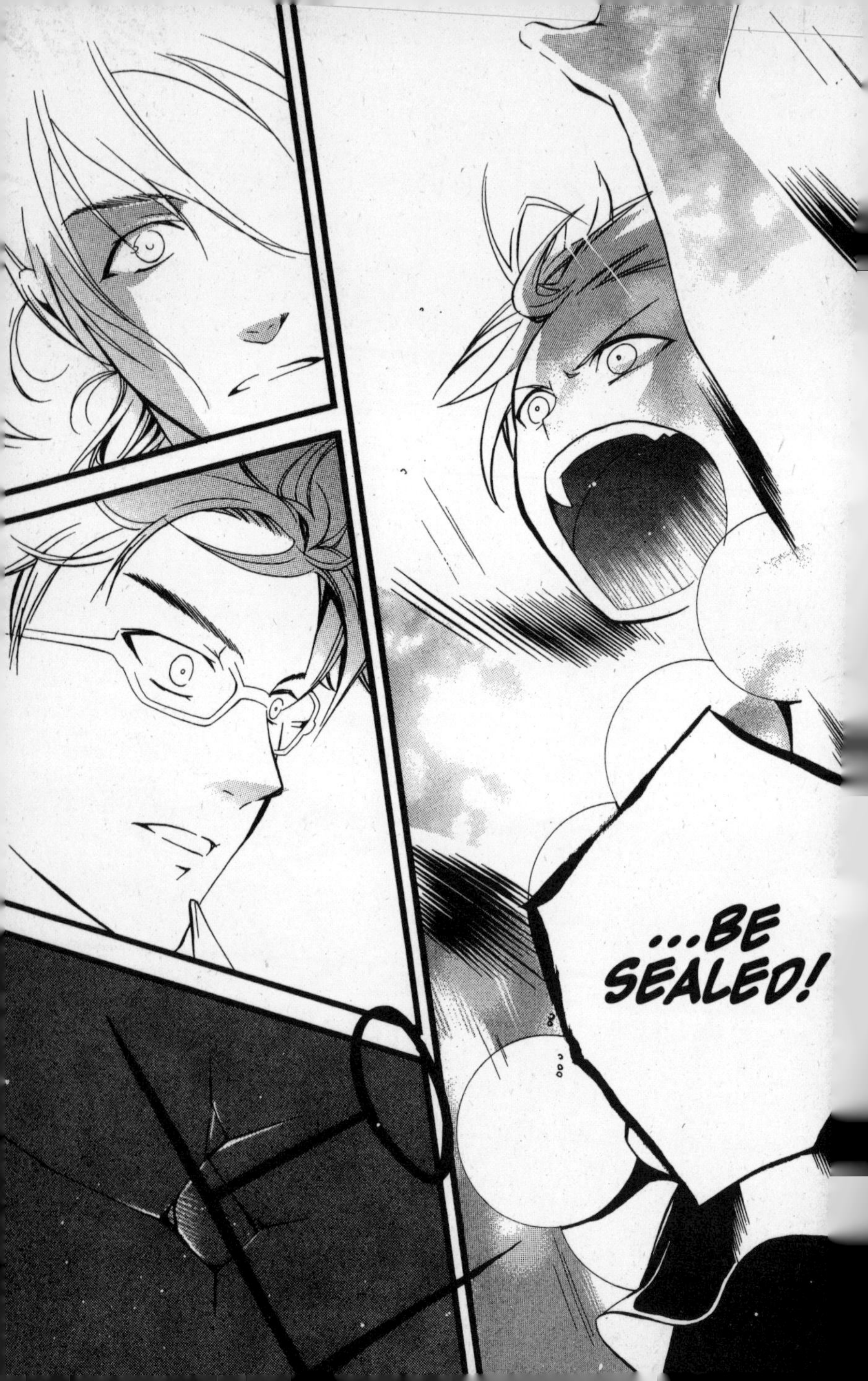
...BE SEALED!

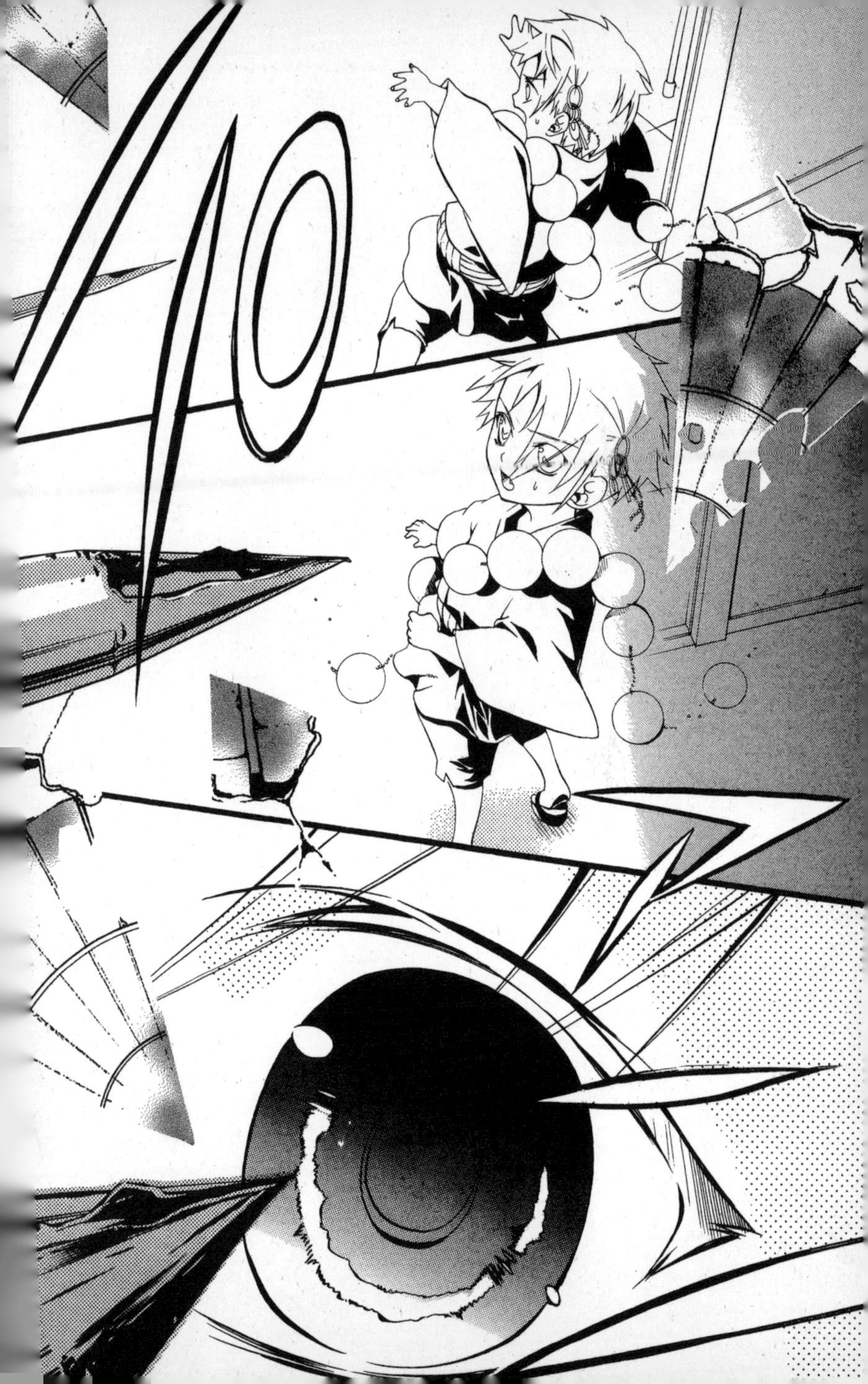

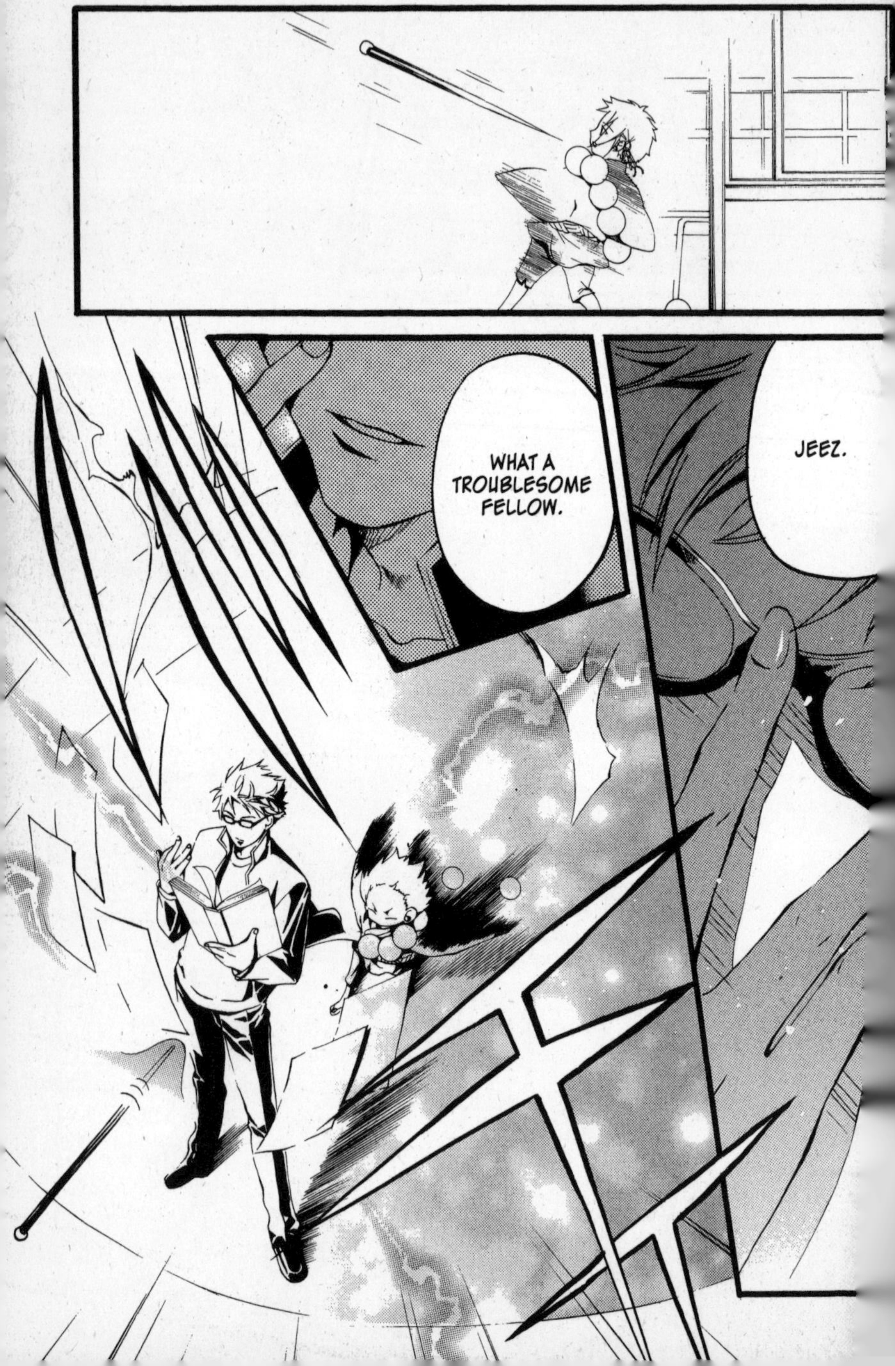
JEEZ.
WHAT A TROUBLESOME FELLOW.

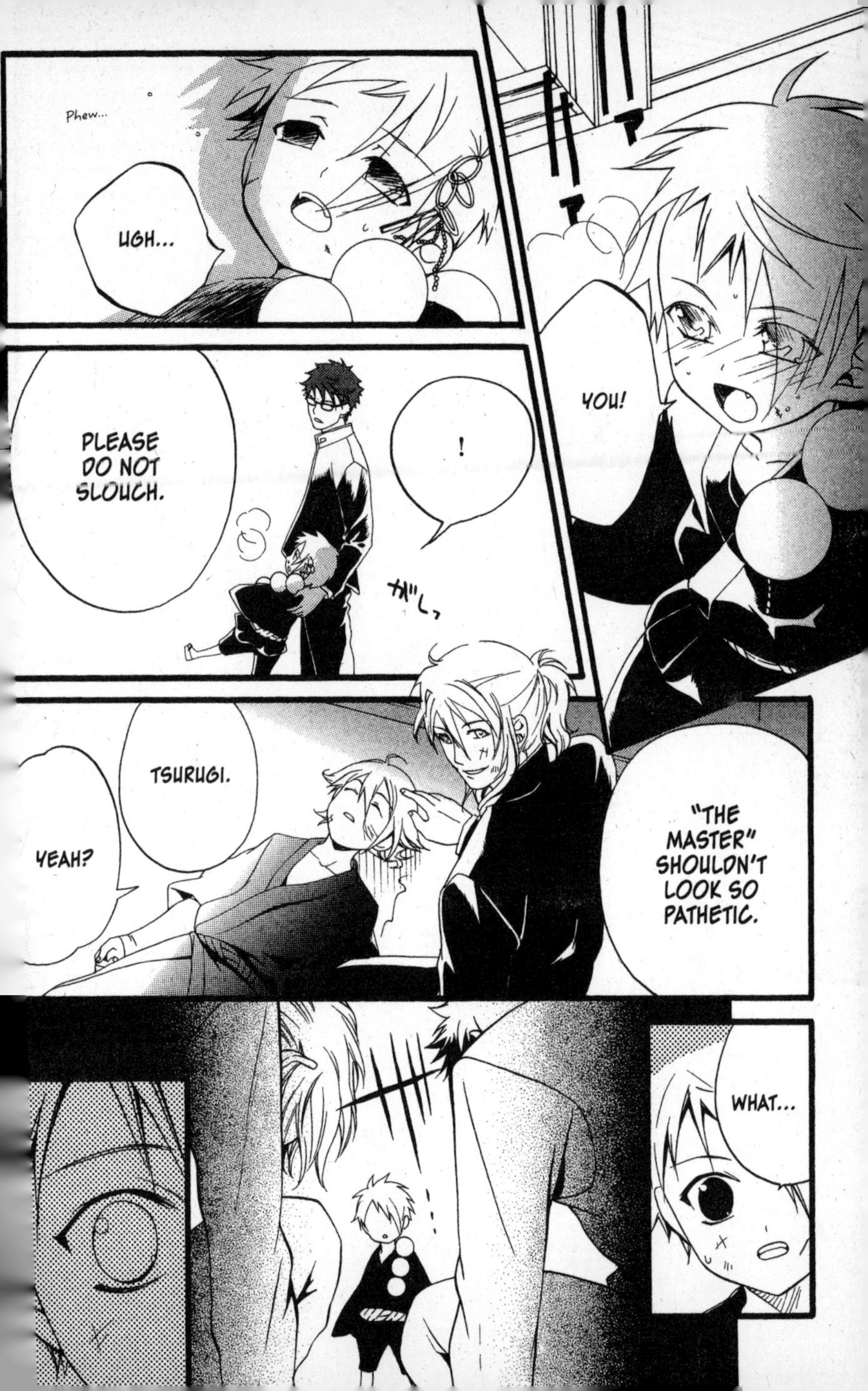
YOU!
Phew...
UGH...
PLEASE DO NOT SLOUCH.
!
ガシッ
"THE MASTER" SHOULDN'T LOOK SO PATHETIC.
TSURUGI.
YEAH?
WHAT...
!
!

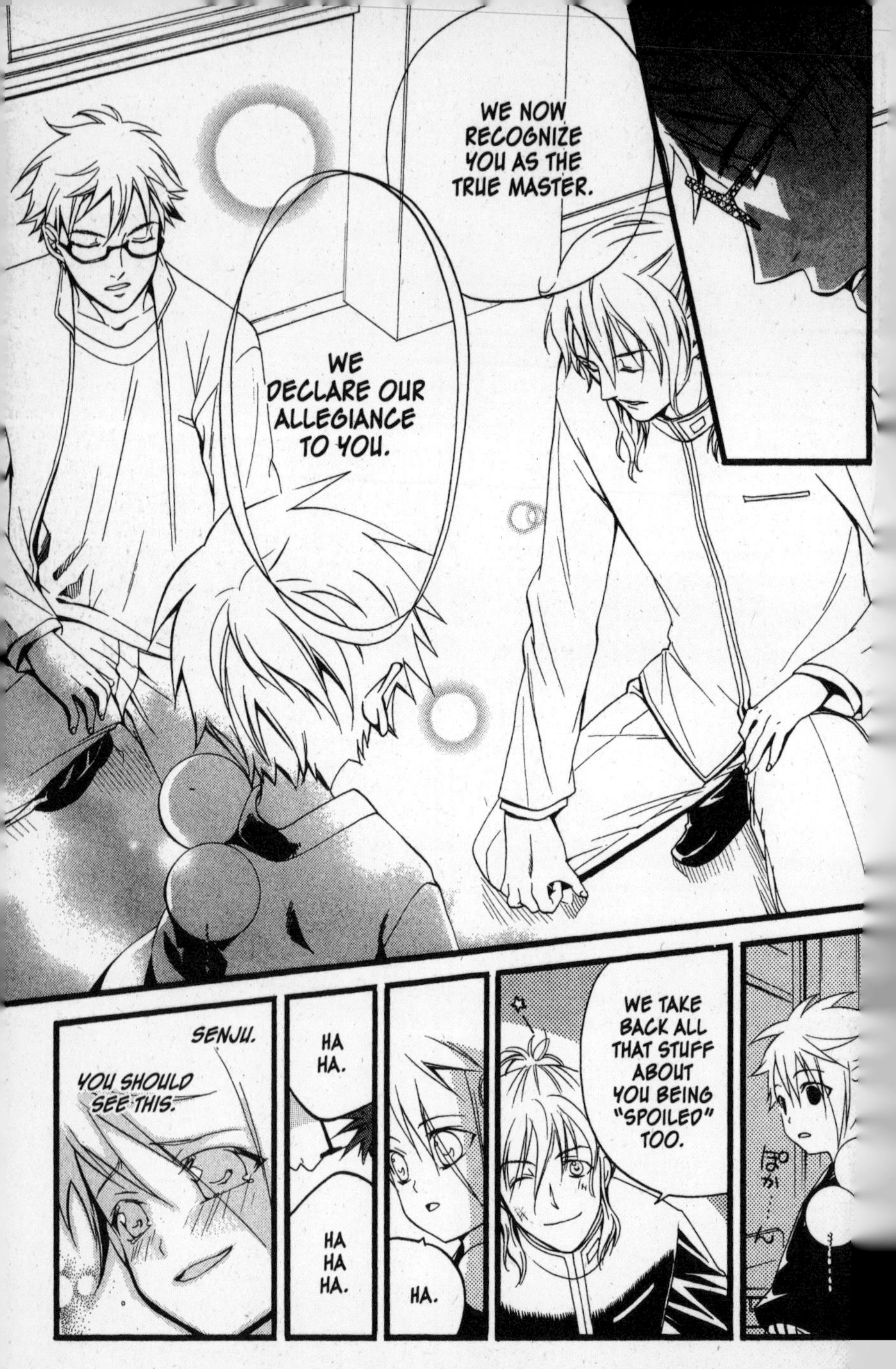
WE NOW RECOGNIZE YOU AS THE TRUE MASTER.
WE DECLARE OUR ALLEGIANCE TO YOU.
ぽか……ん
WE TAKE BACK ALL THAT STUFF ABOUT YOU BEING "SPOILED" TOO.
HA.
HA HA.
HA HA HA.
SENJU.
YOU SHOULD SEE THIS.

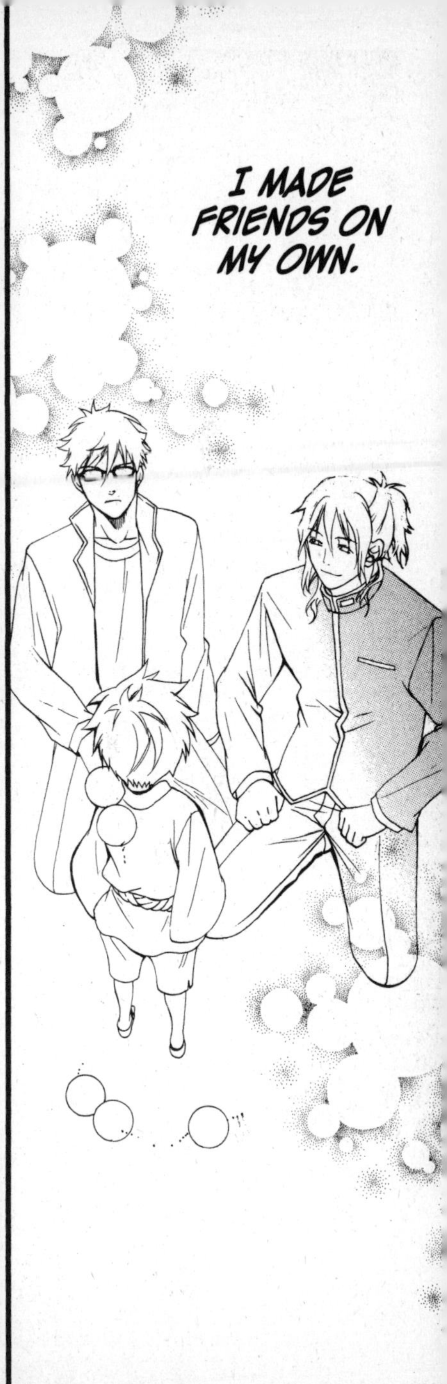
I MADE FRIENDS ON MY OWN.

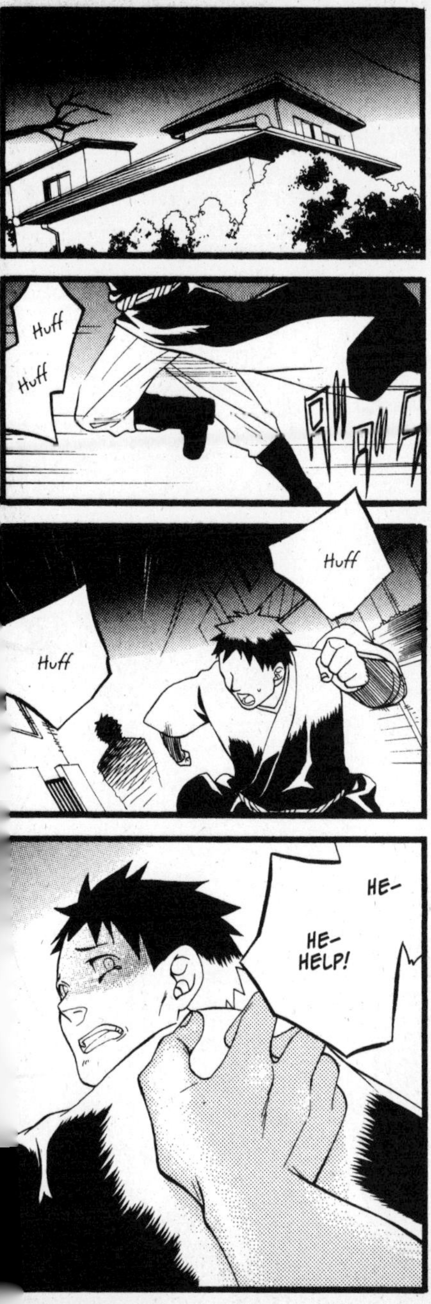
Huff
Huff
Huff
Huff
HE-
HE-HELP!

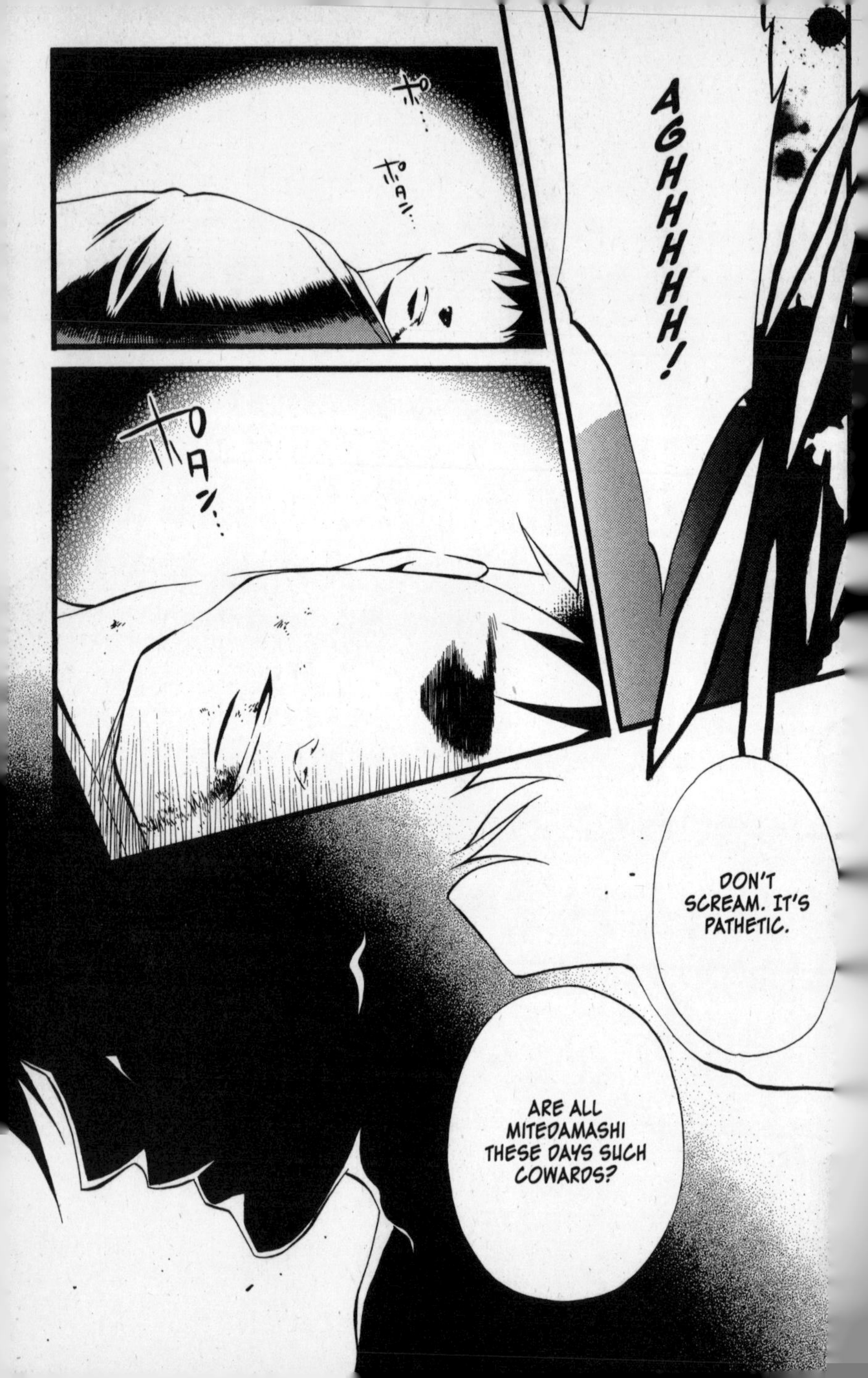
AGHHHHHH!
ポ…
ポタン…
ポタン…
DON'T SCREAM. IT'S PATHETIC.
ARE ALL MITEDAMASHI THESE DAYS SUCH COWARDS?

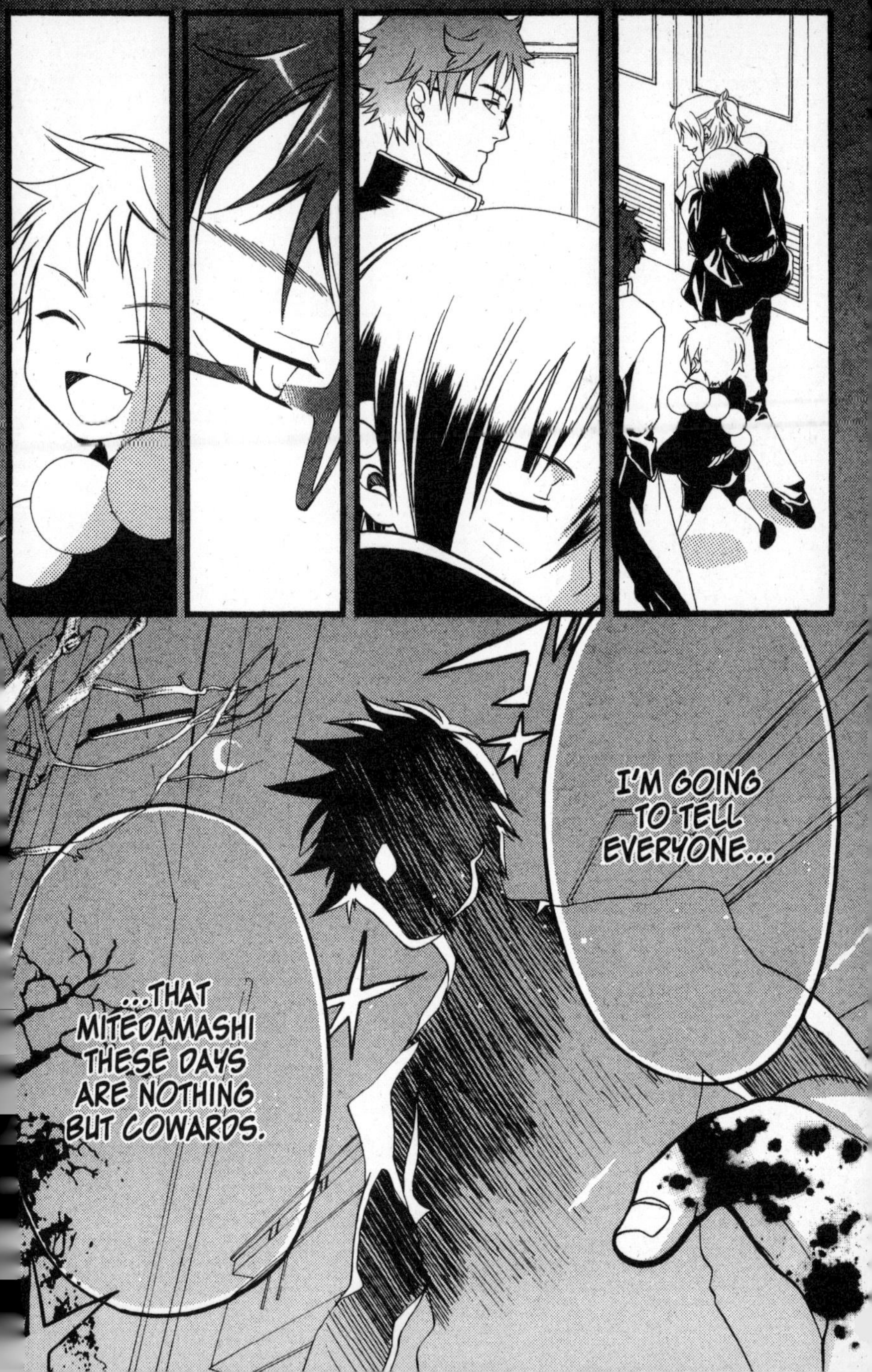
I'M GOING TO TELL EVERYONE...
...THAT MITEDAMASHI THESE DAYS ARE NOTHING BUT COWARDS.

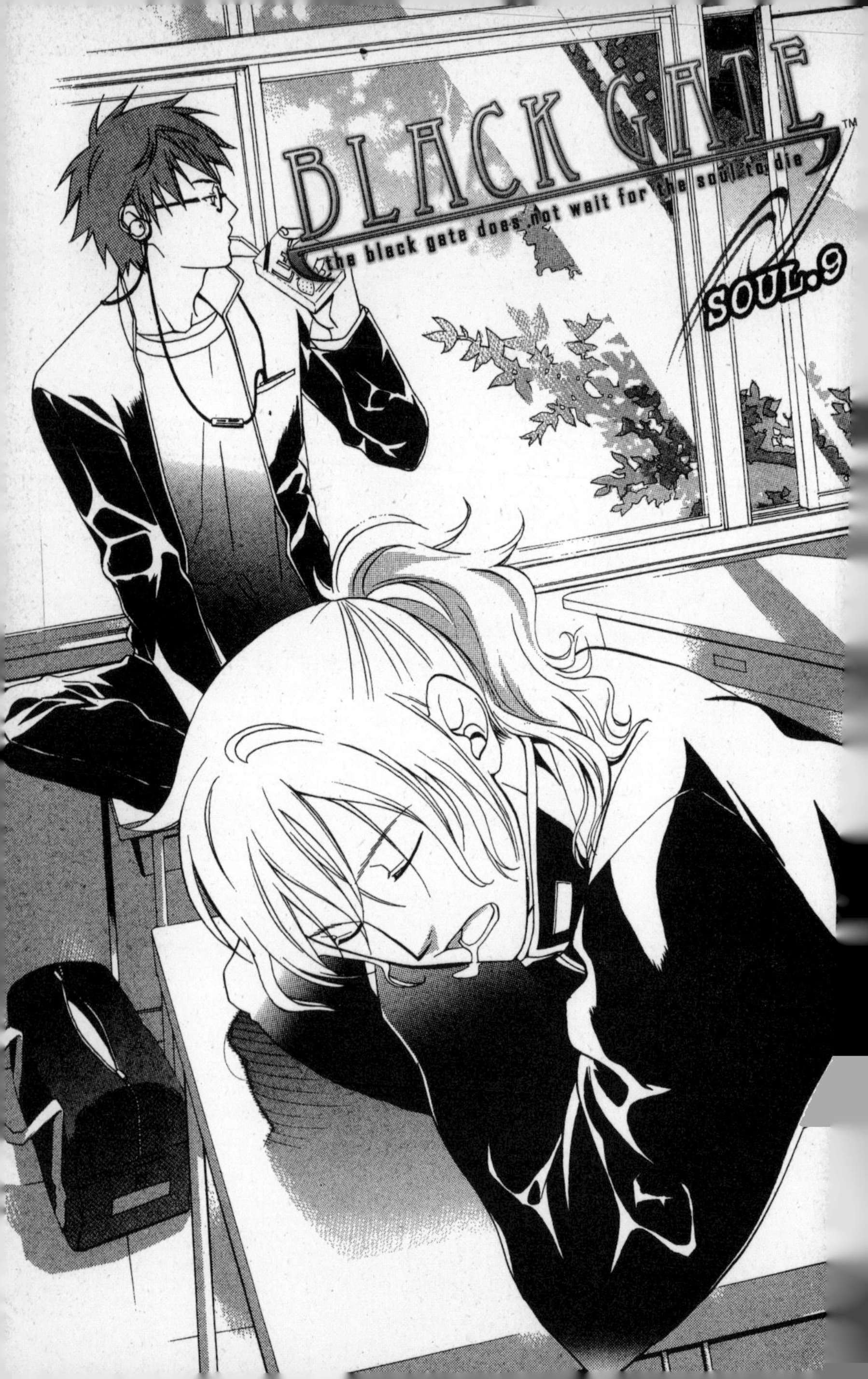
BLACK GATE™
the black gate does not wait for the soul to die
SOUL.9

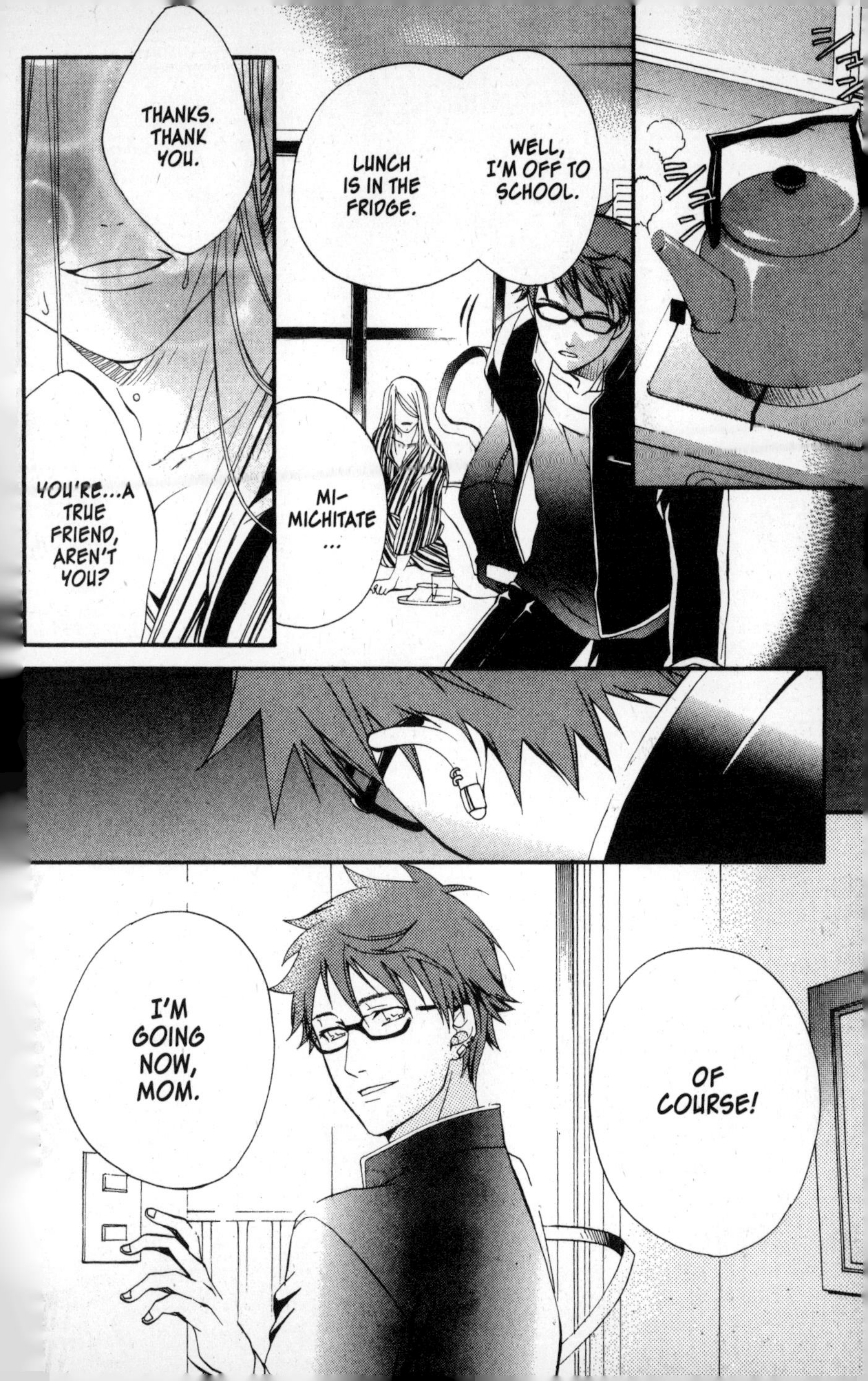
WELL, I'M OFF TO SCHOOL.
LUNCH IS IN THE FRIDGE.
MI-MICHITATE...
THANKS. THANK YOU.
YOU'RE...A TRUE FRIEND, AREN'T YOU?
OF COURSE!
I'M GOING NOW, MOM.

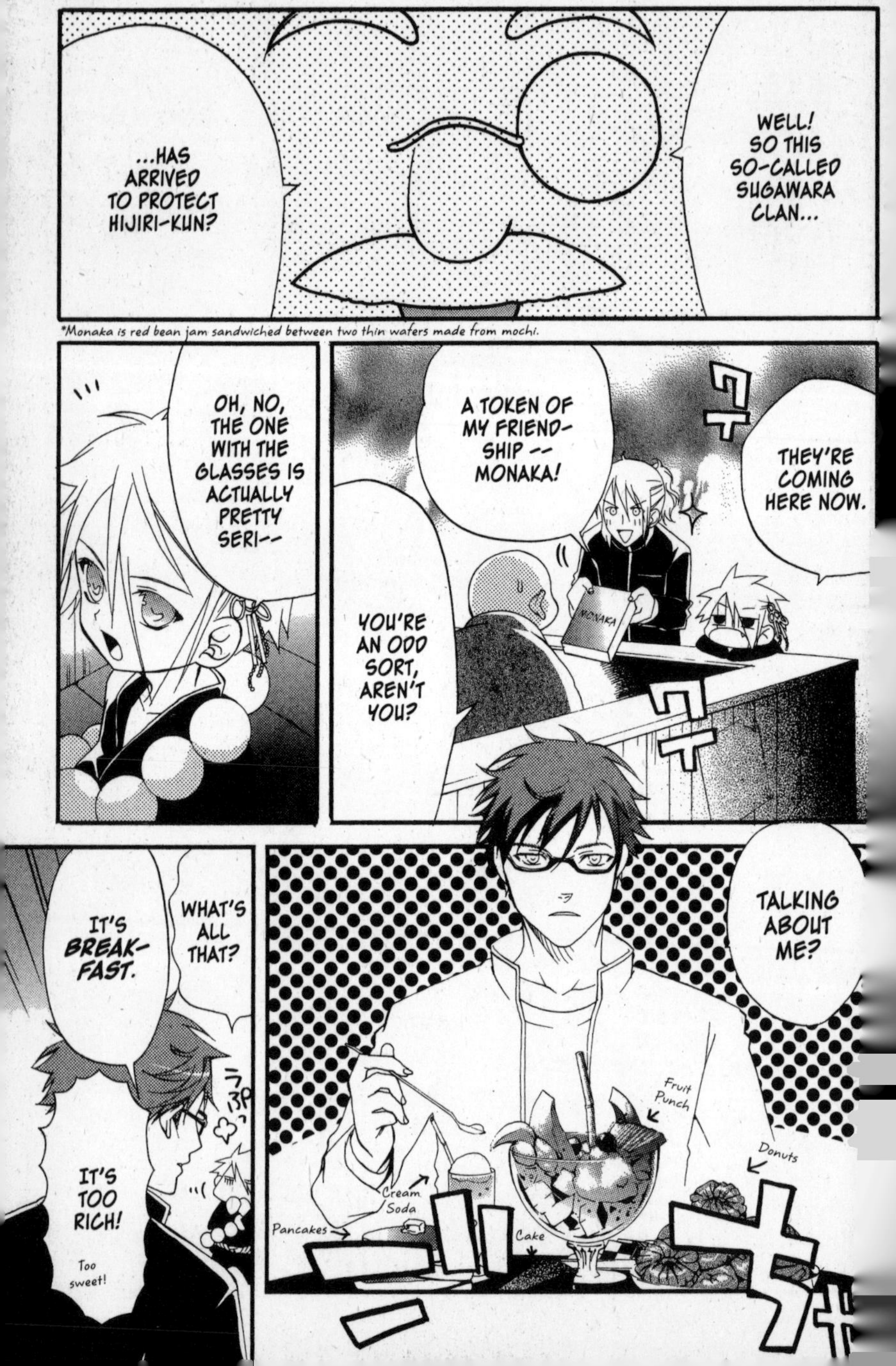
WELL! SO THIS SO-CALLED SUGAWARA CLAN...
...HAS ARRIVED TO PROTECT HIJIRI-KUN?
THEY'RE COMING HERE NOW.
A TOKEN OF MY FRIEND-SHIP -- MONAKA!
MONAKA
YOU'RE AN ODD SORT, AREN'T YOU?
OH, NO, THE ONE WITH THE GLASSES IS ACTUALLY PRETTY SERI--
TALKING ABOUT ME?
Fruit Punch
Donuts
Cream Soda
Cake
Pancakes
WHAT'S ALL THAT?
IT'S BREAKFAST.
IT'S TOO RICH!
Too sweet!

*Monaka is red bean jam sandwiched between two thin wafers made from mochi.

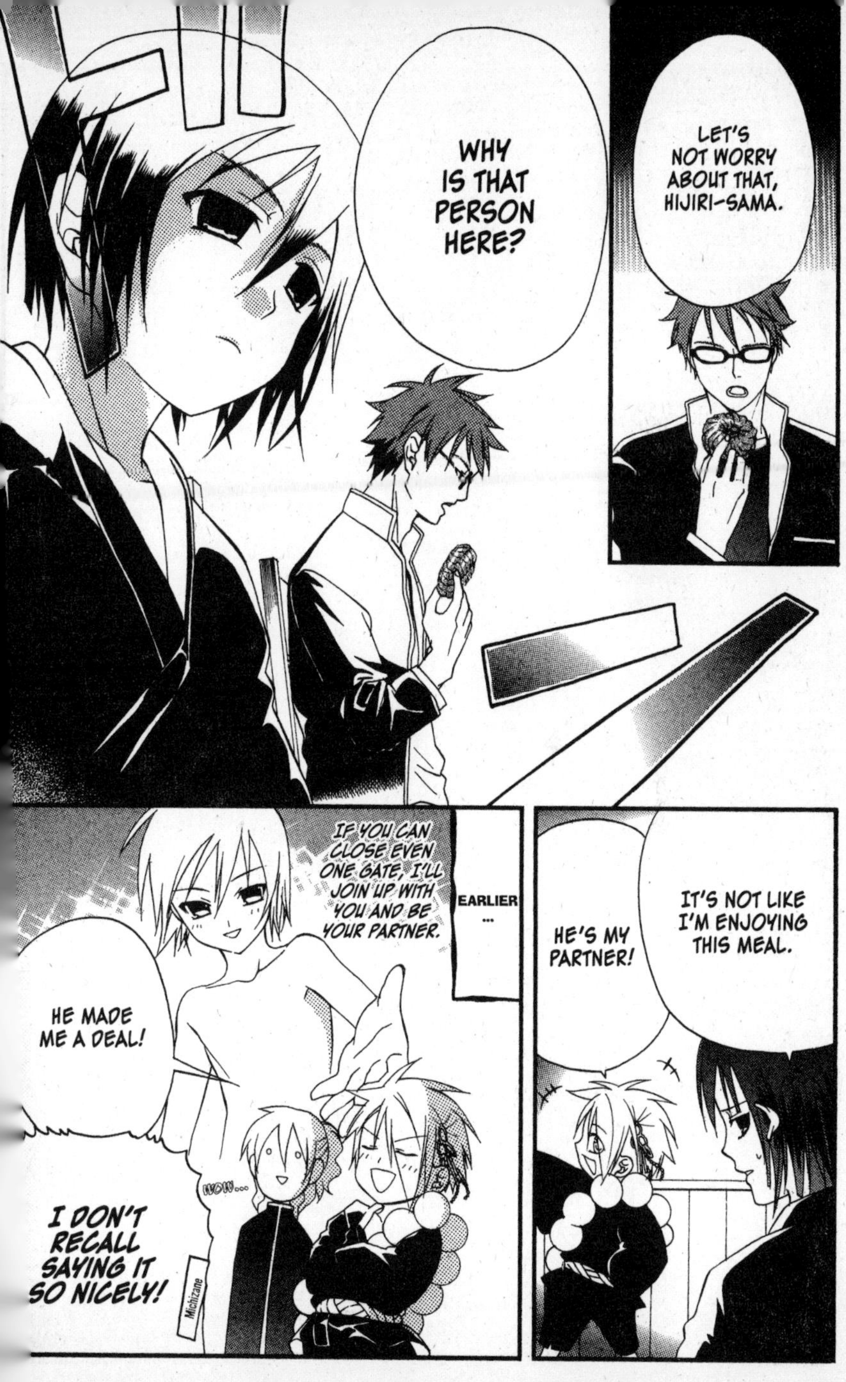
LET'S NOT WORRY ABOUT THAT, HIJIRI-SAMA.
WHY IS THAT PERSON HERE?
IT'S NOT LIKE I'M ENJOYING THIS MEAL.
HE'S MY PARTNER!
EARLIER ...
IF YOU CAN CLOSE EVEN ONE GATE, I'LL JOIN UP WITH YOU AND BE YOUR PARTNER.
HE MADE ME A DEAL!
WOW...
I DON'T RECALL SAYING IT SO NICELY!
Michizane

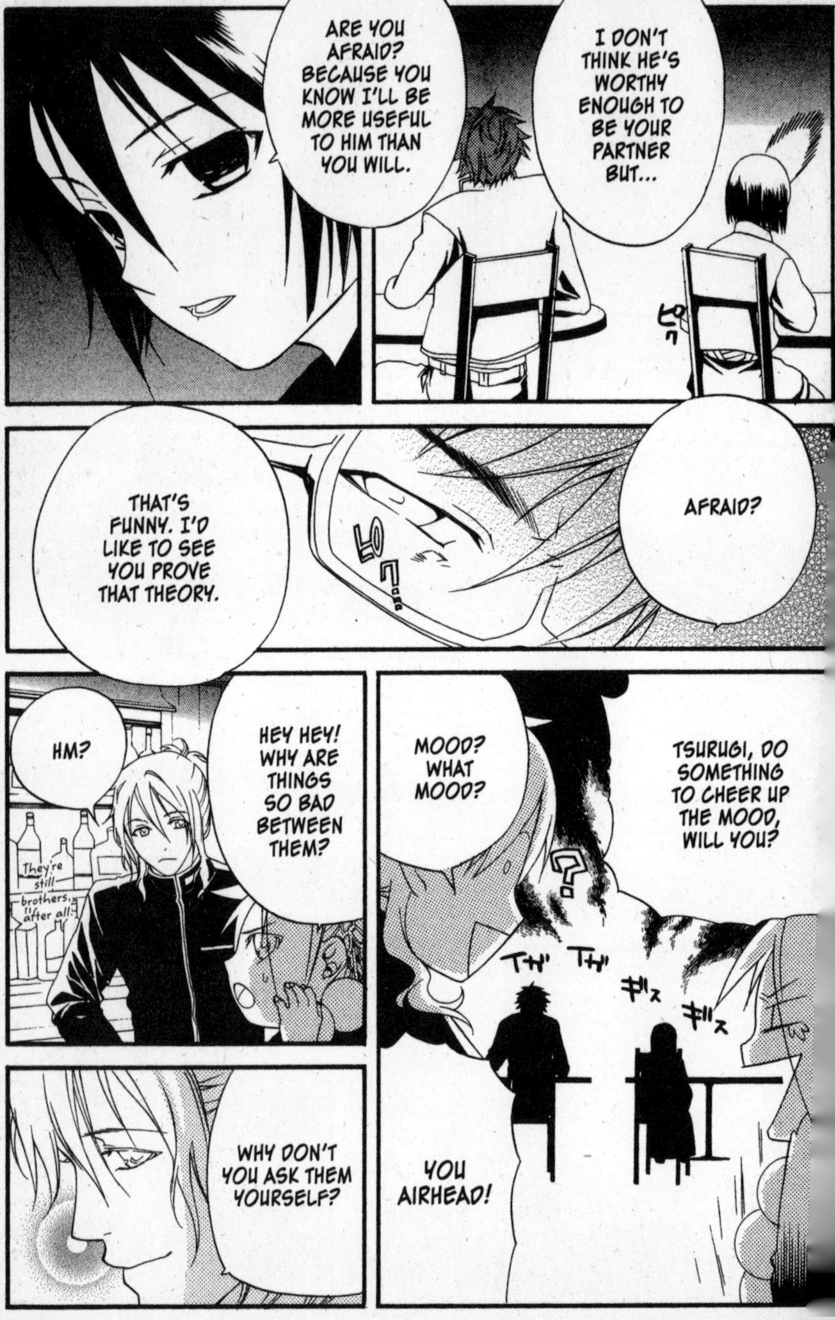
I DON'T THINK HE'S WORTHY ENOUGH TO BE YOUR PARTNER BUT...
ARE YOU AFRAID? BECAUSE YOU KNOW I'LL BE MORE USEFUL TO HIM THAN YOU WILL.
AFRAID?
THAT'S FUNNY. I'D LIKE TO SEE YOU PROVE THAT THEORY.
TSURUGI, DO SOMETHING TO CHEER UP THE MOOD, WILL YOU?
MOOD? WHAT MOOD?
YOU AIRHEAD!
HEY HEY! WHY ARE THINGS SO BAD BETWEEN THEM?
HM?
They're still brothers, after all.
WHY DON'T YOU ASK THEM YOURSELF?

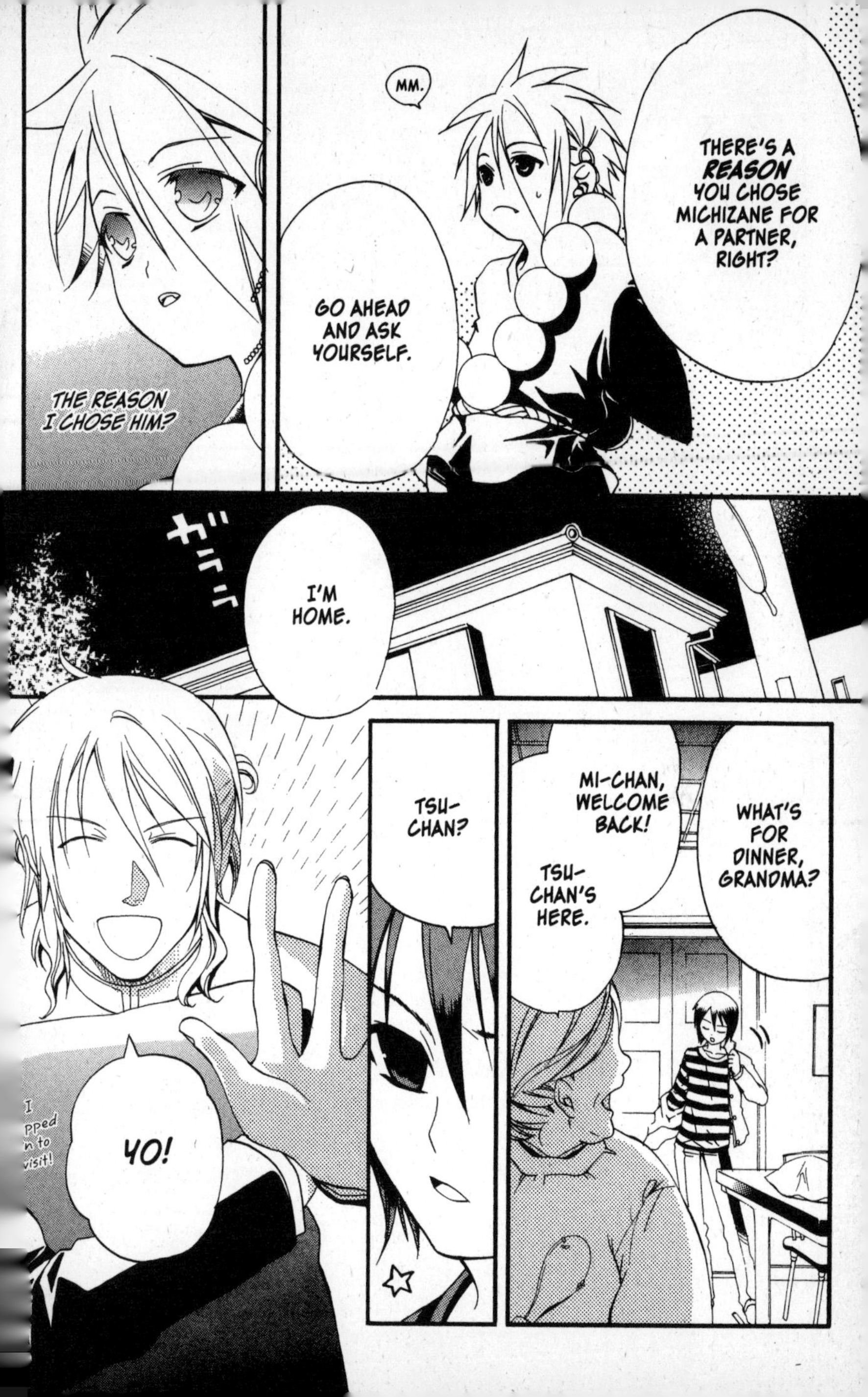
THERE'S A *REASON* YOU CHOSE MICHIZANE FOR A PARTNER, RIGHT?
MM.
GO AHEAD AND ASK YOURSELF.
THE REASON I CHOSE HIM?
I'M HOME.
WHAT'S FOR DINNER, GRANDMA?
MI-CHAN, WELCOME BACK!
TSU-CHAN'S HERE.
TSU-CHAN?
YO!

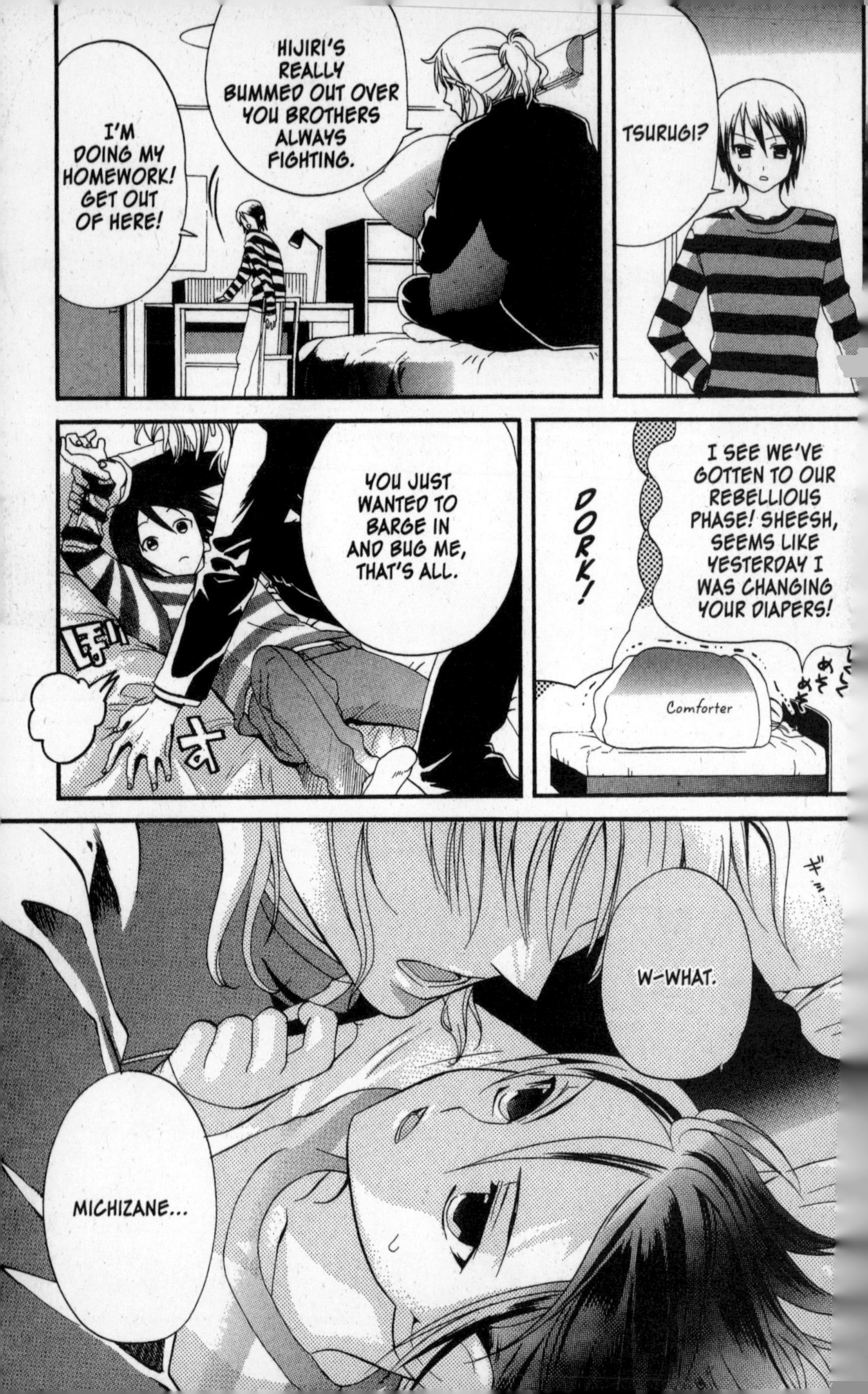
TSURUGI?
HIJIRI'S REALLY BUMMED OUT OVER YOU BROTHERS ALWAYS FIGHTING.
I'M DOING MY HOMEWORK! GET OUT OF HERE!
I SEE WE'VE GOTTEN TO OUR REBELLIOUS PHASE! SHEESH, SEEMS LIKE YESTERDAY I WAS CHANGING YOUR DIAPERS!
DORK!
Comforter
YOU JUST WANTED TO BARGE IN AND BUG ME, THAT'S ALL.
W-WHAT.
MICHIZANE...

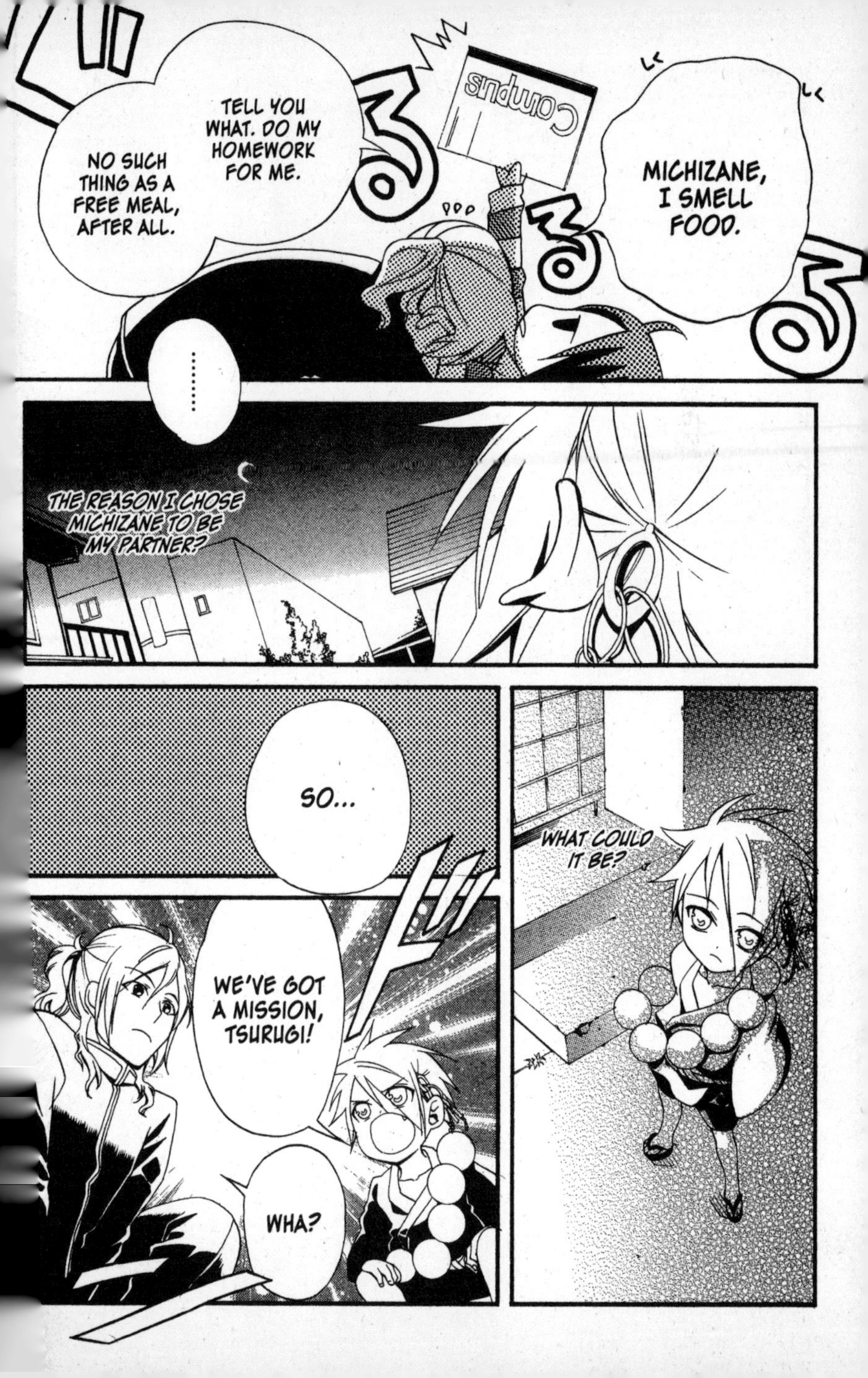
MICHIZANE, I SMELL FOOD.
TELL YOU WHAT. DO MY HOMEWORK FOR ME.
NO SUCH THING AS A FREE MEAL, AFTER ALL.
......
THE REASON I CHOSE MICHIZANE TO BE MY PARTNER?
WHAT COULD IT BE?
SO...
WE'VE GOT A MISSION, TSURUGI!
WHA?

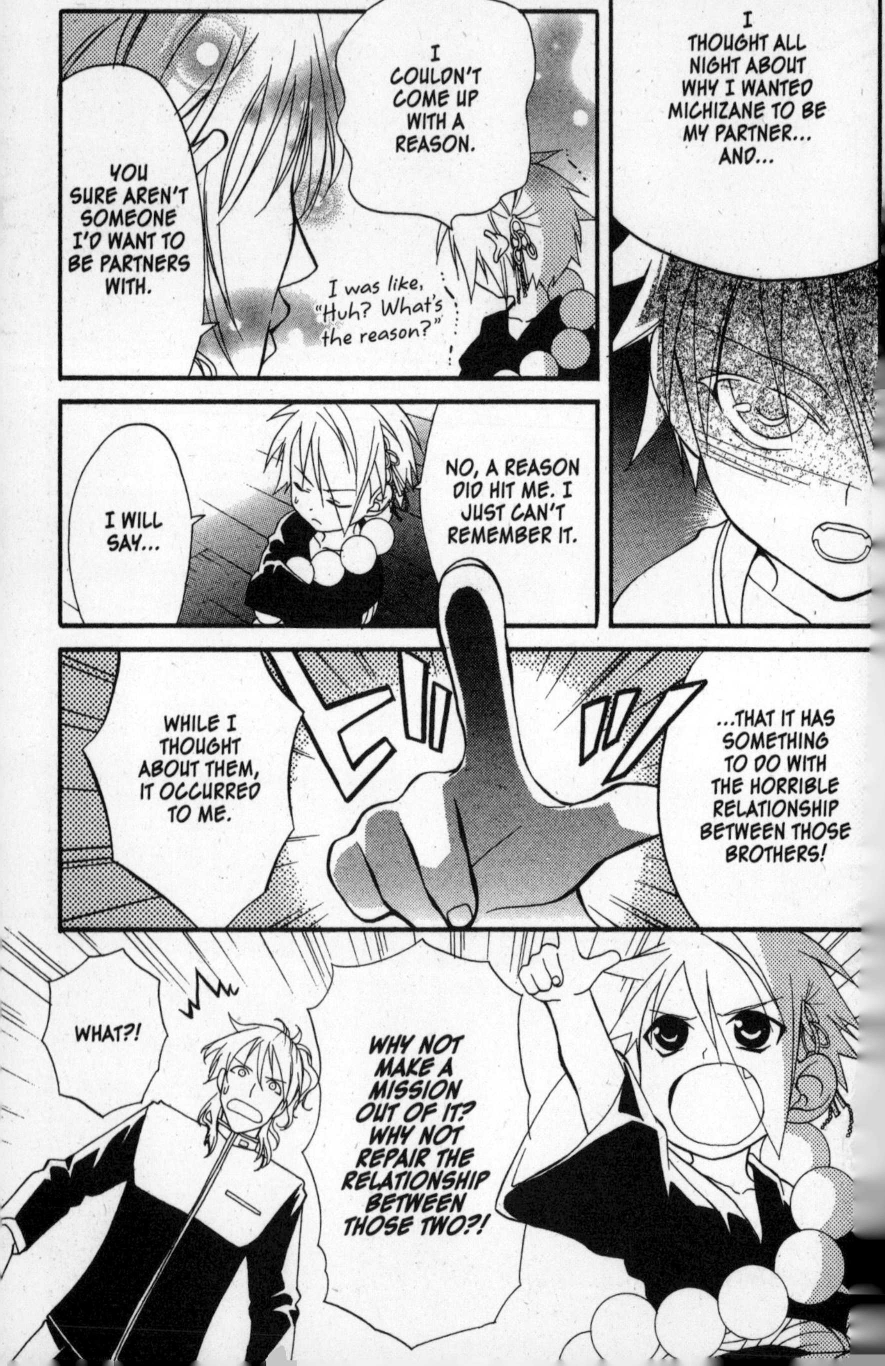
I THOUGHT ALL NIGHT ABOUT WHY I WANTED MICHIZANE TO BE MY PARTNER... AND...
I COULDN'T COME UP WITH A REASON.
I was like, "Huh? What's the reason?"
YOU SURE AREN'T SOMEONE I'D WANT TO BE PARTNERS WITH.
NO, A REASON DID HIT ME. I JUST CAN'T REMEMBER IT.
I WILL SAY...
...THAT IT HAS SOMETHING TO DO WITH THE HORRIBLE RELATIONSHIP BETWEEN THOSE BROTHERS!
WHILE I THOUGHT ABOUT THEM, IT OCCURRED TO ME.
WHY NOT MAKE A MISSION OUT OF IT? WHY NOT REPAIR THE RELATIONSHIP BETWEEN THOSE TWO?!
WHAT?!

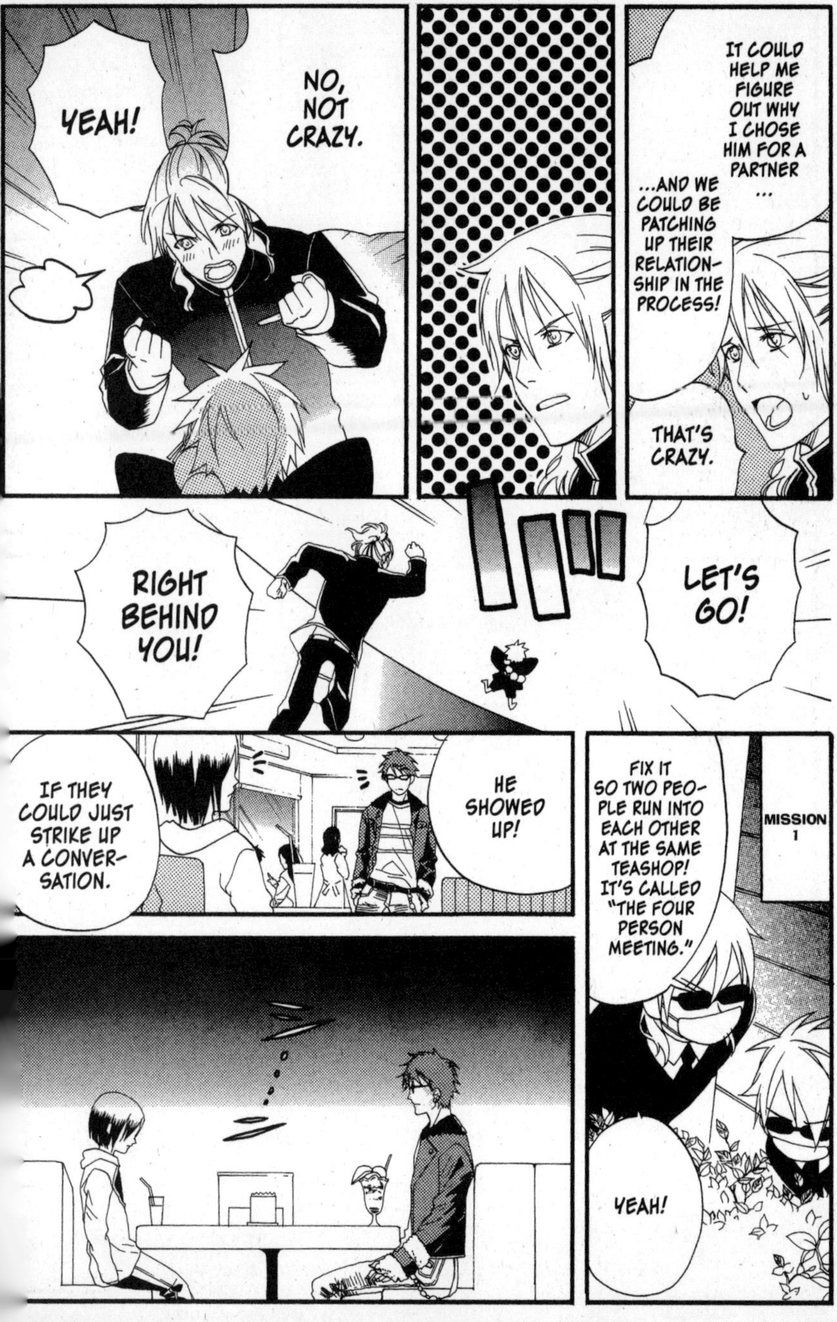
IT COULD HELP ME FIGURE OUT WHY I CHOSE HIM FOR A PARTNER ...
...AND WE COULD BE PATCHING UP THEIR RELATION-SHIP IN THE PROCESS!
THAT'S CRAZY.
NO, NOT CRAZY.
YEAH!
LET'S GO!
RIGHT BEHIND YOU!
MISSION 1
FIX IT SO TWO PEO-PLE RUN INTO EACH OTHER AT THE SAME TEASHOP! IT'S CALLED "THE FOUR PERSON MEETING."
YEAH!
HE SHOWED UP!
IF THEY COULD JUST STRIKE UP A CONVER-SATION.

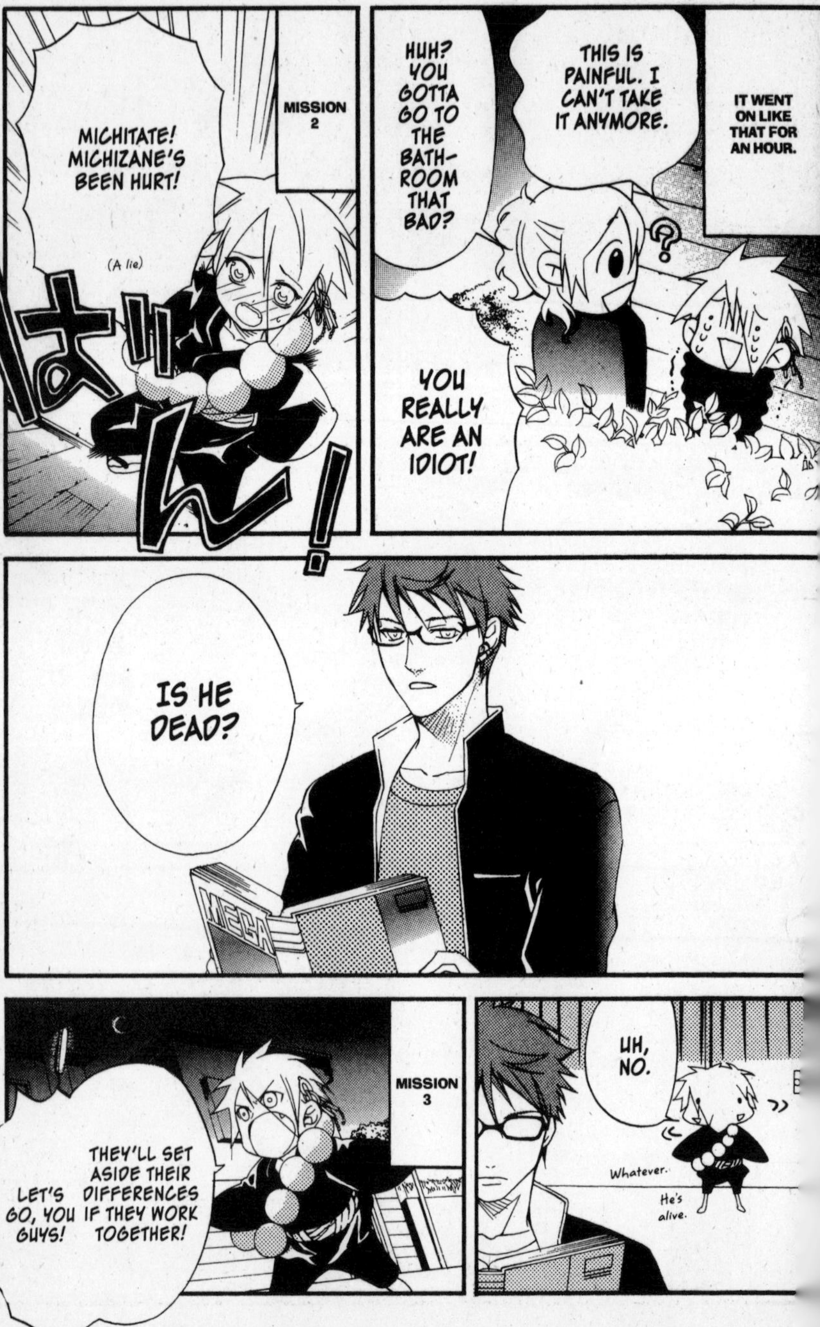
IT WENT ON LIKE THAT FOR AN HOUR.
THIS IS PAINFUL. I CAN'T TAKE IT ANYMORE.
HUH? YOU GOTTA GO TO THE BATHROOM THAT BAD?
YOU REALLY ARE AN IDIOT!
MISSION 2
MICHITATE! MICHIZANE'S BEEN HURT!
(A lie)
IS HE DEAD?
UH, NO.
Whatever.
He's alive.
MISSION 3
THEY'LL SET ASIDE THEIR DIFFERENCES IF THEY WORK TOGETHER!
LET'S GO, YOU GUYS!

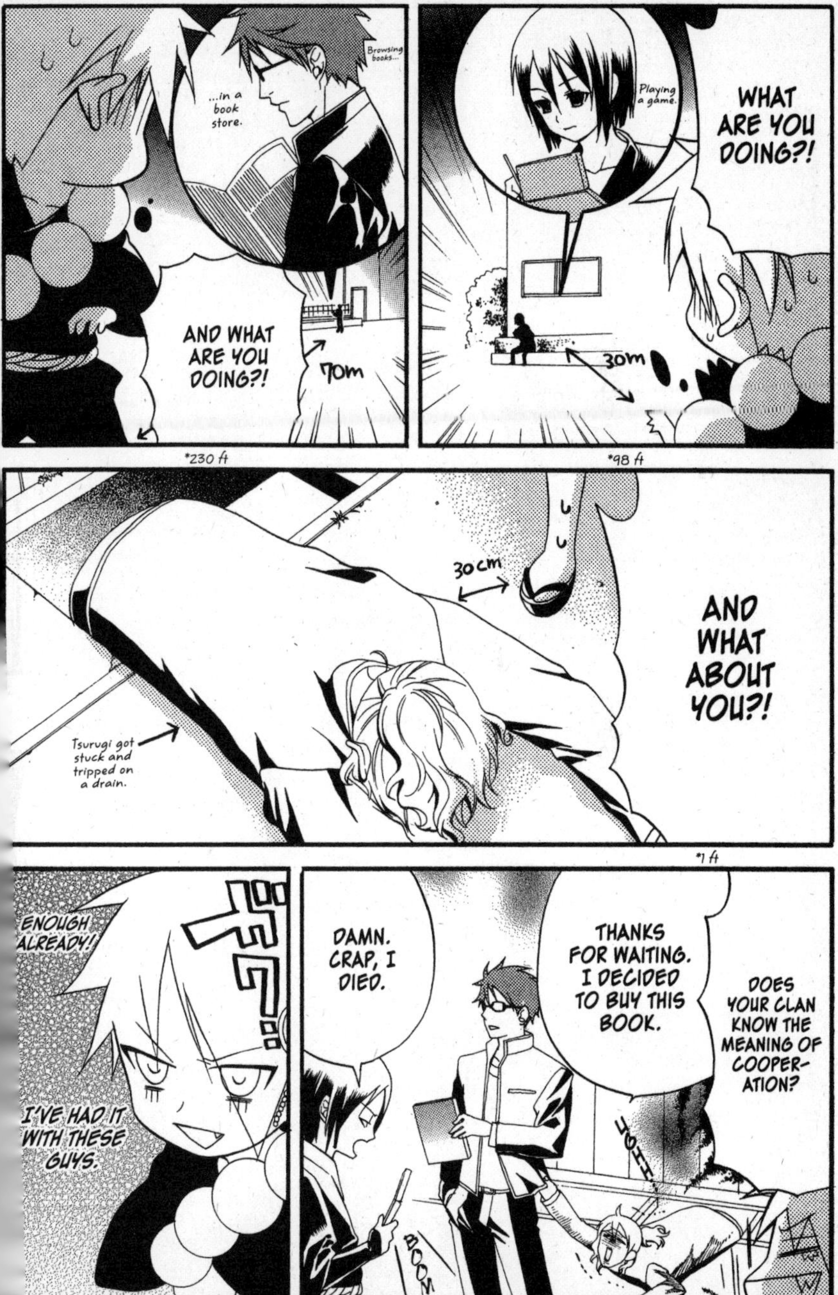
WHAT ARE YOU DOING?!
Playing a game.
30m
*98 ft
Browsing books...
...in a book store.
AND WHAT ARE YOU DOING?!
70m
*230 ft
AND WHAT ABOUT YOU?!
30cm
Tsurugi got stuck and tripped on a drain.
*1 ft
DOES YOUR CLAN KNOW THE MEANING OF COOPER-ATION?
THANKS FOR WAITING. I DECIDED TO BUY THIS BOOK.
DAMN. CRAP, I DIED.
BOOM
ENOUGH ALREADY!
I'VE HAD IT WITH THESE GUYS.

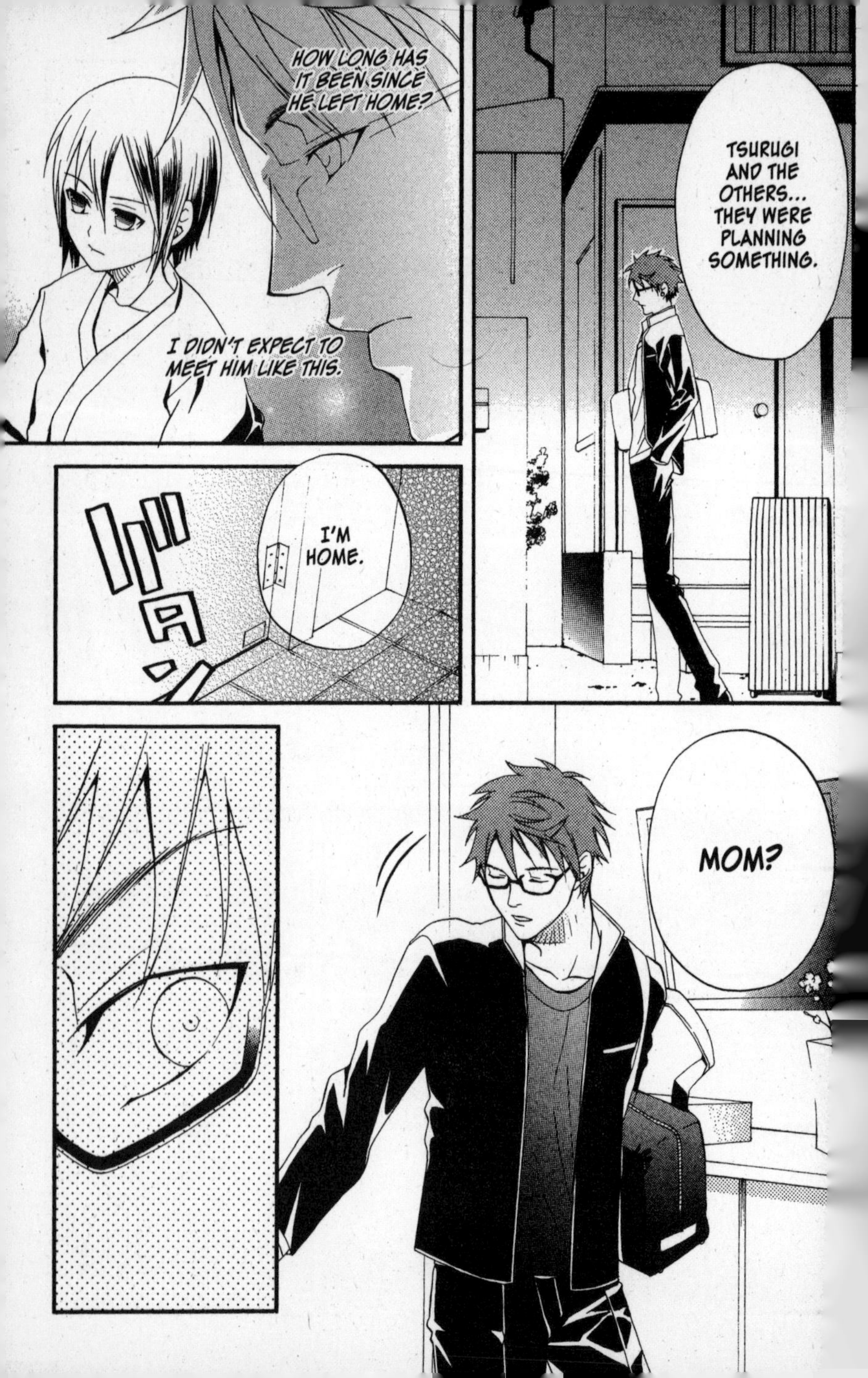
TSURUGI AND THE OTHERS... THEY WERE PLANNING SOMETHING.
HOW LONG HAS IT BEEN SINCE HE LEFT HOME?
I DIDN'T EXPECT TO MEET HIM LIKE THIS.
I'M HOME.
MOM?

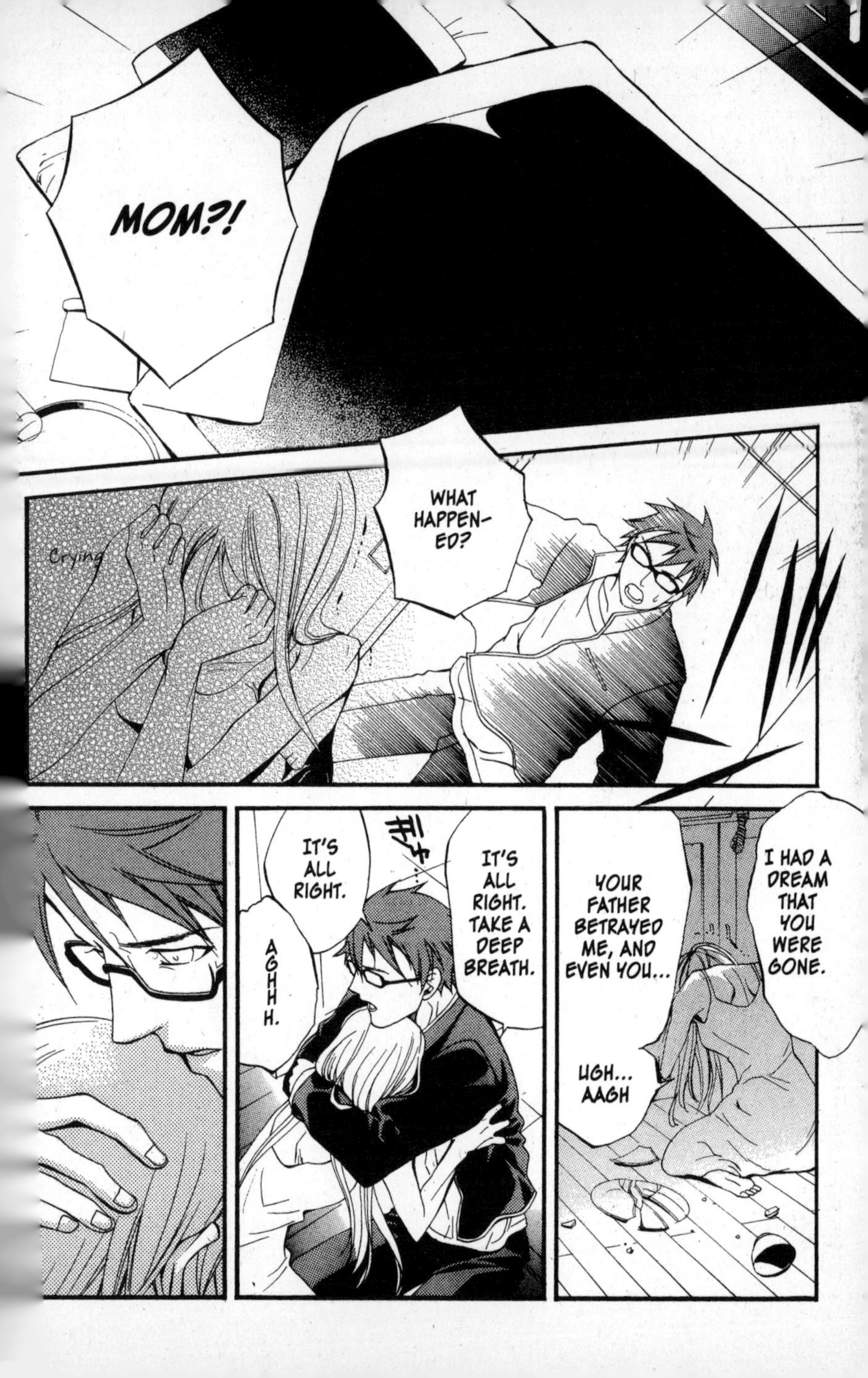
MOM?!
WHAT HAPPEN-ED?
Crying
I HAD A DREAM THAT YOU WERE GONE.
YOUR FATHER BETRAYED ME, AND EVEN YOU...
UGH... AAGH
IT'S ALL RIGHT. TAKE A DEEP BREATH.
IT'S ALL RIGHT.
AGHHH.

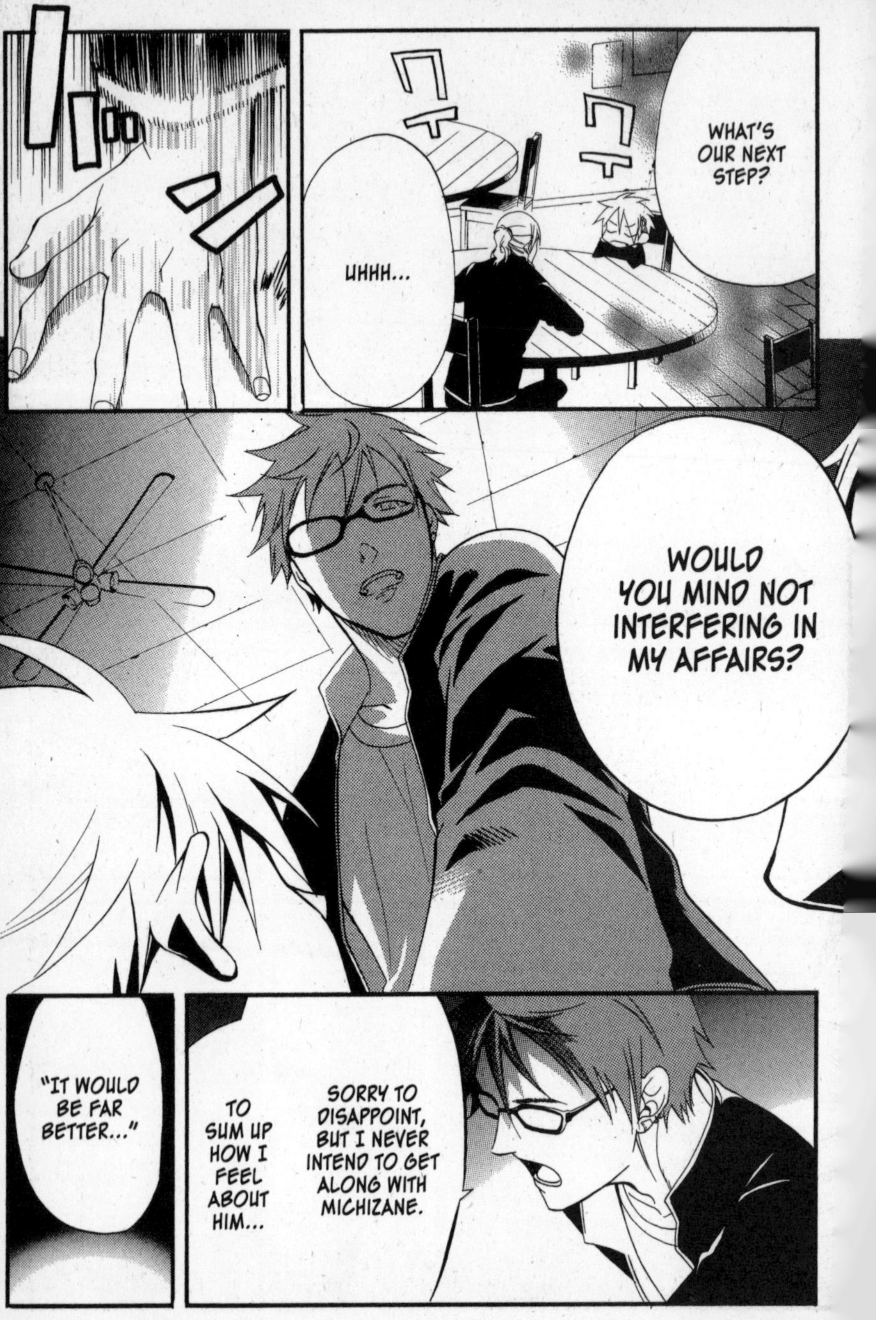
WHAT'S OUR NEXT STEP?
UHHH...
WOULD YOU MIND NOT INTERFERING IN MY AFFAIRS?
SORRY TO DISAPPOINT, BUT I NEVER INTEND TO GET ALONG WITH MICHIZANE.
TO SUM UP HOW I FEEL ABOUT HIM...
"IT WOULD BE FAR BETTER..."

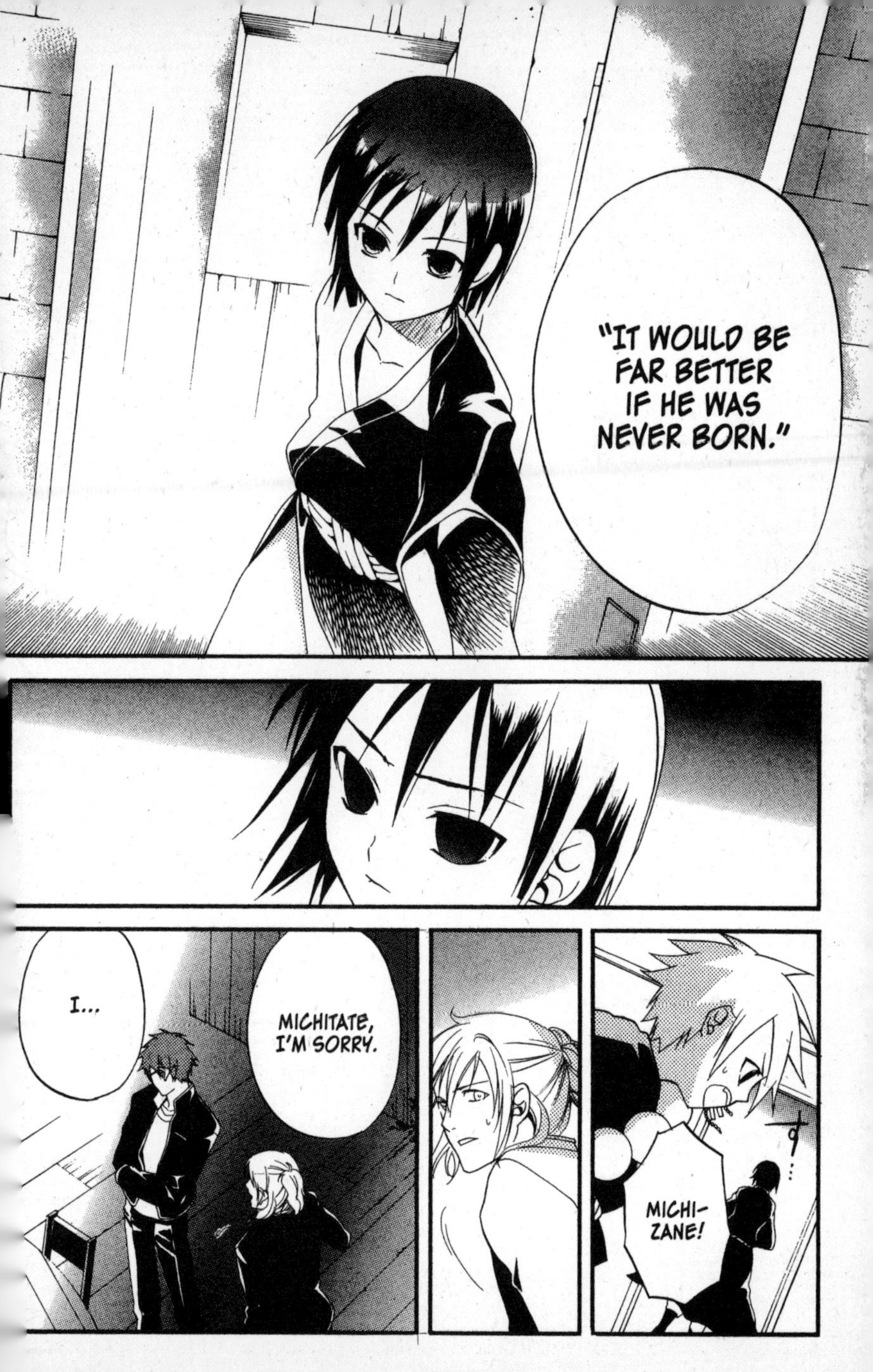
"IT WOULD BE FAR BETTER IF HE WAS NEVER BORN."
す…
MICHI-ZANE!
MICHITATE, I'M SORRY.
I...

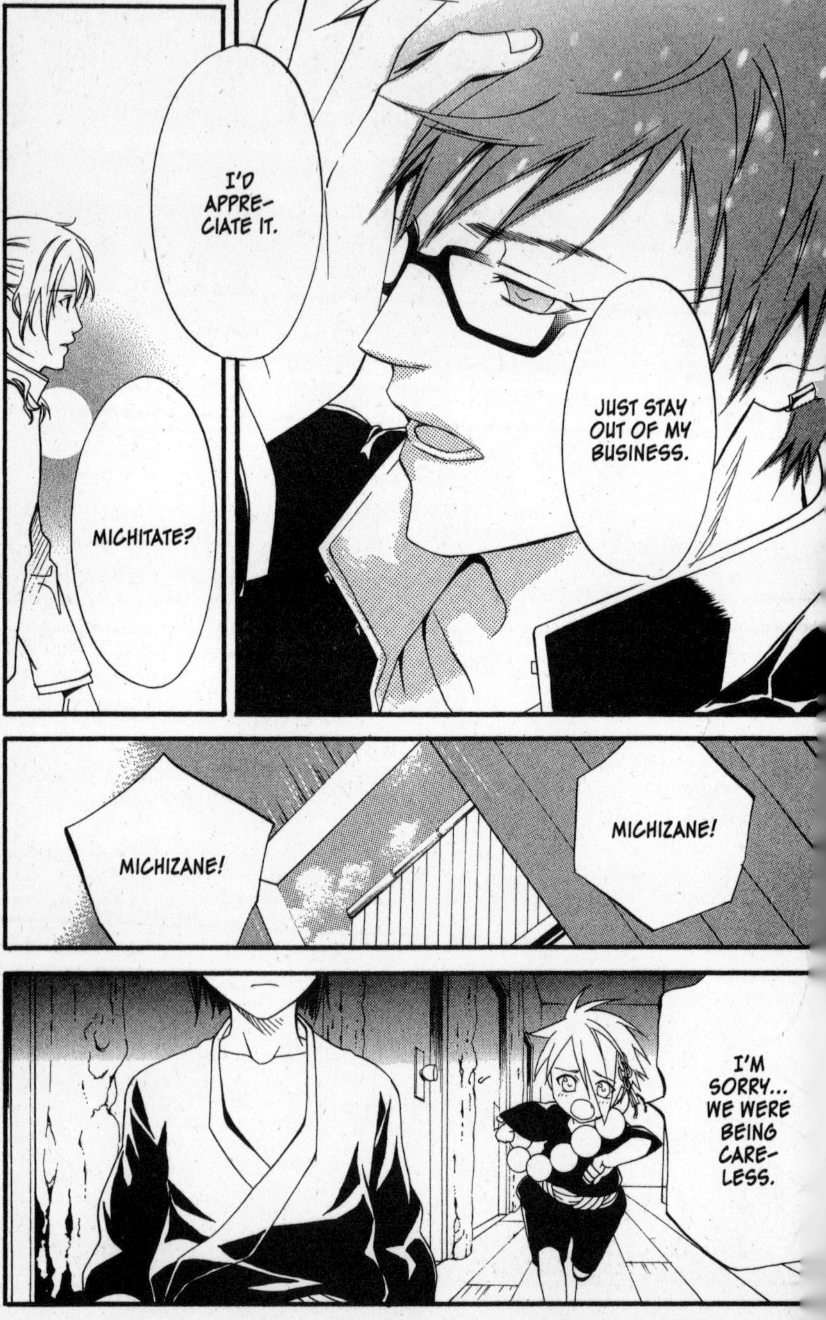
JUST STAY OUT OF MY BUSINESS.
I'D APPRECIATE IT.
MICHITATE?
MICHIZANE!
MICHIZANE!
I'M SORRY... WE WERE BEING CARE- LESS.

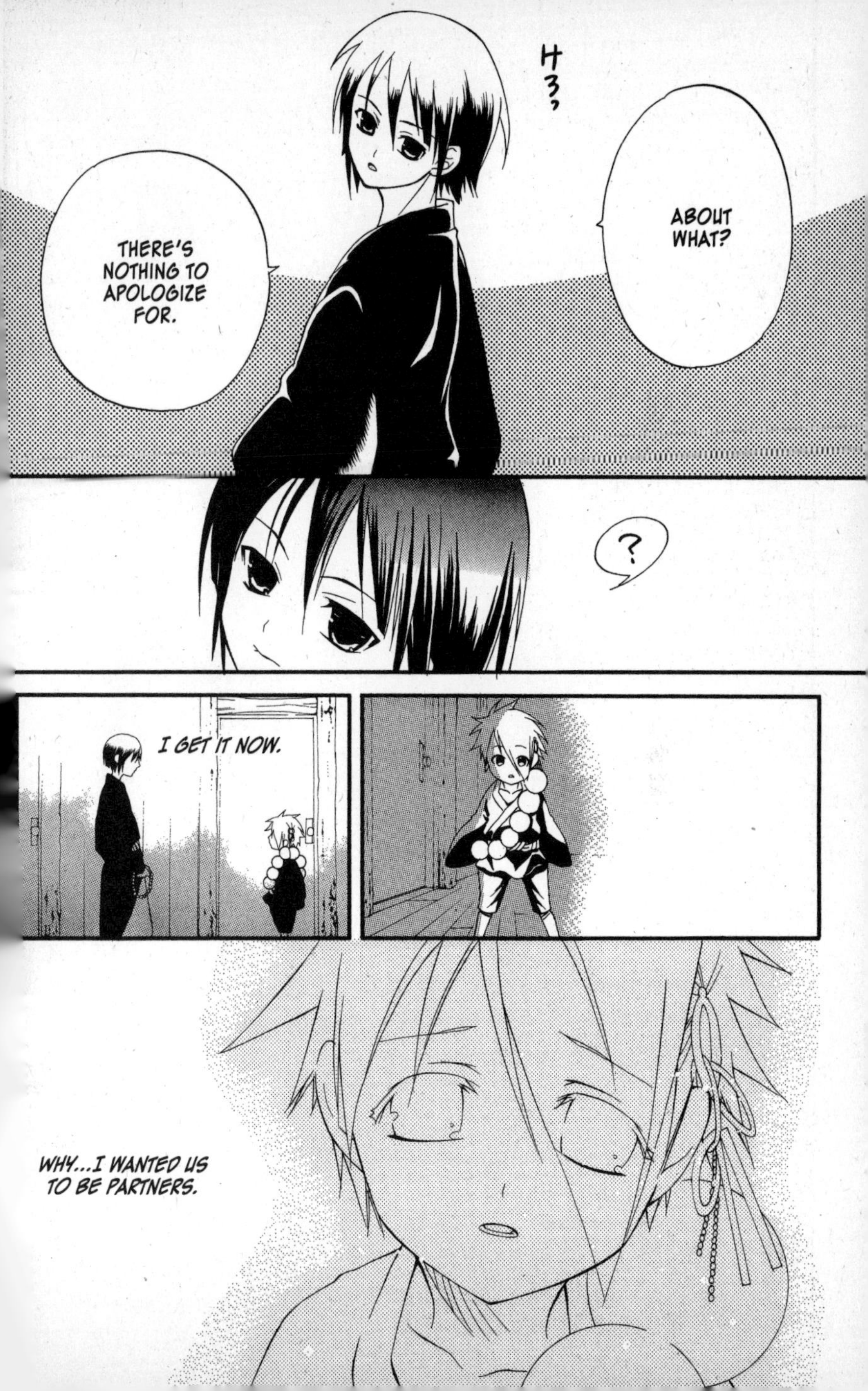
ABOUT WHAT?
THERE'S NOTHING TO APOLOGIZE FOR.
?
I GET IT NOW.
WHY...I WANTED US TO BE PARTNERS.

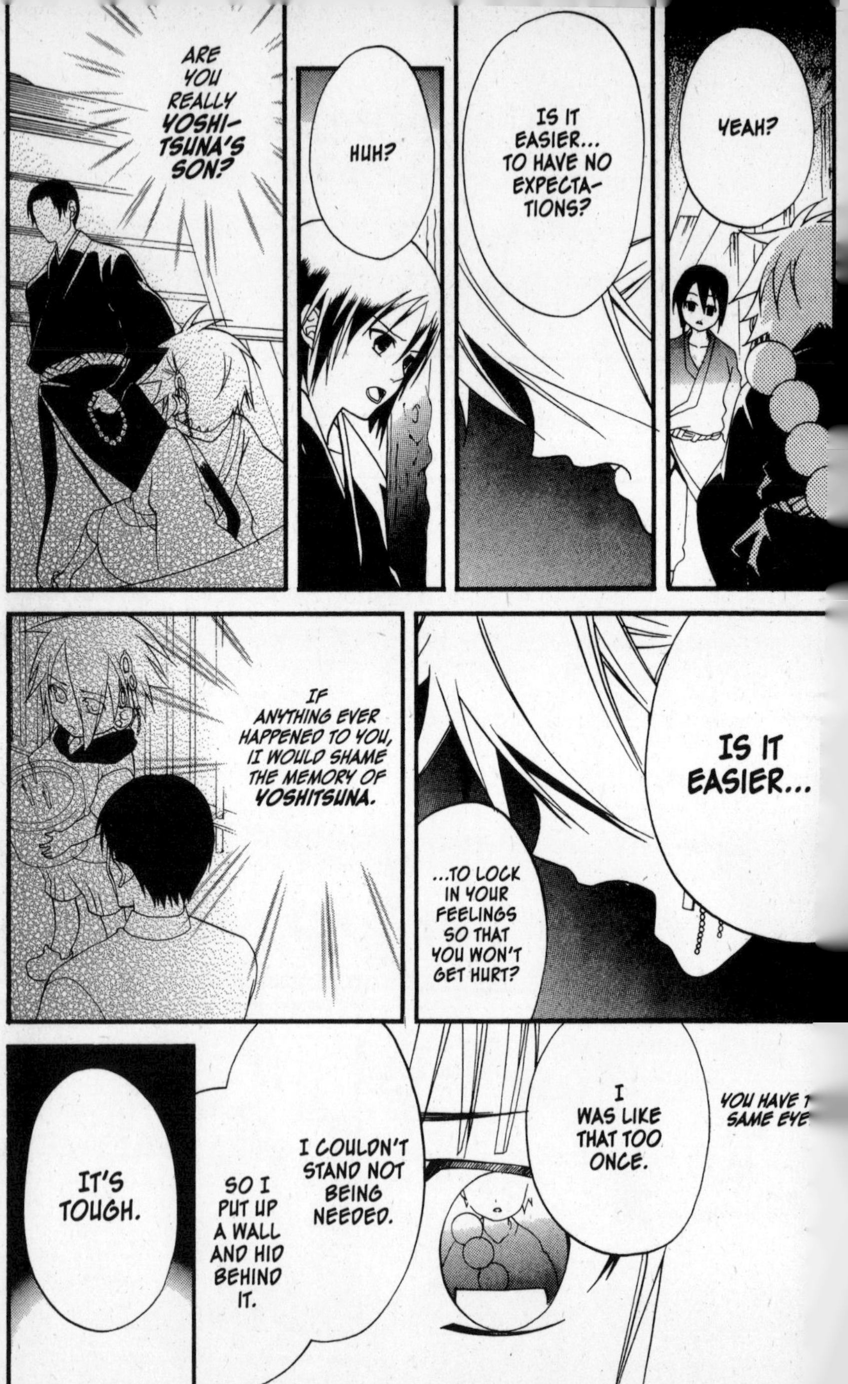
YEAH?
IS IT EASIER... TO HAVE NO EXPECTATIONS?
HUH?
ARE YOU REALLY YOSHITSUNA'S SON?
IS IT EASIER...
...TO LOCK IN YOUR FEELINGS SO THAT YOU WON'T GET HURT?
IF ANYTHING EVER HAPPENED TO YOU, I WOULD SHAME THE MEMORY OF YOSHITSUNA.
YOU HAVE T
SAME EYE
I WAS LIKE THAT TOO ONCE.
I COULDN'T STAND NOT BEING NEEDED.
SO I PUT UP A WALL AND HID BEHIND IT.
IT'S TOUGH.

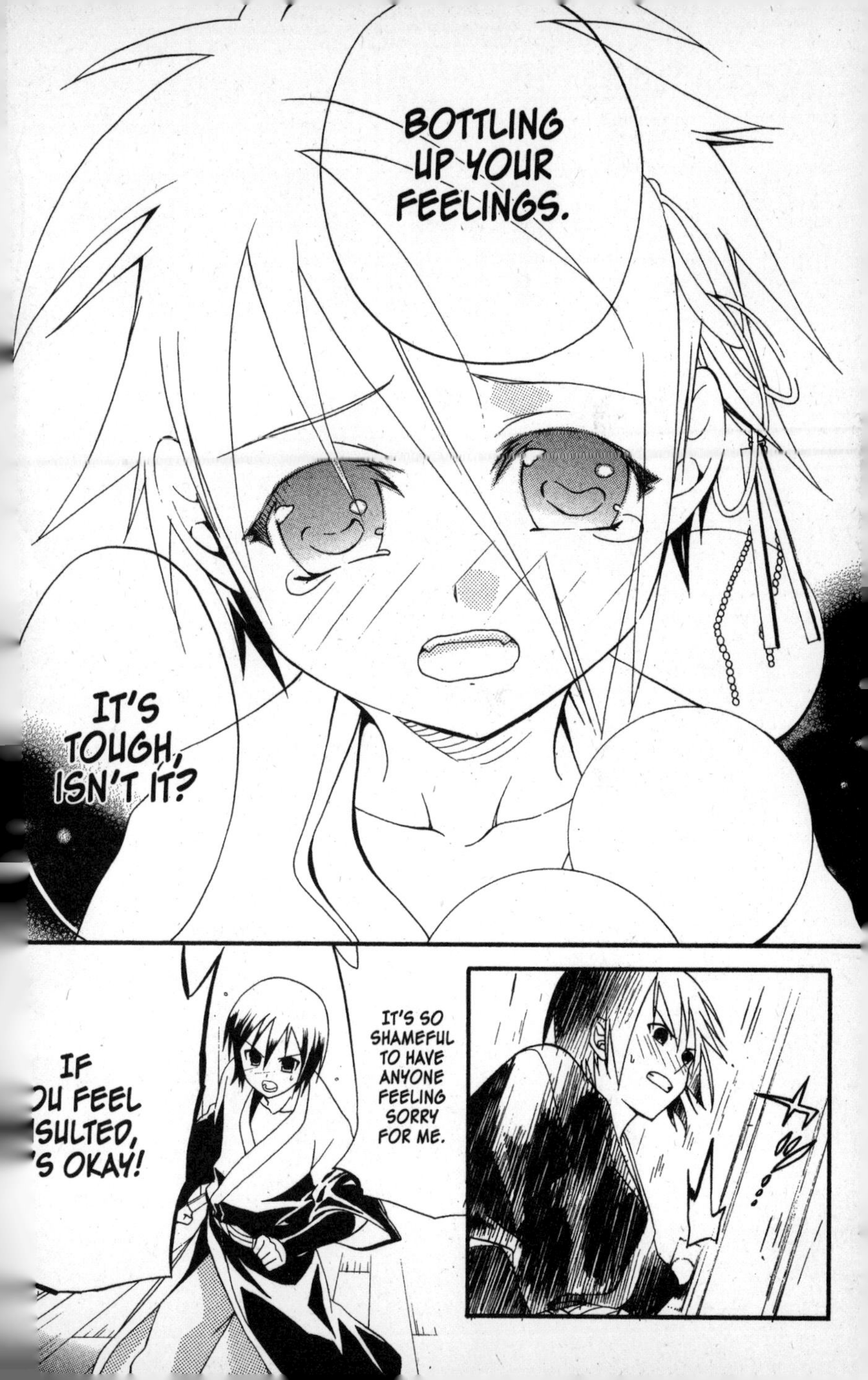
BOTTLING UP YOUR FEELINGS.
IT'S TOUGH, ISN'T IT?
IT'S SO SHAMEFUL TO HAVE ANYONE FEELING SORRY FOR ME.
IF
OU FEEL
SULTED,
'S OKAY!

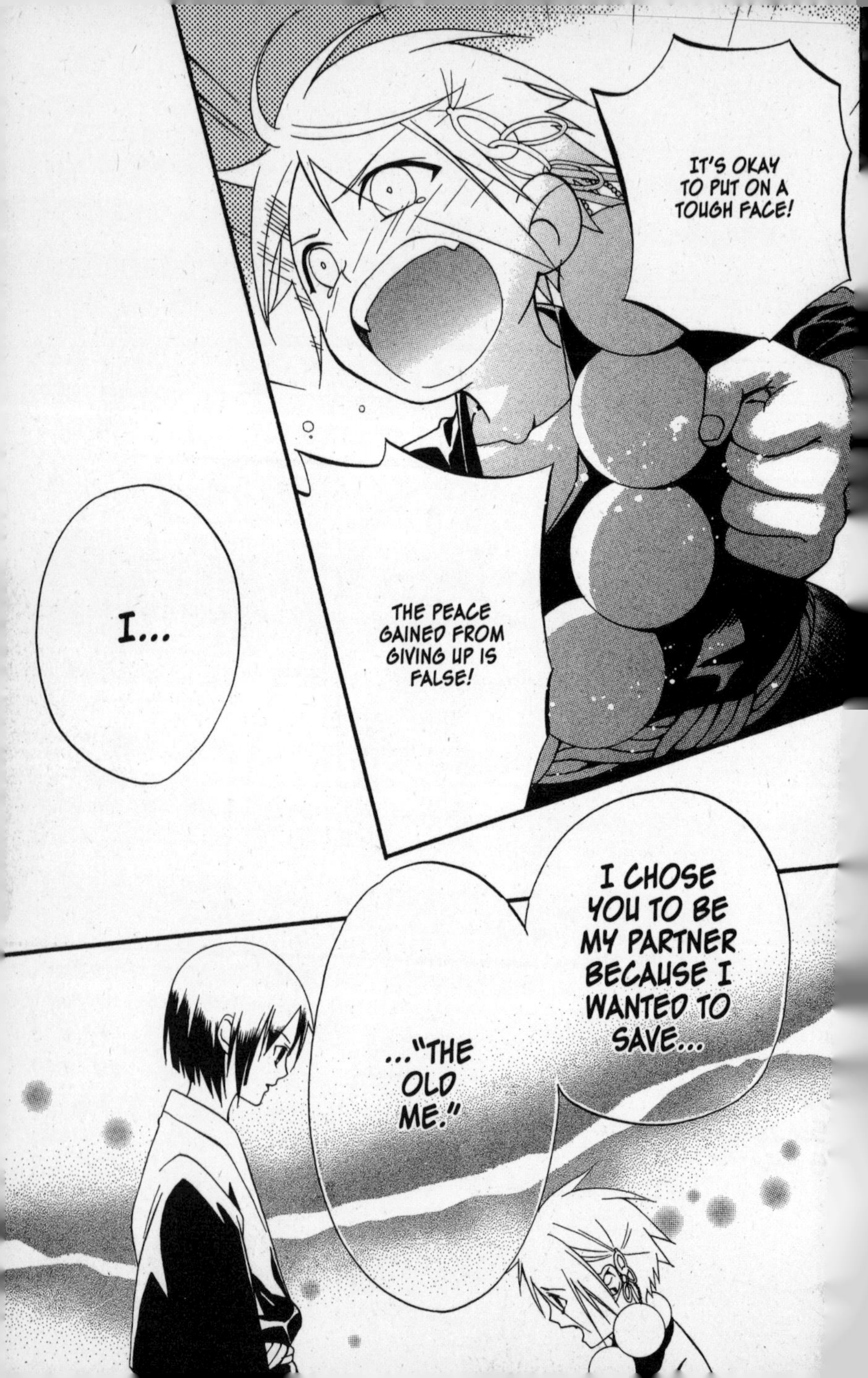
IT'S OKAY TO PUT ON A TOUGH FACE!
THE PEACE GAINED FROM GIVING UP IS FALSE!
I...
I CHOSE YOU TO BE MY PARTNER BECAUSE I WANTED TO SAVE...
..."THE OLD ME."

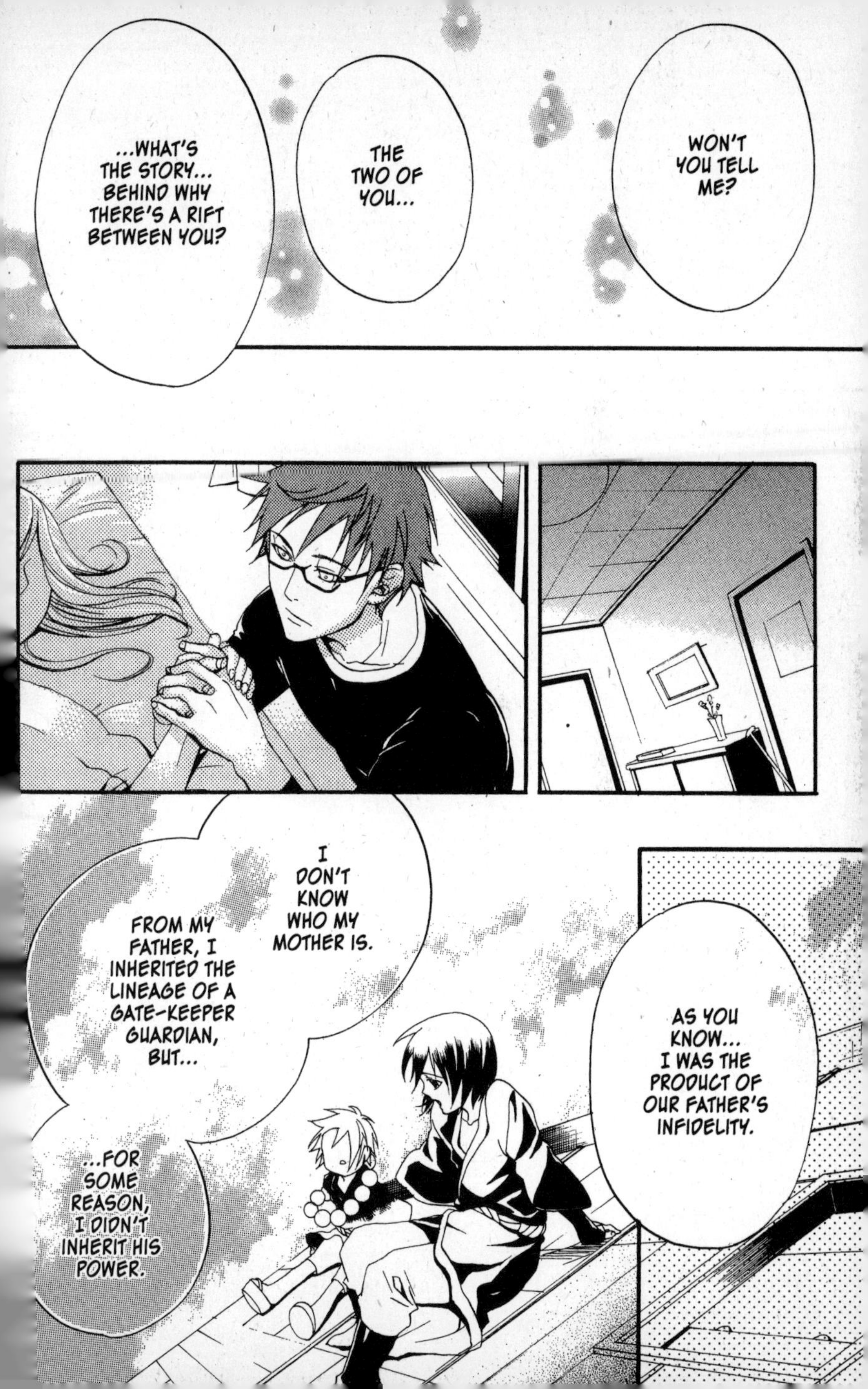
WON'T YOU TELL ME?
THE TWO OF YOU...
...WHAT'S THE STORY... BEHIND WHY THERE'S A RIFT BETWEEN YOU?
AS YOU KNOW... I WAS THE PRODUCT OF OUR FATHER'S INFIDELITY.
I DON'T KNOW WHO MY MOTHER IS.
FROM MY FATHER, I INHERITED THE LINEAGE OF A GATE-KEEPER GUARDIAN, BUT...
...FOR SOME REASON, I DIDN'T INHERIT HIS POWER.

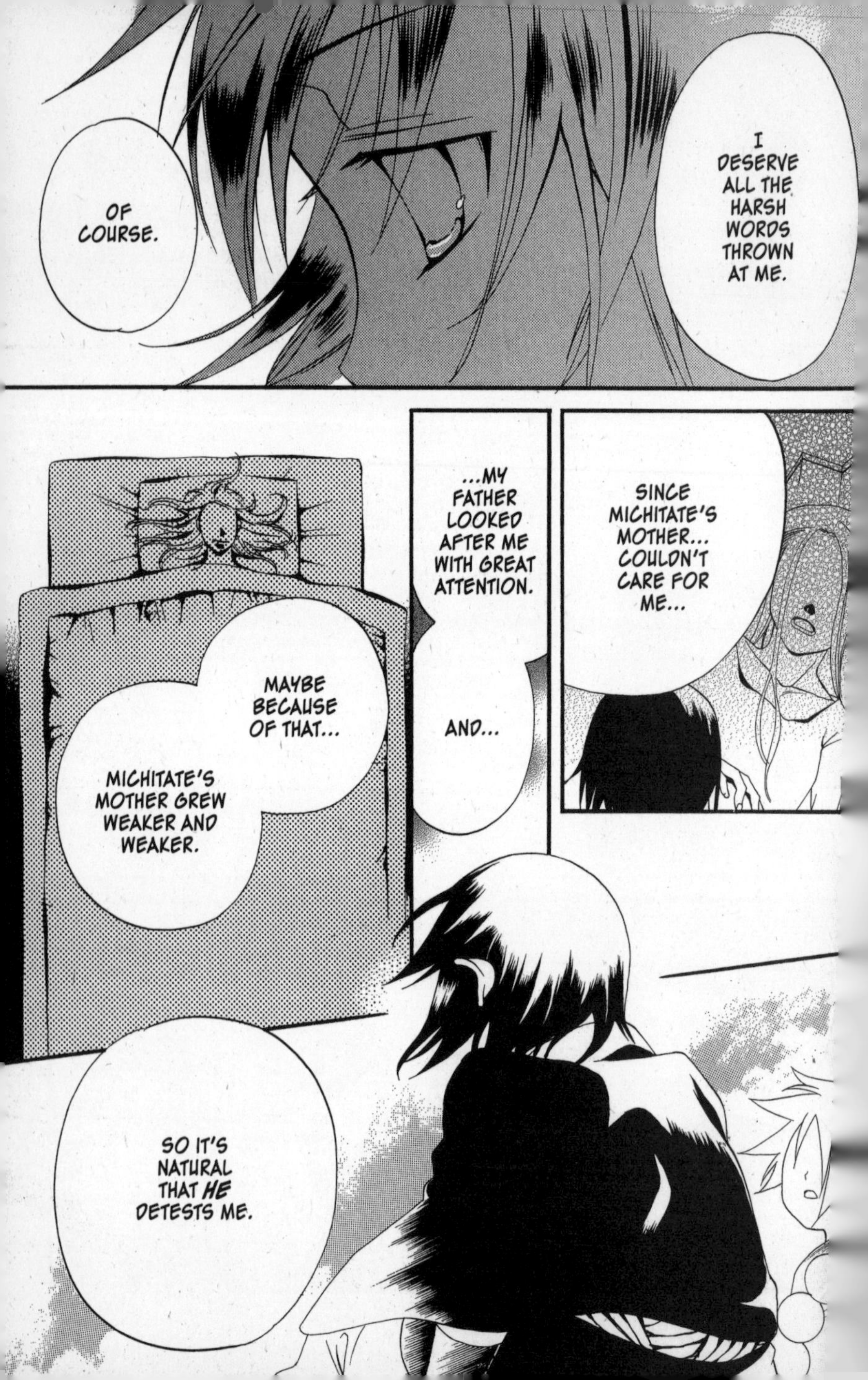
I DESERVE ALL THE HARSH WORDS THROWN AT ME.
OF COURSE.
SINCE MICHITATE'S MOTHER... COULDN'T CARE FOR ME...
...MY FATHER LOOKED AFTER ME WITH GREAT ATTENTION.
AND...
MAYBE BECAUSE OF THAT...
MICHITATE'S MOTHER GREW WEAKER AND WEAKER.
SO IT'S NATURAL THAT *HE* DETESTS ME.

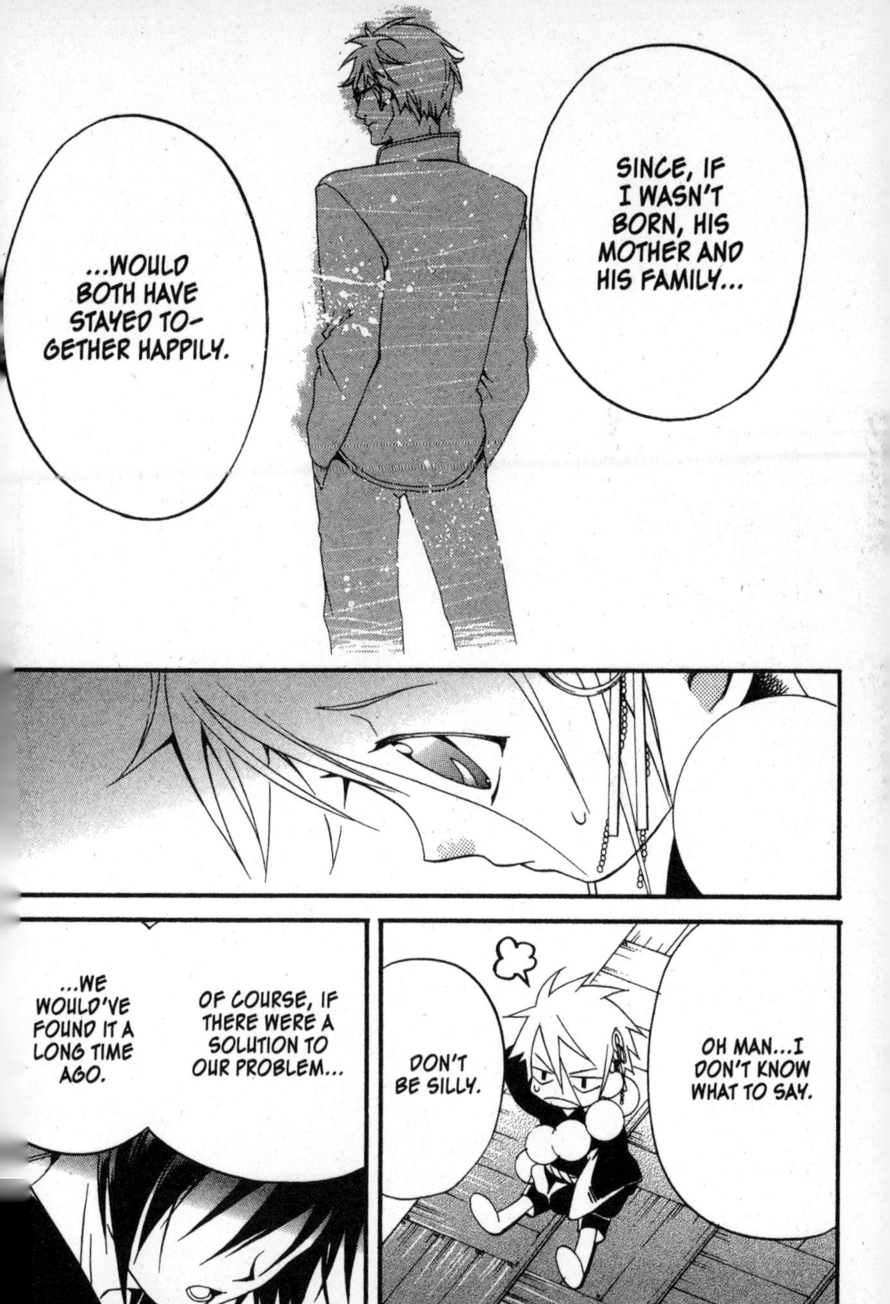
SINCE, IF I WASN'T BORN, HIS MOTHER AND HIS FAMILY...
...WOULD BOTH HAVE STAYED TO-GETHER HAPPILY.
OH MAN...I DON'T KNOW WHAT TO SAY.
DON'T BE SILLY.
OF COURSE, IF THERE WERE A SOLUTION TO OUR PROBLEM...
...WE WOULD'VE FOUND IT A LONG TIME AGO.

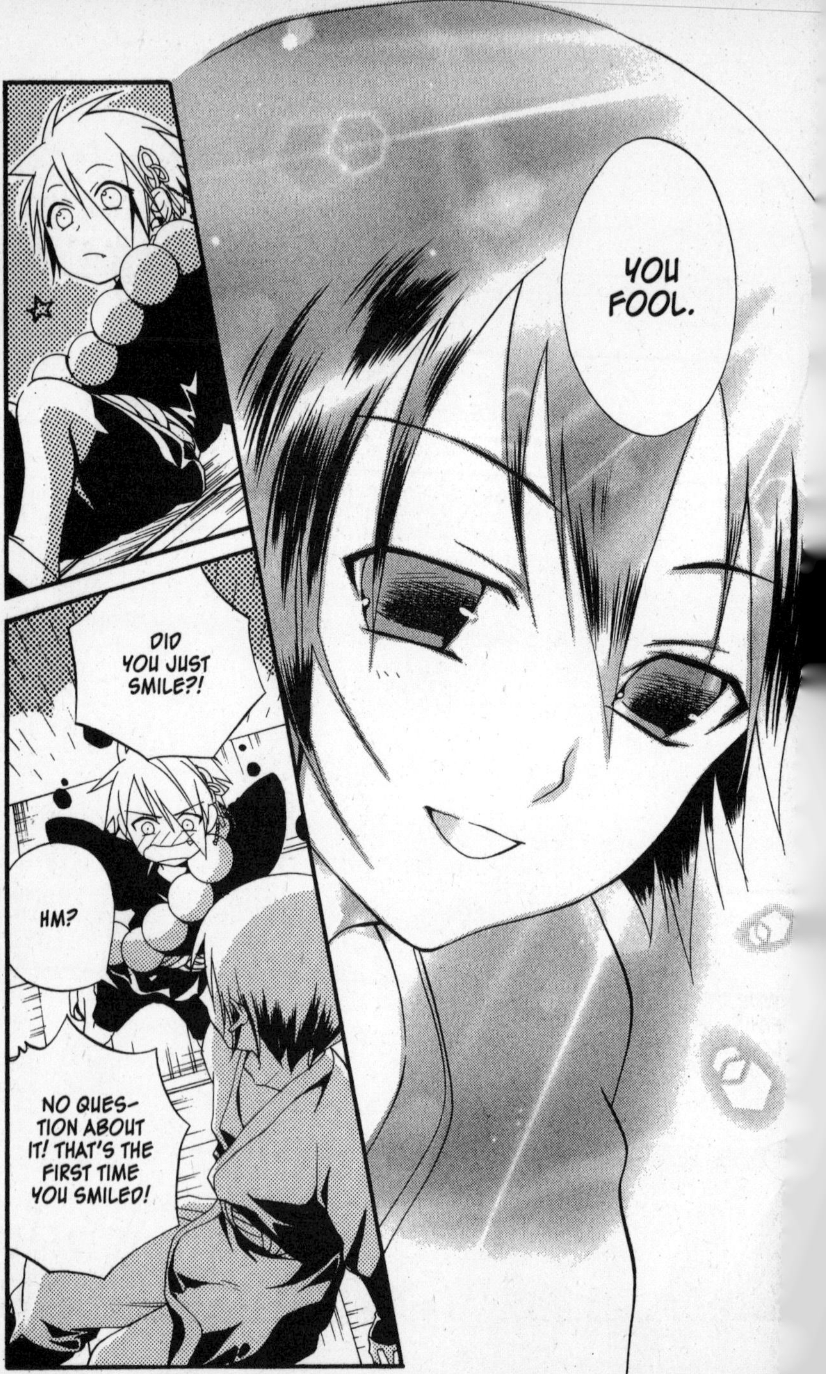
YOU FOOL.
DID YOU JUST SMILE?!
HM?
NO QUES-TION ABOUT IT! THAT'S THE FIRST TIME YOU SMILED!

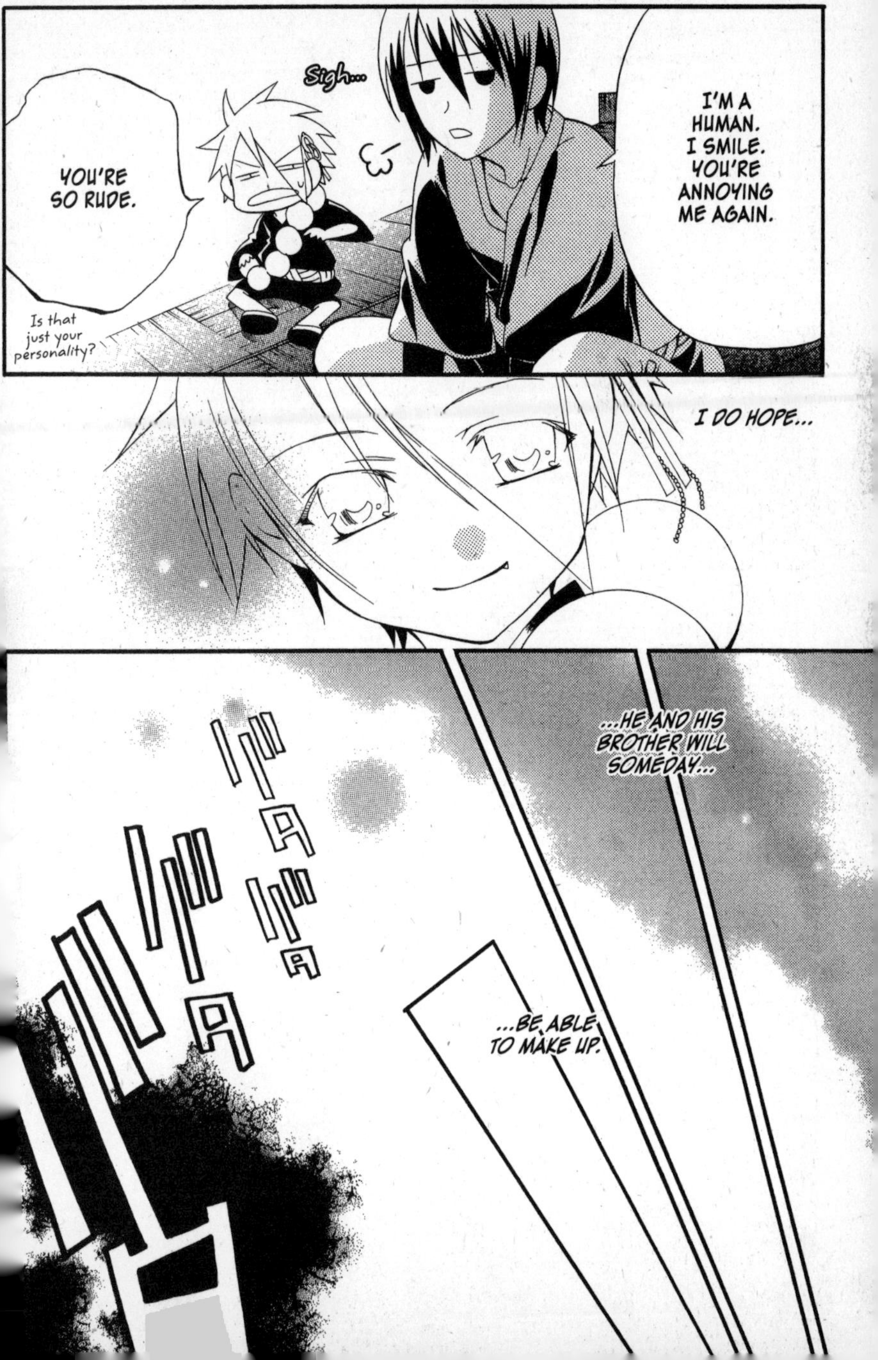
I'M A HUMAN. I SMILE. YOU'RE ANNOYING ME AGAIN.
Sigh...
YOU'RE SO RUDE.
Is that just your personality?
I DO HOPE...
...HE AND HIS BROTHER WILL SOMEDAY...
...BE ABLE TO MAKE UP.

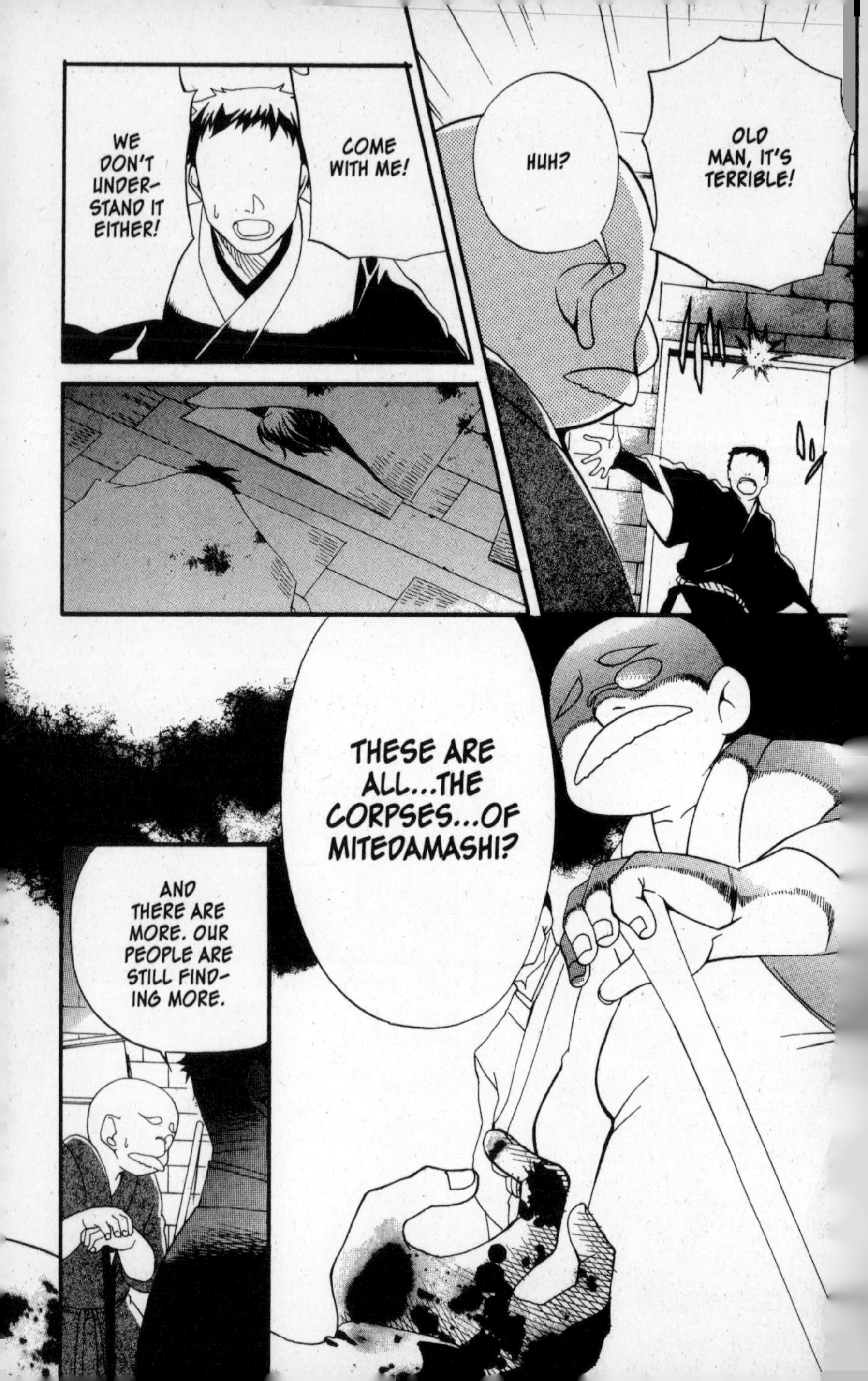
OLD MAN, IT'S TERRIBLE!
HUH?
COME WITH ME!
WE DON'T UNDER-STAND IT EITHER!
THESE ARE ALL...THE CORPSES...OF MITEDAMASHI?
AND THERE ARE MORE. OUR PEOPLE ARE STILL FIND-ING MORE.

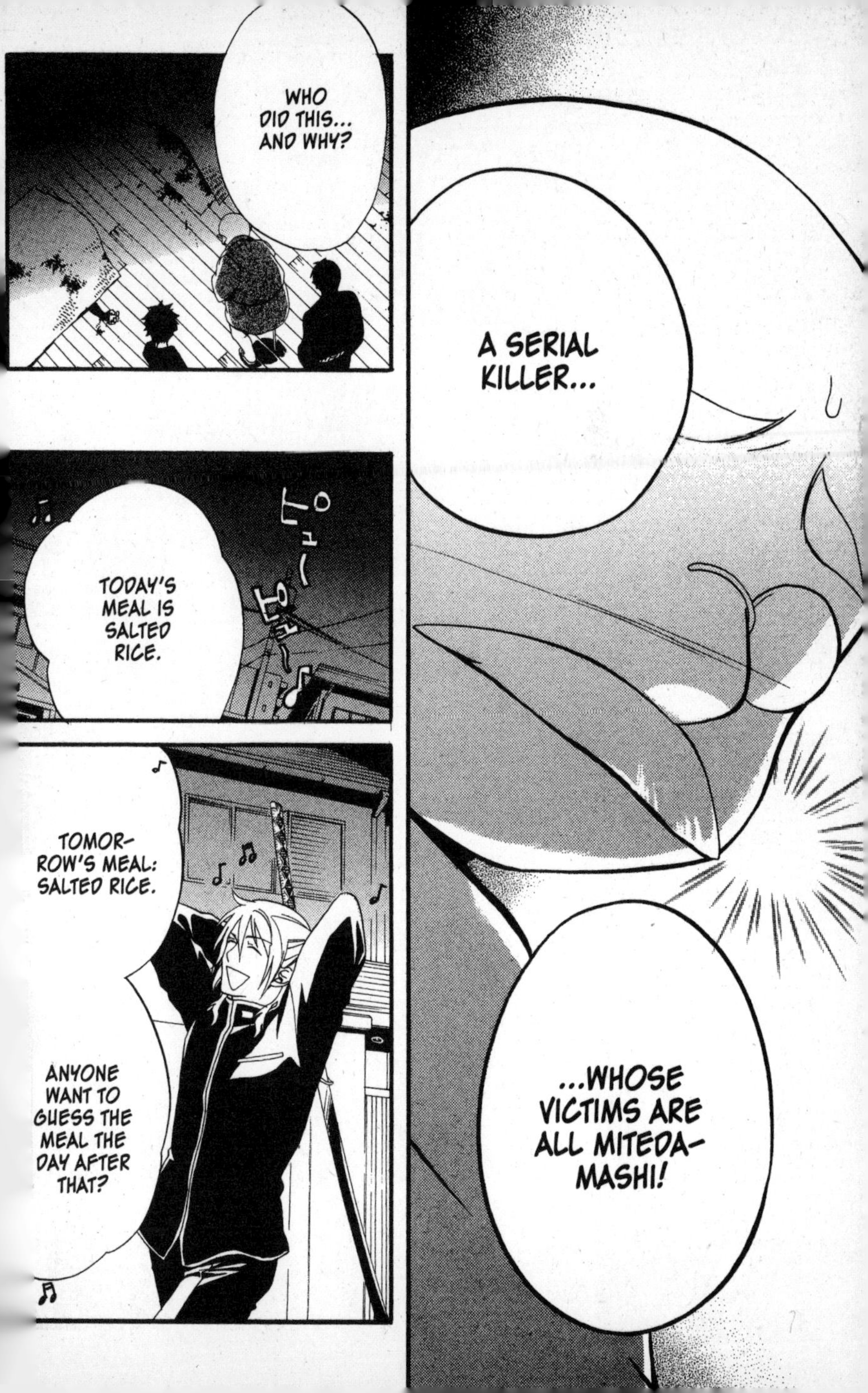
A SERIAL KILLER...
...WHOSE VICTIMS ARE ALL MITEDA-MASHI!
WHO DID THIS... AND WHY?
TODAY'S MEAL IS SALTED RICE.
TOMOR-ROW'S MEAL: SALTED RICE.
ANYONE WANT TO GUESS THE MEAL THE DAY AFTER THAT?

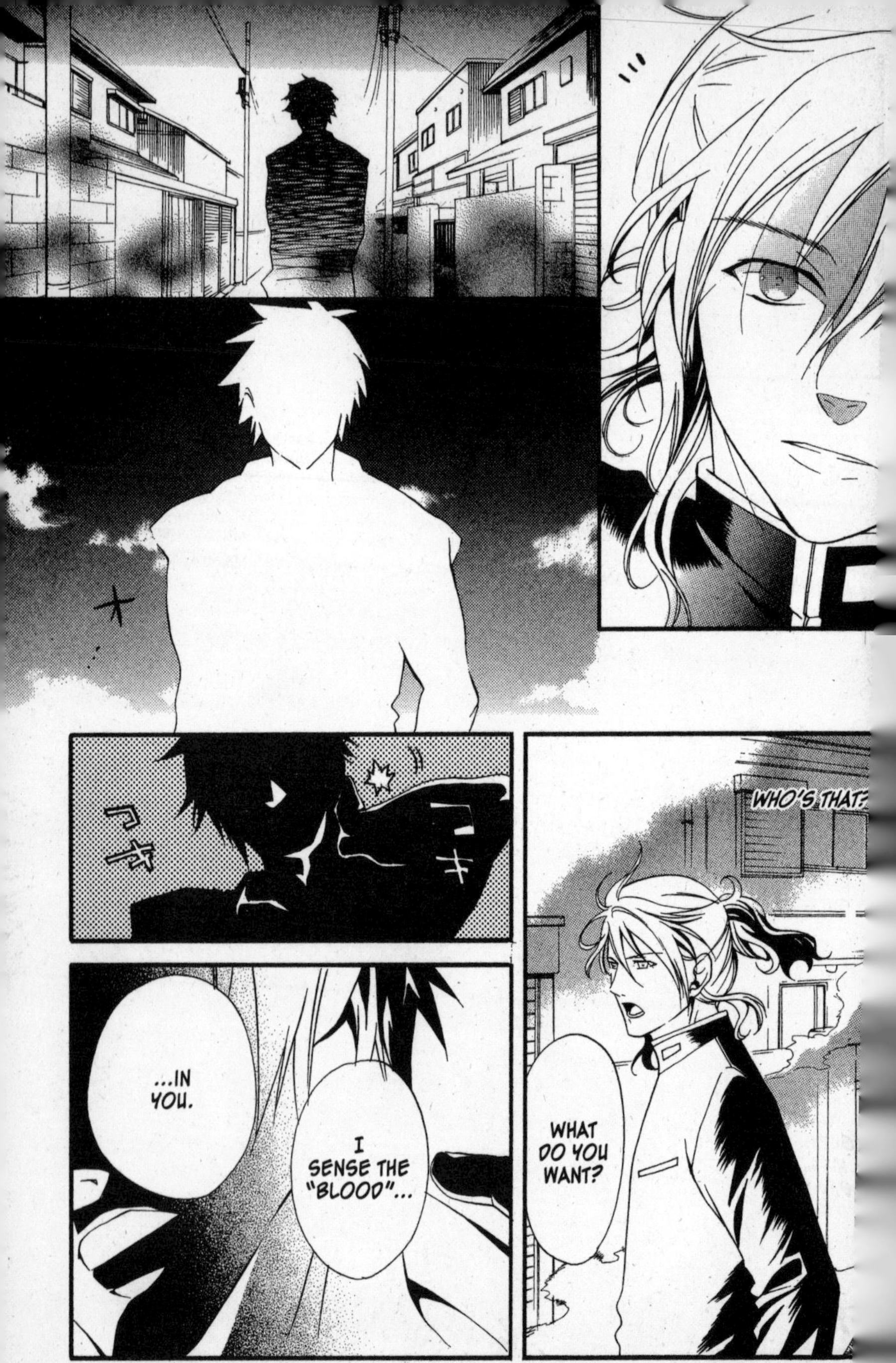
WHO'S THAT?
WHAT DO YOU WANT?
I SENSE THE "BLOOD"...
...IN YOU.

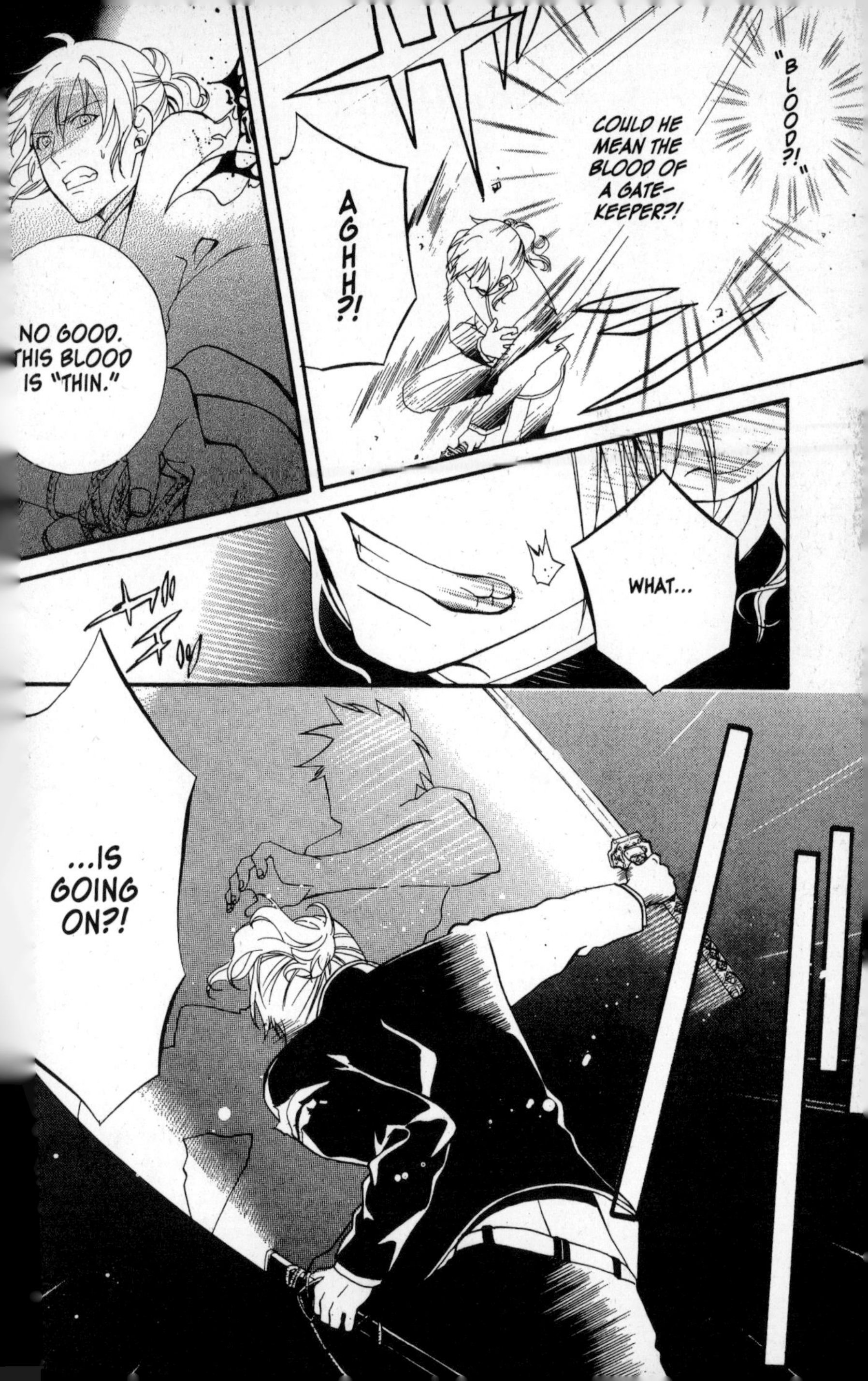
"BLOOD?!"
COULD HE MEAN THE BLOOD OF A GATE-KEEPER?!
AGHH?!
NO GOOD. THIS BLOOD IS "THIN."
WHAT...
...IS GOING ON?!

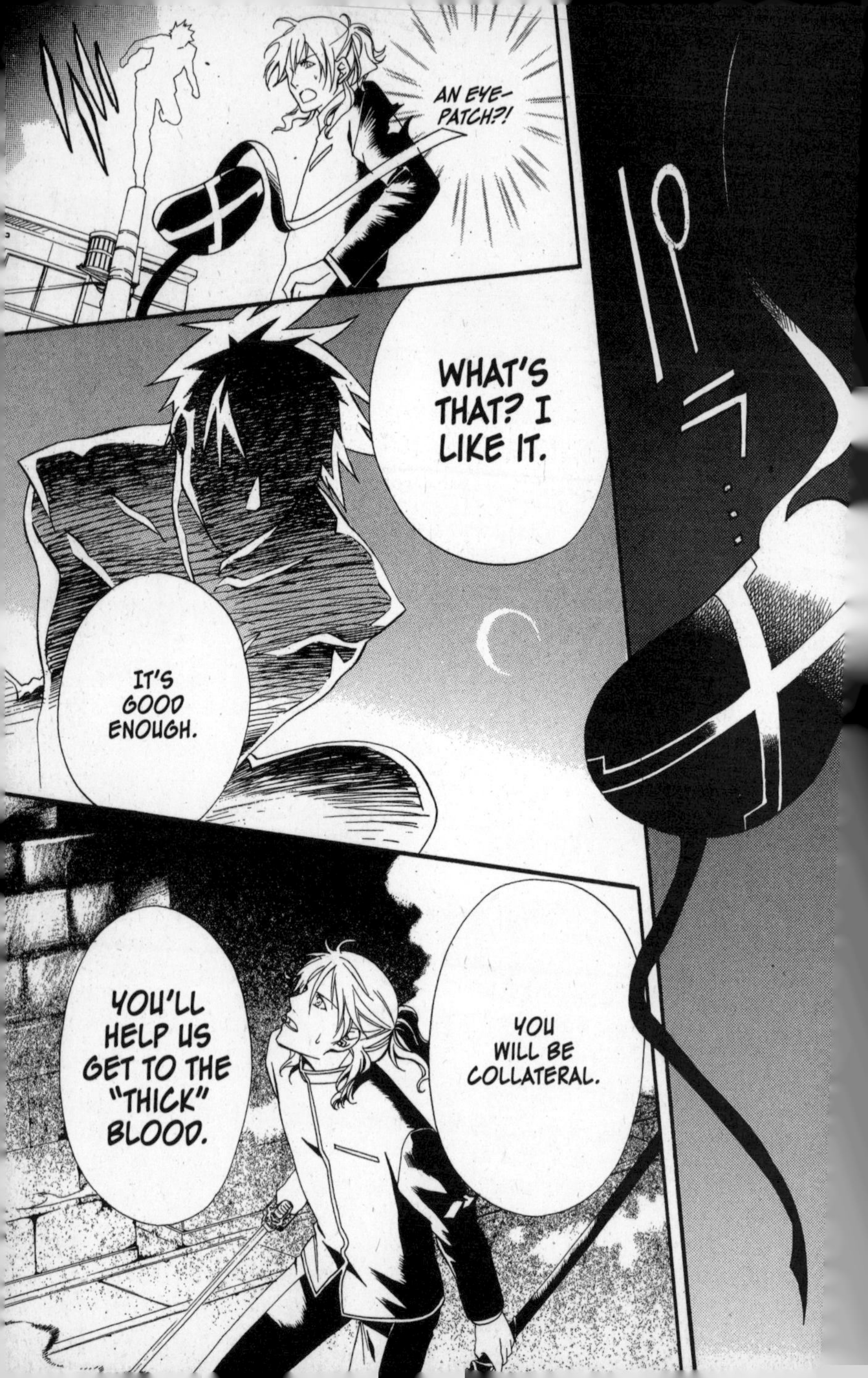
AN EYE-PATCH?!
WHAT'S THAT? I LIKE IT.
IT'S GOOD ENOUGH.
YOU WILL BE COLLATERAL.
YOU'LL HELP US GET TO THE "THICK" BLOOD.

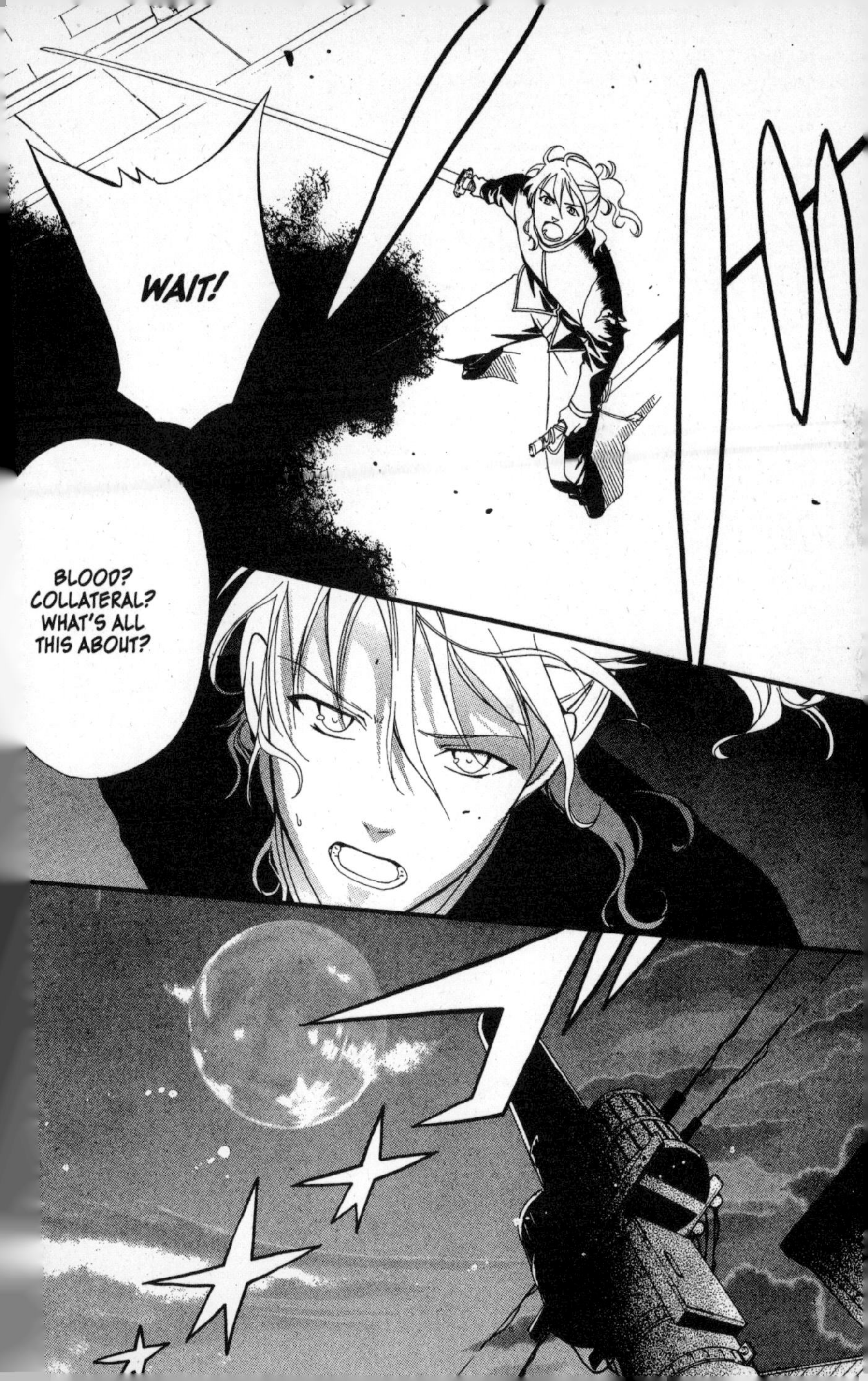
WAIT!
BLOOD? COLLATERAL? WHAT'S ALL THIS ABOUT?

■ TSURUGI SUGAWARA ■

AGE: 17 YEARS OLD/ HEIGHT: 191 CM/ BLOOD TYPE: A/ BIRTHDATE: APRIL 1ST

A SECOND YEAR HIGH SCHOOL STUDENT FROM NAGOYA.
HIS APPEARANCE IS THAT OF A SALUKI (A SLEEK, BEAUTIFUL BREED OF DOG) AND, ON THE INSIDE, HE'S MORE OF A CUDDLY SHIBA.
THAT APPEALING COMBINATION HAS CAUSED COUNTLESS GIRLS TO BURST INTO TEARS OF ADORATION.
AT 191 CM, HE HAS A TALL PHYSIQUE, AND HE CAN FREELY AND EFFORTLESSLY WIELD A LONG SWORD.
HE IS THE DESCENDANT OF A HYBRID RACE CREATED BY A LONG AGO UNION BETWEEN A GATE-KEEPER AND A HUMAN. HENCE, HIS BODY CARRIES A TRACE OF GATE-KEEPER'S BLOOD.
SUPERHUMAN STRENGTH IS HIS INHERITED POWER, ONE THAT HE PUTS TO GOOD USE AS A GUARDIAN.

*HE IS COUSIN TO MICHIZANE AND MICHITATE, AND, FOR A LONG TIME, HE'S HAD A GRUDGING BUT CLOSE-KNIT BOND WITH MICHITATE.
TSURUGI HAS TWO SISTERS, ONE OLDER, THE OTHER YOUNGER.
HE AND MICHITATE CAME FROM NAGOYA TO SEARCH FOR HIJIRI, THE ONE DESTINED TO BE LEADER OF THE GATE-KEEPERS.
HE LOVES ALL KINDS OF FOOD, AND EATS A LOT, ESPECIALLY ODEN.

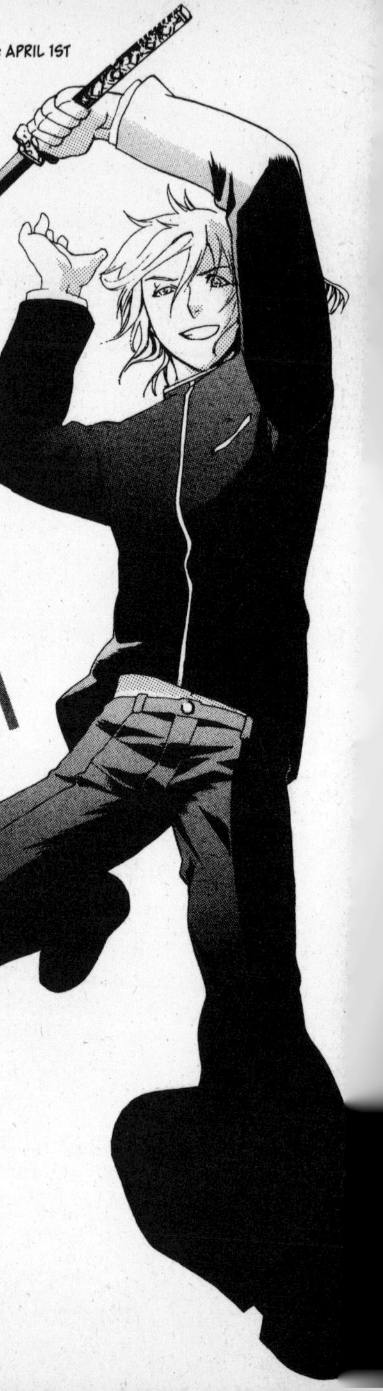

CHARACTER PROFILE:03 TSURUGI

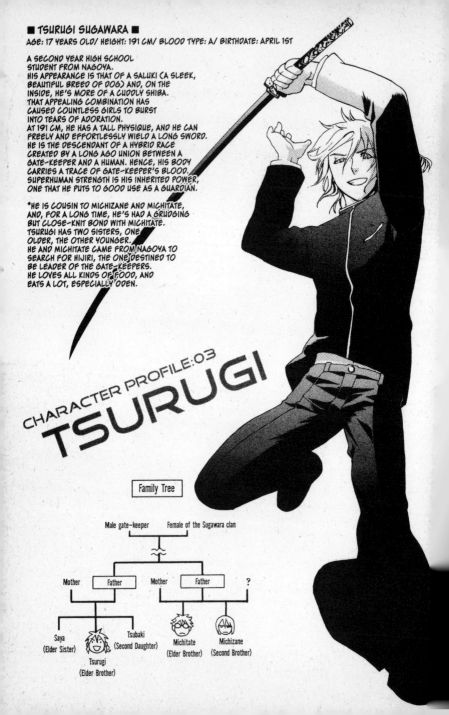

Family Tree

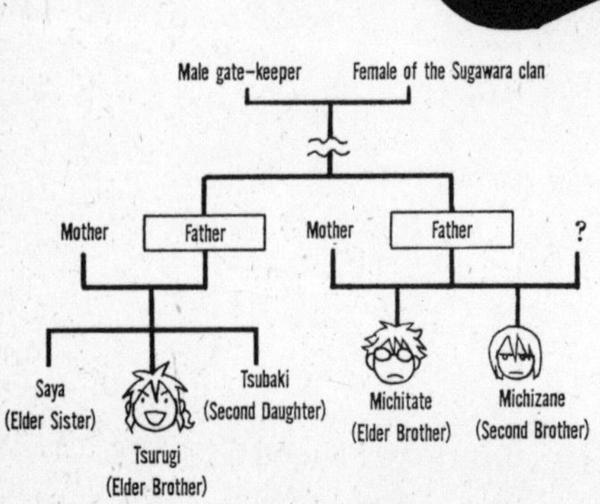
Male gate-keeper
Female of the Sugawara clan
Mother
Father
Mother
Father
?
Saya (Elder Sister)
Tsurugi (Elder Brother)
Tsubaki (Second Daughter)
Michitate (Elder Brother)
Michizane (Second Brother)

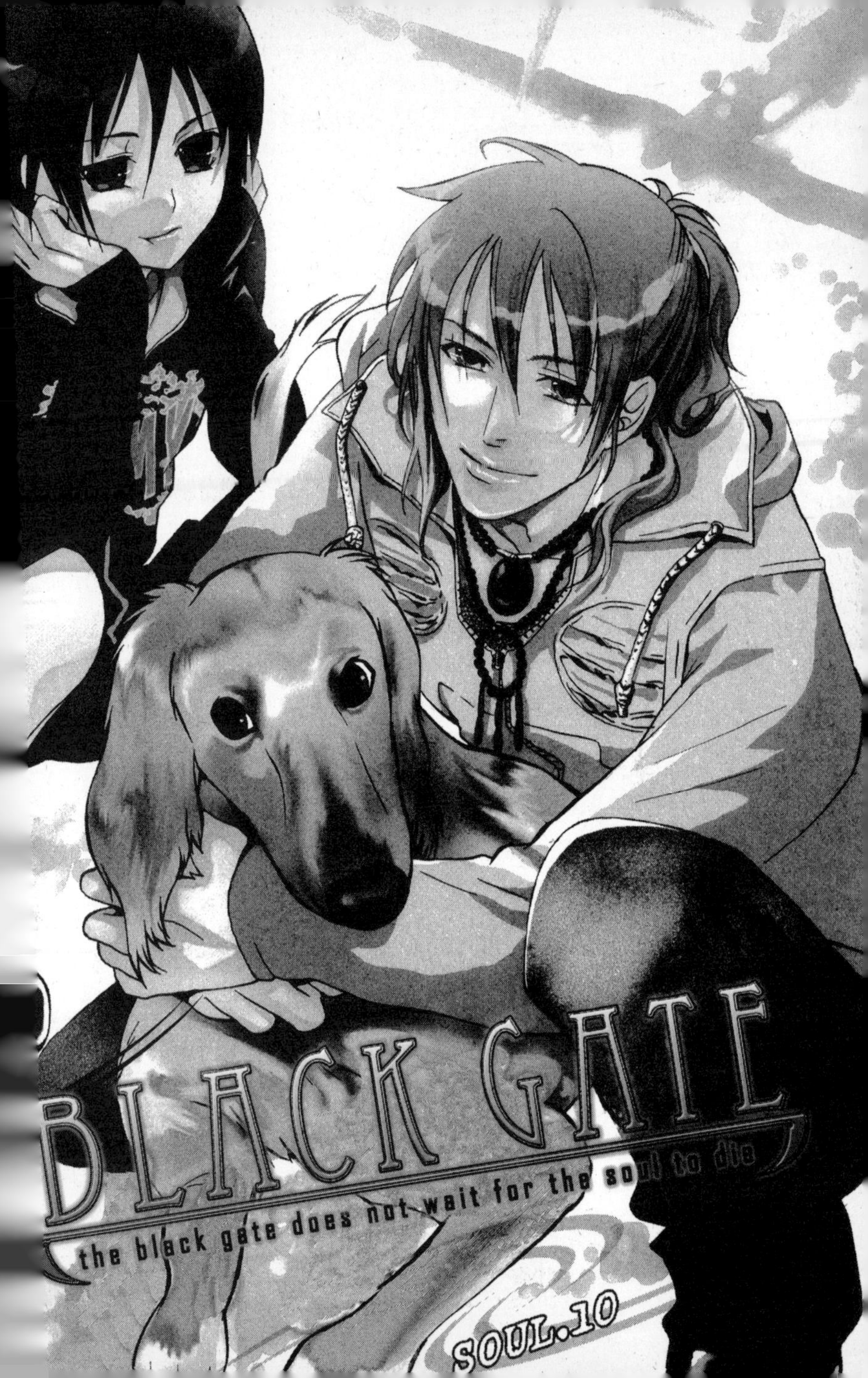
BLACK GATE
the black gate does not wait for the soul to die
SOUL.10

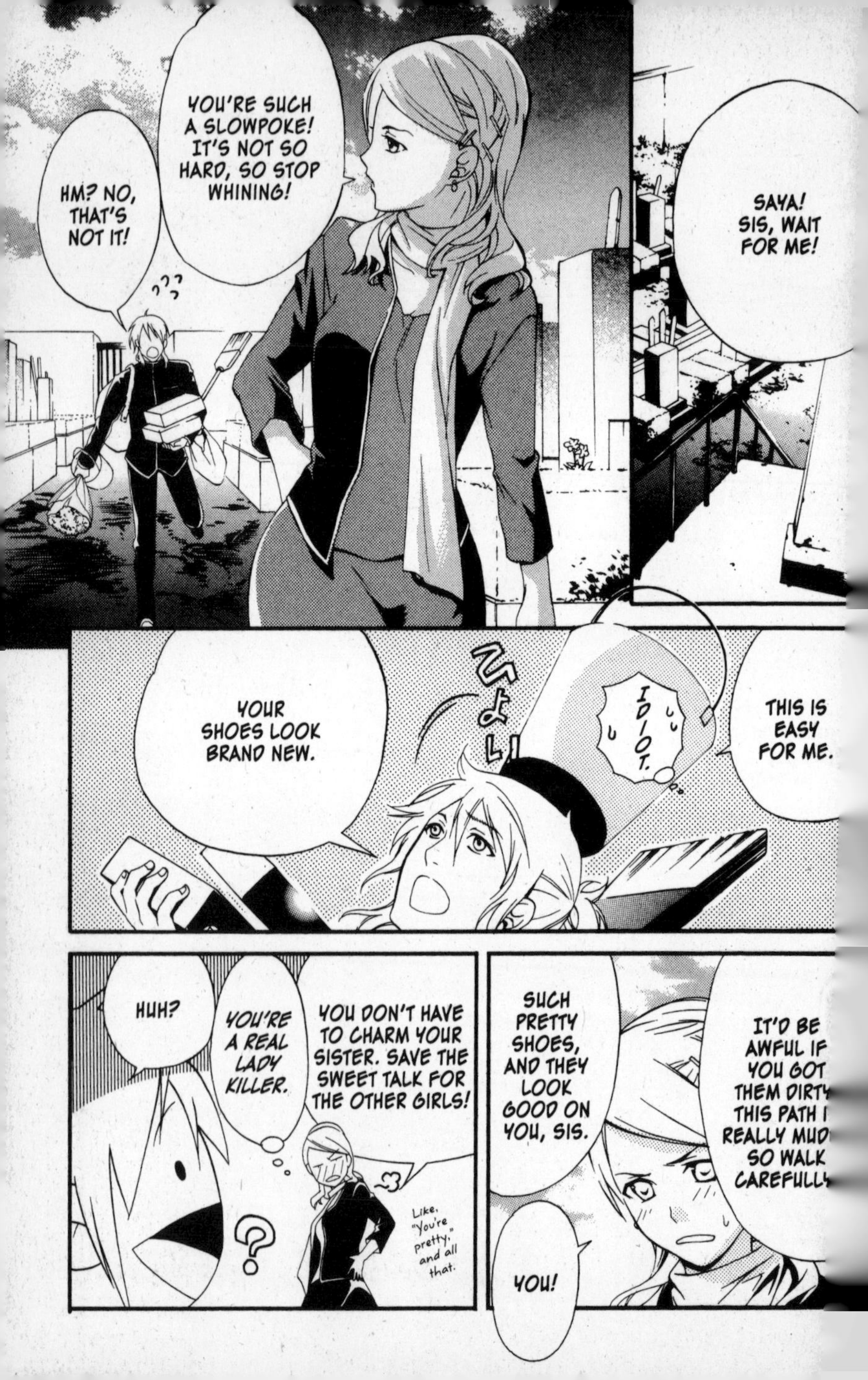
SAYA! SIS, WAIT FOR ME!
YOU'RE SUCH A SLOWPOKE! IT'S NOT SO HARD, SO STOP WHINING!
HM? NO, THAT'S NOT IT!
THIS IS EASY FOR ME.
IDIOT.
ひょい
YOUR SHOES LOOK BRAND NEW.
IT'D BE AWFUL IF YOU GOT THEM DIRTY
THIS PATH I
REALLY MUD
SO WALK CAREFULL
SUCH PRETTY SHOES, AND THEY LOOK GOOD ON YOU, SIS.
YOU!
YOU DON'T HAVE TO CHARM YOUR SISTER. SAVE THE SWEET TALK FOR THE OTHER GIRLS!
YOU'RE A REAL LADY KILLER.
HUH?
Like, "You're pretty," and all that.

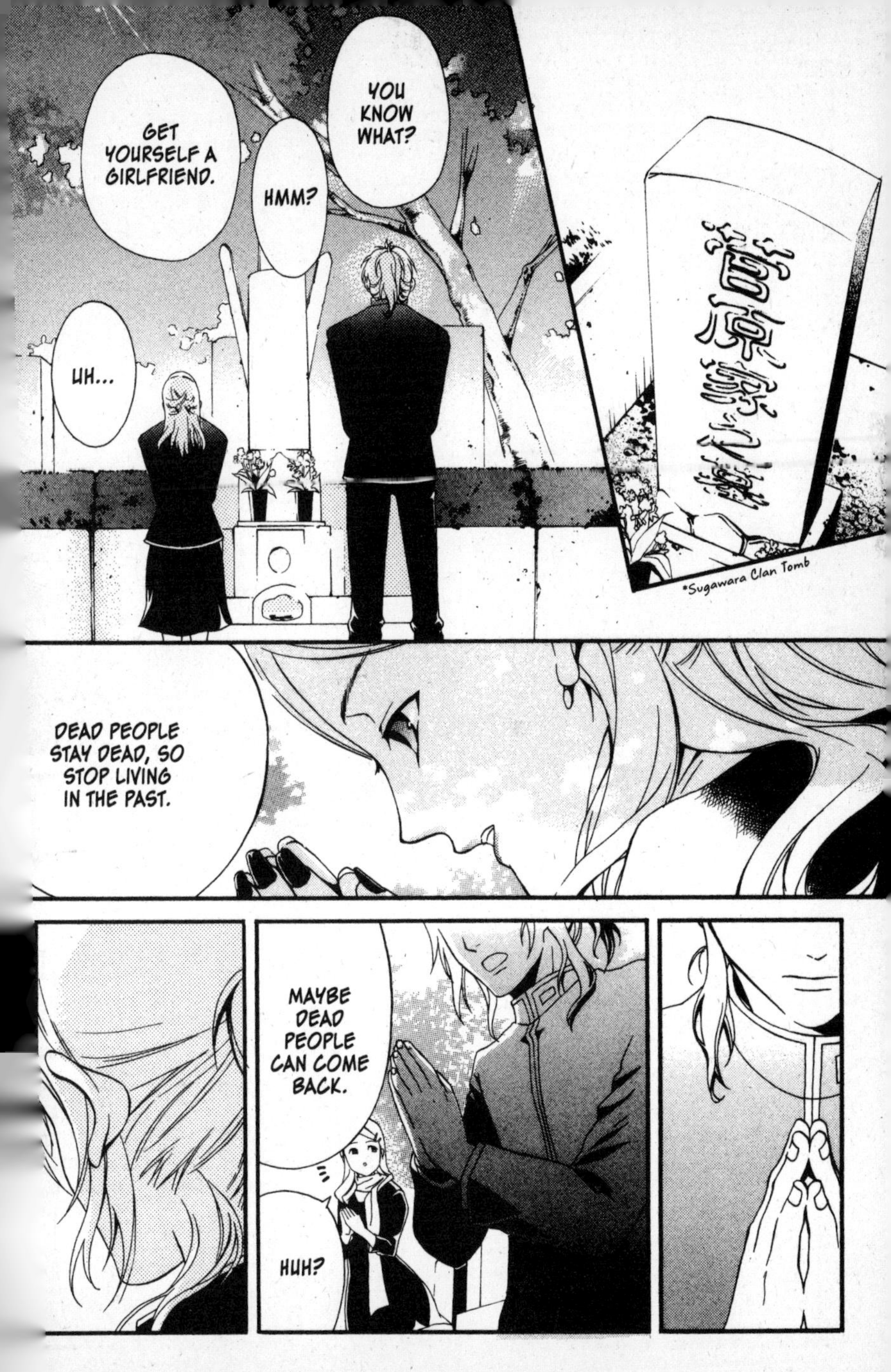
菅原家之墓
*Sugawara Clan Tomb
YOU KNOW WHAT?
HMM?
GET YOURSELF A GIRLFRIEND.
UH...
DEAD PEOPLE STAY DEAD, SO STOP LIVING IN THE PAST.
MAYBE DEAD PEOPLE CAN COME BACK.
HUH?

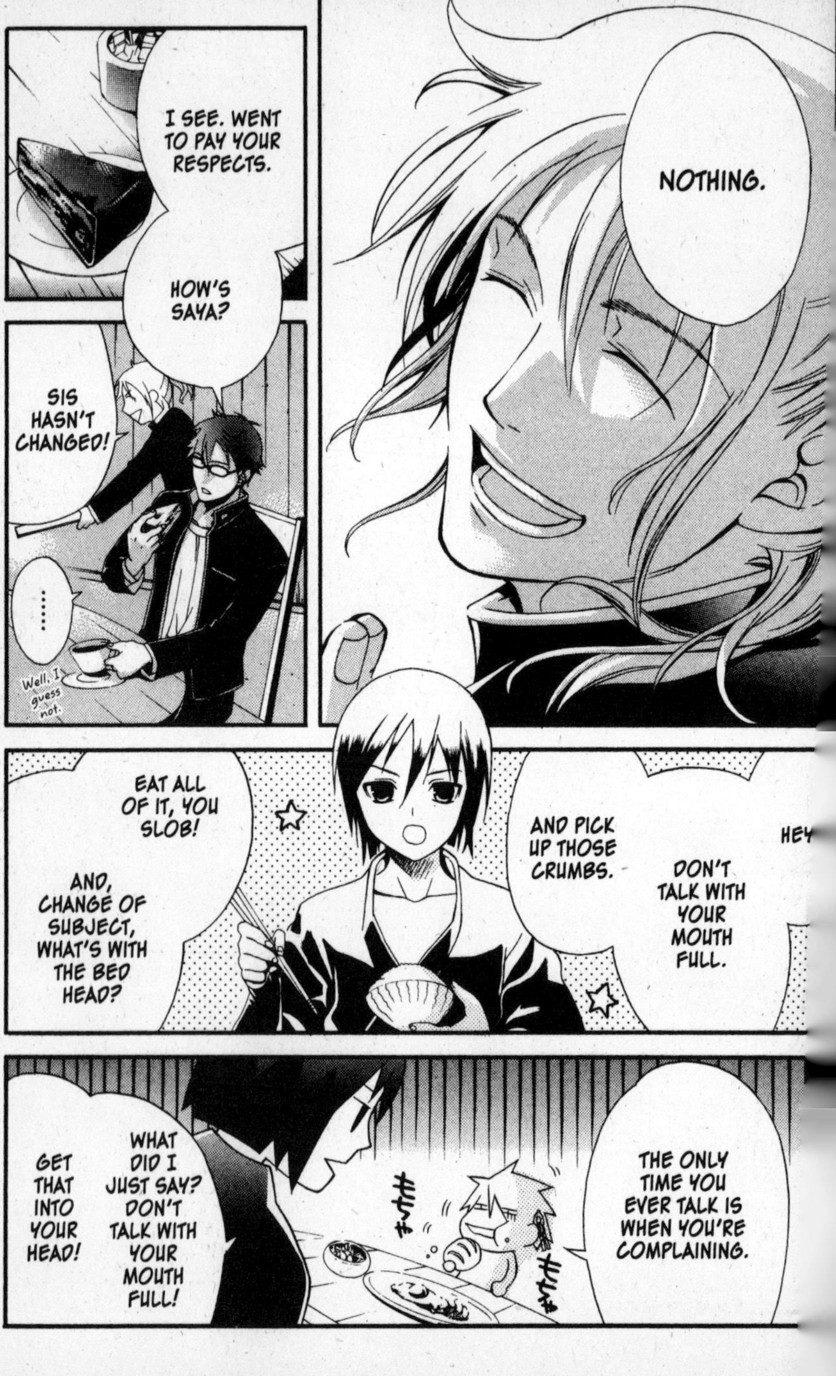
NOTHING.
I SEE. WENT TO PAY YOUR RESPECTS.
HOW'S SAYA?
SIS HASN'T CHANGED!
......
Well, I guess not.
HEY
DON'T TALK WITH YOUR MOUTH FULL.
AND PICK UP THOSE CRUMBS.
EAT ALL OF IT, YOU SLOB!
AND, CHANGE OF SUBJECT, WHAT'S WITH THE BED HEAD?
THE ONLY TIME YOU EVER TALK IS WHEN YOU'RE COMPLAINING.
WHAT DID I JUST SAY? DON'T TALK WITH YOUR MOUTH FULL!
GET THAT INTO YOUR HEAD!

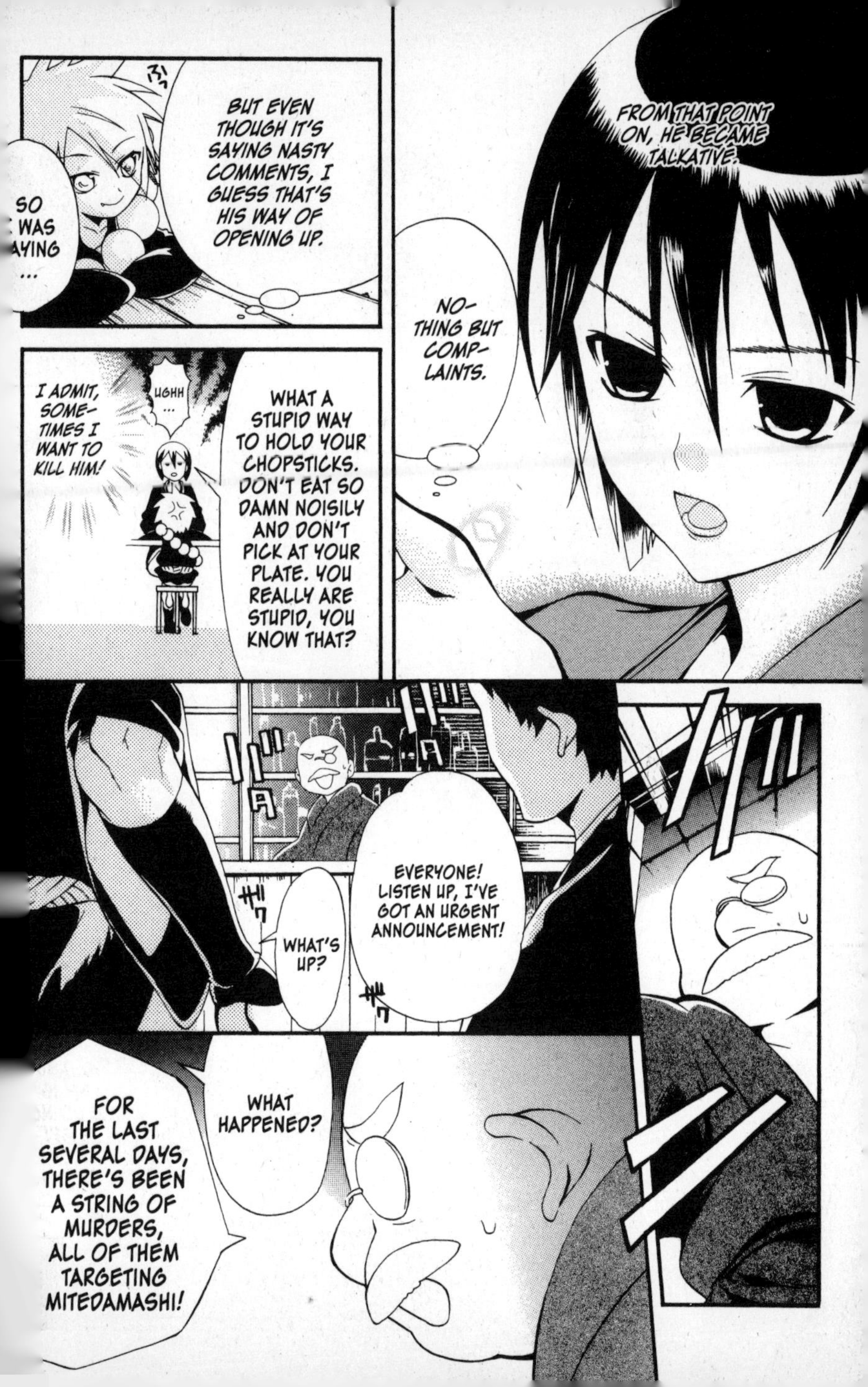
FROM THAT POINT ON, HE BECAME TALKATIVE.
NO-THING BUT COMP-LAINTS.
ぶっ
BUT EVEN THOUGH IT'S SAYING NASTY COMMENTS, I GUESS THAT'S HIS WAY OF OPENING UP.
SO WAS ...
WHAT A STUPID WAY TO HOLD YOUR CHOPSTICKS. DON'T EAT SO DAMN NOISILY AND DON'T PICK AT YOUR PLATE. YOU REALLY ARE STUPID, YOU KNOW THAT?
UGHH ...
I ADMIT, SOME-TIMES I WANT TO KILL HIM!
EVERYONE! LISTEN UP, I'VE GOT AN URGENT ANNOUNCEMENT!
WHAT'S UP?
WHAT HAPPENED?
FOR THE LAST SEVERAL DAYS, THERE'S BEEN A STRING OF MURDERS, ALL OF THEM TARGETING MITEDAMASHI!

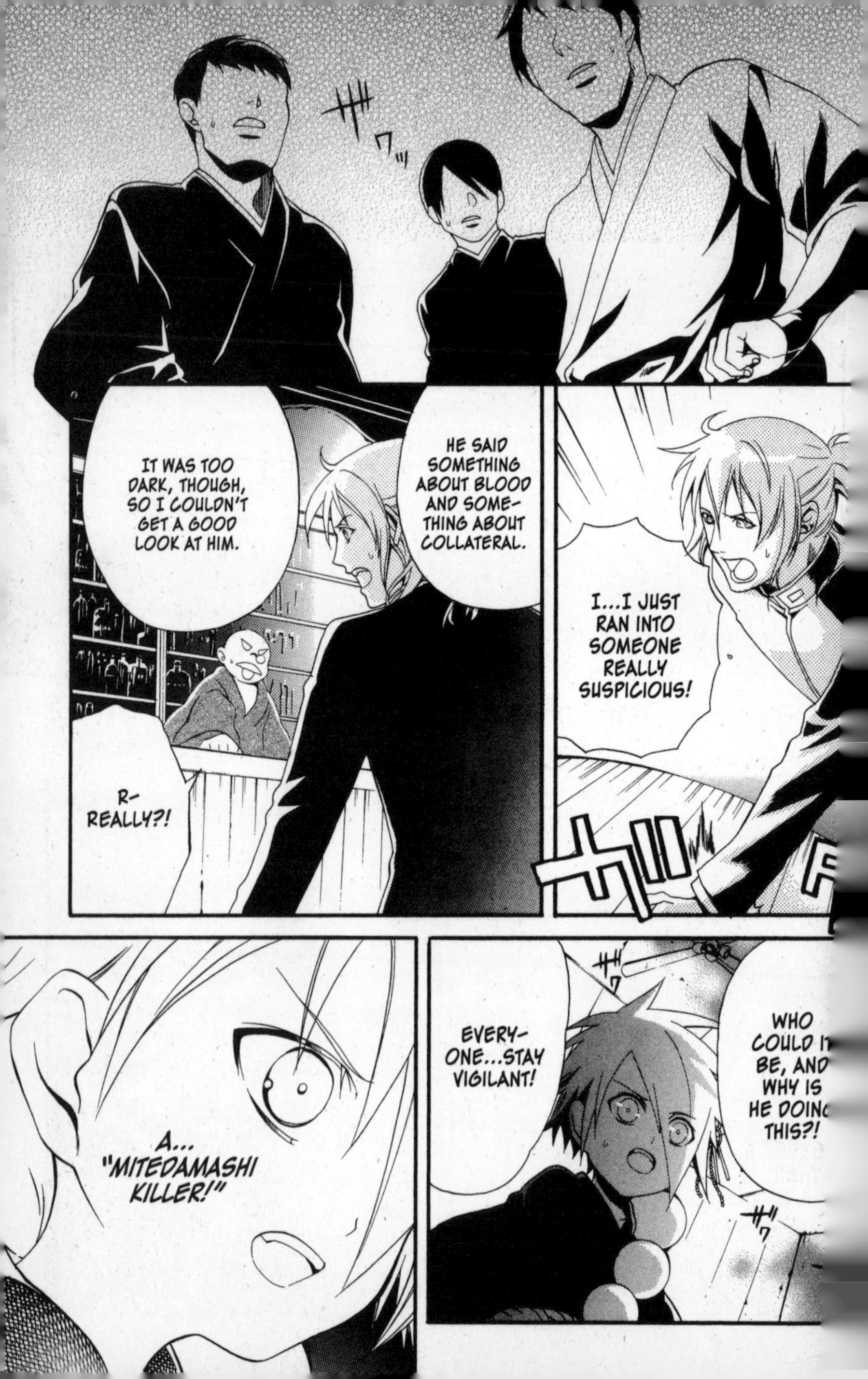
I...I JUST RAN INTO SOMEONE REALLY SUSPICIOUS!
HE SAID SOMETHING ABOUT BLOOD AND SOME-THING ABOUT COLLATERAL.
IT WAS TOO DARK, THOUGH, SO I COULDN'T GET A GOOD LOOK AT HIM.
R-REALLY?!
WHO COULD IT BE, AND WHY IS HE DOING THIS?!
EVERY-ONE...STAY VIGILANT!
A... "MITEDAMASHI KILLER!"

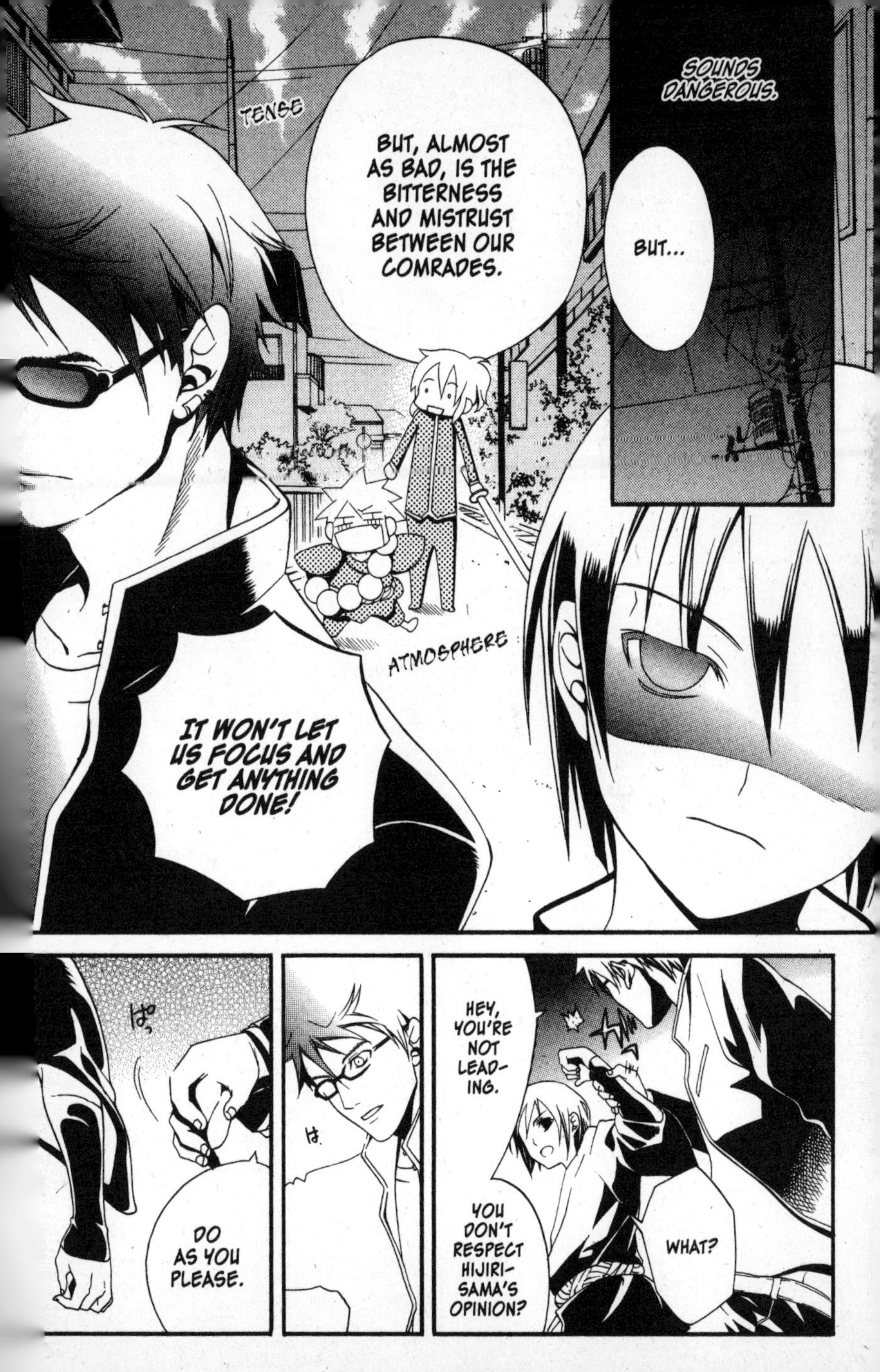
SOUNDS DANGEROUS.
BUT...
BUT, ALMOST AS BAD, IS THE BITTERNESS AND MISTRUST BETWEEN OUR COMRADES.
TENSE
ATMOSPHERE
IT WON'T LET US FOCUS AND GET ANYTHING DONE!
HEY, YOU'RE NOT LEADING.
YOU DON'T RESPECT HIJIRI-SAMA'S OPINION?
WHAT?
は
ぱっ
DO AS YOU PLEASE.

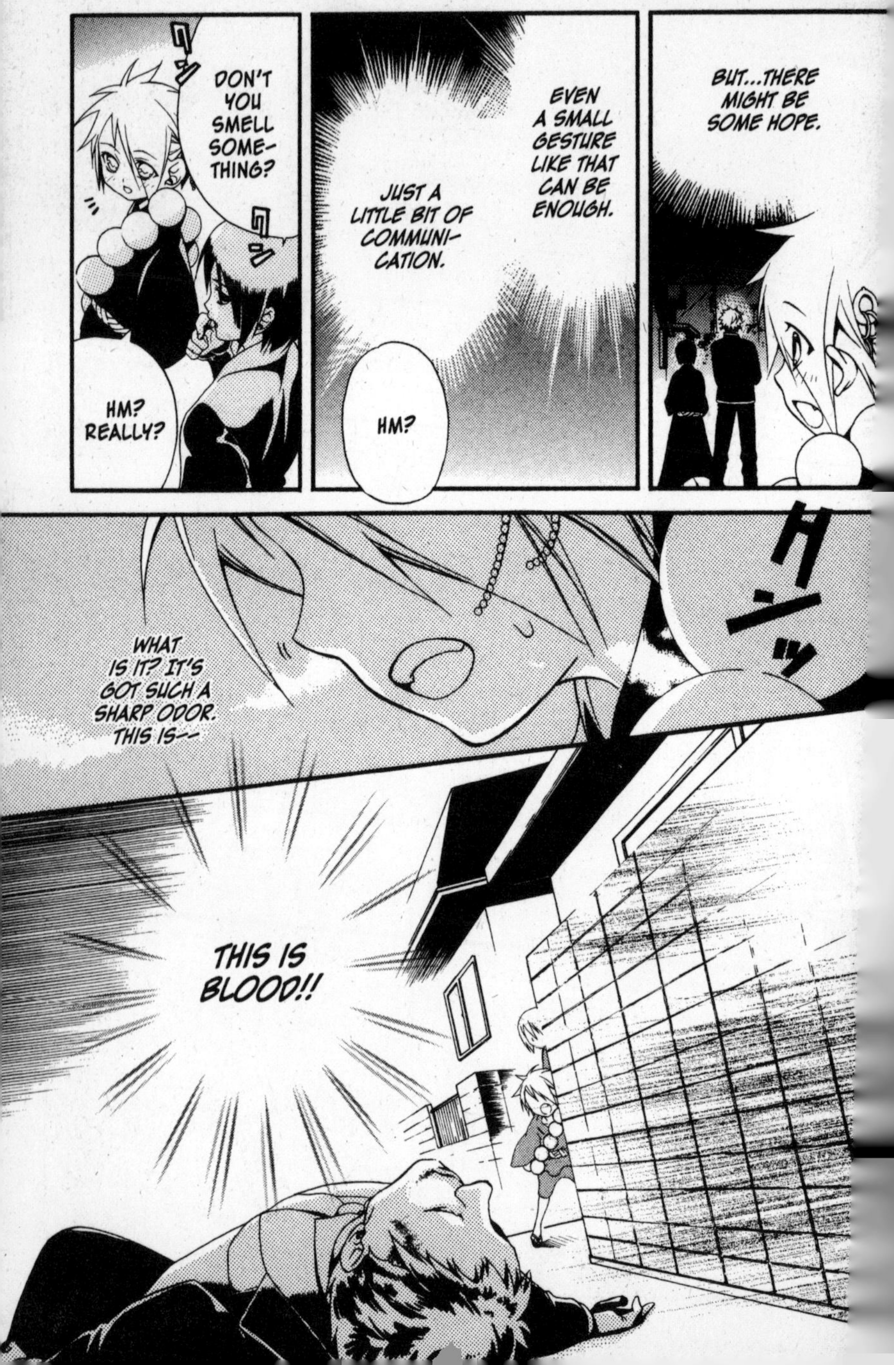
BUT...THERE MIGHT BE SOME HOPE.
EVEN A SMALL GESTURE LIKE THAT CAN BE ENOUGH.
JUST A LITTLE BIT OF COMMUNI-CATION.
HM?
DON'T YOU SMELL SOME-THING?
HM? REALLY?
WHAT IS IT? IT'S GOT SUCH A SHARP ODOR. THIS IS--
THIS IS BLOOD!!

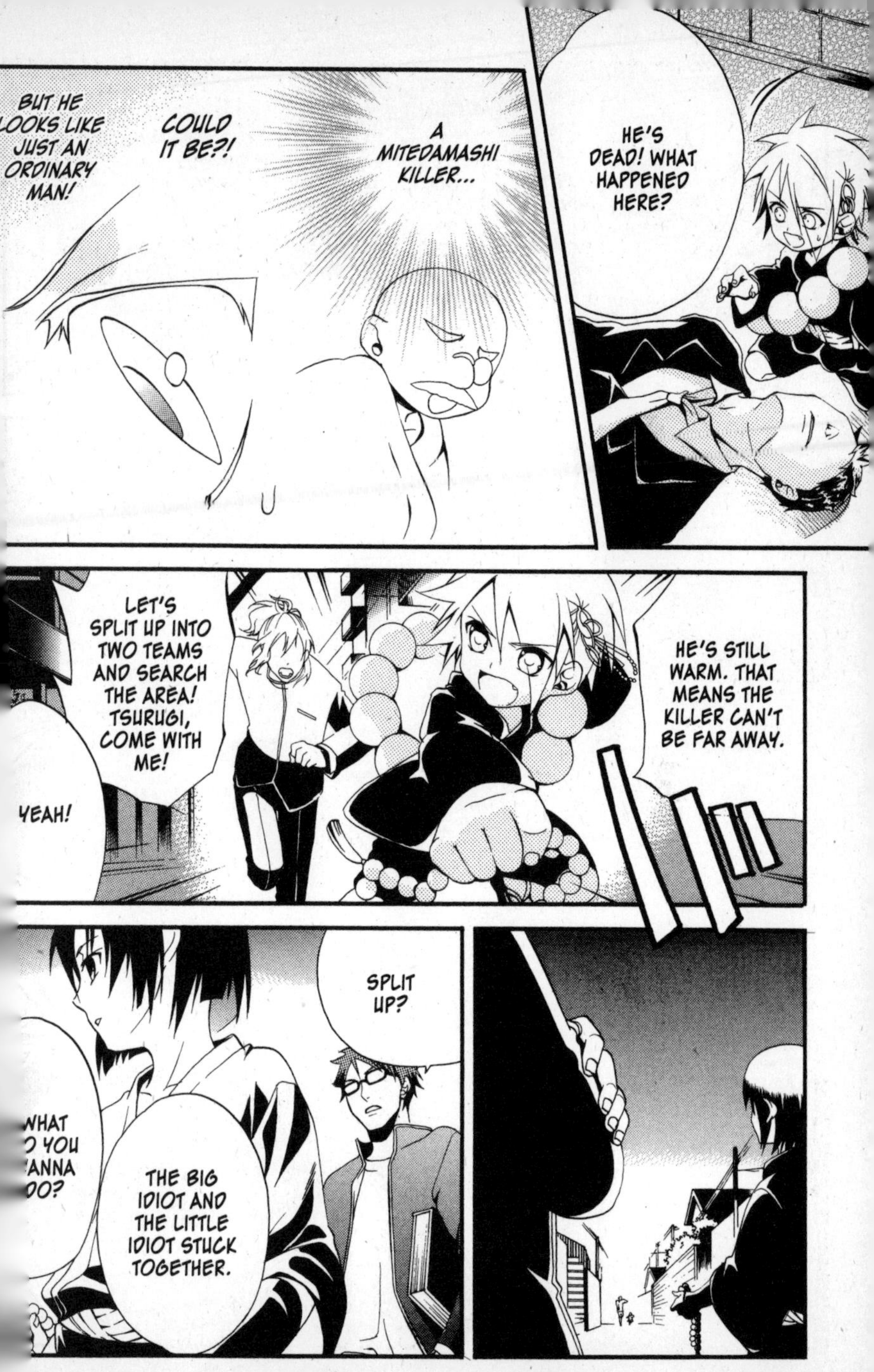
HE'S DEAD! WHAT HAPPENED HERE?
A MITEDAMASHI KILLER...
COULD IT BE?!
BUT HE LOOKS LIKE JUST AN ORDINARY MAN!
HE'S STILL WARM. THAT MEANS THE KILLER CAN'T BE FAR AWAY.
LET'S SPLIT UP INTO TWO TEAMS AND SEARCH THE AREA! TSURUGI, COME WITH ME!
YEAH!
SPLIT UP?
WHAT O YOU ANNA OO?
THE BIG IDIOT AND THE LITTLE IDIOT STUCK TOGETHER.

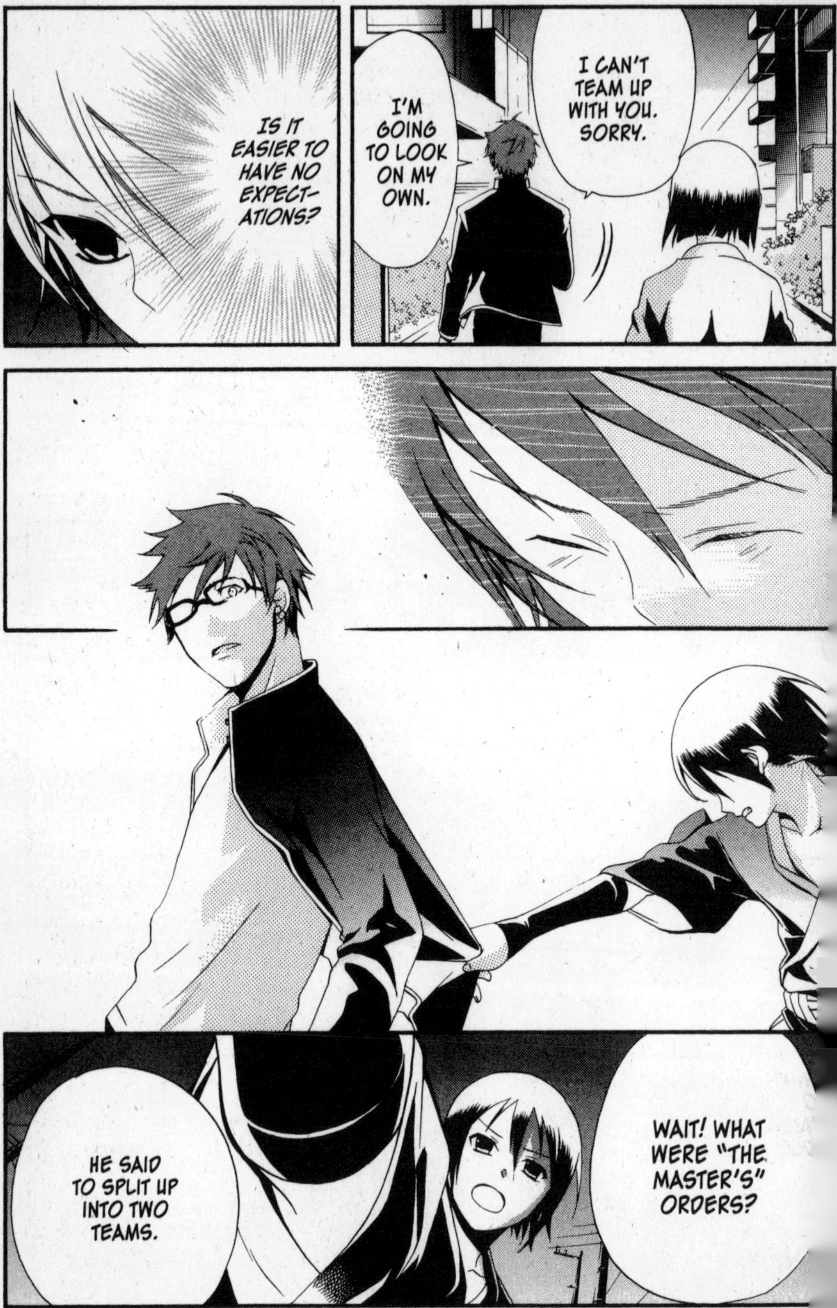
I CAN'T TEAM UP WITH YOU. SORRY.
I'M GOING TO LOOK ON MY OWN.
IS IT EASIER TO HAVE NO EXPECT-ATIONS?
WAIT! WHAT WERE "THE MASTER'S" ORDERS?
HE SAID TO SPLIT UP INTO TWO TEAMS.

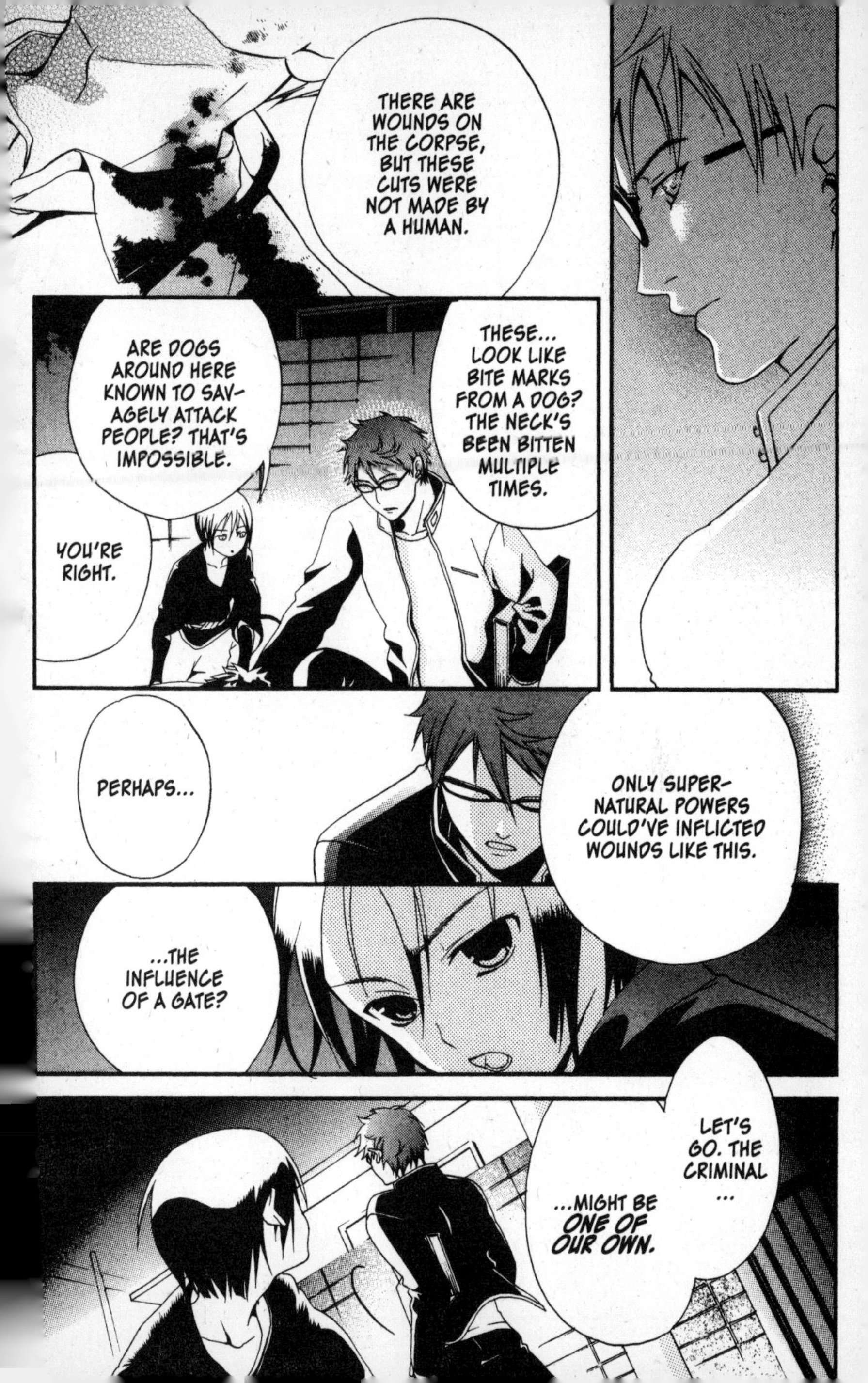
THERE ARE WOUNDS ON THE CORPSE, BUT THESE CUTS WERE NOT MADE BY A HUMAN.
THESE... LOOK LIKE BITE MARKS FROM A DOG? THE NECK'S BEEN BITTEN MULTIPLE TIMES.
ARE DOGS AROUND HERE KNOWN TO SAV-AGELY ATTACK PEOPLE? THAT'S IMPOSSIBLE.
YOU'RE RIGHT.
ONLY SUPER-NATURAL POWERS COULD'VE INFLICTED WOUNDS LIKE THIS.
PERHAPS...
...THE INFLUENCE OF A GATE?
LET'S GO. THE CRIMINAL ...
...MIGHT BE ONE OF OUR OWN.

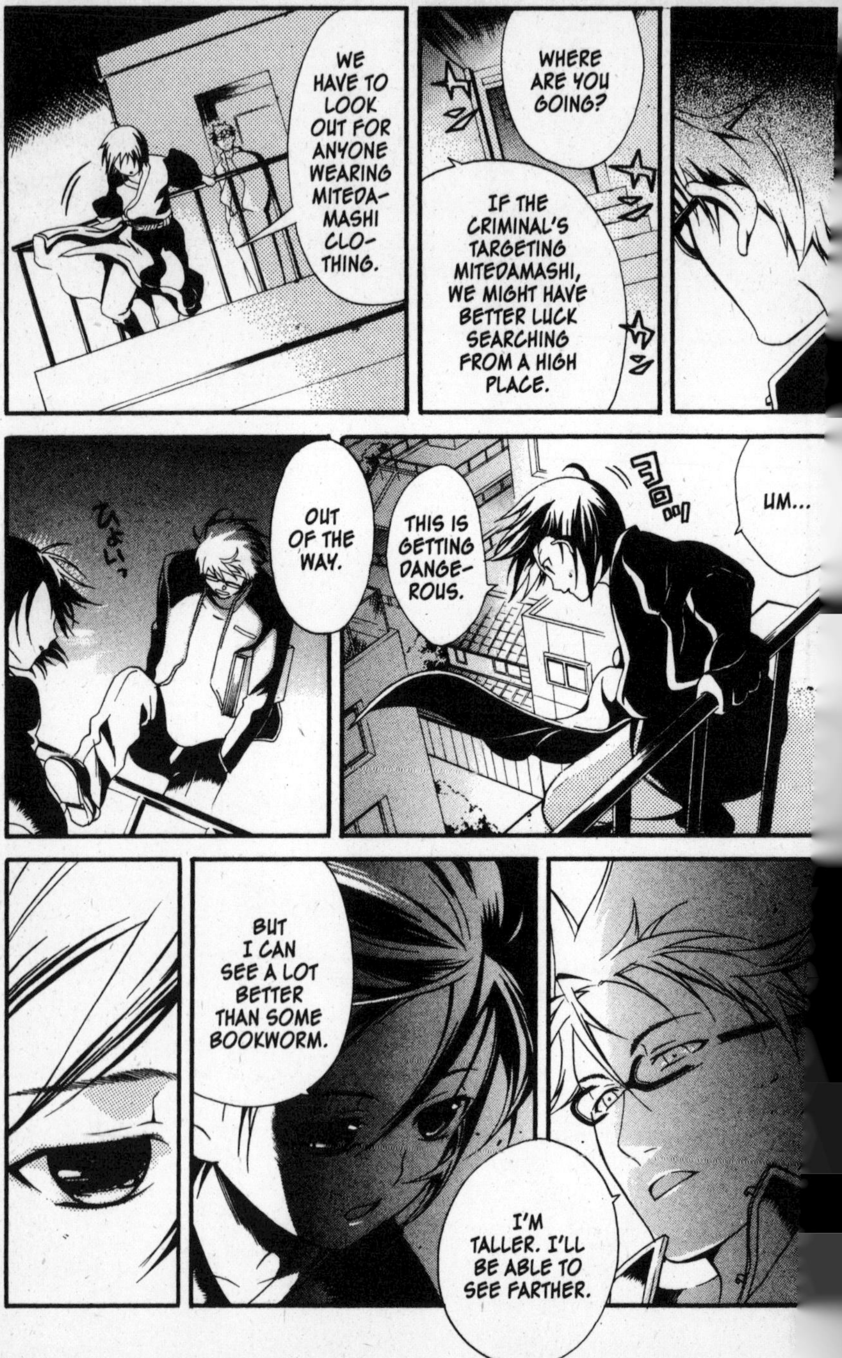
WHERE ARE YOU GOING?
IF THE CRIMINAL'S TARGETING MITEDAMASHI, WE MIGHT HAVE BETTER LUCK SEARCHING FROM A HIGH PLACE.
WE HAVE TO LOOK OUT FOR ANYONE WEARING MITEDA-MASHI CLO-THING.
UM...
ヨロ…
THIS IS GETTING DANGE-ROUS.
OUT OF THE WAY.
ひょい
I'M TALLER. I'LL BE ABLE TO SEE FARTHER.
BUT I CAN SEE A LOT BETTER THAN SOME BOOKWORM.

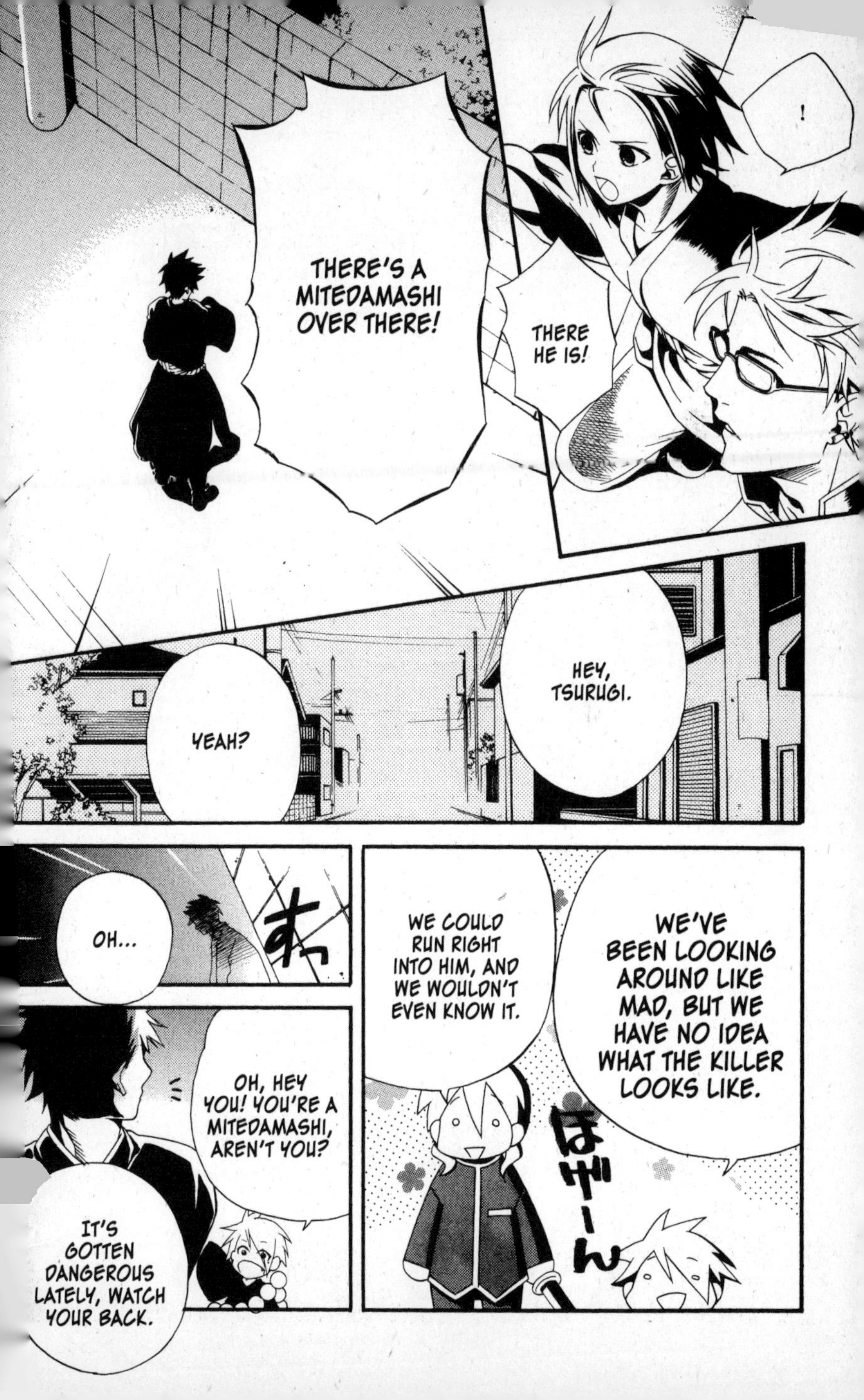

!
THERE HE IS!
THERE'S A MITEDAMASHI OVER THERE!
HEY, TSURUGI.
YEAH?
WE'VE BEEN LOOKING AROUND LIKE MAD, BUT WE HAVE NO IDEA WHAT THE KILLER LOOKS LIKE.
WE COULD RUN RIGHT INTO HIM, AND WE WOULDN'T EVEN KNOW IT.
ほげ～ん
すっ
OH...
OH, HEY YOU! YOU'RE A MITEDAMASHI, AREN'T YOU?
IT'S GOTTEN DANGEROUS LATELY, WATCH YOUR BACK.

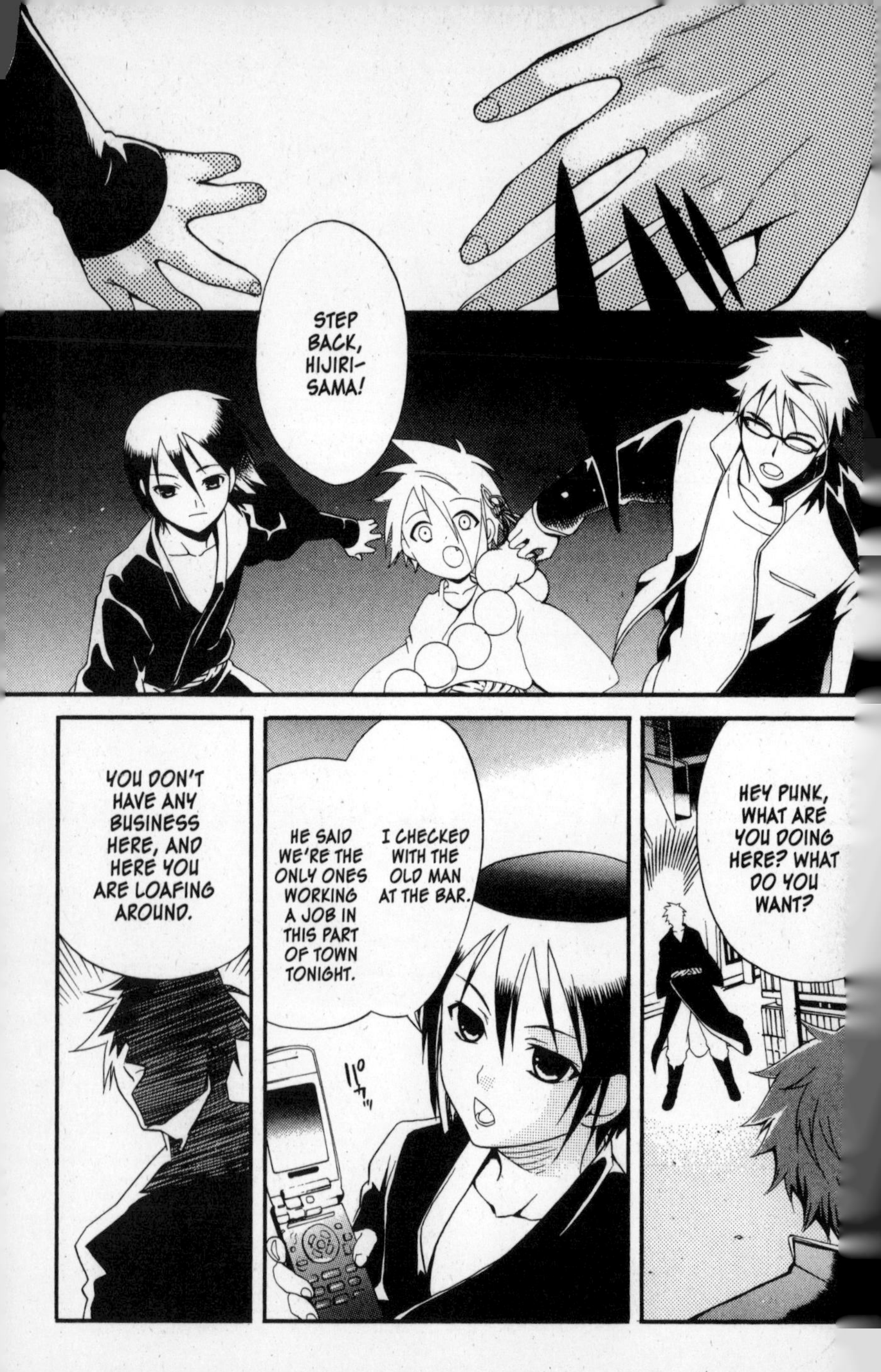
STEP BACK, HIJIRI-SAMA!
HEY PUNK, WHAT ARE YOU DOING HERE? WHAT DO YOU WANT?
I CHECKED WITH THE OLD MAN AT THE BAR.
HE SAID WE'RE THE ONLY ONES WORKING A JOB IN THIS PART OF TOWN TONIGHT.
YOU DON'T HAVE ANY BUSINESS HERE, AND HERE YOU ARE LOAFING AROUND.

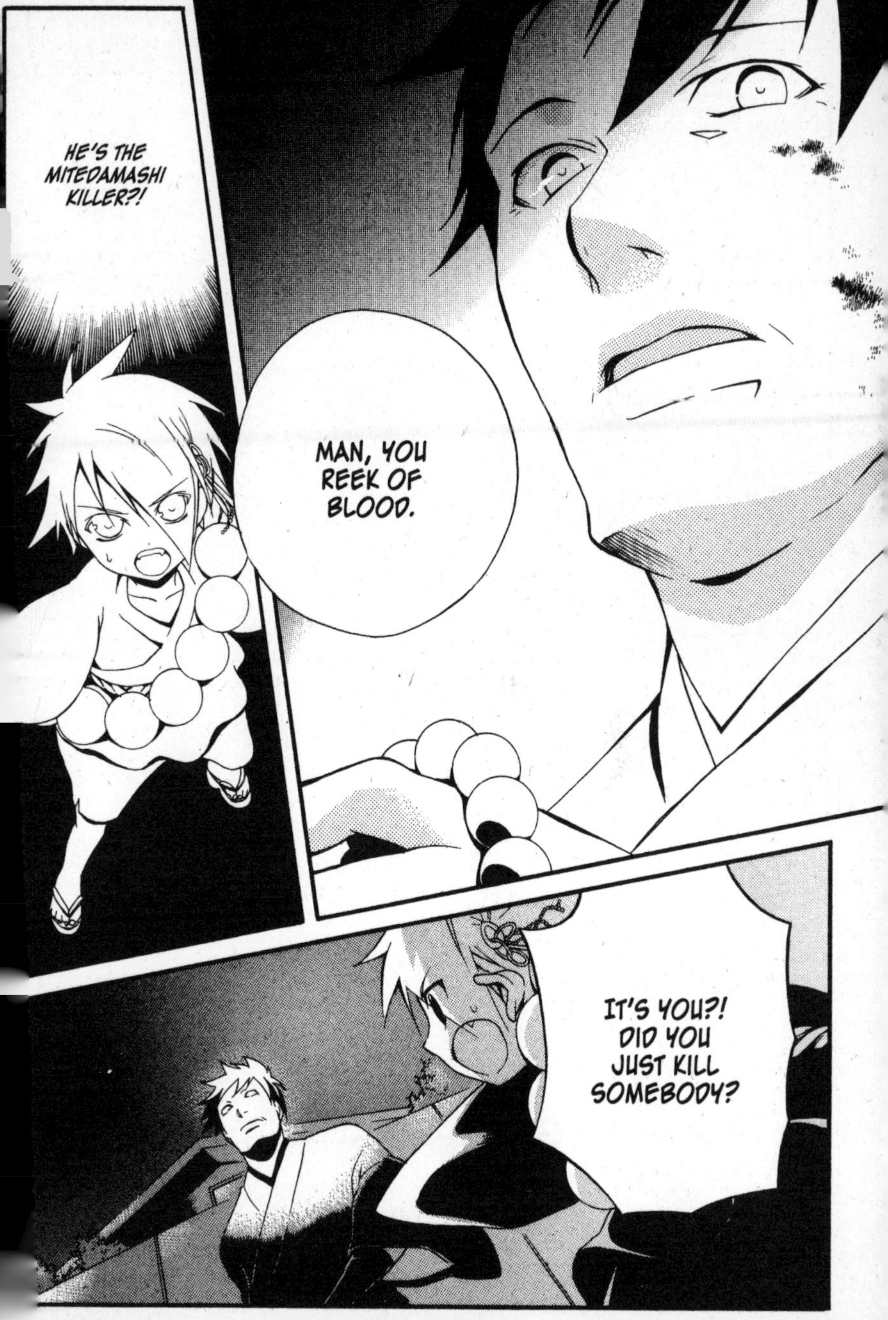
MAN, YOU REEK OF BLOOD.
HE'S THE MITEDAMASHI KILLER?!
IT'S YOU?! DID YOU JUST KILL SOMEBODY?

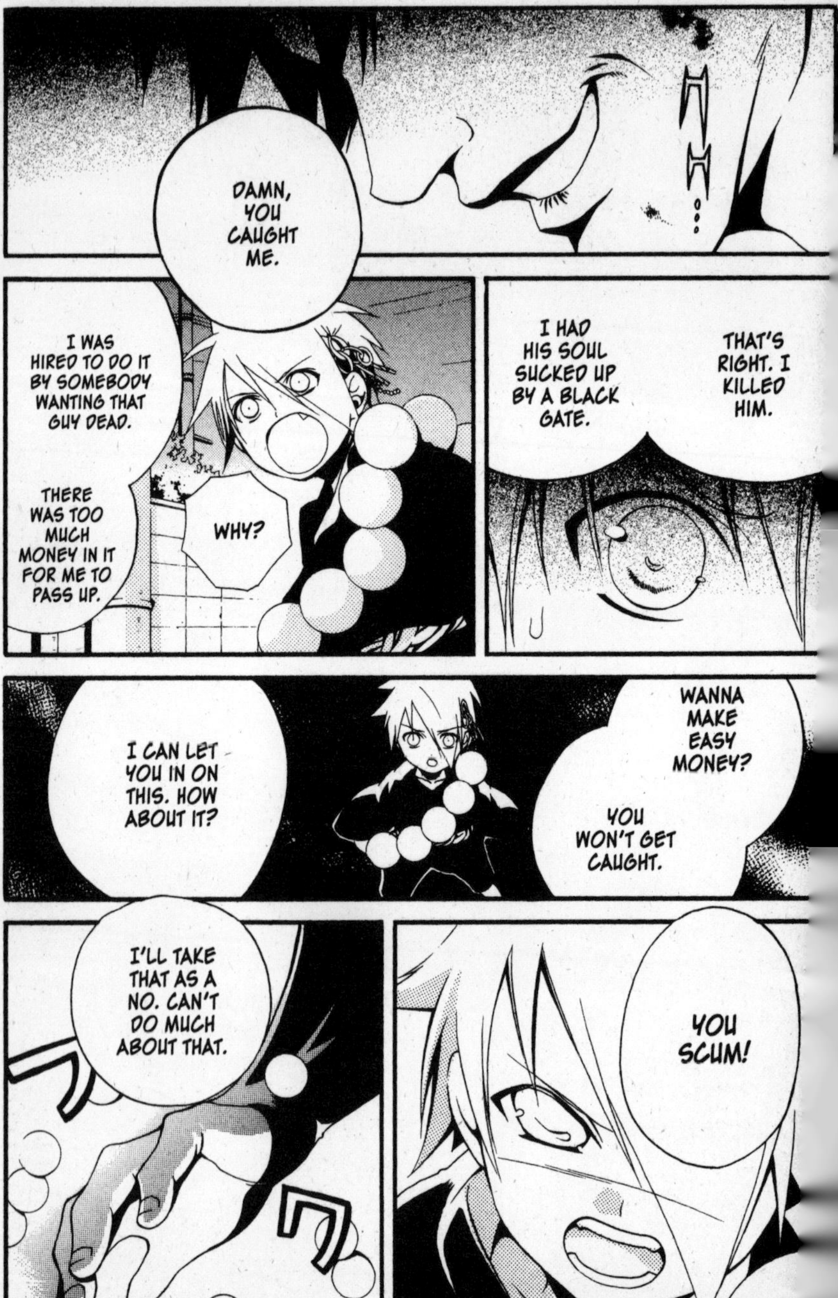
HH...
DAMN, YOU CAUGHT ME.
THAT'S RIGHT. I KILLED HIM.
I HAD HIS SOUL SUCKED UP BY A BLACK GATE.
WHY?
I WAS HIRED TO DO IT BY SOMEBODY WANTING THAT GUY DEAD.
THERE WAS TOO MUCH MONEY IN IT FOR ME TO PASS UP.
WANNA MAKE EASY MONEY?
YOU WON'T GET CAUGHT.
I CAN LET YOU IN ON THIS. HOW ABOUT IT?
YOU SCUM!
I'LL TAKE THAT AS A NO. CAN'T DO MUCH ABOUT THAT.

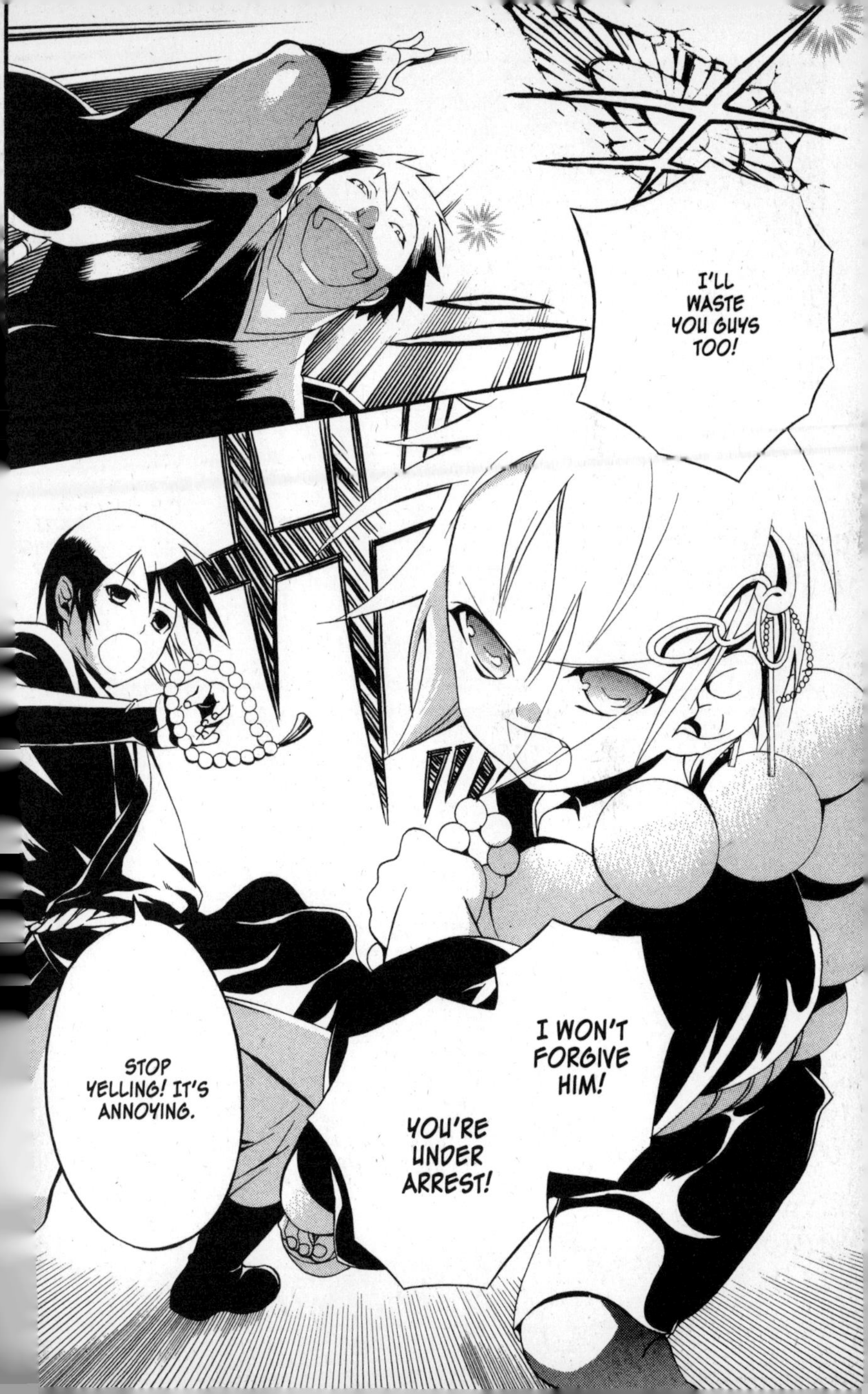
I'LL WASTE YOU GUYS TOO!
I WON'T FORGIVE HIM!
YOU'RE UNDER ARREST!
STOP YELLING! IT'S ANNOYING.

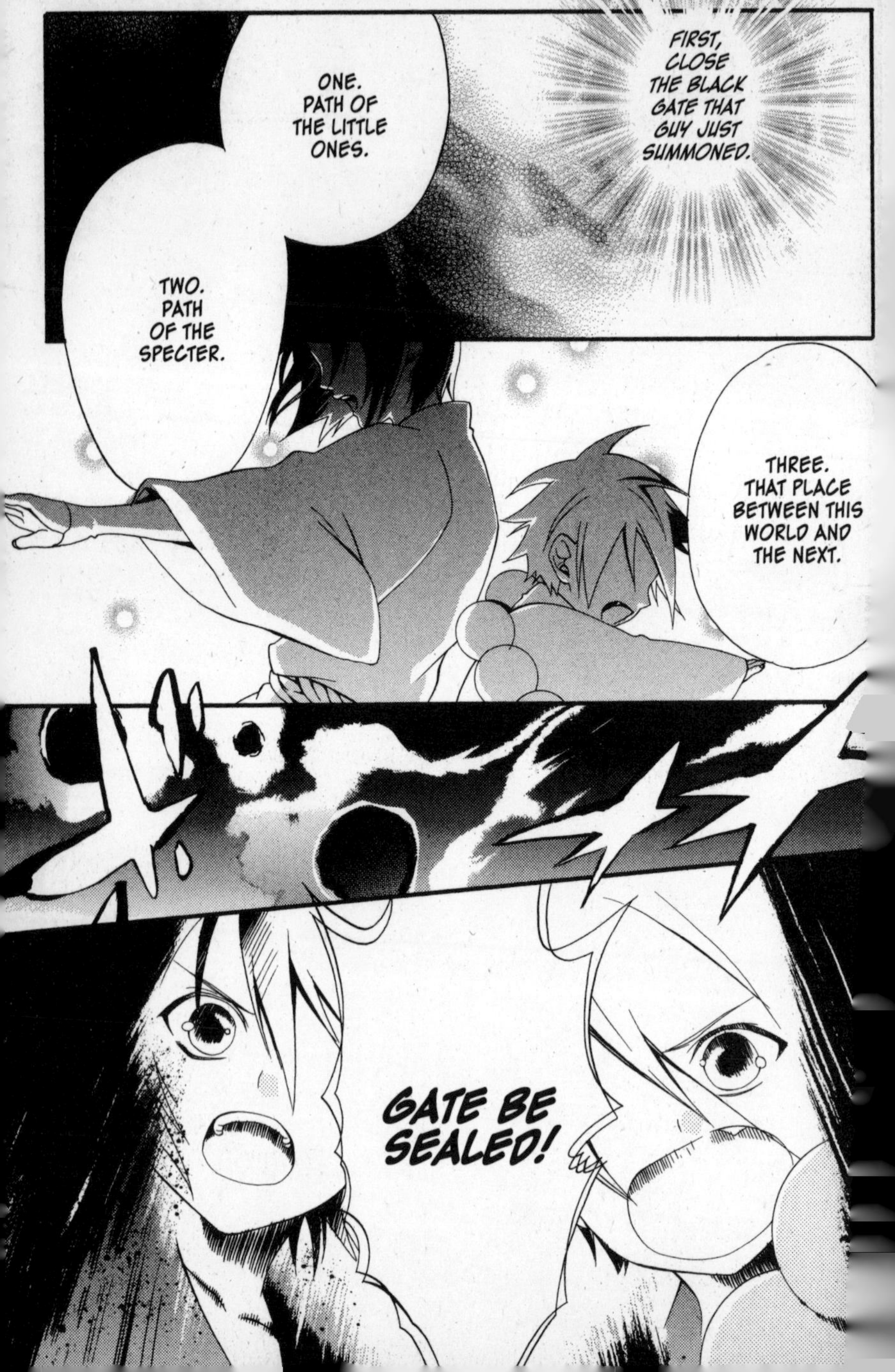
FIRST, CLOSE THE BLACK GATE THAT GUY JUST SUMMONED.
ONE. PATH OF THE LITTLE ONES.
THREE. THAT PLACE BETWEEN THIS WORLD AND THE NEXT.
TWO. PATH OF THE SPECTER.
GATE BE SEALED!

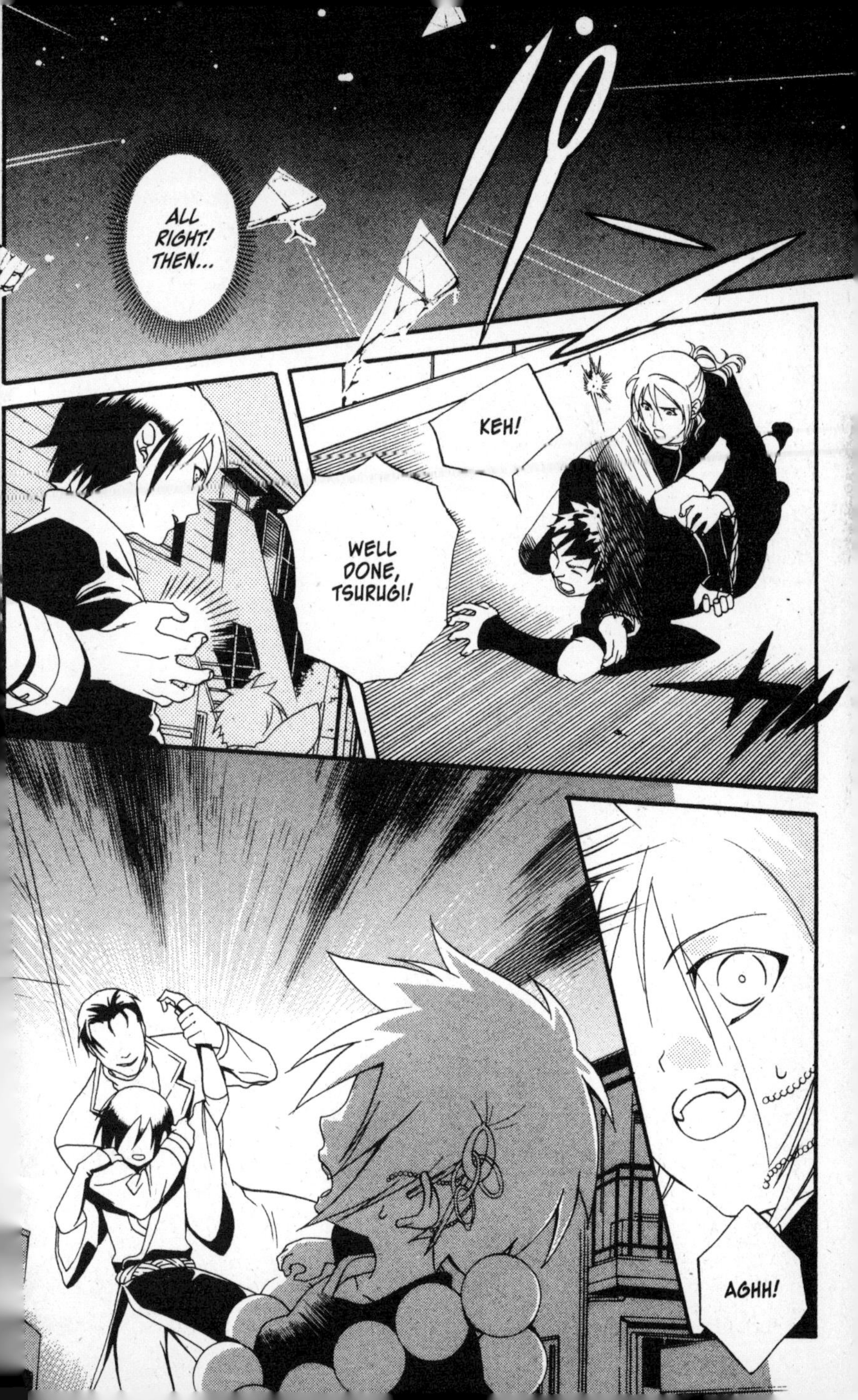
ALL RIGHT! THEN...
KEH!
WELL DONE, TSURUGI!
AGHH!

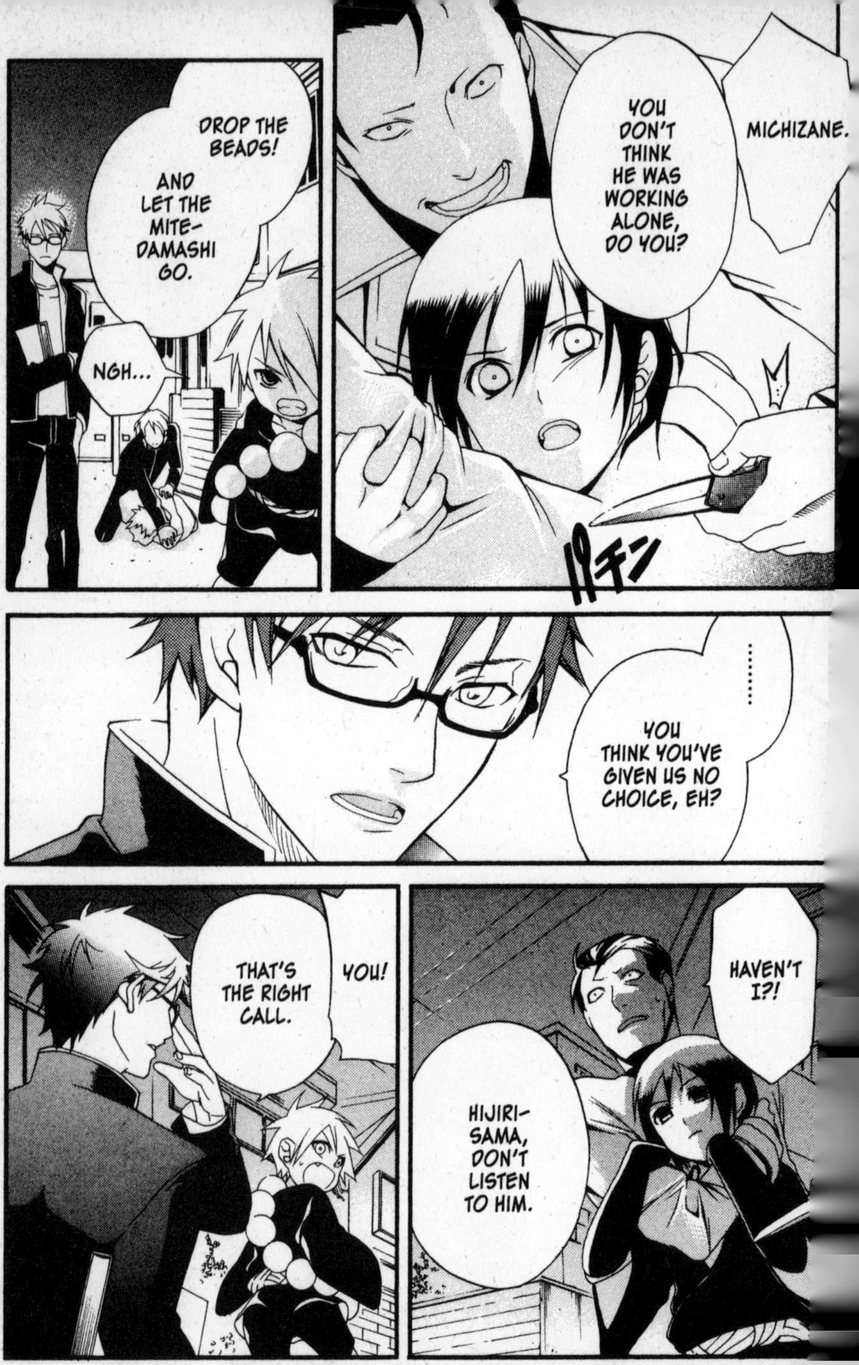
MICHIZANE.
YOU DON'T THINK HE WAS WORKING ALONE, DO YOU?
パチン
DROP THE BEADS!
AND LET THE MITE-DAMASHI GO.
NGH...
......
YOU THINK YOU'VE GIVEN US NO CHOICE, EH?
HAVEN'T I?!
HIJIRI-SAMA, DON'T LISTEN TO HIM.
YOU!
THAT'S THE RIGHT CALL.

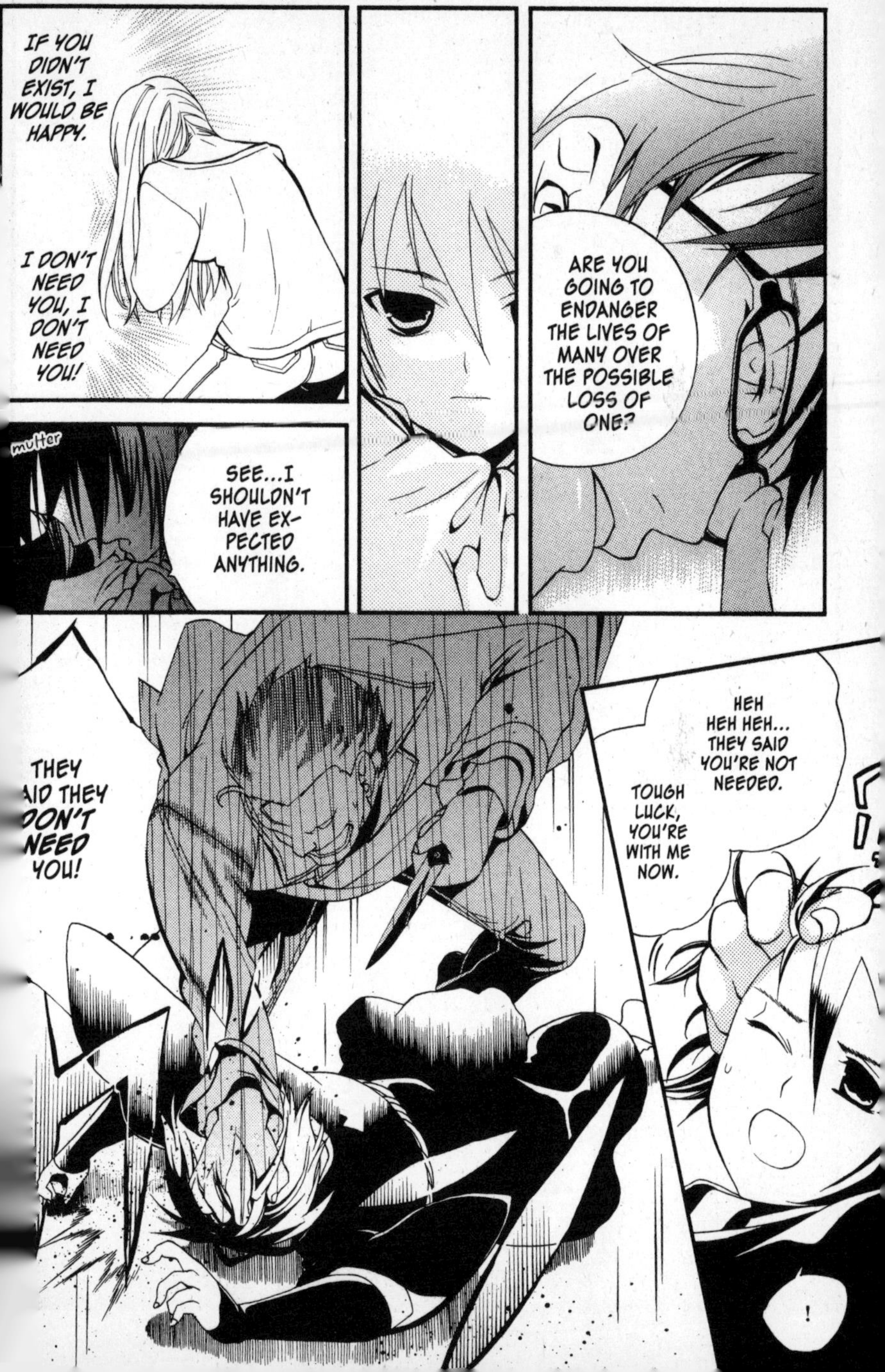
ARE YOU GOING TO ENDANGER THE LIVES OF MANY OVER THE POSSIBLE LOSS OF ONE?
IF YOU DIDN'T EXIST, I WOULD BE HAPPY.
I DON'T NEED YOU, I DON'T NEED YOU!
mutter
SEE...I SHOULDN'T HAVE EX-PECTED ANYTHING.
HEH HEH HEH... THEY SAID YOU'RE NOT NEEDED.
TOUGH LUCK, YOU'RE WITH ME NOW.
!
THEY SAID THEY DON'T NEED YOU!

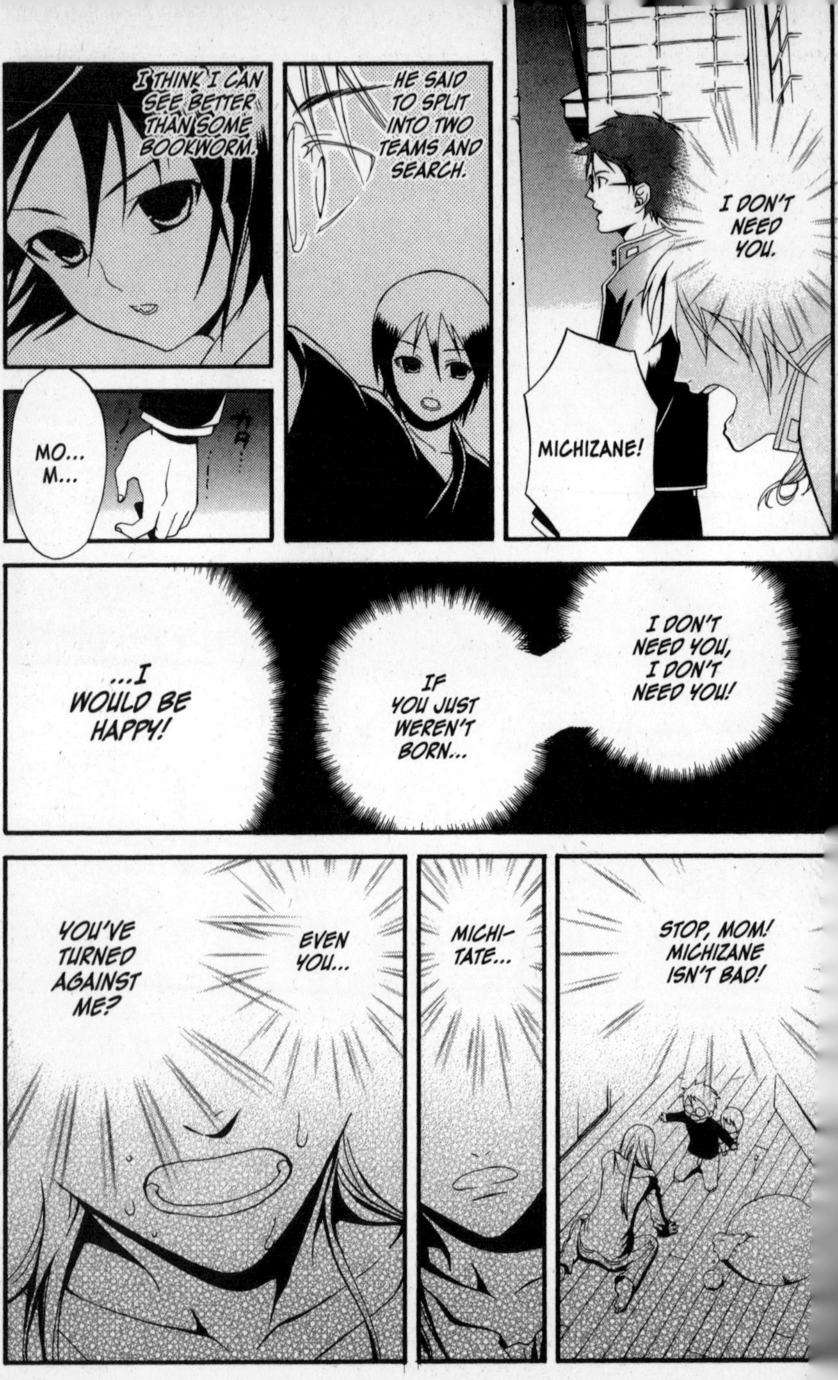
I DON'T NEED YOU.
MICHIZANE!
HE SAID TO SPLIT INTO TWO TEAMS AND SEARCH.
I THINK I CAN SEE BETTER THAN SOME BOOKWORM.
MO... M...
I DON'T NEED YOU, I DON'T NEED YOU!
IF YOU JUST WEREN'T BORN...
...I WOULD BE HAPPY!
STOP, MOM! MICHIZANE ISN'T BAD!
MICHI-TATE...
EVEN YOU...
YOU'VE TURNED AGAINST ME?

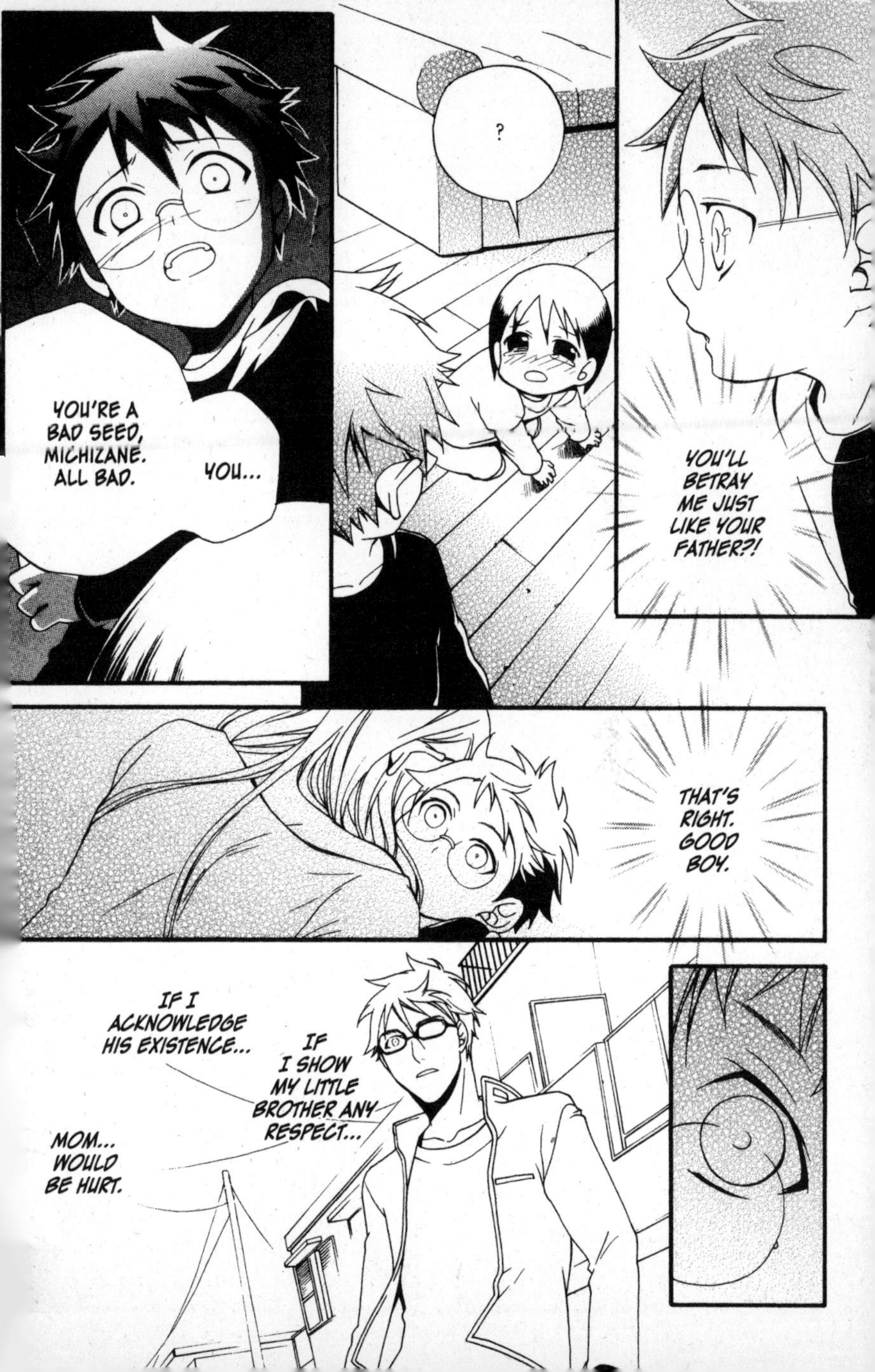
YOU'LL BETRAY ME JUST LIKE YOUR FATHER?!
?
YOU...
YOU'RE A BAD SEED, MICHIZANE. ALL BAD.
THAT'S RIGHT. GOOD BOY.
IF I ACKNOWLEDGE HIS EXISTENCE...
IF I SHOW MY LITTLE BROTHER ANY RESPECT...
MOM... WOULD BE HURT.

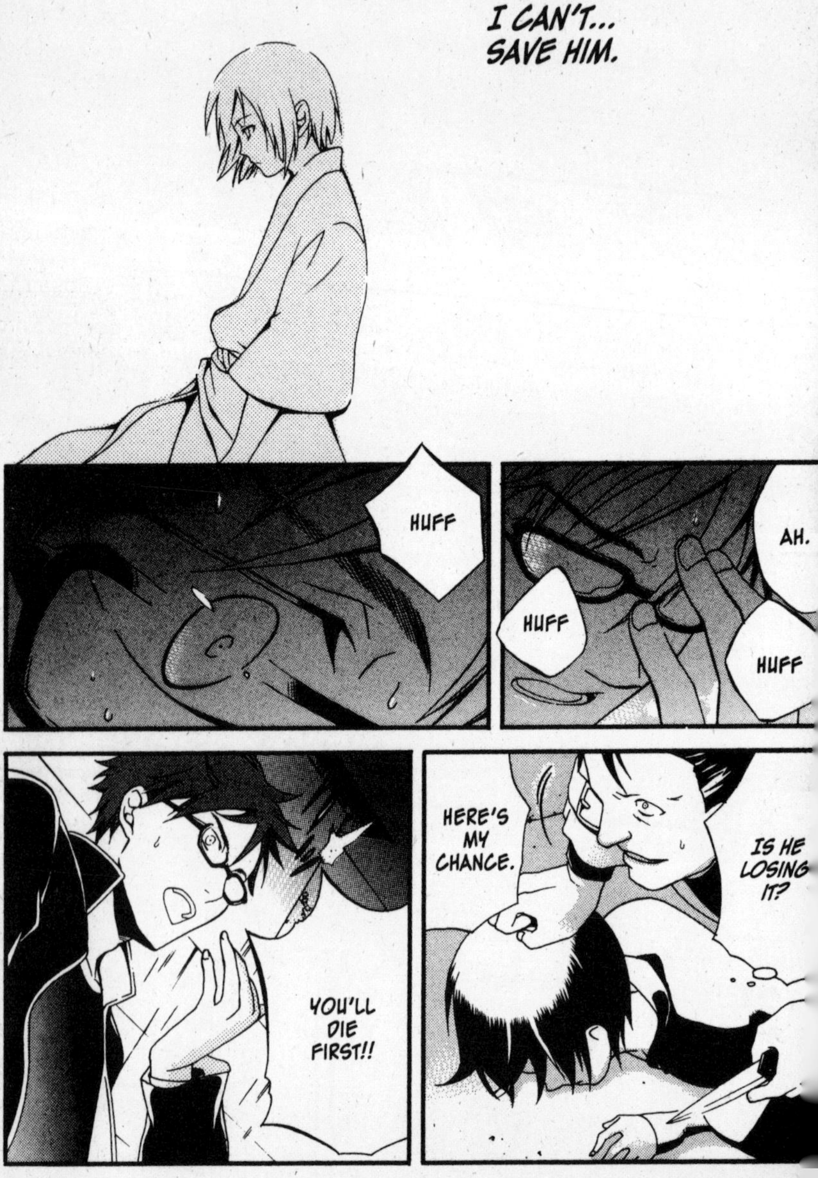
I CAN'T... SAVE HIM.
AH.
HUFF
HUFF
HUFF
IS HE LOSING IT?
HERE'S MY CHANCE.
YOU'LL DIE FIRST!!

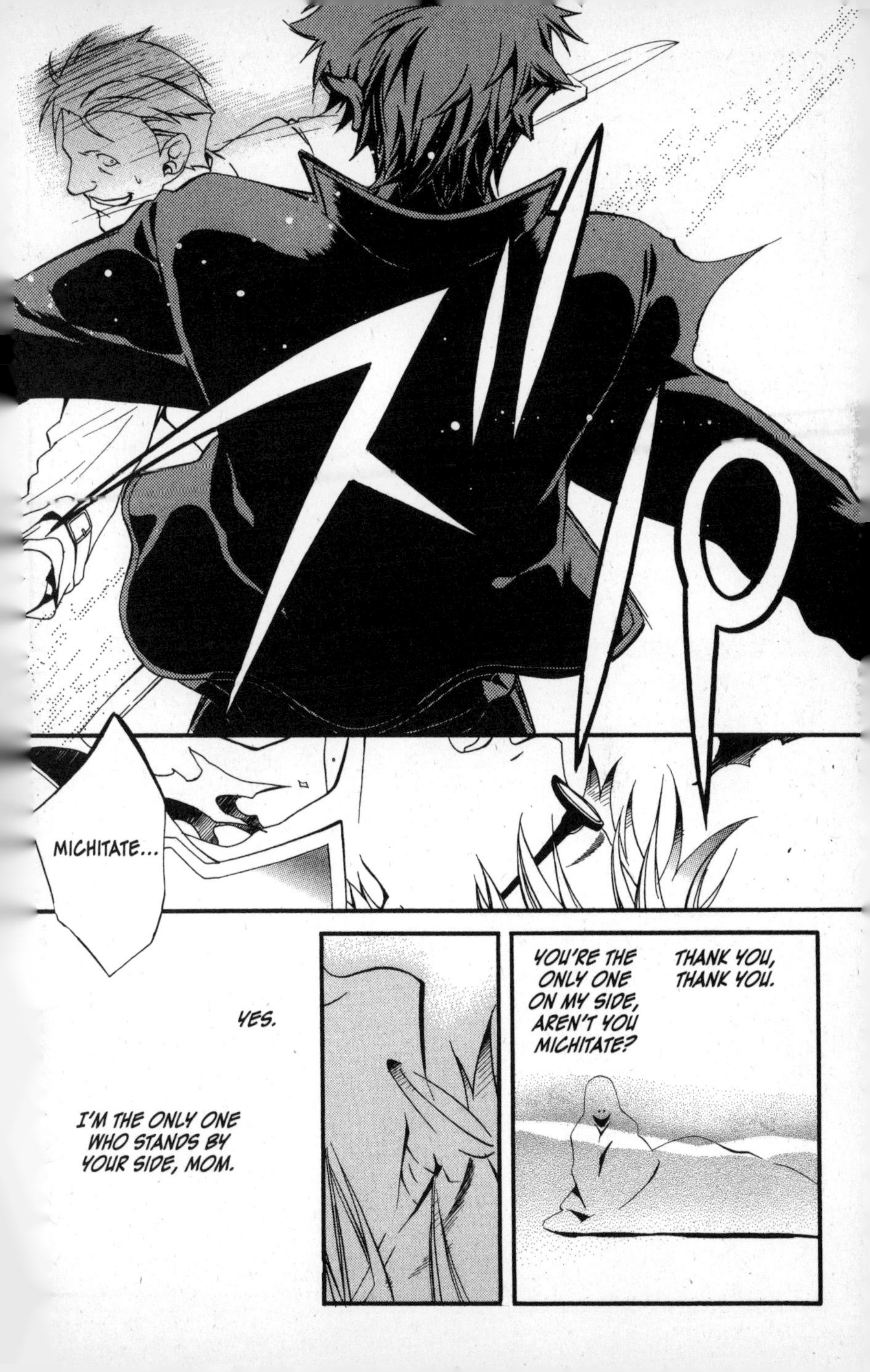
ZAP
MICHITATE...
THANK YOU, THANK YOU.
YOU'RE THE ONLY ONE ON MY SIDE, AREN'T YOU MICHITATE?
YES.
I'M THE ONLY ONE WHO STANDS BY YOUR SIDE, MOM.

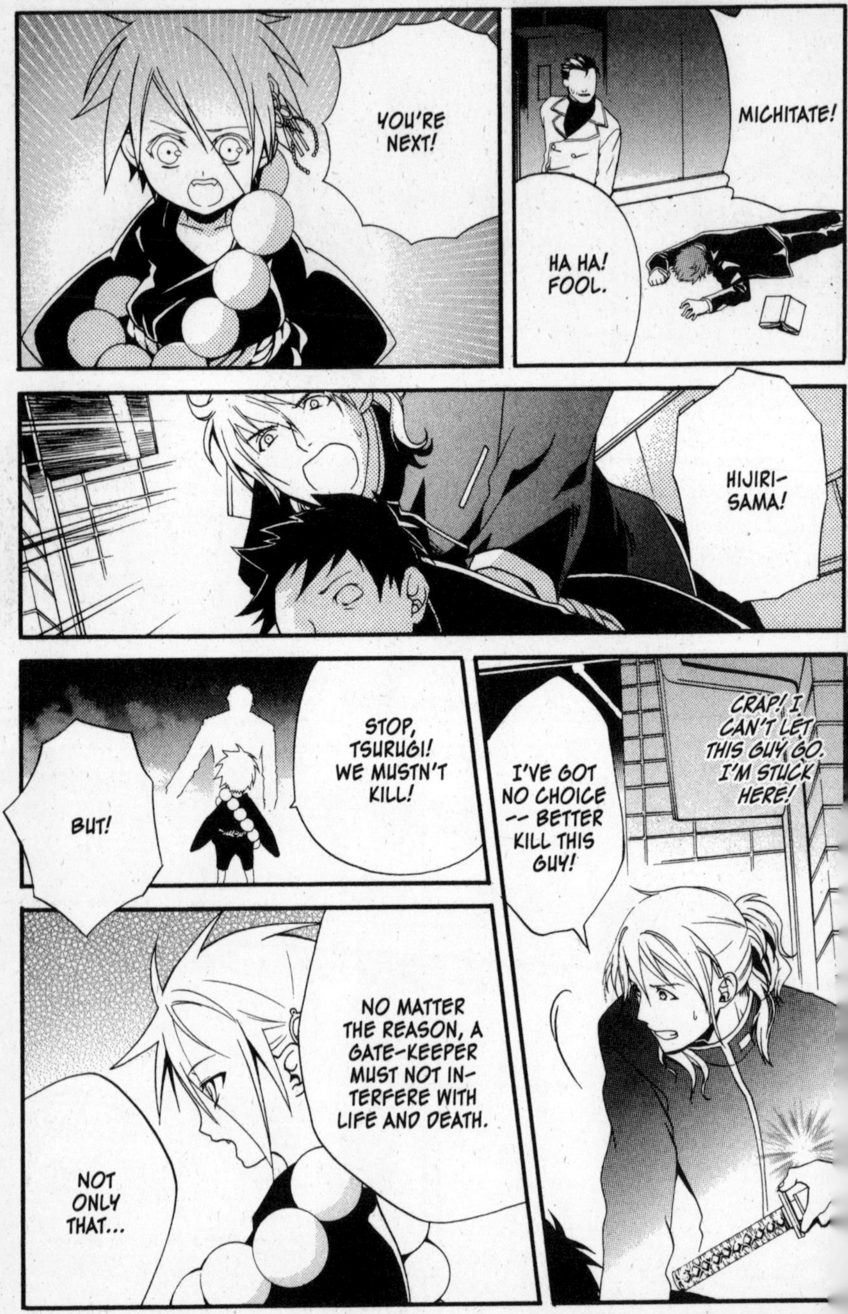
MICHITATE!
HA HA! FOOL.
YOU'RE NEXT!
HIJIRI-SAMA!
CRAP! I CAN'T LET THIS GUY GO. I'M STUCK HERE!
I'VE GOT NO CHOICE -- BETTER KILL THIS GUY!
STOP, TSURUGI! WE MUSTN'T KILL!
BUT!
NO MATTER THE REASON, A GATE-KEEPER MUST NOT INTERFERE WITH LIFE AND DEATH.
NOT ONLY THAT...

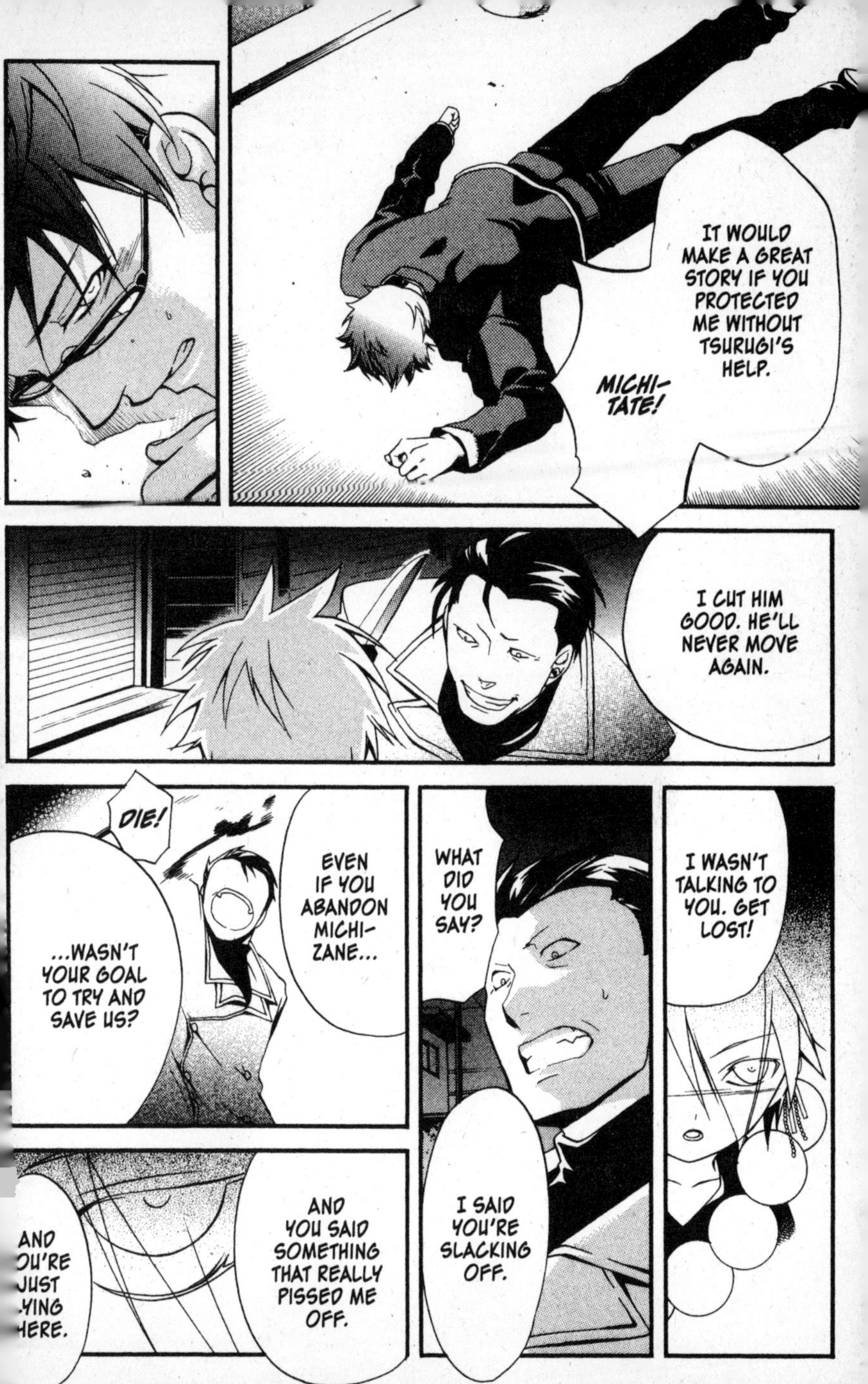
IT WOULD MAKE A GREAT STORY IF YOU PROTECTED ME WITHOUT TSURUGI'S HELP.
MICHI-TATE!
I CUT HIM GOOD. HE'LL NEVER MOVE AGAIN.
I WASN'T TALKING TO YOU. GET LOST!
WHAT DID YOU SAY?
I SAID YOU'RE SLACKING OFF.
EVEN IF YOU ABANDON MICHI-ZANE...
DIE!
...WASN'T YOUR GOAL TO TRY AND SAVE US?
AND YOU SAID SOMETHING THAT REALLY PISSED ME OFF.
AND OU'RE JUST YING HERE.

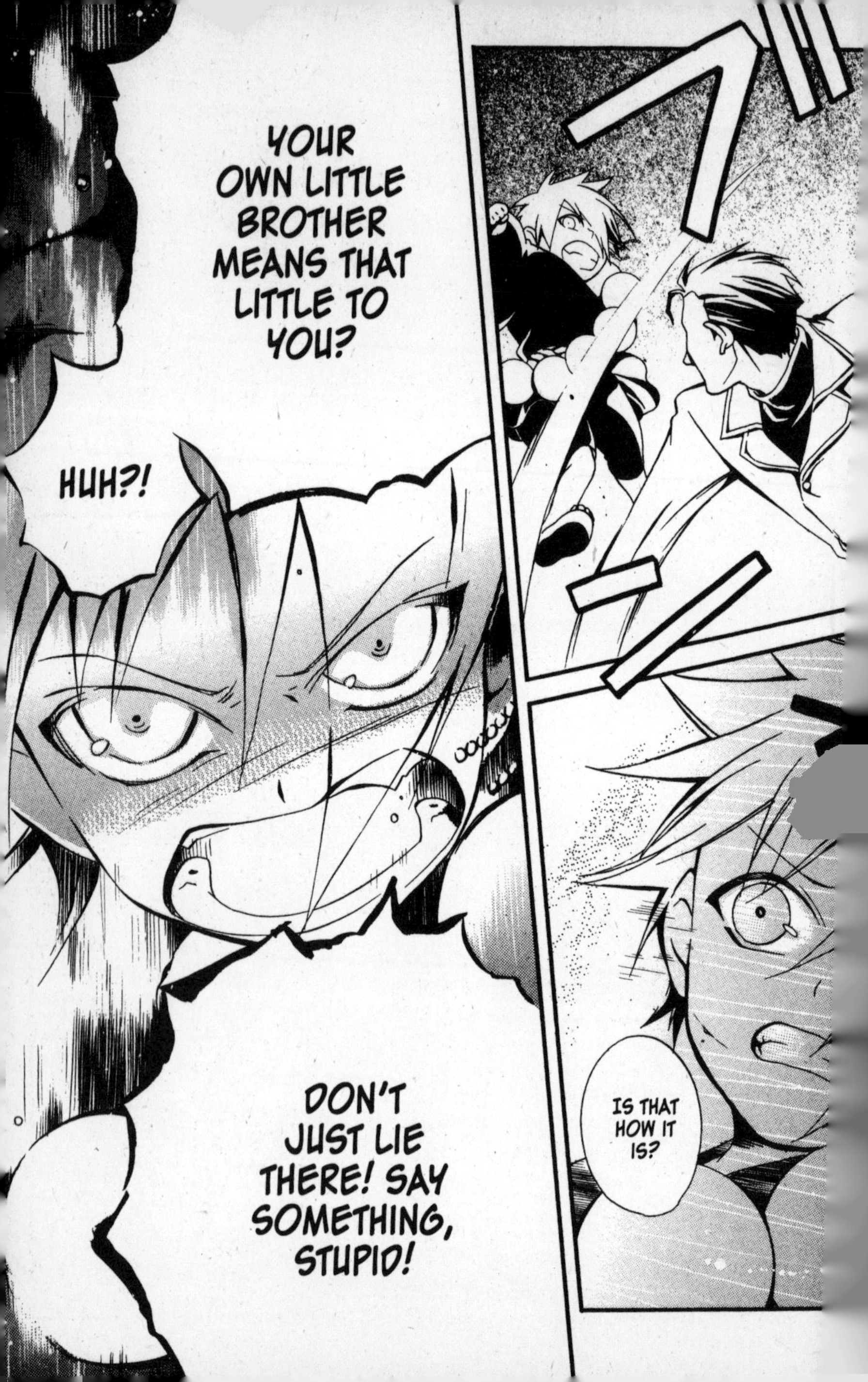
IS THAT HOW IT IS?
YOUR OWN LITTLE BROTHER MEANS THAT LITTLE TO YOU?
HUH?!
DON'T JUST LIE THERE! SAY SOMETHING, STUPID!

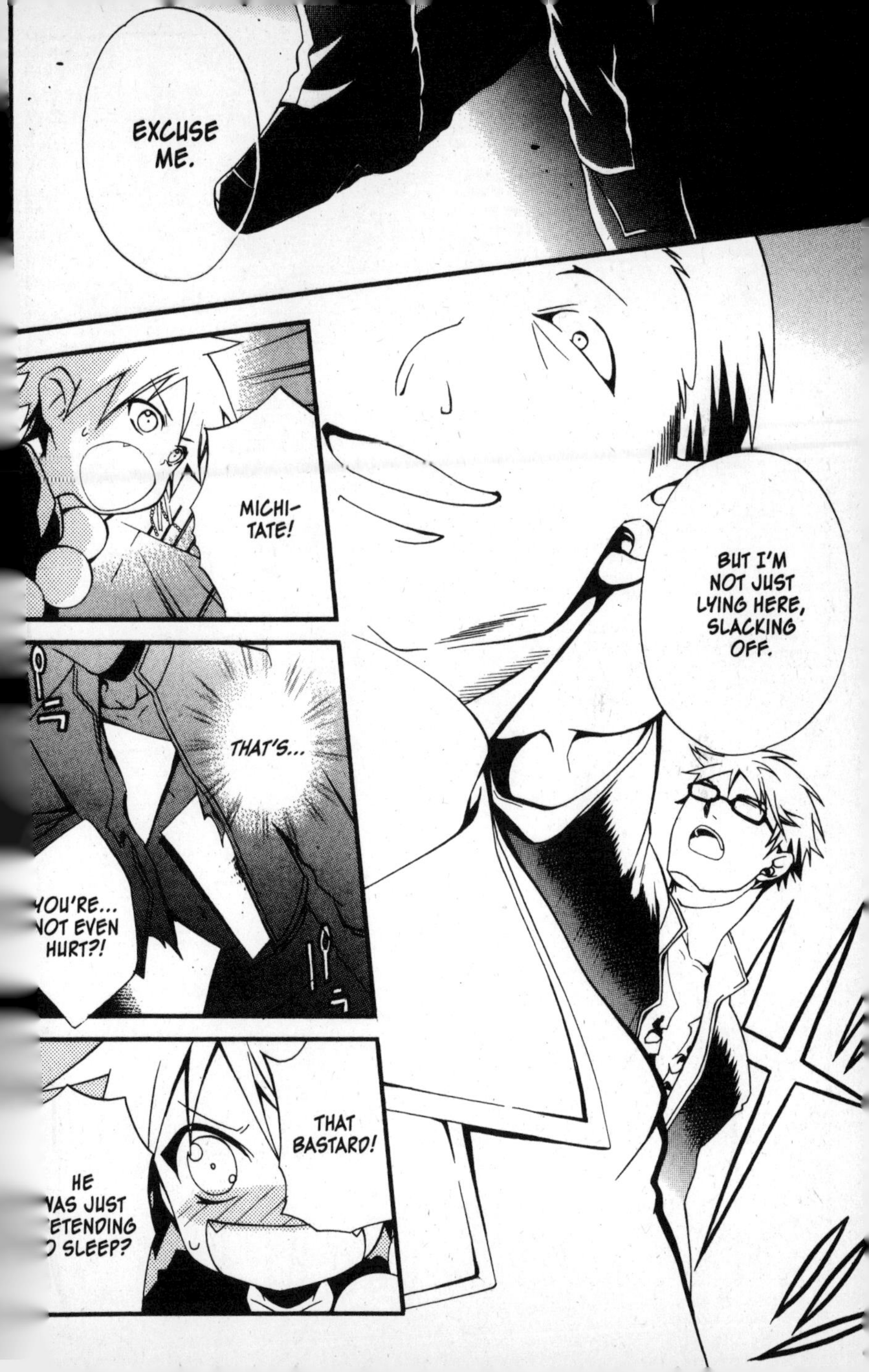
EXCUSE ME.
BUT I'M NOT JUST LYING HERE, SLACKING OFF.
MICHI-TATE!
THAT'S...
YOU'RE... NOT EVEN HURT?!
THAT BASTARD!
HE WAS JUST ETENDING O SLEEP?

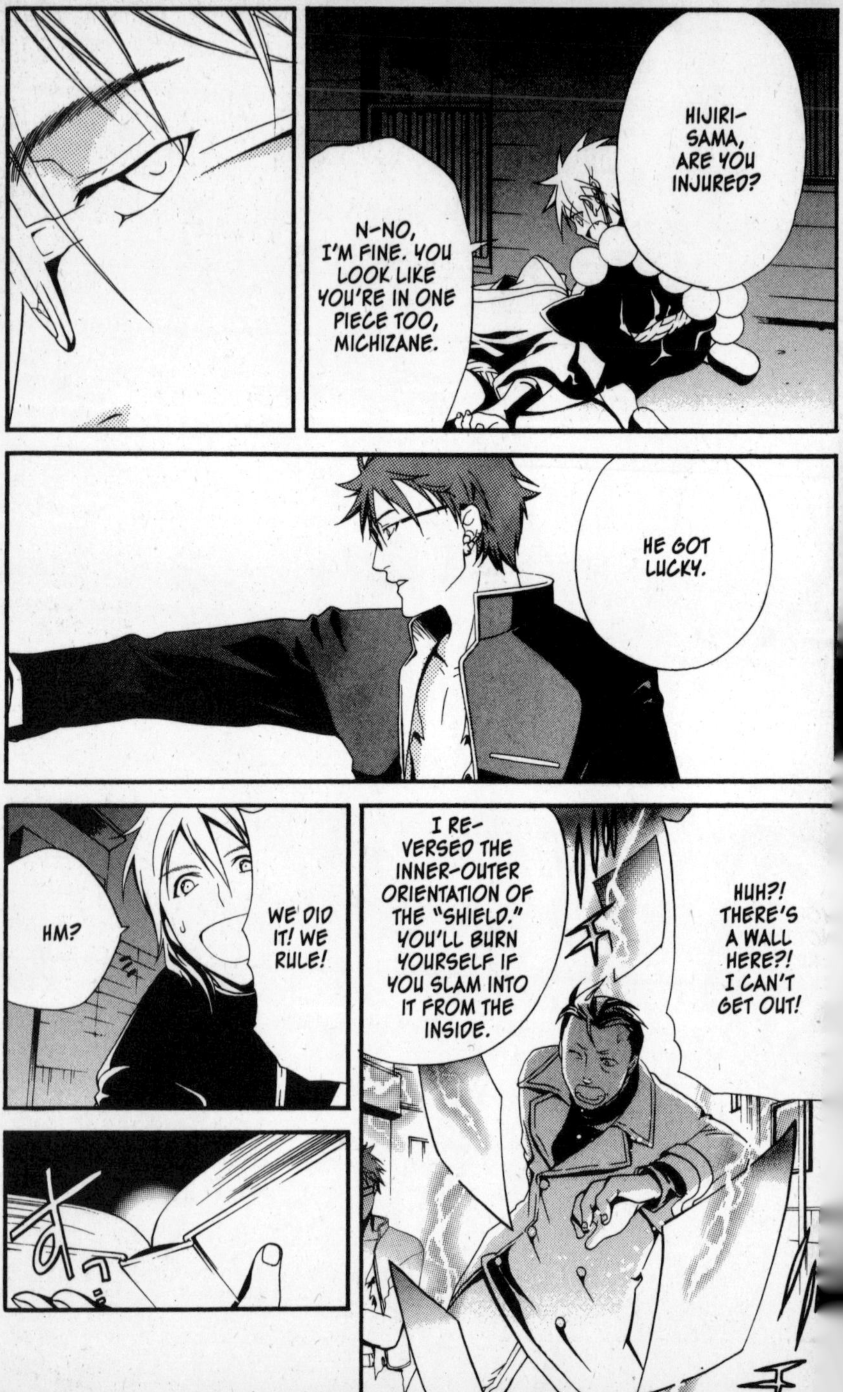
HIJIRI-SAMA, ARE YOU INJURED?
N-NO, I'M FINE. YOU LOOK LIKE YOU'RE IN ONE PIECE TOO, MICHIZANE.
HE GOT LUCKY.
HUH?! THERE'S A WALL HERE?! I CAN'T GET OUT!
I RE-VERSED THE INNER-OUTER ORIENTATION OF THE "SHIELD." YOU'LL BURN YOURSELF IF YOU SLAM INTO IT FROM THE INSIDE.
WE DID IT! WE RULE!
HM?

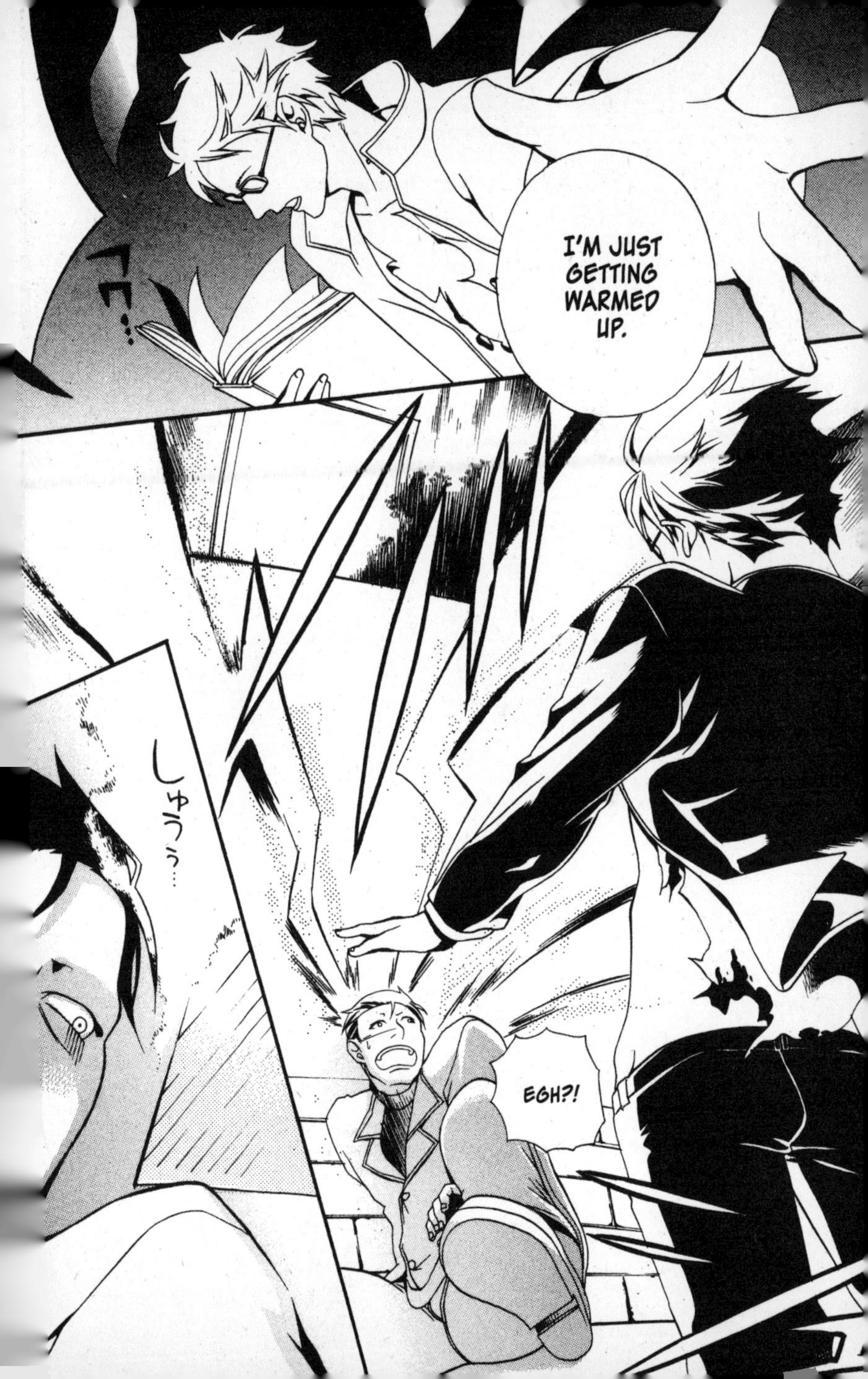
I'M JUST GETTING WARMED UP.
EGH?!
しゅうぅ…

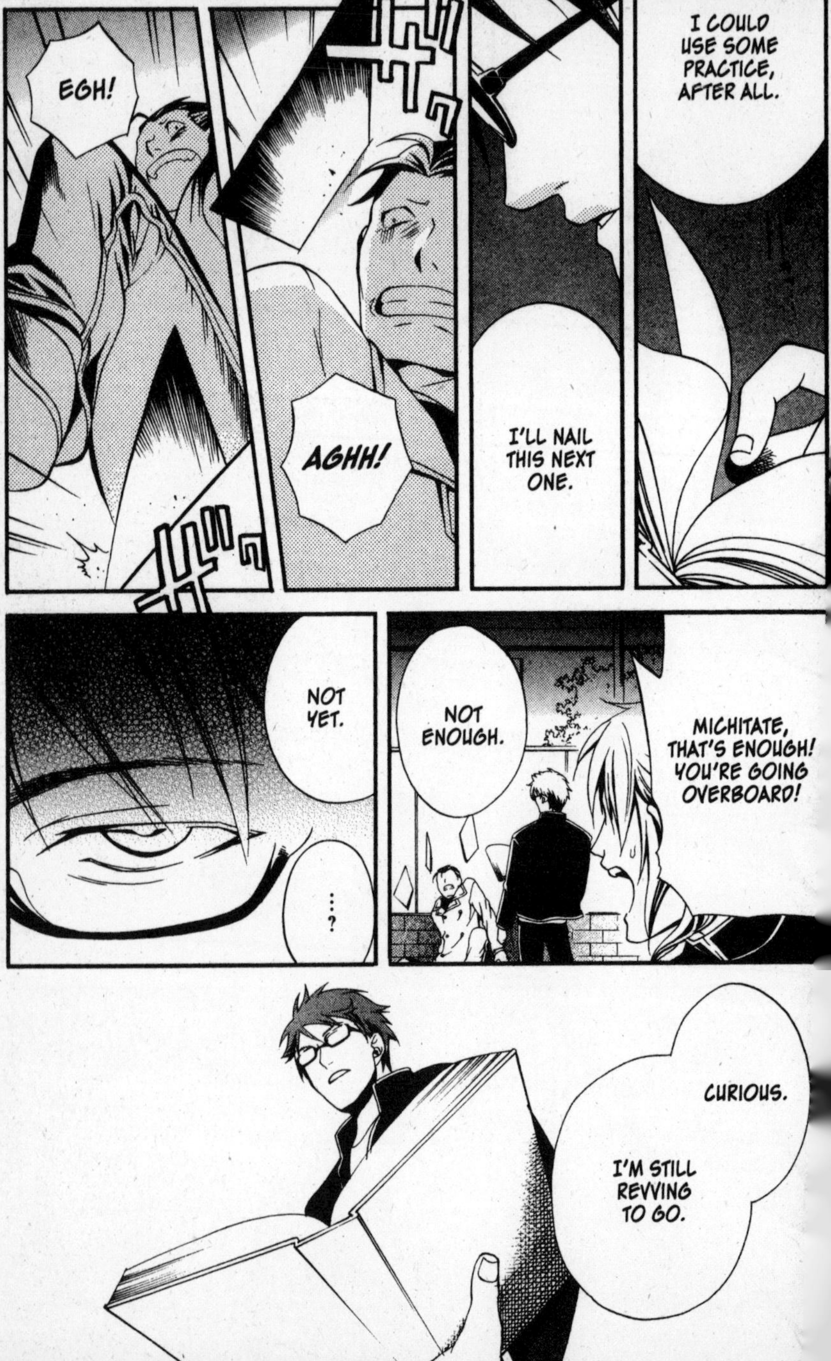
I COULD USE SOME PRACTICE, AFTER ALL.
I'LL NAIL THIS NEXT ONE.
AGHH!
EGH!
MICHITATE, THAT'S ENOUGH! YOU'RE GOING OVERBOARD!
NOT ENOUGH.
NOT YET.
...?
CURIOUS.
I'M STILL REVVING TO GO.

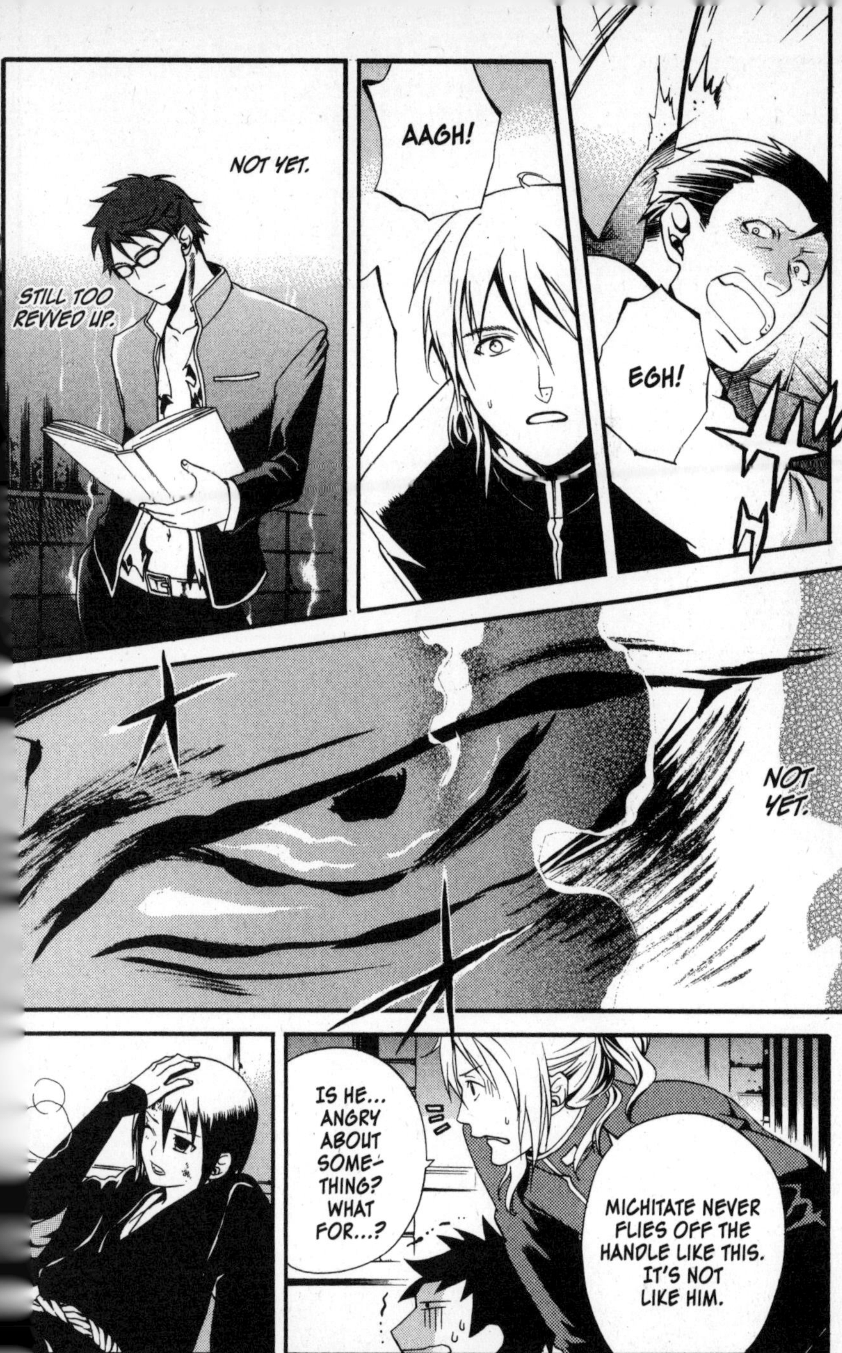
EGH!
AAGH!
NOT YET.
STILL TOO REVVED UP.
NOT YET.
IS HE... ANGRY ABOUT SOME-THING? WHAT FOR...?
MICHITATE NEVER FLIES OFF THE HANDLE LIKE THIS. IT'S NOT LIKE HIM.

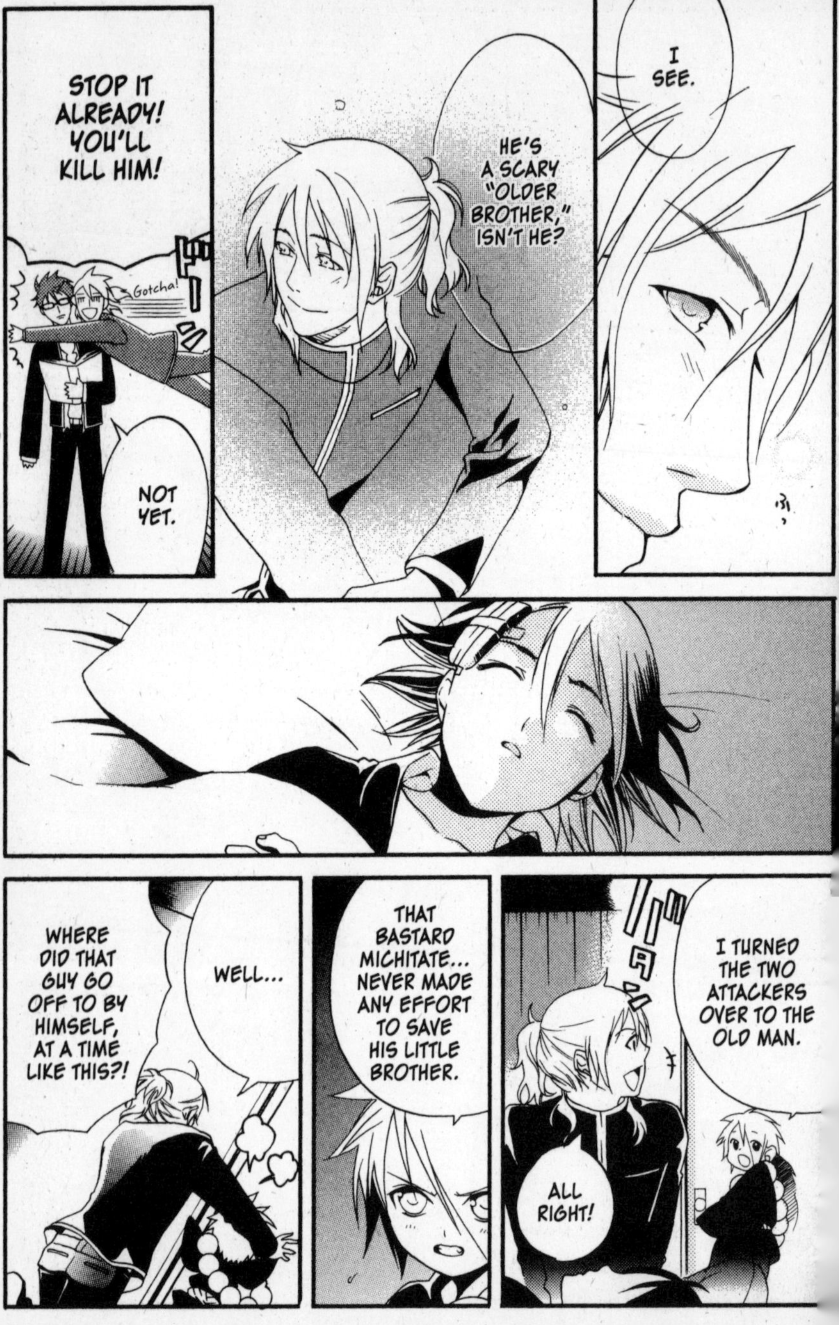
I SEE.
HE'S A SCARY "OLDER BROTHER," ISN'T HE?
STOP IT ALREADY! YOU'LL KILL HIM!
Gotcha!
NOT YET.
I TURNED THE TWO ATTACKERS OVER TO THE OLD MAN.
ALL RIGHT!
THAT BASTARD MICHITATE... NEVER MADE ANY EFFORT TO SAVE HIS LITTLE BROTHER.
WELL...
WHERE DID THAT GUY GO OFF TO BY HIMSELF, AT A TIME LIKE THIS?!

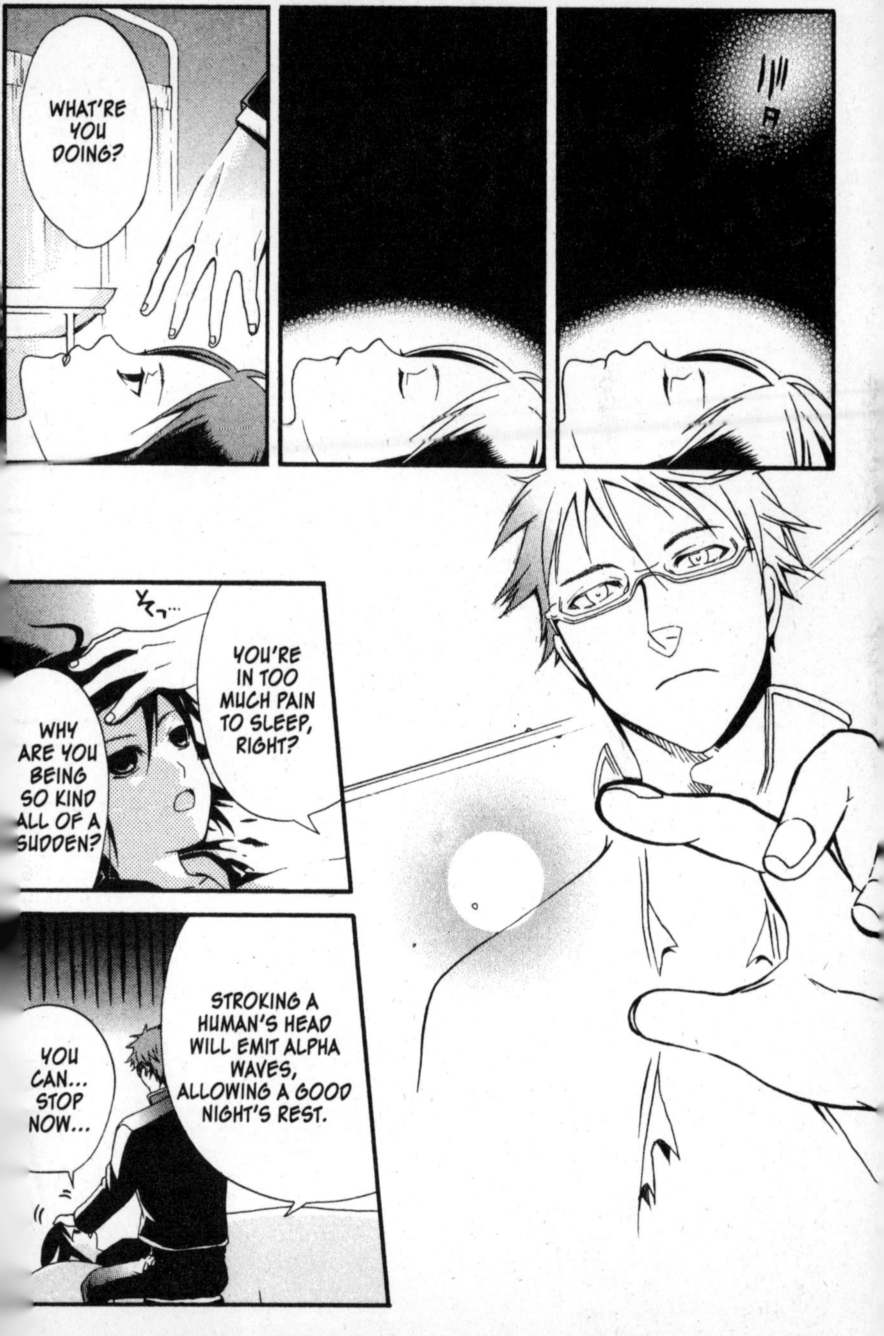
WHAT'RE YOU DOING?
YOU'RE IN TOO MUCH PAIN TO SLEEP, RIGHT?
WHY ARE YOU BEING SO KIND ALL OF A SUDDEN?
STROKING A HUMAN'S HEAD WILL EMIT ALPHA WAVES, ALLOWING A GOOD NIGHT'S REST.
YOU CAN... STOP NOW...

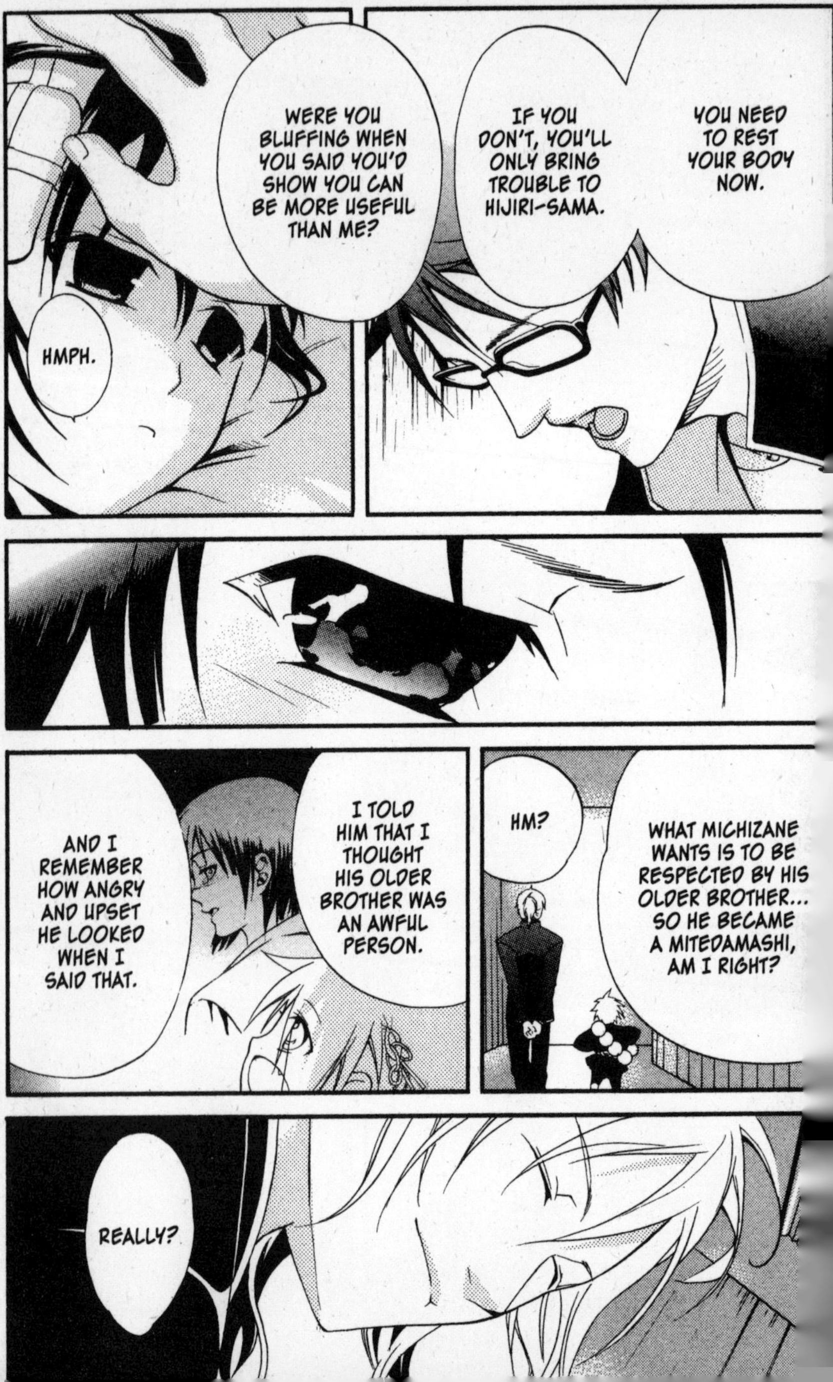
YOU NEED TO REST YOUR BODY NOW.
IF YOU DON'T, YOU'LL ONLY BRING TROUBLE TO HIJIRI-SAMA.
WERE YOU BLUFFING WHEN YOU SAID YOU'D SHOW YOU CAN BE MORE USEFUL THAN ME?
HMPH.
WHAT MICHIZANE WANTS IS TO BE RESPECTED BY HIS OLDER BROTHER... SO HE BECAME A MITEDAMASHI, AM I RIGHT?
HM?
I TOLD HIM THAT I THOUGHT HIS OLDER BROTHER WAS AN AWFUL PERSON.
AND I REMEMBER HOW ANGRY AND UPSET HE LOOKED WHEN I SAID THAT.
REALLY?

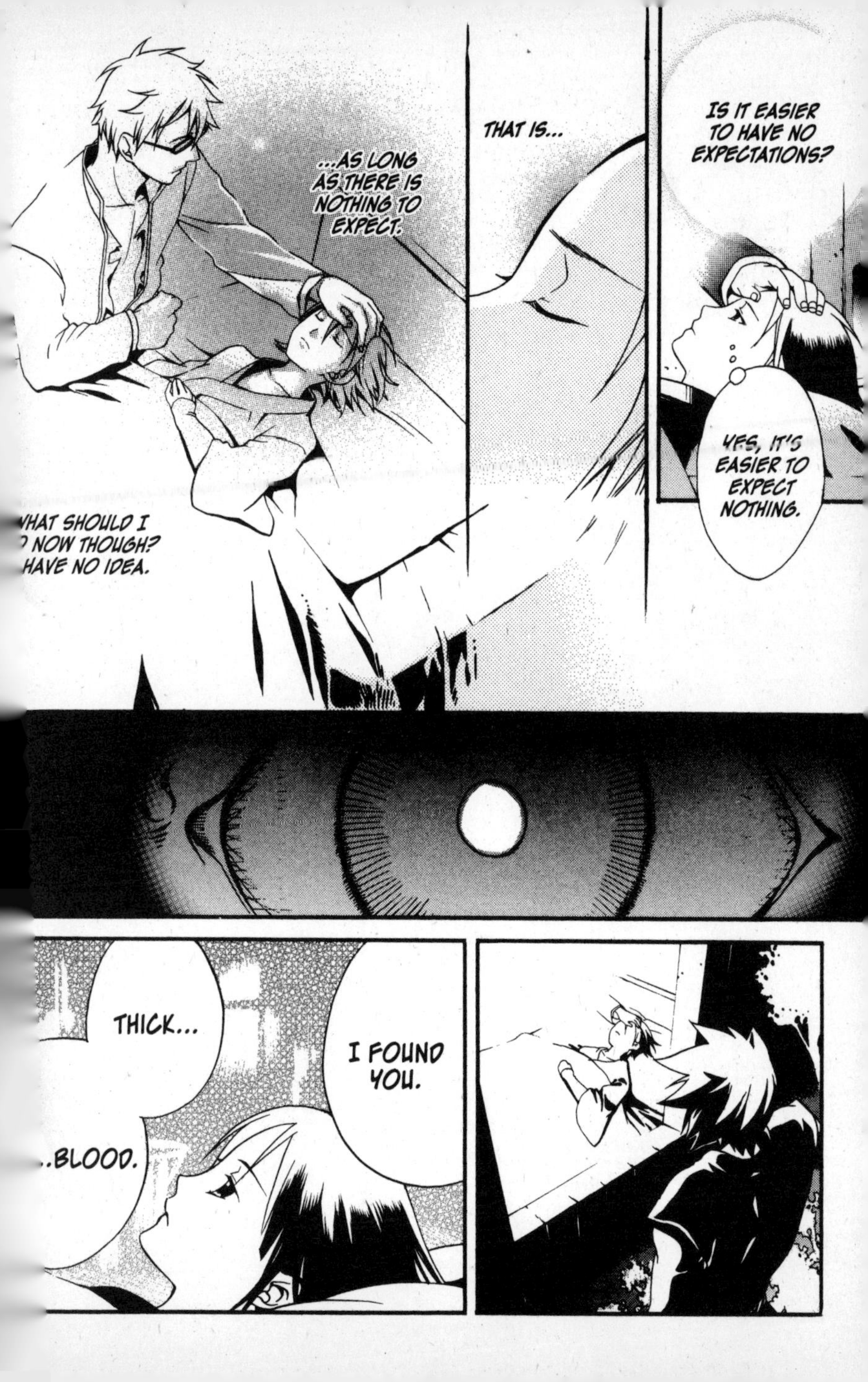
IS IT EASIER TO HAVE NO EXPECTATIONS?
YES, IT'S EASIER TO EXPECT NOTHING.
THAT IS...
...AS LONG AS THERE IS NOTHING TO EXPECT.
WHAT SHOULD I
NOW THOUGH?
HAVE NO IDEA.
I FOUND YOU.
THICK...
..BLOOD.

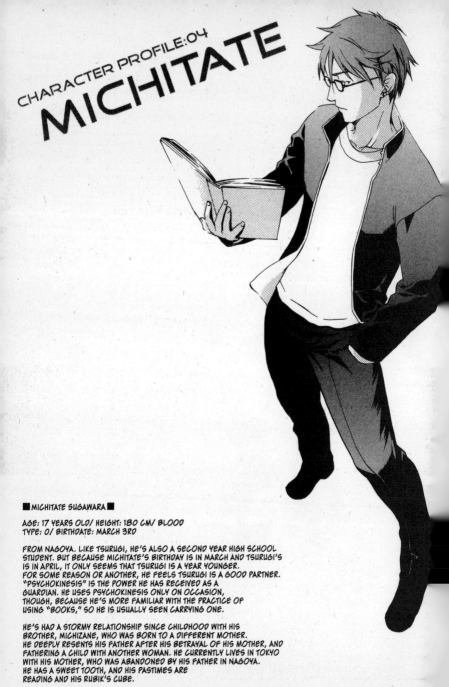

CHARACTER PROFILE:04 MICHITATE

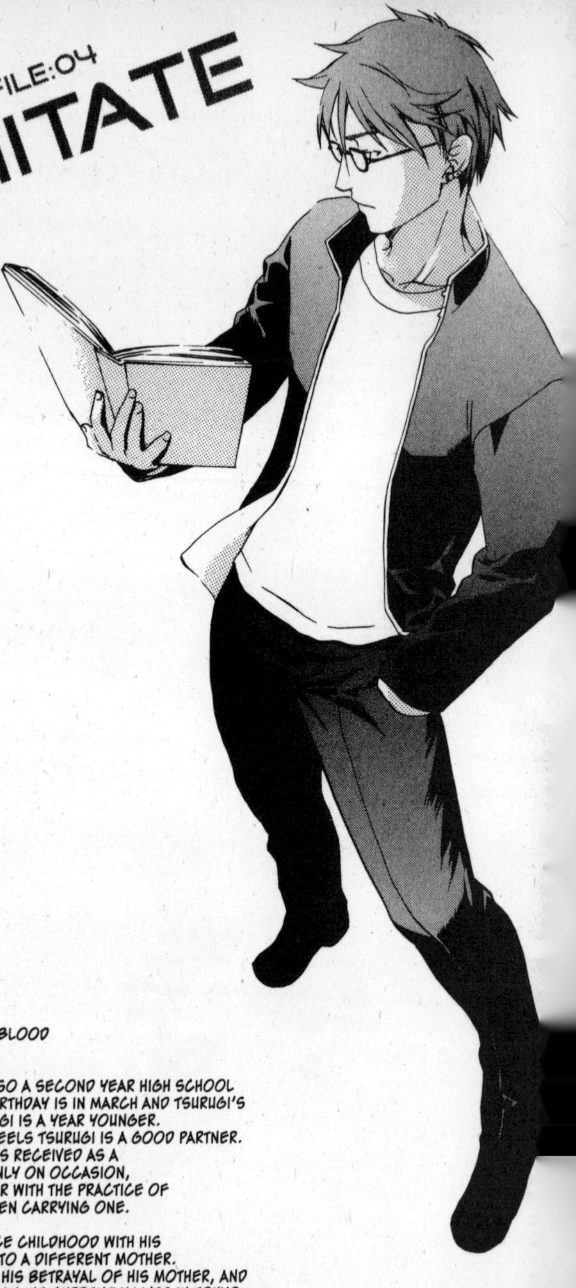

■MICHITATE SUGAWARA■

AGE: 17 YEARS OLD/ HEIGHT: 180 CM/ BLOOD TYPE: O/ BIRTHDATE: MARCH 3RD

FROM NAGOYA. LIKE TSURUGI, HE'S ALSO A SECOND YEAR HIGH SCHOOL STUDENT. BUT BECAUSE MICHITATE'S BIRTHDAY IS IN MARCH AND TSURUGI'S IS IN APRIL, IT ONLY SEEMS THAT TSURUGI IS A YEAR YOUNGER. FOR SOME REASON OR ANOTHER, HE FEELS TSURUGI IS A GOOD PARTNER. "PSYCHOKINESIS" IS THE POWER HE HAS RECEIVED AS A GUARDIAN. HE USES PSYCHOKINESIS ONLY ON OCCASION, THOUGH, BECAUSE HE'S MORE FAMILIAR WITH THE PRACTICE OF USING "BOOKS," SO HE IS USUALLY SEEN CARRYING ONE.

HE'S HAD A STORMY RELATIONSHIP SINCE CHILDHOOD WITH HIS BROTHER, MICHIZANE, WHO WAS BORN TO A DIFFERENT MOTHER. HE DEEPLY RESENTS HIS FATHER AFTER HIS BETRAYAL OF HIS MOTHER, AND FATHERING A CHILD WITH ANOTHER WOMAN. HE CURRENTLY LIVES IN TOKYO WITH HIS MOTHER, WHO WAS ABANDONED BY HIS FATHER IN NAGOYA. HE HAS A SWEET TOOTH, AND HIS PASTIMES ARE READING AND HIS RUBIK'S CUBE.

■ MICHIZANE SUGAWARA ■

AGE: 15 YEARS OLD/ HEIGHT: 161 CM/ BLOOD
TYPE: AB/ BIRTHDATE: FEBRUARY 24TH

MICHITATE'S LITTLE BROTHER, BORN FROM ANOTHER MOTHER.
HE'S A 3RD YEAR JUNIOR HIGH SCHOOL STUDENT, ALSO FROM
NAGOYA. DUE TO FREQUENT FAMILY PROBLEMS, HE OFTEN
MOVED FROM PLACE TO PLACE WITH HIS SINGLE PARENT AS A
CHILD. HE CURRENTLY LIVES WITH HIS GRANDMOTHER IN TOKYO.
SINCE CHILDHOOD, HE'S HAD A QUIET NATURE, AND OFTEN KEEPS
HIS FEELINGS TO HIMSELF. WHEN HE WARMS TO A PERSON, HE
BECOMES MORE TALKATIVE, COMPLAINING AND CRITICIZING FREELY.
INDEED, HIS TONGUE IS SHARPEST TOWARDS THOSE HE FEELS
CLOSEST TO AND MOST COMFORTABLE WITH. HIS HOBBY IS VIDEO
GAMES. HE HATES LOSING, AND EVEN LOSING AT A VIDEO GAME
WILL CAUSE HIM TO GET DRAMATICALLY UPSET. AT A BIT OVER 15
YEARS OLD, HIS MITEDAMASHI SKILLS ARE EXCELLENT, AND HE'S
ALREADY HAD NUMEROUS EXPERIENCES WITH CLOSING GATES.
HOWEVER, UNLIKE OTHERS IN THE SUGAWARA CLAN, HE WASN'T
BORN WITH ANY EXCLUSIVE POWERS AS GUARDIANS NORMALLY
ARE. THE REASON MAY HAVE TO DO WITH A VARIANCE IN HOW
MUCH OF THE "THICK" GATE-KEEPER'S BLOOD HE INHERITED.

CHARACTER PROFILE:05
MICHIZANE

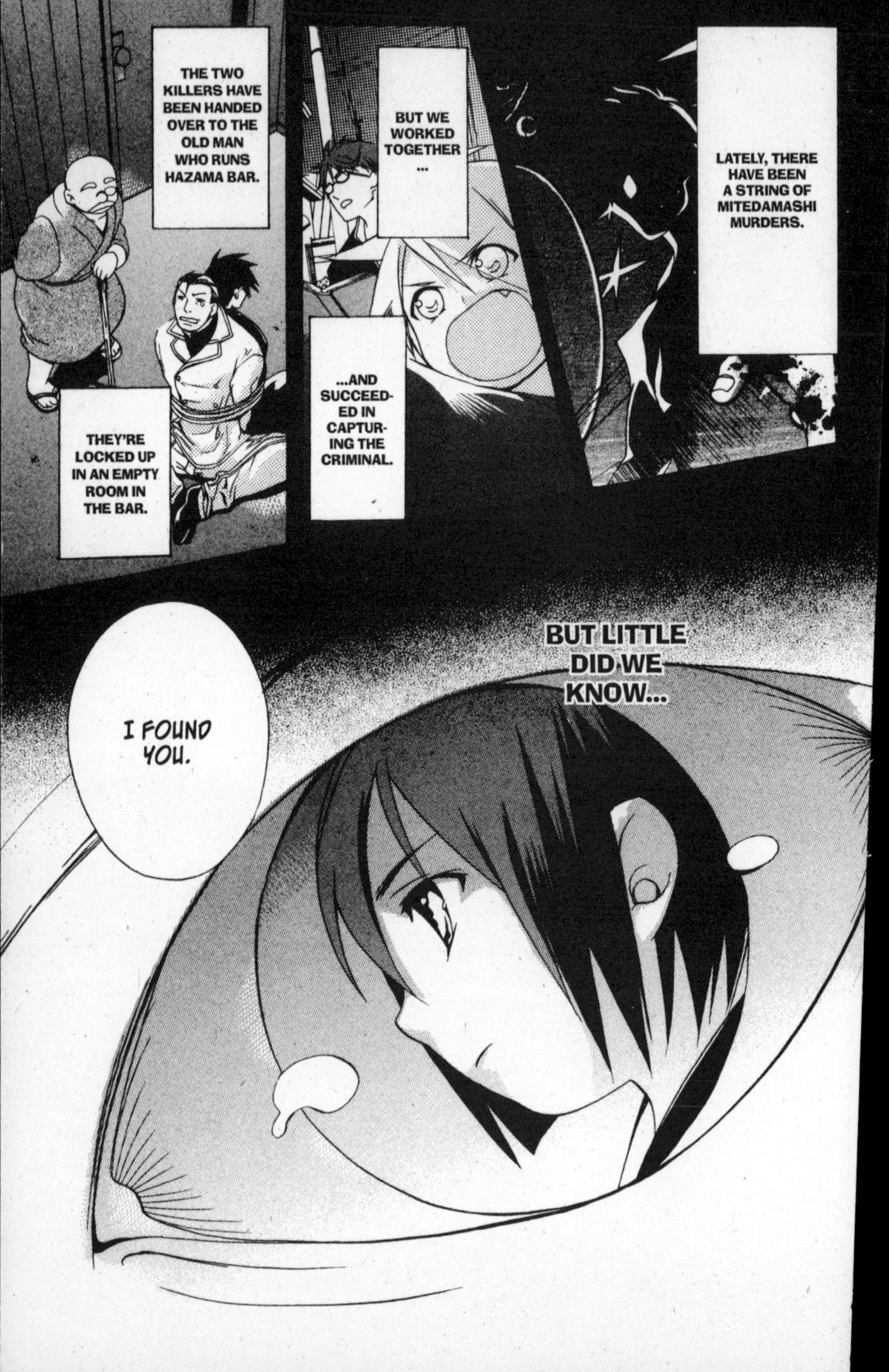
LATELY, THERE HAVE BEEN A STRING OF MITEDAMASHI MURDERS.
BUT WE WORKED TOGETHER ...
...AND SUCCEED-ED IN CAPTUR-ING THE CRIMINAL.
THE TWO KILLERS HAVE BEEN HANDED OVER TO THE OLD MAN WHO RUNS HAZAMA BAR.
THEY'RE LOCKED UP IN AN EMPTY ROOM IN THE BAR.
BUT LITTLE DID WE KNOW...
I FOUND YOU.

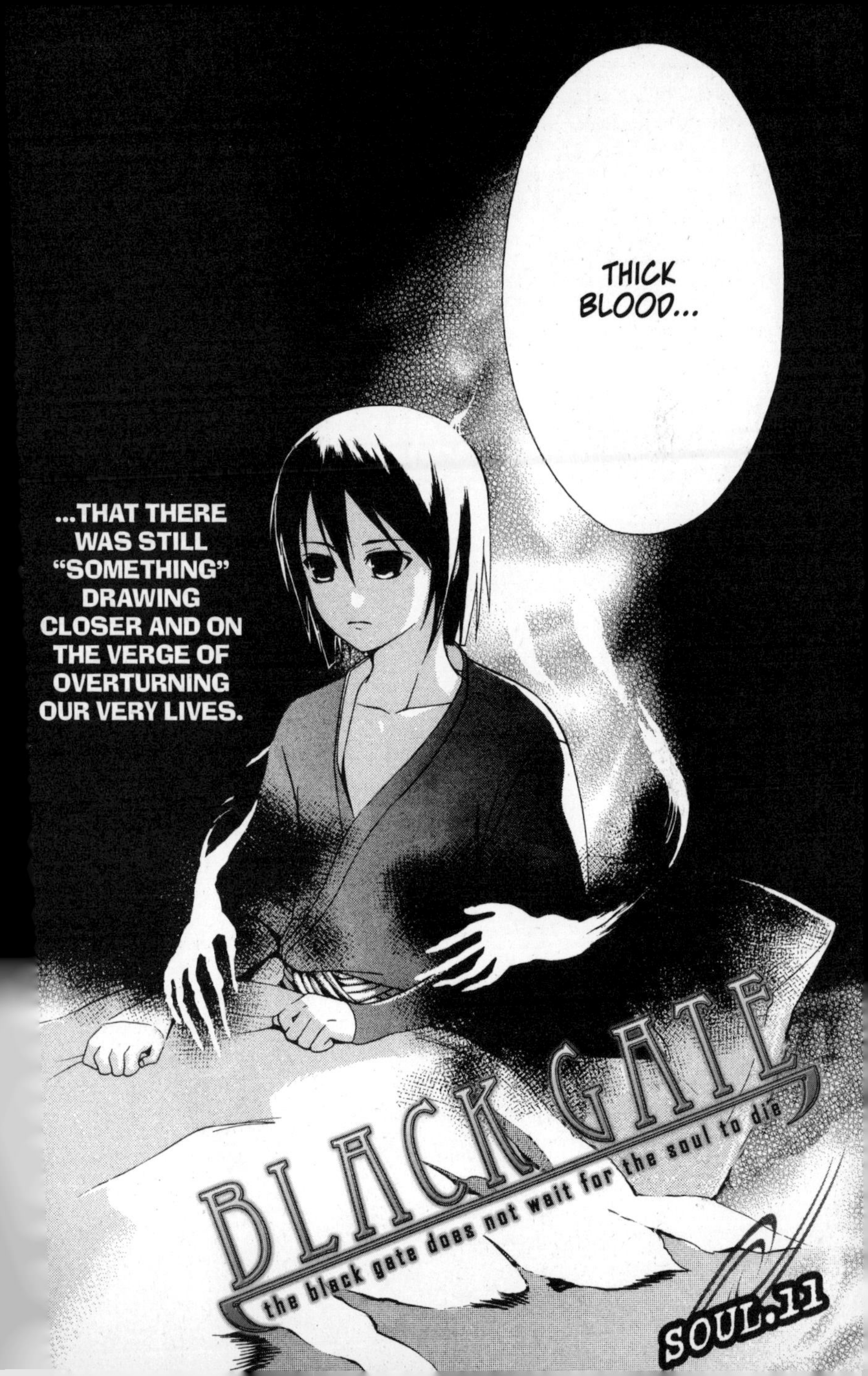
THICK BLOOD...
...THAT THERE WAS STILL "SOMETHING" DRAWING CLOSER AND ON THE VERGE OF OVERTURNING OUR VERY LIVES.
BLACK GATE
the black gate does not wait for the soul to die
SOUL.11

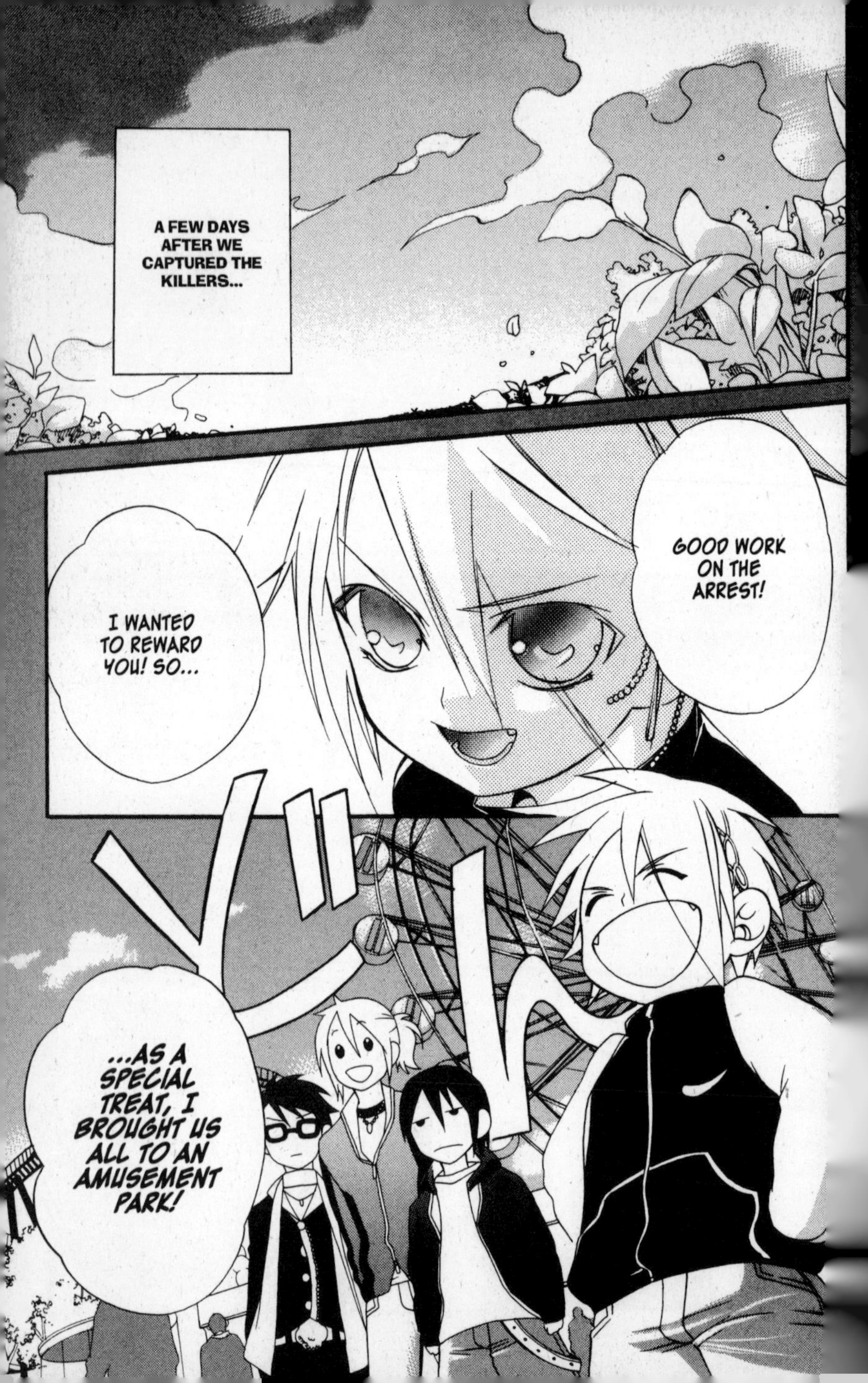
A FEW DAYS AFTER WE CAPTURED THE KILLERS...
GOOD WORK ON THE ARREST!
I WANTED TO REWARD YOU! SO...
...AS A SPECIAL TREAT, I BROUGHT US ALL TO AN AMUSEMENT PARK!

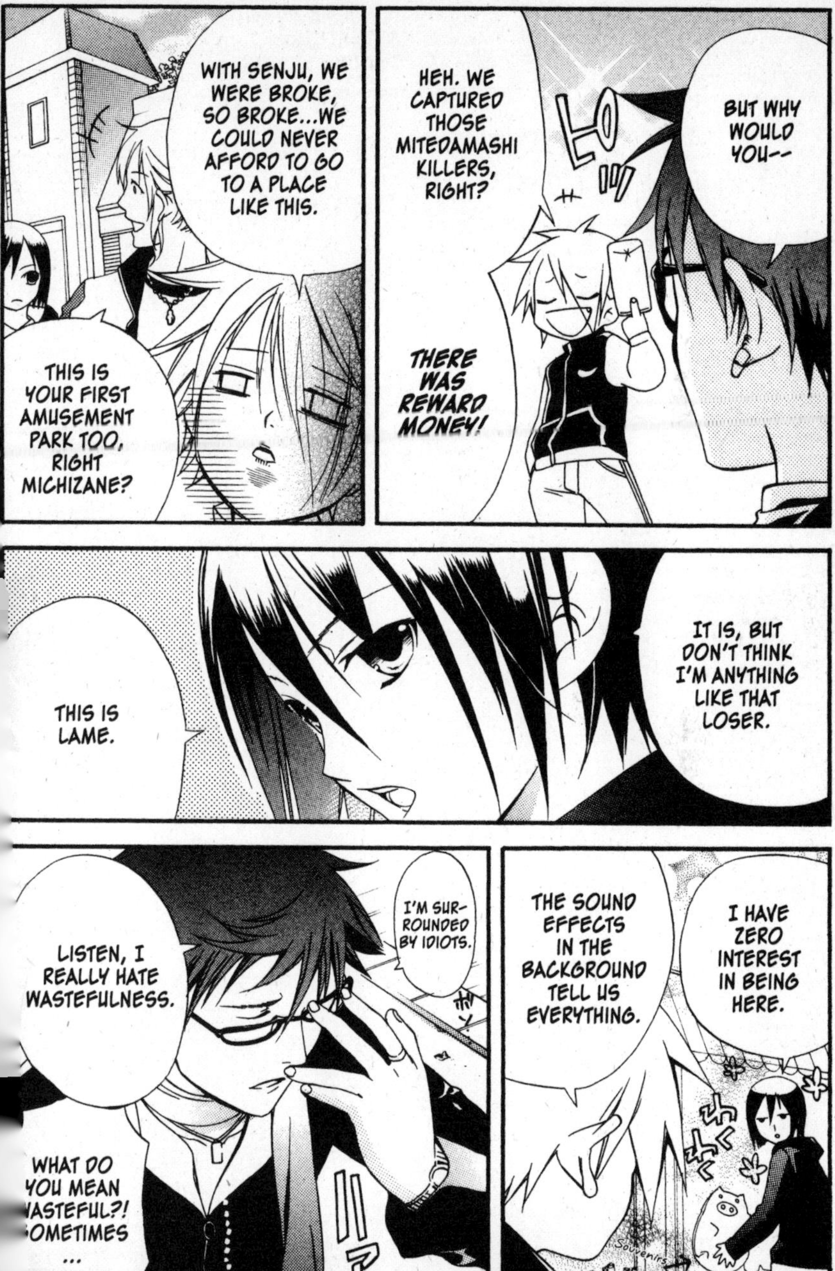
BUT WHY WOULD YOU--
HEH. WE CAPTURED THOSE MITEDAMASHI KILLERS, RIGHT?
THERE WAS REWARD MONEY!
WITH SENJU, WE WERE BROKE, SO BROKE...WE COULD NEVER AFFORD TO GO TO A PLACE LIKE THIS.
THIS IS YOUR FIRST AMUSEMENT PARK TOO, RIGHT MICHIZANE?
IT IS, BUT DON'T THINK I'M ANYTHING LIKE THAT LOSER.
THIS IS LAME.
I HAVE ZERO INTEREST IN BEING HERE.
THE SOUND EFFECTS IN THE BACKGROUND TELL US EVERYTHING.
Souvenirs
I'M SUR-ROUNDED BY IDIOTS.
LISTEN, I REALLY HATE WASTEFULNESS.
WHAT DO YOU MEAN WASTEFUL?! SOMETIMES ...

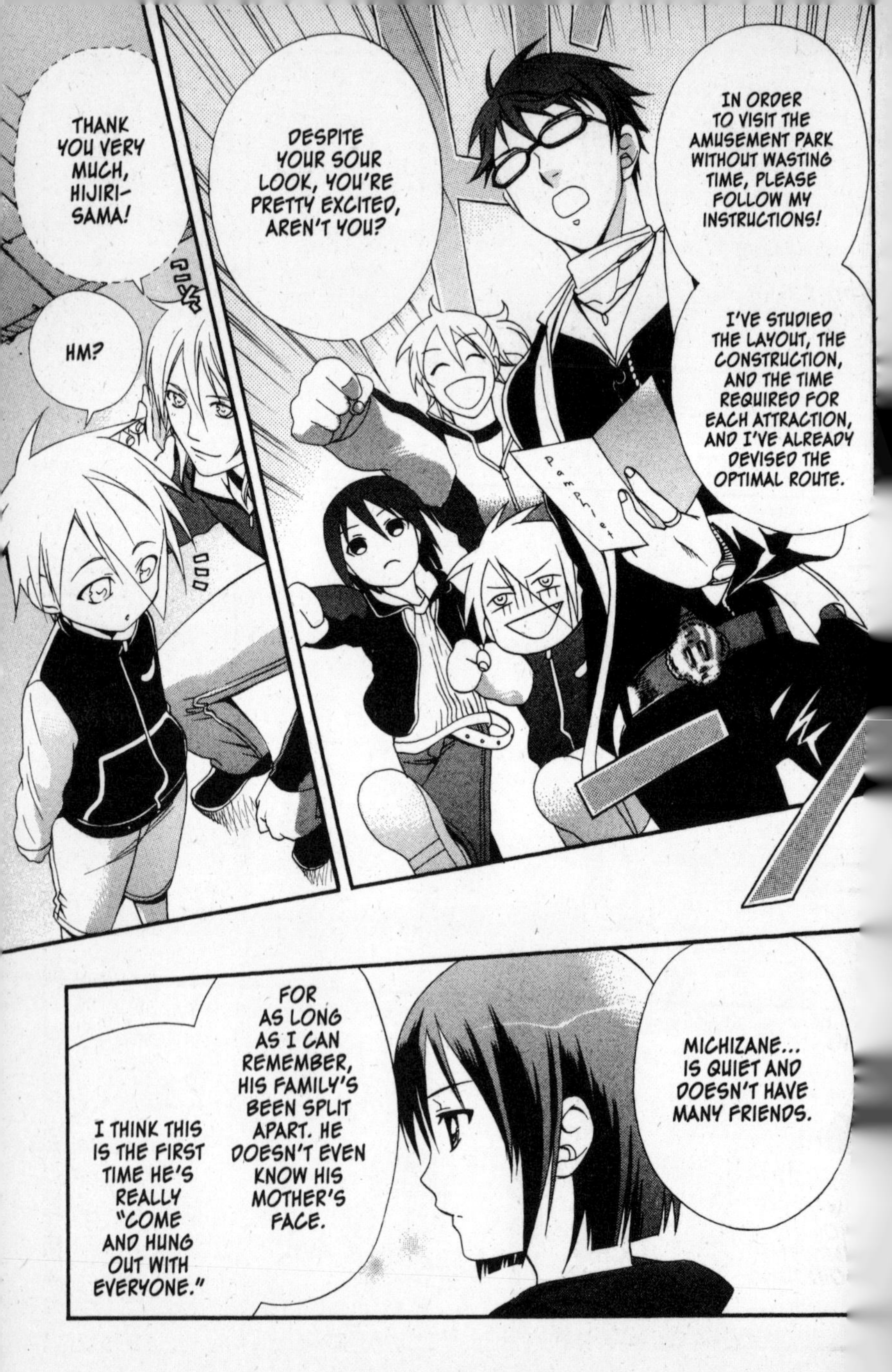
IN ORDER TO VISIT THE AMUSEMENT PARK WITHOUT WASTING TIME, PLEASE FOLLOW MY INSTRUCTIONS!
I'VE STUDIED THE LAYOUT, THE CONSTRUCTION, AND THE TIME REQUIRED FOR EACH ATTRACTION, AND I'VE ALREADY DEVISED THE OPTIMAL ROUTE.
Pamphlet
DESPITE YOUR SOUR LOOK, YOU'RE PRETTY EXCITED, AREN'T YOU?
THANK YOU VERY MUCH, HIJIRI-SAMA!
HM?
MICHIZANE... IS QUIET AND DOESN'T HAVE MANY FRIENDS.
FOR AS LONG AS I CAN REMEMBER, HIS FAMILY'S BEEN SPLIT APART. HE DOESN'T EVEN KNOW HIS MOTHER'S FACE.
I THINK THIS IS THE FIRST TIME HE'S REALLY "COME AND HUNG OUT WITH EVERYONE."

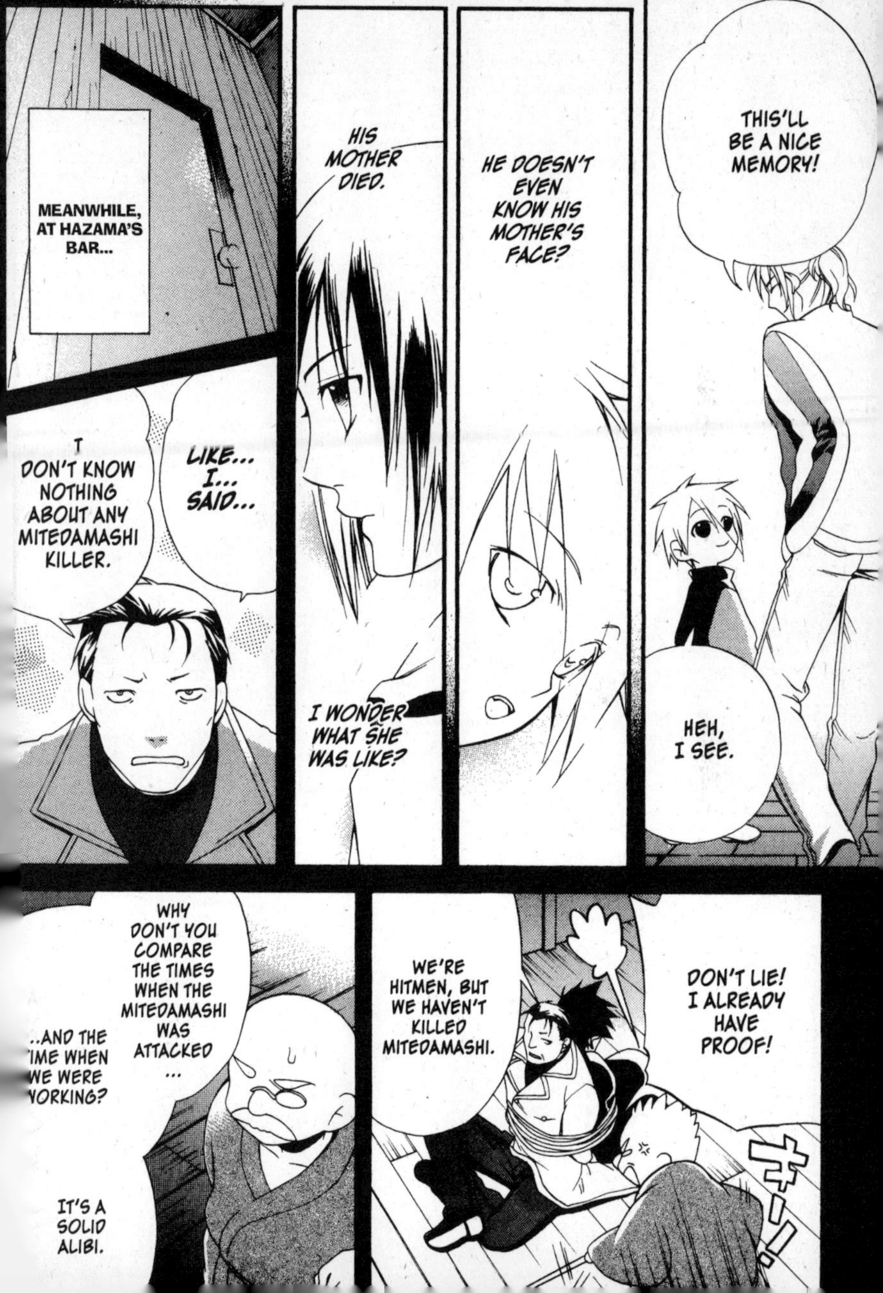
THIS'LL BE A NICE MEMORY!
HEH, I SEE.
HE DOESN'T EVEN KNOW HIS MOTHER'S FACE?
HIS MOTHER DIED.
I WONDER WHAT SHE WAS LIKE?
MEANWHILE, AT HAZAMA'S BAR...
LIKE... I... SAID...
I DON'T KNOW NOTHING ABOUT ANY MITEDAMASHI KILLER.
DON'T LIE! I ALREADY HAVE PROOF!
WE'RE HITMEN, BUT WE HAVEN'T KILLED MITEDAMASHI.
WHY DON'T YOU COMPARE THE TIMES WHEN THE MITEDAMASHI WAS ATTACKED ...
..AND THE TIME WHEN WE WERE WORKING?
IT'S A SOLID ALIBI.

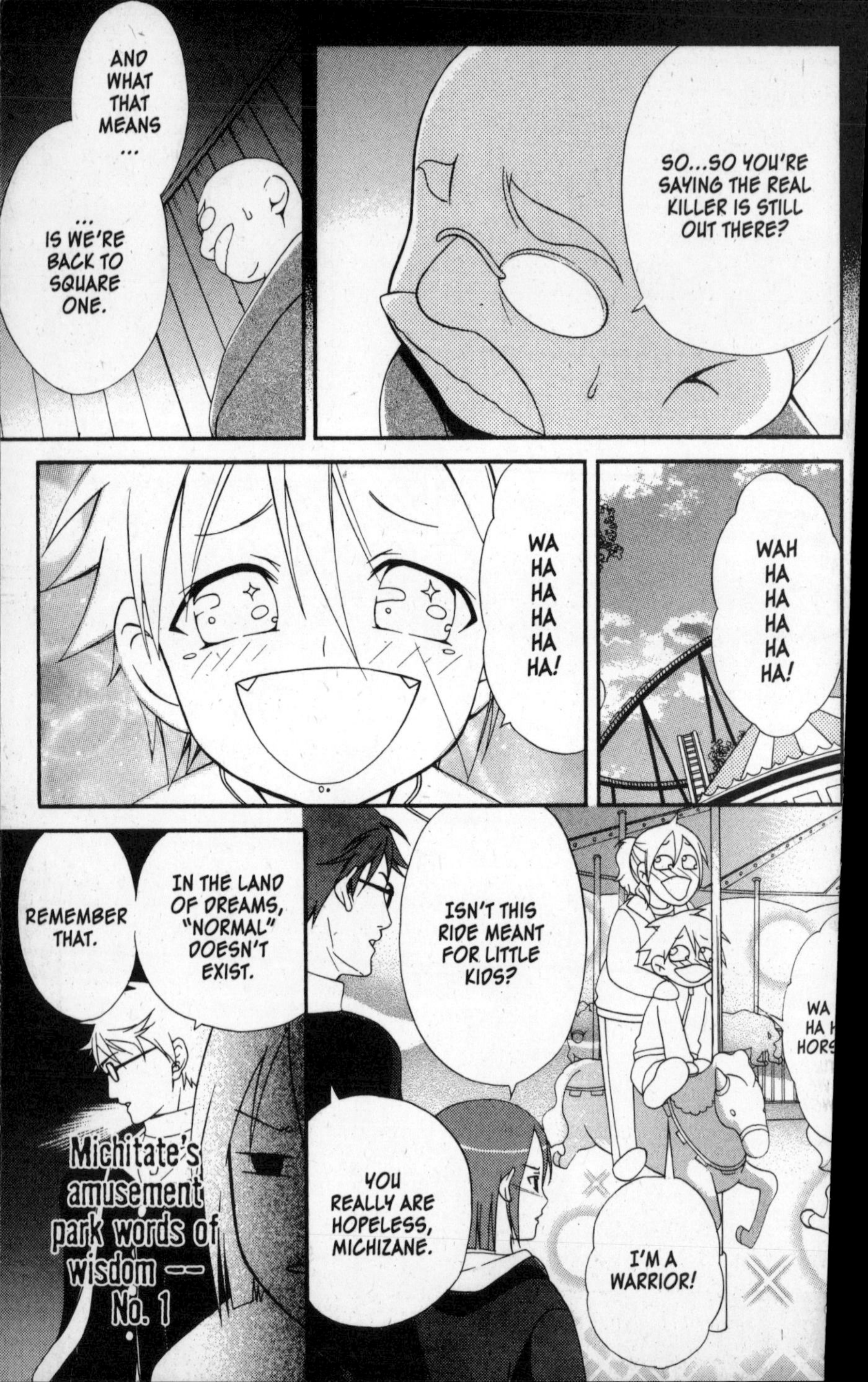
SO...SO YOU'RE SAYING THE REAL KILLER IS STILL OUT THERE?
AND WHAT THAT MEANS ...
... IS WE'RE BACK TO SQUARE ONE.
WAH HA HA HA HA HA HA!
WA HA HA HA HA HA HA!
ISN'T THIS RIDE MEANT FOR LITTLE KIDS?
I'M A WARRIOR!
YOU REALLY ARE HOPELESS, MICHIZANE.
IN THE LAND OF DREAMS, "NORMAL" DOESN'T EXIST.
REMEMBER THAT.
Michitate's amusement park words of wisdom -- No. 1

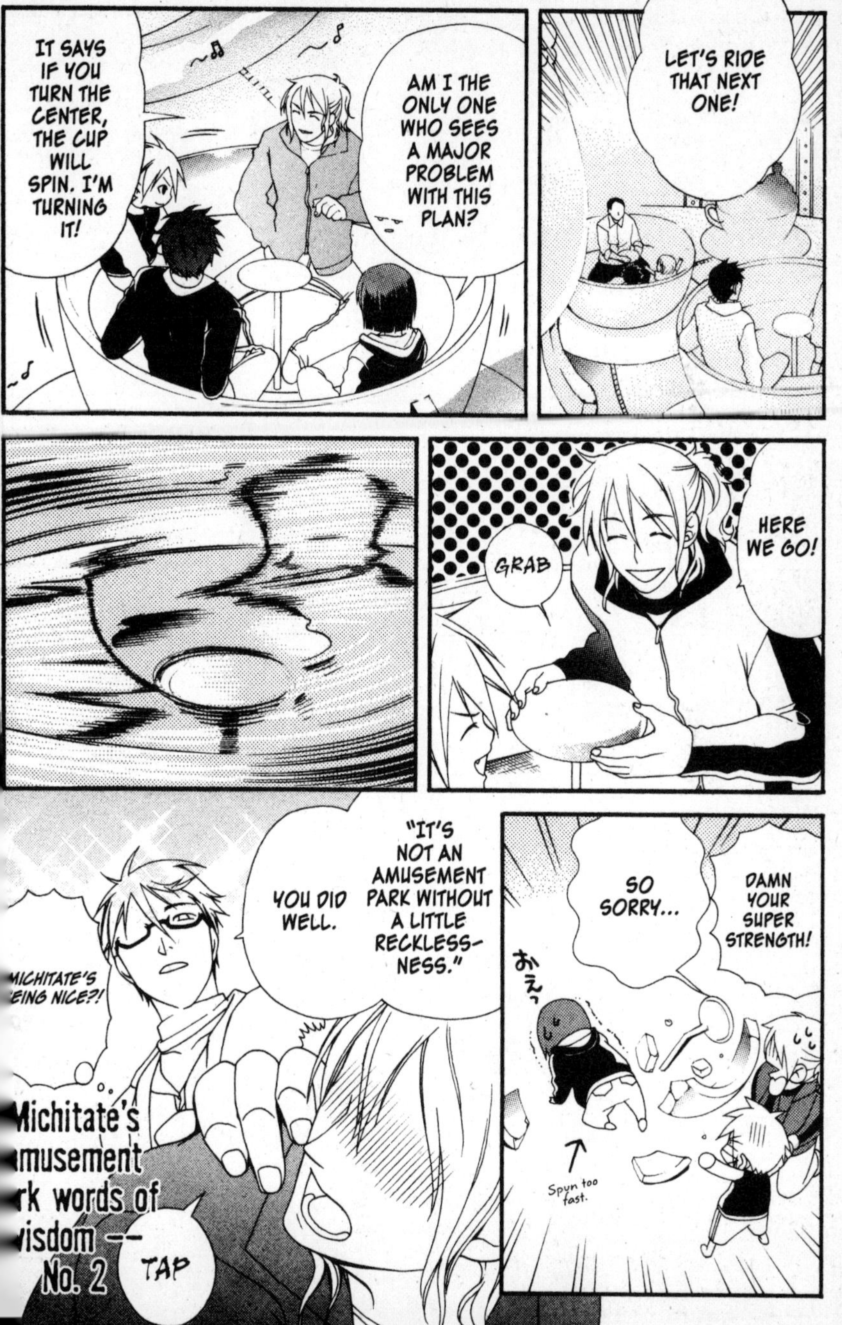
LET'S RIDE THAT NEXT ONE!
AM I THE ONLY ONE WHO SEES A MAJOR PROBLEM WITH THIS PLAN?
IT SAYS IF YOU TURN THE CENTER, THE CUP WILL SPIN. I'M TURNING IT!
HERE WE GO!
GRAB
DAMN YOUR SUPER STRENGTH!
SO SORRY...
おえっ
Spun too fast.
"IT'S NOT AN AMUSEMENT PARK WITHOUT A LITTLE RECKLESS-NESS."
YOU DID WELL.
MICHITATE'S
EING NICE?!
Michitate's
musement
rk words of
visdom --
No. 2
TAP

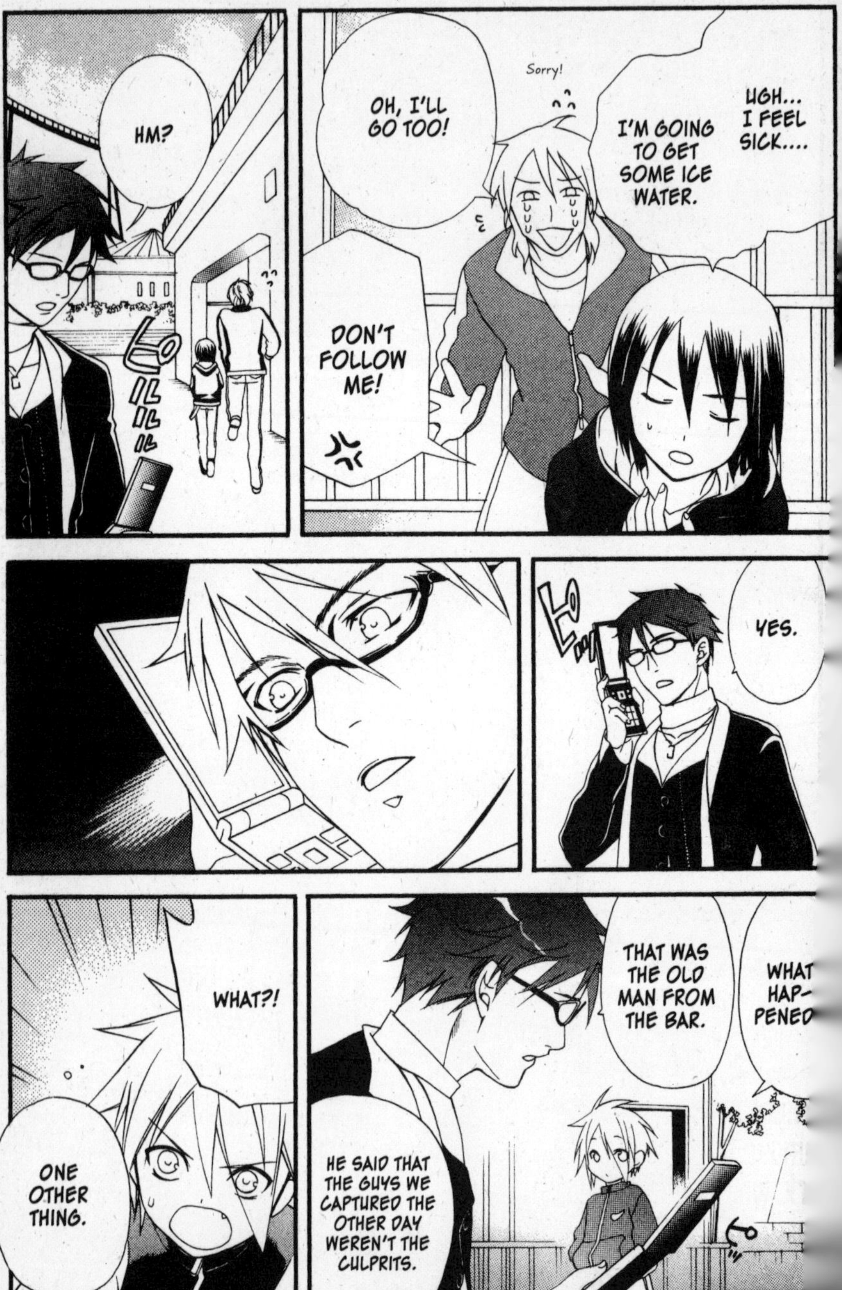
UGH... I FEEL SICK....
I'M GOING TO GET SOME ICE WATER.
Sorry!
OH, I'LL GO TOO!
DON'T FOLLOW ME!
HM?
YES.
WHAT HAP-PENED
THAT WAS THE OLD MAN FROM THE BAR.
HE SAID THAT THE GUYS WE CAPTURED THE OTHER DAY WEREN'T THE CULPRITS.
WHAT?!
ONE OTHER THING.

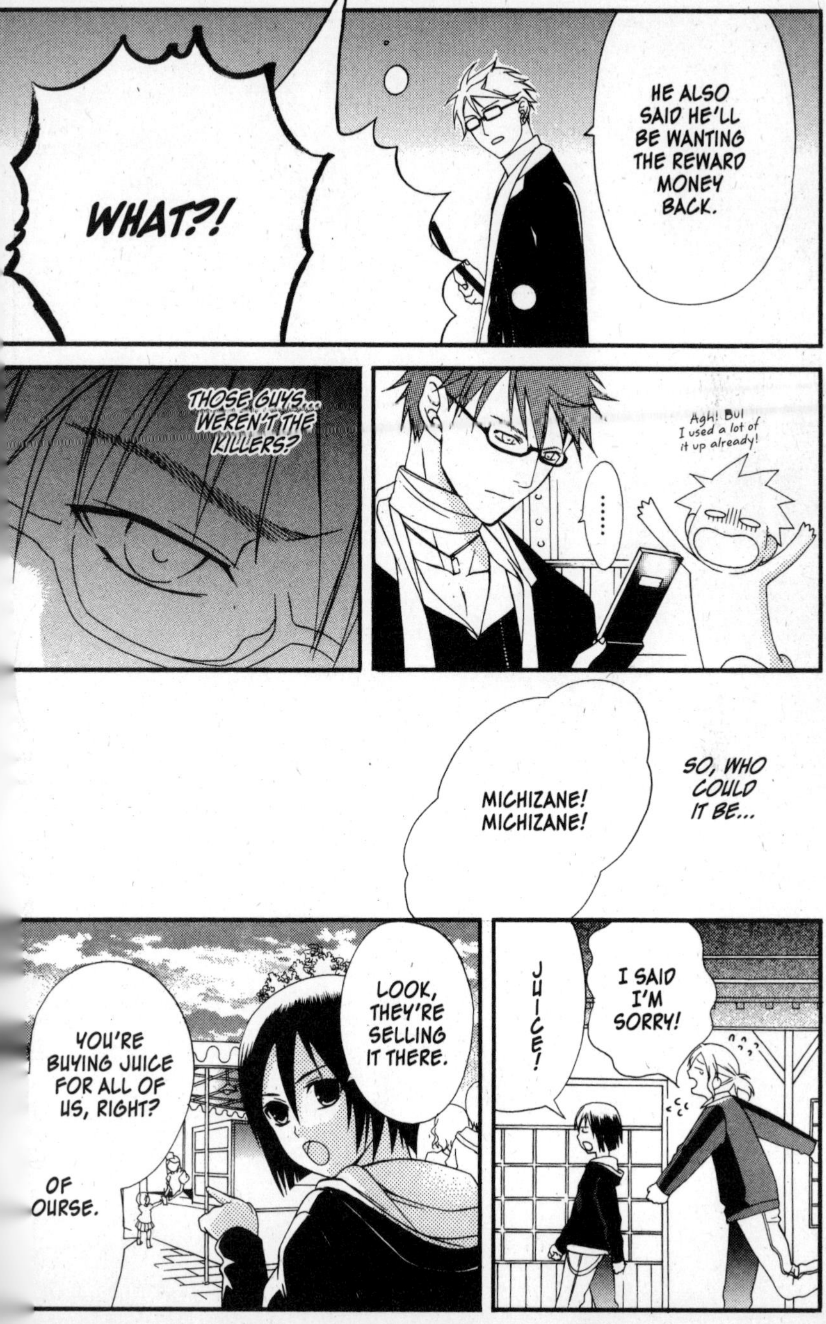
HE ALSO SAID HE'LL BE WANTING THE REWARD MONEY BACK.
WHAT?!
Agh! But I used a lot of it up already!
......
THOSE GUYS... WEREN'T THE KILLERS?
SO, WHO COULD IT BE...
MICHIZANE! MICHIZANE!
I SAID I'M SORRY!
JUICE!
LOOK, THEY'RE SELLING IT THERE.
YOU'RE BUYING JUICE FOR ALL OF US, RIGHT?
OF OURSE.

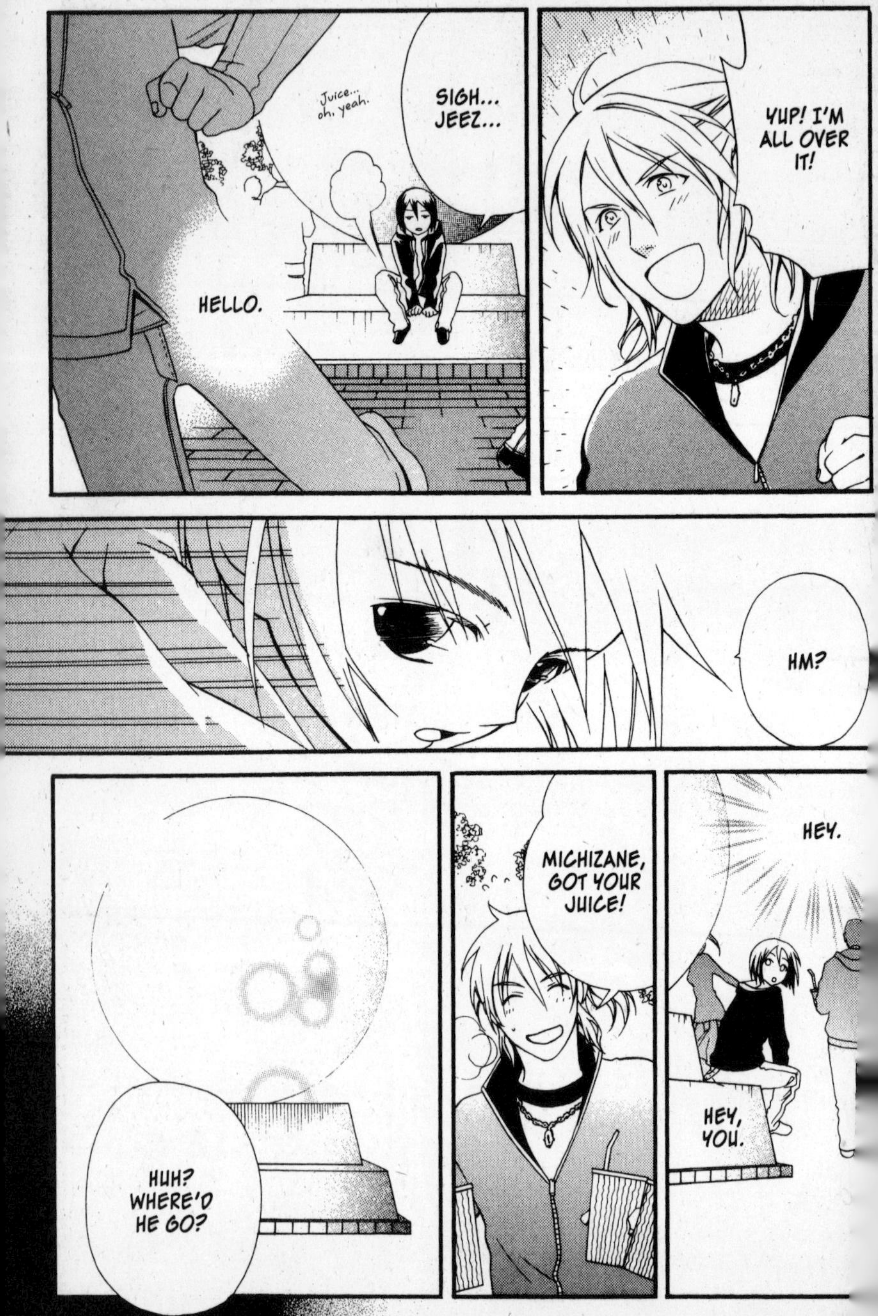
YUP! I'M ALL OVER IT!
SIGH... JEEZ...
Juice... oh, yeah.
HELLO.
HM?
HEY.
HEY, YOU.
MICHIZANE, GOT YOUR JUICE!
HUH? WHERE'D HE GO?

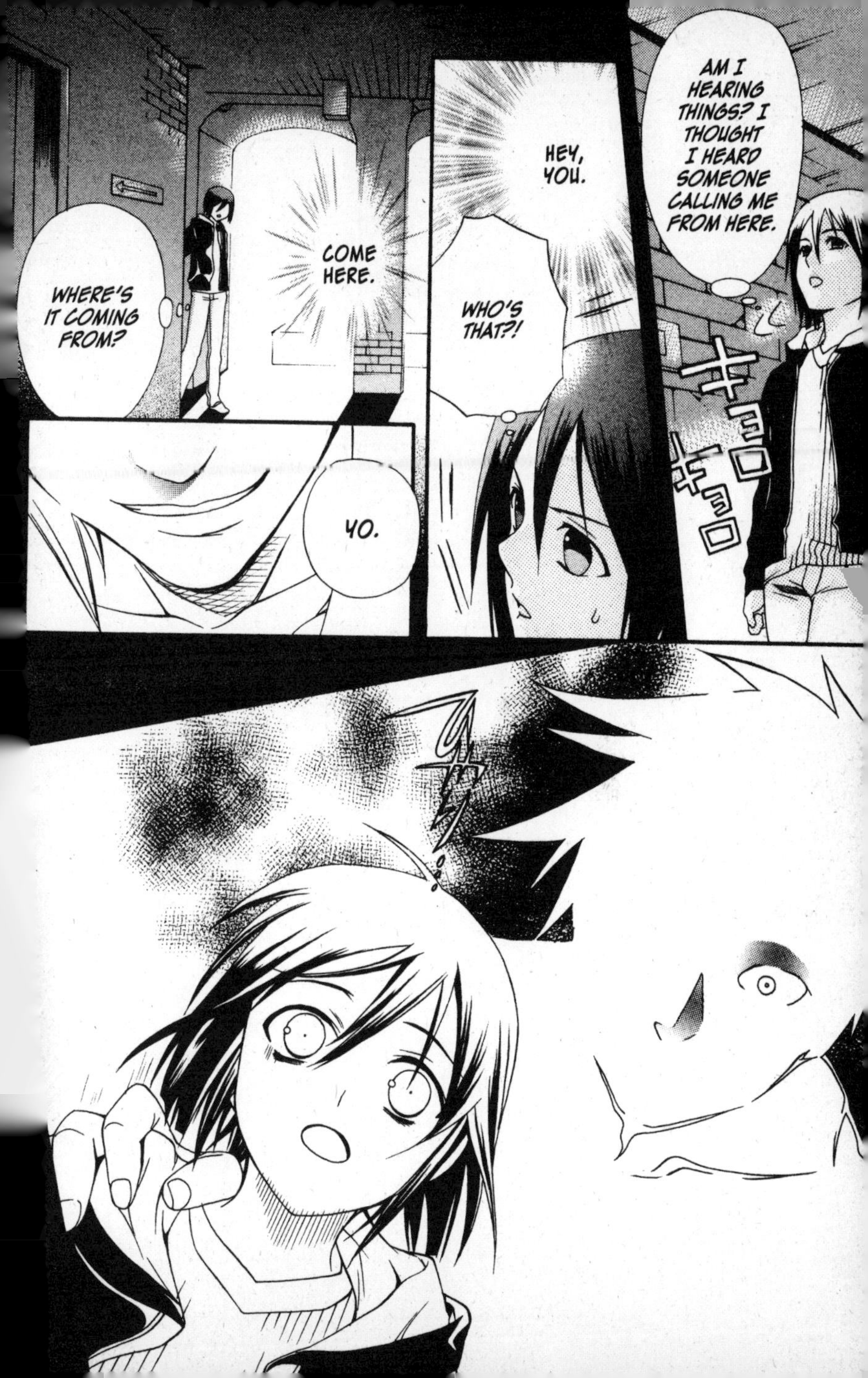
AM I HEARING THINGS? I THOUGHT I HEARD SOMEONE CALLING ME FROM HERE.
キョロキョロ
HEY, YOU.
WHO'S THAT?!
COME HERE.
WHERE'S IT COMING FROM?
YO.

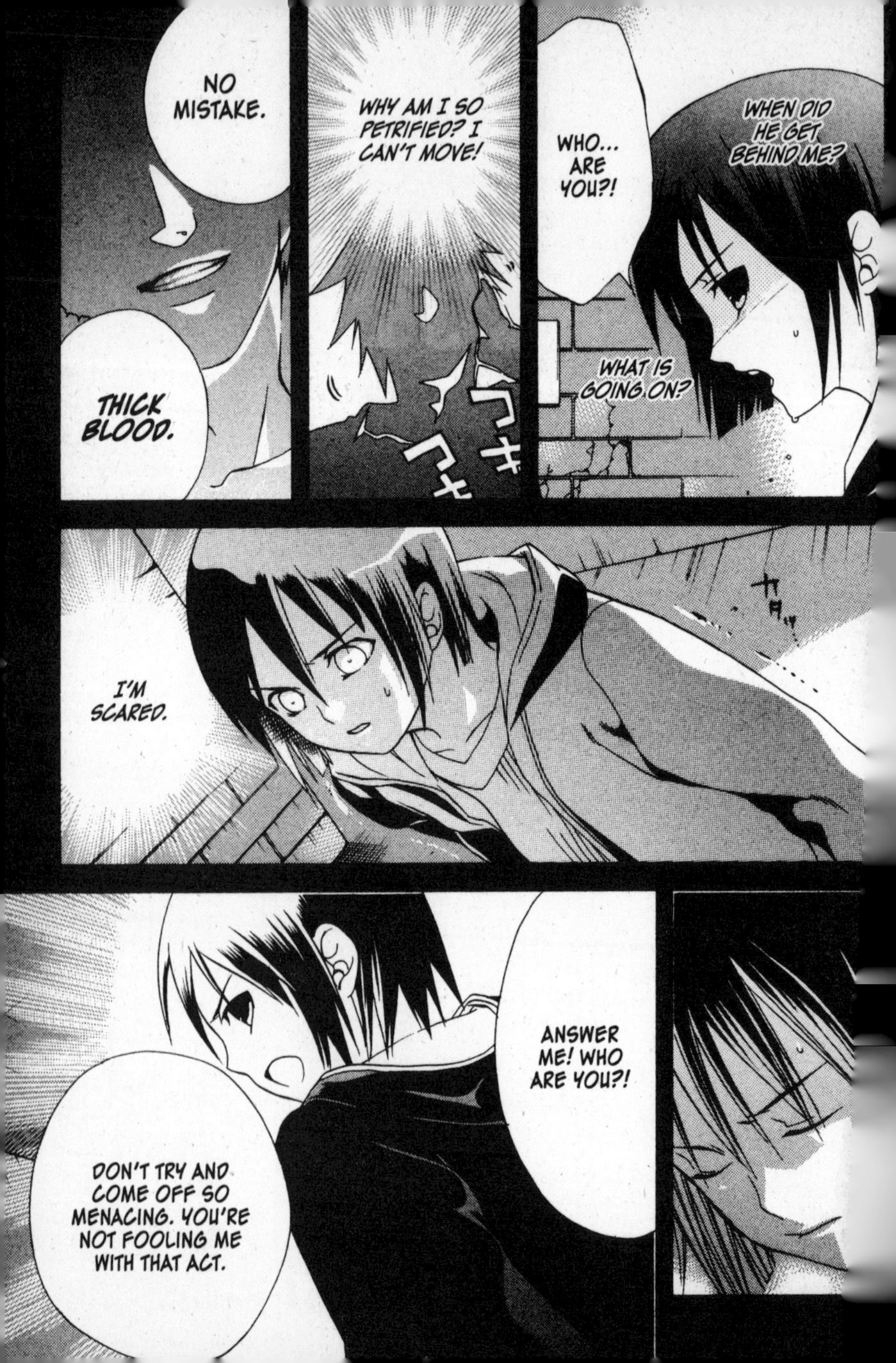
WHEN DID HE GET BEHIND ME?
WHO... ARE YOU?!
WHAT IS GOING ON?
WHY AM I SO PETRIFIED? I CAN'T MOVE!
NO MISTAKE.
THICK BLOOD.
I'M SCARED.
ANSWER ME! WHO ARE YOU?!
DON'T TRY AND COME OFF SO MENACING. YOU'RE NOT FOOLING ME WITH THAT ACT.

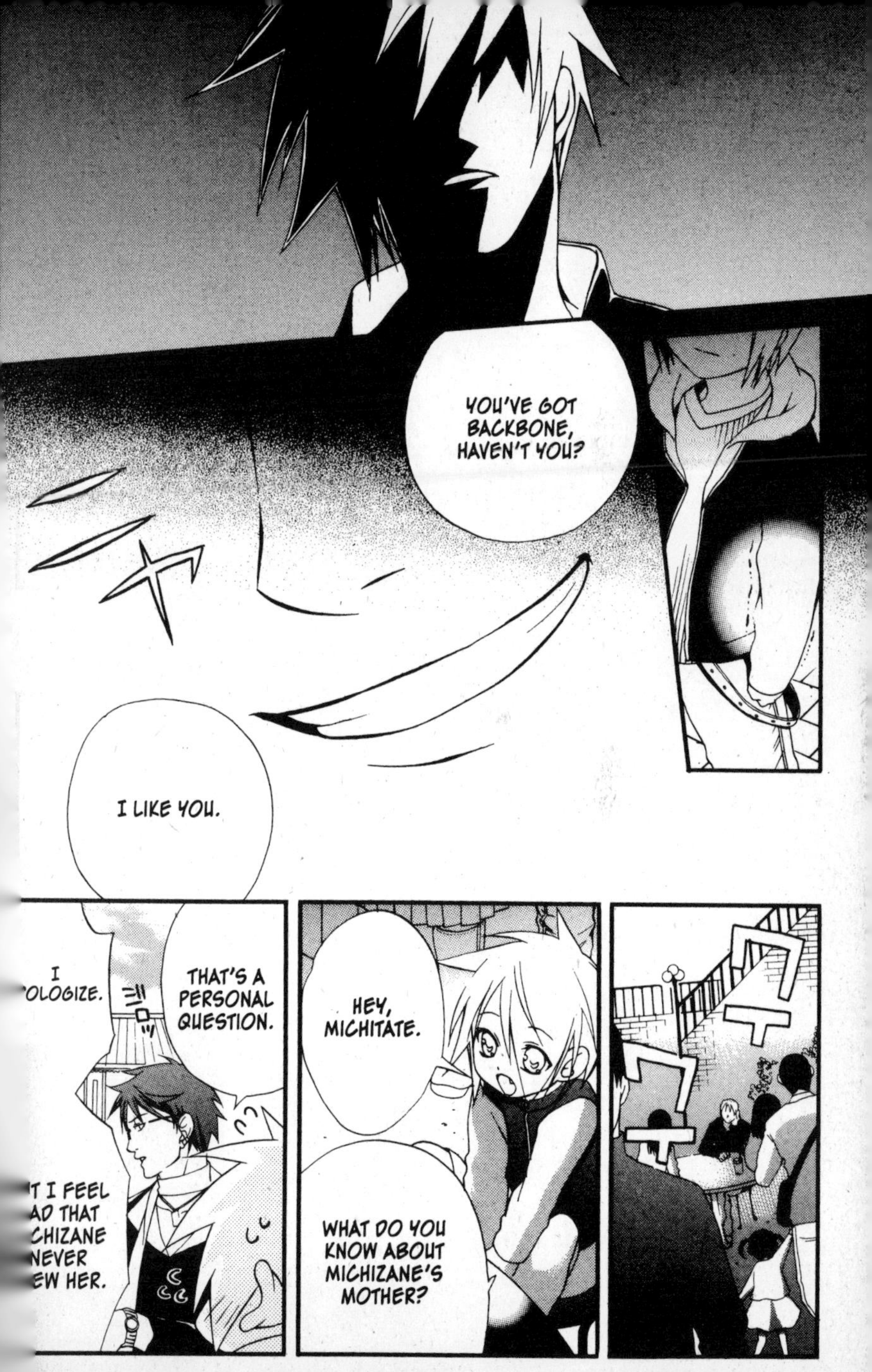
YOU'VE GOT BACKBONE, HAVEN'T YOU?
I LIKE YOU.
HEY, MICHITATE.
WHAT DO YOU KNOW ABOUT MICHIZANE'S MOTHER?
THAT'S A PERSONAL QUESTION.
I OLOGIZE.
T I FEEL AD THAT CHIZANE NEVER EW HER.

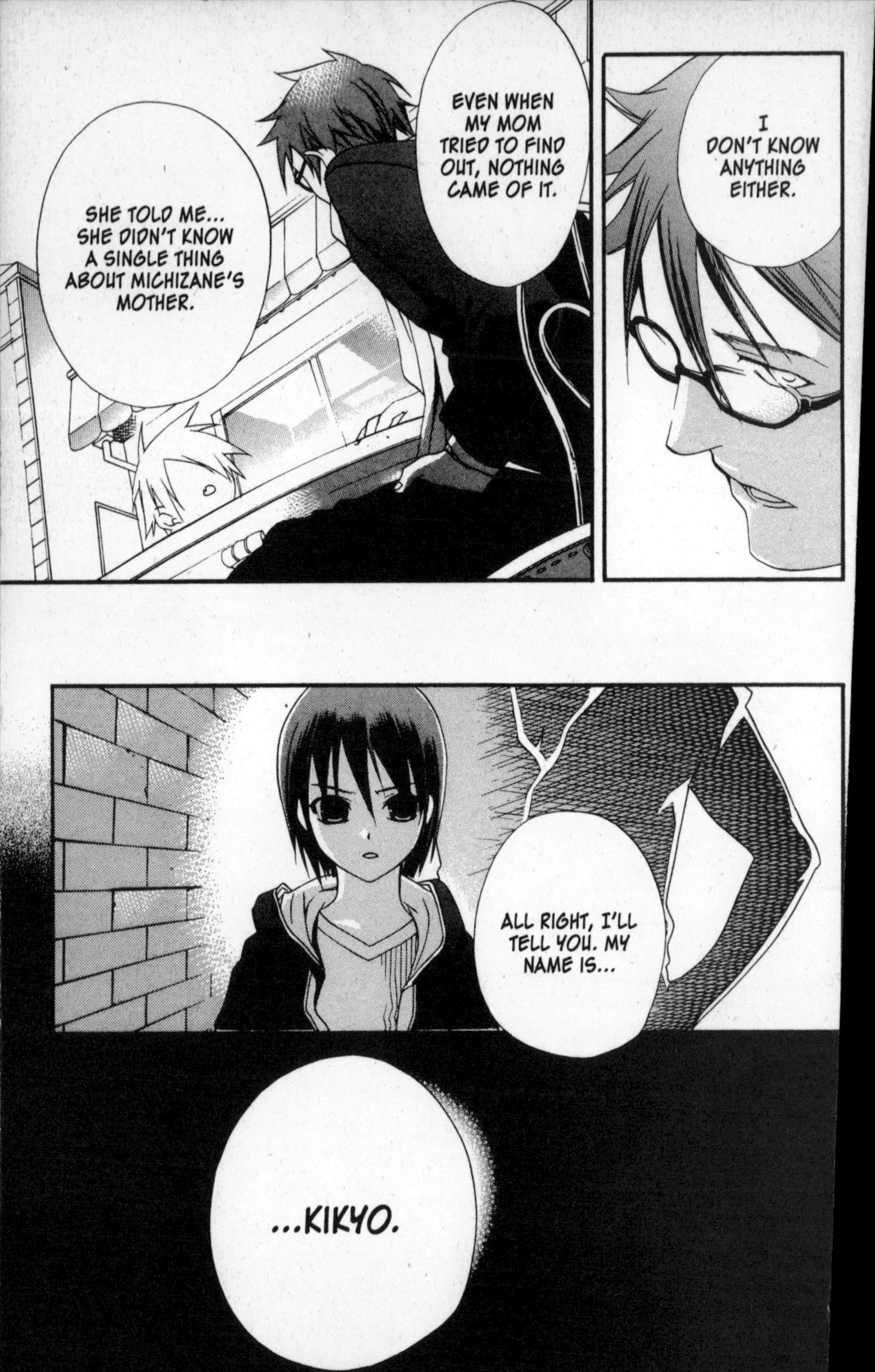
I DON'T KNOW ANYTHING EITHER.
EVEN WHEN MY MOM TRIED TO FIND OUT, NOTHING CAME OF IT.
SHE TOLD ME... SHE DIDN'T KNOW A SINGLE THING ABOUT MICHIZANE'S MOTHER.
ALL RIGHT, I'LL TELL YOU. MY NAME IS...
...KIKYO.

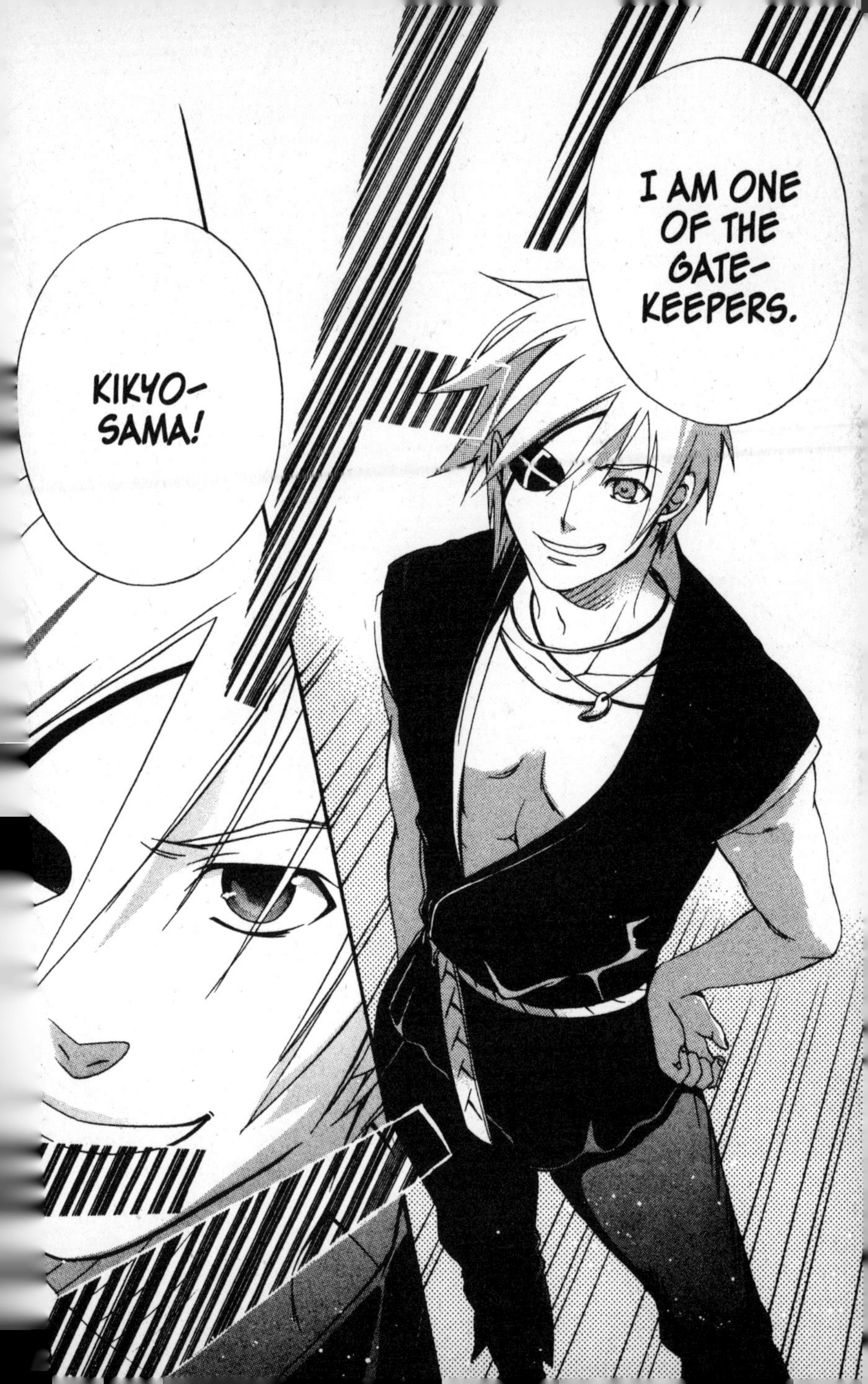
I AM ONE OF THE GATE-KEEPERS.
KIKYO-SAMA!

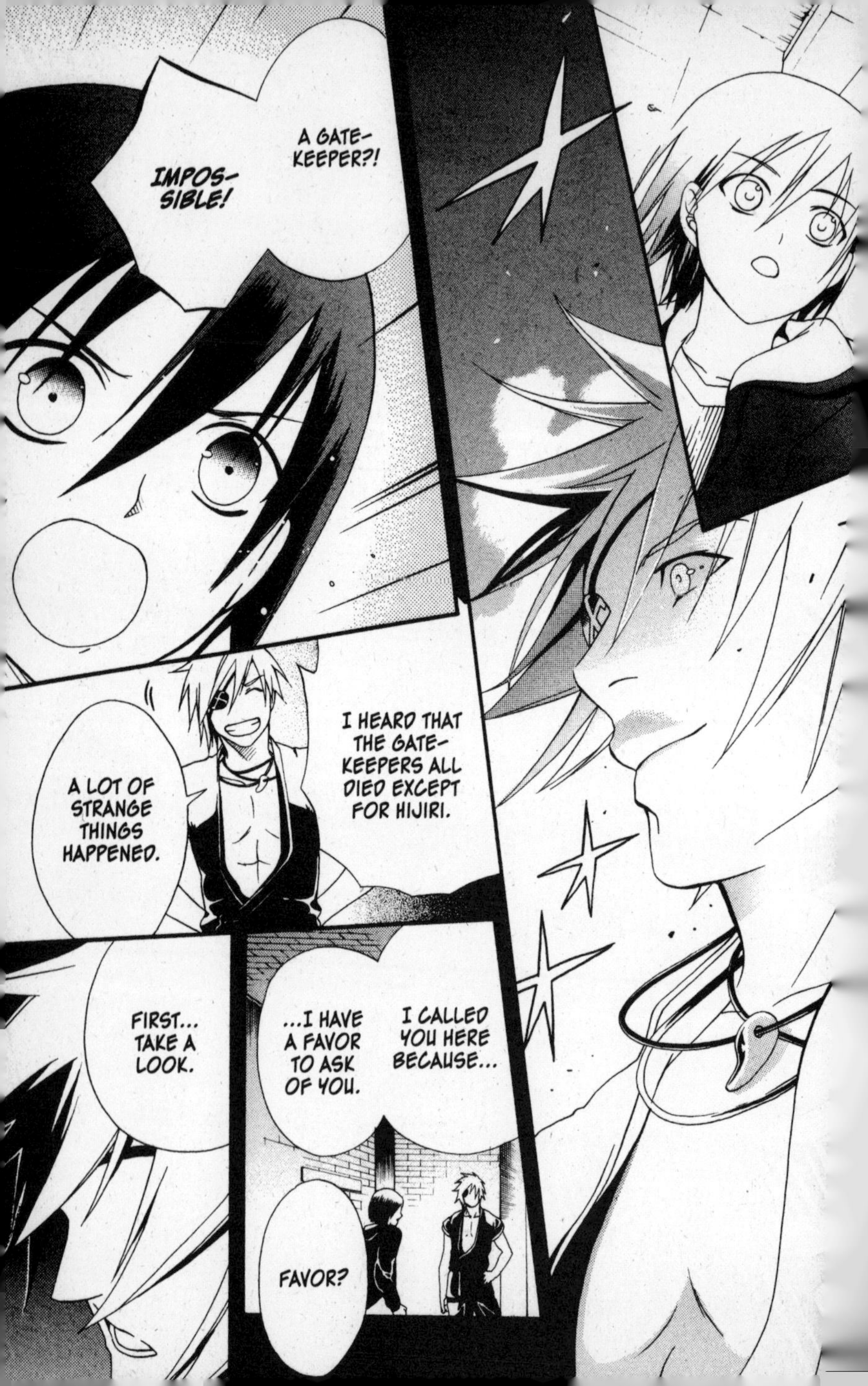
A GATE-KEEPER?!
IMPOSSIBLE!
I HEARD THAT THE GATE-KEEPERS ALL DIED EXCEPT FOR HIJIRI.
A LOT OF STRANGE THINGS HAPPENED.
I CALLED YOU HERE BECAUSE...
...I HAVE A FAVOR TO ASK OF YOU.
FAVOR?
FIRST... TAKE A LOOK.

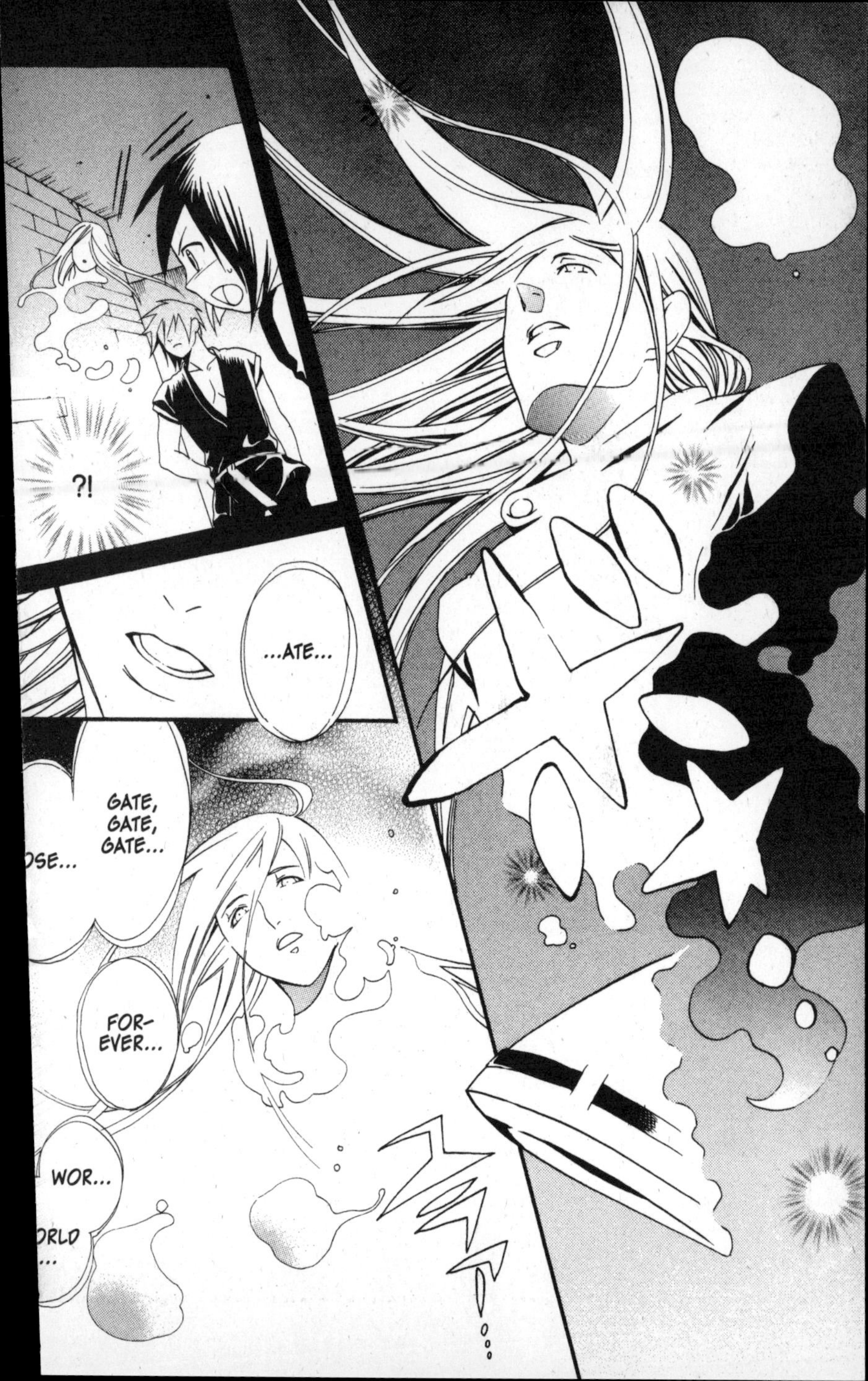

?!
...ATE...
GATE, GATE, GATE...
OSE...
FOR-EVER...
WOR...
ORLD ...

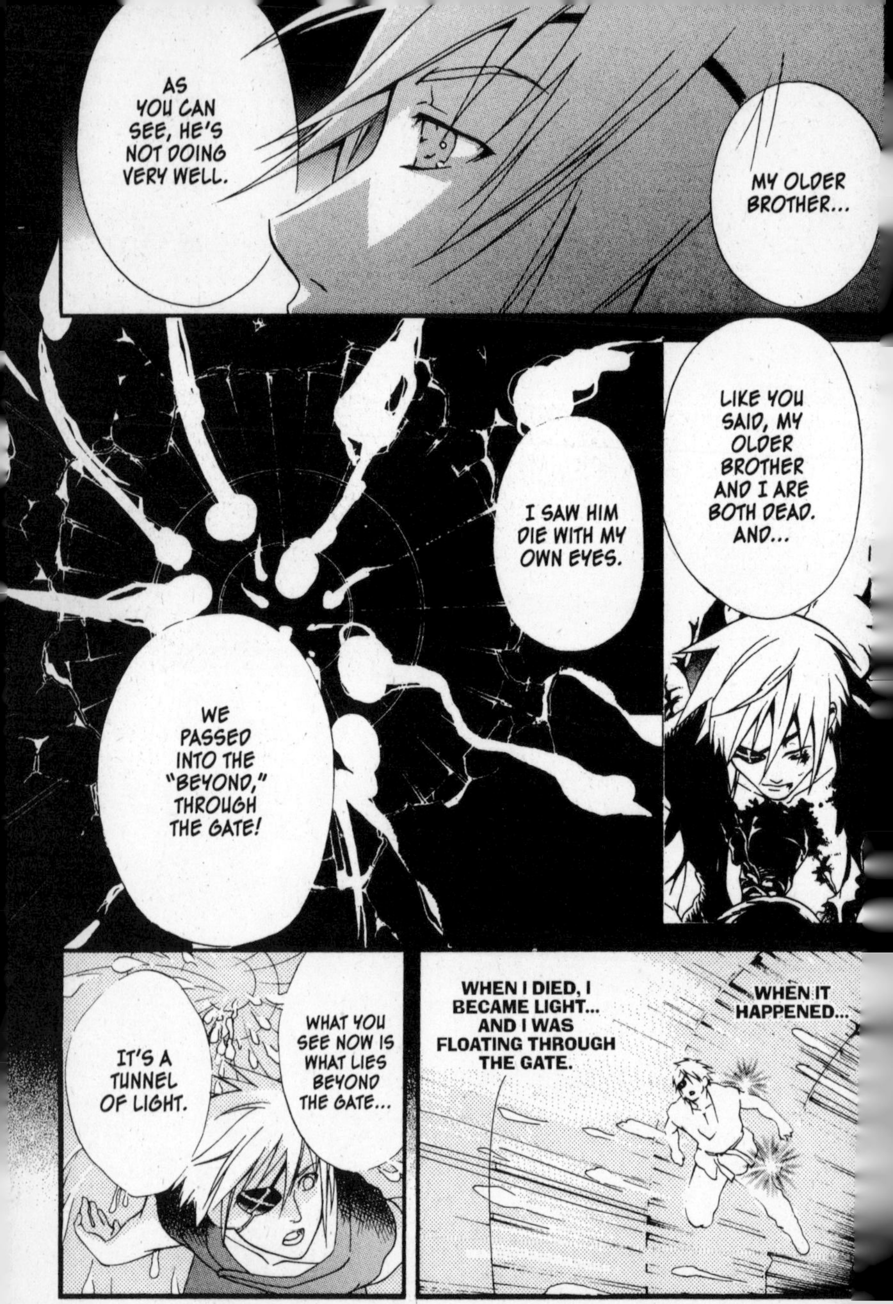
MY OLDER BROTHER...
AS YOU CAN SEE, HE'S NOT DOING VERY WELL.
LIKE YOU SAID, MY OLDER BROTHER AND I ARE BOTH DEAD. AND...
I SAW HIM DIE WITH MY OWN EYES.
WE PASSED INTO THE "BEYOND," THROUGH THE GATE!
WHEN IT HAPPENED...
WHEN I DIED, I BECAME LIGHT... AND I WAS FLOATING THROUGH THE GATE.
WHAT YOU SEE NOW IS WHAT LIES BEYOND THE GATE...
IT'S A TUNNEL OF LIGHT.

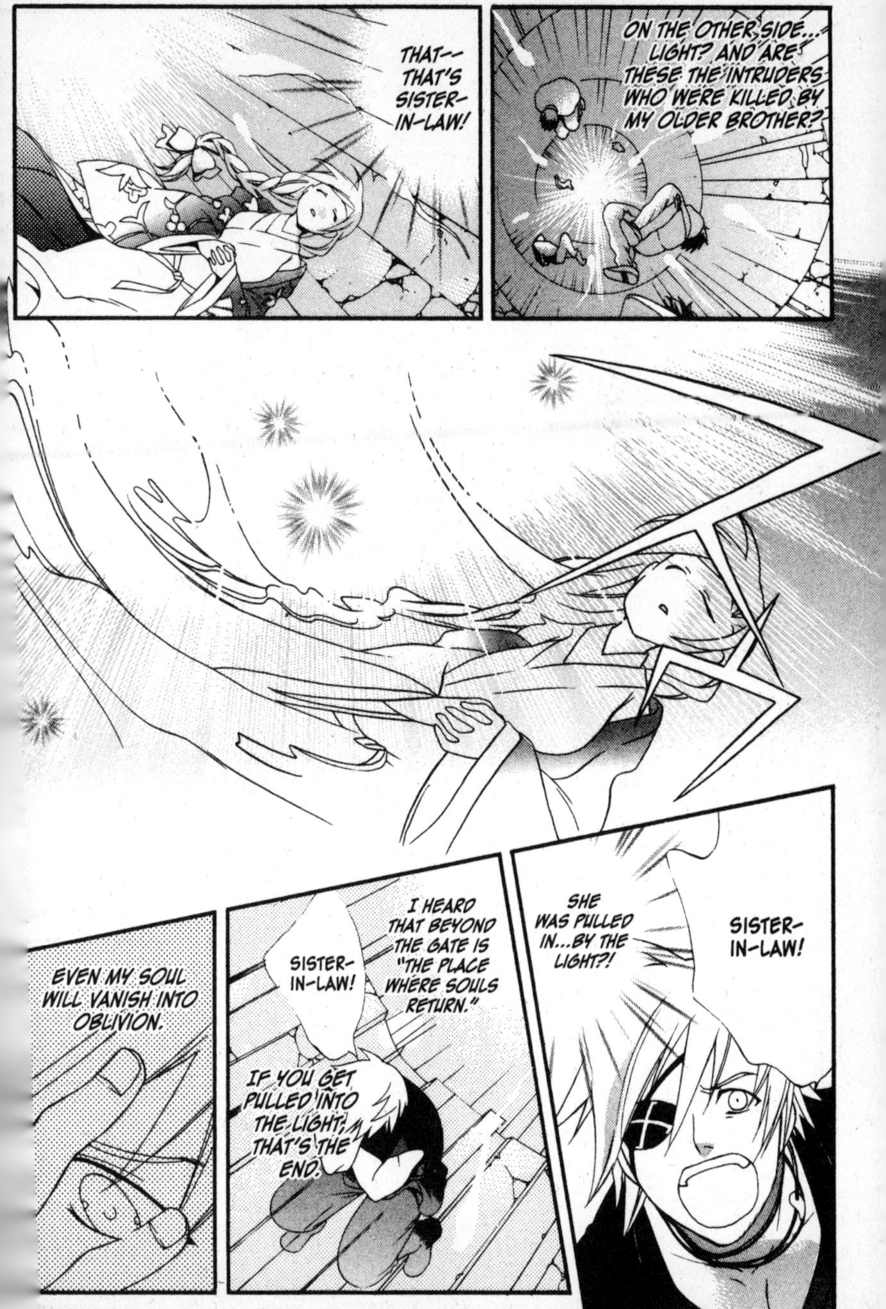
ON THE OTHER SIDE... LIGHT? AND ARE THESE THE INTRUDERS WHO WERE KILLED BY MY OLDER BROTHER?
THAT-- THAT'S SISTER-IN-LAW!
SISTER-IN-LAW!
SHE WAS PULLED IN...BY THE LIGHT?!
I HEARD THAT BEYOND THE GATE IS "THE PLACE WHERE SOULS RETURN."
SISTER-IN-LAW!
IF YOU GET PULLED INTO THE LIGHT, THAT'S THE END.
EVEN MY SOUL WILL VANISH INTO OBLIVION.

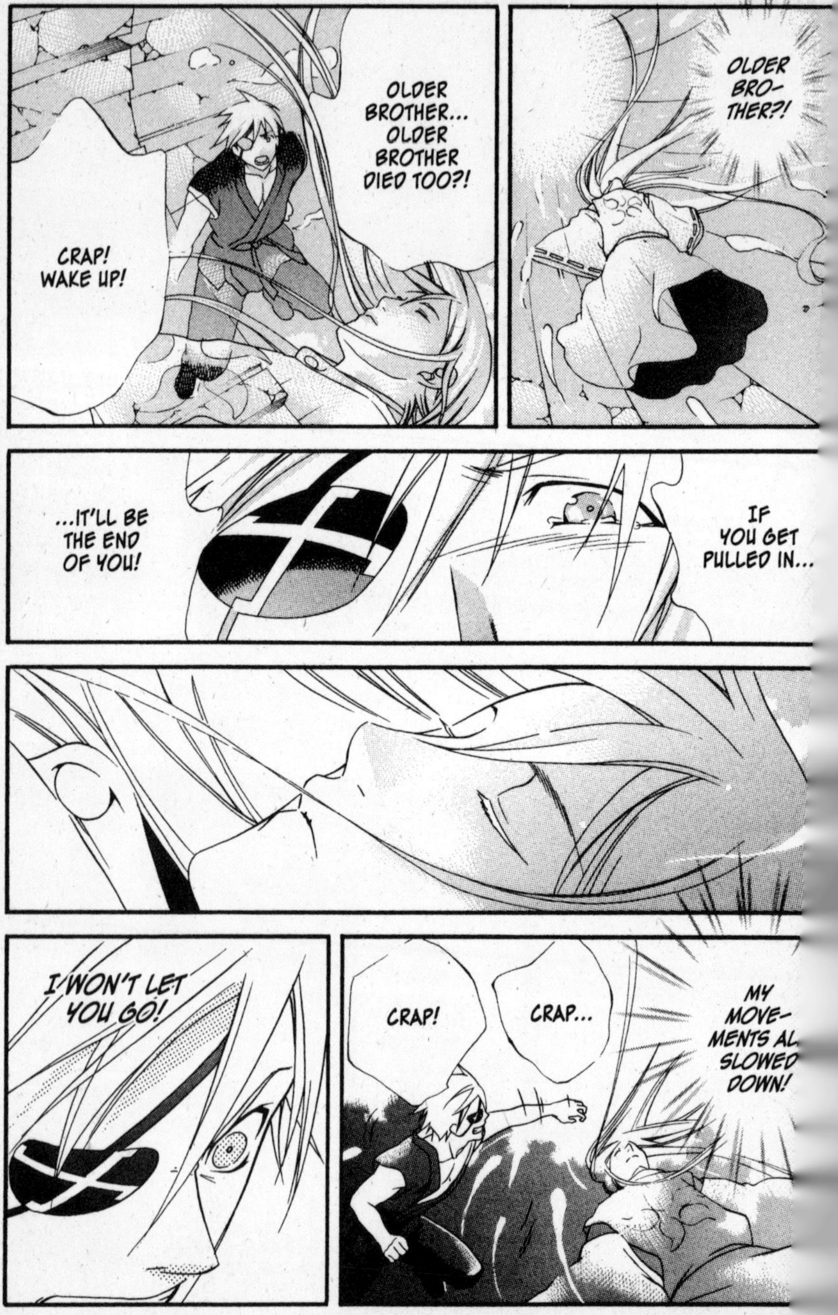
OLDER BRO- THER?!
OLDER BROTHER... OLDER BROTHER DIED TOO?!
CRAP! WAKE UP!
IF YOU GET PULLED IN...
...IT'LL BE THE END OF YOU!
MY MOVE- MENTS AL SLOWED DOWN!
CRAP...
CRAP!
I WON'T LET YOU GO!

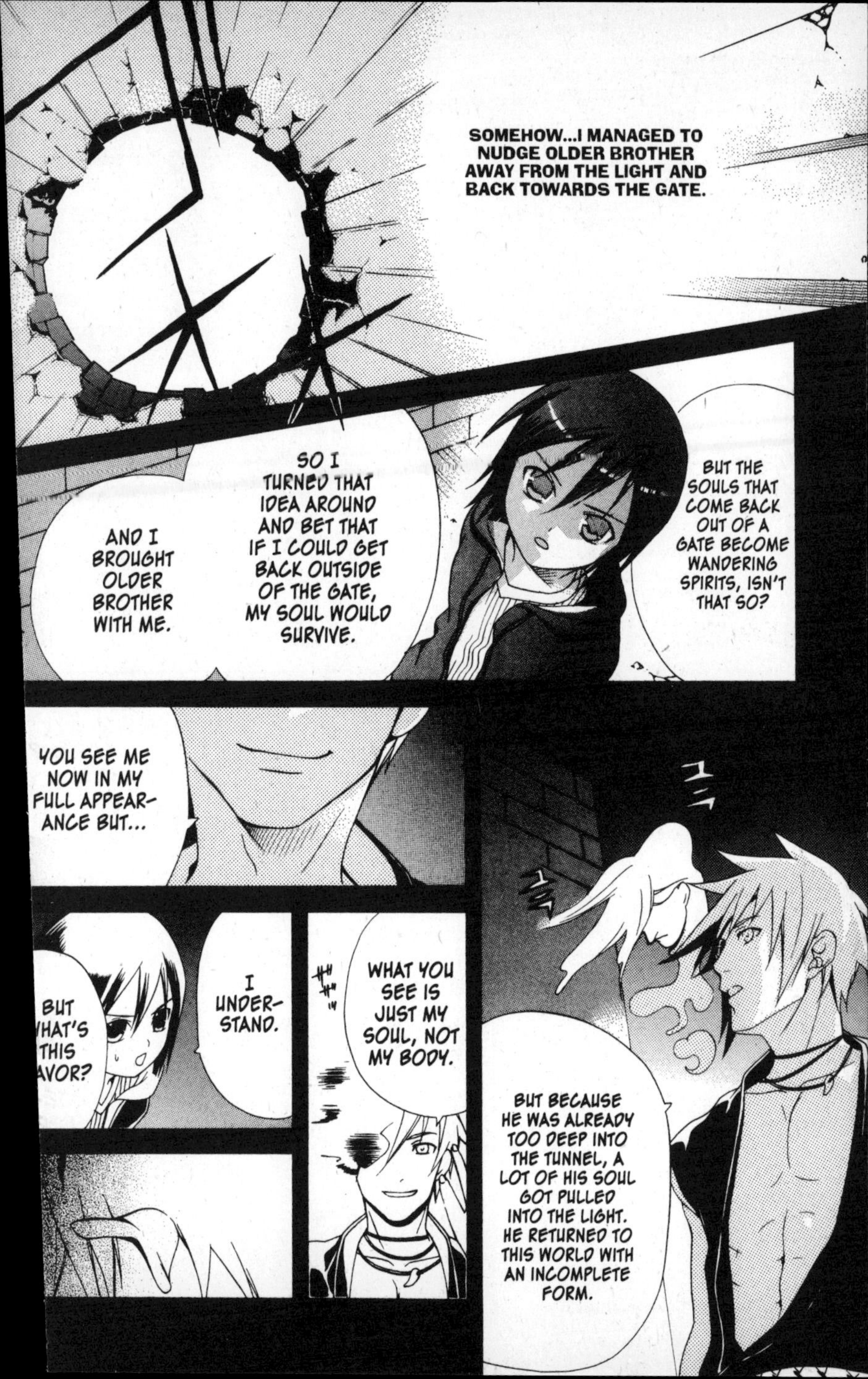
SOMEHOW...I MANAGED TO NUDGE OLDER BROTHER AWAY FROM THE LIGHT AND BACK TOWARDS THE GATE.
BUT THE SOULS THAT COME BACK OUT OF A GATE BECOME WANDERING SPIRITS, ISN'T THAT SO?
SO I TURNED THAT IDEA AROUND AND BET THAT IF I COULD GET BACK OUTSIDE OF THE GATE, MY SOUL WOULD SURVIVE.
AND I BROUGHT OLDER BROTHER WITH ME.
BUT BECAUSE HE WAS ALREADY TOO DEEP INTO THE TUNNEL, A LOT OF HIS SOUL GOT PULLED INTO THE LIGHT. HE RETURNED TO THIS WORLD WITH AN INCOMPLETE FORM.
YOU SEE ME NOW IN MY FULL APPEARANCE BUT...
WHAT YOU SEE IS JUST MY SOUL, NOT MY BODY.
I UNDERSTAND.
BUT HAT'S THIS AVOR?

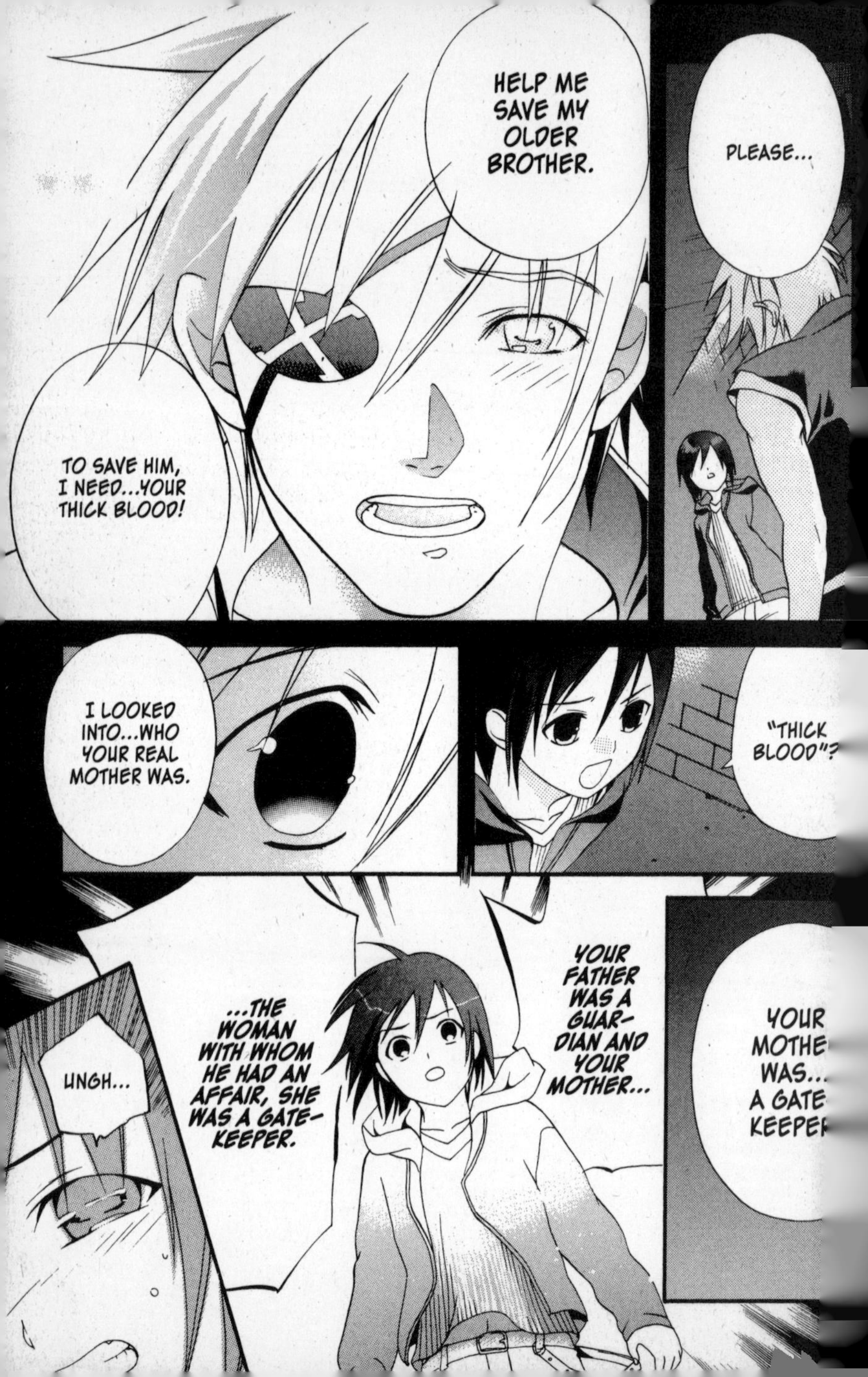
PLEASE...
HELP ME SAVE MY OLDER BROTHER.
TO SAVE HIM, I NEED...YOUR THICK BLOOD!
"THICK BLOOD"?
I LOOKED INTO...WHO YOUR REAL MOTHER WAS.
YOUR MOTHE WAS... A GATE KEEPER
YOUR FATHER WAS A GUARDIAN AND YOUR MOTHER...
...THE WOMAN WITH WHOM HE HAD AN AFFAIR, SHE WAS A GATEKEEPER.
UNGH...

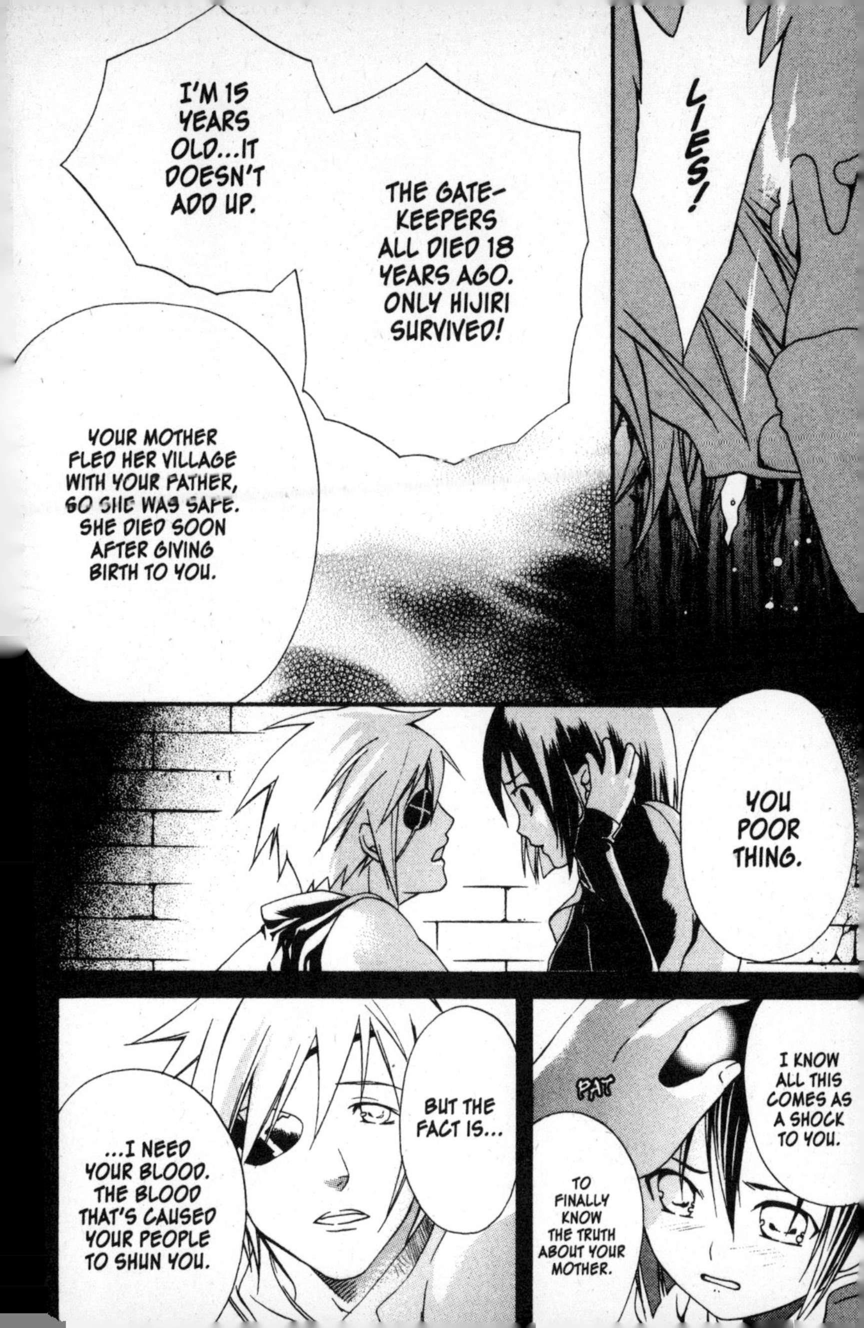
LIES!
THE GATE-KEEPERS ALL DIED 18 YEARS AGO. ONLY HIJIRI SURVIVED!
I'M 15 YEARS OLD...IT DOESN'T ADD UP.
YOUR MOTHER FLED HER VILLAGE WITH YOUR FATHER, SO SHE WAS SAFE. SHE DIED SOON AFTER GIVING BIRTH TO YOU.
YOU POOR THING.
I KNOW ALL THIS COMES AS A SHOCK TO YOU.
PAT
TO FINALLY KNOW THE TRUTH ABOUT YOUR MOTHER.
BUT THE FACT IS...
...I NEED YOUR BLOOD. THE BLOOD THAT'S CAUSED YOUR PEOPLE TO SHUN YOU.

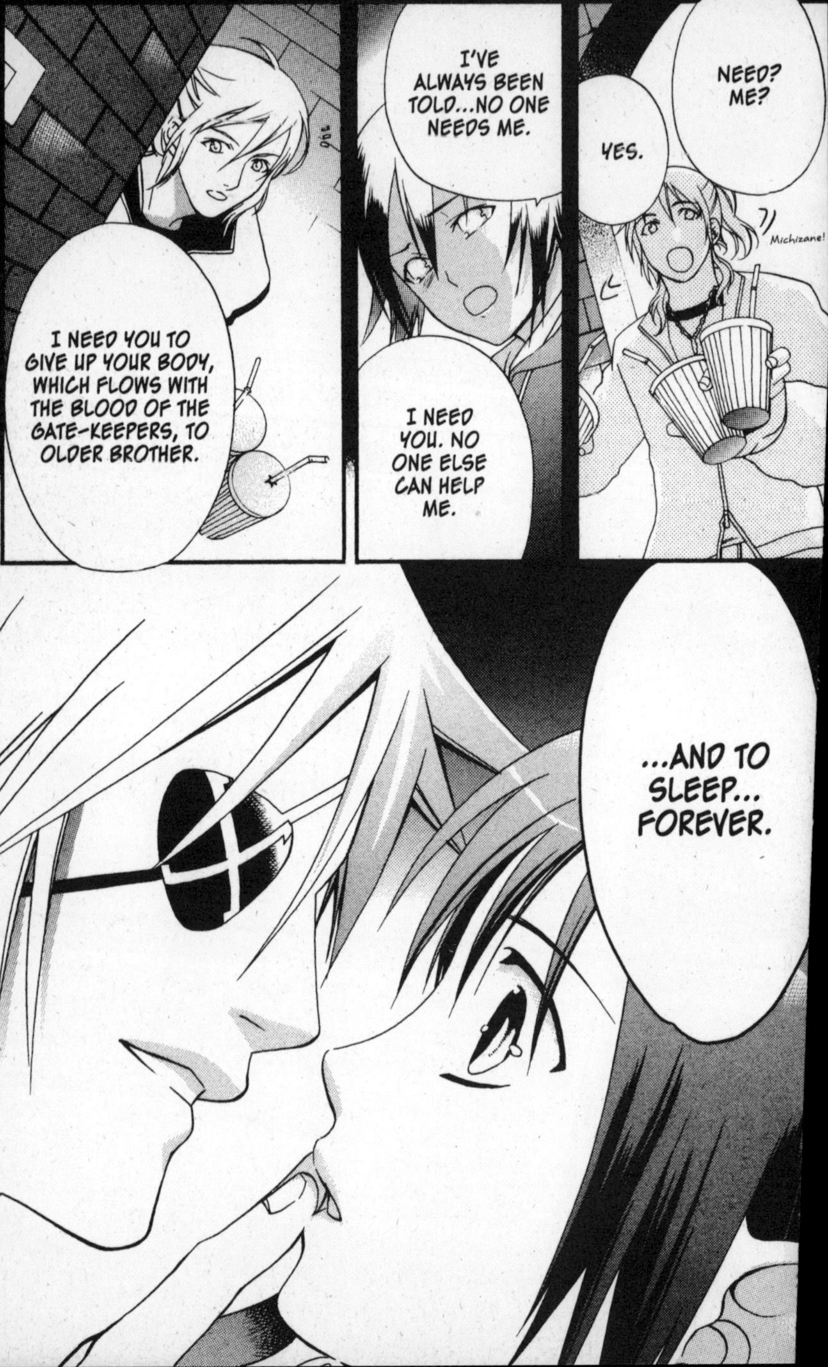
NEED? ME?
YES.
Michizane!
I'VE ALWAYS BEEN TOLD...NO ONE NEEDS ME.
I NEED YOU. NO ONE ELSE CAN HELP ME.
I NEED YOU TO GIVE UP YOUR BODY, WHICH FLOWS WITH THE BLOOD OF THE GATE-KEEPERS, TO OLDER BROTHER.
...AND TO SLEEP... FOREVER.

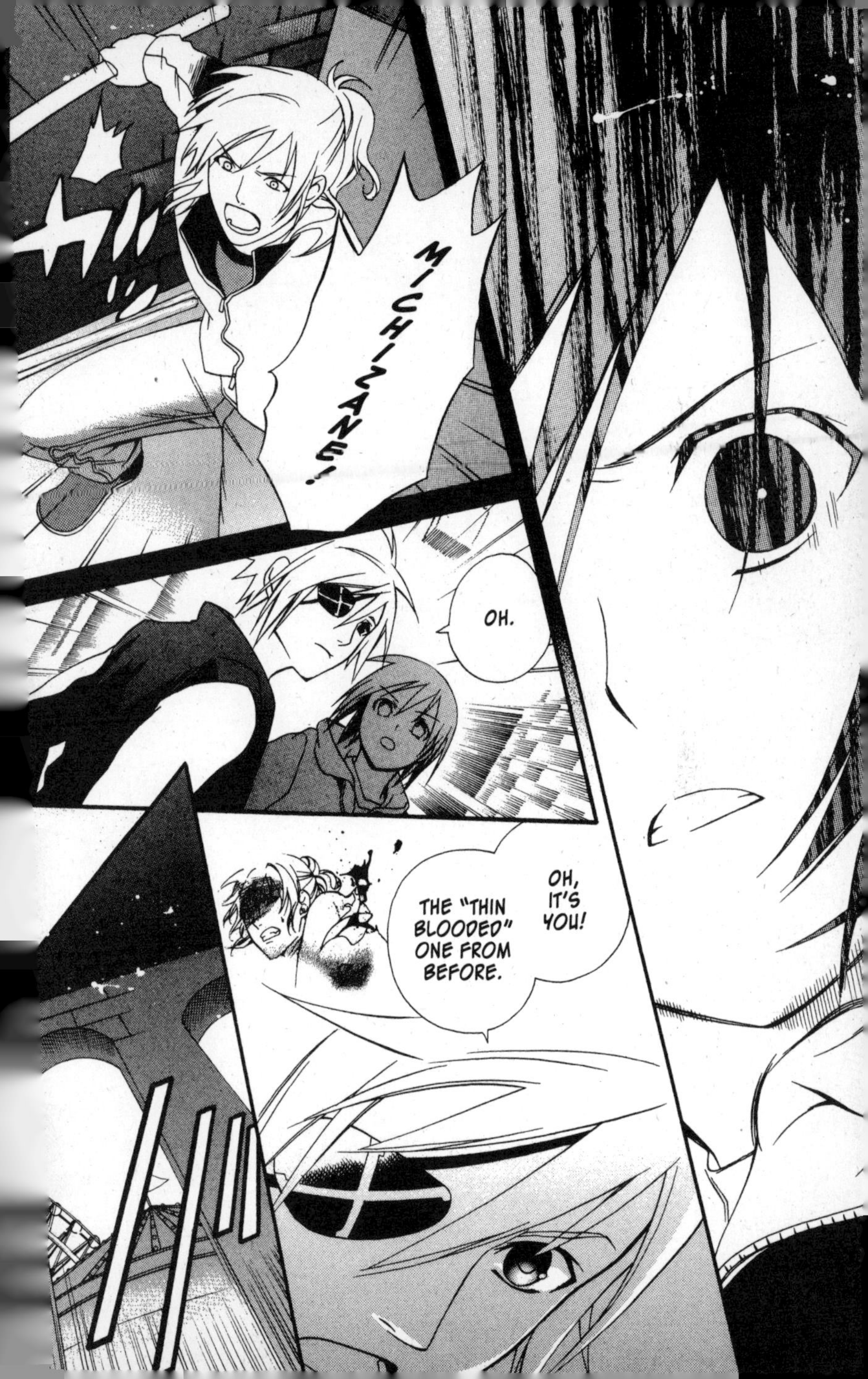
MICHIZANE!
OH.
OH, IT'S YOU!
THE "THIN BLOODED" ONE FROM BEFORE.

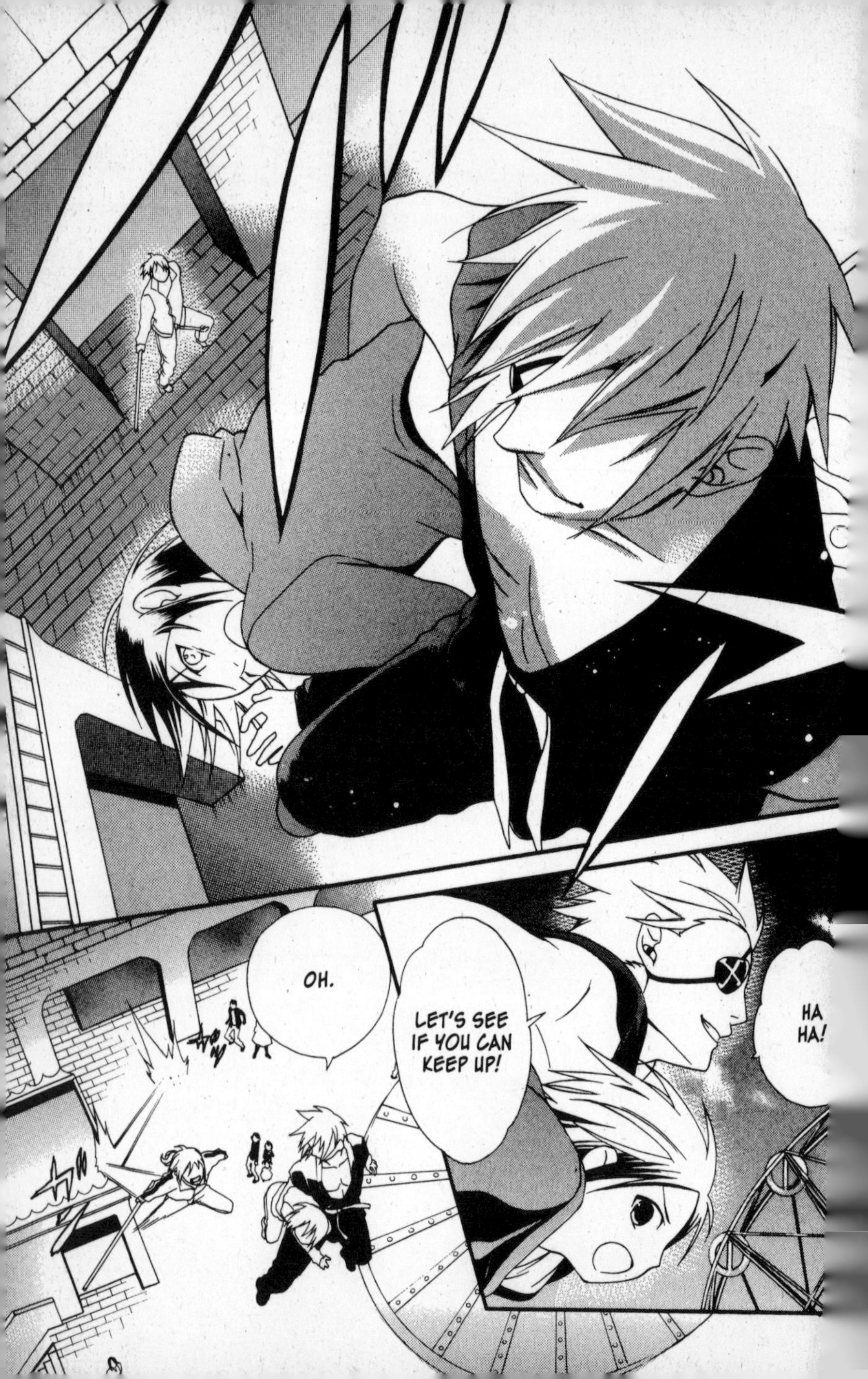
HA HA!
LET'S SEE IF YOU CAN KEEP UP!
OH.

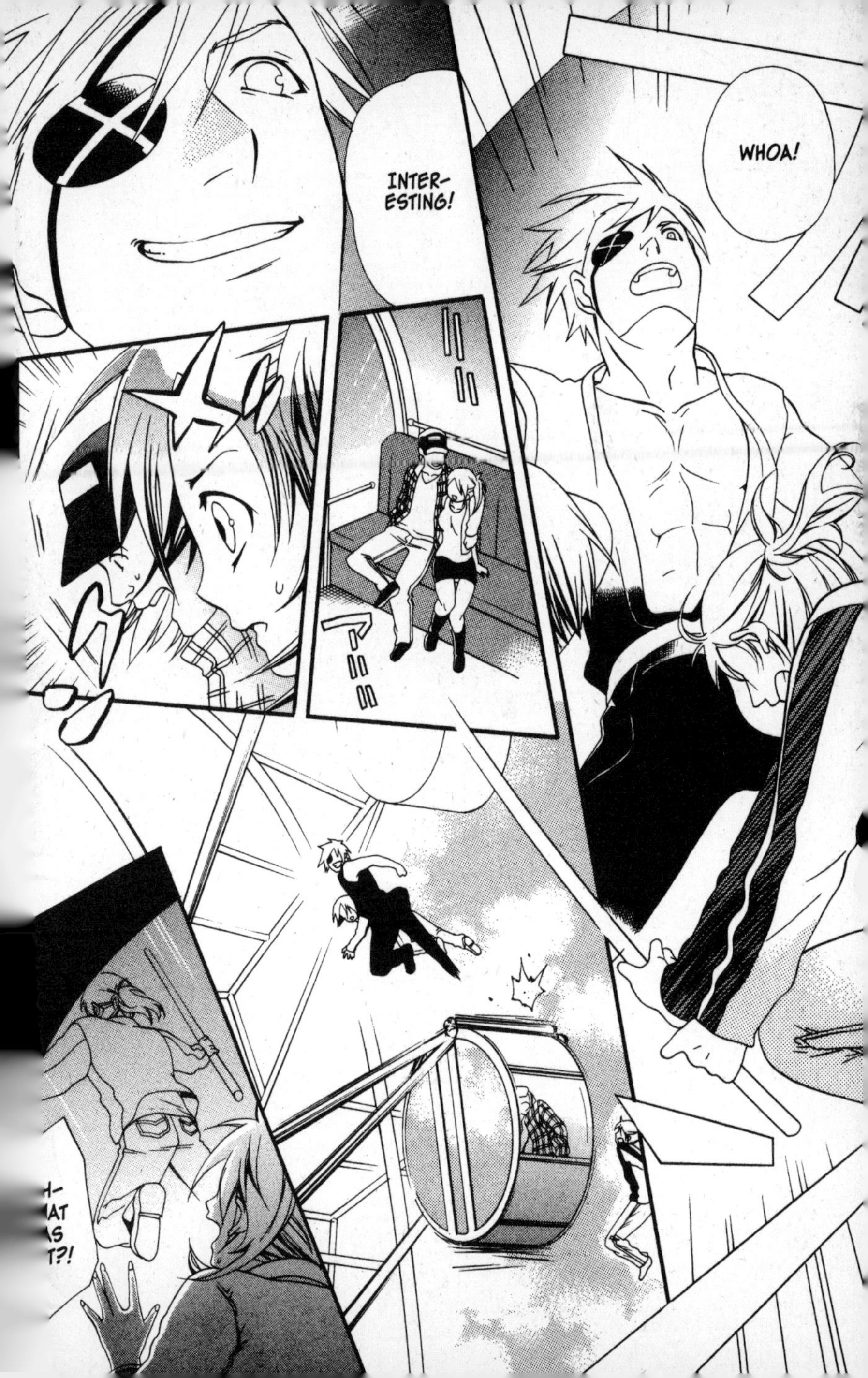
WHOA!
INTER-ESTING!
H- AT S T?!

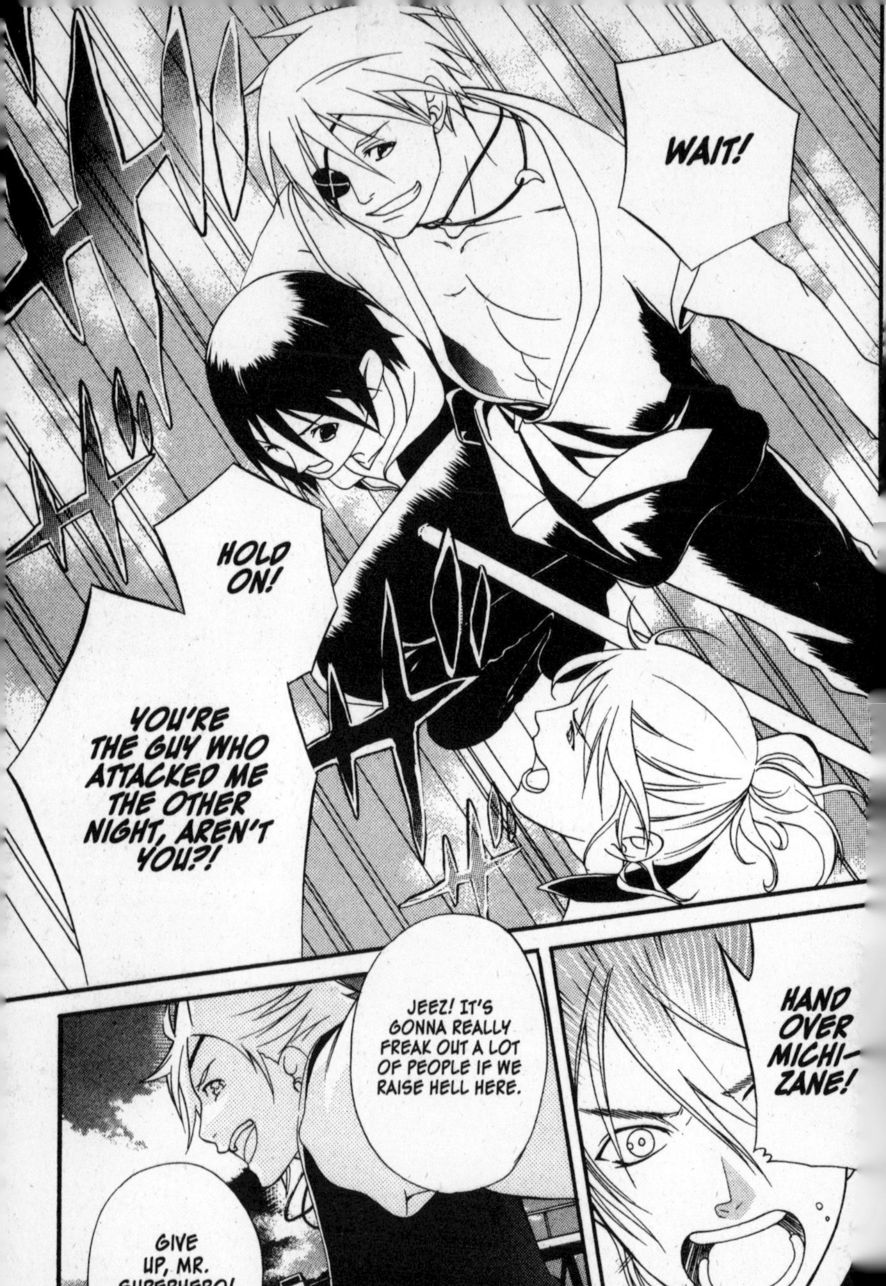
WAIT!
HOLD ON!
YOU'RE THE GUY WHO ATTACKED ME THE OTHER NIGHT, AREN'T YOU?!
HAND OVER MICHI-ZANE!
JEEZ! IT'S GONNA REALLY FREAK OUT A LOT OF PEOPLE IF WE RAISE HELL HERE.
GIVE UP, MR. SUPERHERO!

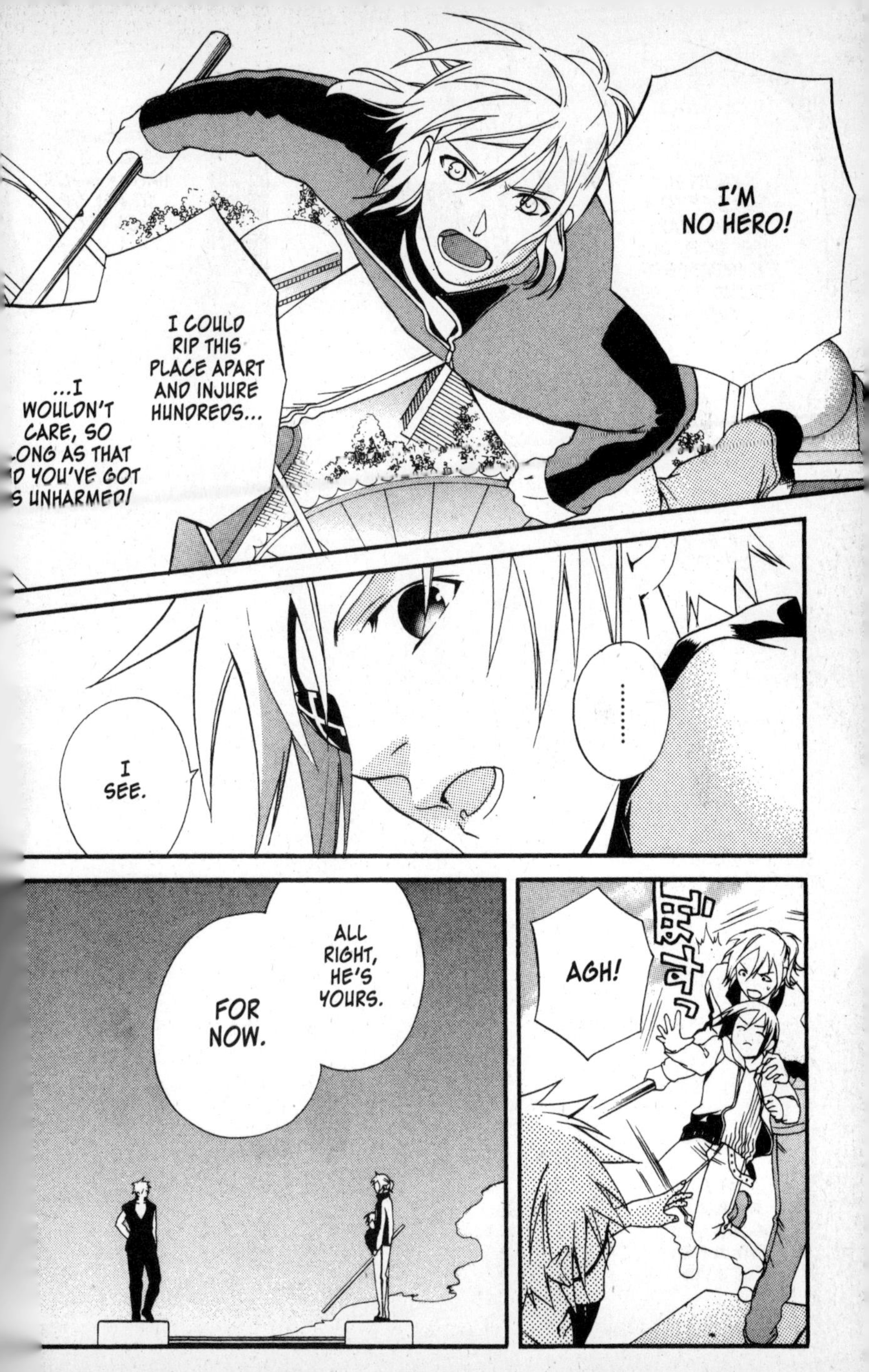
I'M NO HERO!
I COULD RIP THIS PLACE APART AND INJURE HUNDREDS...
...I WOULDN'T CARE, SO
ONG AS THAT
D YOU'VE GOT
S UNHARMED!
......
I SEE.
AGH!
ALL RIGHT, HE'S YOURS.
FOR NOW.

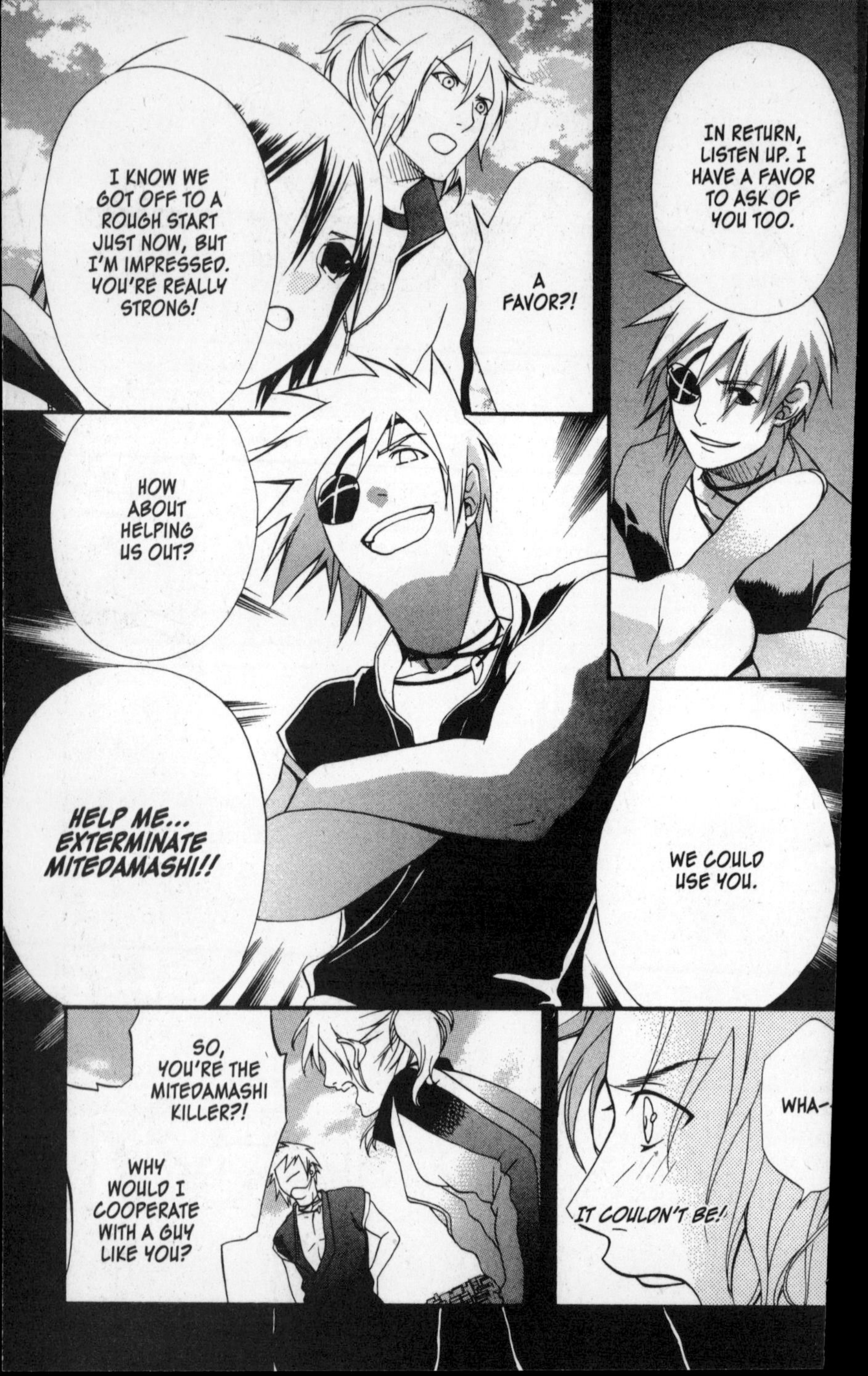
I KNOW WE GOT OFF TO A ROUGH START JUST NOW, BUT I'M IMPRESSED. YOU'RE REALLY STRONG!
IN RETURN, LISTEN UP. I HAVE A FAVOR TO ASK OF YOU TOO.
A FAVOR?!
HOW ABOUT HELPING US OUT?
HELP ME... EXTERMINATE MITEDAMASHI!!
WE COULD USE YOU.
WHA-
IT COULDN'T BE!
SO, YOU'RE THE MITEDAMASHI KILLER?!
WHY WOULD I COOPERATE WITH A GUY LIKE YOU?

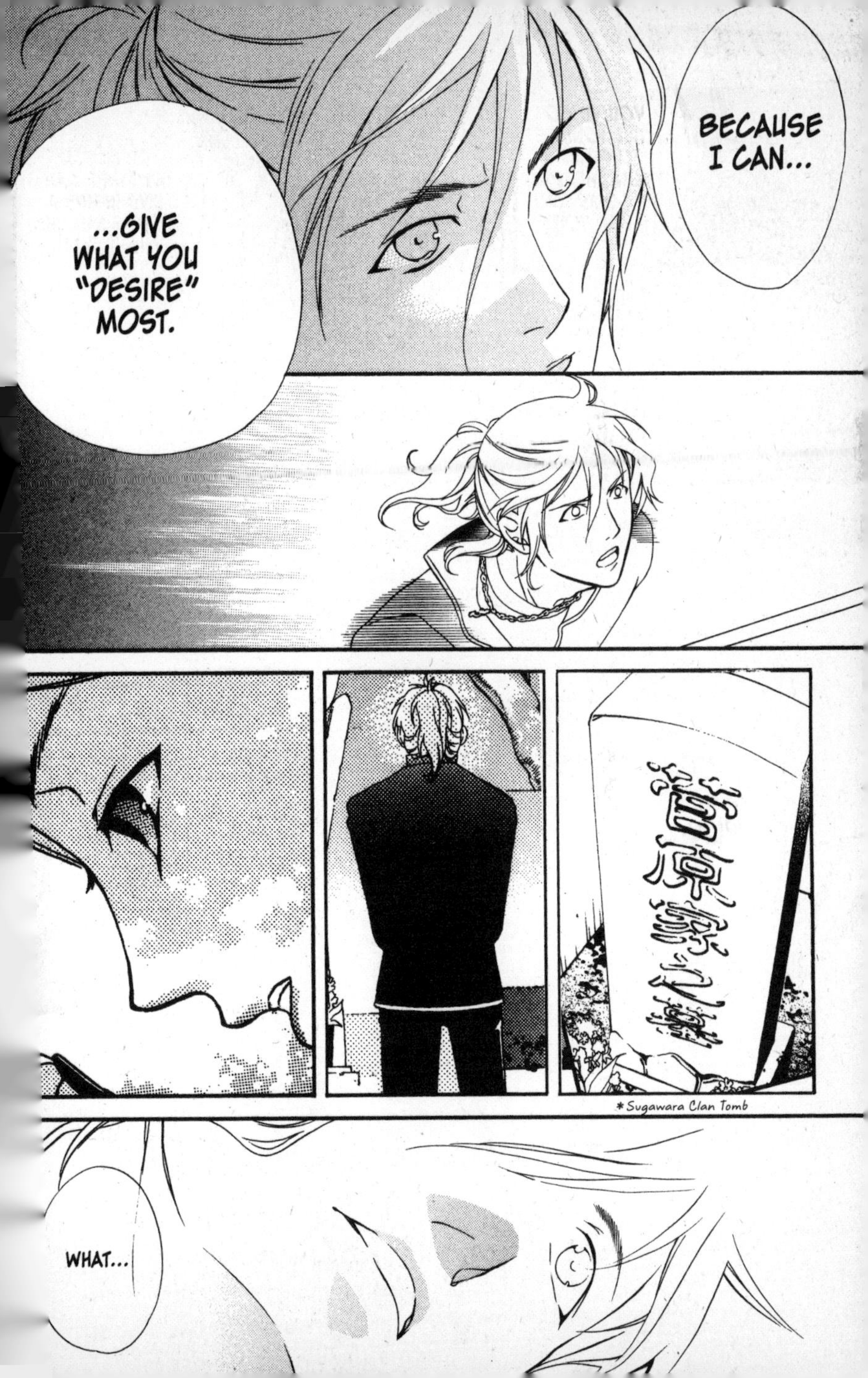
BECAUSE I CAN...
...GIVE WHAT YOU "DESIRE" MOST.
菅原家之墓
*Sugawara Clan Tomb
WHAT...

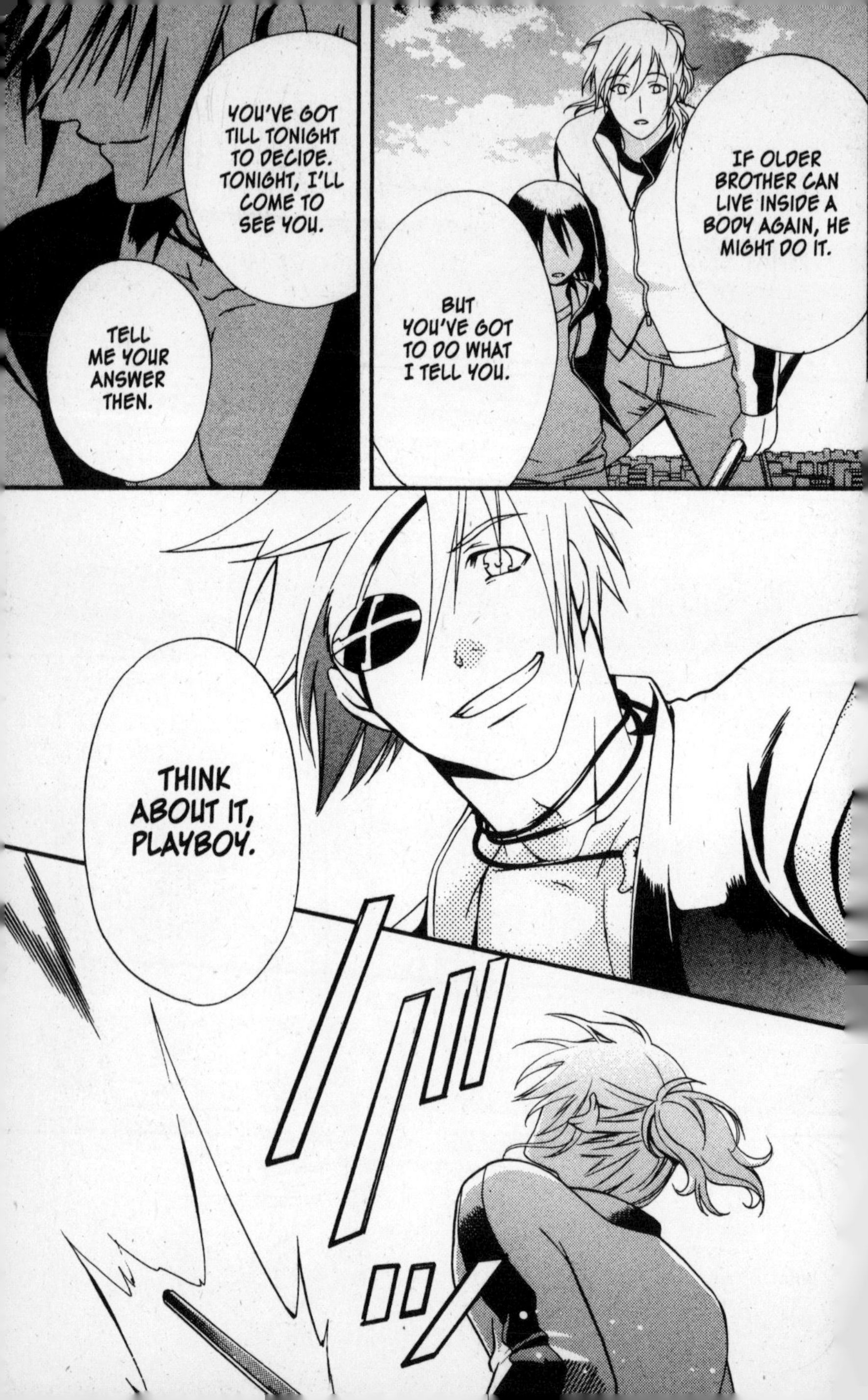
IF OLDER BROTHER CAN LIVE INSIDE A BODY AGAIN, HE MIGHT DO IT.
BUT YOU'VE GOT TO DO WHAT I TELL YOU.
YOU'VE GOT TILL TONIGHT TO DECIDE. TONIGHT, I'LL COME TO SEE YOU.
TELL ME YOUR ANSWER THEN.
THINK ABOUT IT, PLAYBOY.

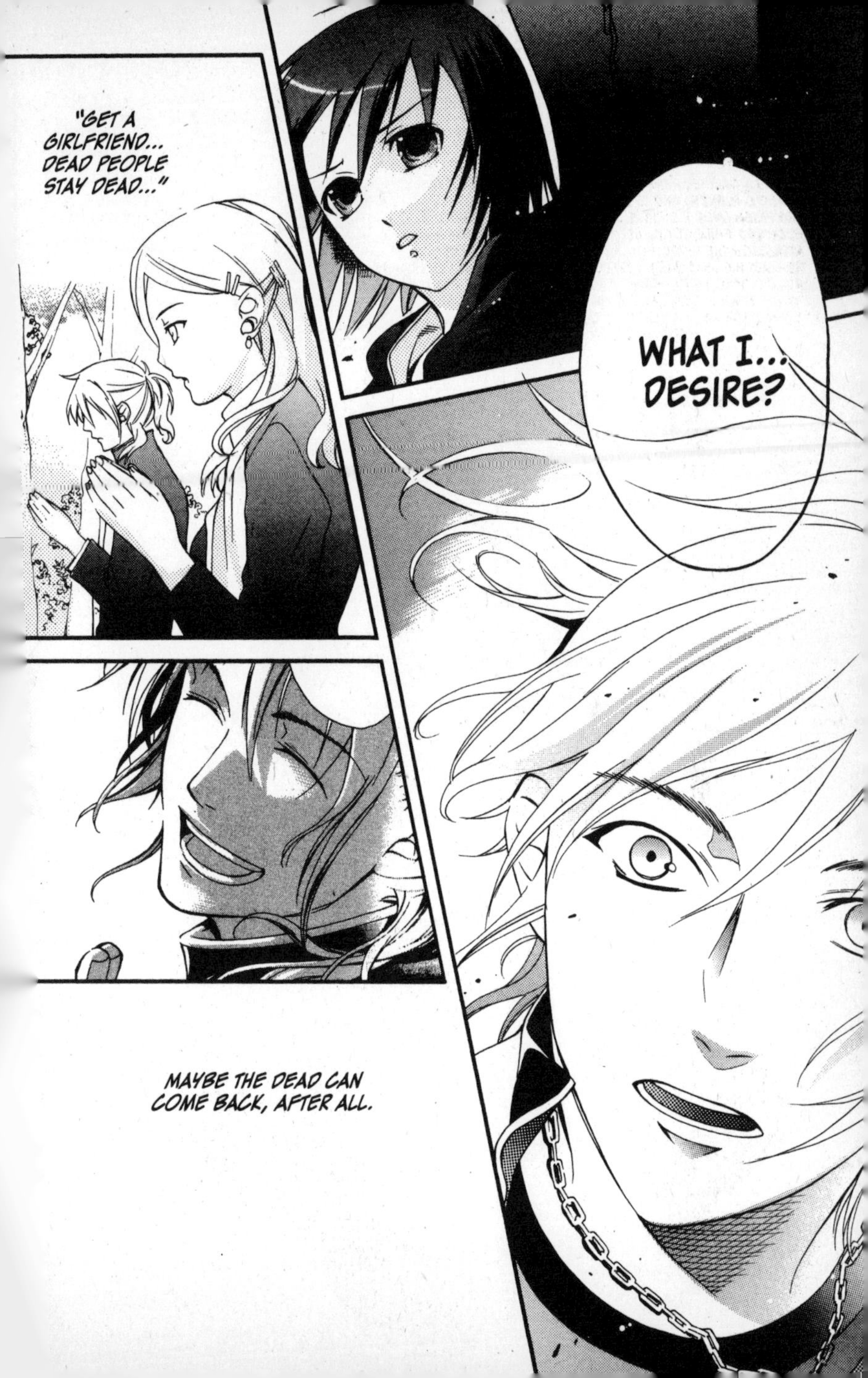
WHAT I... DESIRE?
"GET A GIRLFRIEND... DEAD PEOPLE STAY DEAD..."
MAYBE THE DEAD CAN COME BACK, AFTER ALL.

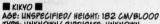

■ KIKYO ■
AGE: UNSPECIFIED/ HEIGHT: 182 CM/BLOOD
TYPE: UNKNOWN/ BIRTHDATE: UNKNOWN

HE HAS A CARING, FRIENDLY, BROTHERLY PERSONALITY,
LOVES CHILDREN, AND IS LIKED BY EVERYONE.
THE PATCH OVER HIS RIGHT EYE COVERS A WOUND HE
RECEIVED WHILE TRYING TO PROTECT CHILDREN DURING AN
ATTACK ON THE HIDDEN VILLAGE OF THE GATE-KEEPERS.
HE LOST HIS LIFE DURING THE SECOND ASSAULT ON THE VILLAGE,
BUT HIS SOUL MANAGED TO ESCAPE BACK OUT THE GATE. HE NOW
EXISTS ONLY IN SOUL FORM. HE CAN NOW SEE OUT OF BOTH
EYES SINCE HE'S NO LONGER LIMITED BY HIS BODILY INJURIES.
CURRENTLY, HE'S ON A MISSION TO HUNT DOWN AND
KILL MITEDAMASHI IN REVENGE FOR THE MURDER
OF HIS MUCH ADORED OLDER BROTHER.
HIS FAVORITE ACTIVITY IS ACTIVITY ITSELF.
HE'S ATHLETIC, AND CRAVES ACTION.

CHARACTER PROFILE:06
KIKYO

CHARACTER PROFILE:07

YOSHITSUNA

■YOSHITSUNA■
AGE: UNSPECIFIED/
HEIGHT: 182 CM/BLOOD
TYPE: UNKNOWN/
BIRTHDATE: UNKNOWN

KIKYO'S BROTHER AND HIJIRI'S FATHER.
AS "LEADER" OF THE GATE-KEEPERS, HIS GENTLE AND QUIET PERSONALITY EARNED HIM TRUST AND RESPECT. HE CAN BE ABSENT-MINDED AT TIMES, HE CRIES OFTEN, AND HE'S OFTEN GIVEN TO KLUTZY ACCIDENTS LIKE HIS WIFE, KUZUNOHA. HOWEVER, HE HAS A STRONG MIND, AND ONCE HE'S SET HIS MIND TO SOMETHING, HIS STUBBORNNESS IS OFTEN UNSHAKEABLE. WHEN THE GATE-KEEPERS' VILLAGE WAS ATTACKED, HE LOST HIS LIFE IN THE BATTLE. A PART OF HIS SOUL WAS LOST TO FORCES WITHIN THE GATE, BUT THE REST OF IT WAS RECOVERED BY KIKYO, AND YOSHITSUNA RETURNED TO THIS WORLD IN AN INCOMPLETE FORM. UNLIKE KIKYO, HE ISN'T QUICK AND NIMBLE. THAT PHYSICAL TRAIT REFLECTS HIS OWN RIGID PERSONALITY, WHICH TENDS TOWARD EXTREME ACTIONS, EVEN VIOLENCE. THE CONSEQUENCES OF THAT TENDENCY LED TO THE TRAGIC INCIDENT AT THE GATE-KEEPERS' VILLAGE.

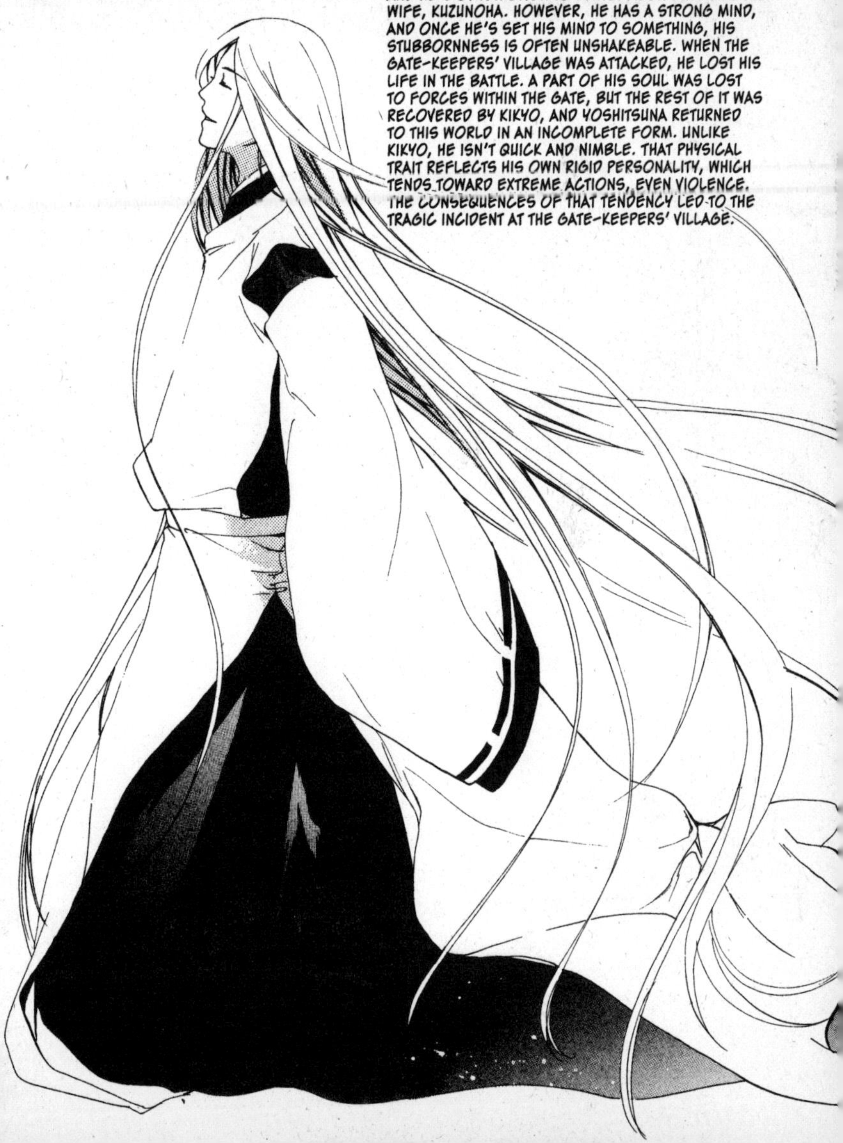

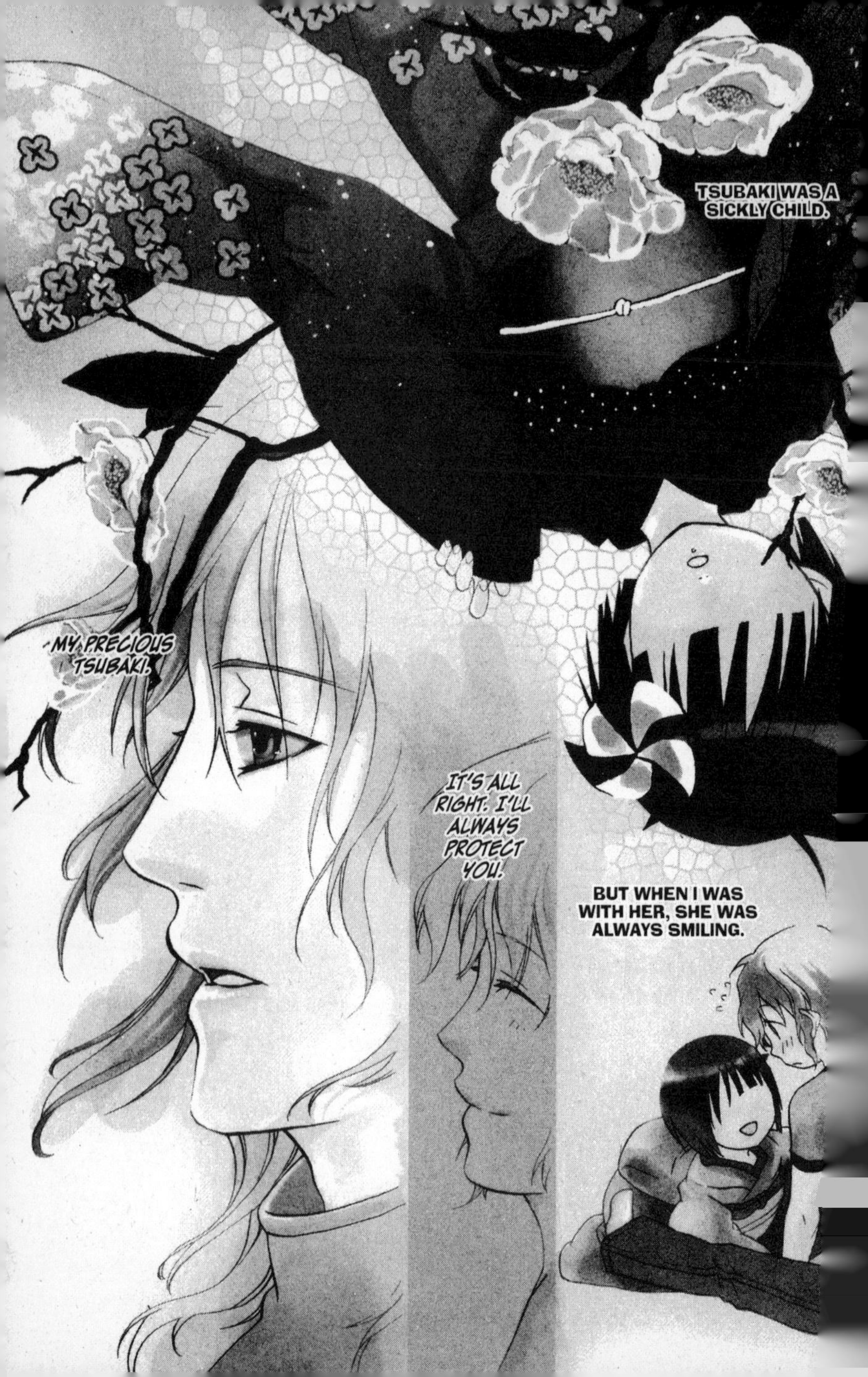
TSUBAKI WAS A SICKLY CHILD.
BUT WHEN I WAS WITH HER, SHE WAS ALWAYS SMILING.
IT'S ALL RIGHT. I'LL ALWAYS PROTECT YOU.
MY PRECIOUS TSUBAKI.

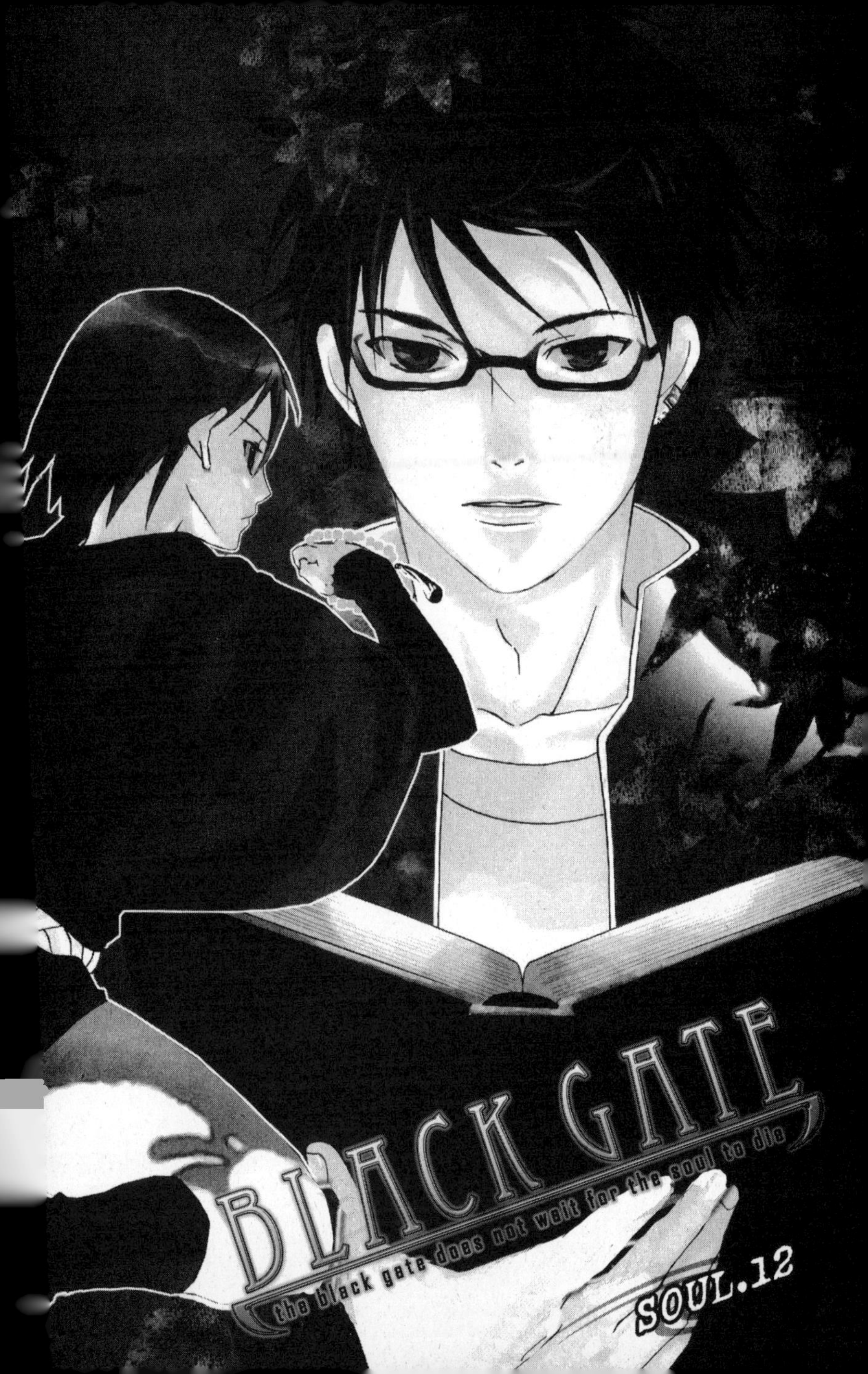
BLACK GATE
the black gate does not wait for the soul to die
SOUL.12

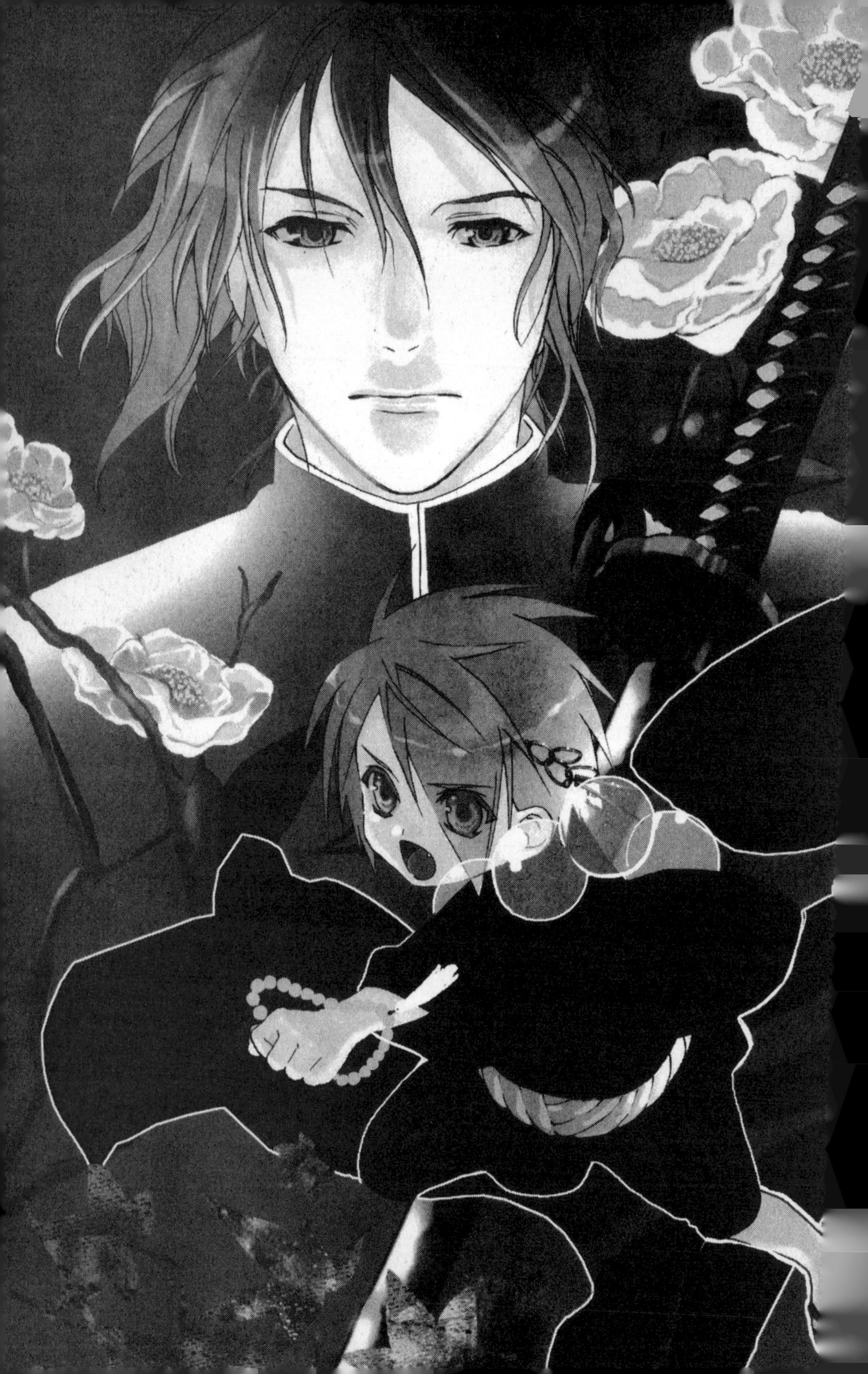

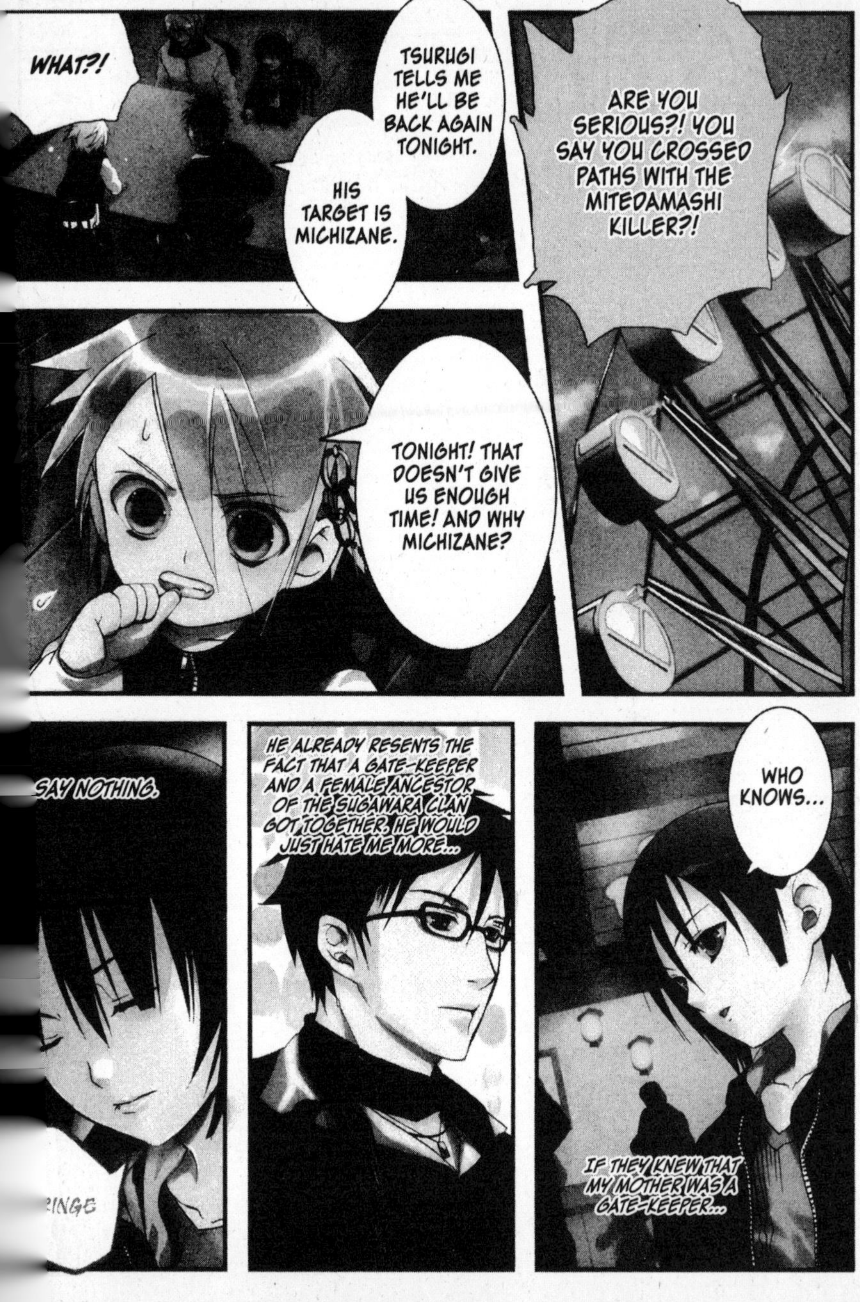
ARE YOU SERIOUS?! YOU SAY YOU CROSSED PATHS WITH THE MITEDAMASHI KILLER?!
TSURUGI TELLS ME HE'LL BE BACK AGAIN TONIGHT.
HIS TARGET IS MICHIZANE.
WHAT?!
TONIGHT! THAT DOESN'T GIVE US ENOUGH TIME! AND WHY MICHIZANE?
WHO KNOWS...
IF THEY KNEW THAT MY MOTHER WAS A GATE-KEEPER...
HE ALREADY RESENTS THE FACT THAT A GATE-KEEPER AND A FEMALE ANCESTOR OF THE SUGAWARA CLAN GOT TOGETHER. HE WOULD JUST HATE ME MORE...
SAY NOTHING.
RINGE

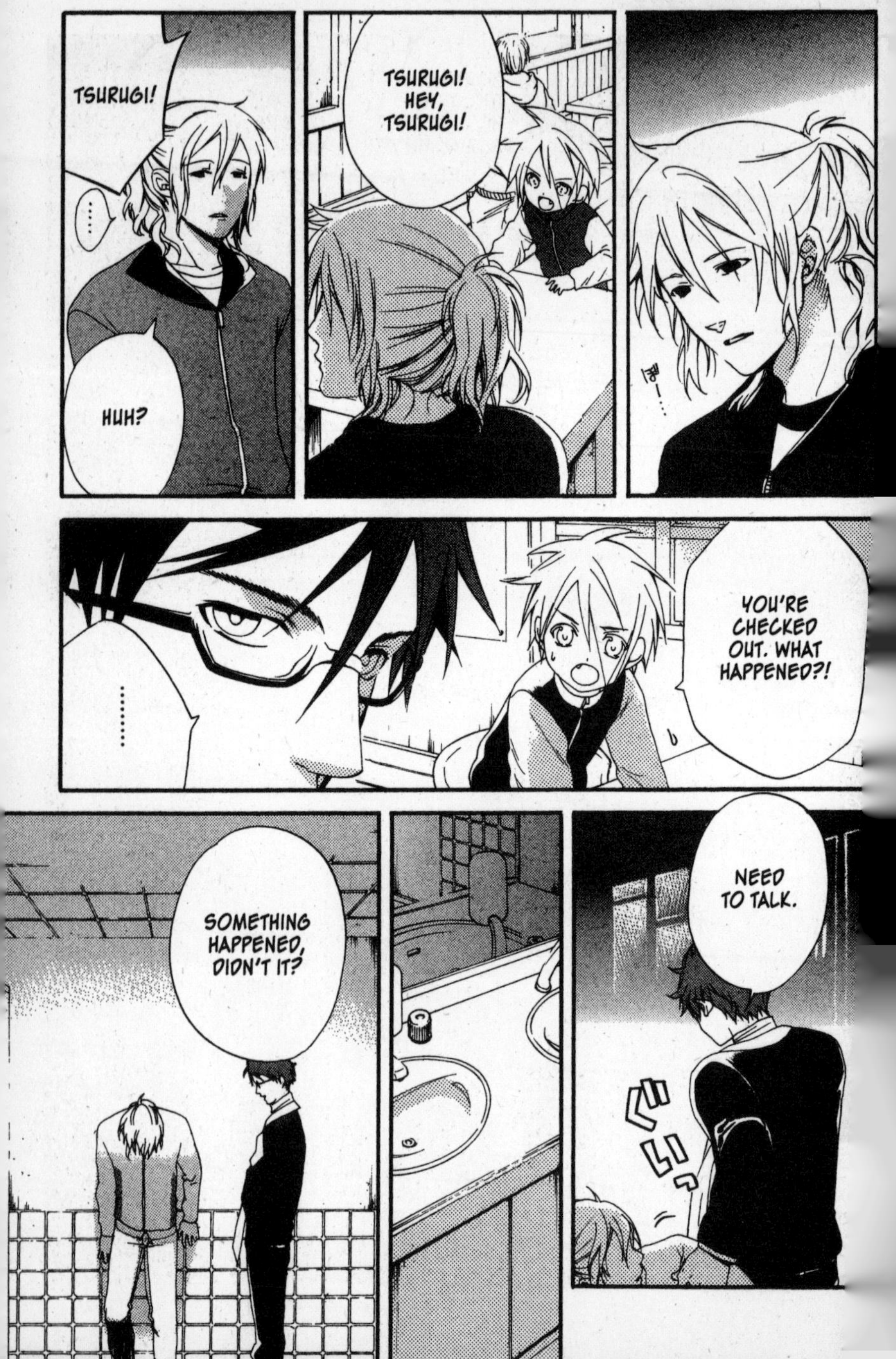
ぼー…
TSURUGI! HEY, TSURUGI!
TSURUGI!
……
HUH?
YOU'RE CHECKED OUT. WHAT HAPPENED?!
……
NEED TO TALK.
ぐいっ
SOMETHING HAPPENED, DIDN'T IT?

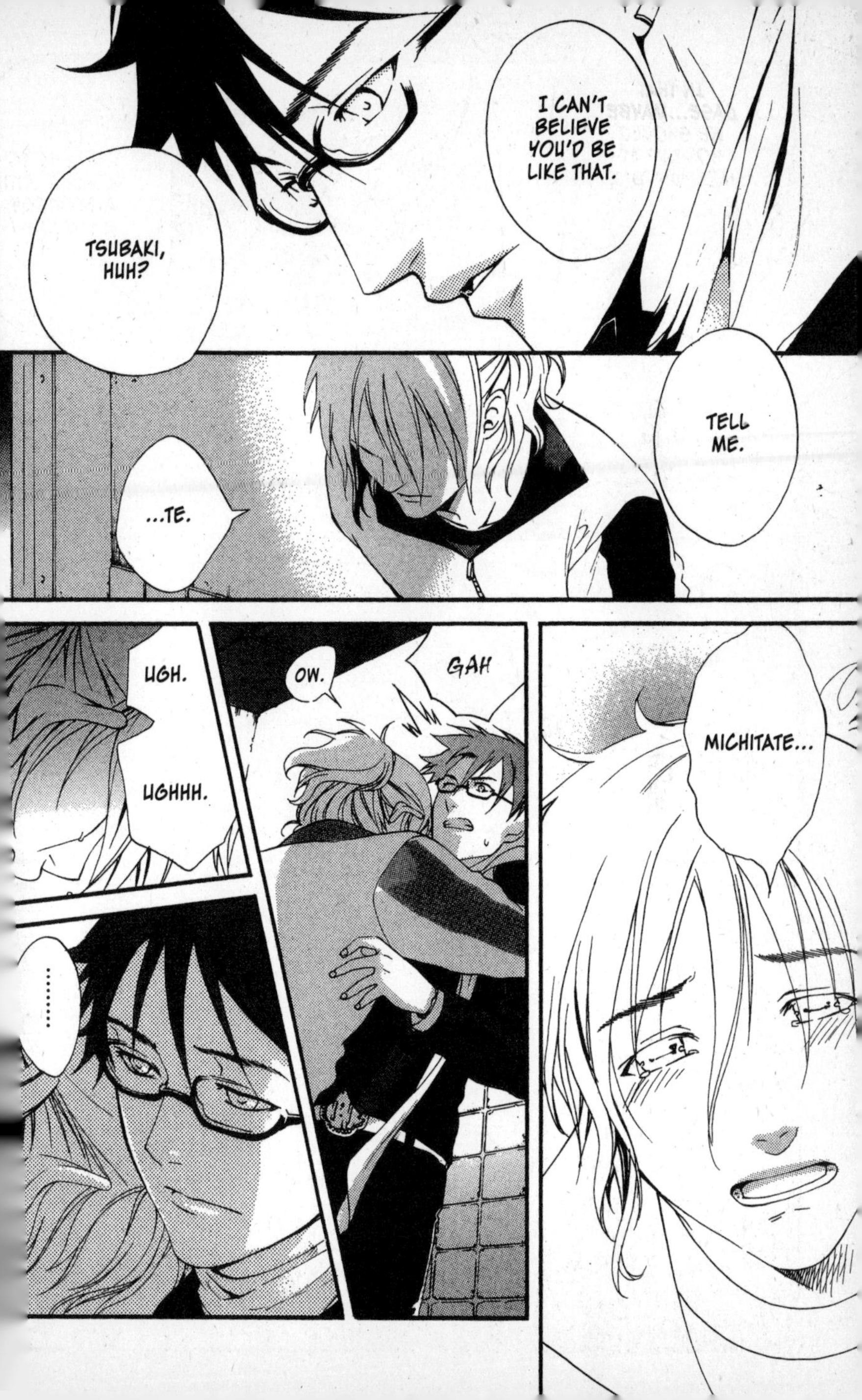
I CAN'T BELIEVE YOU'D BE LIKE THAT.
TSUBAKI, HUH?
TELL ME.
...TE.
MICHITATE...
GAH
OW.
UGH.
UGHHH.
....

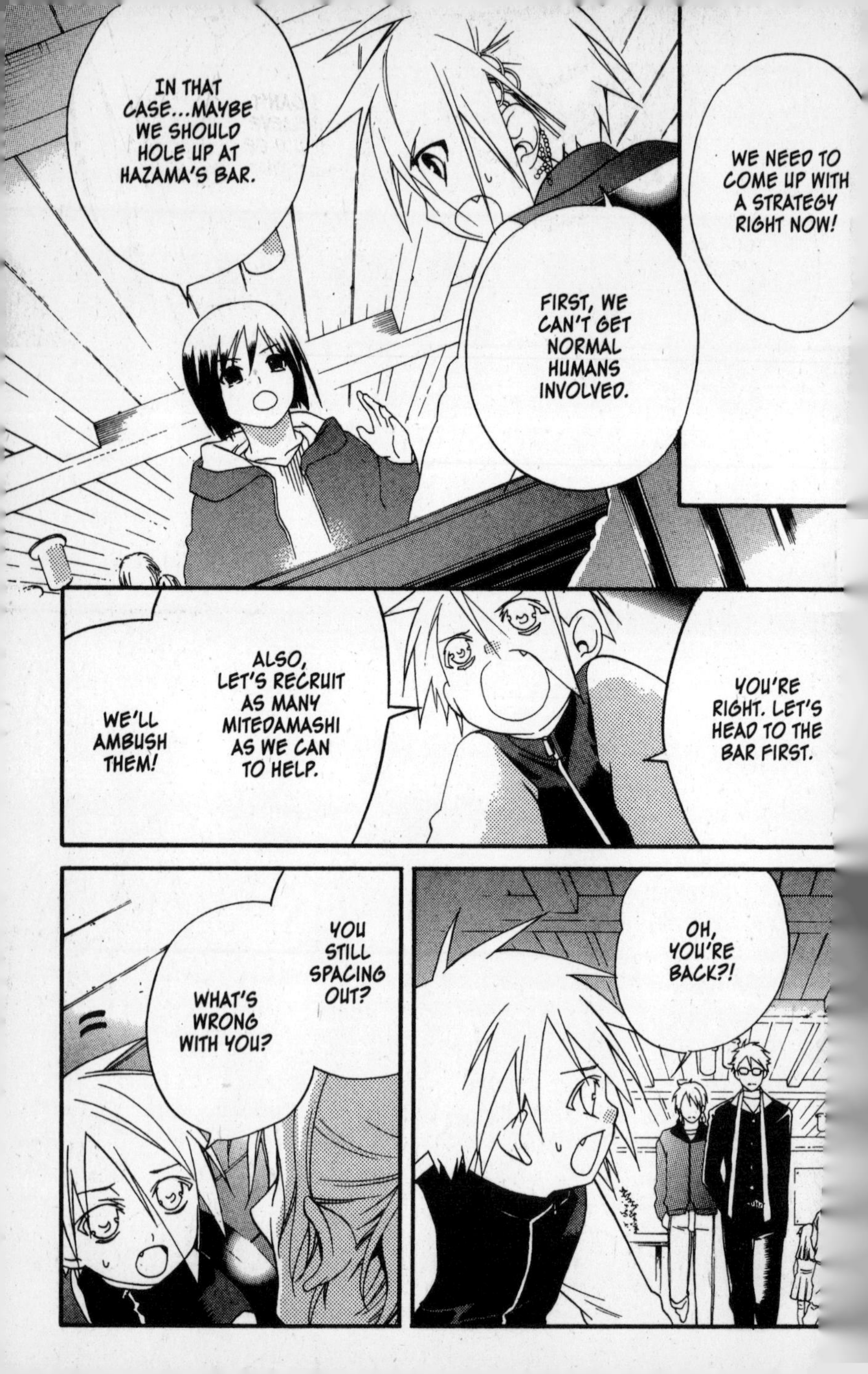
WE NEED TO COME UP WITH A STRATEGY RIGHT NOW!
FIRST, WE CAN'T GET NORMAL HUMANS INVOLVED.
IN THAT CASE...MAYBE WE SHOULD HOLE UP AT HAZAMA'S BAR.
YOU'RE RIGHT. LET'S HEAD TO THE BAR FIRST.
ALSO, LET'S RECRUIT AS MANY MITEDAMASHI AS WE CAN TO HELP.
WE'LL AMBUSH THEM!
OH, YOU'RE BACK?!
YOU STILL SPACING OUT?
WHAT'S WRONG WITH YOU?

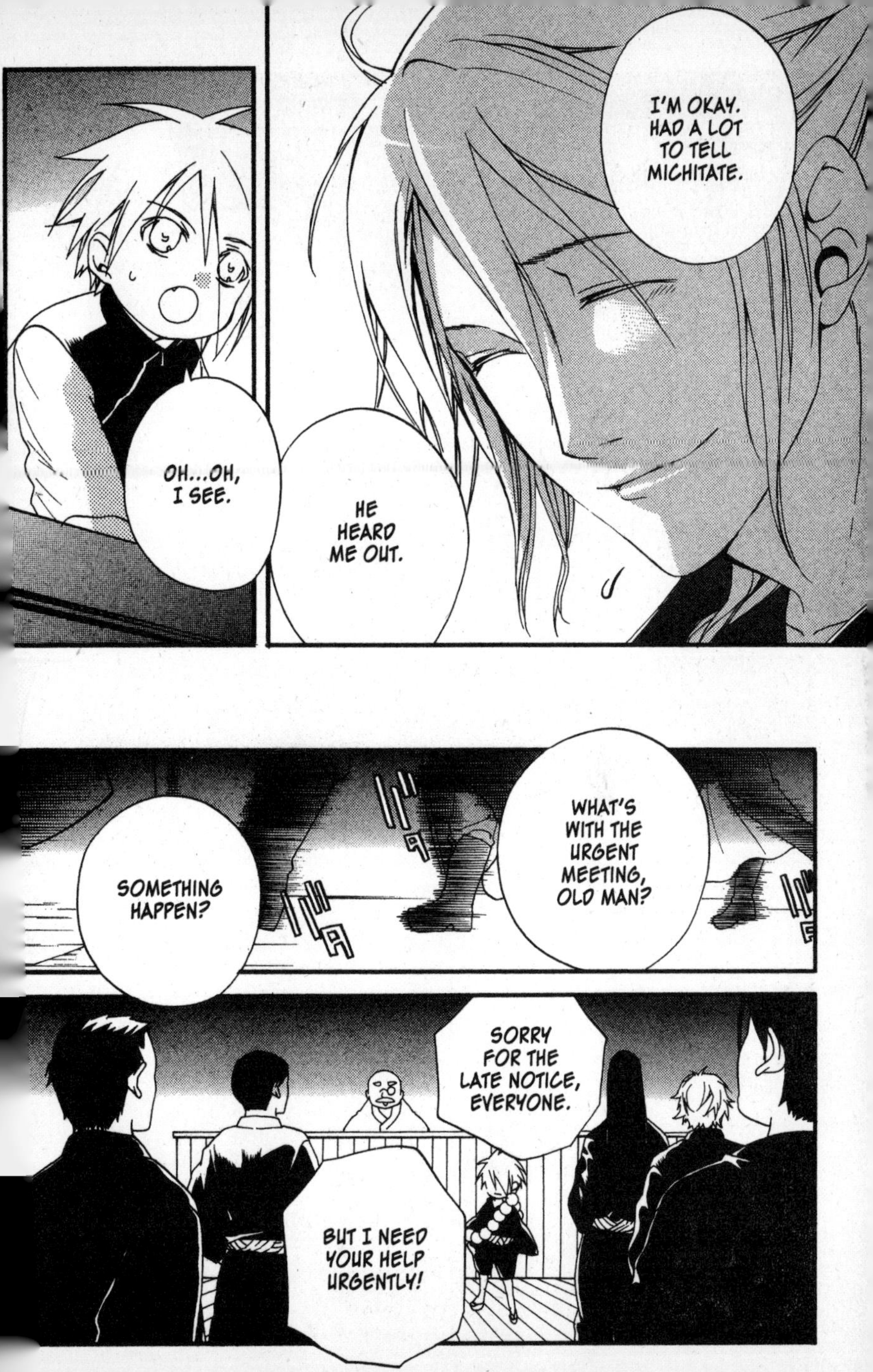
I'M OKAY. HAD A LOT TO TELL MICHITATE.
HE HEARD ME OUT.
OH...OH, I SEE.
WHAT'S WITH THE URGENT MEETING, OLD MAN?
SOMETHING HAPPEN?
SORRY FOR THE LATE NOTICE, EVERYONE.
BUT I NEED YOUR HELP URGENTLY!

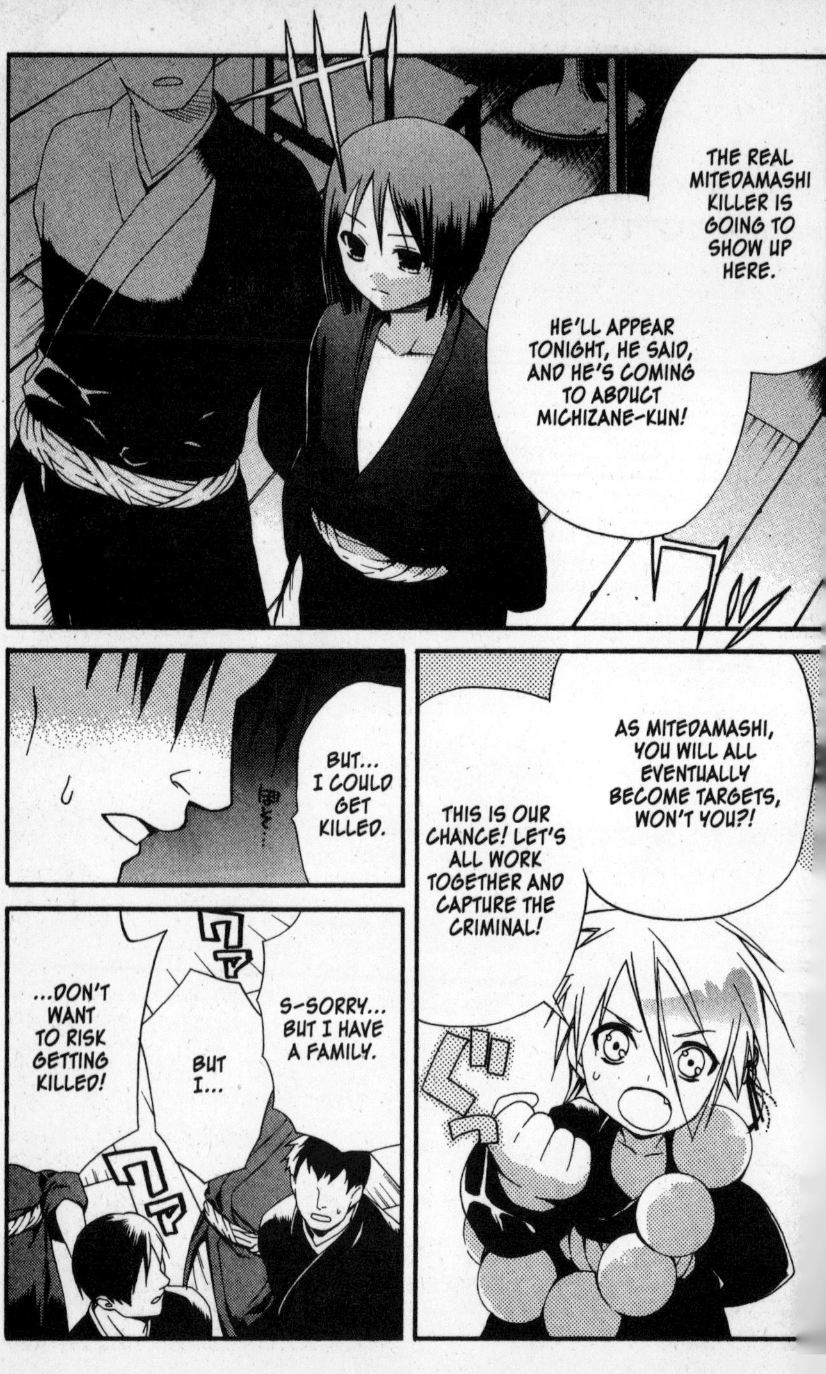
THE REAL MITEDAMASHI KILLER IS GOING TO SHOW UP HERE.
HE'LL APPEAR TONIGHT, HE SAID, AND HE'S COMING TO ABDUCT MICHIZANE-KUN!
AS MITEDAMASHI, YOU WILL ALL EVENTUALLY BECOME TARGETS, WON'T YOU?!
THIS IS OUR CHANCE! LET'S ALL WORK TOGETHER AND CAPTURE THE CRIMINAL!
BUT... I COULD GET KILLED.
S-SORRY... BUT I HAVE A FAMILY.
BUT I...
...DON'T WANT TO RISK GETTING KILLED!

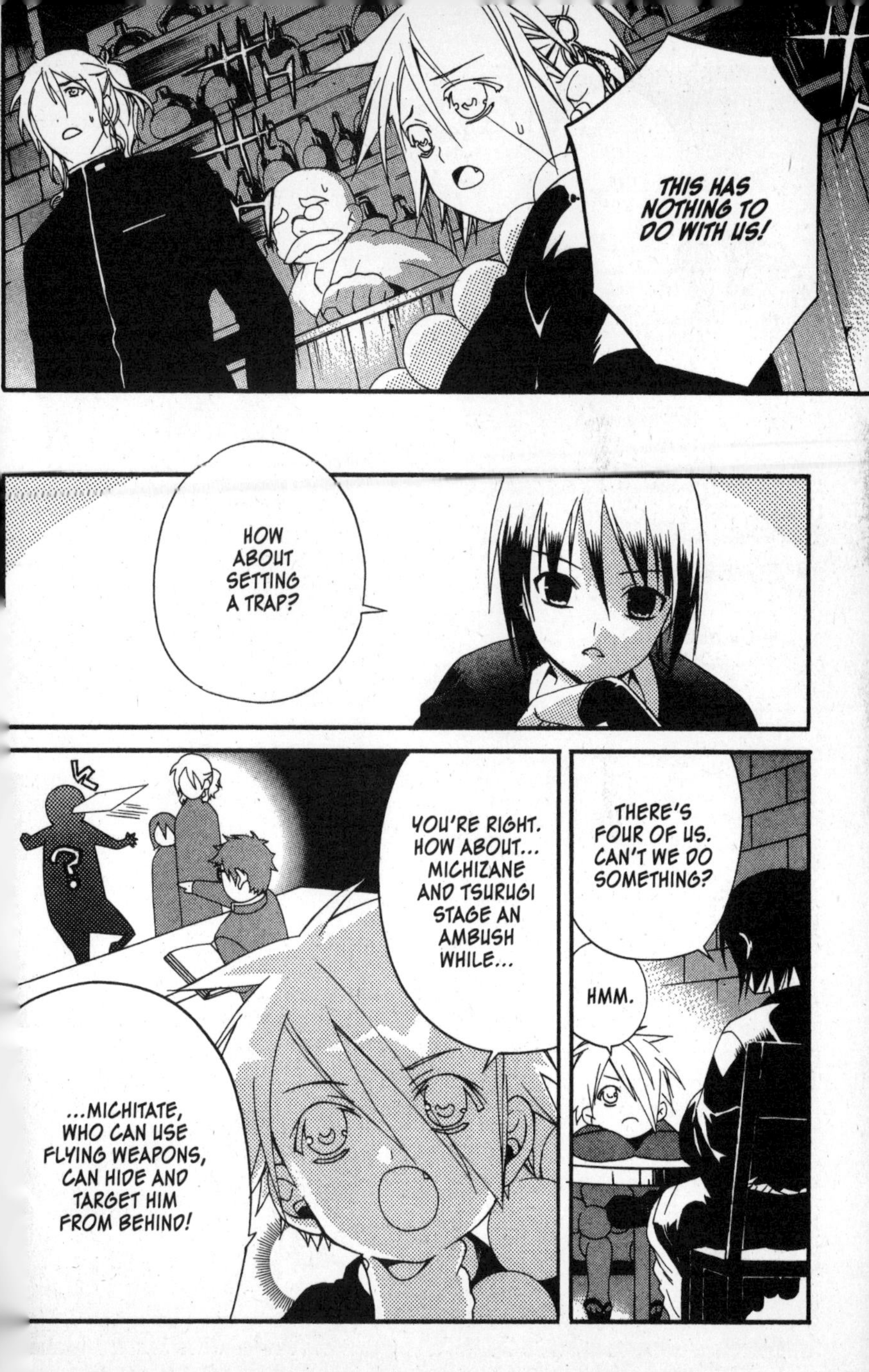
THIS HAS NOTHING TO DO WITH US!
HOW ABOUT SETTING A TRAP?
THERE'S FOUR OF US. CAN'T WE DO SOMETHING?
HMM.
YOU'RE RIGHT. HOW ABOUT... MICHIZANE AND TSURUGI STAGE AN AMBUSH WHILE...
...MICHITATE, WHO CAN USE FLYING WEAPONS, CAN HIDE AND TARGET HIM FROM BEHIND!

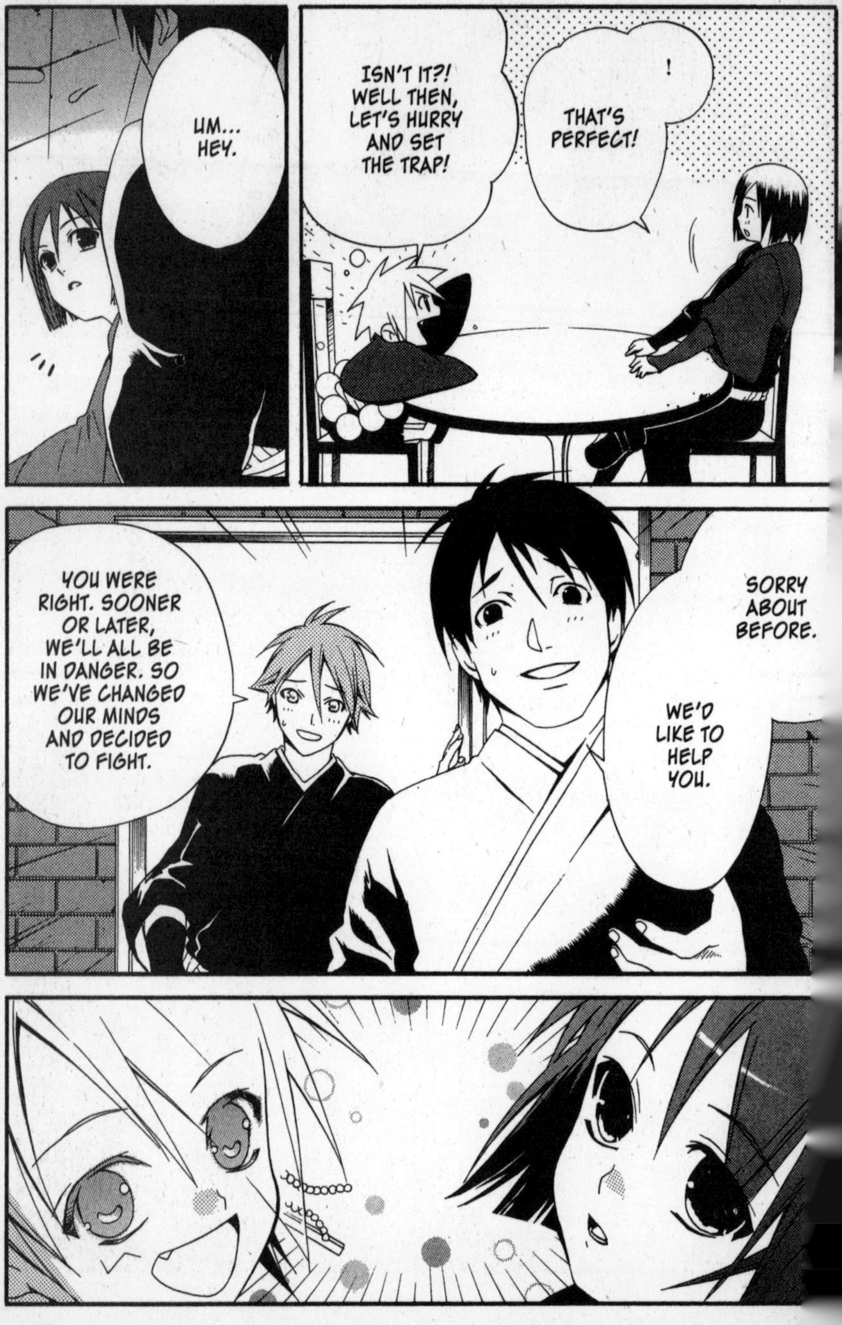
!
THAT'S PERFECT!
ISN'T IT?! WELL THEN, LET'S HURRY AND SET THE TRAP!
UM... HEY.
SORRY ABOUT BEFORE.
WE'D LIKE TO HELP YOU.
YOU WERE RIGHT. SOONER OR LATER, WE'LL ALL BE IN DANGER. SO WE'VE CHANGED OUR MINDS AND DECIDED TO FIGHT.

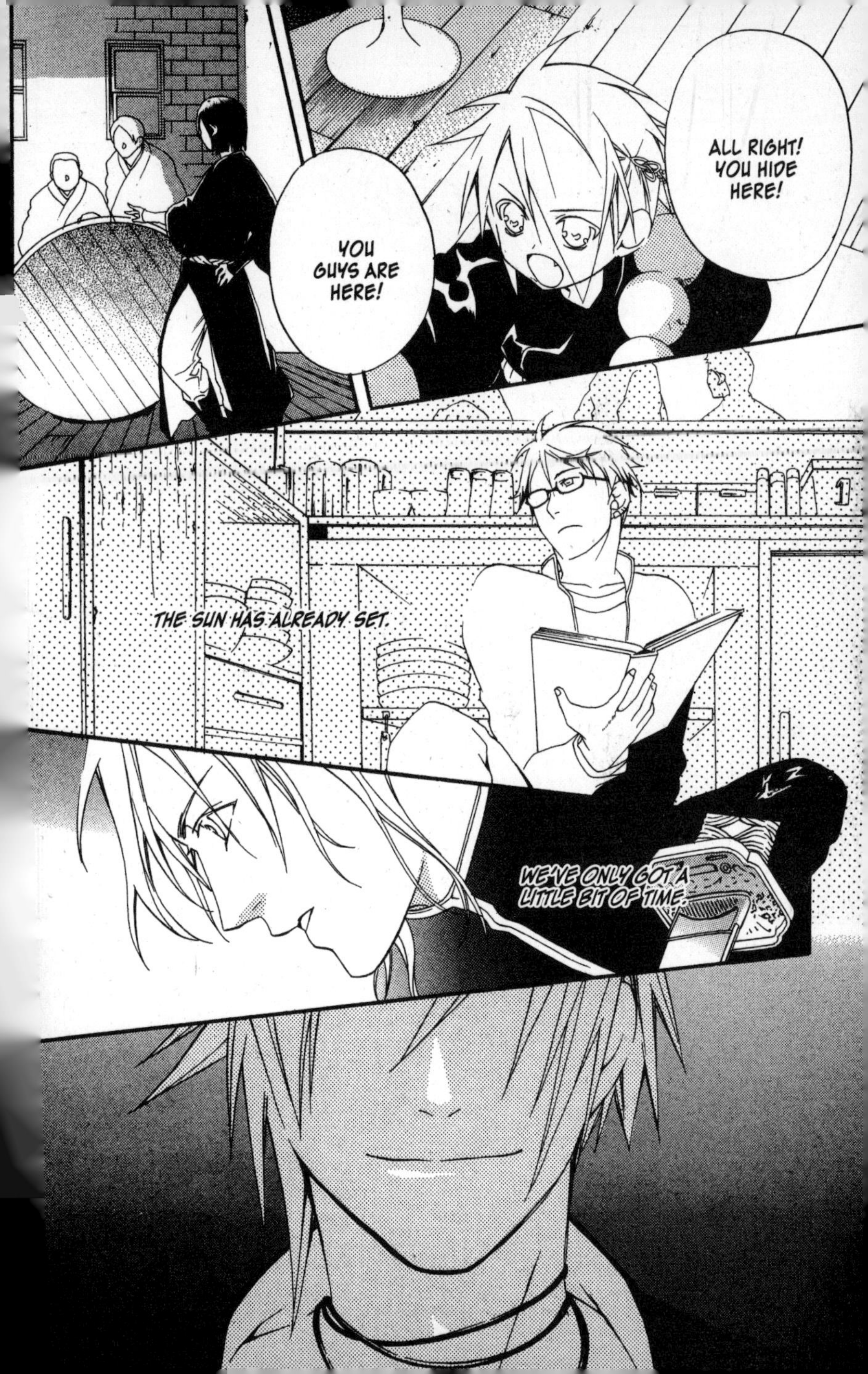
ALL RIGHT! YOU HIDE HERE!
YOU GUYS ARE HERE!
THE SUN HAS ALREADY SET.
WE'VE ONLY GOT A LITTLE BIT OF TIME.

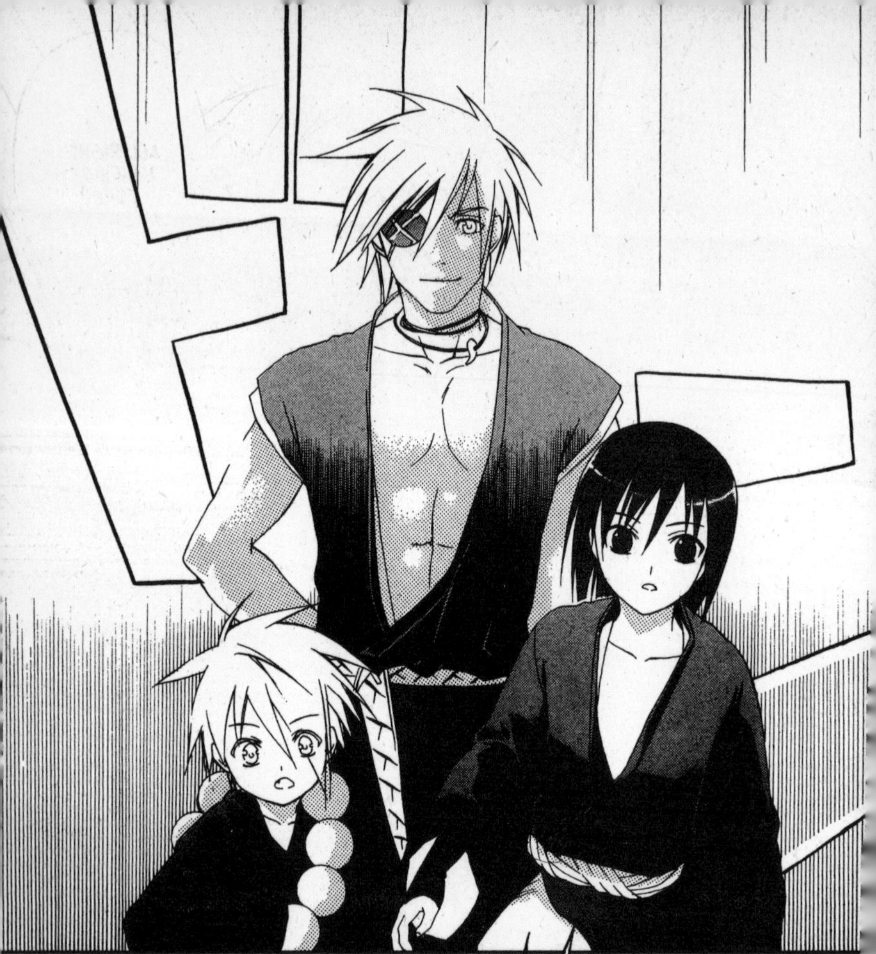

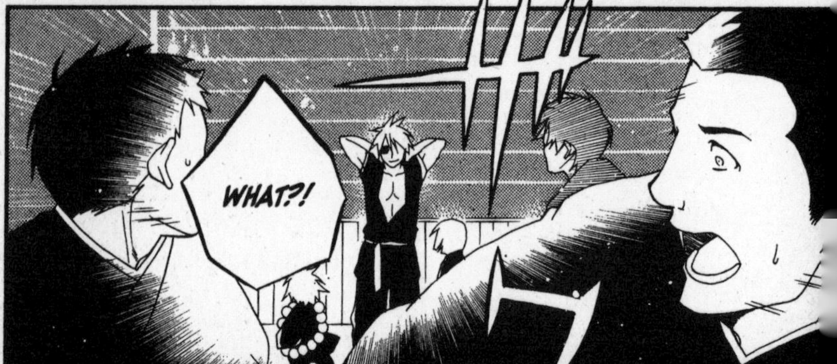
WHAT?!

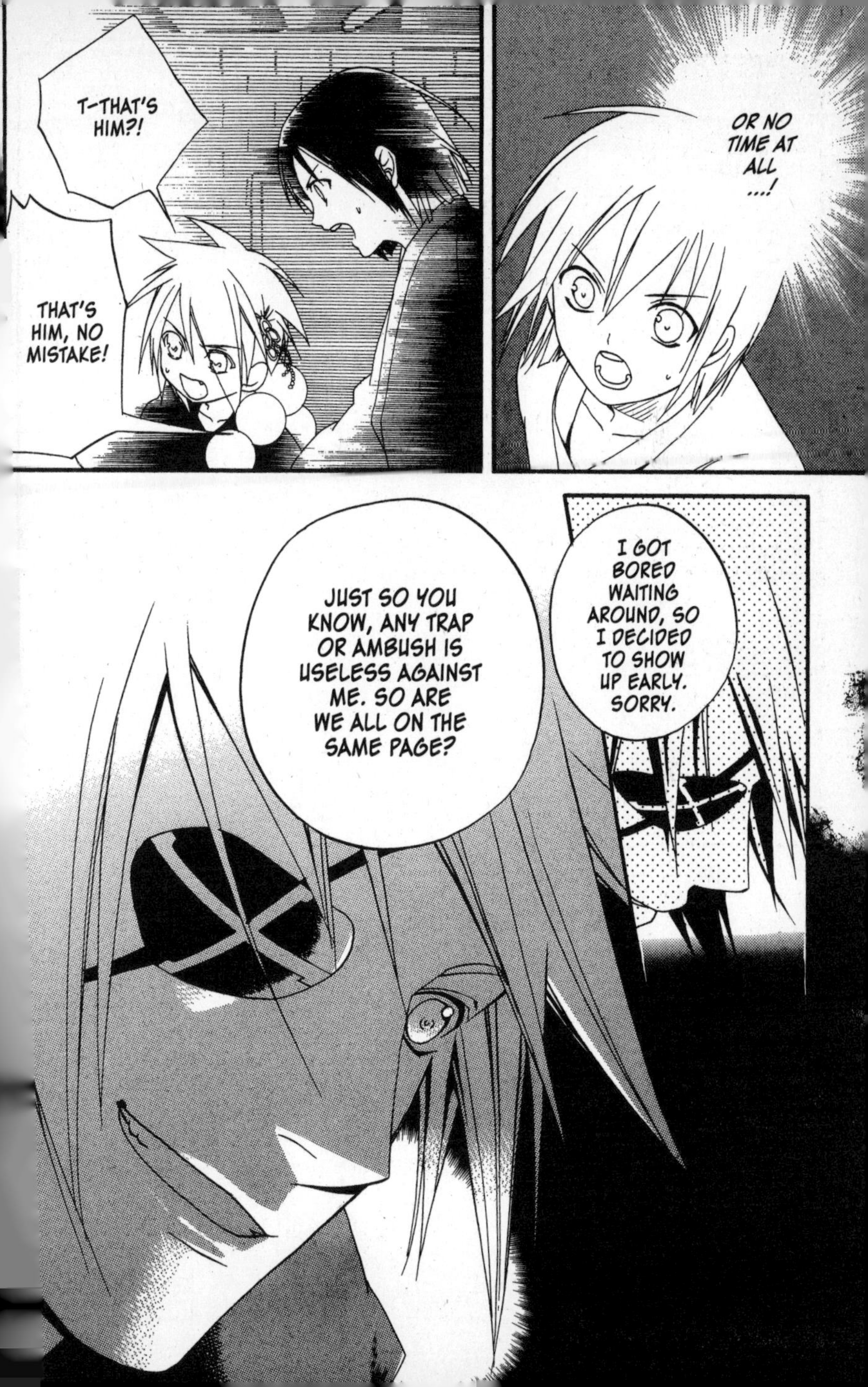
OR NO TIME AT ALL ...!
T-THAT'S HIM?!
THAT'S HIM, NO MISTAKE!
I GOT BORED WAITING AROUND, SO I DECIDED TO SHOW UP EARLY. SORRY.
JUST SO YOU KNOW, ANY TRAP OR AMBUSH IS USELESS AGAINST ME. SO ARE WE ALL ON THE SAME PAGE?

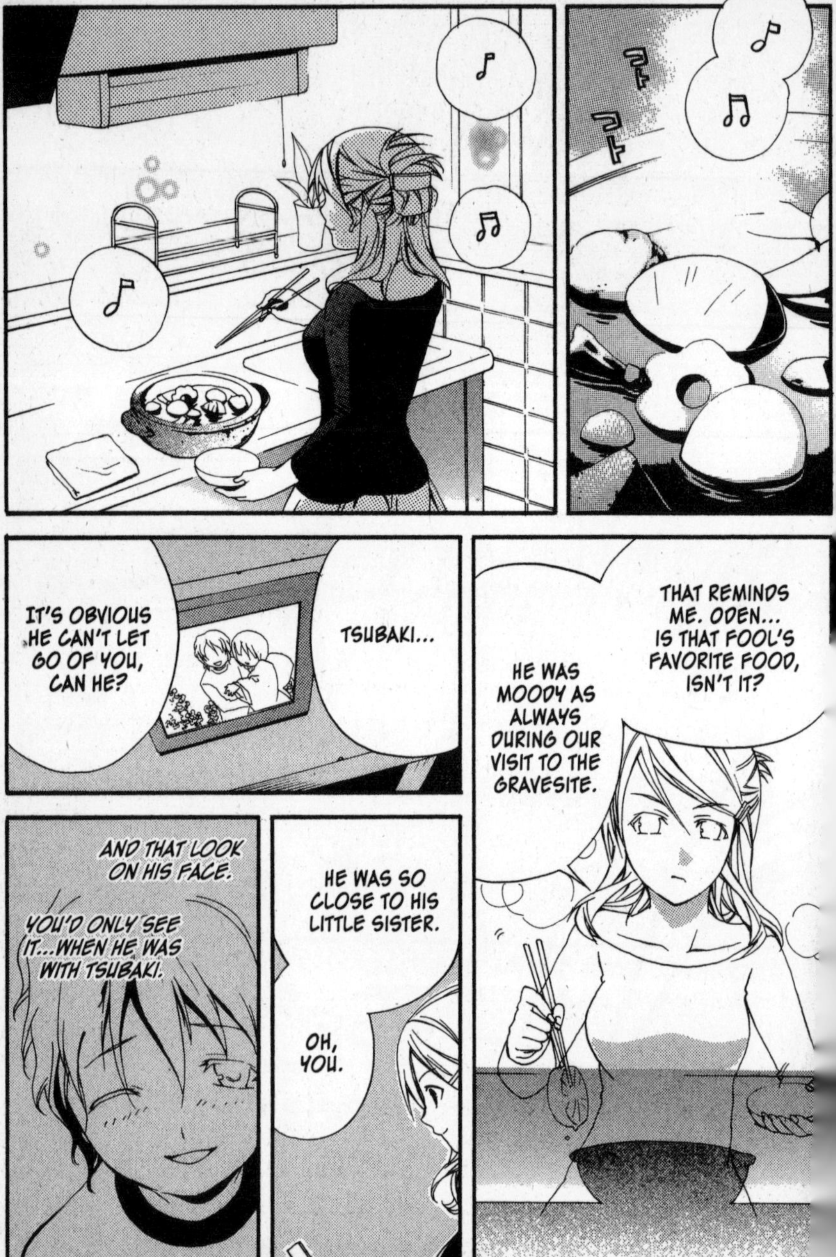
コト
コト
THAT REMINDS ME. ODEN... IS THAT FOOL'S FAVORITE FOOD, ISN'T IT?
HE WAS MOODY AS ALWAYS DURING OUR VISIT TO THE GRAVESITE.
TSUBAKI...
IT'S OBVIOUS HE CAN'T LET GO OF YOU, CAN HE?
HE WAS SO CLOSE TO HIS LITTLE SISTER.
OH, YOU.
AND THAT LOOK ON HIS FACE.
YOU'D ONLY SEE IT...WHEN HE WAS WITH TSUBAKI.

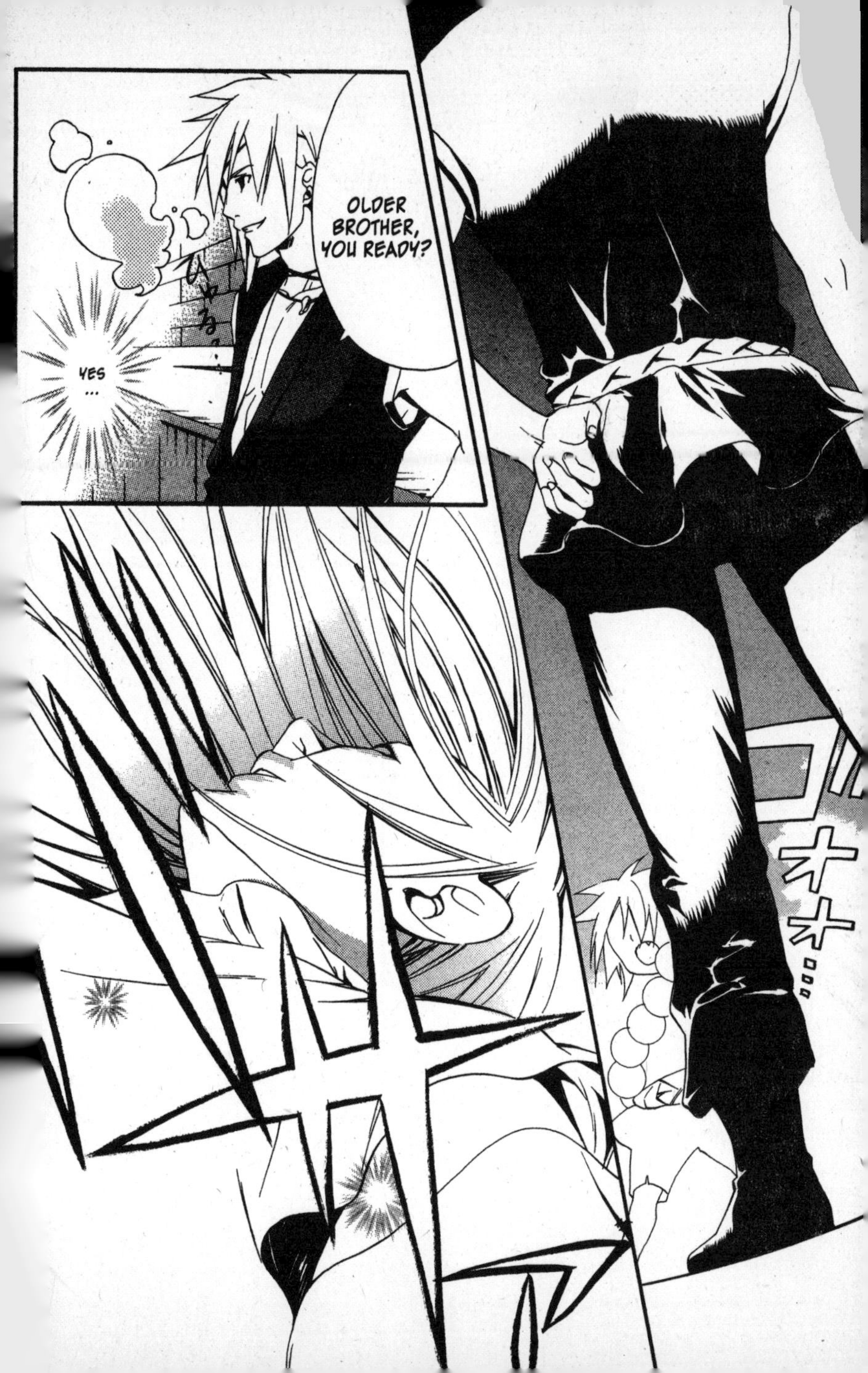
OLDER BROTHER, YOU READY?
YES ...

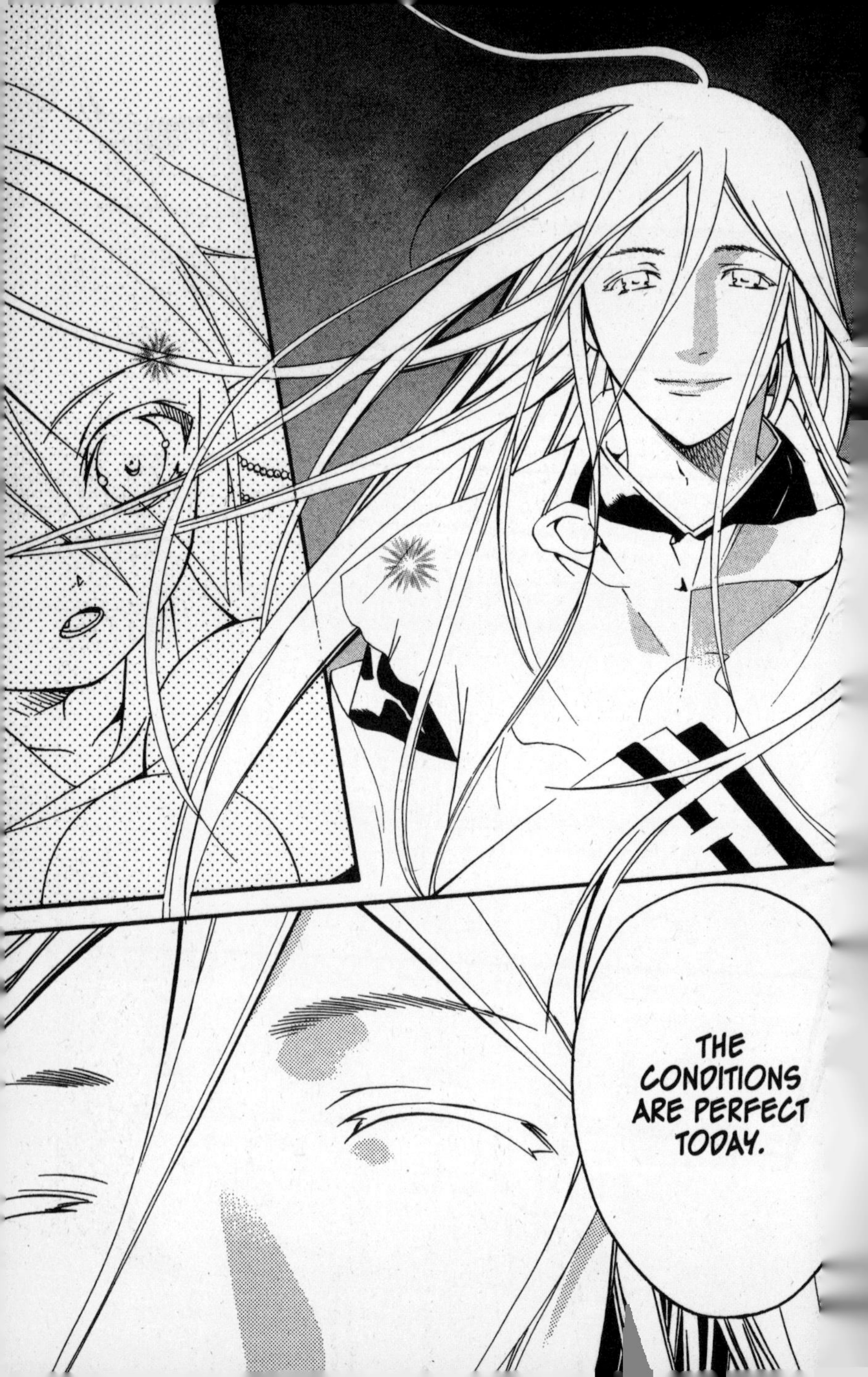
THE CONDITIONS ARE PERFECT TODAY.

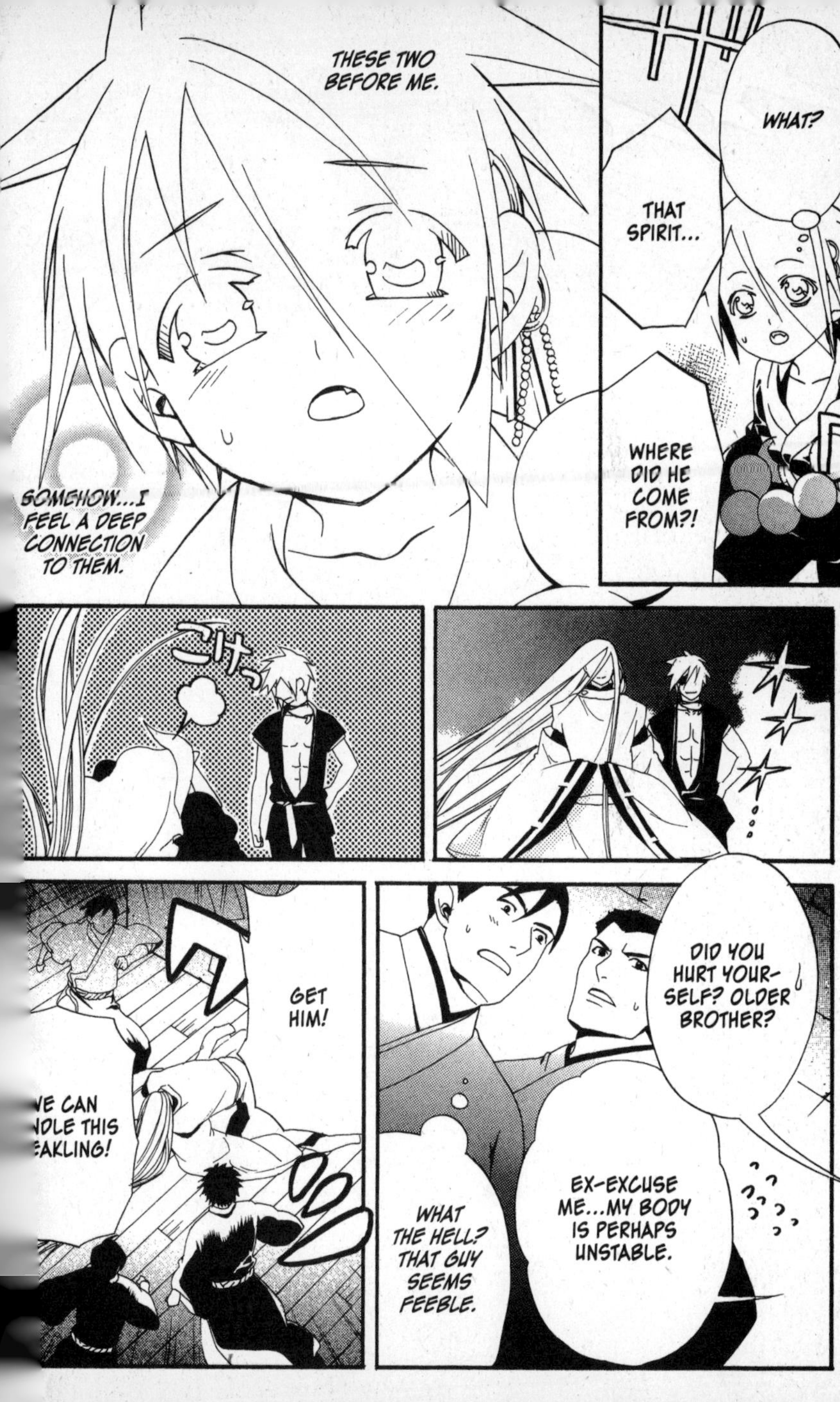
WHAT?
THAT SPIRIT...
WHERE DID HE COME FROM?!
THESE TWO BEFORE ME.
SOMEHOW...I FEEL A DEEP CONNECTION TO THEM.
こけっ
DID YOU HURT YOUR-SELF? OLDER BROTHER?
EX-EXCUSE ME...MY BODY IS PERHAPS UNSTABLE.
WHAT THE HELL? THAT GUY SEEMS FEEBLE.
GET HIM!
E CAN NDLE THIS EAKLING!

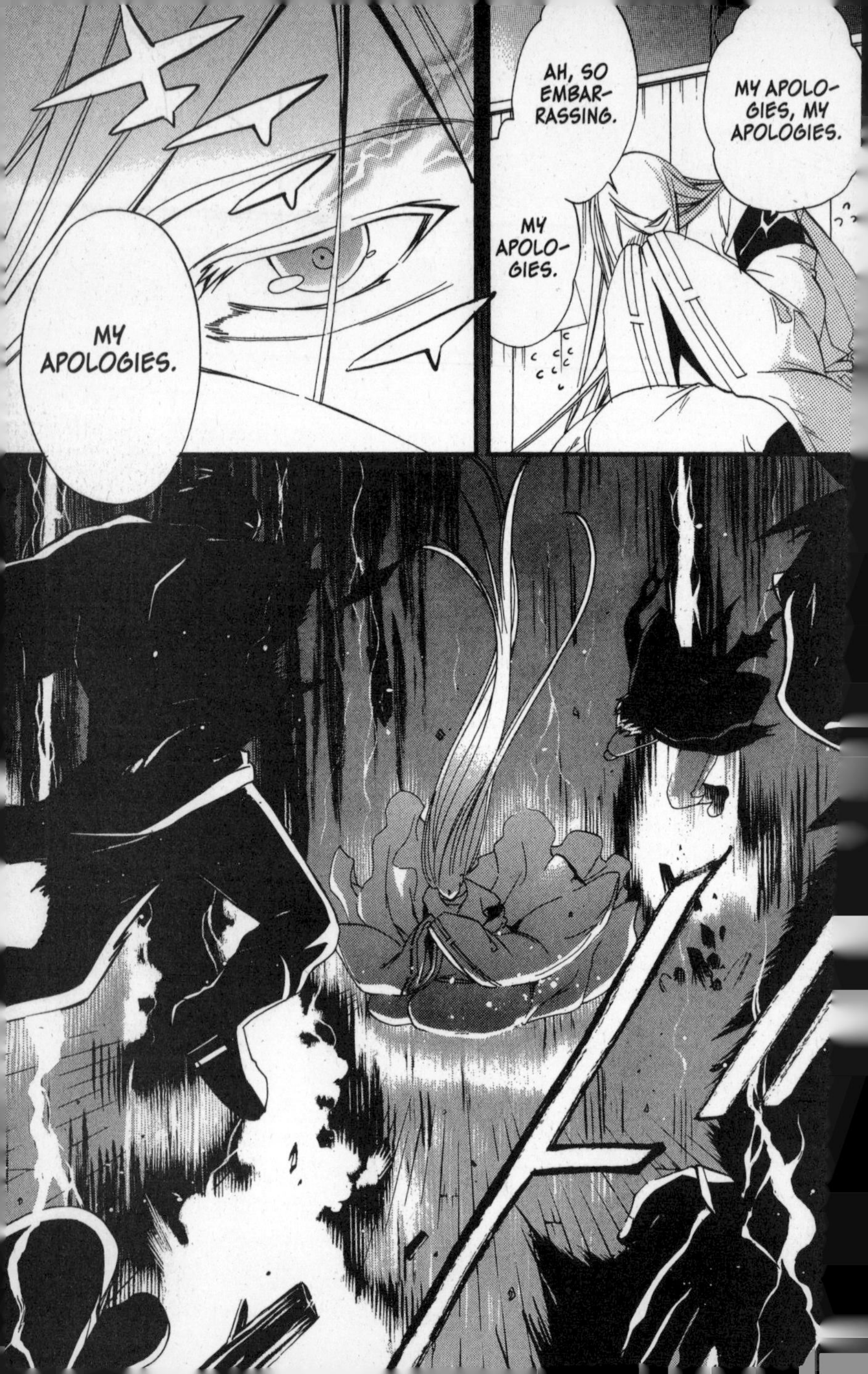
MY APOLOGIES, MY APOLOGIES.
AH, SO EMBARRASSING.
MY APOLOGIES.
MY APOLOGIES.

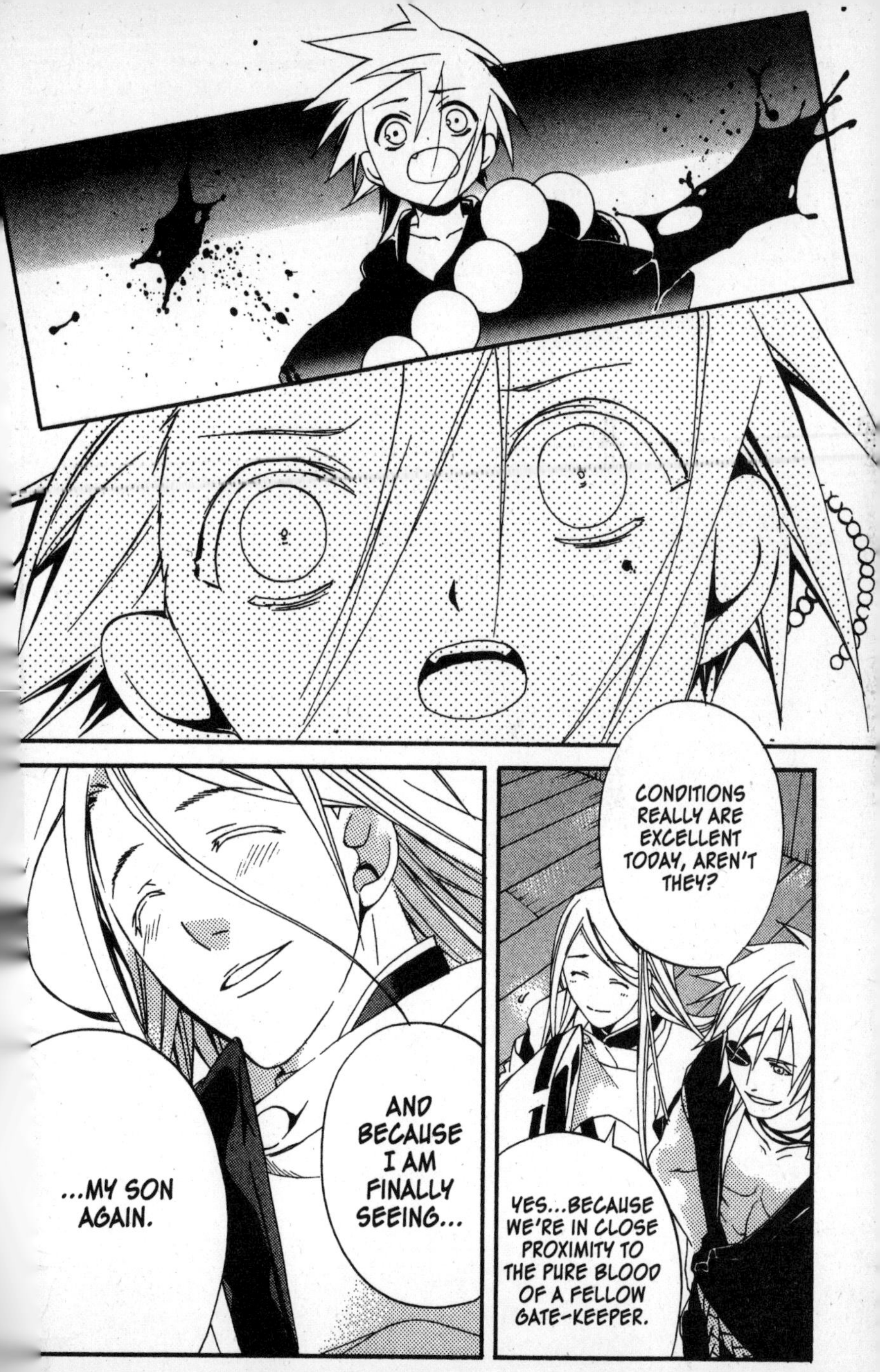
CONDITIONS REALLY ARE EXCELLENT TODAY, AREN'T THEY?
YES...BECAUSE WE'RE IN CLOSE PROXIMITY TO THE PURE BLOOD OF A FELLOW GATE-KEEPER.
AND BECAUSE I AM FINALLY SEEING...
...MY SON AGAIN.

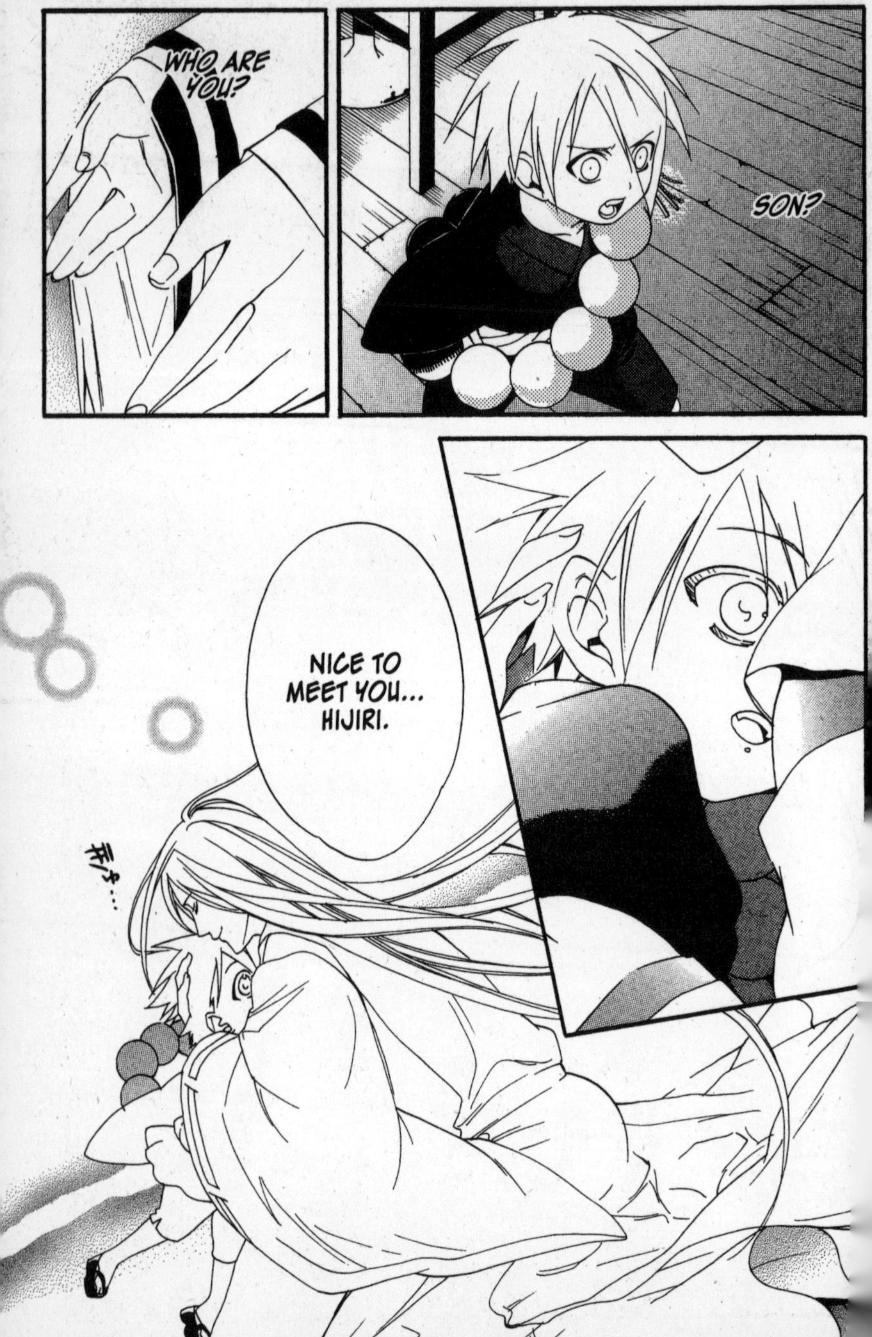
SON?
WHO ARE YOU?
NICE TO MEET YOU... HIJIRI.

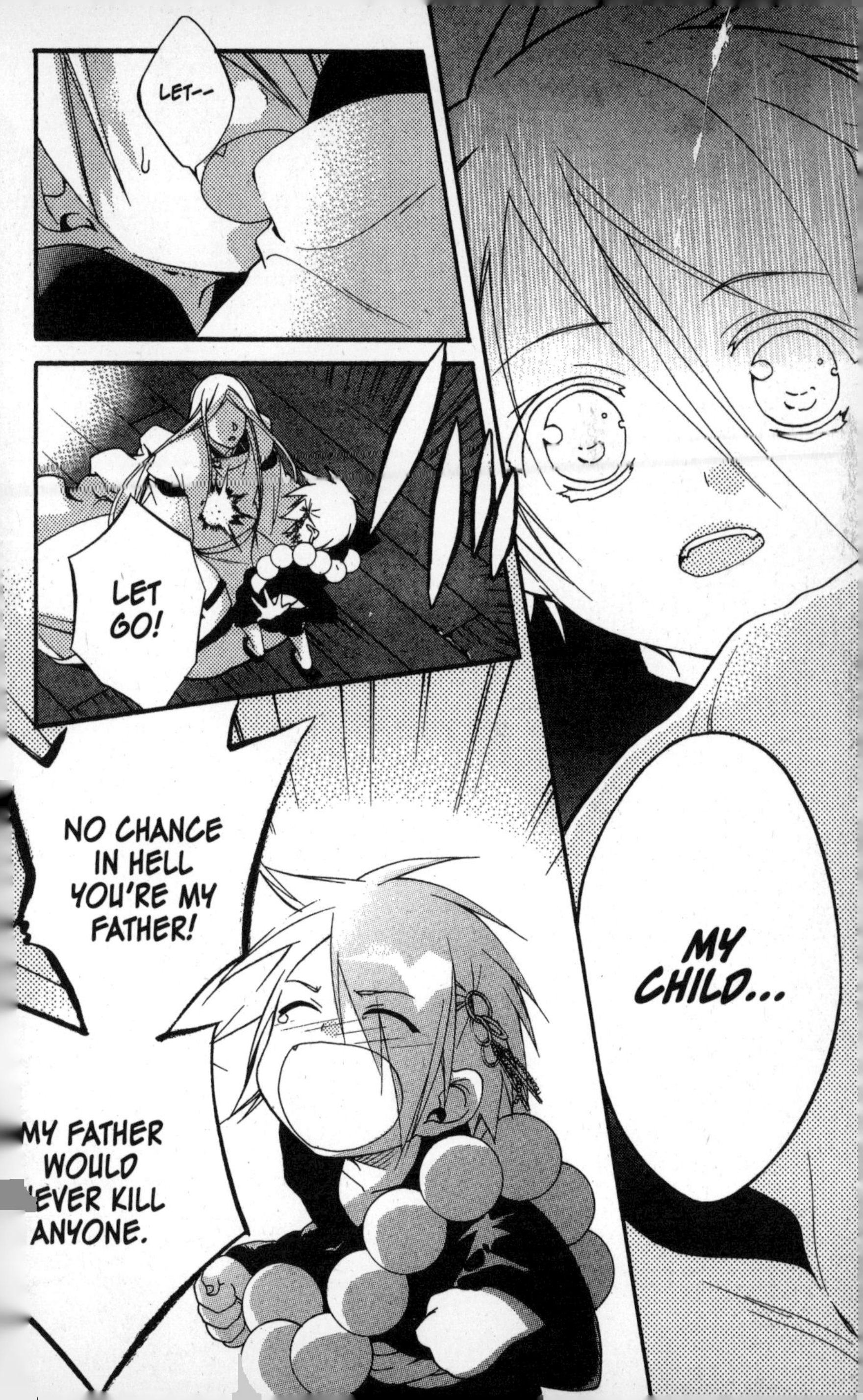
MY CHILD...
LET--
LET GO!
NO CHANCE IN HELL YOU'RE MY FATHER!
MY FATHER WOULD NEVER KILL ANYONE.

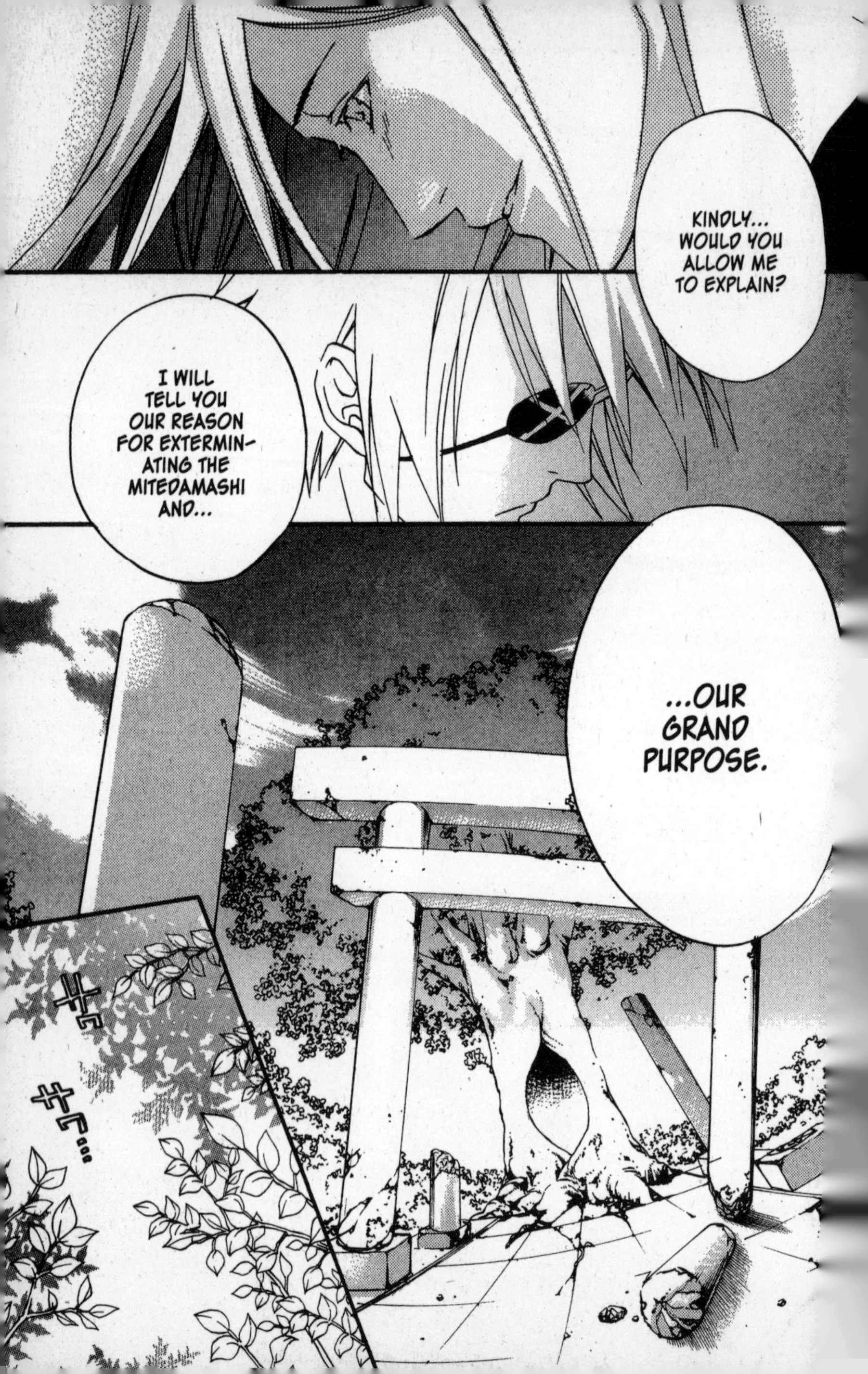
KINDLY... WOULD YOU ALLOW ME TO EXPLAIN?
I WILL TELL YOU OUR REASON FOR EXTERMINATING THE MITEDAMASHI AND...
...OUR GRAND PURPOSE.

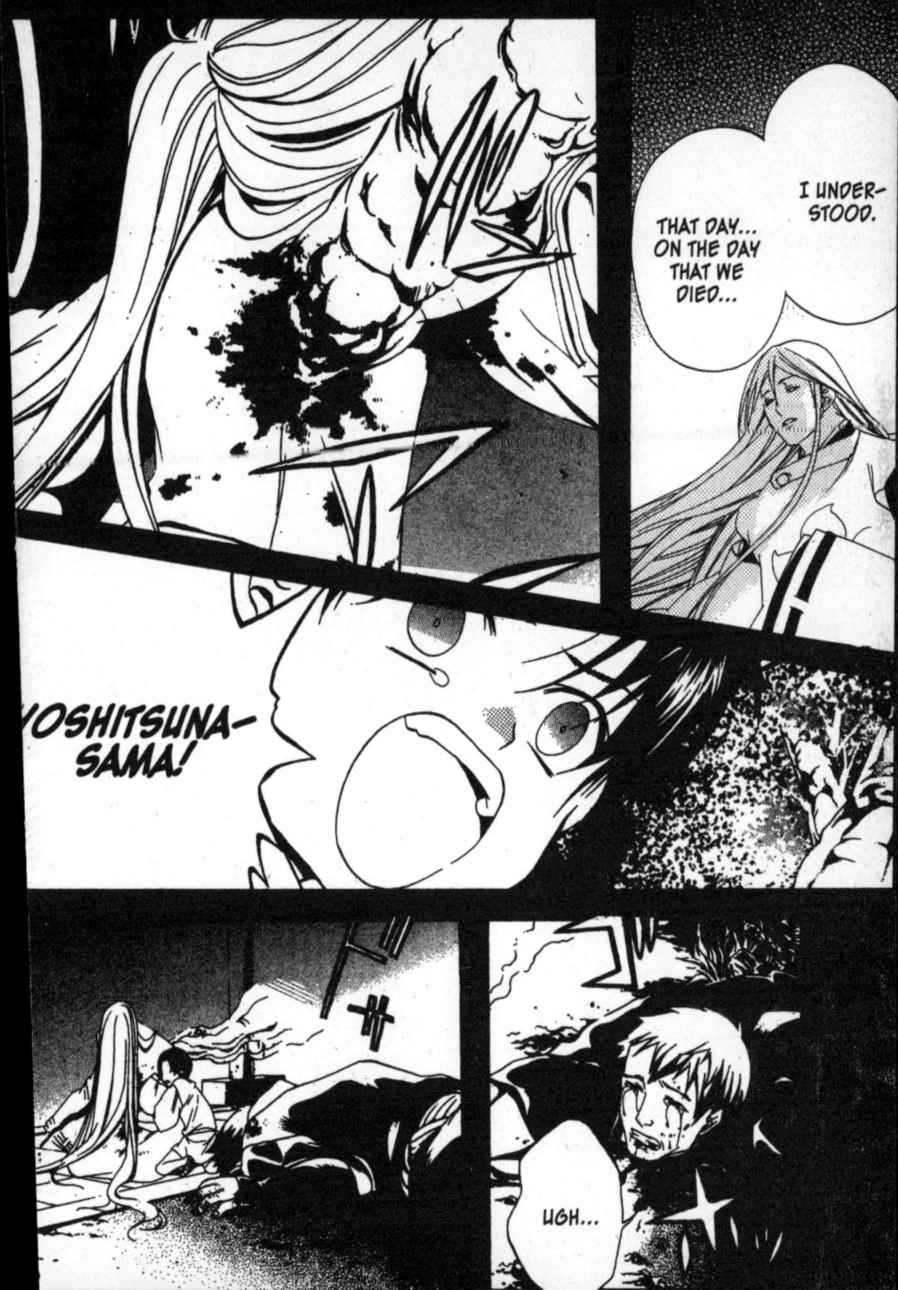
I UNDER-STOOD.
THAT DAY... ON THE DAY THAT WE DIED...
YOSHITSUNA-SAMA!
UGH...

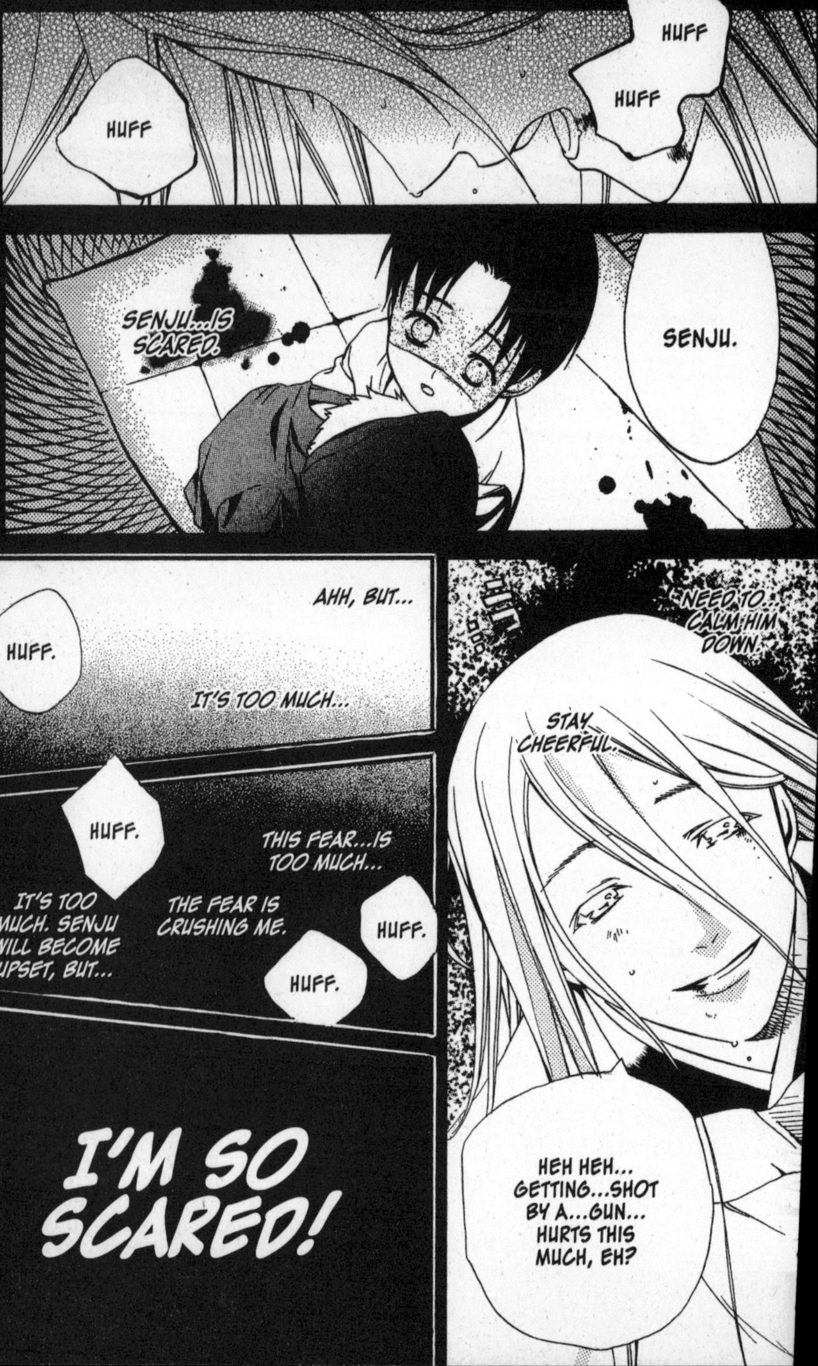
HUFF
HUFF
HUFF
SENJU.
SENJU...IS SCARED.
NEED TO... CALM HIM DOWN.
STAY CHEERFUL.
HEH HEH... GETTING...SHOT BY A...GUN... HURTS THIS MUCH, EH?
AHH, BUT...
HUFF.
IT'S TOO MUCH...
HUFF.
THIS FEAR...IS TOO MUCH...
HUFF.
THE FEAR IS CRUSHING ME.
HUFF.
IT'S TOO MUCH. SENJU WILL BECOME UPSET, BUT...
I'M SO SCARED!

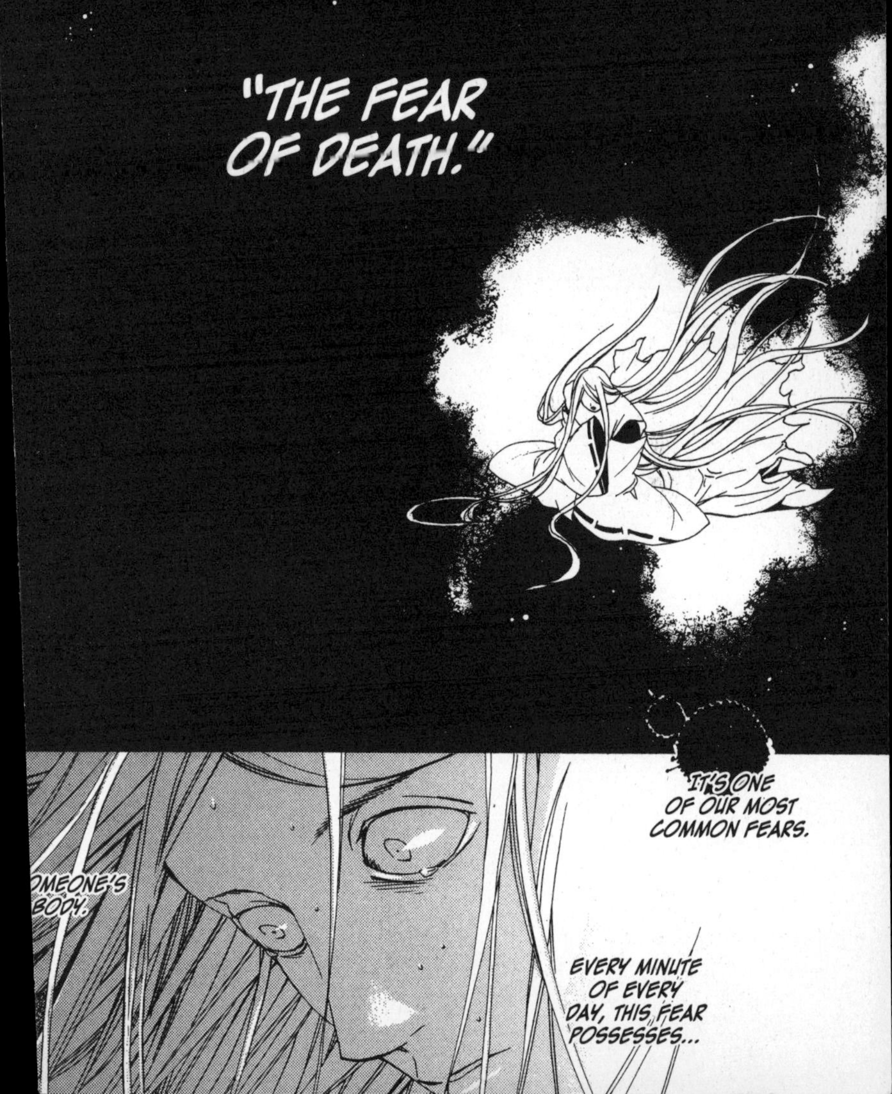
"THE FEAR OF DEATH."
IT'S ONE OF OUR MOST COMMON FEARS.
EVERY MINUTE OF EVERY DAY, THIS FEAR POSSESSES...
OMEONE'S BODY.

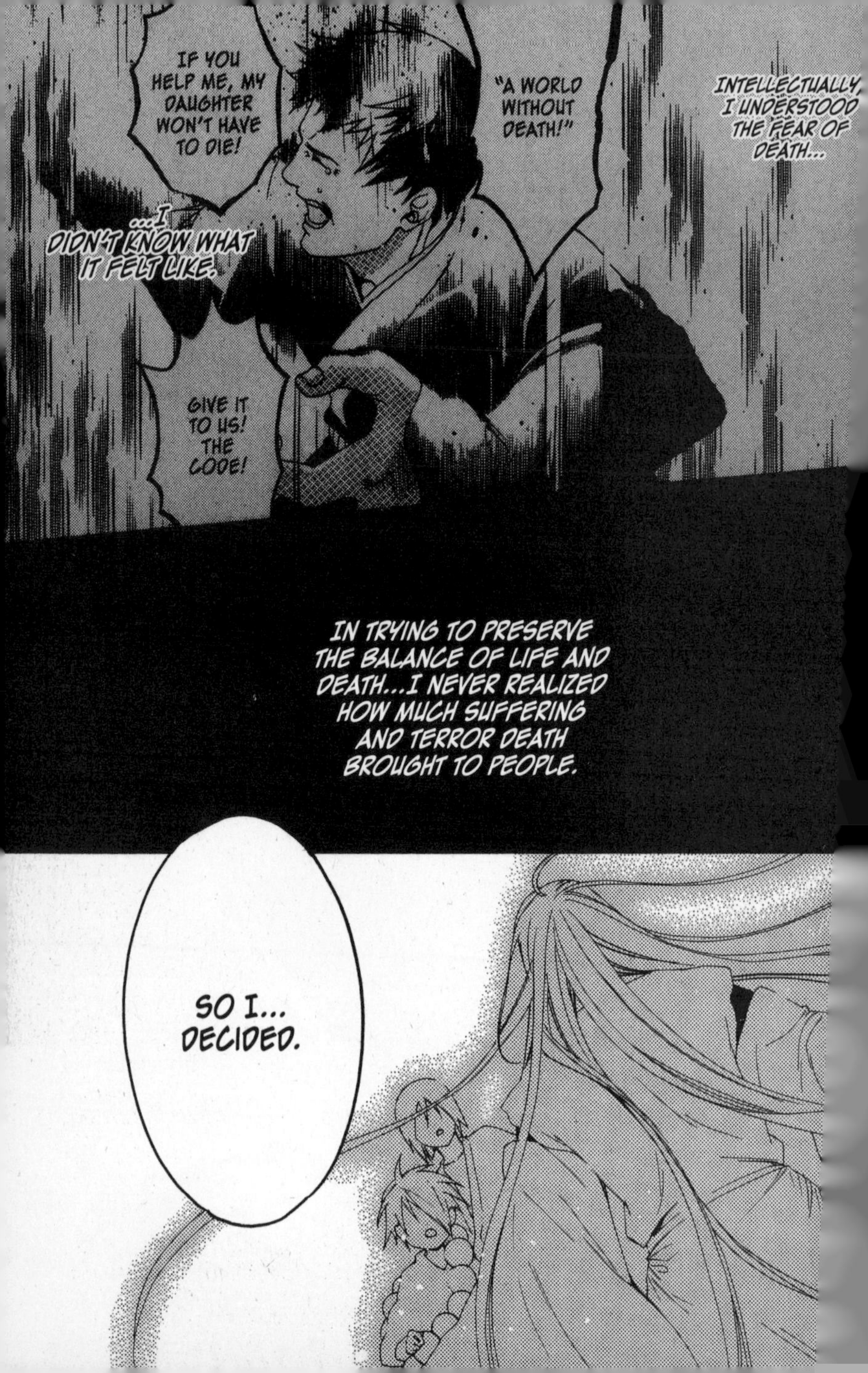
INTELLECTUALLY, I UNDERSTOOD THE FEAR OF DEATH...
"A WORLD WITHOUT DEATH!"
IF YOU HELP ME, MY DAUGHTER WON'T HAVE TO DIE!
...I DIDN'T KNOW WHAT IT FELT LIKE.
GIVE IT TO US! THE CODE!
IN TRYING TO PRESERVE THE BALANCE OF LIFE AND DEATH...I NEVER REALIZED HOW MUCH SUFFERING AND TERROR DEATH BROUGHT TO PEOPLE.
SO I... DECIDED.

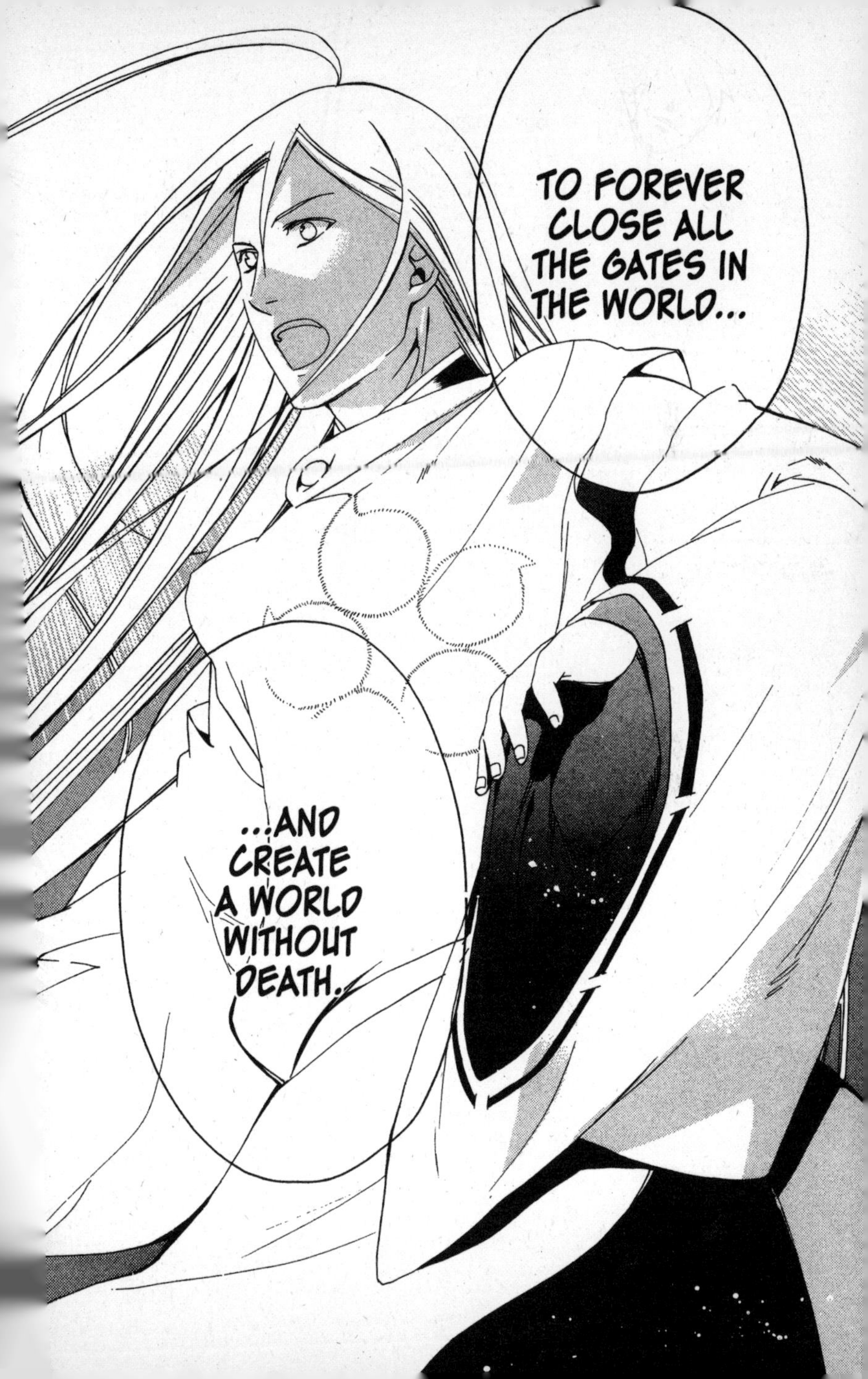
TO FOREVER CLOSE ALL THE GATES IN THE WORLD...
...AND CREATE A WORLD WITHOUT DEATH.

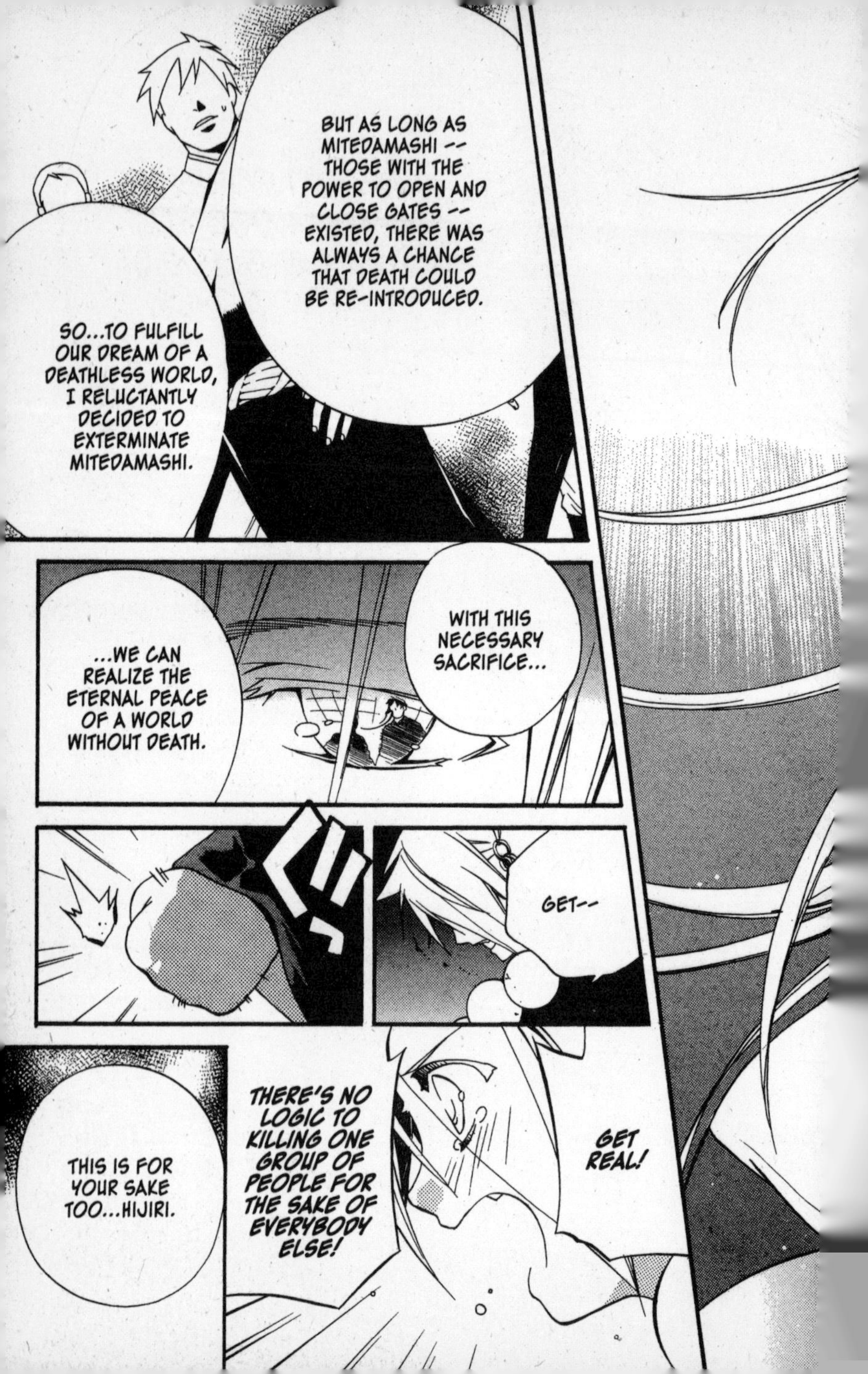
BUT AS LONG AS MITEDAMASHI -- THOSE WITH THE POWER TO OPEN AND CLOSE GATES -- EXISTED, THERE WAS ALWAYS A CHANCE THAT DEATH COULD BE RE-INTRODUCED.
SO...TO FULFILL OUR DREAM OF A DEATHLESS WORLD, I RELUCTANTLY DECIDED TO EXTERMINATE MITEDAMASHI.
WITH THIS NECESSARY SACRIFICE...
...WE CAN REALIZE THE ETERNAL PEACE OF A WORLD WITHOUT DEATH.
GET--
GET REAL!
THERE'S NO LOGIC TO KILLING ONE GROUP OF PEOPLE FOR THE SAKE OF EVERYBODY ELSE!
THIS IS FOR YOUR SAKE TOO...HIJIRI.

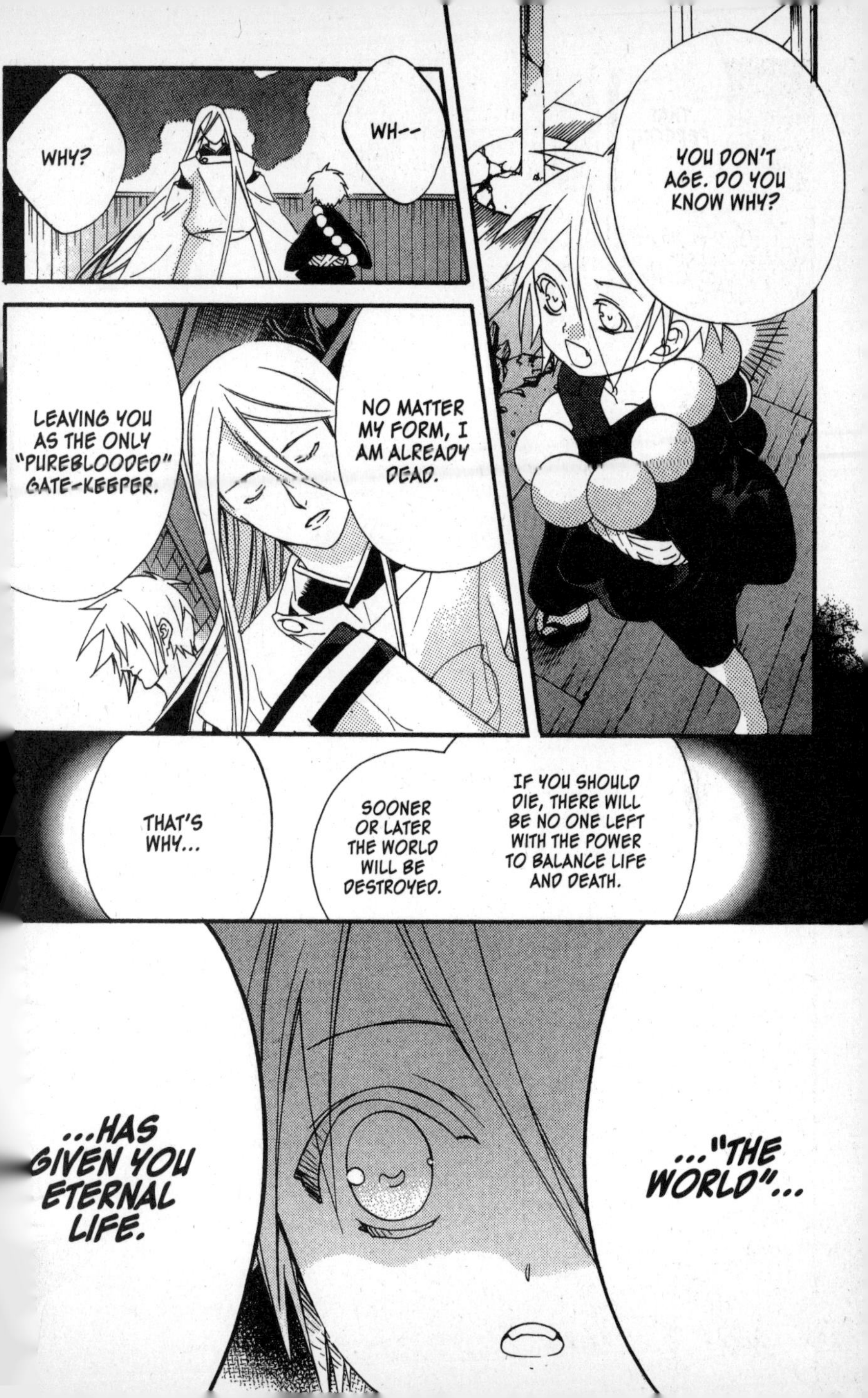
YOU DON'T AGE. DO YOU KNOW WHY?
WH--
WHY?
NO MATTER MY FORM, I AM ALREADY DEAD.
LEAVING YOU AS THE ONLY "PUREBLOODED" GATE-KEEPER.
IF YOU SHOULD DIE, THERE WILL BE NO ONE LEFT WITH THE POWER TO BALANCE LIFE AND DEATH.
SOONER OR LATER THE WORLD WILL BE DESTROYED.
THAT'S WHY...
..."THE WORLD"...
...HAS GIVEN YOU ETERNAL LIFE.

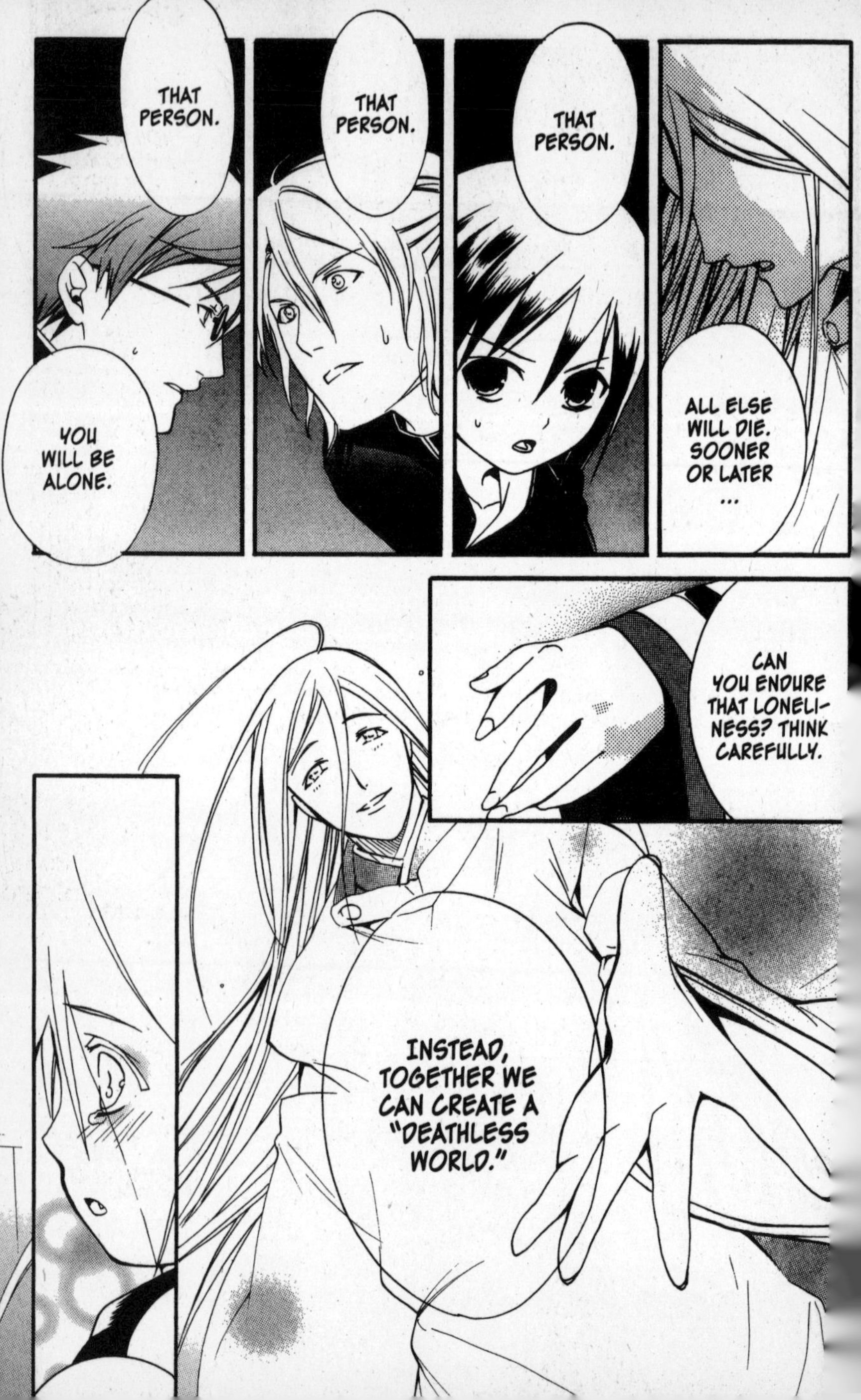
ALL ELSE WILL DIE. SOONER OR LATER ...
THAT PERSON.
THAT PERSON.
THAT PERSON.
YOU WILL BE ALONE.
CAN YOU ENDURE THAT LONELI-NESS? THINK CAREFULLY.
INSTEAD, TOGETHER WE CAN CREATE A "DEATHLESS WORLD."

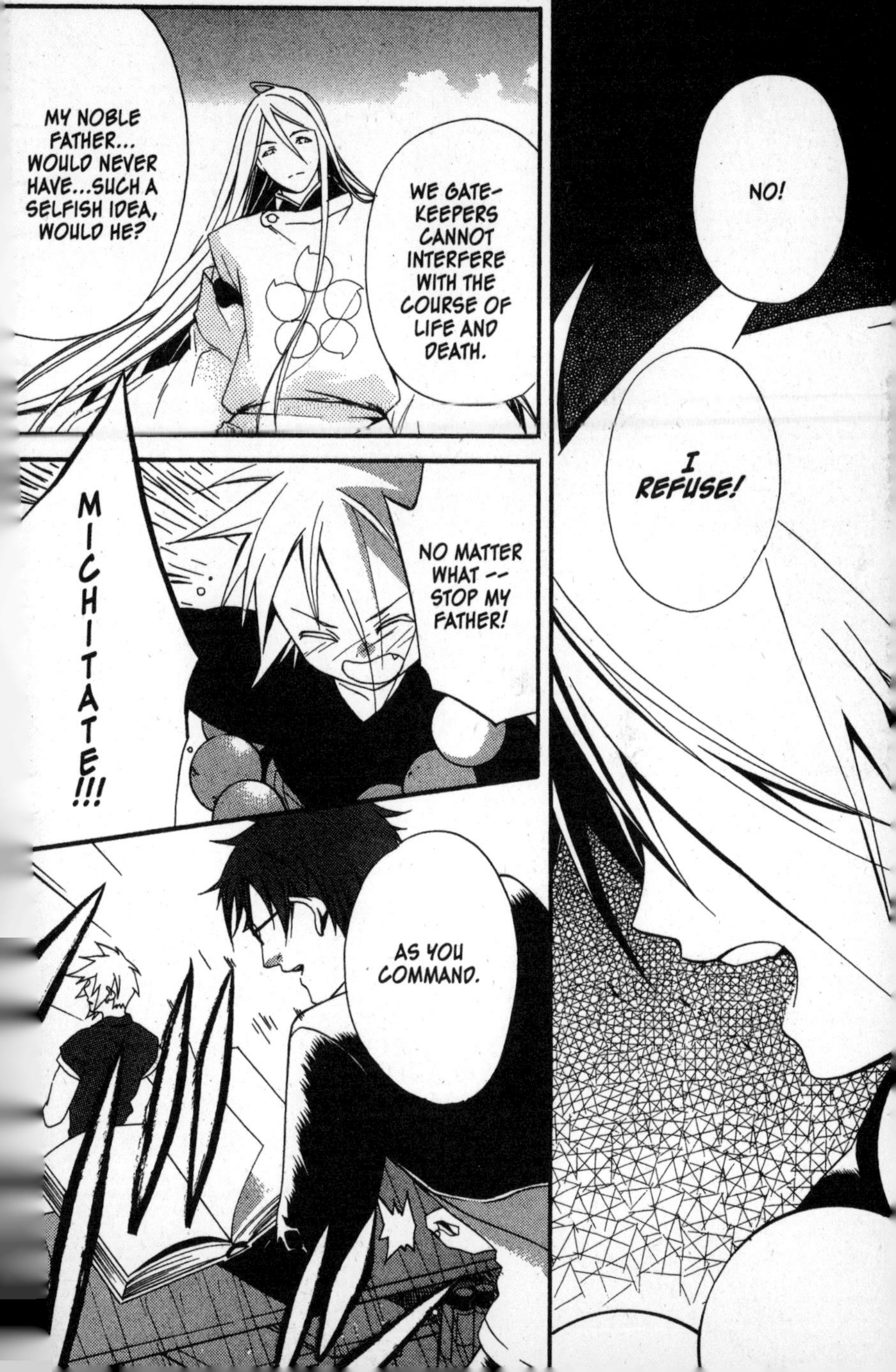
NO!
I REFUSE!
WE GATE-KEEPERS CANNOT INTERFERE WITH THE COURSE OF LIFE AND DEATH.
MY NOBLE FATHER... WOULD NEVER HAVE...SUCH A SELFISH IDEA, WOULD HE?
NO MATTER WHAT -- STOP MY FATHER!
MICHITATE!!!
AS YOU COMMAND.

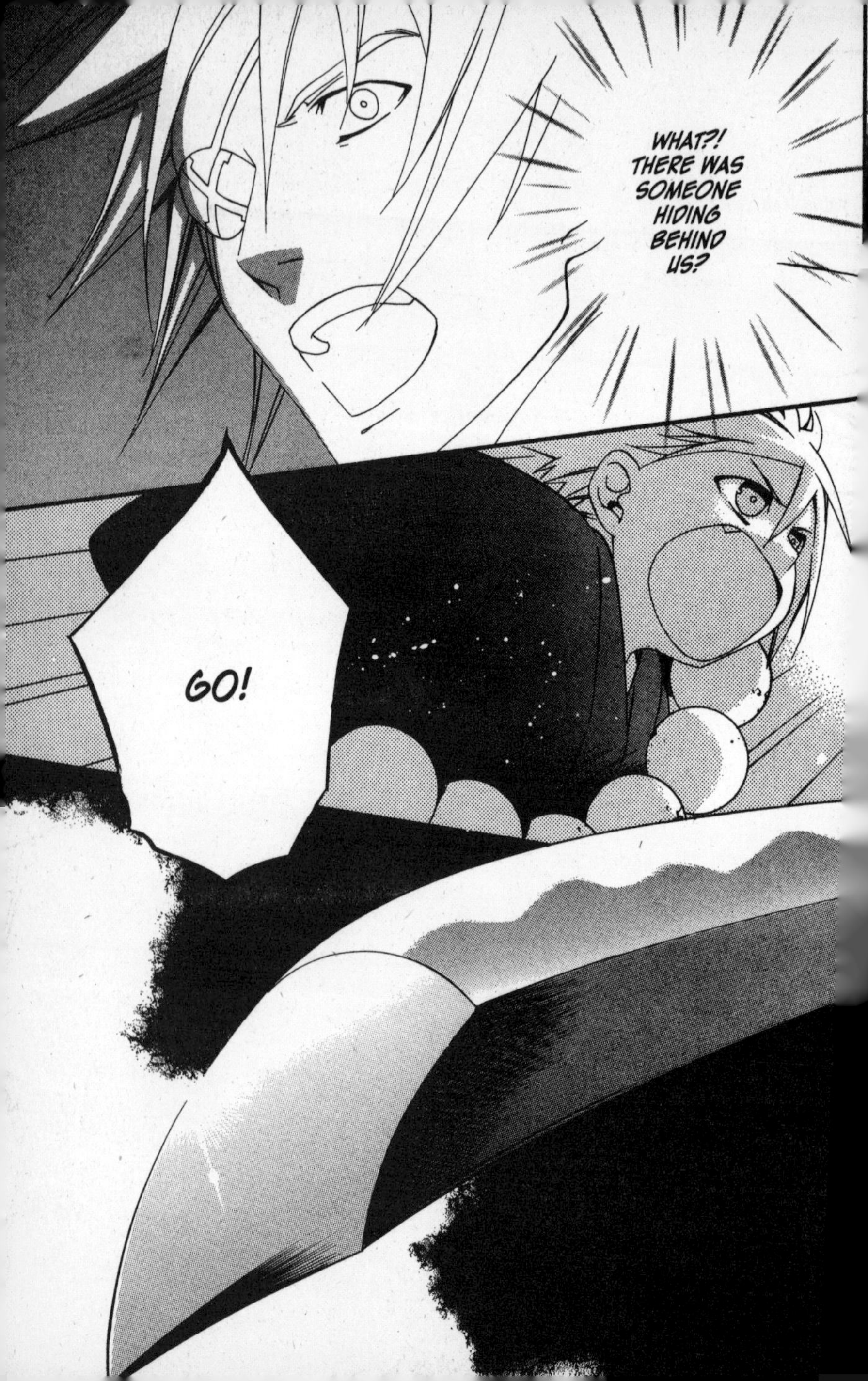
WHAT?! THERE WAS SOMEONE HIDING BEHIND US?
GO!

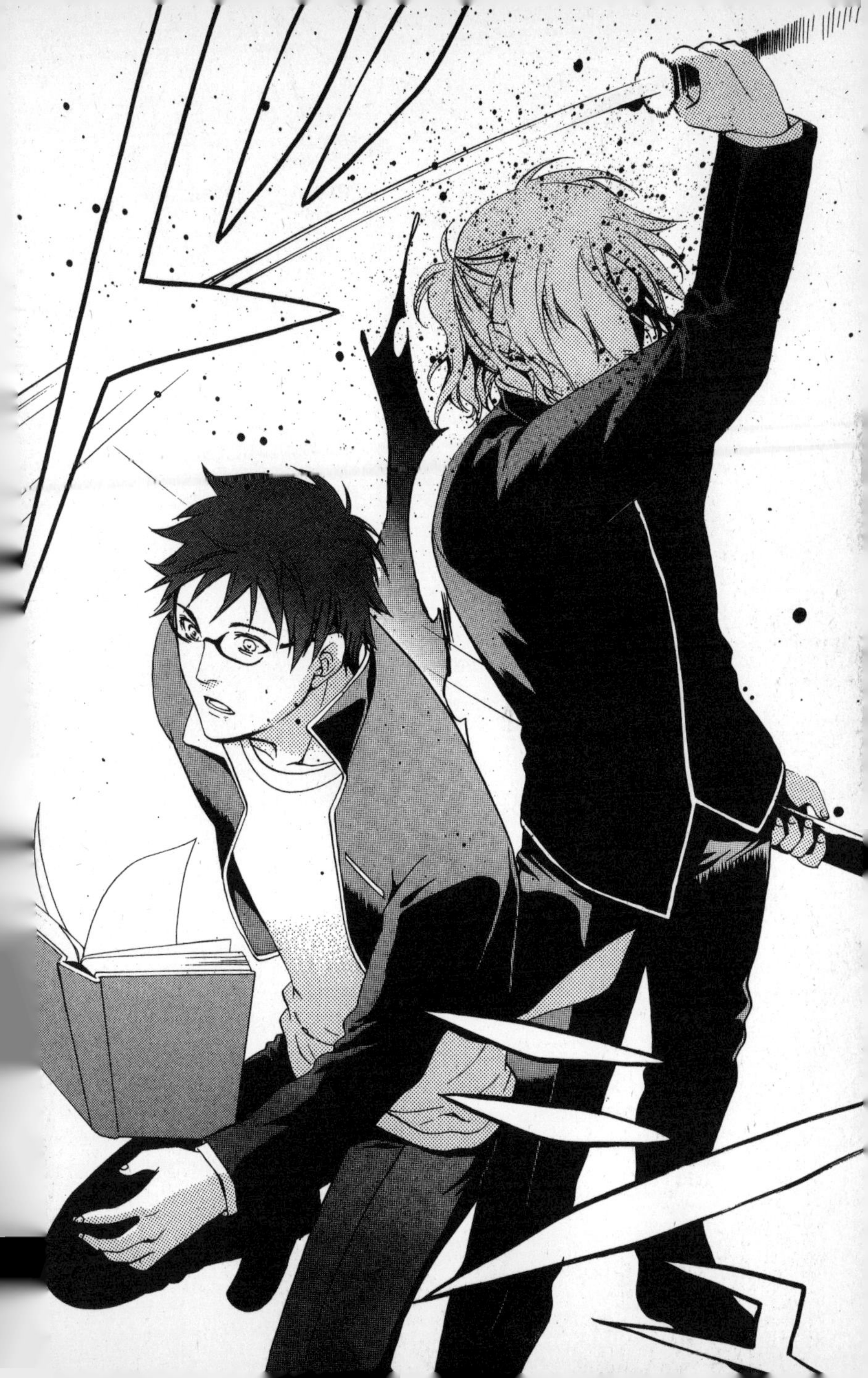

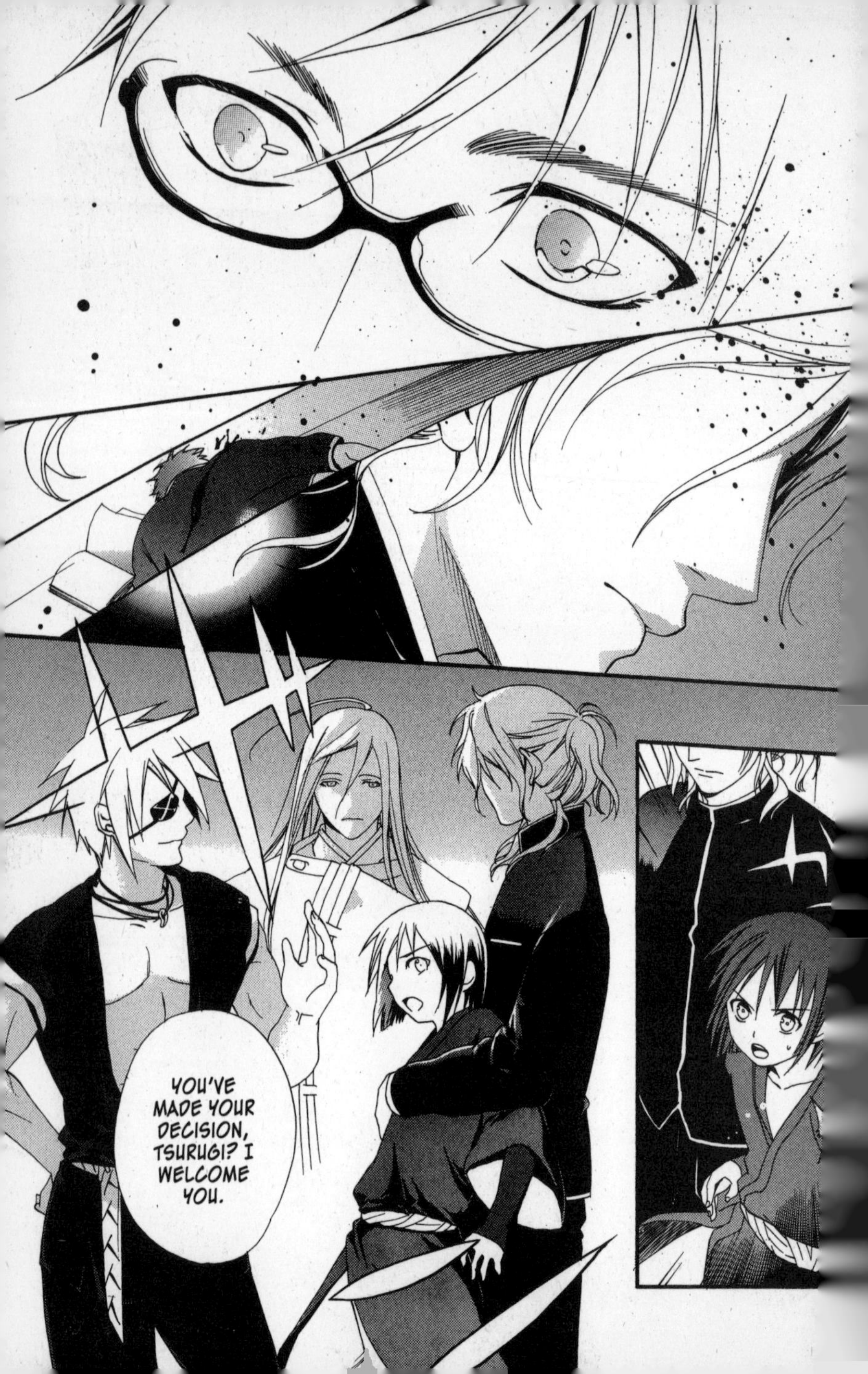
YOU'VE MADE YOUR DECISION, TSURUGI? I WELCOME YOU.

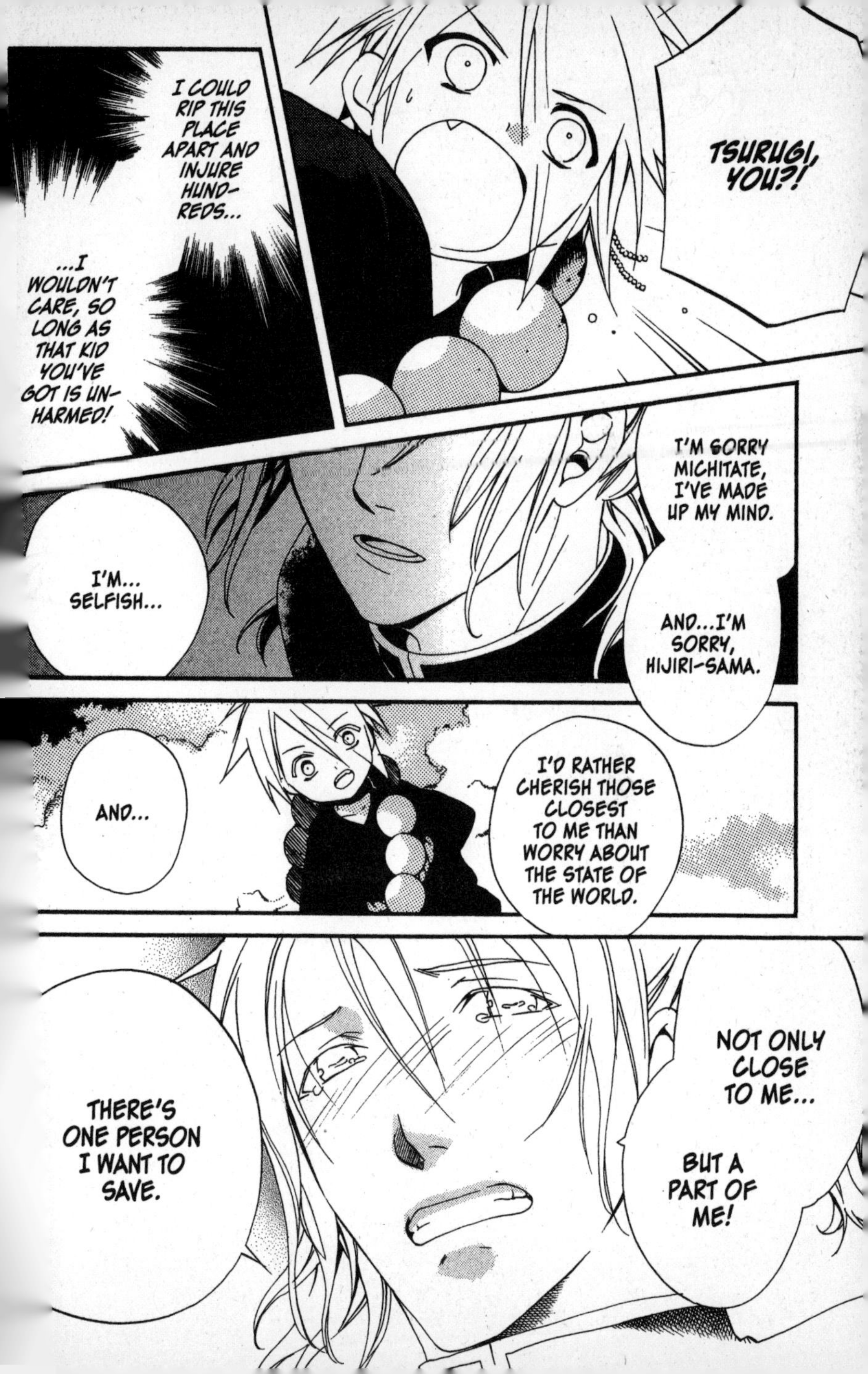
TSURUGI, YOU?!
I COULD RIP THIS PLACE APART AND INJURE HUNDREDS...
...I WOULDN'T CARE, SO LONG AS THAT KID YOU'VE GOT IS UNHARMED!
I'M SORRY MICHITATE, I'VE MADE UP MY MIND.
I'M... SELFISH...
AND...I'M SORRY, HIJIRI-SAMA.
I'D RATHER CHERISH THOSE CLOSEST TO ME THAN WORRY ABOUT THE STATE OF THE WORLD.
AND...
NOT ONLY CLOSE TO ME...
BUT A PART OF ME!
THERE'S ONE PERSON I WANT TO SAVE.

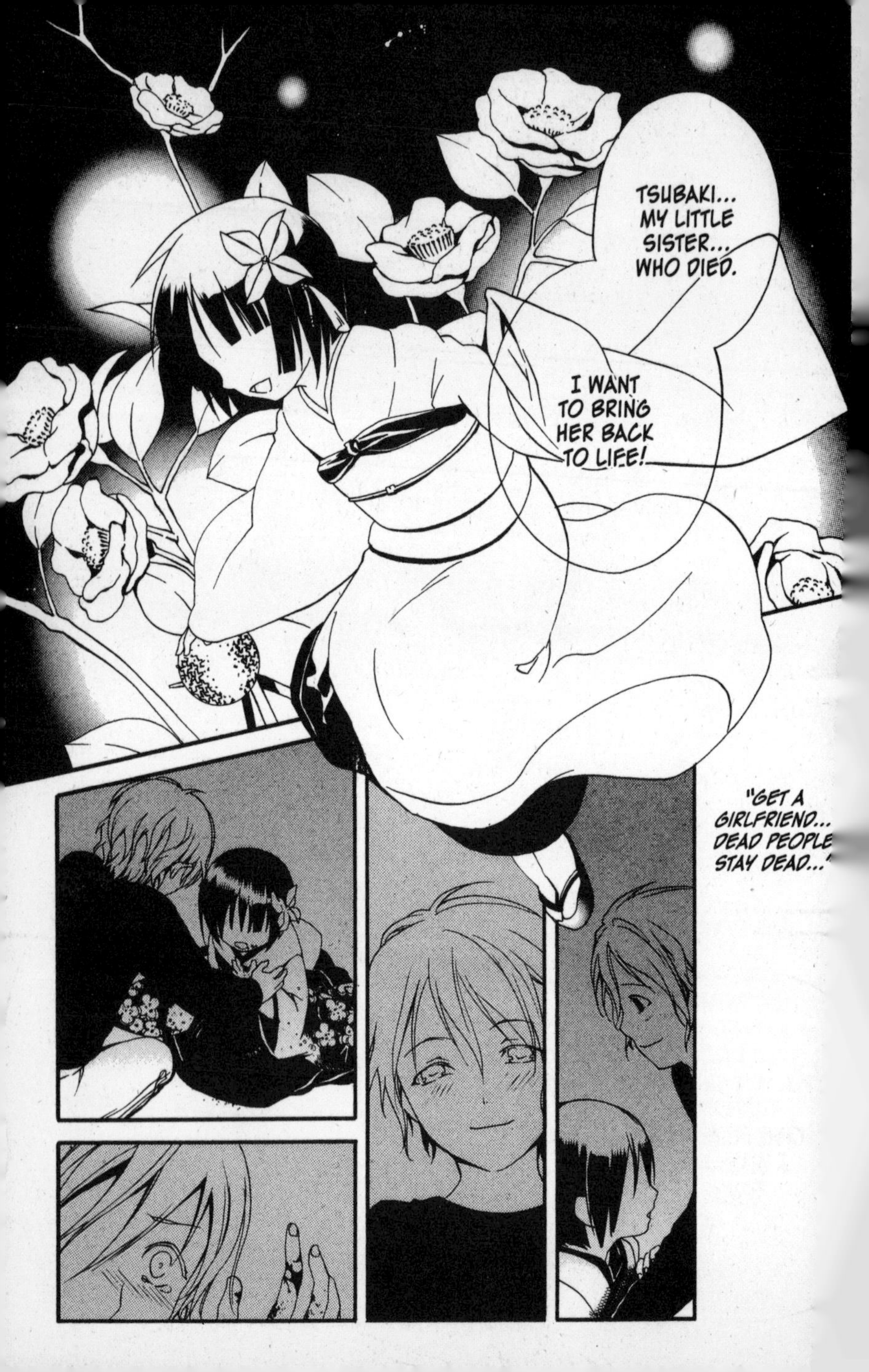
TSUBAKI... MY LITTLE SISTER... WHO DIED.
I WANT TO BRING HER BACK TO LIFE!
"GET A GIRLFRIEND... DEAD PEOPLE STAY DEAD..."

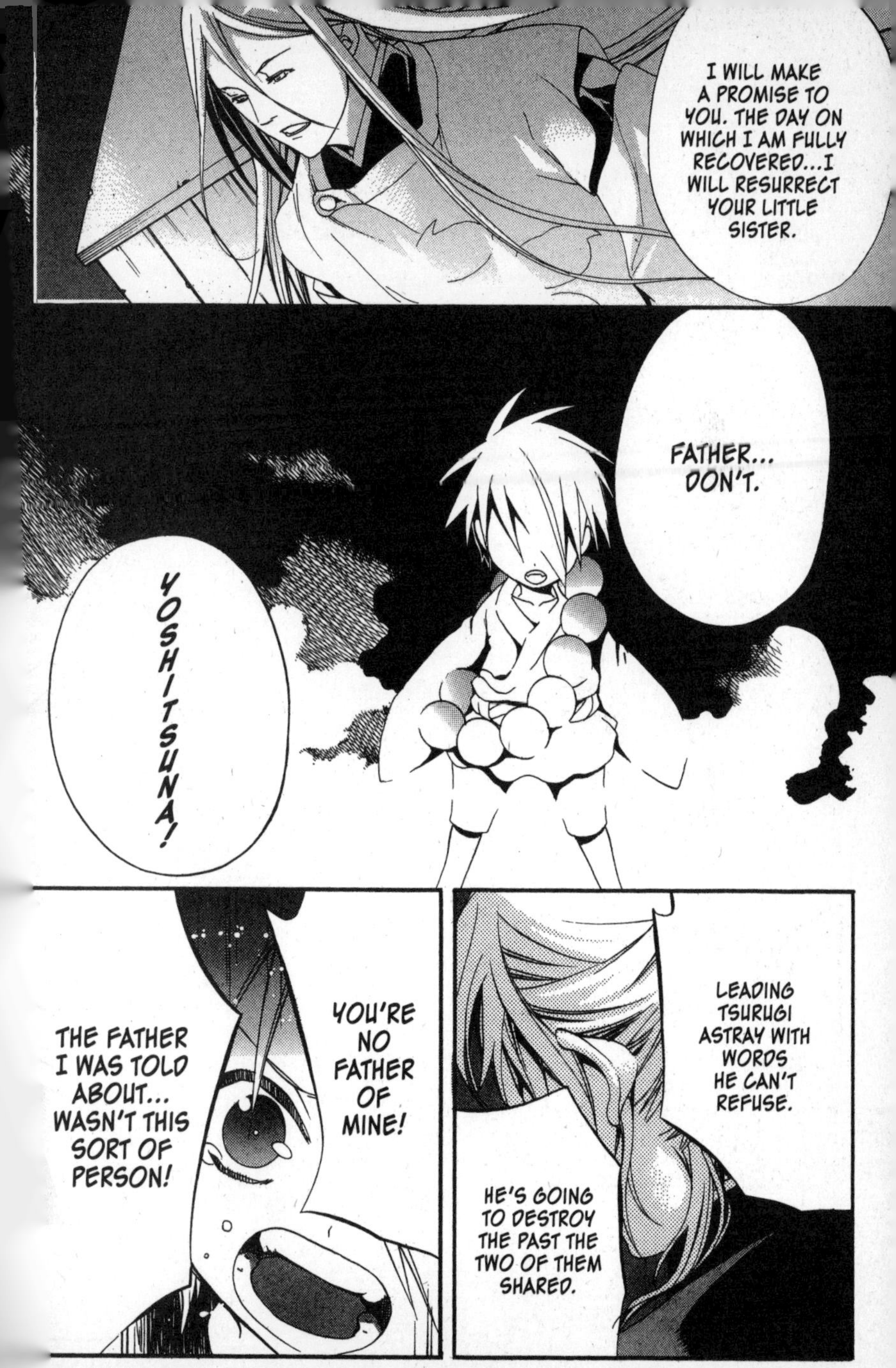
I WILL MAKE A PROMISE TO YOU. THE DAY ON WHICH I AM FULLY RECOVERED...I WILL RESURRECT YOUR LITTLE SISTER.
FATHER... DON'T.
YOSHITSUNA!
LEADING TSURUGI ASTRAY WITH WORDS HE CAN'T REFUSE.
HE'S GOING TO DESTROY THE PAST THE TWO OF THEM SHARED.
YOU'RE NO FATHER OF MINE!
THE FATHER I WAS TOLD ABOUT... WASN'T THIS SORT OF PERSON!

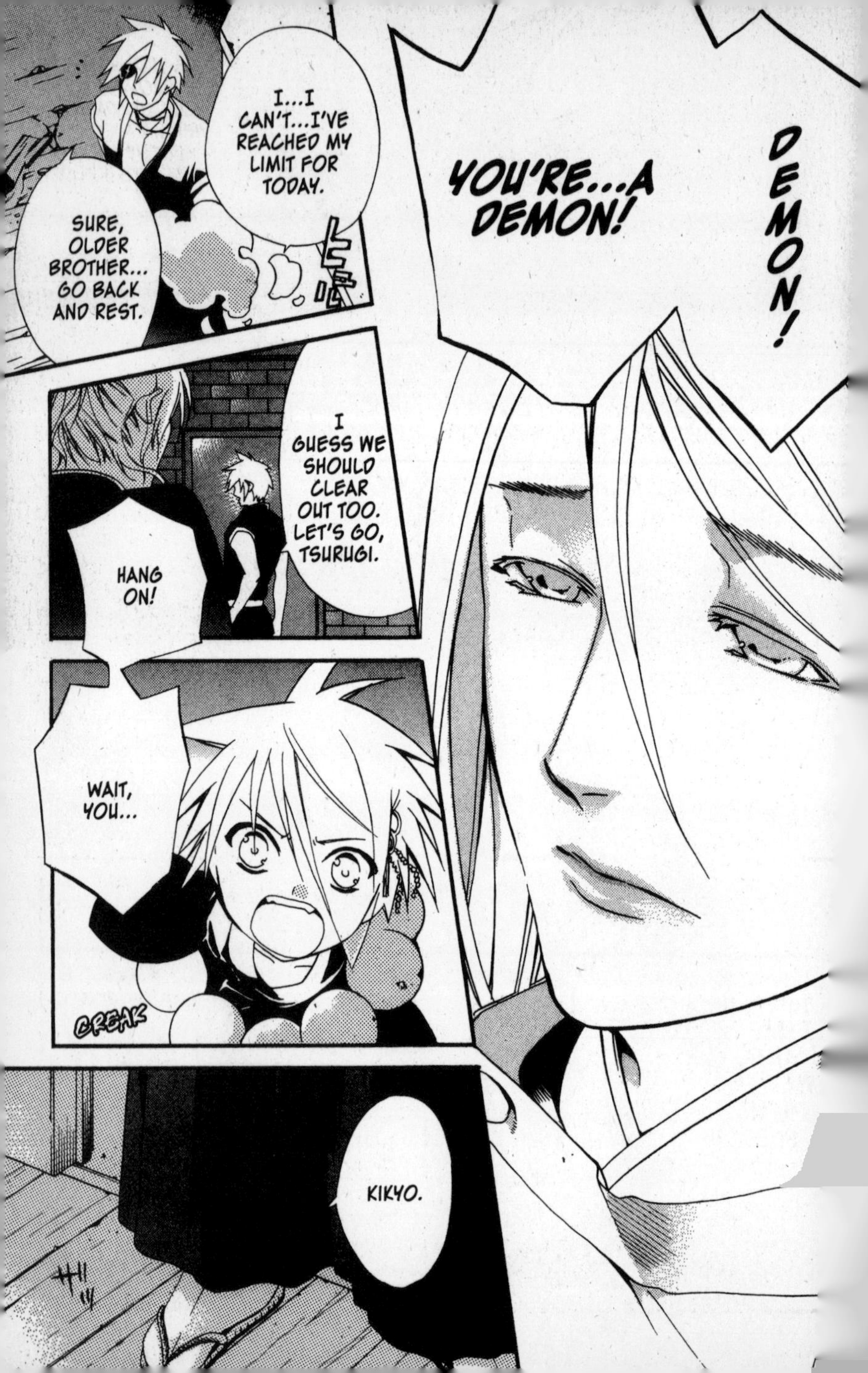

YOU'RE...A DEMON!
DEMON!
I...I CAN'T...I'VE REACHED MY LIMIT FOR TODAY.
SURE, OLDER BROTHER... GO BACK AND REST.
I GUESS WE SHOULD CLEAR OUT TOO. LET'S GO, TSURUGI.
HANG ON!
WAIT, YOU...
CREAK
KIKYO.

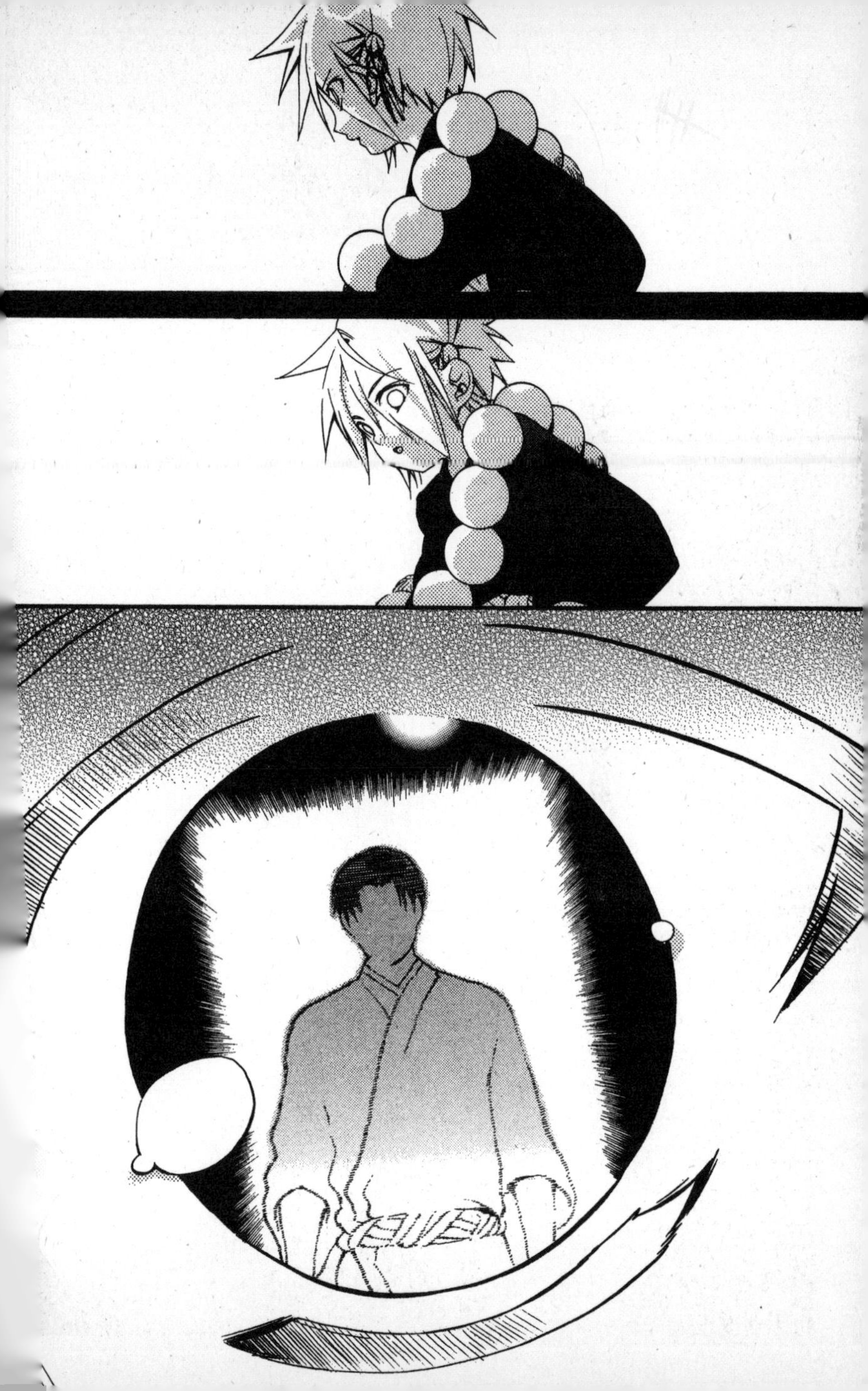

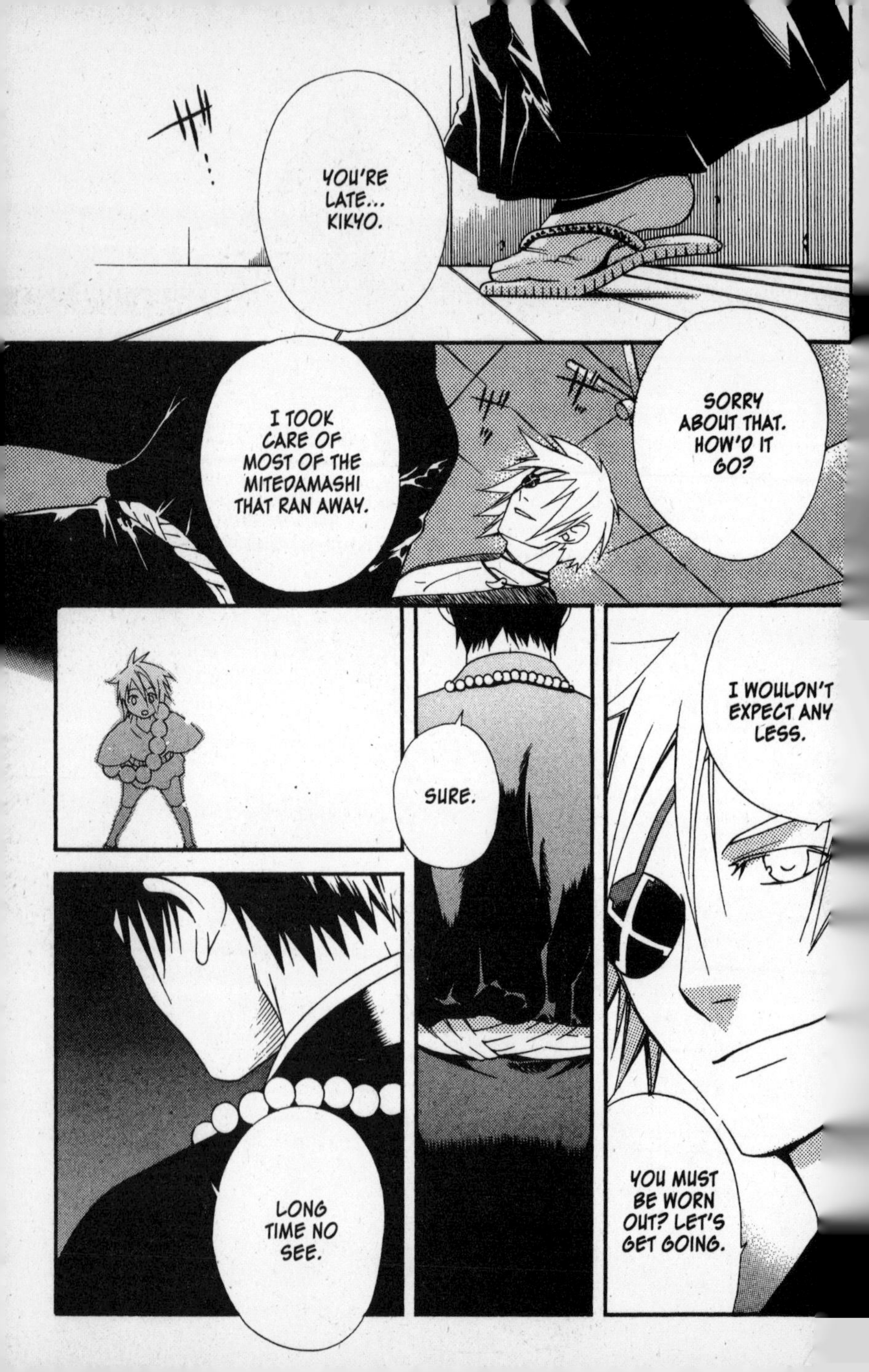
YOU'RE LATE... KIKYO.
SORRY ABOUT THAT. HOW'D IT GO?
I TOOK CARE OF MOST OF THE MITEDAMASHI THAT RAN AWAY.
I WOULDN'T EXPECT ANY LESS.
YOU MUST BE WORN OUT? LET'S GET GOING.
SURE.
LONG TIME NO SEE.

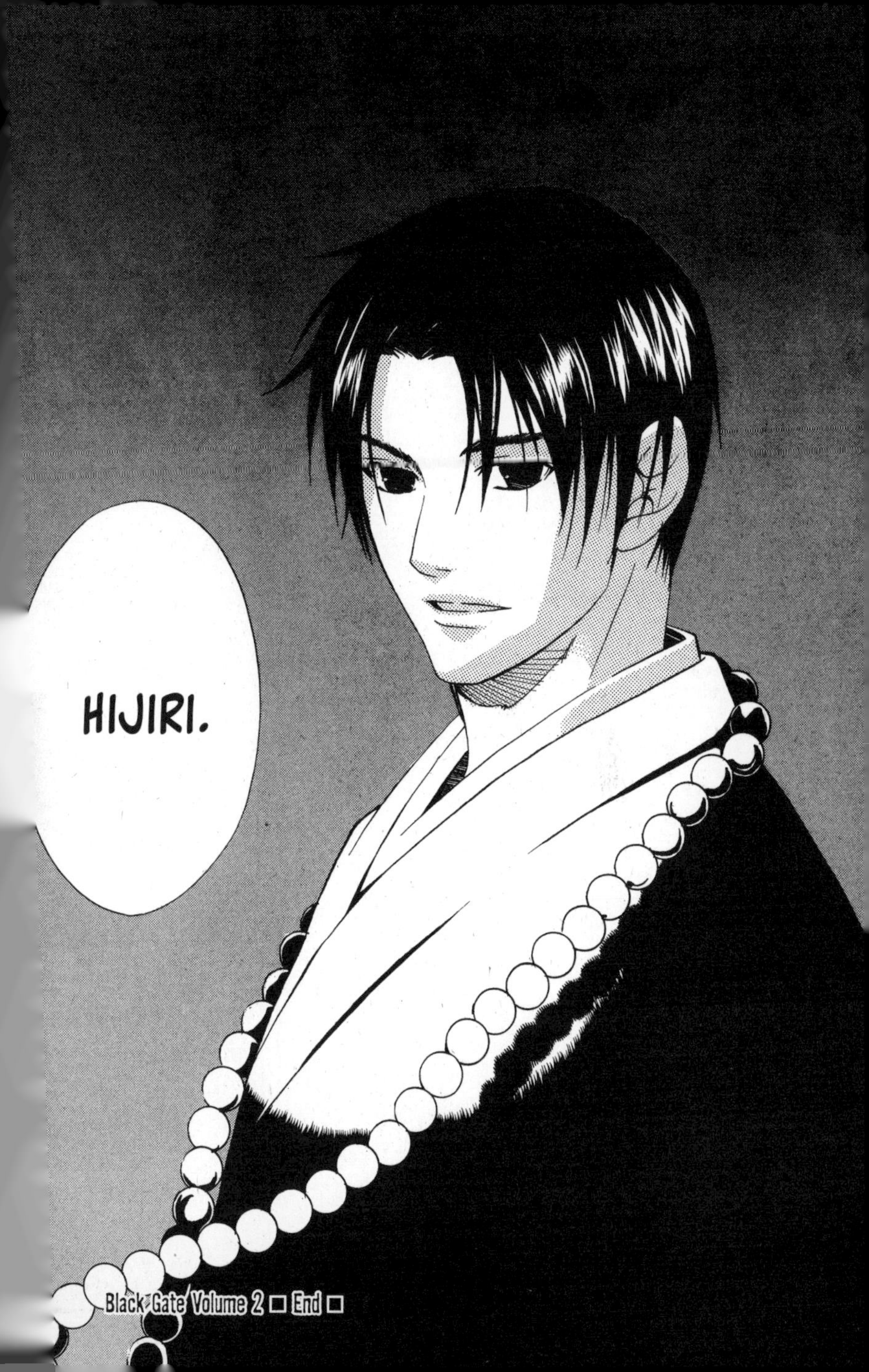
HIJIRI.
Black Gate Volume 2 □ End □

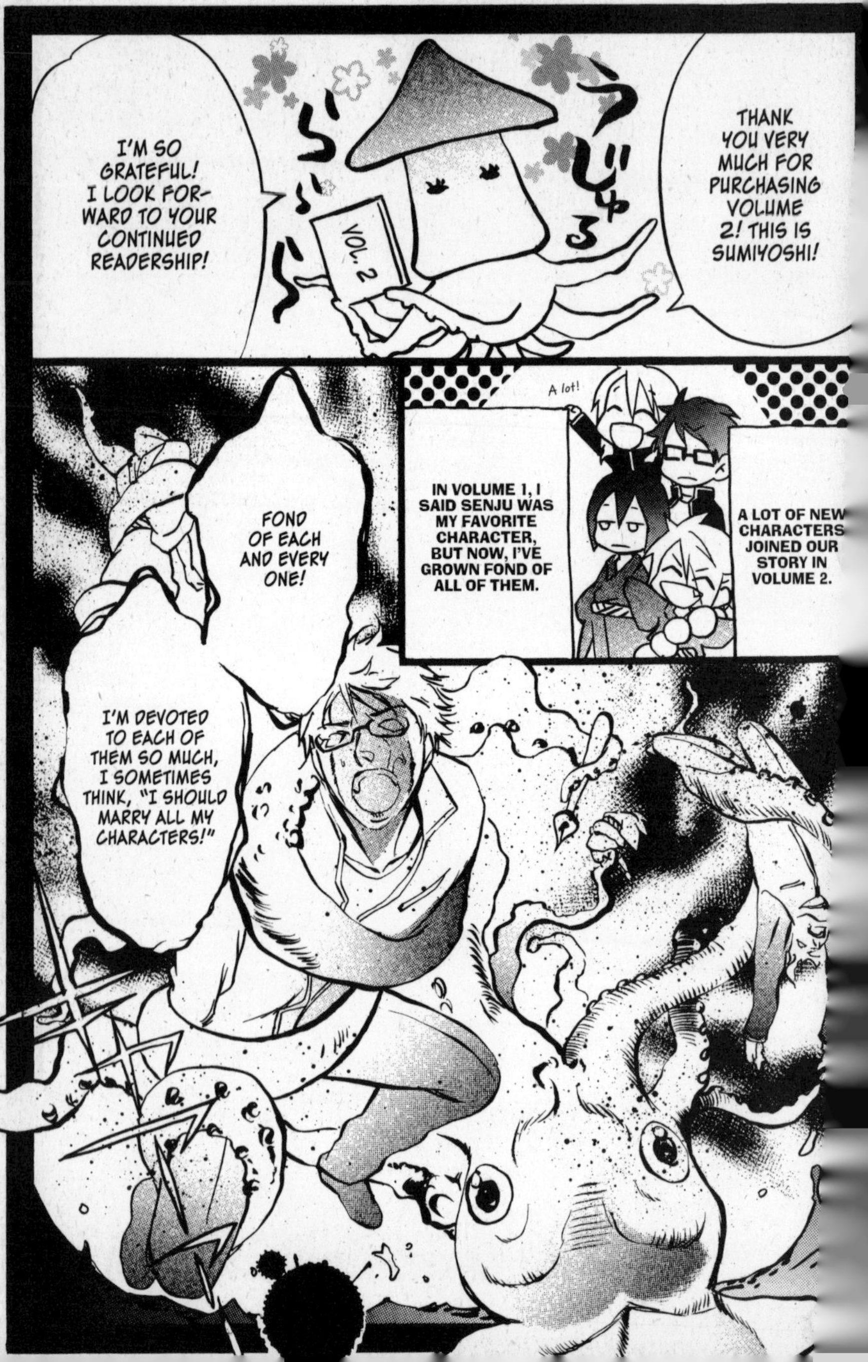
THANK YOU VERY MUCH FOR PURCHASING VOLUME 2! THIS IS SUMIYOSHI!
VOL. 2
I'M SO GRATEFUL! I LOOK FOR-WARD TO YOUR CONTINUED READERSHIP!
A LOT OF NEW CHARACTERS JOINED OUR STORY IN VOLUME 2.
A lot!
IN VOLUME 1, I SAID SENJU WAS MY FAVORITE CHARACTER, BUT NOW, I'VE GROWN FOND OF ALL OF THEM.
FOND OF EACH AND EVERY ONE!
I'M DEVOTED TO EACH OF THEM SO MUCH, I SOMETIMES THINK, "I SHOULD MARRY ALL MY CHARACTERS!"

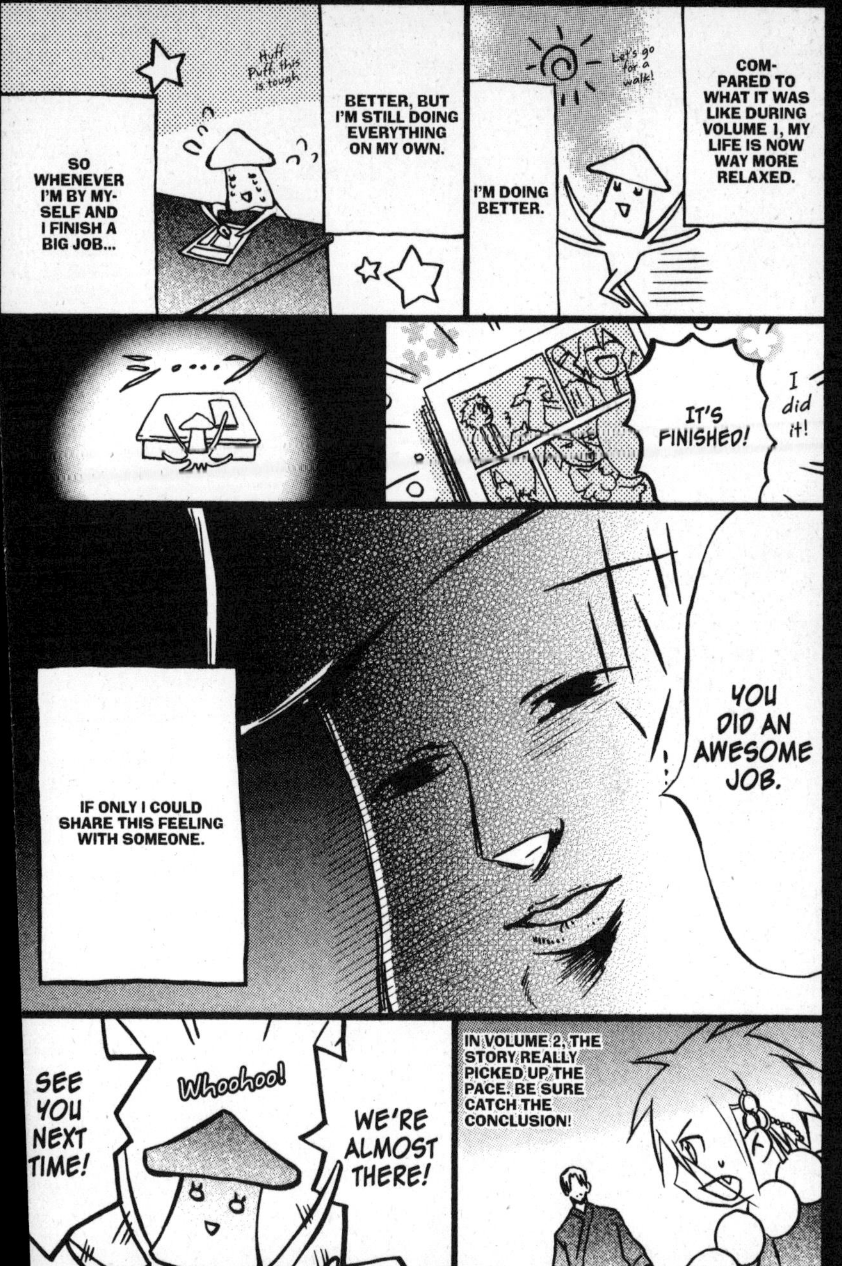
COMPARED TO WHAT IT WAS LIKE DURING VOLUME 1, MY LIFE IS NOW WAY MORE RELAXED.
Let's go for a walk!
I'M DOING BETTER.
BETTER, BUT I'M STILL DOING EVERYTHING ON MY OWN.
Huff Puff this is tough
SO WHENEVER I'M BY MYSELF AND I FINISH A BIG JOB...
I did it!
IT'S FINISHED!
....
YOU DID AN AWESOME JOB.
IF ONLY I COULD SHARE THIS FEELING WITH SOMEONE.
IN VOLUME 2, THE STORY REALLY PICKED UP THE PACE. BE SURE CATCH THE CONCLUSION!
WE'RE ALMOST THERE!
Whoohoo!
SEE YOU NEXT TIME!

ord ■End■

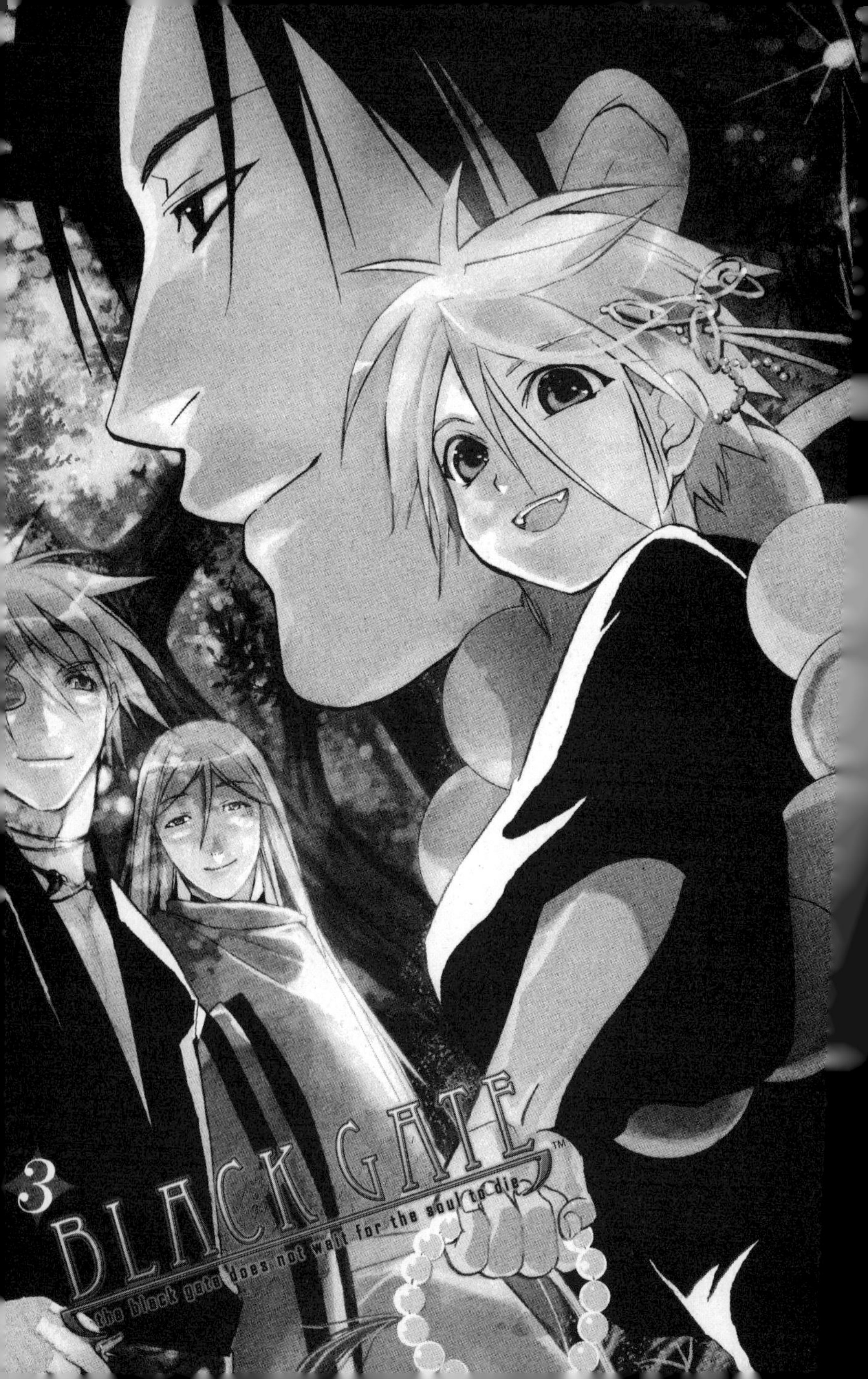
3
BLACK GATE™
the black gate does not wait for the soul to die

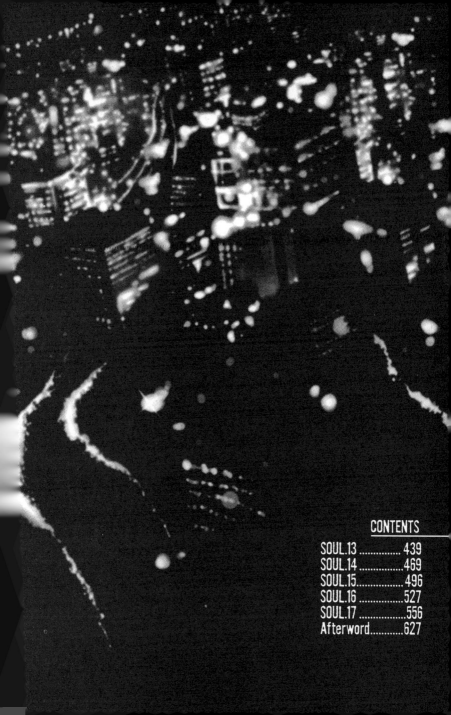

CONTENTS

SOUL.13 439
SOUL.14 469
SOUL.15 496
SOUL.16 527
SOUL.17 556
Afterword 627

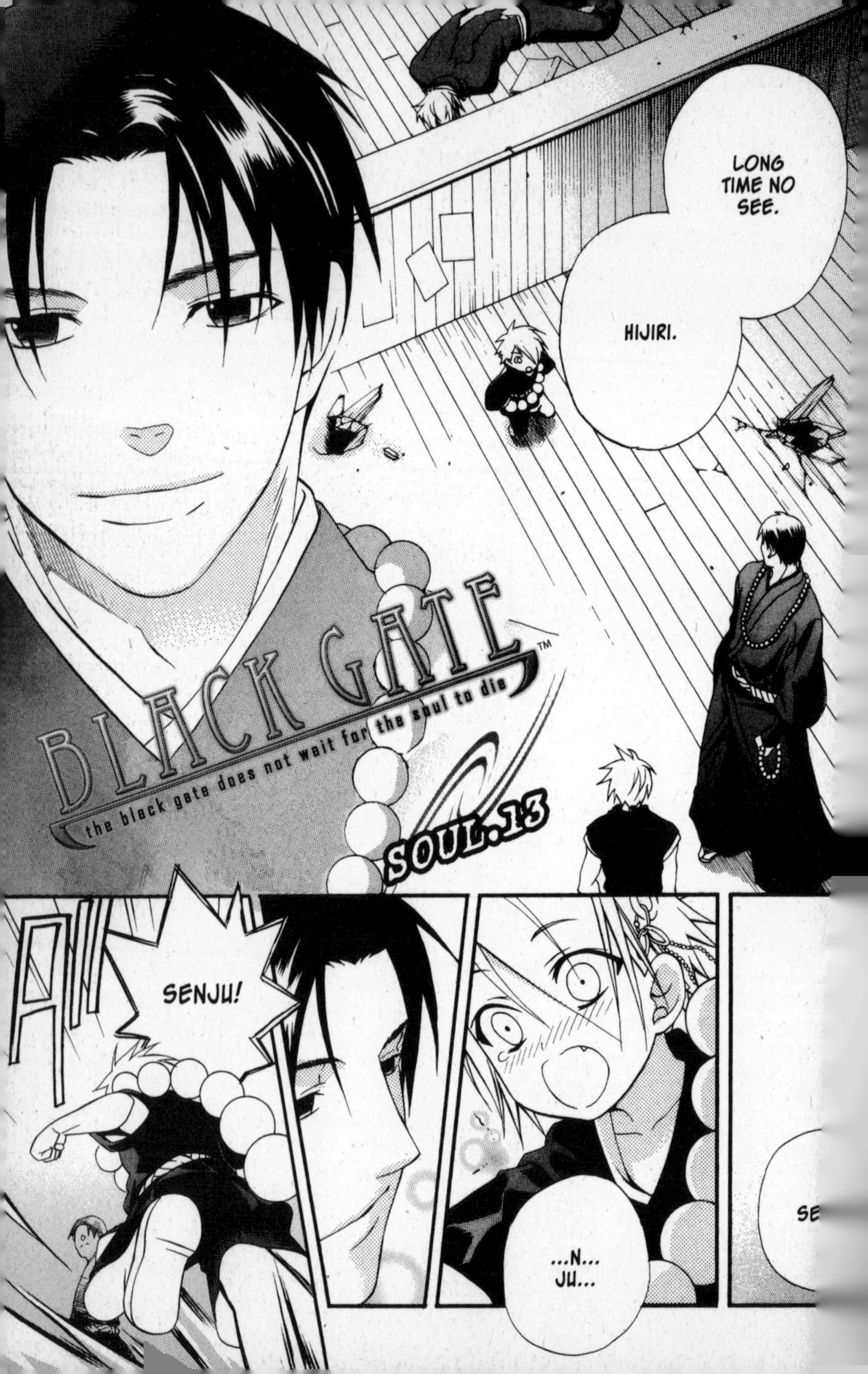
LONG TIME NO SEE.
HIJIRI.
BLACK GATE™
the black gate does not wait for the soul to die
SOUL.13
SE
...N... JU...
SENJU!

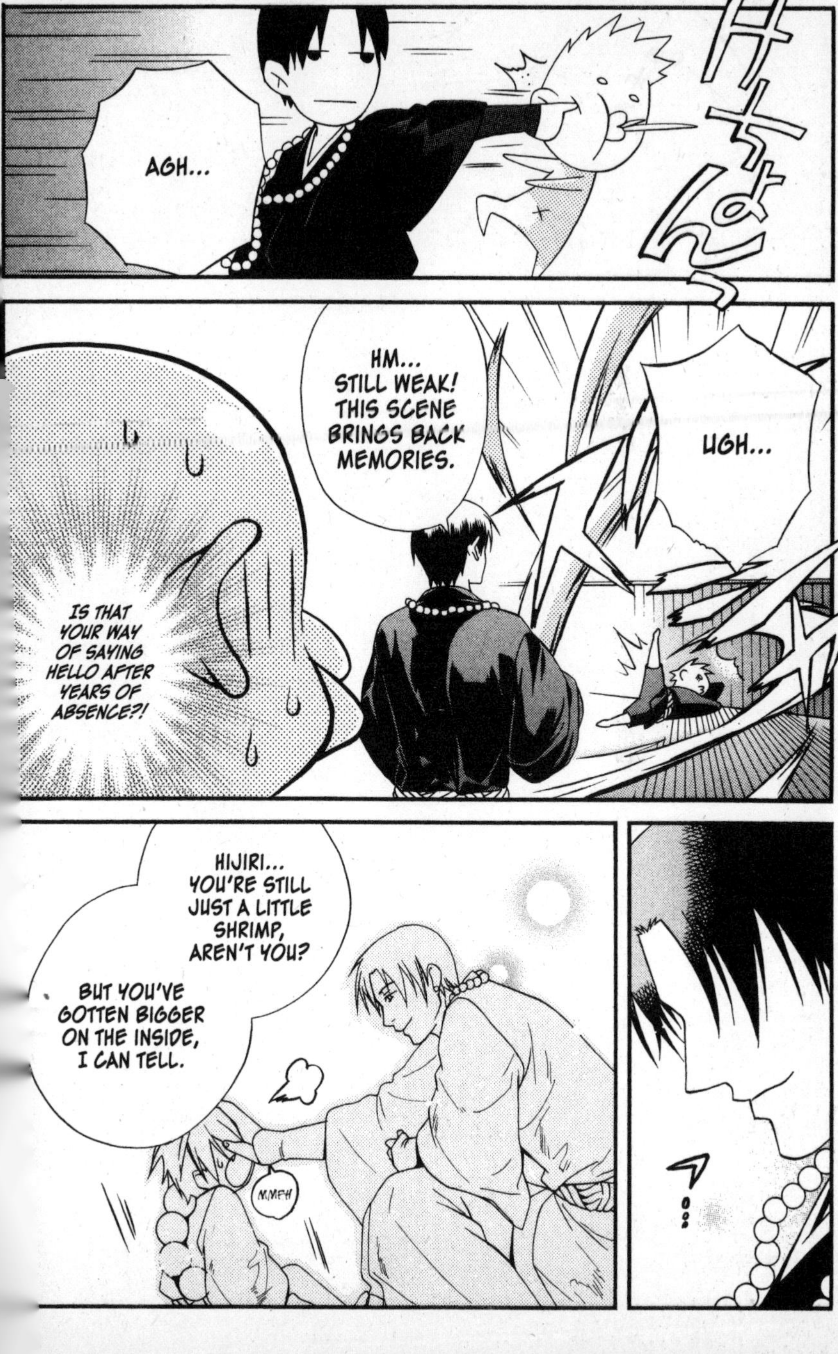
AGH...
UGH...
HM... STILL WEAK! THIS SCENE BRINGS BACK MEMORIES.
IS THAT YOUR WAY OF SAYING HELLO AFTER YEARS OF ABSENCE?!
...
HIJIRI... YOU'RE STILL JUST A LITTLE SHRIMP, AREN'T YOU?
BUT YOU'VE GOTTEN BIGGER ON THE INSIDE, I CAN TELL.
MMFH

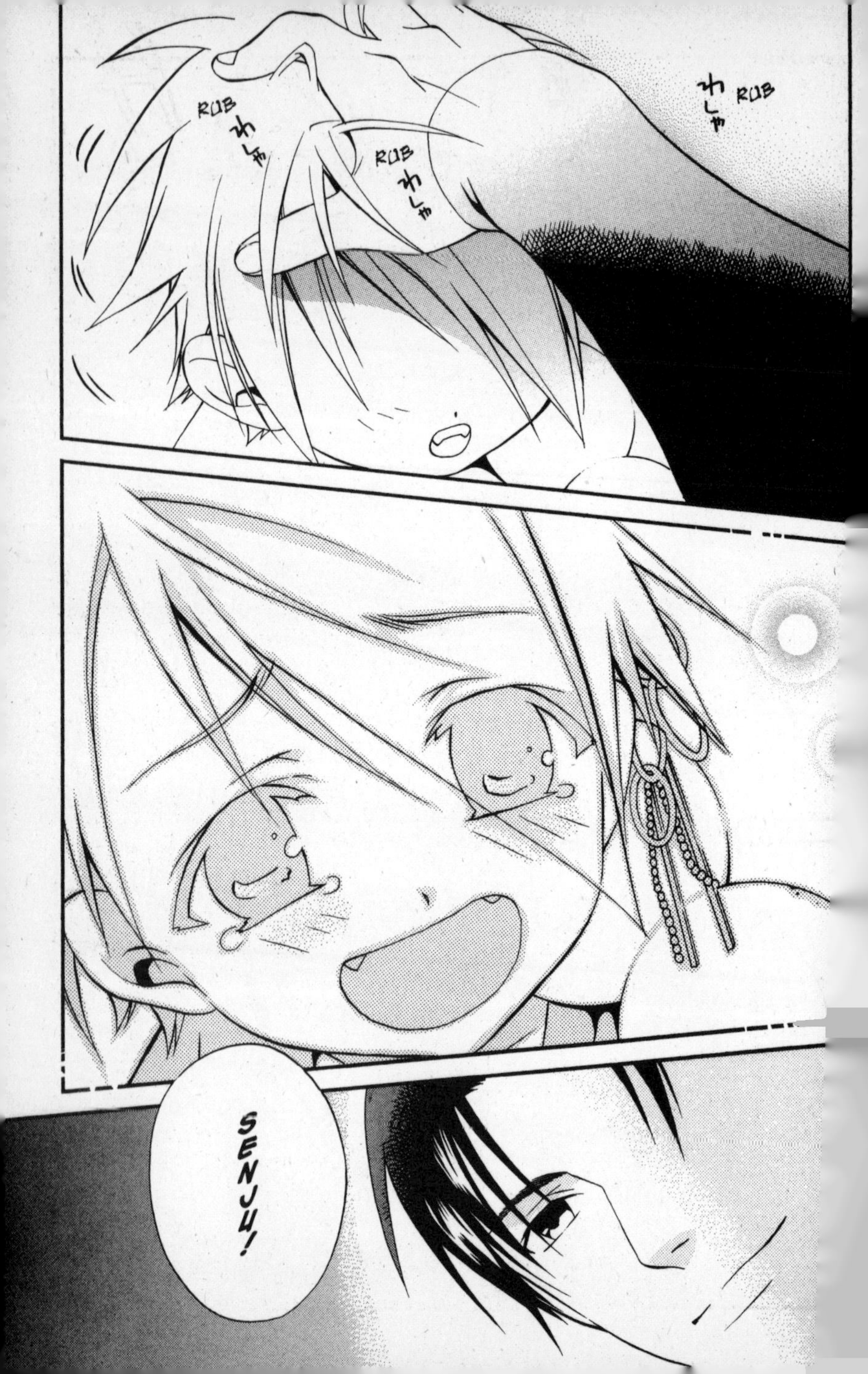

RUB わしゃ
RUB わしゃ
RUB わしゃ
SENJU!

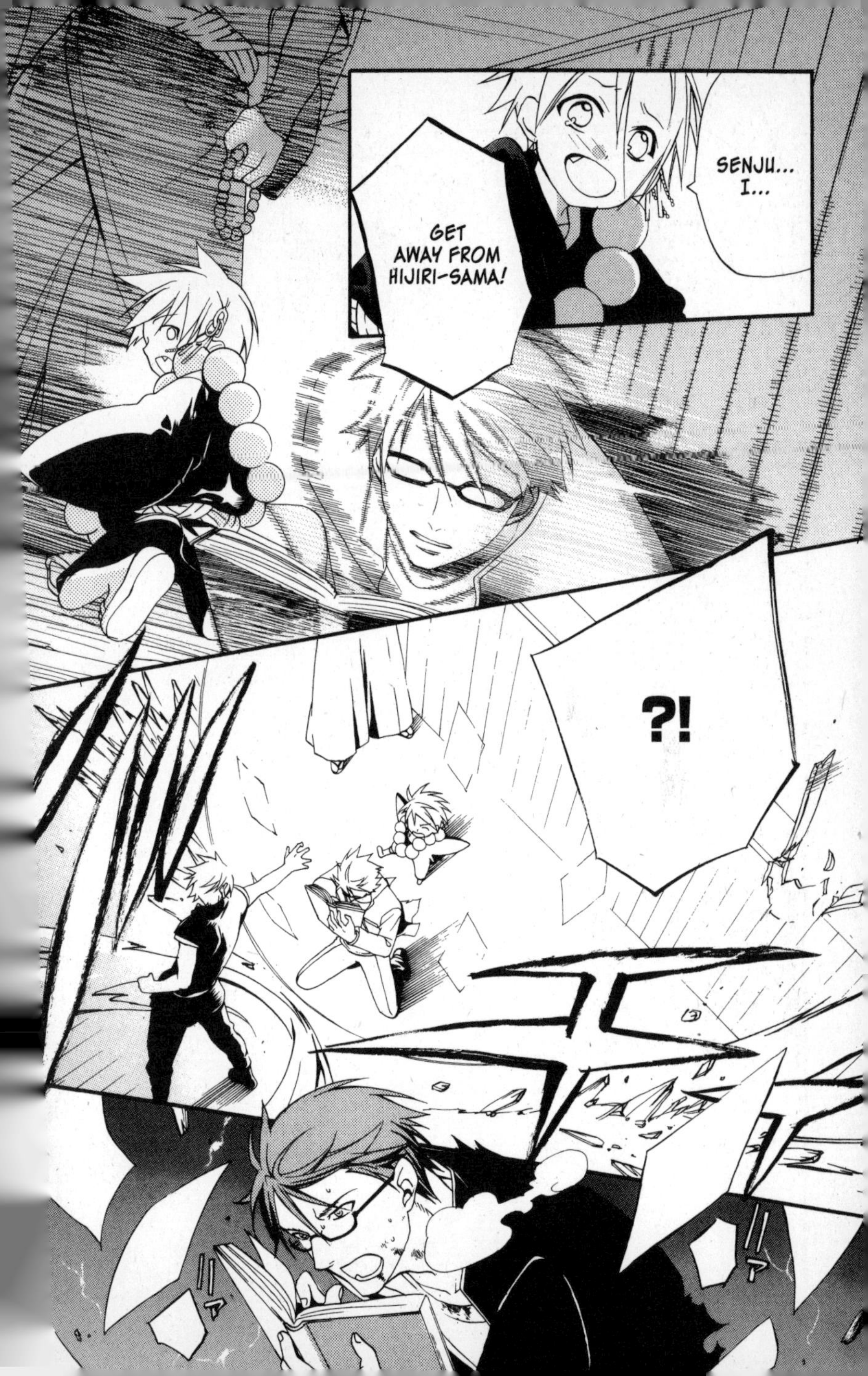
SENJU... I...
GET AWAY FROM HIJIRI-SAMA!
?!

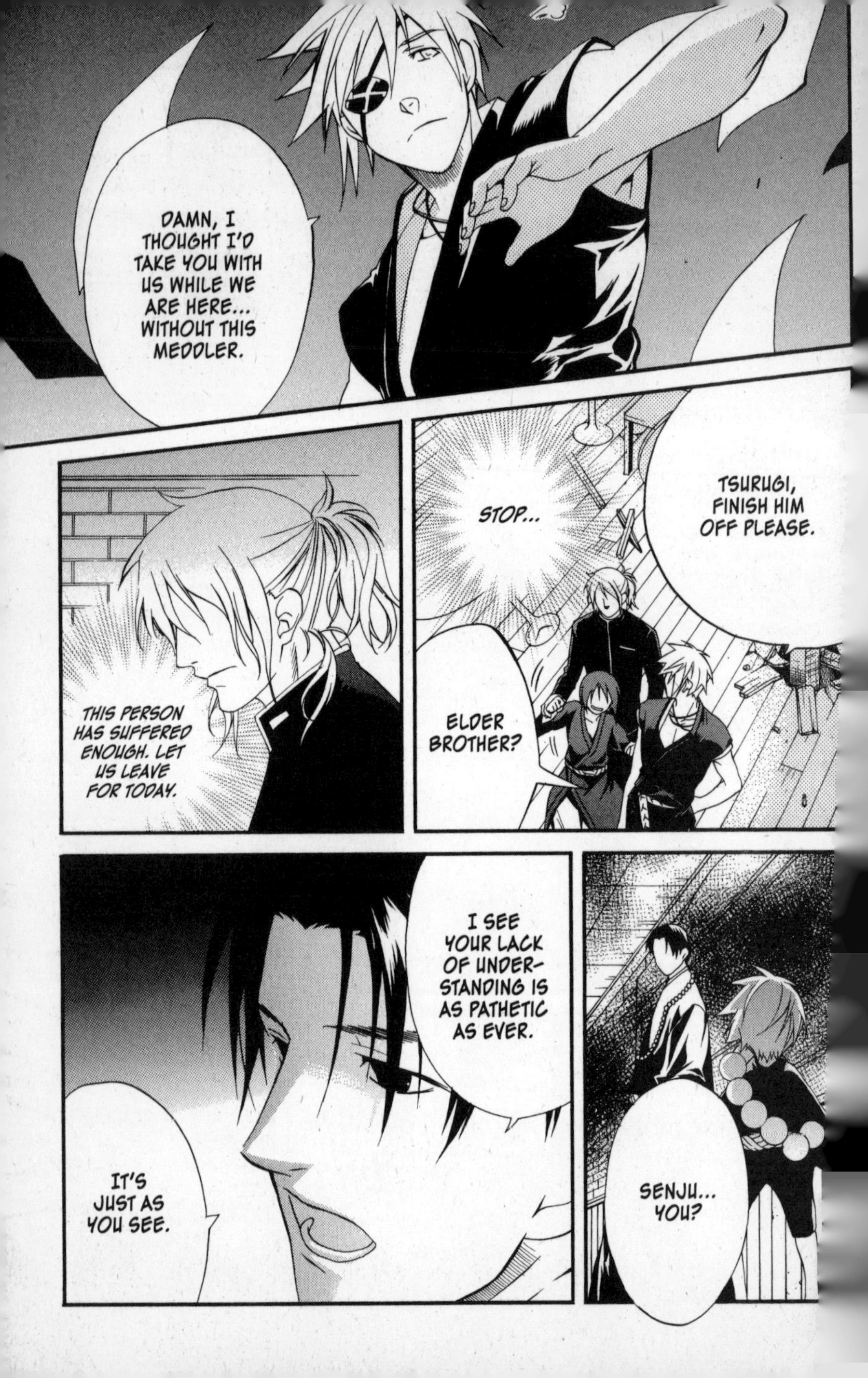
DAMN, I THOUGHT I'D TAKE YOU WITH US WHILE WE ARE HERE... WITHOUT THIS MEDDLER.
TSURUGI, FINISH HIM OFF PLEASE.
STOP...
ELDER BROTHER?
THIS PERSON HAS SUFFERED ENOUGH. LET US LEAVE FOR TODAY.
SENJU... YOU?
I SEE YOUR LACK OF UNDER-STANDING IS AS PATHETIC AS EVER.
IT'S JUST AS YOU SEE.

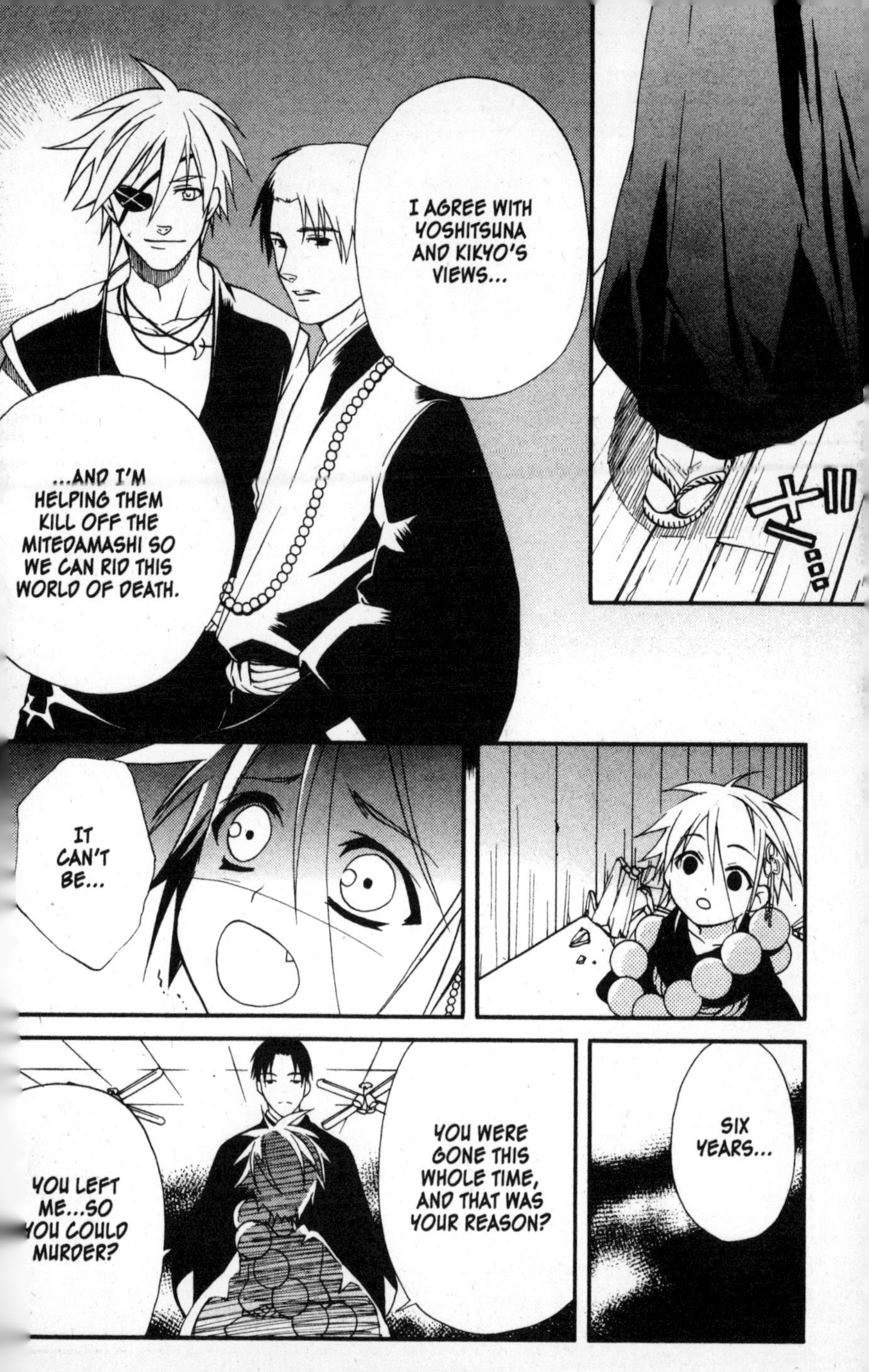
I AGREE WITH YOSHITSUNA AND KIKYO'S VIEWS...
...AND I'M HELPING THEM KILL OFF THE MITEDAMASHI SO WE CAN RID THIS WORLD OF DEATH.
IT CAN'T BE...
SIX YEARS...
YOU WERE GONE THIS WHOLE TIME, AND THAT WAS YOUR REASON?
YOU LEFT ME...SO YOU COULD MURDER?

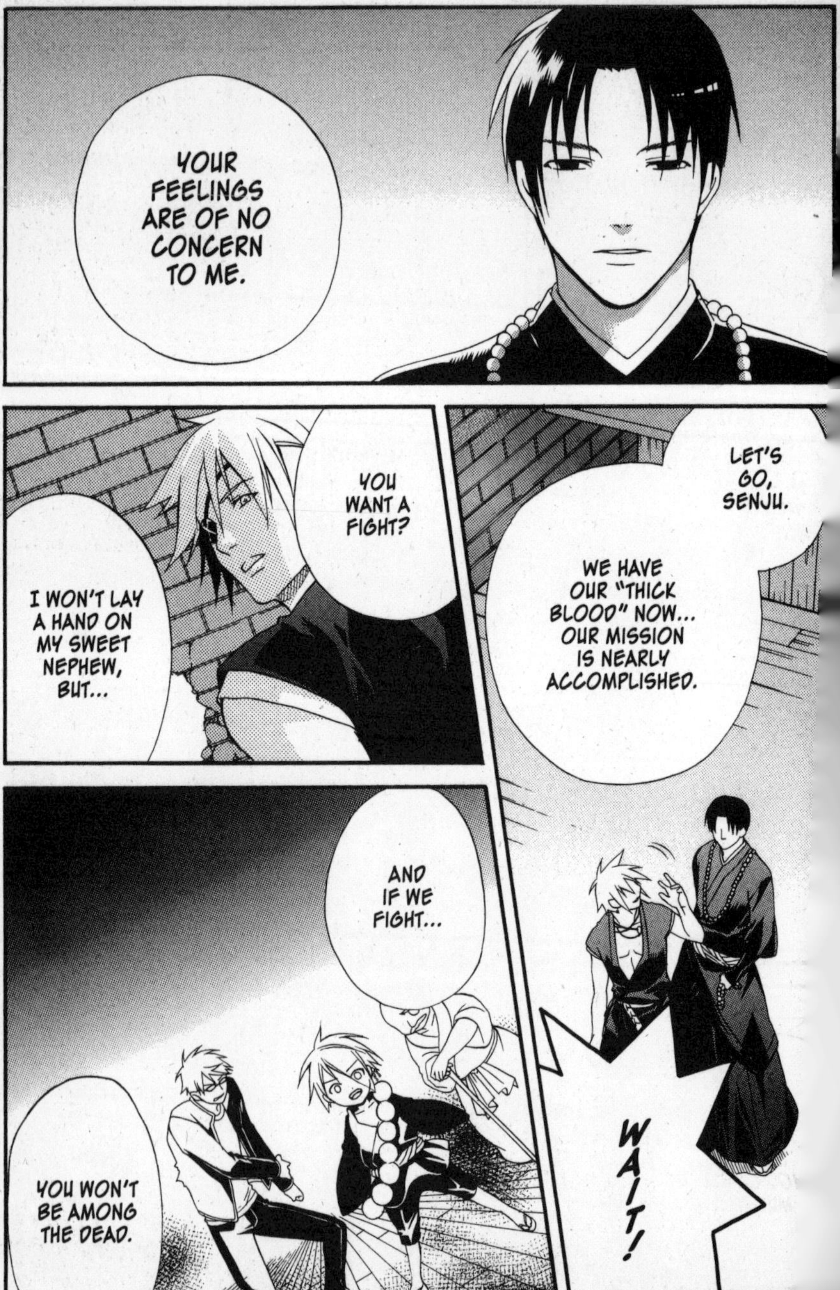
YOUR FEELINGS ARE OF NO CONCERN TO ME.
LET'S GO, SENJU.
WE HAVE OUR "THICK BLOOD" NOW... OUR MISSION IS NEARLY ACCOMPLISHED.
WAIT!
YOU WANT A FIGHT?
I WON'T LAY A HAND ON MY SWEET NEPHEW, BUT...
AND IF WE FIGHT...
YOU WON'T BE AMONG THE DEAD.

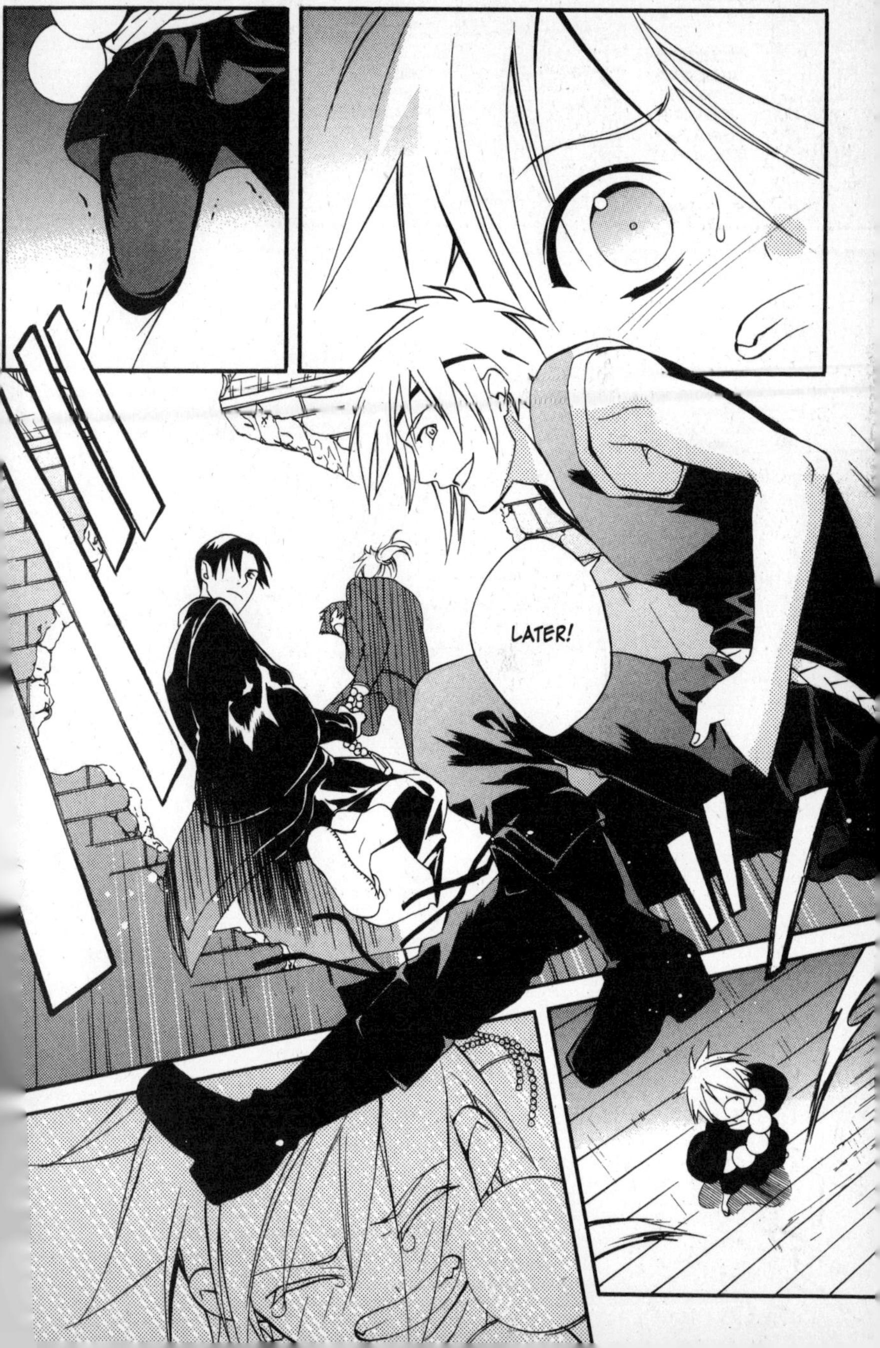
LATER!

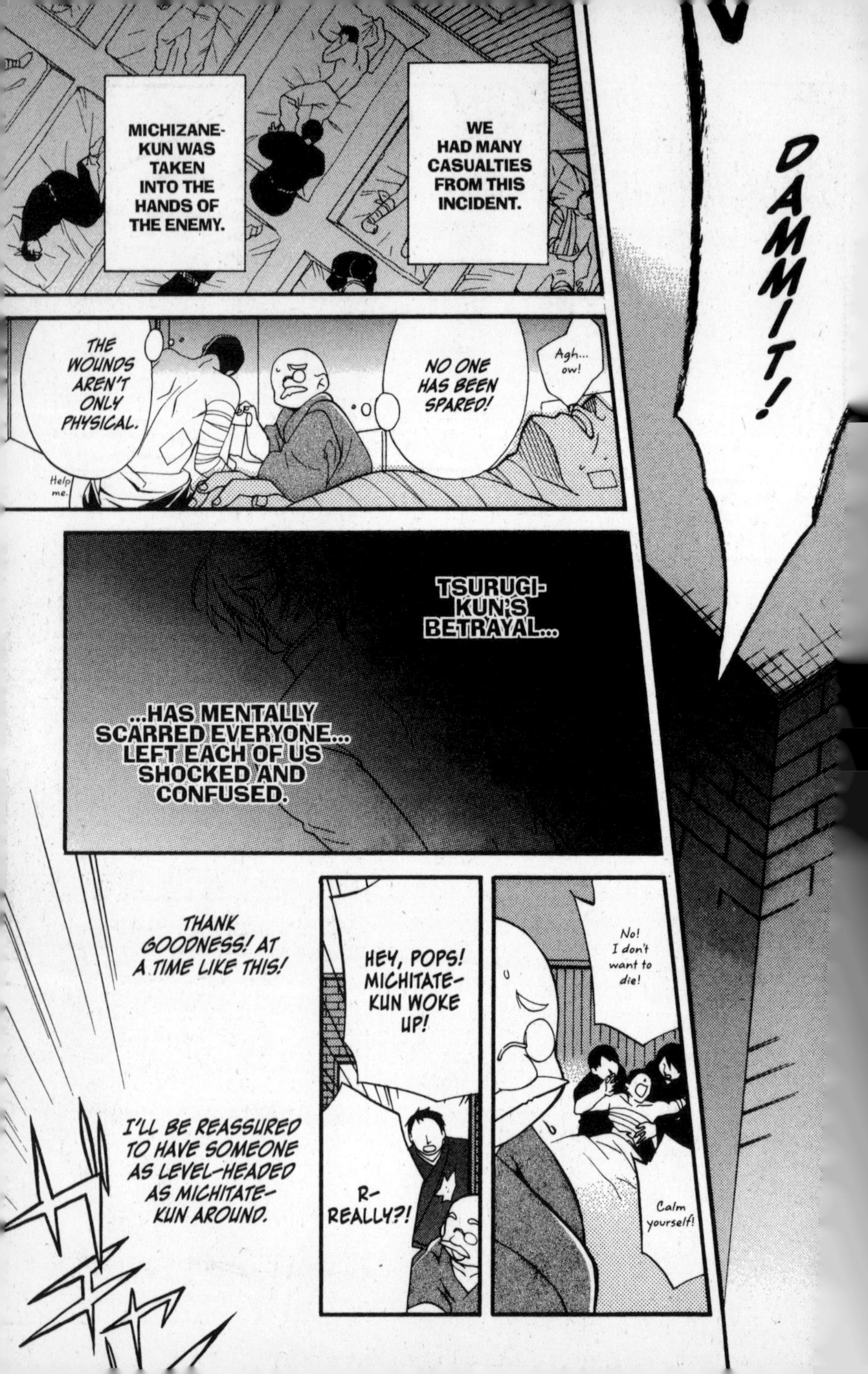
DAMMIT!
WE HAD MANY CASUALTIES FROM THIS INCIDENT.
MICHIZANE-KUN WAS TAKEN INTO THE HANDS OF THE ENEMY.
Agh... ow!
NO ONE HAS BEEN SPARED!
THE WOUNDS AREN'T ONLY PHYSICAL.
Help me.
TSURUGI-KUN'S BETRAYAL...
...HAS MENTALLY SCARRED EVERYONE... LEFT EACH OF US SHOCKED AND CONFUSED.
No! I don't want to die!
Calm yourself!
HEY, POPS! MICHITATE-KUN WOKE UP!
R-REALLY?!
THANK GOODNESS! AT A TIME LIKE THIS!
I'LL BE REASSURED TO HAVE SOMEONE AS LEVEL-HEADED AS MICHITATE-KUN AROUND.

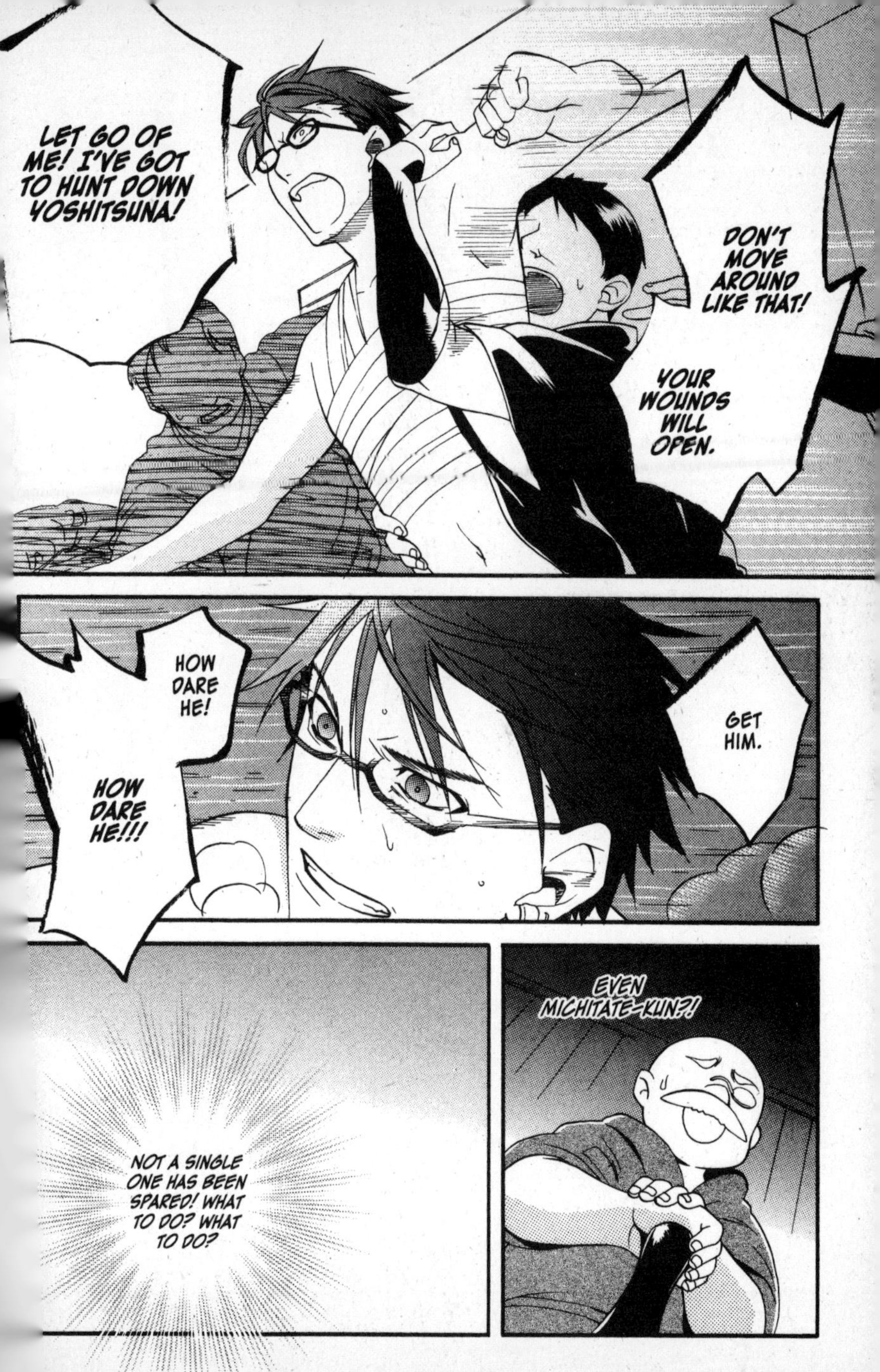
DON'T MOVE AROUND LIKE THAT!
YOUR WOUNDS WILL OPEN.
LET GO OF ME! I'VE GOT TO HUNT DOWN YOSHITSUNA!
GET HIM.
HOW DARE HE!
HOW DARE HE!!!
EVEN MICHITATE-KUN?!
NOT A SINGLE ONE HAS BEEN SPARED! WHAT TO DO? WHAT TO DO?

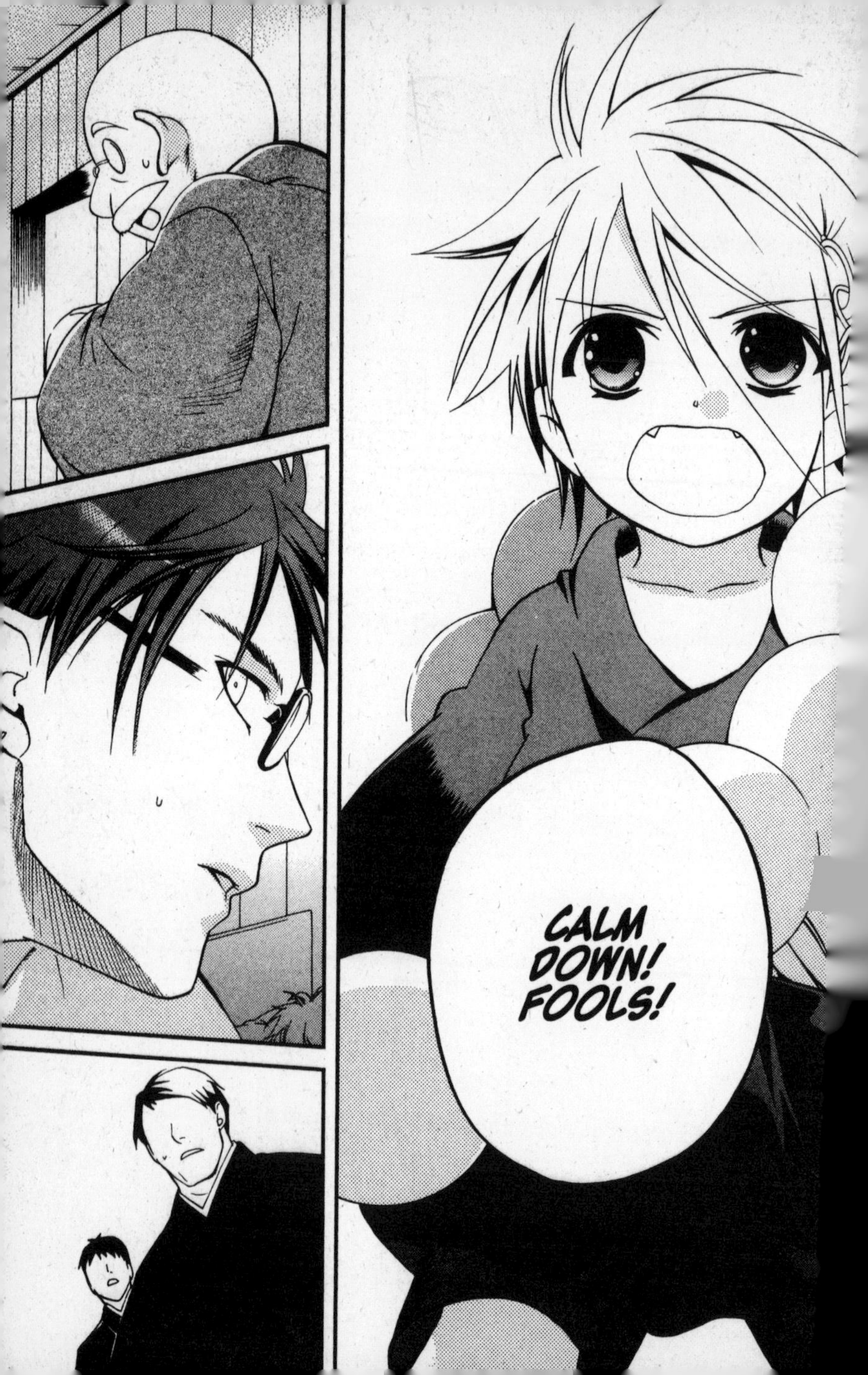
CALM DOWN! FOOLS!

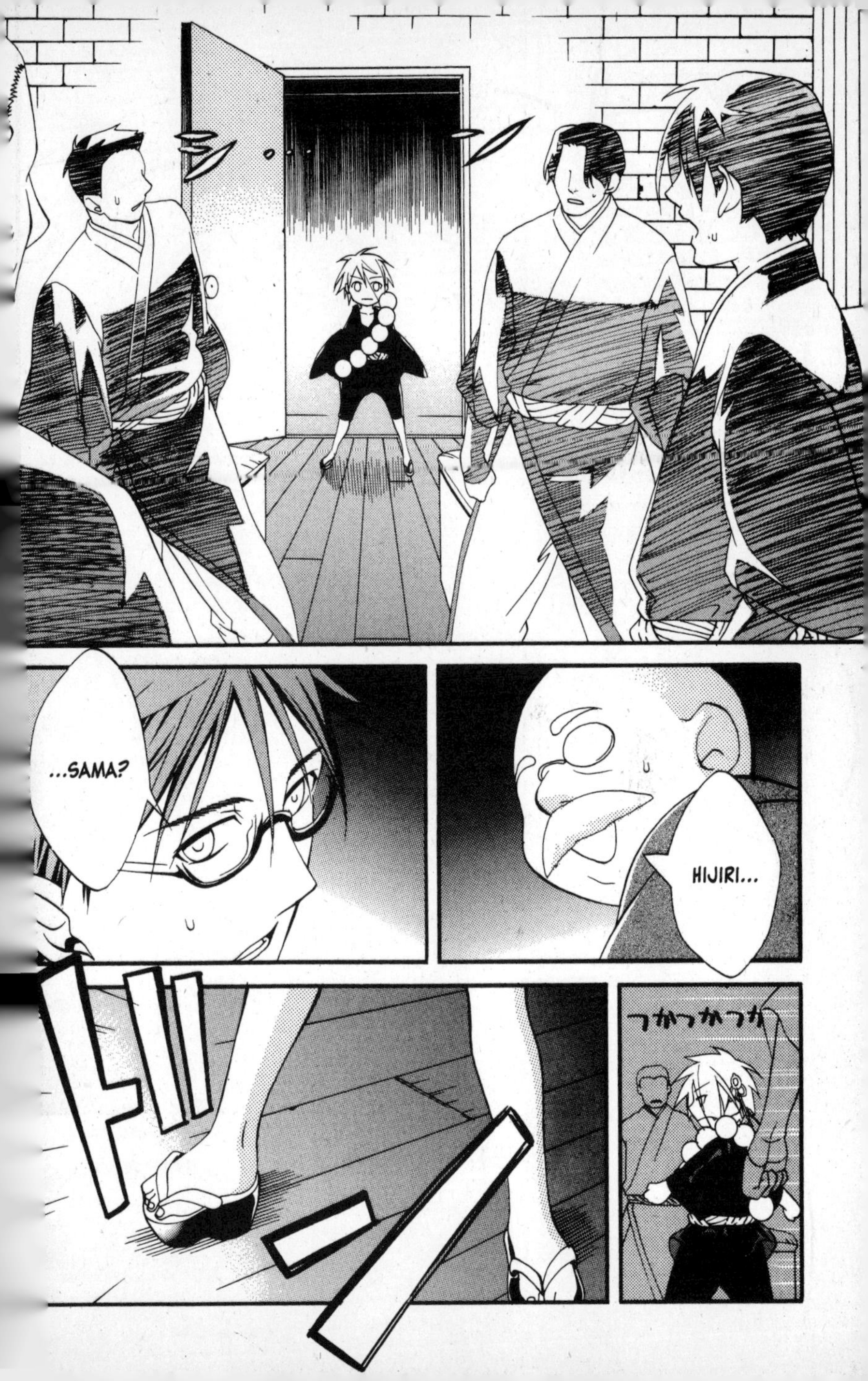
HIJIRI...
...SAMA?

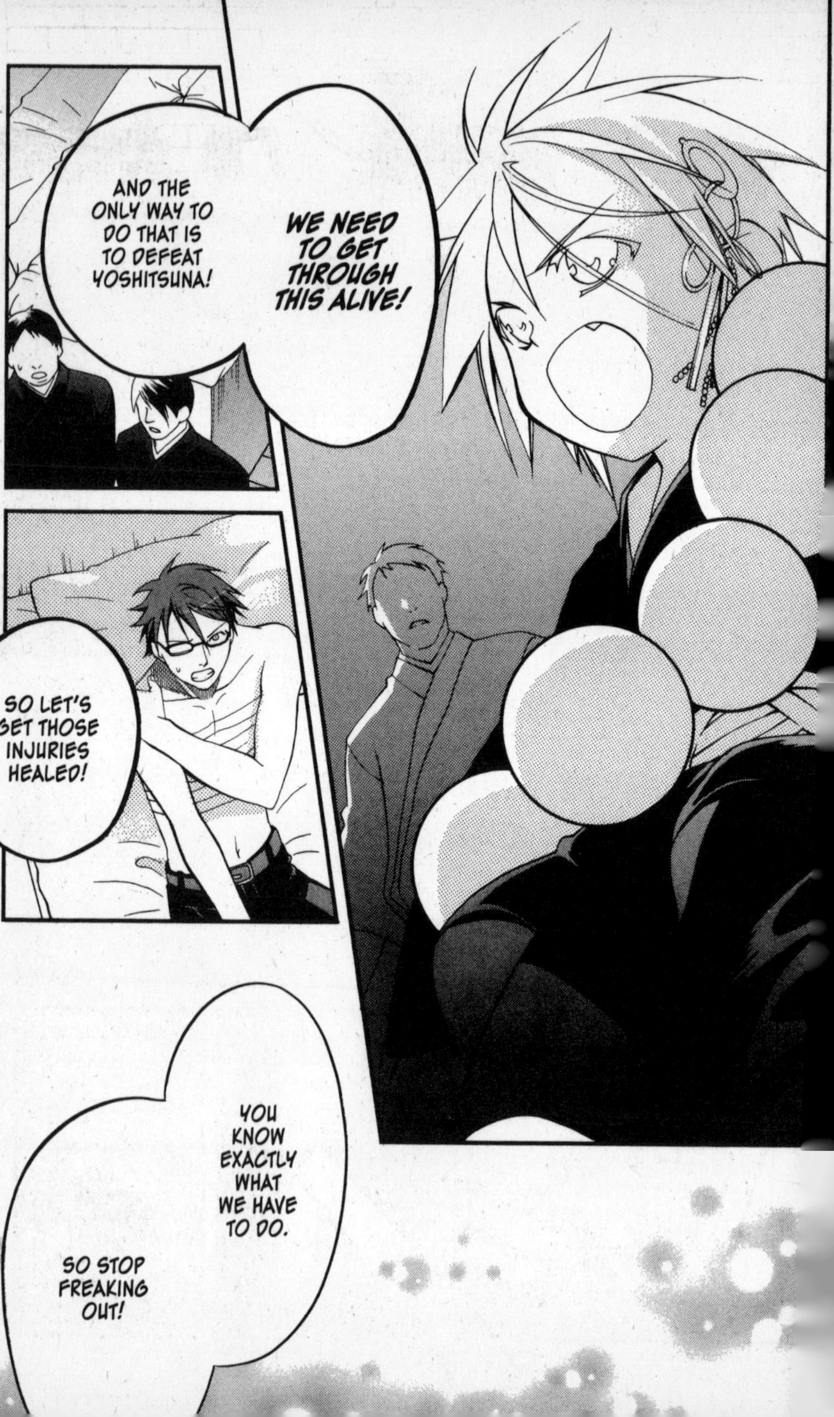
WE NEED TO GET THROUGH THIS ALIVE!
AND THE ONLY WAY TO DO THAT IS TO DEFEAT YOSHITSUNA!
SO LET'S GET THOSE INJURIES HEALED!
YOU KNOW EXACTLY WHAT WE HAVE TO DO.
SO STOP FREAKING OUT!

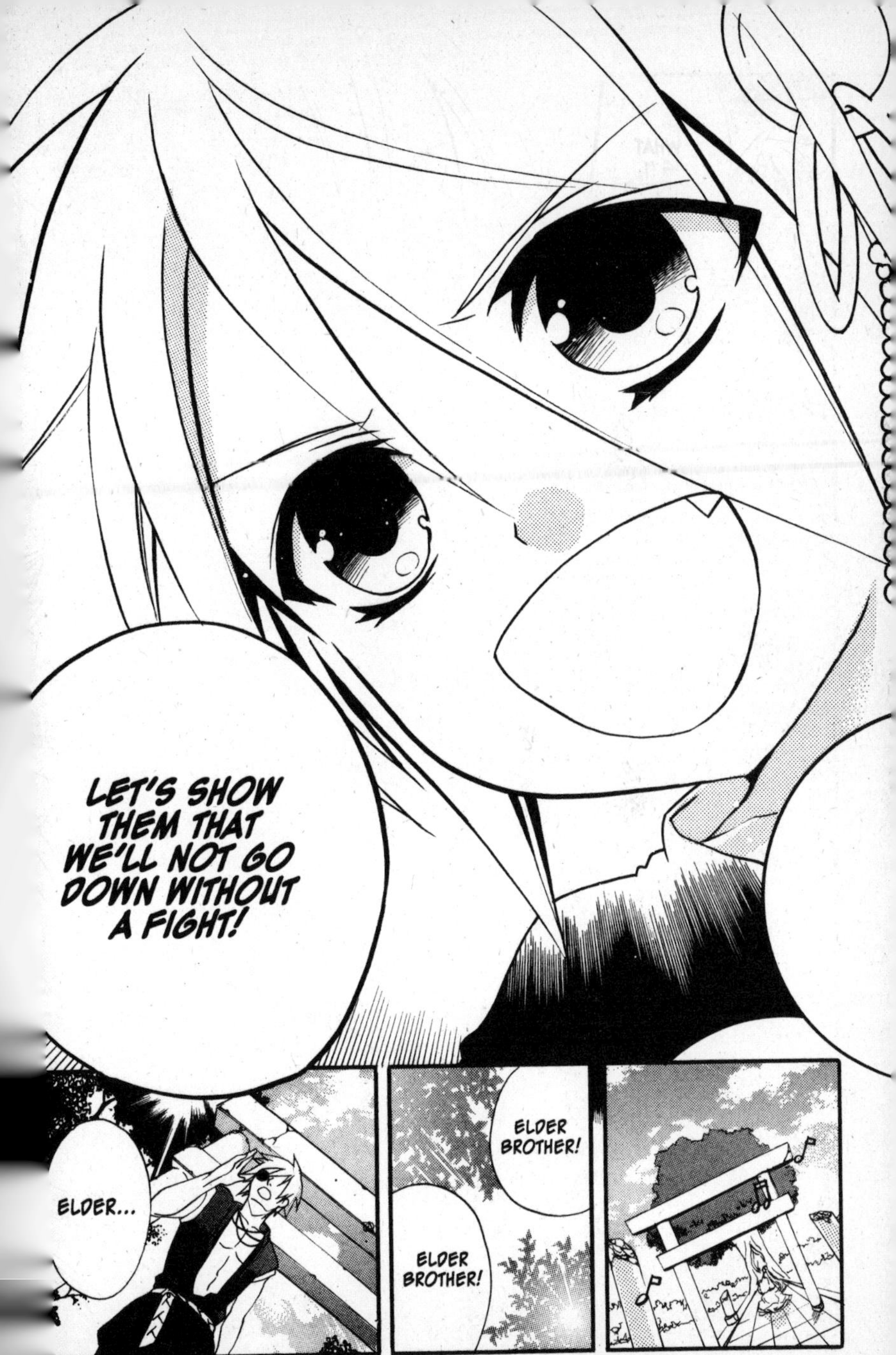
LET'S SHOW THEM THAT WE'LL NOT GO DOWN WITHOUT A FIGHT!
ELDER BROTHER!
ELDER BROTHER!
ELDER...

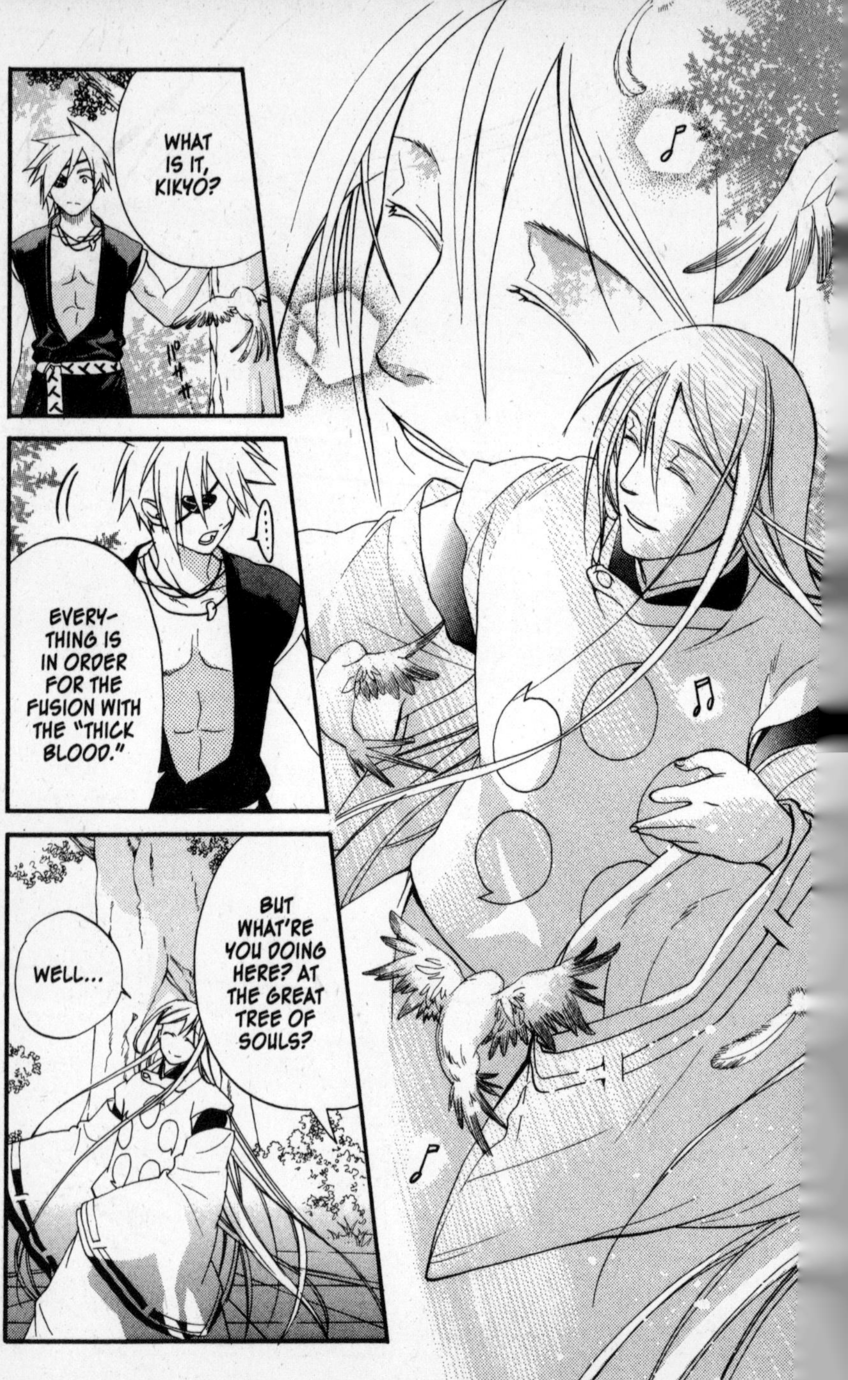
WHAT IS IT, KIKYO?
パサッ
...
EVERY-THING IS IN ORDER FOR THE FUSION WITH THE "THICK BLOOD."
BUT WHAT'RE YOU DOING HERE? AT THE GREAT TREE OF SOULS?
WELL...

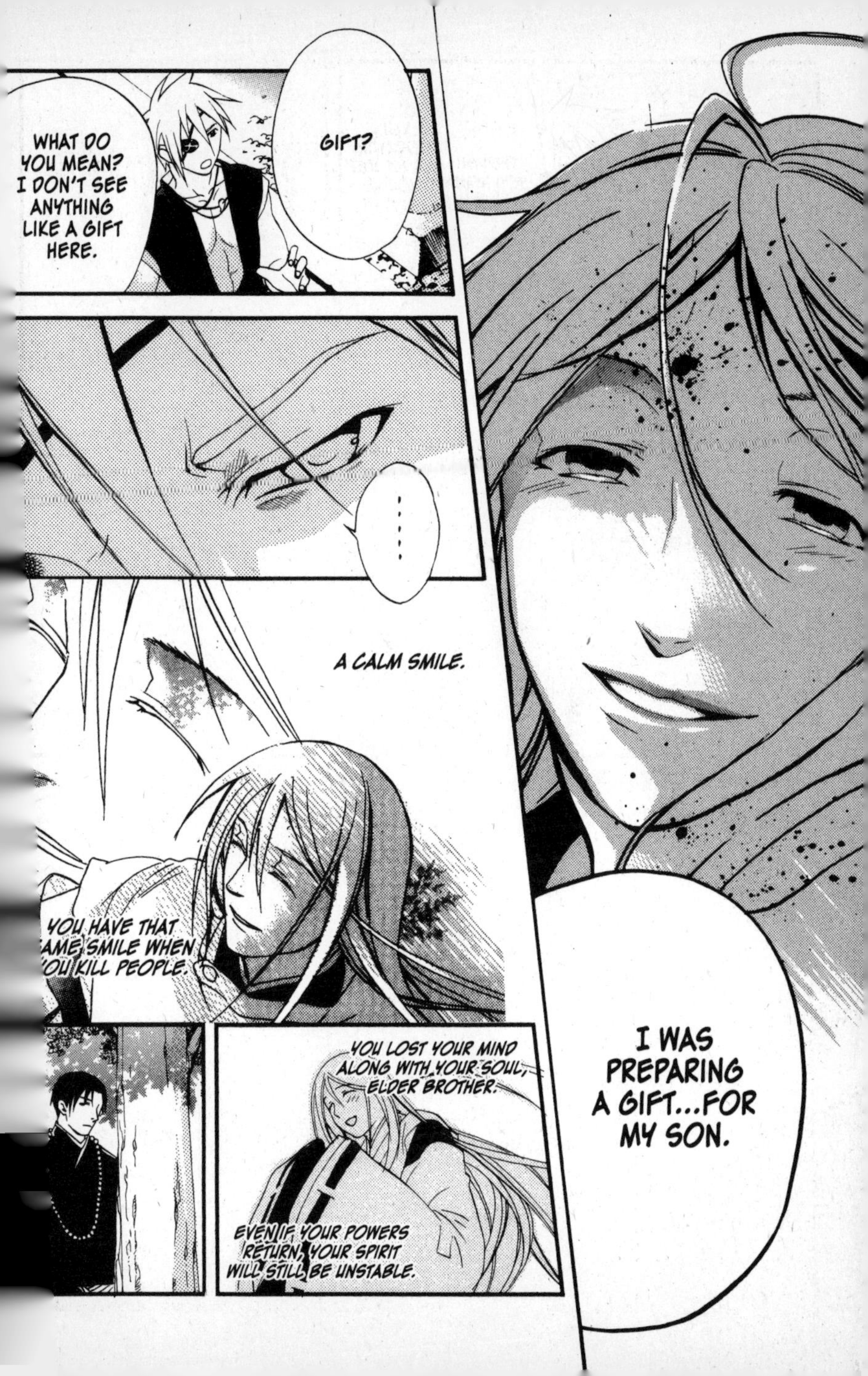
I WAS PREPARING A GIFT...FOR MY SON.
GIFT?
WHAT DO YOU MEAN? I DON'T SEE ANYTHING LIKE A GIFT HERE.
....
A CALM SMILE.
YOU HAVE THAT AME SMILE WHEN OU KILL PEOPLE.
YOU LOST YOUR MIND ALONG WITH YOUR SOUL, ELDER BROTHER.
EVEN IF YOUR POWERS RETURN, YOUR SPIRIT WILL STILL BE UNSTABLE.

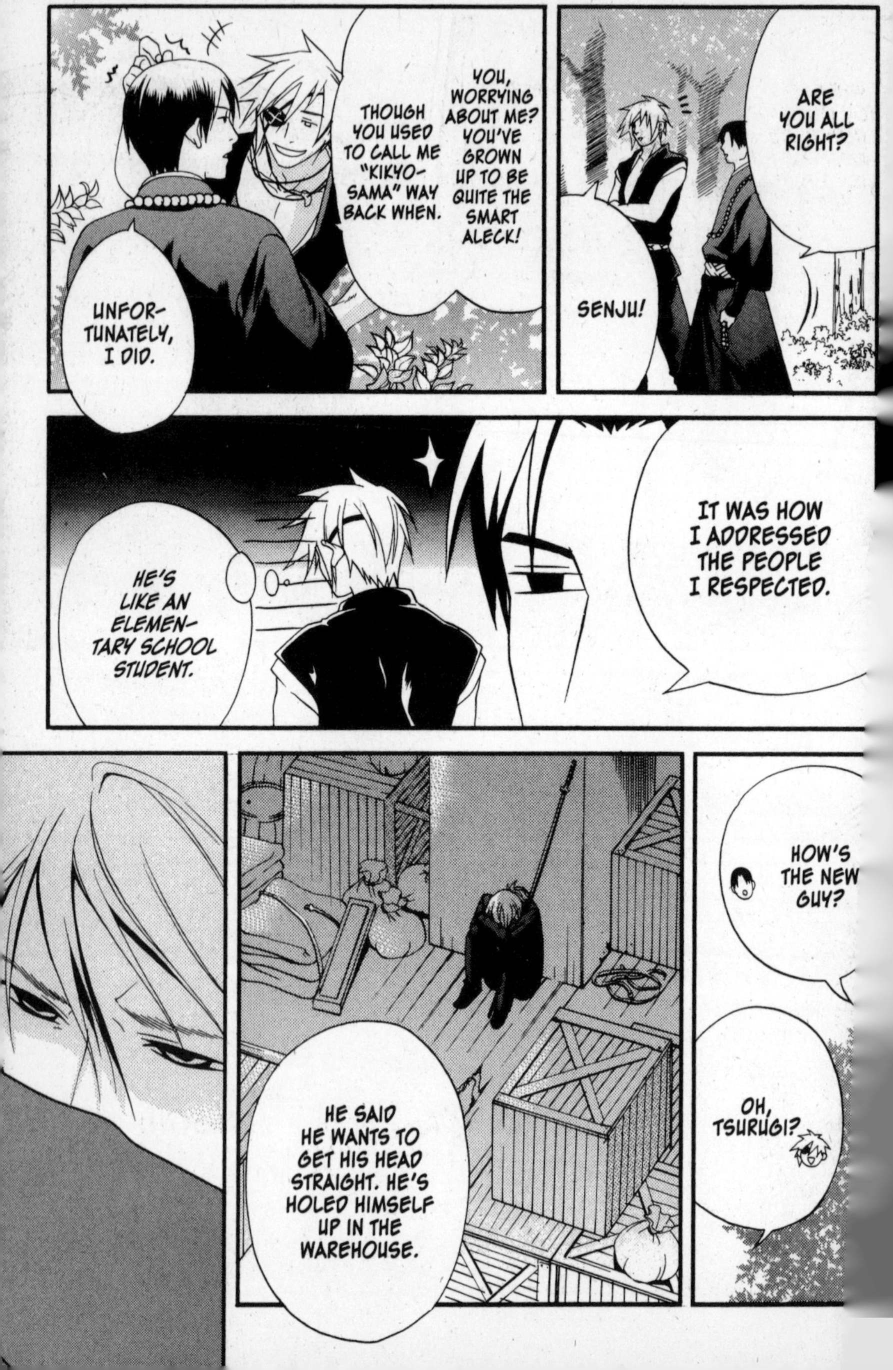
ARE YOU ALL RIGHT?
SENJU!
YOU, WORRYING ABOUT ME? YOU'VE GROWN UP TO BE QUITE THE SMART ALECK!
THOUGH YOU USED TO CALL ME "KIKYO-SAMA" WAY BACK WHEN.
UNFORTUNATELY, I DID.
IT WAS HOW I ADDRESSED THE PEOPLE I RESPECTED.
HE'S LIKE AN ELEMENTARY SCHOOL STUDENT.
HOW'S THE NEW GUY?
OH, TSURUGI?
HE SAID HE WANTS TO GET HIS HEAD STRAIGHT. HE'S HOLED HIMSELF UP IN THE WAREHOUSE.

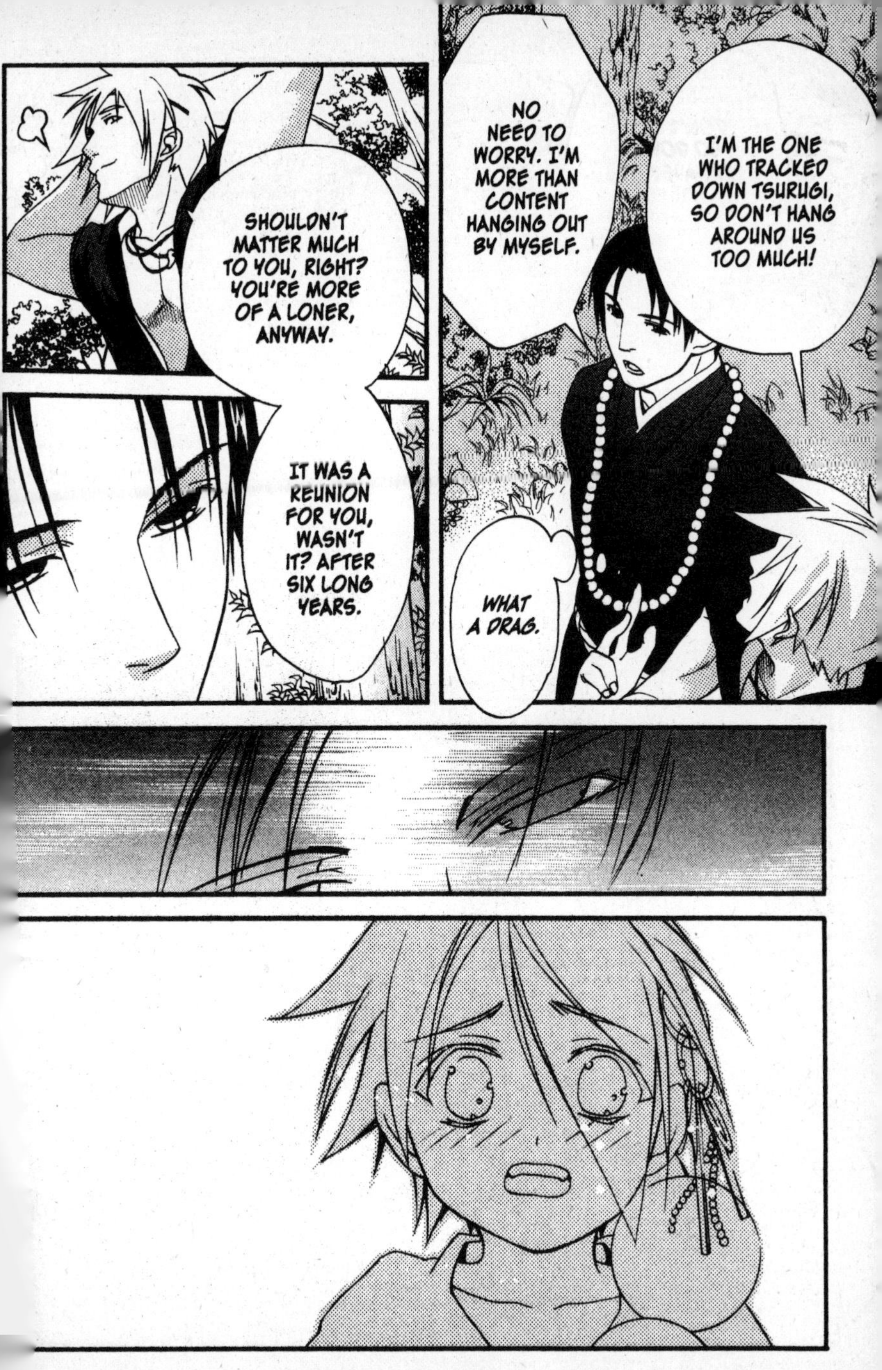
I'M THE ONE WHO TRACKED DOWN TSURUGI, SO DON'T HANG AROUND US TOO MUCH!
NO NEED TO WORRY. I'M MORE THAN CONTENT HANGING OUT BY MYSELF.
WHAT A DRAG.
SHOULDN'T MATTER MUCH TO YOU, RIGHT? YOU'RE MORE OF A LONER, ANYWAY.
IT WAS A REUNION FOR YOU, WASN'T IT? AFTER SIX LONG YEARS.

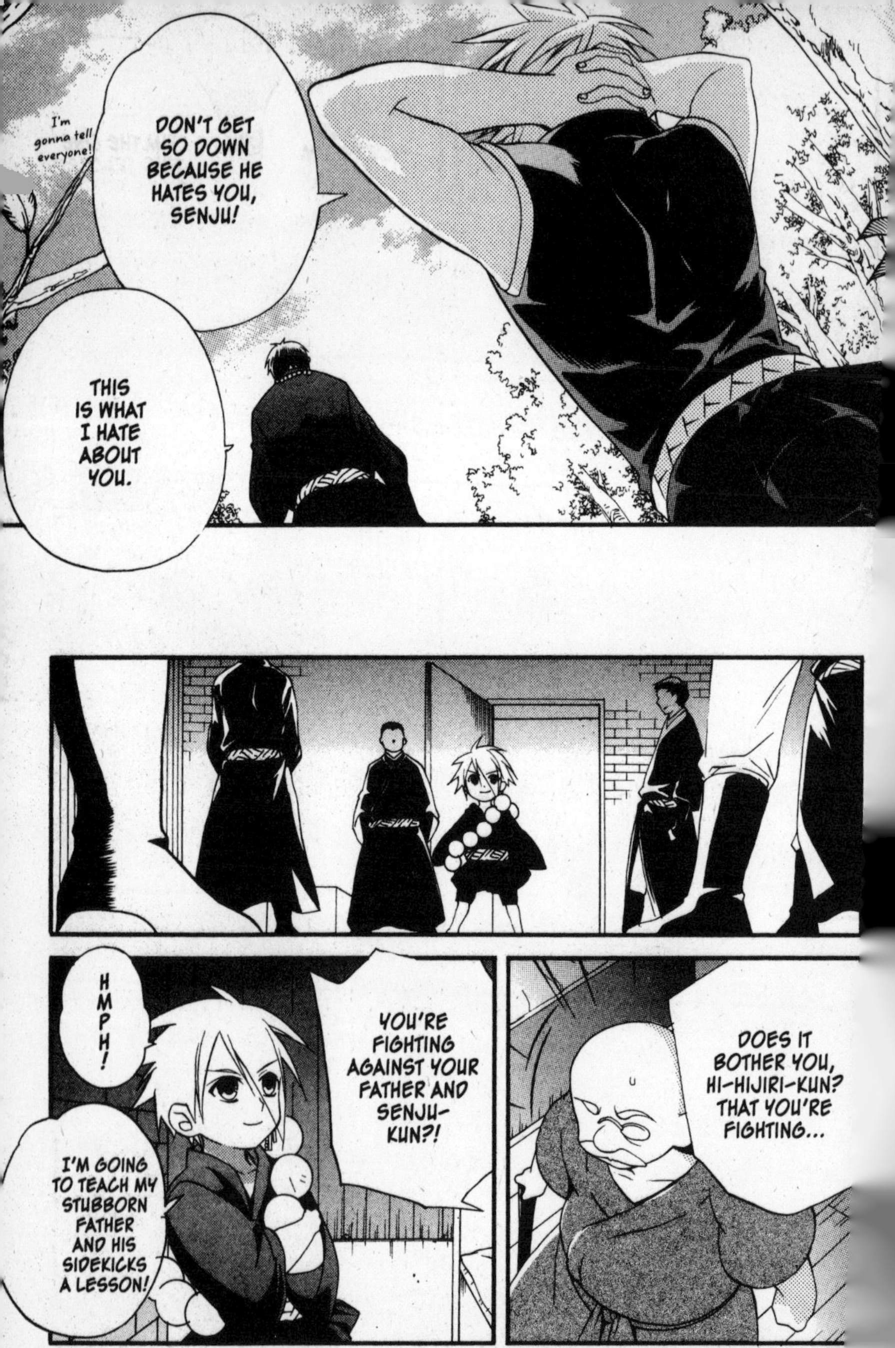

DON'T GET SO DOWN BECAUSE HE HATES YOU, SENJU!
I'm gonna tell everyone!
THIS IS WHAT I HATE ABOUT YOU.
DOES IT BOTHER YOU, HI-HIJIRI-KUN? THAT YOU'RE FIGHTING...
YOU'RE FIGHTING AGAINST YOUR FATHER AND SENJU-KUN?!
HMPH!
I'M GOING TO TEACH MY STUBBORN FATHER AND HIS SIDEKICKS A LESSON!

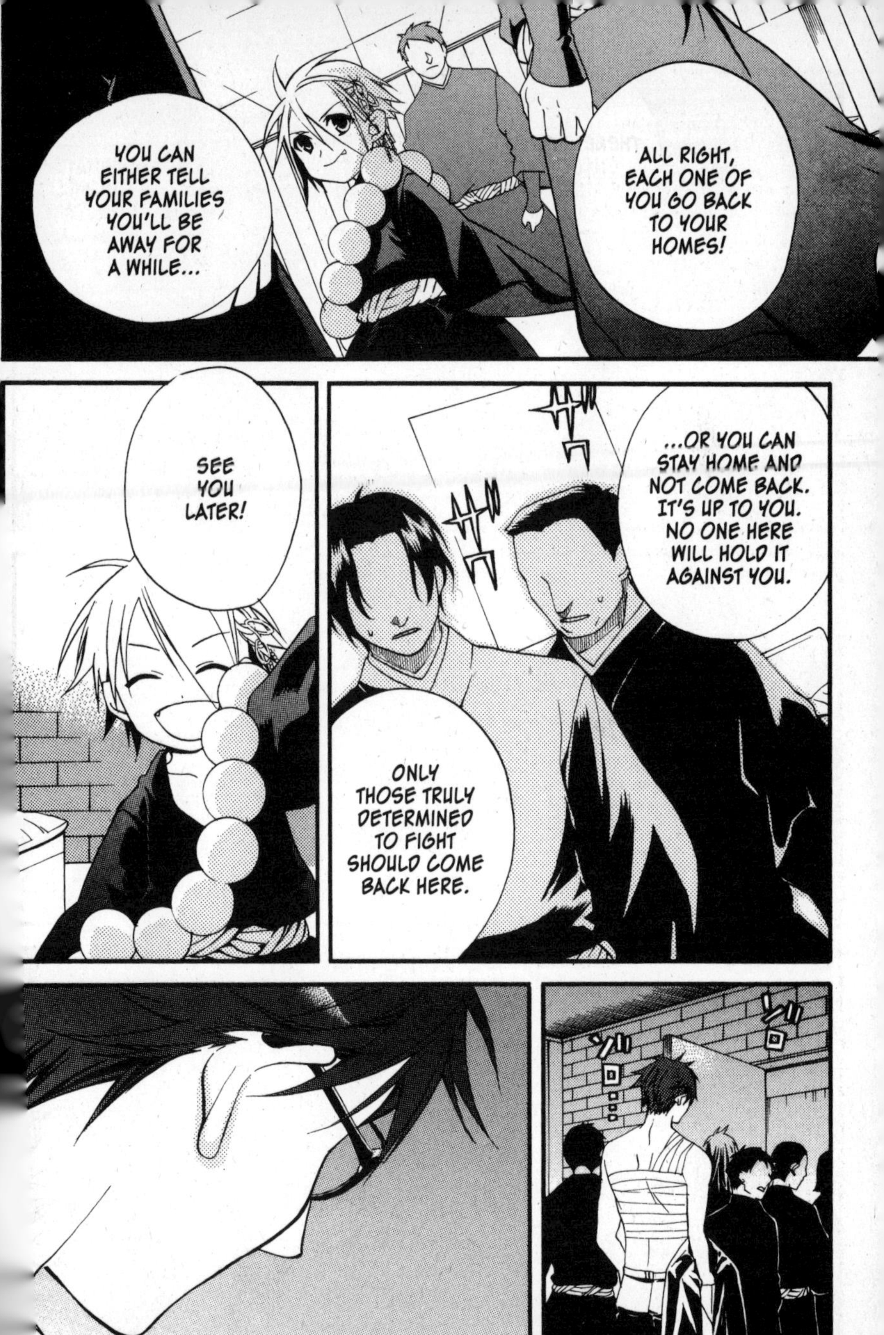
ALL RIGHT, EACH ONE OF YOU GO BACK TO YOUR HOMES!
YOU CAN EITHER TELL YOUR FAMILIES YOU'LL BE AWAY FOR A WHILE...
...OR YOU CAN STAY HOME AND NOT COME BACK. IT'S UP TO YOU. NO ONE HERE WILL HOLD IT AGAINST YOU.
ONLY THOSE TRULY DETERMINED TO FIGHT SHOULD COME BACK HERE.
SEE YOU LATER!

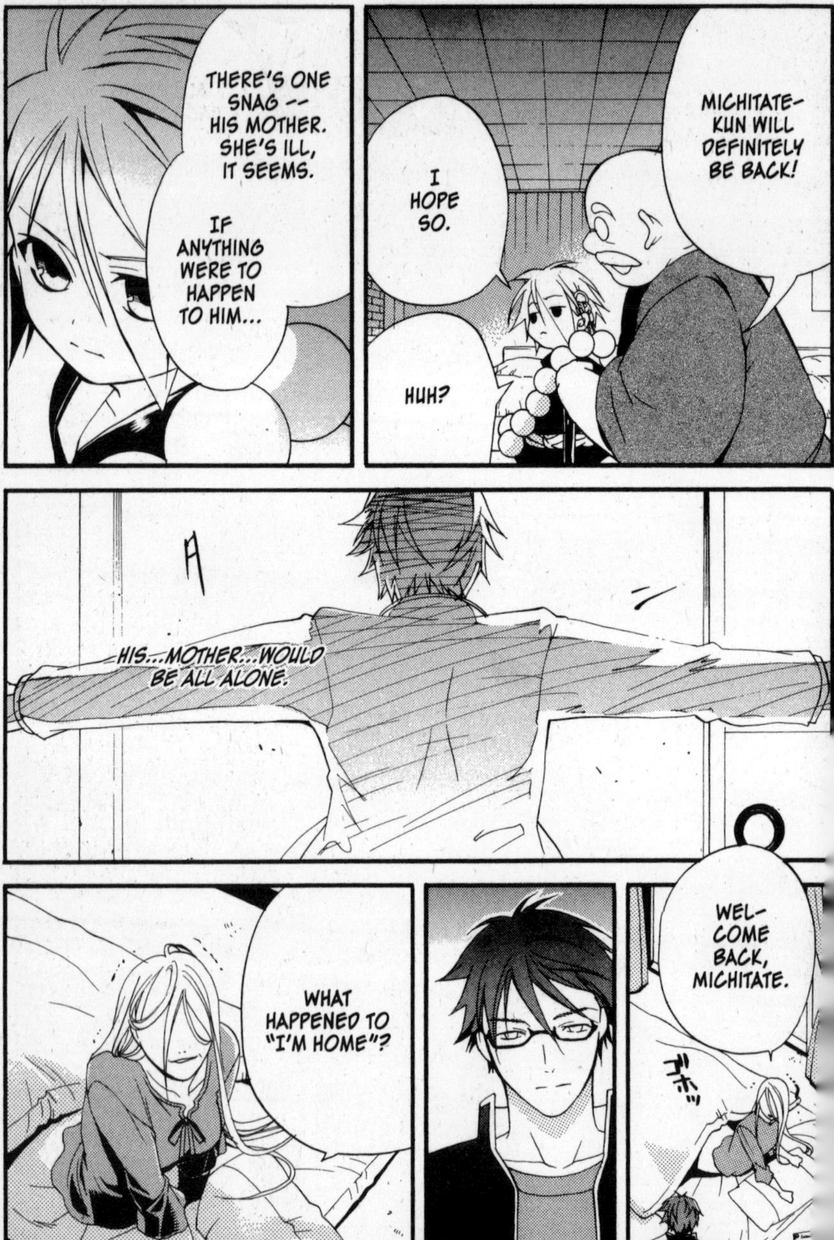
MICHITATE-KUN WILL DEFINITELY BE BACK!
I HOPE SO.
HUH?
THERE'S ONE SNAG -- HIS MOTHER. SHE'S ILL, IT SEEMS.
IF ANYTHING WERE TO HAPPEN TO HIM...
HIS...MOTHER...WOULD BE ALL ALONE.
WEL-COME BACK, MICHITATE.
ゴホッ
WHAT HAPPENED TO "I'M HOME"?

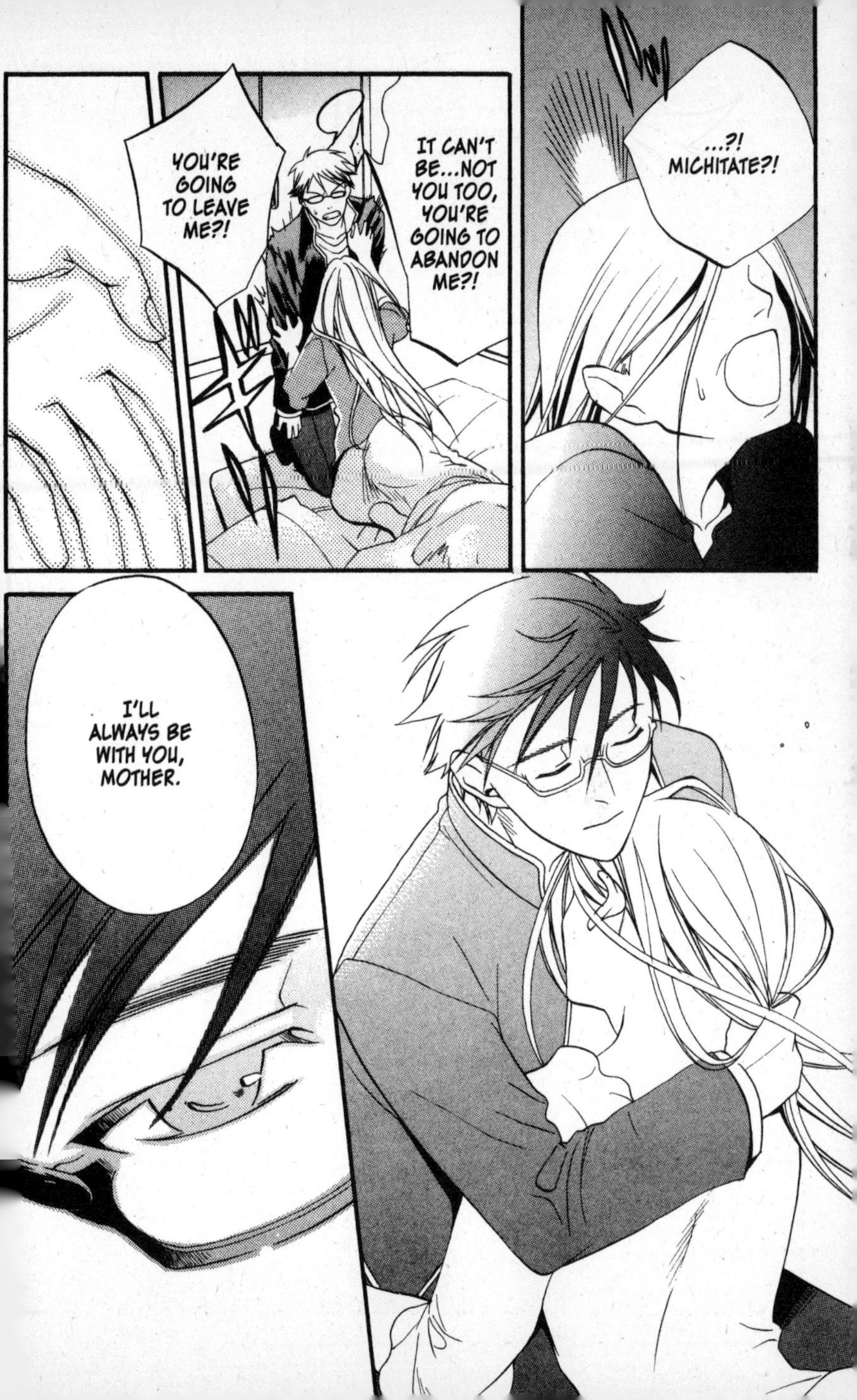
...?! MICHITATE?!
YOU'RE GOING TO LEAVE ME?!
IT CAN'T BE...NOT YOU TOO, YOU'RE GOING TO ABANDON ME?!
I'LL ALWAYS BE WITH YOU, MOTHER.

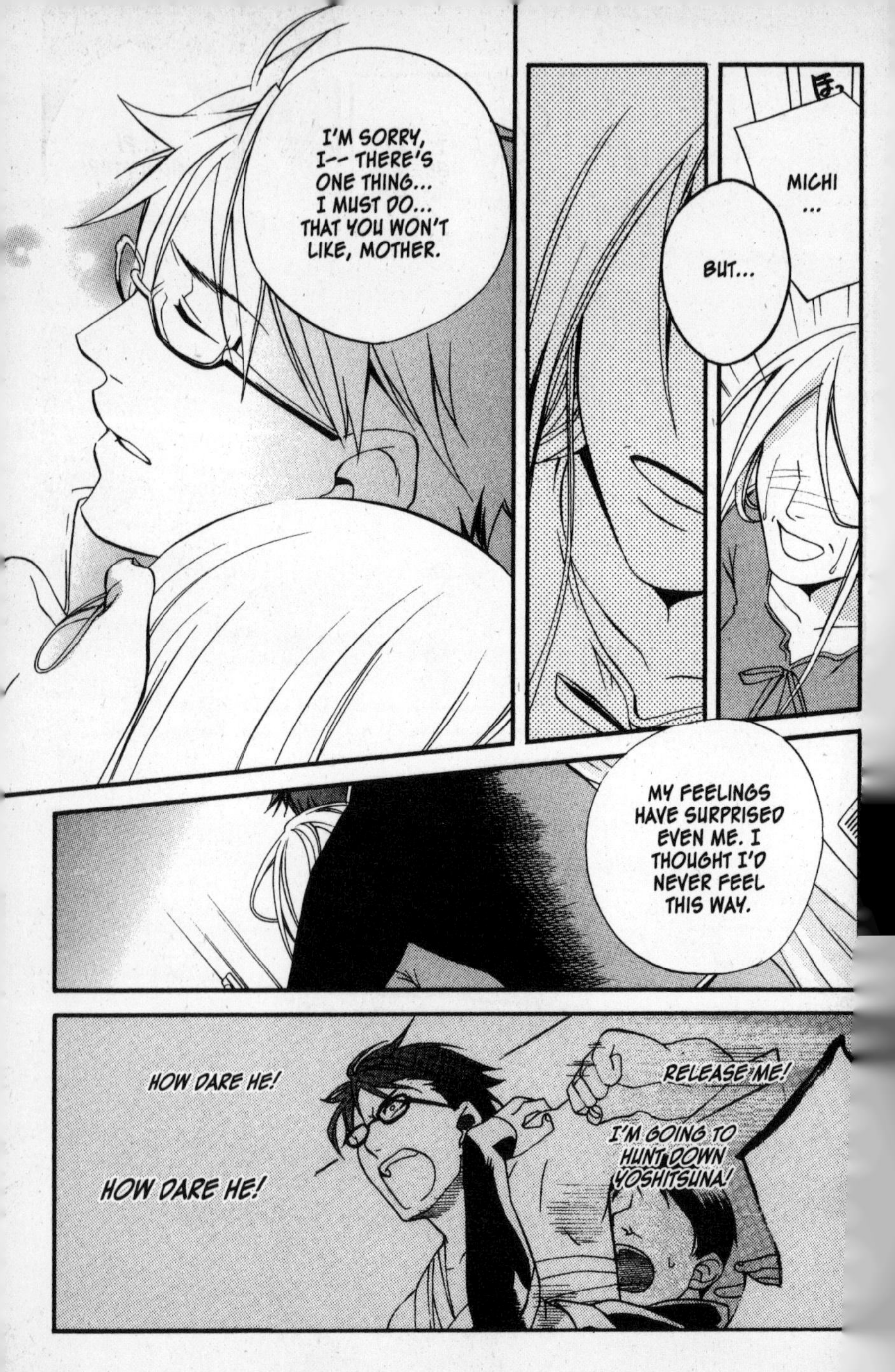
ほっ
MICHI ...
BUT...
I'M SORRY, I-- THERE'S ONE THING... I MUST DO... THAT YOU WON'T LIKE, MOTHER.
MY FEELINGS HAVE SURPRISED EVEN ME. I THOUGHT I'D NEVER FEEL THIS WAY.
RELEASE ME!
I'M GOING TO HUNT DOWN YOSHITSUNA!
HOW DARE HE!
HOW DARE HE!

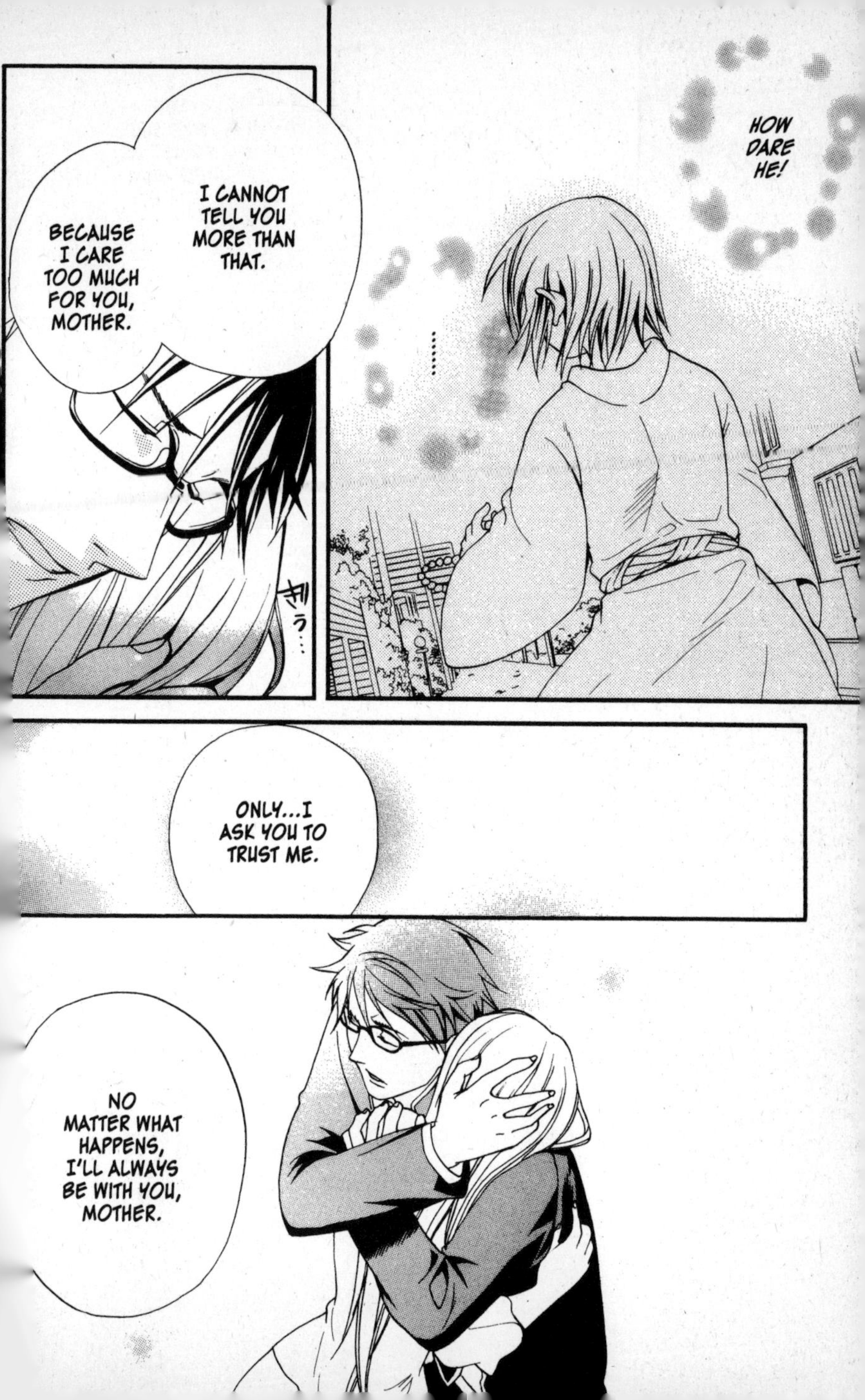
HOW DARE HE!
......
I CANNOT TELL YOU MORE THAN THAT.
BECAUSE I CARE TOO MUCH FOR YOU, MOTHER.
ONLY...I ASK YOU TO TRUST ME.
NO MATTER WHAT HAPPENS, I'LL ALWAYS BE WITH YOU, MOTHER.

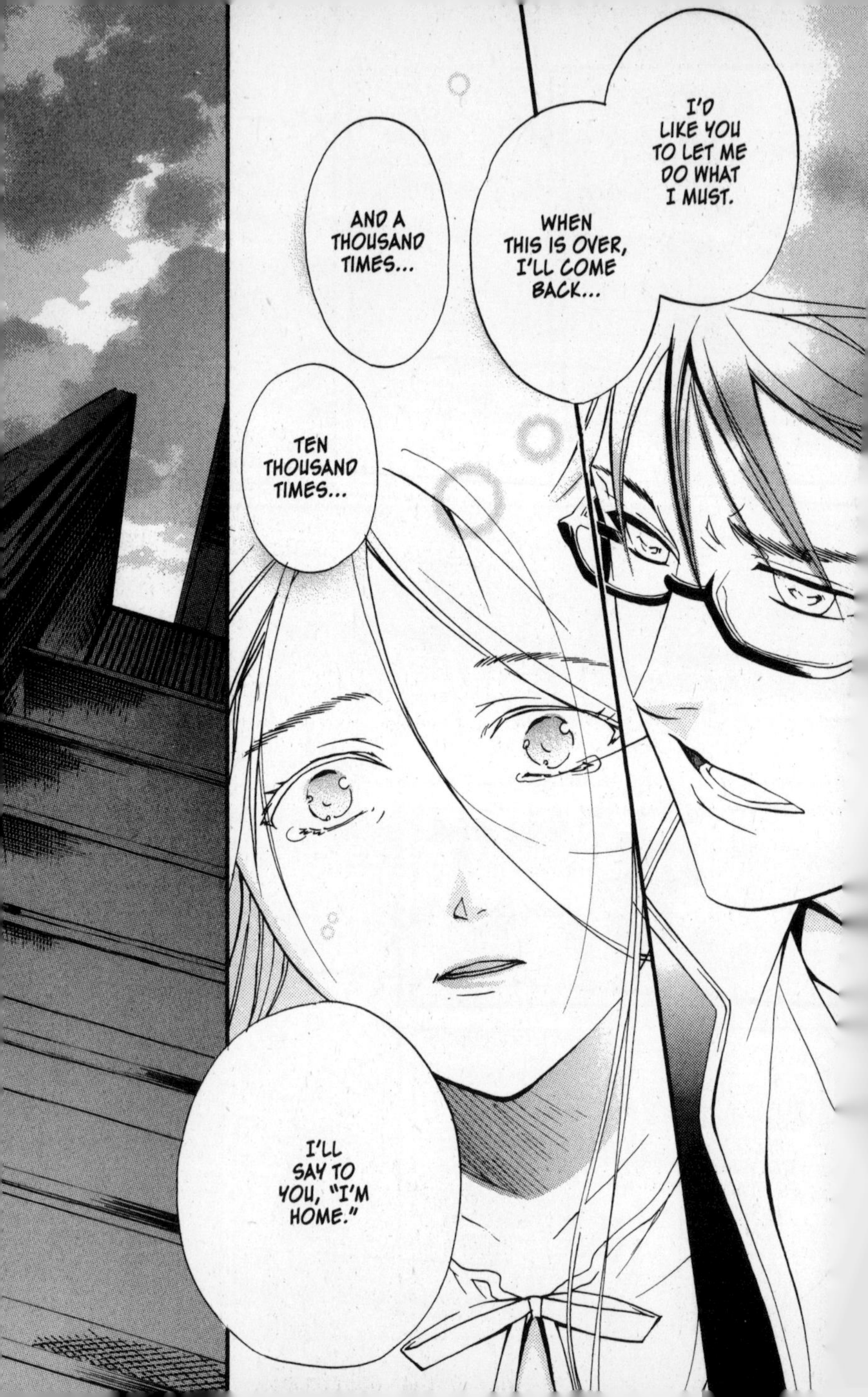
I'D LIKE YOU TO LET ME DO WHAT I MUST.
WHEN THIS IS OVER, I'LL COME BACK...
AND A THOUSAND TIMES...
TEN THOUSAND TIMES...
I'LL SAY TO YOU, "I'M HOME."

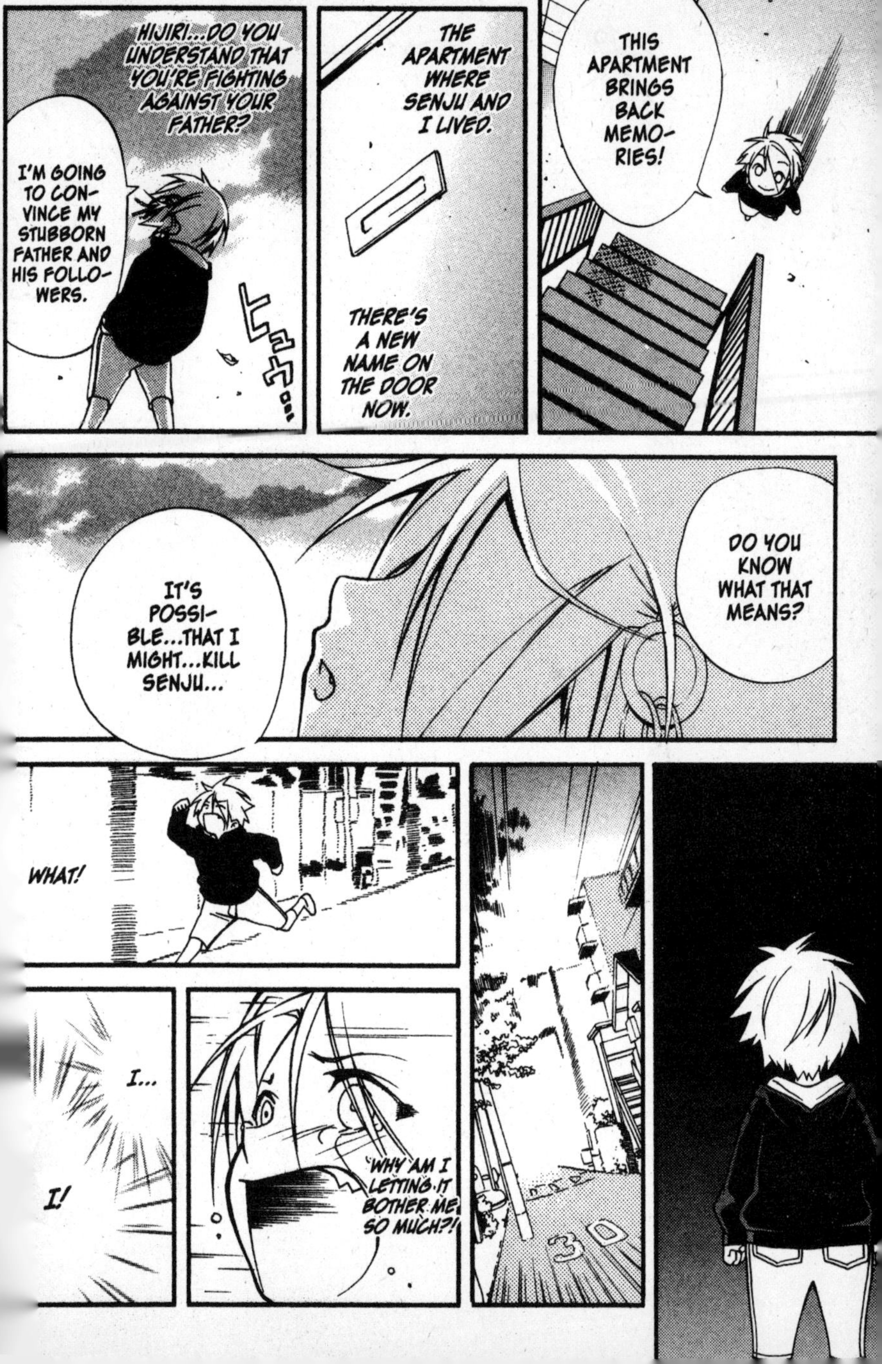
THIS APARTMENT BRINGS BACK MEMORIES!
THE APARTMENT WHERE SENJU AND I LIVED.
THERE'S A NEW NAME ON THE DOOR NOW.
HIJIRI...DO YOU UNDERSTAND THAT YOU'RE FIGHTING AGAINST YOUR FATHER?
I'M GOING TO CONVINCE MY STUBBORN FATHER AND HIS FOLLOWERS.
DO YOU KNOW WHAT THAT MEANS?
IT'S POSSIBLE...THAT I MIGHT...KILL SENJU...
WHAT!
WHY AM I LETTING IT BOTHER ME SO MUCH?!
I...
I!

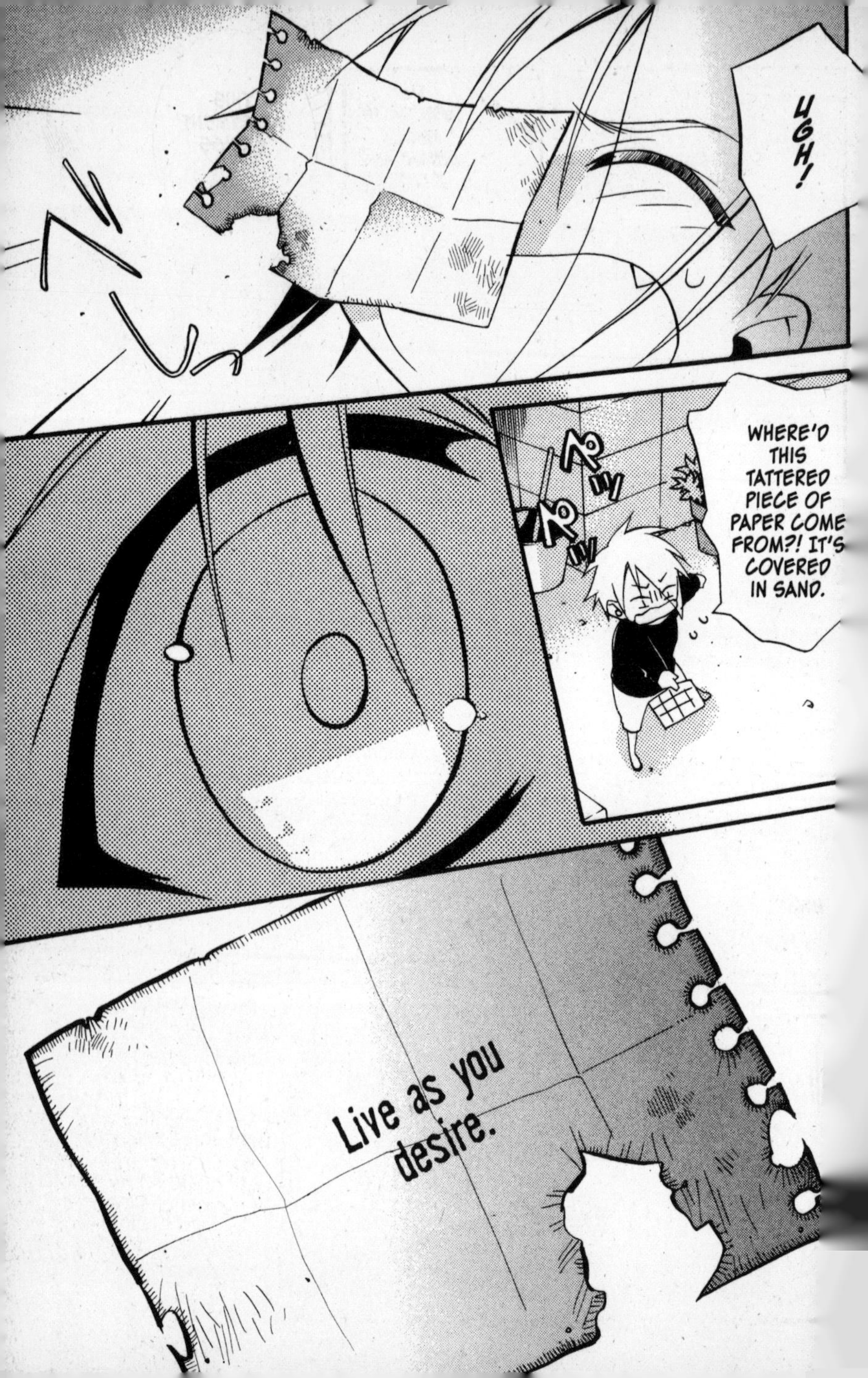
UGH!
WHERE'D THIS TATTERED PIECE OF PAPER COME FROM?! IT'S COVERED IN SAND.
Live as you desire.

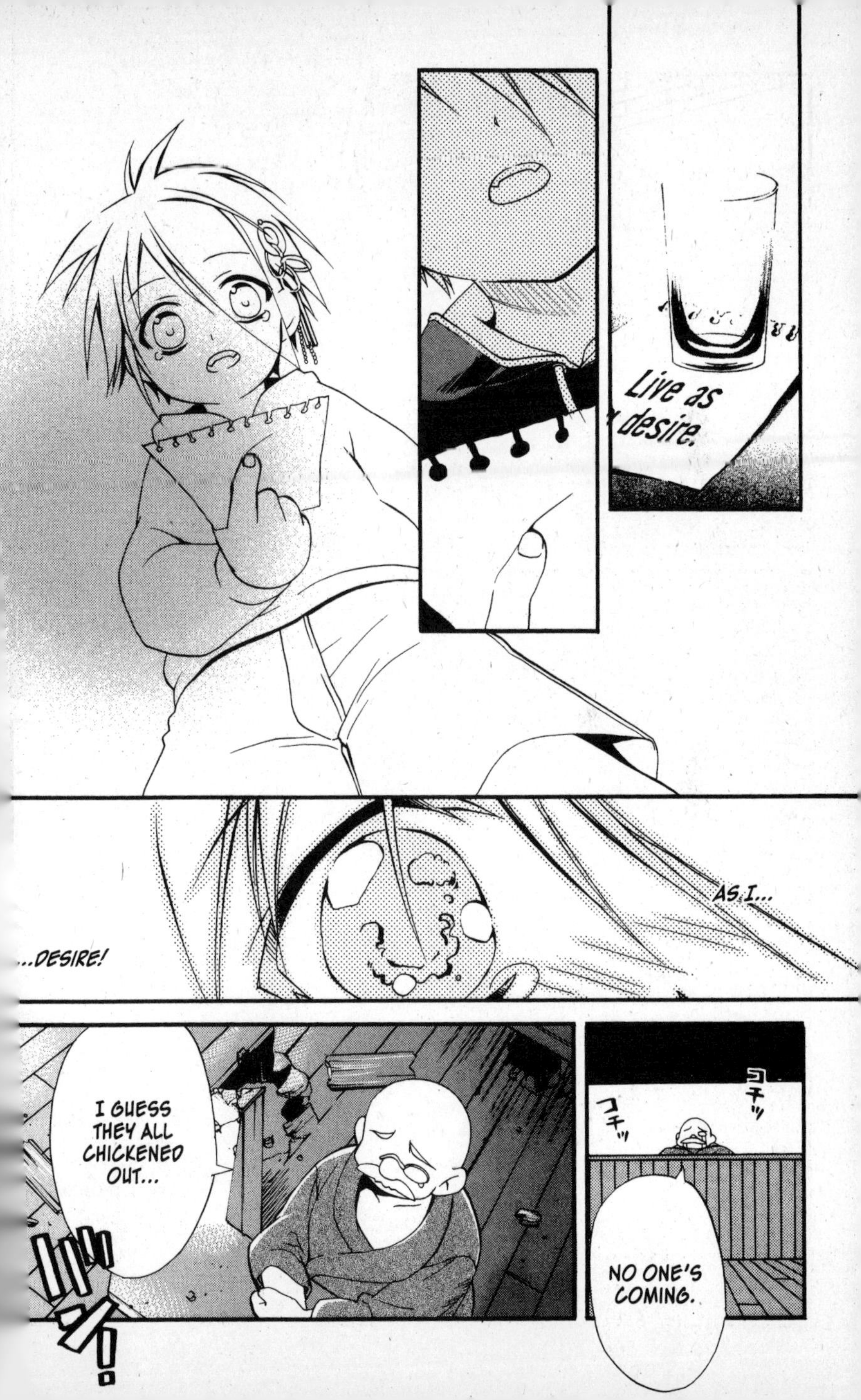
Live as
desire.
AS I...
...DESIRE!
コチッ
コチッ
NO ONE'S COMING.
I GUESS THEY ALL CHICKENED OUT...

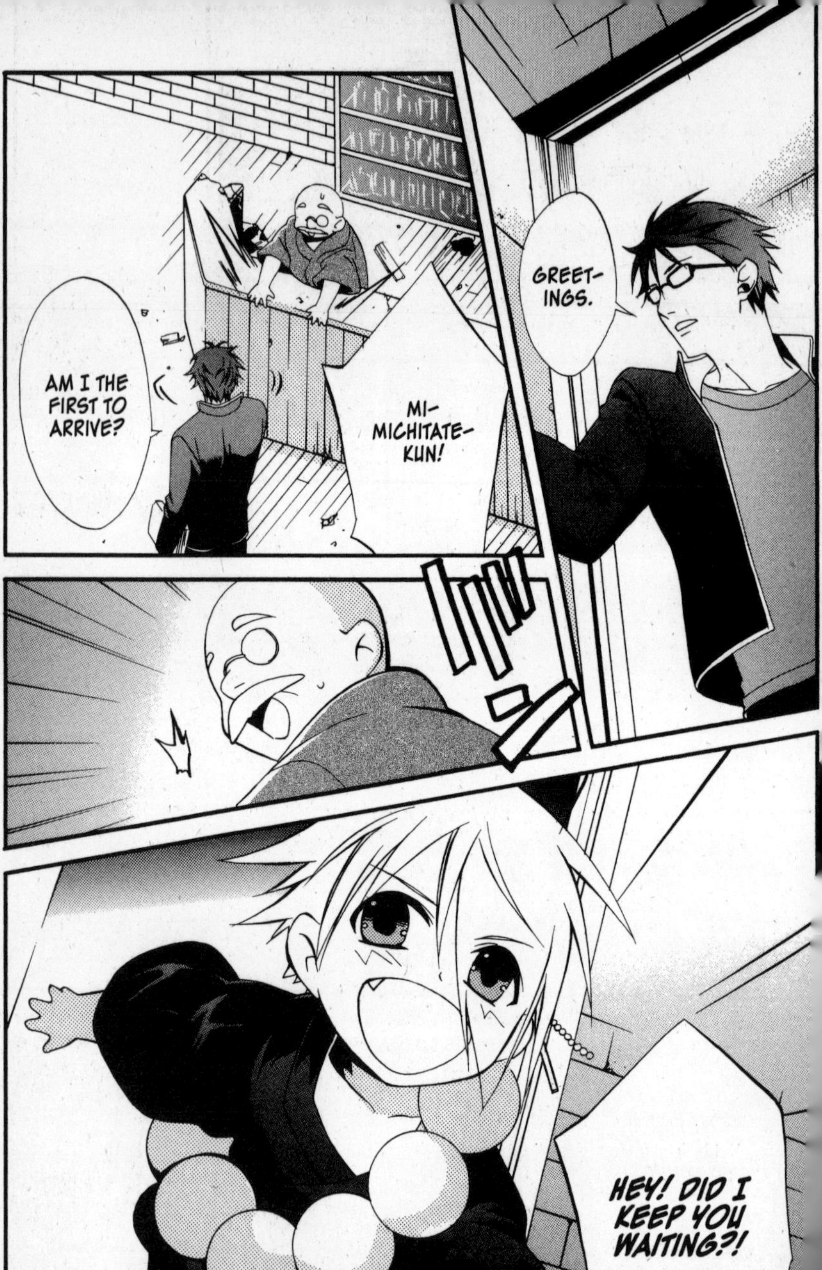
GREET-INGS.
MI-MICHITATE-KUN!
AM I THE FIRST TO ARRIVE?
HEY! DID I KEEP YOU WAITING?!

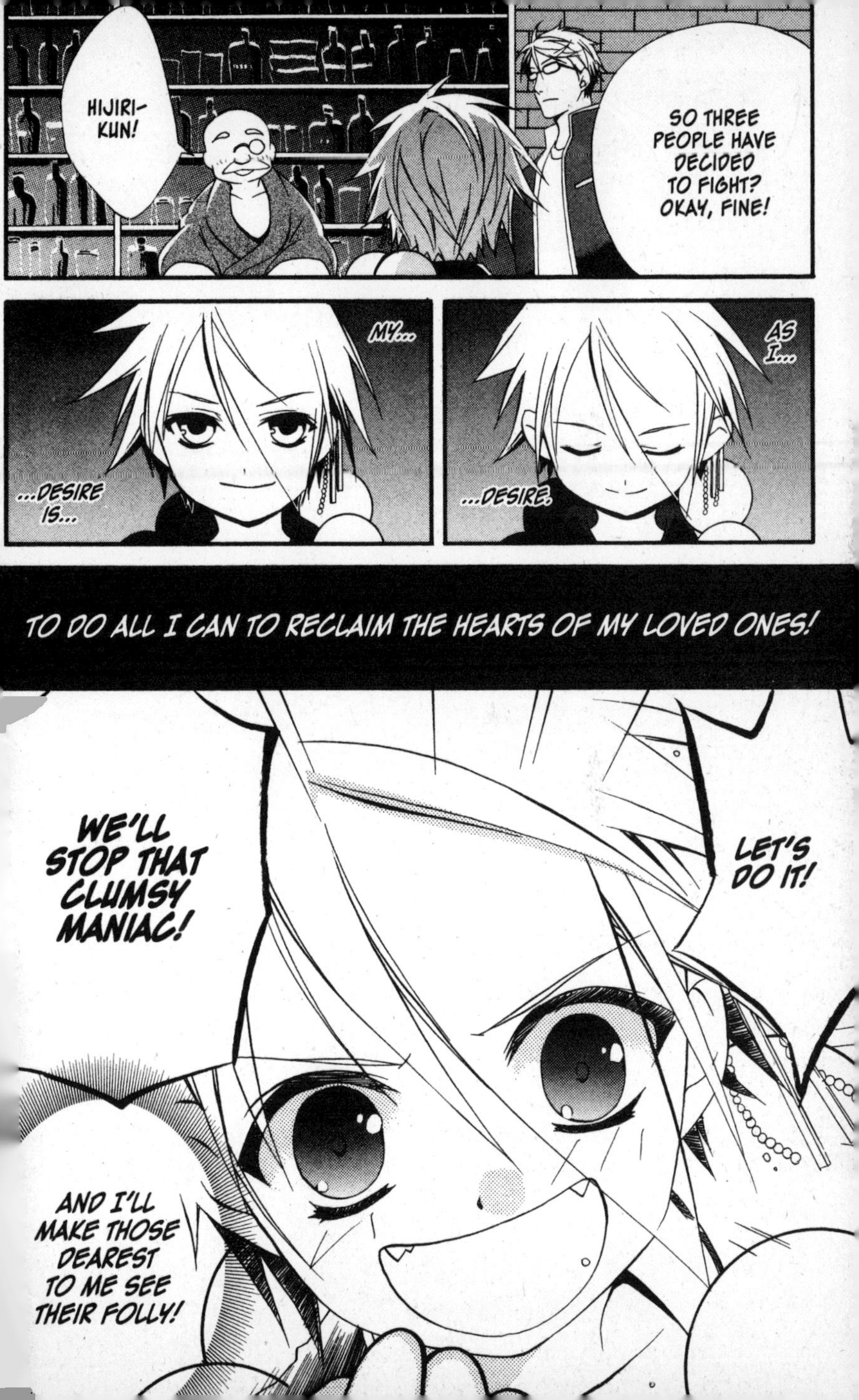
SO THREE PEOPLE HAVE DECIDED TO FIGHT? OKAY, FINE!
HIJIRI-KUN!
AS I...
...DESIRE.
MY...
...DESIRE IS...
TO DO ALL I CAN TO RECLAIM THE HEARTS OF MY LOVED ONES!
LET'S DO IT!
WE'LL STOP THAT CLUMSY MANIAC!
AND I'LL MAKE THOSE DEAREST TO ME SEE THEIR FOLLY!

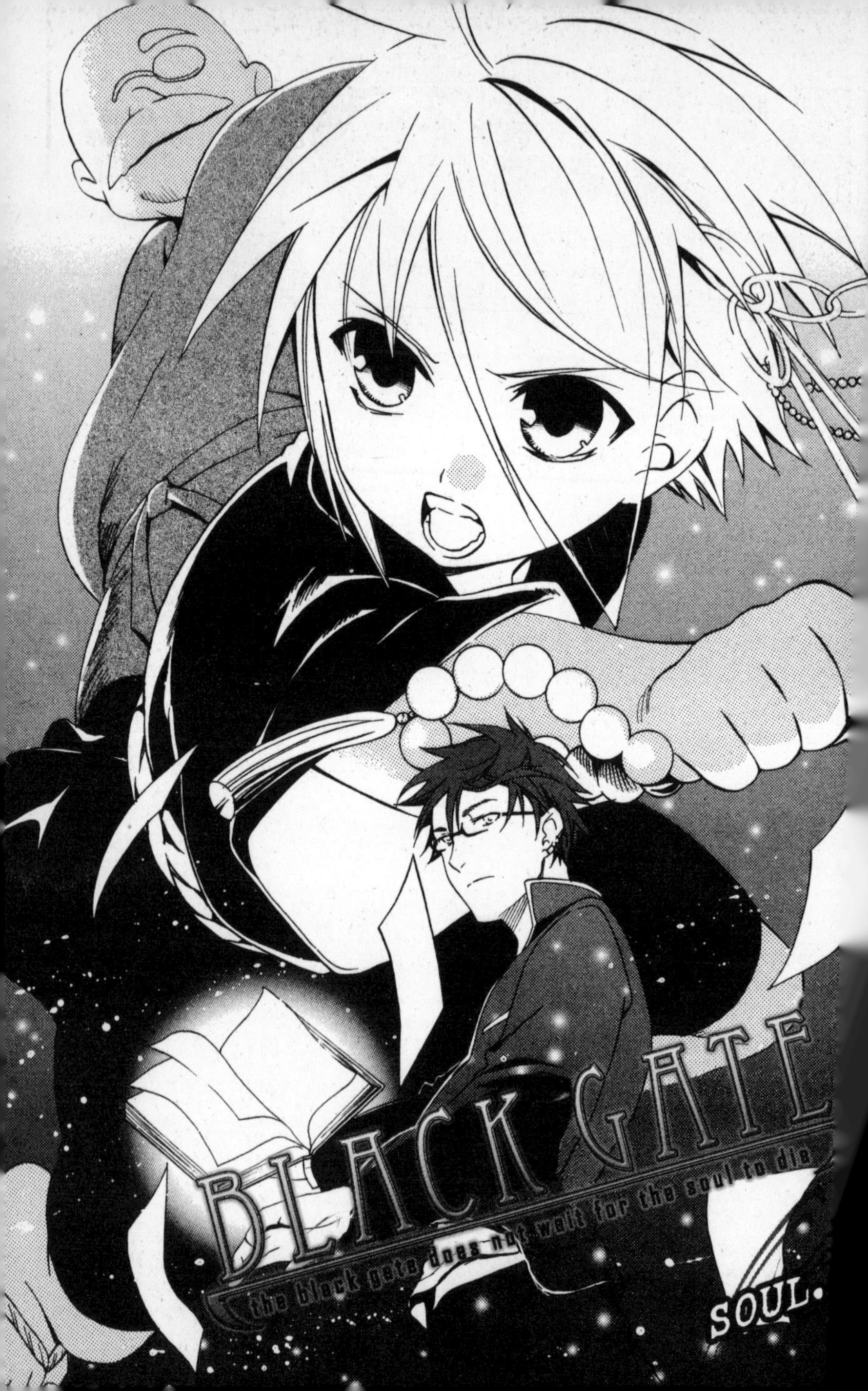
BLACK GATE
the black gate does not wait for the soul to die
SOUL.

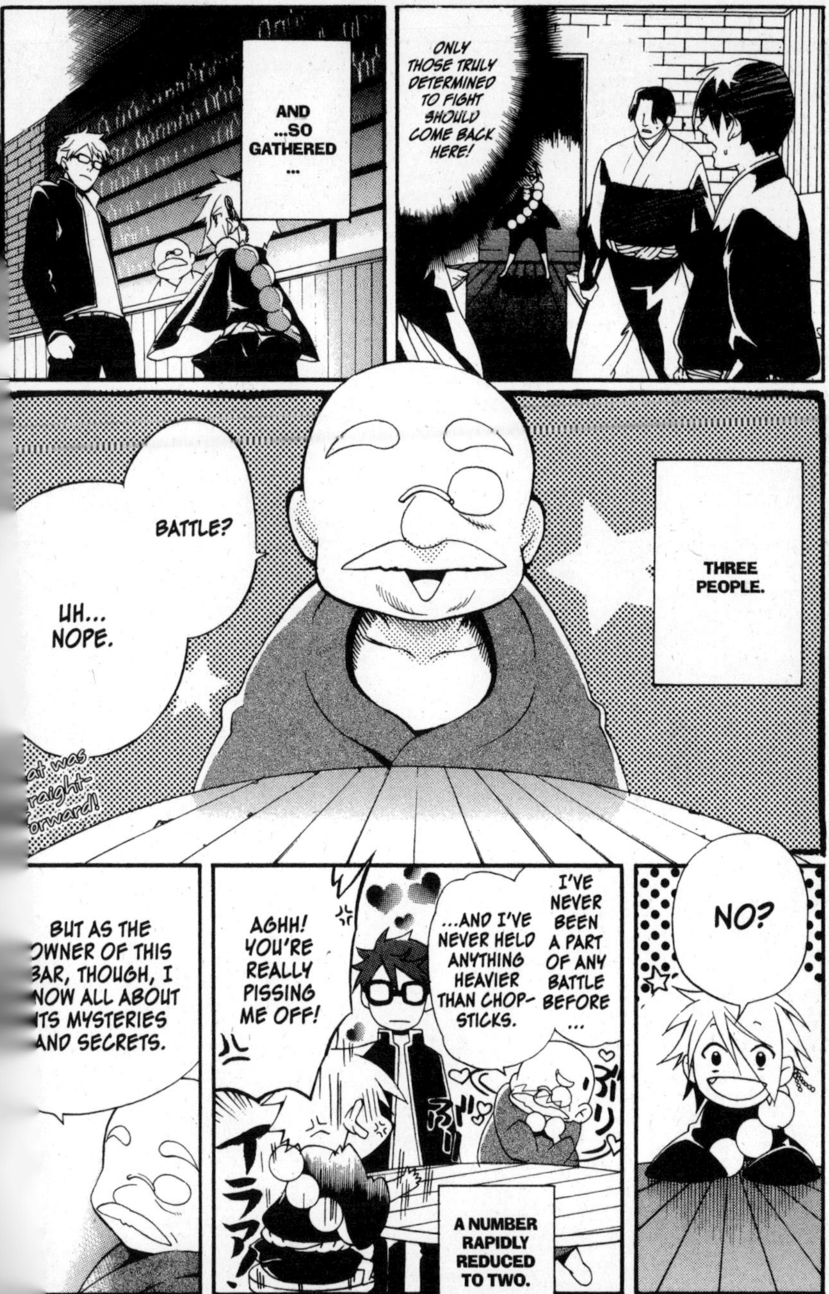

ONLY THOSE TRULY DETERMINED TO FIGHT SHOULD COME BACK HERE!
AND ...SO GATHERED ...
THREE PEOPLE.
BATTLE?
UH... NOPE.
at was straight-forward!
NO?
I'VE NEVER BEEN A PART OF ANY BATTLE BEFORE ...
...AND I'VE NEVER HELD ANYTHING HEAVIER THAN CHOP-STICKS.
AGHH! YOU'RE REALLY PISSING ME OFF!
A NUMBER RAPIDLY REDUCED TO TWO.
BUT AS THE OWNER OF THIS BAR, THOUGH, I KNOW ALL ABOUT ITS MYSTERIES AND SECRETS.

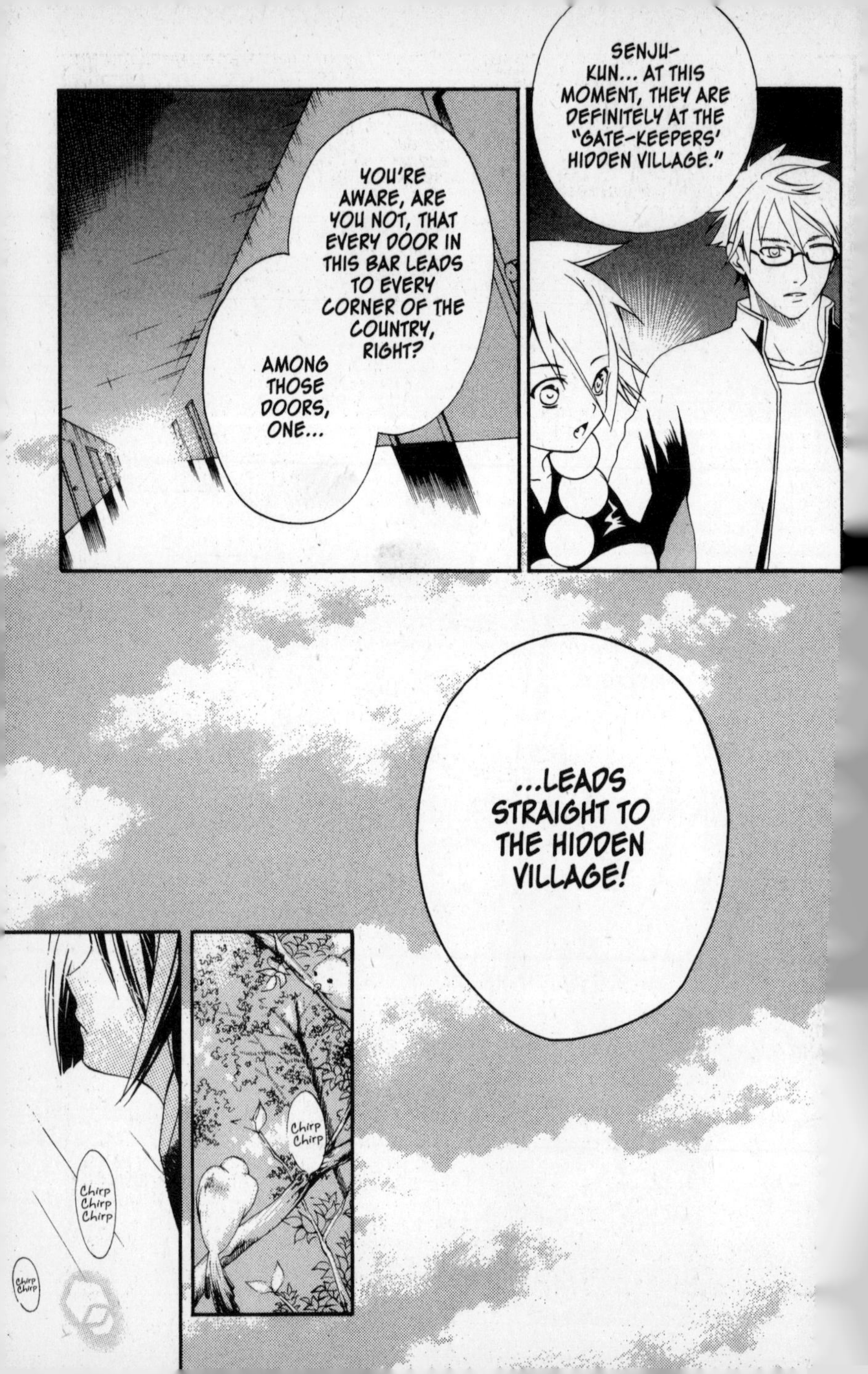
SENJU-KUN... AT THIS MOMENT, THEY ARE DEFINITELY AT THE "GATE-KEEPERS' HIDDEN VILLAGE."
YOU'RE AWARE, ARE YOU NOT, THAT EVERY DOOR IN THIS BAR LEADS TO EVERY CORNER OF THE COUNTRY, RIGHT?
AMONG THOSE DOORS, ONE...
...LEADS STRAIGHT TO THE HIDDEN VILLAGE!
Chirp Chirp
Chirp Chirp Chirp
Chirp Chirp

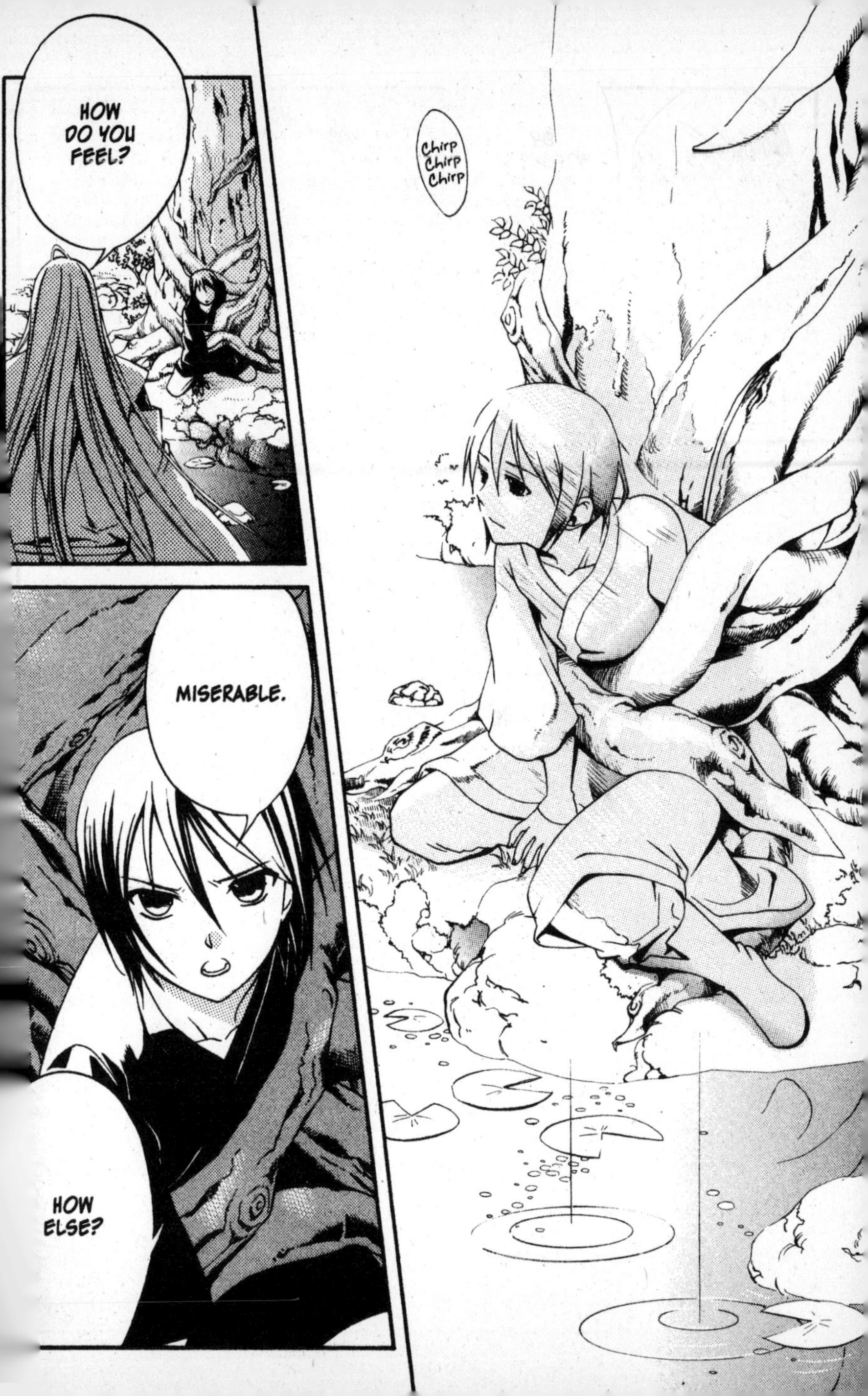
Chirp Chirp Chirp
HOW DO YOU FEEL?
MISERABLE.
HOW ELSE?

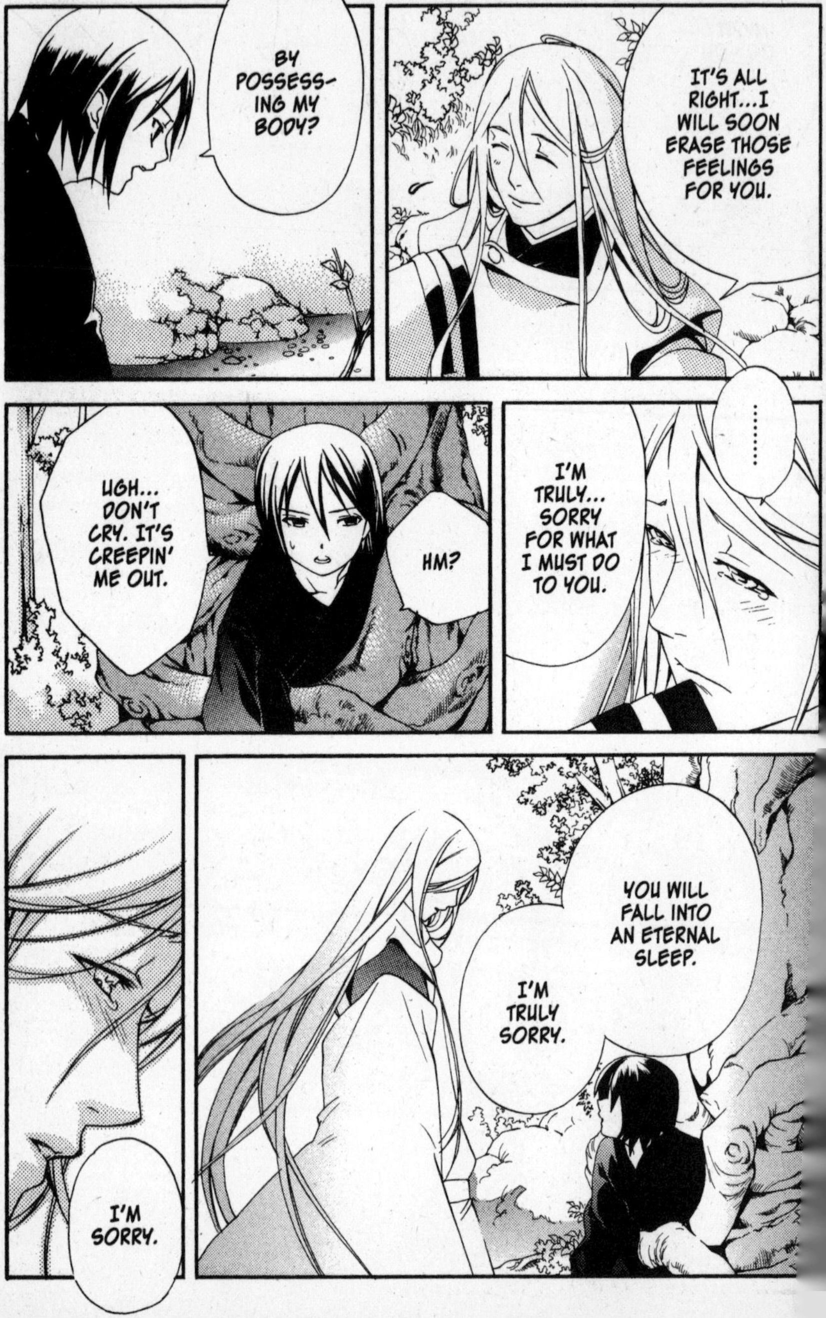
IT'S ALL RIGHT...I WILL SOON ERASE THOSE FEELINGS FOR YOU.
BY POSSESSING MY BODY?
......
I'M TRULY... SORRY FOR WHAT I MUST DO TO YOU.
HM?
UGH... DON'T CRY. IT'S CREEPIN' ME OUT.
YOU WILL FALL INTO AN ETERNAL SLEEP.
I'M TRULY SORRY.
I'M SORRY.

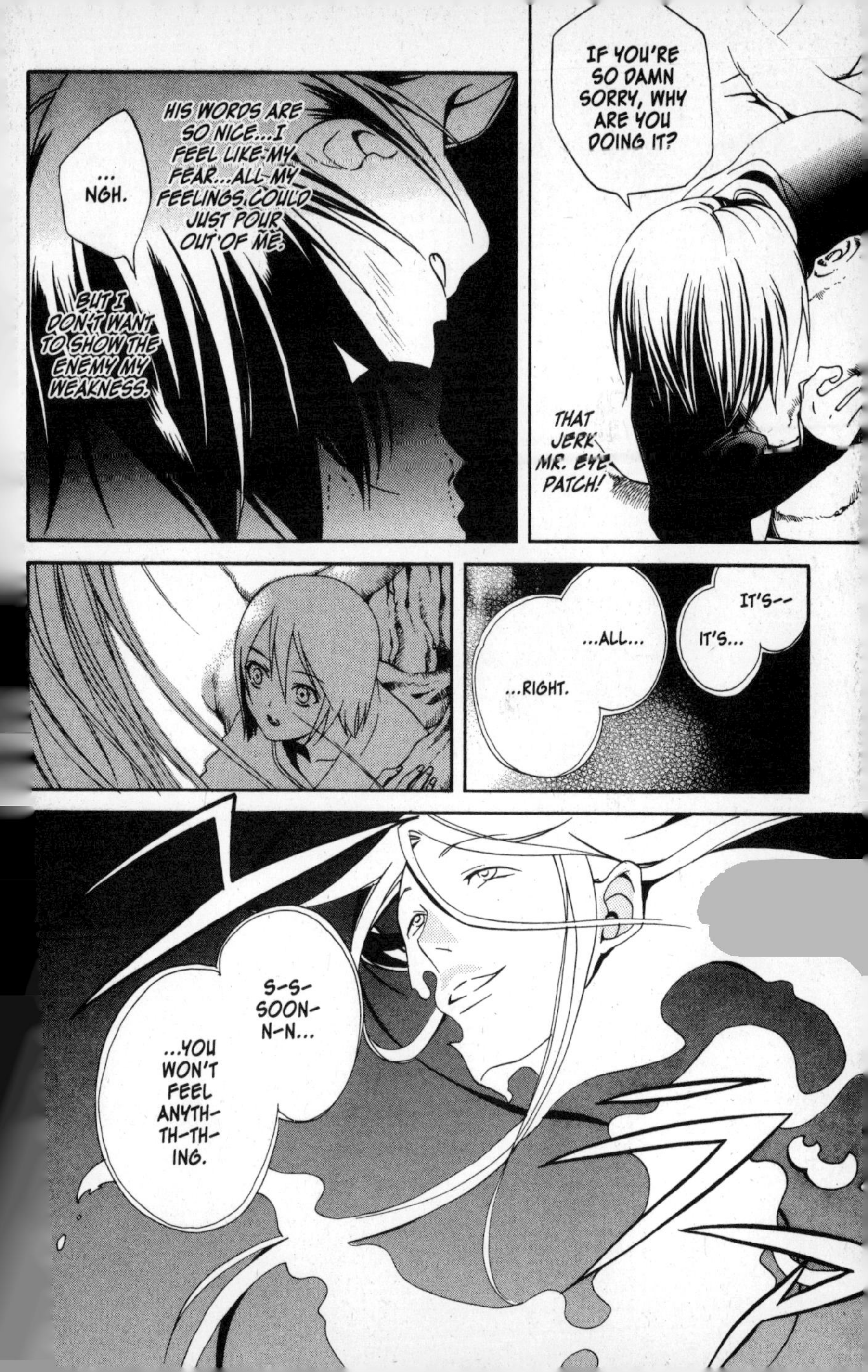
IF YOU'RE SO DAMN SORRY, WHY ARE YOU DOING IT?
THAT JERK MR. EYE-PATCH!
HIS WORDS ARE SO NICE...I FEEL LIKE MY FEAR...ALL MY FEELINGS COULD JUST POUR OUT OF ME.
...NGH.
BUT I DON'T WANT TO SHOW THE ENEMY MY WEAKNESS.
IT'S--
IT'S...
...ALL...
...RIGHT.
S-S-SOON-N-N...
...YOU WON'T FEEL ANYTH-TH-TH-ING.

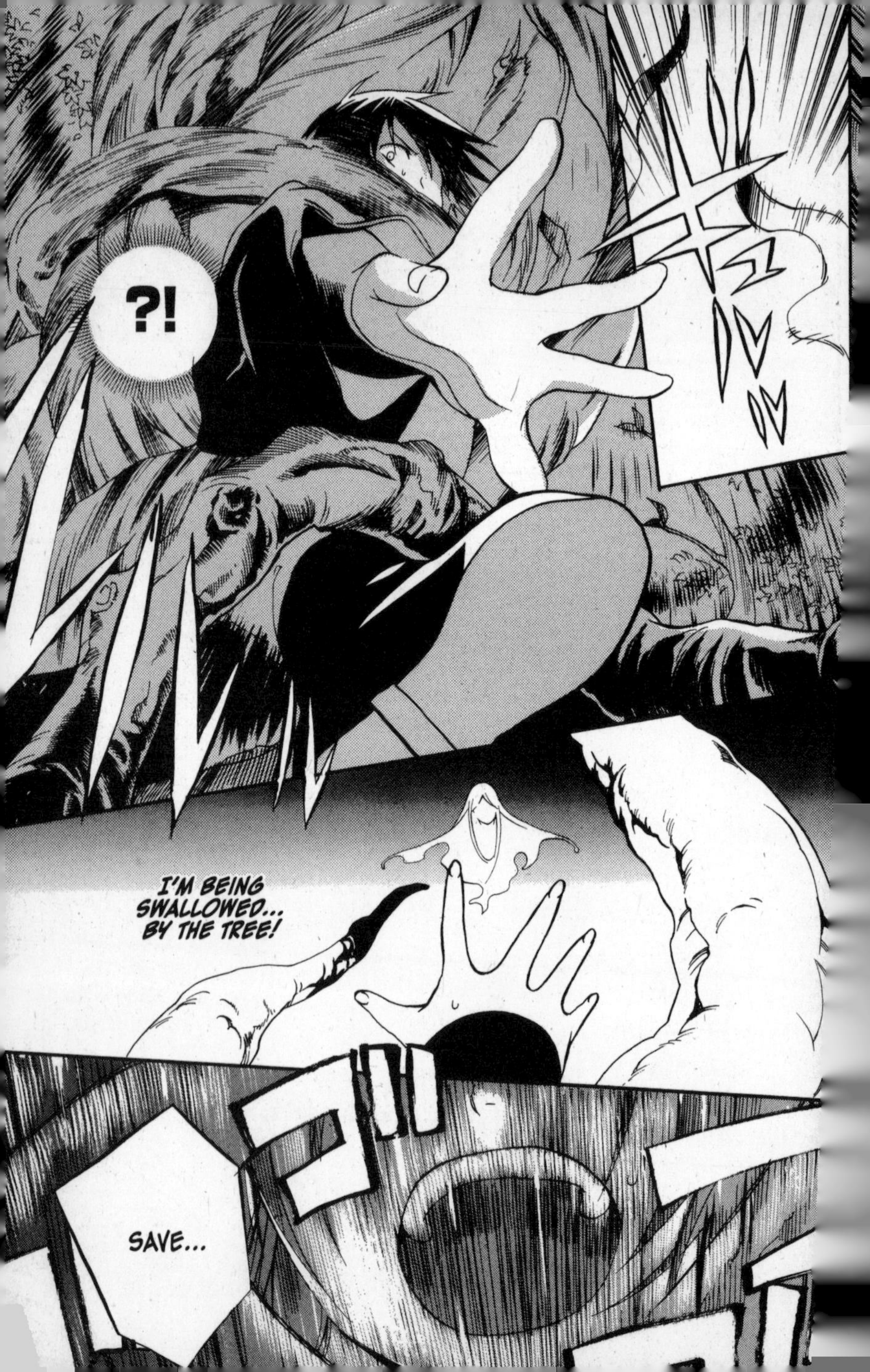
?!
I'M BEING SWALLOWED... BY THE TREE!
SAVE...

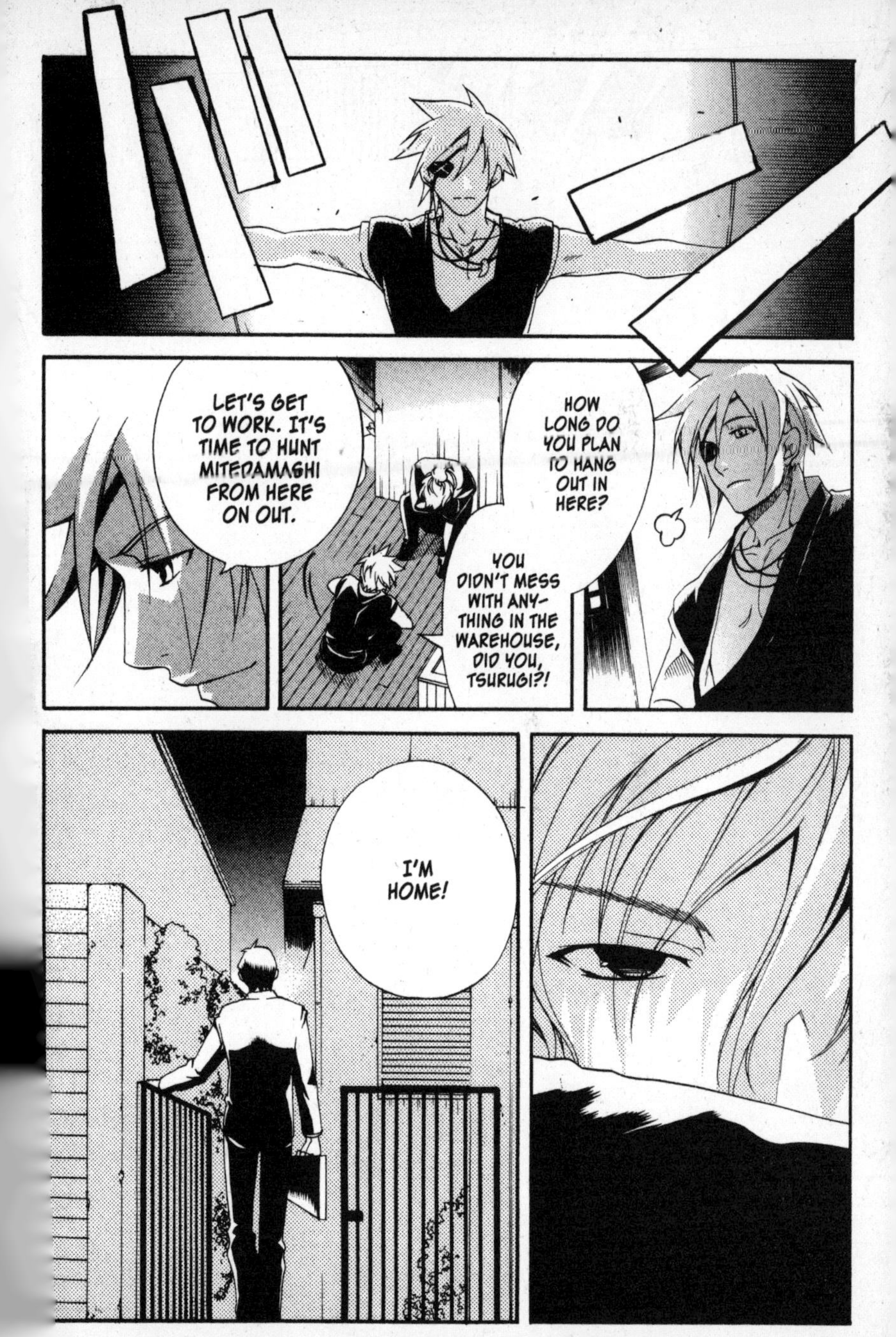
HOW LONG DO YOU PLAN TO HANG OUT IN HERE?
YOU DIDN'T MESS WITH ANY-THING IN THE WAREHOUSE, DID YOU, TSURUGI?!
LET'S GET TO WORK. IT'S TIME TO HUNT MITEDAMAGHI FROM HERE ON OUT.
I'M HOME!

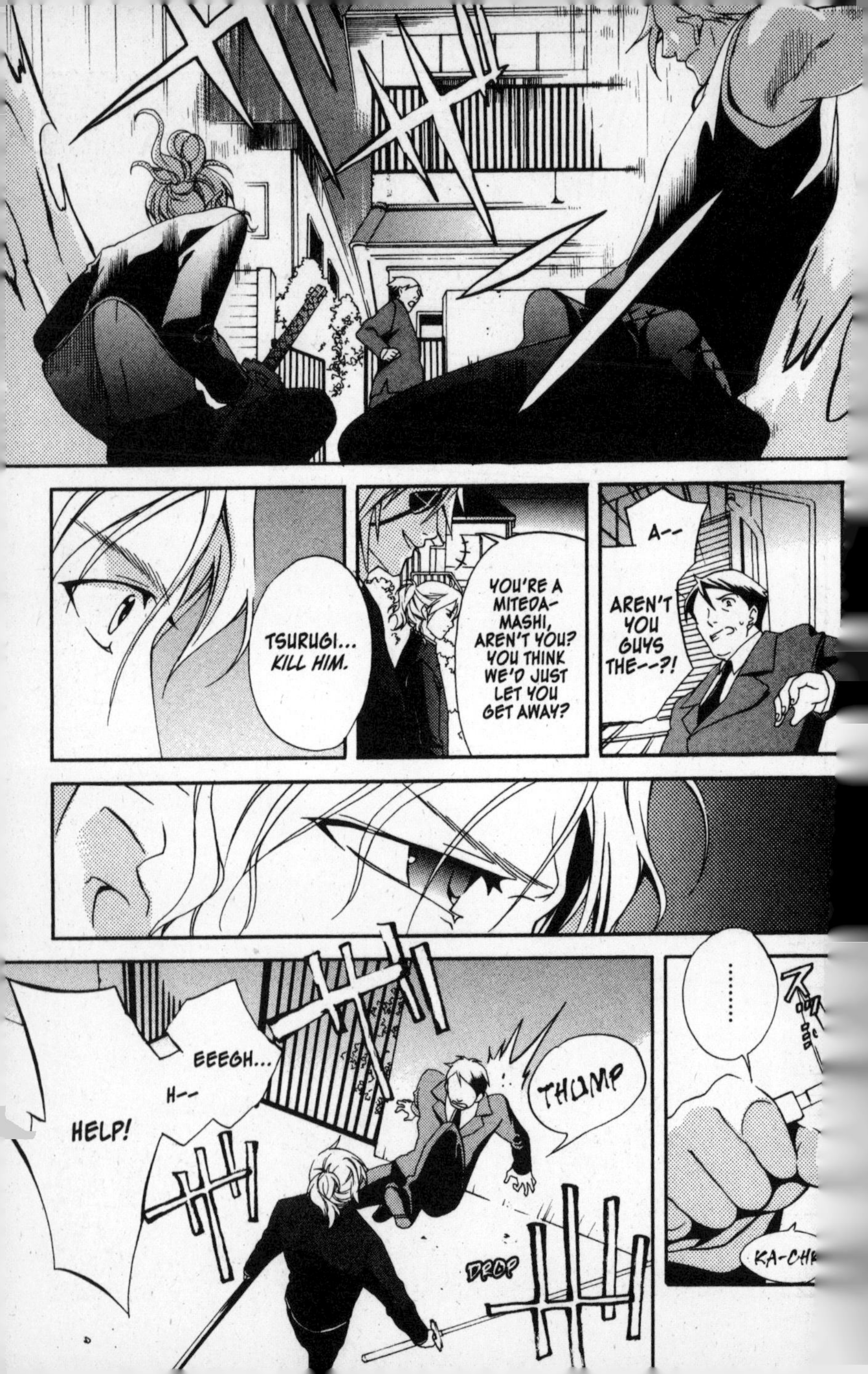
A--
AREN'T YOU GUYS THE--?!
YOU'RE A MITEDA-MASHI, AREN'T YOU? YOU THINK WE'D JUST LET YOU GET AWAY?
TSURUGI... KILL HIM.
......
KA-CH
THUMP
EEEGH...
H--
HELP!
DROP

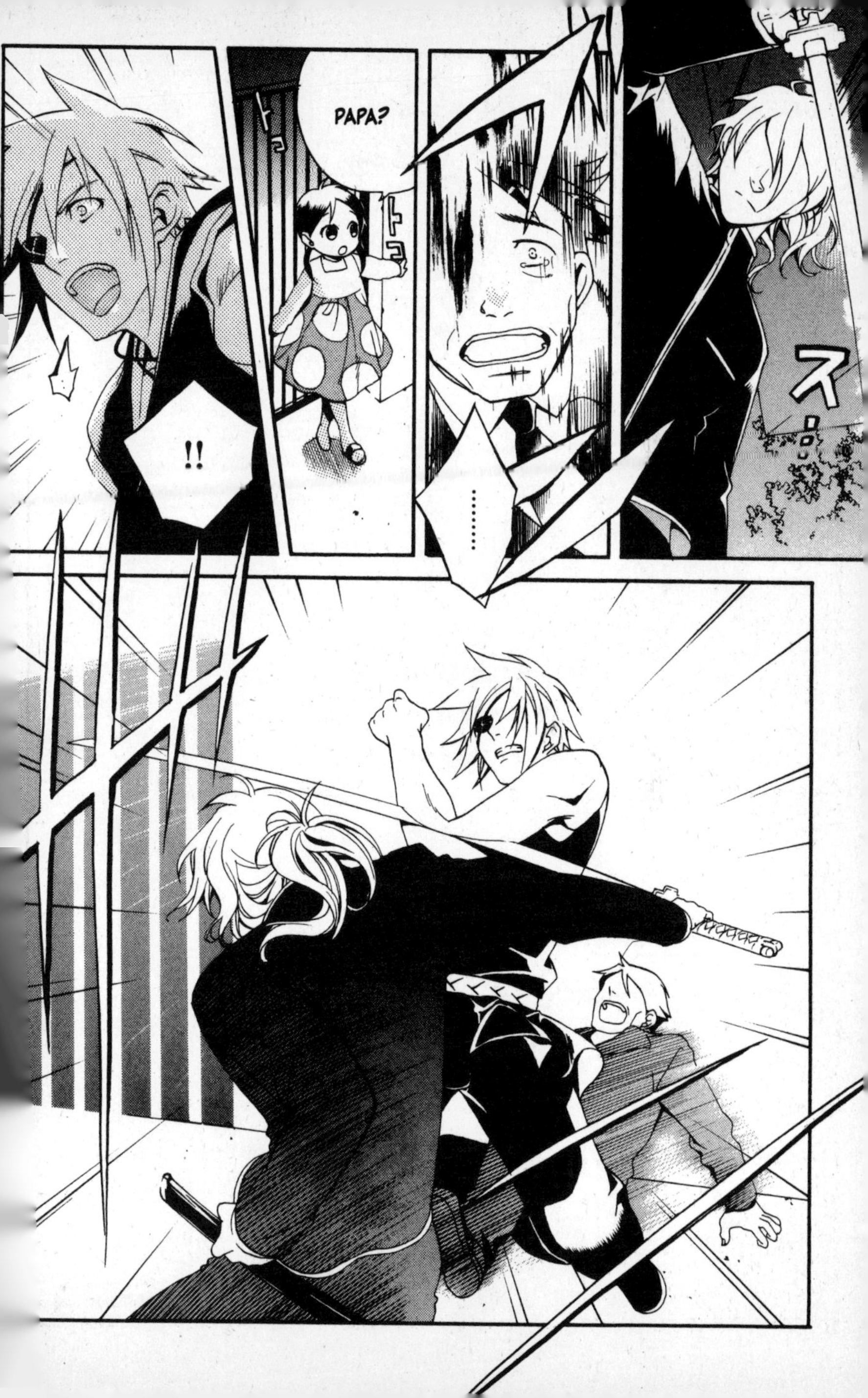
ス
......
PAPA?
トコ
トコ
!!

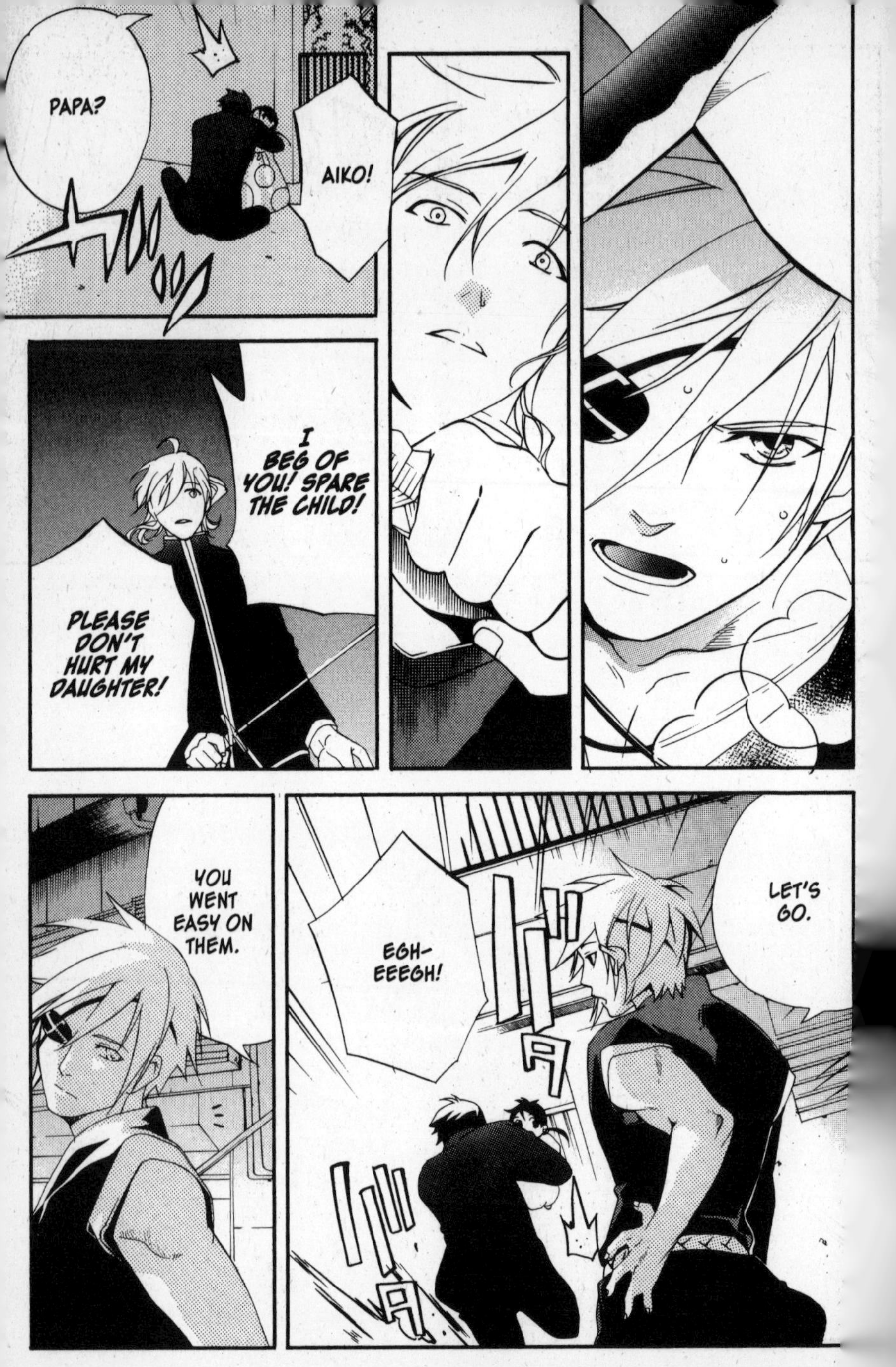
PAPA?
AIKO!
I BEG OF YOU! SPARE THE CHILD!
PLEASE DON'T HURT MY DAUGHTER!
LET'S GO.
EGH-EEEGH!
YOU WENT EASY ON THEM.

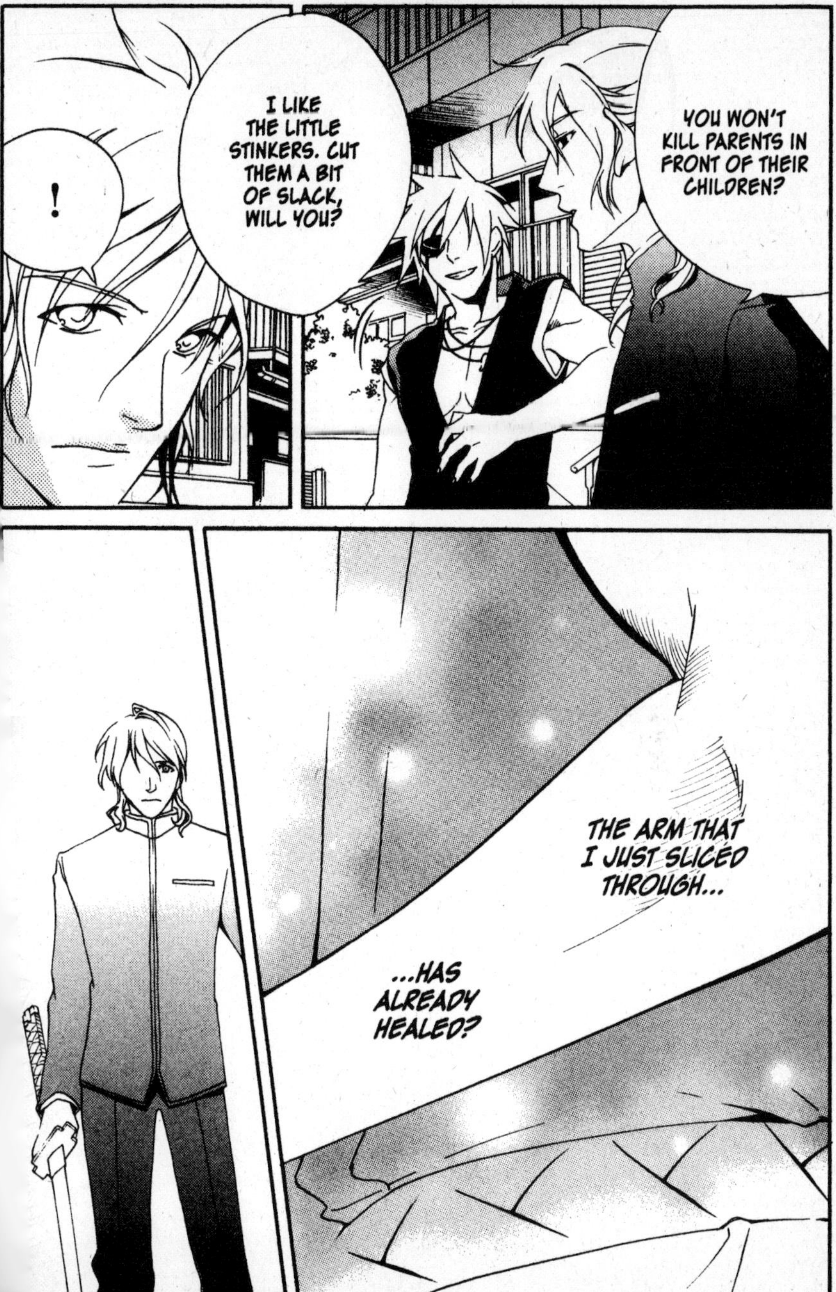
YOU WON'T KILL PARENTS IN FRONT OF THEIR CHILDREN?
I LIKE THE LITTLE STINKERS. CUT THEM A BIT OF SLACK, WILL YOU?
!
THE ARM THAT I JUST SLICED THROUGH...
...HAS ALREADY HEALED?

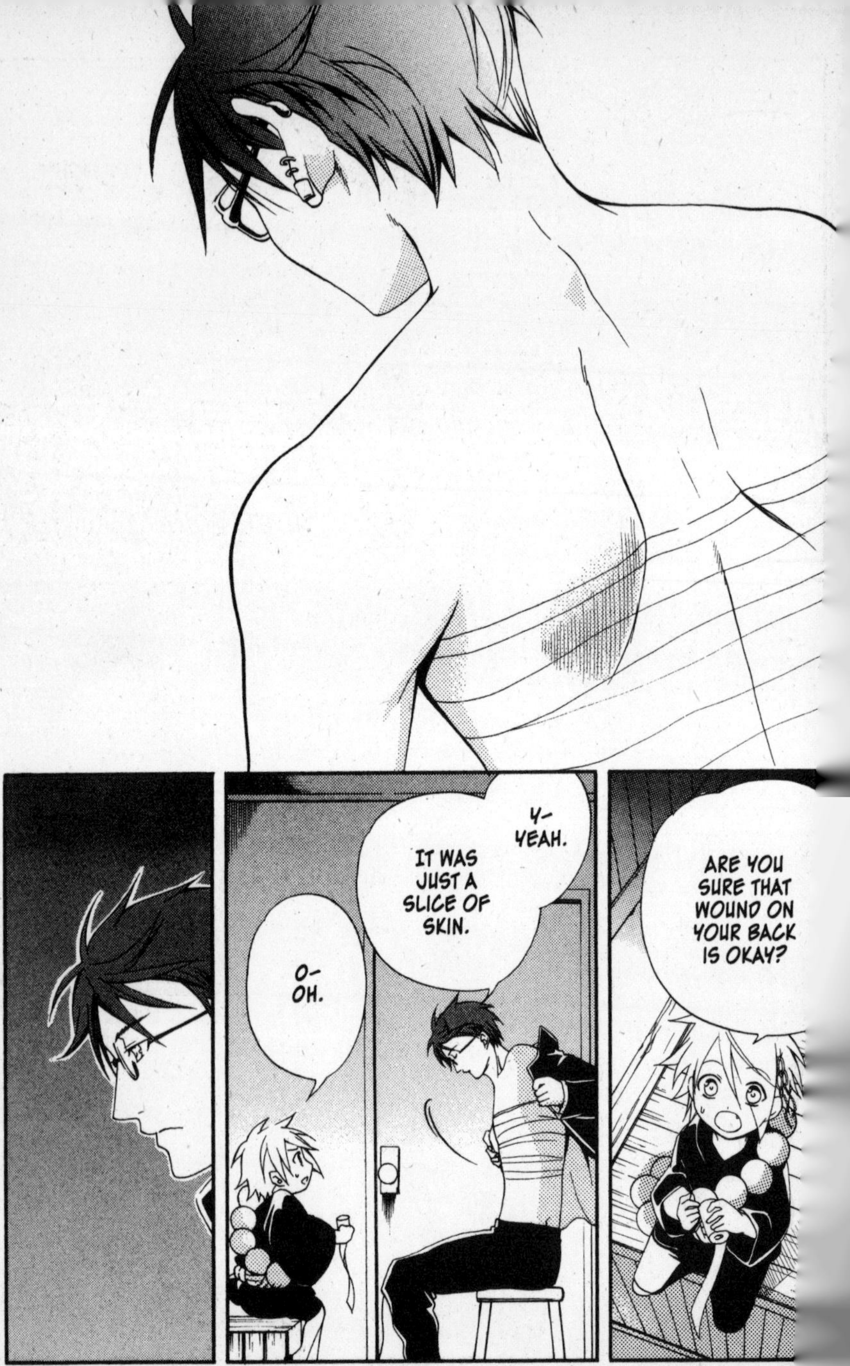
ARE YOU SURE THAT WOUND ON YOUR BACK IS OKAY?
Y-YEAH.
IT WAS JUST A SLICE OF SKIN.
O-OH.

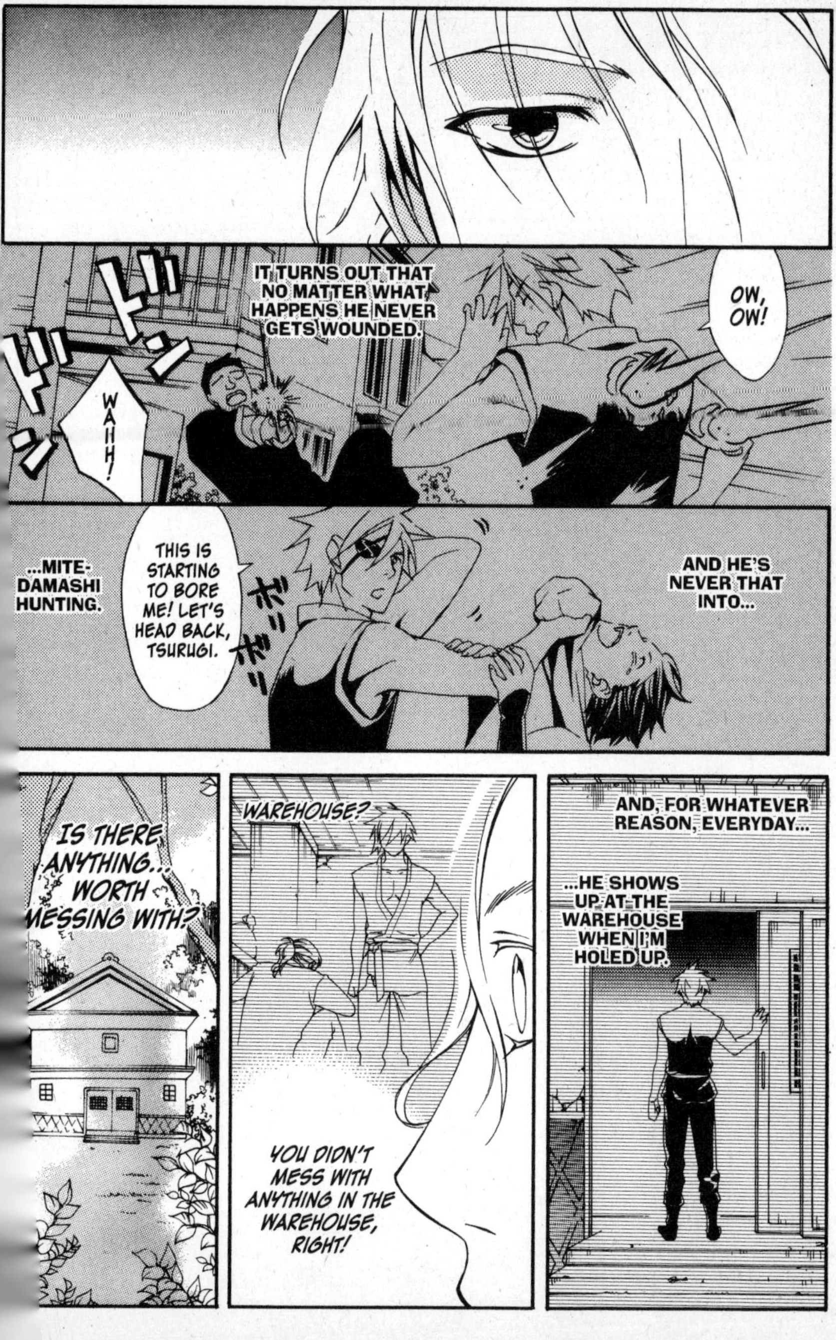
OW, OW!
IT TURNS OUT THAT NO MATTER WHAT HAPPENS HE NEVER GETS WOUNDED.
WAHH!
AND HE'S NEVER THAT INTO...
THIS IS STARTING TO BORE ME! LET'S HEAD BACK, TSURUGI.
...MITE-DAMASHI HUNTING.
AND, FOR WHATEVER REASON, EVERYDAY...
...HE SHOWS UP AT THE WAREHOUSE WHEN I'M HOLED UP.
WAREHOUSE?
YOU DIDN'T MESS WITH ANYTHING IN THE WAREHOUSE, RIGHT!
IS THERE ANYTHING... WORTH MESSING WITH?

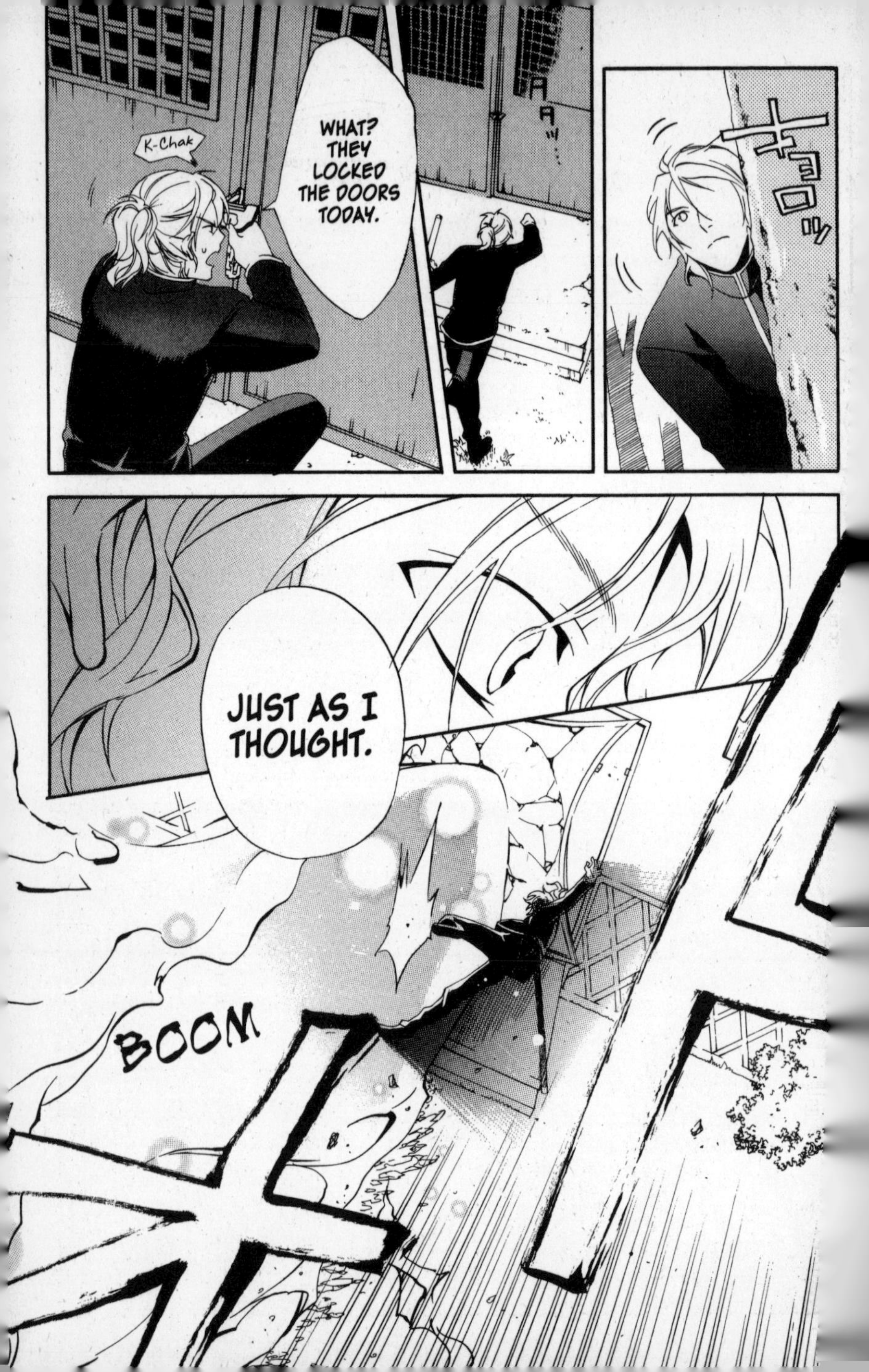
キョロッ
K-Chak
WHAT? THEY LOCKED THE DOORS TODAY.
JUST AS I THOUGHT.
BOOM

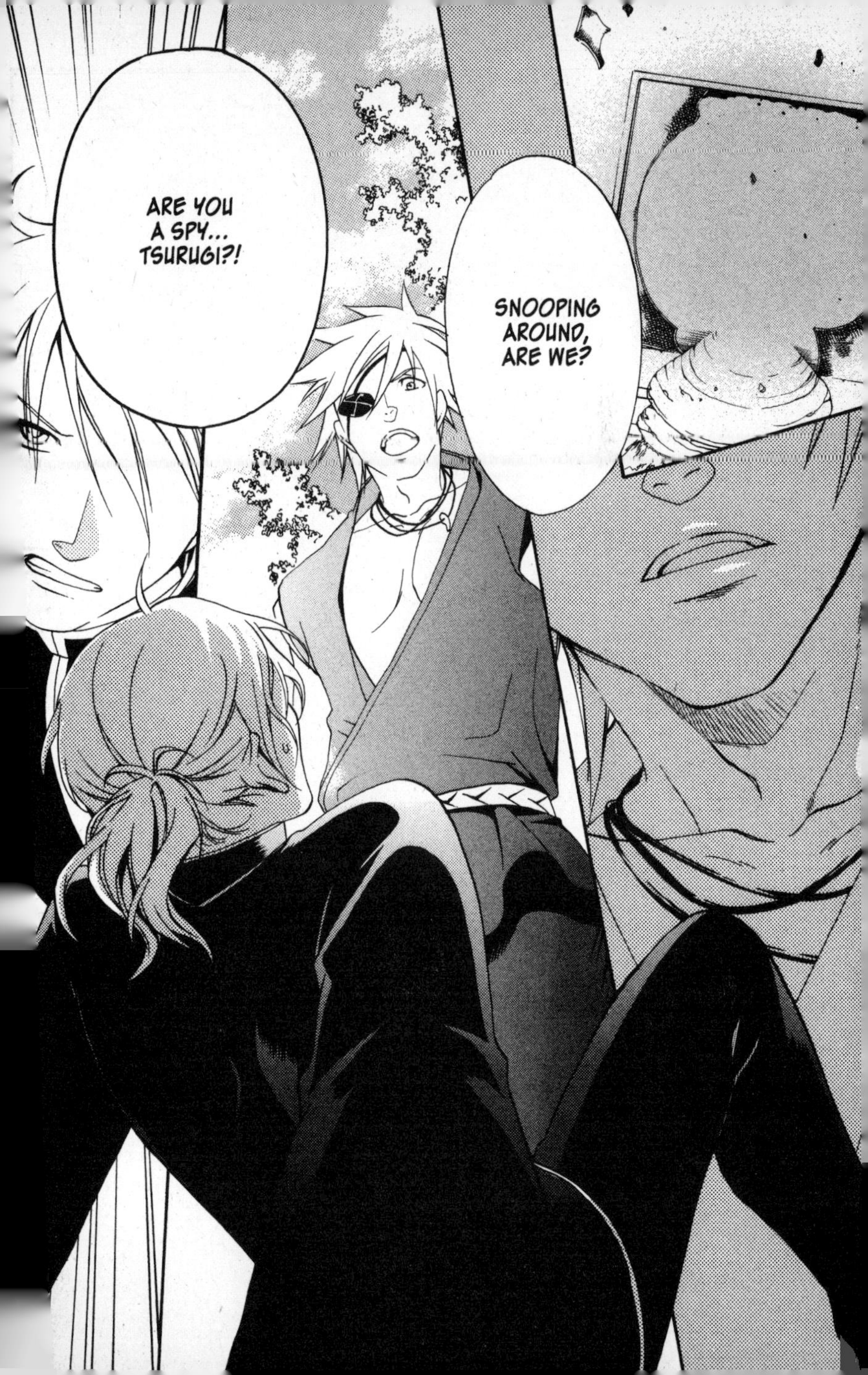
SNOOPING AROUND, ARE WE?
ARE YOU A SPY... TSURUGI?!

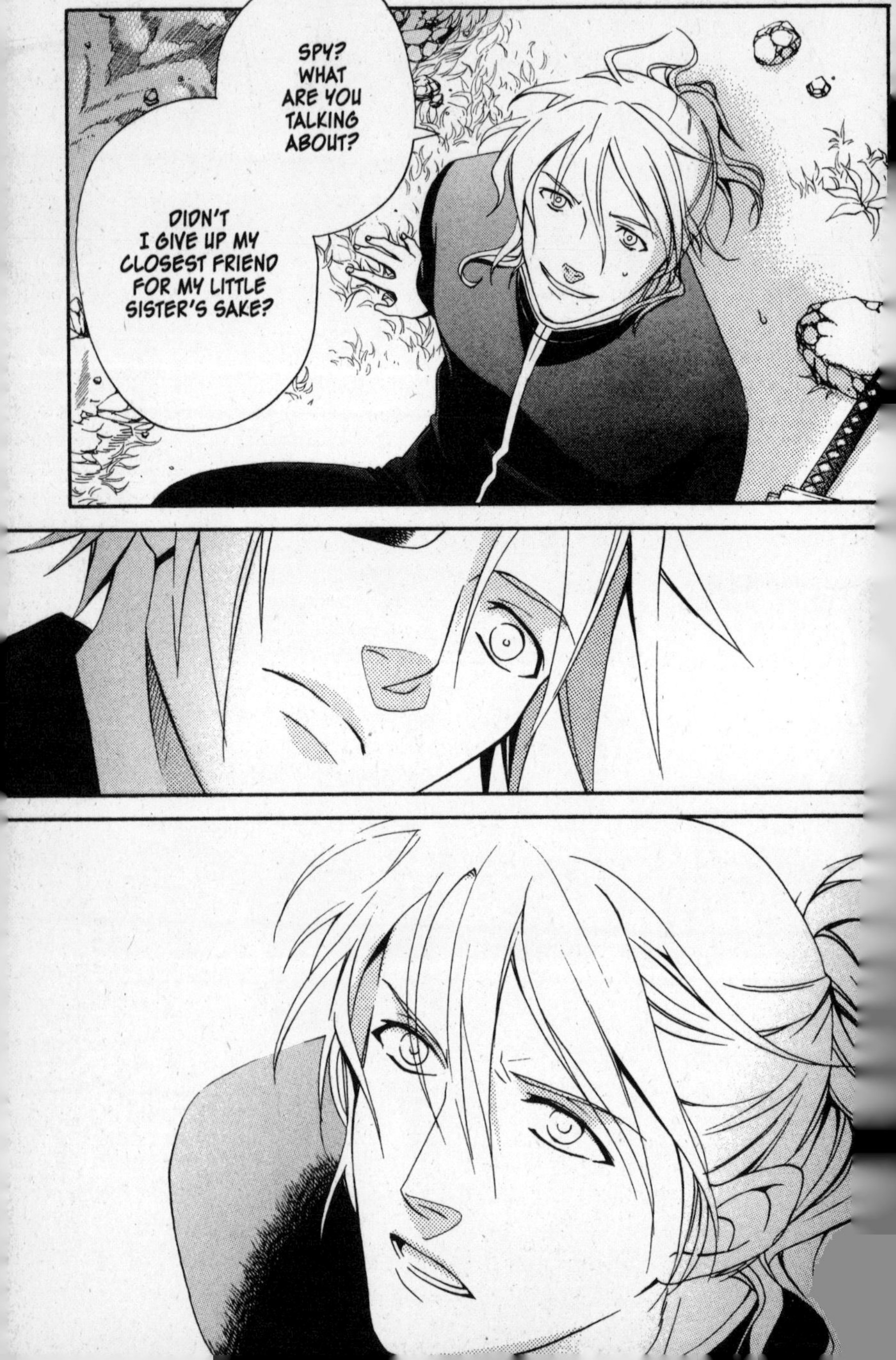
SPY? WHAT ARE YOU TALKING ABOUT?
DIDN'T I GIVE UP MY CLOSEST FRIEND FOR MY LITTLE SISTER'S SAKE?

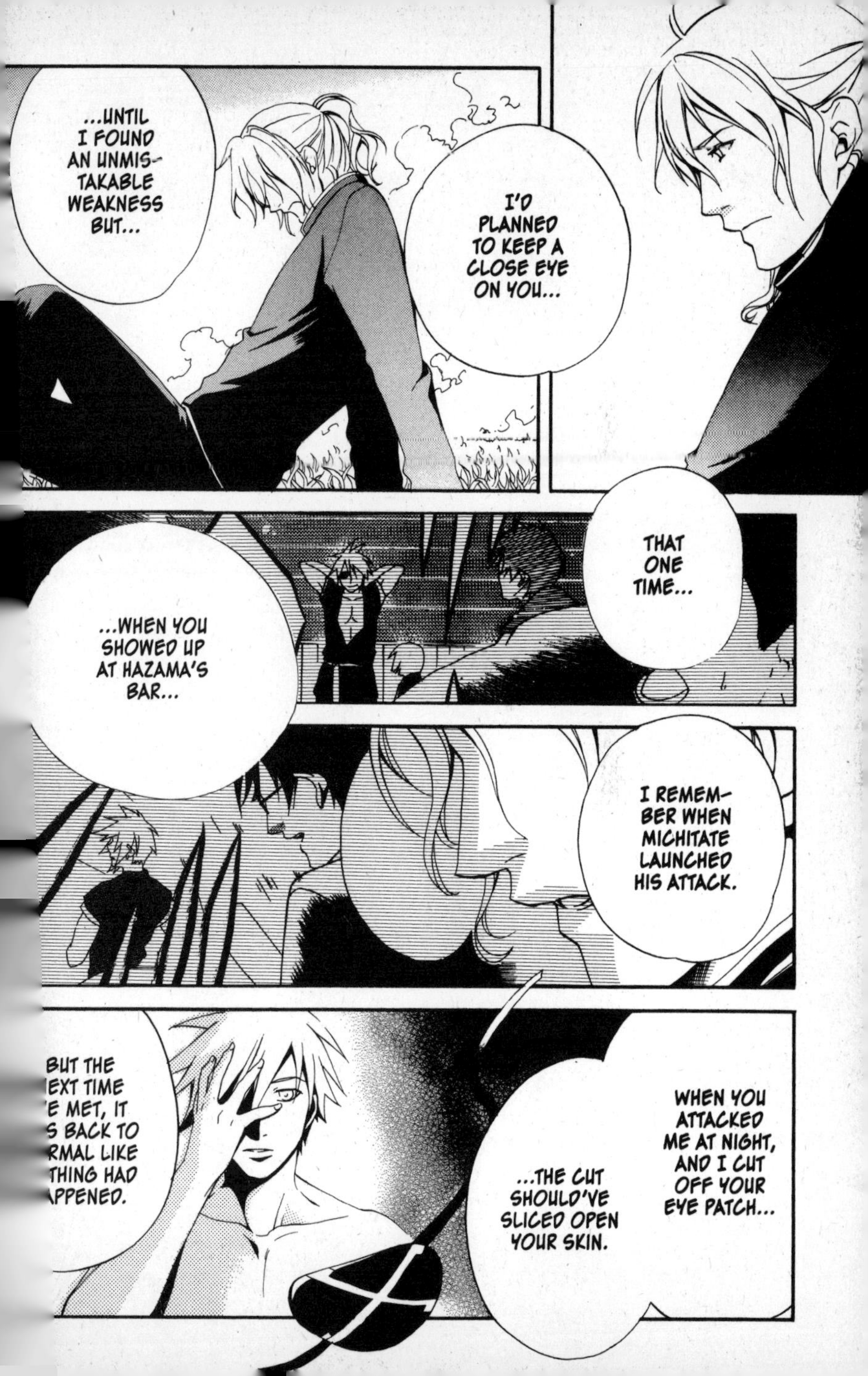
I'D PLANNED TO KEEP A CLOSE EYE ON YOU...
...UNTIL I FOUND AN UNMIS-TAKABLE WEAKNESS BUT...
THAT ONE TIME...
...WHEN YOU SHOWED UP AT HAZAMA'S BAR...
I REMEM-BER WHEN MICHITATE LAUNCHED HIS ATTACK.
WHEN YOU ATTACKED ME AT NIGHT, AND I CUT OFF YOUR EYE PATCH...
...THE CUT SHOULD'VE SLICED OPEN YOUR SKIN.
BUT THE EXT TIME E MET, IT S BACK TO RMAL LIKE THING HAD PPENED.

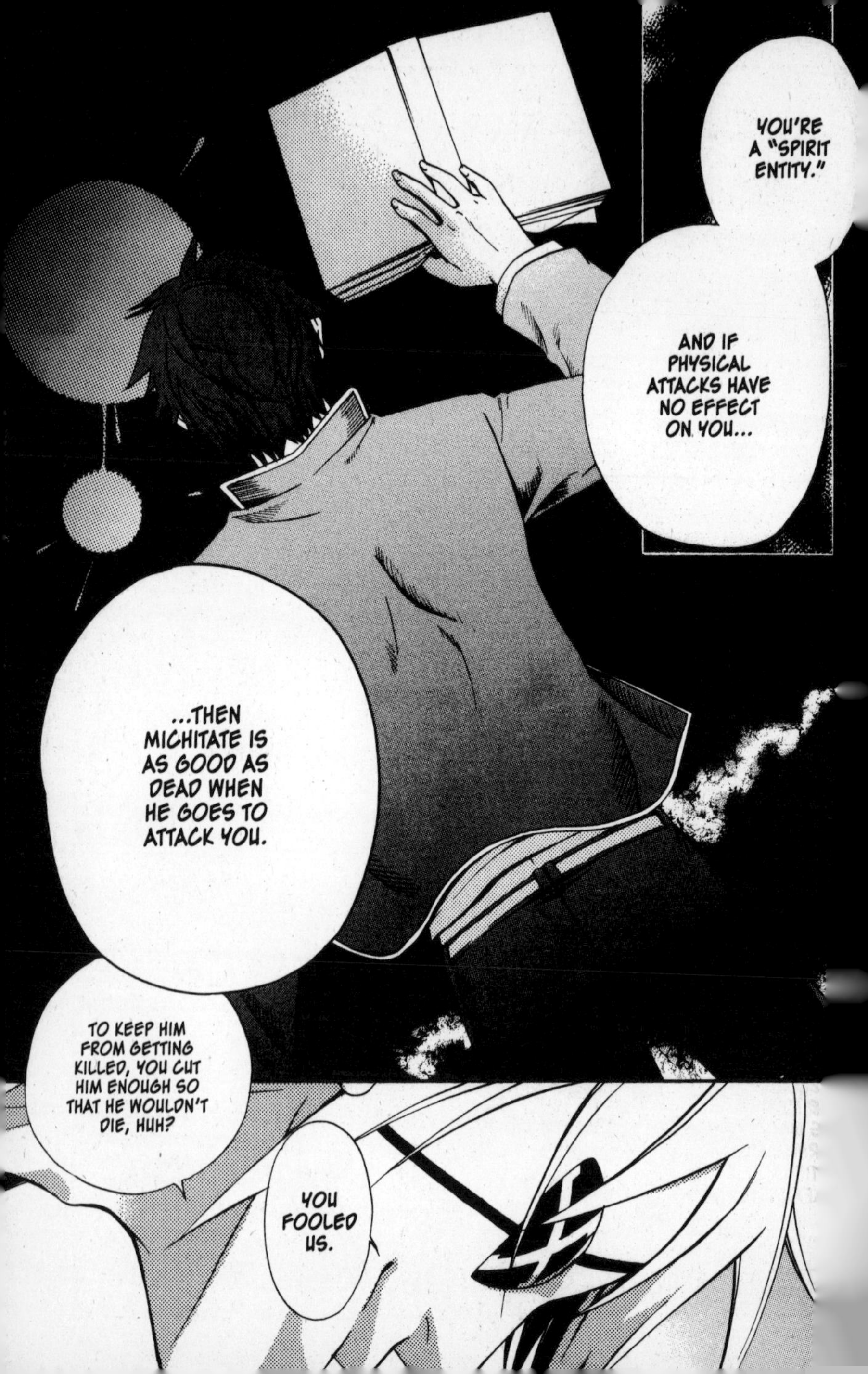
YOU'RE A "SPIRIT ENTITY."
AND IF PHYSICAL ATTACKS HAVE NO EFFECT ON YOU...
...THEN MICHITATE IS AS GOOD AS DEAD WHEN HE GOES TO ATTACK YOU.
TO KEEP HIM FROM GETTING KILLED, YOU CUT HIM ENOUGH SO THAT HE WOULDN'T DIE, HUH?
YOU FOOLED US.

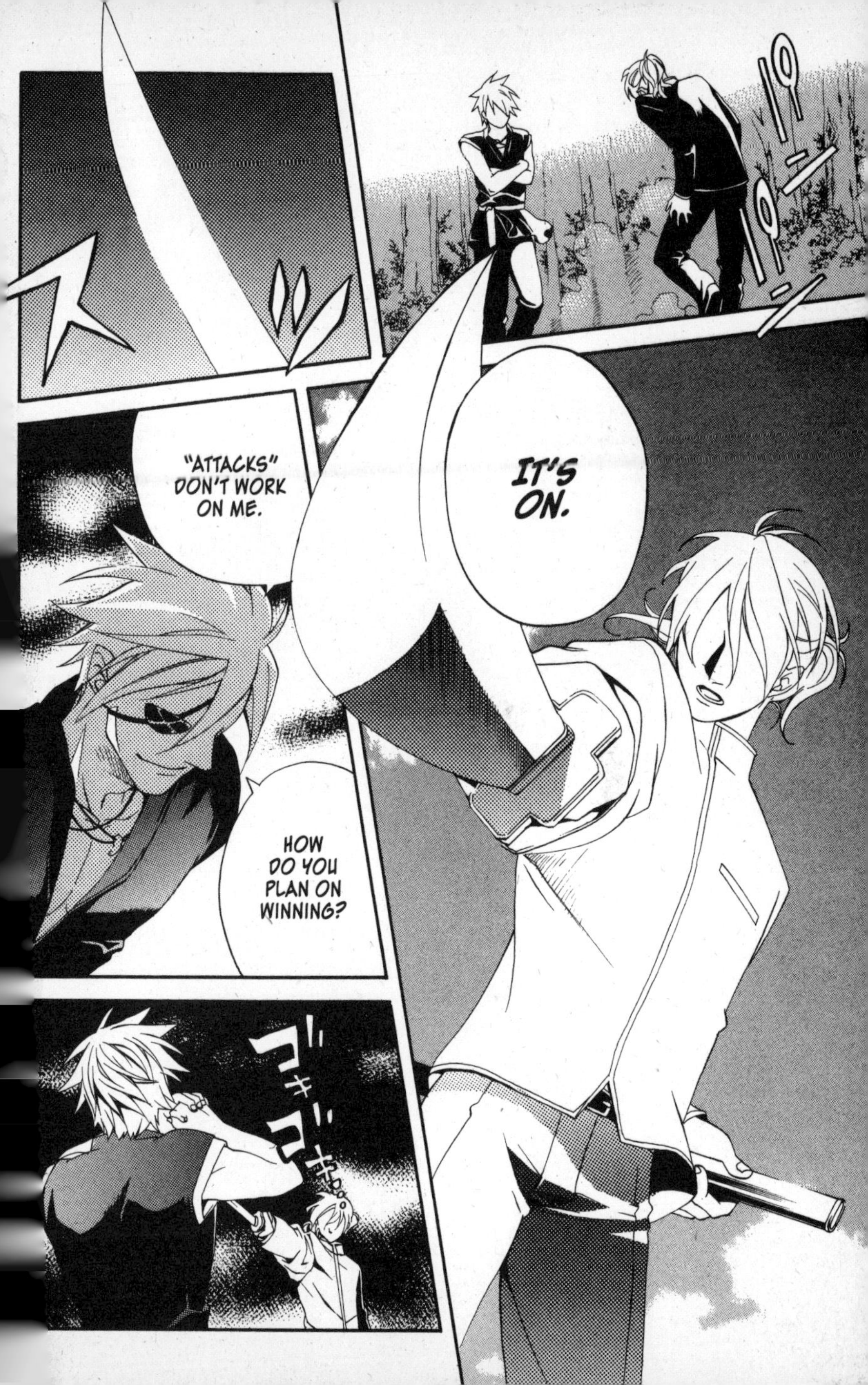
IT'S ON.
"ATTACKS" DON'T WORK ON ME.
HOW DO YOU PLAN ON WINNING?

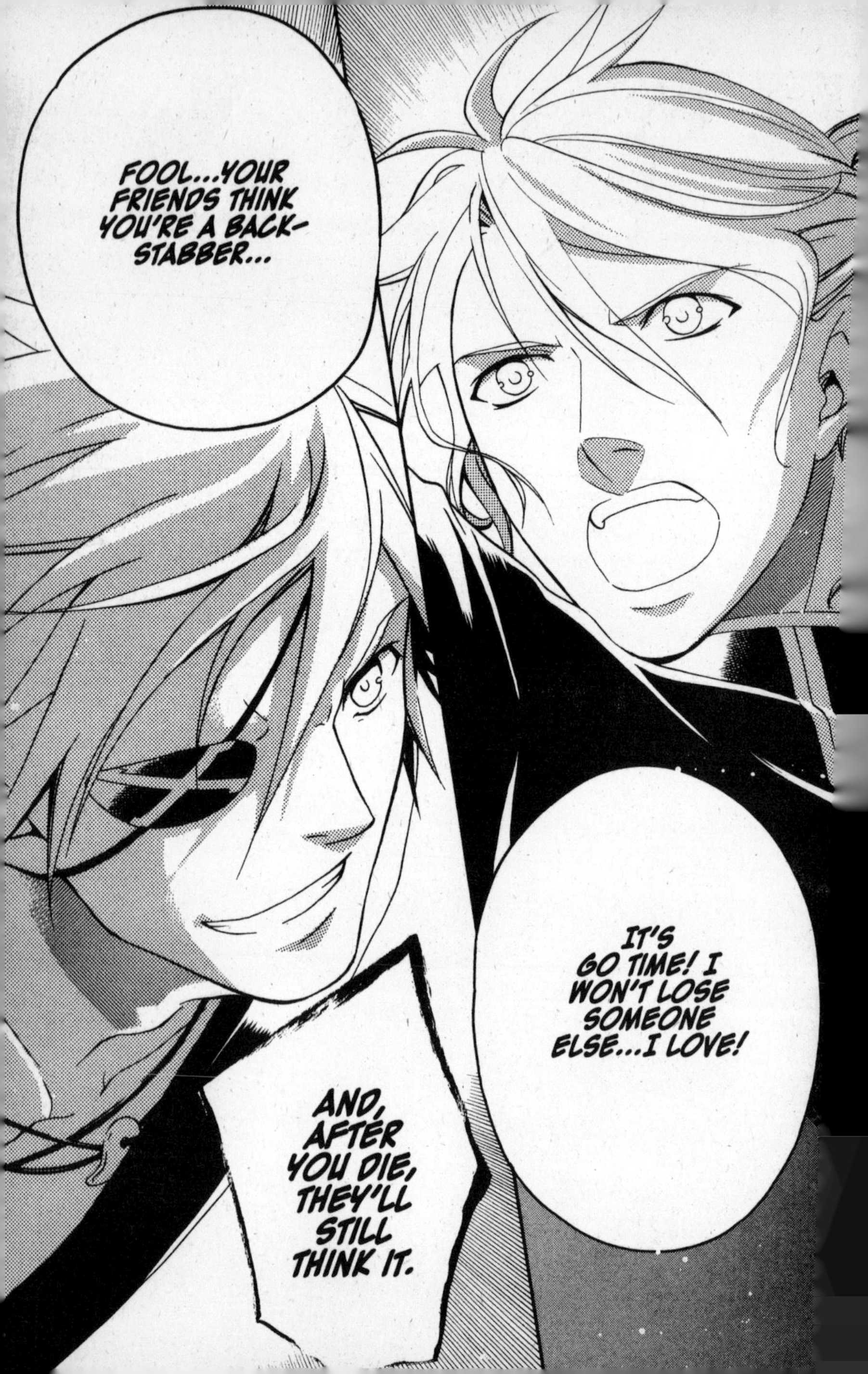
FOOL...YOUR FRIENDS THINK YOU'RE A BACK-STABBER...
IT'S GO TIME! I WON'T LOSE SOMEONE ELSE...I LOVE!
AND, AFTER YOU DIE, THEY'LL STILL THINK IT.

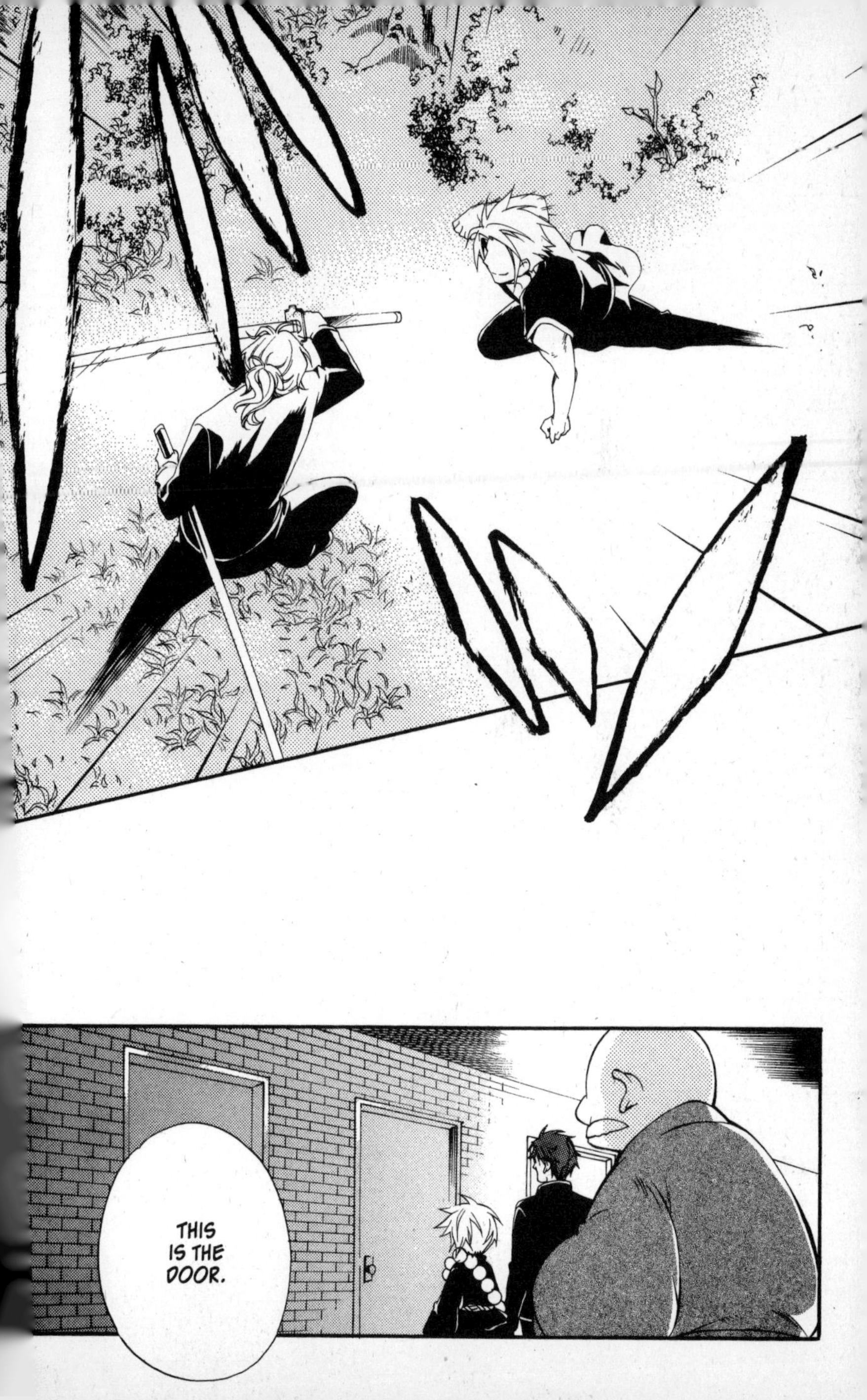
THIS IS THE DOOR.

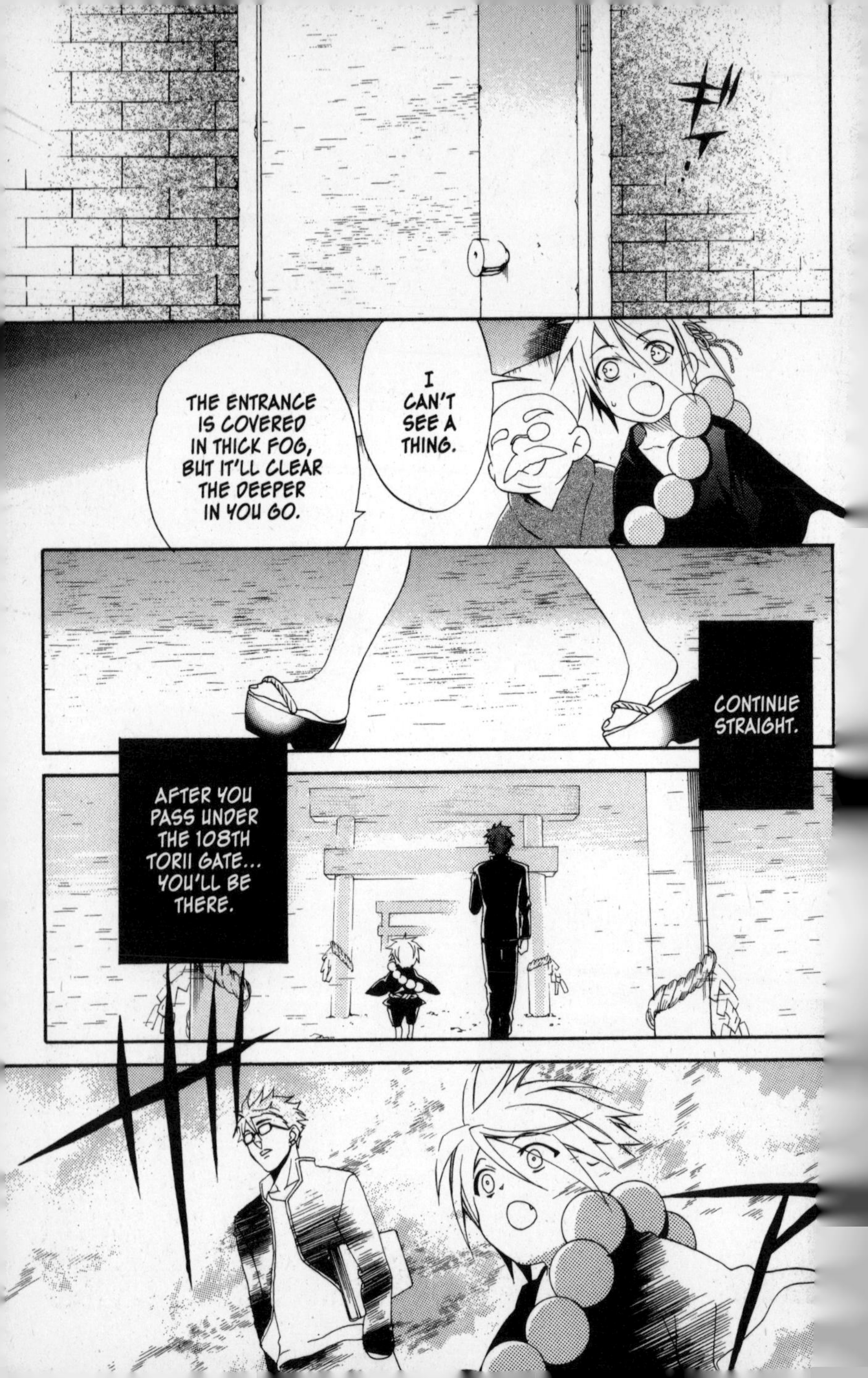
I CAN'T SEE A THING.
THE ENTRANCE IS COVERED IN THICK FOG, BUT IT'LL CLEAR THE DEEPER IN YOU GO.
CONTINUE STRAIGHT.
AFTER YOU PASS UNDER THE 108TH TORII GATE... YOU'LL BE THERE.

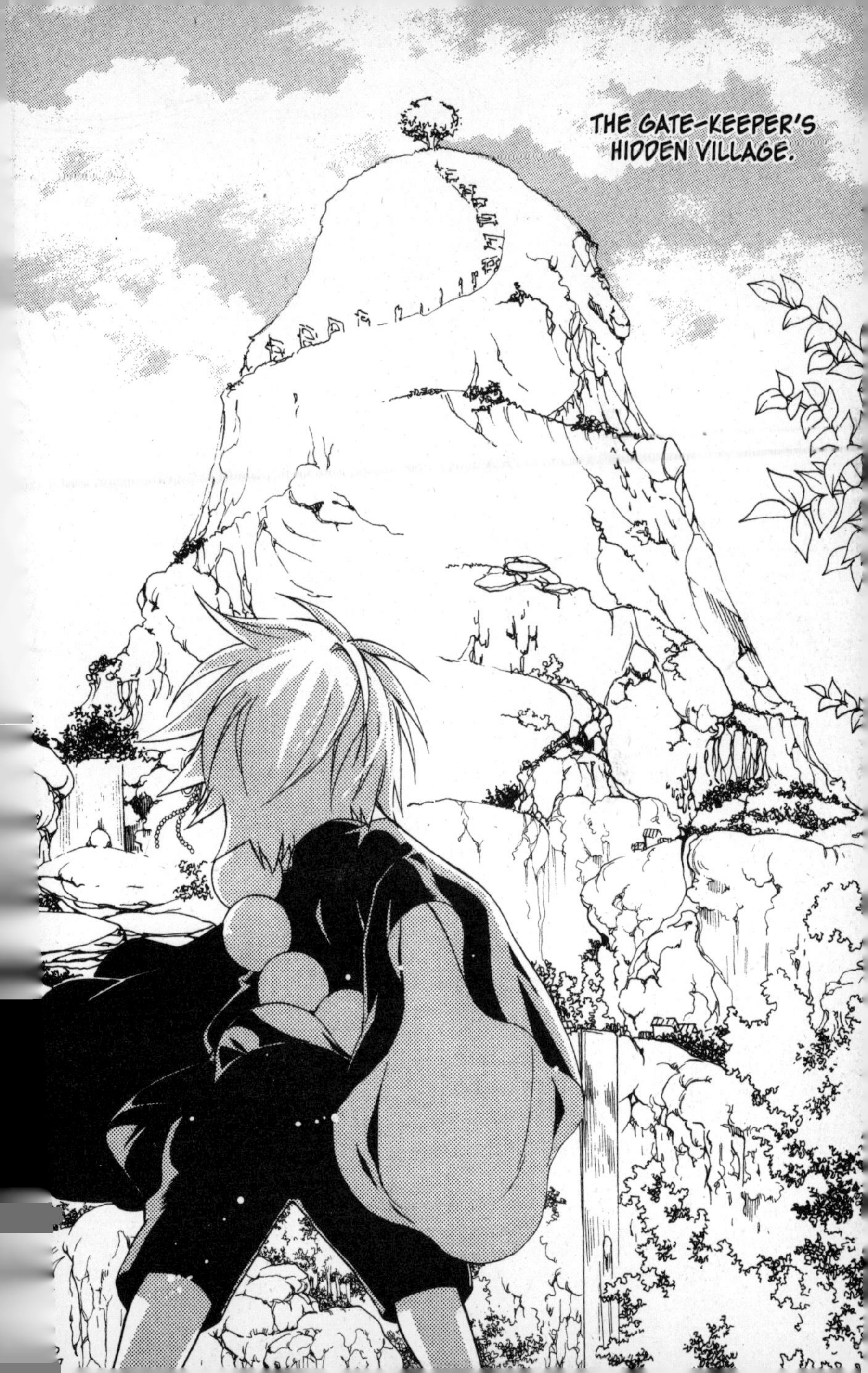
THE GATE-KEEPER'S HIDDEN VILLAGE.

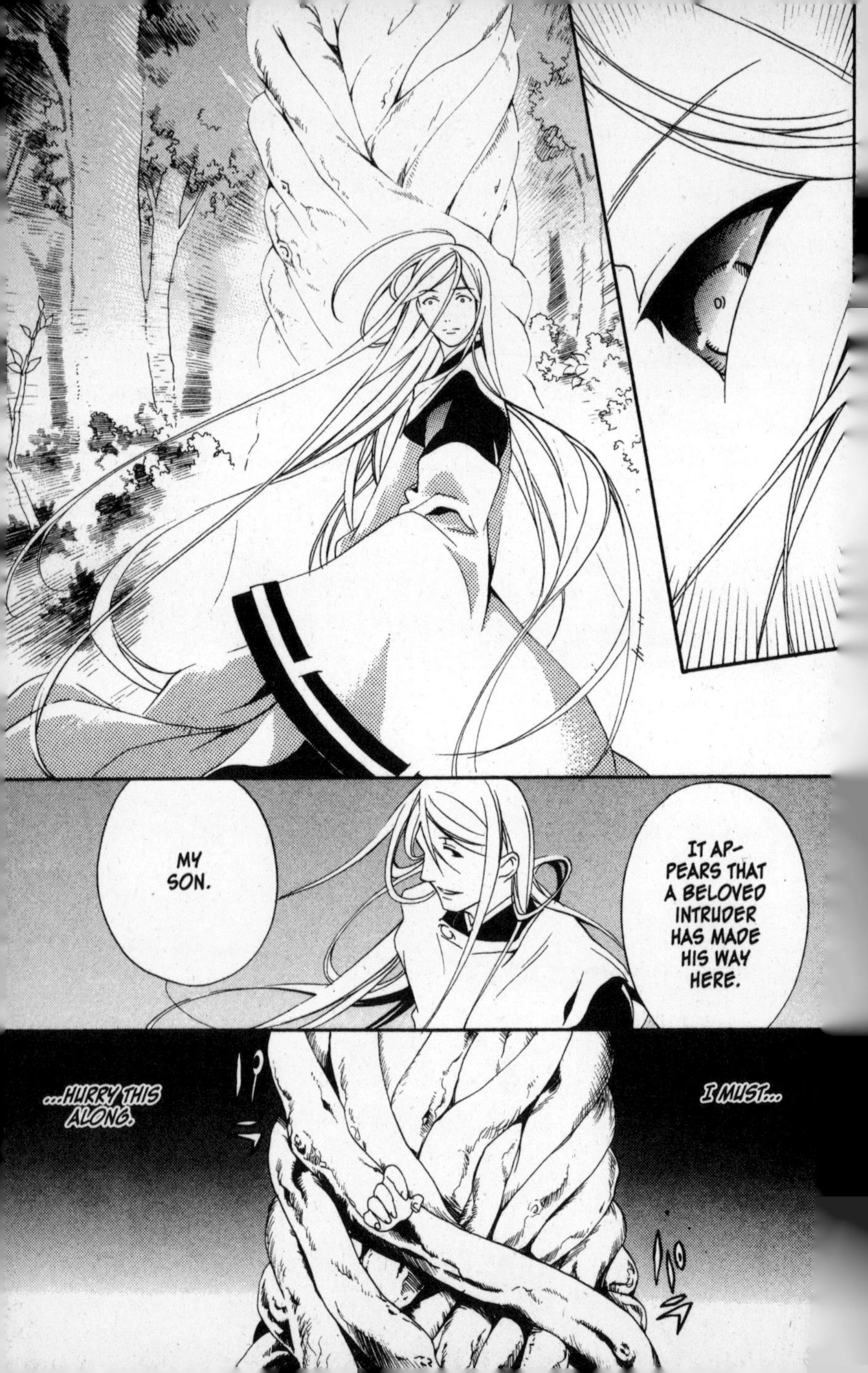
IT AP-PEARS THAT A BELOVED INTRUDER HAS MADE HIS WAY HERE.
MY SON.
I MUST...
...HURRY THIS ALONG.
!?
!?

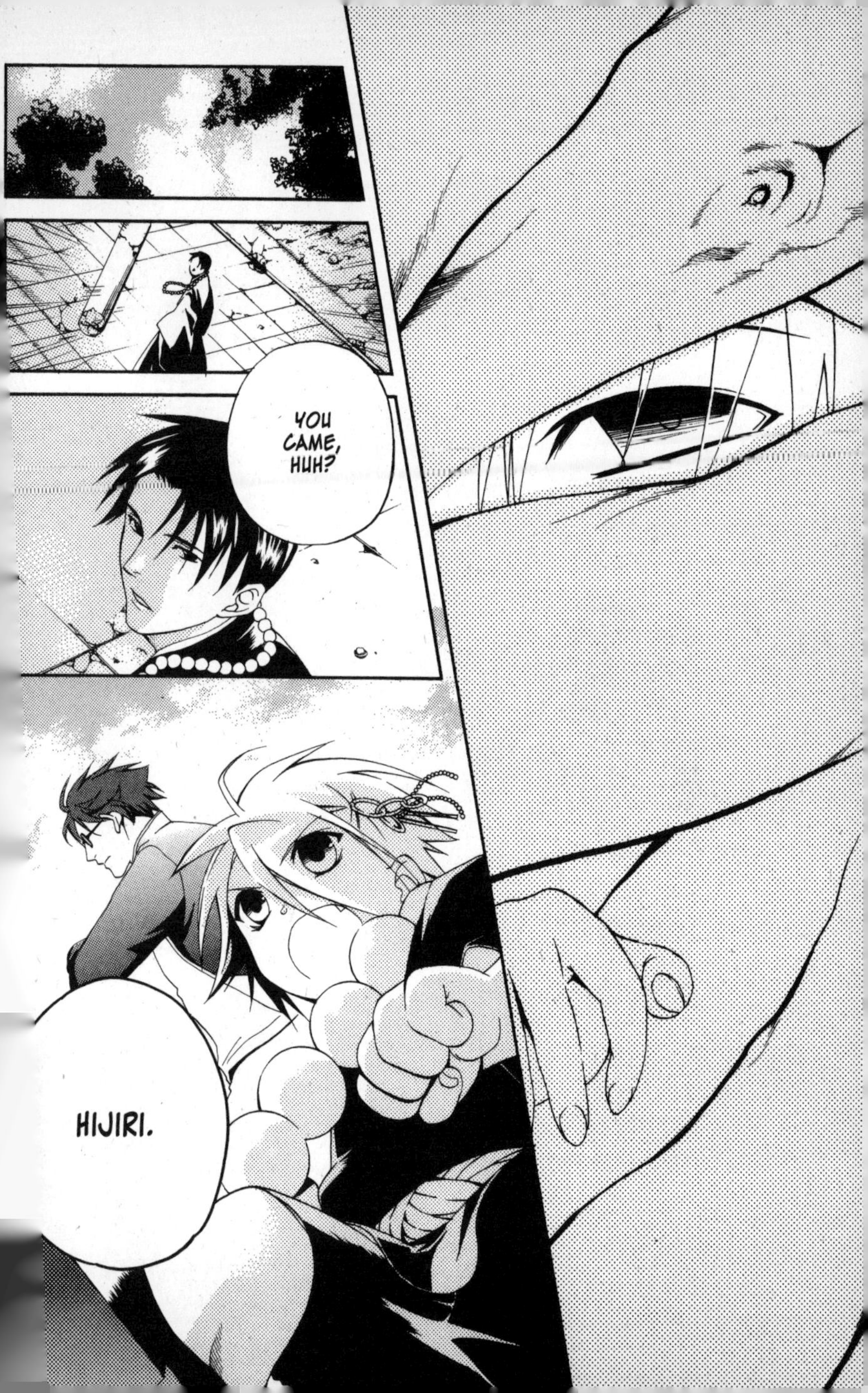
YOU CAME, HUH?
HIJIRI.

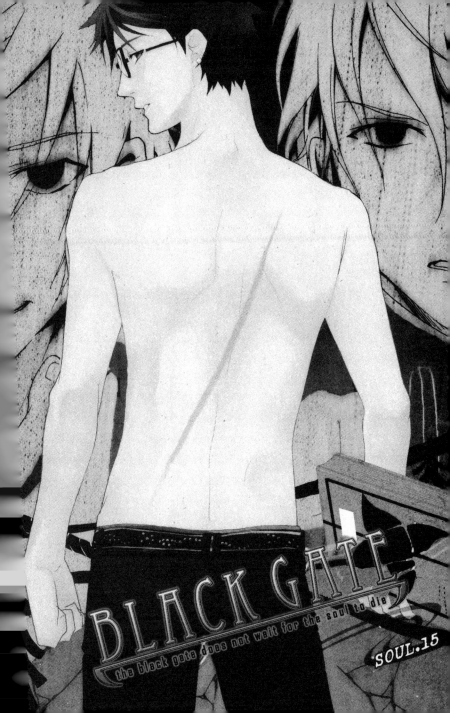

BLACK GATE
the black gate does not wait for the soul to die

SOUL.15

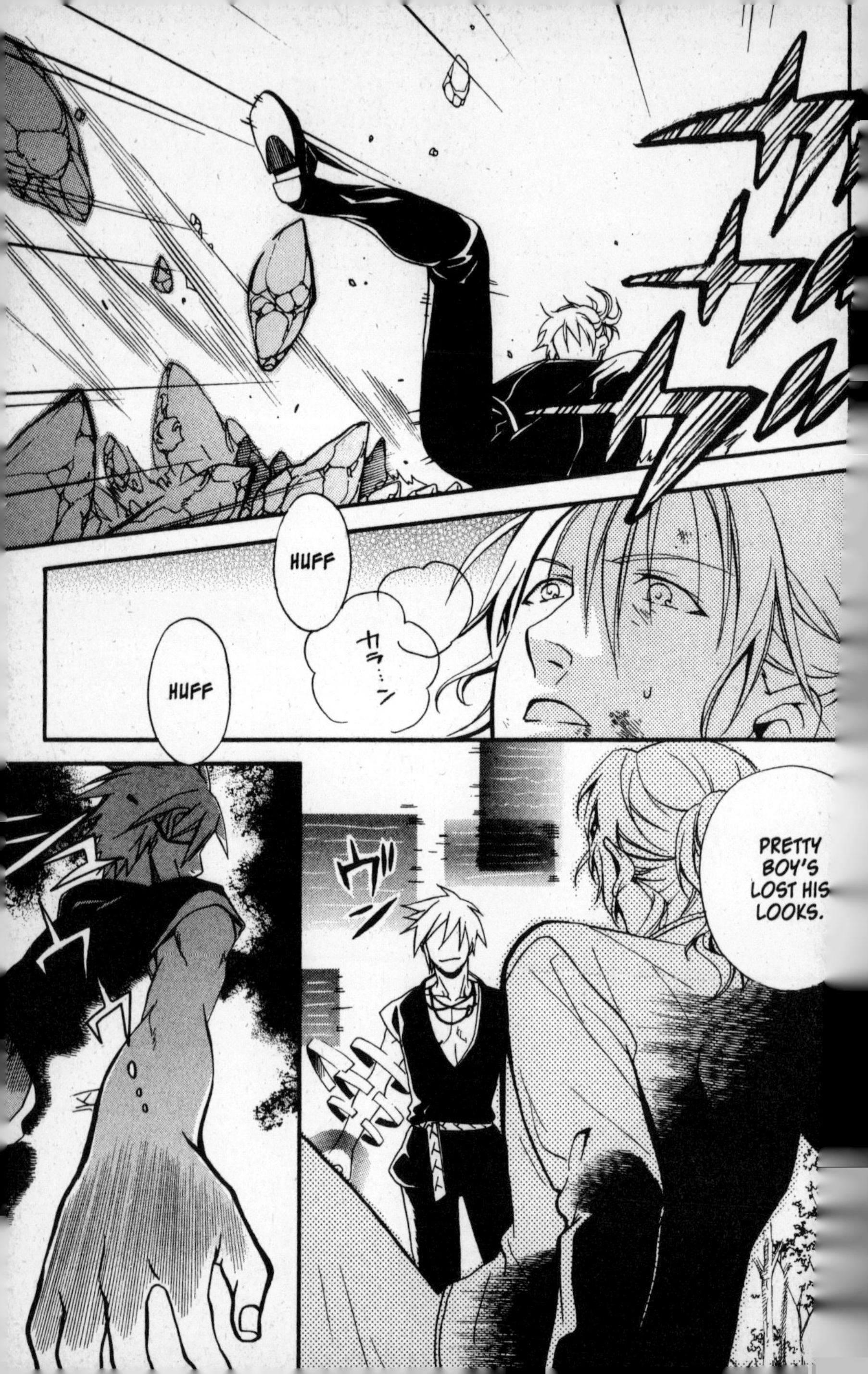
HUFF
カラ…ン
HUFF
PRETTY BOY'S LOST HIS LOOKS.
ヴン

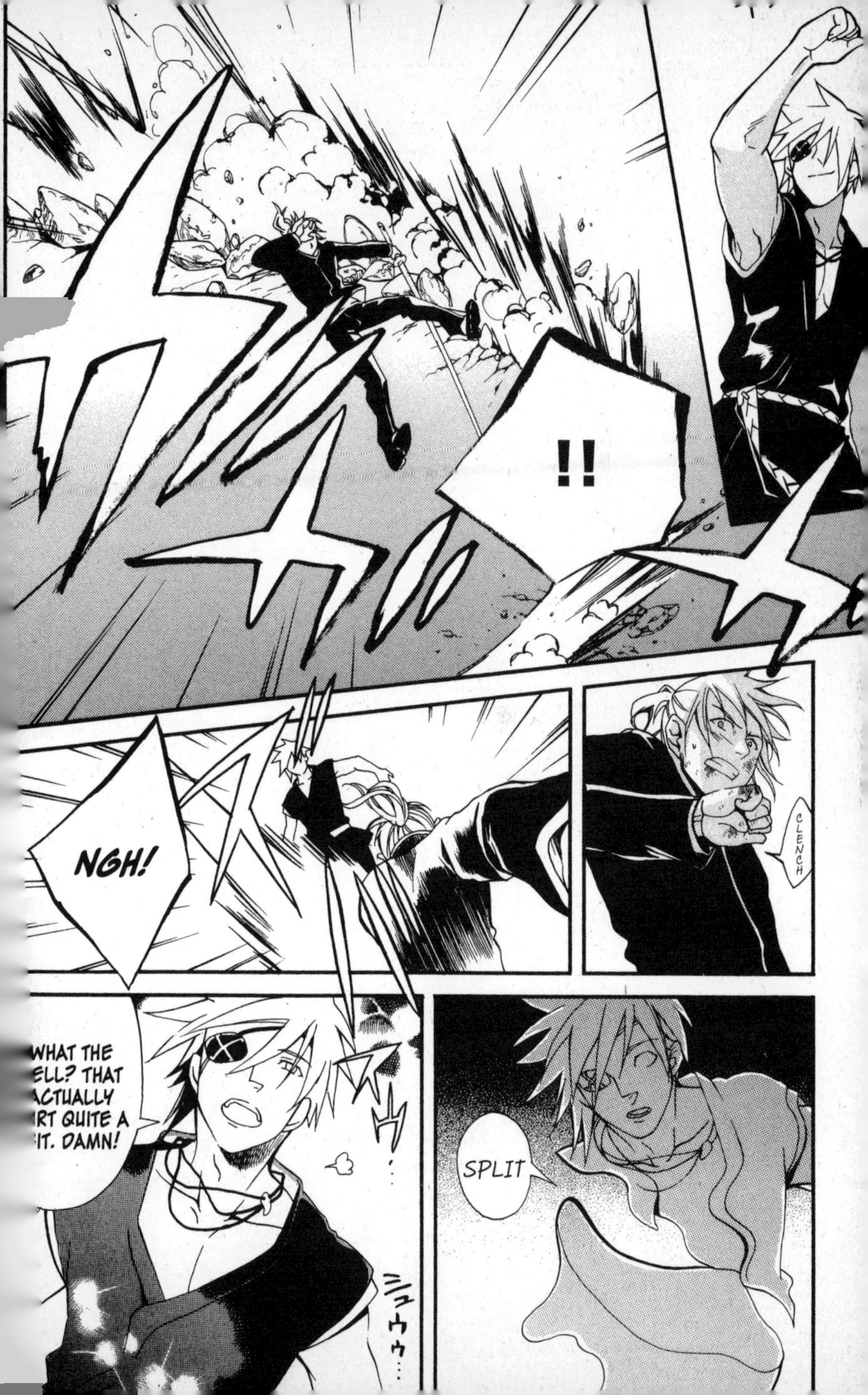
!!
CLENCH
NGH!
SPLIT
WHAT THE ELL? THAT ACTUALLY RT QUITE A IT. DAMN!
シュウウ…

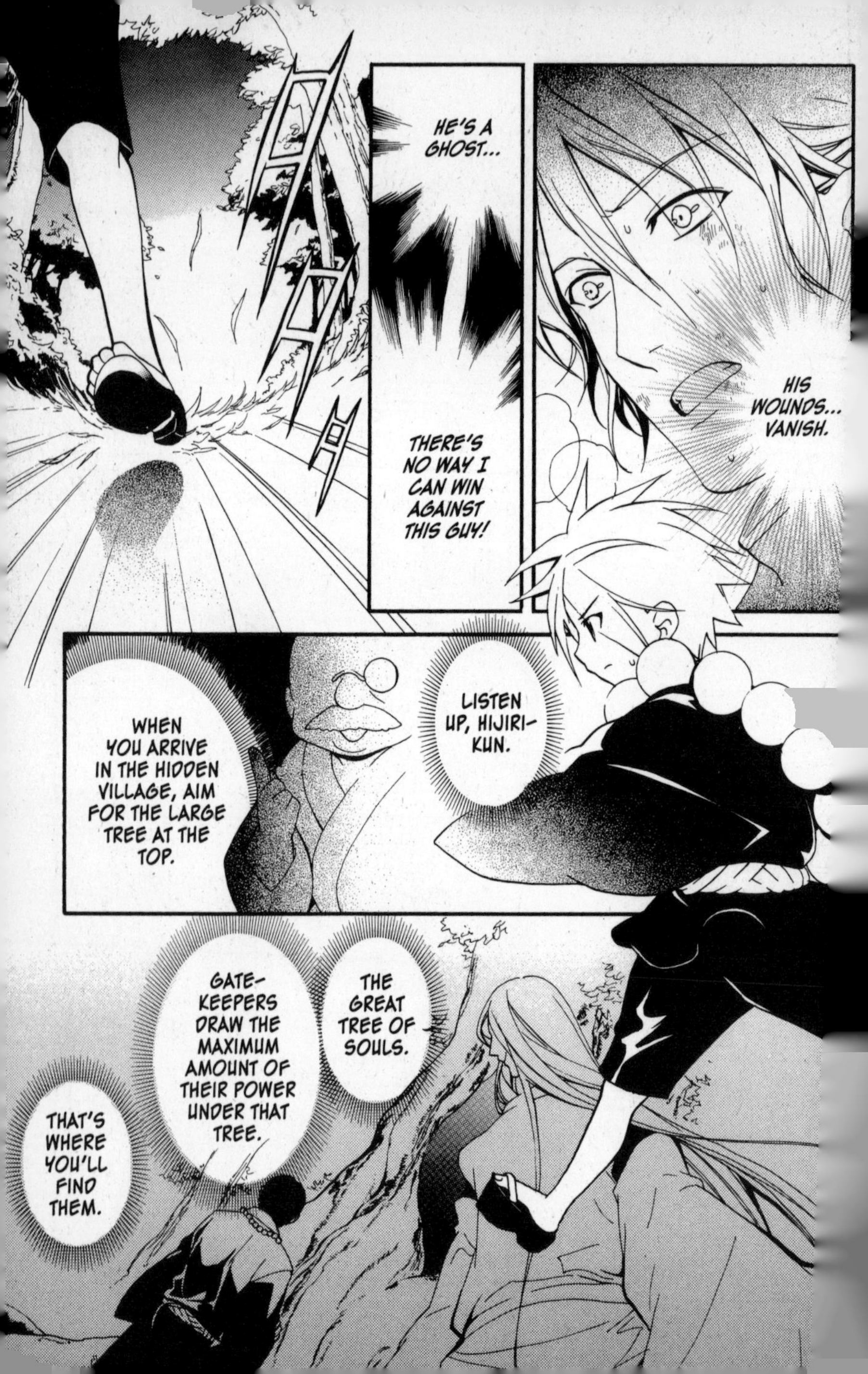
HIS WOUNDS... VANISH.
HE'S A GHOST...
THERE'S NO WAY I CAN WIN AGAINST THIS GUY!
LISTEN UP, HIJIRI-KUN.
WHEN YOU ARRIVE IN THE HIDDEN VILLAGE, AIM FOR THE LARGE TREE AT THE TOP.
THE GREAT TREE OF SOULS.
GATEKEEPERS DRAW THE MAXIMUM AMOUNT OF THEIR POWER UNDER THAT TREE.
THAT'S WHERE YOU'LL FIND THEM.

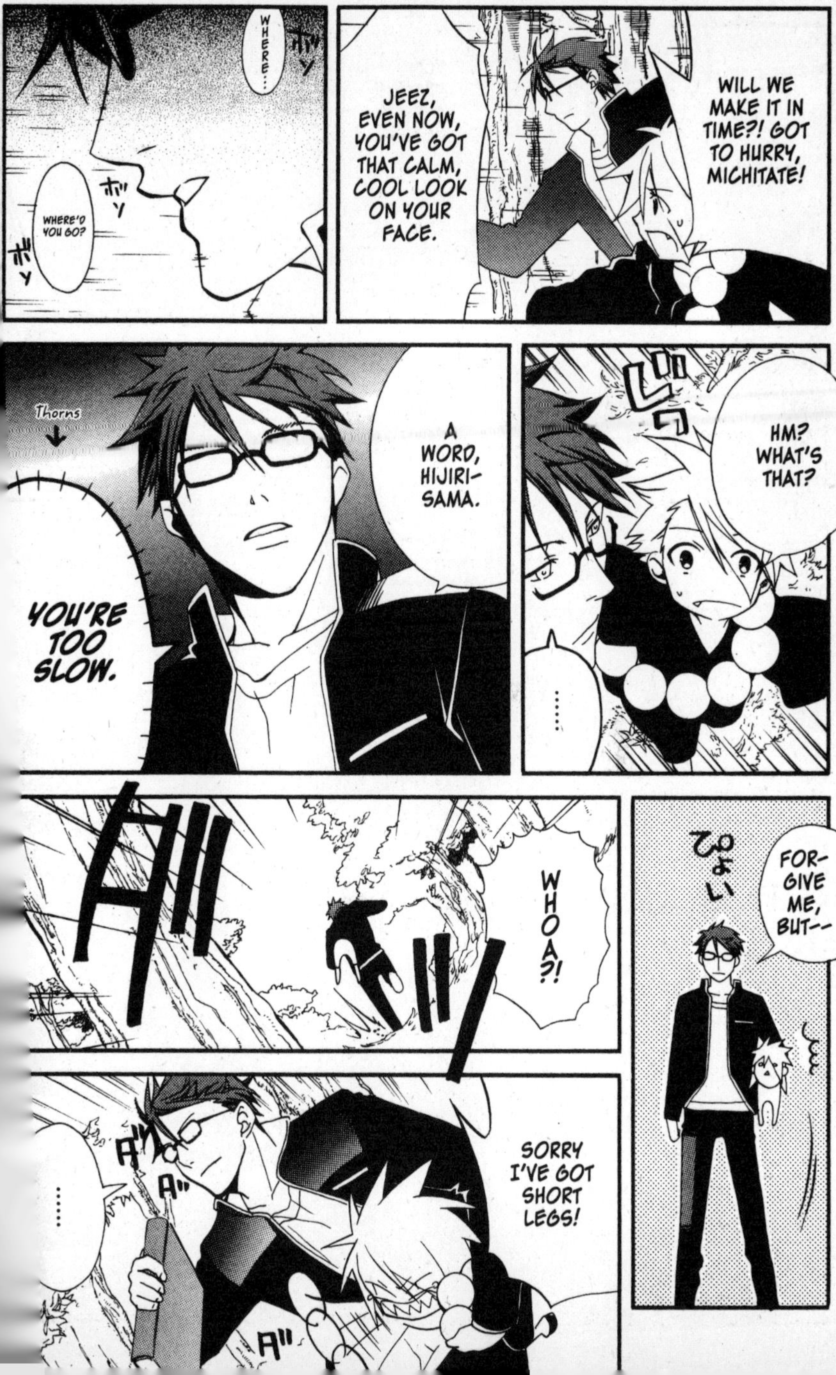
WILL WE MAKE IT IN TIME?! GOT TO HURRY, MICHITATE!
JEEZ, EVEN NOW, YOU'VE GOT THAT CALM, COOL LOOK ON YOUR FACE.
WHERE...
ボソ
WHERE'D YOU GO?
ボソ
ボソ
HM? WHAT'S THAT?
......
A WORD, HIJIRI-SAMA.
Thorns
YOU'RE TOO SLOW.
ぴょい
FOR-GIVE ME, BUT--
WHOA?!
SORRY I'VE GOT SHORT LEGS!
......

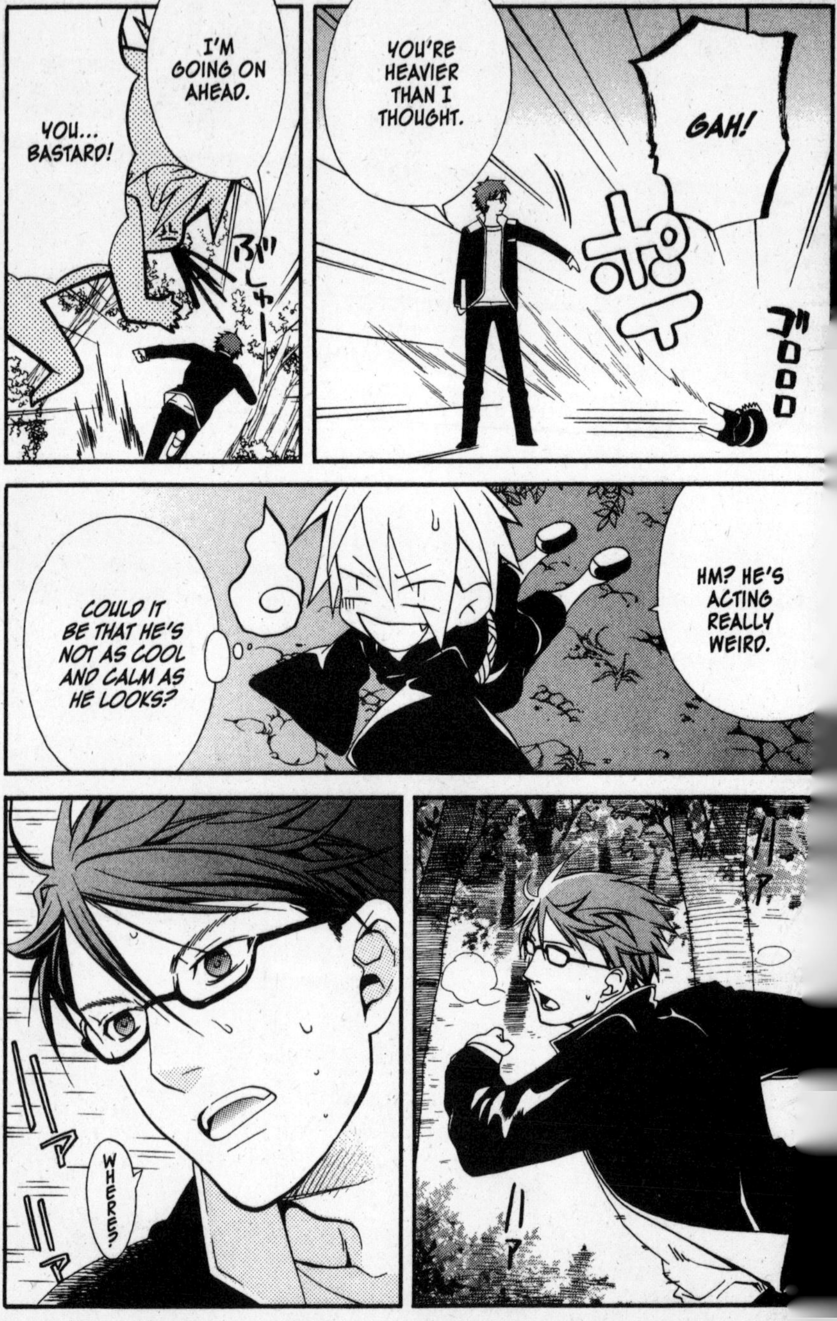
GAH!
ポイ
ゴロロロ
YOU'RE HEAVIER THAN I THOUGHT.
I'M GOING ON AHEAD.
YOU... BASTARD!
ぶしゃー
HM? HE'S ACTING REALLY WEIRD.
COULD IT BE THAT HE'S NOT AS COOL AND CALM AS HE LOOKS?
ハァ
ハァ
ハァ
ハァ
WHERE?

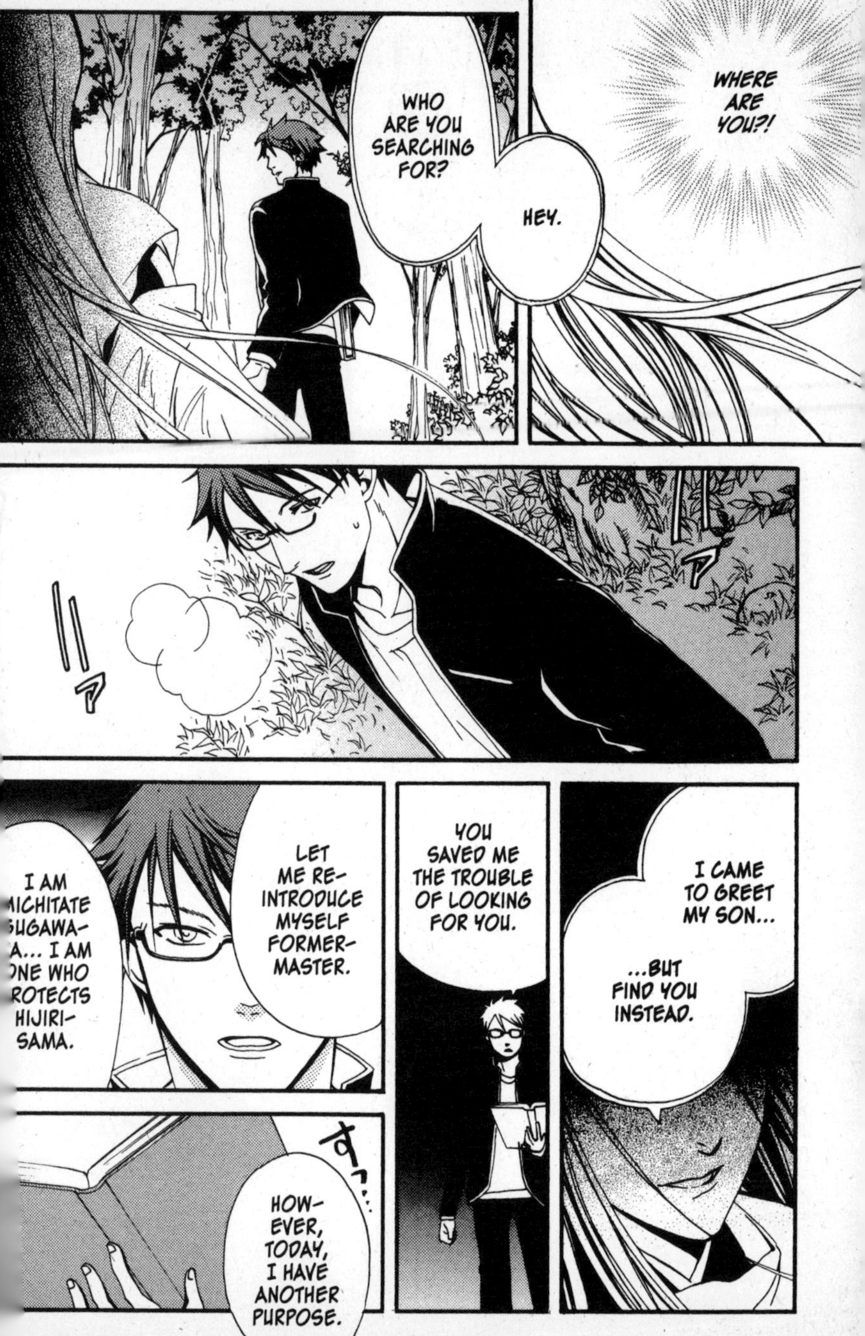
WHERE ARE YOU?!
HEY.
WHO ARE YOU SEARCHING FOR?
ァ
ハァ
I CAME TO GREET MY SON...
...BUT FIND YOU INSTEAD.
YOU SAVED ME THE TROUBLE OF LOOKING FOR YOU.
LET ME RE-INTRODUCE MYSELF FORMER-MASTER.
I AM MICHITATE SUGAWA-A... I AM ONE WHO PROTECTS HIJIRI-SAMA.
すっ...
HOW-EVER, TODAY, I HAVE ANOTHER PURPOSE.

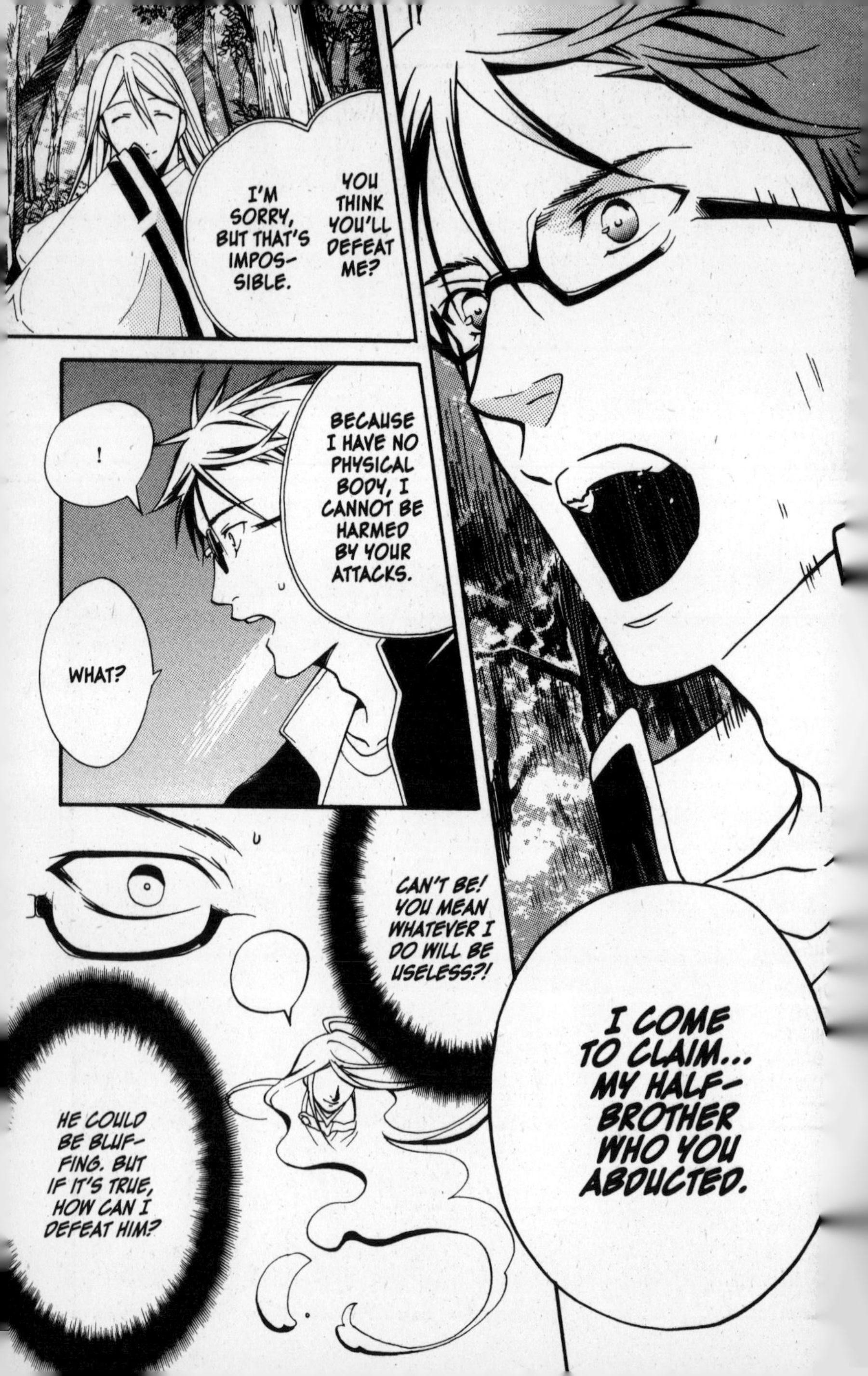
I COME TO CLAIM... MY HALF-BROTHER WHO YOU ABDUCTED.
YOU THINK YOU'LL DEFEAT ME?
I'M SORRY, BUT THAT'S IMPOS-SIBLE.
BECAUSE I HAVE NO PHYSICAL BODY, I CANNOT BE HARMED BY YOUR ATTACKS.
!
WHAT?
CAN'T BE! YOU MEAN WHATEVER I DO WILL BE USELESS?!
HE COULD BE BLUF-FING. BUT IF IT'S TRUE, HOW CAN I DEFEAT HIM?

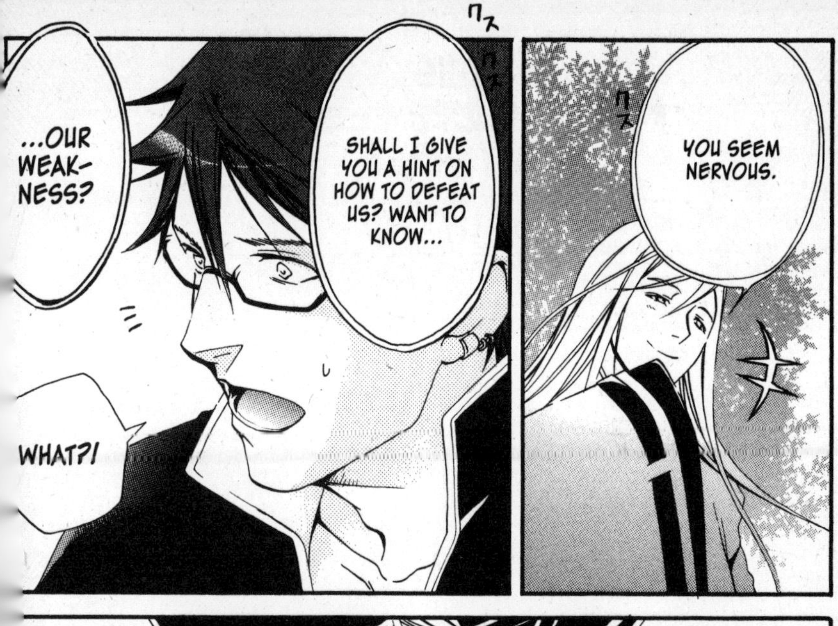
YOU SEEM NERVOUS.
SHALL I GIVE YOU A HINT ON HOW TO DEFEAT US? WANT TO KNOW...
...OUR WEAK-NESS?
WHAT?!
KEEPING A SPIRIT ENTITY IN THIS WORLD REALLY IS A TROUBLESOME AFFAIR. IF WE'RE NOT CAREFUL, WE COULD EASILY GET PULLED INTO A GATE.
YOU SEE, ONCE YOU DIE, IT'S NOT SO EASY TO PRESERVE YOUR HUMAN FORM.

*Yorishiro is from Shinto, and are objects to which a divine spirit has been bound, often they are trees or large rocks.

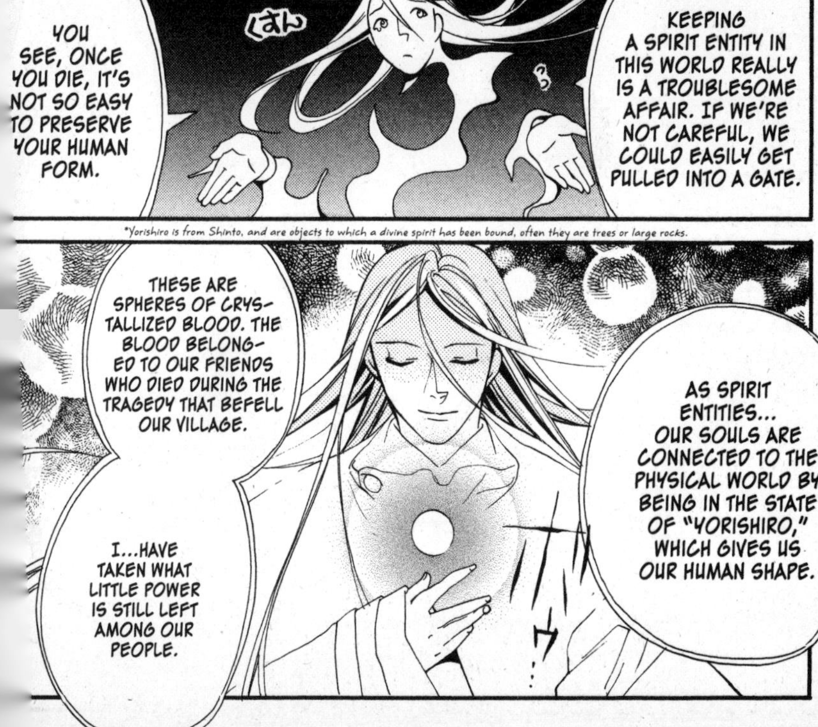
AS SPIRIT ENTITIES... OUR SOULS ARE CONNECTED TO THE PHYSICAL WORLD BY BEING IN THE STATE OF "YORISHIRO," WHICH GIVES US OUR HUMAN SHAPE.
THESE ARE SPHERES OF CRYS-TALLIZED BLOOD. THE BLOOD BELONG-ED TO OUR FRIENDS WHO DIED DURING THE TRAGEDY THAT BEFELL OUR VILLAGE.
I...HAVE TAKEN WHAT LITTLE POWER IS STILL LEFT AMONG OUR PEOPLE.

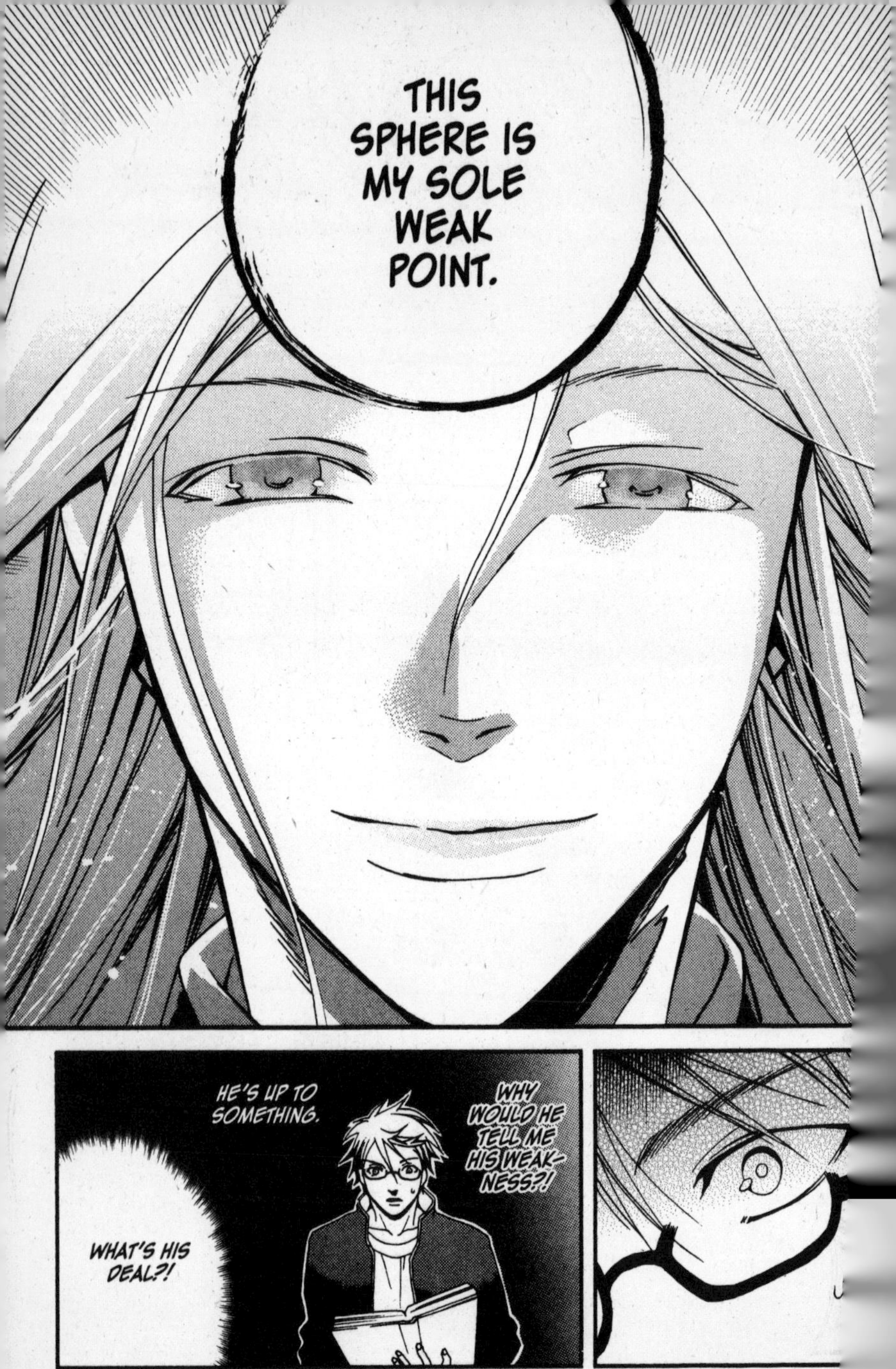
THIS SPHERE IS MY SOLE WEAK POINT.
WHY WOULD HE TELL ME HIS WEAK-NESS?!
HE'S UP TO SOMETHING.
WHAT'S HIS DEAL?!

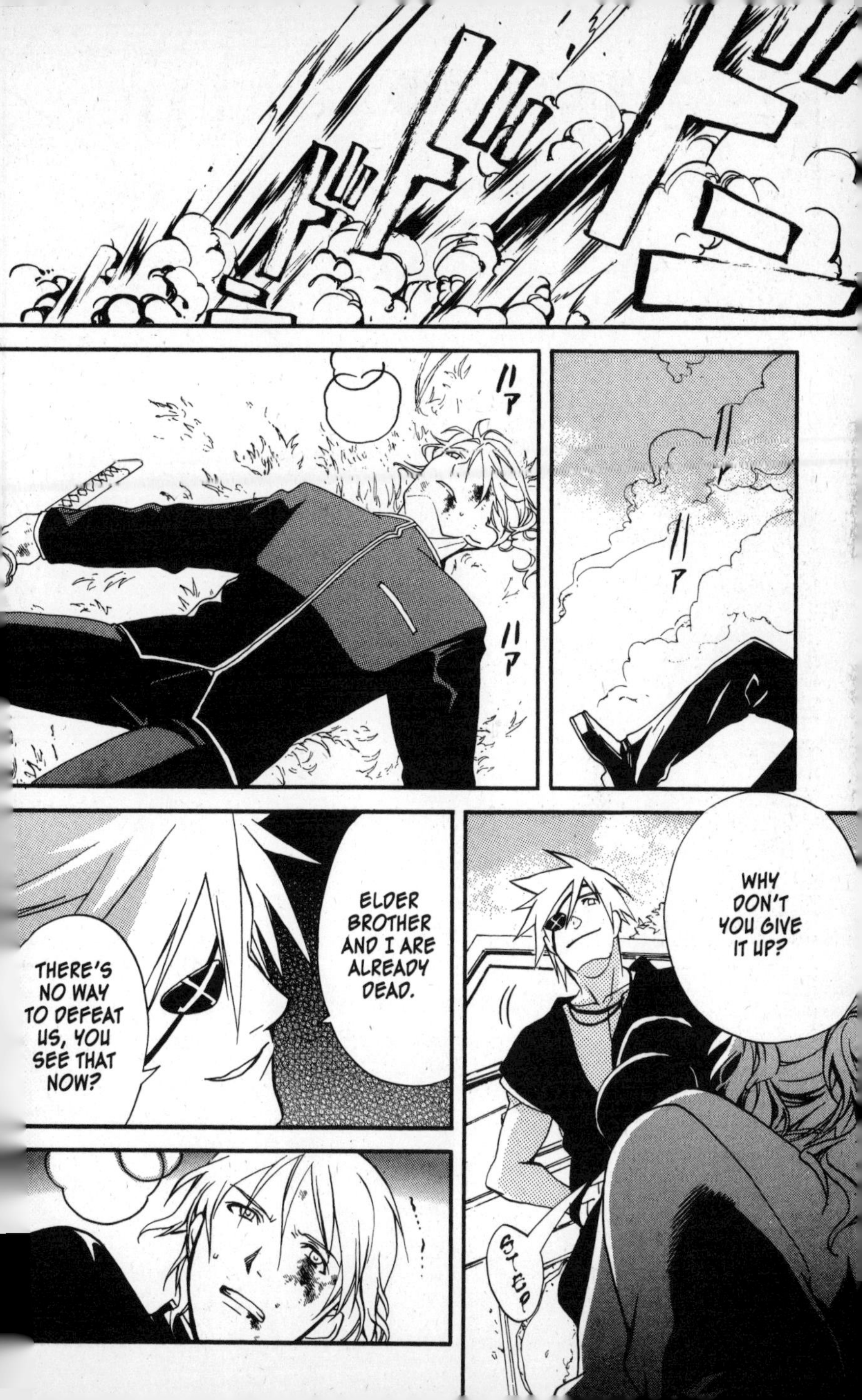
ハァ
ハァ
ハァ
ハァ
WHY DON'T YOU GIVE IT UP?
STEP
ELDER BROTHER AND I ARE ALREADY DEAD.
THERE'S NO WAY TO DEFEAT US, YOU SEE THAT NOW?
......

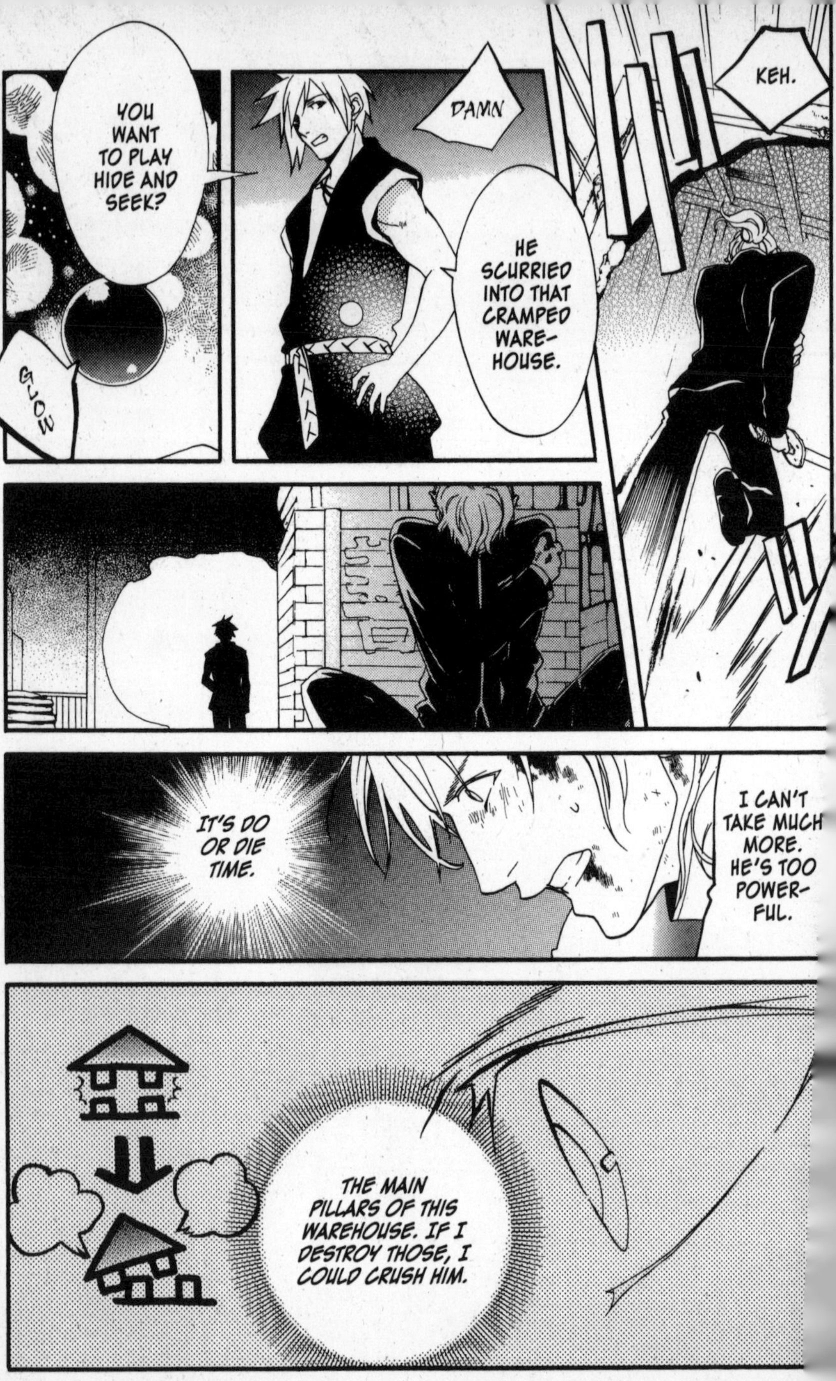
KEH.
DAMN
HE SCURRIED INTO THAT CRAMPED WARE-HOUSE.
YOU WANT TO PLAY HIDE AND SEEK?
GLOW
I CAN'T TAKE MUCH MORE. HE'S TOO POWER-FUL.
IT'S DO OR DIE TIME.
THE MAIN PILLARS OF THIS WAREHOUSE. IF I DESTROY THOSE, I COULD CRUSH HIM.

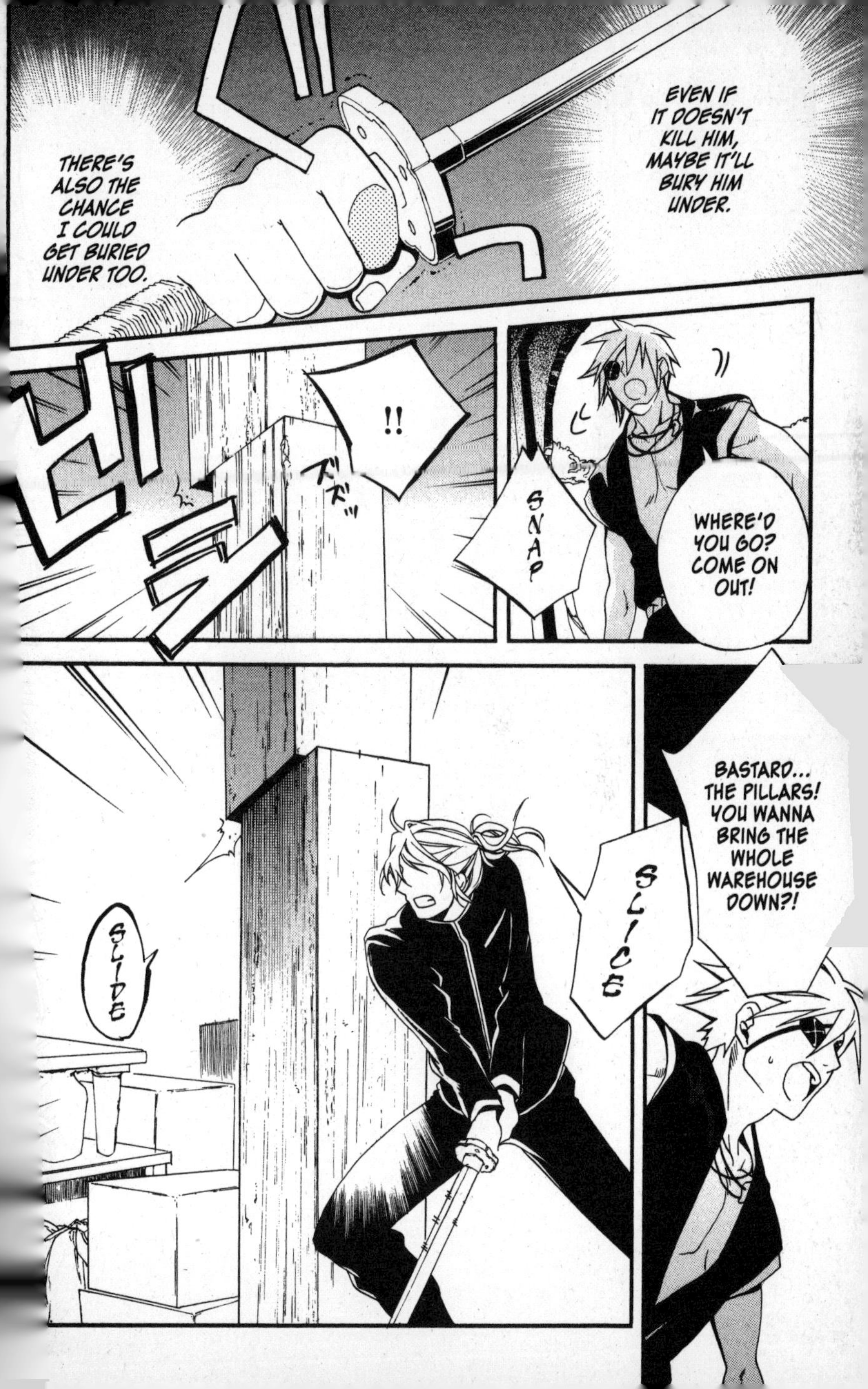
EVEN IF IT DOESN'T KILL HIM, MAYBE IT'LL BURY HIM UNDER.
THERE'S ALSO THE CHANCE I COULD GET BURIED UNDER TOO.
WHERE'D YOU GO? COME ON OUT!
SNAP
!!
BASTARD... THE PILLARS! YOU WANNA BRING THE WHOLE WAREHOUSE DOWN?!
SLICE
SLIDE

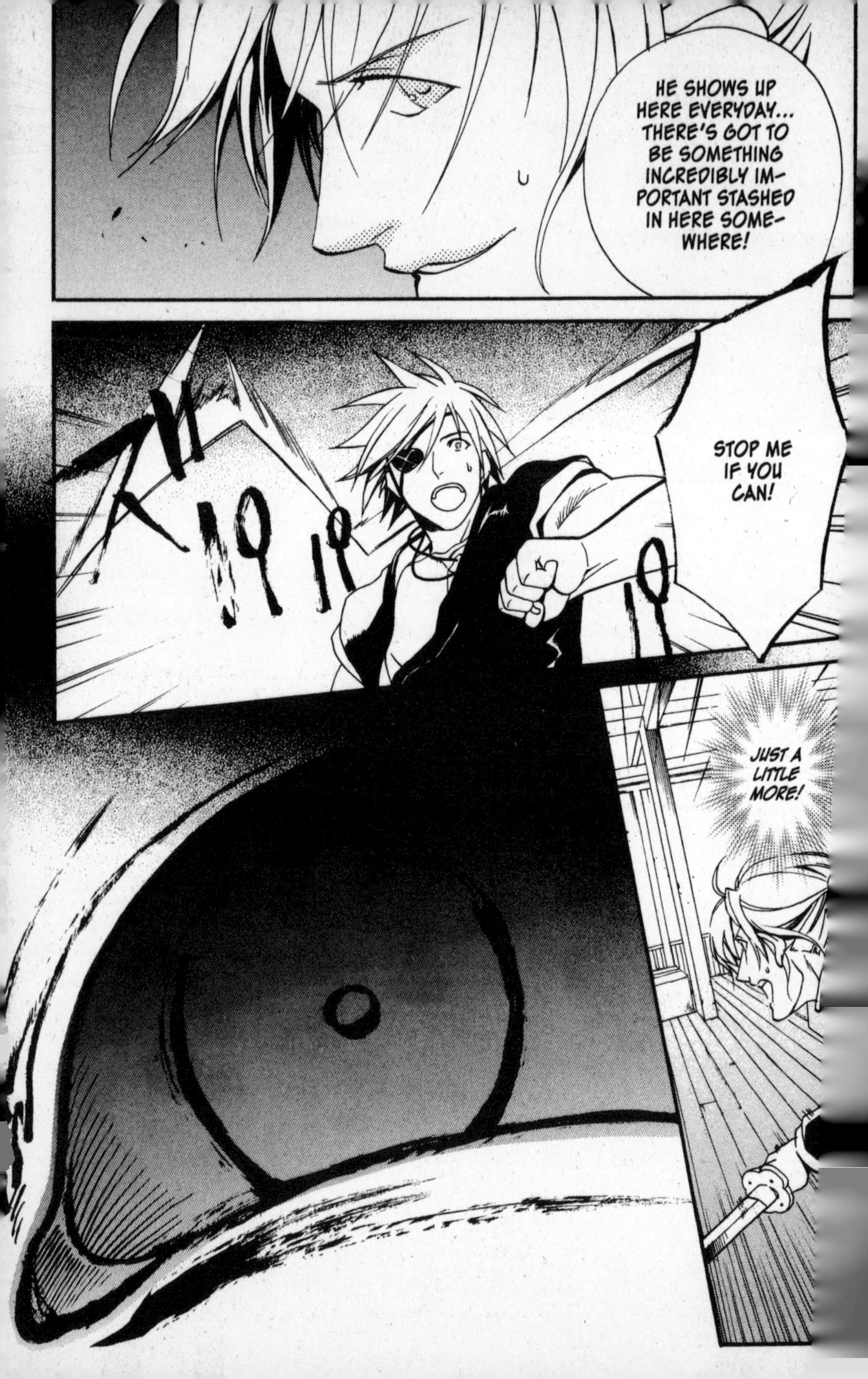
HE SHOWS UP HERE EVERYDAY... THERE'S GOT TO BE SOMETHING INCREDIBLY IM-PORTANT STASHED IN HERE SOME-WHERE!
STOP ME IF YOU CAN!
JUST A LITTLE MORE!

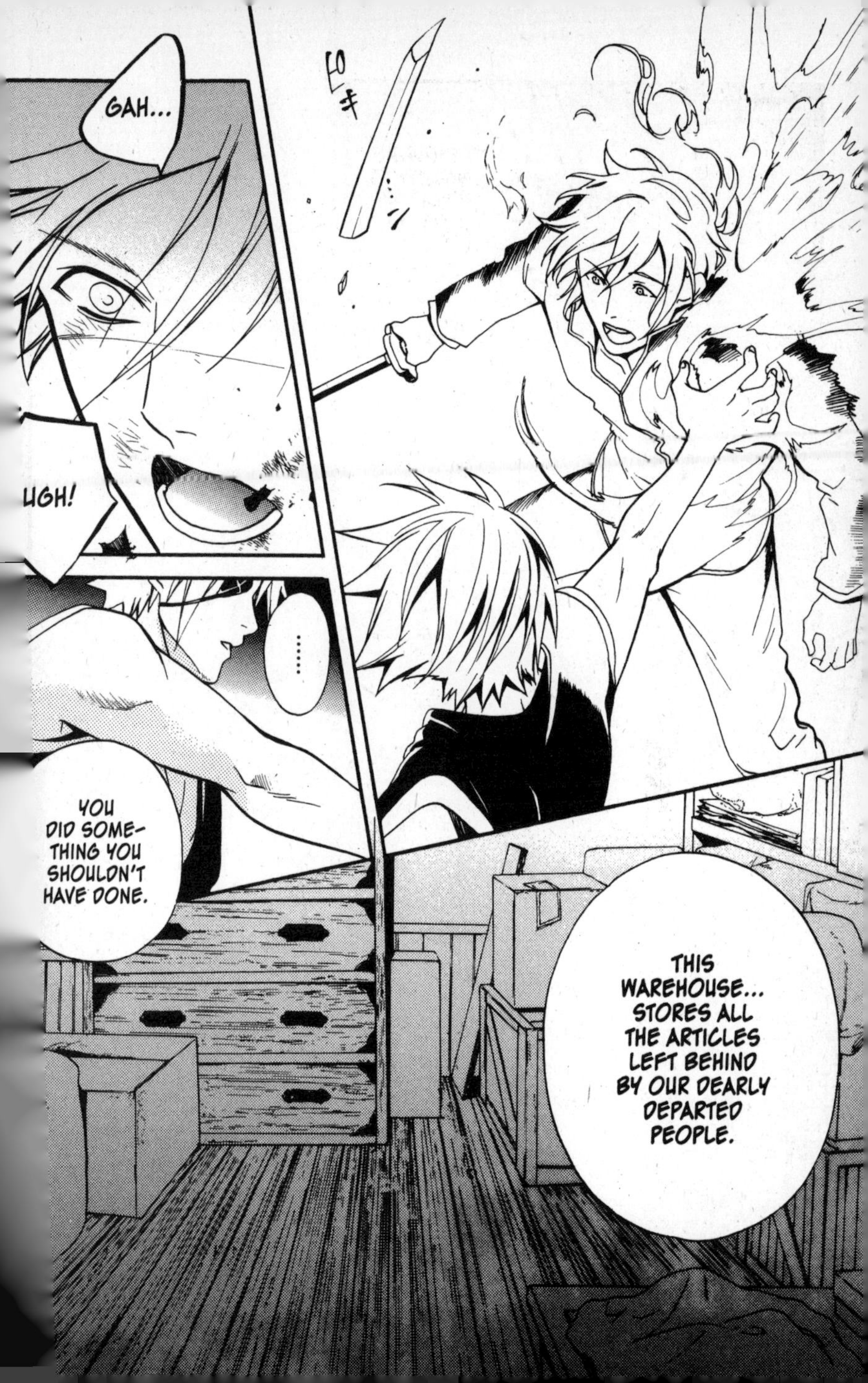
GAH...
UGH!
......
YOU DID SOME-THING YOU SHOULDN'T HAVE DONE.
THIS WAREHOUSE... STORES ALL THE ARTICLES LEFT BEHIND BY OUR DEARLY DEPARTED PEOPLE.

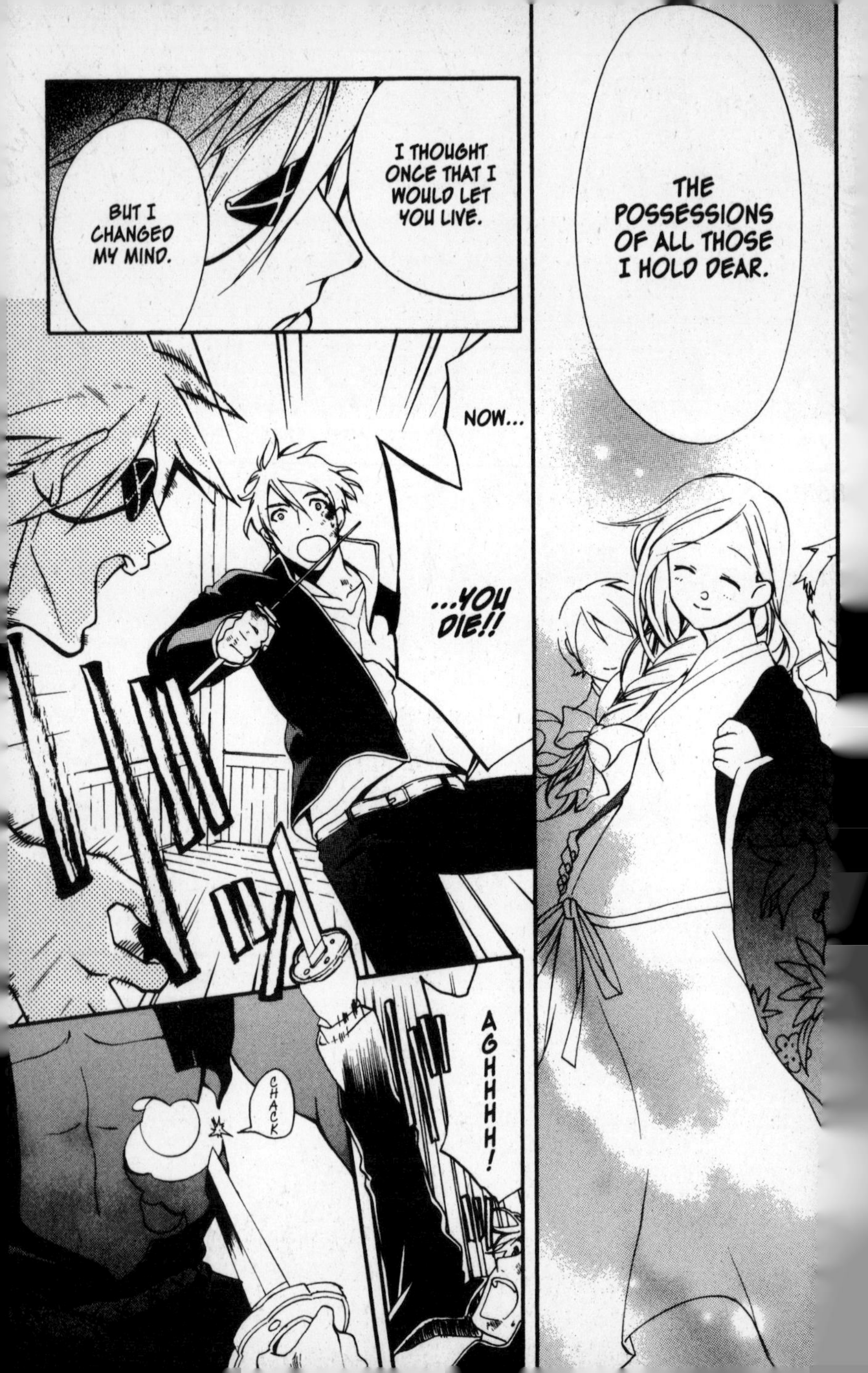
THE POSSESSIONS OF ALL THOSE I HOLD DEAR.
I THOUGHT ONCE THAT I WOULD LET YOU LIVE.
BUT I CHANGED MY MIND.
NOW...
...YOU DIE!!
AGHHHHH!
CHACK

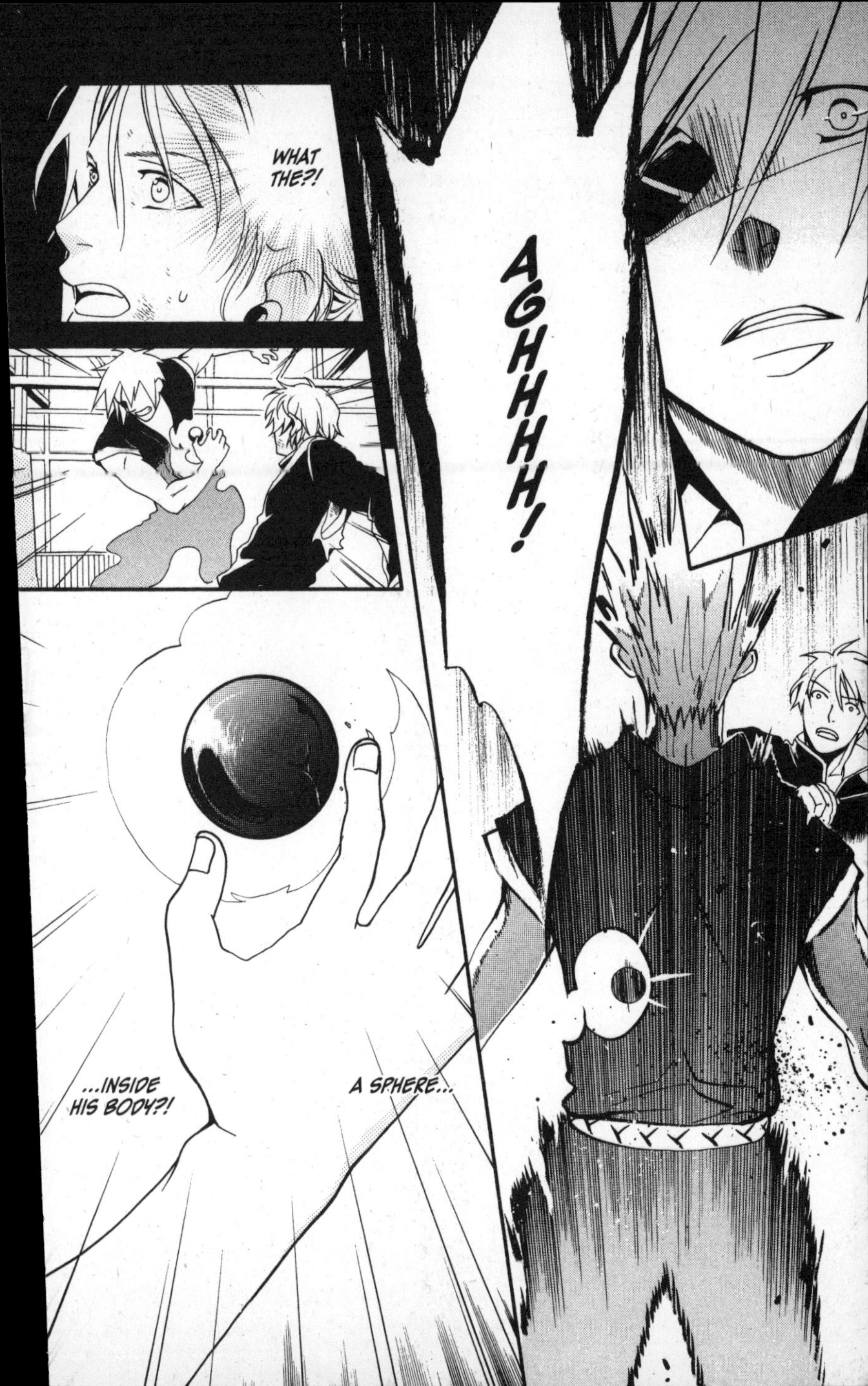
AGHHHHH!
WHAT THE?!
A SPHERE...
...INSIDE HIS BODY?!

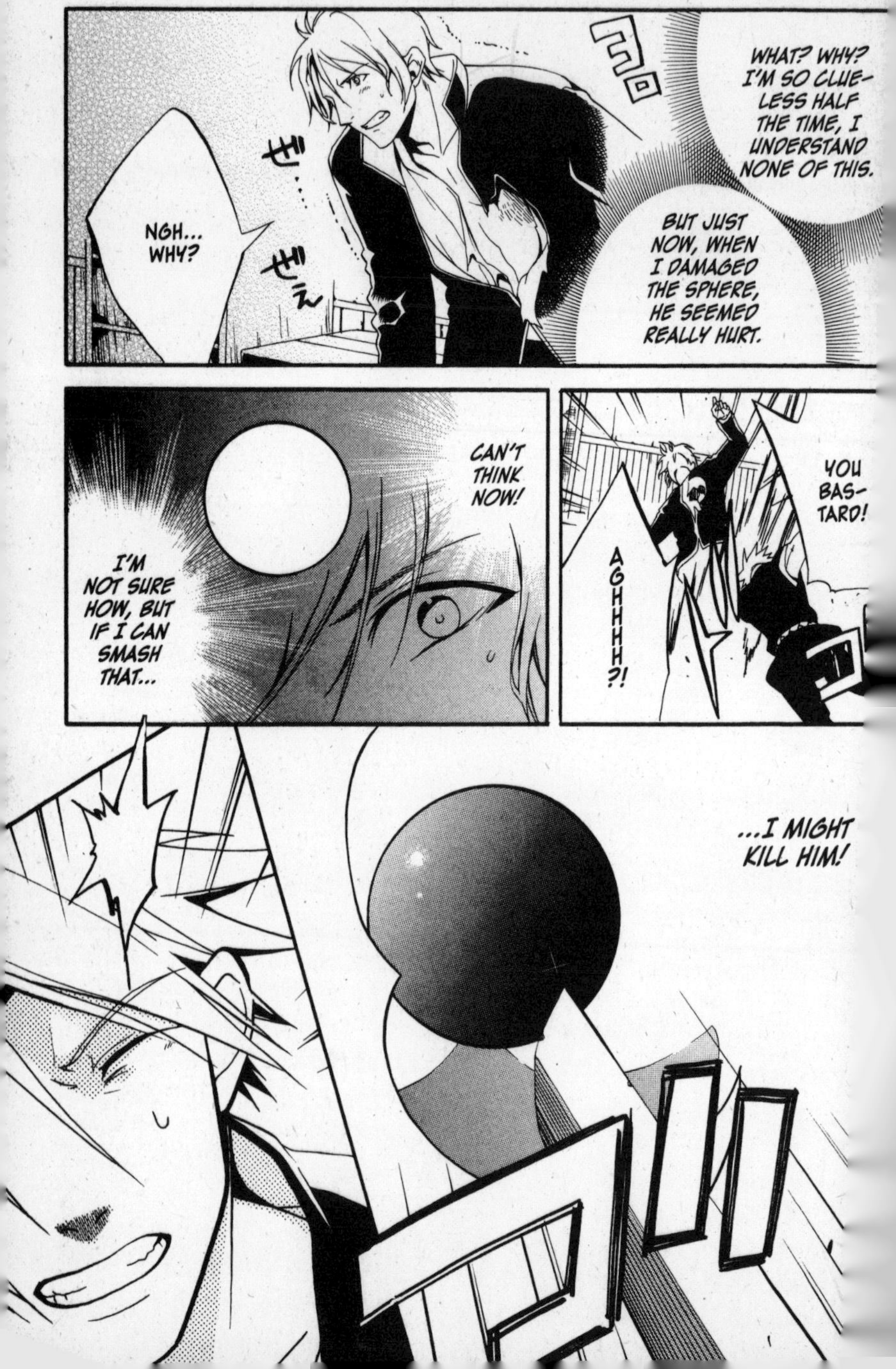
ヨロ
WHAT? WHY? I'M SO CLUE-LESS HALF THE TIME, I UNDERSTAND NONE OF THIS.
BUT JUST NOW, WHEN I DAMAGED THE SPHERE, HE SEEMED REALLY HURT.
ぜ…ぜぇ
NGH... WHY?
YOU BAS-TARD!
AGHHHH?!
CAN'T THINK NOW!
I'M NOT SURE HOW, BUT IF I CAN SMASH THAT...
...I MIGHT KILL HIM!

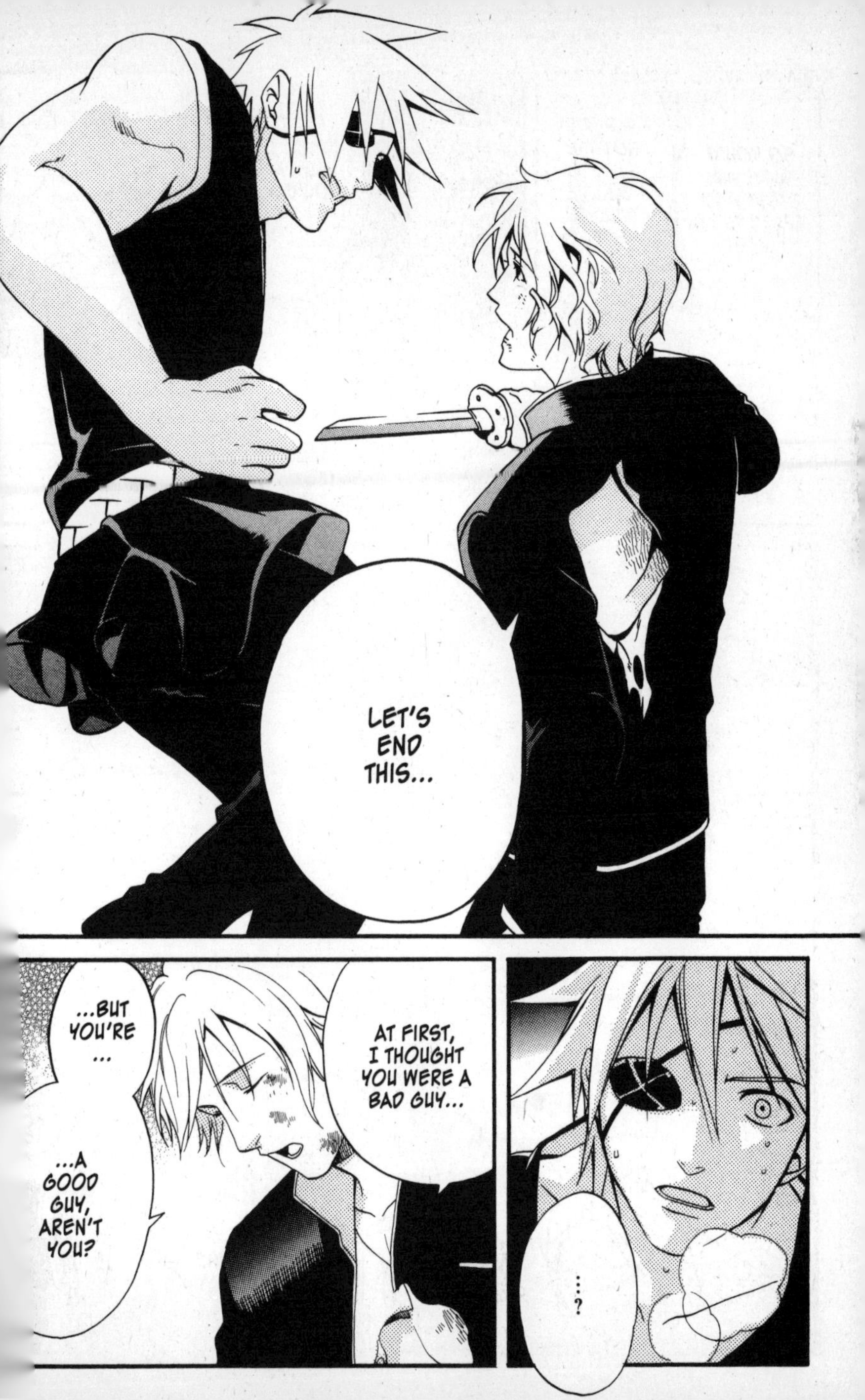
LET'S END THIS...
...?
AT FIRST, I THOUGHT YOU WERE A BAD GUY...
...BUT YOU'RE ...
...A GOOD GUY, AREN'T YOU?

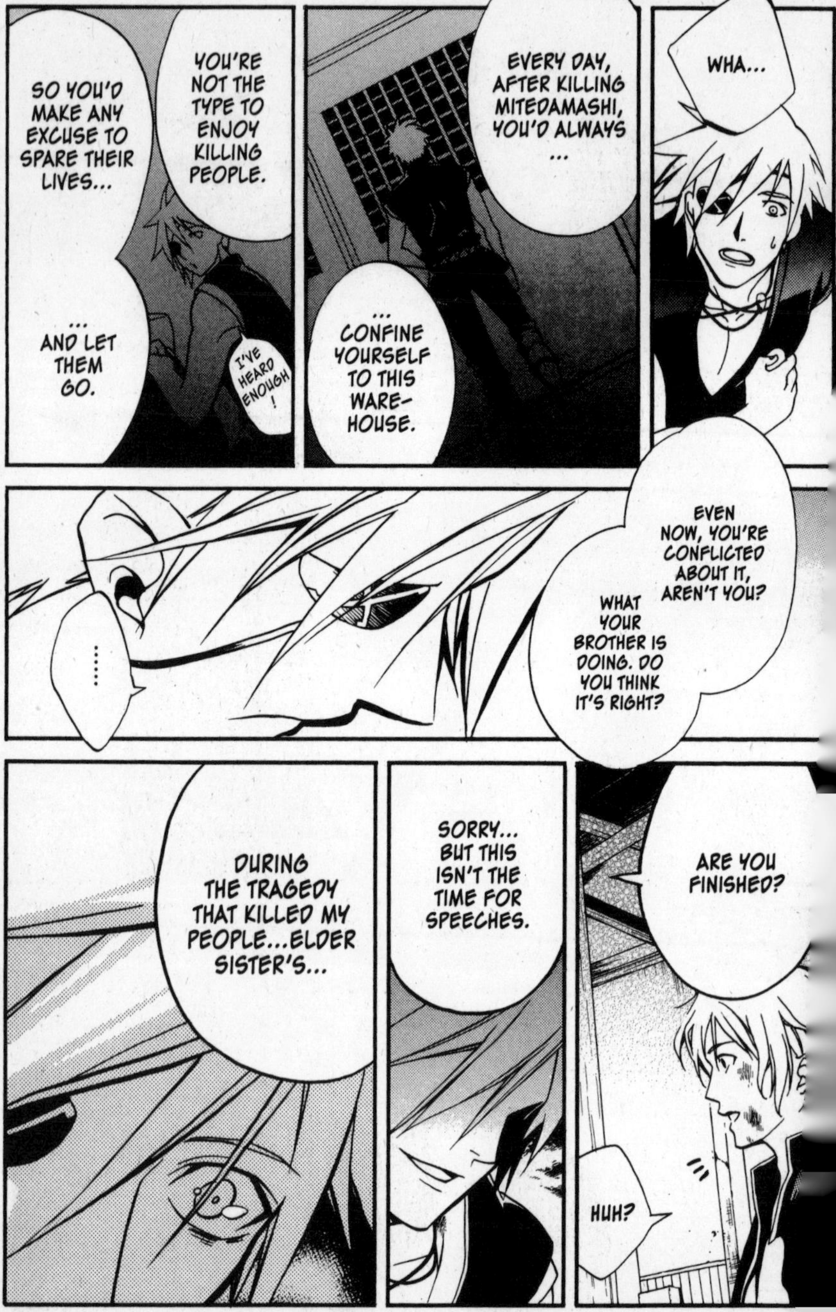
WHA...
EVERY DAY, AFTER KILLING MITEDAMASHI, YOU'D ALWAYS ...
... CONFINE YOURSELF TO THIS WARE-HOUSE.
YOU'RE NOT THE TYPE TO ENJOY KILLING PEOPLE.
SO YOU'D MAKE ANY EXCUSE TO SPARE THEIR LIVES...
I'VE HEARD ENOUGH!
... AND LET THEM GO.
EVEN NOW, YOU'RE CONFLICTED ABOUT IT, AREN'T YOU?
WHAT YOUR BROTHER IS DOING. DO YOU THINK IT'S RIGHT?
......
ARE YOU FINISHED?
HUH?
SORRY... BUT THIS ISN'T THE TIME FOR SPEECHES.
DURING THE TRAGEDY THAT KILLED MY PEOPLE...ELDER SISTER'S...

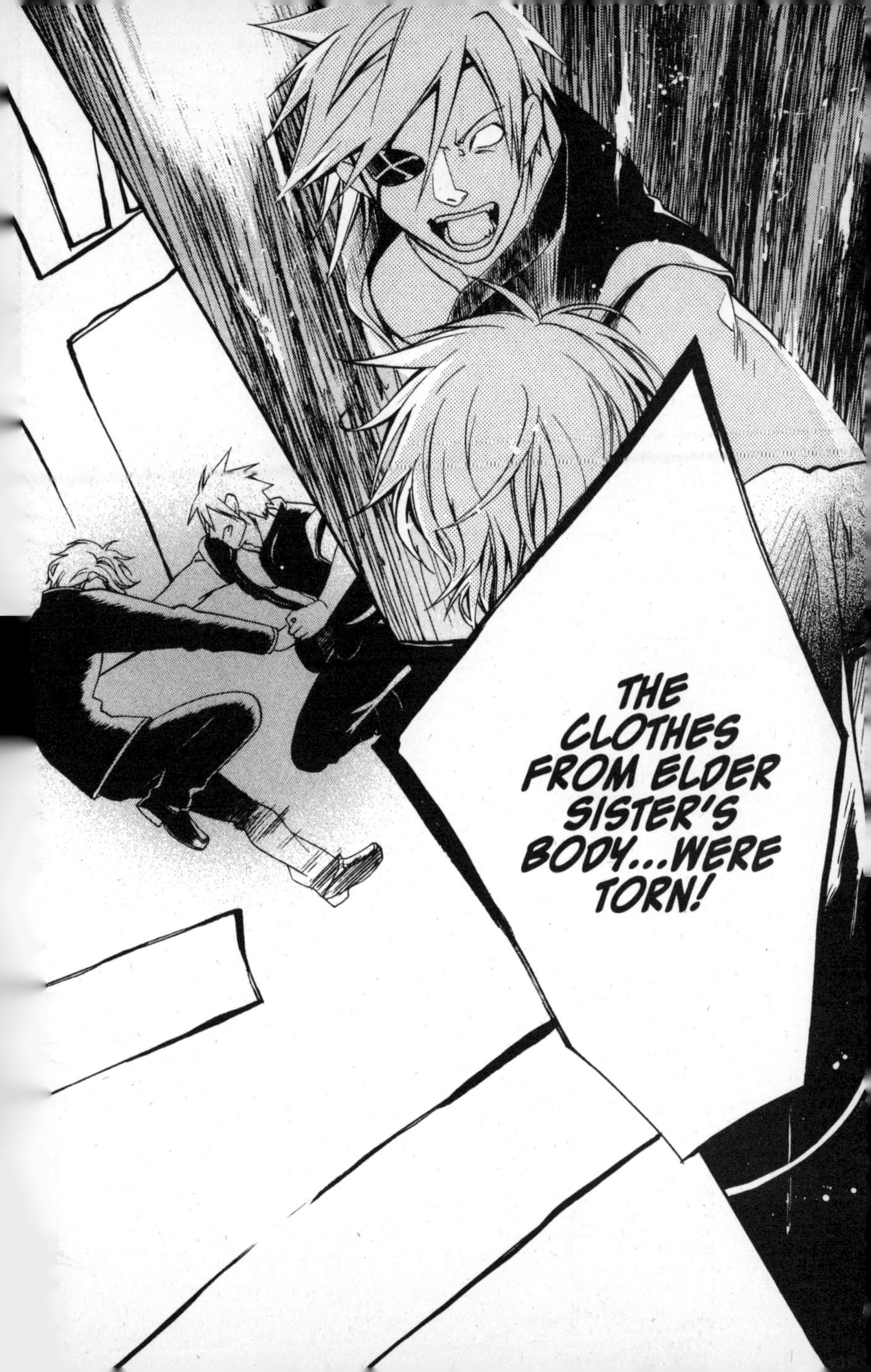
THE CLOTHES FROM ELDER SISTER'S BODY...WERE TORN!

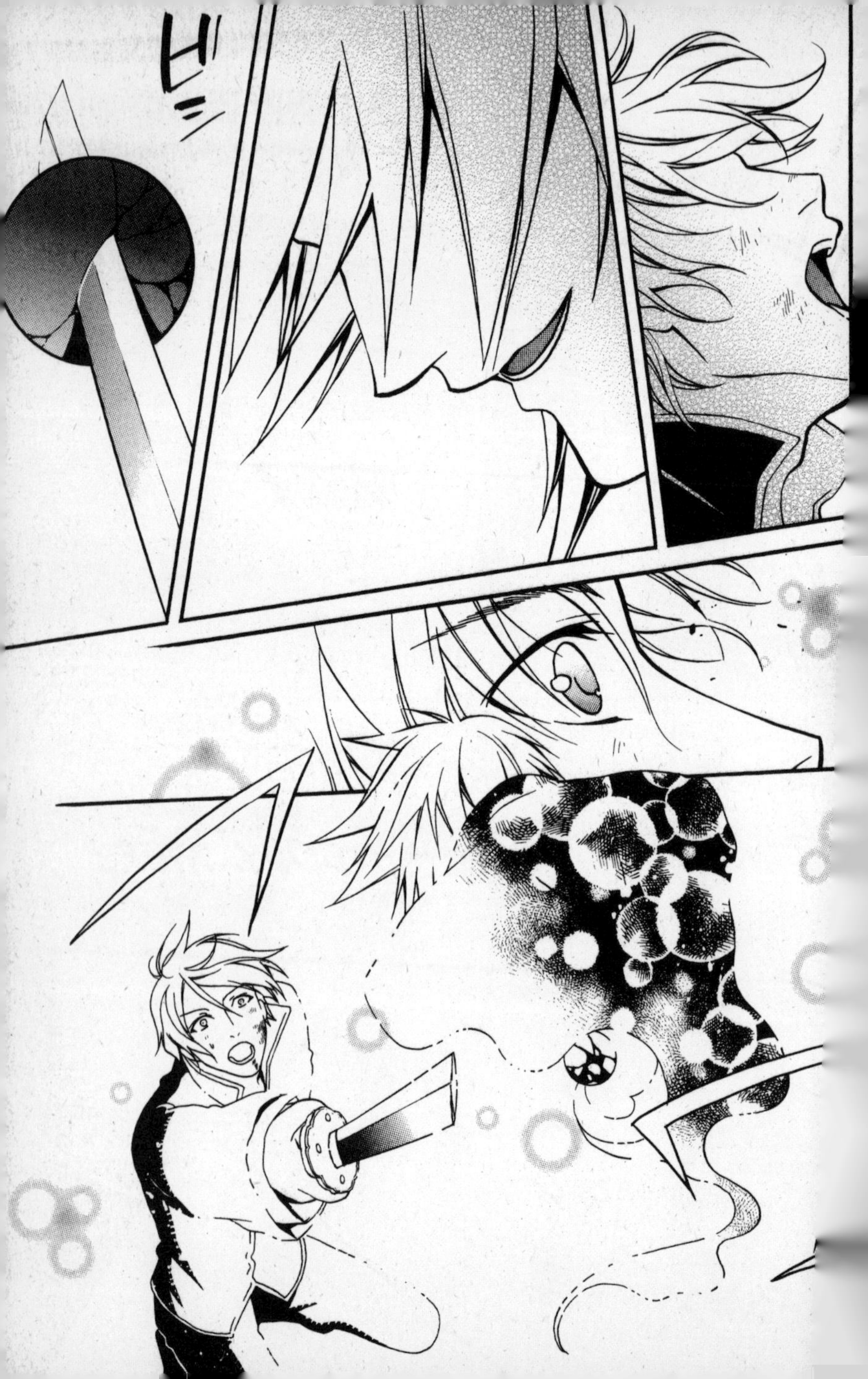
ビシ

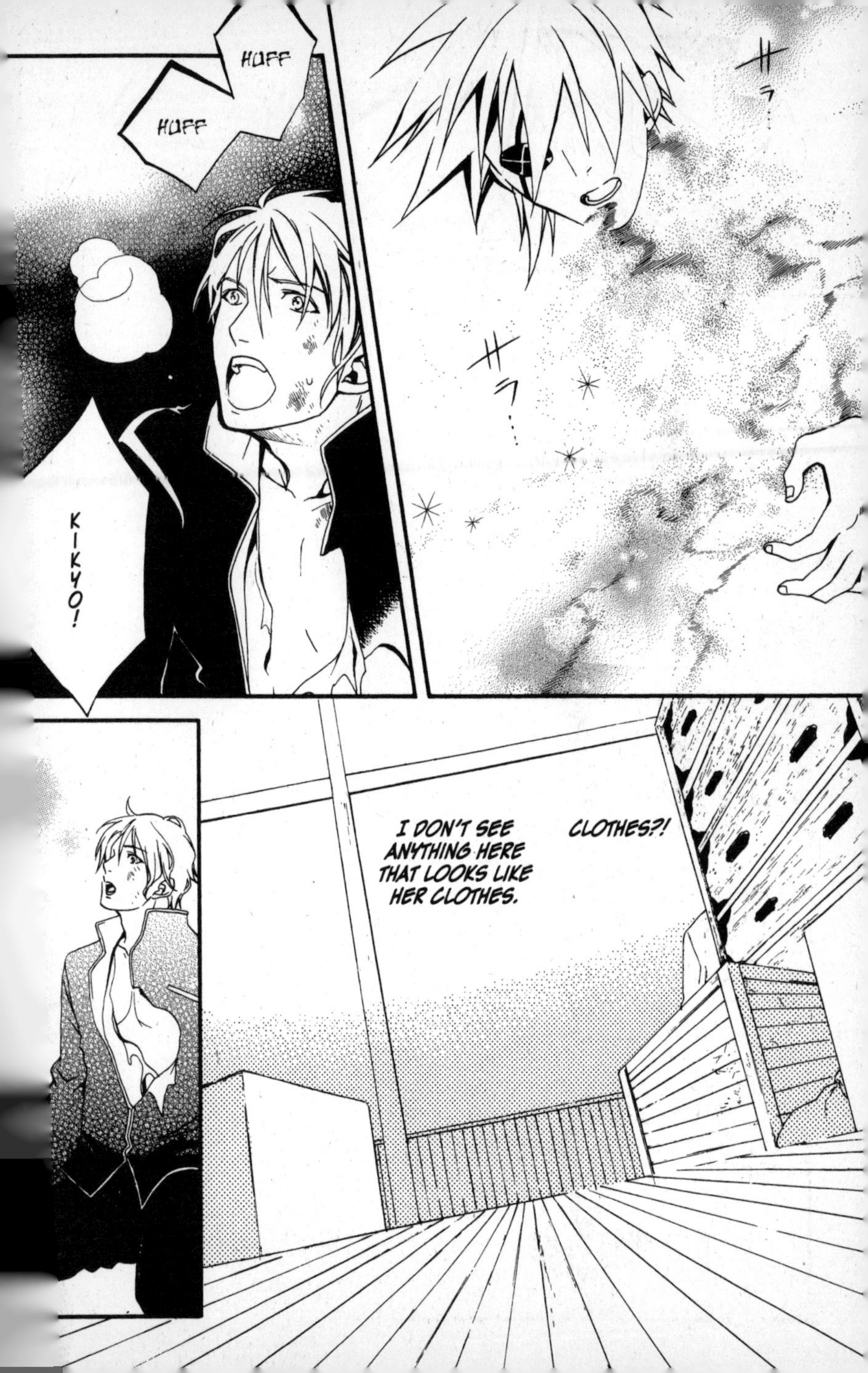
ガラ…
ガラ…
HUFF
HUFF
KIKYO!
CLOTHES?!
I DON'T SEE ANYTHING HERE THAT LOOKS LIKE HER CLOTHES.

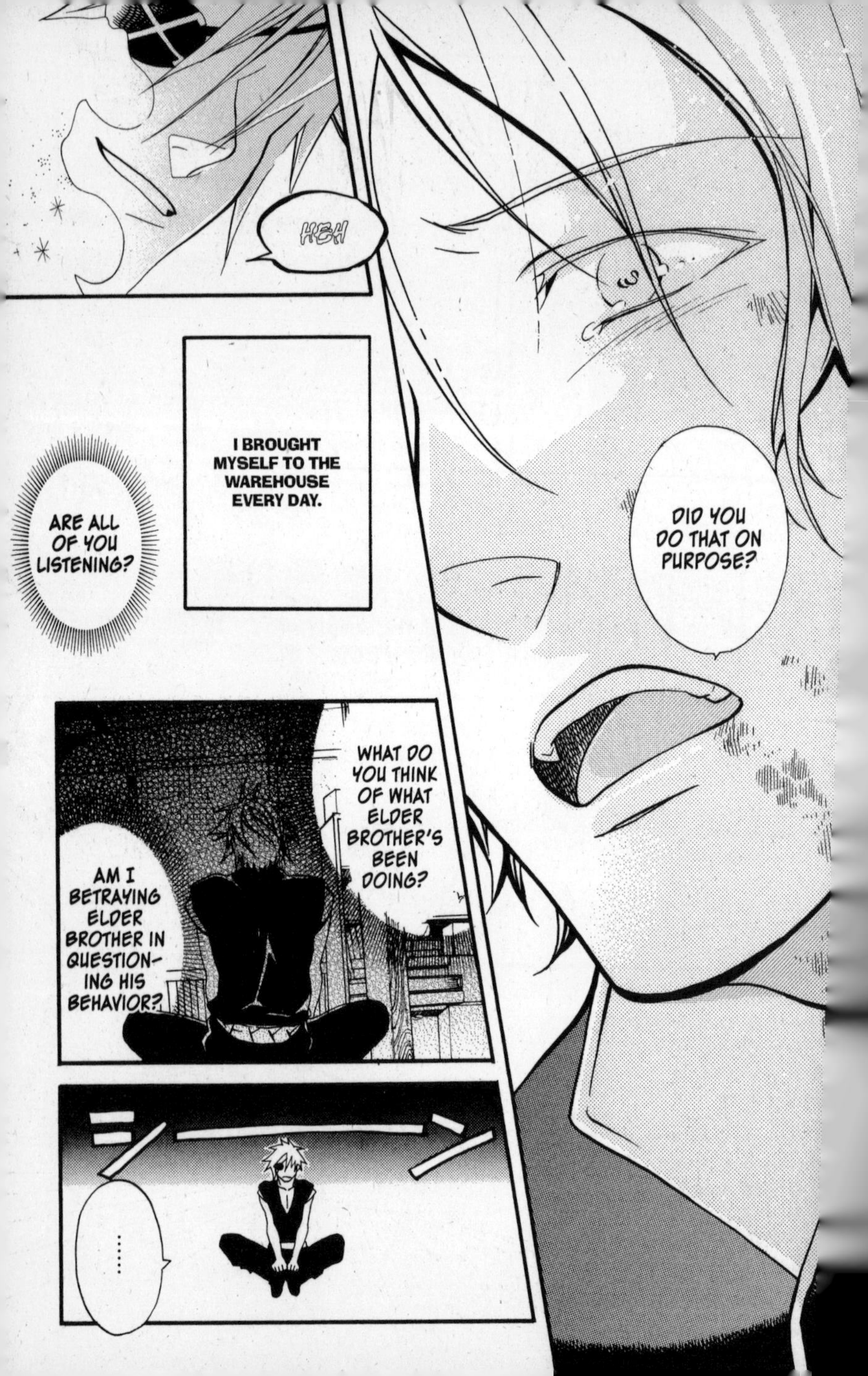
DID YOU DO THAT ON PURPOSE?
HEH
I BROUGHT MYSELF TO THE WAREHOUSE EVERY DAY.
ARE ALL OF YOU LISTENING?
WHAT DO YOU THINK OF WHAT ELDER BROTHER'S BEEN DOING?
AM I BETRAYING ELDER BROTHER IN QUESTIONING HIS BEHAVIOR?
......

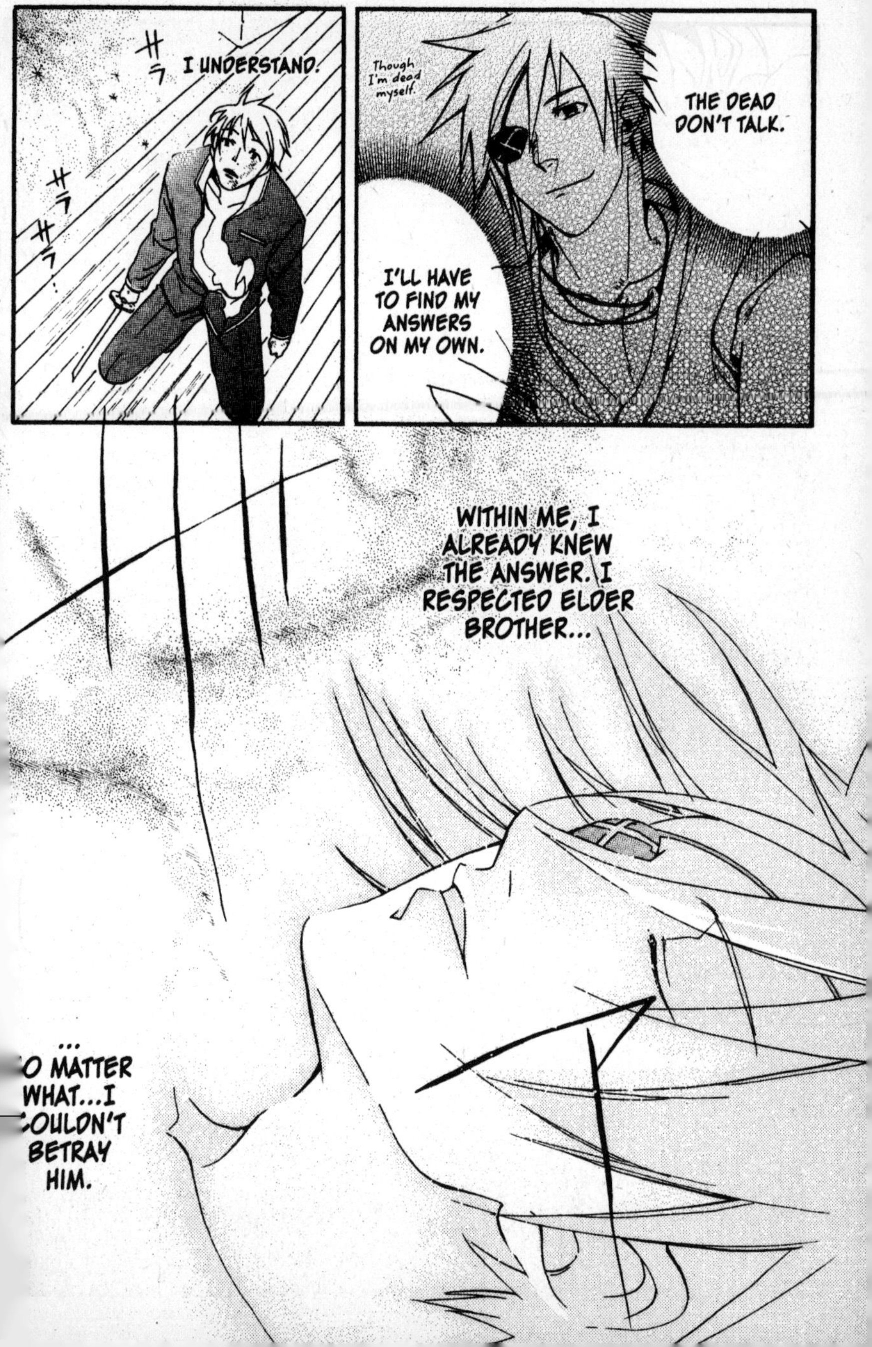
THE DEAD DON'T TALK.
Though I'm dead myself.
I'LL HAVE TO FIND MY ANSWERS ON MY OWN.
I UNDERSTAND.
WITHIN ME, I ALREADY KNEW THE ANSWER. I RESPECTED ELDER BROTHER...
...
O MATTER WHAT...I COULDN'T BETRAY HIM.

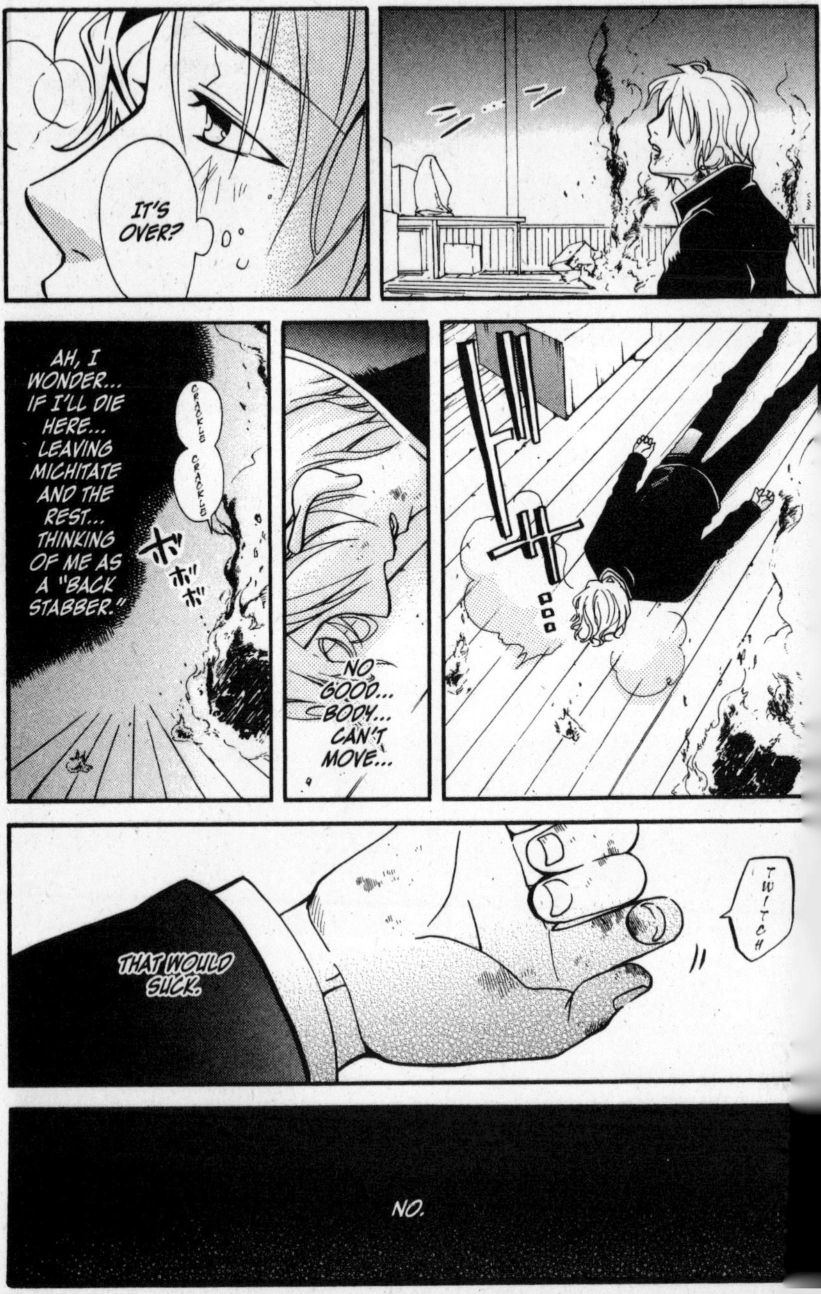
IT'S OVER?
NO GOOD... BODY... CAN'T MOVE...
AH, I WONDER... IF I'LL DIE HERE... LEAVING MICHITATE AND THE REST... THINKING OF ME AS A "BACK STABBER."
CRACKLE CRACKLE
ボボボ
TWITCH
THAT WOULD SUCK.
NO.

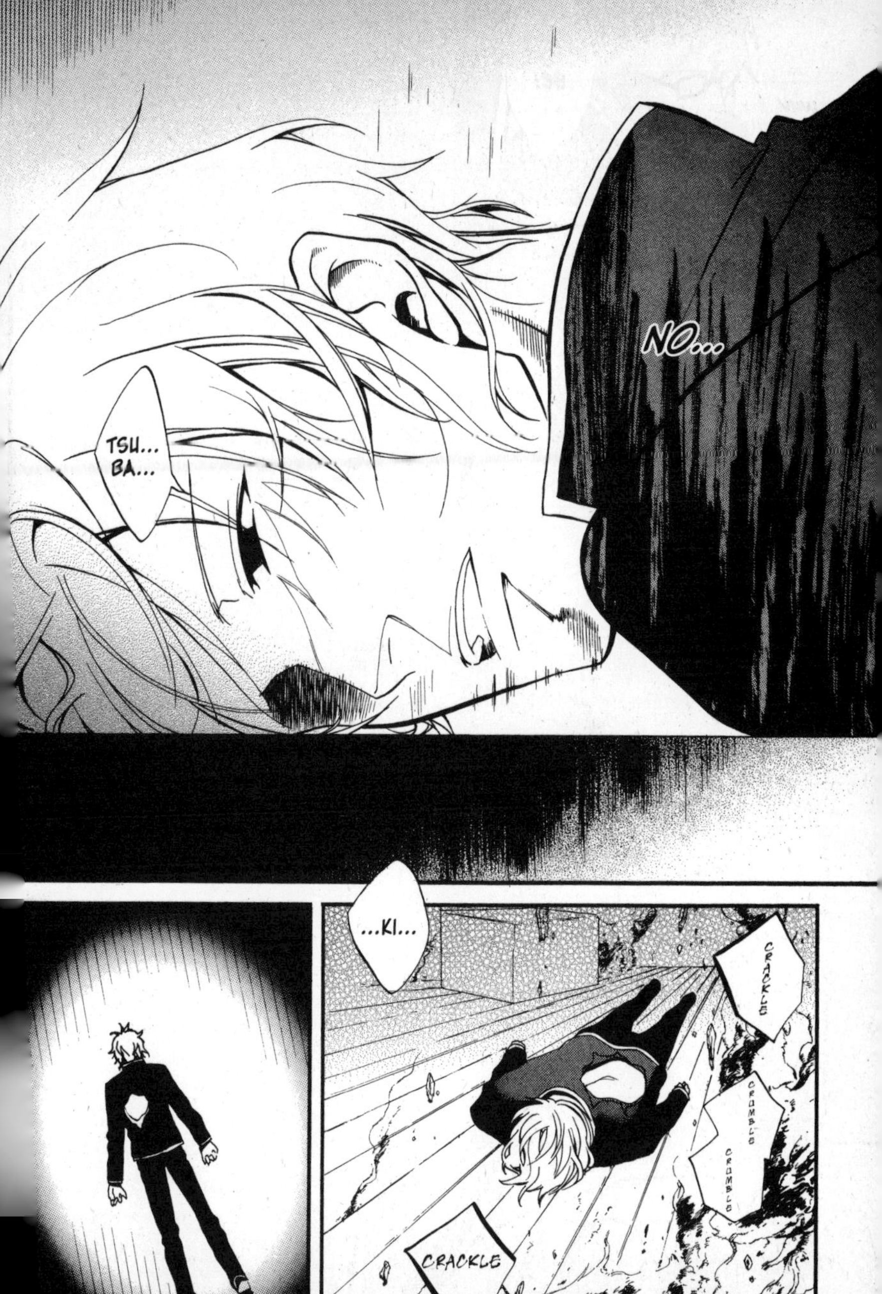
NO...
TSU... BA...
...KI...
CRACKLE
CRUMBLE CRUMBLE
CRACKLE

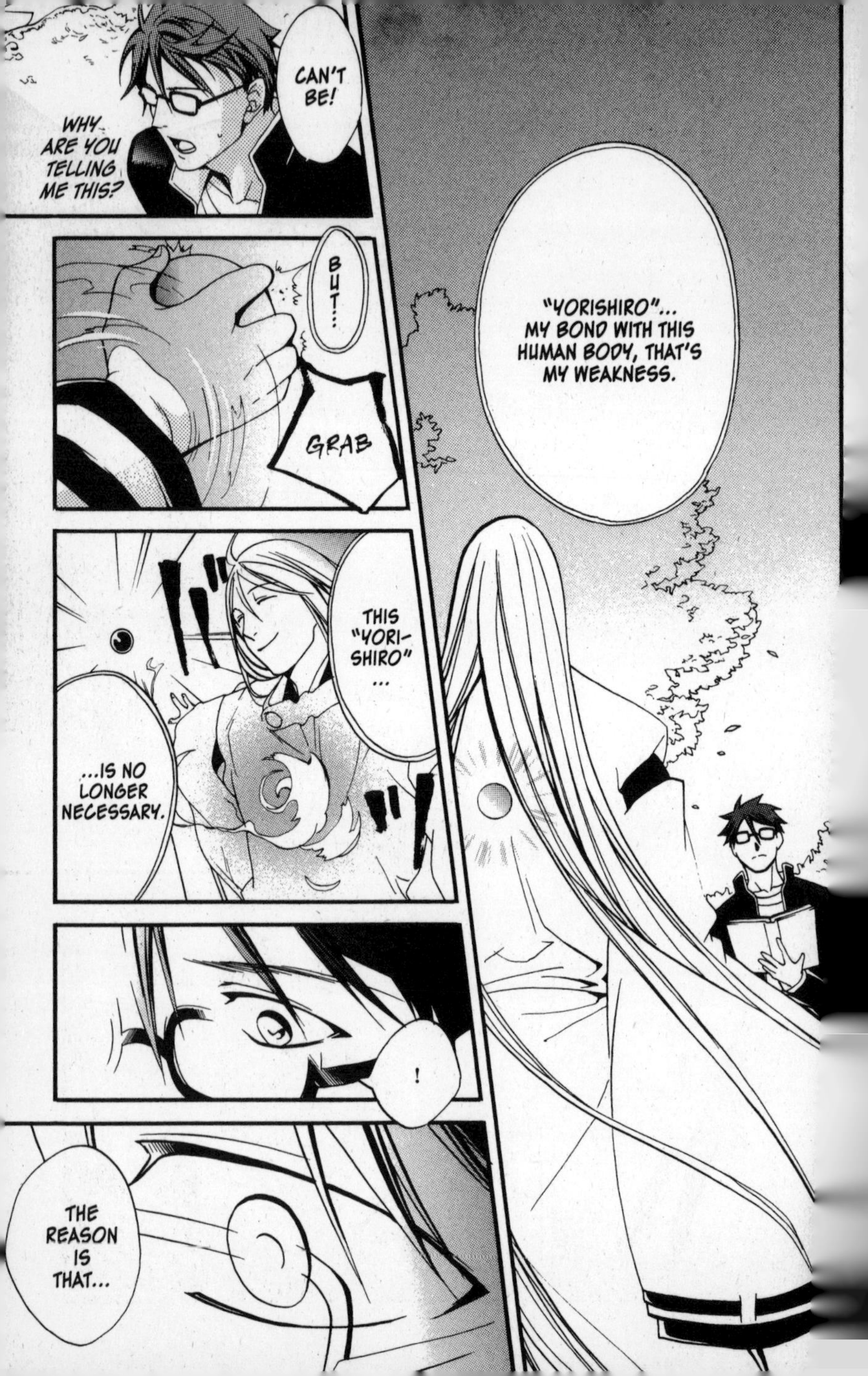
"YORISHIRO"... MY BOND WITH THIS HUMAN BODY, THAT'S MY WEAKNESS.
CAN'T BE!
WHY ARE YOU TELLING ME THIS?
BUT...
GRAB
THIS "YORI-SHIRO" ...
...IS NO LONGER NECESSARY.
!
THE REASON IS THAT...

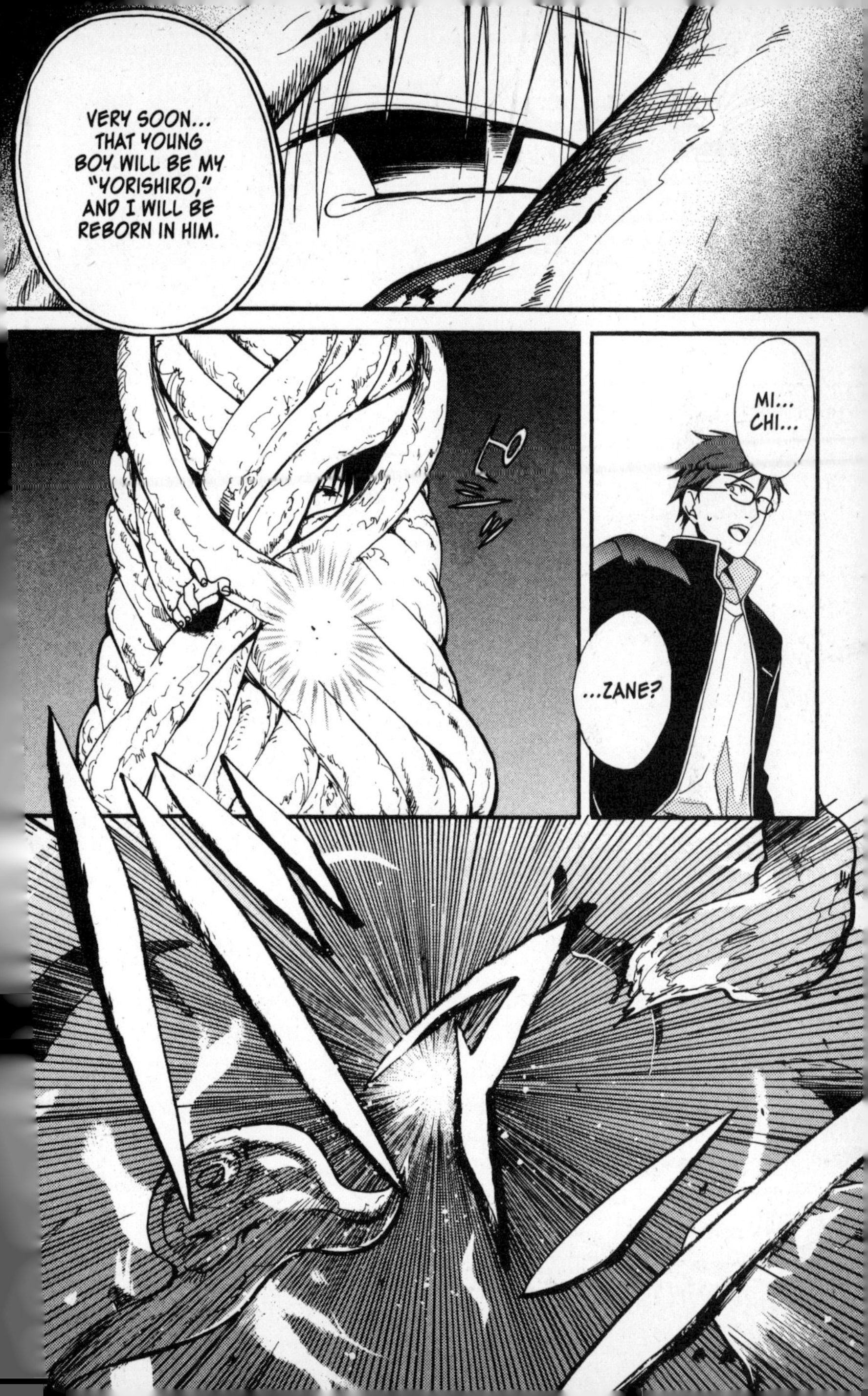
VERY SOON... THAT YOUNG BOY WILL BE MY "YORISHIRO," AND I WILL BE REBORN IN HIM.
MI... CHI...
...ZANE?

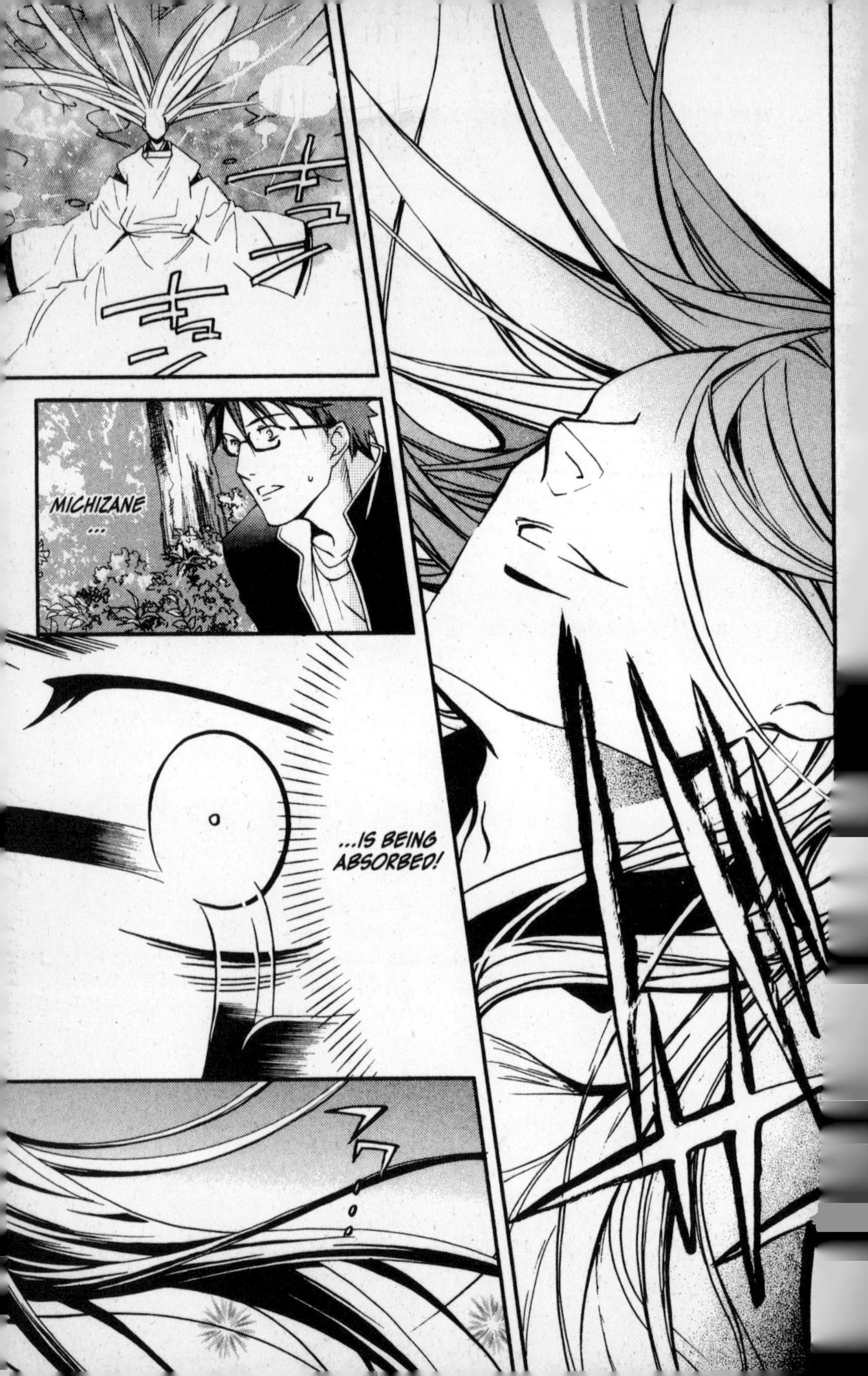
MICHIZANE
...
...IS BEING ABSORBED!

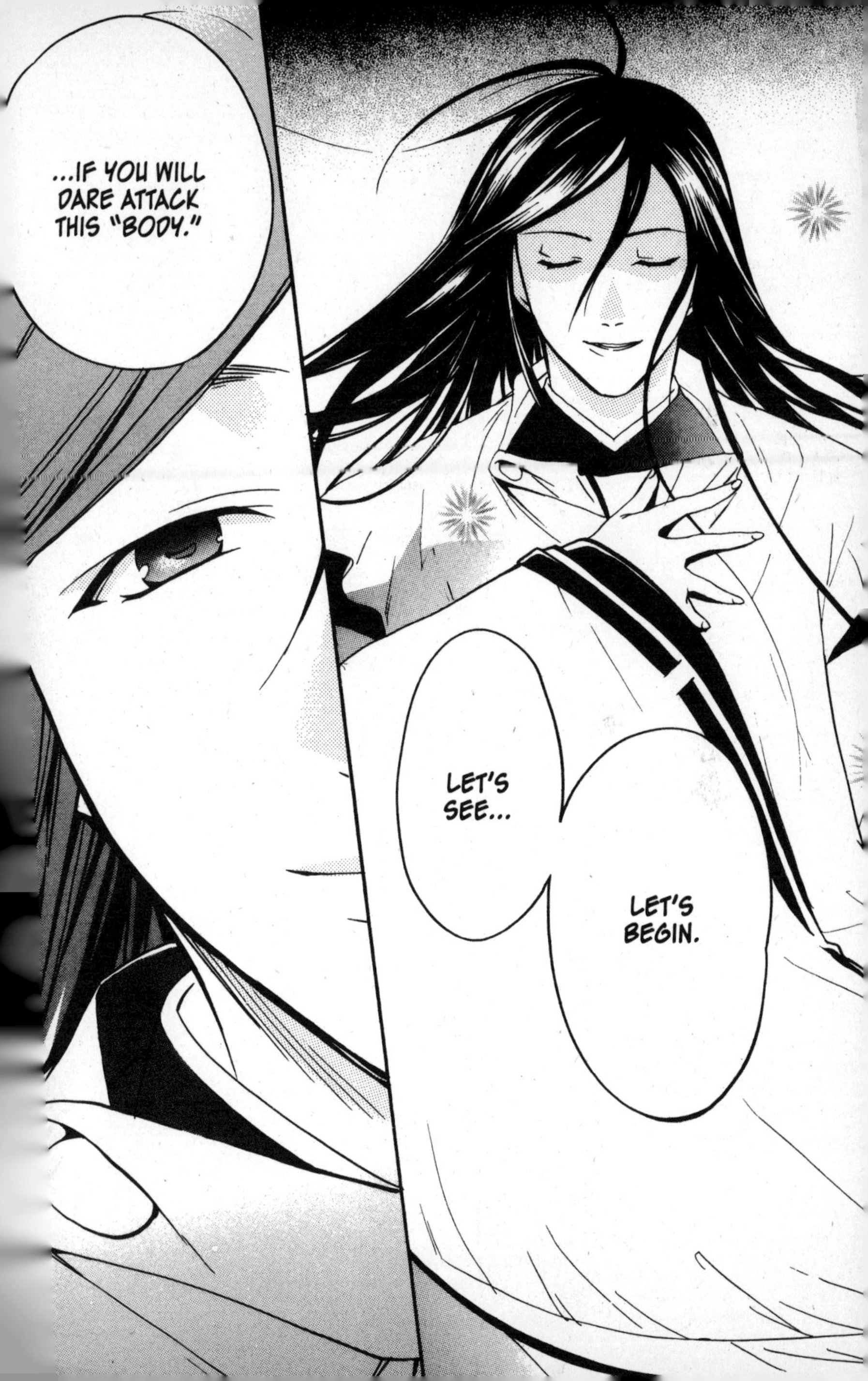
LET'S SEE...
LET'S BEGIN.
...IF YOU WILL DARE ATTACK THIS "BODY."

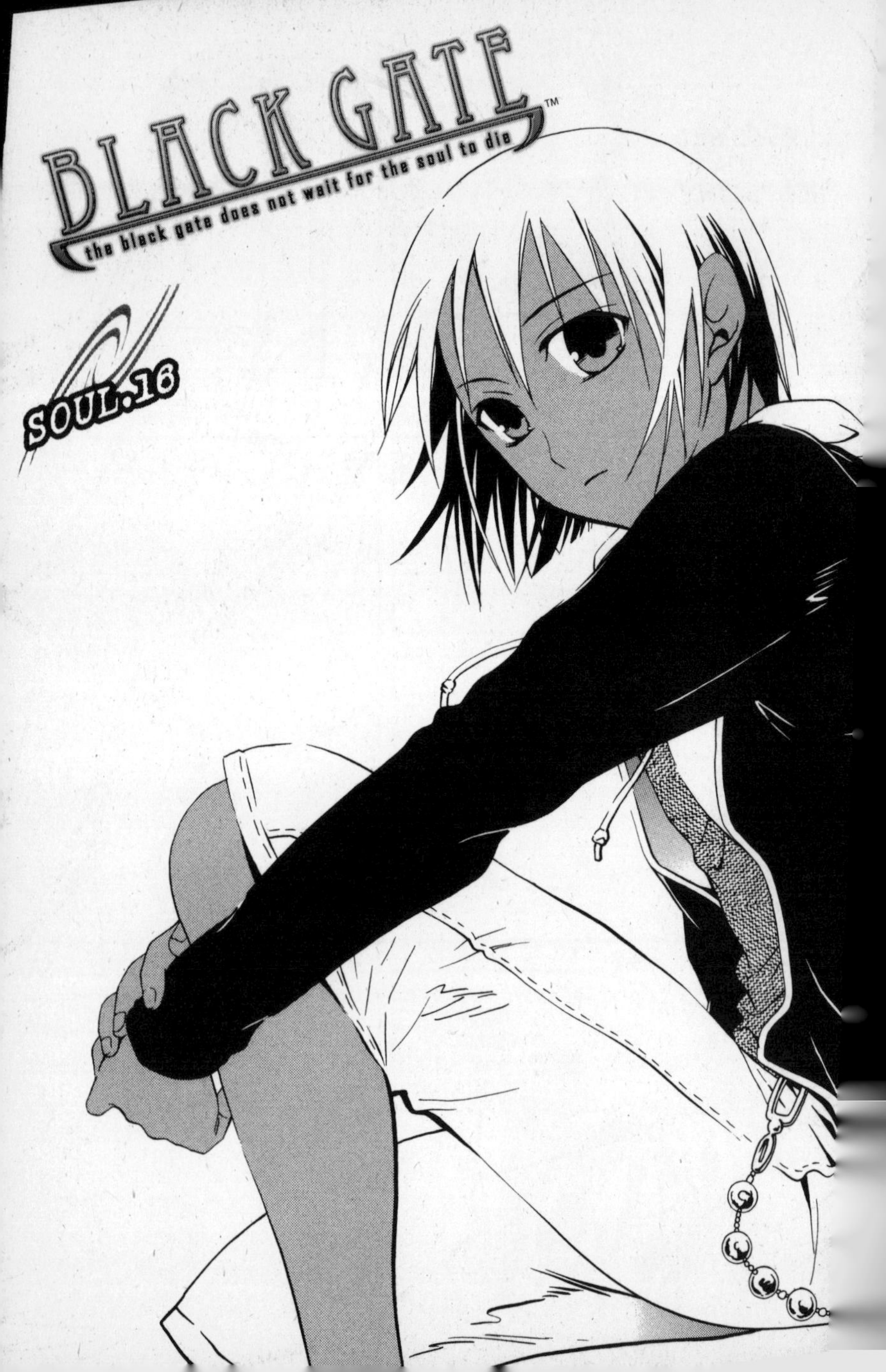
BLACK GATE™
the black gate does not wait for the soul to die
SOUL.16

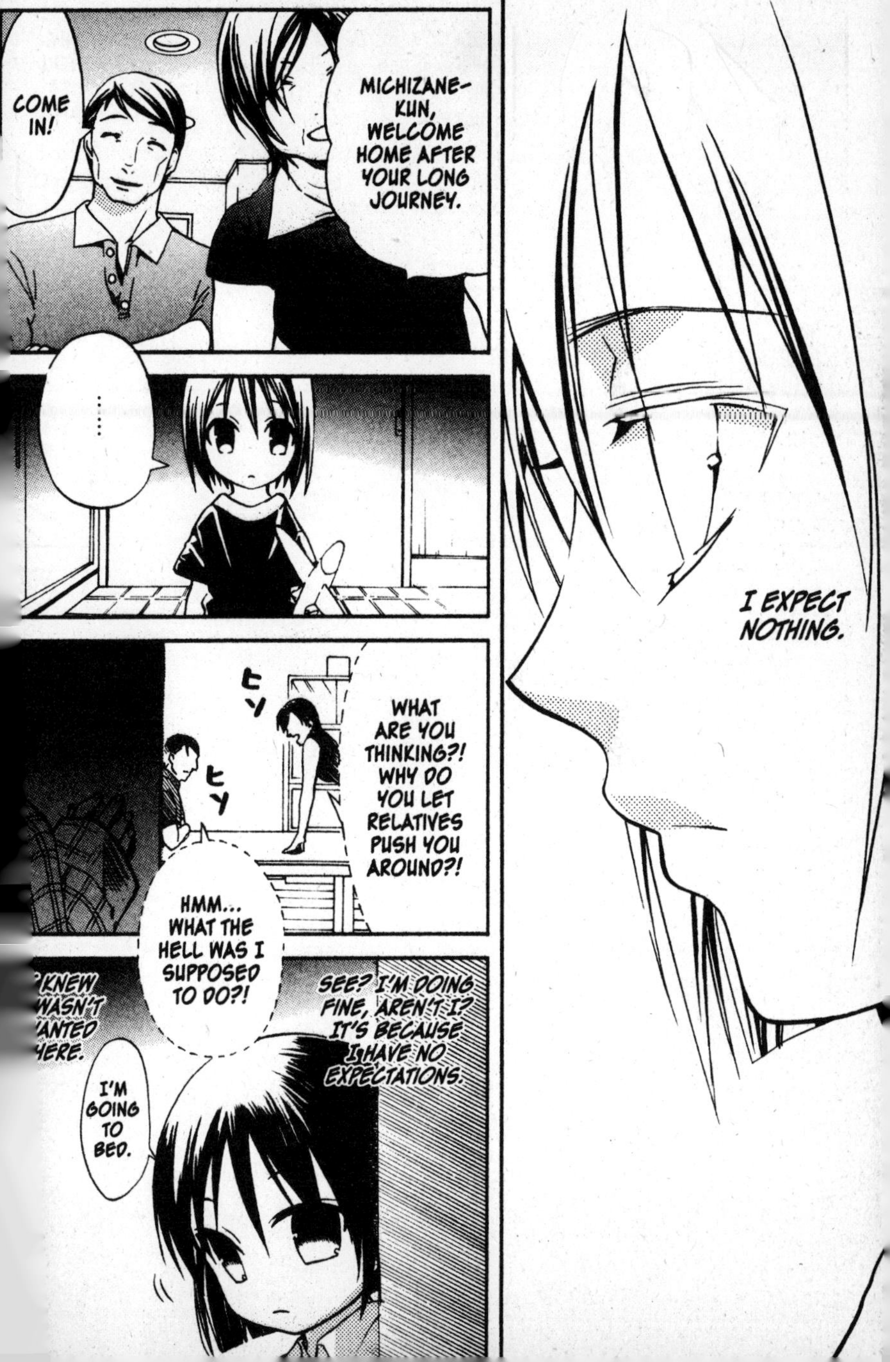
I EXPECT NOTHING.
MICHIZANE-KUN, WELCOME HOME AFTER YOUR LONG JOURNEY.
COME IN!
......
WHAT ARE YOU THINKING?! WHY DO YOU LET RELATIVES PUSH YOU AROUND?!
ヒソ
ヒソ
HMM... WHAT THE HELL WAS I SUPPOSED TO DO?!
SEE? I'M DOING FINE, AREN'T I? IT'S BECAUSE I HAVE NO EXPECTATIONS.
KNEW WASN'T ANTED HERE.
I'M GOING TO BED.

IT'S ALL RIGHT. SOON YOU WON'T FEEL A THING.

SOMEONE... SAVE ME.

AS MUCH AS I SAY I SHOULDN'T EXPECT ANYTHING...

...I STILL DO.

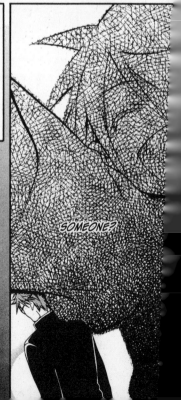

AH...

WHAT'S HAPPENING?

SOMEONE?

WHAT'S THAT?

SOMETHING VERY STRANGE IS GOING ON.

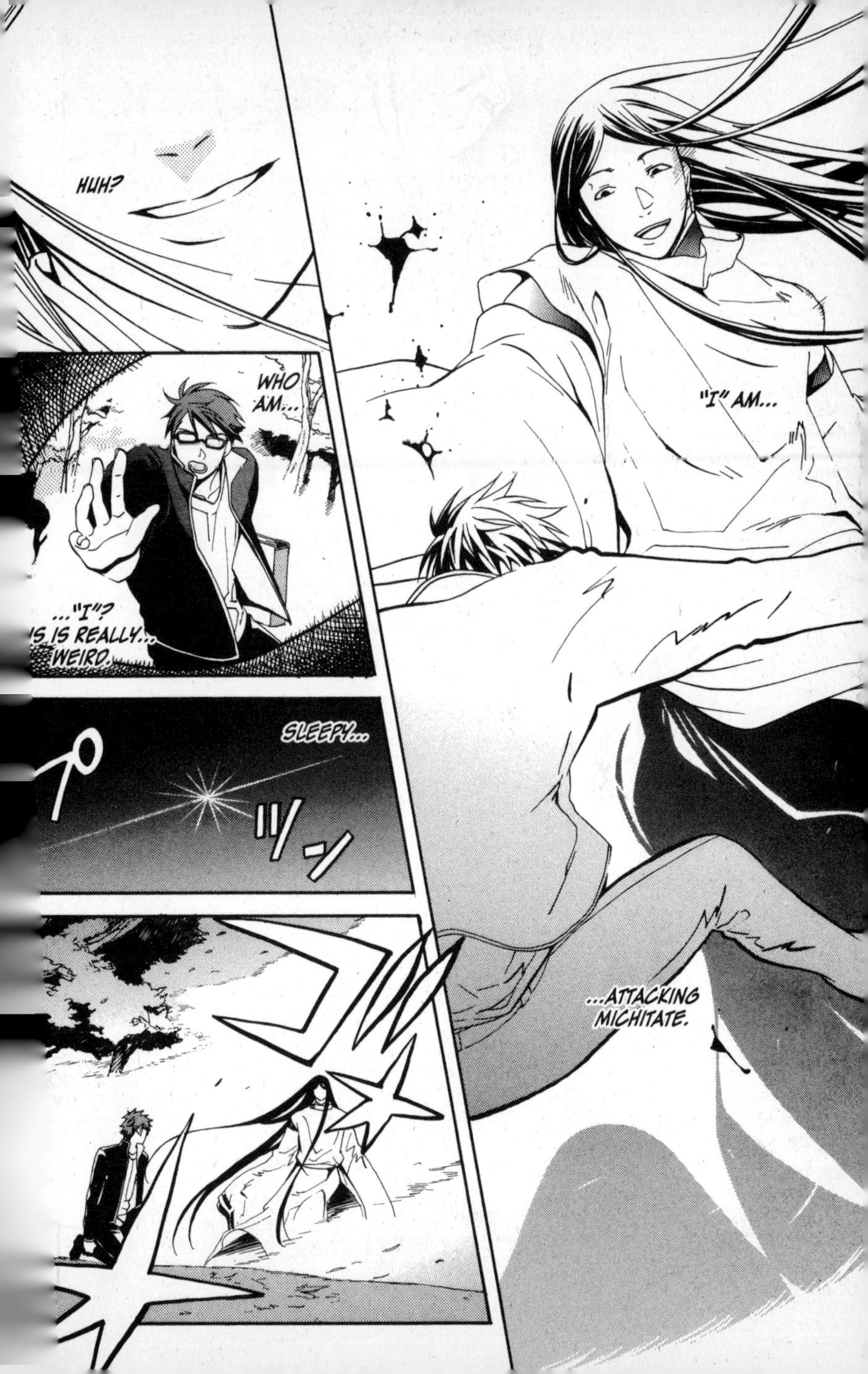
"I" AM...
...ATTACKING MICHITATE.
HUH?
WHO AM...
..."I"?
S IS REALLY... WEIRD.
SLEEPY...

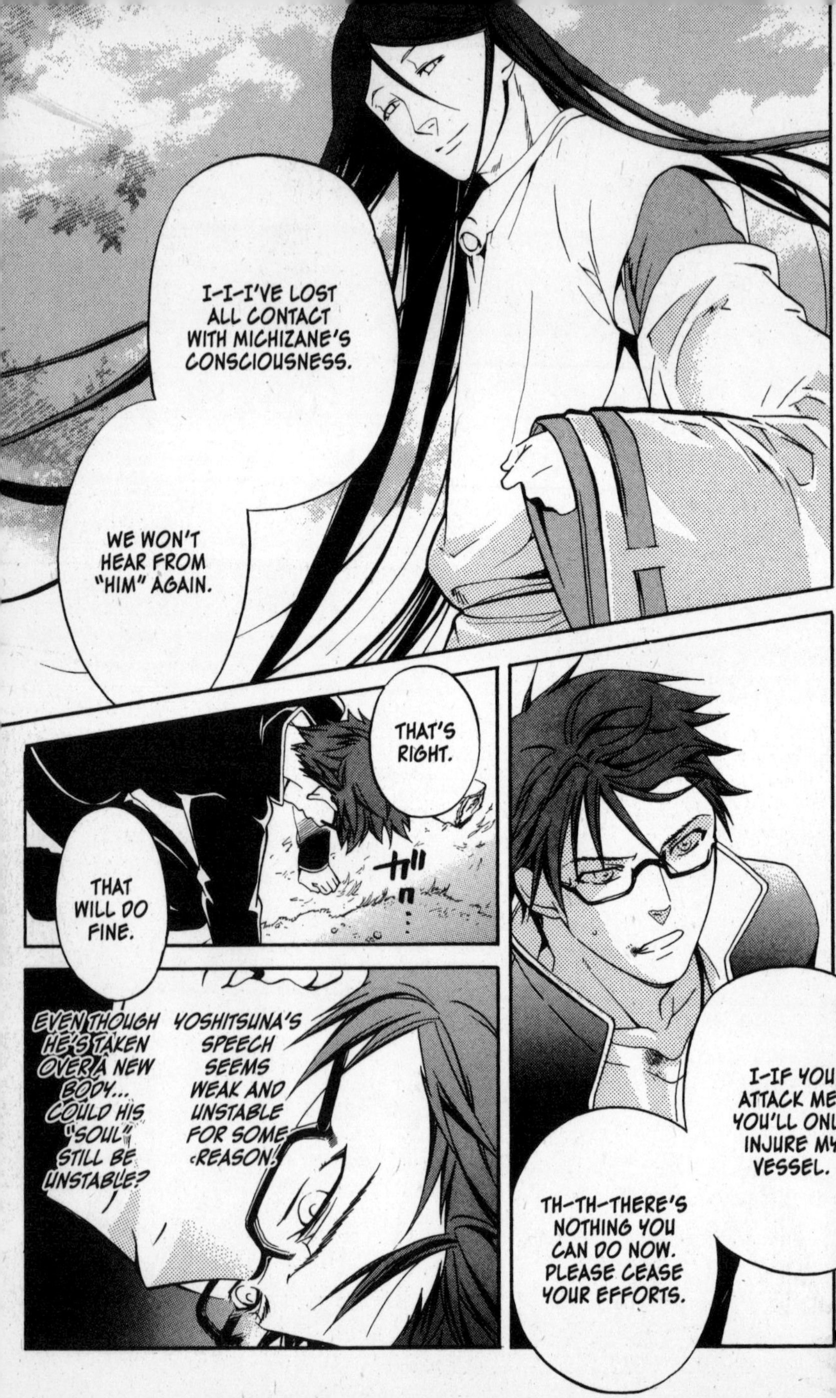
I-I-I'VE LOST ALL CONTACT WITH MICHIZANE'S CONSCIOUSNESS.
WE WON'T HEAR FROM "HIM" AGAIN.
I-IF YOU ATTACK ME, YOU'LL ONLY INJURE MY VESSEL.
TH-TH-THERE'S NOTHING YOU CAN DO NOW. PLEASE CEASE YOUR EFFORTS.
THAT'S RIGHT.
THAT WILL DO FINE.
YOSHITSUNA'S SPEECH SEEMS WEAK AND UNSTABLE FOR SOME REASON!
EVEN THOUGH HE'S TAKEN OVER A NEW BODY... COULD HIS "SOUL" STILL BE UNSTABLE?

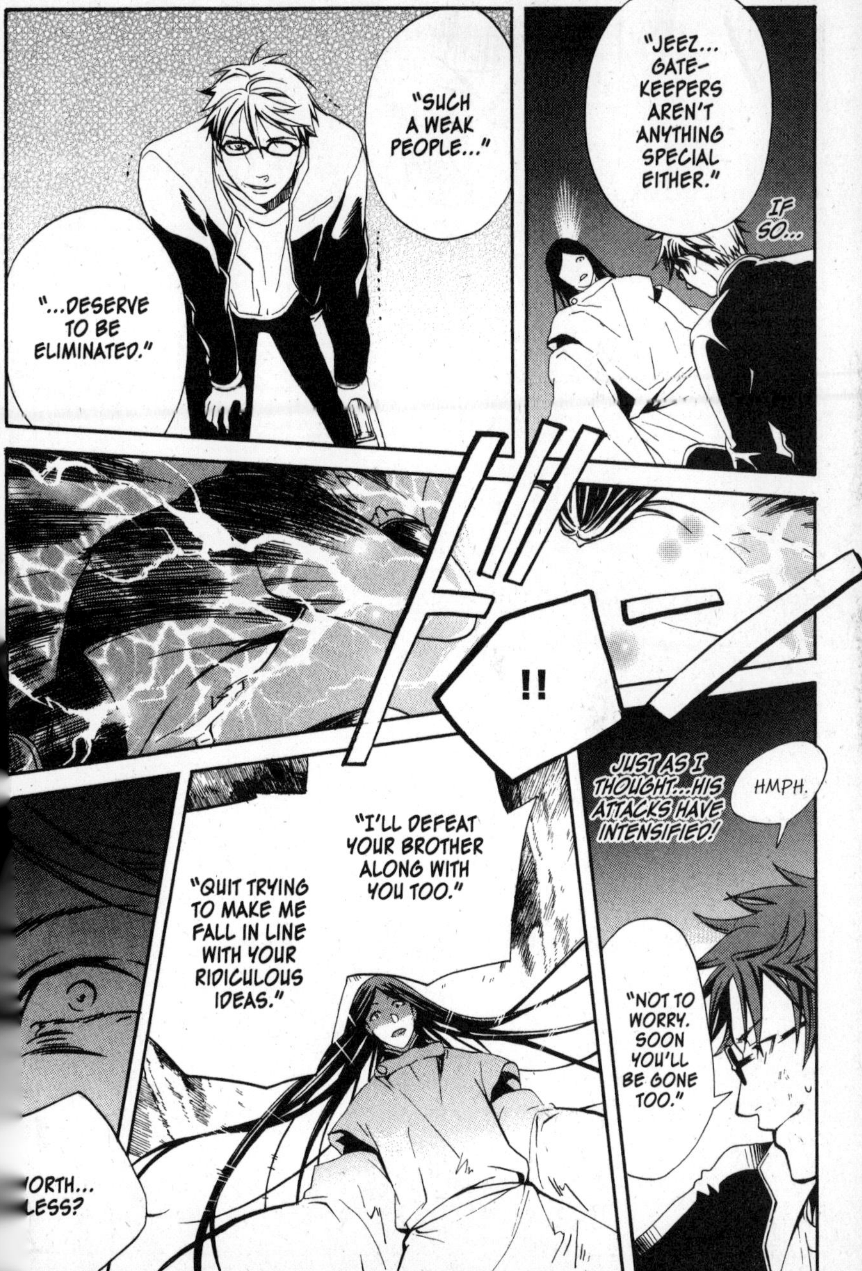
"JEEZ... GATE-KEEPERS AREN'T ANYTHING SPECIAL EITHER."
IF SO...
"SUCH A WEAK PEOPLE..."
"...DESERVE TO BE ELIMINATED."
!!
JUST AS I THOUGHT...HIS ATTACKS HAVE INTENSIFIED!
HMPH.
"NOT TO WORRY. SOON YOU'LL BE GONE TOO."
"I'LL DEFEAT YOUR BROTHER ALONG WITH YOU TOO."
"QUIT TRYING TO MAKE ME FALL IN LINE WITH YOUR RIDICULOUS IDEAS."
ORTH...
LESS?

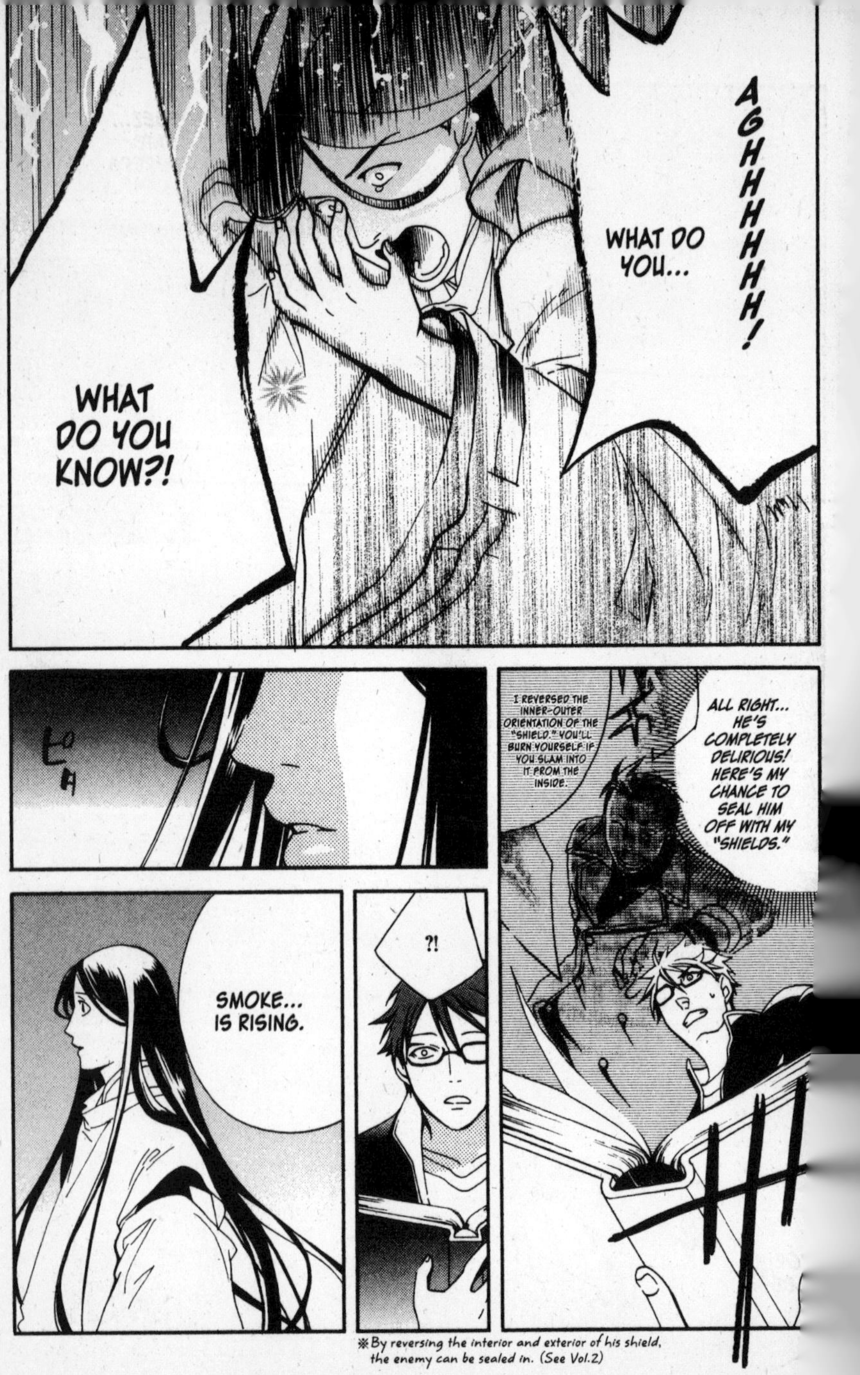
AGHHHHHH!
WHAT DO YOU...
WHAT DO YOU KNOW?!
ALL RIGHT... HE'S COMPLETELY DELIRIOUS! HERE'S MY CHANCE TO SEAL HIM OFF WITH MY "SHIELDS."
I REVERSED THE INNER-OUTER ORIENTATION OF THE "SHIELD." YOU'LL BURN YOURSELF IF YOU SLAM INTO IT FROM THE INSIDE.
?!
SMOKE... IS RISING.

※By reversing the interior and exterior of his shield, the enemy can be sealed in. (See Vol.2)

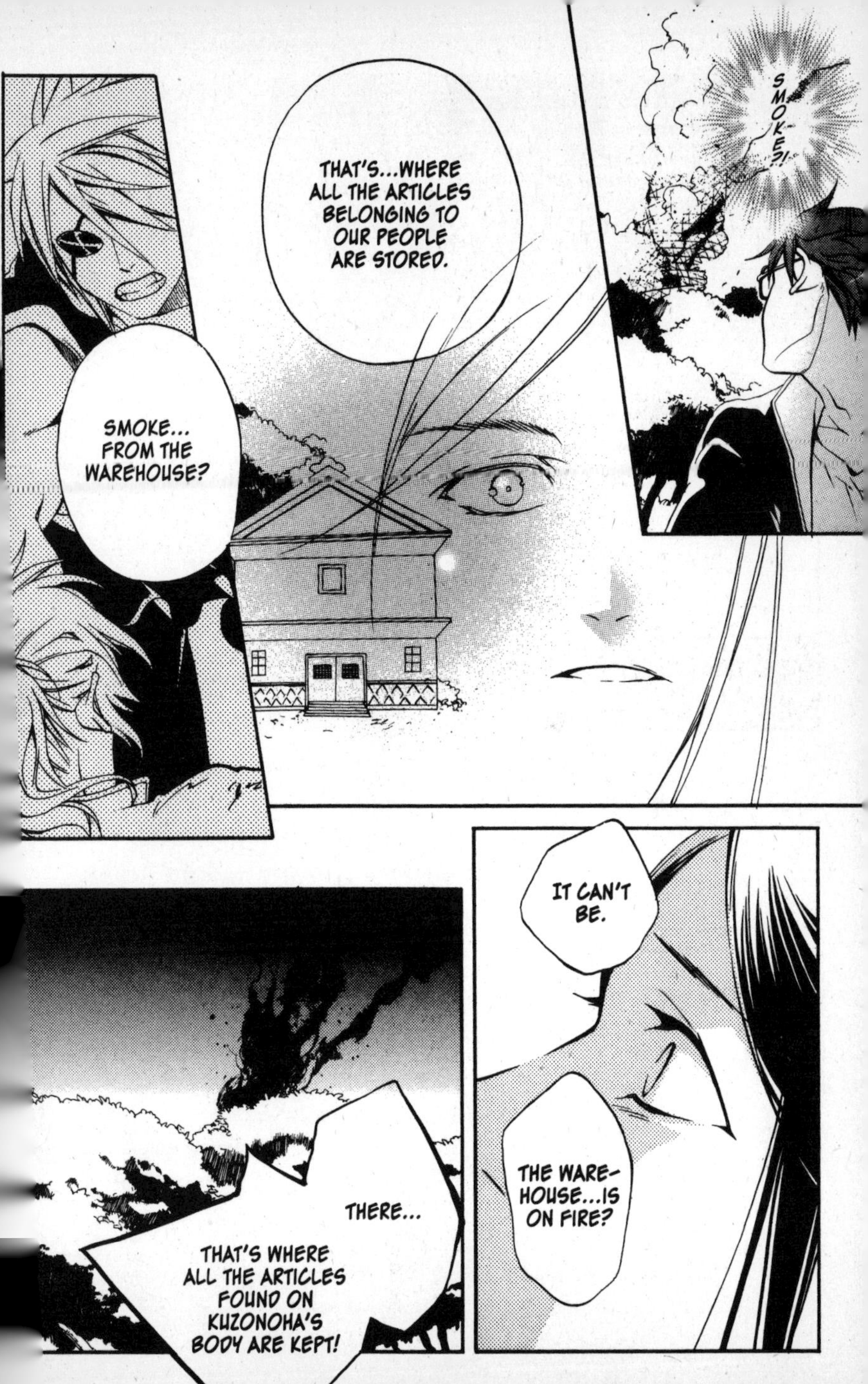
SMOKE?!
THAT'S...WHERE ALL THE ARTICLES BELONGING TO OUR PEOPLE ARE STORED.
SMOKE... FROM THE WAREHOUSE?
IT CAN'T BE.
THE WARE-HOUSE...IS ON FIRE?
THERE...
THAT'S WHERE ALL THE ARTICLES FOUND ON KUZONOHA'S BODY ARE KEPT!

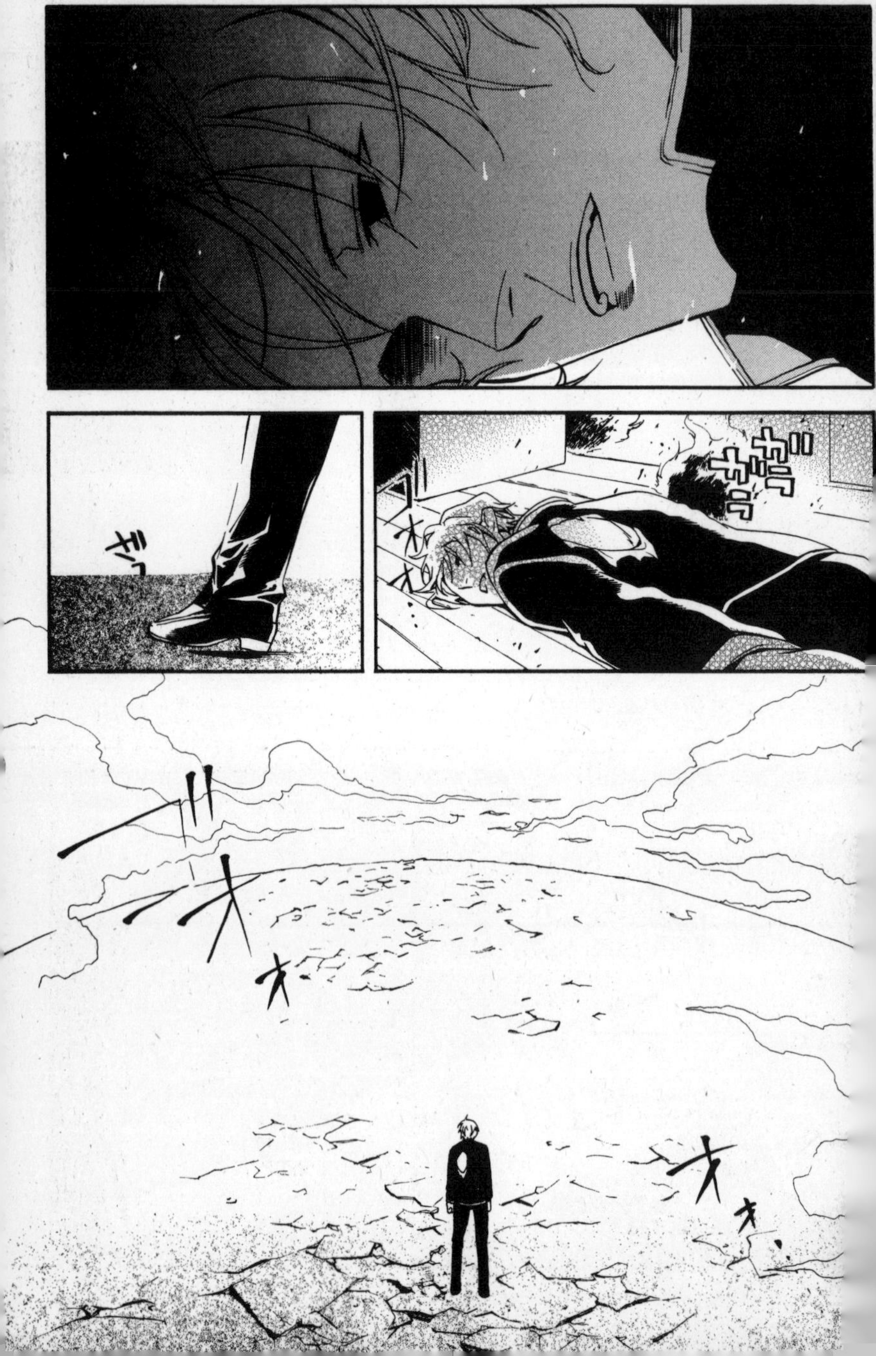
ガラ ガラ
ゴオォ
ギッ
ゴオオォ
オォ…

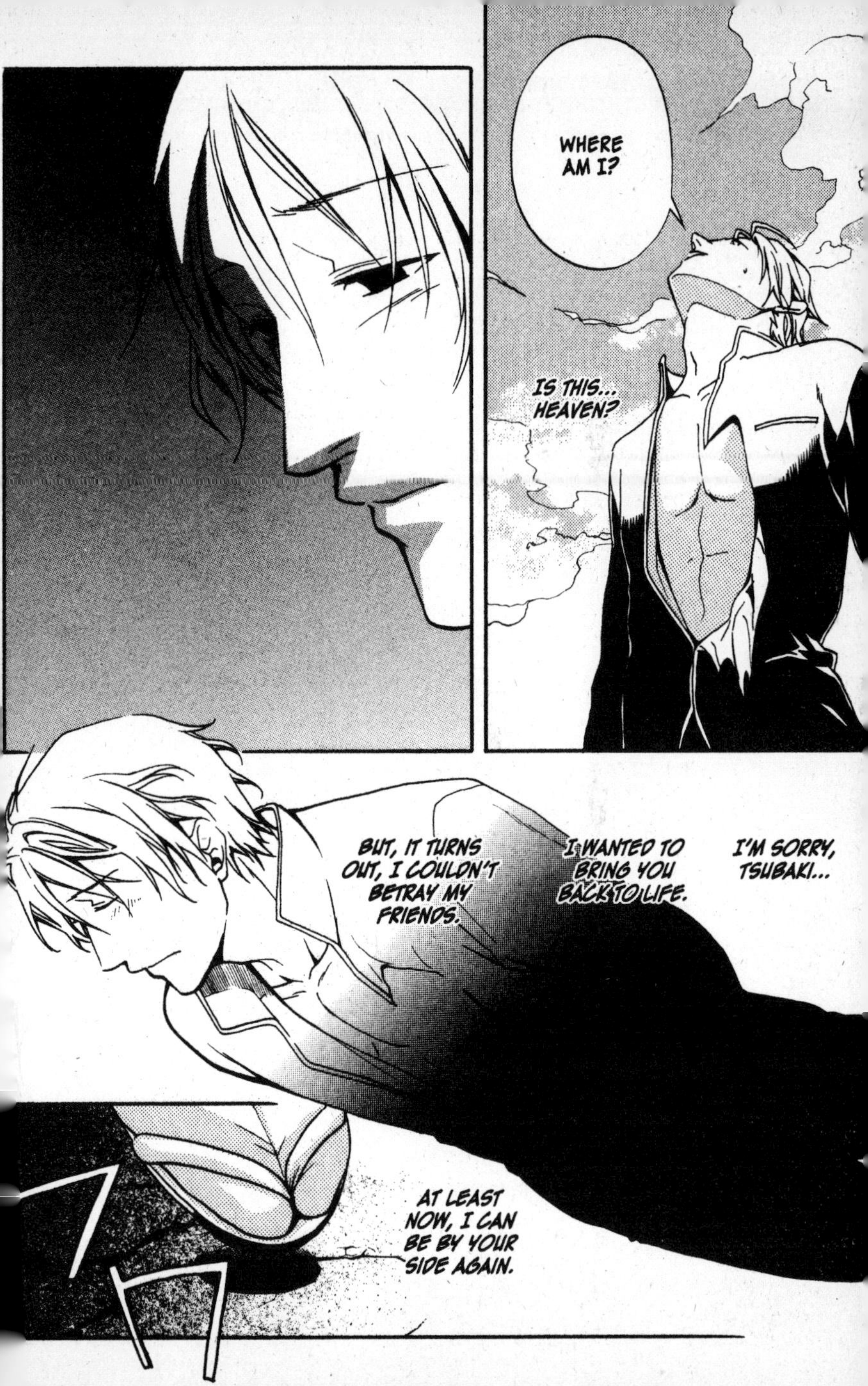
WHERE AM I?
IS THIS... HEAVEN?
I'M SORRY, TSUBAKI...
I WANTED TO BRING YOU BACK TO LIFE.
BUT, IT TURNS OUT, I COULDN'T BETRAY MY FRIENDS.
AT LEAST NOW, I CAN BE BY YOUR SIDE AGAIN.

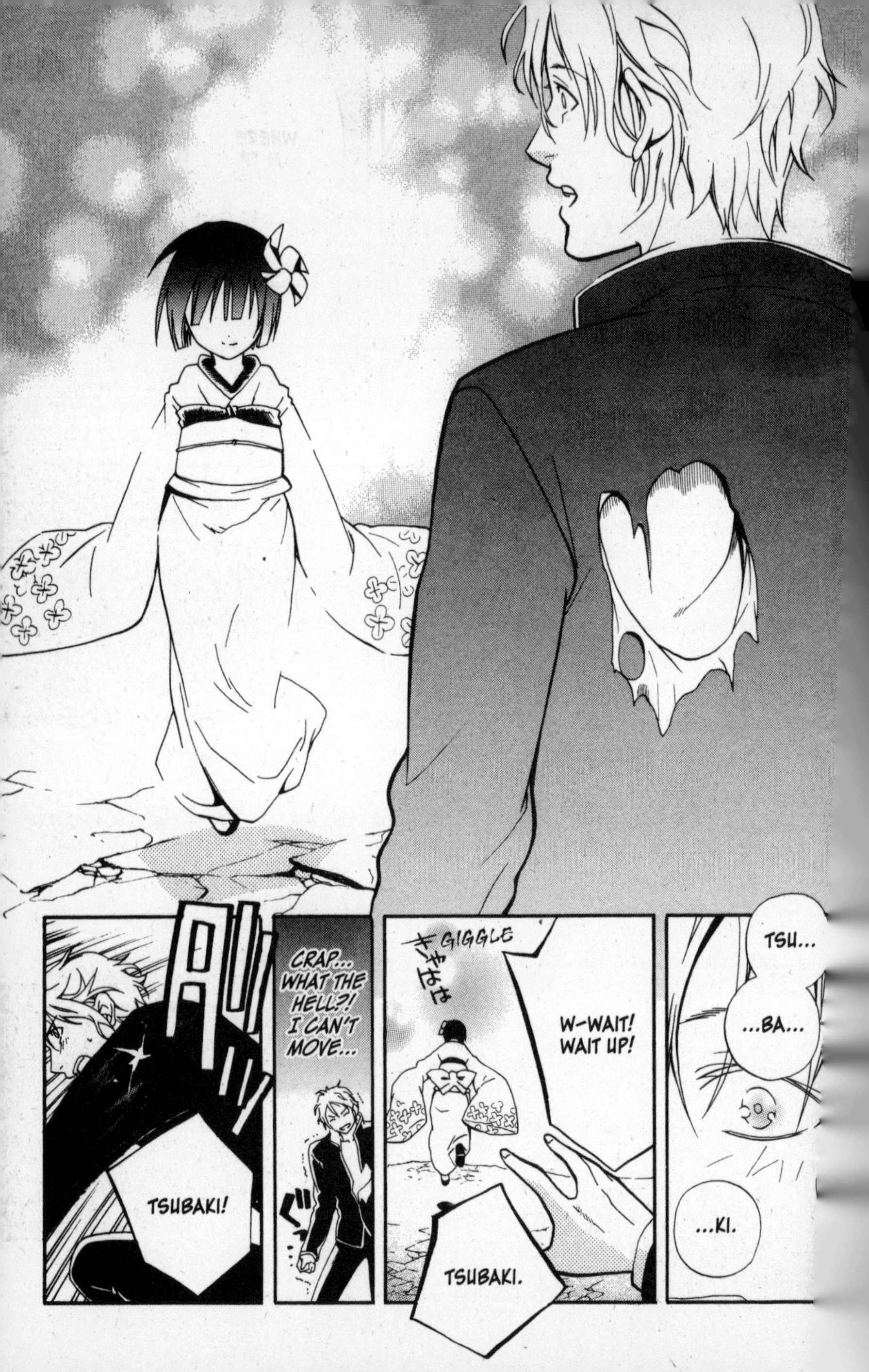
TSU...
...BA...
...KI.
GIGGLE
W-WAIT! WAIT UP!
TSUBAKI.
CRAP... WHAT THE HELL?! I CAN'T MOVE...
TSUBAKI!

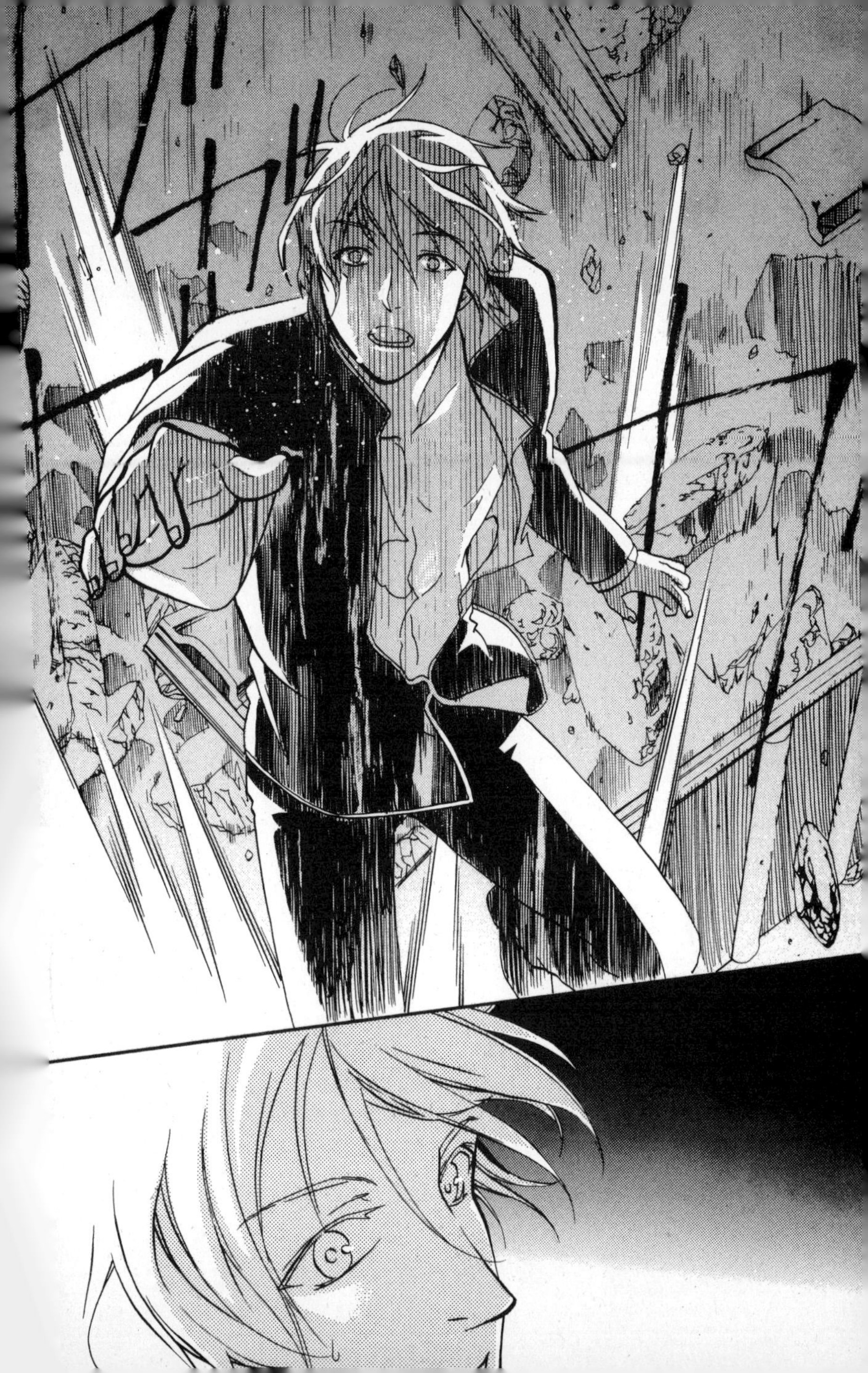

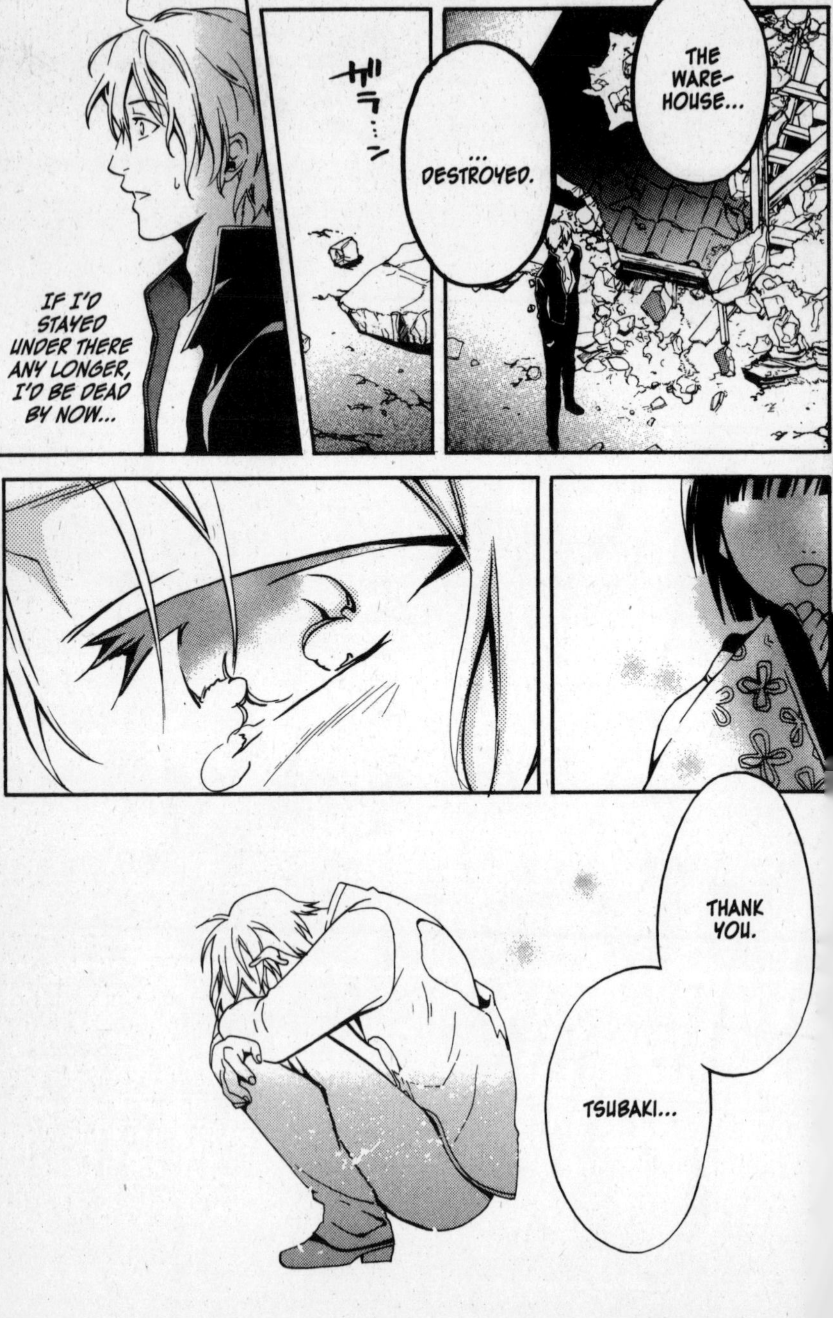
THE WARE-HOUSE...
... DESTROYED.
ガラ…ン
IF I'D STAYED UNDER THERE ANY LONGER, I'D BE DEAD BY NOW...
THANK YOU.
TSUBAKI...

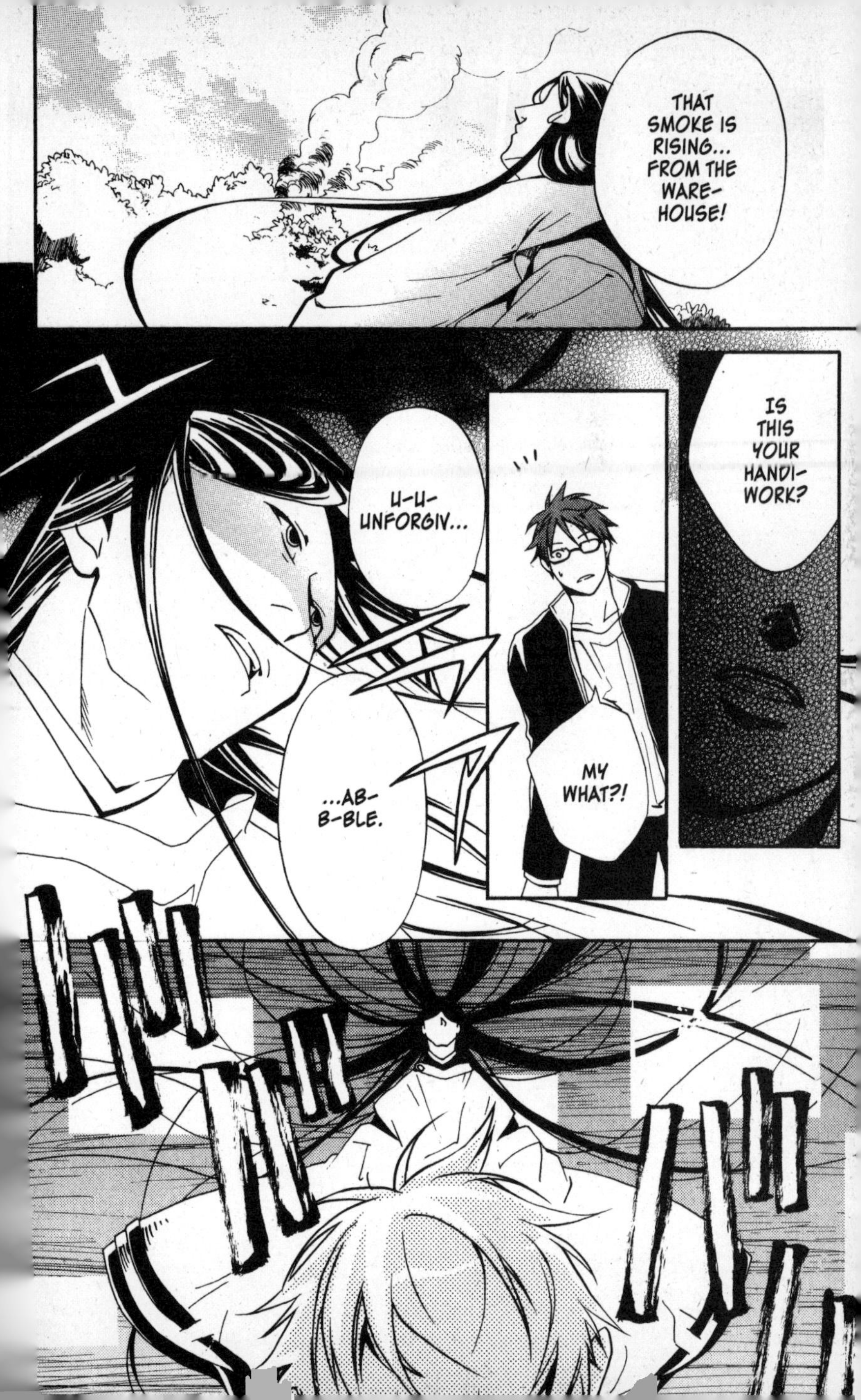
THAT SMOKE IS RISING... FROM THE WARE-HOUSE!
IS THIS YOUR HANDI-WORK?
MY WHAT?!
U-U-UNFORGIV...
...AB-B-BLE.

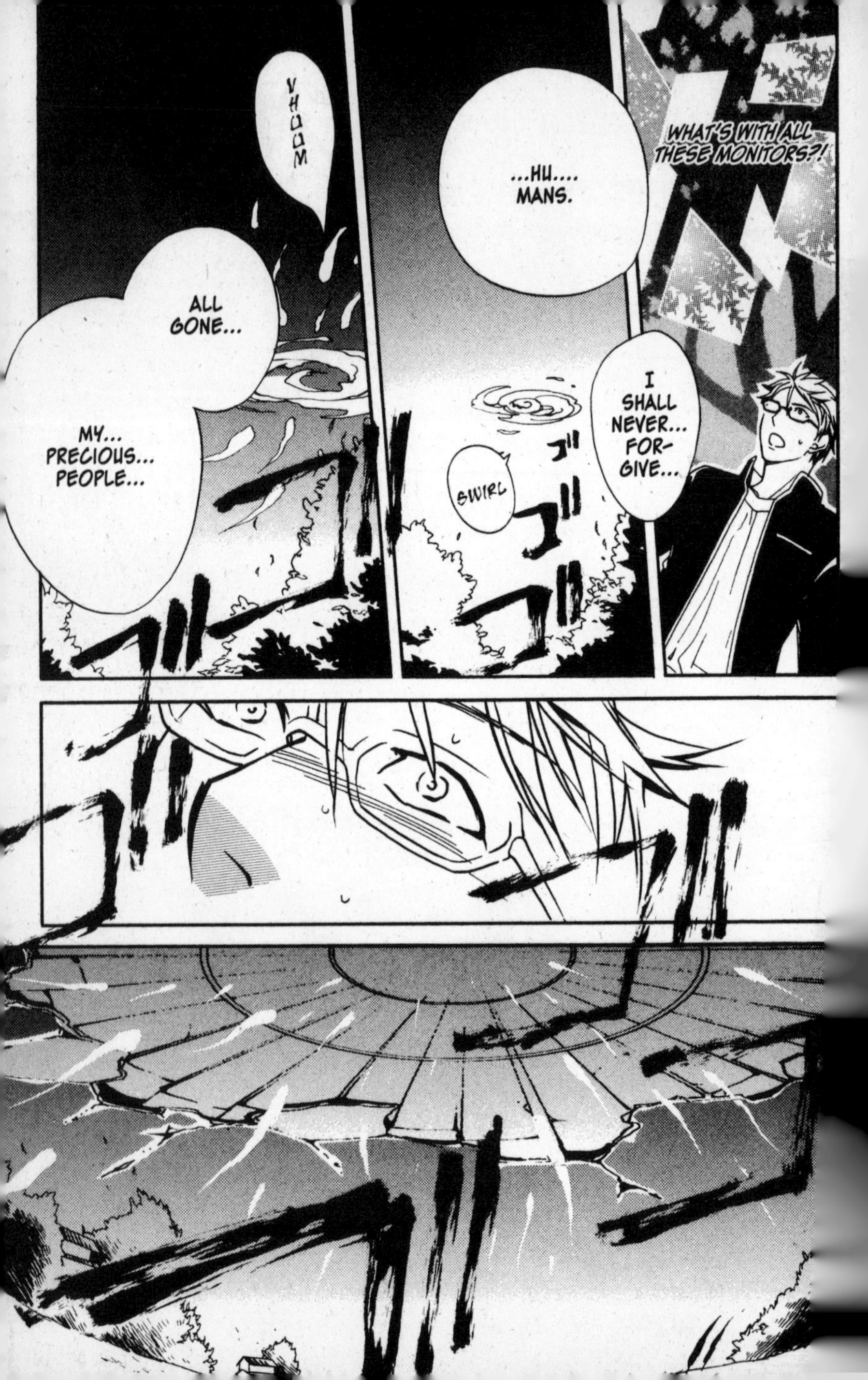

WHAT'S WITH ALL THESE MONITORS?!
I SHALL NEVER... FOR-GIVE...
...HU.... MANS.
SWIRL
VHOOM
ALL GONE...
MY... PRECIOUS... PEOPLE...

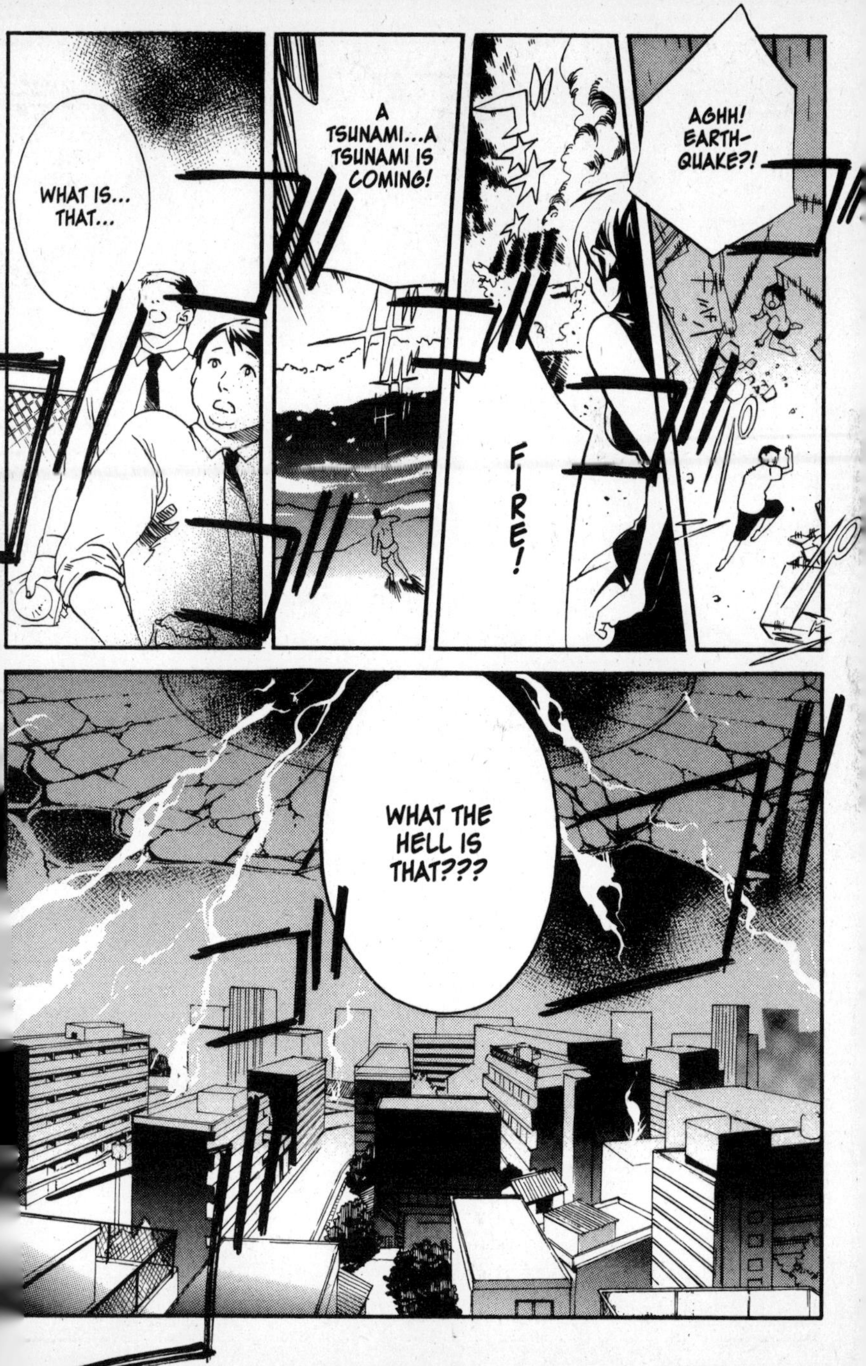
AGHH! EARTH-QUAKE?!
FIRE!
A TSUNAMI...A TSUNAMI IS COMING!
WHAT IS... THAT...
WHAT THE HELL IS THAT???

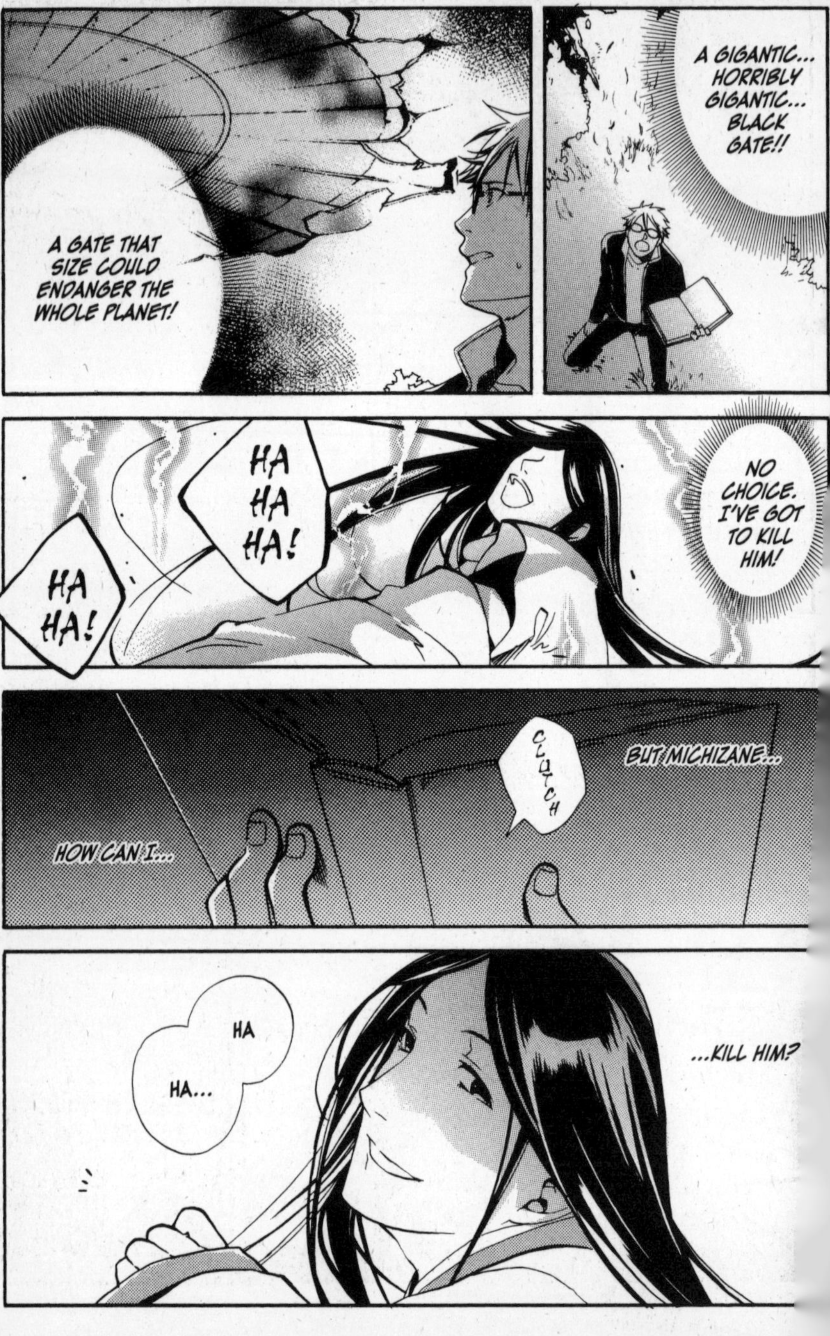
A GIGANTIC... HORRIBLY GIGANTIC... BLACK GATE!!
A GATE THAT SIZE COULD ENDANGER THE WHOLE PLANET!
NO CHOICE. I'VE GOT TO KILL HIM!
HA HA HA!
HA HA!
BUT MICHIZANE...
CLUTCH
HOW CAN I...
...KILL HIM?
HA HA...

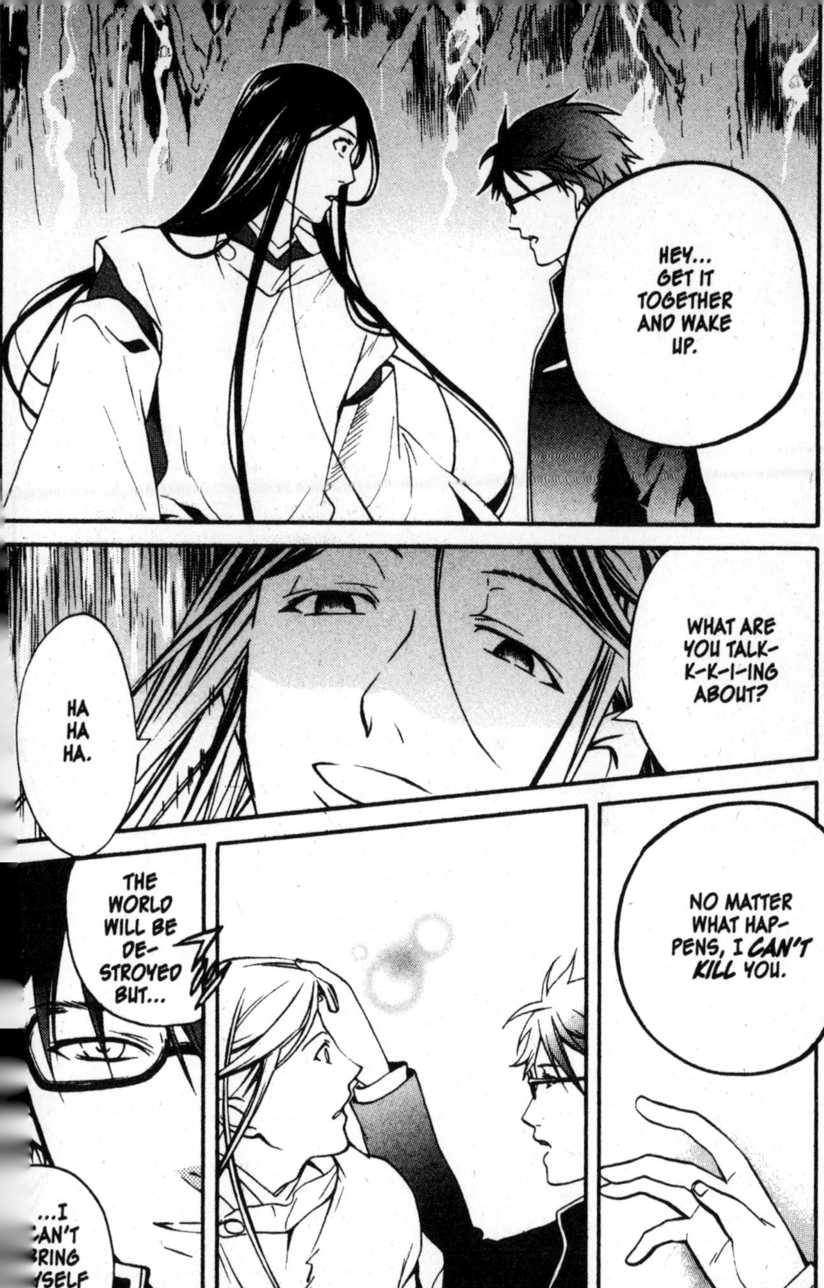
HEY... GET IT TOGETHER AND WAKE UP.
WHAT ARE YOU TALK-K-K-I-ING ABOUT?
HA HA HA.
NO MATTER WHAT HAPPENS, I CAN'T KILL YOU.
THE WORLD WILL BE DESTROYED BUT...
...I CAN'T BRING YSELF DO IT.

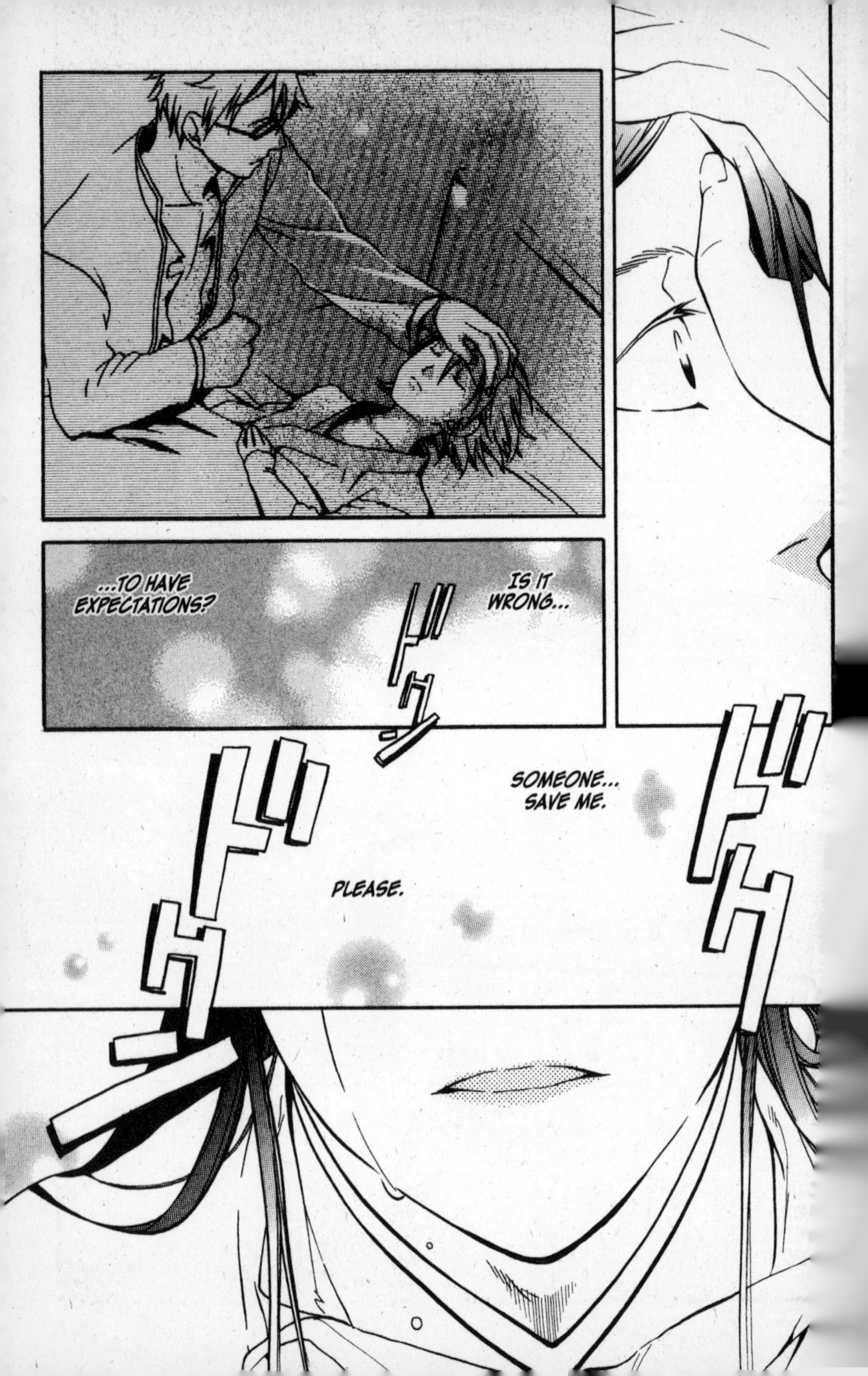
IS IT WRONG...
...TO HAVE EXPECTATIONS?
SOMEONE... SAVE ME.
PLEASE.

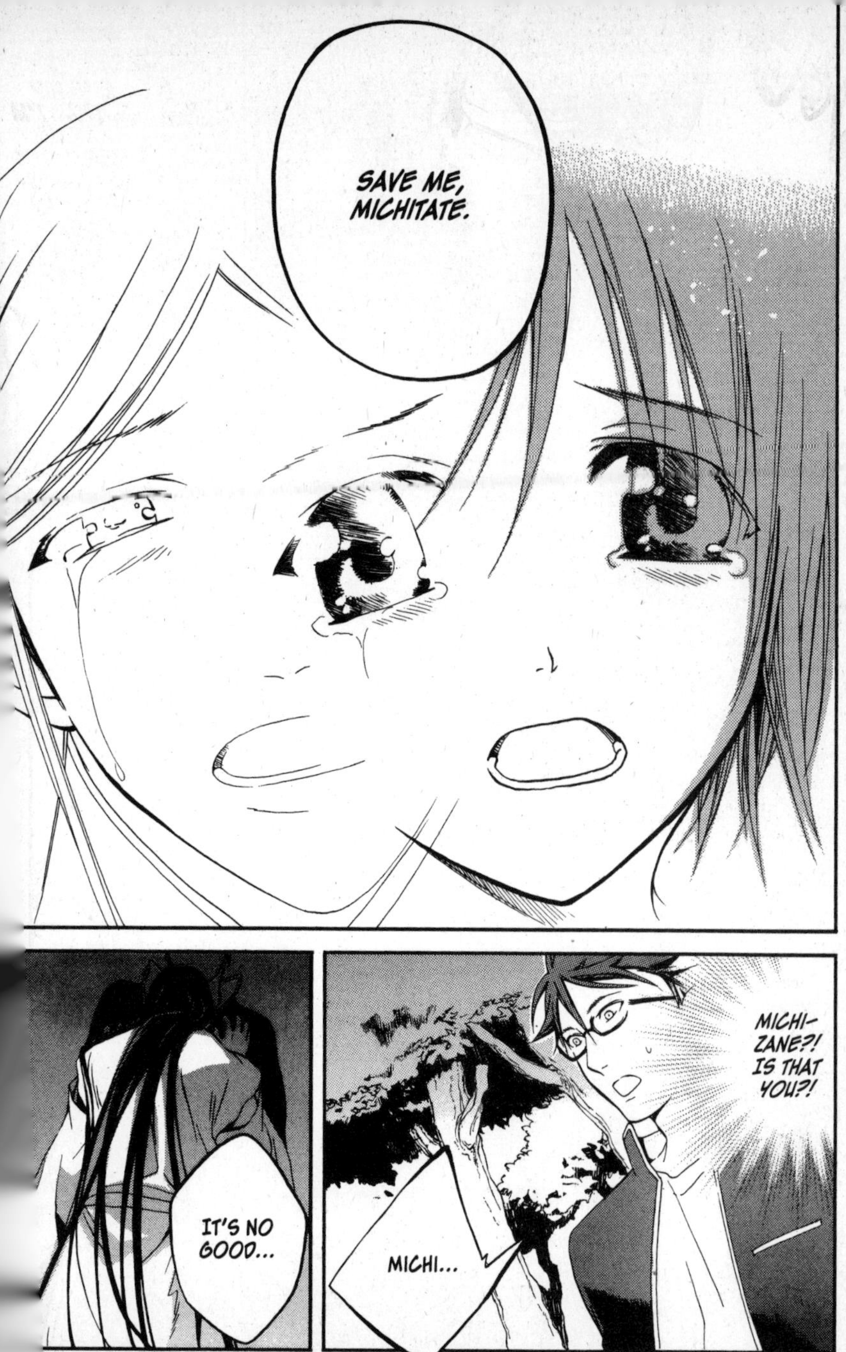
SAVE ME, MICHITATE.
MICHI-ZANE?! IS THAT YOU?!
MICHI...
IT'S NO GOOD...

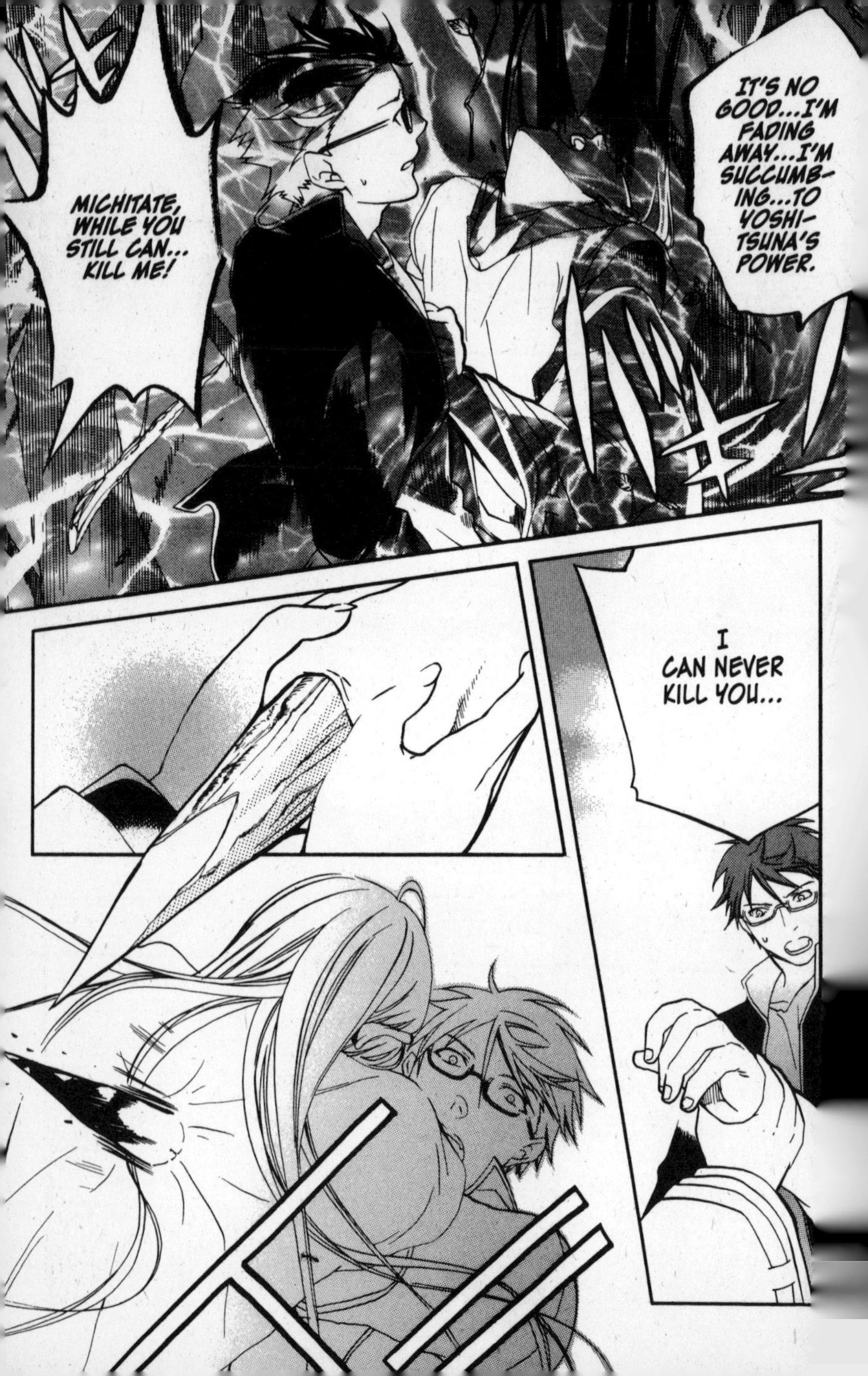
IT'S NO GOOD...I'M FADING AWAY...I'M SUCCUMB-ING...TO YOSHI-TSUNA'S POWER.
MICHITATE, WHILE YOU STILL CAN... KILL ME!
I CAN NEVER KILL YOU...

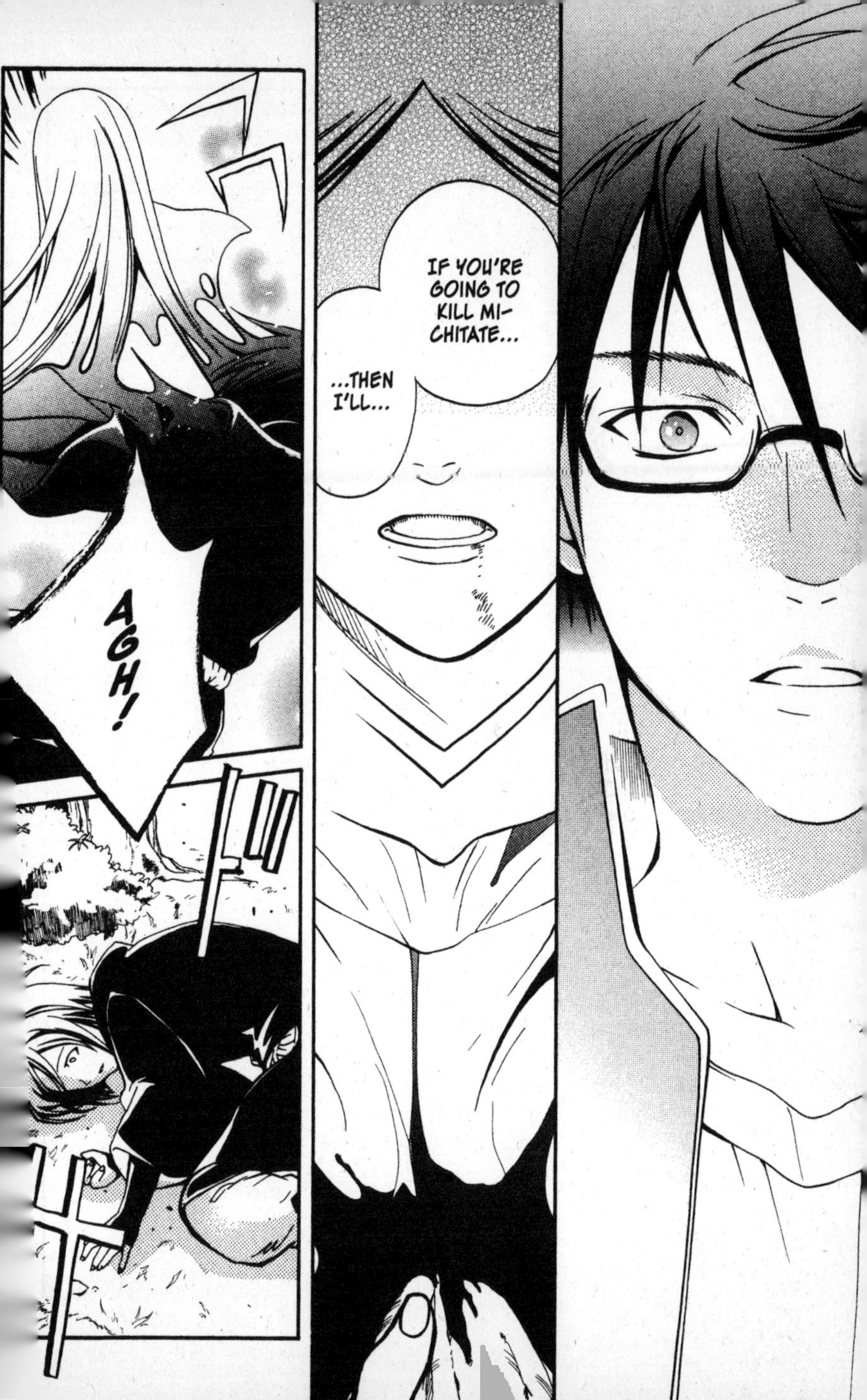
IF YOU'RE GOING TO KILL MI-CHITATE...
...THEN I'LL...
AGH!

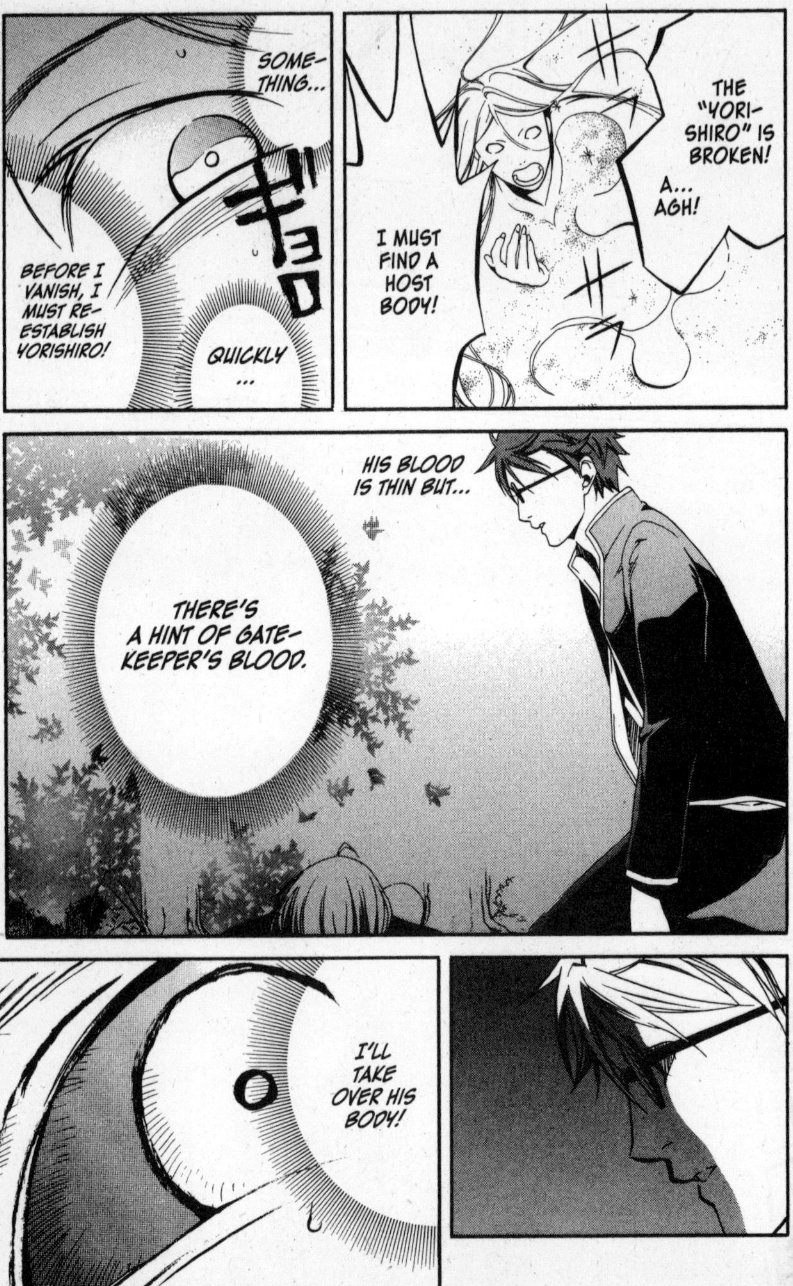
THE "YORI-SHIRO" IS BROKEN!
A... AGH!
I MUST FIND A HOST BODY!
SOME-THING...
ギョロ
QUICKLY ...
BEFORE I VANISH, I MUST RE-ESTABLISH YORISHIRO!
HIS BLOOD IS THIN BUT...
THERE'S A HINT OF GATE-KEEPER'S BLOOD.
I'LL TAKE OVER HIS BODY!

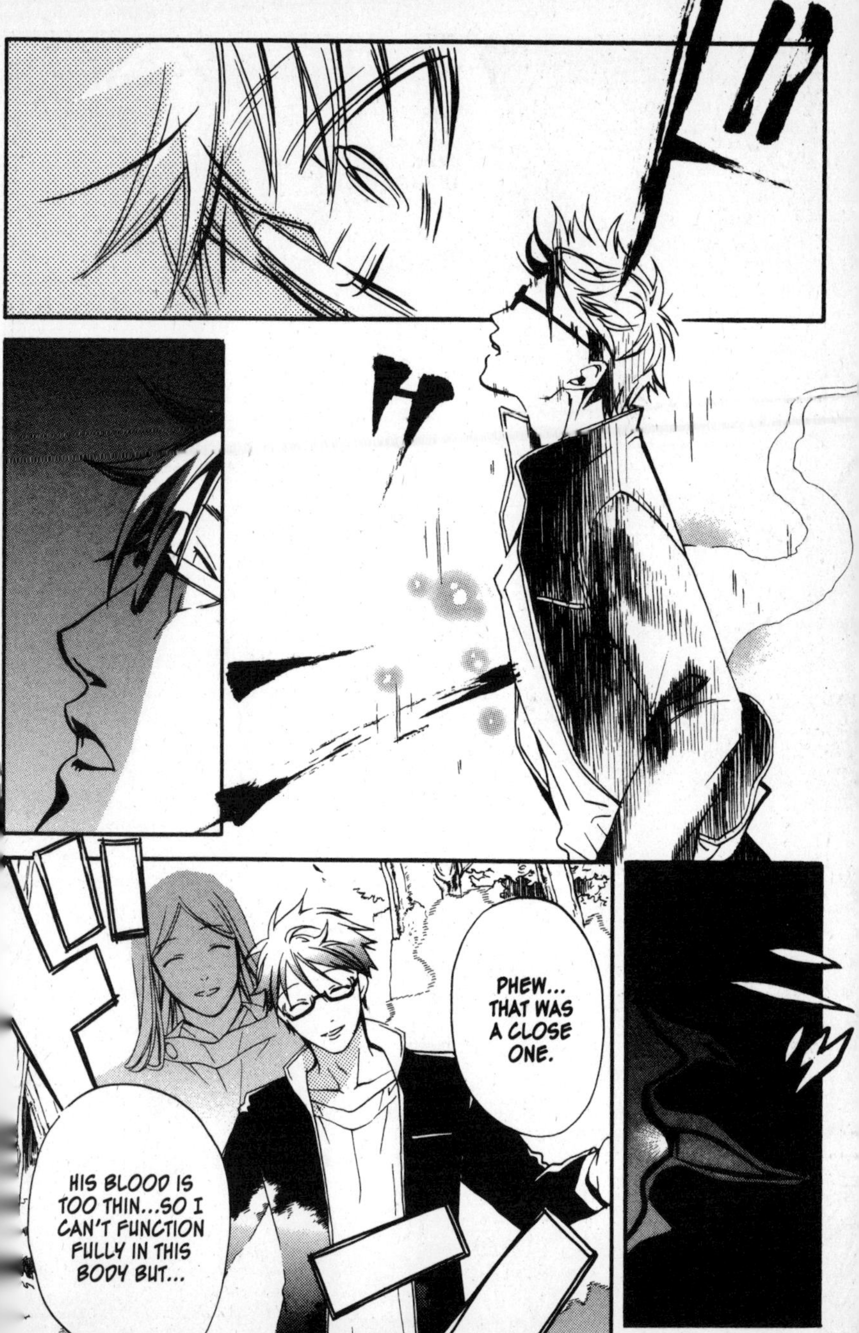
PHEW... THAT WAS A CLOSE ONE.
HIS BLOOD IS TOO THIN...SO I CAN'T FUNCTION FULLY IN THIS BODY BUT...

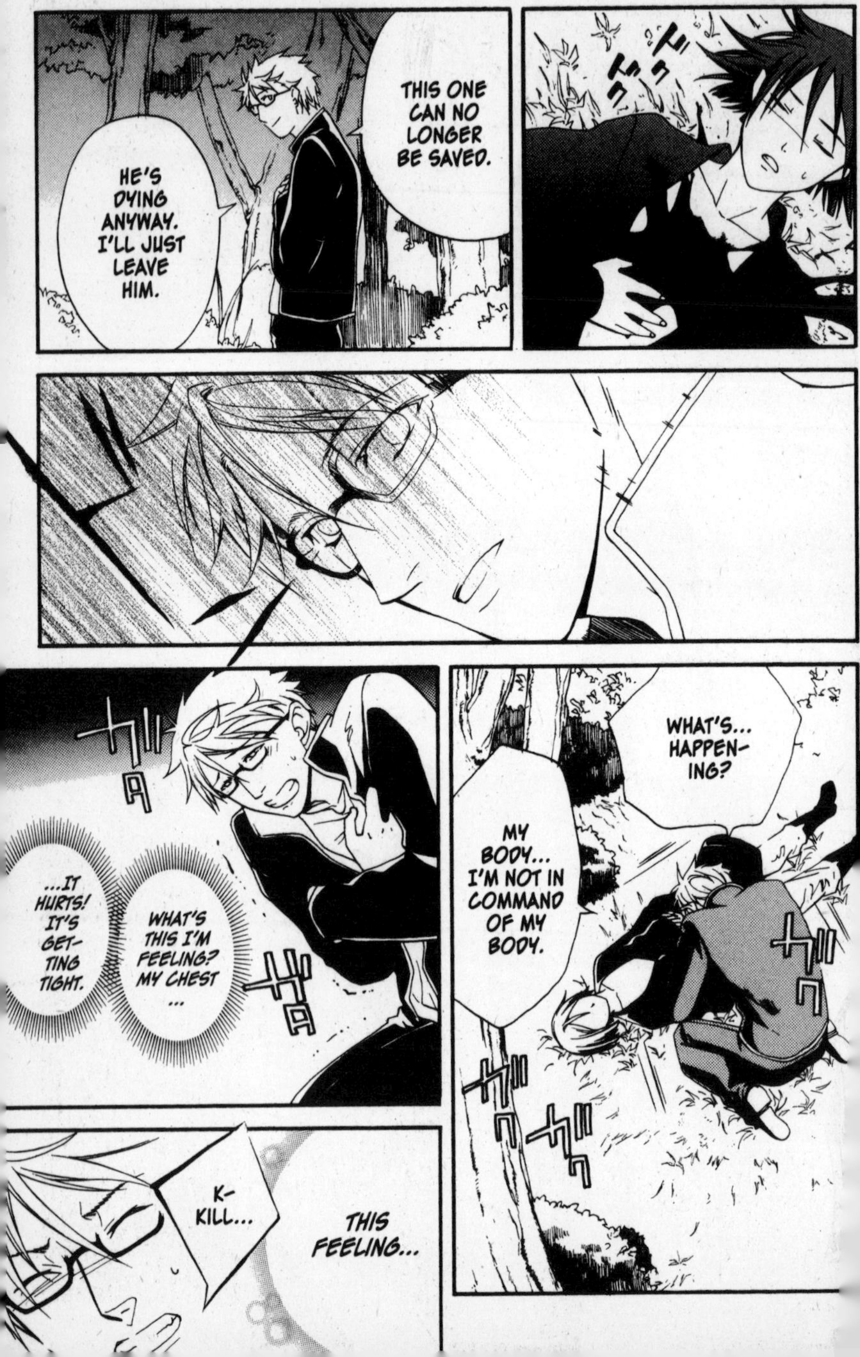
THIS ONE CAN NO LONGER BE SAVED.
HE'S DYING ANYWAY. I'LL JUST LEAVE HIM.
WHAT'S... HAPPEN-ING?
MY BODY... I'M NOT IN COMMAND OF MY BODY.
WHAT'S THIS I'M FEELING? MY CHEST ...
...IT HURTS! IT'S GET-TING TIGHT.
THIS FEELING...
K-KILL...

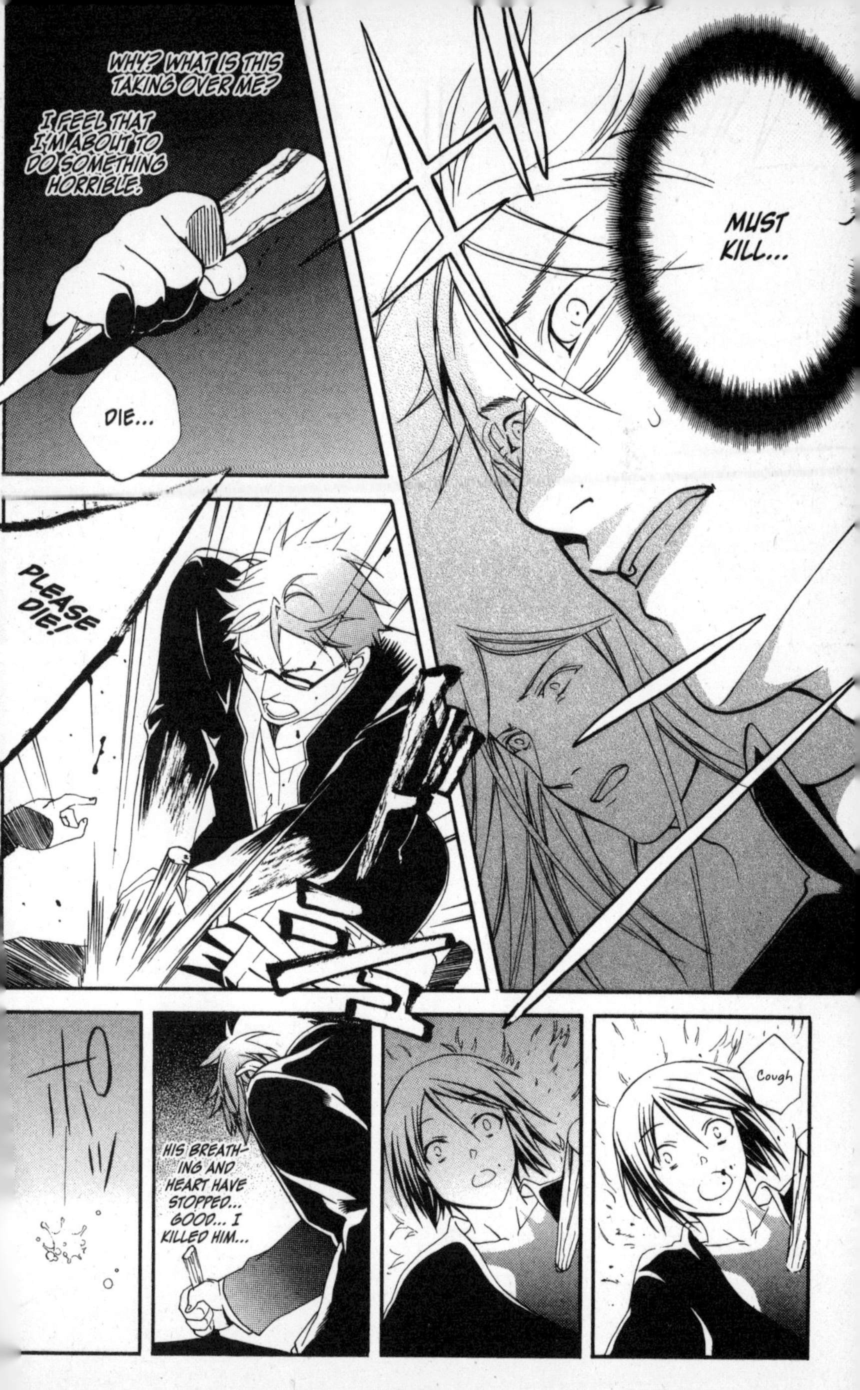
MUST KILL...
WHY? WHAT IS THIS TAKING OVER ME?
I FEEL THAT I'M ABOUT TO DO SOMETHING HORRIBLE.
DIE...
PLEASE DIE!
Cough
HIS BREATH-ING AND HEART HAVE STOPPED... GOOD... I KILLED HIM...

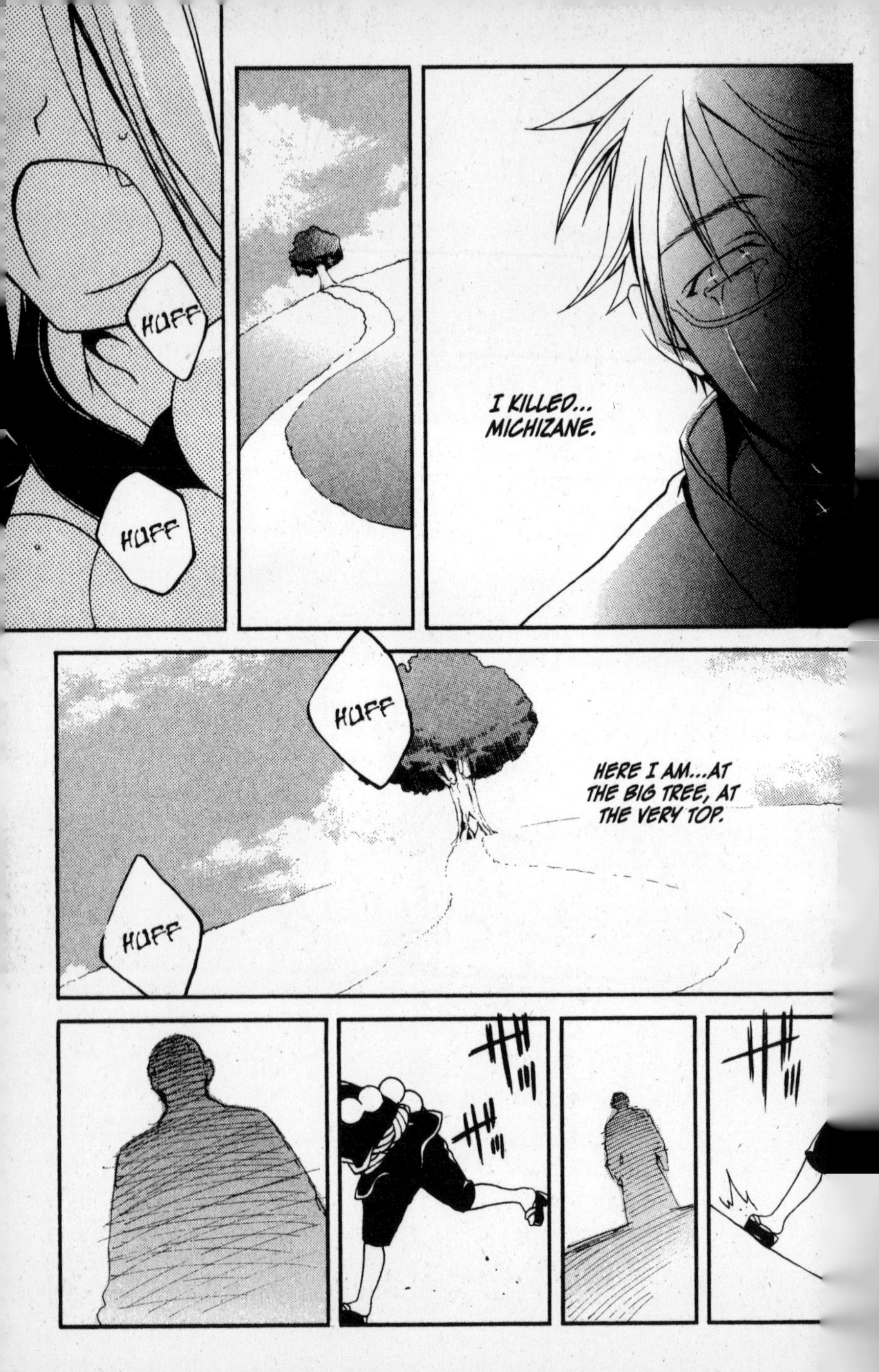
I KILLED... MICHIZANE.
HUFF
HUFF
HERE I AM...AT THE BIG TREE, AT THE VERY TOP.
HUFF
HUFF

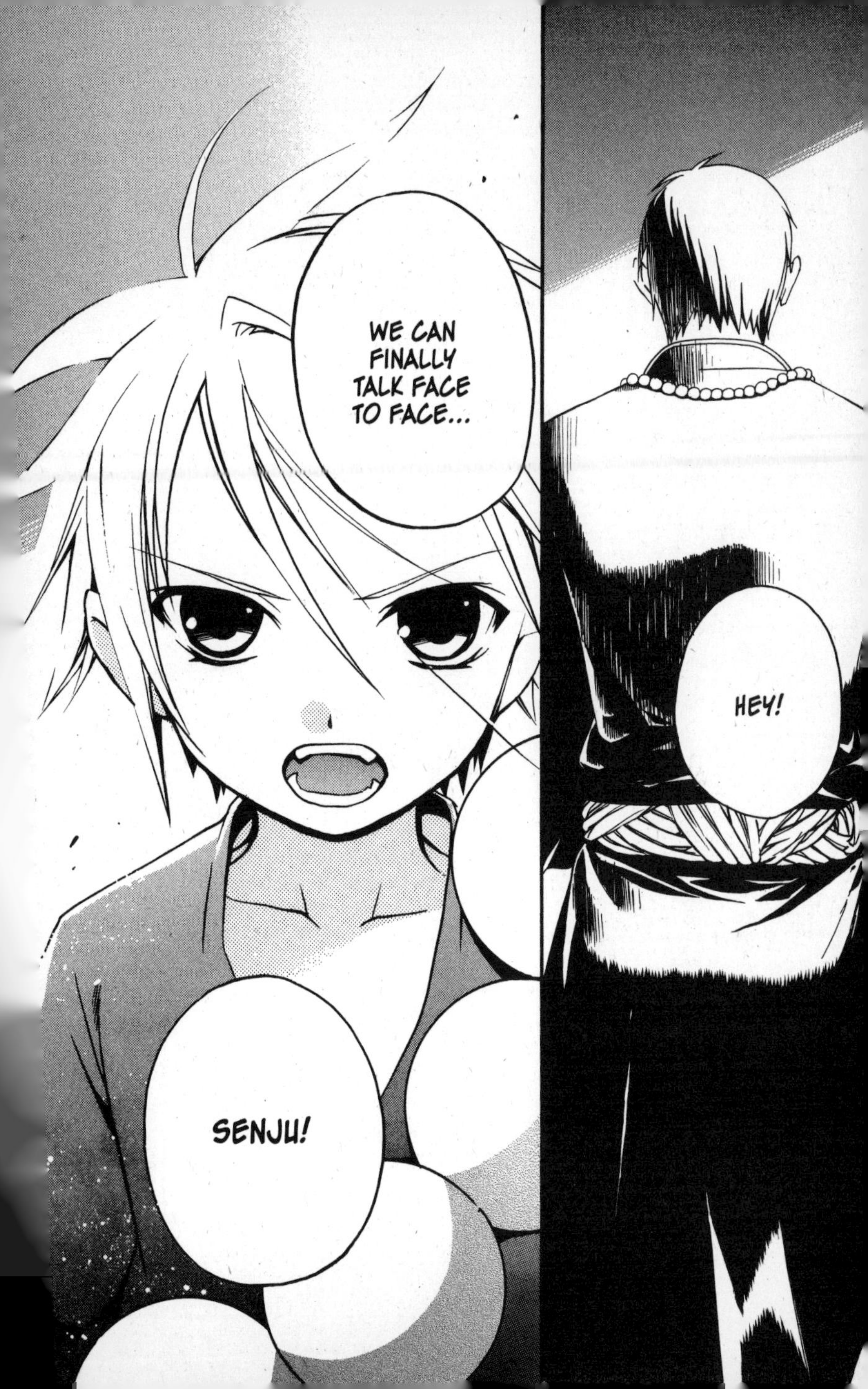
HEY!
WE CAN FINALLY TALK FACE TO FACE...
SENJU!

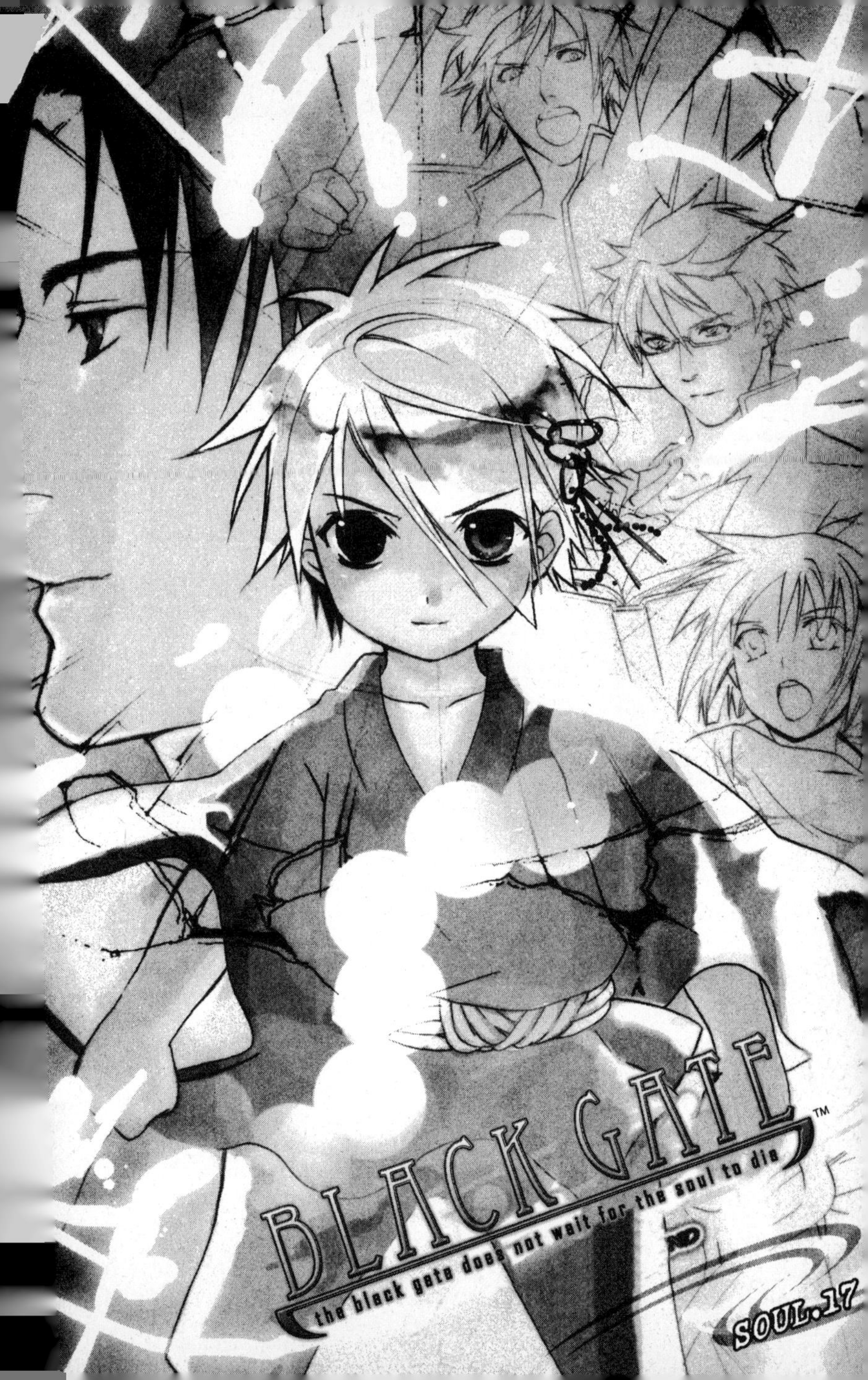
BLACK GATE™
the black gate does not wait for the soul to die
SOUL.17

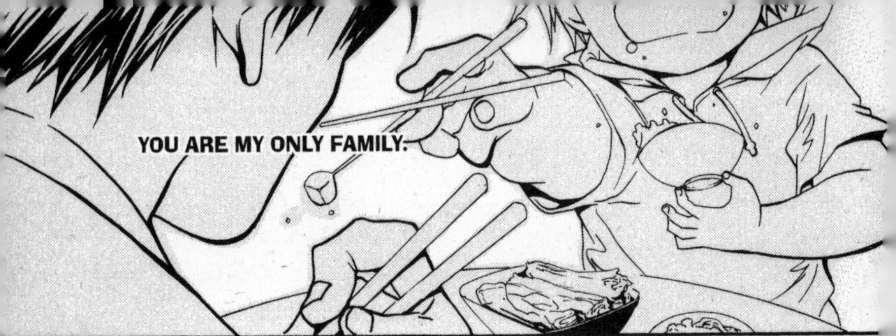
YOU ARE MY ONLY FAMILY.

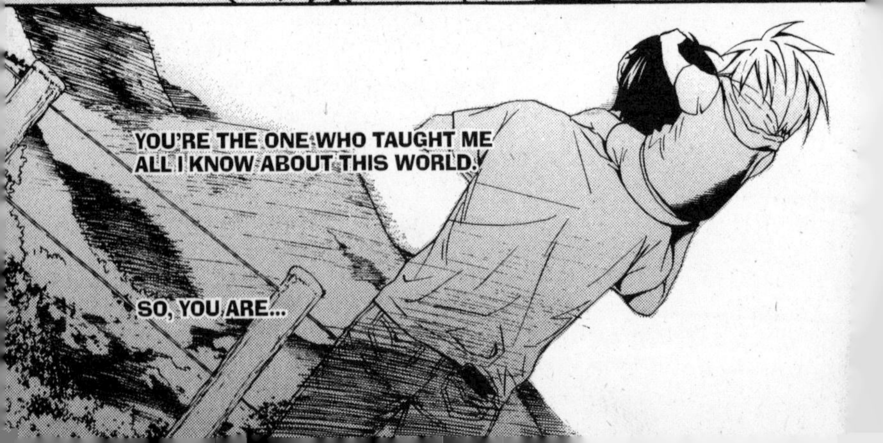
YOU'RE THE ONE WHO TAUGHT ME ALL I KNOW ABOUT THIS WORLD.
SO, YOU ARE...

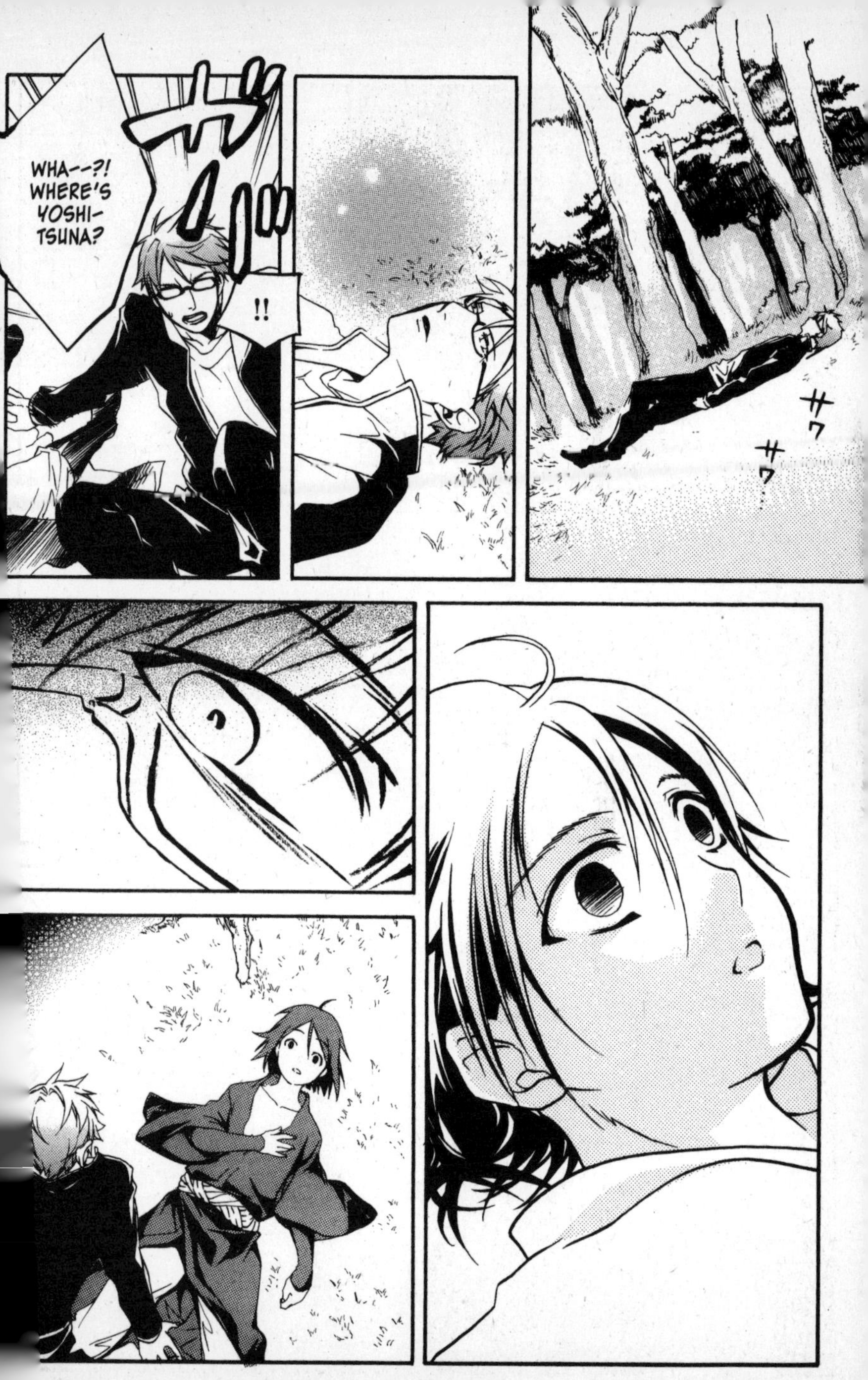
サワ
サワ…
!!
WHA--?! WHERE'S YOSHI-TSUNA?

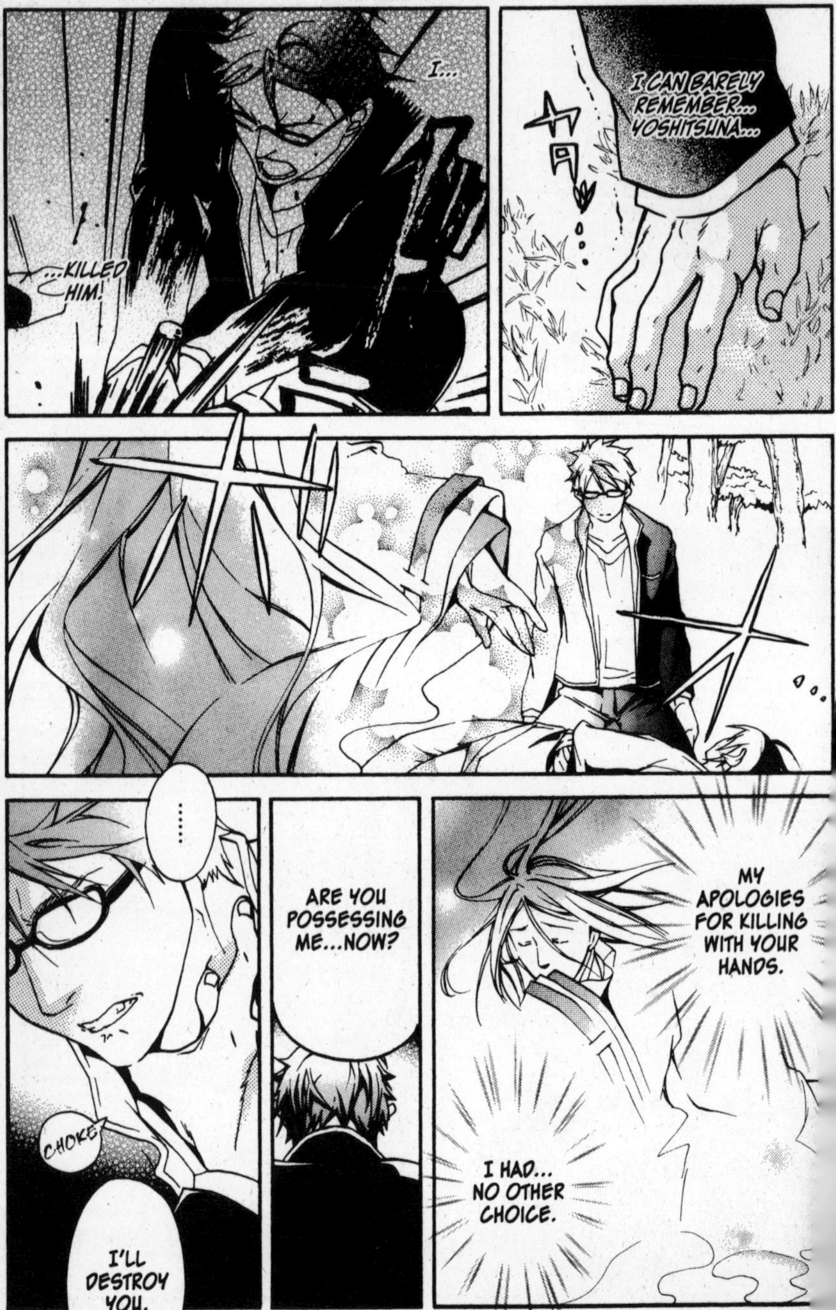
I CAN BARELY REMEMBER... YOSHITSUNA...
I...
...KILLED HIM!
MY APOLOGIES FOR KILLING WITH YOUR HANDS.
I HAD... NO OTHER CHOICE.
ARE YOU POSSESSING ME...NOW?
......
CHOKE
I'LL DESTROY YOU.

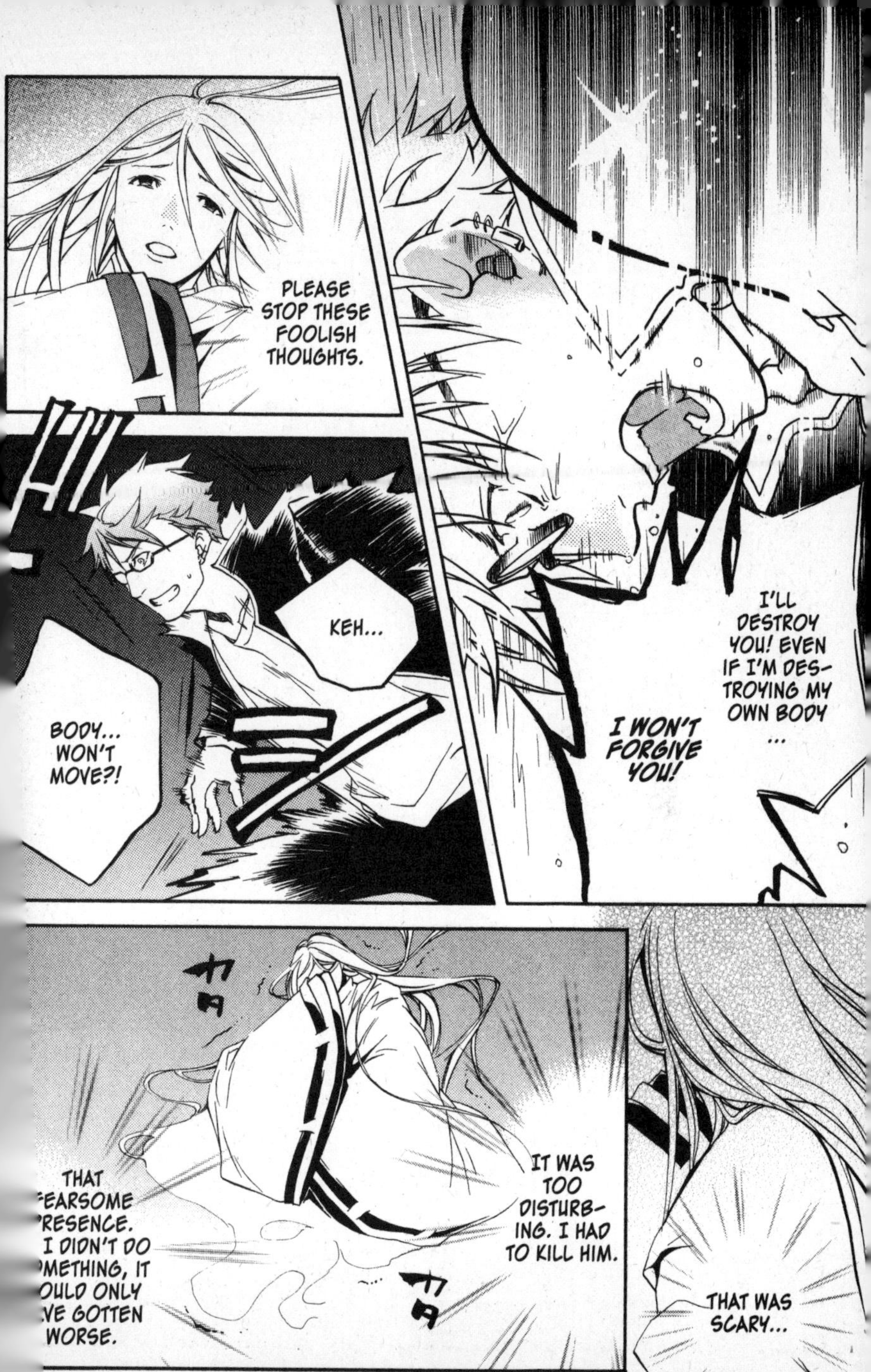

I'LL DESTROY YOU! EVEN IF I'M DES-TROYING MY OWN BODY...
I WON'T FORGIVE YOU!
PLEASE STOP THESE FOOLISH THOUGHTS.
KEH...
BODY... WON'T MOVE?!
THAT WAS SCARY...
IT WAS TOO DISTURB-ING. I HAD TO KILL HIM.
THAT EARSOME RESENCE. I DIDN'T DO OMETHING, IT OULD ONLY VE GOTTEN WORSE.

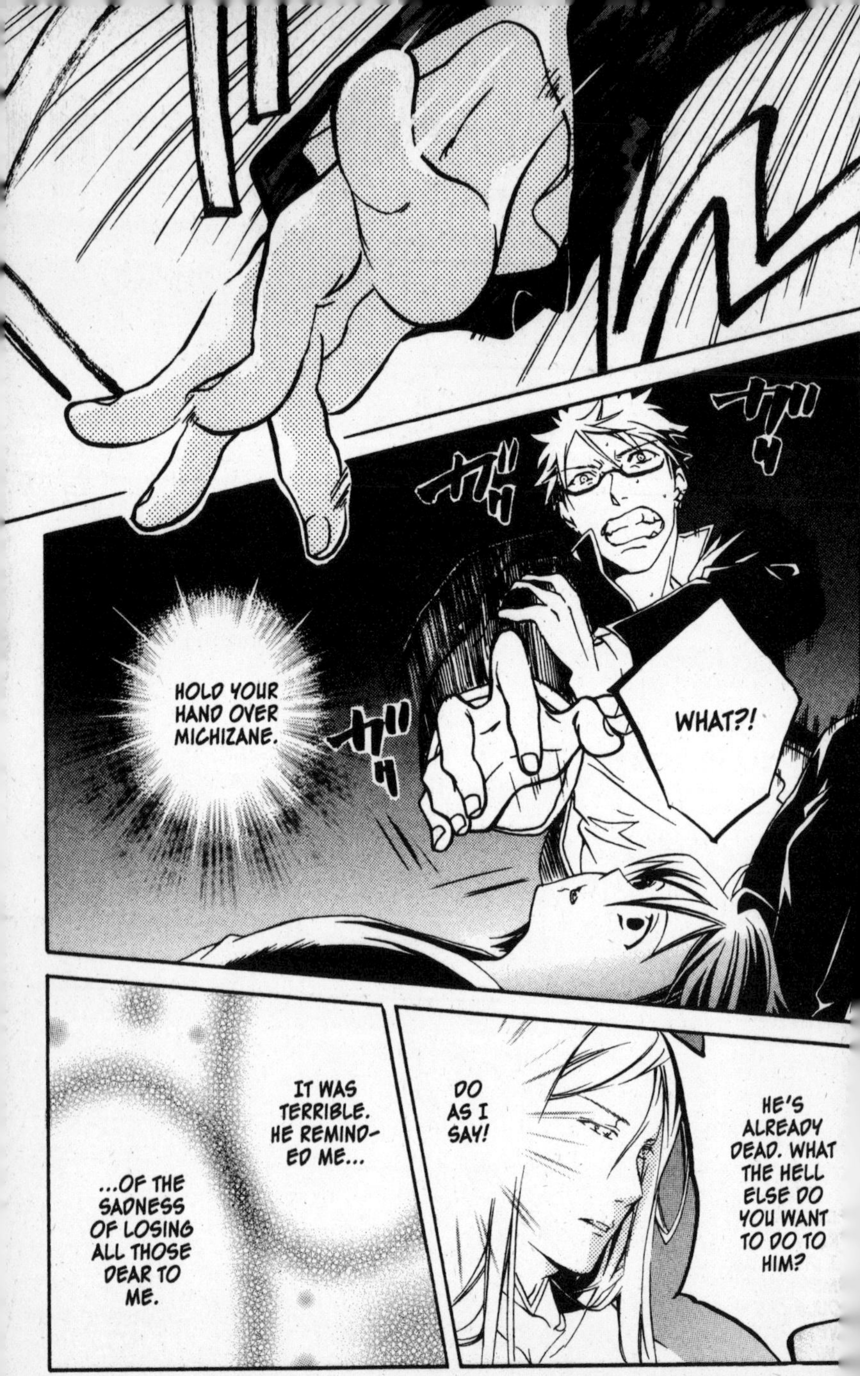
WHAT?!
HOLD YOUR HAND OVER MICHIZANE.
HE'S ALREADY DEAD. WHAT THE HELL ELSE DO YOU WANT TO DO TO HIM?
DO AS I SAY!
IT WAS TERRIBLE. HE REMIND-ED ME...
...OF THE SADNESS OF LOSING ALL THOSE DEAR TO ME.

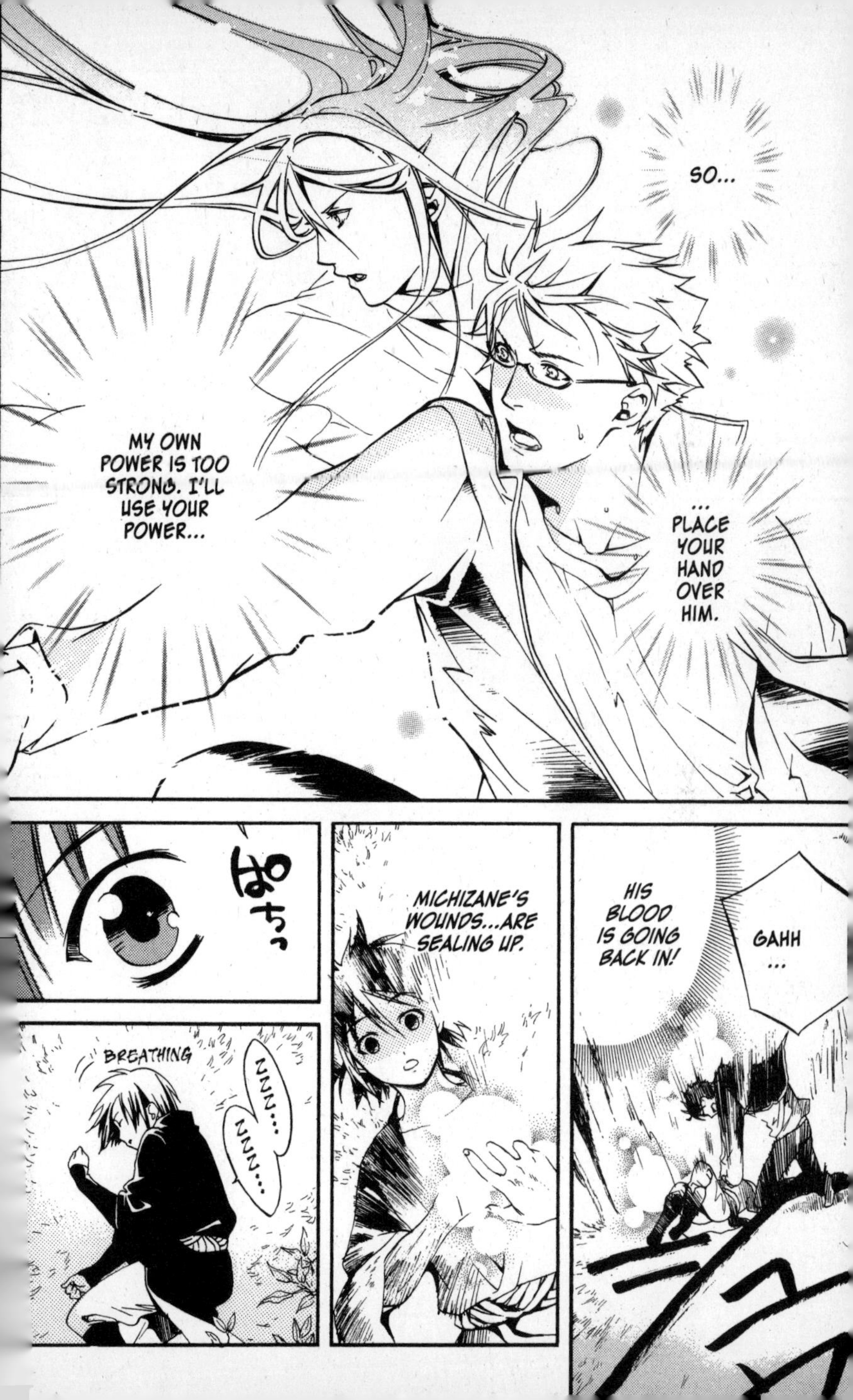
SO...
...PLACE YOUR HAND OVER HIM.
MY OWN POWER IS TOO STRONG. I'LL USE YOUR POWER...
GAHH...
HIS BLOOD IS GOING BACK IN!
MICHIZANE'S WOUNDS...ARE SEALING UP.
ぱちっ
BREATHING
NNN...
NNN...

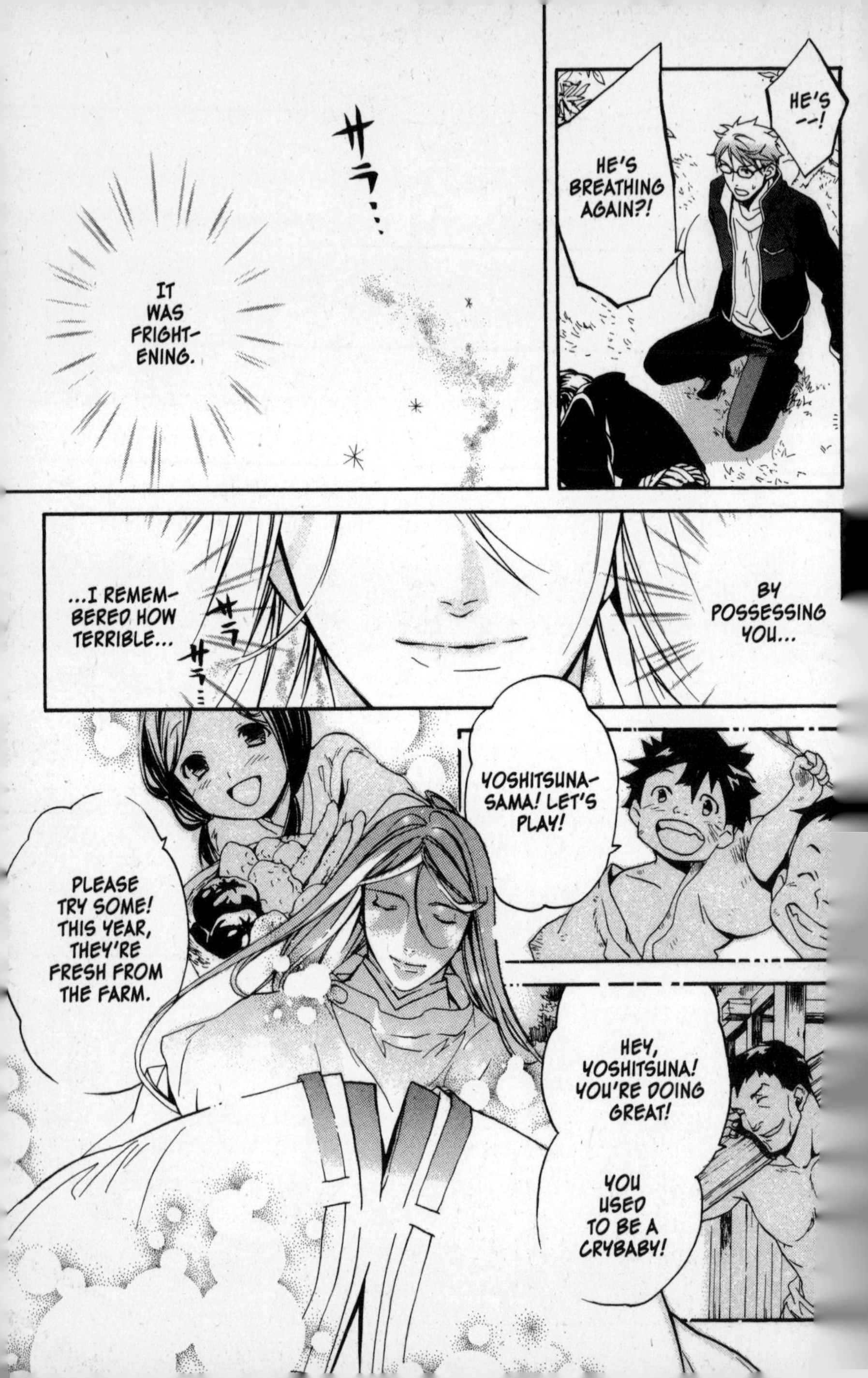
HE'S --!
HE'S BREATHING AGAIN?!
サラ…
IT WAS FRIGHT-ENING.
BY POSSESSING YOU...
...I REMEMBERED HOW TERRIBLE...
サラ
サラ…
YOSHITSUNA-SAMA! LET'S PLAY!
HEY, YOSHITSUNA! YOU'RE DOING GREAT!
YOU USED TO BE A CRYBABY!
PLEASE TRY SOME! THIS YEAR, THEY'RE FRESH FROM THE FARM.

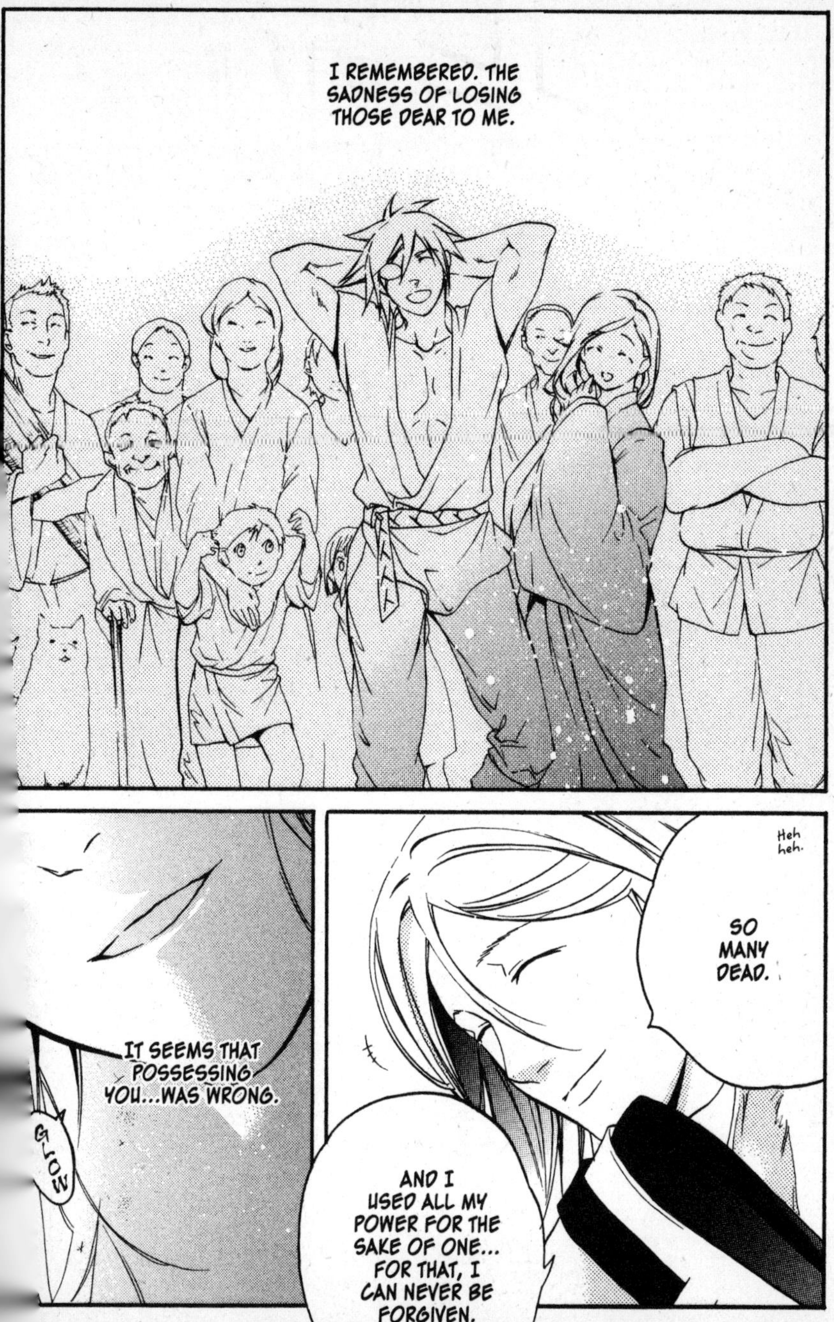
I REMEMBERED. THE SADNESS OF LOSING THOSE DEAR TO ME.
Heh heh.
SO MANY DEAD.
AND I USED ALL MY POWER FOR THE SAKE OF ONE... FOR THAT, I CAN NEVER BE FORGIVEN.
IT SEEMS THAT POSSESSING YOU...WAS WRONG.
GLOW

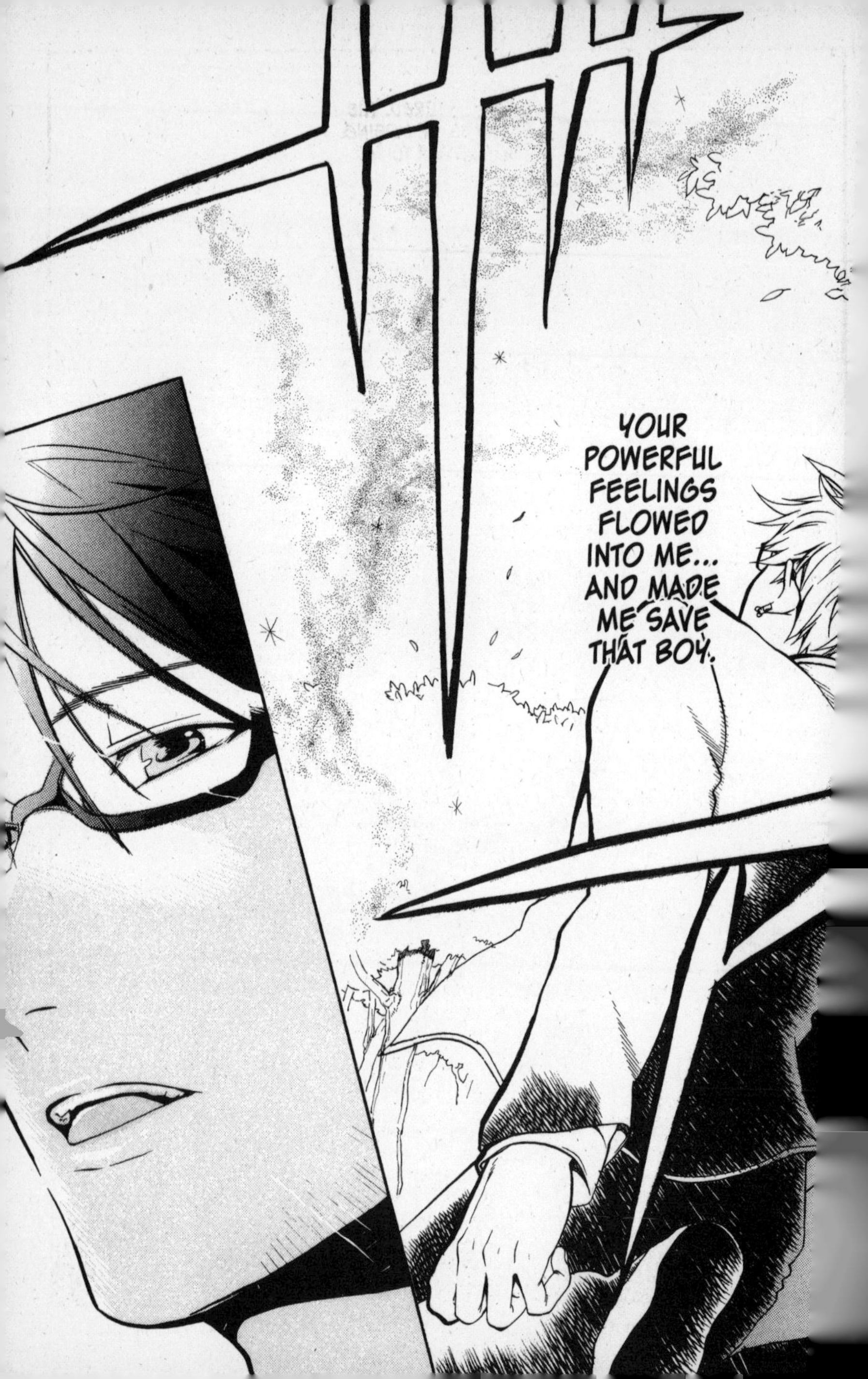
YOUR POWERFUL FEELINGS FLOWED INTO ME... AND MADE ME SAVE THAT BOY.

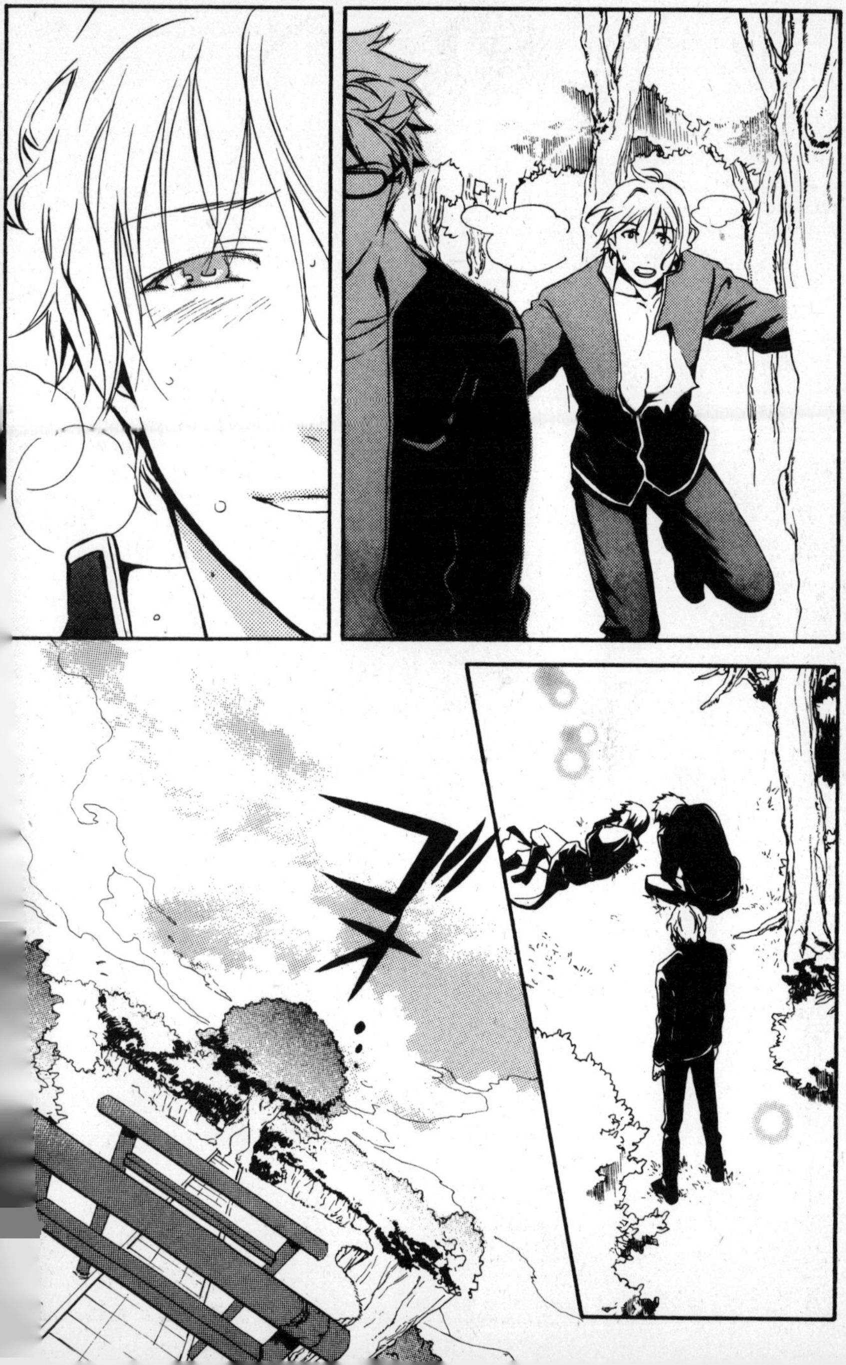

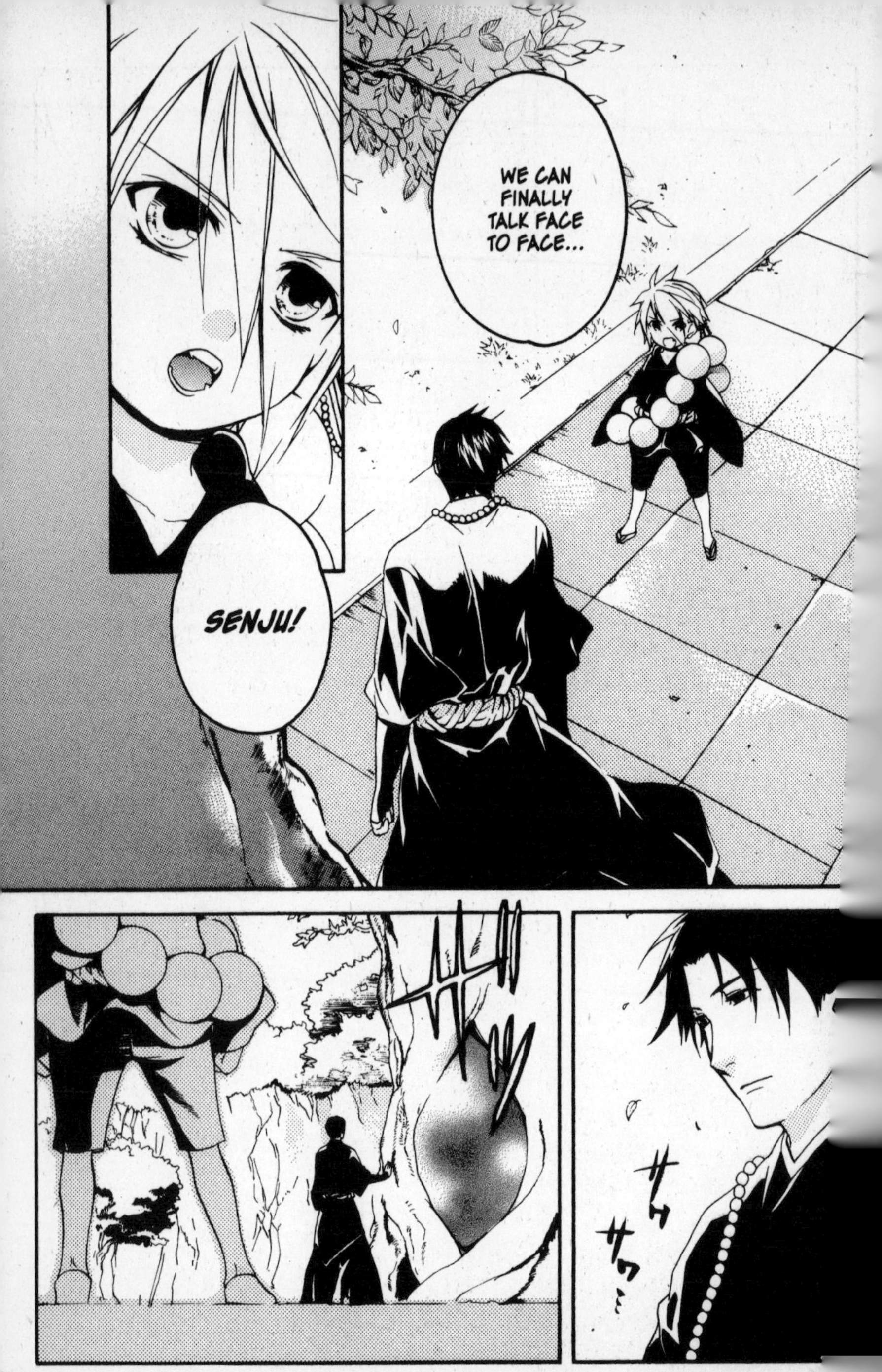
WE CAN FINALLY TALK FACE TO FACE...
SENJU!
サワ サワ

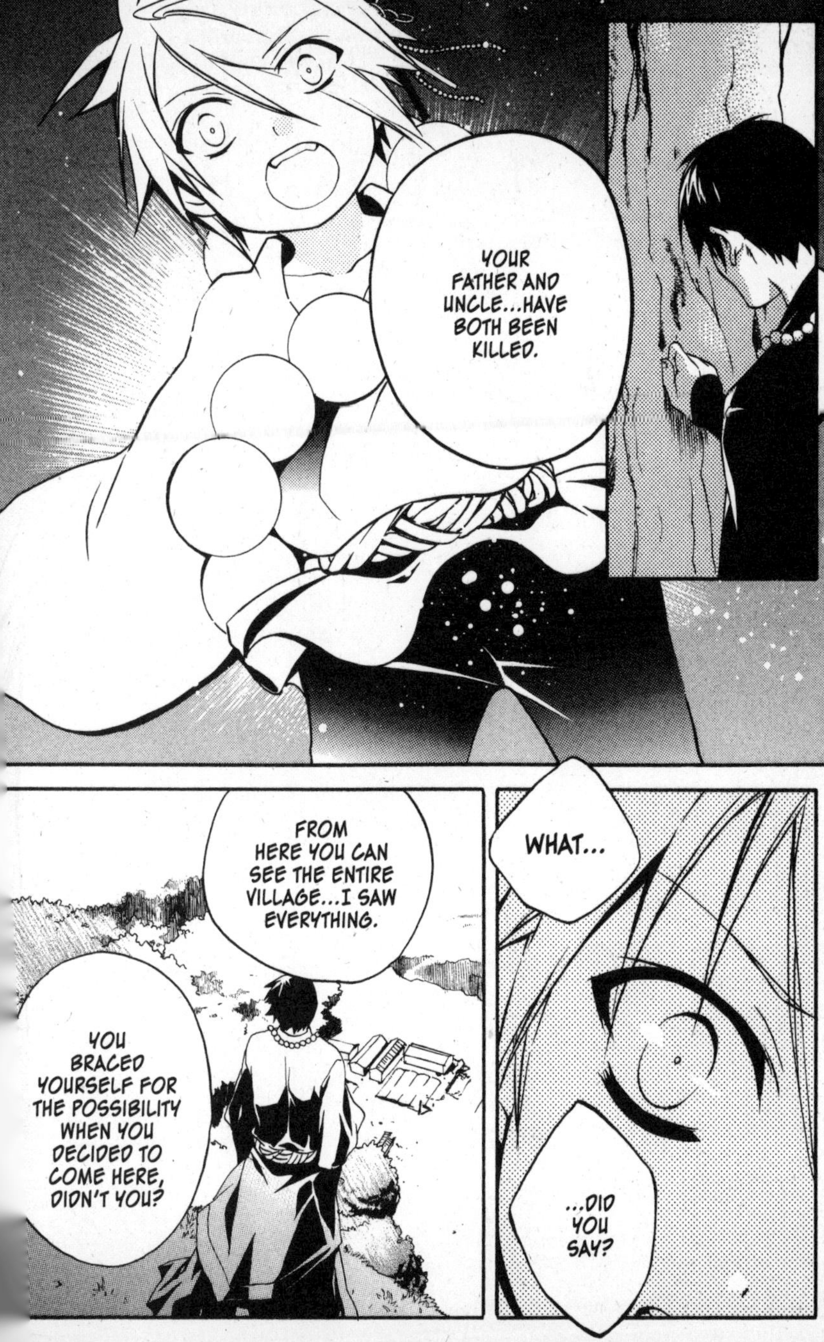
YOUR FATHER AND UNCLE...HAVE BOTH BEEN KILLED.
WHAT...
...DID YOU SAY?
FROM HERE YOU CAN SEE THE ENTIRE VILLAGE...I SAW EVERYTHING.
YOU BRACED YOURSELF FOR THE POSSIBILITY WHEN YOU DECIDED TO COME HERE, DIDN'T YOU?

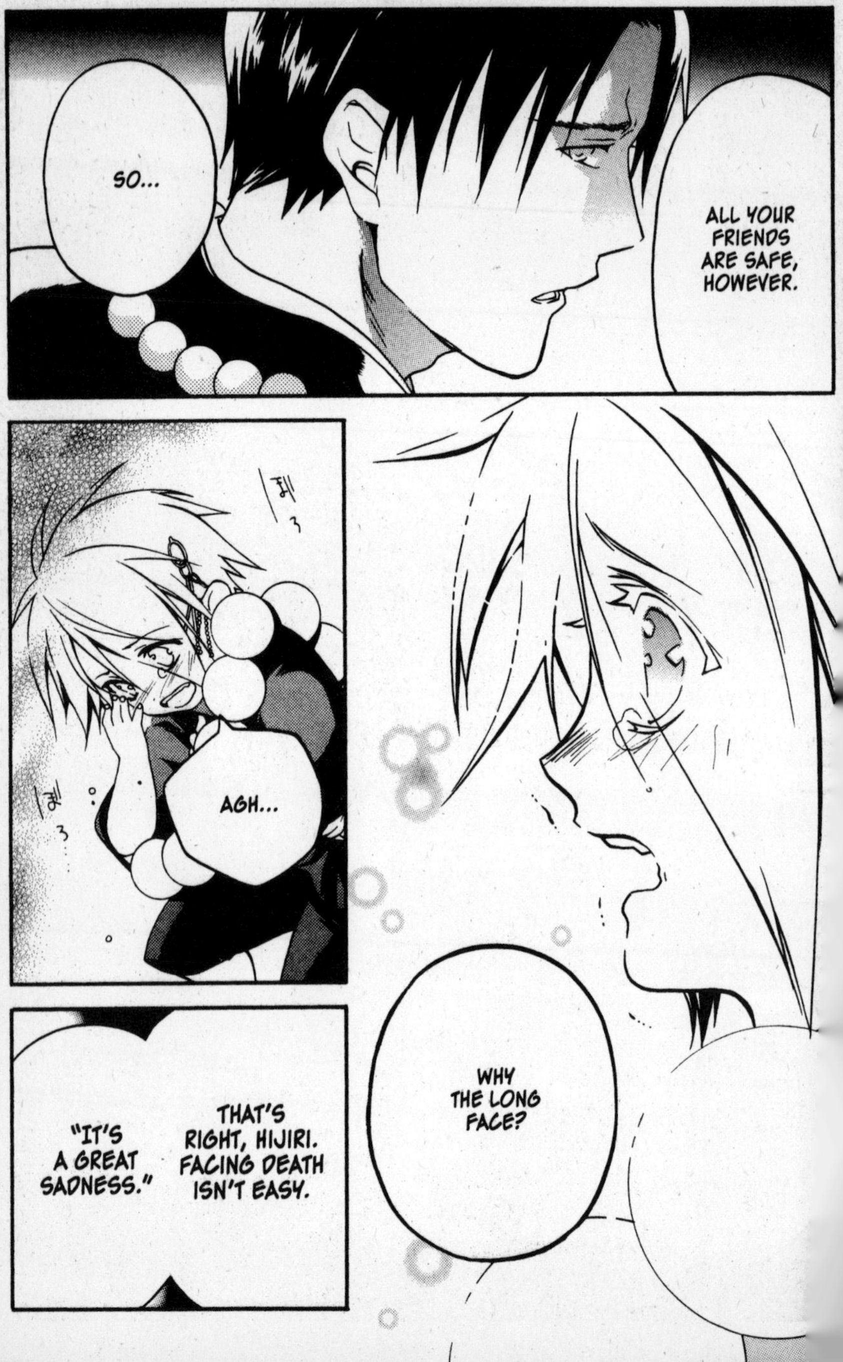
ALL YOUR FRIENDS ARE SAFE, HOWEVER.
SO...
WHY THE LONG FACE?
AGH...
THAT'S RIGHT, HIJIRI. FACING DEATH ISN'T EASY.
"IT'S A GREAT SADNESS."

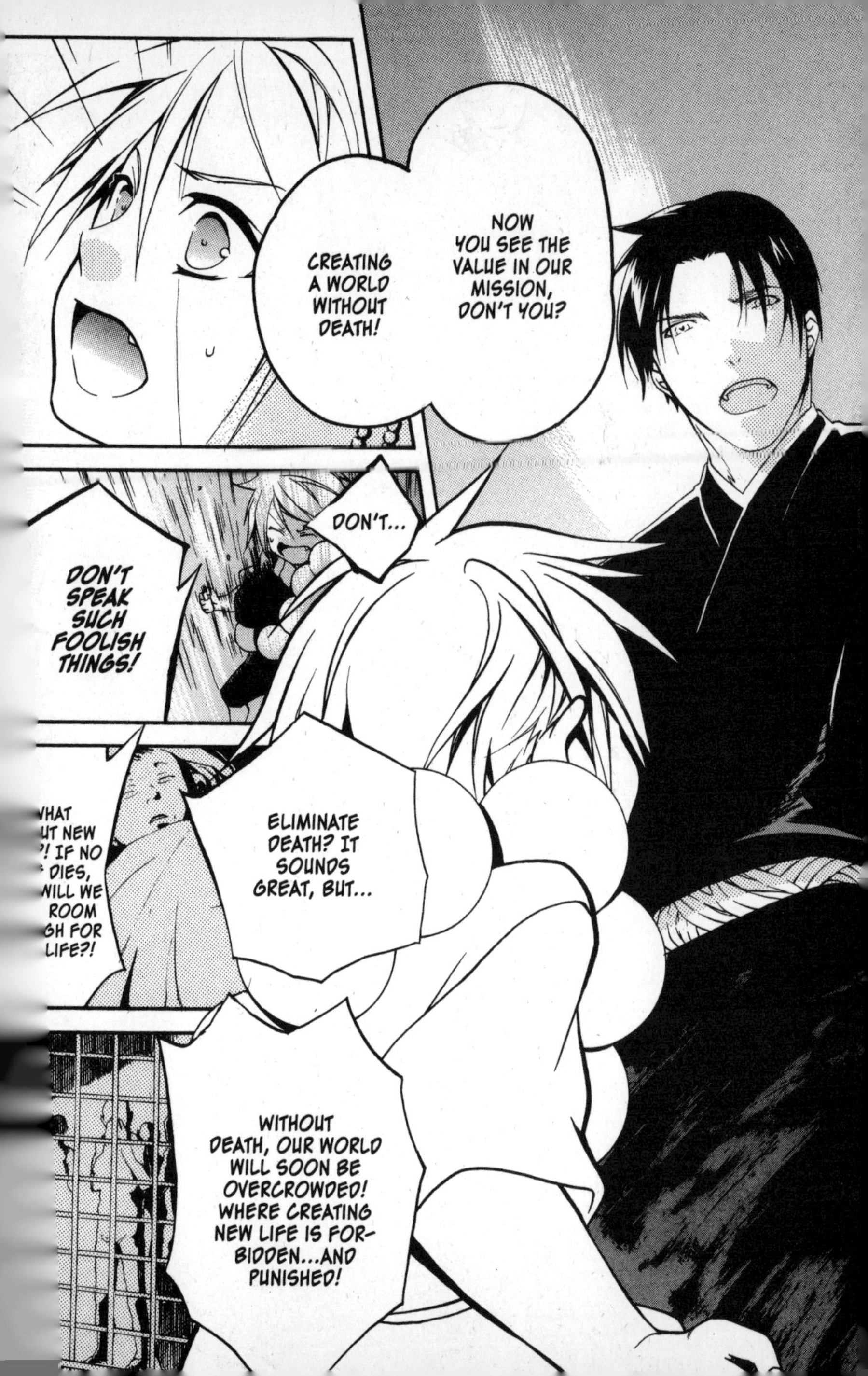
NOW YOU SEE THE VALUE IN OUR MISSION, DON'T YOU?
CREATING A WORLD WITHOUT DEATH!
DON'T...
DON'T SPEAK SUCH FOOLISH THINGS!
ELIMINATE DEATH? IT SOUNDS GREAT, BUT...
WHAT NEW IF NO DIES, WILL WE ROOM FOR LIFE?!
WITHOUT DEATH, OUR WORLD WILL SOON BE OVERCROWDED! WHERE CREATING NEW LIFE IS FOR-BIDDEN...AND PUNISHED!

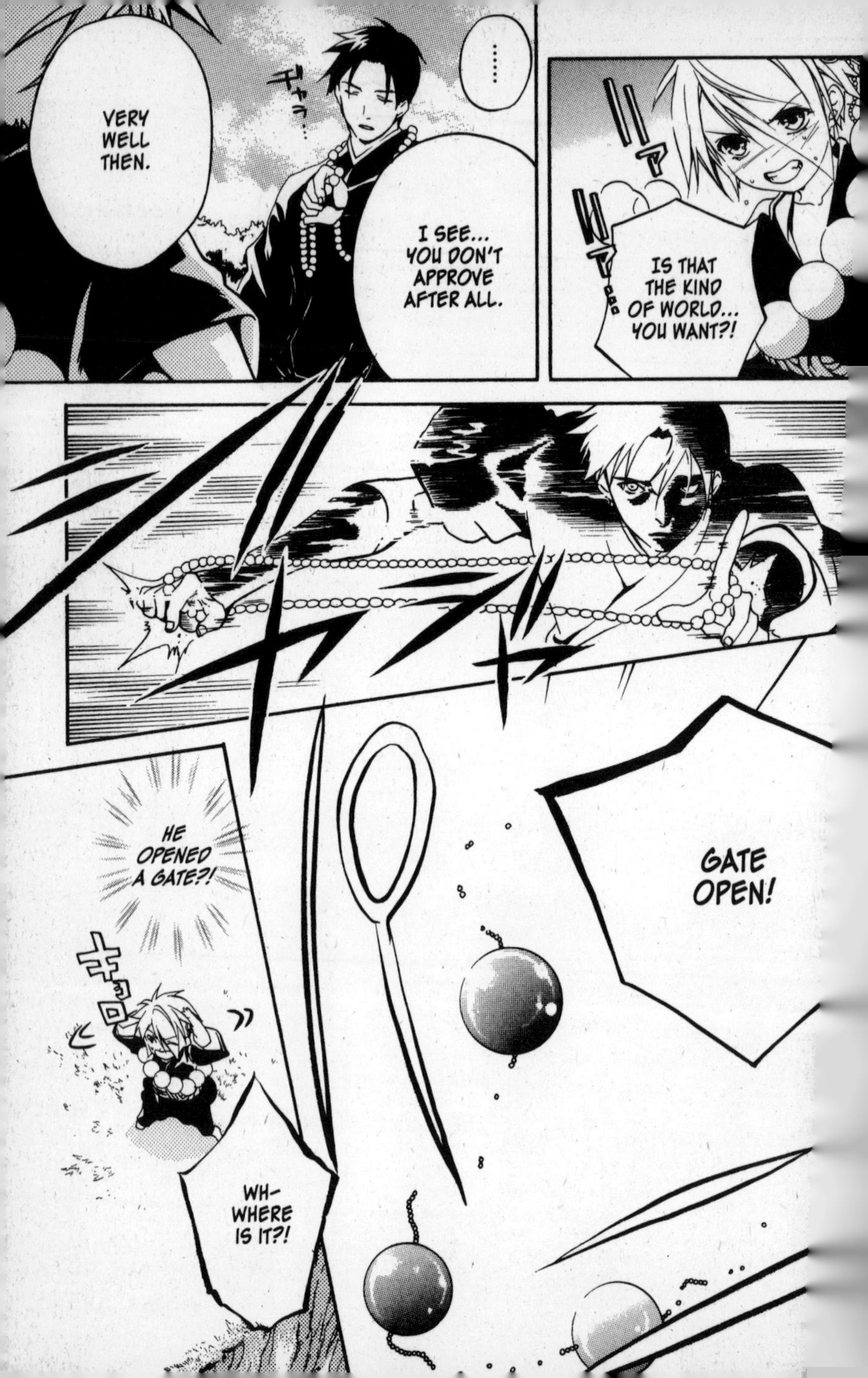
ハァ ハァ
IS THAT THE KIND OF WORLD... YOU WANT?!
......
ジャラ…
I SEE... YOU DON'T APPROVE AFTER ALL.
VERY WELL THEN.
GATE OPEN!
HE OPENED A GATE?!
キョロ
WH- WHERE IS IT?!

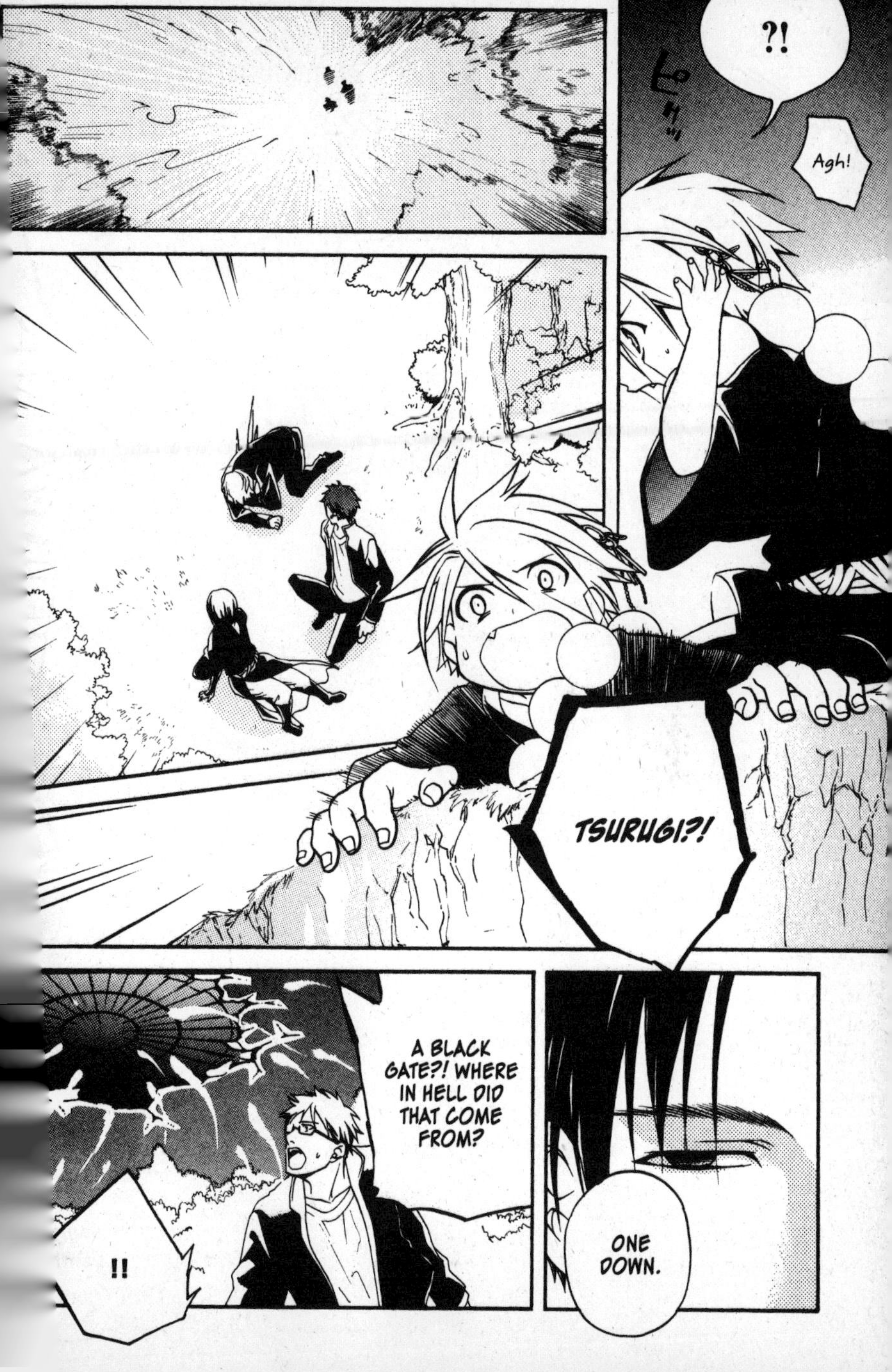
?!
Agh!
TSURUGI?!
ONE DOWN.
A BLACK GATE?! WHERE IN HELL DID THAT COME FROM?
!!

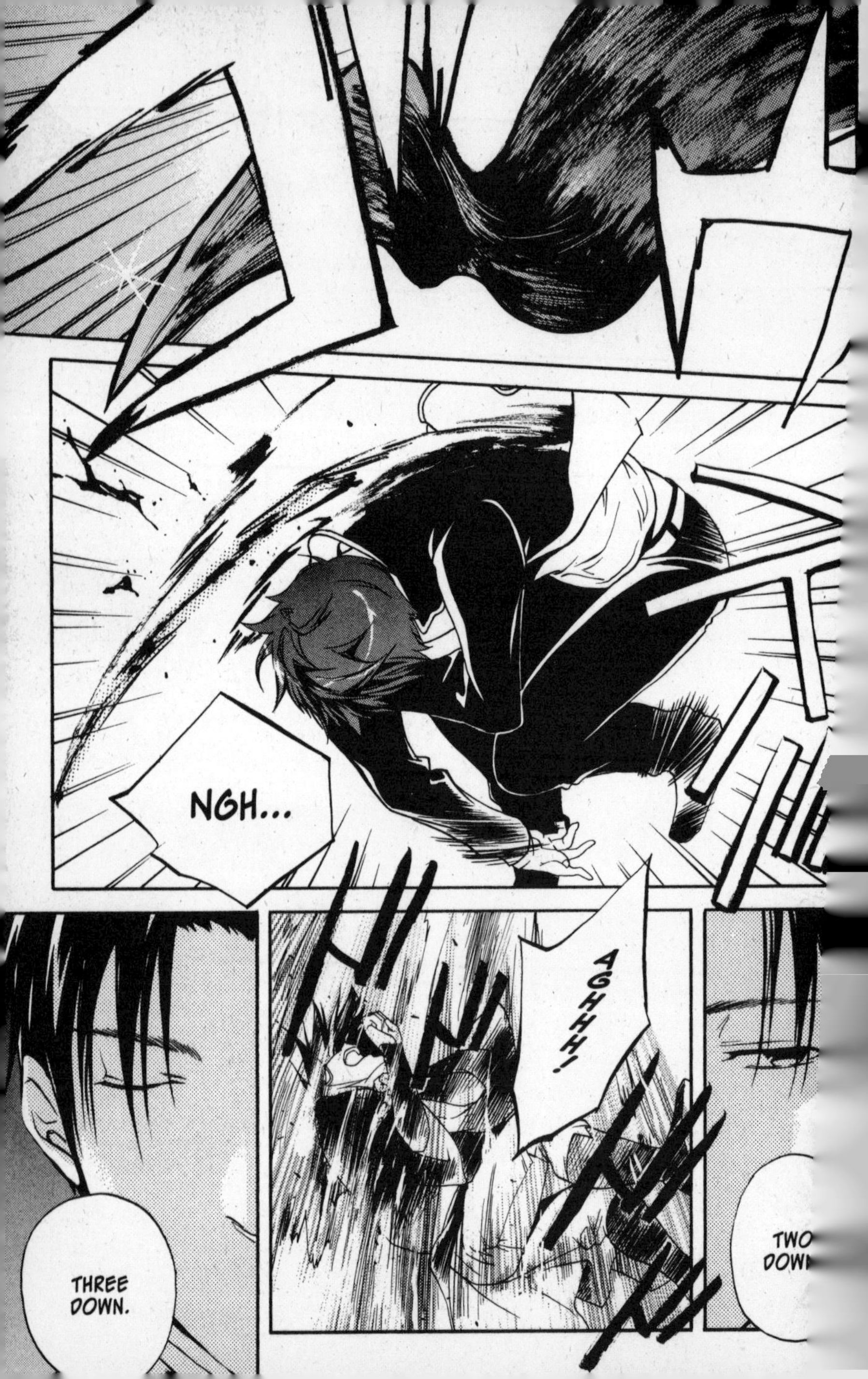
NGH...
TWO DOWN
AGHHH!
THREE DOWN.

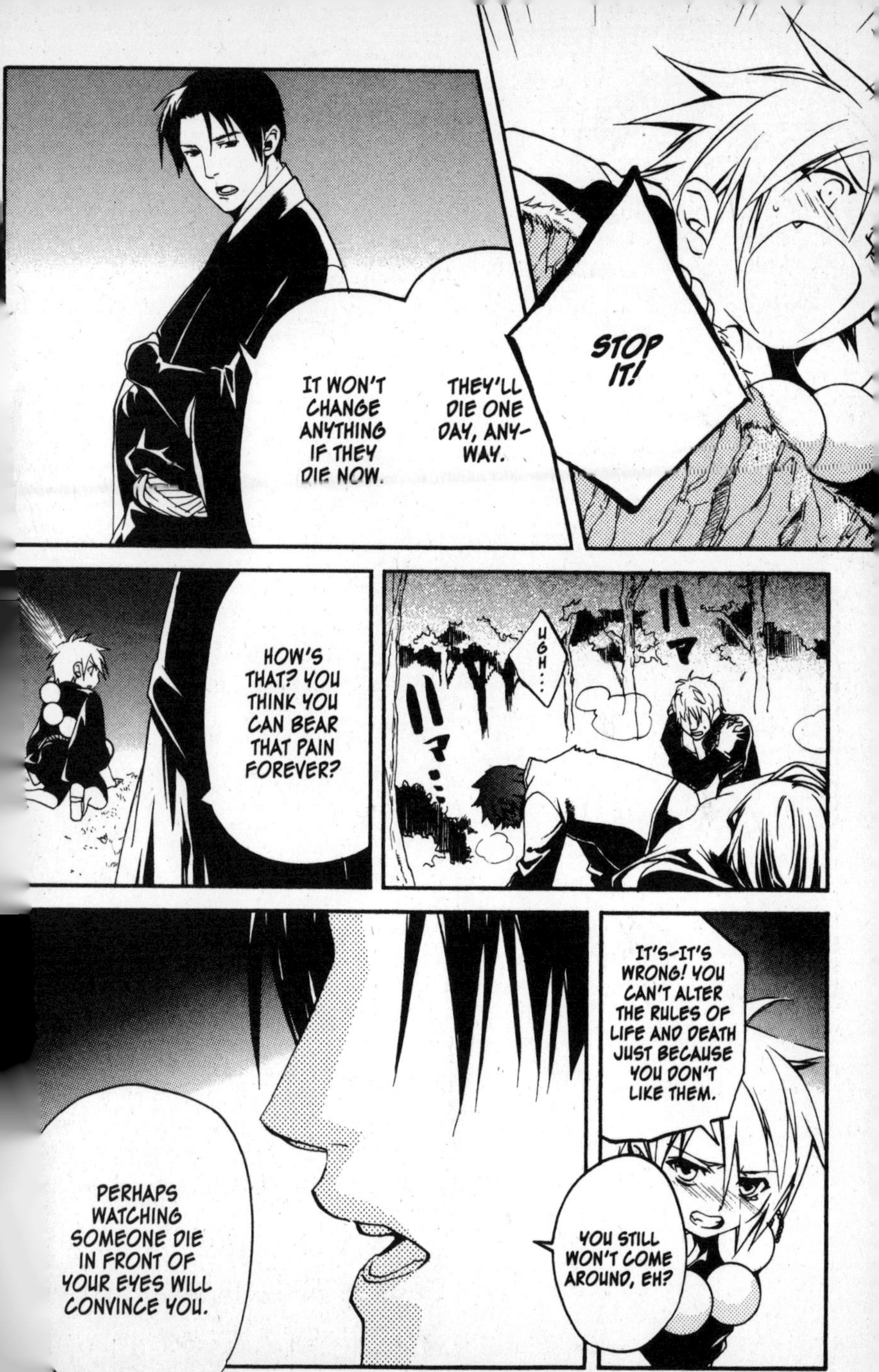
STOP IT!
THEY'LL DIE ONE DAY, ANYWAY.
IT WON'T CHANGE ANYTHING IF THEY DIE NOW.
UGH...
HOW'S THAT? YOU THINK YOU CAN BEAR THAT PAIN FOREVER?
IT'S-IT'S WRONG! YOU CAN'T ALTER THE RULES OF LIFE AND DEATH JUST BECAUSE YOU DON'T LIKE THEM.
YOU STILL WON'T COME AROUND, EH?
PERHAPS WATCHING SOMEONE DIE IN FRONT OF YOUR EYES WILL CONVINCE YOU.

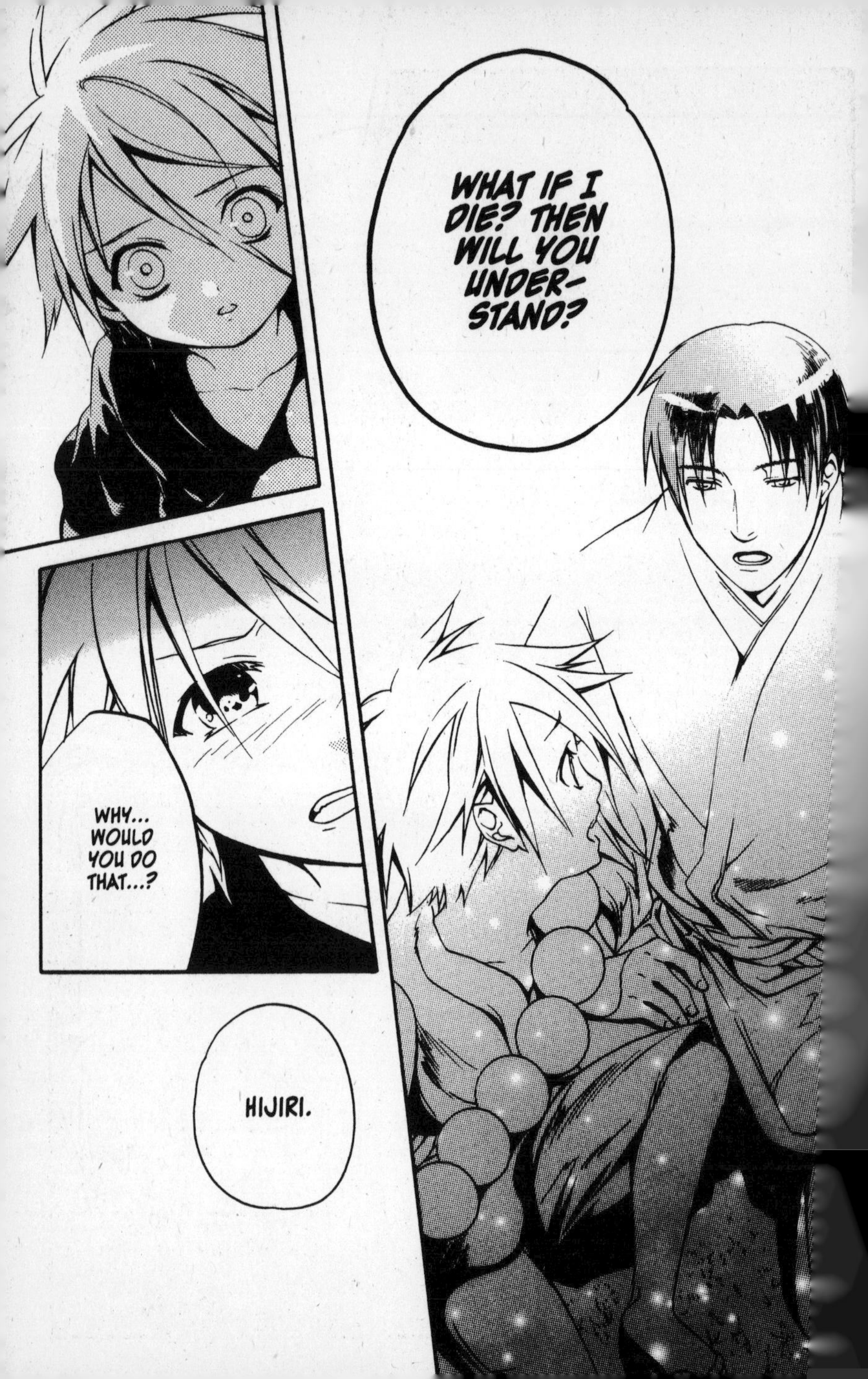
WHAT IF I DIE? THEN WILL YOU UNDER-STAND?
WHY... WOULD YOU DO THAT...?
HIJIRI.

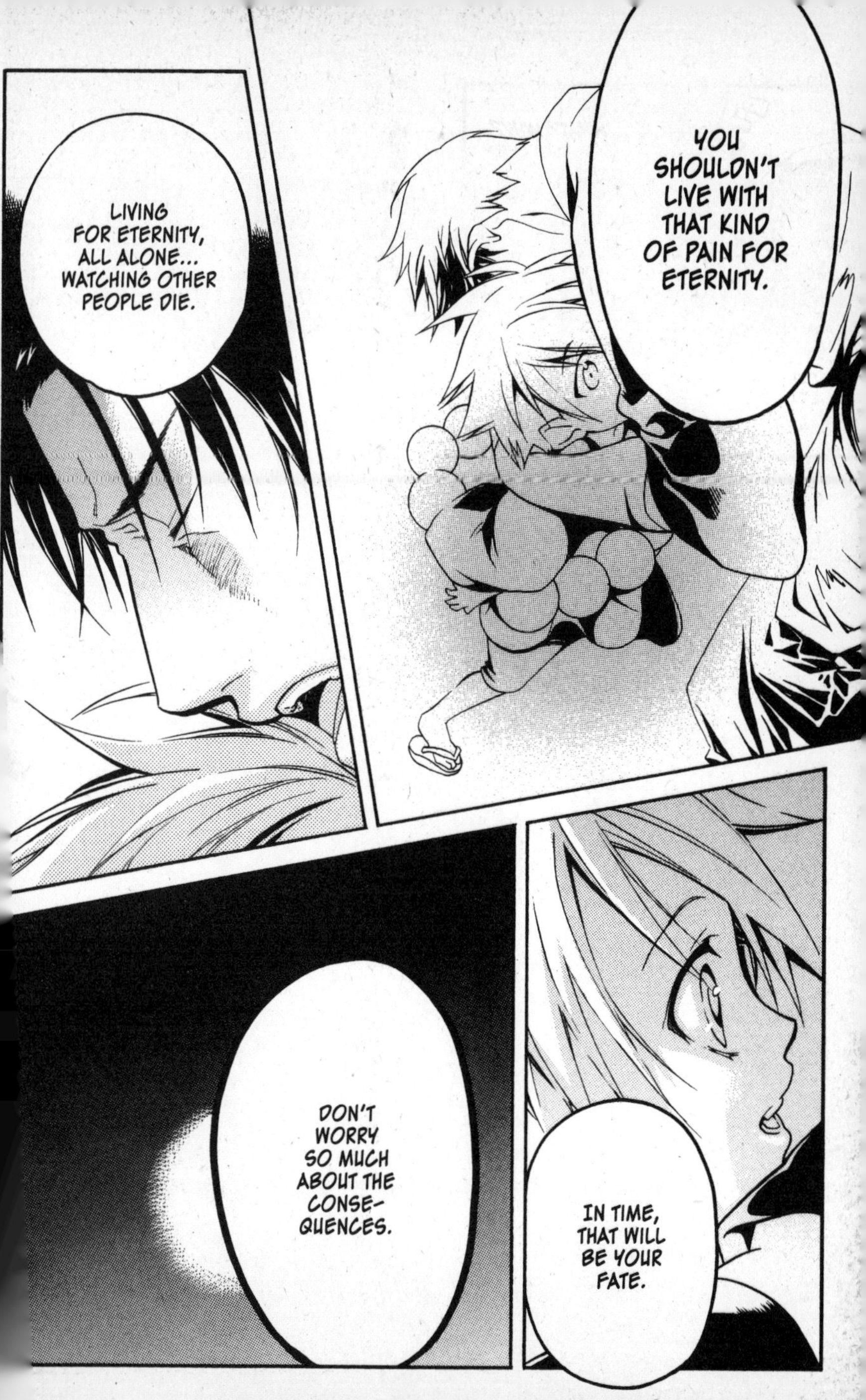
YOU SHOULDN'T LIVE WITH THAT KIND OF PAIN FOR ETERNITY.
LIVING FOR ETERNITY, ALL ALONE... WATCHING OTHER PEOPLE DIE.
IN TIME, THAT WILL BE YOUR FATE.
DON'T WORRY SO MUCH ABOUT THE CONSE-QUENCES.

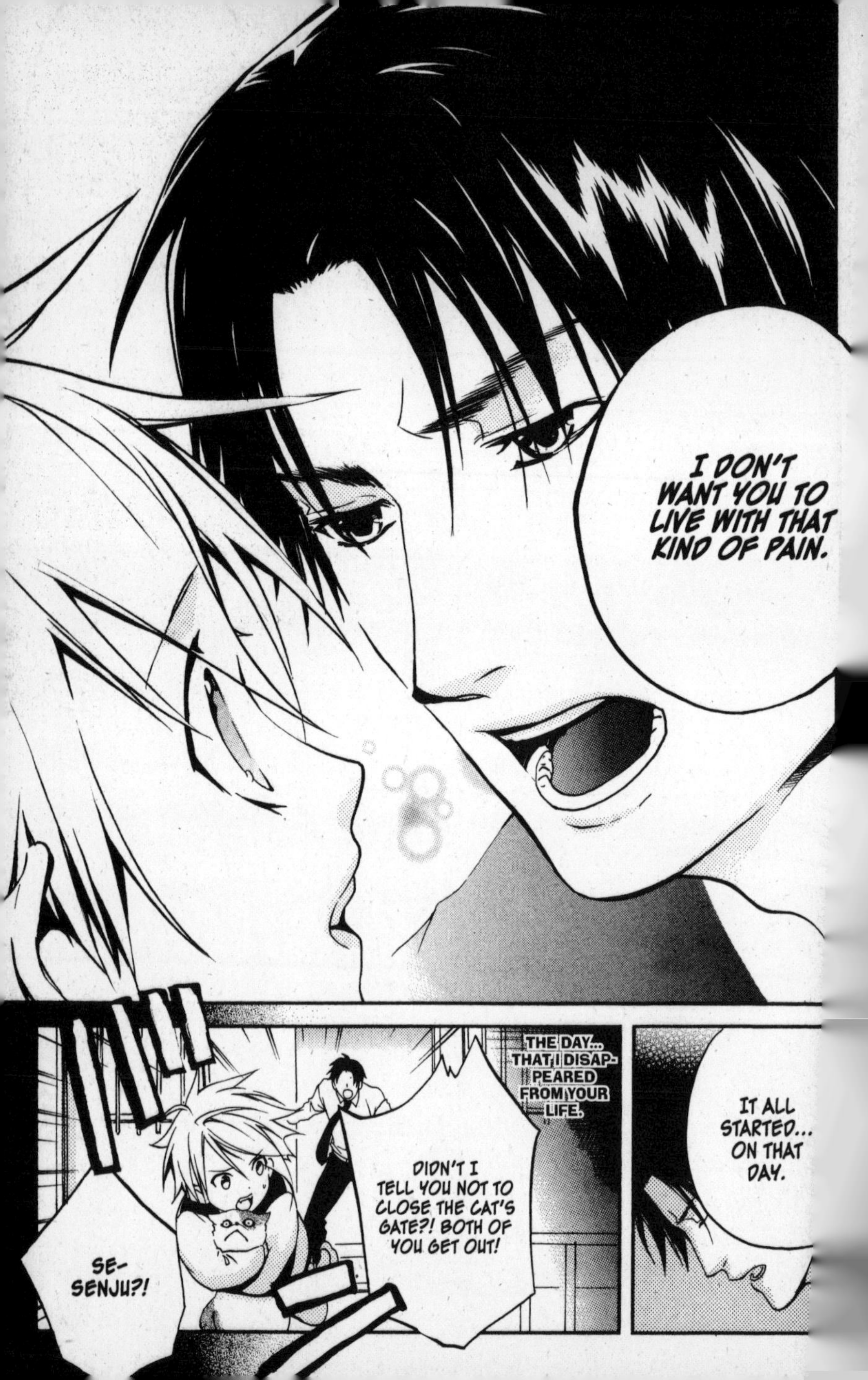
I DON'T WANT YOU TO LIVE WITH THAT KIND OF PAIN.
IT ALL STARTED... ON THAT DAY.
THE DAY... THAT I DISAPPEARED FROM YOUR LIFE.
DIDN'T I TELL YOU NOT TO CLOSE THE CAT'S GATE?! BOTH OF YOU GET OUT!
SE-SENJU?!

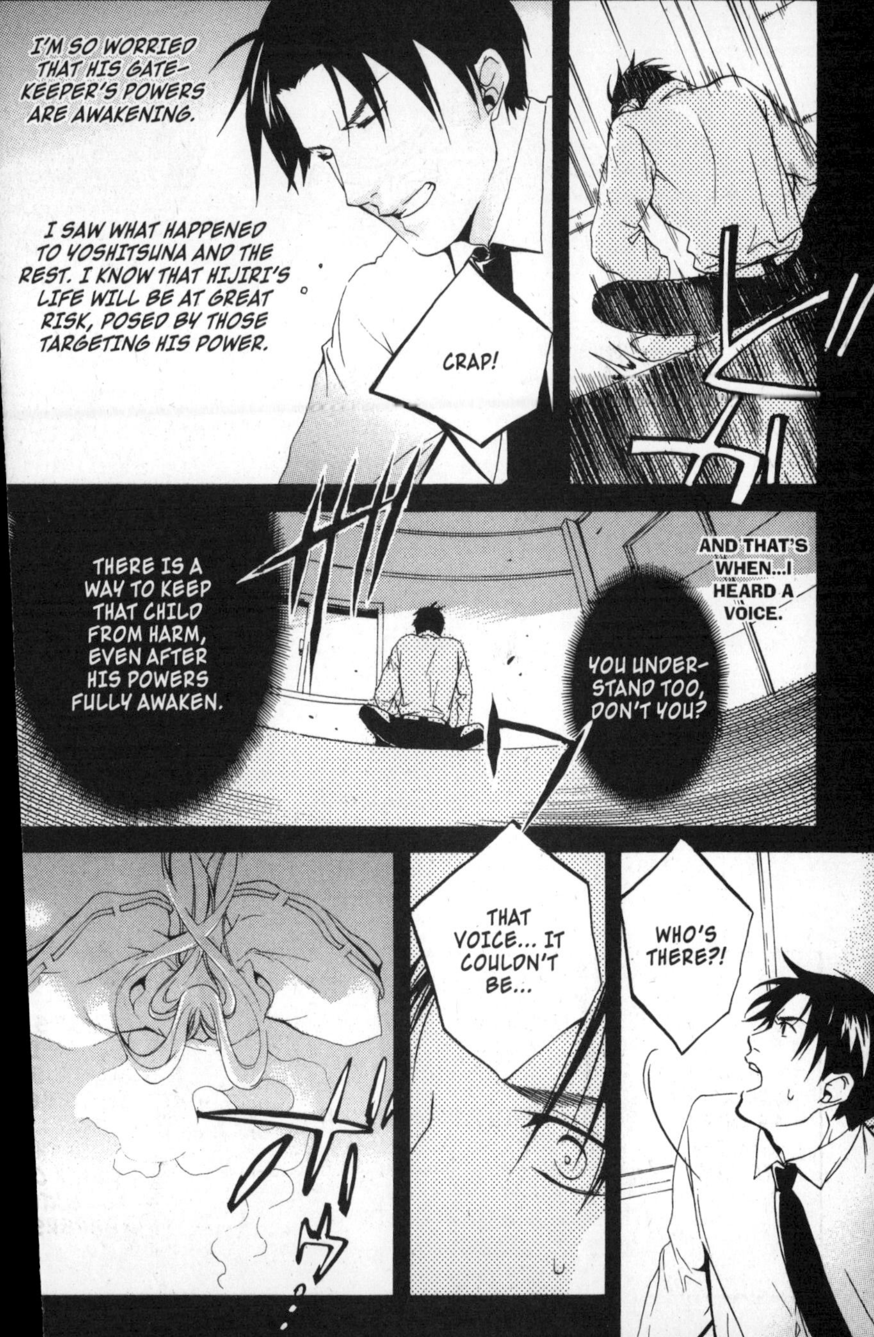
I'M SO WORRIED THAT HIS GATE-KEEPER'S POWERS ARE AWAKENING.
I SAW WHAT HAPPENED TO YOSHITSUNA AND THE REST. I KNOW THAT HIJIRI'S LIFE WILL BE AT GREAT RISK, POSED BY THOSE TARGETING HIS POWER.
CRAP!
AND THAT'S WHEN...I HEARD A VOICE.
YOU UNDER-STAND TOO, DON'T YOU?
THERE IS A WAY TO KEEP THAT CHILD FROM HARM, EVEN AFTER HIS POWERS FULLY AWAKEN.
WHO'S THERE?!
THAT VOICE... IT COULDN'T BE...

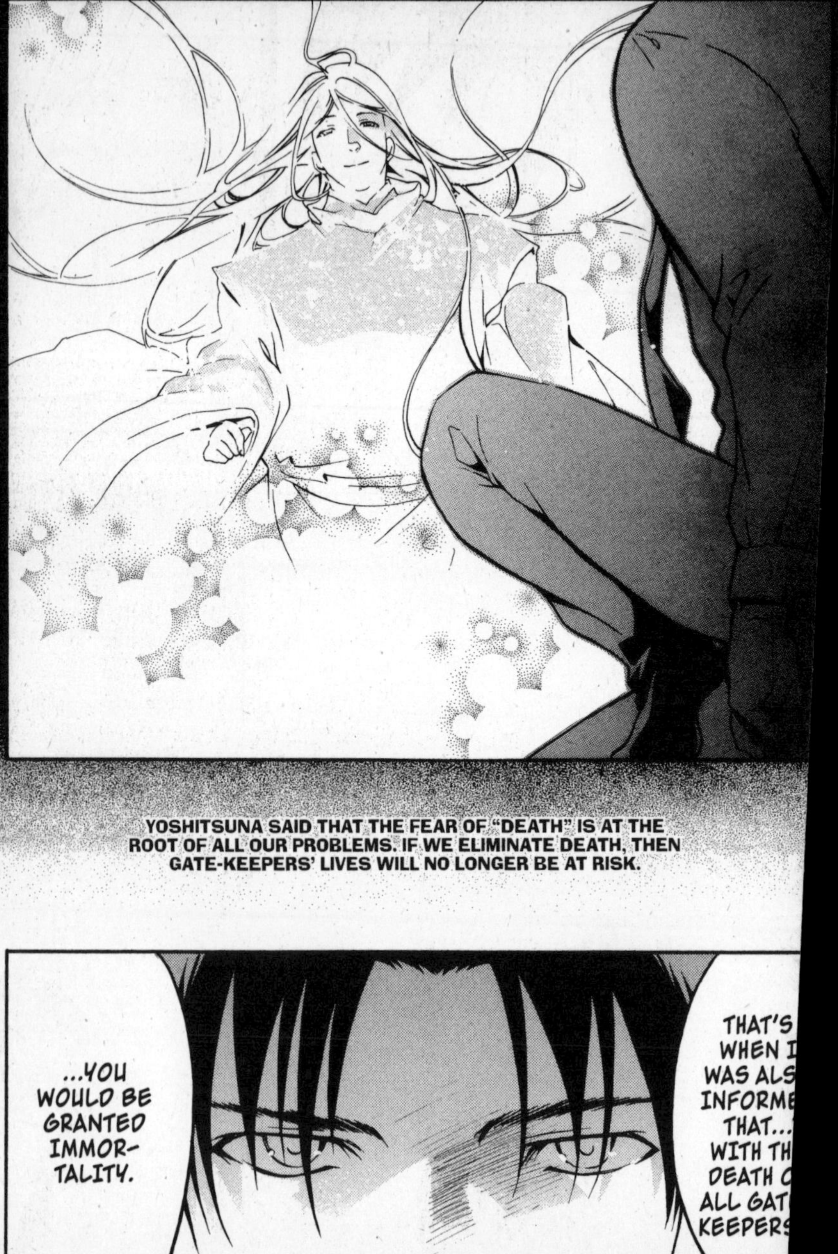
YOSHITSUNA SAID THAT THE FEAR OF "DEATH" IS AT THE ROOT OF ALL OUR PROBLEMS. IF WE ELIMINATE DEATH, THEN GATE-KEEPERS' LIVES WILL NO LONGER BE AT RISK.
THAT'S WHEN I WAS ALS INFORME THAT... WITH TH DEATH O ALL GAT KEEPERS
...YOU WOULD BE GRANTED IMMOR-TALITY.

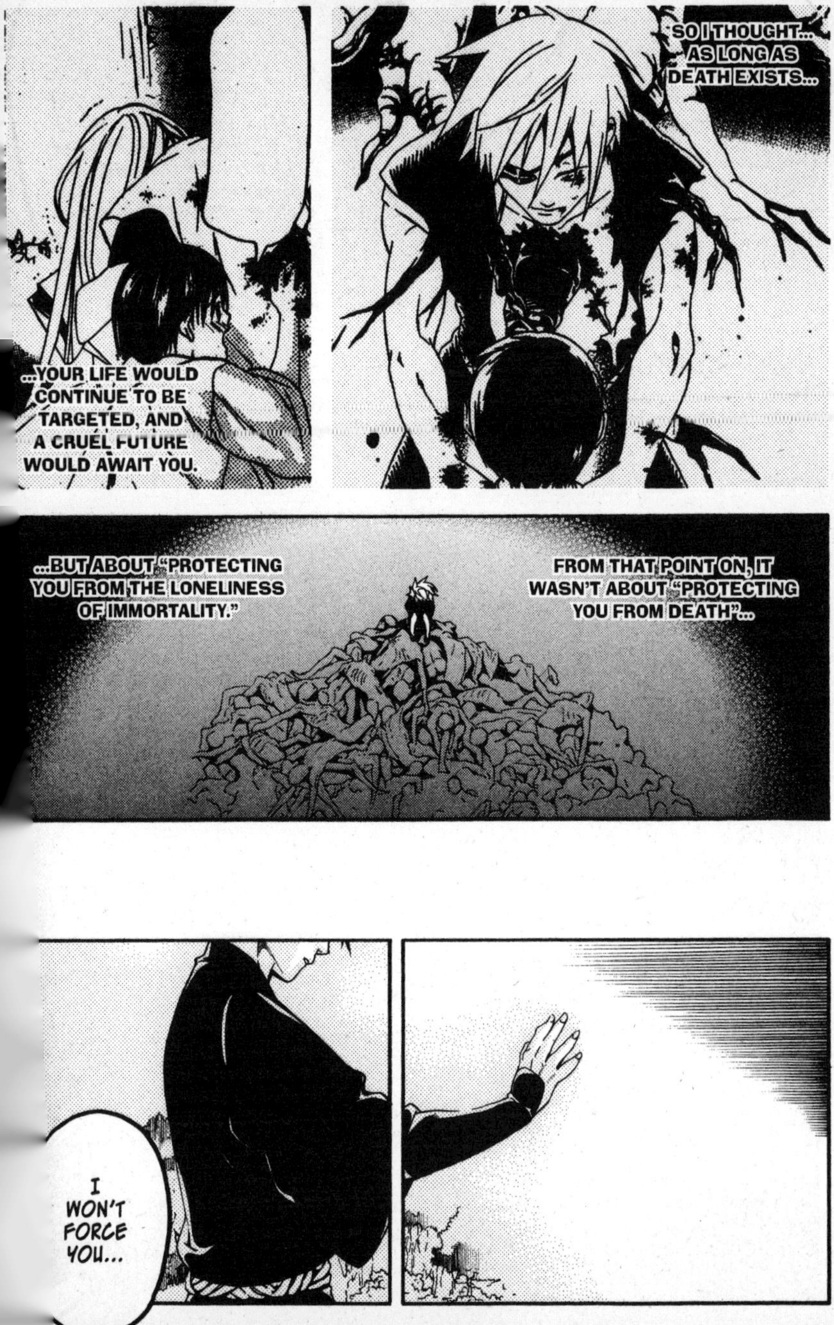
SO I THOUGHT... AS LONG AS DEATH EXISTS...
...YOUR LIFE WOULD CONTINUE TO BE TARGETED, AND A CRUEL FUTURE WOULD AWAIT YOU.
FROM THAT POINT ON, IT WASN'T ABOUT "PROTECTING YOU FROM DEATH"...
...BUT ABOUT "PROTECTING YOU FROM THE LONELINESS OF IMMORTALITY."
I WON'T FORCE YOU...

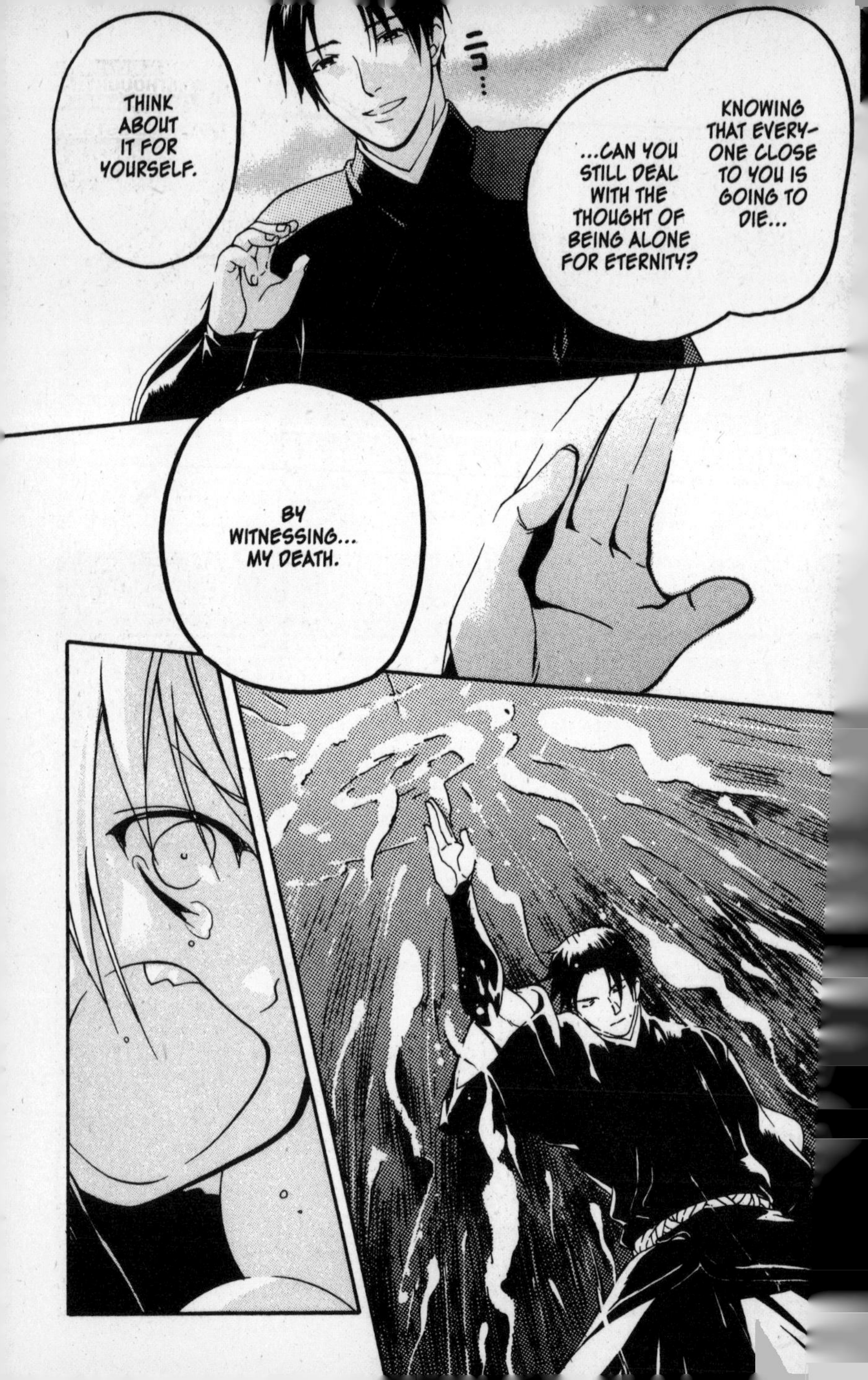
KNOWING THAT EVERY-ONE CLOSE TO YOU IS GOING TO DIE...
...CAN YOU STILL DEAL WITH THE THOUGHT OF BEING ALONE FOR ETERNITY?
THINK ABOUT IT FOR YOURSELF.
BY WITNESSING... MY DEATH.

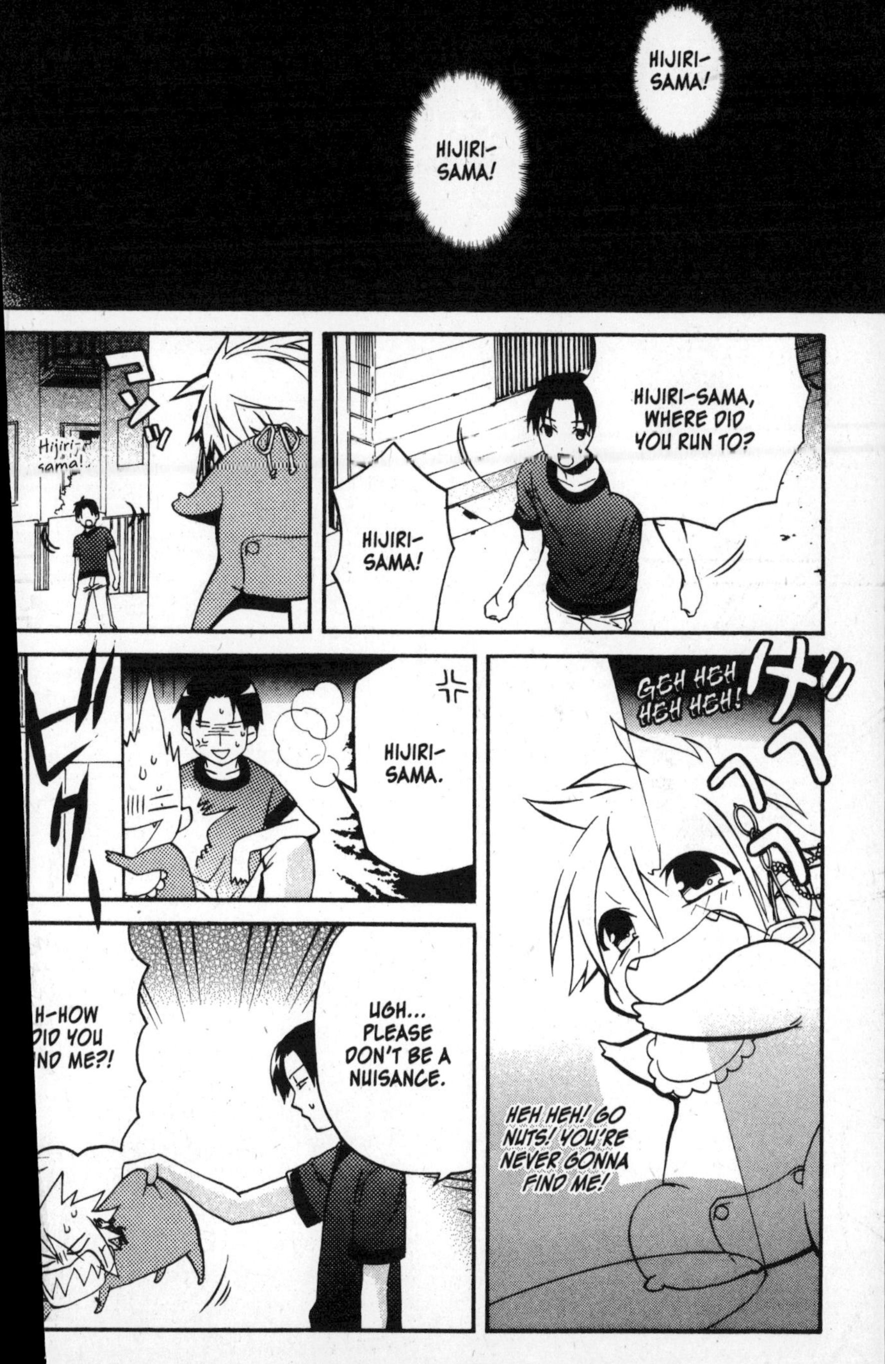
HIJIRI-SAMA!
HIJIRI-SAMA!
HIJIRI-SAMA, WHERE DID YOU RUN TO?
HIJIRI-SAMA!
Hijiri-sama!
GEH HEH HEH HEH!
HEH HEH! GO NUTS! YOU'RE NEVER GONNA FIND ME!
HIJIRI-SAMA.
UGH... PLEASE DON'T BE A NUISANCE.
H-HOW DID YOU IND ME?!

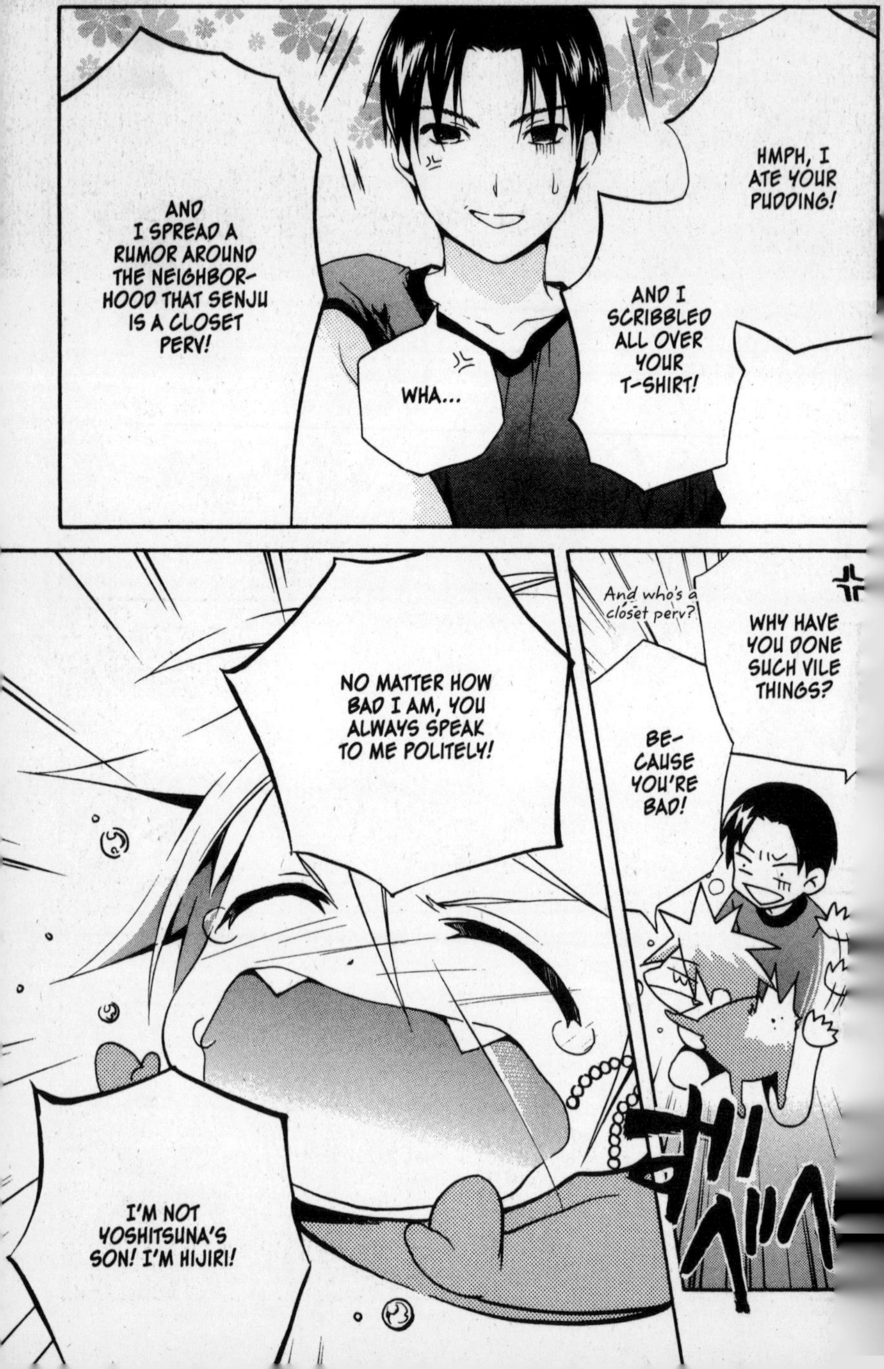
HMPH, I ATE YOUR PUDDING!
AND I SCRIBBLED ALL OVER YOUR T-SHIRT!
WHA...
AND I SPREAD A RUMOR AROUND THE NEIGHBOR-HOOD THAT SENJU IS A CLOSET PERV!
WHY HAVE YOU DONE SUCH VILE THINGS?
And who's a closet perv?
BE-CAUSE YOU'RE BAD!
NO MATTER HOW BAD I AM, YOU ALWAYS SPEAK TO ME POLITELY!
I'M NOT YOSHITSUNA'S SON! I'M HIJIRI!

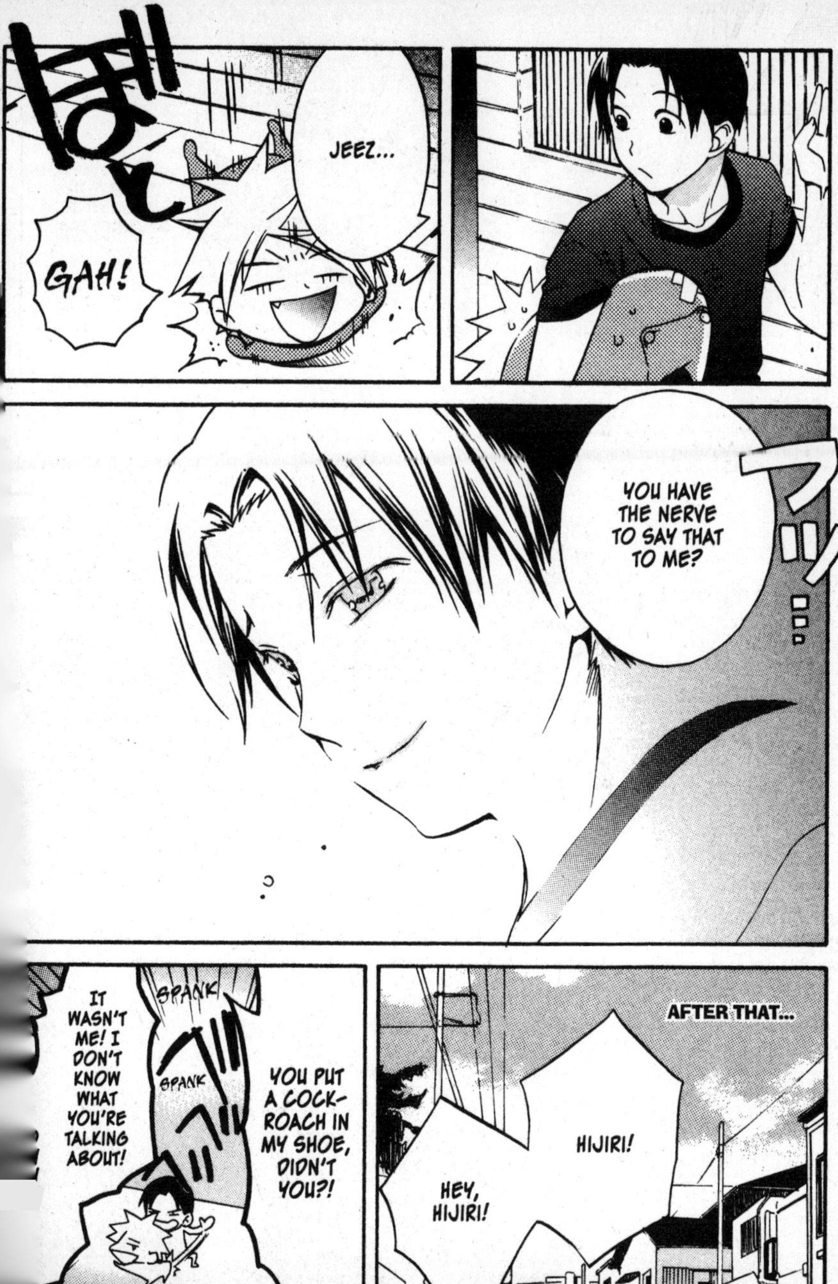
JEEZ...
GAH!
YOU HAVE THE NERVE TO SAY THAT TO ME?
AFTER THAT...
HIJIRI!
HEY, HIJIRI!
YOU PUT A COCK-ROACH IN MY SHOE, DIDN'T YOU?!
SPANK
SPANK
IT WASN'T ME! I DON'T KNOW WHAT YOU'RE TALKING ABOUT!

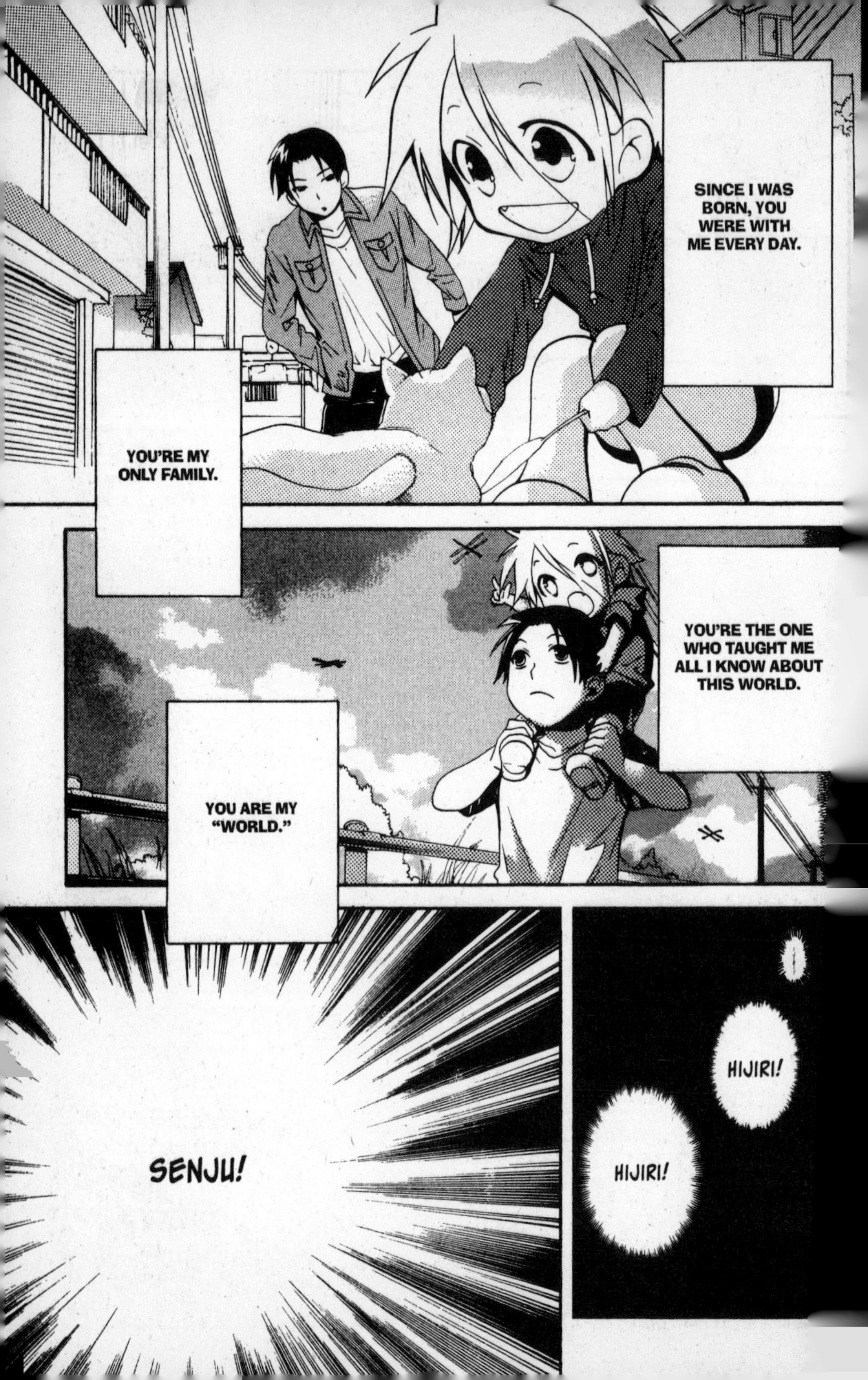
SINCE I WAS BORN, YOU WERE WITH ME EVERY DAY.
YOU'RE MY ONLY FAMILY.
YOU'RE THE ONE WHO TAUGHT ME ALL I KNOW ABOUT THIS WORLD.
YOU ARE MY "WORLD."
!
HIJIRI!
HIJIRI!
SENJU!

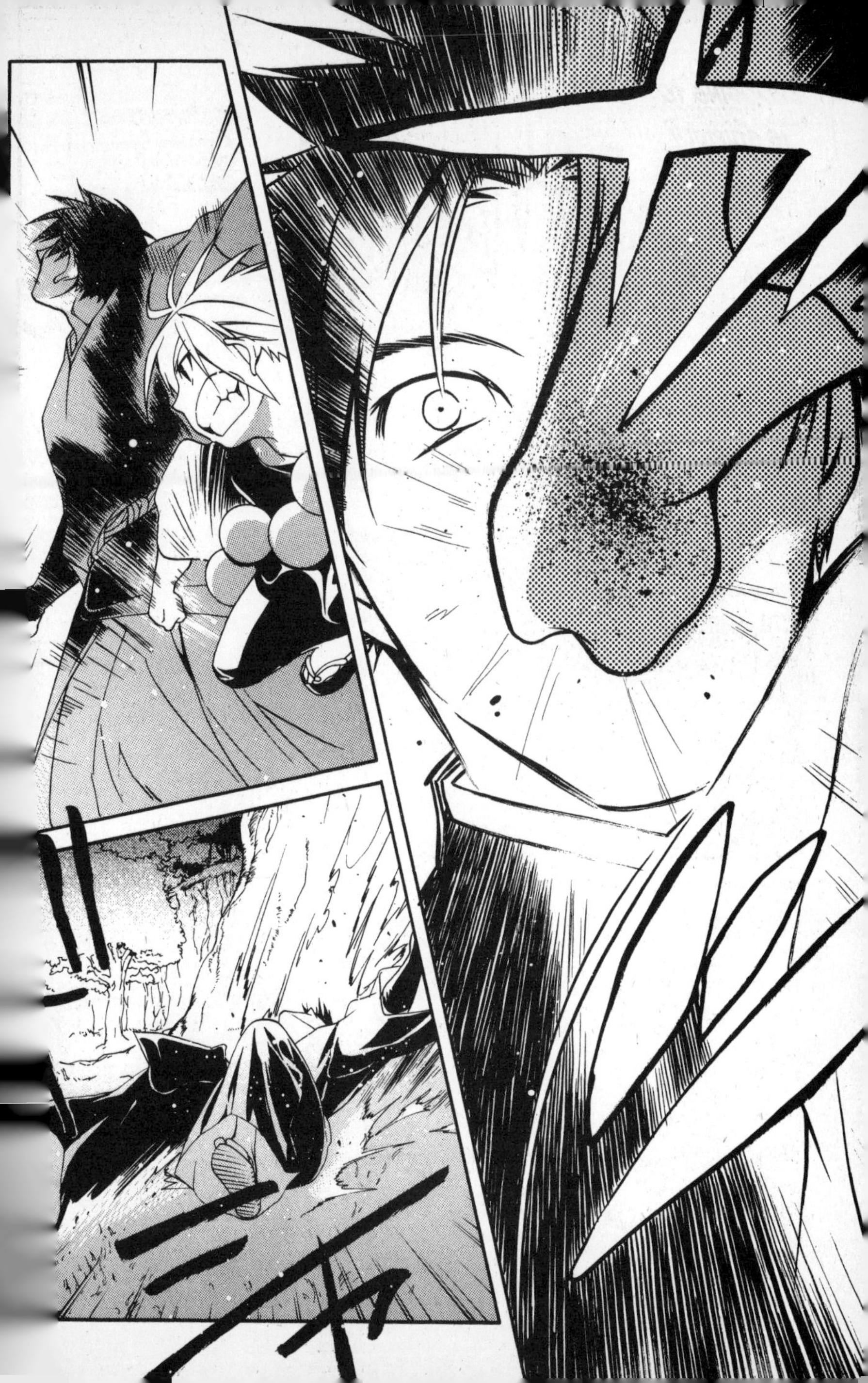

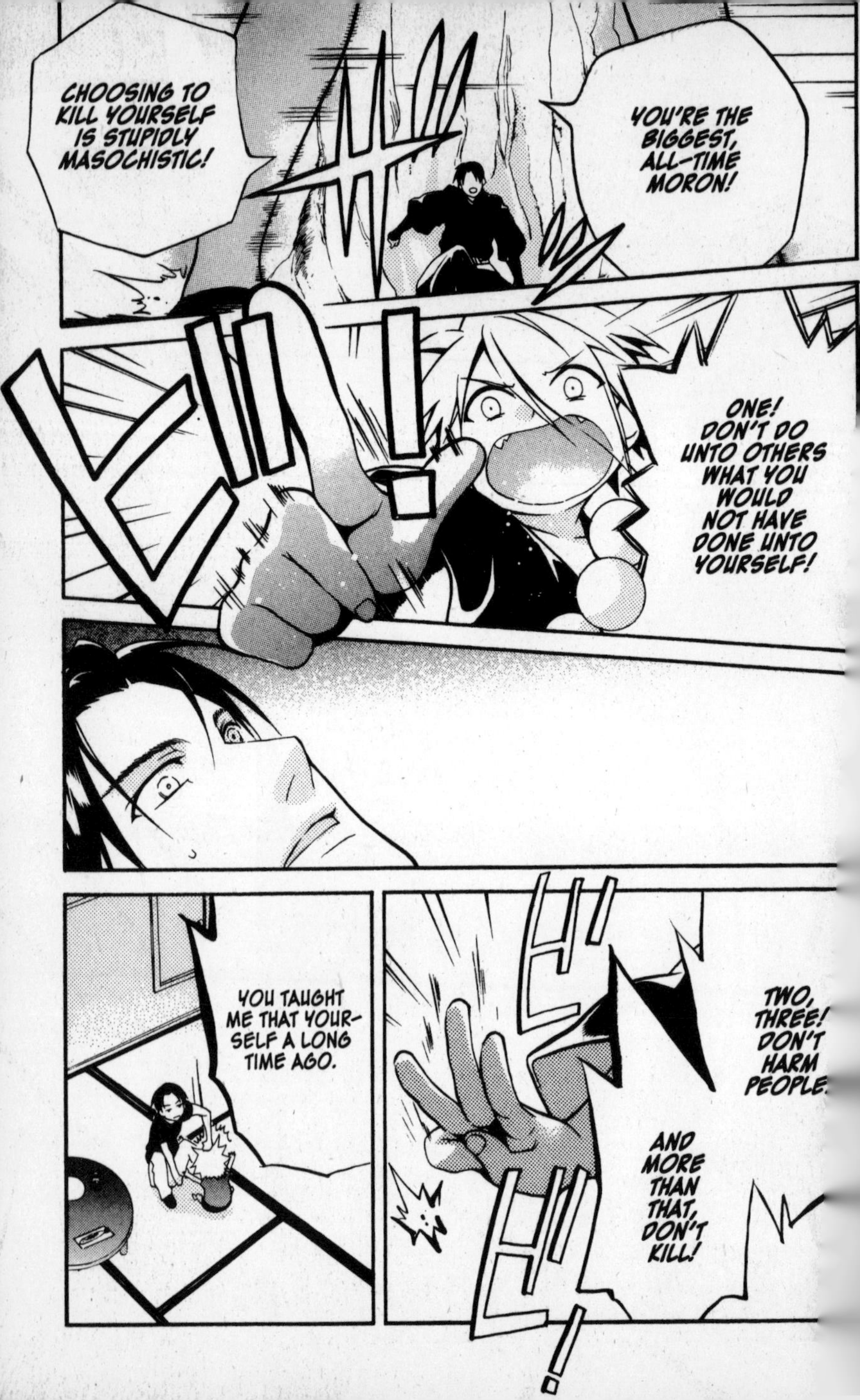
YOU'RE THE BIGGEST, ALL-TIME MORON!
CHOOSING TO KILL YOURSELF IS STUPIDLY MASOCHISTIC!
ONE! DON'T DO UNTO OTHERS WHAT YOU WOULD NOT HAVE DONE UNTO YOURSELF!
TWO, THREE! DON'T HARM PEOPLE.
AND MORE THAN THAT, DON'T KILL!
YOU TAUGHT ME THAT YOUR-SELF A LONG TIME AGO.

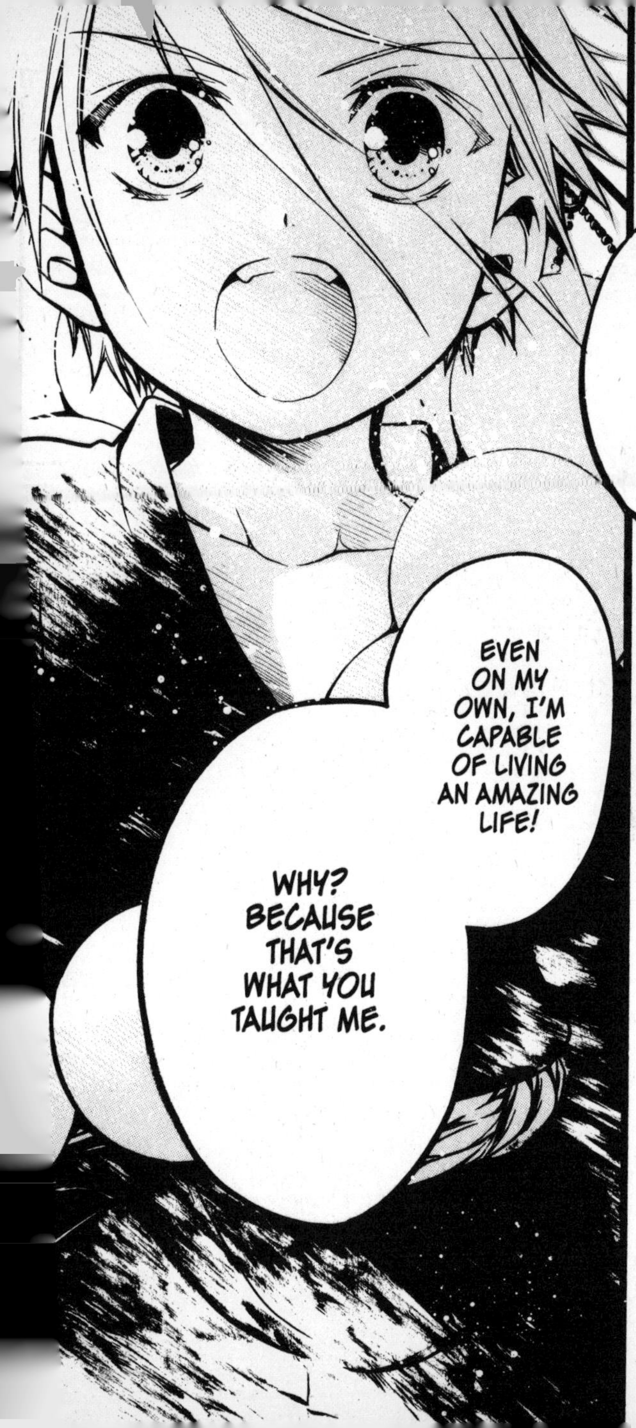
WHO DO YOU THINK RAISED ME?
EVEN ON MY OWN, I'M CAPABLE OF LIVING AN AMAZING LIFE!
WHY? BECAUSE THAT'S WHAT YOU TAUGHT ME.

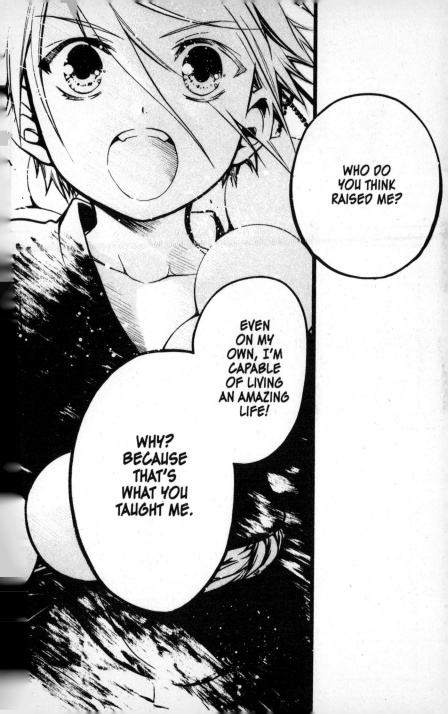

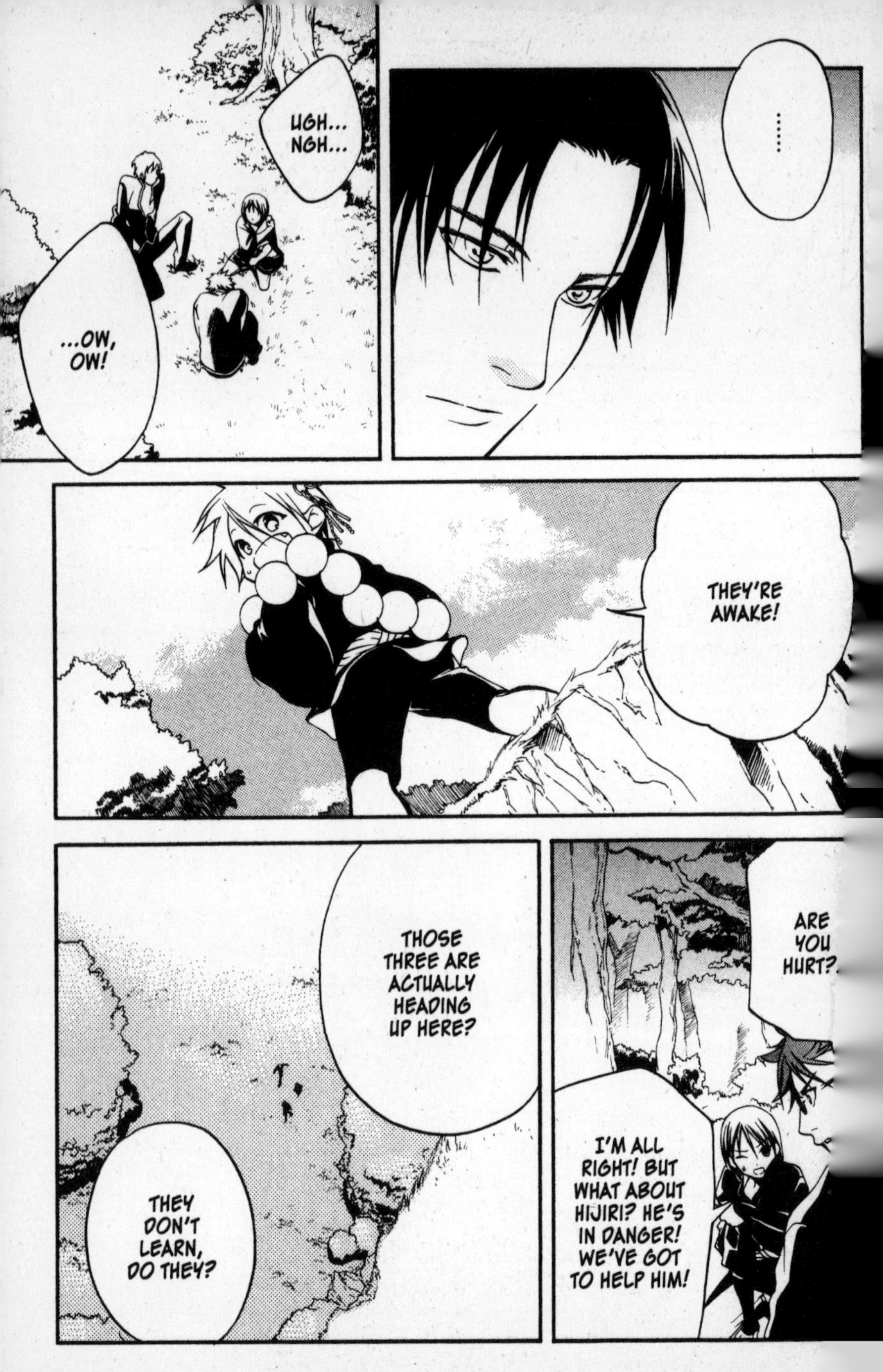
......
UGH... NGH...
...OW, OW!
THEY'RE AWAKE!
ARE YOU HURT?
I'M ALL RIGHT! BUT WHAT ABOUT HIJIRI? HE'S IN DANGER! WE'VE GOT TO HELP HIM!
THOSE THREE ARE ACTUALLY HEADING UP HERE?
THEY DON'T LEARN, DO THEY?

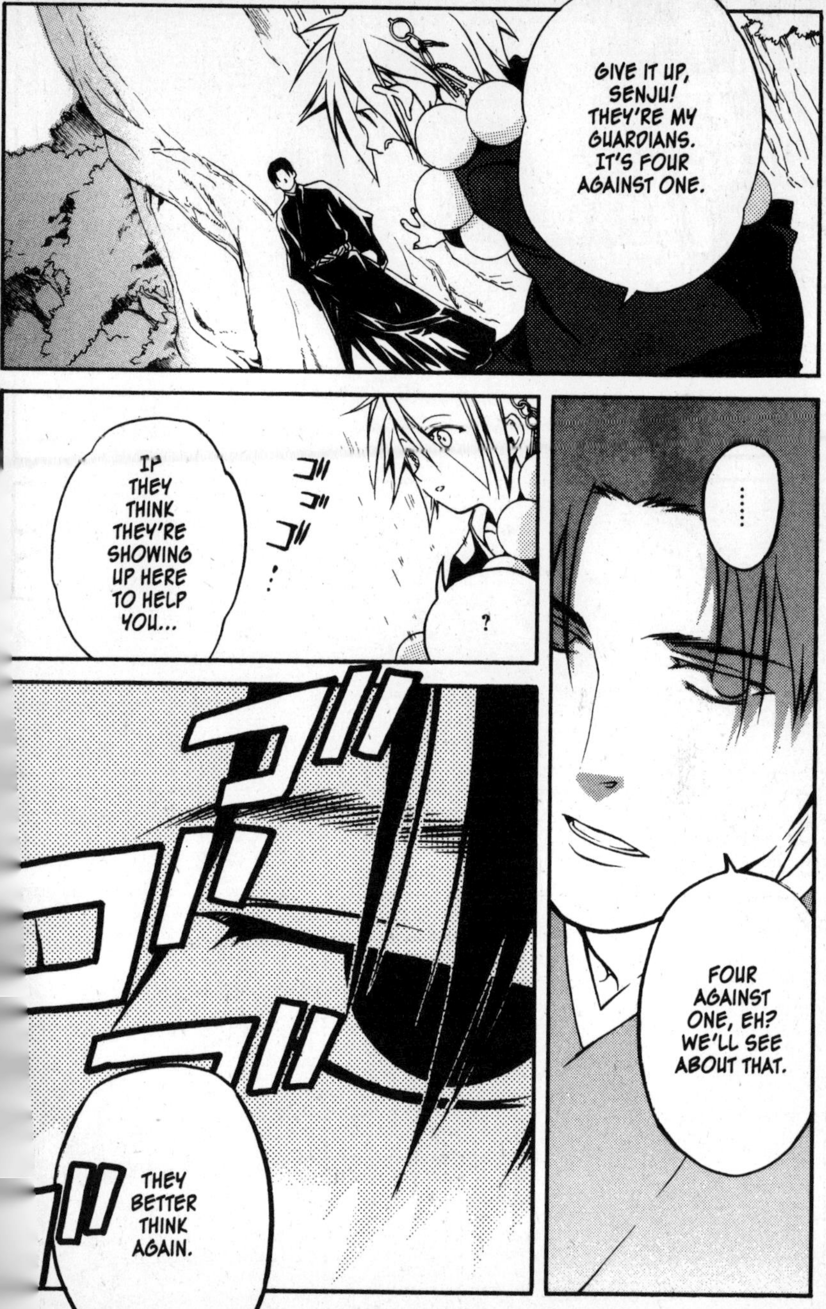
GIVE IT UP, SENJU! THEY'RE MY GUARDIANS. IT'S FOUR AGAINST ONE.
......
FOUR AGAINST ONE, EH? WE'LL SEE ABOUT THAT.
IF THEY THINK THEY'RE SHOWING UP HERE TO HELP YOU...
ゴゴゴ…!
?
THEY BETTER THINK AGAIN.

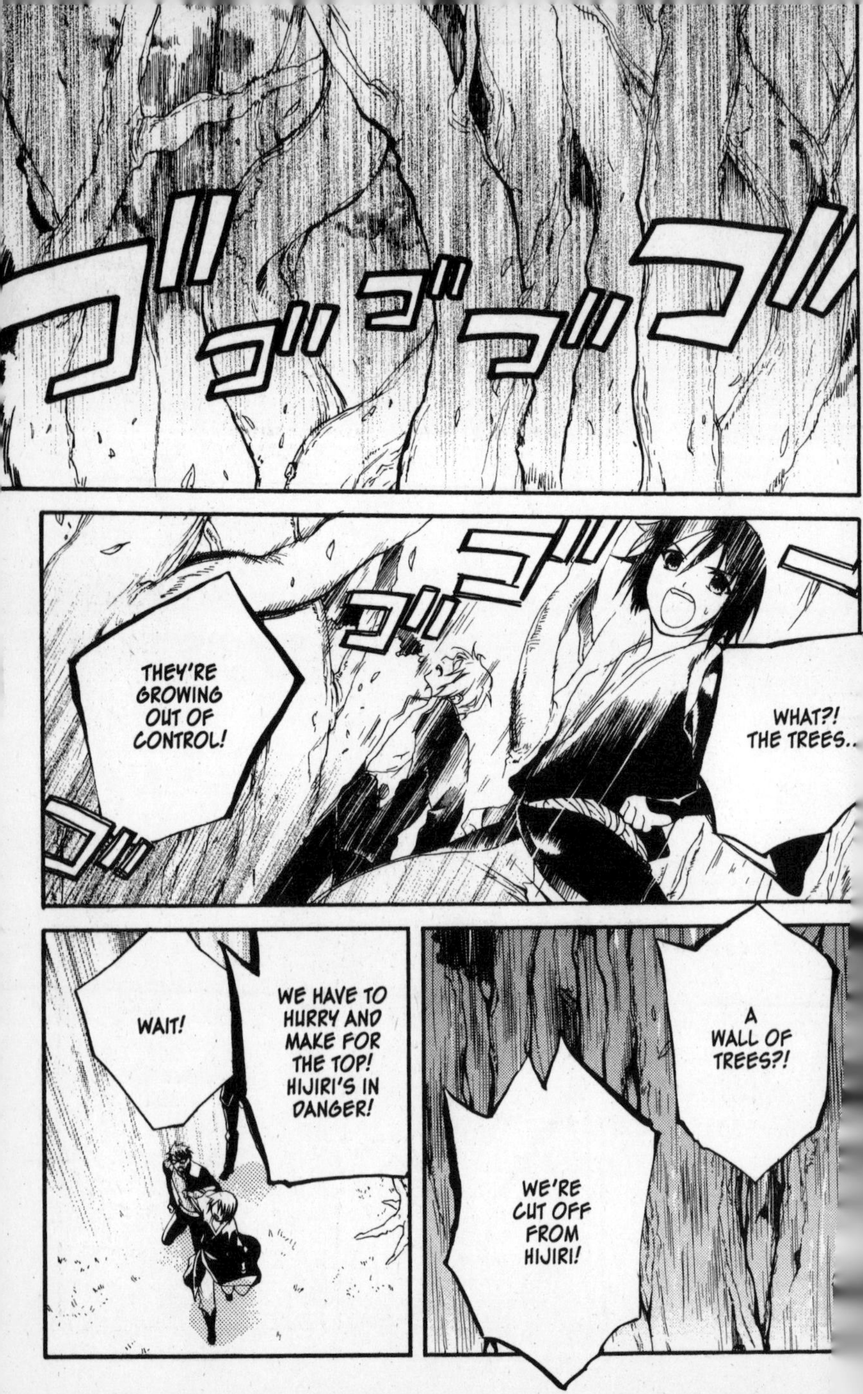
ゴゴゴゴ
WHAT?! THE TREES...
THEY'RE GROWING OUT OF CONTROL!
A WALL OF TREES?!
WE'RE CUT OFF FROM HIJIRI!
WE HAVE TO HURRY AND MAKE FOR THE TOP! HIJIRI'S IN DANGER!
WAIT!

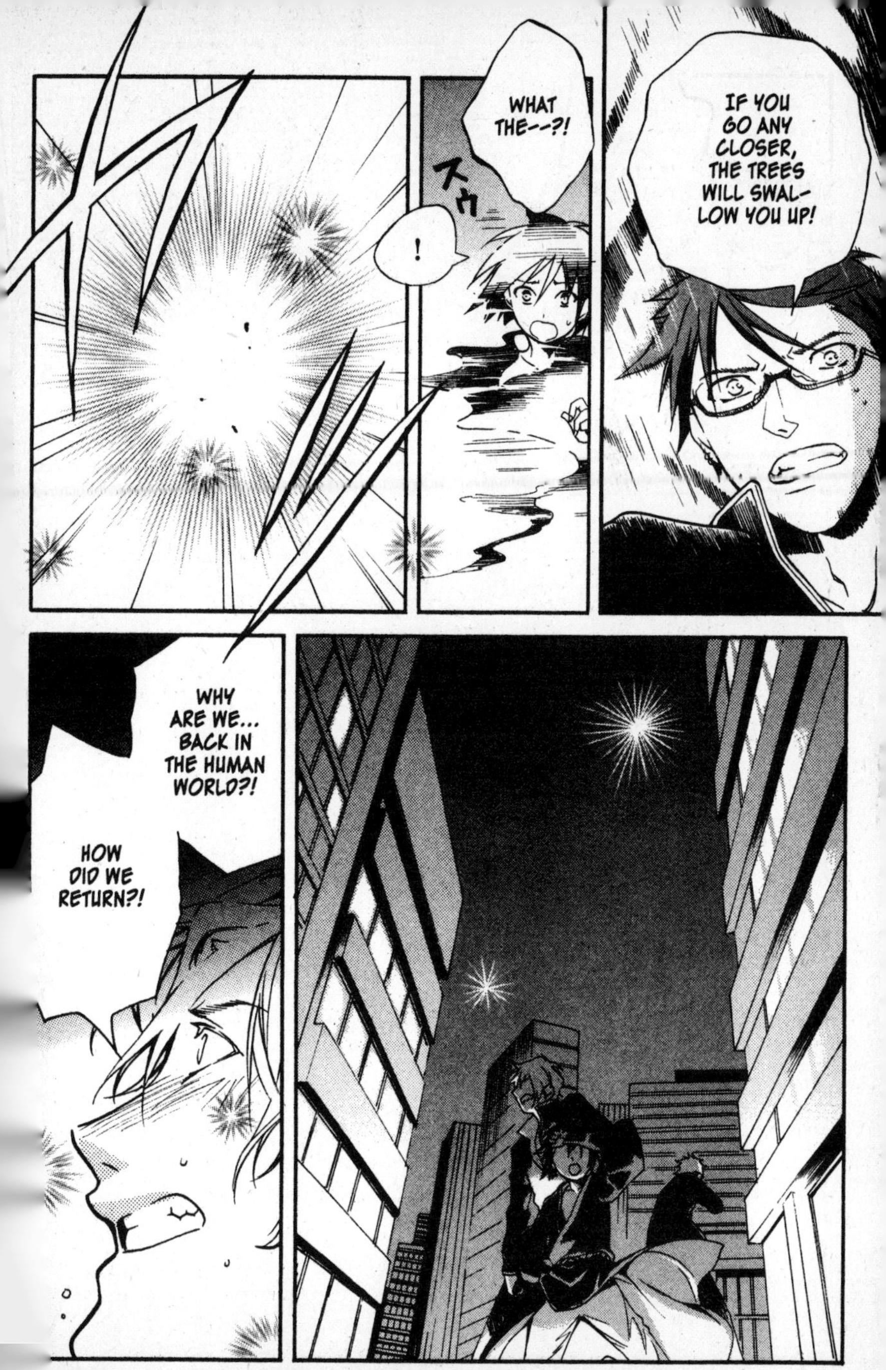
IF YOU GO ANY CLOSER, THE TREES WILL SWAL-LOW YOU UP!
WHAT THE--?!
スゥ
!
WHY ARE WE... BACK IN THE HUMAN WORLD?!
HOW DID WE RETURN?!

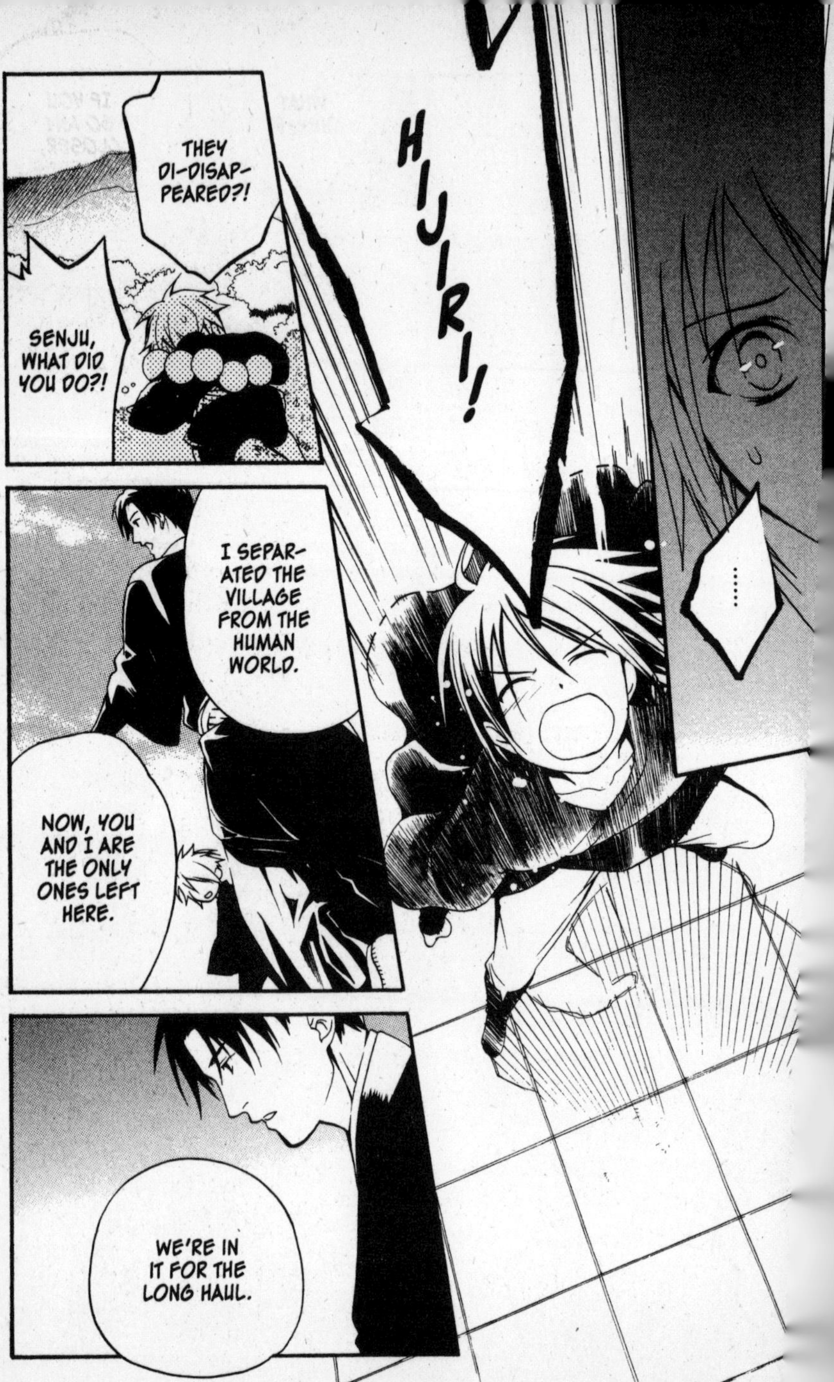
HIJIRI!!
......
THEY DI-DISAP-PEARED?!
SENJU, WHAT DID YOU DO?!
I SEPAR-ATED THE VILLAGE FROM THE HUMAN WORLD.
NOW, YOU AND I ARE THE ONLY ONES LEFT HERE.
WE'RE IN IT FOR THE LONG HAUL.

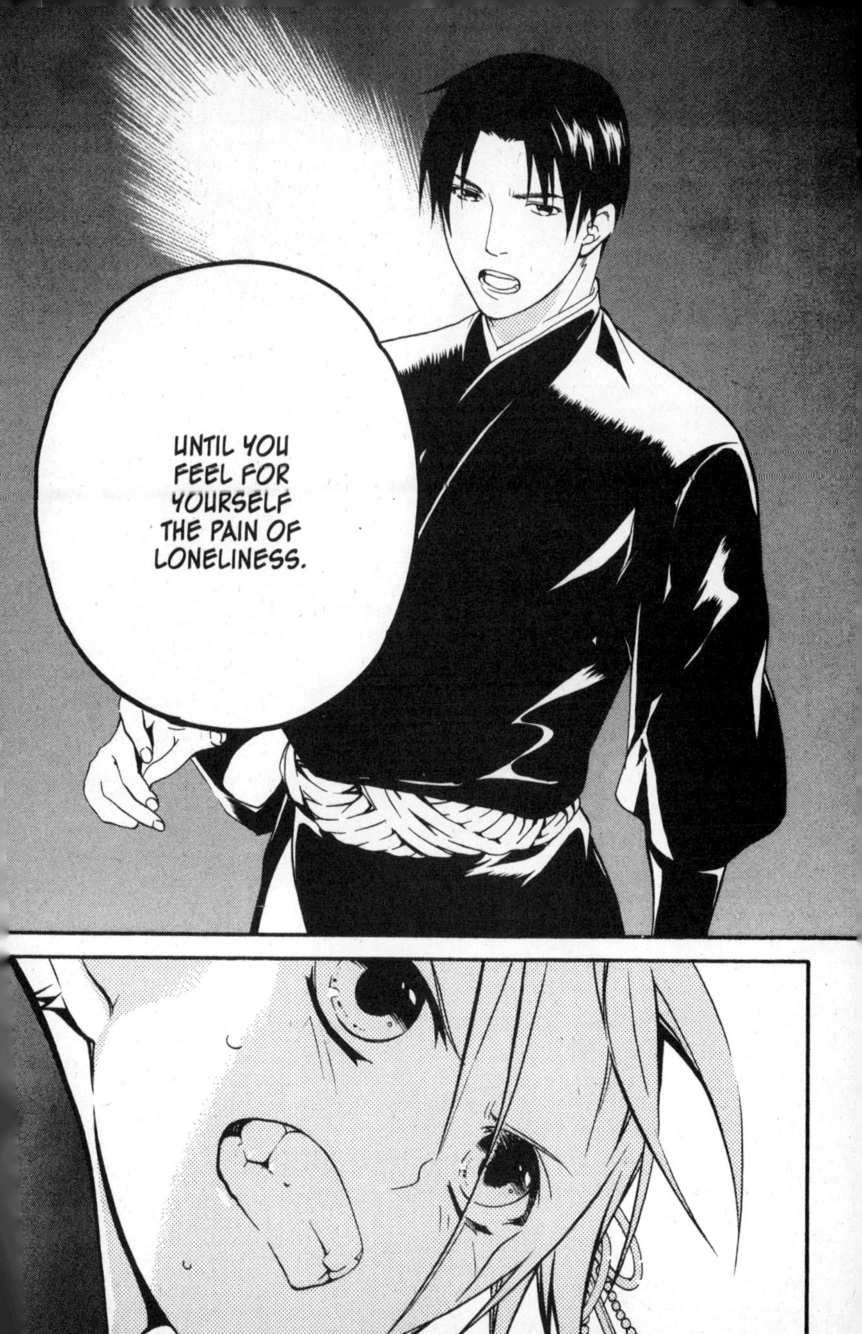
UNTIL YOU FEEL FOR YOURSELF THE PAIN OF LONELINESS.

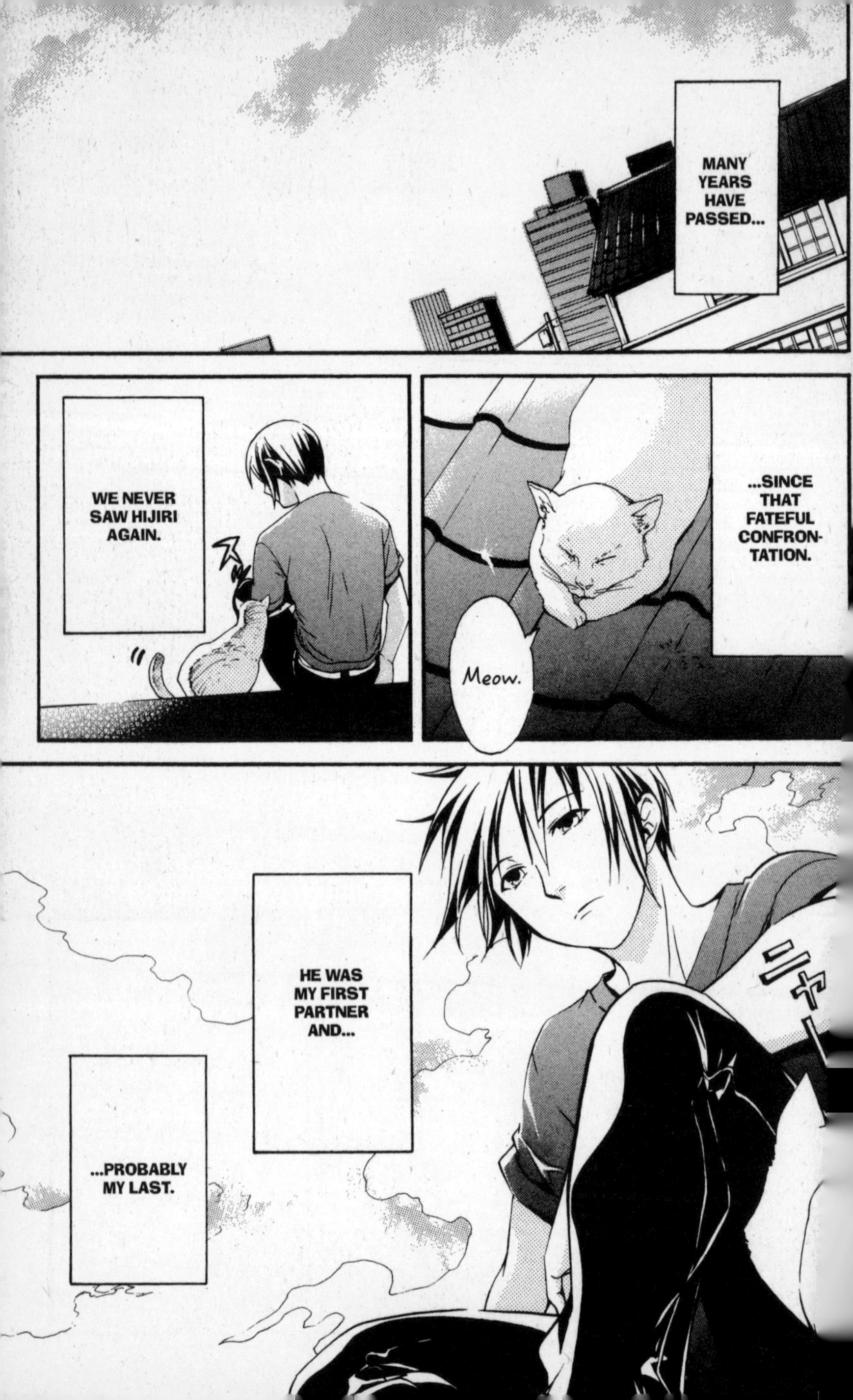
MANY YEARS HAVE PASSED...
...SINCE THAT FATEFUL CONFRONTATION.
Meow.
WE NEVER SAW HIJIRI AGAIN.
ニャー
HE WAS MY FIRST PARTNER AND...
...PROBABLY MY LAST.

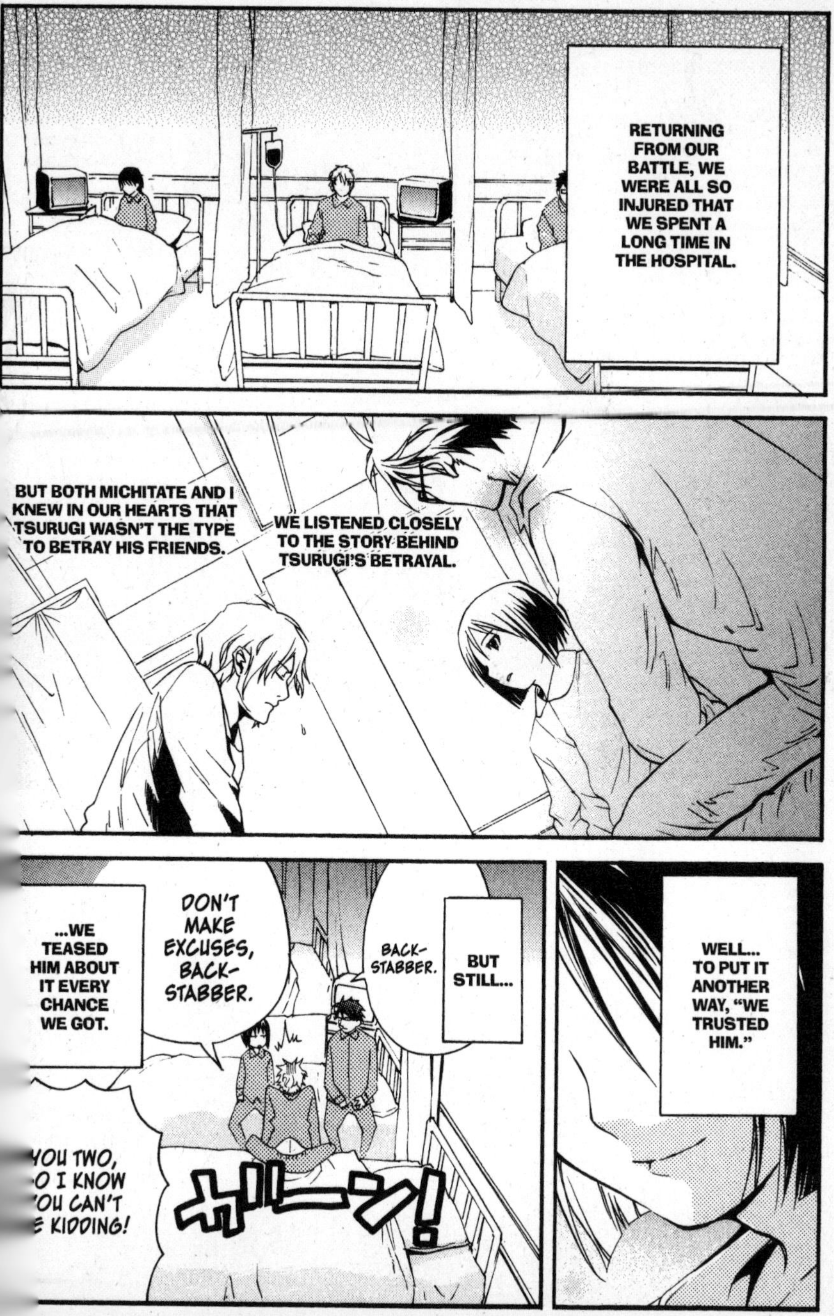
RETURNING FROM OUR BATTLE, WE WERE ALL SO INJURED THAT WE SPENT A LONG TIME IN THE HOSPITAL.
WE LISTENED CLOSELY TO THE STORY BEHIND TSURUGI'S BETRAYAL.
BUT BOTH MICHITATE AND I KNEW IN OUR HEARTS THAT TSURUGI WASN'T THE TYPE TO BETRAY HIS FRIENDS.
WELL... TO PUT IT ANOTHER WAY, "WE TRUSTED HIM."
BUT STILL...
BACK-STABBER.
DON'T MAKE EXCUSES, BACK-STABBER.
...WE TEASED HIM ABOUT IT EVERY CHANCE WE GOT.
カーン!
YOU TWO,
O I KNOW
OU CAN'T
E KIDDING!

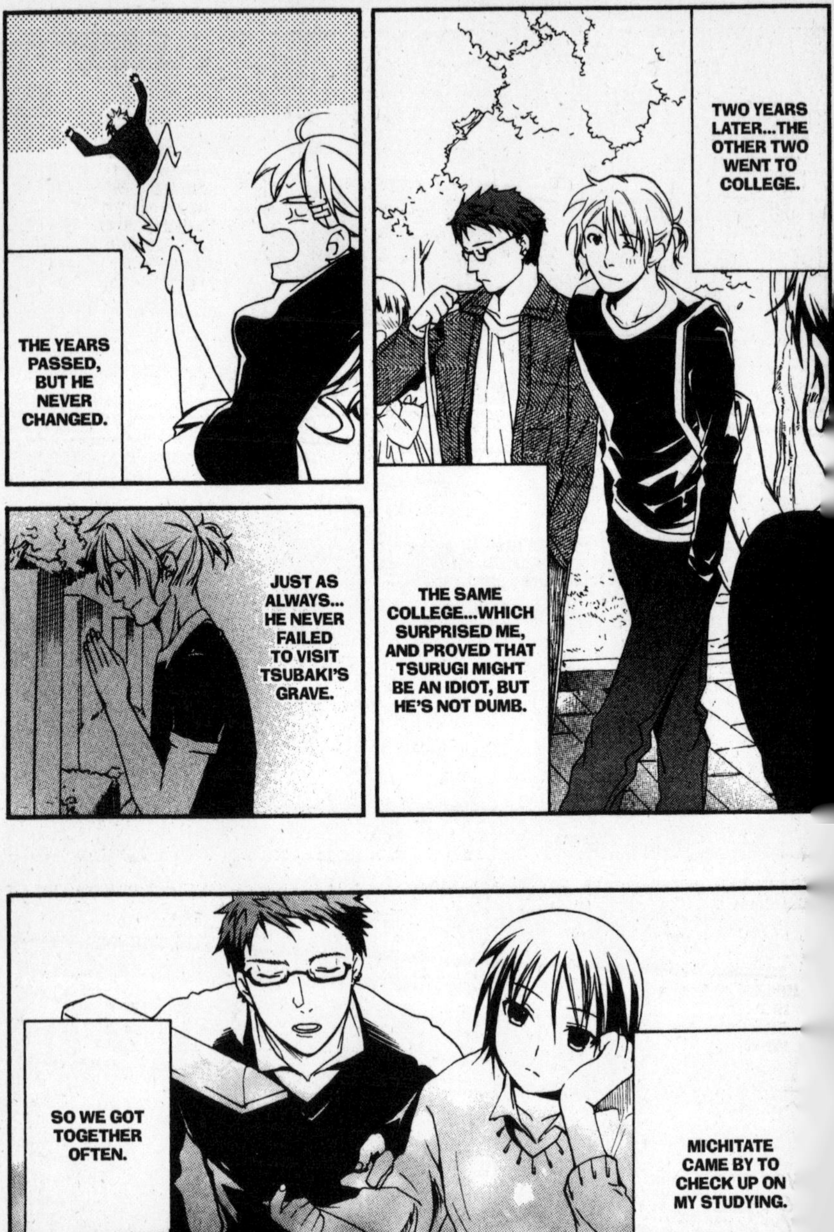
TWO YEARS LATER...THE OTHER TWO WENT TO COLLEGE.
THE SAME COLLEGE...WHICH SURPRISED ME, AND PROVED THAT TSURUGI MIGHT BE AN IDIOT, BUT HE'S NOT DUMB.
THE YEARS PASSED, BUT HE NEVER CHANGED.
JUST AS ALWAYS... HE NEVER FAILED TO VISIT TSUBAKI'S GRAVE.
MICHITATE CAME BY TO CHECK UP ON MY STUDYING.
SO WE GOT TOGETHER OFTEN.

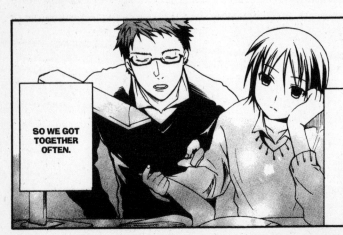

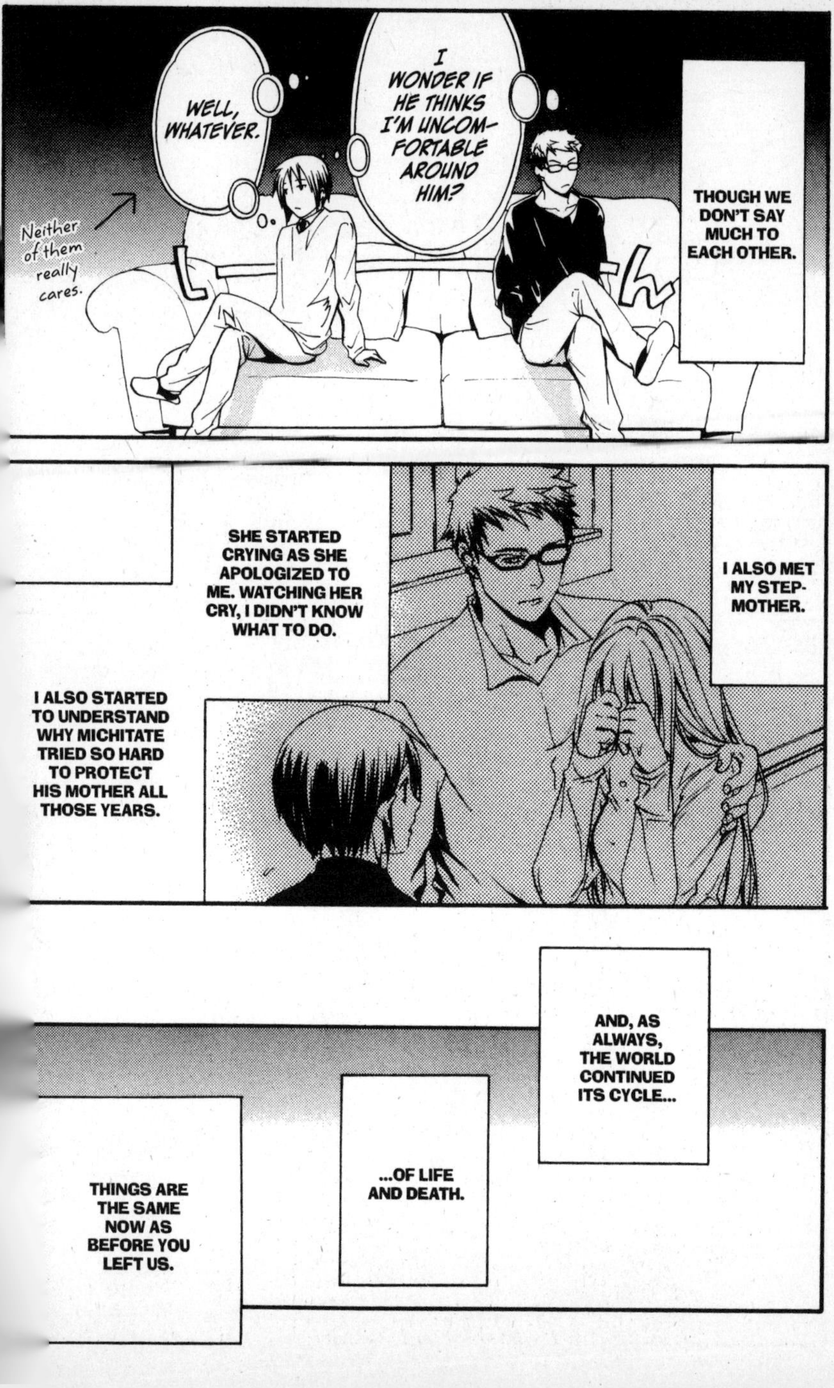
THOUGH WE DON'T SAY MUCH TO EACH OTHER.
I WONDER IF HE THINKS I'M UNCOMFORTABLE AROUND HIM?
WELL, WHATEVER.
Neither of them really cares.
I ALSO MET MY STEPMOTHER.
SHE STARTED CRYING AS SHE APOLOGIZED TO ME. WATCHING HER CRY, I DIDN'T KNOW WHAT TO DO.
I ALSO STARTED TO UNDERSTAND WHY MICHITATE TRIED SO HARD TO PROTECT HIS MOTHER ALL THOSE YEARS.
AND, AS ALWAYS, THE WORLD CONTINUED ITS CYCLE...
...OF LIFE AND DEATH.
THINGS ARE THE SAME NOW AS BEFORE YOU LEFT US.

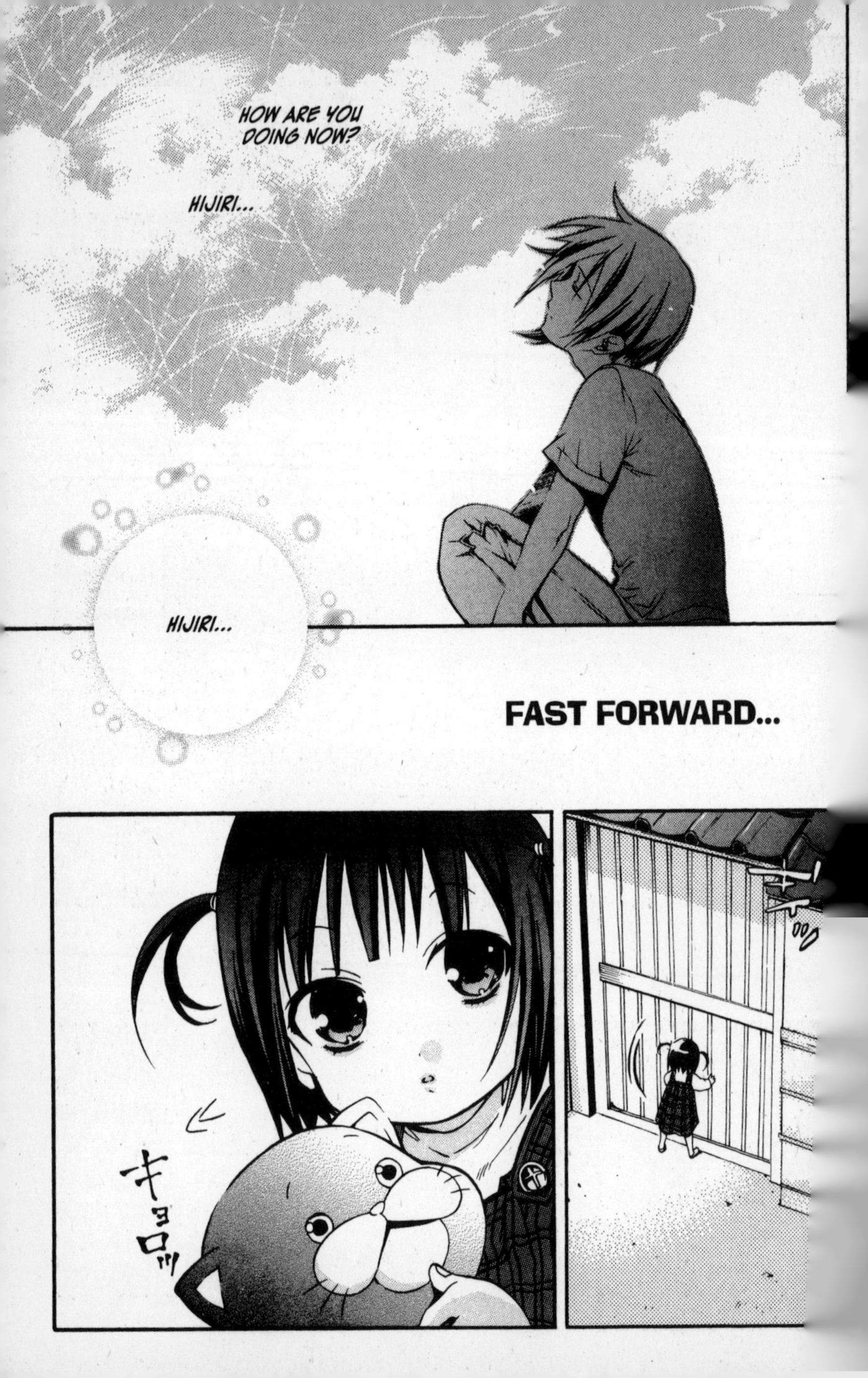
HOW ARE YOU DOING NOW?
HIJIRI...
HIJIRI...
FAST FORWARD...
キョロッ

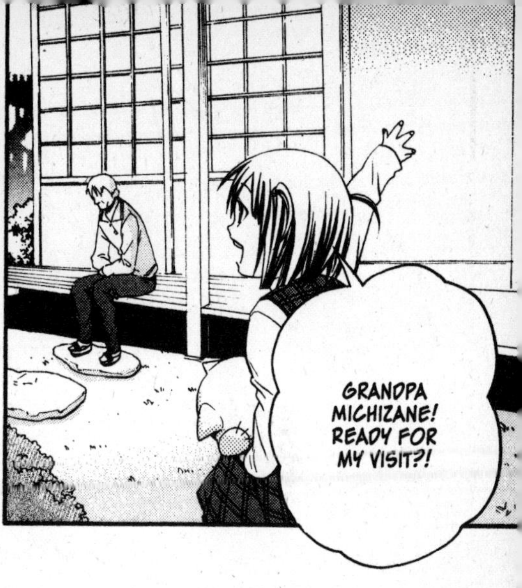
GRANDPA MICHIZANE! READY FOR MY VISIT?!
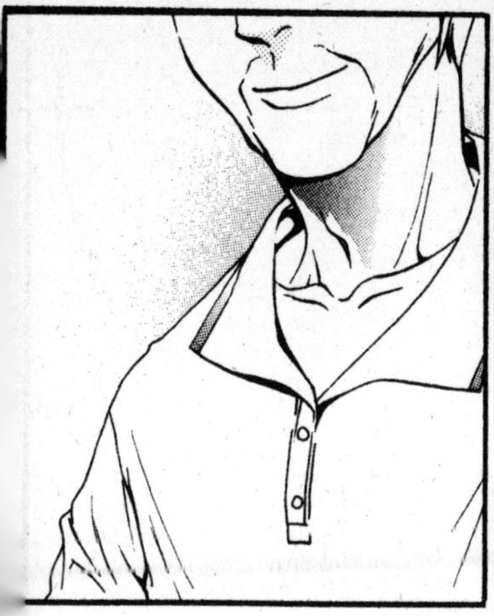
LET'S JUMP AHEAD 60 YEARS OF DAYS, MONTHS, SEASONS...

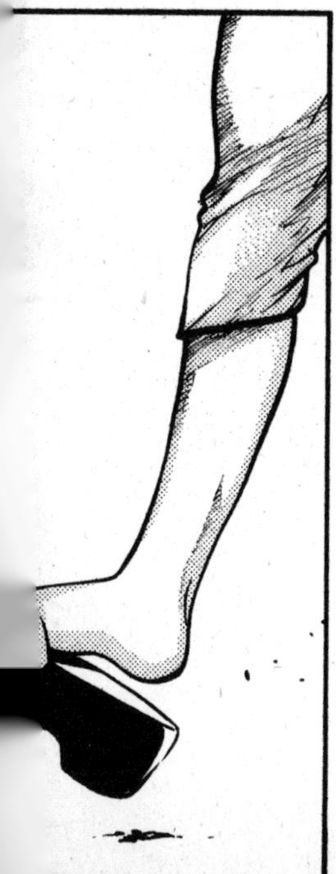

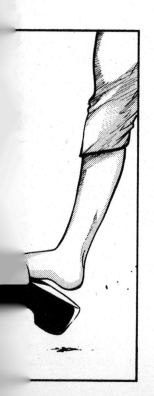

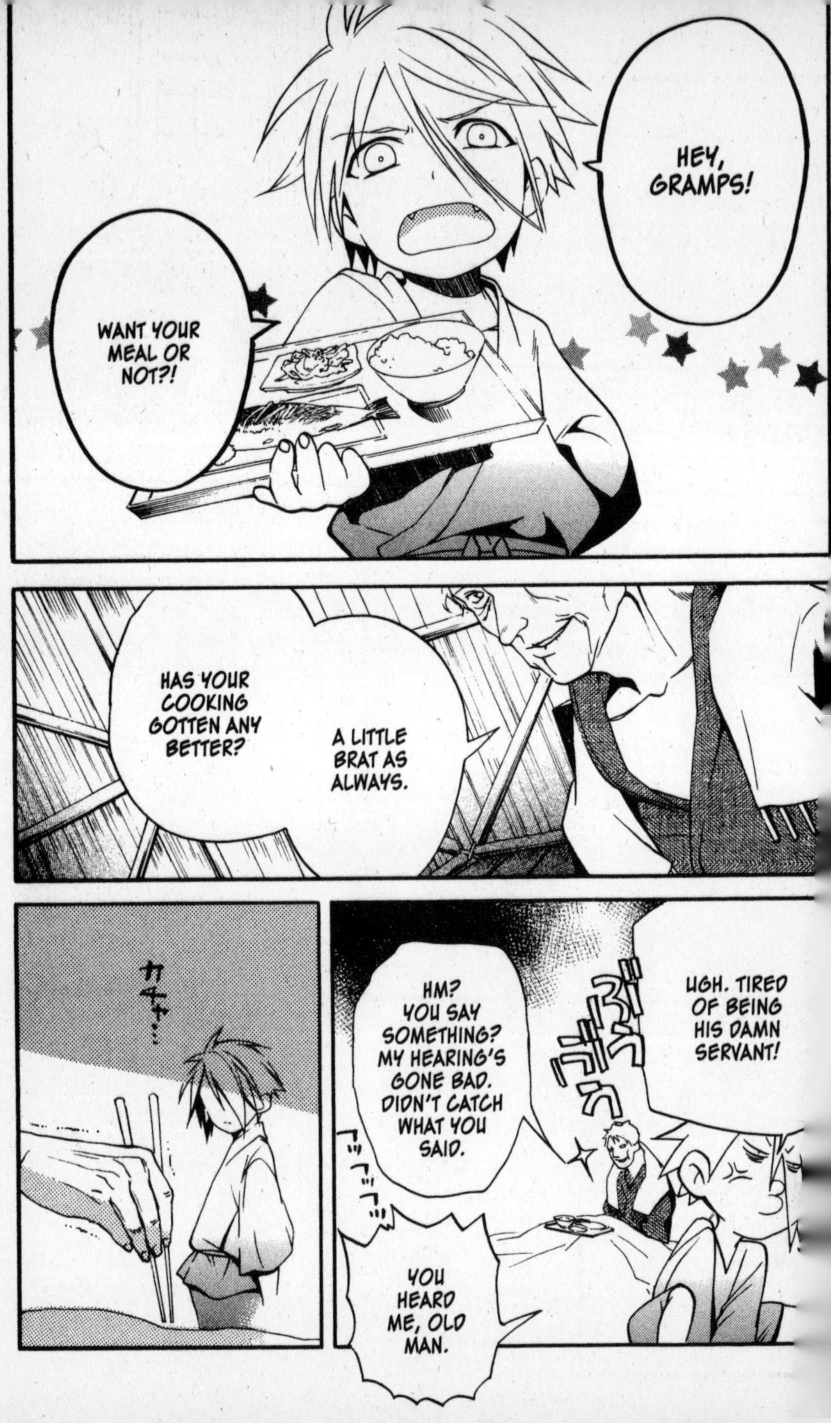
HEY, GRAMPS!
WANT YOUR MEAL OR NOT?!
A LITTLE BRAT AS ALWAYS.
HAS YOUR COOKING GOTTEN ANY BETTER?
UGH. TIRED OF BEING HIS DAMN SERVANT!
HM? YOU SAY SOMETHING? MY HEARING'S GONE BAD. DIDN'T CATCH WHAT YOU SAID.
YOU HEARD ME, OLD MAN.
カチャ…

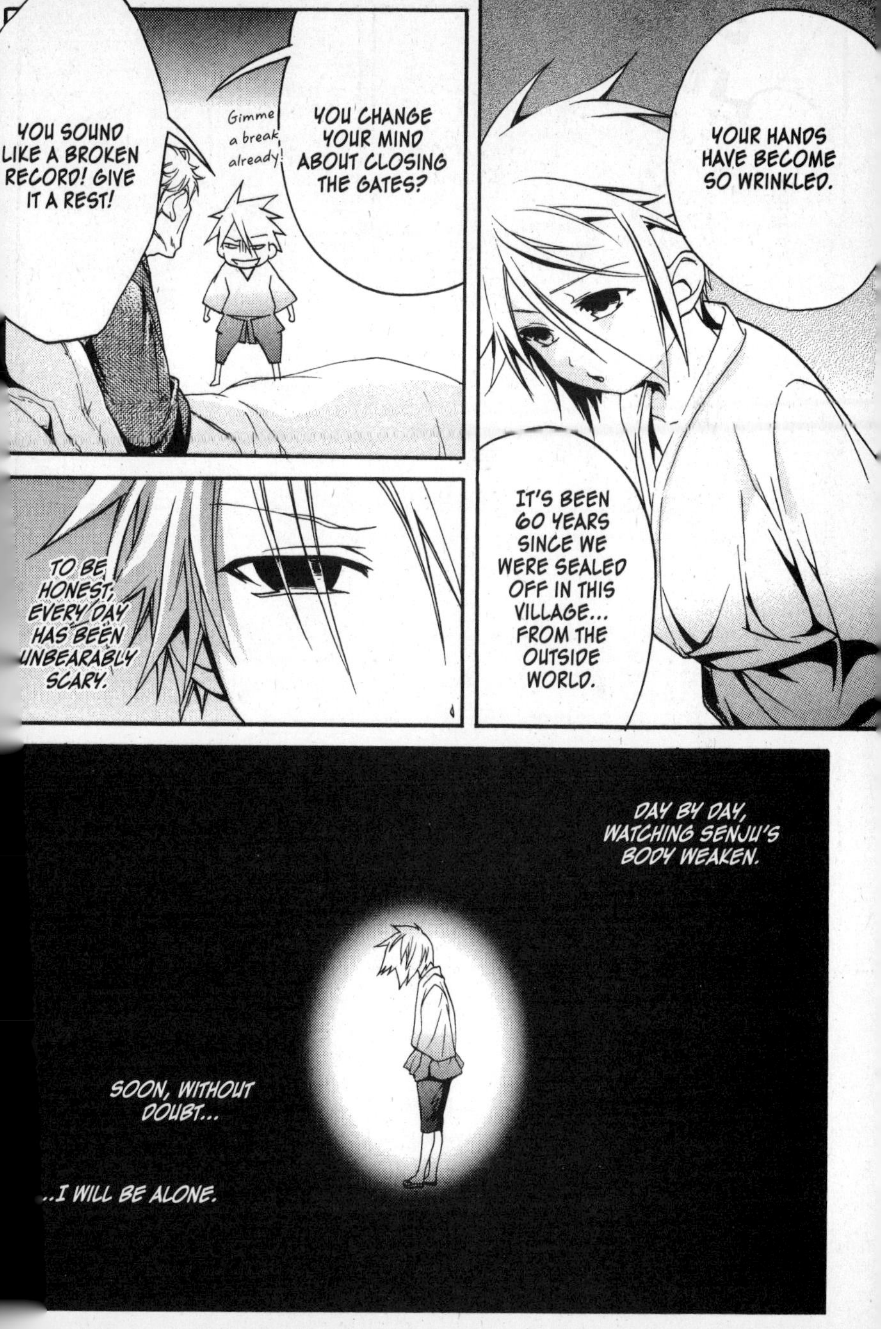
YOUR HANDS HAVE BECOME SO WRINKLED.
IT'S BEEN 60 YEARS SINCE WE WERE SEALED OFF IN THIS VILLAGE... FROM THE OUTSIDE WORLD.
YOU CHANGE YOUR MIND ABOUT CLOSING THE GATES?
Gimme a break, already!
YOU SOUND LIKE A BROKEN RECORD! GIVE IT A REST!
TO BE HONEST, EVERY DAY HAS BEEN UNBEARABLY SCARY.
DAY BY DAY, WATCHING SENJU'S BODY WEAKEN.
SOON, WITHOUT DOUBT...
...I WILL BE ALONE.

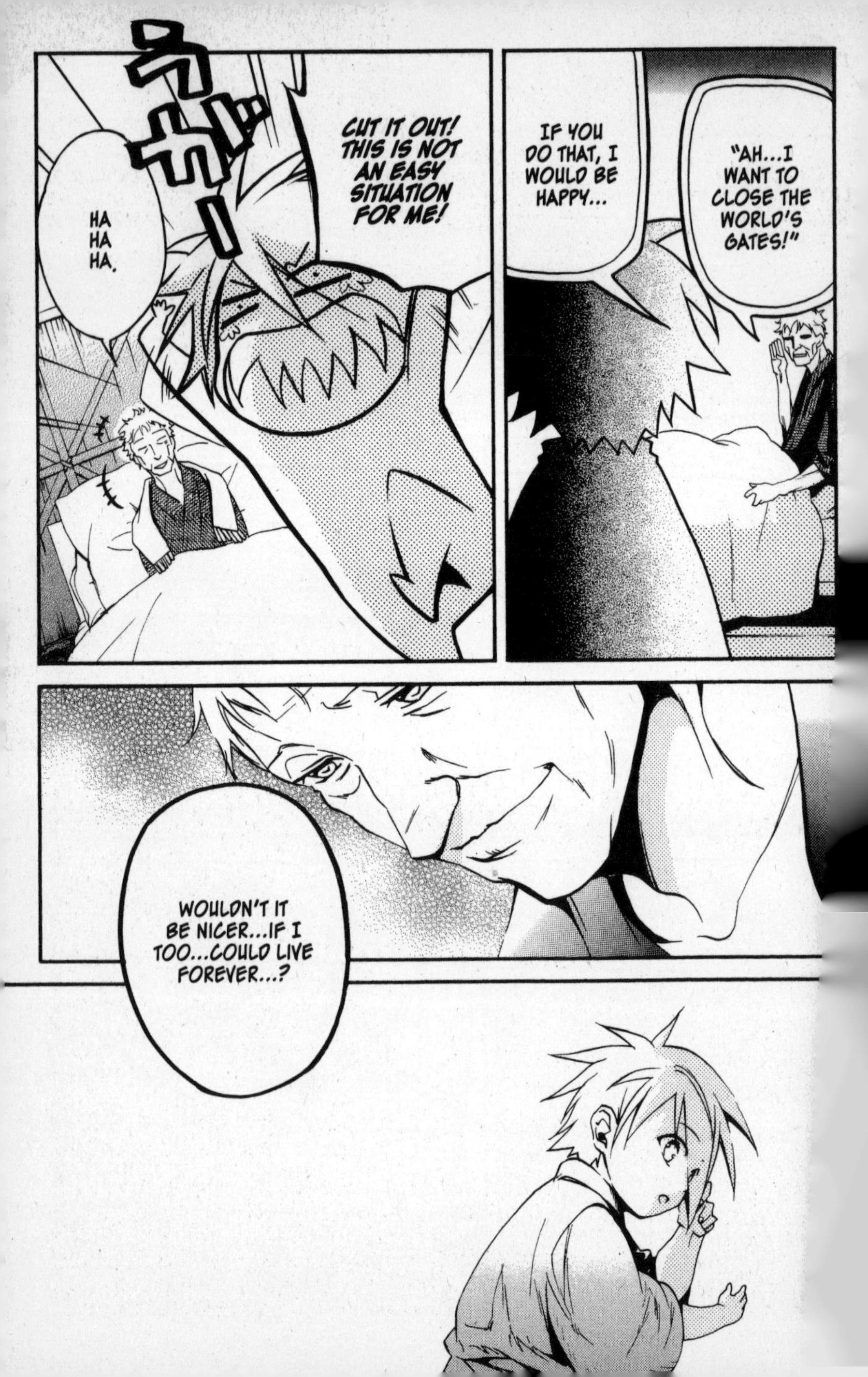
"AH...I WANT TO CLOSE THE WORLD'S GATES!"
IF YOU DO THAT, I WOULD BE HAPPY...
CUT IT OUT! THIS IS NOT AN EASY SITUATION FOR ME!
HA HA HA.
WOULDN'T IT BE NICER...IF I TOO...COULD LIVE FOREVER...?

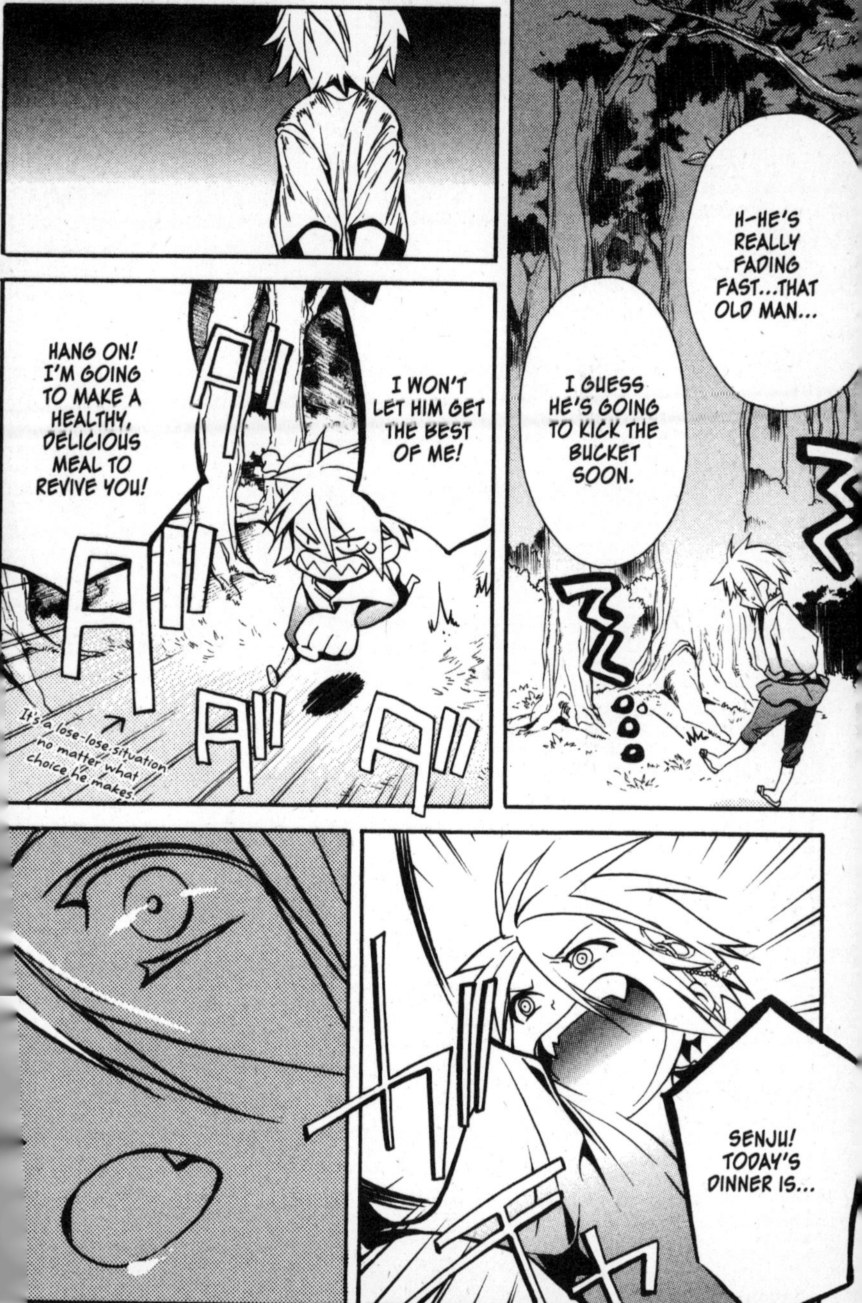
H-HE'S REALLY FADING FAST...THAT OLD MAN...
I GUESS HE'S GOING TO KICK THE BUCKET SOON.
I WON'T LET HIM GET THE BEST OF ME!
HANG ON! I'M GOING TO MAKE A HEALTHY, DELICIOUS MEAL TO REVIVE YOU!
It's a lose-lose situation no matter what choice he makes!
SENJU! TODAY'S DINNER IS...

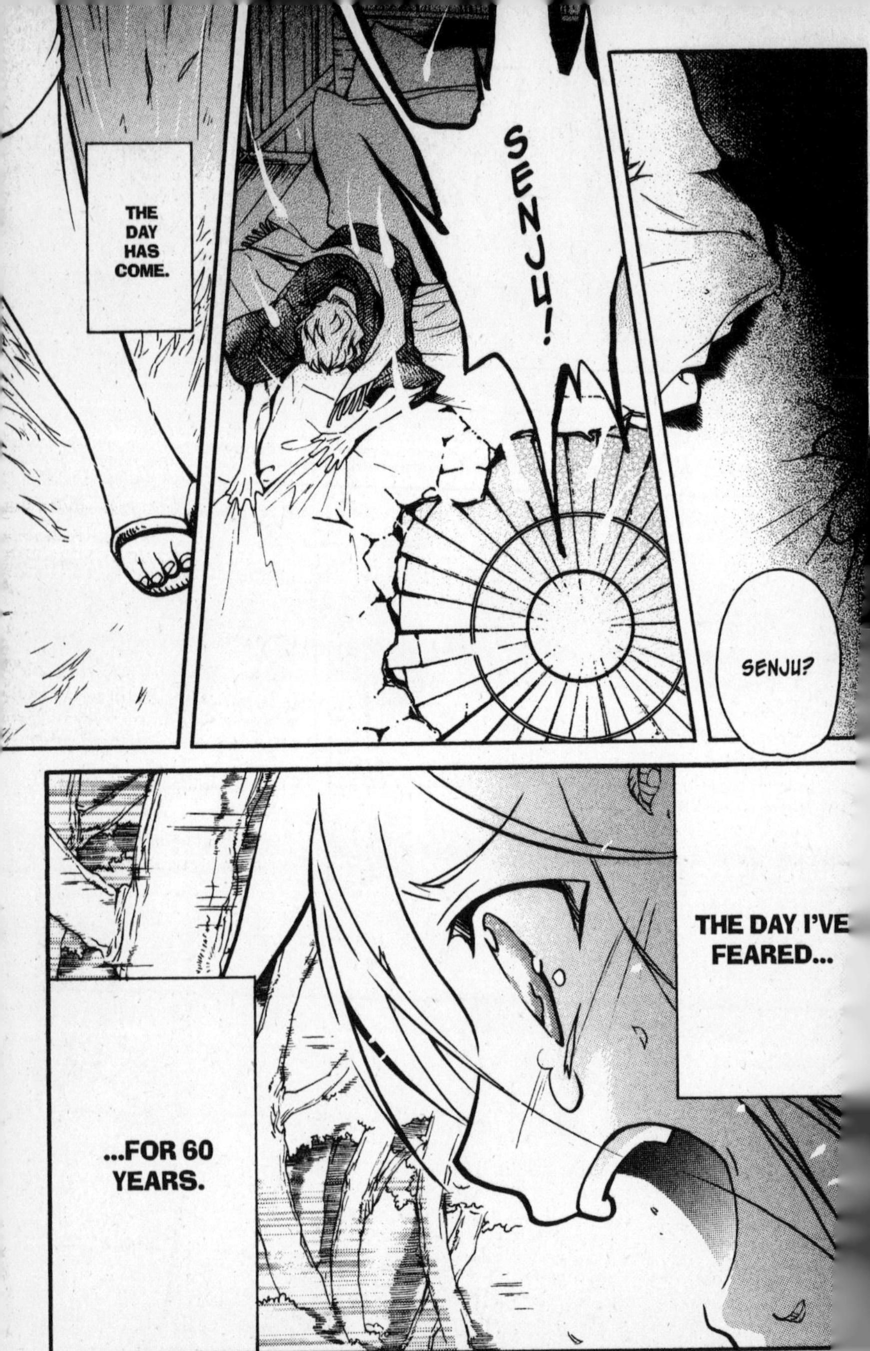
SENJU?
SENJU!
THE DAY HAS COME.
THE DAY I'VE FEARED...
...FOR 60 YEARS.

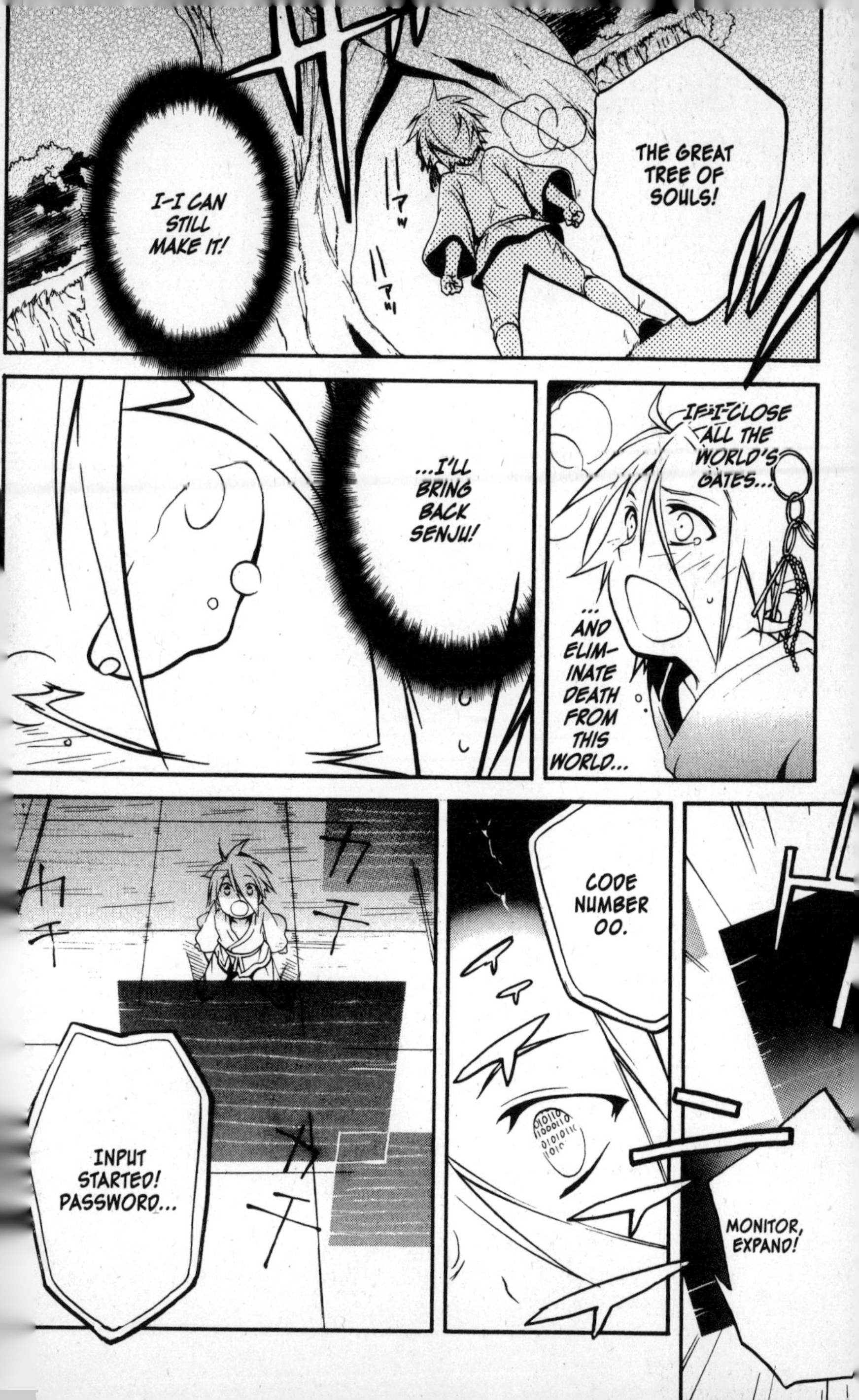
THE GREAT TREE OF SOULS!
I-I CAN STILL MAKE IT!
IF-I-CLOSE ALL THE WORLD'S GATES...
...AND ELIMINATE DEATH FROM THIS WORLD...
...I'LL BRING BACK SENJU!
MONITOR, EXPAND!
CODE NUMBER 00.
INPUT STARTED! PASSWORD...

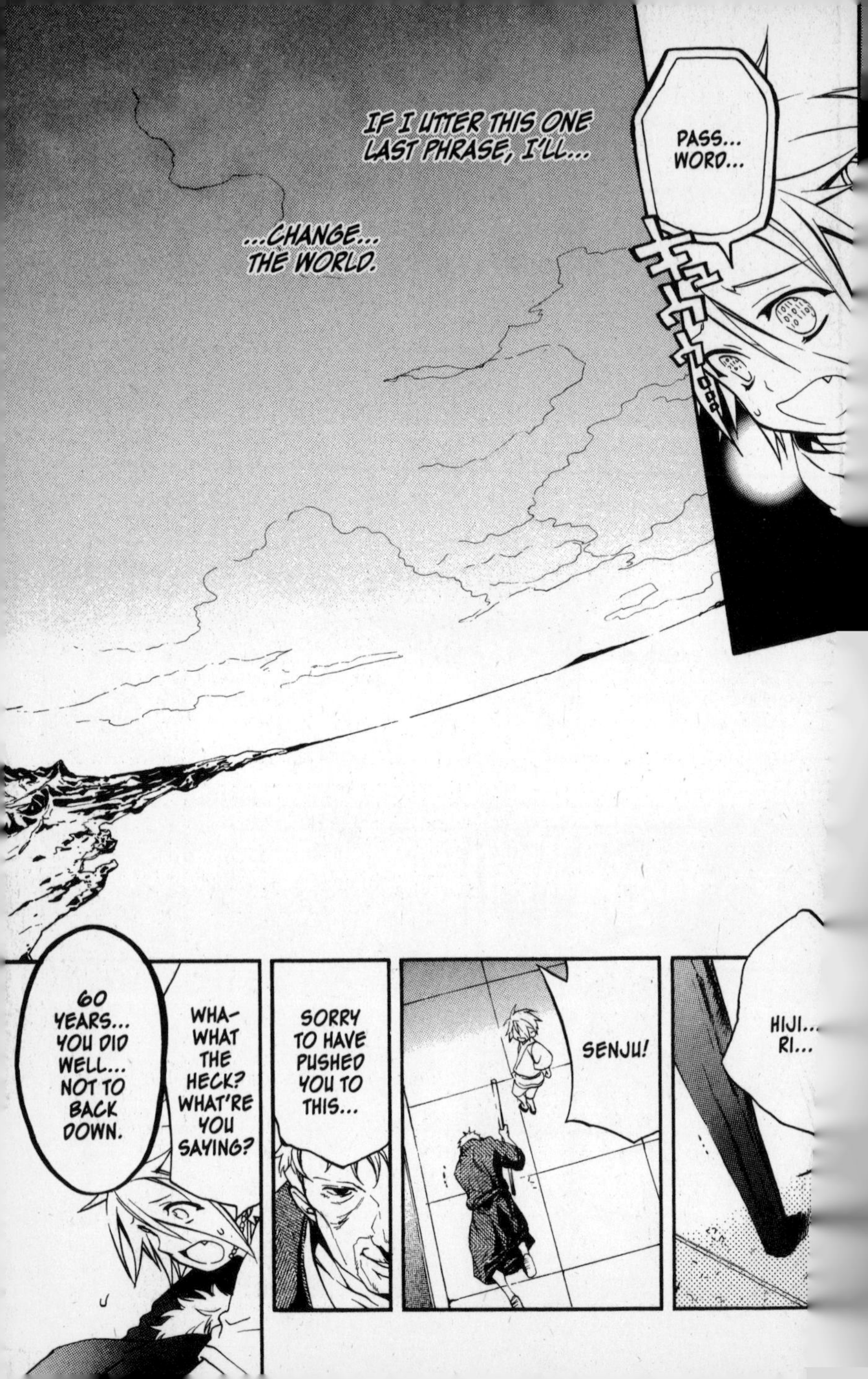
PASS... WORD...
IF I UTTER THIS ONE LAST PHRASE, I'LL...
...CHANGE... THE WORLD.
HIJI... RI...
SENJU!
SORRY TO HAVE PUSHED YOU TO THIS...
WHA-WHAT THE HECK? WHAT'RE YOU SAYING?
60 YEARS... YOU DID WELL... NOT TO BACK DOWN.

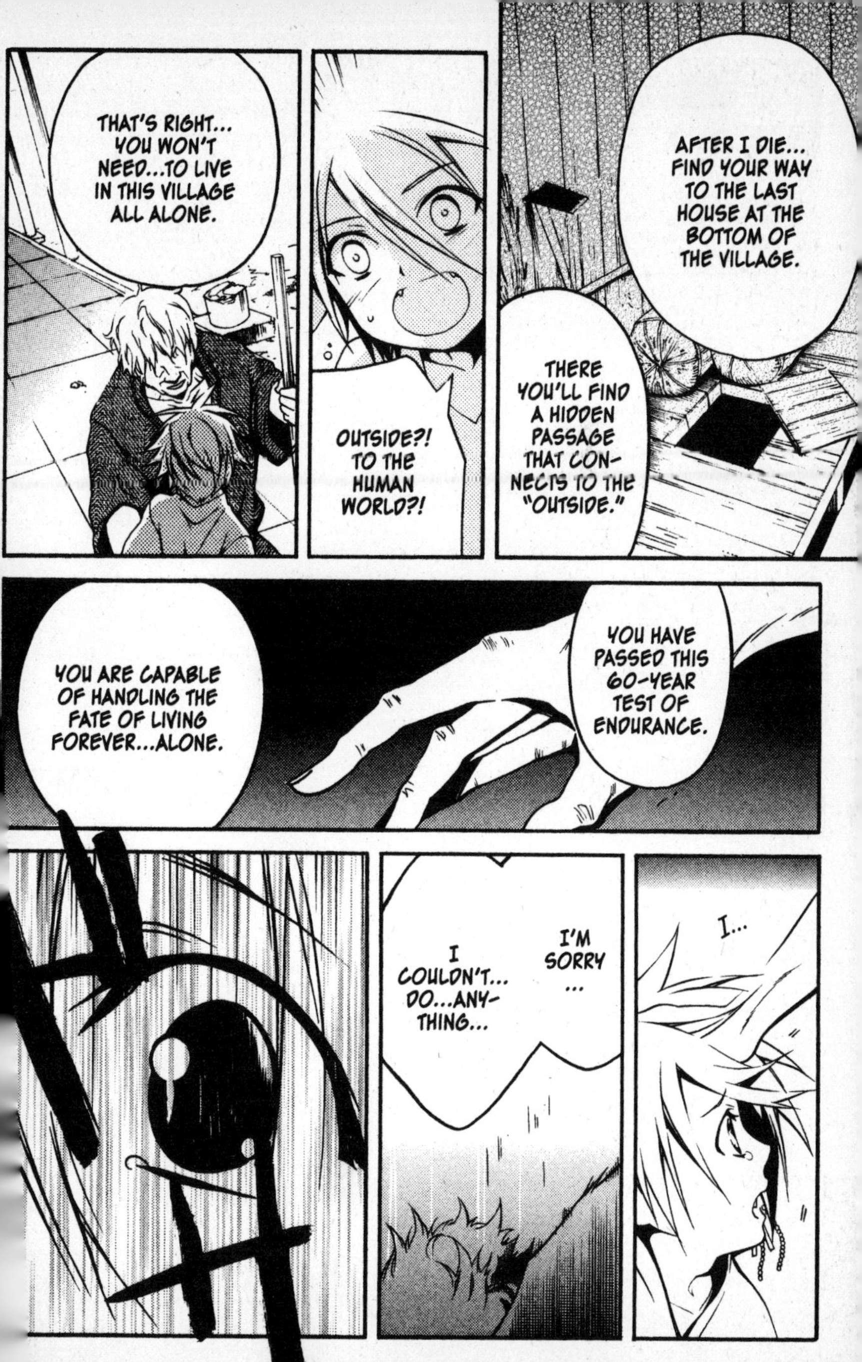
AFTER I DIE... FIND YOUR WAY TO THE LAST HOUSE AT THE BOTTOM OF THE VILLAGE.
THERE YOU'LL FIND A HIDDEN PASSAGE THAT CON-NECTS TO THE "OUTSIDE."
OUTSIDE?! TO THE HUMAN WORLD?!
THAT'S RIGHT... YOU WON'T NEED...TO LIVE IN THIS VILLAGE ALL ALONE.
YOU HAVE PASSED THIS 60-YEAR TEST OF ENDURANCE.
YOU ARE CAPABLE OF HANDLING THE FATE OF LIVING FOREVER...ALONE.
I...
I'M SORRY ...
I COULDN'T... DO...ANY-THING...

NO!

NO!

I-I...

NO!

NO!

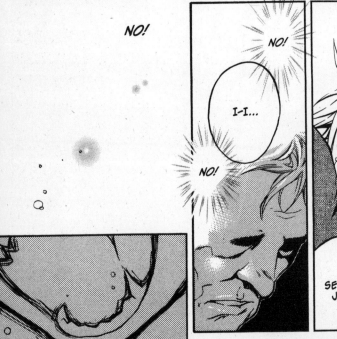

SEN... JU.

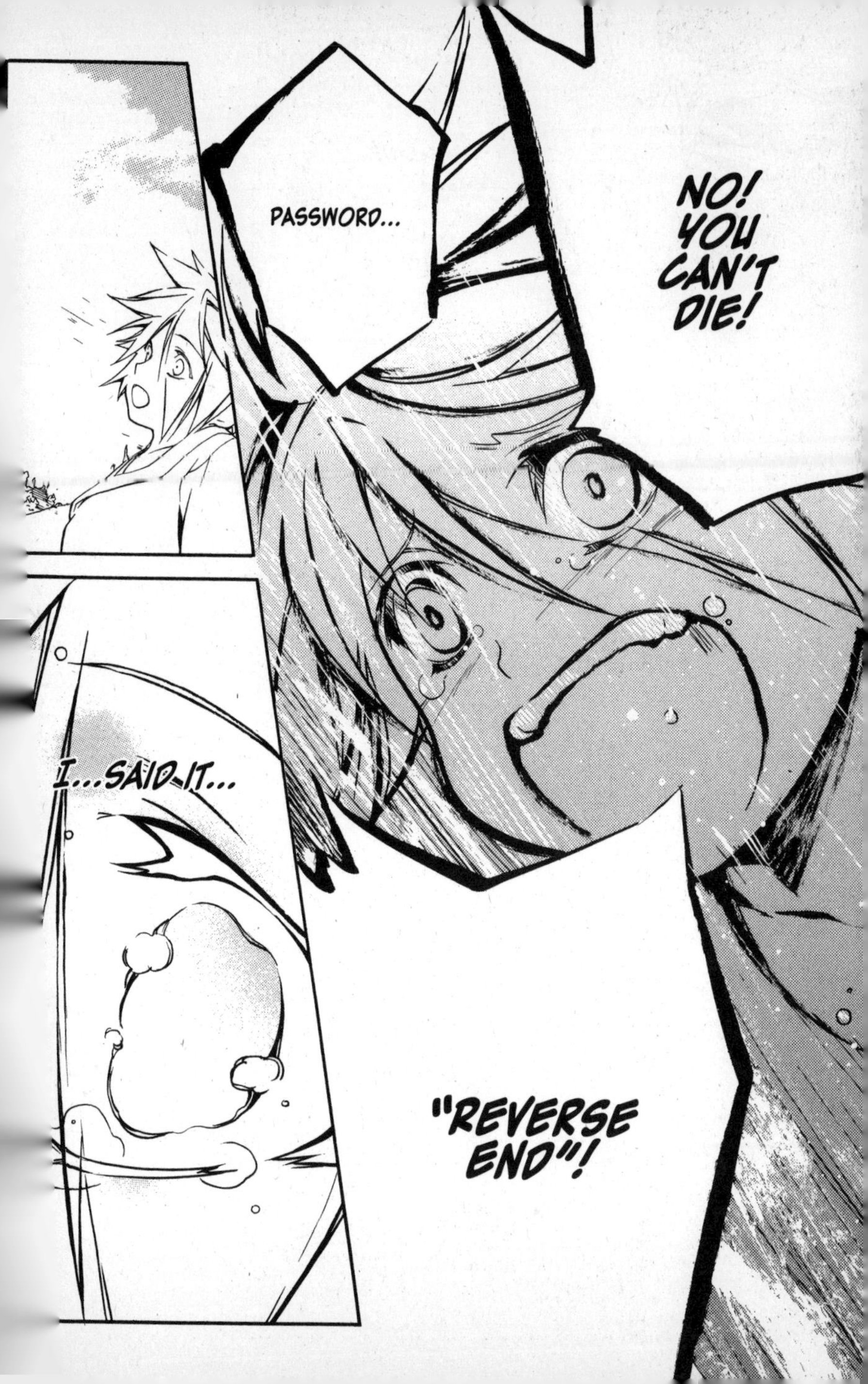
NO! YOU CAN'T DIE!
PASSWORD...
I...SAID IT...
"REVERSE END"!

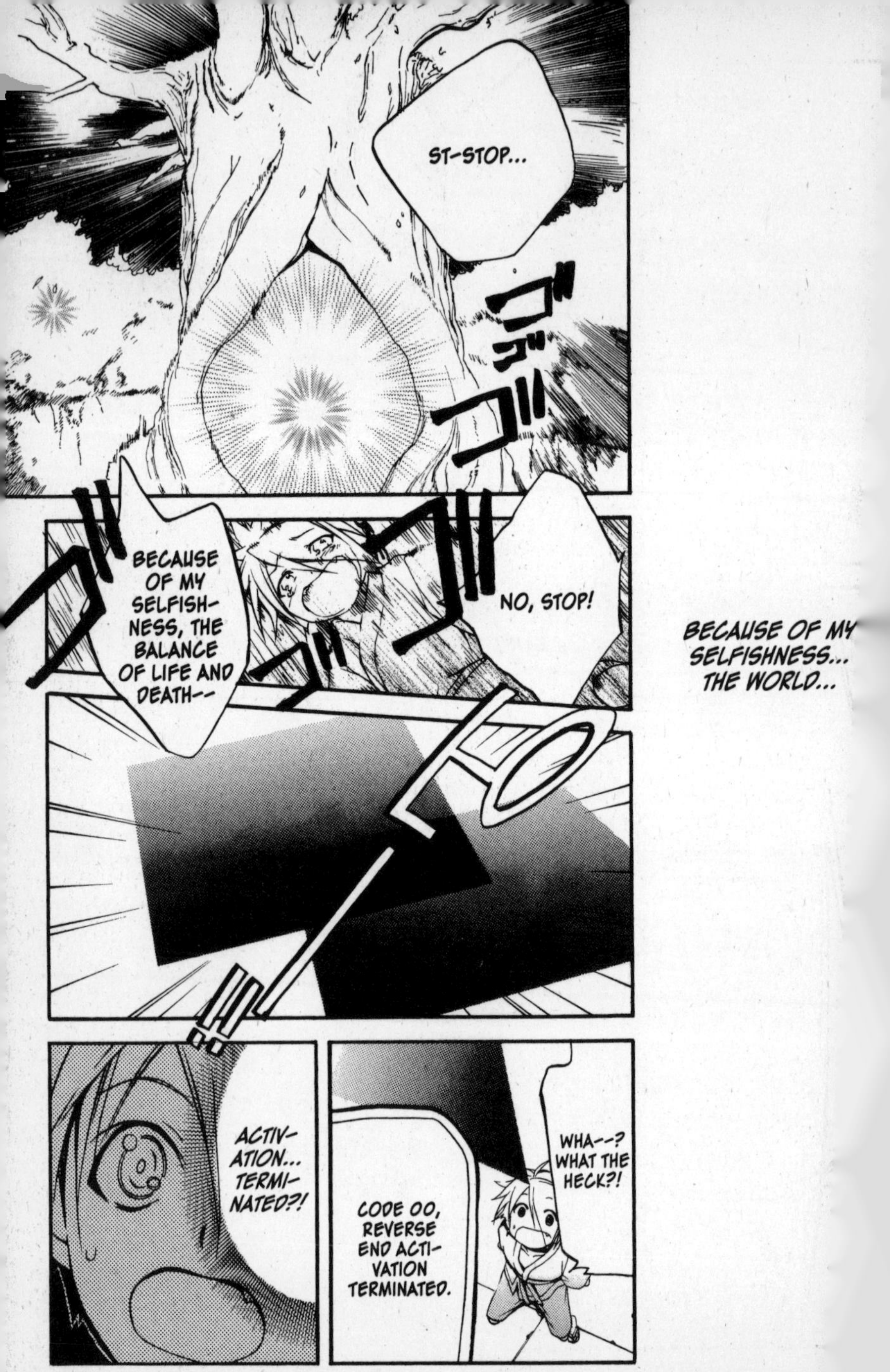
ST-STOP...
ゴゴゴ
BECAUSE OF MY SELFISHNESS... THE WORLD...
NO, STOP!
BECAUSE OF MY SELFISH-NESS, THE BALANCE OF LIFE AND DEATH--
WHA--? WHAT THE HECK?!
CODE 00, REVERSE END ACTI-VATION TERMINATED.
ACTIV-ATION... TERMI-NATED?!

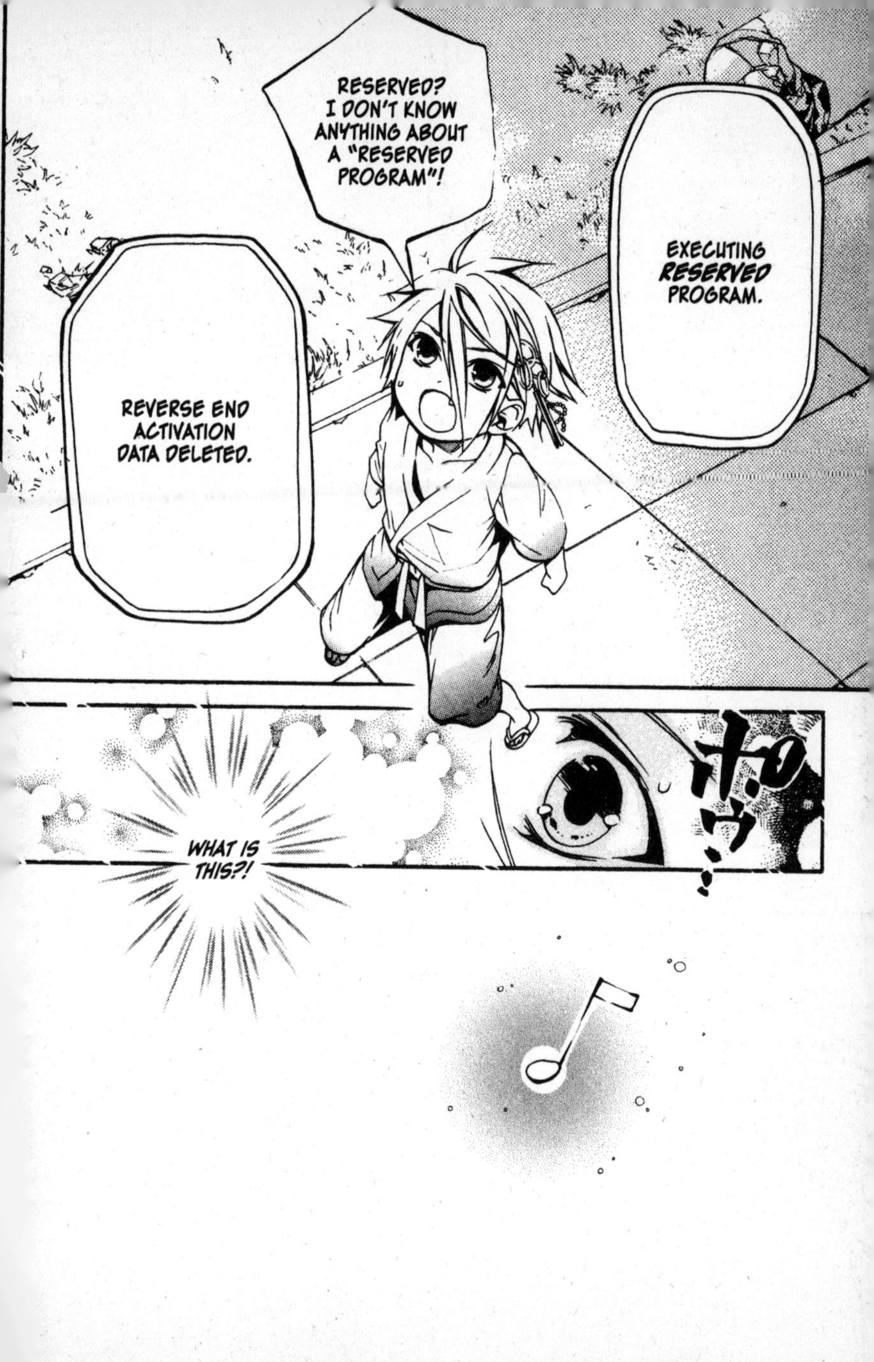
EXECUTING RESERVED PROGRAM.
RESERVED? I DON'T KNOW ANYTHING ABOUT A "RESERVED PROGRAM"!
REVERSE END ACTIVATION DATA DELETED.
ポウ…
WHAT IS THIS?!

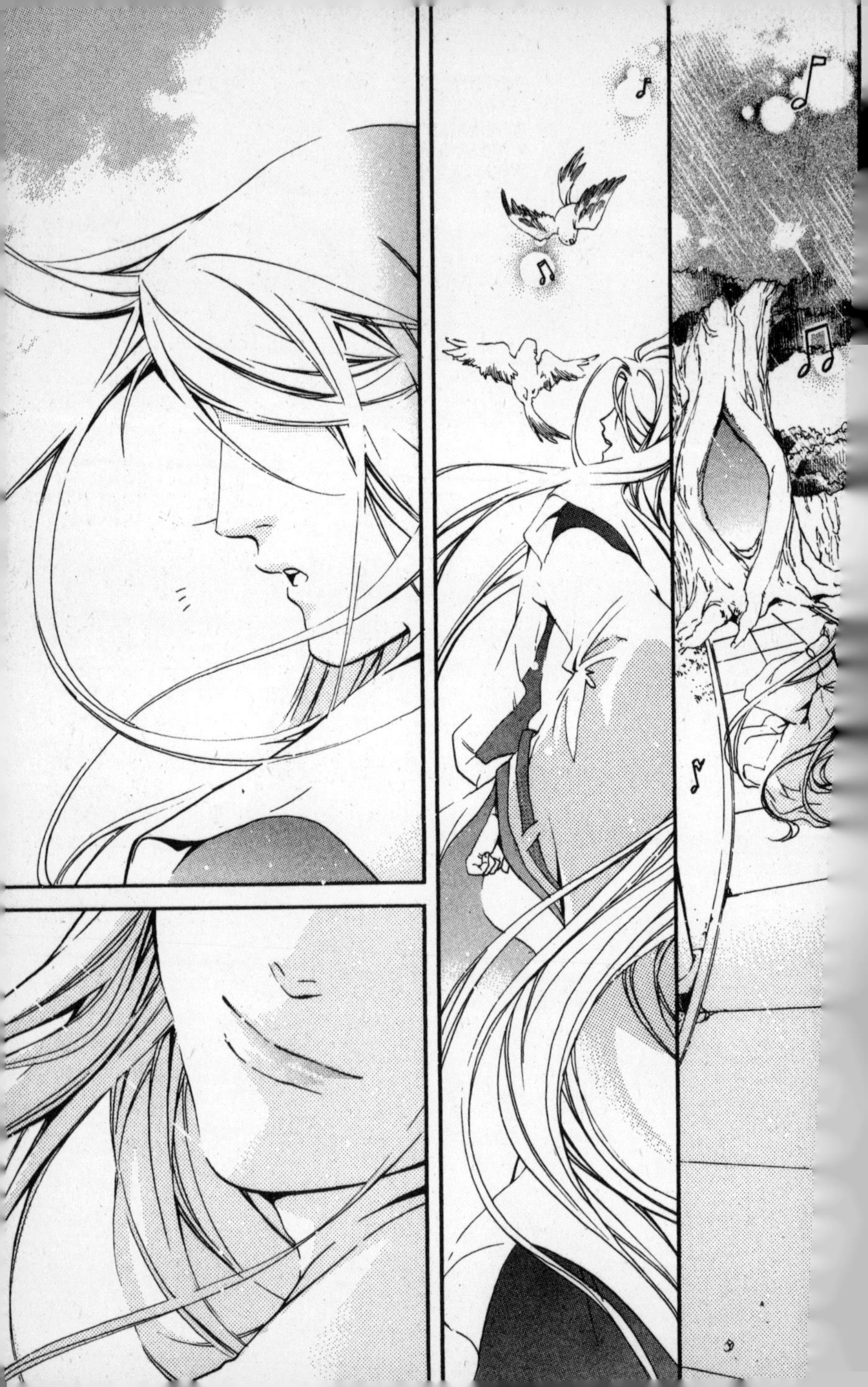

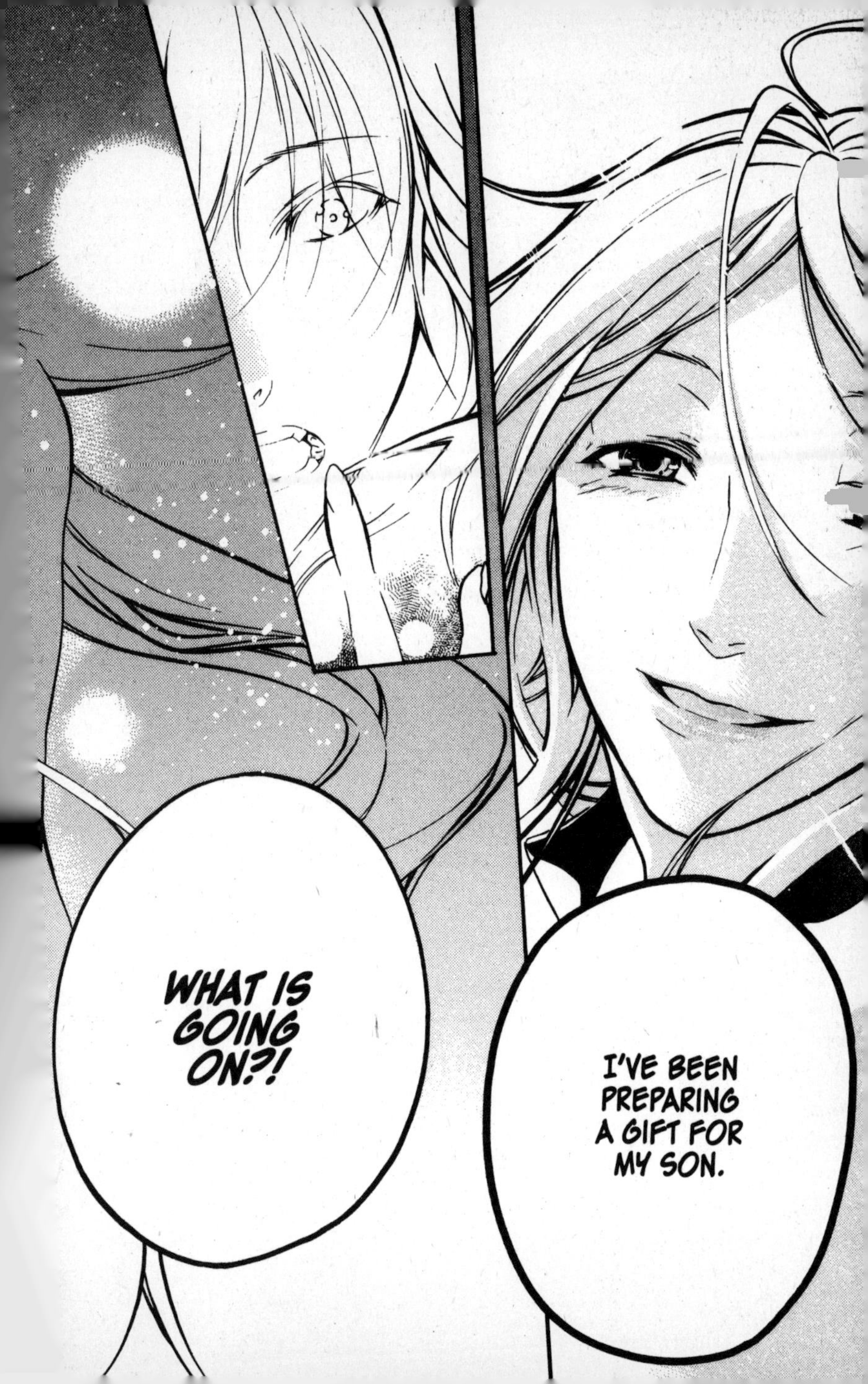
I'VE BEEN PREPARING A GIFT FOR MY SON.
WHAT IS GOING ON?!

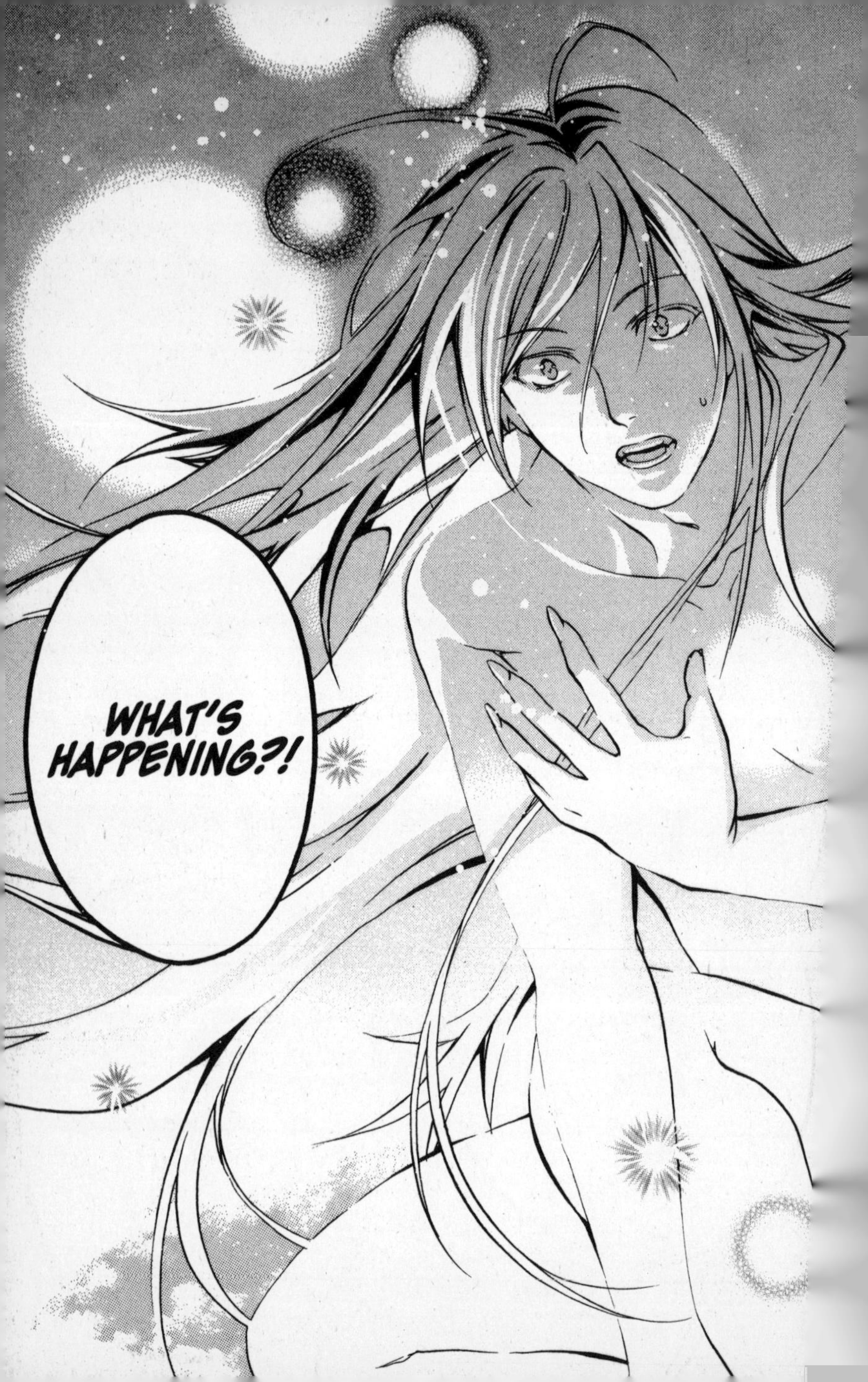
WHAT'S HAPPENING?!

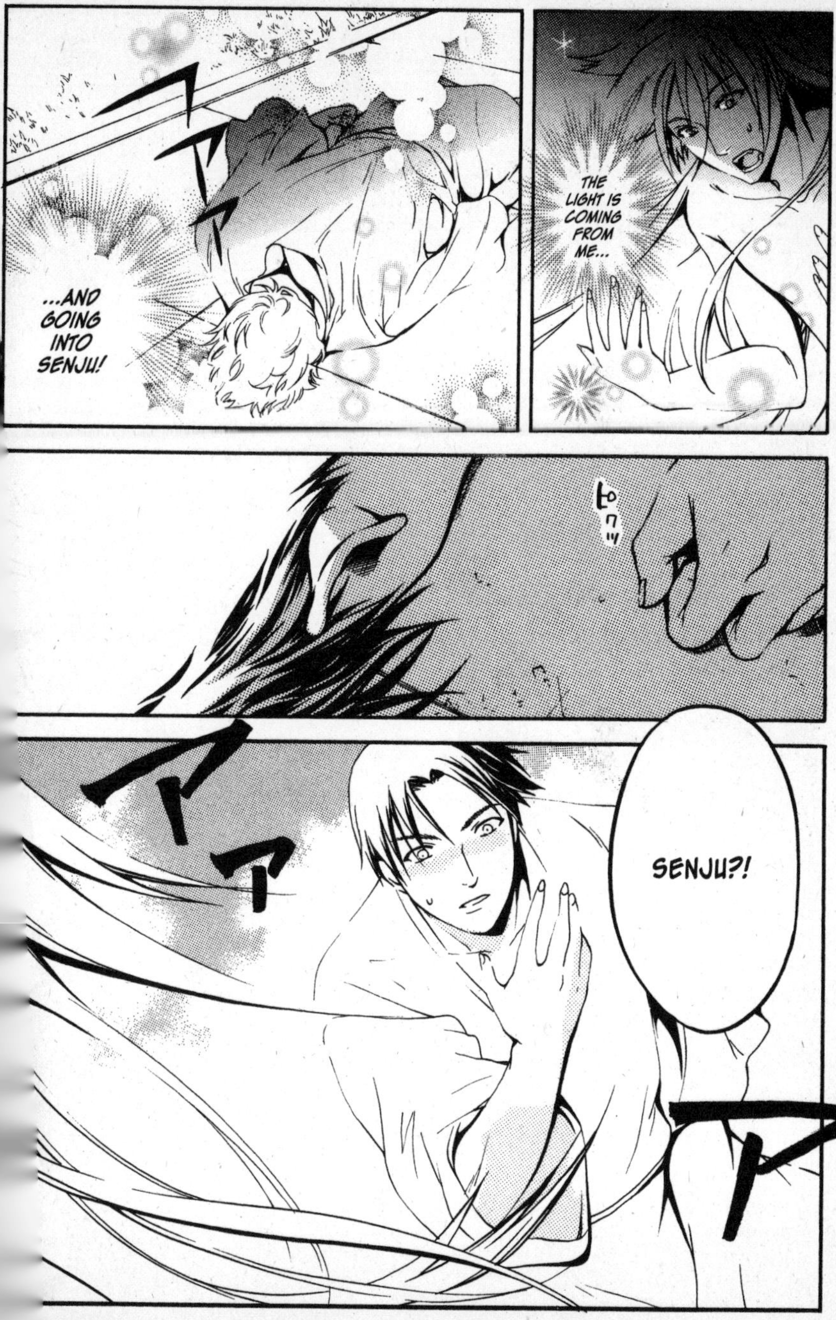
THE LIGHT IS COMING FROM ME...
...AND GOING INTO SENJU!
ピクッ
SENJU?!

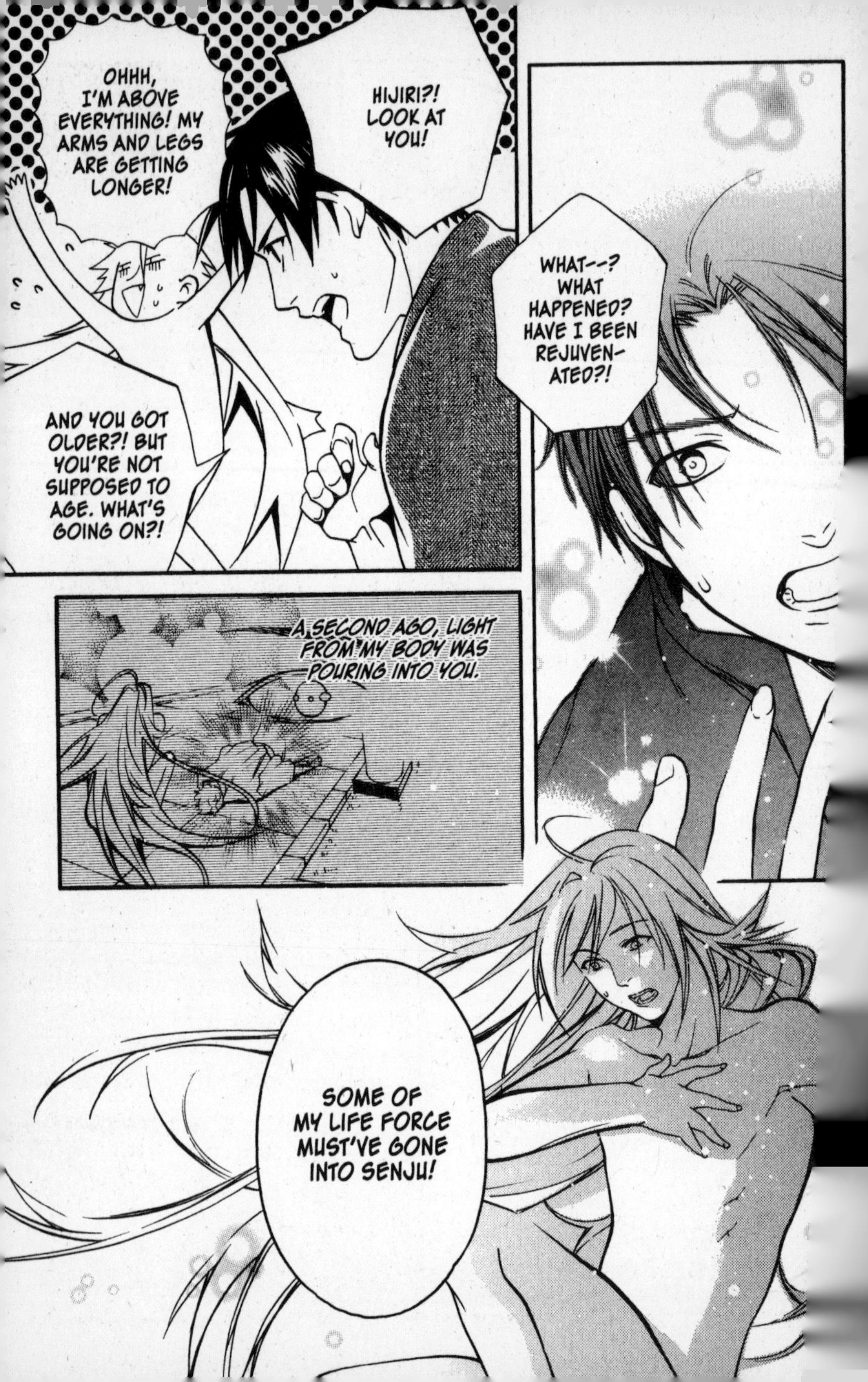
WHAT--? WHAT HAPPENED? HAVE I BEEN REJUVEN-ATED?!
HIJIRI?! LOOK AT YOU!
OHHH, I'M ABOVE EVERYTHING! MY ARMS AND LEGS ARE GETTING LONGER!
AND YOU GOT OLDER?! BUT YOU'RE NOT SUPPOSED TO AGE. WHAT'S GOING ON?!
A SECOND AGO, LIGHT FROM MY BODY WAS POURING INTO YOU.
SOME OF MY LIFE FORCE MUST'VE GONE INTO SENJU!

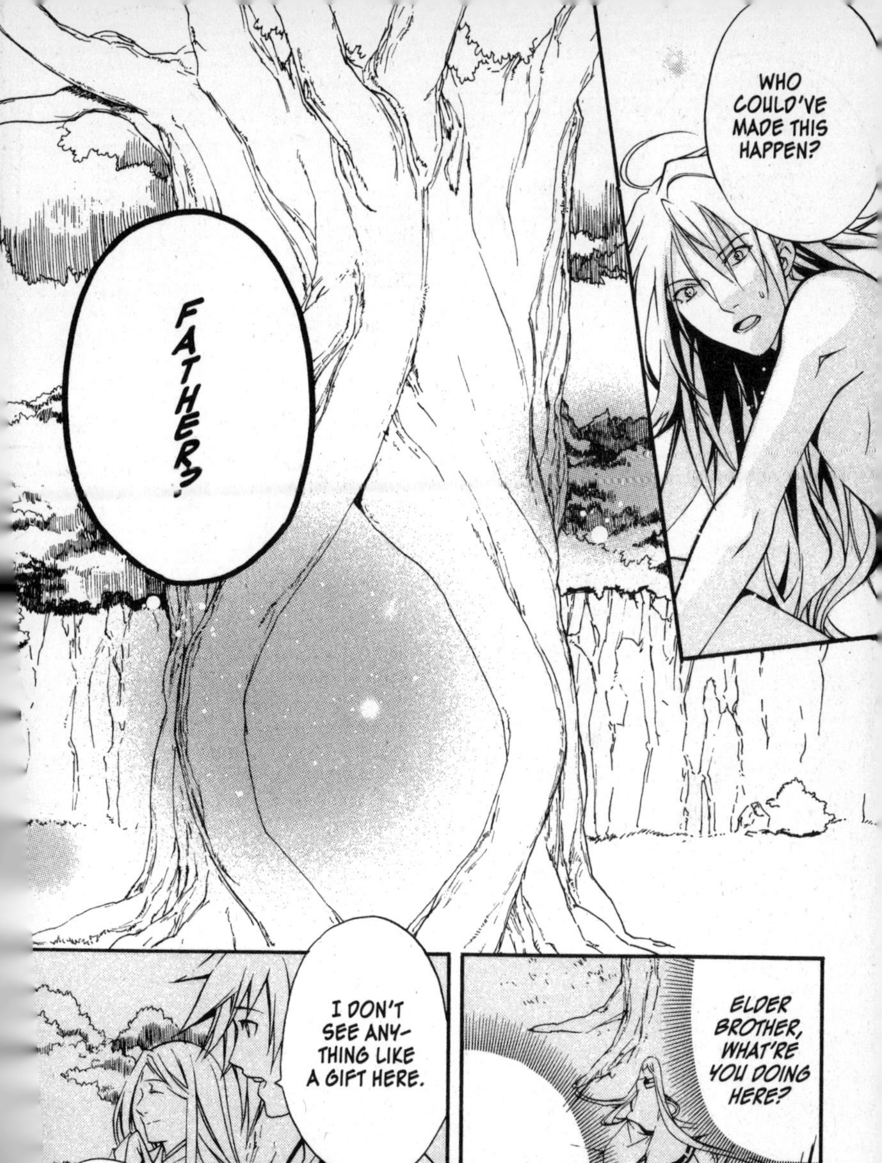
WHO COULD'VE MADE THIS HAPPEN?
FATHER?
ELDER BROTHER, WHAT'RE YOU DOING HERE?
I'VE BEEN PREPARING A GIFT FOR MY SON.
I DON'T SEE ANY-THING LIKE A GIFT HERE.
WELL...

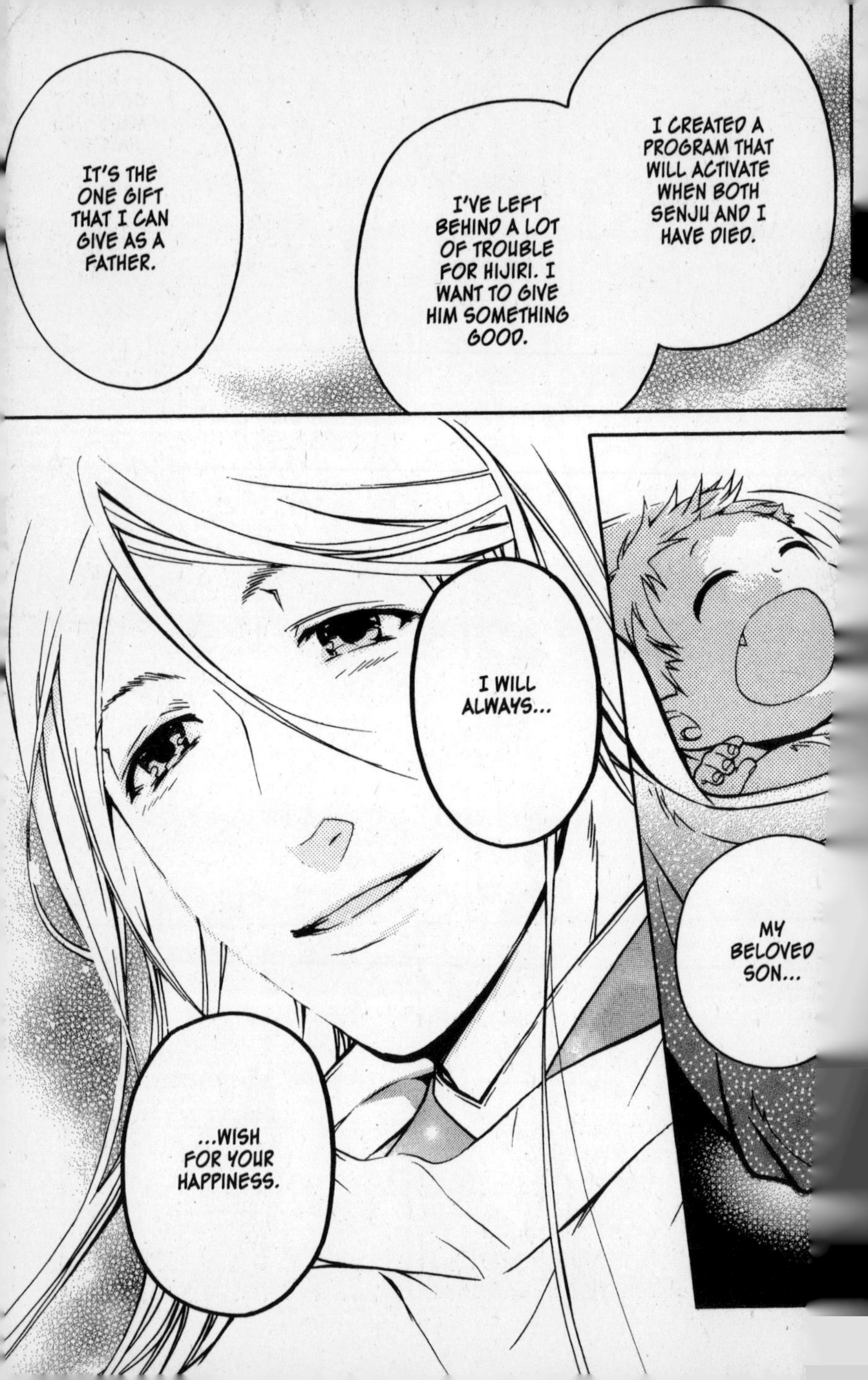
I CREATED A PROGRAM THAT WILL ACTIVATE WHEN BOTH SENJU AND I HAVE DIED.
I'VE LEFT BEHIND A LOT OF TROUBLE FOR HIJIRI. I WANT TO GIVE HIM SOMETHING GOOD.
IT'S THE ONE GIFT THAT I CAN GIVE AS A FATHER.
I WILL ALWAYS...
MY BELOVED SON...
...WISH FOR YOUR HAPPINESS.

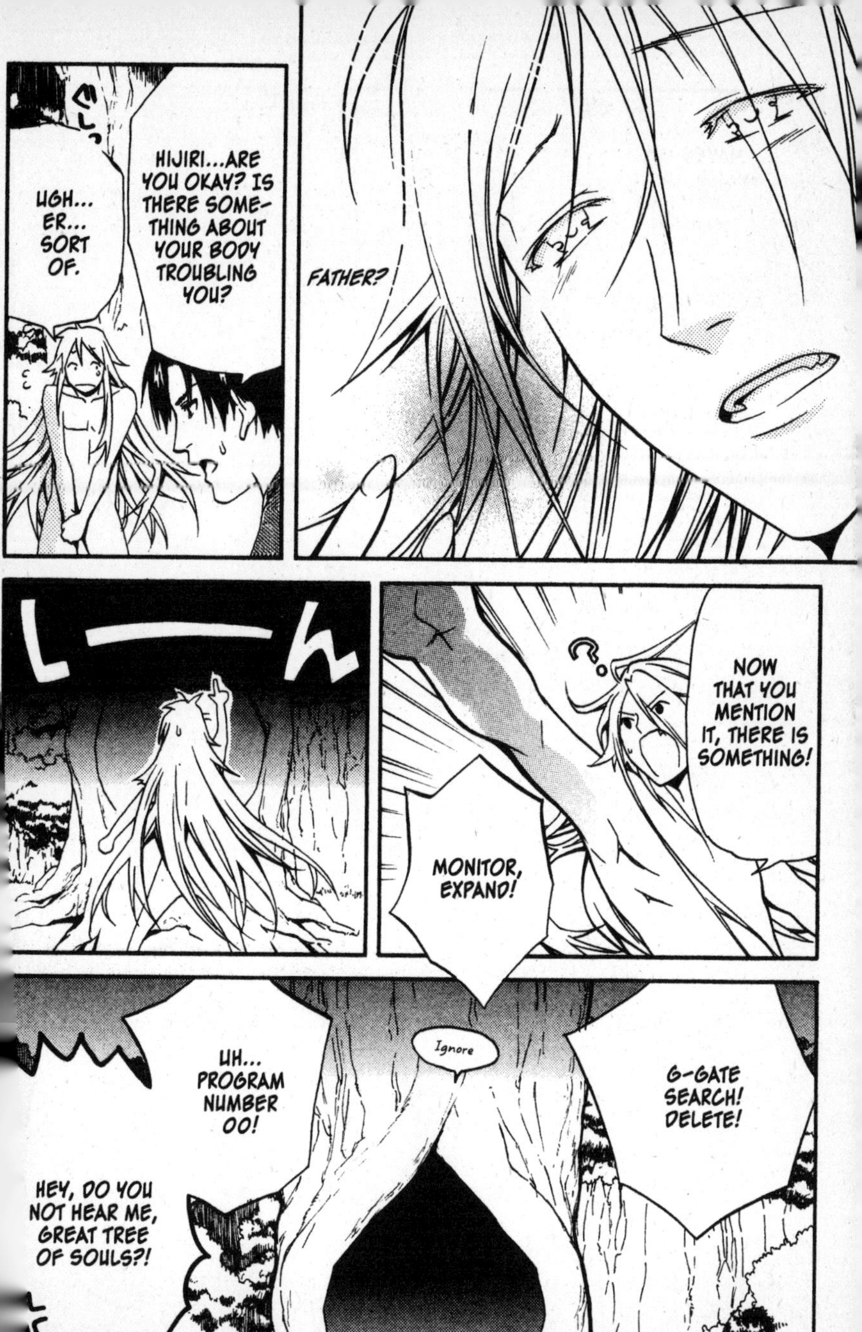
FATHER?
HIJIRI...ARE YOU OKAY? IS THERE SOMETHING ABOUT YOUR BODY TROUBLING YOU?
UGH... ER... SORT OF.
NOW THAT YOU MENTION IT, THERE IS SOMETHING!
MONITOR, EXPAND!
し——ん
G-GATE SEARCH! DELETE!
Ignore
UH... PROGRAM NUMBER OO!
HEY, DO YOU NOT HEAR ME, GREAT TREE OF SOULS?!

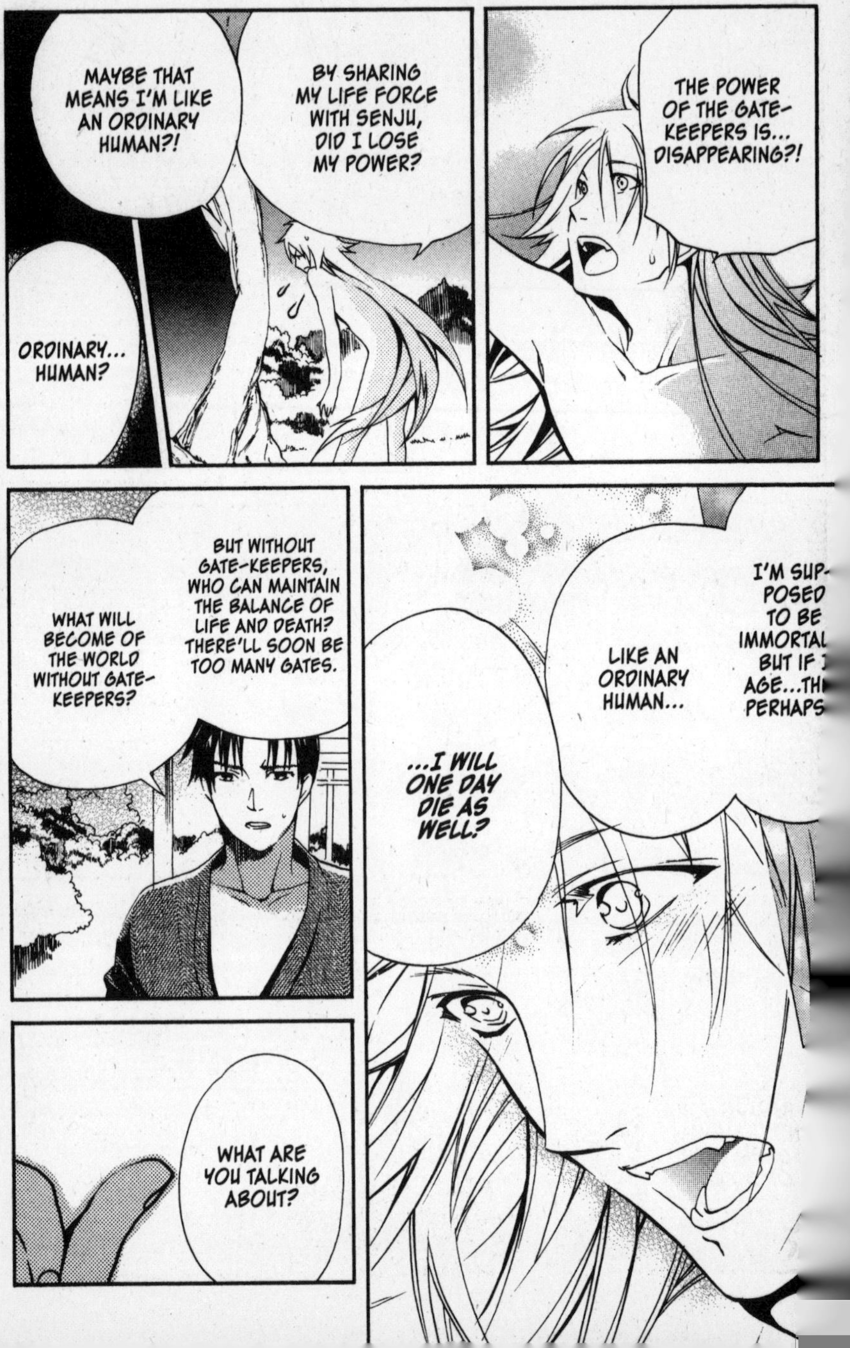
THE POWER OF THE GATE-KEEPERS IS... DISAPPEARING?!
BY SHARING MY LIFE FORCE WITH SENJU, DID I LOSE MY POWER?
MAYBE THAT MEANS I'M LIKE AN ORDINARY HUMAN?!
ORDINARY... HUMAN?
I'M SUP-POSED TO BE IMMORTAL BUT IF AGE...TH PERHAPS
LIKE AN ORDINARY HUMAN...
...I WILL ONE DAY DIE AS WELL?
BUT WITHOUT GATE-KEEPERS, WHO CAN MAINTAIN THE BALANCE OF LIFE AND DEATH? THERE'LL SOON BE TOO MANY GATES.
WHAT WILL BECOME OF THE WORLD WITHOUT GATE-KEEPERS?
WHAT ARE YOU TALKING ABOUT?

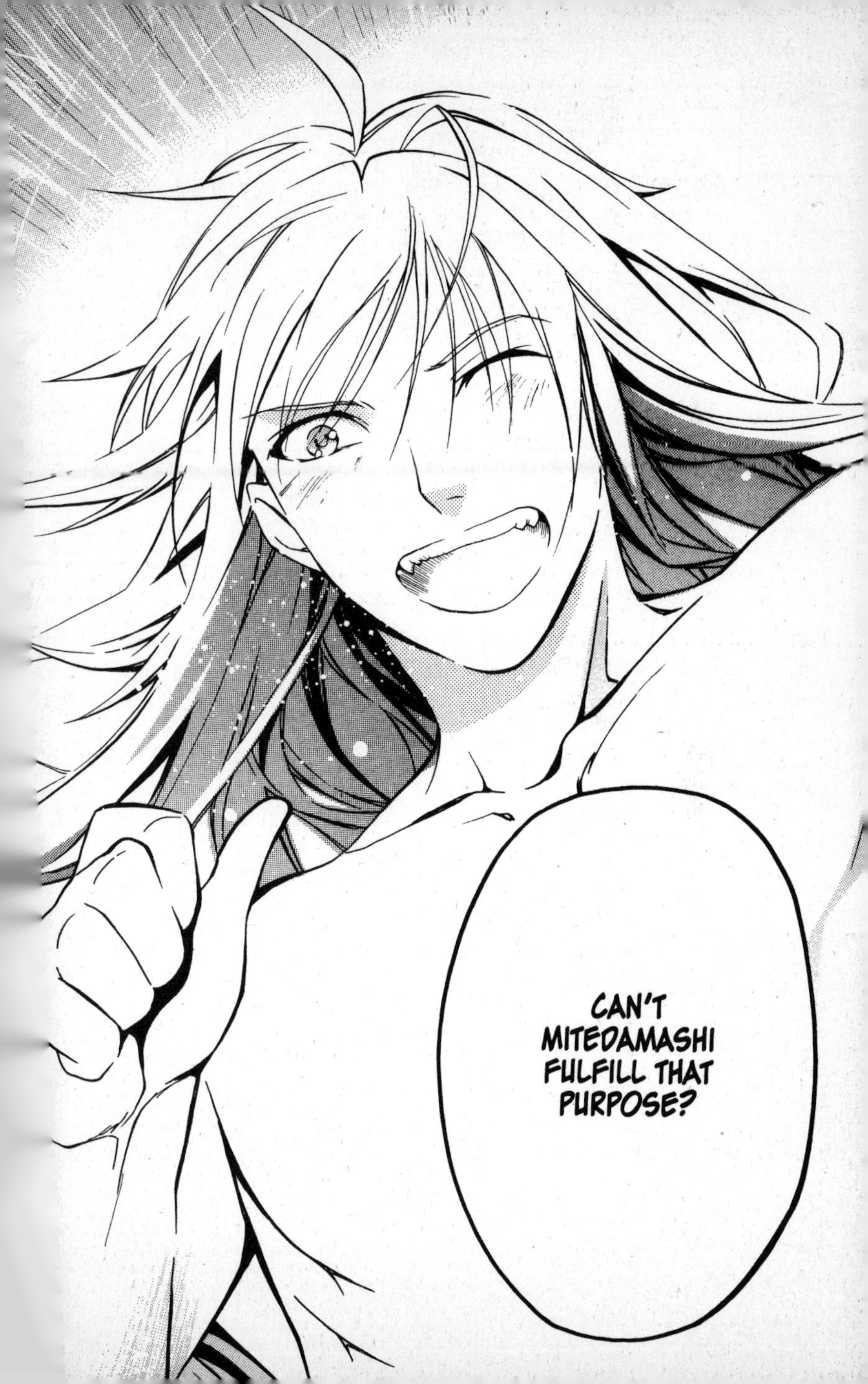
CAN'T MITEDAMASHI FULFILL THAT PURPOSE?

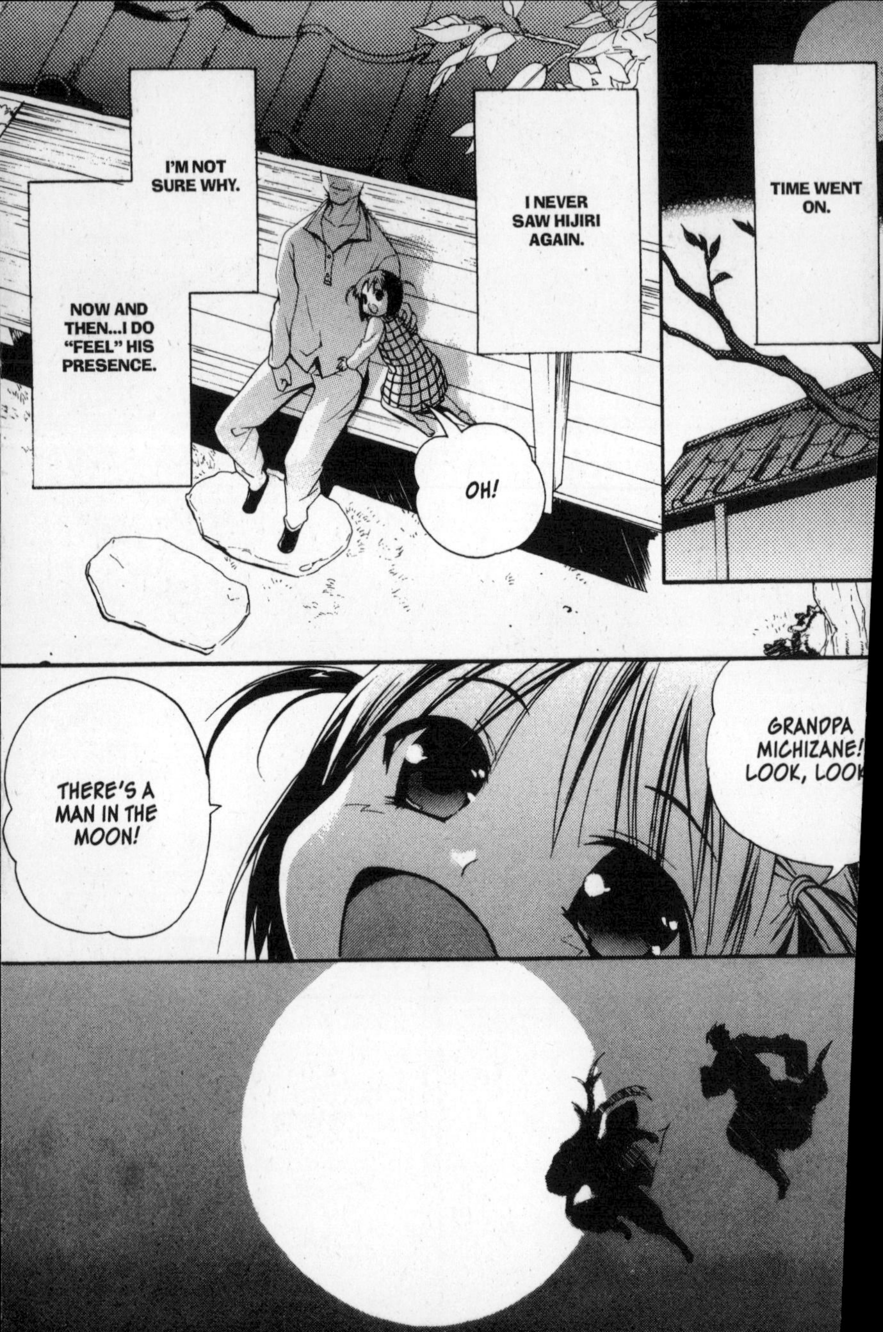
TIME WENT ON.
I NEVER SAW HIJIRI AGAIN.
I'M NOT SURE WHY.
NOW AND THEN...I DO "FEEL" HIS PRESENCE.
OH!
GRANDPA MICHIZANE! LOOK, LOOK
THERE'S A MAN IN THE MOON!

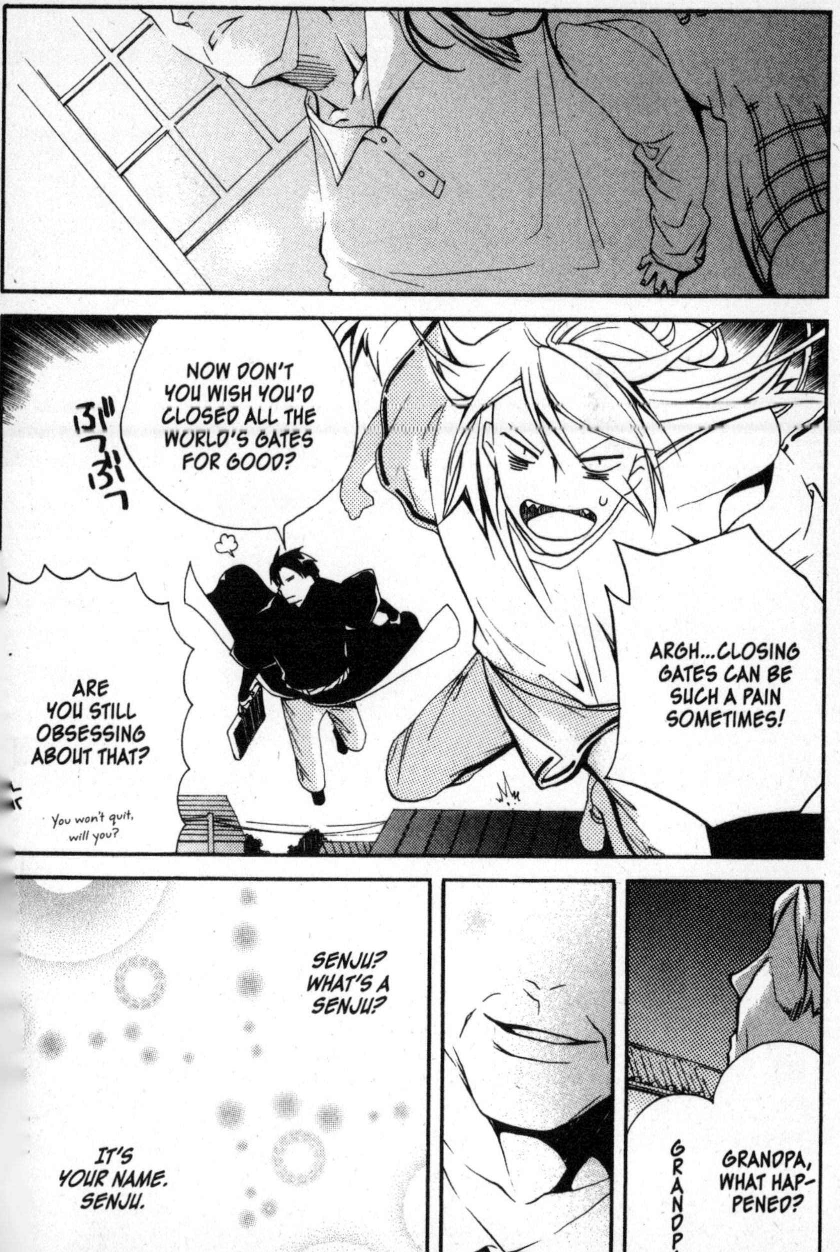
ARGH...CLOSING GATES CAN BE SUCH A PAIN SOMETIMES!
NOW DON'T YOU WISH YOU'D CLOSED ALL THE WORLD'S GATES FOR GOOD?
ぶつぶつ
ARE YOU STILL OBSESSING ABOUT THAT?
You won't quit, will you?
GRANDPA, WHAT HAP-PENED?
GRANDPA?
SENJU? WHAT'S A SENJU?
IT'S YOUR NAME. SENJU.

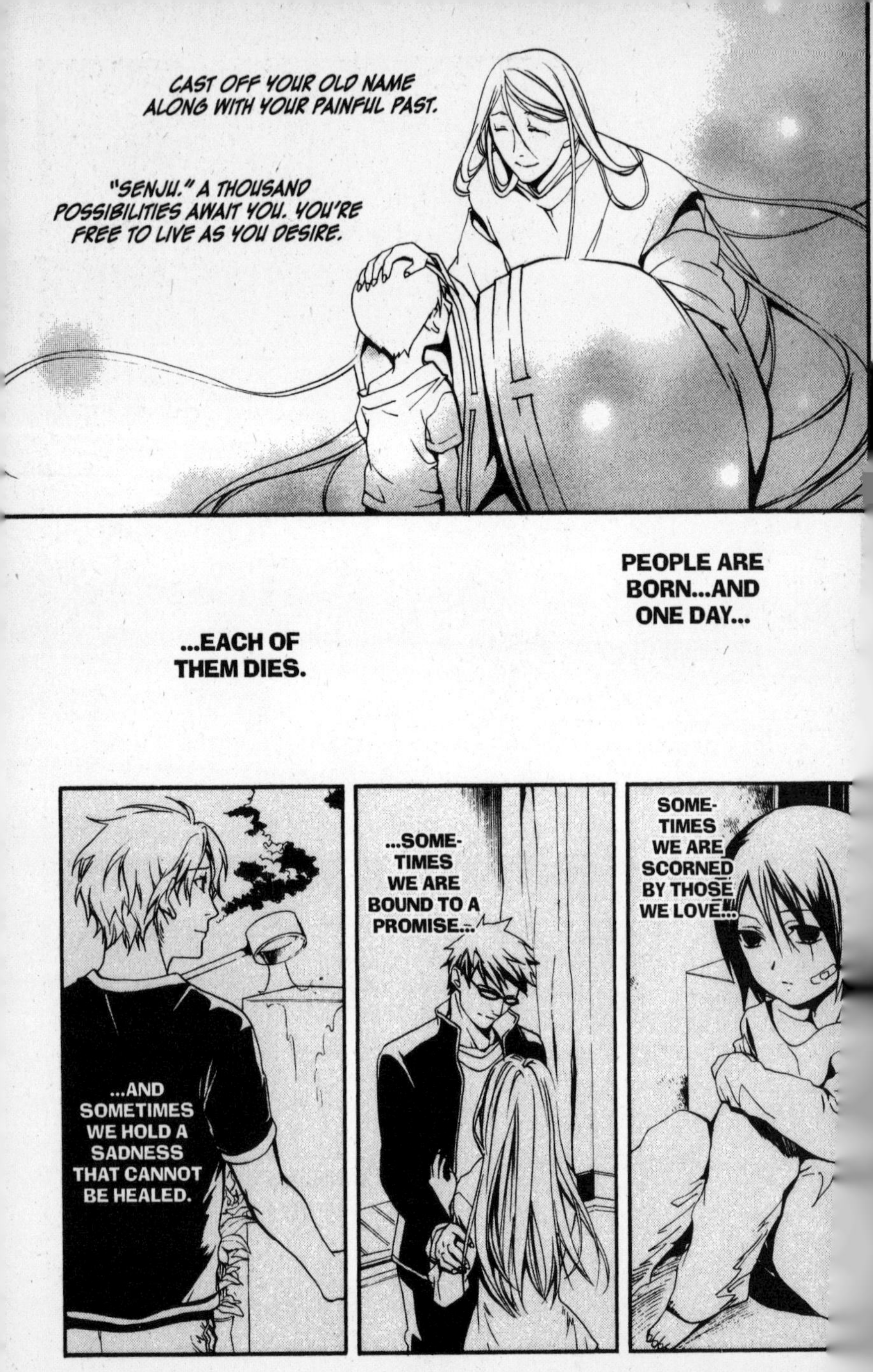
CAST OFF YOUR OLD NAME ALONG WITH YOUR PAINFUL PAST.
"SENJU." A THOUSAND POSSIBILITIES AWAIT YOU. YOU'RE FREE TO LIVE AS YOU DESIRE.
PEOPLE ARE BORN...AND ONE DAY...
...EACH OF THEM DIES.
SOMETIMES WE ARE SCORNED BY THOSE WE LOVE...
...SOMETIMES WE ARE BOUND TO A PROMISE...
...AND SOMETIMES WE HOLD A SADNESS THAT CANNOT BE HEALED.

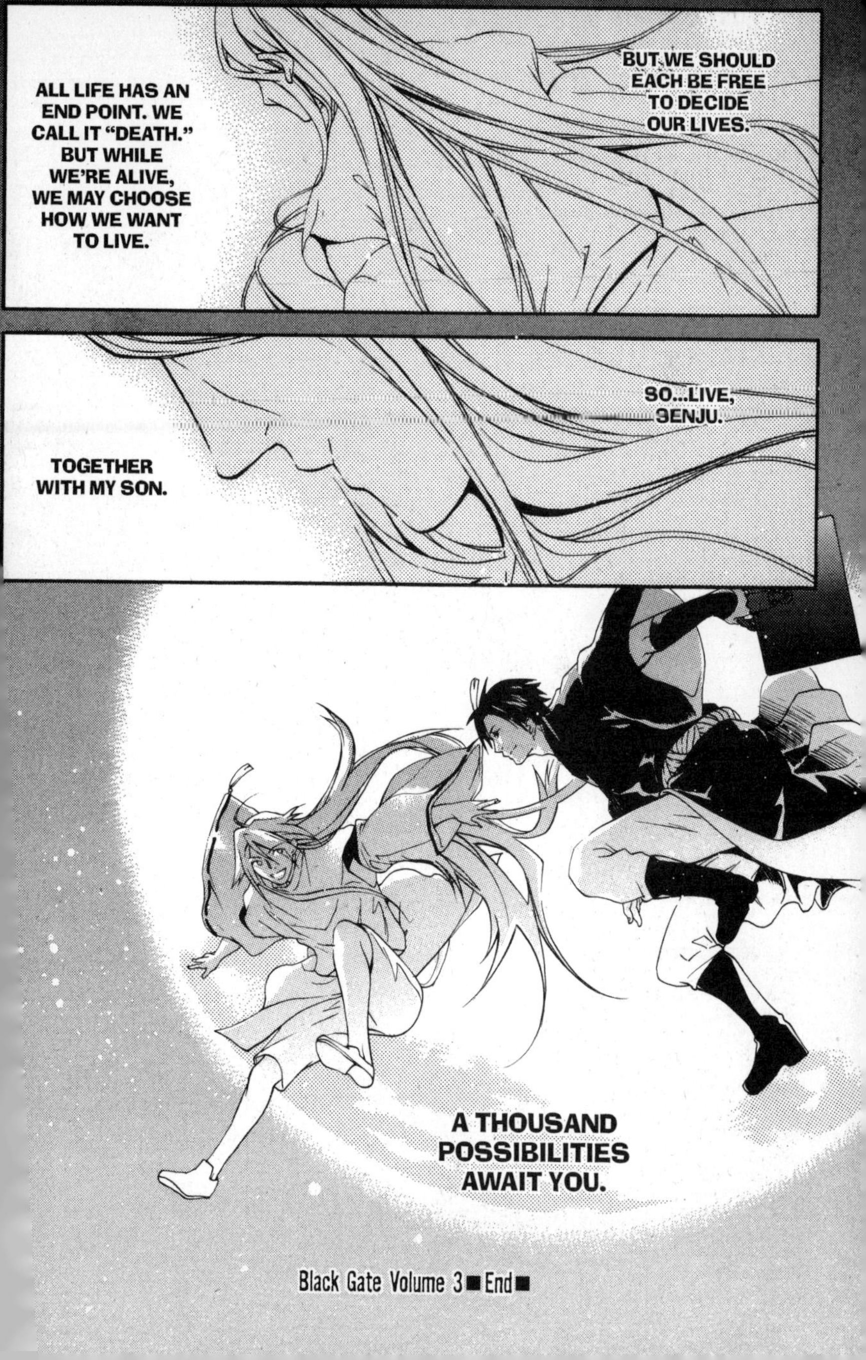
BUT WE SHOULD EACH BE FREE TO DECIDE OUR LIVES.
ALL LIFE HAS AN END POINT. WE CALL IT "DEATH." BUT WHILE WE'RE ALIVE, WE MAY CHOOSE HOW WE WANT TO LIVE.
SO...LIVE, SENJU.
TOGETHER WITH MY SON.
A THOUSAND POSSIBILITIES AWAIT YOU.
Black Gate Volume 3 ■ End ■

Afterword

HELLO, IT'S SUMIYOSHI AGAIN, THANKING YOU FOR PURCHASING THIS FINAL VOLUME.

FIRST OF ALL, I'M GRATEFUL TO HAVE SEEN THIS WORK THROUGH ITS FINAL CHAPTER DESPITE SO MANY PROBLEMS! THIS IS MY FIRST SERIALIZED MANGA STORY.
I WAS SO EXCITED TO DRAW THIS.

SINCE THIS IS THE FINAL VOLUME, I'D LIKE TO EXPLAIN A BIT OF THE STORY'S BACKGROUND.
I GOT THE IDEA FOR IT WHEN I WAS IN HIGH SCHOOL.
IT'S REALLY A REMAKE OF AN "ARABIAN FANTASY BATTLE BETWEEN AN ADULT MALE AND A YOUNG FEMALE."
BUT THIS STORY TURNED OUT NOTHING LIKE IT WAS ORIGINALLY ENVISIONED.

THE WAY IT BEGAN, AND UP 'TIL THE SECOND CHAPTER, HIJIRI WAS SUPPOSED TO "LOOK LIKE A BOY, BUT ACTUALLY BE A GIRL." BUT, DUE TO VARIOUS CONSIDERATIONS, THAT IDEA CHANGED BEFORE LONG, AND I NEVER LOOKED BACK. IT'S SO SURPRISING NOW TO THINK BACK ON MY ORIGINAL IDEA. BUT THAT INITIAL GENDER-BENDING CONCEPT GAVE ME THE NOTION TO DRESS HIJIRI UP IN DRAG IN CHAPTER 3 (LOL). ← (THOUGH, AT FIRST, IT WAS SUPPOSED TO BE HIJIRI, WHO'S REALLY A GIRL, DRESSING UP AS A GIRL.) ANYWAY, THAT WAS THE FIRST TIME I DREW A CHARACTER IN DRAG OUTSIDE OF A GAG COMIC. SO, I WAS REALLY EMBARRASSED, BUT IT ENDED UP BEING SUCH A BLAST (LOL).

THIS BOOK WAS AN ADVENTURE FROM START TO FINISH. IT WAS A HUGE CHALLENGE, AND I GAVE IT MY ALL.
I HOPE YOU'LL THINK OF THIS BOOK AS ONE OF YOUR FAVORITES.

LET'S MEET UP AGAIN IN MY NEXT WORK!

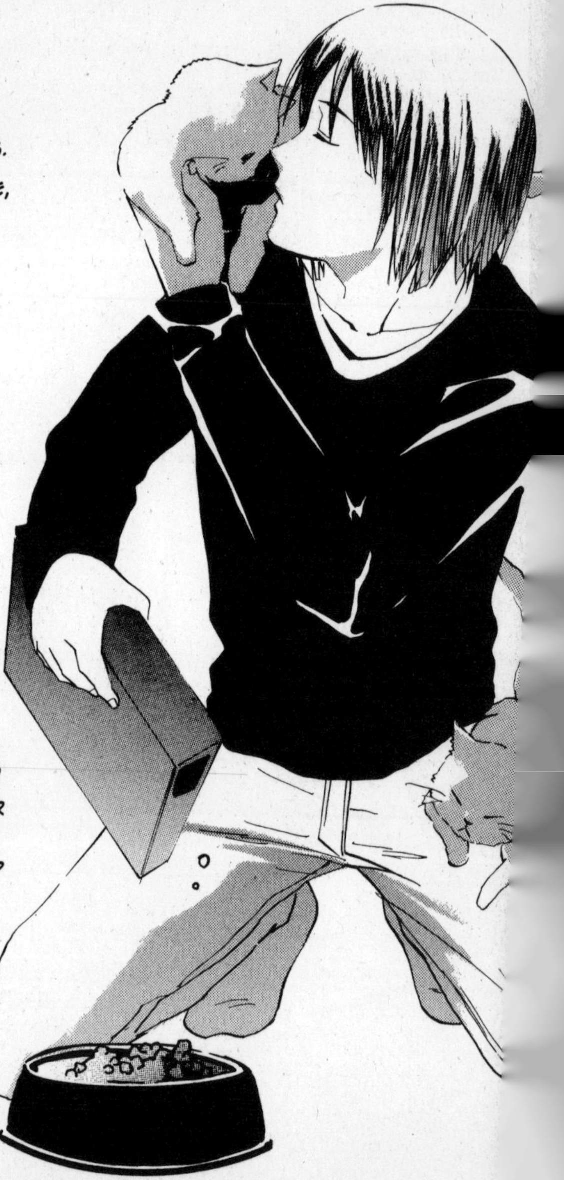

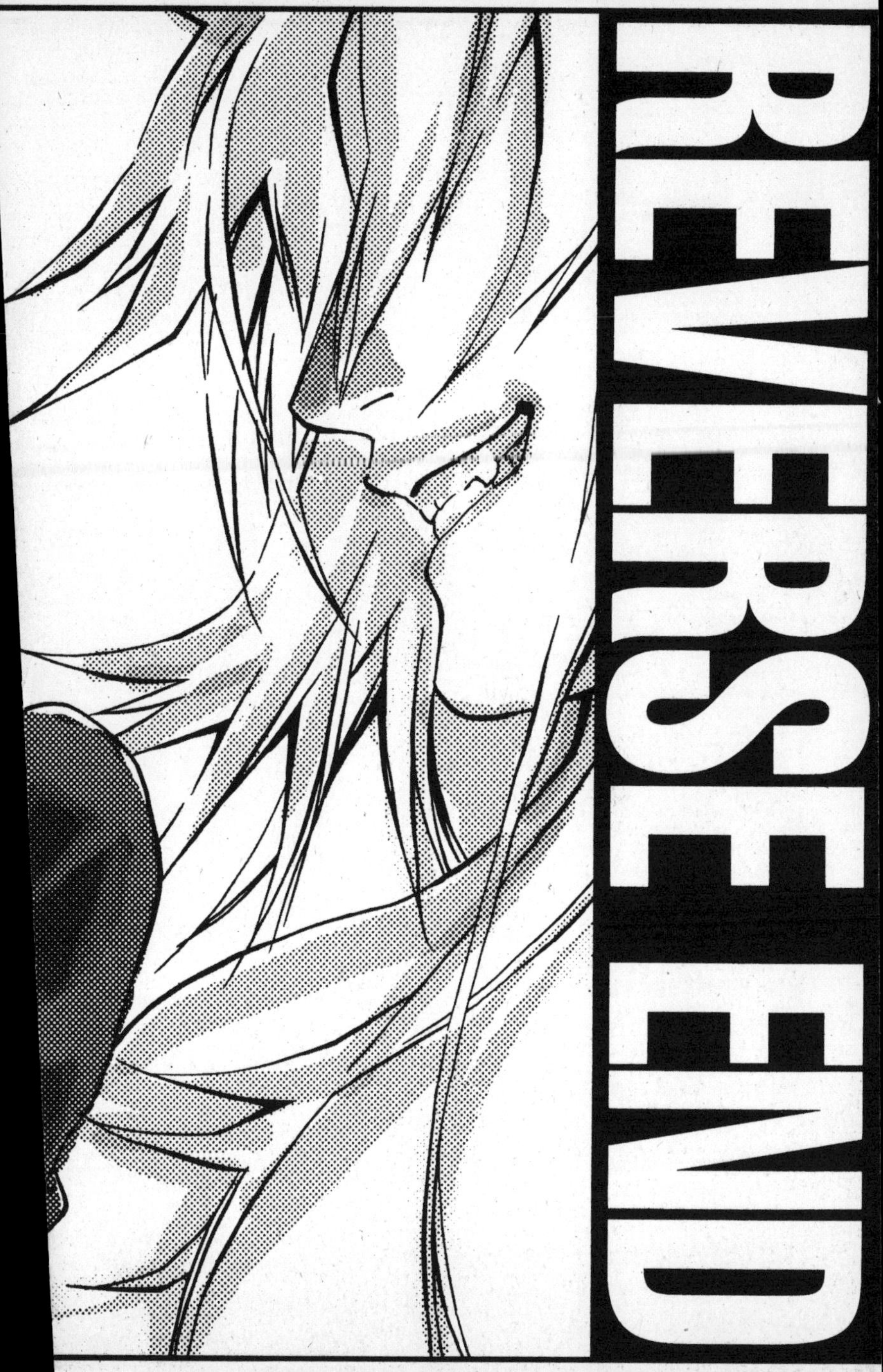
REVERSE END

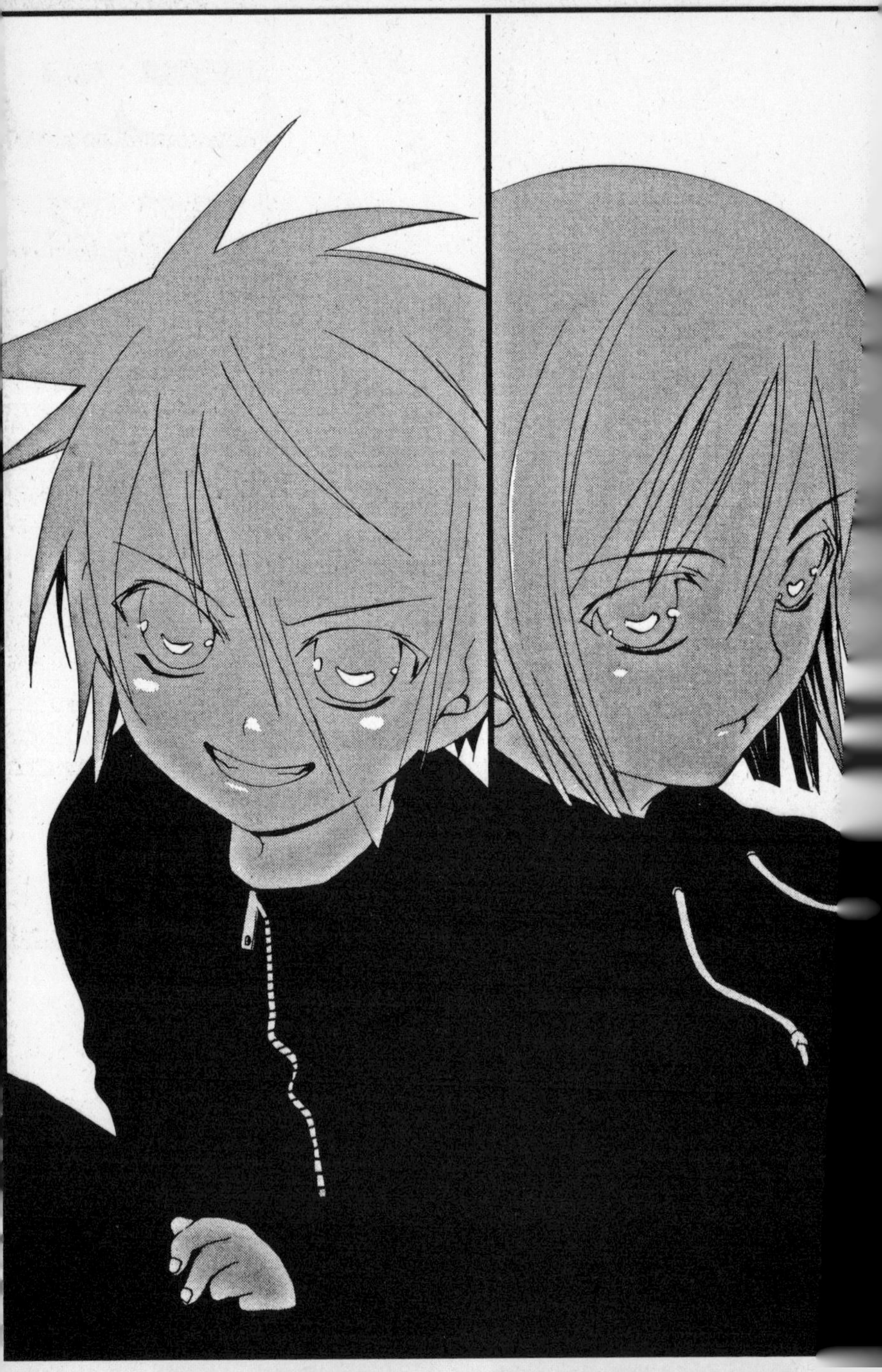

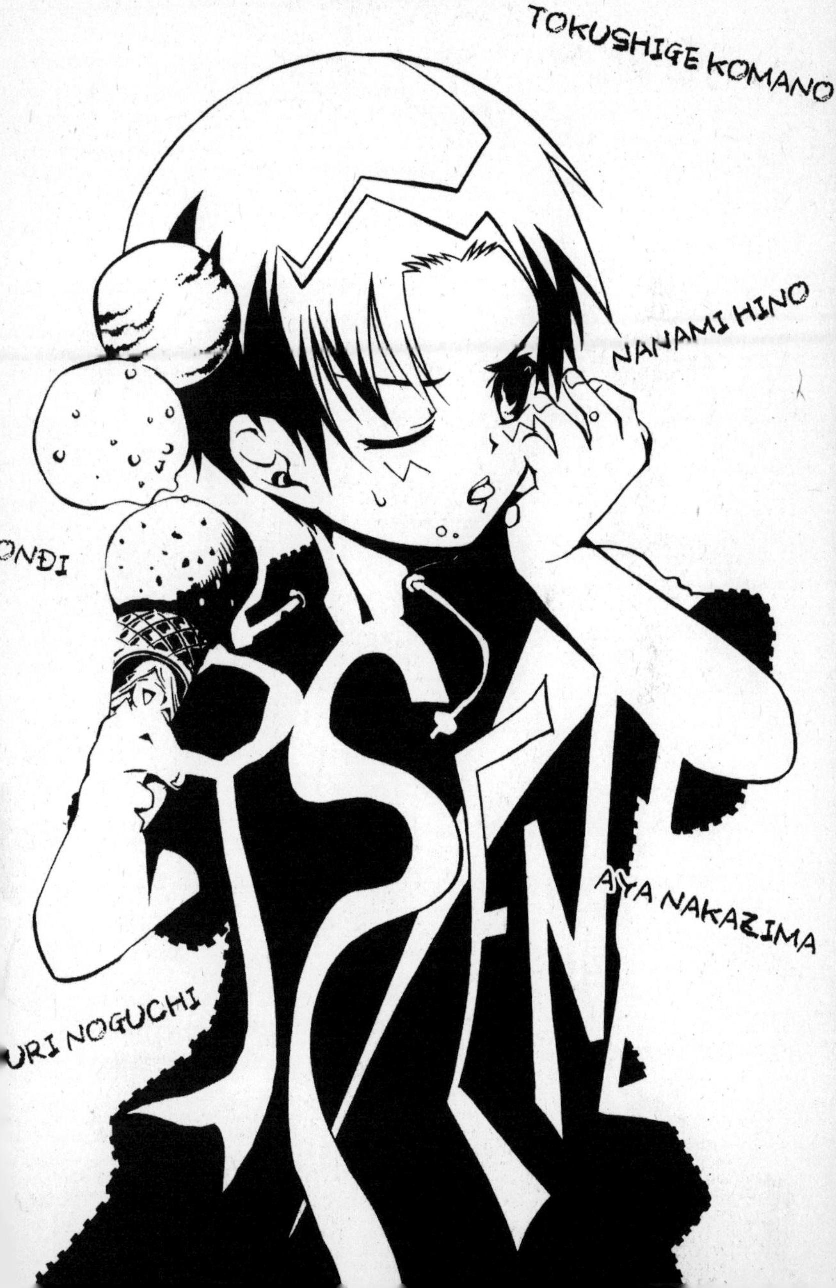
TOKUSHIGE KOMANO
NANAMI HINO
ONDI
AYA NAKAZIMA
URI NOGUCHI

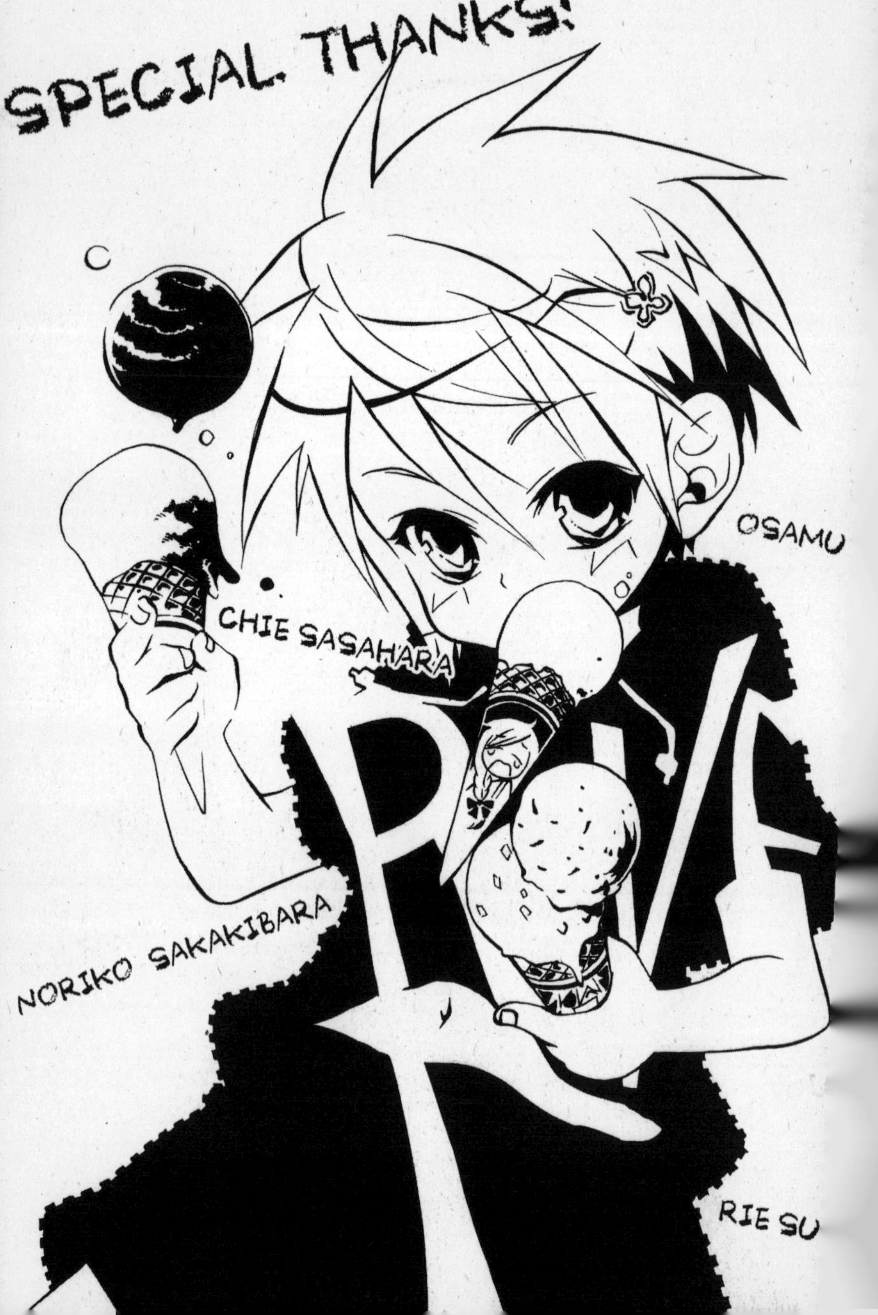
SPECIAL THANKS!
OSAMU
CHIE SASAHARA
NORIKO SAKAKIBARA
RIE SU

RightStuf.com asks...

"What kind of OTAKU are you?"

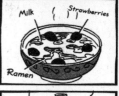

DISCOVER HOW IT ALL BEGAN

AN EVIL, ANCIENT AND HUNGRY, IS ROAMING THE BADLANDS OF THE OLD WEST. IT SPARES NOT MAN, WOMAN NOR CHILD, DEVOURING ALL THAT STAND BEFORE IT. ONLY ONE MAN CAN STOP IT...A MYSTERIOUS PRIEST WITH A CROSS CARVED INTO HIS HEAD. HIS NAME IS IVAN ISAACS, AND HE WILL SMOTE ALL EVIL IN A HAIL OF HOT LEAD. HALLELUJAH.

MIN-WOO HYUNG'S INTERNATIONAL MANWHA SENSATION RETURNS WITH SPECIAL COLLECTOR'S EDITIONS FOR FANS OLD & NEW!

STOP!

This is the back of the book.
You wouldn't want to spoil a great ending!

This book is printed "manga-style," in the authentic Japanese right-to-left format. Since none of the artwork has been flipped or altered, readers get to experience the story just as the creator intended. You've been asking for it, so TOKYOPOP® delivered: authentic, hot-off-the-press, and far more fun!

DIRECTIONS

If this is your first time reading manga-style, here's a quick guide to help you understand how it works.

It's easy... just start in the top right panel and follow the numbers. Have fun, and look for more 100% authentic manga from TOKYOPOP®!